The Mea
The Glorio

An Explanatory Translation by
Mohammed Marmaduke Pickthall

ISLAMIC BOOK TRUST KUALA LUMPUR
2001

© Islamic Book Trust, Kuala Lumpur 2001

ISBN 983-9154-26-5

First published 1930
This edition, with text 2001
First reprint November 2001
Second reprint 2003

Published by
Islamic Book Trust
607 Mutiara Majestic
Jalan Othman
46000 Petaling Jaya, Malaysia

Email: ibtkl@pd.jaring.my
Website: www.ibtbooks.com

Cover design
Habibur Rahman
bounce@tm.net.my

Printed in Malaysia by
Percetakan Zafar Sdn. Bhd. (97878.H)

PUBLISHER'S NOTE

Voices were raised now and then from many quarters, alleging that the English translation of the Holy Qur'an undertaken by the late English Muslim scholar, Mohammed Marmaduke Pickthall, titled *The Meaning of the Glorious Qur'an* contains serious mistakes which need to be looked into and corrected to make the translation serve the purpose for which it was undertaken.

However the original translation, with all the mistakes, is still being published by various publishers throughout the world and is being widely circulated. Perturbed by this, a concerned Muslim brother in Singapore sent us a pamphlet published by one brother, Iqbal Husain Ansari of Karachi, Pakistan, containing a list of 248 corrections in Pickthall's celebrated translation. This has prompted us to undertake this job which we, as an Islamic publisher, consider as our sacred duty.

This edition has incorporated all corrections as listed by Mr. Iqbal, and we hope will have the approval of Muslim scholars and readers of the holy book.

May Allah *subhānahu wa ta'āla* accept the efforts of all of us in this field as a good deed in His service.

Islamic Book Trust,
Kuala Lumpur,
April 2001 / Muharram 1422.

TRANSLITERATION

The following table shows the system which has been followed in transliterating the letters of the Arabic alphabet:

ا	alif	=	a	ف	fā	=	f
		=	ā (*long vowel*)	ق	qāf	=	q
ب	bā	=	b	ك	kāf	=	k
ت	tā	=	t	ل	lām	=	l
ث	thā	=	th	م	mīm	=	m
ج	jīm	=	j	ن	nūn	=	n
ح	ḥā'	=	ḥ	ه	hā	=	h
خ	khā'	=	kh	و	wāw	=	w (*consonantal*)
د	dāl	=	d			=	ū (*long vowel*)
ذ	dhāl	=	dh	ي	yā	=	y (*consonantal*)
ر	rā	=	r			=	ī (*long vowel*)
ز	zāy	=	z	ء	hamza	=	' (*apostrophe*)
س	sīn	=	s				
ش	shīn	=	sh				
ص	ṣād	=	ṣ				
ض	ḍād	=	ḍ				
ط	ṭā	=	ṭ				
ظ	ẓā	=	ẓ				
ع	'ayn	=	' (*inverted apostrophe*)				
غ	ghāyn	=	gh				

Short vowels:

́	(fataḥah)	=	a
́	(dammah)	=	u
̣	(kasrah)	=	i

vii

TRANSLITERATION

The following table shows the system which has been followed in transliterating the letters of the Arabic alphabet.

ا	alif = a		ف	fa = f
ب	ba = b		ق	qaf = q
ت	ta = t		ك	kaf = k
ث	tha = th		ل	lam = l
ج	jim = j		م	mim = m
ح	ḥa = ḥ		ن	nun = n
خ	kha = kh		ه	ha = h
د	dal = d		و	waw = w (consonantal)
ذ	dhal = dh			ū (long vowel)
ر	ra = r		ي	ya = y (consonantal)
ز	za = z			ī (long vowel)
س	sin = s		ء	hamza = ' (interrupted)
ش	shin = sh			
ص	ṣad = ṣ			Short vowels:
ض	ḍad = ḍ			
ط	ṭa = ṭ			(fatḥah) = a
ظ	ẓa = ẓ			
ع	'ayn = ' (inverted apostrophe)			(ḍammah) = u
غ	ghayn = gh			(kasrah) = i

CONTENTS

ix

Translator's Foreword

THE AIM of this work is to present to English readers what Muslims the world over hold to be the meaning of the words of the Qur'an, and the nature of that Book, in not unworthy language and concisely, with a view to the requirements of English Muslims. It may be reasonably claimed that no Holy Scripture can be fairly presented by one who disbelieves its inspiration and its message; and this is the first English translation of the Qur'an by an Englishman who is a Muslim. Some of the translations include commentation offensive to Muslims, and almost all employ a style of language which Muslims at once recognise as unworthy.

The Qur'an cannot be translated. That is the belief of old-fashioned Sheykhs and the view of the present writer. The Book is here rendered almost literally and every effort has been made to choose befitting language. But the result is not the Glorious Qur'an, that inimitable symphony, the very sounds of which move men to tears and ecstasy. It is only an attempt to present the meaning of the Qur'an—and peradventure something of the charm—in English. It can never take the place of the Qur'an in Arabic, nor is it meant to do so.

Before publication the work has been scrutinised word by word and thoroughly revised in Egypt with the help of one whose mother-tongue is Arabic, who has studied the Qur'an and who knows English; and when difficulties were encountered the translator had recourse to perhaps the greatest living authority on the subject. Every care has thus been taken to avoid unwarrantable renderings. On the one or two occasions where there is departure from the traditional interpretation, the traditional rendering will be found in a footnote.

The translator's thanks are due to Lord Lloyd for an introduction of great use in Egypt; to Dr F. Krenkow for supplying him with old

xiii

meanings of Arabic words not to be found in dictionaries; to Muhammad Ahmad Al-Ghamrawī Bey of the Cairo College of Medicine for his invaluable and patient help with the revision of the manuscript, a work which occupied three months; to the Sheykh Mustafā Al-Marāghī, former Rector of Al-Azhar University, for his advice and guidance in the revision; and to His Excellency Fuad Bey Salīm Al-Higāzi, by whose efforts such revision was made possible.

The *mushaf* (copy of the Qur'an) which has been used throughout is a lithograph copy of that written by Al-Hajj Muhammad Shakarzādeh at the command of Sultan Mahmūd of Turkey in 1246 A.H. In the Introduction and the notes to individual sūrahs, Ibn Hishām (Būlāq ed. 1295 A.H.) has been followed, with occasional reference to the much later, much abbreviated, but more critical *Life of the Prophet* by Ibn Khaldūn (published as an appendix to his *Tārīkh,* Būlāq ed.). Other *Sīrahs*, like that of Abū'l-Fidā, late in date and uncritical, have been read but not followed. Of commentators Al-Baydāwī and Zamakhsharī must be mentioned, while for reference during the work of revision, the brief commentary of Al-Jalālayn was kept at hand. Wāhidī's *Asbābu'n-Nuzūl* has been largely consulted, and for the authenticity of Traditions the translator has relied upon Bukhārī.

Introduction

The Meaning of the Glorious Qur'an

PART I
At Makkah

The Prophet's birth

MUHAMMAD, son of 'Abdullah, son of 'Abdul Muttalib, of the tribe of Quraysh, was born at Makkah fifty-three years before the Hijrah. His father died before he was born, and he was protected first by his grandfather, 'Abdul Muttalib, and, after his grandfather's death, by his uncle, Abū Tālib. As a young boy he travelled with his uncle in the merchants' caravan to Syria, and some years afterwards made the same journey in the service of a wealthy widow named Khadījah.

His marriage

So faithfully did he transact the widow's business, and so excellent was the report of his behaviour which she received from her old servant who had accompanied him, that she soon afterwards married her young agent; and the marriage proved a very happy one, though she was fifteen years older than he was. Throughout the twenty-six years of their life together he remained devoted to her; and after her death, when he took other wives he always mentioned her with the greatest love and reverence. This marriage gave him rank among the notables of Makkah, while his conduct earned for him the surname *Al-Amīn*, the "trustworthy."

The Makkans claimed descent from Abraham through Ishmael, and tradition stated that their temple, the Ka'bah, had been built by Abraham for the worship of the One God. It was still called the House of Allah, but the chief objects of worship there were a number of idols; which were called daughters of Allah and intercessors.

xv

The Ḥunafā

The few who felt disgust at this idolatry, which had prevailed for centuries, longed for the religion of Abraham and tried to find out what had been its teaching. Such seekers of the truth were known as Ḥunafā (sing. Ḥanīf) a word originally meaning "those who turn away" (from the existing idol-worship), but coming in the end to have the sense of "upright" or "by nature upright," because such persons held the way of truth to be right conduct. These Ḥunafā did not form a community. They were the agnostics of their day, each seeking truth by the light of his own inner consciousness. Muḥammad son of 'Abdullah became one of these. It was his practice to retire with his family for a month of every year to a cave in the desert for meditation. His place of retreat was Ḥirā, a desert hill not far from Makkah, and his chosen month was Ramaḍān, the month of heat.

The first revelation

It was there one night toward the end of his quiet month that the first revelation came to him when he was forty years old. He was asleep or in a trance when he heard a voice say: "Read!" He said: "I cannot read." The voice again said: "Read!" He said: "I cannot read." A third time the voice, more terrible, commanded: "Read!" He said: "What can I read?" The voice said:

> Read: In the name of thy Lord Who createth.
> Createth man from a clot.
> Read: And it is thy Lord the Most Bountiful
> Who teacheth by the pen,
> Teacheth man that which he knew not. (96:1-5)

The vision of Mount Ḥirā

When he awoke the words remained "as if inscribed upon his heart." He went out of the cave on to the hillside and heard the same awe-inspiring voice say: "O Muḥammad! Thou art Allah's messenger, and I am Gabriel." Then he raised his eyes and saw the angel, in the likeness of a man, standing in the sky above the horizon. And again the dreadful voice said: "O Muhammad! Thou art Allah's messenger, and I am Gabriel." Muhammad (God bless and keep him!) stood quite still, turning away his face from the brightness of the vision, but whithersoever he might turn his face, there always stood the angel confronting him. He remained thus a long while till at length the angel vanished, when he returned in great distress of mind to his wife Khadījah. She did her best to reassure him, saying that his conduct had been such that Allah would not let a harmful spirit come to him and that it was her hope that he was to become the Prophet of his people. On their return to Makkah she took him to her cousin Waraqa ibn Naufal, a very old man, "who knew the Scriptures of the Jews and Christians," who declared his belief that the heavenly messenger who came to Moses of old had come to Muhammad, and that he was chosen as the Prophet of his people.

His distress of mind

To understand the reason of the Prophet's diffidence and his extreme distress of mind after the vision of Mount Ḥirā, it must be remembered that the *Hunafā*, of whom he had been one, sought true religion in the natural and regarded with distrust the intercourse with spirits of which men "avid of the Unseen,"(81:24) sorcerers and soothsayers and even poets, boasted in those days. Moreover, he was a man of humble and devout intelligence, a lover of quiet and solitude, and the very thought of being chosen out of all mankind to face mankind, alone, with such a Message, appalled him at the first. Recognition of the Divine nature of the call he had received involved a change in his whole mental outlook sufficiently disturbing to a sensitive and honest mind, and also the forsaking of his quiet, honoured way of life. The early biographers tell how his wife Khadījah "tried the spirit" which came to him and proved it to be good, and how, with the continuance of the revelations and the conviction that they brought, he at length accepted the tremendous task imposed on him, becoming filled with an enthusiasm of obedience which justifies his proudest title of "The Slave of Allah."

The Qur'an

The words which came to him when in a state of trance are held sacred by the Muslims and are never confounded with those which he uttered when no physical change was apparent in him. The former are the Sacred Book; the latter the *Hadīth* or *Sunnah* of the Prophet. And because the angel on Mt. Hirā bade him "Read!"—insisted on his "Reading" though he was illiterate—the Sacred Book is known as *Al-Qur'ān*, "The Reading,"[1] the Reading of the man who knew not how to read.

First converts

For the first three years, or rather less, of his Mission, the Prophet preached only to his family and his intimate friends, while the people of Makkah as a whole regarded him as one who had become a little mad. The first of all his converts was his wife Khadījah, the second his first cousin 'Alī, whom he had adopted, the third his servant Zayd, a former slave. His old friend Abū Bakr also was among those early converts with some of his slaves and dependents.

Beginning of persecution

At the end of the third year the Prophet received the command to "arise and warn," (74:2) whereupon he began to preach in public, pointing out the wretched folly of idolatry in face of the tremendous laws of day and night, of life and death, of growth and decay, which manifest the power of Allah and attest His sovereignty. It was then, when he began to speak against their gods, that Quraysh became actively hostile, persecuting his poorer disciples, mocking and insulting him. The one consideration

---

1. Or "The Lecture," as it is here translated in passages where the term will bear translation, on the analogy of "Scripture," used for sacred "writing."

which prevented them from killing him was fear of the blood-vengeance of the clan to which his family belonged. Strong in his inspiration, the Prophet went on warning, pleading, threatening, while Quraysh did all they could to ridicule his teaching, and deject his followers.

The flight to Abyssinia

The converts of the first four years were mostly humble folk unable to defend themselves against oppression. So cruel was the persecution they endured that the Prophet advised all who could possibly contrive to do so to emigrate to a Christian country, Abyssinia.[2] And still in spite of persecution and emigration the little company of Muslims grew in number. Quraysh were seriously alarmed. The idol-worship at the Ka'bah, the holy place to which all Arabia made pilgrimage, ranked for them, as guardians of the Ka'bah, as first among their vested interests. At the season of the pilgrimage they posted men on all the roads to warn the tribes against the madman who was preaching in their midst. They tried to bring the Prophet to a compromise, offering to accept his religion if he would so modify it as to make room for their gods as intercessors with Allah, offering to make him their king if he would give up attacking idolatry; and, when their efforts at negotiation failed, they went to his uncle Abū Ṭālib, offering to give him the best of their young men in place of Muhammad, to give him all that he desired, if only he would let them kill Muhammad and have done with him. Abū Ṭālib refused.

The *Saḥīfah* or deed of ostracism

The exasperation of the idolaters was increased by the conversion of 'Umar,[3] one of their stalwarts. They grew more and more embittered, till things came to such a pass that they decided to ostracise the

---

2. See Sūrah 19, introductory note.

3. See Sūrah 20 introductory note.

XX The Meaning of the Glorious Qur'an

Prophet's whole clan, idolaters who protected him as well as Muslims who believed in him. Their chief men caused a document to be drawn up to the effect that none of them or those belonging to them would hold any intercourse with that clan or sell to them or buy from them. This they all signed, and it was deposited in the Ka'bah. Then, for three years, the Prophet was shut up with all his kinsfolk in their stronghold which was situated in one of the gorges which run down to Makkah. Only at the time of pilgrimage could he go out and preach, or did any of his kinsfolk dare to go into the city.

Destruction of the *Saḥīfah*

At length some kinder hearts among Quraysh grew weary of the boycott of old friends and neighbours. They managed to have the document which had been placed in the Ka'bah brought out for reconsideration; when it was found that all the writing had been destroyed by white ants, except the words *Bismika Allāhumma* ("In thy name, O Allah"). When the elders saw that marvel the ban was removed, and the Prophet was again free to go about the city. But meanwhile the opposition to his preaching had grown rigid. He had little success among the Makkans, and an attempt which he made to preach in the city of Ṭā'if was a failure. His Mission was a failure, judged by worldly standards, when, at the season of the yearly pilgrimage, he came upon a little group of men who heard him gladly.

The men from Yathrib

They came from Yathrib, a city more than two hundred miles away, which has since become world famous as *Al-Madīnah*, "the City" *par excellence*. At Yathrib there were Jewish tribes with learned rabbis, who had often spoken to the pagans of a Prophet soon to come among the Arabs, with whom, when he came, the Jews would destroy the pagans as the tribes of 'Ād and Thamūd had been destroyed of old for their idolatry. When the men from Yathrib saw Muḥammad they recognised him as the Prophet whom the Jewish rabbis had described to them. On their return to Yathrib they told what they had seen and heard, with the result that at the next season of pilgrimage a deputation came from Yathrib purposely to meet the Prophet.

First pact of Al-'Aqabah

These swore allegiance to him in the first pact of Al-'Aqabah, the oath they took being that which was afterwards exacted from women converts, with no mention of fighting. They then returned to Yathrib with a Muslim teacher in their company, and soon "there was not a house in Yathrib wherein there was not mention of the messenger of Allah."

Second pact of Al-'Aqabah

In the following year, at the time of pilgrimage, seventy-three Muslims from Yathrib came to Makkah to vow allegiance to the Prophet and invite him to their city. At Al-'Aqabah, by night, they swore to defend him as they would defend their own wives and children. It was then that the Hijrah, the Flight to Yathrib, was decided.

Plot to murder the Prophet

Soon the Muslims who were in a position to do so began to sell their property and to leave Makkah unobtrusively. Quraysh had wind of what was going on. They hated Muhammad in their midst, but dreaded what he might become if he escaped from them. It would be better, they considered, to destroy him now. The death of Abū Ṭālib had removed his chief protector; but still they had to reckon with the vengeance of his clan upon the clan of the murderer. They cast lots and chose a slayer out of every clan. All these were to attack the Prophet simultaneously and strike together, as one man. Thus his blood would be on all Quraysh. It was at this time (Ibn Khaldūn asserts, and it is the only satisfactory explanation of what happened afterwards) that the Prophet received the first revelation ordering him to make war upon his persecutors *"until persecution is no more and religion is for Allah only"*

(8:39).

The Hijrah (June 20th, 622 A.D.)

The last of the able Muslims to remain in Makkah were Abū Bakr, 'Alī
and the Prophet himself. Abū Bakr, a man of wealth, had bought two
riding camels and retained a guide in readiness for the Flight. The
Prophet only waited God's command. It came at length. It was the night
appointed for his murder. The slayers were before his house. He gave
his cloak to 'Alī, bidding him lie down on the bed so that anyone
looking in might think Muḥammad lay there. The slayers were to strike
him as he came out of the house, whether in the night or early morning.
He knew they would not injure 'Alī. Then he left the house and, it is
said, a blindness fell upon the would-be murderers so that he put dust
on their heads as he passed by—without their knowing it. He went to
Abū Bakr's house and called to him, and they two went together to a
cavern in the desert hills and hid there till the hue and cry was past,
Abū Bakr's son and daughter and his herdsman bringing them food and
tidings after nightfall. Once a search-party came quite near them in their
hiding-place, and Abū Bakr was afraid; but the Prophet said: "Fear not!
Allah is with us" (9:40). Then, when the coast was clear, Abū Bakr had
the riding-camels and the guide brought to the cave one night, and they
set out on the long ride to Yathrib.

After travelling for many days by unfrequented paths, the fugitives
reached a suburb of Yathrib, whither, for weeks past, the people of the
city had been going every morning, watching for the Prophet till the
heat drove them to shelter. The travellers arrived in the heat of the day,
after the watchers had retired. It was a Jew who called out to the
Muslims in derisive tones that he whom they expected had at last
arrived.

Such was the Hijrah, the Flight from Makkah to Yathrib, which
counts as the beginning of the Muslim era. The thirteen years of
humiliation, of persecution, of seeming failure, of prophecy still
unfulfilled, were over. The ten years of success, the fullest that has ever

crowned one man's endeavour, had begun. The Hijrah makes a clear division in the story of the Prophet's Mission, which is evident in the Qur'an. Till then he had been a preacher only. Thenceforth he was the ruler of a State, at first a very small one, which grew in ten years to the empire of Arabia. The kind of guidance which he and his people needed after the Hijrah was not the same as that which they had before needed. The Madinah sūrahs differ, therefore, from the Makkan sūrahs. The latter give guidance to the individual soul and to the Prophet as warner; the former give guidance to a growing social and political community and to the Prophet as example, lawgiver and reformer.

Classification of Makkan *sūrahs*

For classification the Makkan sūrahs are here subdivided into four groups: Very Early, Early, Middle and Late. Though the historical data and traditions are insufficient for a strict chronological grouping, the very early sūrahs are, roughly speaking, those revealed before the beginning of the persecution; the early sūrahs those revealed between the beginning of the persecution and the conversion of 'Umar; the middle sūrahs those revealed between the conversion of 'Umar and the destruction of the deed of ostracism; and the late sūrahs those revealed between the raising of the ban of ostracism and the Hijrah.

PART II
At Al-Madīnah

The Jews and Hypocrites

In the first year of his reign at Yathrib the Prophet made a solemn treaty with the Jewish tribes, which secured to them equal rights of citizenship and full religious liberty in return for their support of the new State. But their idea of a Prophet was one who would give them dominion, not one who made the Jews who followed him brothers of every Arab who might happen to believe as they did. When they found that they could not use the Prophet for their own ends, they tried to shake his faith in his Mission and to seduce his followers; behaviour in which they were encouraged secretly by some professing Muslims who considered they had reason to resent the Prophet's coming, since it robbed them of their local influence. In the Madīnah sūrahs there is frequent mention of these Jews and Hypocrites.

The *Qiblah*

Till then the *Qiblah* (the place toward which the Muslims turn their face in prayer) had been Jerusalem. The Jews imagined that the choice implied a leaning toward Judaism and that the Prophet stood in need of their instruction. He received command to change the *Qiblah* (2:144, 149, 150) from Jerusalem to the Ka'bah at Makkah. The whole first part of sūrah 2 relates to this Jewish controversy.

The first expeditions

The Prophet's first concern as ruler was to establish public worship and lay down the constitution of the State; but he did not forget that Quraysh had sworn to make an end of his religion, nor that he had received command to fight against them till they ceased from persecution. After he had been twelve months in Yathrib several small expeditions went out, led either by the Prophet himself or some other of the fugitives from Makkah, for the purpose of reconnoitring and of dissuading other tribes from siding with Quraysh. These are generally represented as warlike but, considering their weakness and the fact that they did not result in fighting, they can hardly have been that, though it is certain that they went out ready to resist attack. It is noteworthy that in those expeditions only fugitives from Makkah were employed, never natives of Yathrib; the reason being (if we accept Ibn Khaldūn's theory, and there is no other explanation) that the command to wage war had been revealed to the Prophet at Makkah after the Yathrib men had sworn their oath of allegiance at Al-'Aqabah, and in their absence. Their oath foresaw fighting in mere defence, not fighting in the field.

Blood was shed and booty taken in only one of those early expeditions, and then it was against the Prophet's orders. One purpose of those expeditions may have been to accustom the Makkan Muslims to going out in warlike trim. For thirteen years they had been strict pacifists, and it is clear, from several passages of the Qur'an (*e.g.*, 2:216), that many of them, including, it may be, the Prophet himself, hated the idea of fighting even in self-defence and had to be inured to it.

The campaign of Badr

In the second year of the Hijrah the Makkan merchants' caravan was returning from Syria as usual by a road which passed not far from Yathrib. As its leader Abū Sufyān approached the territory of Yathrib he heard of the Prophet's design to capture the caravan. At once he sent a camel-rider on to Makkah, who arrived in a worn-out state and shouted frantically from the valley to Quraysh to hasten to the rescue unless they wished to lose both wealth and honour. A force a thousand strong was soon on its way to Yathrib; less, it would seem, with the hope of saving the caravan than with the idea of punishing the raiders, since the Prophet might have taken the caravan before the relief force started from Makkah. Did the Prophet ever intend to raid the caravan? In Ibn Hishām, in the account of the Tabūk expedition, it is stated that the Prophet on that one occasion did not hide his real objective as had been his custom in other campaigns. The caravan was the pretext in the campaign of Badr, the real objective was the Makkan army. He had received command to fight his persecutors, and promise of victory; he was prepared to venture against any odds, as was well seen at Badr. But the Muslims, disinclined and ill-equipped for war, would have despaired if they had known from the first that they were to face a well-armed force three times their number.

The army of Quraysh had advanced more than half-way to Yathrib before the Prophet set out. All three parties—the army of Quraysh, the Muslim army and the caravan—were heading for the water of Badr. Abū Sufyān, the leader of the caravan, heard from one of his scouts that the Muslims were near the water, and turned back to the coast-plain. And the Muslims met the army of Quraysh by the water of Badr. Before the battle the Prophet was prepared still further to increase the odds against him. He gave leave to all the Ansār (natives of Yathrib) to return to their homes unreproached, since their oath did not include the duty of fighting in the field; but the Ansār were only hurt by the suggestion that they could possibly desert him at a time of danger. The battle went at first against the Muslims, but ended in a signal victory for them.[4]

The victory of Badr gave the Prophet new prestige among the Arab tribes; but thenceforth there was the feud of blood between Quraysh and the Islamic State in addition to the old religious hatred. Those passages of the Qur'an which refer to the battle of Badr give warning of much greater struggles yet to come.

The battle of Mount Uḥud

In fact in the following year, an army of three thousand came from Makkah to destroy Yathrib. The Prophet's first idea was merely to defend the city, a plan of which 'Abdullah ibn Ubayy, the leader of "the Hypocrites"(or lukewarm Muslims), strongly approved. But the men who had fought at Badr and believed that God would help them against any odds thought it a shame that they should linger behind walls. The Prophet, approving of their faith and zeal, gave way to them, and set out with an army of one thousand men toward Mt. Uḥud, where the enemy were encamped. 'Abdullah ibn Ubayy was much offended by the change of plan. He thought it unlikely that the Prophet really meant to give battle in conditions so adverse to the Muslims, and was unwilling to take part in a mere demonstration designed to flatter the fanatical extremists. So he withdrew with his men, a fourth of the army.

Despite the heavy odds, the battle on Mt. Uḥud would have been an even greater victory than that at Badr for the Muslims but for the

---

4. See also Sūrah 8, introductory note.

disobedience of a band of fifty archers whom the Prophet set to guard a pass against the enemy cavalry. Seeing their comrades victorious, these men left their post, fearing to lose their share of the spoils. The cavalry of Quraysh rode through the gap and fell on the exultant Muslims. The Prophet himself was wounded and the cry arose that he was slain, till someone recognised him and shouted that he was still living, a shout to which the Muslims rallied. Gathering round the Prophet, they retreated, leaving many dead on the hillside.[5]

On the following day the Prophet again sallied forth with what remained of the army, that Quraysh might hear that he was in the field and so might perhaps be deterred from attacking the city. The stratagem succeeded, thanks to the behaviour of a friendly Bedawi, who met the Muslims and conversed with them and afterwards met the army of Quraysh. Questioned by Abū Sufyān, he said that Muḥammad was in the field, stronger than ever, and thirsting for revenge for yesterday's affair. On that information, Abū Sufyān decided to return to Makkah.

Massacre of Muslims and expulsion of Banī Naḍīr

The reverse which they had suffered on Mt. Uḥud lowered the prestige of the Muslims with the Arab tribes and also with the Jews of Yathrib. Tribes which had inclined toward the Muslims now inclined toward Quraysh. The Prophet's followers were attacked and murdered when they went abroad in little companies. Khubayb, one of his envoys, was captured by a desert tribe and sold to Quraysh, who tortured him to death in Makkah publicly. And the Jews, despite their treaty, now hardly concealed their hostility. They even went so far in flattery of Quraysh as to declare the religion of the pagan Arabs superior to Al-Islām. (4:51) The Prophet was obliged to take punitive action against some of them. The tribe of Banī Naḍīr were besieged in their strong towers, subdued and forced to emigrate. The Hypocrites had sympathised with the Jews and secretly egged them on (Sūrah 59).

---

5. See also Sūrah 3, introductory note.

The War of the Trench

In the fifth year of the Hijrah the idolaters made a great effort to destroy Al-Islām in the War of the Clans or War of the Trench, as it is variously called; when Quraysh with all their clans and the great desert tribe of Ghaṭafān with all their clans, an army of ten thousand men rode against Al-Madīnah (Yathrib). The Prophet (by the advice of Salman the Persian, it is said) caused a deep trench to be dug before the city, and himself led the work of digging it. The army of the clans was stopped by the trench, a novelty in Arab warfare. It seemed impassable for cavalry, which formed their strength. They camped in sight of it and daily showered their arrows on its defenders. While the Muslims were awaiting the assault, news came that Banī Qurayẓah, a Jewish tribe of Yathrib which had till then been loyal, had gone over to the enemy. The case seemed desperate. But the delay caused by the trench had damped the ardour of the clans, and one who was secretly a Muslim managed to sow distrust between Quraysh and their Jewish allies, so that both hesitated to act. Then came a bitter wind from the sea, which blew for three days and nights so terribly that not a tent could be kept standing, not a fire lighted, not a pot boiled. The tribesmen were in utter misery. At length, one night the leader of Quraysh decided that the torment could be borne no longer and gave the order to retire.[6] When Ghaṭafān awoke next morning they found Quraysh had gone and they too took up their baggage and retreated.

Punishment of Banī Qurayẓah

On the day of the return from the trench the Prophet ordered war on the treacherous Banī Qurayẓah, who, conscious of their guilt, had already taken to their towers of refuge. After a siege of nearly a month they had to surrender unconditionally. They only begged that they might be judged by a member of the Arab tribe of which they were adherents.

---

6. See also Sūrah 32, introductory note.

The Prophet granted their request. But the judge, upon whose favour they had counted, condemned their men to death, their women and children to slavery.

The slander against 'Ā'ishah

Early in the sixth year of the Hijrah the Prophet led a campaign against the Banī'l-Mustaliq, a tribe who were preparing to attack the Muslims. It was during the return from that campaign that 'Ā'ishah, his young wife, was left behind and brought back to camp by a young soldier, an incident which gave rise to the scandal denounced in Sūrah 24 (24:11 ff.). It was on this campaign also that 'Abdullah ibn Ubayy, the "Hypocrite" chief, said: "When we return to the city the mightier will soon expel the weaker" (63:8) at sight of a quarrel between Muhājirīn (immigrants from Makkah) and Ansār (natives of Yathrib).

Al-Ḥudaybiyah

In the same year the Prophet had a vision (48:27) in which he found himself entering the holy place at Makkah unopposed; therefore he determined to attempt the pilgrimage. Besides a number of Muslims from Yathrib (which we shall henceforth call Al-Madīnah) he called upon the friendly Arabs, whose numbers had increased since the miraculous (as it was considered) discomfiture of the clans, to accompany him, but most of them did not respond (48:11 ff.). Attired as pilgrims, and taking with them the customary offerings, a company of fourteen hundred men journeyed to Makkah. As they drew near the holy valley, they were met by a friend from the city, who warned the Prophet that Quraysh had put on their leopard skins (the badge of valour) and had sworn to prevent his entering the sanctuary; their cavalry was on the road before him. On that, the Prophet ordered a detour through mountain gorges and the Muslims were tired out when they came down at last into the valley of Makkah and encamped at a spot called Al-Ḥudaybiyah; from thence he tried to open negotiations with Quraysh, explaining that he came only as a pilgrim. The first

messenger he sent towards the city was maltreated and his camel
hamstrung. He returned without delivering his message. Quraysh on
their side sent an envoy who was threatening in tone, and very arrogant.
Another of their envoys was too familiar and had to be reminded sternly
of the respect due to the Prophet. It was he who, on his return to the
city, said: "I have seen Caesar and Chosroes in their pomp, but never
have I seen a man honoured as Muhammad is honoured by his
comrades."

Truce of Al-Ḥudaybiyah

The Prophet sought some messenger who would impose respect.
'Uthmān was finally chosen because of his kinship with the powerful
Umayyad family. While the Muslims were awaiting his return the news
came that he had been murdered. It was then that the Prophet, sitting
under a tree (48:18) in Al-Ḥudaybiyah, took an oath from all his comrades that they would stand or fall together. After a while, however, it
became known that 'Uthmān had not been murdered. A troop which
came out from the city to molest the Muslims in their camp were
captured before they could do any hurt (48:24) and brought before the
Prophet; who forgave them on their promise to renounce hostility. Then
proper envoys came from Quraysh. After some negotiation, the truce of
Al-Ḥudaybiyah was signed. For ten years there were to be no hostilities
between the parties. The Prophet was to return to Al-Madīnah without
visiting the Ka'bah, but in the following year he might perform the
pilgrimage with his comrades, Quraysh promising to evacuate Makkah
for three days to allow of his doing so. Deserters from Quraysh to the
Muslims during the period of the truce were to be returned; not so
deserters from the Muslims to Quraysh. Any tribe or clan who wished
to share in the treaty as allies of the Prophet might do so, and any tribe
or clan who wished to share in the treaty as allies of Quraysh might do
so.

There was dismay among the Muslims at these terms. They asked
one another: "Where is the victory that we were promised?" It was

during the return journey from Al-Ḥudaybiyah that the sūrah entitled "Victory" (Sūrah 48) was revealed. This truce proved, in fact, to be the greatest victory that the Muslims had till then achieved. War had been a barrier between them and the idolaters, but now both parties met and talked together, and the new religion spread more rapidly. In the two years which elapsed between the signing of the truce and the fall of Makkah the number of converts was greater than the total number of all previous converts. The Prophet travelled to Al-Ḥudaybiyah with 1400 men. Two years later, when the Makkans broke the truce, he marched against them with an army of 10,000.

The campaign of Khaybar

In the seventh year of the Hijrah the Prophet led a campaign against Khaybar, the stronghold of the Jewish tribes in North Arabia, which had become a hornets' nest of his enemies. The forts of Khaybar were reduced one by one, and the Jews of Khaybar became thenceforth tenants of the Muslims until the expulsion of the Jews from Arabia in the Caliphate of 'Umar. On the day when the last fort surrendered Ja'far son of Abū Ṭālib, the Prophet's first cousin, arrived with all who remained of the Muslims who had fled to Abyssinia to escape from persecution in the early days. They had been absent from Arabia fifteen years. It was at Khaybar that a Jewess prepared for the Prophet poisoned meat, of which he only tasted a morsel without swallowing it, then warned his comrades that it was poisoned. One Muslim, who had already swallowed a mouthful, died immediately, and the Prophet himself, from the mere taste of it, derived the illness which eventually caused his death. The woman who had cooked the meat was brought before him. When she said that she had done it on account of the humiliation of her people, he forgave her.

Pilgrimage to Makkah

In the same year the Prophet's vision was fulfilled: he visited the holy place at Makkah unopposed. In accordance with the terms of the truce the idolaters evacuated the city, and from the surrounding heights watched the procedure of the Muslims. At the end of the stipulated three days the chiefs of Quraysh sent to remind the Prophet that the time was up. He then withdrew, and the idolaters reoccupied the city.

Mū'tah expedition

In the eighth year of the Hijrah, hearing that the Byzantine emperor was gathering a force in Syria for the destruction of Al-Islām, the Prophet sent three thousand men to Syria under the command of his freedman Zayd. The campaign was unsuccessful except that it impressed the Syrians with a notion of the reckless valour of the Muslims. The three thousand did not hesitate to join battle with a hundred thousand. When all the three leaders appointed by the Prophet had been killed, the survivors obeyed Khālid ibn al-Walīd, who, by his strategy and courage, managed to preserve a remnant and return with them to Al-Madīnah.

Truce broken by Quraysh

In the same year Quraysh broke the truce by attacking a tribe that was in alliance with the Prophet and massacring them even in the sanctuary at Makkah. Afterwards they were afraid because of what they had done. They sent Abū Sufyān to Al-Madīnah to ask for the existing treaty to be renewed and its term prolonged. They hoped that he would arrive before the tidings of the massacre. But a messenger from the injured tribe had been before him, and his embassy was fruitless.

Conquest of Makkah

Then the Prophet summoned all the Muslims capable of bearing arms and marched to Makkah. Quraysh were overawed. Their cavalry put up a show of defence before the town, but were routed without bloodshed; and the Prophet entered his native city as conqueror. The inhabitants expected vengeance for their past misdeeds. The Prophet proclaimed a general amnesty. Only a few known criminals were proscribed, and most of those were in the end forgiven. In their relief and surprise, the whole population of Makkah hastened to swear allegiance. The Prophet caused all the idols which were in the sanctuary to be destroyed, saying: "Truth hath come; darkness hath vanished away;" (17:81) and the Muslim call to prayer was heard in Makkah.

Battle of Ḥunayn

In the same year there was an angry gathering of pagan tribes eager to regain the Ka'bah. The Prophet led twelve thousand men against them. At Ḥunayn, in a deep ravine, his troops were ambushed by the enemy and almost put to flight. It was with difficulty that they were rallied to the Prophet and his bodyguard of faithful comrades who alone stood firm. But the victory, when it came, was complete and the booty enormous, for many of the hostile tribes had brought out with them everything that they possessed.

Conquest of Ṭā'if

The tribe of Thaqīf were among the enemy at Ḥunayn. After that victory their city of Ṭā'if was besieged by the Muslims, and finally reduced. Then the Prophet appointed a governor of Makkah, and himself returned to Al-Madīnah to the boundless joy of the Anṣār, who had feared lest, now that he had regained his native city, he might forsake them and make Makkah the capital.

The Tabūk expedition

In the ninth year of the Hijrah, hearing that an army was again being mustered in Syria, the Prophet called on all the Muslims to support him in a great campaign. The far distance, the hot season, the fact that it was harvest time and the prestige of the enemy caused many to excuse themselves and many more to stay behind without excuse. Those defaulters are denounced in the Qur'an (9:38-99). But the campaign ended peacefully. The army advanced to Tabūk, on the confines of Syria, and there learnt that the enemy had not yet gathered.

Declaration of Immunity

Although Makkah had been conquered and its people were now Muslims, the official order of the pilgrimage had not been changed; the pagan Arabs performing it in their manner, and the Muslims in their manner. It was only after the pilgrims' caravan had left Al-Madinah in the ninth year of the Hijrah, when Al-Islām was dominant in North Arabia, that the Declaration of Immunity, (9:1-12) as it is called, was revealed. The Prophet sent a copy of it by messenger to Abū Bakr, leader of the pilgrimage, with the instruction that 'Alī was to read it to the multitudes at Makkah. Its purport was that after that year Muslims only were to make the pilgrimage, exception being made for such of the idolaters as had a treaty with the Muslims and had never broken their treaty nor supported anyone against them. Such were to enjoy the privileges of their treaty for the term thereof, but when their treaty expired they would be as other idolaters. That proclamation marks the end of idol-worship in Arabia.

The Year of Deputations

The ninth year of the Hijrah is called the Year of Deputations, because from all parts of Arabia deputations came to Al-Madinah (Sūrah 49) to swear allegiance to the Prophet and to hear the Qur'an. The Prophet had become, in fact, the emperor of Arabia, but his way of life remained as simple as before.

The number of the campaigns which he led in person during the last ten years of his life is twenty-seven, in nine of which there was hard fighting. The number of the expeditions which he planned and sent out under other leaders is thirty-eight. He personally controlled every detail of organisation, judged every case and was accessible to every suppliant. In those ten years he destroyed idolatry in Arabia; raised woman from the status of a chattel to complete legal equality with man; effectually stopped the drunkenness and immorality which had till then disgraced the Arabs; made men in love with faith, sincerity and honest dealing; transformed tribes who had been for centuries content with ignorance into a people with the greatest thirst for knowledge; and for the first time in history made universal human brotherhood a fact and principle of common law. And his support and guide in all that work was the Qur'an.

The Farewell Pilgrimage

In the tenth year of the Hijrah he went to Makkah as a pilgrim for the last time—his "pilgrimage of farewell" it is called—when from Mt. 'Arafāt he preached to an enormous throng of pilgrims. He reminded them of all the duties Al-Islām enjoined upon them, and that they would one day have to meet their Lord, who would judge each one of them according to his work. At the end of the discourse, he asked: "Have I not conveyed the Message?" And from that great multitude of men who a few months or years before had all been conscienceless idolaters the shout went up: "O Allah! Yes!" The Prophet said: "O Allah! Be Thou witness!"

Illness and death of the Prophet

It was during that last pilgrimage that the sūrah entitled "Succour" (Sūrah 110) was revealed, which he received as an announcement of approaching death. Soon after his return to Al-Madīnah he fell ill. The tidings of his illness caused dismay throughout Arabia and anguish to the folk of Al-Madīnah, Makkah and Ṭā'if, the hometowns. At early dawn on the last day of his earthly life he came out from his room beside the mosque at Al-Madīnah and joined the public prayer, which Abū Bakr had been leading since his illness. And there was great relief among the people, who supposed him well again. When, later in the day, the rumour grew that he was dead, 'Umar threatened those who spread the rumour with dire punishment, declaring it a crime to think that the Messenger of God could die. He was storming at the people in that strain when Abū Bakr came into the mosque and overheard him. Abū Bakr went to the chamber of his daughter 'Ā'ishah, where the Prophet lay. Having ascertained the fact, and kissed the dead man's

forehead, he went back into the mosque. The people were still listening
to 'Umar, who was saying that the rumour was a wicked lie, that the
Prophet who was all in all to them could not be dead. Abū Bakr went
up to 'Umar and tried to stop him by a whispered word. Then, finding
he would pay no heed, Abū Bakr called to the people, who, recognising
his voice, left 'Umar and came crowding round him. He first gave
praise to Allah, and then said: "O people! Lo! as for him who used to
worship Muḥammad, Muḥammad is dead. But as for him who used to
worship Allah, Allah is Alive and dieth not." He then recited the verse
of the Qur'an:

> *And Muhammad is but a messenger, messengers the like of whom*
> *have passed away before him. Will it be that, when he dieth or is*
> *slain, ye will turn back on your heels? He who turneth back doth*
> *no hurt to Allah, and Allah will reward the thankful.* (3:144).

"And," says the narrator, an eye-witness, "it was as if the people
had not known that such a verse had been revealed till Abū Bakr recited
it." And another witness tells how 'Umar used to say: "Directly I heard
Abū Bakr recite that verse my feet were cut from beneath me and I fell
to the ground, for I knew that Allah's messenger was dead. May Allah
bless and keep him!"

All the sūrahs of the Qur'an had been recorded in writing before
the Prophet's death, and many Muslims had committed the whole
Qur'an to memory. But the written sūrahs were dispersed among the
people; and when, in a battle which took place during the Caliphate of
Abū Bakr—that is to say, within two years of the Prophet's death—a
large number of those who knew the whole Qur'an by heart were killed,
a collection of the whole Qur'an was made and put in writing. In the
Caliphate of 'Uthmān, all existing copies of sūrahs were called in, and
an authoritative version, based on Abū Bakr's collection and the
testimony of those who had the whole Qur'an by heart, was compiled
exactly in the present form and order, which is regarded as traditional
and as the arrangement of the Prophet himself, the Caliph 'Uthmān and

his helpers being Comrades of the Prophet and the most devout students of the Revelation. The Qur'an has thus been very carefully preserved.

The arrangement is not easy to understand. Revelations of various dates and on different subjects are to be found together in one sūrah; verses of Madīnah revelation are found in Makkan sūrahs; some of the Madinah sūrahs, though of late revelation, are placed first and the very early Makkan sūrahs at the end. But the arrangement is not haphazard, as some have hastily supposed. Closer study will reveal a sequence and significance—as, for instance, with regard to the placing of the very early Makkan sūrahs at the end. The inspiration of the Prophet progressed from inmost things to outward things, whereas most people find their way through outward things to things within.

There is another peculiarity which is disconcerting in translation though it proceeds from one of the beauties of the original, and is unavoidable without abolishing the verse-division of great importance for reference. In the Arabic the verses are divided according to the rhythm of the language. When a certain sound which marks the rhythm recurs there is a strong pause and the verse ends naturally, although the sentence may go on to the next verse or to several subsequent verses. That is of the spirit of the Arabic language; but attempts to reproduce such rhythm in English have the opposite effect to that produced by the Arabic. Here only the division is preserved, the verses being divided as in the Qur'an, and numbered.

Al Fātiḥah
(The Opening)

Al Fātiḥah, "The Opening" or *Fātiḥatu'l-Kitāb*, "The Opening of the Scripture" or *Ummu'l-Qur'ān*, "The Essence of the Qur'an," as it is variously named, has been called the Lord's Prayer of the Muslims. It is an essential part of all Muslim worship, public and private, and no solemn contract or transaction is complete unless it is recited. The date of revelation is uncertain, but the fact that it has always, from the very earliest times, formed a part of Muslim worship, there being no record or remembrance of its introduction, or of public prayer without it, makes it clear that it was revealed before the fourth year of the Prophet's Mission (the tenth year before the Hijrah); because we know for certain that by that time regular congregational prayers were offered by the little group of Muslims in Makkah. In that year, as the result of insult and attack[1] by the idolaters, the Prophet arranged for the services, which had till then been held out of doors, to take place in a private house.

This sūrah is also often called *Saba'an min al-Mathāni*, "Seven of the Oft-repeated" ("verses" being understood), sūrah 15: 87, words which are taken as referring to this sūrah.[2]

---

1. Ibn Hishām, *Sīrah* (Cairo Ed.), part I, p.88.

2. See Nöldeke, *Geschichte des Qoráns*, Zweite Auflage, bearbeitet von Fr. Schwally, part I, pp. 110 seq.

Translator's Note: I have retained the word Allah throughout, because there is no corresponding word in English. The word *Allāh* (the stress is in the last syllable) has neither feminine nor plural, and has never been applied to anything other than the unimaginable Supreme Being. I use the word "God" only where the corresponding word *ilāh* is found in the Arabic.

The words in brackets are interpolated to explain the meaning.

سُورَةُ الفَاتِحَةِ

بِسْمِ اللهِ الرَّحْمَنِ الرَّحِيمِ ١

الْحَمْدُ لِلّهِ رَبِّ الْعَالَمِينَ ٢

الرَّحْمَنِ الرَّحِيمِ ٣   مَلِكِ يَوْمِ الدِّينِ ٤

إِيَّاكَ نَعْبُدُ وَإِيَّاكَ نَسْتَعِينُ ٥

اهْدِنَا الصِّرَاطَ الْمُسْتَقِيمَ ٦

صِرَاطَ الَّذِينَ أَنْعَمْتَ عَلَيْهِمْ غَيْرِ

الْمَغْضُوبِ عَلَيْهِمْ وَلَا الضَّالِّينَ ٧

1. In the name of Allah, the Beneficent, the Merciful.

2. Praise be to Allah, Lord of the Worlds,

3. The Beneficent, the Merciful.

4. Owner of the Day of Judgement,

5. Thee (alone) we worship;

Thee (alone) we ask for help.

6. Show us the straight path,

7. The path of those whom Thou hast favoured;

Not (the path) of those who earn Thine anger

nor of those who go astray.

Al Baqarah
(The Cow)

Al Baqarah (The Cow) is so named from the story of the yellow heifer (vv. 67-71). As is the case with many other sūrahs, the title is taken from some word or incident which surprised the listeners. All suggestions to the contrary notwithstanding, it seems probable that the whole of this sūrah was revealed during the first four years after the Hijrah, and that by far the greater portion of it was revealed in the first eighteen months of the Prophet's reign at Al-Madīnah—that is to say, before the battle of Badr.[1]

The Jewish tribes, once paramount in Yathrib had, not very long before the coming of Al-Islām, been reduced by the pagan Arab tribes of Aws and Khazraj, each Jewish tribe becoming an adherent of one or the other. But they had preserved a sort of intellectual ascendancy owing to their possession of the Scripture and their fame for occult science, the pagan Arabs consulting their rabbis on occasions and paying heed to what they said. Before the coming of Al-Islām,[2] these Jewish rabbis had often told their neighbours that a Prophet was about to come, and had often threatened them that, when he came, they (the Jews) would destroy the pagan Arabs as the tribes of 'Ād and Thamūd had been destroyed of old.[3] So plainly did they describe the coming prophet that pilgrims from Yathrib recognised the Prophet, when he addressed them in Makkah, as the same whom the Jewish doctors had described to them. But the Jewish idea of a Prophet was one who would give them dominion, not one who would make them brethren of every

---

1. Th. Nöldeke, *Geschichte des Qorans*, Zweite Auflage, bearbeitet von Fr. Schwally, part I, pp. 173 seq.

2. *Al-Islām means* "The Surrender"-i.e. man's surrender to God's will and purpose.

3. Ibn Hishām (Cairo Ed.), Part I, pp. 180 seq.

3

pagan Arab who chose to accept Al-Islām. When they found that they could not make use of the newcomer, they opposed him and tried to bewilder him with questions from their theology, speaking to him as men who possessed superior wisdom; failing to perceive that, from a Prophet's standpoint, theology is childish nonsense, the very opposite of religion, and its enemy; religion, for the Prophet, being not a matter of conjecture and speech, but of fact and conduct.

Ibn Ishāq[4] states definitely that vv. 1-141 were revealed concerning these Jewish rabbis and such of the new converts to Al-Islām as were half-hearted and inclined to them. There follows the order to change the *Qiblah* (the place toward which the Muslims turn their face in prayer) from Jerusalem to the Ka'bah at Makkah, which was built by Abraham, the choice of Jerusalem having led to a misunderstanding on the part of the Jews that the prophet was groping his way toward their religion and stood in need of their guidance and instruction.

All through the sūrah runs the note of warning, which sounds indeed throughout the whole Qur'an, that it is not the mere profession of a creed, but righteous conduct, which is true religion. There is the repeated announcement that the religion of Abraham, to which Judaism and Christianity(which springs from Judaism) trace their origin, is the only true religion and that that religion consists in the surrender of man's will and purpose to the will and Purpose of the Lord of Creation as manifested in His creation and revealed by way of guidance through successive Prophets. Of sincerity in that religion that one test is conduct, and the standard of that religion is for all alike.

At the time when this sūrah was revealed at Al-Madīnah, the Prophet's own tribe, the pagan Quraysh at Makkah, were preparing to attack the Muslims in their place of refuge. Cruel persecution was the lot of Muslims who had stayed in Makkan territory or who journeyed thither, and Muslims were being prevented from performing the

---

4. *Apud* Ibn Hishām, *Sīrah* (Cairo Ed.), pp. 189 seq.

pilgrimage. The possible necessity of fighting had been forseen in the terms of the oath, taken at Al-'Aqabah by the Muslims of Yathrib before the Flight, to defend the Prophet as they would their own wives and children, and the first commandment to fight was revealed to the Prophet before his flight from Makkah; but there was no actual fighting by the Muslims until the battle of Badr. Many of them were reluctant, having before been subject to a rule of strict non-violence. It was with difficulty that they could accept the idea of fighting even in self-defence, as can be seen from several verses in this sūrah; which contains also rules for fasting and the pilgrimage, bequests, almsgiving, divorce and contracts, and verses which discountenance usury, strong drink and gambling. It concludes with a statement of the universal character of Al-Islām, the religion of Allah's sovereignty, and a prayer for the forgiveness of shortcomings.

This sūrah might be described as the Qur'an in little. It contains mention of all the essential points of the Revelation, which are elaborated elsewhere. This accounts for the precedence given to it in the arrangement of the book.

The period of revelation is the years 1 and 2 A.H. for the most part, certain verses of legislation being considered as of later date.

In the name of Allah, the Beneficent, the Merciful.

1 Alif. Lām. Mīm.[5]

2 This is the Scripture whereof there is no doubt, a guidance unto those who ward off (evil).

3 Who believe in the unseen, and establish worship, and spend of that We have bestowed upon them;

4 And who believe in that which is revealed unto thee (Muhammad) and that which was revealed before thee, and are certain of the Here-after.

5 These depend on guidance from their Lord. These are the successful.

6 As for the disbelievers, whether thou warn them or thou warn them not it is all one for them; they believe not.

---

5. Three letters of the Arabic alphabet. Many sūrahs begin thus with letters of the alphabet. Opinions differ as to thier significance, the prevalent view being that they indicate some mystic words. Some have opined that they are merely the initials of the scribe. They are always included in the text and recited as part of it.

7 Allah has sealed their hearts and their hearing, and on their eyes there is a covering. Theirs will be an awful doom.

خَتَمَ اللّٰهُ عَلٰى قُلُوبِهِمْ وَعَلٰى سَمْعِهِمْ وَعَلٰٓى أَبْصَارِهِمْ غِشَاوَةٌ وَّلَهُمْ عَذَابٌ عَظِيمٌ ۝

8 And of mankind are some who say: We believe in Allah and the Last Day, when they believe not.

وَمِنَ النَّاسِ مَنْ يَّقُوْلُ ءَامَنَّا بِاللّٰهِ وَبِالْيَوْمِ الْاٰخِرِ وَمَا هُمْ بِمُؤْمِنِيْنَ ۝

9 They think to beguile Allah and those who believe, and they beguile none save themselves; but they perceive not.

يُخَادِعُوْنَ اللّٰهَ وَالَّذِيْنَ ءَامَنُوْا وَمَا يَخْدَعُوْنَ إِلَّآ أَنْفُسَهُمْ وَمَا يَشْعُرُوْنَ ۝

10 In their hearts is a disease, and Allah increaseth their disease. A painful doom theirs because they lie.

فِيْ قُلُوْبِهِمْ مَّرَضٌ فَزَادَهُمُ اللّٰهُ مَرَضًا وَّلَهُمْ عَذَابٌ أَلِيْمٌ بِمَا كَانُوْا يَكْذِبُوْنَ ۝

11 And when it is said unto them: Make not mischief in the earth, they say: We are peacemakers only.

وَإِذَا قِيْلَ لَهُمْ لَا تُفْسِدُوْا فِى الْأَرْضِ قَالُوْٓا إِنَّمَا نَحْنُ مُصْلِحُوْنَ ۝

12 Beware! They indeed are the mischief-makers. But they perceive not.

أَلَآ إِنَّهُمْ هُمُ الْمُفْسِدُوْنَ وَلٰكِنْ لَّا يَشْعُرُوْنَ ۝

13 And when it is said unto them: Believe as the people believe, they say: Shall we believe as the foolish believe? Beware! They indeed are the foolish. But they know not.[6]

وَإِذَا قِيْلَ لَهُمْ ءَامِنُوْا كَمَآ ءَامَنَ النَّاسُ قَالُوْٓا أَنُؤْمِنُ كَمَآ ءَامَنَ السُّفَهَآءُ أَلَآ إِنَّهُمْ هُمُ السُّفَهَآءُ وَلٰكِنْ لَّا يَعْلَمُوْنَ ۝

---

6. *i.e.* the people of Al-Madīnah, most of whom were Muslims, vv. 8 to 19 refer to the "Hypocrites" or lukewarm Muslims of Al-Madīnah, whose leader Abdullah ibn Ubayy. They pretended that their aim was to make peace between the Muslims and the Jewish rabbis, but they only embittered the controversy.

14 And when they fall in with
those who believe, they say: We
believe; but when they go apart to
their devils they declare: Lo! we are
with you; verily we did but mock.

وَإِذَا لَقُوا الَّذِينَ ءَامَنُوا قَالُوٓا ءَامَنَّا وَإِذَا
خَلَوْا إِلَىٰ شَيَٰطِينِهِمْ قَالُوٓا إِنَّا مَعَكُمْ إِنَّمَا نَحْنُ
مُسْتَهْزِءُونَ ۝

15 Allah (Himself) doth mock
them, leaving them to wander
blindly on in their contumacy.

اللَّهُ يَسْتَهْزِئُ بِهِمْ وَيَمُدُّهُمْ فِي طُغْيَٰنِهِمْ
يَعْمَهُونَ ۝

16 These are they who purchase
error at the price of guidance, so
their commerce doth not prosper,
neither are they guided.

أُوْلَٰٓئِكَ الَّذِينَ اشْتَرَوُا الضَّلَٰلَةَ بِالْهُدَىٰ فَمَا
رَبِحَت تِّجَٰرَتُهُمْ وَمَا كَانُوا مُهْتَدِينَ ۝

17 Their likeness is as the likeness
of one who kindleth fire, and when
it sheddeth its light around him
Allah taketh away their light and
leaveth them in darkness, where
they cannot see,

مَثَلُهُمْ كَمَثَلِ الَّذِى اسْتَوْقَدَ نَارًا فَلَمَّآ
أَضَآءَتْ مَا حَوْلَهُ ذَهَبَ اللَّهُ بِنُورِهِمْ
وَتَرَكَهُمْ فِي ظُلُمَٰتٍ لَّا يُبْصِرُونَ ۝

18 Deaf, dumb and blind; and they
return not

صُمٌّ بُكْمٌ عُمْىٌ فَهُمْ لَا يَرْجِعُونَ ۝

19 Or like a rainstorm from the
sky, wherein is darkness, thunder
and the flash of lightning. They
thrust their fingers in their ears by
reason of the thunder-claps, for fear
of dead Allah encompasseth the disbelievers (in His guidance).

أَوْ كَصَيِّبٍ مِّنَ السَّمَآءِ فِيهِ ظُلُمَٰتٌ وَرَعْدٌ
وَبَرْقٌ يَجْعَلُونَ أَصَٰبِعَهُمْ فِيٓ ءَاذَانِهِم مِّنَ الصَّوَٰعِقِ
حَذَرَ الْمَوْتِ وَاللَّهُ مُحِيطٌ بِالْكَٰفِرِينَ ۝

20 The lightning almost snatcheth away their sight from them. As often as it flasheth forth for them they walk therein, and when it darkeneth against them they stand still. If Allah willed, He could destroy their hearing and their sight Lo! Allah is Able to do all things.

21 O mankind! Worship your Lord, Who hath created you and those before you, so that ye may ward off (evil).

22 Who hath appointed the earth a resting-place for you, and the sky a canopy; and causeth water to pour down from the sky, thereby producing fruits as food for you. And do not set up rivals to Allah when ye know (better).

23 And if ye are in doubt concerning that which We reveal unto Our slave[7] (Muhammad), then produce a sūrah or the like thereof, and call your witnesses beside Allah if ye are truthful.

24 And if ye do it not—and ye can never do it—then guard yourselves against the fire prepared for disbelievers, whose fuel is of men and stones.

يَكَادُ الْبَرْقُ يَخْطَفُ أَبْصَارَهُمْ كُلَّمَا أَضَاءَ لَهُمْ مَّشَوْا فِيهِ وَإِذَا أَظْلَمَ عَلَيْهِمْ قَامُوا وَلَوْ شَاءَ اللَّهُ لَذَهَبَ بِسَمْعِهِمْ وَأَبْصَارِهِمْ إِنَّ اللَّهَ عَلَى كُلِّ شَيْءٍ قَدِيرٌ ﴿٢٠﴾

يَا أَيُّهَا النَّاسُ اعْبُدُوا رَبَّكُمُ الَّذِي خَلَقَكُمْ وَالَّذِينَ مِن قَبْلِكُمْ لَعَلَّكُمْ تَتَّقُونَ ﴿٢١﴾

الَّذِي جَعَلَ لَكُمُ الْأَرْضَ فِرَاشًا وَالسَّمَاءَ بِنَاءً وَأَنزَلَ مِنَ السَّمَاءِ مَاءً فَأَخْرَجَ بِهِ مِنَ الثَّمَرَاتِ رِزْقًا لَّكُمْ فَلَا تَجْعَلُوا لِلَّهِ أَندَادًا وَأَنتُمْ تَعْلَمُونَ ﴿٢٢﴾

وَإِن كُنتُمْ فِي رَيْبٍ مِّمَّا نَزَّلْنَا عَلَى عَبْدِنَا فَأْتُوا بِسُورَةٍ مِّن مِّثْلِهِ وَادْعُوا شُهَدَاءَكُم مِّن دُونِ اللَّهِ إِن كُنتُمْ صَادِقِينَ ﴿٢٣﴾

فَإِن لَّمْ تَفْعَلُوا وَلَن تَفْعَلُوا فَاتَّقُوا النَّارَ الَّتِي وَقُودُهَا النَّاسُ وَالْحِجَارَةُ أُعِدَّتْ لِلْكَافِرِينَ ﴿٢٤﴾

---

7. To be the slave of Allah is the proudest boast of the Muslim, bondage to Allah liberating from all other servitudes. In the Qur'an mankind are often called God's slaves or bondmen, a stronger and more just expression than the word "servants" generally substituted in translations.

25 And give glad tidings (O
Muhammad) unto those who
believe and do good works; that
theirs are Gardens underneath
which rivers flow; as often as they
are regaled with food of the fruit
thereof, they say: This is what was
given us aforetime;[8] and it is given
to them in resemblance. There for
them are pure companions; there for
ever they abide.

وَبَشِّرِ الَّذِينَ ءَامَنُوا وَعَمِلُوا الصَّـٰلِحَـٰتِ
أَنَّ لَهُمْ جَنَّـٰتٍ تَجْرِى مِن تَحْتِهَا الْأَنْهَـٰرُ
كُلَّمَا رُزِقُوا مِنْهَا مِن ثَمَرَةٍ رِّزْقًا قَالُوا
هَـٰذَا الَّذِى رُزِقْنَا مِن قَبْلُ وَأُتُوا بِهِ مُتَشَـٰبِهًا
وَلَهُمْ فِيهَا أَزْوَٰجٌ مُّطَهَّرَةٌ وَهُمْ فِيهَا
خَـٰلِدُونَ ٢٥

26 Lo! Allah disdaineth not to coin
the similitude even of a gnat or even
anything above that. Those who
believe know that it is the truth
from their Lord; but those who disbelieve say: What doth Allah wish
(to teach) by such a similitude? He
misleadeth many thereby, and He
guideth many thereby; and He
misleadeth thereby only miscreants;

۞ إِنَّ اللَّهَ لَا يَسْتَحْىِۦٓ أَن يَضْرِبَ مَثَلًا مَّا
بَعُوضَةً فَمَا فَوْقَهَا فَأَمَّا الَّذِينَ ءَامَنُوا
فَيَعْلَمُونَ أَنَّهُ الْحَقُّ مِن رَّبِّهِمْ وَأَمَّا الَّذِينَ
كَفَرُوا فَيَقُولُونَ مَاذَآ أَرَادَ اللَّهُ بِهَـٰذَا
مَثَلًا يُضِلُّ بِهِۦ كَثِيرًا وَيَهْدِى بِهِۦ
كَثِيرًا وَمَا يُضِلُّ بِهِۦٓ إِلَّا الْفَـٰسِقِينَ ٢٦

27 Those who break the covenant of
Allah after ratifying it and sever that
which Allah ordered to be joined,
and (who) make mischief in the
earth: Those are they who are the
losers

الَّذِينَ يَنقُضُونَ عَهْدَ اللَّهِ مِنۢ بَعْدِ مِيثَـٰقِهِۦ
وَيَقْطَعُونَ مَآ أَمَرَ اللَّهُ بِهِۦٓ أَن يُوصَلَ
وَيُفْسِدُونَ فِى الْأَرْضِ أُوْلَـٰٓئِكَ هُمُ
الْخَـٰسِرُونَ ٢٧

28 How disbelieve ye in Allah when
ye were dead and He gave life to
you! Then he will give you death,
then life again, and then unto Him
ye will return.

كَيْفَ تَكْفُرُونَ بِاللَّهِ وَكُنتُمْ أَمْوَٰتًا
فَأَحْيَـٰكُمْ ثُمَّ يُمِيتُكُمْ ثُمَّ يُحْيِيكُمْ
ثُمَّ إِلَيْهِ تُرْجَعُونَ ٢٨

---

8. The joys of Paradise will recall, in a rapturous degree, the joys the righteous tasted
in their life on earth.

29 He it is Who created for you all
that is in the earth. Then turned He
to the heaven, and fashioned it as
seven heavens. And He is Knower
of all things.

هُوَ ٱلَّذِى خَلَقَ لَكُم مَّا فِى ٱلْأَرْضِ جَمِيعًا
ثُمَّ ٱسْتَوَىٰٓ إِلَى ٱلسَّمَآءِ فَسَوَّىٰهُنَّ سَبْعَ
سَمَٰوَٰتٍ وَهُوَ بِكُلِّ شَىْءٍ عَلِيمٌ ﴿٢٩﴾

30 And when thy Lord said unto
the angels: Lo! I am about to place
a viceroy in the earth, they said:
wilt Thou place therein one who
will do harm therein and will shed
blood, while we, we hymn Thy
praise and sanctify Thee? He said:
Surely I know that which ye know
not.

وَإِذْ قَالَ رَبُّكَ لِلْمَلَٰٓئِكَةِ إِنِّى جَاعِلٌ فِى
ٱلْأَرْضِ خَلِيفَةً ۖ قَالُوٓا۟ أَتَجْعَلُ فِيهَا مَن يُفْسِدُ
فِيهَا وَيَسْفِكُ ٱلدِّمَآءَ وَنَحْنُ نُسَبِّحُ بِحَمْدِكَ
وَنُقَدِّسُ لَكَ ۖ قَالَ إِنِّىٓ أَعْلَمُ مَا لَا تَعْلَمُونَ ﴿٣٠﴾

31 And He taught Adam all the
names,[9] then showed them to the
angels, saying: Inform me of the
names of these, if ye are truthful.

وَعَلَّمَ ءَادَمَ ٱلْأَسْمَآءَ كُلَّهَا ثُمَّ عَرَضَهُمْ عَلَى
ٱلْمَلَٰٓئِكَةِ فَقَالَ أَنۢبِـُٔونِى بِأَسْمَآءِ هَٰٓؤُلَآءِ
إِن كُنتُمْ صَٰدِقِينَ ﴿٣١﴾

32 They said: Be glorified! We
have no knowledge saving that
which Thou hast taught us. Lo!
Thou, only Thou, art the Knower,
the Wise.

قَالُوا۟ سُبْحَٰنَكَ لَا عِلْمَ لَنَآ إِلَّا مَا عَلَّمْتَنَآ ۖ إِنَّكَ
أَنتَ ٱلْعَلِيمُ ٱلْحَكِيمُ ﴿٣٢﴾

33 He said: O Adam! Inform them
of their names, and when he had
informed them of their names, He
said: Did I not tell you that I know
the secret of the heavens and the
earth? And I know that which ye
disclose and which ye hide.

قَالَ يَٰٓـَٔادَمُ أَنۢبِئْهُم بِأَسْمَآئِهِمْ ۖ فَلَمَّآ أَنۢبَأَهُم
بِأَسْمَآئِهِمْ قَالَ أَلَمْ أَقُل لَّكُمْ إِنِّىٓ أَعْلَمُ غَيْبَ
ٱلسَّمَٰوَٰتِ وَٱلْأَرْضِ وَأَعْلَمُ مَا تُبْدُونَ وَمَا كُنتُمْ
تَكْتُمُونَ ﴿٣٣﴾

---

9. Some especially Sūfīs, hold "the names" to be the attributes of Allah; others, the
names of animals and plants.

34 And when We said unto the angels: Prostrate yourselves before Adam, they fell prostrate, all save Iblīs; he demurred through pride, and so became a disbeliever.

وَإِذْ قُلْنَا لِلْمَلَٰٓئِكَةِ ٱسْجُدُواْ لِأٓدَمَ فَسَجَدُوٓاْ إِلَّآ إِبْلِيسَ أَبَىٰ وَٱسْتَكْبَرَ وَكَانَ مِنَ ٱلْكَٰفِرِينَ ﴿٣٤﴾

35 And We said: O Adam! Dwell thou and thy wife in the Garden, and eat ye[10] freely (of the fruits) thereof where ye will; but come not nigh this tree lest ye become wrong-doers.

وَقُلْنَا يَٰٓـَٔادَمُ ٱسْكُنْ أَنتَ وَزَوْجُكَ ٱلْجَنَّةَ وَكُلَا مِنْهَا رَغَدًا حَيْثُ شِئْتُمَا وَلَا تَقْرَبَا هَٰذِهِ ٱلشَّجَرَةَ فَتَكُونَا مِنَ ٱلظَّٰلِمِينَ ﴿٣٥﴾

36 But Satan caused them to deflect therefrom and expelled them from the (happy) state in which they were; and We said: Fall down,[11] one of you a foe unto the other! There shall be for you on earth a habit-ation and provision for a tune.

فَأَزَلَّهُمَا ٱلشَّيْطَٰنُ عَنْهَا فَأَخْرَجَهُمَا مِمَّا كَانَا فِيهِ وَقُلْنَا ٱهْبِطُواْ بَعْضُكُمْ لِبَعْضٍ عَدُوٌّ وَلَكُمْ فِى ٱلْأَرْضِ مُسْتَقَرٌّ وَمَتَٰعٌ إِلَىٰ حِينٍ ﴿٣٦﴾

37 Then Adam received from his Lord words (of revelation), and He relented toward him. Lo! He is the Relenting, the Merciful.

فَتَلَقَّىٰٓ ءَادَمُ مِن رَّبِّهِۦ كَلِمَٰتٍ فَتَابَ عَلَيْهِ إِنَّهُۥ هُوَ ٱلتَّوَّابُ ٱلرَّحِيمُ ﴿٣٧﴾

38 We said: Go down, all of you, from hence; but verily there cometh unto you from Me a guidance; and whoso followeth My guidance, there shall no fear come upon them neither shall they grieve.

قُلْنَا ٱهْبِطُواْ مِنْهَا جَمِيعًا فَإِمَّا يَأْتِيَنَّكُم مِّنِّى هُدًى فَمَن تَبِعَ هُدَاىَ فَلَا خَوْفٌ عَلَيْهِمْ وَلَا هُمْ يَحْزَنُونَ ﴿٣٨﴾

39 But they who disbelieve, and deny our revelations, such are right-ful owners of the Fire. They will abide therein.

وَٱلَّذِينَ كَفَرُواْ وَكَذَّبُواْ بِـَٔايَٰتِنَآ أُوْلَٰٓئِكَ أَصْحَٰبُ ٱلنَّارِ هُمْ فِيهَا خَٰلِدُونَ ﴿٣٩﴾

---

10. Here the command is in the dual, as addressed to Adam and his wife.

11. Here the command is in the plural, as addressed to Adam's race.

40 O Children of Israel! Remember My favor wherewith I favored you, and fulfil your (part of the) covenant, I shall fulfil My (part of the) covenant and fear Me.

يَٰبَنِىٓ إِسۡرَٰٓءِيلَ ٱذۡكُرُواْ نِعۡمَتِىَ ٱلَّتِىٓ أَنۡعَمۡتُ عَلَيۡكُمۡ وَأَوۡفُواْ بِعَهۡدِىٓ أُوفِ بِعَهۡدِكُمۡ وَإِيَّٰىَ فَٱرۡهَبُونِ ﴿٤٠﴾

41 And believe in that which I reveal, confirming that which ye possess already (of the Scripture), and be not first to disbelieve therein, and part not with My revelations for a trifling price, and keep your duty unto Me.

وَءَامِنُواْ بِمَآ أَنزَلۡتُ مُصَدِّقًا لِّمَا مَعَكُمۡ وَلَا تَكُونُوٓاْ أَوَّلَ كَافِرٍۭ بِهِۦ وَلَا تَشۡتَرُواْ بِـَٔايَٰتِى ثَمَنًا قَلِيلًا وَإِيَّٰىَ فَٱتَّقُونِ ﴿٤١﴾

42 Confound not truth with falsehood, nor knowingly conceal the truth.

وَلَا تَلۡبِسُواْ ٱلۡحَقَّ بِٱلۡبَٰطِلِ وَتَكۡتُمُواْ ٱلۡحَقَّ وَأَنتُمۡ تَعۡلَمُونَ ﴿٤٢﴾

43 Establish worship, pay the poor-due,[12] and bow your heads with those who bow (in worship).

وَأَقِيمُواْ ٱلصَّلَوٰةَ وَءَاتُواْ ٱلزَّكَوٰةَ وَٱرۡكَعُواْ مَعَ ٱلرَّٰكِعِينَ ﴿٤٣﴾

44 Enjoin ye righteousness upon mankind while ye yourselves forget (to practise it)? And ye are readers of the Scripture! Have ye then no sense?

۞ أَتَأۡمُرُونَ ٱلنَّاسَ بِٱلۡبِرِّ وَتَنسَوۡنَ أَنفُسَكُمۡ وَأَنتُمۡ تَتۡلُونَ ٱلۡكِتَٰبَ أَفَلَا تَعۡقِلُونَ ﴿٤٤﴾

45 Seek help in patience and prayer; and truly it is hard save for the humble-minded,

وَٱسۡتَعِينُواْ بِٱلصَّبۡرِ وَٱلصَّلَوٰةِ وَإِنَّهَا لَكَبِيرَةٌ إِلَّا عَلَى ٱلۡخَٰشِعِينَ ﴿٤٥﴾

46 Who know that they will have to meet their Lord, and that unto Him they are returning.

ٱلَّذِينَ يَظُنُّونَ أَنَّهُم مُّلَٰقُواْ رَبِّهِمۡ وَأَنَّهُمۡ إِلَيۡهِ رَٰجِعُونَ ﴿٤٦﴾

47 O Children of Israel! Remember My favor wherewith I favored you and how I preferred you to (all) creatures.

يَٰبَنِىٓ إِسۡرَٰٓءِيلَ ٱذۡكُرُواْ نِعۡمَتِىَ ٱلَّتِىٓ أَنۡعَمۡتُ عَلَيۡكُمۡ وَأَنِّى فَضَّلۡتُكُمۡ عَلَى ٱلۡعَٰلَمِينَ ﴿٤٧﴾

---

12. *Al-Zakāh*: A tax at a fixed rate in proportion to the worth of property, collected from the well-to-do and distributed among the poor Muslims.

48 And guard yourselves against a day when no soul will in aught avail another, nor will intercession be accepted from it, nor will compensation be received from it, nor will they be helped.

وَاتَّقُوا يَوْمًا لَّا تَجْزِى نَفْسٌ عَن نَّفْسٍ شَيْئًا وَلَا يُقْبَلُ مِنْهَا شَفَاعَةٌ وَلَا يُؤْخَذُ مِنْهَا عَدْلٌ وَلَاهُمْ يُنصَرُونَ ۝

49 And (remember) when We did deliver you from Pharaoh's folk, who were afflicting you with dreadful torment, slaying your sons and sparing your women: That was a tremendous trial from your Lord.

وَإِذْ نَجَّيْنَـٰكُم مِّنْ ءَالِ فِرْعَوْنَ يَسُومُونَكُمْ سُوٓءَ ٱلْعَذَابِ يُذَبِّحُونَ أَبْنَآءَكُمْ وَيَسْتَحْيُونَ نِسَآءَكُمْ وَفِى ذَٰلِكُم بَلَآءٌ مِّن رَّبِّكُمْ عَظِيمٌ ۝

50 And when We brought you through the sea and rescued you, and drowned the folk of Pharaoh in your sight.

وَإِذْ فَرَقْنَا بِكُمُ ٱلْبَحْرَ فَأَنجَيْنَـٰكُمْ وَأَغْرَقْنَآ ءَالَ فِرْعَوْنَ وَأَنتُمْ تَنظُرُونَ ۝

51 And when We did appoint for Moses forty nights (of solitude), and then ye chose the calf, when he had gone from you, and were wrong-doers.

وَإِذْ وَٰعَدْنَا مُوسَىٰٓ أَرْبَعِينَ لَيْلَةً ثُمَّ ٱتَّخَذْتُمُ ٱلْعِجْلَ مِنۢ بَعْدِهِۦ وَأَنتُمْ ظَـٰلِمُونَ ۝

52 Then, even after that, We pardoned you in order that ye might give thanks.

ثُمَّ عَفَوْنَا عَنكُم مِّنۢ بَعْدِ ذَٰلِكَ لَعَلَّكُمْ تَشْكُرُونَ ۝

53 And when We gave unto Moses the Scripture and the Criterion (of right and wrong), that ye might be led aright.

وَإِذْ ءَاتَيْنَا مُوسَى ٱلْكِتَـٰبَ وَٱلْفُرْقَانَ لَعَلَّكُمْ تَهْتَدُونَ ۝

54 And when Moses said unto his people: O my people! Ye have wronged yourselves by your choosing of the calf (for worship) so turn in penitence to your Creator, and kill (the guilty) yourselves. That will be best for you with your Creator and He will relent toward you. Lo! He is the Relenting, the Merciful.

وَإِذْ قَالَ مُوسَىٰ لِقَوْمِهِۦ يَـٰقَوْمِ إِنَّكُمْ ظَلَمْتُمْ أَنفُسَكُم بِٱتِّخَاذِكُمُ ٱلْعِجْلَ فَتُوبُوٓا۟ إِلَىٰ بَارِئِكُمْ فَٱقْتُلُوٓا۟ أَنفُسَكُمْ ذَٰلِكُمْ خَيْرٌ لَّكُمْ عِندَ بَارِئِكُمْ فَتَابَ عَلَيْكُمْ إِنَّهُۥ هُوَ ٱلتَّوَّابُ ٱلرَّحِيمُ ۝

55 And when ye said: O Moses! We will not believe in thee till we see Allah plainly; and even while ye gazed the lightning seized you.

56 Then We revived you after your extinction, that ye might give thanks.

57 And We caused the white cloud to overshadow you and sent down on you the manna and the quails, (saying): Eat of the good things wherewith We have provided you They wronged Us not, but they did wrong themselves.

58 "And when We said: Go into this township and eat freely of that which is therein, and enter the gate prostrate, and say: 'Repentance.' We will forgive you your sins and increase (reward) for the right-doers."

59 But those who did wrong changed the word which had been told them for another saying,[13] and We sent down upon the evil-doers wrath from Heaven for their evil doing.

60 And when Moses asked for water for his people, We said: Smite with thy staff the rock. And there gushed out therefrom twelve

وَإِذْ قُلْتُمْ يَمُوسَىٰ لَنْ نُؤْمِنَ لَكَ حَتَّىٰ نَرَى اللّٰهَ جَهْرَةً فَأَخَذَتْكُمُ الصَّٰعِقَةُ وَأَنتُمْ تَنظُرُونَ ۝

ثُمَّ بَعَثْنَٰكُم مِّنۢ بَعْدِ مَوْتِكُمْ لَعَلَّكُمْ تَشْكُرُونَ ۝

وَظَلَّلْنَا عَلَيْكُمُ الْغَمَامَ وَأَنزَلْنَا عَلَيْكُمُ الْمَنَّ وَالسَّلْوَىٰ كُلُوا مِن طَيِّبَٰتِ مَا رَزَقْنَٰكُمْ وَمَا ظَلَمُونَا وَلَٰكِن كَانُوٓا أَنفُسَهُمْ يَظْلِمُونَ ۝

وَإِذْ قُلْنَا ادْخُلُوا هَٰذِهِ الْقَرْيَةَ فَكُلُوا مِنْهَا حَيْثُ شِئْتُمْ رَغَدًا وَادْخُلُوا الْبَابَ سُجَّدًا وَقُولُوا حِطَّةٌ نَّغْفِرْ لَكُمْ خَطَٰيَٰكُمْ وَسَنَزِيدُ الْمُحْسِنِينَ ۝

فَبَدَّلَ الَّذِينَ ظَلَمُوا قَوْلًا غَيْرَ الَّذِى قِيلَ لَهُمْ فَأَنزَلْنَا عَلَى الَّذِينَ ظَلَمُوا رِجْزًا مِّنَ السَّمَآءِ بِمَا كَانُوا يَفْسُقُونَ ۝

وَإِذِ اسْتَسْقَىٰ مُوسَىٰ لِقَوْمِهِ فَقُلْنَا اضْرِب بِّعَصَاكَ الْحَجَرَ فَانفَجَرَتْ مِنْهُ اثْنَتَا عَشْرَةَ

---

13. According to a tradition of the Prophet, *Hittatun* is a word implying submission to Allah and repentance. The evil-doers changed it for a word of rebellion *i.e.* they were disobedient.

springs (so that) each tribe knew their drinking place. Eat and drink of that which Allah hath provided, and do not act corruptly, making mischief in the earth.

عَيۡنًا قَدۡ عَلِمَ كُلُّ أُنَاسٍ مَّشۡرَبَهُمۡ كُلُوۡا وَاشۡرَبُوۡا مِنۡ رِّزۡقِ اللّٰهِ وَلَا تَعۡثَوۡا فِى الۡاَرۡضِ مُفۡسِدِيۡنَ ۝

61 And when ye said: O Moses! We are weary of one kind of food; so call upon thy Lord for us that he bring forth for us of that which the earth groweth of its herbs and its cucumbers and its corn and its lentils and its onions. He said: Would ye exchange that which is higher for that which is lower? Go down to settled country, thus ye shall get that which ye demand. And humiliation and wretchedness were stamped upon them and they were visited with wrath from Allah. That was because they disbelieved in Allah's revelations and slew the prophets wrongfully. That was for their disobedience and transgression.

وَاِذۡ قُلۡتُمۡ يٰمُوۡسٰى لَنۡ نَّصۡبِرَ عَلٰى طَعَامٍ وَّاحِدٍ فَادۡعُ لَنَا رَبَّكَ يُخۡرِجۡ لَنَا مِمَّا تُنۢبِتُ الۡاَرۡضُ مِنۡ بَقۡلِهَا وَقِثَّآئِهَا وَفُوۡمِهَا وَعَدَسِهَا وَبَصَلِهَا ۖ قَالَ اَتَسۡتَبۡدِلُوۡنَ الَّذِىۡ هُوَ اَدۡنٰى بِالَّذِىۡ هُوَ خَيۡرٌ ۚ اِهۡبِطُوۡا مِصۡرًا فَاِنَّ لَكُمۡ مَّا سَاَلۡتُمۡ ۗ وَضُرِبَتۡ عَلَيۡهِمُ الذِّلَّةُ وَالۡمَسۡكَنَةُ ۖ وَبَآءُوۡ بِغَضَبٍ مِّنَ اللّٰهِ ۗ ذٰلِكَ بِاَنَّهُمۡ كَانُوۡا يَكۡفُرُوۡنَ بِاٰيٰتِ اللّٰهِ وَيَقۡتُلُوۡنَ النَّبِيّٖنَ بِغَيۡرِ الۡحَقِّ ۗ ذٰلِكَ بِمَا عَصَوۡا وَّكَانُوۡا يَعۡتَدُوۡنَ ۝

62 Lo! those who believe (in that which is revealed unto thee, Muḥammad), and those who are Jews, and Christians, and Sabaeans whoever believeth in Allah and the Last Day and doeth right surely their reward is with their Lord, and there shall no fear come upon them neither shall they grieve.

اِنَّ الَّذِيۡنَ اٰمَنُوۡا وَالَّذِيۡنَ هَادُوۡا وَالنَّصٰرٰى وَالصّٰبِئِيۡنَ مَنۡ اٰمَنَ بِاللّٰهِ وَالۡيَوۡمِ الۡاٰخِرِ وَعَمِلَ صَالِحًا فَلَهُمۡ اَجۡرُهُمۡ عِنۡدَ رَبِّهِمۡ ۖ وَلَا خَوۡفٌ عَلَيۡهِمۡ وَلَا هُمۡ يَحۡزَنُوۡنَ ۝

63 And (remember, O children of Israel) when We made a covenant with you and caused the Mount to

وَاِذۡ اَخَذۡنَا مِيۡثَاقَكُمۡ وَرَفَعۡنَا فَوۡقَكُمُ الطُّوۡرَ

tower above you, (saying): Hold
fast that which We have given you,
and remember that which is therein,
that ye may ward off (evil).

خُذُوا مَآ ءَاتَيْنَكُم بِقُوَّةٍ وَاذْكُرُوا مَا فِيهِ لَعَلَّكُمْ تَتَّقُونَ ۝

64 Then, even after that, ye turned
away, and if it had not been for the
grace of Allah upon you and His
mercy ye had been among the
losers.

ثُمَّ تَوَلَّيْتُم مِّنۢ بَعْدِ ذَٰلِكَ فَلَوْلَا فَضْلُ ٱللَّهِ عَلَيْكُمْ وَرَحْمَتُهُۥ لَكُنتُم مِّنَ ٱلْخَٰسِرِينَ ۝

65 And ye know of those of you
who broke the Sabbath, how We
said unto them: Be ye apes, despised and hated!

وَلَقَدْ عَلِمْتُمُ ٱلَّذِينَ ٱعْتَدَوْا مِنكُمْ فِى ٱلسَّبْتِ فَقُلْنَا لَهُمْ كُونُوا قِرَدَةً خَٰسِئِينَ ۝

66 And We made it an example to
their own and to succeeding generations, and an admonition to the
God fearing.

فَجَعَلْنَٰهَا نَكَٰلًا لِّمَا بَيْنَ يَدَيْهَا وَمَا خَلْفَهَا وَمَوْعِظَةً لِّلْمُتَّقِينَ ۝

67 And when Moses said unto his
people: Lo! Allah commandeth you
that ye sacrifice a cow, they said:
Dost thou make game of us? He
answered: Allah forbid that I should
be among the foolish!

وَإِذْ قَالَ مُوسَىٰ لِقَوْمِهِۦٓ إِنَّ ٱللَّهَ يَأْمُرُكُمْ أَن تَذْبَحُوا بَقَرَةً قَالُوٓا أَتَتَّخِذُنَا هُزُوًا قَالَ أَعُوذُ بِٱللَّهِ أَنْ أَكُونَ مِنَ ٱلْجَٰهِلِينَ ۝

68 They said: Pray for us unto thy
Lord that He make clear to us what
(cow) she is. (Moses) answered:
Lo! He saith, Verily she is a cow
neither with calf nor immature; (she
is) between the two conditions; so
do that which ye are commanded.

قَالُوا ٱدْعُ لَنَا رَبَّكَ يُبَيِّن لَّنَا مَا هِىَ قَالَ إِنَّهُۥ يَقُولُ إِنَّهَا بَقَرَةٌ لَّا فَارِضٌ وَلَا بِكْرٌ عَوَانٌ بَيْنَ ذَٰلِكَ فَٱفْعَلُوا مَا تُؤْمَرُونَ ۝

69 They said: Pray for us unto thy
Lord that He make clear to us of
what color she is. (Moses) answered: Lo! He saith: Verily she is a
yellow cow. Bright is her color,
gladdening beholders.

قَالُوا ٱدْعُ لَنَا رَبَّكَ يُبَيِّن لَّنَا مَا لَوْنُهَا قَالَ إِنَّهُۥ يَقُولُ إِنَّهَا بَقَرَةٌ صَفْرَآءُ فَاقِعٌ لَّوْنُهَا تَسُرُّ ٱلنَّٰظِرِينَ ۝

70 They said: Pray for us unto thy Lord that He make clear to us what (cow) she is. Lo! cows are much alike to us; and lo! if Allah wills, we may be led aright.

قَالُوا ادْعُ لَنَا رَبَّكَ يُبَيِّن لَّنَا مَا هِيَ إِنَّ الْبَقَرَ تَشَٰبَهَ عَلَيْنَا وَإِنَّا إِن شَآءَ اللَّهُ لَمُهْتَدُونَ ۞

71 (Moses) answered: Lo! He saith: Verily she is a cow unyoked; she plougheth not the soil nor watereth the tilth; whole and without mark. They said: Now thou bringest the truth. So they sacrificed her, though almost they did not.

قَالَ إِنَّهُ يَقُولُ إِنَّهَا بَقَرَةٌ لَّا ذَلُولٌ تُثِيرُ الْأَرْضَ وَلَا تَسْقِى الْحَرْثَ مُسَلَّمَةٌ لَّا شِيَةَ فِيهَا قَالُوا الْـٰٔنَ جِئْتَ بِالْحَقِّ فَذَبَحُوهَا وَمَا كَادُوا يَفْعَلُونَ ۞

72 And (remember) when ye slew a man and disagreed concerning it and Allah brought forth that which ye were hiding.

وَإِذْ قَتَلْتُمْ نَفْسًا فَادَّارَأْتُمْ فِيهَا وَاللَّهُ مُخْرِجٌ مَّا كُنتُمْ تَكْتُمُونَ ۞

73 And We said: Smite him with some of it. Thus Allah bringeth the dead to life and showeth you His portents so that ye may understand.[14]

فَقُلْنَا اضْرِبُوهُ بِبَعْضِهَا كَذَلِكَ يُحْيِ اللَّهُ الْمَوْتَىٰ وَيُرِيكُمْ ءَايَٰتِهِ لَعَلَّكُمْ تَعْقِلُونَ ۞

74 Then, even after that, your hearts were hardened and became as rocks, or worse than rocks, for hardness. For indeed there are rocks from out which rivers gush, and indeed there are rocks which split asunder so that water floweth from them. And indeed there are rocks which fall down for the fear of Allah. Allah is not unaware of what ye do.

ثُمَّ قَسَتْ قُلُوبُكُم مِّنْ بَعْدِ ذَٰلِكَ فَهِيَ كَالْحِجَارَةِ أَوْ أَشَدُّ قَسْوَةً وَإِنَّ مِنَ الْحِجَارَةِ لَمَا يَتَفَجَّرُ مِنْهُ الْأَنْهَٰرُ وَإِنَّ مِنْهَا لَمَا يَشَّقَّقُ فَيَخْرُجُ مِنْهُ الْمَآءُ وَإِنَّ مِنْهَا لَمَا يَهْبِطُ مِنْ خَشْيَةِ اللَّهِ وَمَا اللَّهُ بِغَٰفِلٍ عَمَّا تَعْمَلُونَ ۞

---

14. The old commentators tell various stories by way of explaining vv. 72 and 73; one of them concerning a miracle that happened at Al-Madīnah. For Maulvi Muhammad Ali's exposition of them as referring to the martydom of Jesus Christ (on whom be peace) see the footnote to v. 72 in his translation.

75 Have ye any hope that they will be true to you when a party of them used to listen to the Word of Allah, then used to change it, after they had understood it knowingly?

76 And when they fall in with those who believe, they say: We believe. But when they go apart one with another they say: Prate ye to them of that which Allah hath disclosed to you that they may contend with you before your Lord concerning it? Have ye then no sense?

77 Are they then unaware that Allah knoweth that which they keep hidden and that which they proclaim?

78 Among them are unlettered folk who know the scripture not except from hearsay. They but guess.

79 Therefore woe be unto those who write the Scripture with their hands and then say, "This is from Allah," that they may purchase a small gain therewith. Woe unto them for that their hands have written, and woe unto them for that they earn thereby.

80 And they say: The fire (of punishment) will not touch save for a certain number of days. Say: Have ye received a covenant from Allah truly Allah will not break His covenant or tell ye concerning Allah that which ye know not?

۞ اَفَتَطْمَعُوْنَ اَنْ يُّؤْمِنُوْا لَكُمْ وَقَدْ كَانَ فَرِيْقٌ مِّنْهُمْ يَسْمَعُوْنَ كَلَامَ اللّٰهِ ثُمَّ يُحَرِّفُوْنَهٗ مِنْۢ بَعْدِ مَا عَقَلُوْهُ وَهُمْ يَعْلَمُوْنَ ۝

وَ اِذَا لَقُوا الَّذِيْنَ اٰمَنُوْا قَالُوْا اٰمَنَّا ۖ وَاِذَا خَلَا بَعْضُهُمْ اِلٰى بَعْضٍ قَالُوْۤا اَتُحَدِّثُوْنَهُمْ بِمَا فَتَحَ اللّٰهُ عَلَيْكُمْ لِيُحَاۤجُّوْكُمْ بِهٖ عِنْدَ رَبِّكُمْ ۖ اَفَلَا تَعْقِلُوْنَ ۝

اَوَلَا يَعْلَمُوْنَ اَنَّ اللّٰهَ يَعْلَمُ مَا يُسِرُّوْنَ وَمَا يُعْلِنُوْنَ ۝

وَمِنْهُمْ اُمِّيُّوْنَ لَا يَعْلَمُوْنَ الْكِتٰبَ اِلَّاۤ اَمَانِيَّ وَاِنْ هُمْ اِلَّا يَظُنُّوْنَ ۝

فَوَيْلٌ لِّلَّذِيْنَ يَكْتُبُوْنَ الْكِتٰبَ بِاَيْدِيْهِمْ ثُمَّ يَقُوْلُوْنَ هٰذَا مِنْ عِنْدِ اللّٰهِ لِيَشْتَرُوْا بِهٖ ثَمَنًا قَلِيْلًا ۖ فَوَيْلٌ لَّهُمْ مِّمَّا كَتَبَتْ اَيْدِيْهِمْ وَوَيْلٌ لَّهُمْ مِّمَّا يَكْسِبُوْنَ ۝

وَقَالُوْا لَنْ تَمَسَّنَا النَّارُ اِلَّاۤ اَيَّامًا مَّعْدُوْدَةً ۚ قُلْ اَتَّخَذْتُمْ عِنْدَ اللّٰهِ عَهْدًا فَلَنْ يُّخْلِفَ اللّٰهُ عَهْدَهٗۤ اَمْ تَقُوْلُوْنَ عَلَى اللّٰهِ مَا لَا تَعْلَمُوْنَ ۝

81 Nay, but whosoever hath done evil and his sin surroundeth him; such are rightful owners of the Fire; they will abide therein.

82 And those who believe and do good works: such are rightful owners of the Garden. They will abide therein.

83 And (remember) when We made a covenant with the Children of Israel, (saying): Worship none save Allah (only), and be good to parents and to kindred and to orphans and the needy, and speak kindly to mankind; and establish worship and pay the poor due. Then, after that, ye slid back, save a few of you, being averse.

84 And when We made with you a covenant (saying): Shed not the blood of your people nor turn (a party of) your people out of your dwellings. Then ye ratified (Our covenant) and ye were witnesses (thereto).[15]

85 Yet ye it is who slay each other and drive out a party of your people from their homes, supporting one another against them by sin and

بَلَىٰ مَنْ كَسَبَ سَيِّئَةً وَأَحَاطَتْ بِهِۦ
خَطِيٓـَٔتُهُۥ فَأُو۟لَـٰٓئِكَ أَصْحَـٰبُ ٱلنَّارِ هُمْ
فِيهَا خَـٰلِدُونَ ۝

وَٱلَّذِينَ ءَامَنُوا۟ وَعَمِلُوا۟ ٱلصَّـٰلِحَـٰتِ أُو۟لَـٰٓئِكَ
أَصْحَـٰبُ ٱلْجَنَّةِ هُمْ فِيهَا خَـٰلِدُونَ ۝

وَإِذْ أَخَذْنَا مِيثَـٰقَ بَنِىٓ إِسْرَٰٓءِيلَ لَا تَعْبُدُونَ
إِلَّا ٱللَّهَ وَبِٱلْوَٰلِدَيْنِ إِحْسَانًا وَذِى ٱلْقُرْبَىٰ
وَٱلْيَتَـٰمَىٰ وَٱلْمَسَـٰكِينِ وَقُولُوا۟ لِلنَّاسِ
حُسْنًا وَأَقِيمُوا۟ ٱلصَّلَوٰةَ وَءَاتُوا۟ ٱلزَّكَوٰةَ
ثُمَّ تَوَلَّيْتُمْ إِلَّا قَلِيلًا مِّنكُمْ
وَأَنتُم مُّعْرِضُونَ ۝

وَإِذْ أَخَذْنَا مِيثَـٰقَكُمْ لَا تَسْفِكُونَ دِمَآءَكُمْ
وَلَا تُخْرِجُونَ أَنفُسَكُم مِّن دِيَـٰرِكُمْ ثُمَّ
أَقْرَرْتُمْ وَأَنتُمْ تَشْهَدُونَ ۝

ثُمَّ أَنتُمْ هَـٰٓؤُلَآءِ تَقْتُلُونَ أَنفُسَكُمْ
وَتُخْرِجُونَ فَرِيقًا مِّنكُم مِّن دِيَـٰرِهِم
تَظَـٰهَرُونَ عَلَيْهِم بِٱلْإِثْمِ وَٱلْعُدْوَٰنِ

---

15. v. 83 is generally taken as reffering to the Biblical convenant and v. 84 as reffering to the solemn treaty which the Jews of Al-Madīnah made with the Prophet in the year 1 A.H.

transgression[16]—and if they came to you as captives ye would ransom them, whereas their expulsion was itself unlawful for you. Believe ye in part of the Scripture and disbelieve ye in part thereof? And what is the reward of those who do so save ignominy in the life of the world, and on the Day of Resurrection they will be consigned to the most grievous doom. For Allah is not unaware of what ye do.

وَإِن يَأْتُوكُمْ أُسَٰرَىٰ تُفَٰدُوهُمْ وَهُوَ مُحَرَّمٌ عَلَيْكُمْ إِخْرَاجُهُمْ أَفَتُؤْمِنُونَ بِبَعْضِ الْكِتَٰبِ وَتَكْفُرُونَ بِبَعْضٍ فَمَا جَزَاءُ مَن يَفْعَلُ ذَٰلِكَ مِنكُمْ إِلَّا خِزْيٌ فِى الْحَيَوٰةِ الدُّنْيَا وَيَوْمَ الْقِيَٰمَةِ يُرَدُّونَ إِلَىٰ أَشَدِّ الْعَذَابِ وَمَا اللَّهُ بِغَٰفِلٍ عَمَّا تَعْمَلُونَ ۝

86 Such are those who buy the life of the world at the price of the Hereafter: Their punishment will not be lightened, neither will they have support.

أُوْلَٰٓئِكَ الَّذِينَ اشْتَرَوُا الْحَيَوٰةَ الدُّنْيَا بِالْآخِرَةِ فَلَا يُخَفَّفُ عَنْهُمُ الْعَذَابُ وَلَا هُمْ يُنصَرُونَ ۝

87 And verily We gave unto Moses the Scripture and We caused a train of messengers to follow after him, and We gave unto Jesus, son of Mary, clear proofs (of Allah's sovereignty), and We supported him with the holy Spirit.[17] Is it ever so, that, when there cometh unto you a messenger (from Allah) with that which ye yourselves desire not, ye grow arrogant, and some ye disbelieve and some ye slay?

وَلَقَدْ ءَاتَيْنَا مُوسَى الْكِتَٰبَ وَقَفَّيْنَا مِنۢ بَعْدِهِ بِالرُّسُلِ وَءَاتَيْنَا عِيسَى ابْنَ مَرْيَمَ الْبَيِّنَٰتِ وَأَيَّدْنَٰهُ بِرُوحِ الْقُدُسِ أَفَكُلَّمَا جَاءَكُمْ رَسُولٌۢ بِمَا لَا تَهْوَىٰ أَنفُسُكُمُ اسْتَكْبَرْتُمْ فَفَرِيقًا كَذَّبْتُمْ وَفَرِيقًا تَقْتُلُونَ ۝

---

16. The reference is to the wars between the Arab tribes of Al-Madīnah in which the Jews used to take part as allies of one and the other, Jew waging war upon the Jew.

17. "The holy spirit" is a term for the angel of Revelation, Gabriel (on whom be peace)

88 And they say: Our hearts are hardened. Nay, but Allah hath cursed them for their unbelief. Little is that which they believe.

89 And when there cometh unto them a Scripture from Allah, confirming that in their possession though before that they were asking for a signal triumph over those who disbelieved and when there cometh unto them that which they know (to be the Truth) they disbelieve therein. The curse of Allah is on disbelievers.

90 Evil is that for which they sell their souls: that they should disbelieve in that which Allah hath revealed, grudging that Allah should reveal of His bounty unto whom He will of His bondmen.[18] They have incurred anger upon anger. For disbelievers is a shameful doom.

91 And when it is said unto them. Believe in that which Allah hath revealed, they say: We believe in that which was revealed unto us. And they disbelieve in that which cometh after it, though it is the truth confirming that which they possess. Say (unto them, O Muhammad): Why then slew ye the Prophets of Allah aforetime, if ye are (indeed) believers?

وَقَالُوا۟ قُلُوبُنَا غُلْفٌ ۚ بَل لَّعَنَهُمُ ٱللَّهُ بِكُفْرِهِمْ فَقَلِيلًا مَّا يُؤْمِنُونَ ۝

وَلَمَّا جَآءَهُمْ كِتَٰبٌ مِّنْ عِندِ ٱللَّهِ مُصَدِّقٌ لِّمَا مَعَهُمْ وَكَانُوا۟ مِن قَبْلُ يَسْتَفْتِحُونَ عَلَى ٱلَّذِينَ كَفَرُوا۟ فَلَمَّا جَآءَهُم مَّا عَرَفُوا۟ كَفَرُوا۟ بِهِۦ ۚ فَلَعْنَةُ ٱللَّهِ عَلَى ٱلْكَٰفِرِينَ ۝

بِئْسَمَا ٱشْتَرَوْا۟ بِهِۦٓ أَنفُسَهُمْ أَن يَكْفُرُوا۟ بِمَآ أَنزَلَ ٱللَّهُ بَغْيًا أَن يُنَزِّلَ ٱللَّهُ مِن فَضْلِهِۦ عَلَىٰ مَن يَشَآءُ مِنْ عِبَادِهِۦ ۖ فَبَآءُو بِغَضَبٍ عَلَىٰ غَضَبٍ ۚ وَلِلْكَٰفِرِينَ عَذَابٌ مُّهِينٌ ۝

وَإِذَا قِيلَ لَهُمْ ءَامِنُوا۟ بِمَآ أَنزَلَ ٱللَّهُ قَالُوا۟ نُؤْمِنُ بِمَآ أُنزِلَ عَلَيْنَا وَيَكْفُرُونَ بِمَا وَرَآءَهُۥ وَهُوَ ٱلْحَقُّ مُصَدِّقًا لِّمَا مَعَهُمْ ۗ قُلْ فَلِمَ تَقْتُلُونَ أَنۢبِيَآءَ ٱللَّهِ مِن قَبْلُ إِن كُنتُم مُّؤْمِنِينَ ۝

---

18. See v. 23, footnote.

92 And Moses came unto you with clear proofs (of Allah's sovereignty), yet, while he was away, ye chose the calf (for worship) and ye were wrongdoers.

93 And when We made with you a covenant and caused the Mount to tower above you, (saying): Hold fast by that which We have given you, and hear (Our Word), they said: We hear and we rebel. And (worship of) the calf was made to sink into their hearts because of their rejection (of the Covenant). Say (unto them): Evil is that which your belief enjoineth on you, if ye are believers.

94 Say (unto them): If the abode of the Hereafter in the providence of Allah is indeed for you alone and not for others of mankind (as ye pretend), then long for death (for ye must long for death) if ye are truthful.

95 But they will never long for it, because of that which their own hands have sent before them. Allah is Aware of evildoers.

96 And thou wilt find them greediest of mankind for life and (greedier) than the idolaters. (Each) one of them would like to be allowed to live a thousand years. And to live (a thousand years) would by no means remove him from the doom. Allah is Seer of what they do.

۞ وَلَقَدْ جَآءَكُم مُّوسَىٰ بِالْبَيِّنَٰتِ ثُمَّ ٱتَّخَذْتُمُ ٱلْعِجْلَ مِنۢ بَعْدِهِۦ وَأَنتُمْ ظَٰلِمُونَ ۝

وَإِذْ أَخَذْنَا مِيثَٰقَكُمْ وَرَفَعْنَا فَوْقَكُمُ ٱلطُّورَ خُذُوا۟ مَآ ءَاتَيْنَٰكُم بِقُوَّةٍ وَٱسْمَعُوا۟ قَالُوا۟ سَمِعْنَا وَعَصَيْنَا وَأُشْرِبُوا۟ فِى قُلُوبِهِمُ ٱلْعِجْلَ بِكُفْرِهِمْ قُلْ بِئْسَمَا يَأْمُرُكُم بِهِۦٓ إِيمَٰنُكُمْ إِن كُنتُم مُّؤْمِنِينَ ۝

قُلْ إِن كَانَتْ لَكُمُ ٱلدَّارُ ٱلْءَاخِرَةُ عِندَ ٱللَّهِ خَالِصَةً مِّن دُونِ ٱلنَّاسِ فَتَمَنَّوُا۟ ٱلْمَوْتَ إِن كُنتُمْ صَٰدِقِينَ ۝

وَلَن يَتَمَنَّوْهُ أَبَدًۢا بِمَا قَدَّمَتْ أَيْدِيهِمْ وَٱللَّهُ عَلِيمٌۢ بِٱلظَّٰلِمِينَ ۝

وَلَتَجِدَنَّهُمْ أَحْرَصَ ٱلنَّاسِ عَلَىٰ حَيَوٰةٍ وَمِنَ ٱلَّذِينَ أَشْرَكُوا۟ يَوَدُّ أَحَدُهُمْ لَوْ يُعَمَّرُ أَلْفَ سَنَةٍ وَمَا هُوَ بِمُزَحْزِحِهِۦ مِنَ ٱلْعَذَابِ أَن يُعَمَّرَ وَٱللَّهُ بَصِيرٌۢ بِمَا يَعْمَلُونَ ۝

97 Say (O Muhammad, to mankind): Who is an enemy to Gabriel! For he it is who hath revealed (this Scripture) to thy heart by Allah's leave, confirming that which was (revealed) before it, and a guidance and glad tidings to believers;

قُلْ مَنْ كَانَ عَدُوًّا لِّجِبْرِيلَ فَإِنَّهُ نَزَّلَهُ عَلَىٰ قَلْبِكَ بِإِذْنِ اللَّهِ مُصَدِّقًا لِّمَا بَيْنَ يَدَيْهِ وَهُدًى وَبُشْرَىٰ لِلْمُؤْمِنِينَ ۝

98 Who is an enemy to Allah, and His angels and His messengers, and Gabriel and Michael! Then, lo! Allah (Himself) is an enemy to the disbelievers.

مَنْ كَانَ عَدُوًّا لِّلَّهِ وَمَلَائِكَتِهِ وَرُسُلِهِ وَجِبْرِيلَ وَمِيكَالَ فَإِنَّ اللَّهَ عَدُوٌّ لِّلْكَافِرِينَ ۝

99 Verily We have revealed unto thee clear tokens, and only miscreants will disbelieve in them.

وَلَقَدْ أَنزَلْنَا إِلَيْكَ ءَايَاتٍ بَيِّنَاتٍ وَمَا يَكْفُرُ بِهَا إِلَّا الْفَاسِقُونَ ۝

100 Is it ever so that when they make a covenant a party of them set it aside? The truth is, most of them believe not.

أَوَكُلَّمَا عَاهَدُوا عَهْدًا نَّبَذَهُ فَرِيقٌ مِّنْهُم بَلْ أَكْثَرُهُمْ لَا يُؤْمِنُونَ ۝

101 And when there cometh unto them a messenger from Allah, confirming that which they possess, a party of those who have received the Scripture fling the Scripture of Allah behind their backs as if they knew not,

وَلَمَّا جَاءَهُمْ رَسُولٌ مِّنْ عِندِ اللَّهِ مُصَدِّقٌ لِّمَا مَعَهُمْ نَبَذَ فَرِيقٌ مِّنَ الَّذِينَ أُوتُوا الْكِتَابَ كِتَابَ اللَّهِ وَرَاءَ ظُهُورِهِمْ كَأَنَّهُمْ لَا يَعْلَمُونَ ۝

102 And follow that which the devils falsely related against the kingdom of Solomon. Solomon disbelieved not; but the devils disbelieved, teaching mankind magic and that which was revealed to the two angels in Babel, Hārūt and Mārūt. Nor did they (the two angels) teach it to anyone till they had said: We are only a temptation,

وَاتَّبَعُوا مَا تَتْلُوا الشَّيَاطِينُ عَلَىٰ مُلْكِ سُلَيْمَانَ وَمَا كَفَرَ سُلَيْمَانُ وَلَٰكِنَّ الشَّيَاطِينَ كَفَرُوا يُعَلِّمُونَ النَّاسَ السِّحْرَ وَمَا أُنزِلَ عَلَى الْمَلَكَيْنِ بِبَابِلَ هَارُوتَ وَمَارُوتَ وَمَا يُعَلِّمَانِ مِنْ أَحَدٍ حَتَّىٰ يَقُولَا إِنَّمَا نَحْنُ

therefore disbelieve not (in the guidance of Allah). And from these two (angels) people learn that by which they cause division between man and wife; but they injure thereby no one save by Allah's leave. And they learn that which harmeth them and profiteth them not. And surely they do know that he who trafficketh therein will have no (happy) portion in the Hereafter; and surely evil is the price for which they sell their souls, if they but knew.[19]

103   And if they had believed and kept from evil, a recompense from Allah would be better, if they only knew.

104   O ye who believe, say not (unto the Prophet): "Listen to us" but say "Look upon us,"[20] and be ye listeners. For disbelievers is a painful doom."

105   Neither those who disbelieve among the People of the Scripture[21] nor the idolaters love that there should be sent down unto you any good thing from your Lord. But Allah chooseth for His mercy whom He will, and Allah is of infinite bounty.

فِتْنَةٌ فَلَا تَكْفُرْ فَيَتَعَلَّمُونَ مِنْهُمَا مَا يُفَرِّقُونَ بِهِ بَيْنَ الْمَرْءِ وَزَوْجِهِ وَمَا هُم بِضَآرِّينَ بِهِ مِنْ أَحَدٍ إِلَّا بِإِذْنِ اللَّهِ وَيَتَعَلَّمُونَ مَا يَضُرُّهُمْ وَلَا يَنفَعُهُمْ وَلَقَدْ عَلِمُوا لَمَنِ اشْتَرَاهُ مَا لَهُ فِي الْآخِرَةِ مِنْ خَلَاقٍ وَلَبِئْسَ مَا شَرَوْا بِهِ أَنفُسَهُمْ لَوْ كَانُوا يَعْلَمُونَ ﴿١٠٢﴾

وَلَوْ أَنَّهُمْ ءَامَنُوا وَاتَّقَوْا لَمَثُوبَةٌ مِنْ عِندِ اللَّهِ خَيْرٌ لَوْ كَانُوا يَعْلَمُونَ ﴿١٠٣﴾

يَا أَيُّهَا الَّذِينَ ءَامَنُوا لَا تَقُولُوا رَاعِنَا وَقُولُوا انظُرْنَا وَاسْمَعُوا وَلِلْكَافِرِينَ عَذَابٌ أَلِيمٌ ﴿١٠٤﴾

مَا يَوَدُّ الَّذِينَ كَفَرُوا مِنْ أَهْلِ الْكِتَابِ وَلَا الْمُشْرِكِينَ أَن يُنَزَّلَ عَلَيْكُم مِّنْ خَيْرٍ مِّن رَّبِّكُمْ وَاللَّهُ يَخْتَصُّ بِرَحْمَتِهِ مَن يَشَاءُ وَاللَّهُ ذُو الْفَضْلِ الْعَظِيمِ ﴿١٠٥﴾

---

19. The reference is to the occult science practised by the Jews, the origin of which was ascribed to Solomon.

20. The first word which the Muslims used to call the Prophet's attention respectfully, *Rā'ina*, the Jews could change into an insult by a slight mispronunciation.

21. *i.e.* Jews and Christians.

106   Such of Our revelations as We abrogate or cause to be forgotten, we bring (in place) one better or the like thereof. Knowest thou not that Allah is Able to do all things?

107   Knowest thou not that it is Allah unto Whom belongeth the sovereignty of the heavens and earth; and ye have not, beside Allah, any friend or helper?

108   Or would ye question your messenger as Moses was questioned aforetime? He who chooseth disbelief instead of faith, verily he hath gone astray from a plain road.

109   Many of the People of the Scripture long to make you disbelievers after your belief, through envy on their own account, after the truth hath become manifest unto them. Forgive and be indulgent (toward them) until Allah give command. Lo! Allah is Able to do all things.

110   Establish worship, and pay the poor due;[22] and whatever of good ye send before (you) for your souls, ye will find it with Allah. Lo! Allah is Seer of what ye do.

111   And they say: None entereth Paradise unless he be a Jew or a Christian. These are their own desires. Say: Bring your proof (of what ye state) if ye are truthful.

مَا نَنسَخْ مِنْ ءَايَةٍ أَوْ نُنسِهَا نَأْتِ بِخَيْرٍ مِّنْهَآ أَوْ مِثْلِهَآ ۗ أَلَمْ تَعْلَمْ أَنَّ ٱللَّهَ عَلَىٰ كُلِّ شَيْءٍ قَدِيرٌ ۝

أَلَمْ تَعْلَمْ أَنَّ ٱللَّهَ لَهُۥ مُلْكُ ٱلسَّمَٰوَٰتِ وَٱلْأَرْضِ ۗ وَمَا لَكُم مِّن دُونِ ٱللَّهِ مِن وَلِيٍّ وَلَا نَصِيرٍ ۝

أَمْ تُرِيدُونَ أَن تَسْـَٔلُوا۟ رَسُولَكُمْ كَمَا سُئِلَ مُوسَىٰ مِن قَبْلُ ۗ وَمَن يَتَبَدَّلِ ٱلْكُفْرَ بِٱلْإِيمَٰنِ فَقَدْ ضَلَّ سَوَآءَ ٱلسَّبِيلِ ۝

وَدَّ كَثِيرٌ مِّنْ أَهْلِ ٱلْكِتَٰبِ لَوْ يَرُدُّونَكُم مِّنْ بَعْدِ إِيمَٰنِكُمْ كُفَّارًا حَسَدًا مِّنْ عِندِ أَنفُسِهِم مِّنْ بَعْدِ مَا تَبَيَّنَ لَهُمُ ٱلْحَقُّ ۖ فَٱعْفُوا۟ وَٱصْفَحُوا۟ حَتَّىٰ يَأْتِيَ ٱللَّهُ بِأَمْرِهِۦٓ ۗ إِنَّ ٱللَّهَ عَلَىٰ كُلِّ شَيْءٍ قَدِيرٌ ۝

وَأَقِيمُوا۟ ٱلصَّلَوٰةَ وَءَاتُوا۟ ٱلزَّكَوٰةَ ۚ وَمَا تُقَدِّمُوا۟ لِأَنفُسِكُم مِّنْ خَيْرٍ تَجِدُوهُ عِندَ ٱللَّهِ ۗ إِنَّ ٱللَّهَ بِمَا تَعْمَلُونَ بَصِيرٌ ۝

وَقَالُوا۟ لَن يَدْخُلَ ٱلْجَنَّةَ إِلَّا مَن كَانَ هُودًا أَوْ نَصَٰرَىٰ ۗ تِلْكَ أَمَانِيُّهُمْ ۗ قُلْ هَاتُوا۟ بُرْهَٰنَكُمْ إِن كُنتُمْ صَٰدِقِينَ ۝

---

22. *Al-Zakāh*, a tax at a fixed rate in proportion to the worth of property, collected from the well-to-do and distributed among the poor Muslims.

112 Nay, but whosoever surrendereth his purpose to Allah while
doing good, his reward is with his
Lord; and there shall no fear come
upon them neither shall they grieve.

بَلَىٰ مَنْ أَسْلَمَ وَجْهَهُۥ لِلَّهِ وَهُوَ مُحْسِنٌ فَلَهُۥٓ
أَجْرُهُۥ عِندَ رَبِّهِۦ وَلَا خَوْفٌ عَلَيْهِمْ
وَلَا هُمْ يَحْزَنُونَ ۝

113 And the Jews say the
Christians follow nothing (true), and
the Christians say the Jews follow
nothing (true); yet both are readers of
the Scripture. Even thus speak those
who know not. Allah will judge between them on the Day of Resurrection concerning that wherein they
differ.

وَقَالَتِ ٱلْيَهُودُ لَيْسَتِ ٱلنَّصَٰرَىٰ عَلَىٰ شَىْءٍ
وَقَالَتِ ٱلنَّصَٰرَىٰ لَيْسَتِ ٱلْيَهُودُ عَلَىٰ شَىْءٍ وَهُمْ
يَتْلُونَ ٱلْكِتَٰبَ كَذَٰلِكَ قَالَ ٱلَّذِينَ لَا يَعْلَمُونَ
مِثْلَ قَوْلِهِمْ فَٱللَّهُ يَحْكُمُ بَيْنَهُمْ يَوْمَ ٱلْقِيَٰمَةِ
فِيمَا كَانُوا۟ فِيهِ يَخْتَلِفُونَ ۝

114 And who doth greater wrong
than he who forbiddeth the approach
to the sanctuaries of Allah lest His
name should be mentioned therein,
and striveth for their ruin? As for
such, it was never meant that they
should enter them except in fear.
Theirs in the world is ignominy and
theirs in the Hereafter is an awful
doom.

وَمَنْ أَظْلَمُ مِمَّن مَّنَعَ مَسَٰجِدَ ٱللَّهِ أَن يُذْكَرَ فِيهَا
ٱسْمُهُۥ وَسَعَىٰ فِى خَرَابِهَآ أُو۟لَٰٓئِكَ مَا كَانَ لَهُمْ
أَن يَدْخُلُوهَآ إِلَّا خَآئِفِينَ لَهُمْ فِى ٱلدُّنْيَا
خِزْىٌ وَلَهُمْ فِى ٱلْءَاخِرَةِ عَذَابٌ عَظِيمٌ ۝

115 Unto Allah belong the East
and the West, and whithersoever ye
turn, there is Allah's countenance.
Lo! Allah is All Embracing, All
Knowing.

وَلِلَّهِ ٱلْمَشْرِقُ وَٱلْمَغْرِبُ فَأَيْنَمَا تُوَلُّوا۟ فَثَمَّ وَجْهُ ٱللَّهِ
إِنَّ ٱللَّهَ وَٰسِعٌ عَلِيمٌ ۝

116 And they say: Allah hath
taken unto Himself a Son. Be He
glorified! Nay, but whatsoever is in
the heaven and the earth is His. All
are subservient unto Him.

وَقَالُوا۟ ٱتَّخَذَ ٱللَّهُ وَلَدًا سُبْحَٰنَهُۥ بَل لَّهُۥ
مَا فِى ٱلسَّمَٰوَٰتِ وَٱلْأَرْضِ كُلٌّ لَّهُۥ قَٰنِتُونَ ۝

117 The Originator of the heavens
and the earth! When He decreeth a
thing, He saith unto it only: Be! and
it is.

بَدِيعُ ٱلسَّمَٰوَٰتِ وَٱلْأَرْضِ
وَإِذَا قَضَىٰٓ أَمْرًا فَإِنَّمَا يَقُولُ لَهُۥ كُن فَيَكُونُ ۝

118   And those who have no
knowledge say: Why doth not Allah
speak unto us, or some sign come
unto us? Even thus, as they now
speak, spake those (who were) before
them. Their hearts are all alike. We
have made clear the revelations for
people who are sure.

وَقَالَ الَّذِينَ لَا يَعْلَمُونَ لَوْلَا يُكَلِّمُنَا اللَّهُ
أَوْ تَأْتِينَا آيَةٌ كَذَلِكَ قَالَ الَّذِينَ
مِنْ قَبْلِهِمْ مِثْلَ قَوْلِهِمْ تَشَابَهَتْ قُلُوبُهُمْ
قَدْ بَيَّنَّا الْآيَاتِ لِقَوْمٍ يُوقِنُونَ ۝

119   Lo! We have sent thee (O
Muḥammad) with the truth, a bringer
of glad tidings and a warner. And
thou wilt not be asked about the
owners of hell fire.

إِنَّا أَرْسَلْنَاكَ بِالْحَقِّ بَشِيرًا وَنَذِيرًا
وَلَا تُسْأَلُ عَنْ أَصْحَابِ الْجَحِيمِ ۝

120   And the Jews will not be
pleased with thee, nor will the
Christians, till thou follow their
creed. Say: Lo! the guidance of Allah
(Himself) is Guidance. And if thou
shouldst follow their desires after the
knowledge which hath come unto
thee, then wouldst thou have from
Allah no protecting friend nor helper.

وَلَنْ تَرْضَى عَنْكَ الْيَهُودُ وَلَا النَّصَارَى حَتَّى تَتَّبِعَ
مِلَّتَهُمْ قُلْ إِنَّ هُدَى اللَّهِ هُوَ الْهُدَى وَلَئِنِ
اتَّبَعْتَ أَهْوَاءَهُمْ بَعْدَ الَّذِي جَاءَكَ مِنَ الْعِلْمِ
مَا لَكَ مِنَ اللَّهِ مِنْ وَلِيٍّ وَلَا نَصِيرٍ ۝

121   Those unto whom We have
given the Scripture, who read it with
the right reading, those believe in it.
And whoso disbelieveth in it, those
are they who are the losers.

الَّذِينَ آتَيْنَاهُمُ الْكِتَابَ يَتْلُونَهُ حَقَّ تِلَاوَتِهِ
أُولَئِكَ يُؤْمِنُونَ بِهِ وَمَنْ يَكْفُرْ بِهِ فَأُولَئِكَ
هُمُ الْخَاسِرُونَ ۝

122   O Children of Israel! Remember My favour wherewith I
favoured you and how I preferred
you to (all) creatures.

يَا بَنِي إِسْرَائِيلَ اذْكُرُوا نِعْمَتِيَ الَّتِي أَنْعَمْتُ عَلَيْكُمْ
وَأَنِّي فَضَّلْتُكُمْ عَلَى الْعَالَمِينَ ۝

123   And guard (yourselves against
a day when no soul will naught avail
another, nor will compensation be
accepted from it, nor will intercession
be of use to it; nor will they be
helped.

وَاتَّقُوا يَوْمًا لَا تَجْزِي نَفْسٌ عَنْ نَفْسٍ شَيْئًا وَلَا
يُقْبَلُ مِنْهَا عَدْلٌ وَلَا تَنْفَعُهَا شَفَاعَةٌ وَلَا هُمْ
يُنْصَرُونَ ۝

124 And (remember) when his Lord tried Abraham with (His) commands, and he fulfilled them, He said: Lo! I have appointed thee a leader for mankind. (Abraham) said: And of my offspring (will there be leaders)? He said: My covenant includeth not wrongdoers.

﴾ وَإِذِ ابْتَلَى إِبْرَهِمَ رَبُّهُ بِكَلِمَتٍ فَأَتَمَّهُنَّ قَالَ إِنِّى جَاعِلُكَ لِلنَّاسِ إِمَامًا قَالَ وَمِن ذُرِّيَّتِى قَالَ لَا يَنَالُ عَهْدِى الظَّالِمِينَ ﴿١٢٤﴾

125 And when We made the House (at Makkah) a resort for mankind and a sanctuary, (saying): Take as your place of worship the place where Abraham stood (to pray). And We imposed a duty upon Abraham and Ishmael, (saying): Purify My house for those who go around and those who meditate therein and those who bow down and prostrate themselves (in worship).

وَإِذْ جَعَلْنَا الْبَيْتَ مَثَابَةً لِلنَّاسِ وَأَمْنًا وَاتَّخِذُوا مِن مَّقَامِ إِبْرَهِمَ مُصَلًّى وَعَهِدْنَا إِلَى إِبْرَهِمَ وَإِسْمَعِيلَ أَن طَهِّرَا بَيْتِىَ لِلطَّائِفِينَ وَالْعَاكِفِينَ وَالرُّكَّعِ السُّجُودِ ﴿١٢٥﴾

126 And when Abraham prayed: My Lord! Make this a region of security and bestow upon its people fruits, such of them as believe in Allah and the Last Day, He answered: As for him who disbelieveth, I shall leave him in contentment for a while, then I shall compel him to the doom of fire a hapless journey's end!

وَإِذْ قَالَ إِبْرَهِمُ رَبِّ اجْعَلْ هَذَا بَلَدًا ءَامِنًا وَارْزُقْ أَهْلَهُ مِنَ الثَّمَرَتِ مَنْ ءَامَنَ مِنْهُم بِاللَّهِ وَالْيَوْمِ الْأَخِرِ قَالَ وَمَن كَفَرَ فَأُمَتِّعُهُ قَلِيلًا ثُمَّ أَضْطَرُّهُ إِلَى عَذَابِ النَّارِ وَبِئْسَ الْمَصِيرُ ﴿١٢٦﴾

127 And when Abraham and Ishmael were raising the foundations of the House, (Abraham prayed): Our Lord! Accept from us (this duty). Lo! Thou, only Thou, art the Hearer, the Knower.

وَإِذْ يَرْفَعُ إِبْرَهِمُ الْقَوَاعِدَ مِنَ الْبَيْتِ وَإِسْمَعِيلُ رَبَّنَا تَقَبَّلْ مِنَّا إِنَّكَ أَنتَ السَّمِيعُ الْعَلِيمُ ﴿١٢٧﴾

128   Our Lord! And make us submissive unto Thee and of our seed a
nation submissive unto Thee, and
show us our ways of worship, and
relent toward us. Lo! Thou, only
Thou, art the Relenting, the Merciful.

رَبَّنَا وَاجْعَلْنَا مُسْلِمَيْنِ لَكَ وَمِن ذُرِّيَّتِنَآ أُمَّةً
مُّسْلِمَةً لَّكَ وَأَرِنَا مَنَاسِكَنَا وَتُبْ عَلَيْنَآ
إِنَّكَ أَنتَ التَّوَّابُ الرَّحِيمُ ﴿١٢٨﴾

129   Our Lord! And raise up in
their midst a messenger from among
them who shall recite unto them Thy
revelations, and shall instruct them in
the Scripture and in wisdom and
shall make them grow. Lo! Thou,
only Thou, art the Mighty, Wise.

رَبَّنَا وَابْعَثْ فِيهِمْ رَسُولًا مِّنْهُمْ يَتْلُواْ عَلَيْهِمْ
ءَايَٰتِكَ وَيُعَلِّمُهُمُ الْكِتَٰبَ وَالْحِكْمَةَ
وَيُزَكِّيهِمْ إِنَّكَ أَنتَ الْعَزِيزُ الْحَكِيمُ ﴿١٢٩﴾

130   And who forsaketh the religion of Abraham save him who
befooleth himself? Verily We chose
him in the world, and lo! in the
Hereafter he is among the righteous.

وَمَن يَرْغَبُ عَن مِّلَّةِ إِبْرَٰهِمَ إِلَّا مَن سَفِهَ
نَفْسَهُ وَلَقَدِ اصْطَفَيْنَٰهُ فِي الدُّنْيَا
وَإِنَّهُۥ فِي الْأَخِرَةِ لَمِنَ الصَّٰلِحِينَ ﴿١٣٠﴾

131   When his Lord said unto him:
Surrender! he said: I have surrendered to the Lord of the Worlds.

إِذْ قَالَ لَهُۥ رَبُّهُۥٓ أَسْلِمْ
قَالَ أَسْلَمْتُ لِرَبِّ الْعَٰلَمِينَ ﴿١٣١﴾

132   The same did Abraham enjoin
upon his sons, and also Jacob, (saying): O my sons! Lo! Allah hath
chosen for you the (true) religion;
therefore die not save as men who
have surrendered (unto Him).

وَوَصَّىٰ بِهَآ إِبْرَٰهِمُ بَنِيهِ وَيَعْقُوبُ يَٰبَنِيَّ إِنَّ اللَّهَ
اصْطَفَىٰ لَكُمُ الدِّينَ فَلَا تَمُوتُنَّ إِلَّا
وَأَنتُم مُّسْلِمُونَ ﴿١٣٢﴾

133   Or were ye present when
death came to Jacob, when he said
unto his sons: What will ye worship
after me? They said: We shall worship thy God, the God of thy fathers,
Abraham and Ishmael and Isaac, One
God, and unto Him we have surrendered.

أَمْ كُنتُمْ شُهَدَآءَ إِذْ حَضَرَ يَعْقُوبَ الْمَوْتُ إِذْ
قَالَ لِبَنِيهِ مَا تَعْبُدُونَ مِنۢ بَعْدِى قَالُواْ نَعْبُدُ
إِلَٰهَكَ وَإِلَٰهَ ءَابَآئِكَ إِبْرَٰهِمَ وَإِسْمَٰعِيلَ
وَإِسْحَٰقَ إِلَٰهًا وَٰحِدًا وَنَحْنُ لَهُۥ مُسْلِمُونَ ﴿١٣٣﴾

134   Those are a people who have passed away. Theirs is that which they earned, and yours is that which ye earn. And ye will not be asked of what they used to do.

تِلْكَ أُمَّةٌ قَدْ خَلَتْ لَهَا مَا كَسَبَتْ وَلَكُمْ مَّا كَسَبْتُمْ وَلَا تُسْئَلُونَ عَمَّا كَانُوا يَعْمَلُونَ ۞

135   And they say: Be Jews or Christians, then ye will be rightly guided. Say (unto them, O Muhammad): Nay, but (we follow) the religion of Abraham, the upright, and he was not of the idolaters.

وَقَالُوا كُونُوا هُودًا أَوْ نَصَارَى تَهْتَدُوا قُلْ بَلْ مِلَّةَ إِبْرَهِمَ حَنِيفًا وَمَا كَانَ مِنَ الْمُشْرِكِينَ ۞

136   Say (O Muslims): We believe in Allah and that which is revealed unto Us and that which was revealed unto Abraham, and Ishmael, and Isaac, and Jacob. and the tribes, and that which Moses and Jesus received, and that which the Prophets received from their Lord. We make no distinction between any of them, and unto Him we have surrendered.

قُولُوا ءَامَنَّا بِاللَّهِ وَمَا أُنْزِلَ إِلَيْنَا وَمَا أُنْزِلَ إِلَى إِبْرَهِمَ وَإِسْمَعِيلَ وَإِسْحَقَ وَيَعْقُوبَ وَالْأَسْبَاطِ وَمَا أُوتِيَ مُوسَى وَعِيسَى وَمَا أُوتِيَ النَّبِيُّونَ مِن رَّبِّهِمْ لَا نُفَرِّقُ بَيْنَ أَحَدٍ مِنْهُمْ وَنَحْنُ لَهُ مُسْلِمُونَ ۞

137   And if they believe in the like of that which ye believe, then are they rightly guided. But if they turn away, then are they in schism, and Allah will suffice thee (for defence) against them. He is the Hearer, the Knower.

فَإِنْ ءَامَنُوا بِمِثْلِ مَا ءَامَنتُم بِهِ فَقَدِ اهْتَدُوا وَإِن تَوَلَّوْا فَإِنَّمَا هُمْ فِي شِقَاقٍ فَسَيَكْفِيكَهُمُ اللَّهُ وَهُوَ السَّمِيعُ الْعَلِيمُ ۞

138   (We take our) color from Allah, and who is better than Allah at coloring. We are His worshippers.

صِبْغَةَ اللَّهِ وَمَنْ أَحْسَنُ مِنَ اللَّهِ صِبْغَةً وَنَحْنُ لَهُ عَبِدُونَ ۞

139   Say (unto the People of the Scripture): Dispute ye with us concerning Allah when He is our Lord and your Lord? Ours are our works and yours your works. We look to Him alone.

قُلْ أَتُحَاجُّونَنَا فِي اللَّهِ وَهُوَ رَبُّنَا وَرَبُّكُمْ وَلَنَا أَعْمَالُنَا وَلَكُمْ أَعْمَالُكُمْ وَنَحْنُ لَهُ مُخْلِصُونَ ۞

140   Or say ye that Abraham, and Ishmael, and Isaac, and Jacob, and the tribes were Jews or Christians? Say: Do ye know best, or doth Allah? And who is more unjust than he who hideth a testimony which he hath received from Allah? Allah is not unaware of what ye do.

141   Those are a people who have passed away; theirs is that which they earned and yours that which ye earn. And ye will not be asked of what they used to do.

142   The foolish of the people will say: What hath turned them from the *qiblah*²³ which they formerly observed? Say: Unto Allah belong the East and the West. He guideth whom He will unto a straight path.

143   Thus We have appointed you a middle nation, that ye may be witnesses against mankind. and that the messenger may be a witness against you. And We appointed the *qiblah* which ye formerly observed only that We might know him who followeth the messenger, from him who turneth on his heels. In truth it was a hard (test) save for those

أَمْ تَقُولُونَ إِنَّ إِبْرَاهِيمَ وَإِسْمَاعِيلَ وَإِسْحَاقَ وَيَعْقُوبَ وَالْأَسْبَاطَ كَانُوا هُودًا أَوْ نَصَارَىٰ قُلْ ءَأَنتُمْ أَعْلَمُ أَمِ اللَّهُ وَمَنْ أَظْلَمُ مِمَّن كَتَمَ شَهَادَةً عِندَهُ مِنَ اللَّهِ وَمَا اللَّهُ بِغَافِلٍ عَمَّا تَعْمَلُونَ ۝

تِلْكَ أُمَّةٌ قَدْ خَلَتْ لَهَا مَا كَسَبَتْ وَلَكُم مَّا كَسَبْتُمْ وَلَا تُسْـَٔلُونَ عَمَّا كَانُوا يَعْمَلُونَ ۝

۞ سَيَقُولُ السُّفَهَاءُ مِنَ النَّاسِ مَا وَلَّاهُمْ عَن قِبْلَتِهِمُ الَّتِي كَانُوا عَلَيْهَا قُل لِّلَّهِ الْمَشْرِقُ وَالْمَغْرِبُ يَهْدِي مَن يَشَاءُ إِلَىٰ صِرَاطٍ مُّسْتَقِيمٍ ۝

وَكَذَٰلِكَ جَعَلْنَاكُمْ أُمَّةً وَسَطًا لِّتَكُونُوا شُهَدَاءَ عَلَى النَّاسِ وَيَكُونَ الرَّسُولُ عَلَيْكُمْ شَهِيدًا وَمَا جَعَلْنَا الْقِبْلَةَ الَّتِي كُنتَ عَلَيْهَا إِلَّا لِنَعْلَمَ مَن يَتَّبِعُ الرَّسُولَ مِمَّن يَنقَلِبُ عَلَىٰ عَقِبَيْهِ

---

23. *i.e.* the place towards which the face is turned at prayer. The first *qiblah* of the Muslims was Jerusalem, which gave rise to a misunderstanding on the part of the Jews of Al-Madīnah, who wished to draw the Muslims into Judaism. This was the cause of the Prophet's anxiety mentioned in the next verse but one.

whom Allah guided. But it was not Allah's purpose that your faith should be in vain, for Allah is full of pity, Merciful toward mankind.

144 We have seen the turning of thy face to heaven (for guidance, O Muhammad). And now verily We shall make thee turn (in prayer) toward a *qiblah* which is dear to thee. So turn thy face toward the Inviolable Place of Worship,[24] and ye (O Muslims), wheresoever ye may be, turn your faces when ye pray) toward it. Lo! those who have received the Scripture know that (this Revelation) is the Truth from their Lord. And Allah is not unaware of what they do.

145 And even if thou broughtest unto those who have received the Scripture all kinds of portents, they would not follow thy *qiblah*, nor canst thou be a follower of their *qiblah*; nor are some of them followers of the *qiblah* of others. And if thou shouldst follow their desires after the knowledge which hath come unto thee, then surely wert thou of the evil doers.

146 Those unto whom We gave the Scripture recognize (this revelation) as they recognize their sons. But lo! a party of them knowingly conceal the truth.

وَإِن كَانَتْ لَكَبِيرَةً إِلَّا عَلَى ٱلَّذِينَ هَدَى ٱللَّهُ وَمَا كَانَ ٱللَّهُ لِيُضِيعَ إِيمَٰنَكُمْ إِنَّ ٱللَّهَ بِٱلنَّاسِ لَرَءُوفٌ رَّحِيمٌ ۝

قَدْ نَرَىٰ تَقَلُّبَ وَجْهِكَ فِى ٱلسَّمَآءِ فَلَنُوَلِّيَنَّكَ قِبْلَةً تَرْضَىٰهَا فَوَلِّ وَجْهَكَ شَطْرَ ٱلْمَسْجِدِ ٱلْحَرَامِ وَحَيْثُ مَا كُنتُمْ فَوَلُّوا۟ وُجُوهَكُمْ شَطْرَهُ وَإِنَّ ٱلَّذِينَ أُوتُوا۟ ٱلْكِتَٰبَ لَيَعْلَمُونَ أَنَّهُ ٱلْحَقُّ مِن رَّبِّهِمْ وَمَا ٱللَّهُ بِغَٰفِلٍ عَمَّا يَعْمَلُونَ ۝

وَلَئِنْ أَتَيْتَ ٱلَّذِينَ أُوتُوا۟ ٱلْكِتَٰبَ بِكُلِّ ءَايَةٍ مَّا تَبِعُوا۟ قِبْلَتَكَ وَمَآ أَنتَ بِتَابِعٍ قِبْلَتَهُمْ وَمَا بَعْضُهُم بِتَابِعٍ قِبْلَةَ بَعْضٍ وَلَئِنِ ٱتَّبَعْتَ أَهْوَآءَهُم مِّنۢ بَعْدِ مَا جَآءَكَ مِنَ ٱلْعِلْمِ إِنَّكَ إِذًا لَّمِنَ ٱلظَّٰلِمِينَ ۝

ٱلَّذِينَ ءَاتَيْنَٰهُمُ ٱلْكِتَٰبَ يَعْرِفُونَهُۥ كَمَا يَعْرِفُونَ أَبْنَآءَهُمْ وَإِنَّ فَرِيقًا مِّنْهُمْ لَيَكْتُمُونَ ٱلْحَقَّ وَهُمْ يَعْلَمُونَ ۝

---

24. The Ka'bah at Makkah.

147   It is the Truth from thy Lord
(O Muhammad), so be not thou of
those who waver.

اَلْحَقُّ مِنْ رَّبِّكَ فَلَا تَكُونَنَّ مِنَ الْمُمْتَرِينَ ۝

148   And each one hath a goal
toward which he turneth; so vie
with one another in good works.
Wheresoever ye may be, Allah will
bring you all together. Lo! Allah is
Able to do all things.

وَلِكُلٍّ وِجْهَةٌ هُوَ مُوَلِّيهَا فَاسْتَبِقُوا الْخَيْرَاتِ أَيْنَ
مَا تَكُونُوا يَأْتِ بِكُمُ اللّٰهُ جَمِيعًا إِنَّ اللّٰهَ عَلَى
كُلِّ شَيْءٍ قَدِيرٌ ۝

149   And whencesoever thou
comest forth (for prayer, O
Muhammad) turn thy face toward
the Inviolable Place of Worship.
Lo! it is the Truth from thy Lord
Allah is not unaware of what ye do.

وَمِنْ حَيْثُ خَرَجْتَ فَوَلِّ وَجْهَكَ شَطْرَ
الْمَسْجِدِ الْحَرَامِ وَإِنَّهُ لَلْحَقُّ مِنْ رَّبِّكَ وَمَا
اللّٰهُ بِغَافِلٍ عَمَّا تَعْمَلُونَ ۝

150   Whencesoever thou comest
forth turn thy face toward the
Inviolable Place of Worship; and
wheresoever ye may be (O
Muslims) turn your faces toward it
(when ye pray) so that men may
have no argument against you, save
such of them as do injustice—Fear
them not—but fear Me and so that
I may complete My grace upon
you, and that ye may be guided.

وَمِنْ حَيْثُ خَرَجْتَ فَوَلِّ وَجْهَكَ شَطْرَ الْمَسْجِدِ
الْحَرَامِ وَحَيْثُ مَا كُنْتُمْ فَوَلُّوا وُجُوهَكُمْ
شَطْرَهُ لِئَلَّا يَكُونَ لِلنَّاسِ عَلَيْكُمْ حُجَّةٌ إِلَّا
الَّذِينَ ظَلَمُوا مِنْهُمْ فَلَا تَخْشَوْهُمْ وَاخْشَوْنِي
وَلِأُتِمَّ نِعْمَتِي عَلَيْكُمْ وَلَعَلَّكُمْ تَهْتَدُونَ ۝

151   Even as We have sent unto
you a messenger from among you,
who reciteth unto you Our revelations and causeth you to grow,
and teacheth you the Scripture and
wisdom, and teacheth you that
which ye knew not.[25]

كَمَا أَرْسَلْنَا فِيكُمْ رَسُولًا مِنْكُمْ يَتْلُوا
عَلَيْكُمْ آيَاتِنَا وَيُزَكِّيكُمْ وَيُعَلِّمُكُمُ
الْكِتَابَ وَالْحِكْمَةَ وَيُعَلِّمُكُمْ مَا لَمْ تَكُونُوا
تَعْلَمُونَ ۝

---

25. See Abraham's prayer, Sūrah 5: 129.

152 Therefore remember Me, I will remember you. Give thanks to Me, and reject not Me.

فَاذْكُرُونِىٓ أَذْكُرْكُمْ وَاشْكُرُوا لِى وَلَا تَكْفُرُونِ ۝

153 O ye who believe! Seek help in steadfastness, and prayer. Lo! Allah is with the steadfast.

يَٰٓأَيُّهَا ٱلَّذِينَ ءَامَنُوا ٱسْتَعِينُوا بِٱلصَّبْرِ وَٱلصَّلَوٰةِ إِنَّ ٱللَّهَ مَعَ ٱلصَّٰبِرِينَ ۝

154 "And call not those who are slain in the way of Allah 'dead.' Nay, they are living, only ye perceive not."

وَلَا تَقُولُوا لِمَن يُقْتَلُ فِى سَبِيلِ ٱللَّهِ أَمْوَٰتٌۢ بَلْ أَحْيَآءٌ وَلَٰكِن لَّا تَشْعُرُونَ ۝

155 And surely We shall try you with something of fear and hunger, and loss of wealth and lives and crops; but give glad tidings to the steadfast,

وَلَنَبْلُوَنَّكُم بِشَىْءٍ مِّنَ ٱلْخَوْفِ وَٱلْجُوعِ وَنَقْصٍ مِّنَ ٱلْأَمْوَٰلِ وَٱلْأَنفُسِ وَٱلثَّمَرَٰتِ وَبَشِّرِ ٱلصَّٰبِرِينَ ۝

156 Who say, when a misfortune striketh them: Lo! we are Allah's and Lo! unto Him we are returning.

ٱلَّذِينَ إِذَآ أَصَٰبَتْهُم مُّصِيبَةٌ قَالُوٓا إِنَّا لِلَّهِ وَإِنَّآ إِلَيْهِ رَٰجِعُونَ ۝

157 Such are they on whom are blessings from their Lord, and mercy. Such are the rightly guided.

أُو۟لَٰٓئِكَ عَلَيْهِمْ صَلَوَٰتٌ مِّن رَّبِّهِمْ وَرَحْمَةٌ وَأُو۟لَٰٓئِكَ هُمُ ٱلْمُهْتَدُونَ ۝

158 Lo! (the mountains) Al-Safā and Al-Marwah are among the indications of Allah. It is therefore no sin for him who is on pilgrimage to the House (of God) or visiteth it, to go around them (as the pagan custom is). And he who doeth good of his own accord (for him), Lo! Allah is Responsive, Aware.

۞ إِنَّ ٱلصَّفَا وَٱلْمَرْوَةَ مِن شَعَآئِرِ ٱللَّهِ فَمَنْ حَجَّ ٱلْبَيْتَ أَوِ ٱعْتَمَرَ فَلَا جُنَاحَ عَلَيْهِ أَن يَطَّوَّفَ بِهِمَا وَمَن تَطَوَّعَ خَيْرًا فَإِنَّ ٱللَّهَ شَاكِرٌ عَلِيمٌ ۝

159 Those who hide the proofs and the guidance which We revealed, after We had made it clear in the Scripture: such are accursed of Allah and accursed of those who have the power to curse.

إِنَّ ٱلَّذِينَ يَكْتُمُونَ مَآ أَنزَلْنَا مِنَ ٱلْبَيِّنَٰتِ وَٱلْهُدَىٰ مِنۢ بَعْدِ مَا بَيَّنَّٰهُ لِلنَّاسِ فِى ٱلْكِتَٰبِ أُو۟لَٰٓئِكَ يَلْعَنُهُمُ ٱللَّهُ وَيَلْعَنُهُمُ ٱللَّٰعِنُونَ ۝

160   Except such of them as repent and amend and make manifest (the truth). These it is toward whom I relent. I am the Relenting, the Merciful.

إِلَّا ٱلَّذِينَ تَابُوا۟ وَأَصْلَحُوا۟ وَبَيَّنُوا۟ فَأُو۟لَـٰٓئِكَ أَتُوبُ عَلَيْهِمْ ۚ وَأَنَا ٱلتَّوَّابُ ٱلرَّحِيمُ ﴿١٦٠﴾

161   Lo! those who disbelieve, and die while they are disbelievers; on them is the curse of Allah and of angels and of men combined.

إِنَّ ٱلَّذِينَ كَفَرُوا۟ وَمَاتُوا۟ وَهُمْ كُفَّارٌ أُو۟لَـٰٓئِكَ عَلَيْهِمْ لَعْنَةُ ٱللَّهِ وَٱلْمَلَـٰٓئِكَةِ وَٱلنَّاسِ أَجْمَعِينَ ﴿١٦١﴾

162   They ever dwell therein. The doom will not be lightened for them, neither will they be reprieved.

خَـٰلِدِينَ فِيهَا لَا يُخَفَّفُ عَنْهُمُ ٱلْعَذَابُ وَلَا هُمْ يُنظَرُونَ ﴿١٦٢﴾

163   Your God is One God; there is no God save Him, the Beneficent, the Merciful.

وَإِلَـٰهُكُمْ إِلَـٰهٌ وَٰحِدٌ ۖ لَّآ إِلَـٰهَ إِلَّا هُوَ ٱلرَّحْمَـٰنُ ٱلرَّحِيمُ ﴿١٦٣﴾

164   Lo! in the creation of the heavens and the earth, and the difference of night and day, and the ships which run upon the sea with that which is of use to men, and the water which Allah sendeth down from the sky, thereby reviving the earth after its death, and dispersing all kinds of beasts therein, and (in) the ordinance of the winds, and the clouds obedient between heaven and earth: are signs (of Allah's sovereignty) for people who have sense.

إِنَّ فِى خَلْقِ ٱلسَّمَـٰوَٰتِ وَٱلْأَرْضِ وَٱخْتِلَـٰفِ ٱلَّيْلِ وَٱلنَّهَارِ وَٱلْفُلْكِ ٱلَّتِى تَجْرِى فِى ٱلْبَحْرِ بِمَا يَنفَعُ ٱلنَّاسَ وَمَآ أَنزَلَ ٱللَّهُ مِنَ ٱلسَّمَآءِ مِن مَّآءٍ فَأَحْيَا بِهِ ٱلْأَرْضَ بَعْدَ مَوْتِهَا وَبَثَّ فِيهَا مِن كُلِّ دَآبَّةٍ وَتَصْرِيفِ ٱلرِّيَـٰحِ وَٱلسَّحَابِ ٱلْمُسَخَّرِ بَيْنَ ٱلسَّمَآءِ وَٱلْأَرْضِ لَـَٔايَـٰتٍ لِّقَوْمٍ يَعْقِلُونَ ﴿١٦٤﴾

165   Yet of mankind are some who take unto themselves objects of worship which they set as) rivals to Allah, loving them with a love like (that which is the due) of Allah (only), Those who believe are staun-

وَمِنَ ٱلنَّاسِ مَن يَتَّخِذُ مِن دُونِ ٱللَّهِ أَندَادًا يُحِبُّونَهُمْ كَحُبِّ ٱللَّهِ ۖ وَٱلَّذِينَ ءَامَنُوٓا۟ أَشَدُّ حُبًّا

cher in their love for Allah, that those who do evil had but known, (on the day) when they behold the doom, that power belongeth wholly to Allah, and that Allah is severe in punishment!

لِلَّهِ وَلَوْ يَرَى الَّذِينَ ظَلَمُوا إِذْ يَرَوْنَ الْعَذَابَ أَنَّ الْقُوَّةَ لِلَّهِ جَمِيعًا وَأَنَّ اللَّهَ شَدِيدُ الْعَذَابِ ﴿١٦٥﴾

166 (On the day) when those who were followed disown those who followed (them), and they behold the doom, and all their aims collapse with them.

إِذْ تَبَرَّأَ الَّذِينَ اتُّبِعُوا مِنَ الَّذِينَ اتَّبَعُوا وَرَأَوُا الْعَذَابَ وَتَقَطَّعَتْ بِهِمُ الْأَسْبَابُ ﴿١٦٦﴾

167 And those who were but followers will say: If a return were possible for us, we would disown them even as they have disowned us. Thus will Allah show them their own deeds as anguish for them, and they will not emerge from the Fire.

وَقَالَ الَّذِينَ اتَّبَعُوا لَوْ أَنَّ لَنَا كَرَّةً فَنَتَبَرَّأَ مِنْهُمْ كَمَا تَبَرَّءُوا مِنَّا كَذَلِكَ يُرِيهِمُ اللَّهُ أَعْمَالَهُمْ حَسَرَاتٍ عَلَيْهِمْ وَمَا هُم بِخَارِجِينَ مِنَ النَّارِ ﴿١٦٧﴾

168 O mankind! Eat of that which is lawful and wholesome in the earth, and follow not the footsteps of the devil. Lo! he is an open enemy for you.

يَا أَيُّهَا النَّاسُ كُلُوا مِمَّا فِي الْأَرْضِ حَلَالًا طَيِّبًا وَلَا تَتَّبِعُوا خُطُوَاتِ الشَّيْطَانِ إِنَّهُ لَكُمْ عَدُوٌّ مُّبِينٌ ﴿١٦٨﴾

169 He enjoineth upon you only the evil and the foul, and that ye should tell concerning Allah that which ye know not.

إِنَّمَا يَأْمُرُكُم بِالسُّوءِ وَالْفَحْشَاءِ وَأَن تَقُولُوا عَلَى اللَّهِ مَا لَا تَعْلَمُونَ ﴿١٦٩﴾

170 And when it is said unto them: Follow that which Allah hath revealed, they say: We follow that wherein we found our fathers. What! Even though their fathers were wholly unintelligent and had no guidance?

وَإِذَا قِيلَ لَهُمُ اتَّبِعُوا مَا أَنزَلَ اللَّهُ قَالُوا بَلْ نَتَّبِعُ مَا أَلْفَيْنَا عَلَيْهِ آبَاءَنَا أَوَلَوْ كَانَ آبَاؤُهُمْ لَا يَعْقِلُونَ شَيْئًا وَلَا يَهْتَدُونَ ﴿١٧٠﴾

171　The likeness of those who disbelieve (in relation to the messenger) is as the likeness of one who calleth unto that which heareth naught except a shout and cry. Deaf, dumb, blind, therefore they have no sense.

وَمَثَلُ الَّذِينَ كَفَرُوا كَمَثَلِ الَّذِى يَنْعِقُ بِمَا لَا يَسْمَعُ إِلَّا دُعَاءً وَنِدَاءً ۚ صُمٌّ بُكْمٌ عُمْيٌ فَهُمْ لَا يَعْقِلُونَ ۝

172　O ye who believe! Eat of the good things wherewith We have provided you, and render thanks to Allah if it is (indeed) He whom ye worship.

يَا أَيُّهَا الَّذِينَ آمَنُوا كُلُوا مِن طَيِّبَاتِ مَا رَزَقْنَاكُمْ وَاشْكُرُوا لِلَّهِ إِن كُنتُمْ إِيَّاهُ تَعْبُدُونَ ۝

173　He hath forbidden you only carrion, and blood, and swineflesh, and that which hath been immolated to (the name of) any other than Allah. But he who is driven by necessity, neither craving nor transgressing, it is no sin for him. Lo! Allah is Forgiving, Merciful.

إِنَّمَا حَرَّمَ عَلَيْكُمُ الْمَيْتَةَ وَالدَّمَ وَلَحْمَ الْخِنزِيرِ وَمَا أُهِلَّ بِهِ لِغَيْرِ اللَّهِ ۖ فَمَنِ اضْطُرَّ غَيْرَ بَاغٍ وَلَا عَادٍ فَلَا إِثْمَ عَلَيْهِ ۚ إِنَّ اللَّهَ غَفُورٌ رَّحِيمٌ ۝

174　Lo! those who hide aught of the Scripture which Allah hath revealed, and purchase a small gain therewith, they eat into their bellies nothing else than fire. Allah will not speak to them on the Day of Resurrection, nor will He make them grow. Theirs will be a painful doom.

إِنَّ الَّذِينَ يَكْتُمُونَ مَا أَنزَلَ اللَّهُ مِنَ الْكِتَابِ وَيَشْتَرُونَ بِهِ ثَمَنًا قَلِيلًا ۙ أُولَٰئِكَ مَا يَأْكُلُونَ فِى بُطُونِهِمْ إِلَّا النَّارَ وَلَا يُكَلِّمُهُمُ اللَّهُ يَوْمَ الْقِيَامَةِ وَلَا يُزَكِّيهِمْ وَلَهُمْ عَذَابٌ أَلِيمٌ ۝

175　Those are they who purchase error at the price of guidance, and torment at the price of pardon. How constant are they in their strife to reach the Fire!

أُولَٰئِكَ الَّذِينَ اشْتَرَوُا الضَّلَالَةَ بِالْهُدَىٰ وَالْعَذَابَ بِالْمَغْفِرَةِ ۚ فَمَا أَصْبَرَهُمْ عَلَى النَّارِ ۝

176　That is because Allah hath revealed the Scripture with the truth. Lo! those who find (a cause of) disagreement in the Scripture are in open schism.

ذَٰلِكَ بِأَنَّ اللَّهَ نَزَّلَ الْكِتَابَ بِالْحَقِّ ۗ وَإِنَّ الَّذِينَ اخْتَلَفُوا فِى الْكِتَابِ لَفِى شِقَاقٍ بَعِيدٍ ۝

177 It is not righteousness that ye turn your faces to the East and the West; but righteous is he who believeth in Allah and the Last Day and the angels and the Scripture and the Prophets; and giveth his wealth, for love of Him, to kinsfolk and to orphans and the needy and the wayfarer and to those who ask, and to set slaves free; and observeth proper worship and payeth the poor due.[26] And those who keep their treaty when they make one, and the patient in tribulation and adversity and time of stress. Such are they who are sincere. Such are the God fearing.

178 O ye who believe! Retaliation is prescribed for you in the matter of the murdered; the freeman for the freeman, and the slave for the slave, and the female for the female. And for him who is forgiven somewhat by his (injured) brother, prosecution according to usage and payment unto him in kindness. This is an alleviation and a mercy from your Lord. He who transgresseth after this will have a painful doom.

179 And there is life for you in retaliation, O men of understanding, that ye may ward off (evil).

﷽ لَّيْسَ ٱلْبِرَّ أَن تُوَلُّوا۟ وُجُوهَكُمْ قِبَلَ ٱلْمَشْرِقِ وَٱلْمَغْرِبِ وَلَٰكِنَّ ٱلْبِرَّ مَنْ ءَامَنَ بِٱللَّهِ وَٱلْيَوْمِ ٱلْءَاخِرِ وَٱلْمَلَٰٓئِكَةِ وَٱلْكِتَٰبِ وَٱلنَّبِيِّۦنَ وَءَاتَى ٱلْمَالَ عَلَىٰ حُبِّهِۦ ذَوِى ٱلْقُرْبَىٰ وَٱلْيَتَٰمَىٰ وَٱلْمَسَٰكِينَ وَٱبْنَ ٱلسَّبِيلِ وَٱلسَّآئِلِينَ وَفِى ٱلرِّقَابِ وَأَقَامَ ٱلصَّلَوٰةَ وَءَاتَى ٱلزَّكَوٰةَ وَٱلْمُوفُونَ بِعَهْدِهِمْ إِذَا عَٰهَدُوا۟ۖ وَٱلصَّٰبِرِينَ فِى ٱلْبَأْسَآءِ وَٱلضَّرَّآءِ وَحِينَ ٱلْبَأْسِ أُو۟لَٰٓئِكَ ٱلَّذِينَ صَدَقُوا۟ۖ وَأُو۟لَٰٓئِكَ هُمُ ٱلْمُتَّقُونَ ۝

يَٰٓأَيُّهَا ٱلَّذِينَ ءَامَنُوا۟ كُتِبَ عَلَيْكُمُ ٱلْقِصَاصُ فِى ٱلْقَتْلَى ٱلْحُرُّ بِٱلْحُرِّ وَٱلْعَبْدُ بِٱلْعَبْدِ وَٱلْأُنثَىٰ بِٱلْأُنثَىٰ فَمَنْ عُفِىَ لَهُۥ مِنْ أَخِيهِ شَىْءٌ فَٱتِّبَاعٌۢ بِٱلْمَعْرُوفِ وَأَدَآءٌ إِلَيْهِ بِإِحْسَٰنٍ ذَٰلِكَ تَخْفِيفٌ مِّن رَّبِّكُمْ وَرَحْمَةٌ فَمَنِ ٱعْتَدَىٰ بَعْدَ ذَٰلِكَ فَلَهُۥ عَذَابٌ أَلِيمٌ ۝

وَلَكُمْ فِى ٱلْقِصَاصِ حَيَوٰةٌ يَٰٓأُو۟لِى ٱلْأَلْبَٰبِ لَعَلَّكُمْ تَتَّقُونَ ۝

---

26. See Sūrah 5: 43, footnote.

180   It is prescribed for you, when death approacheth one of you, if he leave wealth, that he bequeath unto parents and near relatives in kindness. (This is) a duty for all those who ward off (evil).

كُتِبَ عَلَيْكُمْ إِذَا حَضَرَ أَحَدَكُمُ الْمَوْتُ إِنْ تَرَكَ خَيْرًا ۖ الْوَصِيَّةُ لِلْوَالِدَيْنِ وَالْأَقْرَبِينَ بِالْمَعْرُوفِ ۖ حَقًّا عَلَى الْمُتَّقِينَ ۞

181   And whoso changeth (the will) after he hath heard it the sin thereof is only upon those who change it. Lo! Allah is Hearer, Knower.

فَمَنْ بَدَّلَهُ بَعْدَمَا سَمِعَهُ فَإِنَّمَا إِثْمُهُ عَلَى الَّذِينَ يُبَدِّلُونَهُ ۚ إِنَّ اللَّهَ سَمِيعٌ عَلِيمٌ ۞

182   But he who feareth from a testator some unjust or sinful clause, and maketh peace between the parties, (it shall be) no sin for him. Lo! Allah is Forgiving, Merciful.

فَمَنْ خَافَ مِنْ مُوصٍ جَنَفًا أَوْ إِثْمًا فَأَصْلَحَ بَيْنَهُمْ فَلَا إِثْمَ عَلَيْهِ ۚ إِنَّ اللَّهَ غَفُورٌ رَحِيمٌ ۞

183   O ye who believe! Fasting is prescribed for you, even as it was prescribed for those before you, that ye may ward off evil);

يَا أَيُّهَا الَّذِينَ آمَنُوا كُتِبَ عَلَيْكُمُ الصِّيَامُ كَمَا كُتِبَ عَلَى الَّذِينَ مِنْ قَبْلِكُمْ لَعَلَّكُمْ تَتَّقُونَ ۞

184   (Fast) a certain number of days; and (for) him who is sick among you, or on a journey, (the same) number of other days; and for those who can afford it there is a ransom: the feeding of a man in need. But whoso doeth good of his own accord, it is better for him: and that ye fast is better for you if ye did but know

أَيَّامًا مَعْدُودَاتٍ ۚ فَمَنْ كَانَ مِنْكُمْ مَرِيضًا أَوْ عَلَىٰ سَفَرٍ فَعِدَّةٌ مِنْ أَيَّامٍ أُخَرَ ۚ وَعَلَى الَّذِينَ يُطِيقُونَهُ فِدْيَةٌ طَعَامُ مِسْكِينٍ ۖ فَمَنْ تَطَوَّعَ خَيْرًا فَهُوَ خَيْرٌ لَهُ ۚ وَأَنْ تَصُومُوا خَيْرٌ لَكُمْ ۖ إِنْ كُنْتُمْ تَعْلَمُونَ ۞

185   The month of Ramadān in which was revealed the Quran, a guidance for mankind, and clear proofs of the guidance, and the Criterion (of right and wrong). And whosoever of you is present, let

شَهْرُ رَمَضَانَ الَّذِي أُنْزِلَ فِيهِ الْقُرْآنُ هُدًى لِلنَّاسِ وَبَيِّنَاتٍ مِنَ الْهُدَىٰ وَالْفُرْقَانِ ۚ فَمَنْ شَهِدَ مِنْكُمُ الشَّهْرَ فَلْيَصُمْهُ

him fast the month, and whosoever of you is sick or on a journey, (let him fast the same) number of other days. Allah desireth for you ease; He desireth not hardship for you; and (He desireth) that ye should complete the period, and that ye should magnify Allah for having guided you, and that peradventure ye may be thankful.

وَمَن كَانَ مَرِيضًا أَوْ عَلَىٰ سَفَرٍ فَعِدَّةٌ مِّنْ أَيَّامٍ أُخَرَ يُرِيدُ ٱللَّهُ بِكُمُ ٱلْيُسْرَ وَلَا يُرِيدُ بِكُمُ ٱلْعُسْرَ وَلِتُكْمِلُوا ٱلْعِدَّةَ وَلِتُكَبِّرُوا ٱللَّهَ عَلَىٰ مَا هَدَاٰكُمْ وَلَعَلَّكُمْ تَشْكُرُونَ ۝

186 And when My servant question thee concerning Me, then surely I am nigh. I answer the prayer of the suppliant when he crieth unto Me. So let them bear My call and let them trust in Me, in order that they may be led aright.

وَإِذَا سَأَلَكَ عِبَادِى عَنِّى فَإِنِّى قَرِيبٌ أُجِيبُ دَعْوَةَ ٱلدَّاعِ إِذَا دَعَانِ فَلْيَسْتَجِيبُوا لِى وَلْيُؤْمِنُوا بِى لَعَلَّهُمْ يَرْشُدُونَ ۝

187 It is made lawful for you to go unto your wives on the night of the fast. They are raiment for you and ye are raiment for them. Allah is aware that ye were deceiving yourselves[27] in this respect and He hath turned in mercy toward you and relieved you. So hold intercourse with them and seek that which Allah hath ordained for you, and eat and drink until the white thread becometh distinct to you from the black thread of the dawn.

أُحِلَّ لَكُمْ لَيْلَةَ ٱلصِّيَامِ ٱلرَّفَثُ إِلَىٰ نِسَآئِكُمْ هُنَّ لِبَاسٌ لَّكُمْ وَأَنتُمْ لِبَاسٌ لَّهُنَّ عَلِمَ ٱللَّهُ أَنَّكُمْ كُنتُمْ تَخْتَانُونَ أَنفُسَكُمْ فَتَابَ عَلَيْكُمْ وَعَفَا عَنكُمْ فَٱلْـَٰٔنَ بَٰشِرُوهُنَّ وَٱبْتَغُوا مَا كَتَبَ ٱللَّهُ لَكُمْ وَكُلُوا وَٱشْرَبُوا حَتَّىٰ يَتَبَيَّنَ لَكُمُ ٱلْخَيْطُ ٱلْأَبْيَضُ مِنَ ٱلْخَيْطِ ٱلْأَسْوَدِ مِنَ ٱلْفَجْرِ ثُمَّ أَتِمُّوا ٱلصِّيَامَ إِلَى ٱلَّيْلِ

---

27. Until this verse was revealed, the Muslims used to fast completely from the evening meal of one day till the evening meal of the next, and if they fell asleep before they had taken their meal they had considered it their duty to abstain from it, with the result that men fainted and came near death. Intercourse with their wives had been similarly restricted.

Then strictly observe the fast till nightfall and touch them not, but be at your devotions in the mosques. These are the limits imposed by Allah, so approach them not. Thus Allah expoundeth His revelations to mankind that they may ward off (evil).

188   And eat not up your property among yourselves in vanity, nor seek by it to gain the hearing of the judges that ye may knowingly devour a portion of the property of others wrongfully.

189   They ask thee, (O Muhammad), of new moons. Say: They are fixed seasons for mankind and for the pilgrimage. It is not right-eousness that ye go to houses by the backs thereof (as do the idolaters at certain seasons), but the righteous man is he who wardeth off (evil). So go to houses by the gates thereof, and observe your duty to Allah, that ye may be successful.

190   Fight in the way of Allah against those who fight against you, but begin not hostilities. Lo! Allah loveth not, aggressors.

191   And slay them wherever ye find them, and drive them out of the places whence they drove you out, for persecution is worse than slaughter. And fight not with them at the Invio-lable Place of Worship until they first attack you there, but if they attack you (there) then slay them. Such is the reward of disbelievers.

192 But if they desist, then lo! Allah is Forgiving, Merciful.

فَإِنِ انْتَهَوْا فَإِنَّ اللَّهَ غَفُورٌ رَحِيمٌ ﴿١٩٢﴾

193 And fight them until persecution is no more, and religion is for Allah. But if they desist, then let there be no hostility except against wrongdoers.

وَقَاتِلُوهُمْ حَتَّى لَا تَكُونَ فِتْنَةٌ وَيَكُونَ الدِّينُ لِلَّهِ فَإِنِ انْتَهَوْا فَلَا عُدْوَانَ إِلَّا عَلَى الظَّالِمِينَ ﴿١٩٣﴾

194 The forbidden month for the forbidden month, and forbidden things in retaliation. And one who attacketh you, attack him like manner as he attacked you. Observe your duty to Allah, and know that Allah is with those who ward off (evil).

الشَّهْرُ الْحَرَامُ بِالشَّهْرِ الْحَرَامِ وَالْحُرُمَاتُ قِصَاصٌ فَمَنِ اعْتَدَى عَلَيْكُمْ فَاعْتَدُوا عَلَيْهِ بِمِثْلِ مَا اعْتَدَى عَلَيْكُمْ وَاتَّقُوا اللَّهَ وَاعْلَمُوا أَنَّ اللَّهَ مَعَ الْمُتَّقِينَ ﴿١٩٤﴾

195 Spend your wealth for the cause of Allah, and cast not (yourselves) by your own hands to ruin; and do good. Lo! Allah loveth the beneficent

وَأَنْفِقُوا فِي سَبِيلِ اللَّهِ وَلَا تُلْقُوا بِأَيْدِيكُمْ إِلَى التَّهْلُكَةِ وَأَحْسِنُوا إِنَّ اللَّهَ يُحِبُّ الْمُحْسِنِينَ ﴿١٩٥﴾

196 Perform the pilgrimage[28] and the visit (to Makkah) for Allah. And if ye are prevented, then send such gifts as can be obtained with ease, and shave not your heads until the gifts have reached their destination. And whoever among you is sick or hath an ailment of the head must pay a ransom of fasting or alms giving or offering. And if ye are in safety, then whosoever contenteth himself with the Visit for the Pilgrimage (shall give) such

وَأَتِمُّوا الْحَجَّ وَالْعُمْرَةَ لِلَّهِ فَإِنْ أُحْصِرْتُمْ فَمَا اسْتَيْسَرَ مِنَ الْهَدْيِ وَلَا تَحْلِقُوا رُءُوسَكُمْ حَتَّى يَبْلُغَ الْهَدْيُ مَحِلَّهُ فَمَنْ كَانَ مِنْكُمْ مَرِيضًا أَوْ بِهِ أَذًى مِنْ رَأْسِهِ فَفِدْيَةٌ مِنْ صِيَامٍ أَوْ صَدَقَةٍ أَوْ نُسُكٍ فَإِذَا أَمِنْتُمْ فَمَنْ تَمَتَّعَ بِالْعُمْرَةِ إِلَى الْحَجِّ فَمَا اسْتَيْسَرَ مِنَ الْهَدْيِ فَمَنْ لَمْ يَجِدْ

---

28. See also Sūrah 22: vv. 26 ff.

gifts as can be had with ease. And
whosoever cannot find (such gifts),
then a fast of three days while on
the pilgrimage, and of seven when
ye have returned; that is, ten in all.
That is for him whose folk are not
present at the Inviolable Place of
Worship. Observe your duty to
Allah, and know that Allah is
severe in punishment.

فَصِيَامُ ثَلَاثَةِ أَيَّامٍ فِي الْحَجِّ وَسَبْعَةٍ إِذَا رَجَعْتُمْ
تِلْكَ عَشَرَةٌ كَامِلَةٌ ذَلِكَ لِمَنْ لَّمْ يَكُنْ أَهْلُهُ حَاضِرِي
الْمَسْجِدِ الْحَرَامِ وَاتَّقُوا اللَّهَ وَاعْلَمُوا أَنَّ اللَّهَ شَدِيدُ
الْعِقَابِ ﴿١٩٦﴾

197   The pilgrimage is (in) the
well known months, and whoever is
minded to perform the pilgrimage
therein (let him remember that)
there is (to be) no lewdness nor
abuse nor angry conversation on the
pilgrimage. And whatsoever good
ye do Allah knoweth it. So make
provision for yourselves (here
after); for the best provision is to
ward off evil. Therefore keep your
duty unto Me, O men of understanding.

الْحَجُّ أَشْهُرٌ مَّعْلُومَاتٌ فَمَن فَرَضَ فِيهِنَّ
الْحَجَّ فَلَا رَفَثَ وَلَا فُسُوقَ وَلَا جِدَالَ فِي الْحَجِّ
وَمَا تَفْعَلُوا مِنْ خَيْرٍ يَعْلَمْهُ اللَّهُ
وَتَزَوَّدُوا فَإِنَّ خَيْرَ الزَّادِ التَّقْوَى
وَاتَّقُونِ يَا أُولِي الْأَلْبَابِ ﴿١٩٧﴾

198   It is no sin for you that ye
seek the bounty of your Lord (by
trading). But, when ye press on in
the multitude from Arafat, remember Allah by the sacred monument. Remember Him as He hath
guided you, although before ye
were of those astray.

لَيْسَ عَلَيْكُمْ جُنَاحٌ أَن تَبْتَغُوا
فَضْلًا مِّن رَّبِّكُمْ فَإِذَا أَفَضْتُم
مِّنْ عَرَفَاتٍ فَاذْكُرُوا اللَّهَ عِندَ
الْمَشْعَرِ الْحَرَامِ وَاذْكُرُوهُ كَمَا
هَدَاكُمْ وَإِن كُنتُم مِّن قَبْلِهِ
لَمِنَ الضَّالِّينَ ﴿١٩٨﴾

199   Then hasten onward from
the place whence the multitude
hasteneth onward, and ask forgiveness of Allah. Lo! Allah is Forgiving, Merciful.

ثُمَّ أَفِيضُوا مِنْ حَيْثُ أَفَاضَ النَّاسُ
وَاسْتَغْفِرُوا اللَّهَ إِنَّ اللَّهَ غَفُورٌ رَّحِيمٌ ﴿١٩٩﴾

200 And when ye have completed your devotions, then remember Allah as ye remember your fathers[29] or with a more lively remembrance. But of mankind is he who saith: "Our Lord! Give unto us in the world," and he hath no portion in the Hereafter.

فَإِذَا قَضَيْتُم مَّنَاسِكَكُمْ فَاذْكُرُواْ اللَّهَ كَذِكْرِكُمْ ءَابَآءَكُمْ أَوْ أَشَدَّ ذِكْرًا فَمِنَ النَّاسِ مَن يَقُولُ رَبَّنَآ ءَاتِنَا فِى الدُّنْيَا وَمَا لَهُۥ فِى الْأَخِرَةِ مِنْ خَلَقٍ ٢٠٠

201 And of them (also) is he who saith: "Our Lord! Give unto us in the world that which is good and in the Hereafter that which is good, and guard us from the doom of Fire."

وَمِنْهُم مَّن يَقُولُ رَبَّنَآ ءَاتِنَا فِى الدُّنْيَا حَسَنَةً وَفِى الْأَخِرَةِ حَسَنَةً وَقِنَا عَذَابَ النَّارِ ٢٠١

202 For them there is in store a goodly portion out of that which they have earned. Allah is swift at reckoning.

أُوْلَٰٓئِكَ لَهُمْ نَصِيبٌ مِّمَّا كَسَبُواْ وَاللَّهُ سَرِيعُ الْحِسَابِ ٢٠٢

203 Remember Allah through the appointed days. Then whoso hasteneth (his departure) by two days, it is no sin for him, and whoso delayeth, it is no sin for him; that is for him who wardeth off (evil). Be careful of your duty to Allah, and know that unto Him ye will be gathered.

۞ وَاذْكُرُواْ اللَّهَ فِى أَيَّامٍ مَّعْدُودَٰتٍ فَمَن تَعَجَّلَ فِى يَوْمَيْنِ فَلَآ إِثْمَ عَلَيْهِ وَمَن تَأَخَّرَ فَلَآ إِثْمَ عَلَيْهِ لِمَنِ اتَّقَىٰ وَاتَّقُواْ اللَّهَ وَاعْلَمُوٓاْ أَنَّكُمْ إِلَيْهِ تُحْشَرُونَ ٢٠٣

204 And of mankind there is he whose conversation on the life of this world pleaseth thee (Muhammad), and he calleth Allah to witness as to that which is in his heart; yet he is the most rigid of opponents.

وَمِنَ النَّاسِ مَن يُعْجِبُكَ قَوْلُهُۥ فِى الْحَيَوٰةِ الدُّنْيَا وَيُشْهِدُ اللَّهَ عَلَىٰ مَا فِى قَلْبِهِۦ وَهُوَ أَلَدُّ الْخِصَامِ ٢٠٤

---

29. It was the custom of the Pagan Arabs to praise their forefathers at the conclusion of the Pilgrimage.

205   And when he turneth away (from thee) his effort in the land is to make mischief therein and to destroy the crops and the cattle; and Allah loveth not mischief.

وَإِذَا تَوَلَّىٰ سَعَىٰ فِى ٱلْأَرْضِ لِيُفْسِدَ فِيهَا وَيُهْلِكَ ٱلْحَرْثَ وَٱلنَّسْلَ وَٱللَّهُ لَا يُحِبُّ ٱلْفَسَادَ ۝

206   And when it is said unto him: Be careful of thy duty to Allah, pride taketh him to sin. Hell will settle his account, an evil resting place.

وَإِذَا قِيلَ لَهُ ٱتَّقِ ٱللَّهَ أَخَذَتْهُ ٱلْعِزَّةُ بِٱلْإِثْمِ فَحَسْبُهُ جَهَنَّمُ وَلَبِئْسَ ٱلْمِهَادُ ۝

207   And of mankind is he who would sell himself, seeking the pleasure of Allah; and Allah hath compassion on (His) bondmen.

وَمِنَ ٱلنَّاسِ مَن يَشْرِى نَفْسَهُ ٱبْتِغَآءَ مَرْضَاتِ ٱللَّهِ وَٱللَّهُ رَءُوفٌ بِٱلْعِبَادِ ۝

208   O ye who believe! Come, all of you, into submission (unto Him); and follow not the footsteps of the devil. Lo! he is an open enemy for you.

يَٰٓأَيُّهَا ٱلَّذِينَ ءَامَنُوا ٱدْخُلُوا فِى ٱلسِّلْمِ كَآفَّةً وَلَا تَتَّبِعُوا خُطُوَٰتِ ٱلشَّيْطَٰنِ إِنَّهُ لَكُمْ عَدُوٌّ مُّبِينٌ ۝

209   And if ye slide back after the clear proofs have come unto you, then know that Allah is Mighty, Wise.

فَإِن زَلَلْتُم مِّنۢ بَعْدِ مَا جَآءَتْكُمُ ٱلْبَيِّنَٰتُ فَٱعْلَمُوٓا أَنَّ ٱللَّهَ عَزِيزٌ حَكِيمٌ ۝

210   Wait they for naught else than that Allah should come unto them in the shadows of the clouds with the angels? Then the case would be already judged. All cases go back to Allah (for judgment).

هَلْ يَنظُرُونَ إِلَّآ أَن يَأْتِيَهُمُ ٱللَّهُ فِى ظُلَلٍ مِّنَ ٱلْغَمَامِ وَٱلْمَلَٰٓئِكَةُ وَقُضِىَ ٱلْأَمْرُ وَإِلَى ٱللَّهِ تُرْجَعُ ٱلْأُمُورُ ۝

211   Ask of the Children of Israel how many a clear revelation We gave them! He who altereth the grace of Allah after it hath come unto him (for him), lo! Allah is severe in punishment.

سَلْ بَنِىٓ إِسْرَٰٓءِيلَ كَمْ ءَاتَيْنَٰهُم مِّنْ ءَايَةٍ بَيِّنَةٍ وَمَن يُبَدِّلْ نِعْمَةَ ٱللَّهِ مِنۢ بَعْدِ مَا جَآءَتْهُ فَإِنَّ ٱللَّهَ شَدِيدُ ٱلْعِقَابِ ۝

212 Beautified is the life of the world for those who disbelieve; they make a jest of the believers. But those who keep their duty to Allah will be above them on the Day of Resurrection. Allah giveth without stint to whom He will.

زُيِّنَ لِلَّذِينَ كَفَرُوا الْحَيَوٰةُ الدُّنْيَا وَيَسْخَرُونَ مِنَ الَّذِينَ ءَامَنُوا وَالَّذِينَ اتَّقَوْا فَوْقَهُمْ يَوْمَ الْقِيَٰمَةِ وَاللَّهُ يَرْزُقُ مَن يَشَاءُ بِغَيْرِ حِسَابٍ ۞

213 Mankind were one community, and Allah sent (unto them) Prophets as bearers of good tidings and as warners, and revealed therewith the Scripture with the truth that it might judge between mankind concerning that wherein they differed. And only those unto whom (the Scripture) was given differed concerning it, after clear proofs had come unto them, through hatred one of another. And Allah by His will guided those who believe unto the truth of that concerning which they differed. Allah guideth whom He will unto a straight path

كَانَ النَّاسُ أُمَّةً وَٰحِدَةً فَبَعَثَ اللَّهُ النَّبِيِّنَ مُبَشِّرِينَ وَمُنذِرِينَ وَأَنزَلَ مَعَهُمُ الْكِتَٰبَ بِالْحَقِّ لِيَحْكُمَ بَيْنَ النَّاسِ فِيمَا اخْتَلَفُوا فِيهِ وَمَا اخْتَلَفَ فِيهِ إِلَّا الَّذِينَ أُوتُوهُ مِنۢ بَعْدِ مَا جَاءَتْهُمُ الْبَيِّنَٰتُ بَغْيًا بَيْنَهُمْ فَهَدَى اللَّهُ الَّذِينَ ءَامَنُوا لِمَا اخْتَلَفُوا فِيهِ مِنَ الْحَقِّ بِإِذْنِهِ وَاللَّهُ يَهْدِى مَن يَشَاءُ إِلَىٰ صِرَٰطٍ مُّسْتَقِيمٍ ۞

214 Or think ye that ye will enter Paradise while yet there hath not come unto you the like of (that which came to) those who passed away before you? Affliction and adversity befell them, they were shaken as with earthquake, till the messenger (of Allah) and those who believed along with him said: When cometh Allah's help? Now surely Allah's help is nigh.

أَمْ حَسِبْتُمْ أَن تَدْخُلُوا الْجَنَّةَ وَلَمَّا يَأْتِكُم مَّثَلُ الَّذِينَ خَلَوْا مِن قَبْلِكُم مَّسَّتْهُمُ الْبَأْسَاءُ وَالضَّرَّاءُ وَزُلْزِلُوا حَتَّىٰ يَقُولَ الرَّسُولُ وَالَّذِينَ ءَامَنُوا مَعَهُ مَتَىٰ نَصْرُ اللَّهِ أَلَا إِنَّ نَصْرَ اللَّهِ قَرِيبٌ ۞

215   They ask thee, (O
Muhammad), what they shall spend.
Say: That which ye spend for good
(must go) to parents and near kindred
and orphans and the needy and the
wayfarer. And whatsoever good ye
do, lo! Allah is Aware of it.

يَسْـَٔلُونَكَ مَاذَا يُنفِقُونَ قُلْ مَا أَنفَقْتُم مِّنْ
خَيْرٍ فَلِلْوَالِدَيْنِ وَالْأَقْرَبِينَ وَالْيَتَـٰمَىٰ وَالْمَسَـٰكِينِ
وَابْنِ السَّبِيلِ وَمَا تَفْعَلُوا مِنْ خَيْرٍ فَإِنَّ اللَّهَ بِهِ
عَلِيمٌ ﴿٢١٥﴾

216   Warfare is ordained for you,
though it is hateful unto you; but it
may happen that ye hate a thing
which is good for you, and it may
happen that ye love a thing which is
bad for you. Allah knoweth, ye know
not.

كُتِبَ عَلَيْكُمُ الْقِتَالُ وَهُوَ كُرْهٌ لَّكُمْ وَعَسَىٰ
أَن تَكْرَهُوا شَيْئًا وَهُوَ خَيْرٌ لَّكُمْ وَعَسَىٰ
أَن تُحِبُّوا شَيْئًا وَهُوَ شَرٌّ لَّكُمْ
وَاللَّهُ يَعْلَمُ وَأَنتُمْ لَا تَعْلَمُونَ ﴿٢١٦﴾

217   They   question   thee   (O
Muhammad) with regard to warfare
in the sacred month. Say: Warfare
therein is a great (transgression), but
to turn (men) from the way of Allah,
and to disbelieve in Him and in the
Inviolable Place of Worship, and to
expel his people thence, is a greater
with Allah; for persecution is worse
than killing. And they will not cease
from fighting against you till they
have made you renegades from your
religion, if they can. And whoso of
you becometh a renegade and dieth in
his disbelief: such are they whose
works have fallen both in the world
and the Hereafter. Such are rightful
owners of the Fire: they will abide
therein.

يَسْـَٔلُونَكَ عَنِ الشَّهْرِ الْحَرَامِ قِتَالٍ فِيهِ قُلْ
قِتَالٌ فِيهِ كَبِيرٌ وَصَدٌّ عَن سَبِيلِ اللَّهِ
وَكُفْرٌ بِهِ وَالْمَسْجِدِ الْحَرَامِ وَإِخْرَاجُ أَهْلِهِ
مِنْهُ أَكْبَرُ عِندَ اللَّهِ وَالْفِتْنَةُ أَكْبَرُ مِنَ الْقَتْلِ
وَلَا يَزَالُونَ يُقَٰتِلُونَكُمْ حَتَّىٰ يَرُدُّوكُمْ عَن دِينِكُمْ
إِنِ اسْتَطَٰعُوا وَمَن يَرْتَدِدْ مِنكُمْ عَن دِينِهِ
فَيَمُتْ وَهُوَ كَافِرٌ فَأُولَـٰئِكَ حَبِطَتْ أَعْمَٰلُهُمْ
فِي الدُّنْيَا وَالْآخِرَةِ وَأُولَـٰئِكَ أَصْحَٰبُ النَّارِ
هُمْ فِيهَا خَٰلِدُونَ ﴿٢١٧﴾

218   Lo! those who believe, and
those who emigrate (to escape the
persecution) and strive in the way of
Allah, these have hope of Allah's
mercy. Allah is Forgiving, Merciful.

إِنَّ الَّذِينَ ءَامَنُوا وَالَّذِينَ هَاجَرُوا وَجَٰهَدُوا
فِي سَبِيلِ اللَّهِ أُولَـٰئِكَ يَرْجُونَ رَحْمَتَ اللَّهِ
وَاللَّهُ غَفُورٌ رَّحِيمٌ ﴿٢١٨﴾

219 They question thee about strong drink and games of chance. Say: In both is great sin, and (some) utility for men; but the sin of them is greater than their usefulness. And they ask thee what they ought to spend. Say: That which is superfluous. Thus Allah maketh plain to you (His) revelations, that haply ye may reflect

ۘ يَسْـَٔلُونَكَ عَنِ ٱلْخَمْرِ وَٱلْمَيْسِرِ ۖ قُلْ فِيهِمَآ إِثْمٌ كَبِيرٌ وَمَنَـٰفِعُ لِلنَّاسِ وَإِثْمُهُمَآ أَكْبَرُ مِن نَّفْعِهِمَا ۗ وَيَسْـَٔلُونَكَ مَاذَا يُنفِقُونَ قُلِ ٱلْعَفْوَ ۗ كَذَٰلِكَ يُبَيِّنُ ٱللَّهُ لَكُمُ ٱلْـَٔايَـٰتِ لَعَلَّكُمْ تَتَفَكَّرُونَ ۝

220 Upon the world and the Hereafter. And they question thee concerning orphans. Say: To improve their lot is best. And if ye mingle your affairs with theirs, then (they are) your brothers. Allah knoweth him who spoileth from him who improveth. Had Allah willed He could have overburdened you. Allah is Mighty, Wise.

فِى ٱلدُّنْيَا وَٱلْـَٔاخِرَةِ ۗ وَيَسْـَٔلُونَكَ عَنِ ٱلْيَتَـٰمَىٰ ۖ قُلْ إِصْلَاحٌ لَّهُمْ خَيْرٌ ۖ وَإِن تُخَالِطُوهُمْ فَإِخْوَٰنُكُمْ ۚ وَٱللَّهُ يَعْلَمُ ٱلْمُفْسِدَ مِنَ ٱلْمُصْلِحِ ۚ وَلَوْ شَآءَ ٱللَّهُ لَأَعْنَتَكُمْ ۚ إِنَّ ٱللَّهَ عَزِيزٌ حَكِيمٌ ۝

221 Wed not idolatresses till they believe; for lo! a believing bondwoman is better than an idolatress though she please you; and give not your daughters in marriage to idolaters till they believe, for lo! a believing slave is better than an idolater though he please you. These invite unto the Fire, and Allah inviteth unto the Garden, and unto forgiveness by His grace, and expoundeth thus His revelations to mankind that haply they may remember.

وَلَا تَنكِحُوا۟ ٱلْمُشْرِكَـٰتِ حَتَّىٰ يُؤْمِنَّ ۚ وَلَأَمَةٌ مُّؤْمِنَةٌ خَيْرٌ مِّن مُّشْرِكَةٍ وَلَوْ أَعْجَبَتْكُمْ ۗ وَلَا تُنكِحُوا۟ ٱلْمُشْرِكِينَ حَتَّىٰ يُؤْمِنُوا۟ ۚ وَلَعَبْدٌ مُّؤْمِنٌ خَيْرٌ مِّن مُّشْرِكٍ وَلَوْ أَعْجَبَكُمْ ۗ أُو۟لَـٰٓئِكَ يَدْعُونَ إِلَى ٱلنَّارِ ۖ وَٱللَّهُ يَدْعُوٓا۟ إِلَى ٱلْجَنَّةِ وَٱلْمَغْفِرَةِ بِإِذْنِهِۦ ۖ وَيُبَيِّنُ ءَايَـٰتِهِۦ لِلنَّاسِ لَعَلَّهُمْ يَتَذَكَّرُونَ ۝

222 They question thee (O Muhammad) concerning menstruation. Say: It is an illness, so let women alone at such time and go not in unto them till they are cleansed. And when they have purified themselves, then go in unto them as Allah hath enjoined upon you. Truly Allah loveth those who turn unto Him, and loveth those who have a care for cleanness.

وَيَسْـَٔلُونَكَ عَنِ ٱلْمَحِيضِ قُلْ هُوَ أَذًى
فَٱعْتَزِلُوا۟ ٱلنِّسَآءَ فِى ٱلْمَحِيضِ وَلَا تَقْرَبُوهُنَّ
حَتَّىٰ يَطْهُرْنَ فَإِذَا تَطَهَّرْنَ فَأْتُوهُنَّ مِنْ حَيْثُ
أَمَرَكُمُ ٱللَّهُ إِنَّ ٱللَّهَ يُحِبُّ ٱلتَّوَّٰبِينَ
وَيُحِبُّ ٱلْمُتَطَهِّرِينَ ۝

223 Your women are a tilth for you (to cultivate) go to your tilth as ye will, and send (good deeds) before you for your souls, and fear Allah, and know that ye will (one day) meet Him. Give glad tidings to believers, (O Muhammad).

نِسَآؤُكُمْ حَرْثٌ لَّكُمْ فَأْتُوا۟ حَرْثَكُمْ أَنَّىٰ شِئْتُمْ
وَقَدِّمُوا۟ لِأَنفُسِكُمْ وَٱتَّقُوا۟ ٱللَّهَ وَٱعْلَمُوٓا۟
أَنَّكُم مُّلَٰقُوهُ وَبَشِّرِ ٱلْمُؤْمِنِينَ ۝

224 And make not Allah, by your oaths, a hindrance to your being righteous and observing your duty unto Him and making peace among mankind. Allah is Hearer, Knower.

وَلَا تَجْعَلُوا۟ ٱللَّهَ عُرْضَةً لِّأَيْمَٰنِكُمْ
أَن تَبَرُّوا۟ وَتَتَّقُوا۟ وَتُصْلِحُوا۟ بَيْنَ ٱلنَّاسِ
وَٱللَّهُ سَمِيعٌ عَلِيمٌ ۝

225 Allah will not take you to task for that which unintentional in your oaths. But He will take you to task for that which your hearts have garnered. Allah is Forgiving, Clement.

لَّا يُؤَاخِذُكُمُ ٱللَّهُ بِٱللَّغْوِ فِىٓ أَيْمَٰنِكُمْ وَلَٰكِن يُؤَاخِذُكُم
بِمَا كَسَبَتْ قُلُوبُكُمْ وَٱللَّهُ غَفُورٌ حَلِيمٌ ۝

226 Those who forswear their wives must wait four months; then, if they change their mind, lo! Allah is Forgiving, Merciful.

لِّلَّذِينَ يُؤْلُونَ مِن نِّسَآئِهِمْ تَرَبُّصُ أَرْبَعَةِ أَشْهُرٍ فَإِن
فَآءُو فَإِنَّ ٱللَّهَ غَفُورٌ رَّحِيمٌ ۝

227 And if they decide upon divorce (let them remember that) Allah is Hearer, Knower.

وَإِنْ عَزَمُوا۟ ٱلطَّلَٰقَ فَإِنَّ ٱللَّهَ سَمِيعٌ عَلِيمٌ ۝

228 Women who are divorced shall wait, keeping themselves apart, three (monthly) courses. And it is not lawful for them that they should conceal that which Allah hath created in their wombs if they are believers in Allah and the Last Day. And their husbands would do better to take them back in that case if they desire a reconciliation. And they (women) have rights similar to those (of men) over them in kindness, and men are a degree above them. Allah is Mighty, Wise.

وَالْمُطَلَّقَاتُ يَتَرَبَّصْنَ بِأَنْفُسِهِنَّ ثَلَاثَةَ قُرُوْءٍ وَلَا يَحِلُّ لَهُنَّ أَنْ يَكْتُمْنَ مَا خَلَقَ اللّٰهُ فِيْ أَرْحَامِهِنَّ إِنْ كُنَّ يُؤْمِنَّ بِاللّٰهِ وَالْيَوْمِ الْآخِرِ وَبُعُوْلَتُهُنَّ أَحَقُّ بِرَدِّهِنَّ فِيْ ذٰلِكَ إِنْ أَرَادُوْا إِصْلَاحًا وَلَهُنَّ مِثْلُ الَّذِيْ عَلَيْهِنَّ بِالْمَعْرُوْفِ وَلِلرِّجَالِ عَلَيْهِنَّ دَرَجَةٌ وَاللّٰهُ عَزِيْزٌ حَكِيْمٌ ۝

229 Divorce must be pronounced twice and then (a woman) must be retained in honor or released in kindness. And it is not lawful for you that ye take from them aught of that which ye have given them; except (in the case) when both fear that they may not be able to keep within the limits (imposed by) Allah. And if ye fear that they may not be able to keep the limits of Allah, in that case it is no sin for either of them if the woman ransom herself. These are the limits (imposed by) Allah. Transgress them not. For whoso transgresseth Allah's limits: such are wrongdoers.

اَلطَّلَاقُ مَرَّتَانِ فَإِمْسَاكٌ بِمَعْرُوْفٍ أَوْ تَسْرِيْحٌ بِإِحْسَانٍ وَلَا يَحِلُّ لَكُمْ أَنْ تَأْخُذُوْا مِمَّا ءَاتَيْتُمُوْهُنَّ شَيْئًا إِلَّا أَنْ يَخَافَا أَلَّا يُقِيْمَا حُدُوْدَ اللّٰهِ فَإِنْ خِفْتُمْ أَلَّا يُقِيْمَا حُدُوْدَ اللّٰهِ فَلَا جُنَاحَ عَلَيْهِمَا فِيْمَا افْتَدَتْ بِهِ تِلْكَ حُدُوْدُ اللّٰهِ فَلَا تَعْتَدُوْهَا وَمَنْ يَتَعَدَّ حُدُوْدَ اللّٰهِ فَأُولٰٓئِكَ هُمُ الظَّالِمُوْنَ ۝

230 And if he hath divorced her (the third time), then she is not lawful unto him thereafter until she hath wedded another husband. Then if he (the other husband) divorce her it is no sin for both of them that they come together again if they consider

فَإِنْ طَلَّقَهَا فَلَا تَحِلُّ لَهُ مِنْ بَعْدُ حَتّٰى تَنْكِحَ زَوْجًا غَيْرَهُ فَإِنْ طَلَّقَهَا فَلَا جُنَاحَ عَلَيْهِمَا أَنْ يَتَرَاجَعَا إِنْ

that they are able to observe the limits of Allah. These are the limits of Allah. He manifesteth them for people who have knowledge.

231 When ye have divorced women, and they have reached their term, then retain them in kindness or release them in kindness. Retain them not to their hurt so that ye transgress (the limits). He who doeth that hath wronged his soul. Make not the revelations of Allah a laughing stock (by your behavior), but re-member Allah's grace upon you and that which He hath revealed unto you of the Scripture and of wisdom, whereby He doth exhort you. Ob-serve your duty to Allah and know that Allah is Aware of all things.

232 And when ye have divorced women and they reach their term, place not difficulties in the way of their marrying their husbands if it is agreed between them in kindness. This is an admonition for him among you who believeth in Allah and the Last Day. That is more virtuous for you, and cleaner. Allah knoweth: ye know not.

233 Mothers shall suckle their children for two whole years; (that is) for those who wish to complete the suckling. The duty of feeding and clothing nursing mothers in a seemly manner is upon the father of the child. No one should be charged beyond his capacity. A mother should

ظَنَّا أَن يُقِيمَا حُدُودَ اللَّهِ وَتِلْكَ حُدُودُ اللَّهِ يُبَيِّنُهَا لِقَوْمٍ يَعْلَمُونَ ۝

وَإِذَا طَلَّقْتُمُ النِّسَاءَ فَبَلَغْنَ أَجَلَهُنَّ فَأَمْسِكُوهُنَّ بِمَعْرُوفٍ أَوْ سَرِّحُوهُنَّ بِمَعْرُوفٍ وَلَا تُمْسِكُوهُنَّ ضِرَارًا لِّتَعْتَدُوا وَمَن يَفْعَلْ ذَلِكَ فَقَدْ ظَلَمَ نَفْسَهُ وَلَا تَتَّخِذُوا ءَايَتِ اللَّهِ هُزُوًا وَاذْكُرُوا نِعْمَتَ اللَّهِ عَلَيْكُمْ وَمَا أَنزَلَ عَلَيْكُم مِّنَ الْكِتَبِ وَالْحِكْمَةِ يَعِظُكُم بِهِ وَاتَّقُوا اللَّهَ وَاعْلَمُوا أَنَّ اللَّهَ بِكُلِّ شَيْءٍ عَلِيمٌ ۝

وَإِذَا طَلَّقْتُمُ النِّسَاءَ فَبَلَغْنَ أَجَلَهُنَّ فَلَا تَعْضُلُوهُنَّ أَن يَنكِحْنَ أَزْوَجَهُنَّ إِذَا تَرَاضَوْا بَيْنَهُم بِالْمَعْرُوفِ ذَلِكَ يُوعَظُ بِهِ مَن كَانَ مِنكُمْ يُؤْمِنُ بِاللَّهِ وَالْيَوْمِ الْأَخِرِ ذَلِكُمْ أَزْكَى لَكُمْ وَأَطْهَرُ وَاللَّهُ يَعْلَمُ وَأَنتُمْ لَا تَعْلَمُونَ ۝

۞ وَالْوَلِدَتُ يُرْضِعْنَ أَوْلَدَهُنَّ حَوْلَيْنِ كَامِلَيْنِ لِمَنْ أَرَادَ أَن يُتِمَّ الرَّضَاعَةَ وَعَلَى الْمَوْلُودِ لَهُ رِزْقُهُنَّ وَكِسْوَتُهُنَّ بِالْمَعْرُوفِ لَا تُكَلَّفُ نَفْسٌ إِلَّا وُسْعَهَا لَا تُضَآرَّ وَلِدَةٌ بِوَلَدِهَا وَلَا مَوْلُودٌ لَّهُ بِوَلَدِهِ

not be made to suffer because of her child, nor should he to whom the child is born (be made to suffer) because of his child. And on the (father's) heir is incumbent the like of that (which was incumbent on the father). If they desire to wean the child by mutual consent and (after) consultation, it is no sin for them; and if ye wish to give your children out to nurse, it is no sin for you, provided that ye pay what is due from you in kindness. Observe your duty to Allah, and know that Allah is Seer of what ye do.

وَعَلَى الْوَارِثِ مِثْلُ ذَٰلِكَ فَإِنْ أَرَادَا فِصَالًا عَنْ تَرَاضٍ مِّنْهُمَا وَتَشَاوُرٍ فَلَا جُنَاحَ عَلَيْهِمَا وَإِنْ أَرَدتُّمْ أَن تَسْتَرْضِعُوٓا أَوْلَٰدَكُمْ فَلَا جُنَاحَ عَلَيْكُمْ إِذَا سَلَّمْتُم مَّآ ءَاتَيْتُم بِالْمَعْرُوفِ وَاتَّقُوا اللَّهَ وَاعْلَمُوٓا أَنَّ اللَّهَ بِمَا تَعْمَلُونَ بَصِيرٌ ۝

234   Such of you as die and leave behind them wives, they (the wives) shall wait, keeping themselves apart, four months and ten days. And when they reach the term (prescribed for them) then there is no sin for you in aught that they may do with themselves in decency. Allah is Informed of what ye do.

وَالَّذِينَ يُتَوَفَّوْنَ مِنكُمْ وَيَذَرُونَ أَزْوَٰجًا يَتَرَبَّصْنَ بِأَنفُسِهِنَّ أَرْبَعَةَ أَشْهُرٍ وَعَشْرًا فَإِذَا بَلَغْنَ أَجَلَهُنَّ فَلَا جُنَاحَ عَلَيْكُمْ فِيمَا فَعَلْنَ فِىٓ أَنفُسِهِنَّ بِالْمَعْرُوفِ وَاللَّهُ بِمَا تَعْمَلُونَ خَبِيرٌ ۝

235   There is no sin for you in that which ye proclaim or hide in your minds concerning your troth with women. Allah knoweth that ye will remember them. But plight not your troth with women except by uttering a recognized form of words. And do not consummate the marriage until (the term) prescribed is run. Know that Allah knoweth what is in your minds, so beware of Him; and know that Allah is Forgiving, Clement.

وَلَا جُنَاحَ عَلَيْكُمْ فِيمَا عَرَّضْتُم بِهِۦ مِنْ خِطْبَةِ النِّسَآءِ أَوْ أَكْنَنتُمْ فِىٓ أَنفُسِكُمْ عَلِمَ اللَّهُ أَنَّكُمْ سَتَذْكُرُونَهُنَّ وَلَٰكِن لَّا تُوَاعِدُوهُنَّ سِرًّا إِلَّآ أَن تَقُولُوا قَوْلًا مَّعْرُوفًا وَلَا تَعْزِمُوا عُقْدَةَ النِّكَاحِ حَتَّىٰ يَبْلُغَ الْكِتَٰبُ أَجَلَهُۥ وَاعْلَمُوٓا أَنَّ اللَّهَ يَعْلَمُ مَا فِىٓ أَنفُسِكُمْ فَاحْذَرُوهُ وَاعْلَمُوٓا أَنَّ اللَّهَ غَفُورٌ حَلِيمٌ ۝

236　It is no sin for you if ye divorce women while yet ye have not touched them, nor appointed unto them a portion. Provide for them, the rich according to his means, and the straitened according to his means, a fair provision. (This is) a bounden duty for those who do good.

لَا جُنَاحَ عَلَيْكُمْ إِن طَلَّقْتُمُ ٱلنِّسَآءَ مَا لَمْ تَمَسُّوهُنَّ أَوْ تَفْرِضُوا۟ لَهُنَّ فَرِيضَةً ۚ وَمَتِّعُوهُنَّ عَلَى ٱلْمُوسِعِ قَدَرُهُۥ وَعَلَى ٱلْمُقْتِرِ قَدَرُهُۥ مَتَٰعًۢا بِٱلْمَعْرُوفِ ۖ حَقًّا عَلَى ٱلْمُحْسِنِينَ ﴿٣٦﴾

237　If ye divorce them before ye have touched them and ye have appointed unto them a portion, then (pay the) half of that which ye appointed, unless they (the women) agree to forgo it, or he agreeth to forgo it in whose hand is the marriage tie.[30] To forgo is nearer to piety; And forget not kindness among yourselves. Allah is Seer of what ye do.

وَإِن طَلَّقْتُمُوهُنَّ مِن قَبْلِ أَن تَمَسُّوهُنَّ وَقَدْ فَرَضْتُمْ لَهُنَّ فَرِيضَةً فَنِصْفُ مَا فَرَضْتُمْ إِلَّآ أَن يَعْفُونَ أَوْ يَعْفُوَا۟ ٱلَّذِى بِيَدِهِۦ عُقْدَةُ ٱلنِّكَاحِ ۚ وَأَن تَعْفُوٓا۟ أَقْرَبُ لِلتَّقْوَىٰ ۚ وَلَا تَنسَوُا۟ ٱلْفَضْلَ بَيْنَكُمْ ۚ إِنَّ ٱللَّهَ بِمَا تَعْمَلُونَ بَصِيرٌ ﴿٣٧﴾

238　Be guardians of your prayers, and of the midmost prayer,[31] and stand up with devotion to Allah.

حَٰفِظُوا۟ عَلَى ٱلصَّلَوَٰتِ وَٱلصَّلَوٰةِ ٱلْوُسْطَىٰ وَقُومُوا۟ لِلَّهِ قَٰنِتِينَ ﴿٣٨﴾

239　And if ye go in fear, then (pray) standing or on horseback. And when ye are again in safety, remember Allah, as He hath taught you that which (heretofore) ye knew not.

فَإِنْ خِفْتُمْ فَرِجَالًا أَوْ رُكْبَانًا ۖ فَإِذَآ أَمِنتُمْ فَٱذْكُرُوا۟ ٱللَّهَ كَمَا عَلَّمَكُم مَّا لَمْ تَكُونُوا۟ تَعْلَمُونَ ﴿٣٩﴾

---

30. *i.e.* the bridegroom.

31. Meaning, probably, the best amid all forms of prayer; but some authorities think the reference is to the 'Aṣr (afternoon) prayer which Muslims are most apt to forget.

240 (In the case of) those of you who are about to die and leave behind them wives, they should bequeath unto their wives a provision for the year without turning them out, but if they go out (of their own accord) there is no sin for you in that which they do of themselves within their rights. Allah is Mighty, Wise.

وَالَّذِينَ يُتَوَفَّوْنَ مِنكُمْ وَيَذَرُونَ أَزْوَٰجًا وَصِيَّةً لِّأَزْوَٰجِهِم مَّتَٰعًا إِلَى ٱلْحَوْلِ غَيْرَ إِخْرَاجٍ فَإِنْ خَرَجْنَ فَلَا جُنَاحَ عَلَيْكُمْ فِى مَا فَعَلْنَ فِىٓ أَنفُسِهِنَّ مِن مَّعْرُوفٍ وَٱللَّهُ عَزِيزٌ حَكِيمٌ ﴿٢٤٠﴾

241 For divorced women is a provision in kindness: a duty for those who ward off (evil).

وَلِلْمُطَلَّقَٰتِ مَتَٰعٌۢ بِٱلْمَعْرُوفِ حَقًّا عَلَى ٱلْمُتَّقِينَ ﴿٢٤١﴾

242 Thus Allah expoundeth unto you His revelations so that ye may understand.

كَذَٰلِكَ يُبَيِّنُ ٱللَّهُ لَكُمْ ءَايَٰتِهِۦ لَعَلَّكُمْ تَعْقِلُونَ ﴿٢٤٢﴾

243 Bethink thee not (O Muhammad) of those of old, who went forth from their habitations in their thousands, fearing death,[32] and Allah said unto them: Die, and then He brought them back to life. Lo! Allah is a Lord of Kindness to mankind, but most of mankind give not thanks.

۞ أَلَمْ تَرَ إِلَى ٱلَّذِينَ خَرَجُوا۟ مِن دِيَٰرِهِمْ وَهُمْ أُلُوفٌ حَذَرَ ٱلْمَوْتِ فَقَالَ لَهُمُ ٱللَّهُ مُوتُوا۟ ثُمَّ أَحْيَٰهُمْ إِنَّ ٱللَّهَ لَذُو فَضْلٍ عَلَى ٱلنَّاسِ وَلَٰكِنَّ أَكْثَرَ ٱلنَّاسِ لَا يَشْكُرُونَ ﴿٢٤٣﴾

244 Fight in the way of Allah, and know that Allah is Hearer, Knower.

وَقَٰتِلُوا۟ فِى سَبِيلِ ٱللَّهِ وَٱعْلَمُوٓا۟ أَنَّ ٱللَّهَ سَمِيعٌ عَلِيمٌ ﴿٢٤٤﴾

245 Who is it that will lend unto Allah a goodly loan,[33] so that He may give it increase manifold for him? Allah straiteneth and enlargeth. Unto Him ye will return.

مَّن ذَا ٱلَّذِى يُقْرِضُ ٱللَّهَ قَرْضًا حَسَنًا فَيُضَٰعِفَهُۥ لَهُۥٓ أَضْعَافًا كَثِيرَةً وَٱللَّهُ يَقْبِضُ وَيَبْصُۜطُ وَإِلَيْهِ تُرْجَعُونَ ﴿٢٤٥﴾

---

32. The reference is to the Exodus.

33. A loan without interest - *i.e.* without thought of gain.

246   Bethink thee of the leaders of
the Children of Israel after Moses,
how they said unto a Prophet whom
they had: Set up for us a King and
we will fight in Allah's way. He
said: Would ye then refrain from
fighting if fighting were prescribed
for you? They said: Why should we
not fight in Allah's way when we
have been driven from our dwellings
with our children? Yet, when fighting was prescribed for them, they
turned away, all save a few of them.
Allah is Aware of evil doers.

أَلَمْ تَرَ إِلَى ٱلْمَلَإِ مِنۢ بَنِىٓ إِسْرَٰٓءِيلَ مِنۢ بَعْدِ
مُوسَىٰٓ إِذْ قَالُوا۟ لِنَبِىٍّ لَّهُمُ ٱبْعَثْ لَنَا مَلِكًا
نُّقَٰتِلْ فِى سَبِيلِ ٱللَّهِ قَالَ هَلْ عَسَيْتُمْ إِن
كُتِبَ عَلَيْكُمُ ٱلْقِتَالُ أَلَّا تُقَٰتِلُوا۟ قَالُوا۟
وَمَا لَنَآ أَلَّا نُقَٰتِلَ فِى سَبِيلِ ٱللَّهِ وَقَدْ
أُخْرِجْنَا مِن دِيَٰرِنَا وَأَبْنَآئِنَا فَلَمَّا كُتِبَ
عَلَيْهِمُ ٱلْقِتَالُ تَوَلَّوْا۟ إِلَّا قَلِيلًا مِّنْهُمْ
وَٱللَّهُ عَلِيمٌۢ بِٱلظَّٰلِمِينَ ۝

247   Their Prophet said unto them:
Lo! Allah hath raised up Saul to be
a king for you. They said: How can
he have kingdom over us when we
are more deserving of the kingdom
than he is, since he hath not been
given wealth enough? He said: Lo!
Allah hath chosen him above you,
and hath increased him abundantly in
wisdom and stature. Allah bestoweth
His sovereignty on whom He will.
Allah is All Embracing, All
Knowing.

وَقَالَ لَهُمْ نَبِيُّهُمْ إِنَّ ٱللَّهَ قَدْ بَعَثَ لَكُمْ
طَالُوتَ مَلِكًا قَالُوٓا۟ أَنَّىٰ يَكُونُ لَهُ ٱلْمُلْكُ
عَلَيْنَا وَنَحْنُ أَحَقُّ بِٱلْمُلْكِ مِنْهُ وَلَمْ يُؤْتَ
سَعَةً مِّنَ ٱلْمَالِ قَالَ إِنَّ ٱللَّهَ ٱصْطَفَىٰهُ
عَلَيْكُمْ وَزَادَهُۥ بَسْطَةً فِى ٱلْعِلْمِ
وَٱلْجِسْمِ وَٱللَّهُ يُؤْتِى مُلْكَهُۥ مَن يَشَآءُ
وَٱللَّهُ وَٰسِعٌ عَلِيمٌ ۝

248   And their Prophet said unto
them: Lo! the token of his kingdom
is that there shall come unto you the
ark wherein is peace of reassurance
from your Lord, and a remnant of
that which the house of Moses and
the house of Aaron left behind, the
angels bearing it. Lo! herein shall be
a token for you if (in truth) ye are
believers.

وَقَالَ لَهُمْ نَبِيُّهُمْ إِنَّ ءَايَةَ مُلْكِهِۦٓ
أَن يَأْتِيَكُمُ ٱلتَّابُوتُ فِيهِ سَكِينَةٌ
مِّن رَّبِّكُمْ وَبَقِيَّةٌ مِّمَّا تَرَكَ ءَالُ مُوسَىٰ
وَءَالُ هَٰرُونَ تَحْمِلُهُ ٱلْمَلَٰٓئِكَةُ إِنَّ فِى ذَٰلِكَ
لَءَايَةً لَّكُمْ إِن كُنتُم مُّؤْمِنِينَ ۝

249 And when Saul set out with the army, he said: Lo! Allah will try you by (the ordeal of) a river. Whosoever therefore drinketh thereof he is not of me, and whosoever tasteth it not he is of me, save him who taketh (thereof) in the hollow of his hand. But they drank thereof, all save a few of them. And after he had crossed (the river), he and those who believed with him, they said: We have no power this day against Goliath and his hosts. But those who knew that they would meet their Lord exclaimed: How many a little company hath overcome a mighty host by Allah's leave! Allah is with the steadfast.

فَلَمَّا فَصَلَ طَالُوتُ بِالْجُنُودِ قَالَ إِنَّ اللّٰهَ مُبْتَلِيكُم بِنَهَرٍ فَمَن شَرِبَ مِنْهُ فَلَيْسَ مِنِّي وَمَن لَّمْ يَطْعَمْهُ فَإِنَّهُ مِنِّي إِلَّا مَنِ اغْتَرَفَ غُرْفَةً بِيَدِهِ فَشَرِبُواْ مِنْهُ إِلَّا قَلِيلًا مِّنْهُمْ فَلَمَّا جَاوَزَهُ هُوَ وَالَّذِينَ ءَامَنُواْ مَعَهُ قَالُواْ لَا طَاقَةَ لَنَا الْيَوْمَ بِجَالُوتَ وَجُنُودِهِ قَالَ الَّذِينَ يَظُنُّونَ أَنَّهُم مُّلَاقُواْ اللّٰهِ كَم مِّن فِئَةٍ قَلِيلَةٍ غَلَبَتْ فِئَةً كَثِيرَةً بِإِذْنِ اللّٰهِ وَاللّٰهُ مَعَ الصَّابِرِينَ ۞

250 And when they went into the field against Goliath and his hosts they said: Our Lord! Bestow on us endurance, make our foothold sure, and give us help against the disbelieving folk.

وَلَمَّا بَرَزُواْ لِجَالُوتَ وَجُنُودِهِ قَالُواْ رَبَّنَا أَفْرِغْ عَلَيْنَا صَبْرًا وَثَبِّتْ أَقْدَامَنَا وَانصُرْنَا عَلَى الْقَوْمِ الْكَافِرِينَ ۞

251 So they routed them by Allah's leave and David slew Goliath; and Allah gave him the kingdom and wisdom, and taught him of that which He willeth. And if Allah had not repelled some men by others the earth would have been corrupted. But Allah is a Lord of Kindness to (His) creatures.

فَهَزَمُوهُم بِإِذْنِ اللّٰهِ وَقَتَلَ دَاوُدُ جَالُوتَ وَءَاتَاهُ اللّٰهُ الْمُلْكَ وَالْحِكْمَةَ وَعَلَّمَهُ مِمَّا يَشَاءُ وَلَوْلَا دَفْعُ اللّٰهِ النَّاسَ بَعْضَهُم بِبَعْضٍ لَّفَسَدَتِ الْأَرْضُ وَلَكِنَّ اللّٰهَ ذُو فَضْلٍ عَلَى الْعَالَمِينَ ۞

252 These are the portents of Allah which We recite unto thee (Muhammad) with truth, and Lo! thou art of the number of (Our) messengers;

تِلْكَ ءَايَاتُ اللّٰهِ نَتْلُوهَا عَلَيْكَ بِالْحَقِّ وَإِنَّكَ لَمِنَ الْمُرْسَلِينَ ۞

253   Of those messengers, some
of whom We have caused to excel
others, and of whom there are some
unto whom Allah spake, while
some of them He exalted (above
others) in degree; and We gave
Jesus, son of Mary, clear proofs (of
Allah's sovereignty) and We supported him with the holy Spirit.[34]
And if Allah had so willed it, those
who followed after them would not
have fought one with another after
the clear proofs had come unto
them. But they differed, some of
them believing and some disbelieving. And if Allah had so willed
it, they would not have fought one
with another; but Allah doeth what
He will.

۞ تِلْكَ الرُّسُلُ فَضَّلْنَا بَعْضَهُمْ عَلَى بَعْضٍ مِّنْهُم
مَّن كَلَّمَ اللَّهُ وَرَفَعَ بَعْضَهُمْ دَرَجَٰتٍ وَءَاتَيْنَا
عِيسَى ابْنَ مَرْيَمَ الْبَيِّنَٰتِ وَأَيَّدْنَٰهُ بِرُوحِ
الْقُدُسِ وَلَوْ شَآءَ اللَّهُ مَا اقْتَتَلَ الَّذِينَ
مِنۢ بَعْدِهِم مِّنۢ بَعْدِ مَا جَآءَتْهُمُ الْبَيِّنَٰتُ
وَلَٰكِنِ اخْتَلَفُوا فَمِنْهُم مَّنْ ءَامَنَ وَمِنْهُم مَّن كَفَرَ
وَلَوْ شَآءَ اللَّهُ مَا اقْتَتَلُوا وَلَٰكِنَّ اللَّهَ يَفْعَلُ
مَا يُرِيدُ ﴿٢٥٣﴾

254   O ye who believe! Spend of
that wherewith We have provided
you ere a day come when there will
be no trafficking, nor friendship,
nor intercession. The disbelievers,
they are the wrong doers.

يَٰٓأَيُّهَا الَّذِينَ ءَامَنُوٓا أَنفِقُوا مِمَّا رَزَقْنَٰكُم
مِّن قَبْلِ أَن يَأْتِيَ يَوْمٌ لَّا بَيْعٌ فِيهِ وَلَا خُلَّةٌ
وَلَا شَفَٰعَةٌ وَالْكَٰفِرُونَ هُمُ الظَّٰلِمُونَ ﴿٢٥٤﴾

255   Allah! There is no God save
Him, the Alive, the Eternal. Neither
slumber nor sleep overtaketh Him.
Unto Him belongeth whatsoever is
in the heavens and whatsoever is in
the earth. Who is he that inter-
cedeth with Him save by His leave?
He knoweth that which is in front

اللَّهُ لَآ إِلَٰهَ إِلَّا هُوَ الْحَيُّ الْقَيُّومُ لَا تَأْخُذُهُۥ سِنَةٌ
وَلَا نَوْمٌ لَّهُۥ مَا فِي السَّمَٰوَٰتِ وَمَا فِي الْأَرْضِ مَن ذَا
الَّذِى يَشْفَعُ عِندَهُۥٓ إِلَّا بِإِذْنِهِۦ يَعْلَمُ مَا بَيْنَ

---

34. *i.e.* the angel Gabriel.

of them and that which is behind them, while they encompass nothing of His knowledge save what He will. His throne includeth the heavens and the earth, and He is never weary of preserving them. He is the Sublime, the Tremendous.

أَيْدِيهِمْ وَمَا خَلْفَهُمْ وَلَا يُحِيطُونَ بِشَيْءٍ مِّنْ عِلْمِهِ إِلَّا بِمَا شَاءَ وَسِعَ كُرْسِيُّهُ السَّمَوَاتِ وَالْأَرْضَ وَلَا يَئُودُهُ حِفْظُهُمَا وَهُوَ الْعَلِيُّ الْعَظِيمُ ۝

256   There is no compulsion in religion. The right direction is henceforth distinct from error. And he who rejecteth false deities and believeth in Allah hath grasped a firm hand hold which will never break. Allah is Hearer, Knower.

لَا إِكْرَاهَ فِى الدِّينِ قَدْ تَبَيَّنَ الرُّشْدُ مِنَ الْغَىِّ فَمَنْ يَكْفُرْ بِالطَّاغُوتِ وَيُؤْمِنْ بِاللّٰهِ فَقَدِ اسْتَمْسَكَ بِالْعُرْوَةِ الْوُثْقَى لَا انْفِصَامَ لَهَا وَاللّٰهُ سَمِيعٌ عَلِيمٌ ۝

257   Allah is the Protecting Friend of those who believe. He bringeth them out of darkness into light. As for those who disbelieve, their patrons are false deities. They bring them out of light into darkness. Such are rightful owners of the Fire. They will abide therein.

اللّٰهُ وَلِىُّ الَّذِينَ ءَامَنُوا يُخْرِجُهُمْ مِنَ الظُّلُمَاتِ إِلَى النُّورِ وَالَّذِينَ كَفَرُوا أَوْلِيَاؤُهُمُ الطَّاغُوتُ يُخْرِجُونَهُمْ مِنَ النُّورِ إِلَى الظُّلُمَاتِ أُولَئِكَ أَصْحَابُ النَّارِ هُمْ فِيهَا خَالِدُونَ ۝

258   Bethink thee not of him who had an argument with Abraham about his Lord, because Allah had given him the kingdom; how, when Abraham said: My Lord is He who giveth life and causeth death, he answered: I give life and cause death. Abraham said: Lo! Allah causeth the sun to rise in the East, so do thou cause it to come up from the West. Thus was the disbeliever abashed. And Allah guideth not wrong doing folk.

أَلَمْ تَرَ إِلَى الَّذِى حَاجَّ إِبْرَاهِيمَ فِى رَبِّهِ أَنْ ءَاتَاهُ اللّٰهُ الْمُلْكَ إِذْ قَالَ إِبْرَاهِيمُ رَبِّيَ الَّذِى يُحْيِ وَيُمِيتُ قَالَ أَنَا أُحْيِ وَأُمِيتُ قَالَ إِبْرَاهِيمُ فَإِنَّ اللّٰهَ يَأْتِى بِالشَّمْسِ مِنَ الْمَشْرِقِ فَأْتِ بِهَا مِنَ الْمَغْرِبِ فَبُهِتَ الَّذِى كَفَرَ وَاللّٰهُ لَا يَهْدِى الْقَوْمَ الظَّالِمِينَ ۝

259   Or (bethink thee of) the like of him who, passing by a township which had fallen into utter ruin, exclaimed: How shall Allah give this township[35] life after its death? And Allah made him die a hundred years, then brought him back to life. He said: How long hast thou tarried? (The man) said: I have tarried a day or part of a day. (He) said: Nay, but thou hast tarried for a hundred years. Just look at thy food and drink which have rotted not! Look at thine ass! And, that We may make thee a token unto mankind, look at the bones, how We adjust them and then cover them with flesh! And when (the matter) became clear unto him, he said: I know now that Allah is Able to do all things.

أَوْ كَالَّذِى مَرَّ عَلَى قَرْيَةٍ وَهِىَ خَاوِيَةٌ عَلَى عُرُوشِهَا قَالَ أَنَّىٰ يُحْىِۦ هَٰذِهِ ٱللَّهُ بَعْدَ مَوْتِهَا فَأَمَاتَهُ ٱللَّهُ مِائَةَ عَامٍ ثُمَّ بَعَثَهُۥ قَالَ كَمْ لَبِثْتَ قَالَ لَبِثْتُ يَوْمًا أَوْ بَعْضَ يَوْمٍ قَالَ بَل لَّبِثْتَ مِائَةَ عَامٍ فَٱنظُرْ إِلَىٰ طَعَامِكَ وَشَرَابِكَ لَمْ يَتَسَنَّهْ وَٱنظُرْ إِلَىٰ حِمَارِكَ وَلِنَجْعَلَكَ ءَايَةً لِّلنَّاسِ وَٱنظُرْ إِلَى ٱلْعِظَامِ كَيْفَ نُنشِزُهَا ثُمَّ نَكْسُوهَا لَحْمًا فَلَمَّا تَبَيَّنَ لَهُۥ قَالَ أَعْلَمُ أَنَّ ٱللَّهَ عَلَىٰ كُلِّ شَىْءٍ قَدِيرٌ ۝

260   And when Abraham said (unto his Lord): My lord! Show me how Thou givest life to the dead, He said: Dost thou not believe? Abraham said: Yea, but (I ask) in order that my heart may be at ease. (His Lord) said: Take four of the birds and cause them to incline unto thee, then place a part of them on each hill, then call them, they will come to thee in haste. And know that Allah is Mighty, Wise.

وَإِذْ قَالَ إِبْرَٰهِـۧمُ رَبِّ أَرِنِى كَيْفَ تُحْىِ ٱلْمَوْتَىٰ قَالَ أَوَلَمْ تُؤْمِن قَالَ بَلَىٰ وَلَٰكِن لِّيَطْمَئِنَّ قَلْبِى قَالَ فَخُذْ أَرْبَعَةً مِّنَ ٱلطَّيْرِ فَصُرْهُنَّ إِلَيْكَ ثُمَّ ٱجْعَلْ عَلَىٰ كُلِّ جَبَلٍ مِّنْهُنَّ جُزْءًا ثُمَّ ٱدْعُهُنَّ يَأْتِينَكَ سَعْيًا وَٱعْلَمْ أَنَّ ٱللَّهَ عَزِيزٌ حَكِيمٌ ۝

---

35. Most of the commentators agree that the reference here is to Jerusalem in the ruins, while following words tell of the vision of Ezekiel.

261 The likeness of those who spend their wealth in Allah's way is as the likeness of a grain which groweth seven ears, in every ear a hundred grains. Allah giveth increase manifold to whom He will. Allah is All Embracing, All Knowing.

مَّثَلُ ٱلَّذِينَ يُنفِقُونَ أَمْوَٰلَهُمْ فِى سَبِيلِ ٱللَّهِ كَمَثَلِ حَبَّةٍ أَنۢبَتَتْ سَبْعَ سَنَابِلَ فِى كُلِّ سُنۢبُلَةٍ مِّائَةُ حَبَّةٍ وَٱللَّهُ يُضَٰعِفُ لِمَن يَشَآءُ وَٱللَّهُ وَٰسِعٌ عَلِيمٌ ﴿٢٦١﴾

262 Those who spend their wealth for the cause of Allah and afterward make not reproach and injury to follow that which they have spent; their reward is with their Lord, and there shall no fear come upon them, neither shall they grieve.

ٱلَّذِينَ يُنفِقُونَ أَمْوَٰلَهُمْ فِى سَبِيلِ ٱللَّهِ ثُمَّ لَا يُتْبِعُونَ مَآ أَنفَقُوا۟ مَنًّا وَلَآ أَذًى لَّهُمْ أَجْرُهُمْ عِندَ رَبِّهِمْ وَلَا خَوْفٌ عَلَيْهِمْ وَلَا هُمْ يَحْزَنُونَ ﴿٢٦٢﴾

263 A kind word with forgiveness is better than alms giving followed by injury. Allah is Absolute, Clement.

۞ قَوْلٌ مَّعْرُوفٌ وَمَغْفِرَةٌ خَيْرٌ مِّن صَدَقَةٍ يَتْبَعُهَآ أَذًى وَٱللَّهُ غَنِىٌّ حَلِيمٌ ﴿٢٦٣﴾

264 O ye who believe! Render not vain your alms giving by reproach and injury, like him who spendeth his wealth only to be seen of men and believeth not in Allah and the Last Day. His likeness is as the likeness of a rock whereon is dust of earth; a rainstorm smiteth it, leaving it smooth and bare. They have no control of aught of that which they have gained. Allah guideth not the disbelieving folk.

يَٰٓأَيُّهَا ٱلَّذِينَ ءَامَنُوا۟ لَا تُبْطِلُوا۟ صَدَقَٰتِكُم بِٱلْمَنِّ وَٱلْأَذَىٰ كَٱلَّذِى يُنفِقُ مَالَهُۥ رِئَآءَ ٱلنَّاسِ وَلَا يُؤْمِنُ بِٱللَّهِ وَٱلْيَوْمِ ٱلْءَاخِرِ فَمَثَلُهُۥ كَمَثَلِ صَفْوَانٍ عَلَيْهِ تُرَابٌ فَأَصَابَهُۥ وَابِلٌ فَتَرَكَهُۥ صَلْدًا لَّا يَقْدِرُونَ عَلَىٰ شَىْءٍ مِّمَّا كَسَبُوا۟ وَٱللَّهُ لَا يَهْدِى ٱلْقَوْمَ ٱلْكَٰفِرِينَ ﴿٢٦٤﴾

265 And the likeness of those who spend their wealth in search of Allah's pleasure, and for the strengthening of their souls, is as the

وَمَثَلُ ٱلَّذِينَ يُنفِقُونَ أَمْوَٰلَهُمُ ٱبْتِغَآءَ مَرْضَاتِ ٱللَّهِ وَتَثْبِيتًا مِّنْ أَنفُسِهِمْ كَمَثَلِ

likeness of a garden on a height.
The rainstorm smiteth it and it bringeth forth its fruit twofold. And if
the rainstorm smite it not, then the
shower. Allah is Seer of what ye do.

266   Would any of you like to
have a garden of palm trees and
vines, with rivers flowing underneath it, with all kinds of fruit for
him therein; and old age hath stri-
cken him and be hath feeble off
spring; and a fiery whirlwind striketh it and it is (all) consumed by
fire. Thus Allah maketh plain His
revelations unto you, in order that
ye may give thought.

267   O ye who believe! Spend of
the good things which ye have
earned, and of that which we bring
forth from the earth for you, and
seek not the bad (with intent) to
spend thereof (in charity) when ye
would not take it for yourselves save
with disdain; and know that Allah is
Absolute, Owner of Praise.

268   The devil promiseth you des-
titution and enjoineth on you lewdness. But Allah promiseth you forgiveness from Himself with bounty.
Allah is All Embracing, All Knowing.

269   He giveth wisdom unto
whom He will, and he unto whom
wisdom is given, he truly hath
received abundant good. But none
remember except men of understanding.

جَنَّةٍ بِرَبْوَةٍ أَصَابَهَا وَابِلٌ فَاٰتَتْ أُكُلَهَا
ضِعْفَيْنِ فَإِن لَّمْ يُصِبْهَا وَابِلٌ فَطَلٌّ
وَٱللّٰهُ بِمَا تَعْمَلُونَ بَصِيرٌ ﴿٢٦٥﴾

أَيَوَدُّ أَحَدُكُمْ أَن تَكُونَ لَهُۥ جَنَّةٌ مِّن نَّخِيلٍ
وَأَعْنَابٍ تَجْرِى مِن تَحْتِهَا ٱلْأَنْهَارُ لَهُۥ
فِيهَا مِن كُلِّ ٱلثَّمَرَٰتِ وَأَصَابَهُ ٱلْكِبَرُ
وَلَهُۥ ذُرِّيَّةٌ ضُعَفَآءُ فَأَصَابَهَآ إِعْصَارٌ فِيهِ نَارٌ
فَٱحْتَرَقَتْ كَذَٰلِكَ يُبَيِّنُ ٱللّٰهُ لَكُمُ ٱلْأٰيَٰتِ
لَعَلَّكُمْ تَتَفَكَّرُونَ ﴿٢٦٦﴾

يَٰٓأَيُّهَا ٱلَّذِينَ ءَامَنُوٓا۟ أَنفِقُوا۟ مِن طَيِّبَٰتِ
مَا كَسَبْتُمْ وَمِمَّآ أَخْرَجْنَا لَكُم مِّنَ ٱلْأَرْضِ
وَلَا تَيَمَّمُوا۟ ٱلْخَبِيثَ مِنْهُ تُنفِقُونَ وَلَسْتُم
بِـَٔاخِذِيهِ إِلَّآ أَن تُغْمِضُوا۟ فِيهِ وَٱعْلَمُوٓا۟ أَنَّ ٱللّٰهَ
غَنِىٌّ حَمِيدٌ ﴿٢٦٧﴾

ٱلشَّيْطَٰنُ يَعِدُكُمُ ٱلْفَقْرَ وَيَأْمُرُكُم
بِٱلْفَحْشَآءِ وَٱللّٰهُ يَعِدُكُم مَّغْفِرَةً مِّنْهُ
وَفَضْلًا وَٱللّٰهُ وَٰسِعٌ عَلِيمٌ ﴿٢٦٨﴾

يُؤْتِى ٱلْحِكْمَةَ مَن يَشَآءُ وَمَن يُؤْتَ
ٱلْحِكْمَةَ فَقَدْ أُوتِىَ خَيْرًا كَثِيرًا
وَمَا يَذَّكَّرُ إِلَّآ أُو۟لُوا۟ ٱلْأَلْبَٰبِ ﴿٢٦٩﴾

270   Whatever alms ye spend or vow ye vow, Lo! Allah knoweth it, Wrongdoers have no helpers.

وَمَا أَنفَقْتُم مِّن نَّفَقَةٍ أَوْ نَذَرْتُم مِّن نَّذْرٍ فَإِنَّ ٱللَّهَ يَعْلَمُهُ ۗ وَمَا لِلظَّٰلِمِينَ مِنْ أَنصَارٍ ۝

271   If ye publish your alms giving, it is well, but if ye hide it and give it to the poor, it will be better for you, and will atone for some of your ill deeds. Allah is Informed of what ye do.

إِن تُبْدُوا۟ ٱلصَّدَقَٰتِ فَنِعِمَّا هِىَ ۖ وَإِن تُخْفُوهَا وَتُؤْتُوهَا ٱلْفُقَرَآءَ فَهُوَ خَيْرٌ لَّكُمْ ۚ وَيُكَفِّرُ عَنكُم مِّن سَيِّـَٔاتِكُمْ ۗ وَٱللَّهُ بِمَا تَعْمَلُونَ خَبِيرٌ ۝

272   The guiding of them is not thy duty (O Muhammad), but Allah guideth whom He will. And whatsoever good thing ye spend, it is for yourselves, when ye spend not save in search of Allah's countenance; and whatsoever good thing ye spend, it will be repaid to you in full, and ye will not be wronged.

۞ لَّيْسَ عَلَيْكَ هُدَىٰهُمْ وَلَٰكِنَّ ٱللَّهَ يَهْدِى مَن يَشَآءُ ۗ وَمَا تُنفِقُوا۟ مِنْ خَيْرٍ فَلِأَنفُسِكُمْ ۚ وَمَا تُنفِقُونَ إِلَّا ٱبْتِغَآءَ وَجْهِ ٱللَّهِ ۚ وَمَا تُنفِقُوا۟ مِنْ خَيْرٍ يُوَفَّ إِلَيْكُمْ وَأَنتُمْ لَا تُظْلَمُونَ ۝

273   (Alms are) for the poor who are straitened for the cause of Allah, who cannot travel in the land (for trade). The unthinking man accounteth them wealthy because of their restraint. Thou shalt know them by their mark: They do not beg of men with importunity. And whatsoever good thing ye spend, lo! Allah knoweth it.

لِلْفُقَرَآءِ ٱلَّذِينَ أُحْصِرُوا۟ فِى سَبِيلِ ٱللَّهِ لَا يَسْتَطِيعُونَ ضَرْبًا فِى ٱلْأَرْضِ يَحْسَبُهُمُ ٱلْجَاهِلُ أَغْنِيَآءَ مِنَ ٱلتَّعَفُّفِ تَعْرِفُهُم بِسِيمَٰهُمْ لَا يَسْـَٔلُونَ ٱلنَّاسَ إِلْحَافًا ۗ وَمَا تُنفِقُوا۟ مِنْ خَيْرٍ فَإِنَّ ٱللَّهَ بِهِ عَلِيمٌ ۝

274   Those who spend their wealth by night and day, by stealth and openly, verily their reward is with their Lord, and there shall no fear come upon them neither shall they grieve.

ٱلَّذِينَ يُنفِقُونَ أَمْوَٰلَهُم بِٱلَّيْلِ وَٱلنَّهَارِ سِرًّا وَعَلَانِيَةً فَلَهُمْ أَجْرُهُمْ عِندَ رَبِّهِمْ وَلَا خَوْفٌ عَلَيْهِمْ وَلَا هُمْ يَحْزَنُونَ ۝

275   Those who swallow usury cannot rise up save as he ariseth whom the devil hath prostrated by (his) touch. That is because they say: Trade is just like usury; whereas Allah permitteth trading and forbiddeth usury. He unto whom an admonition from his Lord cometh, and (he) refraineth (in obedience thereto), he shall keep (the profits of) that which is past, and his affair (henceforth) is with Allah. As for him who returneth (to usury) Such are rightful owners of the Fire. They will abide therein.

الَّذِينَ يَأْكُلُونَ الرِّبَوٰا لَا يَقُومُونَ إِلَّا كَمَا يَقُومُ الَّذِى يَتَخَبَّطُهُ الشَّيْطَنُ مِنَ الْمَسِّ ذَٰلِكَ بِأَنَّهُمْ قَالُوٓا إِنَّمَا الْبَيْعُ مِثْلُ الرِّبَوٰا وَأَحَلَّ اللَّهُ الْبَيْعَ وَحَرَّمَ الرِّبَوٰا فَمَن جَآءَهُ مَوْعِظَةٌ مِّن رَّبِّهِ فَانتَهَىٰ فَلَهُ مَا سَلَفَ وَأَمْرُهُ إِلَى اللَّهِ وَمَنْ عَادَ فَأُوْلَٰئِكَ أَصْحَٰبُ النَّارِ هُمْ فِيهَا خَٰلِدُونَ ۝

276   Allah hath blighted usury and made alms giving fruitful. Allah loveth not the impious and guilty.

يَمْحَقُ اللَّهُ الرِّبَوٰا وَيُرْبِى الصَّدَقَٰتِ وَاللَّهُ لَا يُحِبُّ كُلَّ كَفَّارٍ أَثِيمٍ ۝

277   Lo! those who believe and do good works and establish worship and pay the poor due, their reward is with their Lord and there shall no fear come upon them neither shall they grieve.

إِنَّ الَّذِينَ ءَامَنُوا وَعَمِلُوا الصَّٰلِحَٰتِ وَأَقَامُوا الصَّلَوٰةَ وَءَاتَوُا الزَّكَوٰةَ لَهُمْ أَجْرُهُمْ عِندَ رَبِّهِمْ وَلَا خَوْفٌ عَلَيْهِمْ وَلَا هُمْ يَحْزَنُونَ ۝

278   O ye who believe! Observe your duty to Allah, and give up what remaineth (due to you) from usury, if ye are (in truth) believers.

يَٰٓأَيُّهَا الَّذِينَ ءَامَنُوا اتَّقُوا اللَّهَ وَذَرُوا مَا بَقِىَ مِنَ الرِّبَوٰا إِن كُنتُم مُّؤْمِنِينَ ۝

279   And if ye do not, then be warned of war (against you) from Allah and His messenger. And if ye repent, then ye have your principal (without interest). Wrong not, and ye shall not be wronged,

فَإِن لَّمْ تَفْعَلُوا فَأْذَنُوا بِحَرْبٍ مِّنَ اللَّهِ وَرَسُولِهِ وَإِن تُبْتُمْ فَلَكُمْ رُءُوسُ أَمْوَٰلِكُمْ لَا تَظْلِمُونَ وَلَا تُظْلَمُونَ ۝

280 And if the debtor is in strait-ened circumstances, then (let there be) postponement to (the time of) ease; and that ye remit the debt as alms giving would be better for you if ye did but know.

وَإِن كَانَ ذُو عُسْرَةٍ فَنَظِرَةٌ إِلَىٰ مَيْسَرَةٍ ۚ وَأَن تَصَدَّقُوا خَيْرٌ لَّكُمْ ۖ إِن كُنتُمْ تَعْلَمُونَ ۝

281 And guard yourselves against a day in which ye will be brought back to Allah. Then every soul will be paid in full that which it hath earned, and they will not be wronged.

وَاتَّقُوا يَوْمًا تُرْجَعُونَ فِيهِ إِلَى اللَّهِ ۖ ثُمَّ تُوَفَّىٰ كُلُّ نَفْسٍ مَّا كَسَبَتْ وَهُمْ لَا يُظْلَمُونَ ۝

282 O ye who believe! When ye contract a debt for a fixed term, record it in writing. Let a scribe record it in writing between you in (terms of) equity. No scribe should refuse to write as Allah hath taught him, so let him write, and let him who incurreth the debt dictate, and let him observe his duty to Allah his Lord, and diminish naught thereof. But if he who oweth the debt is of low understanding, or weak, or unable himself to dictate, then let the guardian of his interests dictate in (terms of) equity. And call to witness, from among your men, two witnesses. And if two men be not (at hand) then a man and two women, of such as ye approve as witnesses, so that if one of the two erreth (through forget-fulness) the one of them will re-mind the other. And the witnesses must not refuse when they are

يَا أَيُّهَا الَّذِينَ ءَامَنُوا إِذَا تَدَايَنتُم بِدَيْنٍ إِلَىٰ أَجَلٍ مُّسَمًّى فَاكْتُبُوهُ ۚ وَلْيَكْتُب بَّيْنَكُمْ كَاتِبٌ بِالْعَدْلِ ۚ وَلَا يَأْبَ كَاتِبٌ أَن يَكْتُبَ كَمَا عَلَّمَهُ اللَّهُ ۚ فَلْيَكْتُبْ وَلْيُمْلِلِ الَّذِي عَلَيْهِ الْحَقُّ وَلْيَتَّقِ اللَّهَ رَبَّهُ وَلَا يَبْخَسْ مِنْهُ شَيْئًا ۚ فَإِن كَانَ الَّذِي عَلَيْهِ الْحَقُّ سَفِيهًا أَوْ ضَعِيفًا أَوْ لَا يَسْتَطِيعُ أَن يُمِلَّ هُوَ فَلْيُمْلِلْ وَلِيُّهُ بِالْعَدْلِ ۚ وَاسْتَشْهِدُوا شَهِيدَيْنِ مِن رِّجَالِكُمْ ۖ فَإِن لَّمْ يَكُونَا رَجُلَيْنِ فَرَجُلٌ وَامْرَأَتَانِ مِمَّن تَرْضَوْنَ مِنَ الشُّهَدَاءِ أَن تَضِلَّ إِحْدَاهُمَا فَتُذَكِّرَ إِحْدَاهُمَا الْأُخْرَىٰ ۚ وَلَا يَأْبَ الشُّهَدَاءُ إِذَا مَا دُعُوا ۚ وَلَا تَسْأَمُوا

summoned. Be not averse to writing down (the contract) whether it be small or great, with (record of) the term thereof. That is more equitable in the sight of Allah and more sure for testimony, and the best way of avoiding doubt between you; save only in the case when it is actual merchandise which ye transfer among yourselves from hand to hand. In that case it is no sin for you if ye write it not. And have witnesses when ye sell one to another, and let no harm be done to scribe or witness. If ye do (harm to them) lo! it is a sin in you. Observe your duty to Allah. Allah is teaching you. And Allah is Knower of all things.

أَن تَكۡتُبُوهُ صَغِيرًا أَوۡ كَبِيرًا إِلَىٰ أَجَلِهِۦۚ ذَٰلِكُمۡ أَقۡسَطُ عِندَ ٱللَّهِ وَأَقۡوَمُ لِلشَّهَٰدَةِ وَأَدۡنَىٰٓ أَلَّا تَرۡتَابُوٓاْ إِلَّآ أَن تَكُونَ تِجَٰرَةً حَاضِرَةً تُدِيرُونَهَا بَيۡنَكُمۡ فَلَيۡسَ عَلَيۡكُمۡ جُنَاحٌ أَلَّا تَكۡتُبُوهَاۗ وَأَشۡهِدُوٓاْ إِذَا تَبَايَعۡتُمۡۚ وَلَا يُضَآرَّ كَاتِبٌ وَلَا شَهِيدٌۚ وَإِن تَفۡعَلُواْ فَإِنَّهُۥ فُسُوقٌۢ بِكُمۡۗ وَٱتَّقُواْ ٱللَّهَۖ وَيُعَلِّمُكُمُ ٱللَّهُۗ وَٱللَّهُ بِكُلِّ شَىۡءٍ عَلِيمٌ ۝

283 If ye be on a journey and cannot find a scribe, then a pledge in hand (shall suffice). And if one of you entrusteth to another let him who is trusted deliver up that which is entrusted to him (according to the pact between them) and let him observe his duty to Allah, his Lord. Hide not testimony. He who hideth it, verily his heart is sinful. Allah is Aware of what ye do.

۞ وَإِن كُنتُمۡ عَلَىٰ سَفَرٍ وَلَمۡ تَجِدُواْ كَاتِبًا فَرِهَٰنٌ مَّقۡبُوضَةٌۖ فَإِنۡ أَمِنَ بَعۡضُكُم بَعۡضًا فَلۡيُؤَدِّ ٱلَّذِى ٱؤۡتُمِنَ أَمَٰنَتَهُۥ وَلۡيَتَّقِ ٱللَّهَ رَبَّهُۥۗ وَلَا تَكۡتُمُواْ ٱلشَّهَٰدَةَۚ وَمَن يَكۡتُمۡهَا فَإِنَّهُۥٓ ءَاثِمٌ قَلۡبُهُۥۗ وَٱللَّهُ بِمَا تَعۡمَلُونَ عَلِيمٌ ۝

284 Unto Allah (belongeth) whatsoever is in the heavens and whatsoever is in the earth; and whether ye make known what is in your minds or hide it, Allah will bring you to account for it. He will

لِّلَّهِ مَا فِى ٱلسَّمَٰوَٰتِ وَمَا فِى ٱلۡأَرۡضِۗ وَإِن تُبۡدُواْ مَا فِىٓ أَنفُسِكُمۡ أَوۡ تُخۡفُوهُ يُحَاسِبۡكُم بِهِ ٱللَّهُۖ فَيَغۡفِرُ لِمَن يَشَآءُ وَيُعَذِّبُ مَن يَشَآءُۗ

forgive whom He will and He will punish whom He will. Allah is Able to do all things.

وَاللّٰهُ عَلَىٰ كُلِّ شَىْءٍ قَدِيرٌ ۝

285 The messenger believeth in that which hath been revealed unto him from his Lord and (so do) the believers. Each one believeth in Allah and His angels and His scriptures and His messengers We make no distinction between any of His messengers and they say: We hear, and we obey. (Grant us) Thy forgiveness, our Lord. Unto Thee is the journeying.

ءَامَنَ الرَّسُولُ بِمَآ أُنْزِلَ إِلَيْهِ مِنْ رَّبِّهِ وَالْمُؤْمِنُونَ كُلٌّ ءَامَنَ بِاللّٰهِ وَمَلَٰٓئِكَتِهِ وَكُتُبِهِ وَرُسُلِهِ لَا نُفَرِّقُ بَيْنَ أَحَدٍ مِّنْ رُّسُلِهِ وَقَالُوا سَمِعْنَا وَأَطَعْنَا غُفْرَانَكَ رَبَّنَا وَإِلَيْكَ الْمَصِيرُ ۝

286 Allah tasketh not a soul beyond its scope. For it (is only) that which it hath earned, and against it (only) that which it hath deserved. Our Lord! Condemn us not if we forget, or miss the mark! Our Lord! Lay not on us such a burden as Thou didst lay on those before us! Our Lord! Impose not on us that which we have not the strength to bear! Pardon us, absolve us and have mercy on us, Thou art our Protector, so give us victory over the disbelieving folk.

لَا يُكَلِّفُ اللّٰهُ نَفْسًا إِلَّا وُسْعَهَا لَهَا مَا كَسَبَتْ وَعَلَيْهَا مَا اكْتَسَبَتْ رَبَّنَا لَا تُؤَاخِذْنَآ إِنْ نَّسِينَآ أَوْ أَخْطَأْنَا رَبَّنَا وَلَا تَحْمِلْ عَلَيْنَآ إِصْرًا كَمَا حَمَلْتَهُ عَلَى الَّذِينَ مِنْ قَبْلِنَا رَبَّنَا وَلَا تُحَمِّلْنَا مَا لَا طَاقَةَ لَنَا بِهِ وَاعْفُ عَنَّا وَاغْفِرْ لَنَا وَارْحَمْنَآ أَنْتَ مَوْلَٰنَا فَانْصُرْنَا عَلَى الْقَوْمِ الْكَافِرِينَ ۝

Āli 'Imrān

(The Family of 'Imrān)

Āli 'Imrān takes its title from v. 32, where "the family of 'Imrān" (the father of Moses) occurs as a generic name for all the Hebrew prophets from Moses to John the Baptist and Jesus Christ. This, with the mention of the mother of Mary as "the wife of 'Imrān" (v. 34), and the words "sister of Aaron" addressed to Mary (19: 28), have given rise to a charge of anachronism—absurd because the whole of the rest of the Qu'ran is against it—by Muir and other non-Muslim writers, who say that the Prophet confused Mary, the mother of Jesus, with Miriam, the sister of Moses. Most Muslims believe, on the authority of the Qu'ran, that the grandfather of Jesus Christ was named 'Imrān, which may also have been the name of the father of Moses. In sūrah 19: 28, where Mary is addressed as "sister of Aaron," they hold the ancestral sense to be the more probable, while denying that there is any reason to suppose that the Virgin Mary had not a brother named Aaron.

If vv. 1 to 34 were, as tradition states, revealed on the occasion of the deputation from the Christians of Najrān, which took place in the tenth year of the Hijrah ("the year of deputations," as it is called), then they are of much later date than the rest of the sūrah, but it seems possible that they were only recited by the Prophet on that occasion, having been revealed before.

The Jews have become bolder and more bitter in opposition which, as Nöldeke points out, cannot have been the case, after the signal victory of Badr, until after the Muslims suffered a reverse at Uḥud; a battle to which vv. 120 to 188 largely refer.

In the third year of the Hijrah the Makkans came against Al-Madīnah, with an army of 3000 men to avenge their defeat at Badr in the previous year, and to wipe out the Muslims. The Prophet, against his own first plan, which was to defend Al-Madīnah, at the instance of his companions, went out to meet them on Mount Uḥud, posting his men carefully. He led an army of 1000 men, a third of whom under Abdullah ibn Ubayy (the "Hypocrite" leader) deserted him before the battle, and said afterwards that they did not think there would be any fighting that day. The battle began well for the Muslims but was changed to something near defeat by the disobedience of a band of fifty archers placed to guard a certain point. Seeing the Muslims winning, they feared that they might lose their share of the spoils, and ran to join the others, leaving a way open for the Makkan cavalry. The idolaters then rallied and inflicted considerable loss upon the Muslims, the Prophet himself being wounded in the struggle. A cry arose that the Prophet had been slain, and the Muslims were in despair till someone recognized the Prophet and cried out that he was living. The Muslims then rallied to his side, and retired in some sort of order. The army of Quraysh also retired after the battle.

In this battle the wives of the leaders of Quraysh, who had been brought with the army to give courage by their presence and their chanting, mutilated the Muslim slain, making necklaces and bracelets of ears and noses. Hind, the wife of Abū Sufyān, plucked out the liver of the Prophet's uncle, Hamzah, publicly, and tried to eat it. The Prophet, when he saw the condition of the slain, was moved to vow reprisals. But he was relieved of his vow by a revelation, and mutilation was forbidden to the Muslims.

On the day after the battle of Mount Uḥud, the Prophet again went out with such of the army as survived, in order that Quraysh might hear that he was in the field and haply be deterred from any project of attacking Al-Madīnah in its weakened state. On that occasion many wounded men went out with him. Tradition tells how a friendly nomad met the Muslims and afterwards met the army of Quraysh. Questioned by Abū Sufyān, he said that the Prophet was seeking vengeance with an overwhelming force; and that report determined Abū Sufyān to march back to Makkah.

The period of revelation is the third and fourth years of the Hijrah.

*

In the name of Allah, the Beneficent, the Merciful.

1 Alif. Lām. Mīm.[1]

2 Allah! There is no God save Him, the Alive, the Eternal.

3 He hath revealed unto thee (Muhammad) the Scripture with truth, confirming that which was (revealed) before it, even as He revealed the Torah and the Gospel.

4 Aforetime, for a guidance to mankind; and hath revealed the Criterion (of right and wrong). Lo! those who disbelieve the revelations of Allah, theirs will be a heavy doom. Allah is Mighty, Able to Requite (the wrong).

5 Lo! nothing in the earth or in the heavens is hidden from Allah.

6 He it is who fashioneth you in the wombs as pleaseth Him. There is no God save Him, the Almighty, the Wise.

---

1. See Sūrah 2: 1, footnote.

7 He it is Who hath revealed unto thee (Muḥammad) the Scripture wherein are clear revelations. They are the substance of the Book and others (which are) allegorical. But those in whose hearts is doubt pursue, forsooth, that which is allegorical seeking (to cause) dissension by seeking to explain it. None knoweth its explanation save Allah. And those who are of sound instruction say: We believe therein; the whole is from our Lord; but only men of understanding really heed.

هُوَ الَّذِيٓ أَنزَلَ عَلَيْكَ الْكِتَٰبَ مِنْهُ ءَايَٰتٌ مُّحْكَمَٰتٌ هُنَّ أُمُّ الْكِتَٰبِ وَأُخَرُ مُتَشَٰبِهَٰتٌ ۖ فَأَمَّا الَّذِينَ فِى قُلُوبِهِمْ زَيْغٌ فَيَتَّبِعُونَ مَا تَشَٰبَهَ مِنْهُ ابْتِغَآءَ الْفِتْنَةِ وَابْتِغَآءَ تَأْوِيلِهِۦ ۗ وَمَا يَعْلَمُ تَأْوِيلَهُۥٓ إِلَّا اللَّهُ ۗ وَالرَّٰسِخُونَ فِى الْعِلْمِ يَقُولُونَ ءَامَنَّا بِهِۦ كُلٌّ مِّنْ عِندِ رَبِّنَا ۗ وَمَا يَذَّكَّرُ إِلَّآ أُو۟لُوا الْأَلْبَٰبِ ۝

8 Our Lord! Cause not our hearts to stray after Thou hast guided us, and bestow upon us mercy from Thy Presence. Lo! Thou, only Thou art the Bestower.

رَبَّنَا لَا تُزِغْ قُلُوبَنَا بَعْدَ إِذْ هَدَيْتَنَا وَهَبْ لَنَا مِن لَّدُنكَ رَحْمَةً ۚ إِنَّكَ أَنتَ الْوَهَّابُ ۝

9 Our Lord! it is Thou Who gatherest mankind together to a Day of which there is no doubt. Lo! Allah faileth not to keep the tryst.

رَبَّنَآ إِنَّكَ جَامِعُ النَّاسِ لِيَوْمٍ لَّا رَيْبَ فِيهِ ۚ إِنَّ اللَّهَ لَا يُخْلِفُ الْمِيعَادَ ۝

10 (On that day) neither the riches nor the progeny of those who disbelieve will aught avail them with Allah. They will be fuel for fire.

إِنَّ الَّذِينَ كَفَرُوا لَن تُغْنِىَ عَنْهُمْ أَمْوَٰلُهُمْ وَلَآ أَوْلَٰدُهُم مِّنَ اللَّهِ شَيْـًٔا ۖ وَأُو۟لَٰٓئِكَ هُمْ وَقُودُ النَّارِ ۝

11 Like Pharaoh's folk and those who were before them, they disbelieved Our revelations and so Allah seized them for their sins. And Allah is severe in punishment.

كَدَأْبِ ءَالِ فِرْعَوْنَ وَالَّذِينَ مِن قَبْلِهِمْ ۚ كَذَّبُوا بِـَٔايَٰتِنَا فَأَخَذَهُمُ اللَّهُ بِذُنُوبِهِمْ ۗ وَاللَّهُ شَدِيدُ الْعِقَابِ ۝

12 Say (O Muḥammad) unto those who disbelieve: Ye shall be overcome and gathered unto Hell, an evil resting place.

قُل لِّلَّذِينَ كَفَرُوا سَتُغْلَبُونَ وَتُحْشَرُونَ إِلَىٰ جَهَنَّمَ ۚ وَبِئْسَ الْمِهَادُ ۝

13 There was a token for you in two hosts which met:[2] one army fighting in the way of Allah, and another disbelieving, whom they saw as twice their number, clearly, with their very eyes. Thus Allah strengtheneth with His succour whom He will. Lo! herein verily is a lesson for those who have eyes.

قَدْ كَانَ لَكُمْ ءَايَةٌ فِى فِئَتَيْنِ ٱلْتَقَتَا فِئَةٌ تُقَتِلُ فِى سَبِيلِ ٱللَّهِ وَأُخْرَىٰ كَافِرَةٌ يَرَوْنَهُم مِّثْلَيْهِمْ رَأْىَ ٱلْعَيْنِ وَٱللَّهُ يُؤَيِّدُ بِنَصْرِهِۦ مَن يَشَآءُ إِنَّ فِى ذَٰلِكَ لَعِبْرَةً لِّأُوْلِى ٱلْأَبْصَٰرِ ﴿١٣﴾

14 Beautified for mankind is love of the joys (that come) from women and offspring, and stored up heaps of gold and silver, and horses branded (with their mark), and cattle and land. That is comfort of the life of the world. Allah! With Him is a more excellent abode.

زُيِّنَ لِلنَّاسِ حُبُّ ٱلشَّهَوَٰتِ مِنَ ٱلنِّسَآءِ وَٱلْبَنِينَ وَٱلْقَنَٰطِيرِ ٱلْمُقَنطَرَةِ مِنَ ٱلذَّهَبِ وَٱلْفِضَّةِ وَٱلْخَيْلِ ٱلْمُسَوَّمَةِ وَٱلْأَنْعَٰمِ وَٱلْحَرْثِ ذَٰلِكَ مَتَٰعُ ٱلْحَيَوٰةِ ٱلدُّنْيَا وَٱللَّهُ عِندَهُۥ حُسْنُ ٱلْمَـَٔابِ ﴿١٤﴾

15 Say: Shall I inform you of something better than that? For those who keep from evil, with their Lord, are Gardens underneath which rivers flow wherein they will abide, and pure companions, and contentment from Allah. Allah is Seer of His bondmen,

۞ قُلْ أَؤُنَبِّئُكُم بِخَيْرٍ مِّن ذَٰلِكُمْ لِلَّذِينَ ٱتَّقَوْا عِندَ رَبِّهِمْ جَنَّٰتٌ تَجْرِى مِن تَحْتِهَا ٱلْأَنْهَٰرُ خَٰلِدِينَ فِيهَا وَأَزْوَٰجٌ مُّطَهَّرَةٌ وَرِضْوَٰنٌ مِّنَ ٱللَّهِ وَٱللَّهُ بَصِيرٌ بِٱلْعِبَادِ ﴿١٥﴾

16 Those who say: Our Lord! Lo! we believe. So forgive us our sins and guard us from the punishment of Fire;

ٱلَّذِينَ يَقُولُونَ رَبَّنَآ إِنَّنَآ ءَامَنَّا فَٱغْفِرْ لَنَا ذُنُوبَنَا وَقِنَا عَذَابَ ٱلنَّارِ ﴿١٦﴾

17 The steadfast, and the truthful, and the obedient, those who spend (and hoard not), those who pray for pardon in the watches of the night.

ٱلصَّٰبِرِينَ وَٱلصَّٰدِقِينَ وَٱلْقَٰنِتِينَ وَٱلْمُنفِقِينَ وَٱلْمُسْتَغْفِرِينَ بِٱلْأَسْحَارِ ﴿١٧﴾

---

2. The Reference is to the battle of Badr.

18 Allah (Himself) is witness that there is no God save Him. And the angels and the men of learning (too are witness). Maintaining His creation in justice, there is no God save Him, the Almighty, the Wise.

شَهِدَ اللّٰهُ أَنَّهُ لَاۤ إِلٰهَ إِلَّا هُوَ وَالْمَلٰٓئِكَةُ وَأُولُوا الْعِلْمِ قَآئِمًاۢ بِالْقِسْطِ لَاۤ إِلٰهَ إِلَّا هُوَ الْعَزِيزُ الْحَكِيمُ ۝

19 Lo! religion with Allah (is) The Surrender[3] (to His will and guidance). Those who (formerly) received the Scripture differed only after knowledge came unto them, through transgression among themselves. Whoso disbelieveth the revelations of Allah (will find that) Lo! Allah is swift at reckoning.

إِنَّ الدِّيْنَ عِنْدَ اللّٰهِ الْإِسْلَامُ وَمَا اخْتَلَفَ الَّذِيْنَ أُوْتُوا الْكِتَابَ إِلَّا مِنۢ بَعْدِ مَا جَآءَهُمُ الْعِلْمُ بَغْيًاۢ بَيْنَهُمْ وَمَنْ يَّكْفُرْ بِاٰيٰتِ اللّٰهِ فَإِنَّ اللّٰهَ سَرِيْعُ الْحِسَابِ ۝

20 And if they argue with thee, (O Muhammad), say: I have surrendered my purpose to Allah and (so have) those who follow me. And say unto those who have received the Scripture and those who read not: Have ye (too) surrendered? If they surrender, then truly they are rightly guided, and if they turn away, then it is thy duty only to convey the message (unto them). Allah is Seer of (His) bondmen.

فَإِنْ حَآجُّوْكَ فَقُلْ أَسْلَمْتُ وَجْهِيَ لِلّٰهِ وَمَنِ اتَّبَعَنِ وَقُلْ لِّلَّذِيْنَ أُوْتُوا الْكِتَابَ وَالْأُمِّيِّنَ ءَأَسْلَمْتُمْ فَإِنْ أَسْلَمُوْا فَقَدِ اهْتَدَوْا وَّإِنْ تَوَلَّوْا فَإِنَّمَا عَلَيْكَ الْبَلَاغُ وَاللّٰهُ بَصِيْرٌۢ بِالْعِبَادِ ۝

21 Lo! those who disbelieve the revelations of Allah, and slay the Prophets wrongfully, and slay those of mankind who enjoin equity: promise them a painful doom.

إِنَّ الَّذِيْنَ يَكْفُرُوْنَ بِاٰيٰتِ اللّٰهِ وَيَقْتُلُوْنَ النَّبِيِّيْنَ بِغَيْرِ حَقٍّ وَّيَقْتُلُوْنَ الَّذِيْنَ يَأْمُرُوْنَ بِالْقِسْطِ مِنَ النَّاسِ فَبَشِّرْهُمْ بِعَذَابٍ أَلِيْمٍ ۝

---

3. Ar. *Al-Islām*.

22 Those are they whose works have failed in the world and the Hereafter; and they have no helpers.

أُوْلَـٰٓئِكَ ٱلَّذِينَ حَبِطَتْ أَعْمَالُهُمْ فِى ٱلدُّنْيَا وَٱلْأَخِرَةِ وَمَا لَهُم مِّن نَّـٰصِرِينَ ٢٢

23 Hast thou not seen how those who were given a portion of the Scripture are called to the Scripture of Allah (in their disputes) that it may judge between them; then a faction of them turn away, being opposed (to it)?

أَلَمْ تَرَ إِلَى ٱلَّذِينَ أُوتُوا نَصِيبًا مِّنَ ٱلْكِتَـٰبِ يُدْعَوْنَ إِلَىٰ كِتَـٰبِ ٱللَّهِ لِيَحْكُمَ بَيْنَهُمْ ثُمَّ يَتَوَلَّىٰ فَرِيقٌ مِّنْهُمْ وَهُم مُّعْرِضُونَ ٢٣

24 That is because they say: The Fire will not touch us save for a certain number of days. That which they used to invent hath deceived them regarding their religion.

ذَٰلِكَ بِأَنَّهُمْ قَالُوا لَن تَمَسَّنَا ٱلنَّارُ إِلَّآ أَيَّامًا مَّعْدُودَٰتٍ وَغَرَّهُمْ فِى دِينِهِم مَّا كَانُوا يَفْتَرُونَ ٢٤

25 How (will it be with them) when We have brought them all together to a Day of which there is no doubt, when every soul will be paid in full what it hath earned, and they will not be wronged.

فَكَيْفَ إِذَا جَمَعْنَٰهُمْ لِيَوْمٍ لَّا رَيْبَ فِيهِ وَوُفِّيَتْ كُلُّ نَفْسٍ مَّا كَسَبَتْ وَهُمْ لَا يُظْلَمُونَ ٢٥

26 Say: O Allah! Owner of Sovereignty! Thou givest sovereignty unto whom Thou wilt, and Thou withdrawest sovereignty from whom Thou wilt. Thou exaltest whom Thou wilt and Thou abasest whom Thou wilt. In Thy hand is the good. Lo! Thou art Able to do all things.

قُلِ ٱللَّهُمَّ مَٰلِكَ ٱلْمُلْكِ تُؤْتِى ٱلْمُلْكَ مَن تَشَآءُ وَتَنزِعُ ٱلْمُلْكَ مِمَّن تَشَآءُ وَتُعِزُّ مَن تَشَآءُ وَتُذِلُّ مَن تَشَآءُ بِيَدِكَ ٱلْخَيْرُ إِنَّكَ عَلَىٰ كُلِّ شَىْءٍ قَدِيرٌ ٢٦

27 Thou causest the night to pass into the day, and Thou causest the day to pass into the night. And Thou bringest forth the living from the dead, and Thou bringest forth the dead from the living. And Thou givest sustenance to whom Thou choosest, without stint.

تُولِجُ ٱلَّيْلَ فِى ٱلنَّهَارِ وَتُولِجُ ٱلنَّهَارَ فِى ٱلَّيْلِ وَتُخْرِجُ ٱلْحَىَّ مِنَ ٱلْمَيِّتِ وَتُخْرِجُ ٱلْمَيِّتَ مِنَ ٱلْحَىِّ وَتَرْزُقُ مَن تَشَآءُ بِغَيْرِ حِسَابٍ ٢٧

28 Let not the believers take disbelievers for their friends in preference to believers. Whoso doeth that hath no connection with Allah unless (it be) that ye but guard yourselves against them, taking (as it were) security. Allah biddeth you beware (only) of Himself. Unto Allah is the journeying.

لَا يَتَّخِذِ ٱلْمُؤْمِنُونَ ٱلْكَٰفِرِينَ أَوْلِيَآءَ مِن دُونِ ٱلْمُؤْمِنِينَ وَمَن يَفْعَلْ ذَٰلِكَ فَلَيْسَ مِنَ ٱللَّهِ فِى شَىْءٍ إِلَّآ أَن تَتَّقُوا۟ مِنْهُمْ تُقَىٰةً وَيُحَذِّرُكُمُ ٱللَّهُ نَفْسَهُۥ وَإِلَى ٱللَّهِ ٱلْمَصِيرُ ۝

29 Say, (O Muḥammad): Whether ye hide that which is in your breasts or reveal it, Allah knoweth it. He knoweth that which is in the heavens and that which is in the earth, and Allah is Able to do all things.

قُلْ إِن تُخْفُوا۟ مَا فِى صُدُورِكُمْ أَوْ تُبْدُوهُ يَعْلَمْهُ ٱللَّهُ وَيَعْلَمُ مَا فِى ٱلسَّمَٰوَٰتِ وَمَا فِى ٱلْأَرْضِ وَٱللَّهُ عَلَىٰ كُلِّ شَىْءٍ قَدِيرٌ ۝

30 On the day when every soul will find itself confronted with all that it hath done of good and all that it hath done of evil (every soul) will long that there might be a mighty space of distance between it and that (evil). Allah biddeth you beware of Him. And Allah is full of pity for (His) bondmen.

يَوْمَ تَجِدُ كُلُّ نَفْسٍ مَّا عَمِلَتْ مِنْ خَيْرٍ مُّحْضَرًا وَمَا عَمِلَتْ مِن سُوٓءٍ تَوَدُّ لَوْ أَنَّ بَيْنَهَا وَبَيْنَهُۥٓ أَمَدًۢا بَعِيدًا وَيُحَذِّرُكُمُ ٱللَّهُ نَفْسَهُۥ وَٱللَّهُ رَءُوفٌۢ بِٱلْعِبَادِ ۝

31 Say, (O Muḥammad, to mankind): If ye love Allah, follow me; Allah will love you and forgive you your sins. Allah is Forgiving, Merciful.

قُلْ إِن كُنتُمْ تُحِبُّونَ ٱللَّهَ فَٱتَّبِعُونِى يُحْبِبْكُمُ ٱللَّهُ وَيَغْفِرْ لَكُمْ ذُنُوبَكُمْ وَٱللَّهُ غَفُورٌ رَّحِيمٌ ۝

32 Say: Obey Allah and the messenger. But if they turn away, Lo! Allah loveth not the disbelievers (in His guidance).

قُلْ أَطِيعُوا۟ ٱللَّهَ وَٱلرَّسُولَ فَإِن تَوَلَّوْا۟ فَإِنَّ ٱللَّهَ لَا يُحِبُّ ٱلْكَٰفِرِينَ ۝

33 Lo! Allah preferred Adam and Noah and the Family of Abraham and the Family of 'Imrān above (all His) creatures.

﴿إِنَّ اللَّهَ اصْطَفَىٰٓ ءَادَمَ وَنُوحًا وَءَالَ إِبْرَٰهِيمَ وَءَالَ عِمْرَٰنَ عَلَى الْعَٰلَمِينَ ۝٣٣﴾

34 They were descendants one of another. Allah is Hearer, Knower.

ذُرِّيَّةَۢ بَعْضُهَا مِنۢ بَعْضٍ ۗ وَاللَّهُ سَمِيعٌ عَلِيمٌ ۝٣٤

35 (Remember) when the wife of 'Imrān said: My Lord I have vowed unto Thee that which is in my belly as a consecrated (offering). Accept it from me. Lo! Thou, only Thou, art the Hearer, the Knower!

إِذْ قَالَتِ امْرَأَتُ عِمْرَٰنَ رَبِّ إِنِّي نَذَرْتُ لَكَ مَا فِي بَطْنِي مُحَرَّرًا فَتَقَبَّلْ مِنِّيٓ ۖ إِنَّكَ أَنتَ السَّمِيعُ الْعَلِيمُ ۝٣٥

36 And when she was delivered of her she said: My Lord! Lo! I am delivered of a female—Allah knew best of what she was delivered—the male is not as the female; and Lo! I have named her Mary, and Lo! I crave Thy protection for her and for her offspring from Satan the outcast.

فَلَمَّا وَضَعَتْهَا قَالَتْ رَبِّ إِنِّي وَضَعْتُهَآ أُنثَىٰ وَاللَّهُ أَعْلَمُ بِمَا وَضَعَتْ وَلَيْسَ الذَّكَرُ كَالْأُنثَىٰ ۖ وَإِنِّي سَمَّيْتُهَا مَرْيَمَ وَإِنِّيٓ أُعِيذُهَا بِكَ وَذُرِّيَّتَهَا مِنَ الشَّيْطَٰنِ الرَّجِيمِ ۝٣٦

37 And her Lord accepted her with full acceptance and vouchsafed to her a goodly growth; and made Zachariah her guardian. Whenever Zachariah went into the sanctuary where she was, he found that she had food. He said: O Mary! Whence cometh unto thee this (food)? She answered: It is from Allah. Allah giveth without stint to whom He will.

فَتَقَبَّلَهَا رَبُّهَا بِقَبُولٍ حَسَنٍ وَأَنۢبَتَهَا نَبَاتًا حَسَنًا وَكَفَّلَهَا زَكَرِيَّا ۖ كُلَّمَا دَخَلَ عَلَيْهَا زَكَرِيَّا الْمِحْرَابَ وَجَدَ عِندَهَا رِزْقًا ۖ قَالَ يَٰمَرْيَمُ أَنَّىٰ لَكِ هَٰذَا ۖ قَالَتْ هُوَ مِنْ عِندِ اللَّهِ ۖ إِنَّ اللَّهَ يَرْزُقُ مَن يَشَآءُ بِغَيْرِ حِسَابٍ ۝٣٧

38 Then Zachariah prayed unto his Lord and said: My Lord! Bestow upon me of Thy bounty goodly offspring. Lo! Thou art the Hearer of Prayer.

هُنَالِكَ دَعَا زَكَرِيَّا رَبَّهُ ۖ قَالَ رَبِّ هَبْ لِي مِن لَّدُنكَ ذُرِّيَّةً طَيِّبَةً ۖ إِنَّكَ سَمِيعُ الدُّعَآءِ ۝٣٨

39 And the angels called to him as he stood praying in the sanctuary: Allah giveth thee glad tidings of (a son whose name is) John,[4] (who cometh) to confirm a word from Allah, lordly, chaste, a Prophet of the righteous.

فَنَادَتْهُ ٱلْمَلَٰٓئِكَةُ وَهُوَ قَآئِمٌ يُصَلِّى فِى ٱلْمِحْرَابِ أَنَّ ٱللَّهَ يُبَشِّرُكَ بِيَحْيَىٰ مُصَدِّقًۢا بِكَلِمَةٍ مِّنَ ٱللَّهِ وَسَيِّدًا وَحَصُورًا وَنَبِيًّا مِّنَ ٱلصَّٰلِحِينَ ۝

40 He said: My Lord! How can I have a son when age hath overtaken me already and my wife is barren? (The angel) answered: So (it will be). Allah doeth what He will.

قَالَ رَبِّ أَنَّىٰ يَكُونُ لِى غُلَٰمٌ وَقَدْ بَلَغَنِىَ ٱلْكِبَرُ وَٱمْرَأَتِى عَاقِرٌ قَالَ كَذَٰلِكَ ٱللَّهُ يَفْعَلُ مَا يَشَآءُ ۝

41 He said: My Lord! Appoint a token for me. (The angel) said: The token unto thee (shall be) that thou shalt not speak unto mankind three days except by signs. Remember thy Lord much, and praise (Him) in the early hours of night and morning.

قَالَ رَبِّ ٱجْعَل لِّىٓ ءَايَةً قَالَ ءَايَتُكَ أَلَّا تُكَلِّمَ ٱلنَّاسَ ثَلَٰثَةَ أَيَّامٍ إِلَّا رَمْزًا وَٱذْكُر رَّبَّكَ كَثِيرًا وَسَبِّحْ بِٱلْعَشِىِّ وَٱلْإِبْكَٰرِ ۝

42 And when the angels said: O Mary! Lo! Allah hath chosen thee and made thee pure, and hath preferred thee above (all) the women of creation.

وَإِذْ قَالَتِ ٱلْمَلَٰٓئِكَةُ يَٰمَرْيَمُ إِنَّ ٱللَّهَ ٱصْطَفَىٰكِ وَطَهَّرَكِ وَٱصْطَفَىٰكِ عَلَىٰ نِسَآءِ ٱلْعَٰلَمِينَ ۝

43 O Mary! Be obedient to thy Lord, prostrate thyself and bow with those who bow (in worship).

يَٰمَرْيَمُ ٱقْنُتِى لِرَبِّكِ وَٱسْجُدِى وَٱرْكَعِى مَعَ ٱلرَّٰكِعِينَ ۝

44 This is of the tidings of things hidden. We reveal it unto thee (Muhammad). Thou wast not present with them when they threw

ذَٰلِكَ مِنْ أَنۢبَآءِ ٱلْغَيْبِ نُوحِيهِ إِلَيْكَ وَمَا كُنتَ لَدَيْهِمْ إِذْ يُلْقُونَ أَقْلَٰمَهُمْ أَيُّهُمْ يَكْفُلُ

---

4. Ar. *Yahyā*.

their pens (to know) which of them should be the guardian of Mary, nor wast thou present with them when they quarrelled (thereupon).

مَرْيَمَ وَمَا كُنْتَ لَدَيْهِمْ إِذْ يَخْتَصِمُونَ ٤٤

45 (And remember) when the angels said: O Mary! Allah giveth thee glad tidings of a word from Him, whose name is the Messiah, Jesus, son of Mary, illustrious in the world and the Hereafter, and one of those brought near (unto Allah).

إِذْ قَالَتِ الْمَلَئِكَةُ يَمَرْيَمُ إِنَّ اللَّهَ يُبَشِّرُكِ بِكَلِمَةٍ مِّنْهُ اسْمُهُ الْمَسِيحُ عِيسَى ابْنُ مَرْيَمَ وَجِيهًا فِي الدُّنْيَا وَالْآخِرَةِ وَمِنَ الْمُقَرَّبِينَ ٤٥

46 He will speak unto mankind in his cradle and in his manhood, and he is of the righteous.

وَيُكَلِّمُ النَّاسَ فِي الْمَهْدِ وَكَهْلًا وَمِنَ الصَّالِحِينَ ٤٦

47 She said: My Lord! How can I have a child when no mortal hath touched me? He said: So (it will be). Allah createth what He will. If He decreeth a thing, He saith unto it only: Be! and it is.

قَالَتْ رَبِّ أَنَّى يَكُونُ لِي وَلَدٌ وَلَمْ يَمْسَسْنِي بَشَرٌ قَالَ كَذَلِكِ اللَّهُ يَخْلُقُ مَا يَشَاءُ إِذَا قَضَى أَمْرًا فَإِنَّمَا يَقُولُ لَهُ كُنْ فَيَكُونُ ٤٧

48 And He will teach him the Scripture and wisdom, and the Torah and the Gospel.

وَيُعَلِّمُهُ الْكِتَابَ وَالْحِكْمَةَ وَالتَّوْرَاةَ وَالْإِنْجِيلَ ٤٨

49 And will make him a messenger unto the children of Israel, (saying): Lo! I come unto you with a sign from your Lord. Lo! I fashion for you out of clay the likeness of a bird, and I breathe into it and it is a bird, by Allah's leave. I heal him who was born blind, and the leper, and I raise the dead, by Allah's leave. And I announce unto you what ye eat and what ye store up in your houses. Lo! herein verily is a portent for you, if ye are believers.

وَرَسُولًا إِلَى بَنِي إِسْرَائِيلَ أَنِّي قَدْ جِئْتُكُمْ بِآيَةٍ مِنْ رَبِّكُمْ أَنِّي أَخْلُقُ لَكُمْ مِنَ الطِّينِ كَهَيْئَةِ الطَّيْرِ فَأَنْفُخُ فِيهِ فَيَكُونُ طَيْرًا بِإِذْنِ اللَّهِ وَأُبْرِئُ الْأَكْمَهَ وَالْأَبْرَصَ وَأُحْيِي الْمَوْتَى بِإِذْنِ اللَّهِ وَأُنَبِّئُكُمْ بِمَا تَأْكُلُونَ وَمَا تَدَّخِرُونَ فِي بُيُوتِكُمْ إِنَّ فِي ذَلِكَ لَآيَةً لَكُمْ إِنْ كُنْتُمْ مُؤْمِنِينَ ٤٩

50 And (I come) confirming that which was before me of the Torah, and to make lawful some of that which was forbidden unto you. I come unto you with a sign from your Lord, so keep your duty to Allah and obey me.

وَمُصَدِّقًا لِّمَا بَيْنَ يَدَيَّ مِنَ التَّوْرَاةِ وَلِأُحِلَّ لَكُم بَعْضَ الَّذِي حُرِّمَ عَلَيْكُمْ وَجِئْتُكُم بِآيَةٍ مِّن رَّبِّكُمْ فَاتَّقُوا اللَّهَ وَأَطِيعُونِ ۝

51 Lo! Allah is my Lord and your Lord, so worship Him. That is a straight path.

إِنَّ اللَّهَ رَبِّي وَرَبُّكُمْ فَاعْبُدُوهُ ۚ هَٰذَا صِرَاطٌ مُّسْتَقِيمٌ ۝

52 But when Jesus became conscious of their disbelief, he cried: Who will be my helpers in the cause of Allah? The disciples said: We will be Allah's helpers. We believe in Allah, and bear thou witness that we have surrendered⁵ (unto Him).

۞ فَلَمَّا أَحَسَّ عِيسَىٰ مِنْهُمُ الْكُفْرَ قَالَ مَنْ أَنصَارِي إِلَى اللَّهِ ۖ قَالَ الْحَوَارِيُّونَ نَحْنُ أَنصَارُ اللَّهِ آمَنَّا بِاللَّهِ وَاشْهَدْ بِأَنَّا مُسْلِمُونَ ۝

53 Our Lord! We believe in that which Thou hast revealed and we follow him whom Thou hast sent. Enroll us among those who witness (to the truth).

رَبَّنَا آمَنَّا بِمَا أَنزَلْتَ وَاتَّبَعْنَا الرَّسُولَ فَاكْتُبْنَا مَعَ الشَّاهِدِينَ ۝

54 And they (the disbelievers) schemed, and Allah schemed (against them): and Allah is the best of schemers.

وَمَكَرُوا وَمَكَرَ اللَّهُ ۖ وَاللَّهُ خَيْرُ الْمَاكِرِينَ ۝

55 (And remember) when Allah said: O Jesus! Lo! I am gathering thee and causing thee to ascend unto Me, and am cleansing thee of those who disbelieve and am setting those who follow thee above those who disbelieve until the Day of Resurrection. Then unto Me ye will (all) return,

إِذْ قَالَ اللَّهُ يَا عِيسَىٰ إِنِّي مُتَوَفِّيكَ وَرَافِعُكَ إِلَيَّ وَمُطَهِّرُكَ مِنَ الَّذِينَ كَفَرُوا وَجَاعِلُ الَّذِينَ اتَّبَعُوكَ فَوْقَ الَّذِينَ كَفَرُوا إِلَىٰ يَوْمِ الْقِيَامَةِ ثُمَّ إِلَيَّ مَرْجِعُكُمْ فَأَحْكُمُ بَيْنَكُمْ فِيمَا

---

5. Or "are Muslims".

and I shall judge between you as to that wherein ye used to differ.

كُنْتُمْ فِيهِ تَخْتَلِفُونَ ۝

56 As for those who disbelieve I shall chastise them with a heavy chastisement in the world and the Hereafter; and they will have no helpers.

فَأَمَّا الَّذِينَ كَفَرُوا فَأُعَذِّبُهُمْ عَذَابًا شَدِيدًا فِي الدُّنْيَا وَالْآخِرَةِ وَمَا لَهُمْ مِنْ نَاصِرِينَ ۝

57 And as for those who believe and do good works, He will pay them their wages in full. Allah loveth not wrong-doers.

وَأَمَّا الَّذِينَ ءَامَنُوا وَعَمِلُوا الصَّالِحَاتِ فَيُوَفِّيهِمْ أُجُورَهُمْ وَاللَّهُ لَا يُحِبُّ الظَّالِمِينَ ۝

58 This (which) We recite unto thee is a revelation and a wise reminder.

ذَلِكَ نَتْلُوهُ عَلَيْكَ مِنَ الْآيَاتِ وَالذِّكْرِ الْحَكِيمِ ۝

59 Lo! the likeness of Jesus with Allah is as the likeness of Adam. He created him of dust, then He said unto him: Be! and he is.

إِنَّ مَثَلَ عِيسَى عِنْدَ اللَّهِ كَمَثَلِ ءَادَمَ خَلَقَهُ مِنْ تُرَابٍ ثُمَّ قَالَ لَهُ كُنْ فَيَكُونُ ۝

60 (This is) the truth from thy Lord (O Muhammad), so be not thou of those who waver.

الْحَقُّ مِنْ رَبِّكَ فَلَا تَكُنْ مِنَ الْمُمْتَرِينَ ۝

61 And whoso disputeth with thee concerning him, after the knowledge which hath come unto thee, say (unto him): Come! We will summon our sons and your sons, and our women and your women, and ourselves and yourselves, then we will pray humbly (to our Lord) and (solemnly) invoke the curse of Allah upon those who lie.

فَمَنْ حَاجَّكَ فِيهِ مِنْ بَعْدِ مَا جَاءَكَ مِنَ الْعِلْمِ فَقُلْ تَعَالَوْا نَدْعُ أَبْنَاءَنَا وَأَبْنَاءَكُمْ وَنِسَاءَنَا وَنِسَاءَكُمْ وَأَنْفُسَنَا وَأَنْفُسَكُمْ ثُمَّ نَبْتَهِلْ فَنَجْعَلْ لَعْنَتَ اللَّهِ عَلَى الْكَاذِبِينَ ۝

62 Lo! This verily is the true narrative. There is no God save Allah, and lo! Allah is the Mighty, the Wise.

إِنَّ هَذَا لَهُوَ الْقَصَصُ الْحَقُّ وَمَا مِنْ إِلَهٍ إِلَّا اللَّهُ وَإِنَّ اللَّهَ لَهُوَ الْعَزِيزُ الْحَكِيمُ ۝

63 And if they turn away, then lo! Allah is Aware of (who are) the corrupters.

فَإِنْ تَوَلَّوْا فَإِنَّ اللَّهَ عَلِيمٌ بِالْمُفْسِدِينَ ۝

64 Say: O People of the Scripture![6]
Come to an agreement between us
and you: that we shall worship none
but Allah, and that we shall ascribe
no partners unto Him, and that none
of us shall take others for lords beside Allah. And if they turn away,
then say: Bear witness that we are
they who have surrendered[7] (unto
Him).

قُلْ يَـٰٓأَهْلَ ٱلْكِتَـٰبِ تَعَالَوْا۟ إِلَىٰ كَلِمَةٍ سَوَآءٍ
بَيْنَنَا وَبَيْنَكُمْ أَلَّا نَعْبُدَ إِلَّا ٱللَّهَ وَلَا نُشْرِكَ
بِهِۦ شَيْـًٔا وَلَا يَتَّخِذَ بَعْضُنَا بَعْضًا أَرْبَابًا
مِّن دُونِ ٱللَّهِ فَإِن تَوَلَّوْا۟ فَقُولُوا۟ ٱشْهَدُوا۟ بِأَنَّا
مُسْلِمُونَ ﴿٦٤﴾

65 O People of the Scripture! Why
will ye argue about Abraham, when
the Torah and the Gospel were not
revealed till after him? Have ye
then no sense?

يَـٰٓأَهْلَ ٱلْكِتَـٰبِ لِمَ تُحَآجُّونَ فِىٓ إِبْرَٰهِيمَ
وَمَآ أُنزِلَتِ ٱلتَّوْرَىٰةُ وَٱلْإِنجِيلُ إِلَّا مِنۢ بَعْدِهِۦٓ
أَفَلَا تَعْقِلُونَ ﴿٦٥﴾

66 Lo! ye are those who argue
about that whereof ye have some
knowledge: Why then argue ye concerning that whereof ye have no
knowledge? Allah knoweth. Ye
know not.

هَـٰٓأَنتُمْ هَـٰٓؤُلَآءِ حَـٰجَجْتُمْ فِيمَا لَكُم بِهِۦ
عِلْمٌ فَلِمَ تُحَآجُّونَ فِيمَا لَيْسَ لَكُم بِهِۦ عِلْمٌ
وَٱللَّهُ يَعْلَمُ وَأَنتُمْ لَا تَعْلَمُونَ ﴿٦٦﴾

67 Abraham was not a Jew, nor yet
a Christian; but he was an upright
man who had surrendered (to Allah),
and he was not of the idolaters.

مَا كَانَ إِبْرَٰهِيمُ يَهُودِيًّا وَلَا نَصْرَانِيًّا وَلَـٰكِن كَانَ
حَنِيفًا مُّسْلِمًا وَمَا كَانَ مِنَ ٱلْمُشْرِكِينَ ﴿٦٧﴾

68 Lo! those of mankind who have
the best claim to Abraham are those
who followed him, and this Prophet
and those who believe (with him);
and Allah is the Protecting Friend of
the believers.

إِنَّ أَوْلَى ٱلنَّاسِ بِإِبْرَٰهِيمَ لَلَّذِينَ ٱتَّبَعُوهُ وَهَـٰذَا
ٱلنَّبِىُّ وَٱلَّذِينَ ءَامَنُوا۟ وَٱللَّهُ وَلِىُّ ٱلْمُؤْمِنِينَ ﴿٦٨﴾

---

6. Jews and Christians.

7. Ar. *muslimūm*.

69 A party of the people of the Scripture long to make you go astray; and they make none to go astray except themselves, but they perceive not.

وَدَّت طَّآئِفَةٌ مِّنْ أَهْلِ ٱلْكِتَٰبِ لَوْ يُضِلُّونَكُمْ وَمَا يُضِلُّونَ إِلَّآ أَنفُسَهُمْ وَمَا يَشْعُرُونَ ٦٩

70 O People of the Scripture! Why disbelieve ye in the revelations of Allah, when ye (yourselves) bear witness (to their truth)?

يَٰٓأَهْلَ ٱلْكِتَٰبِ لِمَ تَكْفُرُونَ بِـَٔايَٰتِ ٱللَّهِ وَأَنتُمْ تَشْهَدُونَ ٧٠

71 O People of the Scripture! Why confound ye truth with falsehood and knowingly conceal the truth?

يَٰٓأَهْلَ ٱلْكِتَٰبِ لِمَ تَلْبِسُونَ ٱلْحَقَّ بِٱلْبَٰطِلِ وَتَكْتُمُونَ ٱلْحَقَّ وَأَنتُمْ تَعْلَمُونَ ٧١

72 And a party of the People of the Scripture say: Believe in that which hath been revealed, unto those who believe at the opening of the day, and disbelieve at the end thereof, in order that they may return;[8]

وَقَالَت طَّآئِفَةٌ مِّنْ أَهْلِ ٱلْكِتَٰبِ ءَامِنُوا بِٱلَّذِىٓ أُنزِلَ عَلَى ٱلَّذِينَ ءَامَنُوا وَجْهَ ٱلنَّهَارِ وَٱكْفُرُوٓا ءَاخِرَهُۥ لَعَلَّهُمْ يَرْجِعُونَ ٧٢

73 And believe not save in one who followeth your religion—Say (O Muhammad): Lo! the guidance is Allah's guidance—that any one is given the like of that which was given unto you or that they may argue with you in the presence of your Lord. Say (O Muhammad): Lo! the bounty is in Allah's hand. He bestoweth it on whom He will. Allah is All Embracing, All Knowing.

وَلَا تُؤْمِنُوٓا إِلَّا لِمَن تَبِعَ دِينَكُمْ قُلْ إِنَّ ٱلْهُدَىٰ هُدَى ٱللَّهِ أَن يُؤْتَىٰٓ أَحَدٌ مِّثْلَ مَآ أُوتِيتُمْ أَوْ يُحَآجُّوكُمْ عِندَ رَبِّكُمْ قُلْ إِنَّ ٱلْفَضْلَ بِيَدِ ٱللَّهِ يُؤْتِيهِ مَن يَشَآءُ وَٱللَّهُ وَٰسِعٌ عَلِيمٌ ٧٣

74 He selecteth for His mercy whom He will. Allah is of infinite bounty.

يَخْتَصُّ بِرَحْمَتِهِۦ مَن يَشَآءُ وَٱللَّهُ ذُو ٱلْفَضْلِ ٱلْعَظِيمِ ٧٤

---

8. The reference is to some Jews of Al-Madīnah, who feigned an interest in Al-Islām only in the hope of detaching some Muslims by their subtle arguments.

75 Among the People of the Scripture there is he who, if thou trust him with a weight of treasure, will return it to thee. And among them there is he who, if thou trust him with a piece of gold, will not return it to thee unless thou keep standing over him. That is because they say: We have no duty to the Gentiles. They speak a lie concerning Allah knowingly.

۞ وَمِنْ أَهْلِ الْكِتَابِ مَنْ إِنْ تَأْمَنْهُ بِقِنطَارٍ يُؤَدِّهِ إِلَيْكَ وَمِنْهُم مَّنْ إِن تَأْمَنْهُ بِدِينَارٍ لَّا يُؤَدِّهِ إِلَيْكَ إِلَّا مَا دُمْتَ عَلَيْهِ قَآئِمًا ذَٰلِكَ بِأَنَّهُمْ قَالُوا لَيْسَ عَلَيْنَا فِى الْأُمِّيِّنَ سَبِيلٌ وَيَقُولُونَ عَلَى اللَّهِ الْكَذِبَ وَهُمْ يَعْلَمُونَ ۝

76 Nay, but (the chosen of Allah is) he who fulfilleth his pledge and wardeth off (evil); for lo! Allah loveth those who ward off (evil).

بَلَىٰ مَنْ أَوْفَىٰ بِعَهْدِهِ وَاتَّقَىٰ فَإِنَّ اللَّهَ يُحِبُّ الْمُتَّقِينَ ۝

77 Lo! those who purchase a small gain at the cost of Allah's covenant and their oaths,[9] they have no portion in the Hereafter. Allah will neither speak to them nor look upon them on the Day of Resurrection, nor will He make them grow. Theirs will be a painful doom.

إِنَّ الَّذِينَ يَشْتَرُونَ بِعَهْدِ اللَّهِ وَأَيْمَانِهِمْ ثَمَنًا قَلِيلًا أُوْلَٰئِكَ لَا خَلَاقَ لَهُمْ فِى الْآخِرَةِ وَلَا يُكَلِّمُهُمُ اللَّهُ وَلَا يَنظُرُ إِلَيْهِمْ يَوْمَ الْقِيَٰمَةِ وَلَا يُزَكِّيهِمْ وَلَهُمْ عَذَابٌ أَلِيمٌ ۝

78 And Lo! there is a party of them who distort the Scripture with their tongues, that ye may think that what they say is from the Scripture, when it is not from the Scripture. And they say: It is from Allah, when it is not from Allah; and they speak a lie concerning Allah knowingly.

وَإِنَّ مِنْهُمْ لَفَرِيقًا يَلْوُونَ أَلْسِنَتَهُم بِالْكِتَٰبِ لِتَحْسَبُوهُ مِنَ الْكِتَٰبِ وَمَا هُوَ مِنَ الْكِتَٰبِ وَيَقُولُونَ هُوَ مِنْ عِندِ اللَّهِ وَمَا هُوَ مِنْ عِندِ اللَّهِ وَيَقُولُونَ عَلَى اللَّهِ الْكَذِبَ وَهُمْ يَعْلَمُونَ ۝

---

9. The Jews of Al-Madīnah had made a solemn treaty with the Prophet in the year 1 A.H.

79 It is not (possible) for any human being unto whom Allah had given the Scripture and wisdom and the Prophethood that he should afterwards have said unto mankind: Be slaves of me instead of Allah; but (what he said was): Be ye faithful servants of the Lord by virtue of your constant teaching of the Scripture and of your constant study thereof.

مَاكَانَ لِبَشَرٍ أَن يُؤْتِيَهُ اللّٰهُ الْكِتَبَ وَالْحُكْمَ وَالنُّبُوَّةَ ثُمَّ يَقُولَ لِلنَّاسِ كُونُوا عِبَادًا لِّى مِن دُونِ اللّٰهِ وَلَكِن كُونُوا رَبَّنِيّنَ بِمَا كُنتُمْ تُعَلِّمُونَ الْكِتَبَ وَبِمَا كُنتُمْ تَدْرُسُونَ ۝

80 And he commanded you not that ye should take the angels and the Prophets for lords. Would he command you to disbelieve after ye had surrendered (to Allah)?

وَلَا يَأْمُرَكُمْ أَن تَتَّخِذُوا الْمَلَئِكَةَ وَالنَّبِيّنَ أَرْبَابًا أَيَأْمُرُكُم بِالْكُفْرِ بَعْدَ إِذْ أَنتُم مُّسْلِمُونَ ۝

81 When Allah made (His) covenant with the Prophets, (He said): Behold that which I have given you of the Scripture and knowledge. And afterward there will come unto you a messenger, confirming that which ye possess. Ye shall believe in him and ye shall help him. He said: Do ye agree, and will ye take up My burden (which I lay upon you) in this (matter)? They answered: We agree. He said: Then bear ye witness. I will be a witness with you.

وَإِذْ أَخَذَ اللّٰهُ مِيثَقَ النَّبِيّنَ لَمَا ءَاتَيْتُكُم مِّن كِتَبٍ وَحِكْمَةٍ ثُمَّ جَاءَكُمْ رَسُولٌ مُّصَدِّقٌ لِّمَا مَعَكُمْ لَتُؤْمِنُنَّ بِهِ وَلَتَنصُرُنَّهُ قَالَ ءَأَقْرَرْتُمْ وَأَخَذْتُمْ عَلَى ذَلِكُمْ إِصْرِى قَالُوا أَقْرَرْنَا قَالَ فَاشْهَدُوا وَأَنَا مَعَكُم مِّنَ الشَّهِدِينَ ۝

82 Then whosoever after this shall turn away: they will be miscreants.

83 Seek they other than the religion of Allah, when unto Him submitteth whosoever is in the heavens and the earth, willingly, or unwillingly, and unto Him they will be returned.

فَمَن تَوَلَّى بَعْدَ ذَلِكَ فَأُوْلَئِكَ هُمُ الْفَسِقُونَ ۝ أَفَغَيْرَ دِينِ اللّٰهِ يَبْغُونَ وَلَهُ أَسْلَمَ مَن فِى السَّمَوَتِ وَالْأَرْضِ طَوْعًا وَكَرْهًا وَإِلَيْهِ يُرْجَعُونَ ۝

84 Say (O Muhammad): We believe in Allah and that which is revealed unto us and that which was revealed unto Abraham and Ishmael and Isaac and Jacob and the tribes, and that which was vouchsafed unto Moses and Jesus and the Prophets from their Lord. We make no distinction between any of them, and unto Him we have surrendered.[10]

قُلْ ءَامَنَّا بِاللَّهِ وَمَا أُنزِلَ عَلَيْنَا وَمَا أُنزِلَ عَلَىٰ إِبْرَٰهِيمَ وَإِسْمَٰعِيلَ وَإِسْحَٰقَ وَيَعْقُوبَ وَالْأَسْبَاطِ وَمَا أُوتِيَ مُوسَىٰ وَعِيسَىٰ وَالنَّبِيُّونَ مِن رَّبِّهِمْ لَا نُفَرِّقُ بَيْنَ أَحَدٍ مِّنْهُمْ وَنَحْنُ لَهُ مُسْلِمُونَ ۝

85 And whoso seeketh as religion other than the Surrender[11] (to Allah) it will not be accepted from him, and he will be a loser in the Hereafter.

وَمَن يَبْتَغِ غَيْرَ الْإِسْلَٰمِ دِينًا فَلَن يُقْبَلَ مِنْهُ وَهُوَ فِي الْآخِرَةِ مِنَ الْخَٰسِرِينَ ۝

86 How shall Allah guide a people who disbelieved after their belief and (after) they bore witness that the messenger is true and after clear proofs (of Allah's sovereignty) had come unto them. And Allah guideth not wrongdoing folk.

كَيْفَ يَهْدِي اللَّهُ قَوْمًا كَفَرُوا بَعْدَ إِيمَٰنِهِمْ وَشَهِدُوا أَنَّ الرَّسُولَ حَقٌّ وَجَاءَهُمُ الْبَيِّنَٰتُ وَاللَّهُ لَا يَهْدِي الْقَوْمَ الظَّٰلِمِينَ ۝

87 As for such, their guerdon is that on them rests the curse of Allah and of angels and of men combined.

أُو۟لَٰٓئِكَ جَزَآؤُهُمْ أَنَّ عَلَيْهِمْ لَعْنَةَ اللَّهِ وَالْمَلَٰٓئِكَةِ وَالنَّاسِ أَجْمَعِينَ ۝

88 They will abide therein. Their doom will not be lightened, neither will they be reprieved;

خَٰلِدِينَ فِيهَا لَا يُخَفَّفُ عَنْهُمُ الْعَذَابُ وَلَا هُمْ يُنظَرُونَ ۝

89 Save those who afterward repent and do right. Lo! Allah is Forgiving, Merciful.

إِلَّا الَّذِينَ تَابُوا مِن بَعْدِ ذَٰلِكَ وَأَصْلَحُوا فَإِنَّ اللَّهَ غَفُورٌ رَّحِيمٌ ۝

---

10. Almost identical with Sūrah 2: 136.

11. Ar. *Al-Islām*.

90 Lo! those who disbelieve after their (profession of) belief, and afterward grow violent in disbelief: their repentance will not be accepted. And such are those who are astray.

إِنَّ الَّذِينَ كَفَرُوا بَعْدَ إِيمَٰنِهِمْ ثُمَّ ازْدَادُوا كُفْرًا لَّن تُقْبَلَ تَوْبَتُهُمْ وَأُوْلَٰٓئِكَ هُمُ الضَّآلُّونَ ۝

91 Lo! those who disbelieve, and die in disbelief, the (whole) earth full of gold would not be accepted from such a one if it were offered as a ransom (for his soul). Theirs will be a painful doom and they will have no helpers.

إِنَّ الَّذِينَ كَفَرُوا وَمَاتُوا وَهُمْ كُفَّارٌ فَلَن يُقْبَلَ مِنْ أَحَدِهِم مِّلْءُ الْأَرْضِ ذَهَبًا وَلَوِ افْتَدَىٰ بِهِۦٓ أُوْلَٰٓئِكَ لَهُمْ عَذَابٌ أَلِيمٌ وَمَا لَهُم مِّن نَّٰصِرِينَ ۝

92 Ye will not attain unto piety until ye spend of that which ye love. And whatsoever ye spend, Allah is aware thereof.

لَن تَنَالُوا الْبِرَّ حَتَّىٰ تُنفِقُوا مِمَّا تُحِبُّونَ وَمَا تُنفِقُوا مِن شَيْءٍ فَإِنَّ اللَّهَ بِهِۦ عَلِيمٌ ۝

93 All food was lawful unto the children of Israel, save that which Israel forbade himself, (in days) before the Torah was revealed. Say: Produce the Torah and read it (unto us) if ye are truthful.

۞ كُلُّ الطَّعَامِ كَانَ حِلًّا لِّبَنِىٓ إِسْرَٰٓءِيلَ إِلَّا مَا حَرَّمَ إِسْرَٰٓءِيلُ عَلَىٰ نَفْسِهِۦ مِن قَبْلِ أَن تُنَزَّلَ التَّوْرَىٰةُ قُلْ فَأْتُوا بِالتَّوْرَىٰةِ فَاتْلُوهَآ إِن كُنتُمْ صَٰدِقِينَ ۝

94 And whoever shall invent a falsehood after that concerning Allah, such will be wrong-doers.

فَمَنِ افْتَرَىٰ عَلَى اللَّهِ الْكَذِبَ مِنۢ بَعْدِ ذَٰلِكَ فَأُوْلَٰٓئِكَ هُمُ الظَّٰلِمُونَ ۝

95 Say: Allah speaketh truth. So follow the religion of Abraham, the upright. He was not of the idolaters.

قُلْ صَدَقَ اللَّهُ فَاتَّبِعُوا مِلَّةَ إِبْرَٰهِيمَ حَنِيفًا وَمَا كَانَ مِنَ الْمُشْرِكِينَ ۝

96 Lo! the first Sanctuary appointed for mankind was that at Becca,[12] a blessed place, a guidance to the peoples;

إِنَّ أَوَّلَ بَيْتٍ وُضِعَ لِلنَّاسِ لَلَّذِى بِبَكَّةَ مُبَارَكًا وَهُدًى لِّلْعَٰلَمِينَ ۝

---

12. Makkah.

97 Wherein are plain memorials (of Allah's guidance); the place where Abraham stood up to pray; and whosoever entereth it is safe. And pilgrimage to the House is a duty unto Allah for mankind, for him who can find a way thither. As for him who disbelieveth, (let him know that) lo! Allah is Independent of (all) creatures.

فِيهِ ءَايَتُ بَيِّنَتُ مَّقَامُ إِبْرَٰهِيمَ وَمَن دَخَلَهُۥ كَانَ ءَامِنًا وَلِلَّهِ عَلَى ٱلنَّاسِ حِجُّ ٱلْبَيْتِ مَنِ ٱسْتَطَاعَ إِلَيْهِ سَبِيلًا وَمَن كَفَرَ فَإِنَّ ٱللَّهَ غَنِىٌّ عَنِ ٱلْعَٰلَمِينَ ۝

98 Say: O People of the Scripture! Why disbelieve ye in the revelations of Allah, when Allah (Himself) is Witness of what ye do?

قُلْ يَٰٓأَهْلَ ٱلْكِتَٰبِ لِمَ تَكْفُرُونَ بِـَٔايَٰتِ ٱللَّهِ وَٱللَّهُ شَهِيدٌ عَلَىٰ مَا تَعْمَلُونَ ۝

99 Say: O People of the Scripture! Why drive ye back believers from the way of Allah, seeking to make it crooked, when ye are witnesses (to Allah's guidance)? Allah is not unaware of what ye do.

قُلْ يَٰٓأَهْلَ ٱلْكِتَٰبِ لِمَ تَصُدُّونَ عَن سَبِيلِ ٱللَّهِ مَنْ ءَامَنَ تَبْغُونَهَا عِوَجًا وَأَنتُمْ شُهَدَآءُ وَمَا ٱللَّهُ بِغَٰفِلٍ عَمَّا تَعْمَلُونَ ۝

100 O ye who believe! If ye obey a party of those who have received the Scripture they will make you disbelievers after your belief.

يَٰٓأَيُّهَا ٱلَّذِينَ ءَامَنُوٓا۟ إِن تُطِيعُوا۟ فَرِيقًا مِّنَ ٱلَّذِينَ أُوتُوا۟ ٱلْكِتَٰبَ يَرُدُّوكُم بَعْدَ إِيمَٰنِكُمْ كَٰفِرِينَ ۝

101 How can ye disbelieve, when Allah's revelations are recited unto you, and His messenger is in your midst? He who holdeth fast to Allah, he indeed is guided unto a right path.

وَكَيْفَ تَكْفُرُونَ وَأَنتُمْ تُتْلَىٰ عَلَيْكُمْ ءَايَٰتُ ٱللَّهِ وَفِيكُمْ رَسُولُهُۥ وَمَن يَعْتَصِم بِٱللَّهِ فَقَدْ هُدِىَ إِلَىٰ صِرَٰطٍ مُّسْتَقِيمٍ ۝

102 O ye who believe! Observe your duty to Allah with right observance, and die not save as those who have surrendered (unto Him);

يَٰٓأَيُّهَا ٱلَّذِينَ ءَامَنُوا۟ ٱتَّقُوا۟ ٱللَّهَ حَقَّ تُقَاتِهِۦ وَلَا تَمُوتُنَّ إِلَّا وَأَنتُم مُّسْلِمُونَ ۝

103   And hold fast, all of you together, to the cable of Allah, and do not separate. And remember Allah's favour unto you: how ye were enemies and He made friendship between your hearts so that ye became as brothers by His grace; and (how) ye were upon the brink of an abyss of fire, and He did save you from it. Thus Allah maketh clear His revelations unto you, that haply ye may be guided,

وَاعْتَصِمُوا بِحَبْلِ اللّٰهِ جَمِيعًا وَّلَا تَفَرَّقُوا ۚ وَاذْكُرُوا نِعْمَتَ اللّٰهِ عَلَيْكُمْ إِذْ كُنْتُمْ أَعْدَآءً فَأَلَّفَ بَيْنَ قُلُوبِكُمْ فَأَصْبَحْتُمْ بِنِعْمَتِهٖٓ إِخْوَانًا ۚ وَكُنْتُمْ عَلٰى شَفَا حُفْرَةٍ مِّنَ النَّارِ فَأَنْقَذَكُمْ مِّنْهَا ۗ كَذٰلِكَ يُبَيِّنُ اللّٰهُ لَكُمْ ءَايٰتِهٖ لَعَلَّكُمْ تَهْتَدُونَ ۝

104   And there may spring from you a nation who invite to goodness, and enjoin right conduct and forbid indecency. Such are they who are successful.

وَلْتَكُنْ مِّنْكُمْ أُمَّةٌ يَّدْعُونَ إِلَى الْخَيْرِ وَيَأْمُرُونَ بِالْمَعْرُوفِ وَيَنْهَوْنَ عَنِ الْمُنْكَرِ ۚ وَأُولٰٓئِكَ هُمُ الْمُفْلِحُونَ ۝

105   And be ye not as those who separated and disputed after the clear proofs had come unto them. For such there is an awful doom,

وَلَا تَكُونُوا كَالَّذِينَ تَفَرَّقُوا وَاخْتَلَفُوا مِنْ بَعْدِ مَا جَآءَهُمُ الْبَيِّنٰتُ ۚ وَأُولٰٓئِكَ لَهُمْ عَذَابٌ عَظِيمٌ ۝

106   On the day when (some) faces will be whitened and (some) faces will be blackened; and as for those whose faces have been blackened, it will be said unto them: Disbelieved ye after your (profession of) belief? Then taste the punishment for that ye disbelieved.

يَوْمَ تَبْيَضُّ وُجُوهٌ وَّتَسْوَدُّ وُجُوهٌ ۚ فَأَمَّا الَّذِينَ اسْوَدَّتْ وُجُوهُهُمْ أَكَفَرْتُمْ بَعْدَ إِيمَانِكُمْ فَذُوقُوا الْعَذَابَ بِمَا كُنْتُمْ تَكْفُرُونَ ۝

107   As for those whose faces have been whitened, lo! in the mercy of Allah they dwell forever.

108   These are revelations of Allah. We recite them unto thee in truth. Allah willeth no injustice to (His) creatures.

وَأَمَّا الَّذِينَ ابْيَضَّتْ وُجُوهُهُمْ فَفِي رَحْمَةِ اللّٰهِ ۖ هُمْ فِيهَا خَالِدُونَ ۝

تِلْكَ ءَايٰتُ اللّٰهِ نَتْلُوهَا عَلَيْكَ بِالْحَقِّ ۗ وَمَا اللّٰهُ يُرِيدُ ظُلْمًا لِّلْعَالَمِينَ ۝

109 Unto Allah belongeth whatsoever is in the heavens and whatsoever is in the earth; and unto Allah all things are returned.

وَلِلَّهِ مَا فِى السَّمَوَاتِ وَمَا فِى الْأَرْضِ وَإِلَى اللَّهِ تُرْجَعُ الْأُمُورُ ۝

110 Ye are the best community that hath been raised up for mankind. Ye enjoin right conduct and forbid indecency; and ye believe in Allah. And if the People of the Scripture had believed it had been better for them. Some of them are believers; but most of them are evil-livers.

كُنتُمْ خَيْرَ أُمَّةٍ أُخْرِجَتْ لِلنَّاسِ تَأْمُرُونَ بِالْمَعْرُوفِ وَتَنْهَوْنَ عَنِ الْمُنكَرِ وَتُؤْمِنُونَ بِاللَّهِ وَلَوْ ءَامَنَ أَهْلُ الْكِتَبِ لَكَانَ خَيْرًا لَّهُم مِّنْهُمُ الْمُؤْمِنُونَ وَأَكْثَرُهُمُ الْفَسِقُونَ ۝

111 They will not harm you save a trifling hurt, and if they fight against you they will turn and flee. And afterward they will not be helped.

لَن يَضُرُّوكُمْ إِلَّا أَذًى وَإِن يُقَتِلُوكُمْ يُوَلُّوكُمُ الْأَدْبَارَ ثُمَّ لَا يُنصَرُونَ ۝

112 Ignominy shall be their portion wheresoever they are found save (where they grasp) a rope from Allah and a rope from men.[13] They have incurred anger from their Lord, and wretchedness is laid upon them. That is because they used to disbelieve the revelations of Allah, and slew the Prophets wrongfully. That is because they were rebellious and used to transgress.

ضُرِبَتْ عَلَيْهِمُ الذِّلَّةُ أَيْنَ مَا ثُقِفُوا إِلَّا بِحَبْلٍ مِّنَ اللَّهِ وَحَبْلٍ مِّنَ النَّاسِ وَبَاءُو بِغَضَبٍ مِّنَ اللَّهِ وَضُرِبَتْ عَلَيْهِمُ الْمَسْكَنَةُ ذَلِكَ بِأَنَّهُمْ كَانُوا يَكْفُرُونَ بِـَٔايَتِ اللَّهِ وَيَقْتُلُونَ الْأَنبِيَاءَ بِغَيْرِ حَقٍّ ذَلِكَ بِمَا عَصَوا وَّكَانُوا يَعْتَدُونَ ۝

113 They are not all alike. Of the People of the Scripture there is a staunch community who recite the

۞ لَيْسُوا سَوَاءً مِّنْ أَهْلِ الْكِتَبِ أُمَّةٌ قَائِمَةٌ

---

13. *i.e.* when they keep the convenant which the Prophet had made with the Jews of Al-Madīnah.

revelations of Allah in the night season, falling prostrate (before Him).

يَتْلُونَ ءَايَتِ اللَّهِ ءَانَآءَ الَّيْلِ وَهُمْ يَسْجُدُونَ ۝

114   They believe in Allah and the Last Day, and enjoin right conduct and forbid indecency, and vie one with another in good works. They are of the righteous.

يُؤْمِنُونَ بِاللَّهِ وَالْيَوْمِ الْأَخِرِ وَيَأْمُرُونَ بِالْمَعْرُوفِ وَيَنْهَوْنَ عَنِ الْمُنكَرِ وَيُسَرِعُونَ فِى الْخَيْرَتِ وَأُوْلَتِكَ مِنَ الصَّلِحِينَ ۝

115   And whatever good they do, they will not be denied the meed thereof. Allah is Aware of those who ward off (evil).

وَمَا يَفْعَلُواْ مِنْ خَيْرٍ فَلَن يُكْفَرُوهُ وَاللَّهُ عَلِيمٌ بِالْمُتَّقِينَ ۝

116   Lo! the riches and the progeny of those who disbelieve will not avail them aught against Allah; and such are rightful owners of the Fire. They will abide therein.

إِنَّ الَّذِينَ كَفَرُواْ لَن تُغْنِىَ عَنْهُمْ أَمْوَلُهُمْ وَلَآ أَوْلَدُهُم مِّنَ اللَّهِ شَيْـًا وَأُوْلَتِكَ أَصْحَبُ النَّارِ هُمْ فِيهَا خَلِدُونَ ۝

117   The likeness of that which they spend in this life of the world is as the likeness of a biting, icy wind which smiteth the harvest of a people who have wronged themselves, and devastateth it. Allah wronged them not, but they did wrong themselves.

مَثَلُ مَا يُنفِقُونَ فِى هَذِهِ الْحَيَوةِ الدُّنْيَا كَمَثَلِ رِيحٍ فِيهَا صِرٌّ أَصَابَتْ حَرْثَ قَوْمٍ ظَلَمُواْ أَنفُسَهُمْ فَأَهْلَكَتْهُ وَمَا ظَلَمَهُمُ اللَّهُ وَلَكِنْ أَنفُسَهُمْ يَظْلِمُونَ ۝

118   O ye who believe! Take not for intimates others than your own folk, who would spare no pains to ruin you; they love to hamper you. Hatred is revealed by (the utterance of) their mouths, but that which their breasts hide is greater. We have made plain for you the revelations if ye will understand.

يَتَأَيُّهَا الَّذِينَ ءَامَنُواْ لَا تَتَّخِذُواْ بِطَانَةً مِّن دُونِكُمْ لَا يَأْلُونَكُمْ خَبَالًا وَدُّواْ مَا عَنِتُّمْ قَدْ بَدَتِ الْبَغْضَآءُ مِنْ أَفْوَهِهِمْ وَمَا تُخْفِى صُدُورُهُمْ أَكْبَرُ قَدْ بَيَّنَّا لَكُمُ الْأَيَتِ إِن كُنتُمْ تَعْقِلُونَ ۝

119   O ye are those who love them though they love you not, and ye believe in all the Scripture. When they fall in with you they say: We believe; but when they go apart they bite their finger tips at you, for rage. Say: Perish in your rage! Lo! Allah is Aware of what is hidden in (your) breasts.

هَاۤأَنتُمۡ أُوۡلَآءِ تُحِبُّونَهُمۡ وَلَا يُحِبُّونَكُمۡ وَتُؤۡمِنُونَ بِٱلۡكِتَٰبِ كُلِّهِۦ ۖ وَإِذَا لَقُوكُمۡ قَالُوۤاْ ءَامَنَّا وَإِذَا خَلَوۡاْ عَضُّوۡاْ عَلَيۡكُمُ ٱلۡأَنَامِلَ مِنَ ٱلۡغَيۡظِ ۚ قُلۡ مُوتُواْ بِغَيۡظِكُمۡ ۗ إِنَّ ٱللَّهَ عَلِيمٌۢ بِذَاتِ ٱلصُّدُورِ ﴿١١٩﴾

120   If a lucky chance befall you, it is evil unto them, and if disaster strike you they rejoice thereat. But if ye persevere and keep from evil their guile will never harm you. Lo! Allah is Surrounding what they do.

إِن تَمۡسَسۡكُمۡ حَسَنَةٌ تَسُؤۡهُمۡ وَإِن تُصِبۡكُمۡ سَيِّئَةٌ يَفۡرَحُواْ بِهَا ۖ وَإِن تَصۡبِرُواْ وَتَتَّقُواْ لَا يَضُرُّكُمۡ كَيۡدُهُمۡ شَيۡـًٔا ۗ إِنَّ ٱللَّهَ بِمَا يَعۡمَلُونَ مُحِيطٌ ﴿١٢٠﴾

121   And remember when thou settedst forth at daybreak from thy housefolk to assign to the believers their positions for the battle,[14] Allah was Hearer, Knower.

وَإِذۡ غَدَوۡتَ مِنۡ أَهۡلِكَ تُبَوِّئُ ٱلۡمُؤۡمِنِينَ مَقَٰعِدَ لِلۡقِتَالِ ۗ وَٱللَّهُ سَمِيعٌ عَلِيمٌ ﴿١٢١﴾

122   When two parties of you almost fell away, and Allah was their Protecting Friend. In Allah do believers put their trust.

إِذۡ هَمَّت طَّآئِفَتَانِ مِنكُمۡ أَن تَفۡشَلَا وَٱللَّهُ وَلِيُّهُمَا ۗ وَعَلَى ٱللَّهِ فَلۡيَتَوَكَّلِ ٱلۡمُؤۡمِنُونَ ﴿١٢٢﴾

123   Allah had already given you the victory at Badr, when ye were contemptible. So observe your duty to Allah in order that ye may be thankful.

وَلَقَدۡ نَصَرَكُمُ ٱللَّهُ بِبَدۡرٍ وَأَنتُمۡ أَذِلَّةٌ ۖ فَٱتَّقُواْ ٱللَّهَ لَعَلَّكُمۡ تَشۡكُرُونَ ﴿١٢٣﴾

124   And when thou didst say unto the believers: Is it not sufficient for you that your Lord should support you with three thousand angels sent down (to your help)?

إِذۡ تَقُولُ لِلۡمُؤۡمِنِينَ أَلَن يَكۡفِيَكُمۡ أَن يُمِدَّكُمۡ رَبُّكُم بِثَلَٰثَةِ ءَالَٰفٍ مِّنَ ٱلۡمَلَٰٓئِكَةِ مُنزَلِينَ ﴿١٢٤﴾

---

14. The battle of Mt. Uḥud near Al-Madīnah in the third year of the Hijrah. (see introduction to this Sūrah)

125   Nay, but if ye persevere, and keep from evil, and (the enemy) attack you suddenly, your Lord will help you with five thousand angels sweeping on.

126   Allah ordained this only as a message of good cheer for you, and that thereby your hearts might be at rest. Victory cometh only from Allah, the Mighty, the Wise.

127   That He may cut off a part of those who disbelieve, or overwhelm them so that they retire, frustrated.

128   It is no concern at all of thee (Muhammad) whether He relent toward them or punish them; for they are evil-doers.

129   Unto Allah belongeth whatsoever is in the heavens and whatsoever is in the earth. He forgiveth whom He will, and punisheth whom He will. Allah is Forgiving, Merciful.

130   O ye who believe! Devour not usury, doubling and quadrupling (the sum lent). Observe your duty to Allah, that ye may be successful.

131   And ward off (from yourselves) the Fire prepared for disbelievers.

132   And obey Allah and the messenger, that ye may find mercy.

بَلَىٰٓ إِن تَصۡبِرُواْ وَتَتَّقُواْ وَيَأۡتُوكُم مِّن فَوۡرِهِمۡ هَٰذَا يُمۡدِدۡكُمۡ رَبُّكُم بِخَمۡسَةِ ءَالَٰفٍ مِّنَ ٱلۡمَلَٰٓئِكَةِ مُسَوِّمِينَ ۝

وَمَا جَعَلَهُ ٱللَّهُ إِلَّا بُشۡرَىٰ لَكُمۡ وَلِتَطۡمَئِنَّ قُلُوبُكُم بِهِۦۗ وَمَا ٱلنَّصۡرُ إِلَّا مِنۡ عِندِ ٱللَّهِ ٱلۡعَزِيزِ ٱلۡحَكِيمِ ۝

لِيَقۡطَعَ طَرَفًا مِّنَ ٱلَّذِينَ كَفَرُوٓاْ أَوۡ يَكۡبِتَهُمۡ فَيَنقَلِبُواْ خَآئِبِينَ ۝

لَيۡسَ لَكَ مِنَ ٱلۡأَمۡرِ شَيۡءٌ أَوۡ يَتُوبَ عَلَيۡهِمۡ أَوۡ يُعَذِّبَهُمۡ فَإِنَّهُمۡ ظَٰلِمُونَ ۝

وَلِلَّهِ مَا فِي ٱلسَّمَٰوَٰتِ وَمَا فِي ٱلۡأَرۡضِ يَغۡفِرُ لِمَن يَشَآءُ وَيُعَذِّبُ مَن يَشَآءُۚ وَٱللَّهُ غَفُورٌ رَّحِيمٌ ۝

يَٰٓأَيُّهَا ٱلَّذِينَ ءَامَنُواْ لَا تَأۡكُلُواْ ٱلرِّبَوٰٓاْ أَضۡعَٰفًا مُّضَٰعَفَةًۖ وَٱتَّقُواْ ٱللَّهَ لَعَلَّكُمۡ تُفۡلِحُونَ ۝

وَٱتَّقُواْ ٱلنَّارَ ٱلَّتِيٓ أُعِدَّتۡ لِلۡكَٰفِرِينَ ۝

وَأَطِيعُواْ ٱللَّهَ وَٱلرَّسُولَ لَعَلَّكُمۡ تُرۡحَمُونَ ۝

133   And vie one with another for forgiveness from your Lord, and for a Paradise as wide as are the heavens and the earth, prepared for those who ward off (evil);

﴿ وَسَارِعُوٓا إِلَىٰ مَغْفِرَةٍ مِّن رَّبِّكُمْ وَجَنَّةٍ عَرْضُهَا ٱلسَّمَٰوَٰتُ وَٱلْأَرْضُ أُعِدَّتْ لِلْمُتَّقِينَ ﴾

134   Those who spend (of that which Allah hath given them) in ease and in adversity, those who control their wrath and are forgiving toward mankind; Allah loveth the good;

ٱلَّذِينَ يُنفِقُونَ فِى ٱلسَّرَّآءِ وَٱلضَّرَّآءِ وَٱلْكَٰظِمِينَ ٱلْغَيْظَ وَٱلْعَافِينَ عَنِ ٱلنَّاسِ وَٱللَّهُ يُحِبُّ ٱلْمُحْسِنِينَ ﴿١٣٤﴾

135   And those who, when they do an evil thing or wrong themselves, remember Allah and implore forgiveness for their sins. Who forgiveth sins save Allah only?—and will not knowingly repeat (the wrong) they did.

وَٱلَّذِينَ إِذَا فَعَلُوا فَٰحِشَةً أَوْ ظَلَمُوٓا أَنفُسَهُمْ ذَكَرُوا ٱللَّهَ فَٱسْتَغْفَرُوا لِذُنُوبِهِمْ وَمَن يَغْفِرُ ٱلذُّنُوبَ إِلَّا ٱللَّهُ وَلَمْ يُصِرُّوا عَلَىٰ مَا فَعَلُوا وَهُمْ يَعْلَمُونَ ﴿١٣٥﴾

136   The reward of such will be forgiveness from their Lord, and Gardens underneath which rivers flow, wherein they will abide forever—a bountiful reward for workers!

أُوْلَٰٓئِكَ جَزَآؤُهُم مَّغْفِرَةٌ مِّن رَّبِّهِمْ وَجَنَّٰتٌ تَجْرِى مِن تَحْتِهَا ٱلْأَنْهَٰرُ خَٰلِدِينَ فِيهَا وَنِعْمَ أَجْرُ ٱلْعَٰمِلِينَ ﴿١٣٦﴾

137   Systems have passed away before you. Do but travel in the land and see the nature of the consequence for those who did deny (the messengers).

قَدْ خَلَتْ مِن قَبْلِكُمْ سُنَنٌ فَسِيرُوا فِى ٱلْأَرْضِ فَٱنظُرُوا كَيْفَ كَانَ عَٰقِبَةُ ٱلْمُكَذِّبِينَ ﴿١٣٧﴾

138   This is a declaration for mankind, a guidance and an admonition unto those who ward off (evil).

هَٰذَا بَيَانٌ لِّلنَّاسِ وَهُدًى وَمَوْعِظَةٌ لِّلْمُتَّقِينَ ﴿١٣٨﴾

139   Faint not nor grieve, for ye will overcome them if ye are (indeed) believers.

وَلَا تَهِنُوا وَلَا تَحْزَنُوا وَأَنتُمُ ٱلْأَعْلَوْنَ إِن كُنتُم مُّؤْمِنِينَ ﴿١٣٩﴾

140   If ye have received a blow, the (disbelieving) people have received a blow the like thereof.[15] These are (only) the vicissitudes which We cause to follow one another for mankind, to the end that Allah may know those who believe and may choose witnesses[16] from among you; and Allah loveth not wrong-doers.

إِن يَمْسَسْكُمْ قَرْحٌ فَقَدْ مَسَّ ٱلْقَوْمَ قَرْحٌ مِّثْلُهُۥ وَتِلْكَ ٱلْأَيَّامُ نُدَاوِلُهَا بَيْنَ ٱلنَّاسِ وَلِيَعْلَمَ ٱللَّهُ ٱلَّذِينَ ءَامَنُوا۟ وَيَتَّخِذَ مِنكُمْ شُهَدَآءَ وَٱللَّهُ لَا يُحِبُّ ٱلظَّـٰلِمِينَ ۝

141   And that Allah may prove those who believe, and may blight the disbelievers.

وَلِيُمَحِّصَ ٱللَّهُ ٱلَّذِينَ ءَامَنُوا۟ وَيَمْحَقَ ٱلْكَـٰفِرِينَ ۝

142   Or deemed ye that ye would enter Paradise while yet Allah knoweth not those of you who really strive, nor knoweth those (of you) who are steadfast?

أَمْ حَسِبْتُمْ أَن تَدْخُلُوا۟ ٱلْجَنَّةَ وَلَمَّا يَعْلَمِ ٱللَّهُ ٱلَّذِينَ جَـٰهَدُوا۟ مِنكُمْ وَيَعْلَمَ ٱلصَّـٰبِرِينَ ۝

143   And verily ye used to wish for death before ye met it (in the field). Now ye have seen it with your eyes!

وَلَقَدْ كُنتُمْ تَمَنَّوْنَ ٱلْمَوْتَ مِن قَبْلِ أَن تَلْقَوْهُ فَقَدْ رَأَيْتُمُوهُ وَأَنتُمْ تَنظُرُونَ ۝

144   Muhammad is but a messenger, messengers (the like of whom) have passed away before him. Will it be that, when he dieth or is slain, ye will turn back on your heels? He who turneth back doth no hurt to Allah, and Allah will reward the thankful.[17]

وَمَا مُحَمَّدٌ إِلَّا رَسُولٌ قَدْ خَلَتْ مِن قَبْلِهِ ٱلرُّسُلُ أَفَإِي۟ن مَّاتَ أَوْ قُتِلَ ٱنقَلَبْتُمْ عَلَىٰٓ أَعْقَـٰبِكُمْ وَمَن يَنقَلِبْ عَلَىٰ عَقِبَيْهِ فَلَن يَضُرَّ ٱللَّهَ شَيْـًٔا وَسَيَجْزِى ٱللَّهُ ٱلشَّـٰكِرِينَ ۝

---

15. At Badr.

16. Or *martyrs*.

17. On the morning when the Prophet died, Abū Bakr came into the mosque at Al-Madīnah and found the people all distracted, and 'Umar telling them that it was a sin to say that he was dead. Abū Bakr went and ascertained the truth, and coming back into the

145 No soul can ever die except by Allah's leave and at a term appointed. Whoso desireth the reward of the world, We bestow on him thereof; and whoso desireth the reward of the Hereafter, We bestow on him thereof. We shall reward the thankful.

وَمَا كَانَ لِنَفْسٍ أَن تَمُوتَ إِلَّا بِإِذْنِ اللَّهِ كِتَابًا مُّؤَجَّلًا ۗ وَمَن يُرِدْ ثَوَابَ الدُّنْيَا نُؤْتِهِ مِنْهَا وَمَن يُرِدْ ثَوَابَ الْآخِرَةِ نُؤْتِهِ مِنْهَا ۚ وَسَنَجْزِي الشَّاكِرِينَ ﴿١٤٥﴾

146 And with how many a prophet have there been a number of devoted men who fought (beside him). They quailed not for aught that befell them in the way of Allah, nor did they weaken, nor were they brought low. Allah loveth the steadfast.

وَكَأَيِّن مِّن نَّبِيٍّ قَاتَلَ مَعَهُ رِبِّيُّونَ كَثِيرٌ فَمَا وَهَنُوا لِمَا أَصَابَهُمْ فِي سَبِيلِ اللَّهِ وَمَا ضَعُفُوا وَمَا اسْتَكَانُوا ۗ وَاللَّهُ يُحِبُّ الصَّابِرِينَ ﴿١٤٦﴾

147 Their cry was only that they said: Our Lord! Forgive us for our sins and wasted efforts, make our foothold sure, and give us victory over the disbelieving folk.

وَمَا كَانَ قَوْلَهُمْ إِلَّا أَن قَالُوا رَبَّنَا اغْفِرْ لَنَا ذُنُوبَنَا وَإِسْرَافَنَا فِي أَمْرِنَا وَثَبِّتْ أَقْدَامَنَا وَانصُرْنَا عَلَى الْقَوْمِ الْكَافِرِينَ ﴿١٤٧﴾

148 So Allah gave them the reward of the world and the good reward of the Hereafter. Allah loveth those whose deeds are good.

فَآتَاهُمُ اللَّهُ ثَوَابَ الدُّنْيَا وَحُسْنَ ثَوَابِ الْآخِرَةِ ۗ وَاللَّهُ يُحِبُّ الْمُحْسِنِينَ ﴿١٤٨﴾

149 O ye who believe! If ye obey those who disbelieve, they will make you turn back on your heels, and ye turn back as losers.

يَا أَيُّهَا الَّذِينَ آمَنُوا إِن تُطِيعُوا الَّذِينَ كَفَرُوا يَرُدُّوكُمْ عَلَى أَعْقَابِكُمْ فَتَنقَلِبُوا خَاسِرِينَ ﴿١٤٩﴾

150 But Allah is your Protector, and He is the best of helpers.

بَلِ اللَّهُ مَوْلَاكُمْ ۖ وَهُوَ خَيْرُ النَّاصِرِينَ ﴿١٥٠﴾

---

mosque, cried: "Lo! as for him who worshipped Muhammad, Muhammad is dead, but as for him who worshippeth Allah, Allah is alive and dieth not." Then he recited this verse "and it was as if the people had not known till then that such verse had been revealed."

151   We shall cast terror into the hearts of those who disbelieve because they ascribe unto Allah partners, for which no warrant hath been revealed. Their habitation is the Fire, and hapless the abode of the wrong-doers.

سَنُلْقِى فِى قُلُوبِ الَّذِينَ كَفَرُوا الرُّعْبَ بِمَآ أَشْرَكُوا بِاللَّهِ مَا لَمْ يُنَزِّلْ بِهِ سُلْطَانًا وَمَأْوَاهُمُ النَّارُ وَبِئْسَ مَثْوَى الظَّالِمِينَ ۝

152   Allah verily made good His promise unto you when ye routed them by His leave, until (the moment) when your courage failed you, and ye disagreed about the order and ye disobeyed, after He had shown you that for which ye long.[18] Some of you desired the world, and some of you desired the Hereafter. Therefore He made you flee from them, that He might try you. Yet now He hath forgiven you. Allah is a Lord of Kindness to believers.

وَلَقَدْ صَدَقَكُمُ اللَّهُ وَعْدَهُ إِذْ تَحُسُّونَهُم بِإِذْنِهِ حَتَّى إِذَا فَشِلْتُمْ وَتَنَازَعْتُمْ فِى الْأَمْرِ وَعَصَيْتُم مِّنْ بَعْدِ مَآ أَرَاكُم مَّا تُحِبُّونَ مِنكُم مَّن يُرِيدُ الدُّنْيَا وَمِنكُم مَّن يُرِيدُ الْآخِرَةَ ثُمَّ صَرَفَكُمْ عَنْهُمْ لِيَبْتَلِيَكُمْ وَلَقَدْ عَفَا عَنكُمْ وَاللَّهُ ذُو فَضْلٍ عَلَى الْمُؤْمِنِينَ ۝

153   When ye climbed (the hill) and paid no heed to anyone, while the messenger, in your rear, was calling you (to fight). Therefor He rewarded you grief for (his) grief, that (He might teach) you not to sorrow either for that which ye missed or for that which befell you. Allah is Aware of what ye do.

۞ إِذْ تُصْعِدُونَ وَلَا تَلْوُونَ عَلَى أَحَدٍ وَالرَّسُولُ يَدْعُوكُمْ فِى أُخْرَاكُمْ فَأَثَابَكُمْ غَمًّا بِغَمٍّ لِّكَيْلَا تَحْزَنُوا عَلَى مَا فَاتَكُمْ وَلَا مَآ أَصَابَكُمْ وَاللَّهُ خَبِيرٌ بِمَا تَعْمَلُونَ ۝

---

18. When the archers deserted their post to share in the spoils, thinking that the day was won.

154   Then, after grief, He sent down security for you. As slumber did it overcome a party of you, while (the other) party, who were anxious on their own account, thought wrongly of Allah, the thought of ignorance. They said: Have we any part in the cause? Say (O Muhammad): The cause belongeth wholly to Allah. They hide within themselves (a thought) which they reveal not unto thee, saying: Had we had any part in the cause we should not have been slain here. Say: Even though ye had been in your houses, those appointed to be slain would have gone forth to the places where they were to lie. (All this hath been) in order that Allah might try what is in your breasts and prove what is in your hearts. Allah is Aware of what is hidden in the breasts (of men).

ثُمَّ أَنزَلَ عَلَيْكُم مِّنۢ بَعْدِ ٱلْغَمِّ أَمَنَةً نُّعَاسًا يَغْشَىٰ طَآئِفَةً مِّنكُمْ ۖ وَطَآئِفَةٌ قَدْ أَهَمَّتْهُمْ أَنفُسُهُمْ يَظُنُّونَ بِٱللَّهِ غَيْرَ ٱلْحَقِّ ظَنَّ ٱلْجَٰهِلِيَّةِ ۖ يَقُولُونَ هَل لَّنَا مِنَ ٱلْأَمْرِ مِن شَىْءٍ ۗ قُلْ إِنَّ ٱلْأَمْرَ كُلَّهُۥ لِلَّهِ ۗ يُخْفُونَ فِىٓ أَنفُسِهِم مَّا لَا يُبْدُونَ لَكَ ۖ يَقُولُونَ لَوْ كَانَ لَنَا مِنَ ٱلْأَمْرِ شَىْءٌ مَّا قُتِلْنَا هَٰهُنَا ۗ قُل لَّوْ كُنتُمْ فِى بُيُوتِكُمْ لَبَرَزَ ٱلَّذِينَ كُتِبَ عَلَيْهِمُ ٱلْقَتْلُ إِلَىٰ مَضَاجِعِهِمْ ۖ وَلِيَبْتَلِىَ ٱللَّهُ مَا فِى صُدُورِكُمْ وَلِيُمَحِّصَ مَا فِى قُلُوبِكُمْ ۗ وَٱللَّهُ عَلِيمٌۢ بِذَاتِ ٱلصُّدُورِ ۝

155   Lo! those of you who turned back on the day when the two hosts met, Satan alone it was who caused them to backslide, because of some of that which they have earned. Now Allah hath forgiven them. Lo! Allah is Forgiving, Clement.

إِنَّ ٱلَّذِينَ تَوَلَّوْاْ مِنكُمْ يَوْمَ ٱلْتَقَى ٱلْجَمْعَانِ إِنَّمَا ٱسْتَزَلَّهُمُ ٱلشَّيْطَٰنُ بِبَعْضِ مَا كَسَبُواْ ۖ وَلَقَدْ عَفَا ٱللَّهُ عَنْهُمْ ۗ إِنَّ ٱللَّهَ غَفُورٌ حَلِيمٌ ۝

156   O ye who believe! Be not as those who disbelieved and said of their brethren who went abroad in the land or were fighting in the field: If they had been (here) with us they would not have died or

يَٰٓأَيُّهَا ٱلَّذِينَ ءَامَنُواْ لَا تَكُونُواْ كَٱلَّذِينَ كَفَرُواْ وَقَالُواْ لِإِخْوَٰنِهِمْ إِذَا ضَرَبُواْ فِى ٱلْأَرْضِ أَوْ كَانُواْ غُزًّى لَّوْ كَانُواْ عِندَنَا مَا مَاتُواْ وَمَا قُتِلُواْ لِيَجْعَلَ ٱللَّهُ ذَٰلِكَ

been killed; that Allah may make it
anguish in their hearts. Allah giveth
life and causeth death; and Allah is
Seer of what ye do.

حَسْرَةً فِى قُلُوبِهِمْ وَاللّٰهُ يُحْىِ وَيُمِيتُ
وَاللّٰهُ بِمَا تَعْمَلُونَ بَصِيرٌ ﴿١٥٦﴾

157   And what though ye be slain
in Allah's way or die therein? Surely pardon from Allah and mercy are
better than all that they amass.

وَلَئِنْ قُتِلْتُمْ فِى سَبِيلِ اللّٰهِ أَوْ مُتُّمْ لَمَغْفِرَةٌ
مِنَ اللّٰهِ وَرَحْمَةٌ خَيْرٌ مِّمَّا يَجْمَعُونَ ﴿١٥٧﴾

158   What though ye be slain or
die, when unto Allah ye are gathered?

وَلَئِنْ مُّتُّمْ أَوْ قُتِلْتُمْ لَإِلَى اللّٰهِ تُحْشَرُونَ ﴿١٥٨﴾

159   It was by the mercy of Allah
that thou wast lenient with them (O
Muhammad), for if thou hadst been
stern and fierce of heart they would
have dispersed from round about
thee. So pardon them and ask forgiveness for them and consult with
them upon the conduct of affairs.
And when thou art resolved, then
put thy trust in Allah. Lo! Allah
loveth those who put their trust (in
Him).

فَبِمَا رَحْمَةٍ مِّنَ اللّٰهِ لِنْتَ لَهُمْ وَلَوْ كُنْتَ فَظًّا غَلِيظَ
الْقَلْبِ لَانْفَضُّوا مِنْ حَوْلِكَ فَاعْفُ عَنْهُمْ وَاسْتَغْفِرْ
لَهُمْ وَشَاوِرْهُمْ فِى الْأَمْرِ فَإِذَا عَزَمْتَ فَتَوَكَّلْ
عَلَى اللّٰهِ إِنَّ اللّٰهَ يُحِبُّ الْمُتَوَكِّلِينَ ﴿١٥٩﴾

160   If Allah is your helper none
can overcome you, and if He withdraw His help from you, who is
there who can help you? In Allah
let believers put their trust.

إِنْ يَنْصُرْكُمُ اللّٰهُ فَلَا غَالِبَ لَكُمْ وَإِنْ يَخْذُلْكُمْ
فَمَنْ ذَا الَّذِى يَنْصُرُكُمْ مِنْ بَعْدِهِ وَعَلَى اللّٰهِ
فَلْيَتَوَكَّلِ الْمُؤْمِنُونَ ﴿١٦٠﴾

161   It is not for any Prophet to
deceive (mankind). Whoso deceiveth will bring his deceit with him
on the Day of Resurrection. Then
every soul will be paid in full what
it hath earned; and they will not be
wronged.

وَمَا كَانَ لِنَبِىٍّ أَنْ يَغُلَّ وَمَنْ يَغْلُلْ يَأْتِ بِمَا غَلَّ
يَوْمَ الْقِيٰمَةِ ثُمَّ تُوَفّٰى كُلُّ نَفْسٍ مَّا كَسَبَتْ
وَهُمْ لَا يُظْلَمُونَ ﴿١٦١﴾

162   Is one who followeth the pleasure of Allah as one who hath earned condemnation from Allah, whose habitation is the Fire, a hapless journey's end?

أَفَمَنِ ٱتَّبَعَ رِضْوَانَ ٱللَّهِ كَمَنۢ بَآءَ بِسَخَطٍ مِّنَ ٱللَّهِ وَمَأْوَىٰهُ جَهَنَّمُ وَبِئْسَ ٱلْمَصِيرُ ﴿١٦٢﴾

163   They are (in different) degrees (of grace and reprobation) with Allah, and Allah is Seer of what ye do.

هُمْ دَرَجَٰتٌ عِندَ ٱللَّهِ وَٱللَّهُ بَصِيرٌۢ بِمَا يَعْمَلُونَ ﴿١٦٣﴾

164   Allah verily hath shown grace to the believers by sending unto them a messenger of their own who reciteth unto them His revelations, and causeth them to grow, and teacheth them the Scripture and wisdom;[19] although before (he came to them) they were in flagrant error.

لَقَدْ مَنَّ ٱللَّهُ عَلَى ٱلْمُؤْمِنِينَ إِذْ بَعَثَ فِيهِمْ رَسُولًا مِّنْ أَنفُسِهِمْ يَتْلُواْ عَلَيْهِمْ ءَايَٰتِهِۦ وَيُزَكِّيهِمْ وَيُعَلِّمُهُمُ ٱلْكِتَٰبَ وَٱلْحِكْمَةَ وَإِن كَانُواْ مِن قَبْلُ لَفِى ضَلَٰلٍ مُّبِينٍ ﴿١٦٤﴾

165   And was it so, when a disaster smote you, though ye had smitten (them with a disaster) twice (as great),[20] that ye said: How is this? Say (unto them, O Muhammad): It is from yourselves. Lo! Allah is Able to do all things.

أَوَلَمَّآ أَصَٰبَتْكُم مُّصِيبَةٌ قَدْ أَصَبْتُم مِّثْلَيْهَا قُلْتُمْ أَنَّىٰ هَٰذَا قُلْ هُوَ مِنْ عِندِ أَنفُسِكُمْ إِنَّ ٱللَّهَ عَلَىٰ كُلِّ شَىْءٍ قَدِيرٌ ﴿١٦٥﴾

166   That which befell you, on the day when the two armies met, was by permission of Allah; that He might know the true believers;

وَمَآ أَصَٰبَكُمْ يَوْمَ ٱلْتَقَى ٱلْجَمْعَانِ فَبِإِذْنِ ٱللَّهِ وَلِيَعْلَمَ ٱلْمُؤْمِنِينَ ﴿١٦٦﴾

---

19. In fulfilment of the prayer of Abraham (Sūrah 2: 129).

20. At Badr.

167   And that He might know the
hypocrites, unto whom it was said:
Come, fight in the way of Allah, or
defend yourselves. They answered:
If we knew aught of fighting we
would follow you. On that day they
were nearer disbelief than faith.
They utter with their mouths a
thing which is not in their hearts.
Allah is best aware of what they
hide.

وَلِيَعْلَمَ الَّذِينَ نَافَقُوا وَقِيلَ لَهُمْ تَعَالَوْا قَاتِلُوا
فِي سَبِيلِ اللَّهِ أَوِ ادْفَعُوا قَالُوا لَوْ نَعْلَمُ قِتَالًا
لَّاتَّبَعْنَاكُمْ هُمْ لِلْكُفْرِ يَوْمَئِذٍ أَقْرَبُ مِنْهُمْ
لِلْإِيمَانِ يَقُولُونَ بِأَفْوَاهِهِم مَّا لَيْسَ
فِي قُلُوبِهِمْ وَاللَّهُ أَعْلَمُ بِمَا يَكْتُمُونَ ۝

168   Those who, while they sat at
home, said of their brethren (who
were fighting for the cause of
Allah): If they had obeyed Us; they
would not have been slain. Say
(unto them, O Muhammad): Then
avert death from yourselves if ye
are truthful.

الَّذِينَ قَالُوا لِإِخْوَانِهِمْ وَقَعَدُوا لَوْ أَطَاعُونَا
مَا قُتِلُوا قُلْ فَادْرَءُوا عَنْ أَنفُسِكُمُ الْمَوْتَ
إِن كُنتُمْ صَادِقِينَ ۝

169   Think not of those, who are
slain in the way of Allah, as dead.
Nay, they are living. With their
Lord they have provision.

وَلَا تَحْسَبَنَّ الَّذِينَ قُتِلُوا فِي سَبِيلِ اللَّهِ أَمْوَاتًا بَلْ
أَحْيَاءٌ عِندَ رَبِّهِمْ يُرْزَقُونَ ۝

170   Jubilant (are they) because
of that which Allah hath bestowed
upon them of His bounty, rejoicing
for the sake of those who have not
joined them but are left behind: that
there shall no fear come upon them
neither shall they grieve.

فَرِحِينَ بِمَا آتَاهُمُ اللَّهُ مِن فَضْلِهِ
وَيَسْتَبْشِرُونَ بِالَّذِينَ لَمْ يَلْحَقُوا بِهِم مِّنْ خَلْفِهِمْ
أَلَّا خَوْفٌ عَلَيْهِمْ وَلَا هُمْ يَحْزَنُونَ ۝

171   They rejoice because of
favour from Allah and kindness,
and that Allah wasteth not the wage
of the believers.

۞ يَسْتَبْشِرُونَ بِنِعْمَةٍ مِّنَ اللَّهِ وَفَضْلٍ وَأَنَّ اللَّهَ
لَا يُضِيعُ أَجْرَ الْمُؤْمِنِينَ ۝

172 As for those who heard the call of Allah and His messenger after the harm befell them (in the fight); for such of them as do right and ward off (evil), there is great reward,

الَّذِينَ اسْتَجَابُوا لِلَّهِ وَالرَّسُولِ مِنْ بَعْدِ مَا أَصَابَهُمُ الْقَرْحُ لِلَّذِينَ أَحْسَنُوا مِنْهُمْ وَاتَّقَوْا أَجْرٌ عَظِيمٌ ۝

173 Those unto whom men said: Lo! the people have gathered against you, therefor fear them. (The threat of danger) but increased the faith of them and they cried: Allah is sufficient for us! Most Excellent is He in Whom we trust!

الَّذِينَ قَالَ لَهُمُ النَّاسُ إِنَّ النَّاسَ قَدْ جَمَعُوا لَكُمْ فَاخْشَوْهُمْ فَزَادَهُمْ إِيمَانًا وَقَالُوا حَسْبُنَا اللَّهُ وَنِعْمَ الْوَكِيلُ ۝

174 So they returned with grace and favour from Allah, and no harm touched them. They followed the good pleasure of Allah, and Allah is of infinite bounty.

فَانْقَلَبُوا بِنِعْمَةٍ مِنَ اللَّهِ وَفَضْلٍ لَمْ يَمْسَسْهُمْ سُوءٌ وَاتَّبَعُوا رِضْوَانَ اللَّهِ وَاللَّهُ ذُو فَضْلٍ عَظِيمٍ ۝

175 It is only the devil who would make (men) fear his partisans. Fear them not; fear Me, if ye are true believers.

إِنَّمَا ذَلِكُمُ الشَّيْطَانُ يُخَوِّفُ أَوْلِيَاءَهُ فَلَا تَخَافُوهُمْ وَخَافُونِ إِنْ كُنْتُمْ مُؤْمِنِينَ ۝

176 Let not their conduct grieve thee, who run easily to disbelief, for lo! they injure Allah not at all. It is Allah's will to assign them no portion in the Hereafter, and theirs will be an awful doom.

وَلَا يَحْزُنْكَ الَّذِينَ يُسَارِعُونَ فِي الْكُفْرِ إِنَّهُمْ لَنْ يَضُرُّوا اللَّهَ شَيْئًا يُرِيدُ اللَّهُ أَلَّا يَجْعَلَ لَهُمْ حَظًّا فِي الْآخِرَةِ وَلَهُمْ عَذَابٌ عَظِيمٌ ۝

177 Those who purchase disbelief at the price of faith harm Allah not at all, but theirs will be a painful doom.

إِنَّ الَّذِينَ اشْتَرَوُا الْكُفْرَ بِالْإِيمَانِ لَنْ يَضُرُّوا اللَّهَ شَيْئًا وَلَهُمْ عَذَابٌ أَلِيمٌ ۝

178 And let not those who disbelieve imagine that the rein We give them bodeth good unto their

وَلَا يَحْسَبَنَّ الَّذِينَ كَفَرُوا أَنَّمَا نُمْلِي لَهُمْ خَيْرٌ

souls. We only give them rein that
they may grow in sinfulness. And
theirs will be a shameful doom.

179   It is not (the purpose) of
Allah to leave you in your present
state till He shall separate the wicked from the good. And it is not
(the purpose of) Allah to let you
know the unseen. But Allah chooseth of His messengers whom He
will, (to receive knowledge thereof). So believe in Allah and His
messengers. If ye believe and ward
off (evil), yours will be a vast
reward.

180   And let not those who hoard
up that which Allah hath bestowed
upon them of His bounty think that
it is better for them. Nay, it is
worse for them. That which they
hoard will be their collar on the
Day of Resurrection. Allah's is the
heritage of the heavens and the
earth, And Allah is Aware of what
ye do.

181   Verily Allah heard the saying
of those who said, (when asked for
contributions to the war): "Allah,
forsooth, is poor, and we are rich!"[21]
We shall record their saying with
their slaying of the Prophets wrongfully and We shall say: Taste ye the
punishment of burning!

لِأَنفُسِهِمْ إِنَّمَا نُمْلِى لَهُمْ لِيَزْدَادُوٓاْ إِثْمًا
وَلَهُمْ عَذَابٌ مُّهِينٌ ۝

مَّا كَانَ ٱللَّهُ لِيَذَرَ ٱلْمُؤْمِنِينَ عَلَىٰ مَآ أَنتُمْ عَلَيْهِ حَتَّىٰ
يَمِيزَ ٱلْخَبِيثَ مِنَ ٱلطَّيِّبِ وَمَا كَانَ ٱللَّهُ لِيُطْلِعَكُمْ
عَلَى ٱلْغَيْبِ وَلَٰكِنَّ ٱللَّهَ يَجْتَبِى مِن رُّسُلِهِ مَن يَشَآءُ
فَـَٔامِنُواْ بِٱللَّهِ وَرُسُلِهِ وَإِن تُؤْمِنُواْ وَتَتَّقُواْ فَلَكُمْ
أَجْرٌ عَظِيمٌ ۝

وَلَا يَحْسَبَنَّ ٱلَّذِينَ يَبْخَلُونَ بِمَآ ءَاتَىٰهُمُ ٱللَّهُ مِن
فَضْلِهِ هُوَ خَيْرًا لَّهُم بَلْ هُوَ شَرٌّ لَّهُمْ سَيُطَوَّقُونَ
مَا بَخِلُواْ بِهِ يَوْمَ ٱلْقِيَٰمَةِ وَلِلَّهِ مِيرَٰثُ
ٱلسَّمَٰوَٰتِ وَٱلْأَرْضِ وَٱللَّهُ بِمَا تَعْمَلُونَ خَبِيرٌ ۝

لَّقَدْ سَمِعَ ٱللَّهُ قَوْلَ ٱلَّذِينَ قَالُوٓاْ إِنَّ ٱللَّهَ فَقِيرٌ
وَنَحْنُ أَغْنِيَآءُ سَنَكْتُبُ مَا قَالُواْ وَقَتْلَهُمُ
ٱلْأَنۢبِيَآءَ بِغَيْرِ حَقٍّ وَنَقُولُ ذُوقُواْ عَذَابَ
ٱلْحَرِيقِ ۝

---

21. A saying of some Jews of Al-Madīnah.

182   This is on account of that which your own hands have sent before (you to the judgment). Allah is no oppressor of (His) bondmen.

ذٰلِكَ بِمَا قَدَّمَتْ أَيْدِيكُمْ وَأَنَّ اللّٰهَ لَيْسَ بِظَلَّامٍ لِّلْعَبِيدِ ۝

183   (The same are) those who say: Lo! Allah hath charged us that we believe not in any messenger until he bring us an offering which fire (from heaven) shall devour. Say (unto them, O Muhammad): Messengers came unto you before me with miracles, and with that (very miracle) which ye describe. Why then did ye slay them? (Answer that) if ye are truthful!

ٱلَّذِينَ قَالُوٓاْ إِنَّ ٱللّٰهَ عَهِدَ إِلَيْنَآ أَلَّا نُؤْمِنَ لِرَسُولٍ حَتَّىٰ يَأْتِيَنَا بِقُرْبَانٍ تَأْكُلُهُ ٱلنَّارُ قُلْ قَدْ جَآءَكُمْ رُسُلٌ مِّن قَبْلِي بِٱلْبَيِّنَٰتِ وَبِٱلَّذِي قُلْتُمْ فَلِمَ قَتَلْتُمُوهُمْ إِن كُنتُمْ صَٰدِقِينَ ۝

184   And if they deny thee, even so did they deny messengers who were before thee, who came with miracles and with the Psalms and with the Scripture giving light.

فَإِن كَذَّبُوكَ فَقَدْ كُذِّبَ رُسُلٌ مِّن قَبْلِكَ جَآءُو بِٱلْبَيِّنَٰتِ وَٱلزُّبُرِ وَٱلْكِتَٰبِ ٱلْمُنِيرِ ۝

185   Every soul will taste of death. And ye will be paid on the Day of Resurrection only that which ye have fairly earned. Whoso is removed from the Fire and is made to enter Paradise, he indeed is triumphant. The life of this world is but comfort of illusion.

كُلُّ نَفْسٍ ذَآئِقَةُ ٱلْمَوْتِ وَإِنَّمَا تُوَفَّوْنَ أُجُورَكُمْ يَوْمَ ٱلْقِيَٰمَةِ فَمَن زُحْزِحَ عَنِ ٱلنَّارِ وَأُدْخِلَ ٱلْجَنَّةَ فَقَدْ فَازَ وَمَا ٱلْحَيَوٰةُ ٱلدُّنْيَآ إِلَّا مَتَٰعُ ٱلْغُرُورِ ۝

186   Assuredly ye will be tried in your property and in your persons, and ye will hear much wrong from those who were given the Scripture before you, and from the idolaters. But if ye persevere and ward off (evil), then that is of the steadfast heart of things.

۞ لَتُبْلَوُنَّ فِىٓ أَمْوَٰلِكُمْ وَأَنفُسِكُمْ وَلَتَسْمَعُنَّ مِنَ ٱلَّذِينَ أُوتُواْ ٱلْكِتَٰبَ مِن قَبْلِكُمْ وَمِنَ ٱلَّذِينَ أَشْرَكُوٓاْ أَذًى كَثِيرًا وَإِن تَصْبِرُواْ وَتَتَّقُواْ فَإِنَّ ذَٰلِكَ مِنْ عَزْمِ ٱلْأُمُورِ ۝

187   And (remember) when Allah laid a charge on those who had received the Scripture (He said): Ye are to expound it to mankind and not to hide it. But they flung it behind their backs and bought thereby a little gain. Verily evil is that which they have gained thereby.

وَإِذْ أَخَذَ اللّٰهُ مِيثَاقَ الَّذِينَ أُوتُوا الْكِتَبَ لَتُبَيِّنُنَّهُ لِلنَّاسِ وَلَا تَكْتُمُونَهُ فَنَبَذُوهُ وَرَآءَ ظُهُورِهِمْ وَاشْتَرَوْا بِهِ ثَمَنًا قَلِيلًا فَبِئْسَ مَا يَشْتَرُونَ ۝

188   Think not that those who exult in what they have given, and love to be praised for what they have not done—Think not, they are in safety from the doom. A painful doom is theirs.

لَا تَحْسَبَنَّ الَّذِينَ يَفْرَحُونَ بِمَا أَتَوْا وَيُحِبُّونَ أَنْ يُحْمَدُوا بِمَا لَمْ يَفْعَلُوا فَلَا تَحْسَبَنَّهُمْ بِمَفَازَةٍ مِنَ الْعَذَابِ وَلَهُمْ عَذَابٌ أَلِيمٌ ۝

189   Unto Allah belongeth the Sovereignty of the heavens and the earth. Allah is Able to do all things.

وَلِلّٰهِ مُلْكُ السَّمَوَاتِ وَالْأَرْضِ وَاللّٰهُ عَلَى كُلِّ شَيْءٍ قَدِيرٌ ۝

190   Lo! In the creation of the heavens and the earth and (in) the difference of night and day are tokens (of His sovereignty) for men of understanding,

إِنَّ فِي خَلْقِ السَّمَوَاتِ وَالْأَرْضِ وَاخْتِلَافِ الَّيْلِ وَالنَّهَارِ لَآيَاتٍ لِأُولِي الْأَلْبَابِ ۝

191   Such as remember Allah, standing, sitting, and reclining, and consider the creation of the heavens and the earth, (and say): Our Lord! Thou createdst not this in vain. Glory be to Thee! Preserve us from the doom of Fire.

الَّذِينَ يَذْكُرُونَ اللّٰهَ قِيَامًا وَقُعُودًا وَعَلَى جُنُوبِهِمْ وَيَتَفَكَّرُونَ فِي خَلْقِ السَّمَوَاتِ وَالْأَرْضِ رَبَّنَا مَا خَلَقْتَ هَذَا بَاطِلًا سُبْحَانَكَ فَقِنَا عَذَابَ النَّارِ ۝

192   Our Lord! Whom Thou causest to enter the Fire: him indeed Thou hast confounded. For evil-doers there will be no helpers.

رَبَّنَا إِنَّكَ مَنْ تُدْخِلِ النَّارَ فَقَدْ أَخْزَيْتَهُ وَمَا لِلظَّالِمِينَ مِنْ أَنْصَارٍ ۝

193 Our Lord! Lo! we have heard a crier calling unto Faith: "Believe ye in your Lord!" So we believed. Our Lord! Therefor forgive us our sins, and remit from us our evil deeds, and make us die the death of the righteous.

رَبَّنَا إِنَّنَا سَمِعْنَا مُنَادِيًا يُنَادِي لِلْإِيمَنِ أَنْ ءَامِنُوا بِرَبِّكُمْ فَـَٔامَنَّا رَبَّنَا فَاغْفِرْ لَنَا ذُنُوبَنَا وَكَفِّرْ عَنَّا سَيِّئَاتِنَا وَتَوَفَّنَا مَعَ الْأَبْرَارِ ۝

194 Our Lord! And give us that which Thou hast promised to us by Thy messengers. Confound us not upon the Day of Resurrection. Lo! Thou breakest not the tryst.

رَبَّنَا وَءَاتِنَا مَا وَعَدتَّنَا عَلَى رُسُلِكَ وَلَا تُخْزِنَا يَوْمَ الْقِيَمَةِ إِنَّكَ لَا تُخْلِفُ الْمِيعَادَ ۝

195 And their Lord hath heard them (and He saith): Lo! I suffer not the work of any worker, male or female, to be lost. Ye proceed one from another.[22] So those who fled and were driven forth from their homes and suffered damage for My cause, and fought and were slain, verily I shall remit their evil deeds from them and verily I shall bring them into Gardens underneath which rivers flow—A reward from Allah. And with Allah is the fairest of rewards.

فَاسْتَجَابَ لَهُمْ رَبُّهُمْ أَنِّي لَا أُضِيعُ عَمَلَ عَمِلٍ مِّنكُم مِّن ذَكَرٍ أَوْ أُنثَى بَعْضُكُم مِّنۢ بَعْضٍ فَالَّذِينَ هَاجَرُوا وَأُخْرِجُوا مِن دِيَرِهِمْ وَأُوذُوا فِي سَبِيلِي وَقَتَلُوا وَقُتِلُوا لَأُكَفِّرَنَّ عَنْهُمْ سَيِّئَاتِهِمْ وَلَأُدْخِلَنَّهُمْ جَنَّتٍ تَجْرِي مِن تَحْتِهَا الْأَنْهَرُ ثَوَابًا مِّنْ عِندِ اللَّهِ وَاللَّهُ عِندَهُۥ حُسْنُ الثَّوَابِ ۝

196 Let not the vicissitude (of the success) of those who disbelieve, in the land, deceive thee (O Muḥammad).

لَا يَغُرَّنَّكَ تَقَلُّبُ الَّذِينَ كَفَرُوا فِي الْبِلَدِ ۝

---

22. This expression, which recurs in the Qur'an, is a reminder to men that women are of the same human status as themselves.

197   It is but a brief comfort.
And afterward their habitation will
be hell, an ill abode.

متَاعٌ قَلِيلٌ ثُمَّ مَأْوَاهُمْ جَهَنَّمُ وَبِئْسَ الْمِهَادُ ۝

198   But those who keep their
duty to their Lord, for them are
Gardens underneath which rivers
flow, wherein they will be safe forever. A gift of welcome from their
Lord. That which Allah hath in
store is better for the righteous.

لَكِنِ الَّذِينَ اتَّقَوْا رَبَّهُمْ لَهُمْ جَنَّاتٌ تَجْرِى
مِن تَحْتِهَا الْأَنْهَارُ خَالِدِينَ فِيهَا نُزُلًا مِّنْ عِندِ
اللَّهِ وَمَا عِندَ اللَّهِ خَيْرٌ لِّلْأَبْرَارِ ۝

199   And lo! of the People of the
Scripture there are some who
believe in Allah and that which is
revealed unto you and that which
was revealed unto them, humbling
themselves before Allah. They
purchase not a trifling gain at the
price of the revelations of Allah.
Verily their reward is with their
Lord, and lo! Allah is swift to take
account.

وَإِنَّ مِنْ أَهْلِ الْكِتَابِ لَمَن يُؤْمِنُ بِاللَّهِ
وَمَا أُنزِلَ إِلَيْكُمْ وَمَا أُنزِلَ إِلَيْهِمْ خَاشِعِينَ
لِلَّهِ لَا يَشْتَرُونَ بِآيَاتِ اللَّهِ ثَمَنًا قَلِيلًا
أُوْلَئِكَ لَهُمْ أَجْرُهُمْ عِندَ رَبِّهِمْ إِنَّ
اللَّهَ سَرِيعُ الْحِسَابِ ۝

200   O ye who believe! Endure,
outdo all others in endurance, be
ready, and observe your duty to
Allah, in order that ye may succeed.

يَا أَيُّهَا الَّذِينَ آمَنُوا اصْبِرُوا وَصَابِرُوا
وَرَابِطُوا وَاتَّقُوا اللَّهَ لَعَلَّكُمْ تُفْلِحُونَ ۝

An Nisā
(Women)

An Nisā, "Women," is so-called because it deals largely with women's rights. The period of revelation is the months following the battle of Uhud, or, as Nöldeke, a careful critic, puts it, "between the end of the third year and the end of the fifth year"[1] of the Prophet's reign at Al-Madīnah. As the sūrah contains no reference to the siege of Al-Madīnah ("The War of the Trench") by the allied tribes, which took place in the fifth year, I should rather say, between the end of the third year and the beginning of the fifth year.

Many Muslims were killed at the battle of Uhud, hence the concern for orphans and widows in the opening verses which lead on to a declaration of some rights of women of which they were deprived among the pagan Arabs. The defection of the Hypocrites—as the lukewarm or purely time-serving adherents were called—had been the chief cause of the reverse at Uhud; and after that reverse some of the Jewish tribes, who had till then observed the letter of their treaty with the Prophet, became avowed supporters of the enemy, even going so far as to declare that the old Arab idolatry was preferable to Al-Islām as a religion, and giving help and information to Quraysh, so that in the end the Muslims were obliged to make war on them. Both the Hypocrites and the rebellious Jews are dealt with incidentlly in this sūrah, the former at some length. There is a reference to Christian belief in vv. 171-172.

The period of revelation is the fourth year of the Hijrah.

---

1. Nöldeke, *Geschichte des Qorāns* (2nd ed.), part I, p.195.

In the name of Allah, the
Beneficent, the Merciful.

بِسْمِ اللهِ الرَّحْمٰنِ الرَّحِيمِ

1   O mankind! Be careful of your
duty to your Lord Who created you
from a single soul and from it
created its mate and from them
twain hath spread abroad a multitude of men and women. Be careful
of your duty toward Allah in
Whom ye claim (your rights) of
one another, and toward the wombs
(that bare you). Lo! Allah hath been
a Watcher over you.

يَٰٓأَيُّهَا ٱلنَّاسُ ٱتَّقُوا۟ رَبَّكُمُ ٱلَّذِى خَلَقَكُم مِّن نَّفْسٍ
وَٰحِدَةٍ وَخَلَقَ مِنْهَا زَوْجَهَا وَبَثَّ مِنْهُمَا رِجَالًا كَثِيرًا
وَنِسَآءً ۚ وَٱتَّقُوا۟ ٱللَّهَ ٱلَّذِى تَسَآءَلُونَ بِهِۦ وَٱلْأَرْحَامَ ۚ
إِنَّ ٱللَّهَ كَانَ عَلَيْكُمْ رَقِيبًا ۝

2   Give unto orphans their wealth.
Exchange not the good for the bad
(in your management thereof) nor
absorb their wealth into your own
wealth. Lo! that would be a great
sin.

وَءَاتُوا۟ ٱلْيَتَٰمَىٰٓ أَمْوَٰلَهُمْ ۖ وَلَا تَتَبَدَّلُوا۟ ٱلْخَبِيثَ بِٱلطَّيِّبِ ۖ
وَلَا تَأْكُلُوٓا۟ أَمْوَٰلَهُمْ إِلَىٰٓ أَمْوَٰلِكُمْ ۚ إِنَّهُۥ كَانَ حُوبًا
كَبِيرًا ۝

3   And if ye fear that ye will not
deal fairly by the orphans, marry of
the women, who seem good to you,
two or three or four; and if ye fear
that ye cannot do justice (to so
many) then one (only) or (the captives) that your right hands possess.
Thus it is more likely that ye will
not do injustice.

وَإِنْ خِفْتُمْ أَلَّا تُقْسِطُوا۟ فِى ٱلْيَتَٰمَىٰ فَٱنكِحُوا۟ مَا طَابَ
لَكُم مِّنَ ٱلنِّسَآءِ مَثْنَىٰ وَثُلَٰثَ وَرُبَٰعَ ۖ فَإِنْ خِفْتُمْ
أَلَّا تَعْدِلُوا۟ فَوَٰحِدَةً أَوْ مَا مَلَكَتْ أَيْمَٰنُكُمْ ۚ ذَٰلِكَ أَدْنَىٰٓ
أَلَّا تَعُولُوا۟ ۝

4 And give unto the women, (whom ye marry) free gift of their marriage portions; but if they of their own accord remit unto you a part thereof, then ye are welcome to absorb it (in your wealth).

وَءَاتُواالنِّسَاءَصَدُقَٰتِهِنَّ نِحْلَةً فَإِن طِبْنَ لَكُمْ عَن
شَيْءٍ مِّنْهُ نَفْسًا فَكُلُوهُ هَنِيٓئًامَّرِيٓئًا ۝

5 Give not unto the foolish (what is in) your (keeping of their) wealth, which Allah hath given you to maintain; but feed and clothe them from it, and speak kindly unto them.

وَلَاتُؤْتُواالسُّفَهَاءَأَمْوَالَكُمُ الَّتِي جَعَلَ اللّٰهُ لَكُمْ قِيَٰمًا
وَارْزُقُوهُمْ فِيهَاوَاكْسُوهُمْ وَقُولُوالَهُمْ قَوْلًامَّعْرُوفًا ۝

6 Prove orphans till they reach the marriageable age; then, if ye find them of sound judgment, deliver over unto them their fortune; and devour it not squandering and in haste lest they should grow up. Whoso (of the guardians) is rich, let him abstain generously (from taking of the property of orphans); and whoso is poor let him take thereof in reason (for his guardianship). And when ye deliver up their fortune unto orphans, have (the transaction) witnessed in their presence. Allah sufficeth as a Reckoner.

وَابْتَلُواالْيَتَٰمَىٰ حَتَّىٰٓ إِذَابَلَغُواالنِّكَاحَ فَإِنْ ءَانَسْتُم
مِّنْهُمْ رُشْدًافَادْفَعُوٓاإِلَيْهِمْ أَمْوَالَهُمْ وَلَاتَأْكُلُوهَآ
إِسْرَافًاوَبِدَارًا أَن يَكْبَرُوا وَمَن كَانَ غَنِيًّا
فَلْيَسْتَعْفِفْ وَمَن كَانَ فَقِيرًافَلْيَأْكُلْ بِالْمَعْرُوفِ
فَإِذَادَفَعْتُمْ إِلَيْهِمْ أَمْوَالَهُمْ فَأَشْهِدُواعَلَيْهِمْ
وَكَفَىٰ بِاللّٰهِ حَسِيبًا ۝

7 Unto the men (of a family) belongeth a share of that which parents and near kindred leave, and unto the women a share of that which parents and near kindred leave, whether it be little or much—a legal share.

لِلرِّجَالِ نَصِيبٌ مِّمَّاتَرَكَ الْوَٰلِدَانِ وَالْأَقْرَبُونَ
وَلِلنِّسَاءِ نَصِيبٌ مِّمَّاتَرَكَ الْوَٰلِدَانِ وَالْأَقْرَبُونَ
مِمَّاقَلَّ مِنْهُ أَوْكَثُرَ نَصِيبًامَّفْرُوضًا ۝

8 And when kinsfolk and orphans and the needy are present at the division (of the heritage), bestow on them therefrom and speak kindly unto them.

وَإِذَاحَضَرَالْقِسْمَةَ أُولُواالْقُرْبَىٰ وَالْيَتَٰمَىٰ
وَالْمَسَٰكِينُ فَارْزُقُوهُم مِّنْهُ وَقُولُوالَهُمْ
قَوْلًامَّعْرُوفًا ۝

9 And let those fear (in their behaviour toward orphans) who if they left behind them weak offspring would be afraid for them. So let them mind their duty to Allah, and speak justly.

وَلْيَخْشَ الَّذِينَ لَوْ تَرَكُوا مِنْ خَلْفِهِمْ ذُرِّيَّةً ضِعَافًا خَافُوا عَلَيْهِمْ فَلْيَتَّقُوا اللّٰهَ وَلْيَقُولُوا قَوْلًا سَدِيدًا ۝

10 Lo! Those who devour the wealth of orphans wrongfully, they do but swallow fire into their bellies, and they will be exposed to burning flame.

إِنَّ الَّذِينَ يَأْكُلُونَ أَمْوَالَ الْيَتَامَىٰ ظُلْمًا إِنَّمَا يَأْكُلُونَ فِي بُطُونِهِمْ نَارًا وَسَيَصْلَوْنَ سَعِيرًا ۝

11 Allah chargeth you concerning (the provision for) your children: to the male the equivalent of the portion of two females, and if there be women more than two, then theirs is two-thirds of the inheritance, and if there be one (only) then for her is the half. And to his[2] parents a sixth of the inheritance, if he have a son; and if he have no son and his parents are his heirs, then to his mother appertaineth the third; and if he have brethren, then to his mother appertaineth the sixth, after any legacy he may have bequeathed, or debt (hath been paid). Your parents or your children: Ye know not which of them is nearer unto you in usefulness. It is an injunction from Allah. Lo! Allah is Knower, Wise.

يُوصِيكُمُ اللّٰهُ فِي أَوْلَادِكُمْ لِلذَّكَرِ مِثْلُ حَظِّ الْأُنْثَيَيْنِ فَإِنْ كُنَّ نِسَاءً فَوْقَ اثْنَتَيْنِ فَلَهُنَّ ثُلُثَا مَا تَرَكَ وَإِنْ كَانَتْ وَاحِدَةً فَلَهَا النِّصْفُ وَلِأَبَوَيْهِ لِكُلِّ وَاحِدٍ مِنْهُمَا السُّدُسُ مِمَّا تَرَكَ إِنْ كَانَ لَهُ وَلَدٌ فَإِنْ لَمْ يَكُنْ لَهُ وَلَدٌ وَوَرِثَهُ أَبَوَاهُ فَلِأُمِّهِ الثُّلُثُ فَإِنْ كَانَ لَهُ إِخْوَةٌ فَلِأُمِّهِ السُّدُسُ مِنْ بَعْدِ وَصِيَّةٍ يُوصِي بِهَا أَوْ دَيْنٍ ءَابَاؤُكُمْ وَأَبْنَاؤُكُمْ لَا تَدْرُونَ أَيُّهُمْ أَقْرَبُ لَكُمْ نَفْعًا فَرِيضَةً مِنَ اللّٰهِ إِنَّ اللّٰهَ كَانَ عَلِيمًا حَكِيمًا ۝

---

2. The deceased.

12 And unto you belongeth a half of that which your wives leave, if they have no child; but if they have a child then unto you the fourth of that which they leave, after any legacy they may have bequeathed, or debt (they may have contracted, hath been paid). And unto them belongeth the fourth of that which ye leave if ye have no child, but if ye have a child then the eighth of that which ye leave, after any legacy ye may have bequeathed, or debt (ye may have contracted, hath been paid). And if a man or a woman have a distant heir (having left neither parent nor child), and he (or she) have a brother or a sister (only on the mother's side) then to each of them twain (the brother and the sister) the sixth, and if they be more than two, then they shall be sharers in the third, after any legacy that may have been bequeathed or debt (contracted) not injuring (the heirs by willing away more than a third of the heritage) hath been paid. A commandment from Allah. Allah is knower, Indulgent.

13 These are the limits (imposed by) Allah. Whoso obeyeth Allah and His messenger, He will make him enter Gardens underneath which rivers flow, where such will dwell forever. That will be the great success.

وَلَكُمْ نِصْفُ مَا تَرَكَ أَزْوَاجُكُمْ إِنْ لَمْ يَكُنْ لَهُنَّ وَلَدٌ فَإِنْ كَانَ لَهُنَّ وَلَدٌ فَلَكُمُ الرُّبُعُ مِمَّا تَرَكْنَ مِنْ بَعْدِ وَصِيَّةٍ يُوصِينَ بِهَا أَوْ دَيْنٍ وَلَهُنَّ الرُّبُعُ مِمَّا تَرَكْتُمْ إِنْ لَمْ يَكُنْ لَكُمْ وَلَدٌ فَإِنْ كَانَ لَكُمْ وَلَدٌ فَلَهُنَّ الثُّمُنُ مِمَّا تَرَكْتُمْ مِنْ بَعْدِ وَصِيَّةٍ تُوصُونَ بِهَا أَوْ دَيْنٍ وَإِنْ كَانَ رَجُلٌ يُورَثُ كَلَالَةً أَوِ امْرَأَةٌ وَلَهُ أَخٌ أَوْ أُخْتٌ فَلِكُلِّ وَاحِدٍ مِنْهُمَا السُّدُسُ فَإِنْ كَانُوا أَكْثَرَ مِنْ ذَلِكَ فَهُمْ شُرَكَاءُ فِي الثُّلُثِ مِنْ بَعْدِ وَصِيَّةٍ يُوصَى بِهَا أَوْ دَيْنٍ غَيْرَ مُضَارٍّ وَصِيَّةً مِنَ اللَّهِ وَاللَّهُ عَلِيمٌ حَلِيمٌ ﴿١٢﴾

تِلْكَ حُدُودُ اللَّهِ وَمَنْ يُطِعِ اللَّهَ وَرَسُولَهُ يُدْخِلْهُ جَنَّاتٍ تَجْرِي مِنْ تَحْتِهَا الْأَنْهَارُ خَالِدِينَ فِيهَا وَذَلِكَ الْفَوْزُ الْعَظِيمُ ﴿١٣﴾

14 And whoso disobeyeth Allah
and His messenger and transgresseth His limits, He will make
him enter Fire, where such will
dwell forever; his will be a shameful doom.

15 As for those of your women
who are guilty of lewdness, call to
witness four of you against them.
And if they testify (to the truth of
the allegation) then confine them to
the houses until death take them or
(until) Allah appoint for them a
way (through new legislation).[3]

16 And as for the two of you who
are guilty thereof, punish them
both. And if they repent and improve, then let them be. Lo! Allah
is Relenting, Merciful.

17 Forgiveness is only incumbent
on Allah toward those who do evil
in ignorance (and) then turn quickly
(in repentance) to Allah. These are
they toward whom Allah relenteth.
Allah is ever Knower, Wise.

18 The forgiveness is not for those
who do ill deeds until, when death
attendeth upon one of them, he
saith: Lo! I repent now; nor yet for
those who die while they are disbelievers. For such We have prepared
a painful doom.

وَمَن يَعْصِ اللَّهَ وَرَسُولَهُ وَيَتَعَدَّ
حُدُودَهُ يُدْخِلْهُ نَارًا خَالِدًا فِيهَا وَلَهُۥ
عَذَابٌ مُّهِينٌ ۝

وَالَّتِي يَأْتِينَ الْفَٰحِشَةَ مِن نِّسَآئِكُمْ
فَاسْتَشْهِدُوا عَلَيْهِنَّ أَرْبَعَةً مِّنكُمْ فَإِن
شَهِدُوا فَأَمْسِكُوهُنَّ فِي الْبُيُوتِ حَتَّىٰ
يَتَوَفَّاهُنَّ الْمَوْتُ أَوْ يَجْعَلَ اللَّهُ لَهُنَّ سَبِيلًا ۝

وَالَّذَانِ يَأْتِيَانِهَا مِنكُمْ فَـَٔاذُوهُمَا
فَإِن تَابَا وَأَصْلَحَا فَأَعْرِضُوا عَنْهُمَا
إِنَّ اللَّهَ كَانَ تَوَّابًا رَّحِيمًا ۝

إِنَّمَا التَّوْبَةُ عَلَى اللَّهِ لِلَّذِينَ يَعْمَلُونَ السُّوٓءَ
بِجَهَٰلَةٍ ثُمَّ يَتُوبُونَ مِن قَرِيبٍ فَأُو۟لَٰٓئِكَ يَتُوبُ
اللَّهُ عَلَيْهِمْ وَكَانَ اللَّهُ عَلِيمًا حَكِيمًا ۝

وَلَيْسَتِ التَّوْبَةُ لِلَّذِينَ يَعْمَلُونَ
السَّيِّئَاتِ حَتَّىٰ إِذَا حَضَرَ أَحَدَهُمُ الْمَوْتُ
قَالَ إِنِّي تُبْتُ الْـَٰٔنَ وَلَا الَّذِينَ يَمُوتُونَ
وَهُمْ كُفَّارٌ أُو۟لَٰٓئِكَ أَعْتَدْنَا لَهُمْ عَذَابًا
أَلِيمًا ۝

---

3. See Sūrah 24: 2-10.

19 O ye who believe! It is not lawful for you forcibly to inherit the women (of your deceased kinsmen), nor (that) ye should put constraint upon them that ye may take away a part of that which ye have given them, unless they be guilty of flagrant lewdness. But consort with them in kindness, for if ye hate them it may happen that ye hate a thing wherein Allah hath placed much good.

يَـٰٓأَيُّهَا ٱلَّذِينَ ءَامَنُوا۟ لَا يَحِلُّ لَكُمْ أَن تَرِثُوا۟ ٱلنِّسَآءَ كَرْهًا ۖ وَلَا تَعْضُلُوهُنَّ لِتَذْهَبُوا۟ بِبَعْضِ مَآ ءَاتَيْتُمُوهُنَّ إِلَّآ أَن يَأْتِينَ بِفَـٰحِشَةٍ مُّبَيِّنَةٍ ۚ وَعَاشِرُوهُنَّ بِٱلْمَعْرُوفِ ۚ فَإِن كَرِهْتُمُوهُنَّ فَعَسَىٰٓ أَن تَكْرَهُوا۟ شَيْـًٔا وَيَجْعَلَ ٱللَّهُ فِيهِ خَيْرًا كَثِيرًا ﴿١٩﴾

20 And if ye wish to exchange one wife for another and ye have given unto one of them a sum of money (however great), take nothing from it. Would ye take it by the way of calumny and open wrong?

وَإِنْ أَرَدتُّمُ ٱسْتِبْدَالَ زَوْجٍ مَّكَانَ زَوْجٍ وَءَاتَيْتُمْ إِحْدَىٰهُنَّ قِنطَارًا فَلَا تَأْخُذُوا۟ مِنْهُ شَيْـًٔا ۚ أَتَأْخُذُونَهُۥ بُهْتَـٰنًا وَإِثْمًا مُّبِينًا ﴿٢٠﴾

21 How can ye take it (back) after one of you hath gone in unto the other, and they have taken a strong pledge from you?

وَكَيْفَ تَأْخُذُونَهُۥ وَقَدْ أَفْضَىٰ بَعْضُكُمْ إِلَىٰ بَعْضٍ وَأَخَذْنَ مِنكُم مِّيثَـٰقًا غَلِيظًا ﴿٢١﴾

22 And marry not those women whom your fathers married, except what hath already happened (of that nature) in the past. Lo! it was ever lewdness and abomination, and an evil way.

وَلَا تَنكِحُوا۟ مَا نَكَحَ ءَابَآؤُكُم مِّنَ ٱلنِّسَآءِ إِلَّا مَا قَدْ سَلَفَ ۚ إِنَّهُۥ كَانَ فَـٰحِشَةً وَمَقْتًا وَسَآءَ سَبِيلًا ﴿٢٢﴾

23 Forbidden unto you are your mothers, and your daughters, and your sisters, and your father's sisters, and your mother's sisters, and your brother's daughters and your sister's daughters, and your foster mothers, and your foster sisters, and your mothers-in-law, and your step-

حُرِّمَتْ عَلَيْكُمْ أُمَّهَـٰتُكُمْ وَبَنَاتُكُمْ وَأَخَوَٰتُكُمْ وَعَمَّـٰتُكُمْ وَخَـٰلَـٰتُكُمْ وَبَنَاتُ ٱلْأَخِ وَبَنَاتُ ٱلْأُخْتِ وَأُمَّهَـٰتُكُمُ ٱلَّـٰتِىٓ أَرْضَعْنَكُمْ وَأَخَوَٰتُكُم مِّنَ ٱلرَّضَـٰعَةِ وَأُمَّهَـٰتُ نِسَآئِكُمْ وَرَبَـٰٓئِبُكُمُ ٱلَّـٰتِى

daughters who are under your protection (born) of your women unto
whom ye have gone in—but if ye
have not gone in unto them, then it
is no sin for you (to marry their
daughters)—and the wives of your
sons who (spring) from your own
loins. And (it is forbidden unto
you) that ye should have two sisters
together, except what hath already
happened (of that nature) in the
past. Lo! Allah is ever Forgiving,
Merciful.

فِى حُجُورِكُمْ مِّنْ نِّسَآئِكُمُ الَّتِى
دَخَلْتُمْ بِهِنَّ فَإِنْ لَّمْ تَكُونُوا دَخَلْتُمْ
بِهِنَّ فَلَا جُنَاحَ عَلَيْكُمْ وَحَلَآئِلُ
أَبْنَآئِكُمُ الَّذِينَ مِنْ أَصْلَابِكُمْ
وَأَنْ تَجْمَعُوا بَيْنَ الْأُخْتَيْنِ إِلَّا مَا قَدْ
سَلَفَ إِنَّ اللَّهَ كَانَ غَفُورًا رَّحِيمًا ۝

24 And all married women (are
forbidden unto you save those (captives) whom your right hands possess. It is a decree of Allah for you.
Lawful unto you are all beyond
those mentioned, so that ye seek
them with your wealth in honest
wedlock, not debauchery. And those
of whom ye seek content (by marrying them), give unto them their
portions as a duty. And there is no
sin for you in what ye do by mutual agreement after the duty (hath
been done). Lo! Allah is ever
Knower, Wise.

۞ وَالْمُحْصَنَاتُ مِنَ النِّسَآءِ إِلَّا مَا مَلَكَتْ
أَيْمَانُكُمْ كِتَابَ اللَّهِ عَلَيْكُمْ وَأُحِلَّ لَكُم
مَّا وَرَآءَ ذَلِكُمْ أَنْ تَبْتَغُوا بِأَمْوَالِكُم مُّحْصِنِينَ
غَيْرَ مُسَافِحِينَ فَمَا اسْتَمْتَعْتُم بِهِ مِنْهُنَّ
فَآتُوهُنَّ أُجُورَهُنَّ فَرِيضَةً وَلَا جُنَاحَ
عَلَيْكُمْ فِيمَا تَرَاضَيْتُم بِهِ مِنْ بَعْدِ الْفَرِيضَةِ
إِنَّ اللَّهَ كَانَ عَلِيمًا حَكِيمًا ۝

25 And whoso is not able to afford
to marry free, believing women, let
them marry from the believing maids whom your right hands possess.
Allah knoweth best (concerning)
your faith. Ye (proceed) one from

وَمَنْ لَّمْ يَسْتَطِعْ مِنْكُمْ طَوْلًا أَنْ يَنْكِحَ
الْمُحْصَنَاتِ الْمُؤْمِنَاتِ فَمِنْ مَّا مَلَكَتْ
أَيْمَانُكُم مِّنْ فَتَيَاتِكُمُ الْمُؤْمِنَاتِ وَاللَّهُ أَعْلَمُ
بِإِيمَانِكُم بَعْضُكُم مِّنْ بَعْضٍ فَانْكِحُوهُنَّ

another;[4] so wed them by permission of their folk, and give unto them their portions in kindness, they being honest, not debauched nor of loose conduct. And if when they are honorably married they commit lewdness they shall incur the half of the punishment (prescribed) for free women (in that case). This is for him among you who feareth to commit sin. But to have patience would be better for you. Allah is Forgiving, Merciful.

بِإِذْنِ أَهْلِهِنَّ وَءَاتُوهُنَّ أُجُورَهُنَّ بِٱلْمَعْرُوفِ مُحْصَنَٰتٍ غَيْرَ مُسَٰفِحَٰتٍ وَلَا مُتَّخِذَٰتِ أَخْدَانٍ فَإِذَآ أُحْصِنَّ فَإِنْ أَتَيْنَ بِفَٰحِشَةٍ فَعَلَيْهِنَّ نِصْفُ مَا عَلَى ٱلْمُحْصَنَٰتِ مِنَ ٱلْعَذَابِ ذَٰلِكَ لِمَنْ خَشِيَ ٱلْعَنَتَ مِنكُمْ وَأَن تَصْبِرُوا۟ خَيْرٌ لَّكُمْ وَٱللَّهُ غَفُورٌ رَّحِيمٌ ۝

26 Allah would explain to you and guide you by the examples of those who were before you, and would turn to you in mercy. Allah is Knower, Wise.

يُرِيدُ ٱللَّهُ لِيُبَيِّنَ لَكُمْ وَيَهْدِيَكُمْ سُنَنَ ٱلَّذِينَ مِن قَبْلِكُمْ وَيَتُوبَ عَلَيْكُمْ وَٱللَّهُ عَلِيمٌ حَكِيمٌ ۝

27 And Allah would turn to you in mercy; but those who follow vain desires would have you go tremendously astray.

وَٱللَّهُ يُرِيدُ أَن يَتُوبَ عَلَيْكُمْ وَيُرِيدُ ٱلَّذِينَ يَتَّبِعُونَ ٱلشَّهَوَٰتِ أَن تَمِيلُوا۟ مَيْلًا عَظِيمًا ۝

28 Allah would make the burden light for you, for man was created weak.

يُرِيدُ ٱللَّهُ أَن يُخَفِّفَ عَنكُمْ وَخُلِقَ ٱلْإِنسَٰنُ ضَعِيفًا ۝

29 O ye who believe! Squander not your wealth among yourselves in vanity, except it be a trade by mutual consent, and kill not one another. Lo! Allah is ever Merciful unto you.

يَٰٓأَيُّهَا ٱلَّذِينَ ءَامَنُوا۟ لَا تَأْكُلُوٓا۟ أَمْوَٰلَكُم بَيْنَكُم بِٱلْبَٰطِلِ إِلَّآ أَن تَكُونَ تِجَٰرَةً عَن تَرَاضٍ مِّنكُمْ وَلَا تَقْتُلُوٓا۟ أَنفُسَكُمْ إِنَّ ٱللَّهَ كَانَ بِكُمْ رَحِيمًا ۝

---

4. This expression, which recurs in the Qur'an, is a reminder to men that women are of the same human status as themselves.

30 Whoso doeth that through aggr-
ession and injustice, We shall cast
him into Fire, and that is ever easy
for Allah.

وَمَنْ يَّفْعَلْ ذٰلِكَ عُدْوَانًا وَّظُلْمًا فَسَوْفَ
نُصْلِيْهِ نَارًا ۖ وَكَانَ ذٰلِكَ عَلَى اللّٰهِ
يَسِيْرًا ۝

31 If ye avoid the great (things)
which ye are forbidden, We will
remit from you your evil deeds and
make you enter at a noble gate.

إِنْ تَجْتَنِبُوْا كَبَآئِرَ مَا تُنْهَوْنَ عَنْهُ نُكَفِّرْ
عَنْكُمْ سَيِّاٰتِكُمْ وَنُدْخِلْكُمْ مُّدْخَلًا
كَرِيْمًا ۝

32 And covet not the thing in which
Allah hath made some of you excel
others. Unto men a fortune from that
which they have earned, and unto
women a fortune from that which
they have earned. (Envy not one
another) but ask Allah of His bounty. Lo! Allah is ever Knower of all
things.

وَلَا تَتَمَنَّوْا مَا فَضَّلَ اللّٰهُ بِهٖ بَعْضَكُمْ
عَلٰى بَعْضٍ ۚ لِلرِّجَالِ نَصِيْبٌ مِّمَّا اكْتَسَبُوْا ۚ
وَلِلنِّسَآءِ نَصِيْبٌ مِّمَّا اكْتَسَبْنَ ۚ وَسْـَٔلُوا اللّٰهَ
مِنْ فَضْلِهٖ ۚ إِنَّ اللّٰهَ كَانَ بِكُلِّ شَيْءٍ
عَلِيْمًا ۝

33 And unto each We have appointed heirs of that which parents and
near kindred leave; and as for those
with whom your right hands have
made a covenant, give them their
due. Lo! Allah is ever Witness over
all things.

وَلِكُلٍّ جَعَلْنَا مَوَالِيَ مِمَّا تَرَكَ الْوَالِدَانِ
وَالْأَقْرَبُوْنَ ۚ وَالَّذِيْنَ عَقَدَتْ أَيْمَانُكُمْ
فَاٰتُوْهُمْ نَصِيْبَهُمْ ۚ إِنَّ اللّٰهَ كَانَ عَلٰى كُلِّ
شَيْءٍ شَهِيْدًا ۝

34 Men are in charge of women,
because Allah hath made the one of
them to excel the other, and because
they spend of their property (for the
support of women). So good women
are the obedient, guarding in secret
that which Allah hath guarded. As
for those from whom ye fear rebellion, admonish them and banish them
to beds apart, and scourge them.
Then if they obey you, seek not a
way against them. Lo! Allah is ever
High Exalted, Great.

الرِّجَالُ قَوَّامُوْنَ عَلَى النِّسَآءِ بِمَا فَضَّلَ اللّٰهُ
بَعْضَهُمْ عَلٰى بَعْضٍ وَّبِمَآ أَنْفَقُوْا مِنْ أَمْوَالِهِمْ ۚ
فَالصّٰلِحٰتُ قٰنِتٰتٌ حٰفِظٰتٌ لِّلْغَيْبِ
بِمَا حَفِظَ اللّٰهُ ۚ وَالّٰتِيْ تَخَافُوْنَ نُشُوْزَهُنَّ
فَعِظُوْهُنَّ وَاهْجُرُوْهُنَّ فِى الْمَضَاجِعِ
وَاضْرِبُوْهُنَّ ۚ فَإِنْ أَطَعْنَكُمْ فَلَا تَبْغُوْا عَلَيْهِنَّ
سَبِيْلًا ۚ إِنَّ اللّٰهَ كَانَ عَلِيًّا كَبِيْرًا ۝

35 And if ye fear a breach between them twain (the man and wife), appoint an arbiter from his folk and an arbiter from her folk. If they desire amendment Allah will make them of one mind. Lo! Allah is ever Knower, Aware.

وَإِنْ خِفْتُمْ شِقَاقَ بَيْنِهِمَا فَابْعَثُوا حَكَمًا مِنْ أَهْلِهِ وَحَكَمًا مِنْ أَهْلِهَا إِنْ يُرِيدَا إِصْلَاحًا يُوَفِّقِ اللَّهُ بَيْنَهُمَا إِنَّ اللَّهَ كَانَ عَلِيمًا خَبِيرًا ﴿٣٥﴾

36 And serve Allah. Ascribe no thing as partner unto Him. (Show) kindness unto parents, and unto near kindred, and orphans, and the needy, and into the neighbor who is of kin (unto you) and the neighbor who is not of kin and the fellow traveller and the wayfarer and (the slaves) whom your right hands possess. Lo! Allah loveth not such as are proud and boastful,

۞ وَاعْبُدُوا اللَّهَ وَلَا تُشْرِكُوا بِهِ شَيْئًا وَبِالْوَالِدَيْنِ إِحْسَانًا وَبِذِى الْقُرْبَى وَالْيَتَامَى وَالْمَسَاكِينِ وَالْجَارِ ذِى الْقُرْبَى وَالْجَارِ الْجُنُبِ وَالصَّاحِبِ بِالْجَنْبِ وَابْنِ السَّبِيلِ وَمَا مَلَكَتْ أَيْمَانُكُمْ إِنَّ اللَّهَ لَا يُحِبُّ مَنْ كَانَ مُخْتَالًا فَخُورًا ﴿٣٦﴾

37 Who hoard their wealth and enjoin avarice on others, and hide that which Allah hath bestowed upon them of His bounty. For disbelievers We prepare a shameful doom;

الَّذِينَ يَبْخَلُونَ وَيَأْمُرُونَ النَّاسَ بِالْبُخْلِ وَيَكْتُمُونَ مَا آتَاهُمُ اللَّهُ مِنْ فَضْلِهِ وَأَعْتَدْنَا لِلْكَافِرِينَ عَذَابًا مُهِينًا ﴿٣٧﴾

38 And (also) those who spend their wealth in order to be seen of men, and believe not in Allah nor the Last Day. Whoso taketh Satan for a comrade, a bad comrade hath he.

وَالَّذِينَ يُنْفِقُونَ أَمْوَالَهُمْ رِئَاءَ النَّاسِ وَلَا يُؤْمِنُونَ بِاللَّهِ وَلَا بِالْيَوْمِ الْآخِرِ وَمَنْ يَكُنِ الشَّيْطَانُ لَهُ قَرِينًا فَسَاءَ قَرِينًا ﴿٣٨﴾

39 What have they (to fear) if they believe in Allah and the Last Day and spend (aright) of that which Allah hath bestowed upon them, when Allah is ever Aware of them (and all they do)?

وَمَاذَا عَلَيْهِمْ لَوْ آمَنُوا بِاللَّهِ وَالْيَوْمِ الْآخِرِ وَأَنْفَقُوا مِمَّا رَزَقَهُمُ اللَّهُ وَكَانَ اللَّهُ بِهِمْ عَلِيمًا ﴿٣٩﴾

40 Lo! Allah wrongeth not even of the weight of an ant; and if there is a good deed, He will double it and will give (the doer) from His presence an immense reward.

إِنَّ اللّٰهَ لَا يَظْلِمُ مِثْقَالَ ذَرَّةٍ وَإِن تَكُ حَسَنَةً يُّضَاعِفْهَا وَيُؤْتِ مِن لَّدُنْهُ أَجْرًا عَظِيمًا ﴿٤٠﴾

41 But how (will it be with them) when we bring of every people a witness, and We bring thee (O Muhammad) a witness against these?

فَكَيْفَ إِذَا جِئْنَا مِن كُلِّ أُمَّةٍ بِشَهِيدٍ وَجِئْنَا بِكَ عَلَىٰ هَٰؤُلَاءِ شَهِيدًا ﴿٤١﴾

42 On that day those who disbelieved and disobeyed the messenger will wish that they were level with the ground, and they can hide no fact from Allah!

يَوْمَئِذٍ يَّوَدُّ الَّذِينَ كَفَرُوا وَعَصَوُا الرَّسُولَ لَوْ تُسَوَّىٰ بِهِمُ الْأَرْضُ وَلَا يَكْتُمُونَ اللّٰهَ حَدِيثًا ﴿٤٢﴾

43 O ye who believe! Draw not near unto prayer when ye are drunken, till ye know that which ye utter, nor when ye are polluted, save when journeying upon the road, till ye have bathed. And if ye be ill, or on a journey, or one of you cometh from the closet, or ye have touched women, and ye find not water, than go to high clean soil and rub your faces and your hands (therewith). Lo! Allah is Benign, Forgiving.

يَا أَيُّهَا الَّذِينَ آمَنُوا لَا تَقْرَبُوا الصَّلَاةَ وَأَنتُمْ سُكَارَىٰ حَتَّىٰ تَعْلَمُوا مَا تَقُولُونَ وَلَا جُنُبًا إِلَّا عَابِرِي سَبِيلٍ حَتَّىٰ تَغْتَسِلُوا وَإِن كُنتُم مَّرْضَىٰ أَوْ عَلَىٰ سَفَرٍ أَوْ جَاءَ أَحَدٌ مِّنكُم مِّنَ الْغَائِطِ أَوْ لَامَسْتُمُ النِّسَاءَ فَلَمْ تَجِدُوا مَاءً فَتَيَمَّمُوا صَعِيدًا طَيِّبًا فَامْسَحُوا بِوُجُوهِكُمْ وَأَيْدِيكُمْ إِنَّ اللّٰهَ كَانَ عَفُوًّا غَفُورًا ﴿٤٣﴾

44 Seest thou not those unto whom a portion of the Scripture hath been given, how they purchase error, and seek to make you (Muslims) err from the right way?

أَلَمْ تَرَ إِلَى الَّذِينَ أُوتُوا نَصِيبًا مِّنَ الْكِتَابِ يَشْتَرُونَ الضَّلَالَةَ وَيُرِيدُونَ أَن تَضِلُّوا السَّبِيلَ ﴿٤٤﴾

45 Allah knoweth best (who are) your enemies. Allah is sufficient as a Friend, and Allah is sufficient as a Helper.

وَاللّٰهُ أَعْلَمُ بِأَعْدَائِكُمْ وَكَفَىٰ بِاللّٰهِ وَلِيًّا وَكَفَىٰ بِاللّٰهِ نَصِيرًا ﴿٤٥﴾

46 Some of those who are Jews change words from their context and say: "We hear and disobey; hear thou as one who cannot be made to hear" and "Listen to us!"[5] distorting with their tongues and slandering religion. If they had said: "We hear and we obey; hear thou, and look at us" it had been better for them, and more upright. But Allah hath cursed them for their disbelief, so they believe not, save a few.

مِنَ ٱلَّذِينَ هَادُوا۟ يُحَرِّفُونَ ٱلْكَلِمَ عَن مَّوَاضِعِهِۦ وَيَقُولُونَ سَمِعْنَا وَعَصَيْنَا وَٱسْمَعْ غَيْرَ مُسْمَعٍ وَرَٰعِنَا لَيًّۢا بِأَلْسِنَتِهِمْ وَطَعْنًا فِى ٱلدِّينِ وَلَوْ أَنَّهُمْ قَالُوا۟ سَمِعْنَا وَأَطَعْنَا وَٱسْمَعْ وَٱنظُرْنَا لَكَانَ خَيْرًا لَّهُمْ وَأَقْوَمَ وَلَٰكِن لَّعَنَهُمُ ٱللَّهُ بِكُفْرِهِمْ فَلَا يُؤْمِنُونَ إِلَّا قَلِيلًا ﴿٤٦﴾

47 O ye unto whom the Scripture hath been given! Believe in what We have revealed concerning that which ye possess, before We destroy countenances so as to confound them, or curse them as We cursed the Sabbath breakers (of old time). The commandment of Allah is always executed.

يَٰٓأَيُّهَا ٱلَّذِينَ أُوتُوا۟ ٱلْكِتَٰبَ ءَامِنُوا۟ بِمَا نَزَّلْنَا مُصَدِّقًا لِّمَا مَعَكُم مِّن قَبْلِ أَن نَّطْمِسَ وُجُوهًا فَنَرُدَّهَا عَلَىٰٓ أَدْبَارِهَآ أَوْ نَلْعَنَهُمْ كَمَا لَعَنَّآ أَصْحَٰبَ ٱلسَّبْتِ وَكَانَ أَمْرُ ٱللَّهِ مَفْعُولًا ﴿٤٧﴾

48 Lo! Allah forgiveth not that a partner should be ascribed unto Him. He forgiveth (all) save that to whom He will. Whoso ascribeth partners to Allah, he hath indeed invented a tremendous sin.

إِنَّ ٱللَّهَ لَا يَغْفِرُ أَن يُشْرَكَ بِهِۦ وَيَغْفِرُ مَا دُونَ ذَٰلِكَ لِمَن يَشَآءُ وَمَن يُشْرِكْ بِٱللَّهِ فَقَدِ ٱفْتَرَىٰٓ إِثْمًا عَظِيمًا ﴿٤٨﴾

49 Hast thou not seen those who praise themselves for purity? Nay, Allah purifieth whom He will, and

أَلَمْ تَرَ إِلَى ٱلَّذِينَ يُزَكُّونَ أَنفُسَهُم بَلِ ٱللَّهُ يُزَكِّى

---

5. Devices of some of the Jews of Al-Madīnah to annoy the Muslims by distorting words of Scripture. *Rā'inā* (meaning "listen to us"), by which the Muslims used to call the Prophet's notice, they turned by slight mispronunciation into a Hebrew word of insult (cf. 2: 104, footnote).

they will not be wronged even the hair upon a date-stone.

50 See, how they invent lies about Allah! That of itself is flagrant sin.

51 Hast thou not seen those unto whom a portion of the Scripture hath been given, how they believe in idols and false deities, and how they say of those (idolaters) who disbelieve: "These are more rightly guided than those who believe?"

52 Those are they whom Allah hath cursed, and he whom Allah hath cursed, thou (O Muhammad) wilt find for him no helper.

53 Or have they even a share in the Sovereignty? Then in that case, they would not give mankind even the speck on a date stone.

54 Or are they jealous of mankind because of that which Allah of His bounty hath bestowed upon them? For We bestowed upon the house of Abraham (of old) the Scripture and Wisdom, and We bestowed on them a mighty kingdom.

55 And of them were (some) who believed therein and of them were (some) who disbelieved therein. Hell is sufficient for (their) burning.

56 Lo! Those who disbelieve Our revelations, We shall expose them to the Fire. As often as their skins are consumed We shall exchange them for fresh skins that they may taste the torment. Lo! Allah is ever Mighty, Wise.

مَن يَشَآءُ وَلَا يُظْلَمُونَ فَتِيلًا ﴿٤٩﴾

أَنظُرْ كَيْفَ يَفْتَرُونَ عَلَى ٱللَّهِ ٱلْكَذِبَ وَكَفَىٰ بِهِۦٓ إِثْمًا مُّبِينًا ﴿٥٠﴾

أَلَمْ تَرَ إِلَى ٱلَّذِينَ أُوتُوا۟ نَصِيبًا مِّنَ ٱلْكِتَٰبِ يُؤْمِنُونَ بِٱلْجِبْتِ وَٱلطَّٰغُوتِ وَيَقُولُونَ لِلَّذِينَ كَفَرُوا۟ هَٰٓؤُلَآءِ أَهْدَىٰ مِنَ ٱلَّذِينَ ءَامَنُوا۟ سَبِيلًا ﴿٥١﴾

أُو۟لَٰٓئِكَ ٱلَّذِينَ لَعَنَهُمُ ٱللَّهُ وَمَن يَلْعَنِ ٱللَّهُ فَلَن تَجِدَ لَهُۥ نَصِيرًا ﴿٥٢﴾

أَمْ لَهُمْ نَصِيبٌ مِّنَ ٱلْمُلْكِ فَإِذًا لَّا يُؤْتُونَ ٱلنَّاسَ نَقِيرًا ﴿٥٣﴾

أَمْ يَحْسُدُونَ ٱلنَّاسَ عَلَىٰ مَآ ءَاتَىٰهُمُ ٱللَّهُ مِن فَضْلِهِۦ فَقَدْ ءَاتَيْنَآ ءَالَ إِبْرَٰهِيمَ ٱلْكِتَٰبَ وَٱلْحِكْمَةَ وَءَاتَيْنَٰهُم مُّلْكًا عَظِيمًا ﴿٥٤﴾

فَمِنْهُم مَّنْ ءَامَنَ بِهِۦ وَمِنْهُم مَّن صَدَّ عَنْهُ وَكَفَىٰ بِجَهَنَّمَ سَعِيرًا ﴿٥٥﴾

إِنَّ ٱلَّذِينَ كَفَرُوا۟ بِـَٔايَٰتِنَا سَوْفَ نُصْلِيهِمْ نَارًا كُلَّمَا نَضِجَتْ جُلُودُهُم بَدَّلْنَٰهُمْ جُلُودًا غَيْرَهَا لِيَذُوقُوا۟ ٱلْعَذَابَ إِنَّ ٱللَّهَ كَانَ عَزِيزًا حَكِيمًا ﴿٥٦﴾

57 And as for those who believe and do good works, We shall make them enter Gardens underneath which rivers flow to dwell therein forever; there for them are pure companions and We shall make them enter plenteous shade.

وَٱلَّذِينَ ءَامَنُوا۟ وَعَمِلُوا۟ ٱلصَّٰلِحَٰتِ سَنُدْخِلُهُمْ جَنَّٰتٍ تَجْرِى مِن تَحْتِهَا ٱلْأَنْهَٰرُ خَٰلِدِينَ فِيهَآ أَبَدًا لَّهُمْ فِيهَآ أَزْوَٰجٌ مُّطَهَّرَةٌ وَنُدْخِلُهُمْ ظِلًّا ظَلِيلًا ﴿٥٧﴾

58 Lo! Allah commandeth you that ye restore deposits to their owners, and, if ye judge between mankind, that ye judge justly. Lo! comely is this which Allah admonisheth you. Lo! Allah is ever Hearer, Seer.

۞ إِنَّ ٱللَّهَ يَأْمُرُكُمْ أَن تُؤَدُّوا۟ ٱلْأَمَٰنَٰتِ إِلَىٰٓ أَهْلِهَا وَإِذَا حَكَمْتُم بَيْنَ ٱلنَّاسِ أَن تَحْكُمُوا۟ بِٱلْعَدْلِ إِنَّ ٱللَّهَ نِعِمَّا يَعِظُكُم بِهِۦٓ إِنَّ ٱللَّهَ كَانَ سَمِيعًا بَصِيرًا ﴿٥٨﴾

59 O ye who believe! Obey Allah, and obey the messenger and those of you who are in authority; and if ye have a dispute concerning any matter, refer it to Allah and the messenger if ye are (in truth) believers in Allah and the Last Day. That is better and more seemly in the end.

يَٰٓأَيُّهَا ٱلَّذِينَ ءَامَنُوٓا۟ أَطِيعُوا۟ ٱللَّهَ وَأَطِيعُوا۟ ٱلرَّسُولَ وَأُو۟لِى ٱلْأَمْرِ مِنكُمْ فَإِن تَنَٰزَعْتُمْ فِى شَىْءٍ فَرُدُّوهُ إِلَى ٱللَّهِ وَٱلرَّسُولِ إِن كُنتُمْ تُؤْمِنُونَ بِٱللَّهِ وَٱلْيَوْمِ ٱلْءَاخِرِ ذَٰلِكَ خَيْرٌ وَأَحْسَنُ تَأْوِيلًا ﴿٥٩﴾

60 Hast thou not seen those who pretend that they believe in that which is revealed unto thee and that which was revealed before thee, how they would go for judgment (in their disputes) to false deities when they have been ordered to abjure them? Satan would mislead them far astray.

أَلَمْ تَرَ إِلَى ٱلَّذِينَ يَزْعُمُونَ أَنَّهُمْ ءَامَنُوا۟ بِمَآ أُنزِلَ إِلَيْكَ وَمَآ أُنزِلَ مِن قَبْلِكَ يُرِيدُونَ أَن يَتَحَاكَمُوٓا۟ إِلَى ٱلطَّٰغُوتِ وَقَدْ أُمِرُوٓا۟ أَن يَكْفُرُوا۟ بِهِۦ وَيُرِيدُ ٱلشَّيْطَٰنُ أَن يُضِلَّهُمْ ضَلَٰلًۢا بَعِيدًا ﴿٦٠﴾

61 And then it is said unto them: Come unto that which Allah hath revealed and unto the messenger, thou seest the hypocrites turn from thee with aversion.

وَإِذَا قِيلَ لَهُمْ تَعَالَوْا۟ إِلَىٰ مَآ أَنزَلَ ٱللَّهُ وَإِلَى ٱلرَّسُولِ رَأَيْتَ ٱلْمُنَٰفِقِينَ يَصُدُّونَ عَنكَ صُدُودًا ﴿٦١﴾

62 How would it be if a misfortune smote them because of that which their own hands have sent before (them)? Then would they come unto thee, swearing by Allah that they were seeking naught but harmony and kindness.

فَكَيْفَ إِذَا أَصَابَتْهُمْ مُّصِيبَةٌ بِمَا قَدَّمَتْ أَيْدِيهِمْ ثُمَّ جَاءُوكَ يَحْلِفُونَ بِاللَّهِ إِنْ أَرَدْنَا إِلَّا إِحْسَانًا وَتَوْفِيقًا ٦٢

63 Those are they, the secrets of whose hearts Allah knoweth. So oppose them and admonish them, and address them in plain terms about their souls.

أُولَٰئِكَ الَّذِينَ يَعْلَمُ اللَّهُ مَا فِي قُلُوبِهِمْ فَأَعْرِضْ عَنْهُمْ وَعِظْهُمْ وَقُلْ لَّهُمْ فِي أَنفُسِهِمْ قَوْلًا بَلِيغًا ٦٣

64 We sent; no messenger save that he should be obeyed by Allah's leave. And if, when they had wronged themselves, they had but come unto thee and asked forgiveness of Allah, and the messenger (also) asked forgiveness for them, they would have found Allah Forgiving, Merciful.

وَمَا أَرْسَلْنَا مِن رَّسُولٍ إِلَّا لِيُطَاعَ بِإِذْنِ اللَّهِ وَلَوْ أَنَّهُمْ إِذ ظَّلَمُوا أَنفُسَهُمْ جَاءُوكَ فَاسْتَغْفَرُوا اللَّهَ وَاسْتَغْفَرَ لَهُمُ الرَّسُولُ لَوَجَدُوا اللَّهَ تَوَّابًا رَّحِيمًا ٦٤

65 But nay, by thy Lord, they will not believe (in truth) until they make thee judge of what is in dispute between them and find within themselves no dislike of that which thou decidest, and submit with full submission.

فَلَا وَرَبِّكَ لَا يُؤْمِنُونَ حَتَّىٰ يُحَكِّمُوكَ فِيمَا شَجَرَ بَيْنَهُمْ ثُمَّ لَا يَجِدُوا فِي أَنفُسِهِمْ حَرَجًا مِّمَّا قَضَيْتَ وَيُسَلِّمُوا تَسْلِيمًا ٦٥

66 And if We had decreed for them: Lay down your lives or go forth from your dwellings, but few of them would have done it; though if they did what they are exhorted to do, it would be better for them, and more strengthening;

وَلَوْ أَنَّا كَتَبْنَا عَلَيْهِمْ أَنِ اقْتُلُوا أَنفُسَكُمْ أَوِ اخْرُجُوا مِن دِيَارِكُم مَّا فَعَلُوهُ إِلَّا قَلِيلٌ مِّنْهُمْ وَلَوْ أَنَّهُمْ فَعَلُوا مَا يُوعَظُونَ بِهِ لَكَانَ خَيْرًا لَّهُمْ وَأَشَدَّ تَثْبِيتًا ٦٦

67 And then We should bestow upon them from Our presence an immense reward,

وَإِذًا لَّآتَيْنَاهُم مِّن لَّدُنَّآ أَجْرًا عَظِيمًا ۝

68 And should guide them unto a straight path.

وَلَهَدَيْنَاهُمْ صِرَاطًا مُّسْتَقِيمًا ۝

69 Whoso obeyeth Allah and the messenger, they are with those unto whom Allah hath shown favour, of the Prophets and the saints and the martyrs and the righteous. The best of company are they!

وَمَن يُطِعِ اللَّهَ وَالرَّسُولَ فَأُوْلَـٰئِكَ مَعَ الَّذِينَ أَنْعَمَ اللَّهُ عَلَيْهِم مِّنَ النَّبِيِّـٰنَ وَالصِّدِّيقِينَ وَالشُّهَدَآءِ وَالصَّـٰلِحِينَ ۚ وَحَسُنَ أُوْلَـٰئِكَ رَفِيقًا ۝

70 Such is the bounty of Allah, and Allah sufficeth as Knower.

ذَٰلِكَ الْفَضْلُ مِنَ اللَّهِ ۚ وَكَفَىٰ بِاللَّهِ عَلِيمًا ۝

71 O ye who believe! Take your precautions, then move on as separate units, or advance all together.

يَـٰٓأَيُّهَا الَّذِينَ ءَامَنُوا خُذُوا حِذْرَكُمْ فَانفِرُوا ثُبَاتٍ أَوِ انفِرُوا جَمِيعًا ۝

72 Lo! among you there is he who loitereth; and if disaster overtook you, he would say: Allah hath been gracious unto me since I was not present with them.

وَإِنَّ مِنكُمْ لَمَن لَّيُبَطِّئَنَّ فَإِنْ أَصَابَتْكُم مُّصِيبَةٌ قَالَ قَدْ أَنْعَمَ اللَّهُ عَلَيَّ إِذْ لَمْ أَكُن مَّعَهُمْ شَهِيدًا ۝

73 And if a bounty from Allah befell you, he would surely cry, as if there had been no love between you and him: Oh, would that I had been with them, then should I have achieved a great success!

وَلَئِنْ أَصَابَكُمْ فَضْلٌ مِّنَ اللَّهِ لَيَقُولَنَّ كَأَن لَّمْ تَكُن بَيْنَكُمْ وَبَيْنَهُ مَوَدَّةٌ يَـٰلَيْتَنِى كُنتُ مَعَهُمْ فَأَفُوزَ فَوْزًا عَظِيمًا ۝

74 Let those fight in the way of Allah who sell the life of this world for the other. Whoso fighteth in the way of Allah, be he slain or be he victorious, on him We shall bestow a vast reward.

۞ فَلْيُقَـٰتِلْ فِى سَبِيلِ اللَّهِ الَّذِينَ يَشْرُونَ الْحَيَوٰةَ الدُّنْيَا بِالْأَخِرَةِ ۚ وَمَن يُقَـٰتِلْ فِى سَبِيلِ اللَّهِ فَيُقْتَلْ أَوْ يَغْلِبْ فَسَوْفَ نُؤْتِيهِ أَجْرًا عَظِيمًا ۝

75 How should ye not fight for the cause of Allah and of the feeble among men and of the women and the children who are crying: Our Lord! Bring us forth from out this town[6] of which the people are oppressors! Oh, give us from Thy presence some protecting friend! Oh, give us from Thy presence some defender!

وَمَا لَكُمْ لَا تُقَاتِلُونَ فِى سَبِيلِ اللّٰهِ وَالْمُسْتَضْعَفِينَ مِنَ الرِّجَالِ وَالنِّسَاءِ وَالْوِلْدَانِ الَّذِينَ يَقُولُونَ رَبَّنَآ أَخْرِجْنَا مِنْ هٰذِهِ الْقَرْيَةِ الظَّالِمِ أَهْلُهَا وَاجْعَلْ لَّنَا مِنْ لَّدُنْكَ وَلِيًّا وَّاجْعَلْ لَّنَا مِنْ لَّدُنْكَ نَصِيرًا ۝

76 Those who believe do battle for the cause of Allah; and those who disbelieve do battle for the cause of idols. So fight the minions of the devil. Lo! the devil's strategy is ever weak.

اَلَّذِينَ اٰمَنُوا يُقَاتِلُونَ فِى سَبِيلِ اللّٰهِ وَالَّذِينَ كَفَرُوا يُقَاتِلُونَ فِى سَبِيلِ الطَّاغُوتِ فَقَاتِلُوا أَوْلِيَآءَ الشَّيْطٰنِ إِنَّ كَيْدَ الشَّيْطٰنِ كَانَ ضَعِيفًا ۝

77 Hast thou not seen those unto whom it was said: Withhold your hands, establish worship and pay the poor due, but when fighting was prescribed for them behold! a party of them fear mankind even as their fear of Allah or with greater fear, and say: Our Lord! Why hast thou ordained fighting for us? If only Thou wouldst give us respite yet a while! Say (unto them, O Muhammad): The comfort of this world is scant; the Hereafter will be better for him who wardeth off (evil); and ye will not be wronged the down upon a date-stone.

أَلَمْ تَرَ إِلَى الَّذِينَ قِيلَ لَهُمْ كُفُّوا أَيْدِيَكُمْ وَأَقِيمُوا الصَّلٰوةَ وَاٰتُوا الزَّكٰوةَ فَلَمَّا كُتِبَ عَلَيْهِمُ الْقِتَالُ إِذَا فَرِيقٌ مِّنْهُمْ يَخْشَوْنَ النَّاسَ كَخَشْيَةِ اللّٰهِ أَوْ أَشَدَّ خَشْيَةً وَقَالُوا رَبَّنَا لِمَ كَتَبْتَ عَلَيْنَا الْقِتَالَ لَوْلَا أَخَّرْتَنَآ إِلَىٰ أَجَلٍ قَرِيبٍ قُلْ مَتَاعُ الدُّنْيَا قَلِيلٌ وَالْاٰخِرَةُ خَيْرٌ لِّمَنِ اتَّقَى وَلَا تُظْلَمُونَ فَتِيلًا ۝

---

6. Makkah.

78 Wheresoever ye may be, death will overtake you, even though ye were in lofty towers. Yet if a happy thing befalleth them they say: This is from Allah; and if an evil thing befalleth them they say: This is of thy doing (O Muhammad). Say (unto them): All is from Allah. What is amiss with these people that they come not nigh to understand a happening?[7]

79 Whatever of good befalleth thee (O man) it is from Allah, and whatever of ill befalleth thee it is from thyself. We have sent thee (Muhammad) as a messenger unto mankind and Allah is sufficient as witness.

80 Whoso obeyeth the messenger obeyeth Allah, and whoso turneth away: We have not sent thee as a warder over them.

81 And they say: (It is) obedience; but when they have gone forth from thee a party of them spend the night in planning other than what thou sayest. Allah recordeth what they plan by night. So ignore them and put thy trust in Allah. Allah is sufficient as Trustee.

82 Will they not then ponder on the Qur'an? If it had been from other than Allah they would have found therein much incongruity.

أَيْنَمَا تَكُوْنُوْا يُدْرِكْكُّمُ الْمَوْتُ وَلَوْ كُنْتُمْ فِىْ بُرُوْجٍ مُّشَيَّدَةٍ ۗ وَإِنْ تُصِبْهُمْ حَسَنَةٌ يَّقُوْلُوْا هٰذِهٖ مِنْ عِنْدِ اللّٰهِ ۚ وَإِنْ تُصِبْهُمْ سَيِّئَةٌ يَّقُوْلُوْا هٰذِهٖ مِنْ عِنْدِكَ ۚ قُلْ كُلٌّ مِّنْ عِنْدِ اللّٰهِ ۖ فَمَالِ هٰٓؤُلَاۤءِ الْقَوْمِ لَا يَكَادُوْنَ يَفْقَهُوْنَ حَدِيْثًا ۝

مَّاۤ أَصَابَكَ مِنْ حَسَنَةٍ فَمِنَ اللّٰهِ ۖ وَمَاۤ أَصَابَكَ مِنْ سَيِّئَةٍ فَمِنْ نَّفْسِكَ ۚ وَأَرْسَلْنَاكَ لِلنَّاسِ رَسُوْلًا ۚ وَكَفٰى بِاللّٰهِ شَهِيْدًا ۝

مَنْ يُّطِعِ الرَّسُوْلَ فَقَدْ أَطَاعَ اللّٰهَ ۚ وَمَنْ تَوَلّٰى فَمَاۤ أَرْسَلْنَاكَ عَلَيْهِمْ حَفِيْظًا ۝

وَيَقُوْلُوْنَ طَاعَةٌ ۖ فَإِذَا بَرَزُوْا مِنْ عِنْدِكَ بَيَّتَ طَاۤئِفَةٌ مِّنْهُمْ غَيْرَ الَّذِىْ تَقُوْلُ ۚ وَاللّٰهُ يَكْتُبُ مَا يُبَيِّتُوْنَ ۖ فَأَعْرِضْ عَنْهُمْ وَتَوَكَّلْ عَلَى اللّٰهِ ۚ وَكَفٰى بِاللّٰهِ وَكِيْلًا ۝

أَفَلَا يَتَدَبَّرُوْنَ الْقُرْآنَ ۚ وَلَوْ كَانَ مِنْ عِنْدِ غَيْرِ اللّٰهِ لَوَجَدُوْا فِيْهِ اخْتِلَافًا كَثِيْرًا ۝

---

7. The reference is to the reverse which the Muslims suffered at Mt. Uhud which was caused by thier own disobedience to the Prophets orders.

83 And if any tidings, whether of safety or fear, come unto them, they noise it abroad, whereas if they had referred it to the messenger and such of them as are in authority, those among them who are able to think out the matter would have known it. If it had not been for the grace of Allah and His mercy ye would have followed Satan, save a few (of you).

وَإِذَا جَآءَهُمْ أَمْرٌ مِّنَ الْأَمْنِ أَوِ الْخَوْفِ أَذَاعُوا بِهِ ۖ وَلَوْ رَدُّوهُ إِلَى الرَّسُولِ وَإِلَىٰ أُولِي الْأَمْرِ مِنْهُمْ لَعَلِمَهُ الَّذِينَ يَسْتَنۢبِطُونَهُ مِنْهُمْ ۗ وَلَوْلَا فَضْلُ اللَّهِ عَلَيْكُمْ وَرَحْمَتُهُ لَاتَّبَعْتُمُ الشَّيْطَٰنَ إِلَّا قَلِيلًا ﴿٨٣﴾

84 So fight (O Muhammad) in the way of Allah—Thou art not taxed (with the responsibility for anyone) except for thyself and urge on the believers. Peradventure Allah will restrain the might of those who disbelieve. Allah is stronger in might and stronger in inflicting punishment.

فَقَٰتِلْ فِى سَبِيلِ اللَّهِ لَا تُكَلَّفُ إِلَّا نَفْسَكَ ۚ وَحَرِّضِ الْمُؤْمِنِينَ ۖ عَسَى اللَّهُ أَن يَكُفَّ بَأْسَ الَّذِينَ كَفَرُوا ۚ وَاللَّهُ أَشَدُّ بَأْسًا وَأَشَدُّ تَنكِيلًا ﴿٨٤﴾

85 Whoso interveneth in a good cause will have the reward thereof, and whoso interveneth in an evil cause will bear the consequence thereof Allah overseeth all things.

مَّن يَشْفَعْ شَفَٰعَةً حَسَنَةً يَكُن لَّهُ نَصِيبٌ مِّنْهَا ۖ وَمَن يَشْفَعْ شَفَٰعَةً سَيِّئَةً يَكُن لَّهُ كِفْلٌ مِّنْهَا ۗ وَكَانَ اللَّهُ عَلَىٰ كُلِّ شَىْءٍ مُّقِيتًا ﴿٨٥﴾

86 When ye are greeted with a greeting, greet ye with a better than it or return it. Lo! Allah taketh count of all things.

وَإِذَا حُيِّيتُم بِتَحِيَّةٍ فَحَيُّوا بِأَحْسَنَ مِنْهَآ أَوْ رُدُّوهَآ ۗ إِنَّ اللَّهَ كَانَ عَلَىٰ كُلِّ شَىْءٍ حَسِيبًا ﴿٨٦﴾

87 Allah! There is no God save Him. He gathereth you all unto a Day of Resurrection whereof there is no doubt. Who is more true in statement than Allah?

اللَّهُ لَا إِلَٰهَ إِلَّا هُوَ ۚ لَيَجْمَعَنَّكُمْ إِلَىٰ يَوْمِ الْقِيَٰمَةِ لَا رَيْبَ فِيهِ ۗ وَمَنْ أَصْدَقُ مِنَ اللَّهِ حَدِيثًا ﴿٨٧﴾

88 What aileth you that ye are become two parties regarding the hypocrites,[8] when Allah cast them back (to disbelief) because of what they earned? Seek ye to guide him whom Allah hath sent astray? He whom Allah sendeth astray, for him thou (O Muḥammad) canst not find a road.

﴿ فَمَا لَكُمْ فِى ٱلْمُنَٰفِقِينَ فِئَتَيْنِ وَٱللَّهُ أَرْكَسَهُم بِمَا كَسَبُوٓا۟ أَتُرِيدُونَ أَن تَهْدُوا۟ مَنْ أَضَلَّ ٱللَّهُ وَمَن يُضْلِلِ ٱللَّهُ فَلَن تَجِدَ لَهُۥ سَبِيلًا ٨٨ ﴾

89 They long that ye should disbelieve even as they disbelieve, that ye may be upon a level (with them). So choose not friends from them till they forsake their homes in the way of Allah; if they turn back (to enmity) then take them and kill them wherever ye find them, and choose no friend nor helper from among them,

وَدُّوا۟ لَوْ تَكْفُرُونَ كَمَا كَفَرُوا۟ فَتَكُونُونَ سَوَآءً فَلَا تَتَّخِذُوا۟ مِنْهُمْ أَوْلِيَآءَ حَتَّىٰ يُهَاجِرُوا۟ فِى سَبِيلِ ٱللَّهِ فَإِن تَوَلَّوْا۟ فَخُذُوهُمْ وَٱقْتُلُوهُمْ حَيْثُ وَجَدتُّمُوهُمْ وَلَا تَتَّخِذُوا۟ مِنْهُمْ وَلِيًّا وَلَا نَصِيرًا ٨٩ ﴾

90 Except those who seek refuge with a people between whom and you there is a covenant, or (those who) come unto you because their hearts forbid them to make war on you or make war on their own folk. Had Allah willed He could have given them power over you so that assuredly they would have fought you. So, if they hold aloof from you and wage not war against you and offer you peace, Allah alloweth you no way against them.

إِلَّا ٱلَّذِينَ يَصِلُونَ إِلَىٰ قَوْمٍ بَيْنَكُمْ وَبَيْنَهُم مِّيثَٰقٌ أَوْ جَآءُوكُمْ حَصِرَتْ صُدُورُهُمْ أَن يُقَٰتِلُوكُمْ أَوْ يُقَٰتِلُوا۟ قَوْمَهُمْ وَلَوْ شَآءَ ٱللَّهُ لَسَلَّطَهُمْ عَلَيْكُمْ فَلَقَٰتَلُوكُمْ فَإِنِ ٱعْتَزَلُوكُمْ فَلَمْ يُقَٰتِلُوكُمْ وَأَلْقَوْا۟ إِلَيْكُمُ ٱلسَّلَمَ فَمَا جَعَلَ ٱللَّهُ لَكُمْ عَلَيْهِمْ سَبِيلًا ٩٠ ﴾

---

8. According to Tradition, the reference here is not to the lukewarm section of the Muslims of Al-Madīnah, but to a particular group of alleged converts from among the Arabs, who afterwards relapsed into idolatry, and concerning whom there were two opinions among the Muslims.

91 Ye will find others who desire
that they should have security from
you, and security from their own
folk. So often as they are returned
to hostility they are plunged therein.
If they keep not aloof from you nor
offer you peace nor hold their
hands, then take them and kill them
wherever ye find them. Against
such We have given you clear warrant.

سَتَجِدُونَ ءَاخَرِينَ يُرِيدُونَ أَن يَأْمَنُوكُمْ وَيَأْمَنُوا
قَوْمَهُمْ كُلَّ مَا رُدُّوٓا إِلَى ٱلْفِتْنَةِ أُرْكِسُوا فِيهَا فَإِن
لَّمْ يَعْتَزِلُوكُمْ وَيُلْقُوٓا إِلَيْكُمُ ٱلسَّلَمَ وَيَكُفُّوٓا أَيْدِيَهُمْ
فَخُذُوهُمْ وَٱقْتُلُوهُمْ حَيْثُ ثَقِفْتُمُوهُمْ
وَأُوْلَٰٓئِكُمْ جَعَلْنَا لَكُمْ عَلَيْهِمْ سُلْطَٰنًا مُّبِينًا ٩١

92 It is not for a believer to kill a
believer unless (it be) by mistake.
He who hath killed a believer by
mistake must set free a believing
slave, and pay the blood money to
the family of the slain, unless they
remit it as a charity. If he (the victim) be of a people hostile unto
you, and he is a believer, then (the
penance is) to set free a believing
slave. And if he cometh of a folk
between whom and you there is a
covenant, then the blood money
must be paid unto his folk and
(also) a believing slave must be set
free. And whoso hath not the
wherewithal must fast two consecu-
tive months. A penance from Allah.
Allah is Knower, Wise.

وَمَا كَانَ لِمُؤْمِنٍ أَن يَقْتُلَ مُؤْمِنًا إِلَّا خَطَـًٔا
وَمَن قَتَلَ مُؤْمِنًا خَطَـًٔا فَتَحْرِيرُ رَقَبَةٍ مُّؤْمِنَةٍ
وَدِيَةٌ مُّسَلَّمَةٌ إِلَىٰٓ أَهْلِهِۦٓ إِلَّآ أَن يَصَّدَّقُوا
فَإِن كَانَ مِن قَوْمٍ عَدُوٍّ لَّكُمْ وَهُوَ مُؤْمِنٌ
فَتَحْرِيرُ رَقَبَةٍ مُّؤْمِنَةٍ وَإِن كَانَ
مِن قَوْمٍ بَيْنَكُمْ وَبَيْنَهُم مِّيثَٰقٌ فَدِيَةٌ
مُّسَلَّمَةٌ إِلَىٰٓ أَهْلِهِۦ وَتَحْرِيرُ رَقَبَةٍ مُّؤْمِنَةٍ
فَمَن لَّمْ يَجِدْ فَصِيَامُ شَهْرَيْنِ
مُتَتَابِعَيْنِ تَوْبَةً مِّنَ ٱللَّهِ وَكَانَ ٱللَّهُ
عَلِيمًا حَكِيمًا ٩٢

93 Whoso slayeth a believer of set
purpose, his reward is Hell forever.
Allah is wroth against him and He
hath cursed him and prepared for
him an awful doom.

وَمَن يَقْتُلْ مُؤْمِنًا مُّتَعَمِّدًا فَجَزَآؤُهُۥ
جَهَنَّمُ خَٰلِدًا فِيهَا وَغَضِبَ ٱللَّهُ عَلَيْهِ
وَلَعَنَهُۥ وَأَعَدَّ لَهُۥ عَذَابًا عَظِيمًا ٩٣

94 "O ye who believe! When ye go forth (to fight) in the way of Allah, be careful to discriminate, and say not unto one who offereth you peace: 'Thou are not a believer;' seeking the chance profits of this life (so that ye may despoil him). With Allah are plenteous spoils. Even thus (as he now is) were ye before; but Allah hath since then been gracious unto you. Therefore take care to discriminate. Allah is ever Aware of what you do."

يَـٰٓأَيُّهَا ٱلَّذِينَ ءَامَنُوٓا۟ إِذَا ضَرَبْتُمْ فِى سَبِيلِ ٱللَّهِ فَتَبَيَّنُوا۟ وَلَا تَقُولُوا۟ لِمَنْ أَلْقَىٰٓ إِلَيْكُمُ ٱلسَّلَـٰمَ لَسْتَ مُؤْمِنًا تَبْتَغُونَ عَرَضَ ٱلْحَيَوٰةِ ٱلدُّنْيَا فَعِندَ ٱللَّهِ مَغَانِمُ كَثِيرَةٌ كَذَٰلِكَ كُنتُم مِّن قَبْلُ فَمَنَّ ٱللَّهُ عَلَيْكُمْ فَتَبَيَّنُوٓا۟ إِنَّ ٱللَّهَ كَانَ بِمَا تَعْمَلُونَ خَبِيرًا ﴿٩٤﴾

95 Those of the believers who sit still, other than those who have a (disabling) hurt, are not on an equality with those who strive in the way of Allah with their wealth and lives. Allah hath conferred on those who strive with their wealth and lives a rank above the sedentary. Unto each Allah hath promised good, but He hath bestowed on those who strive a great reward above the sedentary;

لَّا يَسْتَوِى ٱلْقَـٰعِدُونَ مِنَ ٱلْمُؤْمِنِينَ غَيْرُ أُو۟لِى ٱلضَّرَرِ وَٱلْمُجَـٰهِدُونَ فِى سَبِيلِ ٱللَّهِ بِأَمْوَٰلِهِمْ وَأَنفُسِهِمْ فَضَّلَ ٱللَّهُ ٱلْمُجَـٰهِدِينَ بِأَمْوَٰلِهِمْ وَأَنفُسِهِمْ عَلَى ٱلْقَـٰعِدِينَ دَرَجَةً وَكُلًّا وَعَدَ ٱللَّهُ ٱلْحُسْنَىٰ وَفَضَّلَ ٱللَّهُ ٱلْمُجَـٰهِدِينَ عَلَى ٱلْقَـٰعِدِينَ أَجْرًا عَظِيمًا ﴿٩٥﴾

96 Degrees of rank from Him, and forgiveness and mercy. Allah is ever Forgiving, Merciful.

دَرَجَـٰتٍ مِّنْهُ وَمَغْفِرَةً وَرَحْمَةً وَكَانَ ٱللَّهُ غَفُورًا رَّحِيمًا ﴿٩٦﴾

97 Lo! as for those whom the angels take (in death) while they wrong themselves, (the angels) will ask: In what were ye engaged? They will say: We were oppressed in the land. (The angels) will say: Was not Allah's earth spacious that ye could have migrated therein? As for such, their habitation will be hell, an evil journey's end;

إِنَّ ٱلَّذِينَ تَوَفَّىٰهُمُ ٱلْمَلَـٰٓئِكَةُ ظَالِمِىٓ أَنفُسِهِمْ قَالُوا۟ فِيمَ كُنتُمْ قَالُوا۟ كُنَّا مُسْتَضْعَفِينَ فِى ٱلْأَرْضِ قَالُوٓا۟ أَلَمْ تَكُنْ أَرْضُ ٱللَّهِ وَٰسِعَةً فَتُهَاجِرُوا۟ فِيهَا فَأُو۟لَـٰٓئِكَ مَأْوَىٰهُمْ جَهَنَّمُ وَسَآءَتْ مَصِيرًا ﴿٩٧﴾

98 Except the feeble among men, and the women, and the children, who are unable to devise a plan and are not shown a way.

إِلَّا ٱلْمُسْتَضْعَفِينَ مِنَ ٱلرِّجَالِ وَٱلنِّسَآءِ وَٱلْوِلْدَانِ لَا يَسْتَطِيعُونَ حِيلَةً وَلَا يَهْتَدُونَ سَبِيلًا ۝

99 As for such, it may be that Allah will pardon them. Allah is ever Clement, Forgiving.

فَأُوْلَٰٓئِكَ عَسَى ٱللَّهُ أَن يَعْفُوَ عَنْهُمْ وَكَانَ ٱللَّهُ عَفُوًّا غَفُورًا ۝

100 Whoso migrateth for the cause of Allah will find much refuge and abundance in the earth, and whoso forsaketh his home, a fugitive unto Allah and His messenger, and death overtaketh him, his reward is then incumbent on Allah. Allah is ever Forgiving, Merciful.

۞ وَمَن يُهَاجِرْ فِي سَبِيلِ ٱللَّهِ يَجِدْ فِي ٱلْأَرْضِ مُرَٰغَمًا كَثِيرًا وَسَعَةً وَمَن يَخْرُجْ مِنۢ بَيْتِهِ مُهَاجِرًا إِلَى ٱللَّهِ وَرَسُولِهِ ثُمَّ يُدْرِكْهُ ٱلْمَوْتُ فَقَدْ وَقَعَ أَجْرُهُ عَلَى ٱللَّهِ وَكَانَ ٱللَّهُ غَفُورًا رَّحِيمًا ۝

101 And when ye go forth in the land, it is no sin for you to curtail (your) worship if ye fear that those who disbelieve may attack you. In truth the disbelievers are an open enemy to you.

وَإِذَا ضَرَبْتُمْ فِي ٱلْأَرْضِ فَلَيْسَ عَلَيْكُمْ جُنَاحٌ أَن تَقْصُرُواْ مِنَ ٱلصَّلَوٰةِ إِنْ خِفْتُمْ أَن يَفْتِنَكُمُ ٱلَّذِينَ كَفَرُوٓاْ إِنَّ ٱلْكَٰفِرِينَ كَانُواْ لَكُمْ عَدُوًّا مُّبِينًا ۝

102 And when thou (O Muhammad) art among them and arrangest (their) worship for them, let only a party of them stand with thee (to worship) and let them take their arms. Then when they have performed their prostrations let them fall to the rear of you and let another party come that hath not worshipped and let them worship with thee, and let them take their precaution and their arms. Those who disbelieve long for you to neglect your arms and your baggage

وَإِذَا كُنتَ فِيهِمْ فَأَقَمْتَ لَهُمُ ٱلصَّلَوٰةَ فَلْتَقُمْ طَآئِفَةٌ مِّنْهُم مَّعَكَ وَلْيَأْخُذُوٓاْ أَسْلِحَتَهُمْ فَإِذَا سَجَدُواْ فَلْيَكُونُواْ مِن وَرَآئِكُمْ وَلْتَأْتِ طَآئِفَةٌ أُخْرَىٰ لَمْ يُصَلُّواْ فَلْيُصَلُّواْ مَعَكَ وَلْيَأْخُذُواْ حِذْرَهُمْ وَأَسْلِحَتَهُمْ وَدَّ ٱلَّذِينَ كَفَرُواْ لَوْ تَغْفُلُونَ عَنْ أَسْلِحَتِكُمْ وَأَمْتِعَتِكُمْ

that they may attack you once for all. It is no sin for you to lay aside your arms, if rain impedeth you or ye are sick. But take your precaution. Lo! Allah prepareth for the disbelievers shameful punishment.

فَيَمِيلُونَ عَلَيْكُم مَّيْلَةً وَاحِدَةً وَلَا جُنَاحَ عَلَيْكُمْ إِن كَانَ بِكُمْ أَذًى مِّن مَّطَرٍ أَوْ كُنتُم مَّرْضَىٰ أَن تَضَعُوٓا أَسْلِحَتَكُمْ وَخُذُوا حِذْرَكُمْ إِنَّ ٱللَّهَ أَعَدَّ لِلْكَـٰفِرِينَ عَذَابًا مُّهِينًا ۝

103   When ye have performed the act of worship, remember Allah, standing, sitting and reclining. And when ye are in safety, observe proper worship. Worship at fixed hours hath been enjoined on the believers.

فَإِذَا قَضَيْتُمُ ٱلصَّلَوٰةَ فَٱذْكُرُوا ٱللَّهَ قِيَـٰمًا وَقُعُودًا وَعَلَىٰ جُنُوبِكُمْ فَإِذَا ٱطْمَأْنَنتُمْ فَأَقِيمُوا ٱلصَّلَوٰةَ إِنَّ ٱلصَّلَوٰةَ كَانَتْ عَلَى ٱلْمُؤْمِنِينَ كِتَـٰبًا مَّوْقُوتًا ۝

104   Relent not in pursuit of the (hostile) people. If ye are suffering, lo! they suffer even as ye suffer and ye hope from Allah that for which they cannot hope. Allah is ever Knower, Wise.

وَلَا تَهِنُوا فِي ٱبْتِغَآءِ ٱلْقَوْمِ إِن تَكُونُوا تَأْلَمُونَ فَإِنَّهُمْ يَأْلَمُونَ كَمَا تَأْلَمُونَ وَتَرْجُونَ مِنَ ٱللَّهِ مَا لَا يَرْجُونَ وَكَانَ ٱللَّهُ عَلِيمًا حَكِيمًا ۝

105   Lo! We reveal unto thee the Scripture with the truth, that thou mayst judge between mankind by that which Allah showeth thee. And be not thou a pleader for the treacherous;

إِنَّا أَنزَلْنَآ إِلَيْكَ ٱلْكِتَـٰبَ بِٱلْحَقِّ لِتَحْكُمَ بَيْنَ ٱلنَّاسِ بِمَآ أَرَىٰكَ ٱللَّهُ وَلَا تَكُن لِّلْخَآئِنِينَ خَصِيمًا ۝

106   And seek forgiveness of Allah. Lo! Allah is ever Forgiving, Merciful.

وَٱسْتَغْفِرِ ٱللَّهَ إِنَّ ٱللَّهَ كَانَ غَفُورًا رَّحِيمًا ۝

107   And plead not on behalf of (people) who deceive themselves. Lo! Allah loveth not one who is treacherous and sinful.

وَلَا تُجَـٰدِلْ عَنِ ٱلَّذِينَ يَخْتَانُونَ أَنفُسَهُمْ إِنَّ ٱللَّهَ لَا يُحِبُّ مَن كَانَ خَوَّانًا أَثِيمًا ۝

108   They seek to hide from men and seek not to hide from Allah. He is with them when by night they hold discourse displeasing unto Him. Allah ever surroundeth what they do.

يَسْتَخْفُونَ مِنَ ٱلنَّاسِ وَلَا يَسْتَخْفُونَ مِنَ ٱللَّهِ وَهُوَ مَعَهُمْ إِذْ يُبَيِّتُونَ مَا لَا يَرْضَىٰ مِنَ ٱلْقَوْلِ وَكَانَ ٱللَّهُ بِمَا يَعْمَلُونَ مُحِيطًا ۝

109   Lo! ye are they who pleaded for them in the life of the world. But who will plead with Allah for them on the Day of Resurrection, or who will then be their defender?

هَآأَنتُمْ هَٰٓؤُلَآءِ جَٰدَلْتُمْ عَنْهُمْ فِى ٱلْحَيَوٰةِ ٱلدُّنْيَا فَمَن يُجَٰدِلُ ٱللَّهَ عَنْهُمْ يَوْمَ ٱلْقِيَٰمَةِ أَم مَّن يَكُونُ عَلَيْهِمْ وَكِيلًا ۝

110   Yet whoso doeth evil or wrongeth his own soul, then seeketh pardon of Allah, will find Allah Forgiving, Merciful.

وَمَن يَعْمَلْ سُوٓءًا أَوْ يَظْلِمْ نَفْسَهُۥ ثُمَّ يَسْتَغْفِرِ ٱللَّهَ يَجِدِ ٱللَّهَ غَفُورًا رَّحِيمًا ۝

111   Whoso committeth sin; committeth it only against himself. Allah is ever Knower, Wise.

وَمَن يَكْسِبْ إِثْمًا فَإِنَّمَا يَكْسِبُهُۥ عَلَىٰ نَفْسِهِۦ وَكَانَ ٱللَّهُ عَلِيمًا حَكِيمًا ۝

112   And whoso committeth a delinquency or crime, then throweth (the blame) thereof upon the innocent, hath burdened himself with falsehood and a flagrant crime.

وَمَن يَكْسِبْ خَطِيٓئَةً أَوْ إِثْمًا ثُمَّ يَرْمِ بِهِۦ بَرِيٓئًا فَقَدِ ٱحْتَمَلَ بُهْتَٰنًا وَإِثْمًا مُّبِينًا ۝

113   But for the grace of Allah upon thee (Muhammad), and His mercy, a party of them had resolved to mislead thee, but they will mislead only themselves and they will hurt thee not at all. Allah revealeth unto thee the Scripture and wisdom, and teacheth thee that which thou knewest not. The grace of Allah toward thee hath been great.

وَلَوْلَا فَضْلُ ٱللَّهِ عَلَيْكَ وَرَحْمَتُهُۥ لَهَمَّت طَّآئِفَةٌ مِّنْهُمْ أَن يُضِلُّوكَ وَمَا يُضِلُّونَ إِلَّآ أَنفُسَهُمْ وَمَا يَضُرُّونَكَ مِن شَىْءٍ وَأَنزَلَ ٱللَّهُ عَلَيْكَ ٱلْكِتَٰبَ وَٱلْحِكْمَةَ وَعَلَّمَكَ مَا لَمْ تَكُن تَعْلَمُ وَكَانَ فَضْلُ ٱللَّهِ عَلَيْكَ عَظِيمًا ۝

114   There is no good in much of their secret conferences save (in) him who enjoineth alms giving and kindness and peace making among the people. Whoso doeth that, seeking the good pleasure of Allah, We shall bestow on him a vast reward.

۞ لَّا خَيْرَ فِى كَثِيرٍ مِّن نَّجْوَىٰهُمْ إِلَّا مَنْ أَمَرَ بِصَدَقَةٍ أَوْ مَعْرُوفٍ أَوْ إِصْلَٰحٍ بَيْنَ ٱلنَّاسِ وَمَن يَفْعَلْ ذَٰلِكَ ٱبْتِغَآءَ مَرْضَاتِ ٱللَّهِ فَسَوْفَ نُؤْتِيهِ أَجْرًا عَظِيمًا ۝

115   And whoso opposeth the messenger after the guidance (of Allah) hath been manifested unto him, and followeth other than the believer's way, We appoint for him that unto which he himself hath turned, and expose him unto hell a hapless journey's end!

وَمَنْ يُشَاقِقِ الرَّسُولَ مِنْ بَعْدِ مَا تَبَيَّنَ لَهُ الْهُدَىٰ وَيَتَّبِعْ غَيْرَ سَبِيلِ الْمُؤْمِنِينَ نُوَلِّهِ مَا تَوَلَّىٰ وَنُصْلِهِ جَهَنَّمَ وَسَاءَتْ مَصِيرًا ۝

116   Lo! Allah pardoneth not that partners should be ascribed unto him. He pardoneth all save that to whom He will. Whoso ascribeth partners unto Allah hath wandered far astray.

إِنَّ اللَّهَ لَا يَغْفِرُ أَنْ يُشْرَكَ بِهِ وَيَغْفِرُ مَا دُونَ ذَٰلِكَ لِمَنْ يَشَاءُ وَمَنْ يُشْرِكْ بِاللَّهِ فَقَدْ ضَلَّ ضَلَالًا بَعِيدًا ۝

117   They invoke in His stead only females;[9] they pray to none else than Satan, a rebel;

إِنْ يَدْعُونَ مِنْ دُونِهِ إِلَّا إِنَاثًا وَإِنْ يَدْعُونَ إِلَّا شَيْطَانًا مَرِيدًا ۝

118   Whom Allah cursed, and he said: Surely I will take of Thy bondmen an appointed portion,

لَعَنَهُ اللَّهُ وَقَالَ لَأَتَّخِذَنَّ مِنْ عِبَادِكَ نَصِيبًا مَفْرُوضًا ۝

119   And surely I will lead them astray, and surely I will arouse desires in them, and surely I will command them and they will cut the cattle's ears, and surely I will command them and they will change Allah's creation. Whoso chooseth Satan for a patron instead of Allah is verily a loser and his loss is manifest.

وَلَأُضِلَّنَّهُمْ وَلَأُمَنِّيَنَّهُمْ وَلَآمُرَنَّهُمْ فَلَيُبَتِّكُنَّ ءَاذَانَ الْأَنْعَامِ وَلَآمُرَنَّهُمْ فَلَيُغَيِّرُنَّ خَلْقَ اللَّهِ وَمَنْ يَتَّخِذِ الشَّيْطَانَ وَلِيًّا مِنْ دُونِ اللَّهِ فَقَدْ خَسِرَ خُسْرَانًا مُبِينًا ۝

120   He promiseth them and stirreth up desires in them, and Satan promiseth them only to beguile.

يَعِدُهُمْ وَيُمَنِّيهِمْ وَمَا يَعِدُهُمُ الشَّيْطَانُ إِلَّا غُرُورًا ۝

---

9. The Idols that the pagan Arabs worshipped were all female.

121   For such, their habitation
will be hell, and they will find no
refuge therefrom.

أُوْلَٰٓئِكَ مَأْوَىٰهُمْ جَهَنَّمُ وَلَا يَجِدُونَ عَنْهَا
مَحِيصًا ۝

122   But as for those who believe
and do good works We shall bring
them into gardens underneath which
rivers flow, wherein they will abide
forever. It is a promise from Allah
in truth; and who can be more
truthful than Allah in utterance?

وَالَّذِينَ ءَامَنُوا۟ وَعَمِلُوا۟ ٱلصَّٰلِحَٰتِ
سَنُدْخِلُهُمْ جَنَّٰتٍ تَجْرِى مِن تَحْتِهَا
ٱلْأَنْهَٰرُ خَٰلِدِينَ فِيهَآ أَبَدًا ۖ وَعْدَ ٱللَّهِ حَقًّا ۚ
وَمَنْ أَصْدَقُ مِنَ ٱللَّهِ قِيلًا ۝

123   It will not be in accordance
with your desires, nor the desires of
the People of the Scripture.[10] He
who doeth wrong will have the recompense thereof, and will not find
against Allah any protecting friend
or helper.

لَّيْسَ بِأَمَانِيِّكُمْ وَلَآ أَمَانِىِّ أَهْلِ ٱلْكِتَٰبِ ۗ
مَن يَعْمَلْ سُوٓءًا يُجْزَ بِهِۦ وَلَا يَجِدْ لَهُۥ مِن
دُونِ ٱللَّهِ وَلِيًّا وَلَا نَصِيرًا ۝

124   And whoso doeth good
works, whether of male or female,
and he (or she) is a believer, such
will enter paradise and they will not
be wronged the dint in a date-stone.

وَمَن يَعْمَلْ مِنَ ٱلصَّٰلِحَٰتِ مِن ذَكَرٍ
أَوْ أُنثَىٰ وَهُوَ مُؤْمِنٌ فَأُوْلَٰٓئِكَ يَدْخُلُونَ ٱلْجَنَّةَ
وَلَا يُظْلَمُونَ نَقِيرًا ۝

125   Who is better in religion
than he who surrendereth his purpose to Allah while doing good (to
men) and followeth the tradition of
Abraham, the upright? Allah (Himself) chose Abraham for friend.

وَمَنْ أَحْسَنُ دِينًا مِّمَّنْ أَسْلَمَ وَجْهَهُۥ لِلَّهِ
وَهُوَ مُحْسِنٌ وَٱتَّبَعَ مِلَّةَ إِبْرَٰهِيمَ حَنِيفًا ۗ
وَٱتَّخَذَ ٱللَّهُ إِبْرَٰهِيمَ خَلِيلًا ۝

126   Unto Allah belongeth whatsoever is in the heavens and whatsoever is in the earth. Allah ever
surroundeth all things.

وَلِلَّهِ مَا فِى ٱلسَّمَٰوَٰتِ وَمَا فِى ٱلْأَرْضِ ۚ
وَكَانَ ٱللَّهُ بِكُلِّ شَىْءٍ مُّحِيطًا ۝

---

10. Jews and Christians.

127   They consult thee concerning women. Say: Allah give to you decree concerning them, and the Scripture which hath been recited unto you (giveth decree), concerning female orphans unto whom ye give not that which is ordained for them though ye desire to marry them, and (concerning) the weak among children, and that ye should deal justly with orphans. Whatever good ye do, lo! Allah is ever Aware of it.

وَيَسْتَفْتُونَكَ فِى ٱلنِّسَآءِ قُلِ ٱللَّهُ يُفْتِيكُمْ فِيهِنَّ وَمَا يُتْلَىٰ عَلَيْكُمْ فِى ٱلْكِتَٰبِ فِى يَتَٰمَى ٱلنِّسَآءِ ٱلَّٰتِى لَا تُؤْتُونَهُنَّ مَا كُتِبَ لَهُنَّ وَتَرْغَبُونَ أَن تَنكِحُوهُنَّ وَٱلْمُسْتَضْعَفِينَ مِنَ ٱلْوِلْدَٰنِ وَأَن تَقُومُوا۟ لِلْيَتَٰمَىٰ بِٱلْقِسْطِ وَمَا تَفْعَلُوا۟ مِنْ خَيْرٍ فَإِنَّ ٱللَّهَ كَانَ بِهِۦ عَلِيمًا ﴿١٢٧﴾

128   If a woman feareth ill treatment from her husband, or desertion, it is no sin for them twain if they make terms of peace between themselves. Peace is better. But greed hath been made present in the minds (of men). If ye do good and keep from evil, Lo! Allah is ever Aware of what ye do.

وَإِنِ ٱمْرَأَةٌ خَافَتْ مِنۢ بَعْلِهَا نُشُوزًا أَوْ إِعْرَاضًا فَلَا جُنَاحَ عَلَيْهِمَآ أَن يُصْلِحَا بَيْنَهُمَا صُلْحًا وَٱلصُّلْحُ خَيْرٌ وَأُحْضِرَتِ ٱلْأَنفُسُ ٱلشُّحَّ وَإِن تُحْسِنُوا۟ وَتَتَّقُوا۟ فَإِنَّ ٱللَّهَ كَانَ بِمَا تَعْمَلُونَ خَبِيرًا ﴿١٢٨﴾

129   Ye will not be able to deal equally between (your) wives, however much ye wish (to do so): But turn not altogether away (from one), leaving her as in suspense. If ye do good and keep from evil, lo! Allah is ever Forgiving, Merciful.

وَلَن تَسْتَطِيعُوٓا۟ أَن تَعْدِلُوا۟ بَيْنَ ٱلنِّسَآءِ وَلَوْ حَرَصْتُمْ فَلَا تَمِيلُوا۟ كُلَّ ٱلْمَيْلِ فَتَذَرُوهَا كَٱلْمُعَلَّقَةِ وَإِن تُصْلِحُوا۟ وَتَتَّقُوا۟ فَإِنَّ ٱللَّهَ كَانَ غَفُورًا رَّحِيمًا ﴿١٢٩﴾

130   But if they separate, Allah will compensate each out of His abundance. Allah is ever All Embracing, All Knowing.

وَإِن يَتَفَرَّقَا يُغْنِ ٱللَّهُ كُلًّا مِّن سَعَتِهِۦ وَكَانَ ٱللَّهُ وَٰسِعًا حَكِيمًا ﴿١٣٠﴾

131   Unto Allah belongeth whatsoever is in the heavens and whatsoever is in the earth And We charged those who received the Scr-

وَلِلَّهِ مَا فِى ٱلسَّمَٰوَٰتِ وَمَا فِى ٱلْأَرْضِ وَلَقَدْ وَصَّيْنَا ٱلَّذِينَ أُوتُوا۟ ٱلْكِتَٰبَ مِن قَبْلِكُمْ

ipture before you, and (We charge) you, that ye keep your duty toward Allah. And if ye disbelieve, lo! unto Allah belongeth whatsoever is in the heavens and whatsoever is in the earth, and Allah is ever Absolute, Owner of Praise.

وَإِيَّاكُمْ أَنِ اتَّقُوا اللَّهَ وَإِن تَكْفُرُوا فَإِنَّ لِلَّهِ مَا فِى السَّمَوَاتِ وَمَا فِى الْأَرْضِ وَكَانَ اللَّهُ غَنِيًّا حَمِيدًا ۝

132   Unto Allah belongeth whatsoever is in the heavens and whatsoever is in the earth. And Allah is sufficient as Defender.

وَلِلَّهِ مَا فِى السَّمَوَاتِ وَمَا فِى الْأَرْضِ وَكَفَى بِاللَّهِ وَكِيلًا ۝

133   If He will, He can remove you, O people, and produce others (in your stead). Allah is Able to do that.

إِن يَشَأْ يُذْهِبْكُمْ أَيُّهَا النَّاسُ وَيَأْتِ بِآخَرِينَ وَكَانَ اللَّهُ عَلَى ذَلِكَ قَدِيرًا ۝

134   Whoso desireth the reward of the world, (let him know that) with Allah is the reward of the world and the Hereafter. Allah is ever Hearer, Seer.

مَن كَانَ يُرِيدُ ثَوَابَ الدُّنْيَا فَعِندَ اللَّهِ ثَوَابُ الدُّنْيَا وَالْآخِرَةِ وَكَانَ اللَّهُ سَمِيعًا بَصِيرًا ۝

135   O ye who believe! Be ye staunch in justice, witnesses for Allah, even though it be against yourselves or (your) parents or (your) kindred, whether (the case be of) a rich man or a poor man, for Allah is nearer unto both (than ye are). So follow not passion lest ye lapse (from truth) and if ye lapse or fall away, then lo! Allah is ever Informed of what ye do.

۞ يَا أَيُّهَا الَّذِينَ آمَنُوا كُونُوا قَوَّامِينَ بِالْقِسْطِ شُهَدَاءَ لِلَّهِ وَلَوْ عَلَى أَنفُسِكُمْ أَوِ الْوَالِدَيْنِ وَالْأَقْرَبِينَ إِن يَكُنْ غَنِيًّا أَوْ فَقِيرًا فَاللَّهُ أَوْلَى بِهِمَا فَلَا تَتَّبِعُوا الْهَوَى أَن تَعْدِلُوا وَإِن تَلْوُوا أَوْ تُعْرِضُوا فَإِنَّ اللَّهَ كَانَ بِمَا تَعْمَلُونَ خَبِيرًا ۝

136   O ye who believe! Believe in Allah and His messenger and the Scripture which He hath revealed unto His messenger, and the Scripture which He revealed aforetime.

يَا أَيُّهَا الَّذِينَ آمَنُوا آمِنُوا بِاللَّهِ وَرَسُولِهِ وَالْكِتَابِ الَّذِى نَزَّلَ عَلَى رَسُولِهِ وَالْكِتَابِ الَّذِى أَنزَلَ مِن قَبْلُ وَمَن يَكْفُرْ

Whoso disbelieveth in Allah and His angels and His scriptures and His messengers and the Last Day, he verily hath wandered far astray.

بِٱللَّهِ وَمَلَـٰٓئِكَتِهِۦ وَكُتُبِهِۦ وَرُسُلِهِۦ وَٱلْيَوْمِ ٱلْءَاخِرِ فَقَدْ ضَلَّ ضَلَـٰلَۢا بَعِيدًا ﴿١٣٦﴾

137   Lo! those who believe, then disbelieve and then (again) believe, then disbelieve, and then increase in disbelief, Allah will never pardon them, nor will He guide them unto a way.

إِنَّ ٱلَّذِينَ ءَامَنُوا۟ ثُمَّ كَفَرُوا۟ ثُمَّ ءَامَنُوا۟ ثُمَّ كَفَرُوا۟ ثُمَّ ٱزْدَادُوا۟ كُفْرًا لَّمْ يَكُنِ ٱللَّهُ لِيَغْفِرَ لَهُمْ وَلَا لِيَهْدِيَهُمْ سَبِيلَۢا ﴿١٣٧﴾

138   Bear unto the hypocrites the tidings that for them there is a painful doom;

بَشِّرِ ٱلْمُنَـٰفِقِينَ بِأَنَّ لَهُمْ عَذَابًا أَلِيمًا ﴿١٣٨﴾

139   Those who choose disbelievers for their friends instead of believers! Do they look for power at their hands? Lo! all power appertaineth to Allah.

ٱلَّذِينَ يَتَّخِذُونَ ٱلْكَـٰفِرِينَ أَوْلِيَآءَ مِن دُونِ ٱلْمُؤْمِنِينَ أَيَبْتَغُونَ عِندَهُمُ ٱلْعِزَّةَ فَإِنَّ ٱلْعِزَّةَ لِلَّهِ جَمِيعًا ﴿١٣٩﴾

140   He hath already revealed unto you in the Scripture that, when ye hear the revelations of Allah rejected and derided, (ye) sit not with them (who disbelieve and mock) until they engage in some other conversation. Lo! in that case (if ye stayed) ye would be like unto them. Lo! Allah will gather hypocrites and disbelievers, all together, into hell;

وَقَدْ نَزَّلَ عَلَيْكُمْ فِى ٱلْكِتَـٰبِ أَنْ إِذَا سَمِعْتُمْ ءَايَـٰتِ ٱللَّهِ يُكْفَرُ بِهَا وَيُسْتَهْزَأُ بِهَا فَلَا تَقْعُدُوا۟ مَعَهُمْ حَتَّىٰ يَخُوضُوا۟ فِى حَدِيثٍ غَيْرِهِۦٓ إِنَّكُمْ إِذًا مِّثْلُهُمْ إِنَّ ٱللَّهَ جَامِعُ ٱلْمُنَـٰفِقِينَ وَٱلْكَـٰفِرِينَ فِى جَهَنَّمَ جَمِيعًا ﴿١٤٠﴾

141   Those who wait upon occasion in regard to you and, if a victory cometh unto you from Allah, say: Are we not with you? and if the disbelievers meet with a success say: Had we not the mastery of you, and did we not protect you

ٱلَّذِينَ يَتَرَبَّصُونَ بِكُمْ فَإِن كَانَ لَكُمْ فَتْحٌ مِّنَ ٱللَّهِ قَالُوٓا۟ أَلَمْ نَكُن مَّعَكُمْ وَإِن كَانَ لِلْكَـٰفِرِينَ نَصِيبٌ قَالُوٓا۟ أَلَمْ نَسْتَحْوِذْ عَلَيْكُمْ وَنَمْنَعْكُم

from the believers? Allah will judge between you at the Day of Resurrection, and Allah will not give the disbelievers any way (of success) against the believers.

مِنَ ٱلْمُؤْمِنِينَ فَٱللَّهُ يَحْكُمُ بَيْنَكُمْ يَوْمَ
ٱلْقِيَامَةِ وَلَن يَجْعَلَ ٱللَّهُ لِلْكَافِرِينَ عَلَى
ٱلْمُؤْمِنِينَ سَبِيلًا ﴿١٤١﴾

142 Lo! the hypocrites seek to beguile Allah, but it is Allah who beguileth them. When they stand up to worship they perform it languidly and to be seen of men, and are mindful of Allah but little;

إِنَّ ٱلْمُنَافِقِينَ يُخَادِعُونَ ٱللَّهَ وَهُوَ خَادِعُهُمْ
وَإِذَا قَامُوٓاْ إِلَى ٱلصَّلَوٰةِ قَامُواْ كُسَالَىٰ يُرَآءُونَ
ٱلنَّاسَ وَلَا يَذْكُرُونَ ٱللَّهَ إِلَّا قَلِيلًا ﴿١٤٢﴾

143 Swaying between this (and that), (belonging) neither to these nor to those. He whom Allah causeth to go astray, thou (O Muhammad) wilt not find a way for him:

مُّذَبْذَبِينَ بَيْنَ ذَٰلِكَ لَآ إِلَىٰ هَٰٓؤُلَآءِ وَلَآ إِلَىٰ هَٰٓؤُلَآءِ
وَمَن يُضْلِلِ ٱللَّهُ فَلَن تَجِدَ لَهُۥ سَبِيلًا ﴿١٤٣﴾

144 O ye who believe! Choose not disbelievers for (your) friends in place of believers. Would ye give Allah a clear warrant against you?

يَٰٓأَيُّهَا ٱلَّذِينَ ءَامَنُواْ لَا تَتَّخِذُواْ ٱلْكَافِرِينَ
أَوْلِيَآءَ مِن دُونِ ٱلْمُؤْمِنِينَ أَتُرِيدُونَ
أَن تَجْعَلُواْ لِلَّهِ عَلَيْكُمْ سُلْطَٰنًا مُّبِينًا ﴿١٤٤﴾

145 Lo! the hypocrites (will be) in the lowest deep of the fire, and thou wilt find no helper for them;

إِنَّ ٱلْمُنَافِقِينَ فِي ٱلدَّرْكِ ٱلْأَسْفَلِ مِنَ ٱلنَّارِ
وَلَن تَجِدَ لَهُمْ نَصِيرًا ﴿١٤٥﴾

146 Save those who repent and amend and hold fast to Allah and make their religion pure for Allah (only). Those are with the believers. And Allah will bestow on the believers an immense reward.

إِلَّا ٱلَّذِينَ تَابُواْ وَأَصْلَحُواْ وَٱعْتَصَمُواْ
بِٱللَّهِ وَأَخْلَصُواْ دِينَهُمْ لِلَّهِ فَأُوْلَٰٓئِكَ مَعَ
ٱلْمُؤْمِنِينَ وَسَوْفَ يُؤْتِ ٱللَّهُ ٱلْمُؤْمِنِينَ
أَجْرًا عَظِيمًا ﴿١٤٦﴾

147 What concern hath Allah for your punishment if ye are thankful (for His mercies) and believe (in Him)? Allah was ever Responsive, Aware.

مَّا يَفْعَلُ ٱللَّهُ بِعَذَابِكُمْ إِن شَكَرْتُمْ
وَءَامَنتُمْ وَكَانَ ٱللَّهُ شَاكِرًا عَلِيمًا ﴿١٤٧﴾

148   Allah loveth not the utterance of harsh speech save by one
who hath been wronged. Allah is
ever Hearer, Knower.

149   If ye do good openly or keep
it secret, or forgive evil, lo! Allah
is Forgiving, Powerful.

150   Lo! those who disbelieve in
Allah and His messengers, and seek
to make distinction between Allah
and His messengers, and say: We
believe in some and disbelieve in
others, and seek to choose a way in
between;

151   Such are disbelievers in truth;
and for disbelievers We prepare a
shameful doom.

152   But those who believe in
Allah and His messengers and make
no distinction between any of them,
unto them Allah will give their
wages; and Allah was ever Forgiving,
Merciful.

153   The People of the Scripture
ask of thee that thou shouldst cause
an (actual) Book to descend upon
them from heaven. They asked a greater thing of Moses aforetime, for
they said: Show us Allah plainly.
The storm of lightning seized them
for their wickedness. Then (even
after that) they chose the calf (for
worship) after clear proofs (of
Allah's Sovereignty) had come unto
them. And We forgave them that!
And We bestowed on Moses evident
authority.

154   And We caused the Mount to tower above them at (the taking of) their covenant: and We bade them: Enter the gate, prostrate! and we bade them: Transgress not the Sabbath! and We took from them a firm covenant.

وَرَفَعْنَا فَوْقَهُمُ الطُّورَ بِمِيثَٰقِهِمْ وَقُلْنَا لَهُمُ ادْخُلُوا الْبَابَ سُجَّدًا وَقُلْنَا لَهُمْ لَا تَعْدُوا فِي السَّبْتِ وَأَخَذْنَا مِنْهُم مِّيثَٰقًا غَلِيظًا ﴿١٥٤﴾

155   Then because of their breaking of their covenant, and their disbelieving in the revelations of Allah, and their slaying of the Prophets wrongfully, and their saying: Our hearts are hardened Nay, but Allah hath set a seal upon them for their disbelief, so that they believe not save a few;

فَبِمَا نَقْضِهِم مِّيثَٰقَهُمْ وَكُفْرِهِم بِـَٔايَٰتِ اللَّهِ وَقَتْلِهِمُ الْأَنۢبِيَآءَ بِغَيْرِ حَقٍّ وَقَوْلِهِمْ قُلُوبُنَا غُلْفٌ بَلْ طَبَعَ اللَّهُ عَلَيْهَا بِكُفْرِهِمْ فَلَا يُؤْمِنُونَ إِلَّا قَلِيلًا ﴿١٥٥﴾

156   And because of their disbelief and of their speaking against Mary a tremendous calumny;

وَبِكُفْرِهِمْ وَقَوْلِهِمْ عَلَىٰ مَرْيَمَ بُهْتَٰنًا عَظِيمًا ﴿١٥٦﴾

157   And because of their saying: We slew the Messiah Jesus son of Mary, Allah's messenger; They slew him not nor crucified, but it appeared so unto them; and lo! those who disagree concerning it are in doubt thereof; they have no knowledge thereof save pursuit of a conjecture; they slew him not for certain.

وَقَوْلِهِمْ إِنَّا قَتَلْنَا الْمَسِيحَ عِيسَى ابْنَ مَرْيَمَ رَسُولَ اللَّهِ وَمَا قَتَلُوهُ وَمَا صَلَبُوهُ وَلَٰكِن شُبِّهَ لَهُمْ وَإِنَّ الَّذِينَ اخْتَلَفُوا فِيهِ لَفِي شَكٍّ مِّنْهُ مَا لَهُم بِهِ مِنْ عِلْمٍ إِلَّا اتِّبَاعَ الظَّنِّ وَمَا قَتَلُوهُ يَقِينًا ﴿١٥٧﴾

158   But Allah took him up unto Himself. Allah is ever Mighty, Wise.

بَل رَّفَعَهُ اللَّهُ إِلَيْهِ وَكَانَ اللَّهُ عَزِيزًا حَكِيمًا ﴿١٥٨﴾

159   There is not one of the People of the Scripture but will believe in him before his death, and on the Day of Resurrection he will be a witness against them;

وَإِن مِّنْ أَهْلِ الْكِتَٰبِ إِلَّا لَيُؤْمِنَنَّ بِهِ قَبْلَ مَوْتِهِ وَيَوْمَ الْقِيَٰمَةِ يَكُونُ عَلَيْهِمْ شَهِيدًا ﴿١٥٩﴾

160   Because of the wrongdoing of the Jews We forbade them good things which were (before) made lawful unto them, and because of their much hindering from Allah's way,

فَبِظُلْمٍ مِّنَ الَّذِينَ هَادُوا حَرَّمْنَا عَلَيْهِمْ طَيِّبَٰتٍ أُحِلَّتْ لَهُمْ وَبِصَدِّهِمْ عَن سَبِيلِ اللَّهِ كَثِيرًا ﴿١٦٠﴾

161   And of their taking usury when they were forbidden it, and of their devouring people's wealth by false pretences. We have prepared for those of them who disbelieve a painful doom.

وَأَخْذِهِمُ الرِّبَوٰا وَقَدْ نُهُوا عَنْهُ وَأَكْلِهِمْ أَمْوَٰلَ النَّاسِ بِالْبَٰطِلِ وَأَعْتَدْنَا لِلْكَٰفِرِينَ مِنْهُمْ عَذَابًا أَلِيمًا ﴿١٦١﴾

162   But those of them who are firm in knowledge and the believers believe in that which is revealed unto thee, and that which was revealed before thee, especially the diligent in prayer and those who pay the poor due, the believers in Allah and the Last Day. Upon these We shall bestow immense reward.

لَّٰكِنِ الرَّٰسِخُونَ فِي الْعِلْمِ مِنْهُمْ وَالْمُؤْمِنُونَ يُؤْمِنُونَ بِمَا أُنزِلَ إِلَيْكَ وَمَا أُنزِلَ مِن قَبْلِكَ وَالْمُقِيمِينَ الصَّلَوٰةَ وَالْمُؤْتُونَ الزَّكَوٰةَ وَالْمُؤْمِنُونَ بِاللَّهِ وَالْيَوْمِ الْآخِرِ أُوْلَٰئِكَ سَنُؤْتِيهِمْ أَجْرًا عَظِيمًا ﴿١٦٢﴾

163   Lo! We inspire thee as We inspired Noah and the prophets after him, as We inspired Abraham and Ishmael and Isaac and Jacob and the tribes, and Jesus and Job and Jonah and Aaron and Solomon, and as we imparted unto David the Psalms;

۞ إِنَّا أَوْحَيْنَا إِلَيْكَ كَمَا أَوْحَيْنَا إِلَىٰ نُوحٍ وَالنَّبِيِّـۧنَ مِنۢ بَعْدِهِ وَأَوْحَيْنَا إِلَىٰ إِبْرَٰهِيمَ وَإِسْمَٰعِيلَ وَإِسْحَٰقَ وَيَعْقُوبَ وَالْأَسْبَاطِ وَعِيسَىٰ وَأَيُّوبَ وَيُونُسَ وَهَٰرُونَ وَسُلَيْمَٰنَ وَءَاتَيْنَا دَاوُۥدَ زَبُورًا ﴿١٦٣﴾

164   And messengers We have mentioned unto thee before and messengers We have not mentioned unto thee; and Allah spake directly unto Moses;

وَرُسُلًا قَدْ قَصَصْنَٰهُمْ عَلَيْكَ مِن قَبْلُ وَرُسُلًا لَّمْ نَقْصُصْهُمْ عَلَيْكَ وَكَلَّمَ اللَّهُ مُوسَىٰ تَكْلِيمًا ﴿١٦٤﴾

165   Messengers of good cheer
and of warning, in order that mankind might have no argument against Allah after the messengers.
Allah is ever Mighty, Wise.

رُسُلًا مُّبَشِّرِينَ وَمُنذِرِينَ لِئَلَّا يَكُونَ لِلنَّاسِ
عَلَى اللَّهِ حُجَّةٌۢ بَعْدَ الرُّسُلِ وَكَانَ اللَّهُ عَزِيزًا
حَكِيمًا ۝

166   But Allah (Himself) testi-
fieth concerning that which He hath
revealed unto thee; in His knowledge hath He revealed it; and the
Angels also testify. And Allah is
sufficient witness.

لَّٰكِنِ اللَّهُ يَشْهَدُ بِمَآ أَنزَلَ إِلَيْكَ أَنزَلَهُ
بِعِلْمِهِ وَالْمَلَٰٓئِكَةُ يَشْهَدُونَ وَكَفَىٰ
بِاللَّهِ شَهِيدًا ۝

167   Lo! those who disbelieve
and hinder (others) from the way of
Allah, they verily have wandered
far astray.

إِنَّ الَّذِينَ كَفَرُوا وَصَدُّوا عَن سَبِيلِ اللَّهِ قَدْ
ضَلُّوا ضَلَٰلًۢا بَعِيدًا ۝

168   Lo! those who disbelieve
and deal in wrong, Allah will never
forgive them, neither will He guide
them unto a road.

إِنَّ الَّذِينَ كَفَرُوا وَظَلَمُوا لَمْ يَكُنِ اللَّهُ لِيَغْفِرَ
لَهُمْ وَلَا لِيَهْدِيَهُمْ طَرِيقًا ۝

169   Except the road of hell,
wherein they will abide forever.
And that is ever easy for Allah.

إِلَّا طَرِيقَ جَهَنَّمَ خَٰلِدِينَ فِيهَآ أَبَدًا وَكَانَ ذَٰلِكَ
عَلَى اللَّهِ يَسِيرًا ۝

170   O mankind! The messenger
hath come unto you with the truth
from your Lord. Therefor believe;
(it is) better for you. But if ye disbelieve, still, lo! unto Allah belongeth whatsoever is in the heavens
and the earth. Allah is ever Knower, Wise.

يَٰٓأَيُّهَا النَّاسُ قَدْ جَآءَكُمُ الرَّسُولُ بِالْحَقِّ
مِن رَّبِّكُمْ فَـَٔامِنُوا خَيْرًا لَّكُمْ وَإِن تَكْفُرُوا
فَإِنَّ لِلَّهِ مَا فِي السَّمَٰوَٰتِ وَالْأَرْضِ وَكَانَ اللَّهُ
عَلِيمًا حَكِيمًا ۝

171   O People of the Scripture!
Do not exaggerate in your religion
nor utter aught concerning Allah
save the truth. The Messiah, Jesus
son of Mary, was only a messenger

يَٰٓأَهْلَ الْكِتَٰبِ لَا تَغْلُوا فِي دِينِكُمْ
وَلَا تَقُولُوا عَلَى اللَّهِ إِلَّا الْحَقَّ إِنَّمَا الْمَسِيحُ
عِيسَى ابْنُ مَرْيَمَ رَسُولُ اللَّهِ وَكَلِمَتُهُ

of Allah, and His word which He
conveyed unto Mary, and a spirit
from Him. So believe in Allah and
His messengers, and say not
"Three". Cease! (it is) better for
you! Allah is only One God. Far is
it removed from His transcendent
majesty that he should have a son.
His is all that is in the heavens and
all that is in the earth. And Allah is
sufficient as Defender.

أَلْقَاهَا إِلَىٰ مَرْيَمَ وَرُوحٌ مِّنْهُ ۖ فَآمِنُوا بِاللَّهِ
وَرُسُلِهِ ۖ وَلَا تَقُولُوا ثَلَاثَةٌ ۚ انتَهُوا خَيْرًا
لَّكُمْ ۚ إِنَّمَا اللَّهُ إِلَٰهٌ وَاحِدٌ ۖ سُبْحَانَهُ أَن
يَكُونَ لَهُ وَلَدٌ ۘ لَّهُ مَا فِي السَّمَاوَاتِ
وَمَا فِي الْأَرْضِ ۗ وَكَفَىٰ بِاللَّهِ وَكِيلًا ﴿١٧١﴾

172   The Messiah will never
scorn to be a slave unto Allah, nor
will the favoured angels. Whoso
scorneth His service and is proud,
all such will He assemble unto
Him;

لَّن يَسْتَنكِفَ الْمَسِيحُ أَن يَكُونَ عَبْدًا
لِّلَّهِ وَلَا الْمَلَائِكَةُ الْمُقَرَّبُونَ ۚ وَمَن يَسْتَنكِفْ
عَنْ عِبَادَتِهِ وَيَسْتَكْبِرْ فَسَيَحْشُرُهُمْ
إِلَيْهِ جَمِيعًا ﴿١٧٢﴾

173   Then, as for those who believed and did good works, unto
them will He pay their wages in
full, adding unto them of His bounty; and as for those who were
scornful and proud, them will He
punish with a painful doom. And
they will not find for them, against
Allah, any protecting friend or
helper.

فَأَمَّا الَّذِينَ آمَنُوا وَعَمِلُوا الصَّالِحَاتِ
فَيُوَفِّيهِمْ أُجُورَهُمْ وَيَزِيدُهُم مِّن فَضْلِهِ ۖ
وَأَمَّا الَّذِينَ اسْتَنكَفُوا وَاسْتَكْبَرُوا
فَيُعَذِّبُهُمْ عَذَابًا أَلِيمًا وَلَا يَجِدُونَ لَهُم
مِّن دُونِ اللَّهِ وَلِيًّا وَلَا نَصِيرًا ﴿١٧٣﴾

174   O mankind! Now hath a
proof from your Lord come unto
you, and We have sent down unto
you a clear light;

يَا أَيُّهَا النَّاسُ قَدْ جَاءَكُم بُرْهَانٌ مِّن رَّبِّكُمْ
وَأَنزَلْنَا إِلَيْكُمْ نُورًا مُّبِينًا ﴿١٧٤﴾

175   As for those who believe in
Allah, and hold fast unto Him, them
He will cause to enter into His
mercy and grace, and will guide
them unto Him by a straight road.

فَأَمَّا الَّذِينَ آمَنُوا بِاللَّهِ وَاعْتَصَمُوا بِهِ
فَسَيُدْخِلُهُمْ فِي رَحْمَةٍ مِّنْهُ وَفَضْلٍ وَيَهْدِيهِمْ
إِلَيْهِ صِرَاطًا مُّسْتَقِيمًا ﴿١٧٥﴾

176   They ask thee for a pronouncement. Say: Allah hath pronounced for you concerning distant kindred. If a man die childless and he have a sister, hers is half the heritage, and he would have inherited from her had she died childless. And if there be two sisters, then theirs are two-thirds of the heritage, and if they be brethren, men and women, unto the male is the equivalent of the share of two females. Allah expoundeth unto you, so that ye err not. Allah is Knower of all things.

يَسْتَفْتُونَكَ قُلِ اللَّهُ يُفْتِيكُمْ فِي الْكَلَالَةِ
إِنِ امْرُؤٌا هَلَكَ لَيْسَ لَهُ وَلَدٌ وَلَهُ أُخْتٌ فَلَهَا
نِصْفُ مَا تَرَكَ وَهُوَ يَرِثُهَا إِنْ لَمْ يَكُنْ لَهَا
وَلَدٌ فَإِنْ كَانَتَا اثْنَتَيْنِ فَلَهُمَا الثُّلُثَانِ مِمَّا تَرَكَ
وَإِنْ كَانُوا إِخْوَةً رِجَالًا وَنِسَاءً فَلِلذَّكَرِ مِثْلُ
حَظِّ الْأُنْثَيَيْنِ يُبَيِّنُ اللَّهُ لَكُمْ أَنْ تَضِلُّوا
وَاللَّهُ بِكُلِّ شَيْءٍ عَلِيمٌ ﴿١٧٦﴾

Al Mā'idah
(The Table Spread)

Al Mā'idah, "The Table Spread," derives its name from vv. 112 ff., where it is told how the disciples of Jesus asked that a table spread with food might be sent down from Heaven, and their prayer was granted, a passage in which some have seen an allusion to the Eucharist. Many authorities regard it as the last sūrah in order of revelation, and Rodwell has so placed it in his chronological arrangement; but the claim can only be established in the case of verse 3, which announces the completion of their religion for the Muslims, and the choice for them of Al-Islām (the Surrender to Allah) as their religion. That verse is undoubtedly the latest of the whole Qur'an. It was revealed during the Prophet's last pilgrimage ("The Farewell Pilgrimage," as it is called) to Makkah, and spoken by him in the course of his address to the assembled thousands at 'Arafāt, when all Arabia had embraced Al-Islām, only a little while before his death. It is possible that, as Nöldeke supposes, two other verses near to it are of the same date, but the remainder of the revelations contained in this sūrah belong rather to the period between the fourth and seventh years of the Hijrah. Its subject is observance of religious duties. The followers of former prophets had failed through breaking their covenant, and so the Muslims are adjured to keep their covenant with God and all their obligations watchfully, because God's covenant is only with those who do right. There is more mention of the Christians here than in the former sūrahs, from which some writers infer that this sūrah must have been revealed at the time when the Prophet was at war with certain Christian tribes belonging to the Eastern Roman Empire. But there is no evidence for that either in Tradition or in the text itself.

The period of revelation is between the fifth and tenth years of the Hijrah.

In the name of Allah, the Beneficent, the Merciful.

1 O ye who believe! Fulfil your undertakings. The beast of cattle is made lawful unto you (for food) except that which is announced unto you (herein), game being unlawful when ye are on pilgrimage. Lo! Allah ordaineth that which pleaseth Him.

2 O ye who believe! Profane not Allah's monuments, nor the Sacred Month, nor the offerings, nor the collared (animals of sacrifice), nor those repairing to the Sacred House,[1] seeking the grace and pleasure of Allah. But when ye have left the sacred territory, then go hunting (if ye will). And let not your hatred of a folk who (once) stopped your going to the Inviolable Place of Worship seduce you to transgress; but help ye one another unto righteousness and pious duty. Help not one another unto sin and transgression, but keep your duty to Allah. Lo! Allah is severe in punishment.

---

1. *i.e.* the Ka'bah at Makkah.

3 Forbidden unto you (for food) are carrion and blood and swine-flesh, and that which hath been dedicated unto any other than Allah, and the strangled, and the dead through beating, and the dead through falling from a height, and that which hath been killed by (the goring of) horns, and the devoured of wild beasts, saving that which ye make lawful (by the death-stroke), and that which hath been immolated unto idols. And (forbidden is it) that ye apportion by the divining arrows. This is an abomination. This day are those who disbelieve in despair of (ever harming) your religion; so fear them not, fear Me! This day have I perfected your religion for you and completed My favour unto you, and have chosen for you as religion AL-ISLĀM.[2] Whoso is forced by hunger, not by will, to sin: (for him) lo! Allah is Forgiving, Merciful.

حُرِّمَتْ عَلَيْكُمُ ٱلْمَيْتَةُ وَٱلدَّمُ وَلَحْمُ ٱلْخِنزِيرِ وَمَآ أُهِلَّ لِغَيْرِ ٱللَّهِ بِهِۦ وَٱلْمُنْخَنِقَةُ وَٱلْمَوْقُوذَةُ وَٱلْمُتَرَدِّيَةُ وَٱلنَّطِيحَةُ وَمَآ أَكَلَ ٱلسَّبُعُ إِلَّا مَا ذَكَّيْتُمْ وَمَا ذُبِحَ عَلَى ٱلنُّصُبِ وَأَن تَسْتَقْسِمُوا۟ بِٱلْأَزْلَٰمِ ذَٰلِكُمْ فِسْقٌ ٱلْيَوْمَ يَئِسَ ٱلَّذِينَ كَفَرُوا۟ مِن دِينِكُمْ فَلَا تَخْشَوْهُمْ وَٱخْشَوْنِ ٱلْيَوْمَ أَكْمَلْتُ لَكُمْ دِينَكُمْ وَأَتْمَمْتُ عَلَيْكُمْ نِعْمَتِى وَرَضِيتُ لَكُمُ ٱلْإِسْلَٰمَ دِينًا فَمَنِ ٱضْطُرَّ فِى مَخْمَصَةٍ غَيْرَ مُتَجَانِفٍ لِّإِثْمٍ فَإِنَّ ٱللَّهَ غَفُورٌ رَّحِيمٌ ۝٣

4 They ask thee (O Muḥammad) what is made lawful for them. Say: (all) good things are made lawful for you. And those beasts and birds of prey which ye have trained as hounds are trained, ye teach them that which Allah taught you; so eat of that which they catch for you

يَسْـَٔلُونَكَ مَاذَآ أُحِلَّ لَهُمْ قُلْ أُحِلَّ لَكُمُ ٱلطَّيِّبَٰتُ وَمَا عَلَّمْتُم مِّنَ ٱلْجَوَارِحِ مُكَلِّبِينَ تُعَلِّمُونَهُنَّ مِمَّا عَلَّمَكُمُ ٱللَّهُ فَكُلُوا۟ مِمَّآ أَمْسَكْنَ عَلَيْكُمْ وَٱذْكُرُوا۟ ٱسْمَ

---

2. *i.e.* "The Surrender" to Allah. Thus solemnly the religion which the Prophet had established received its name.

اللَّهِ عَلَيْهِ وَاتَّقُوا اللَّهَ إِنَّ اللَّهَ سَرِيعُ الْحِسَابِ ۞

and mention Allah's name upon it,
and observe your duty to Allah. Lo!
Allah is swift to take account.

5 This day are (all) good things
made lawful for you. The food of
those who have received the Scripture is lawful for you, and your
food is lawful for them. And so are
the virtuous women of the believers
and the virtuous women of those
who received the Scripture before
you (lawful for you) when ye give
them their marriage portions and
live with them in honour, not in
fornication, nor taking them as
secret concubines. Whoso denieth
the faith, his work is vain and he
will be among the losers in the
Hereafter.

الْيَوْمَ أُحِلَّ لَكُمُ الطَّيِّبَاتُ وَطَعَامُ الَّذِينَ أُوتُوا
الْكِتَابَ حِلٌّ لَكُمْ وَطَعَامُكُمْ حِلٌّ لَهُمْ وَالْمُحْصَنَاتُ
مِنَ الْمُؤْمِنَاتِ وَالْمُحْصَنَاتُ مِنَ الَّذِينَ أُوتُوا الْكِتَابَ
مِن قَبْلِكُمْ إِذَا آتَيْتُمُوهُنَّ أُجُورَهُنَّ مُحْصِنِينَ
غَيْرَ مُسَافِحِينَ وَلَا مُتَّخِذِي أَخْدَانٍ وَمَن يَكْفُرْ
بِالْإِيمَانِ فَقَدْ حَبِطَ عَمَلُهُ وَهُوَ فِي
الْآخِرَةِ مِنَ الْخَاسِرِينَ ۞

6 O ye who believe! When ye rise
up for prayer, wash your faces, and
your hands up to the elbows, and
lightly rub your heads and (wash)
your feet up to the ankles. And if
ye are unclean, purify yourselves.
And if ye are sick or on a journey,
or one of you cometh from the
closet, or ye have had contact with
women, and ye find not water, then
go to clean, high ground and rub
your faces and your hands with
some of it. Allah doth not wish to
place a burden on you, but He
wishes to purify you and would
perfect His grace upon you, that ye
may give thanks.

يَا أَيُّهَا الَّذِينَ آمَنُوا إِذَا قُمْتُمْ إِلَى الصَّلَوٰةِ
فَاغْسِلُوا وُجُوهَكُمْ وَأَيْدِيَكُمْ إِلَى الْمَرَافِقِ
وَامْسَحُوا بِرُءُوسِكُمْ وَأَرْجُلَكُمْ إِلَى
الْكَعْبَيْنِ وَإِن كُنتُمْ جُنُبًا فَاطَّهَّرُوا وَإِن كُنتُم
مَّرْضَى أَوْ عَلَى سَفَرٍ أَوْ جَاءَ أَحَدٌ مِّنكُم مِّنَ الْغَائِطِ
أَوْ لَامَسْتُمُ النِّسَاءَ فَلَمْ تَجِدُوا مَاءً فَتَيَمَّمُوا
صَعِيدًا طَيِّبًا فَامْسَحُوا بِوُجُوهِكُمْ
وَأَيْدِيكُم مِّنْهُ مَا يُرِيدُ اللَّهُ لِيَجْعَلَ
عَلَيْكُم مِّنْ حَرَجٍ وَلَٰكِن يُرِيدُ لِيُطَهِّرَكُمْ
وَلِيُتِمَّ نِعْمَتَهُ عَلَيْكُمْ لَعَلَّكُمْ
تَشْكُرُونَ ۞

7 Remember Allah's grace upon you and His covenant by which He bound you when ye said: We hear and we obey; and keep your duty to Allah. Lo! Allah knoweth what is in the breasts (of men).

8 O ye who believe! Be steadfast witnesses for Allah in equity, and let not hatred of any people seduce you that ye deal not justly. Deal justly, that is nearer to your duty. Observe your duty to Allah. Lo! Allah is Aware of what you do.

9 Allah hath promised those who believe and do good works: Theirs will be forgiveness and immense reward.

10 And they who disbelieve and deny Our revelations, such are rightful owners of hell.

11 O ye who believe! Remember Allah's favour unto you, how a people were minded to stretch out their hands against you but He withheld their hands from you; and keep your duty to Allah. In Allah let believers put their trust.

12 Allah made a covenant of old with the Children of Israel and We raised among them twelve chieftains, and Allah said: Lo! I am with you. If ye establish worship and pay the poor due, and believe in My messengers and support them,

وَاذْكُرُوا نِعْمَةَ اللّٰهِ عَلَيْكُمْ وَمِيثَاقَهُ الَّذِى وَاثَقَكُمْ بِهِ إِذْ قُلْتُمْ سَمِعْنَا وَأَطَعْنَا وَاتَّقُوا اللّٰهَ إِنَّ اللّٰهَ عَلِيمٌ بِذَاتِ الصُّدُورِ ٧

يَا أَيُّهَا الَّذِينَ ءَامَنُوا كُونُوا قَوّٰمِينَ لِلّٰهِ شُهَدَآءَ بِالْقِسْطِ وَلَا يَجْرِمَنَّكُمْ شَنَآنُ قَوْمٍ عَلَى أَلَّا تَعْدِلُوا اعْدِلُوا هُوَ أَقْرَبُ لِلتَّقْوٰى وَاتَّقُوا اللّٰهَ إِنَّ اللّٰهَ خَبِيرٌ بِمَا تَعْمَلُونَ ٨

وَعَدَ اللّٰهُ الَّذِينَ ءَامَنُوا وَعَمِلُوا الصّٰلِحٰتِ لَهُمْ مَغْفِرَةٌ وَأَجْرٌ عَظِيمٌ ٩

وَالَّذِينَ كَفَرُوا وَكَذَّبُوا بِآيٰتِنَا أُولَٰئِكَ أَصْحٰبُ الْجَحِيمِ ١٠

يَا أَيُّهَا الَّذِينَ ءَامَنُوا اذْكُرُوا نِعْمَتَ اللّٰهِ عَلَيْكُمْ إِذْ هَمَّ قَوْمٌ أَن يَبْسُطُوا إِلَيْكُمْ أَيْدِيَهُمْ فَكَفَّ أَيْدِيَهُمْ عَنكُمْ وَاتَّقُوا اللّٰهَ وَعَلَى اللّٰهِ فَلْيَتَوَكَّلِ الْمُؤْمِنُونَ ١١

۞ وَلَقَدْ أَخَذَ اللّٰهُ مِيثَاقَ بَنِى إِسْرَٰئِيلَ وَبَعَثْنَا مِنْهُمُ اثْنَىْ عَشَرَ نَقِيبًا وَقَالَ اللّٰهُ إِنِّى مَعَكُمْ لَئِنْ أَقَمْتُمُ الصَّلَوٰةَ وَءَاتَيْتُمُ الزَّكَوٰةَ وَءَامَنتُم بِرُسُلِى وَعَزَّرْتُمُوهُمْ

and lend unto Allah a kindly loan,[3] surely I shall remit your sins, and surely I shall bring you into gardens underneath which rivers flow. Whoso among you disbelieveth after this will go astray from a plain road.

وَأَقْرَضْتُمُ ٱللَّهَ قَرْضًا حَسَنًا لَّأُكَفِّرَنَّ عَنكُمْ سَيِّئَاتِكُمْ وَلَأُدْخِلَنَّكُمْ جَنَّٰتٍ تَجْرِى مِن تَحْتِهَا ٱلْأَنْهَٰرُ فَمَن كَفَرَ بَعْدَ ذَٰلِكَ مِنكُمْ فَقَدْ ضَلَّ سَوَآءَ ٱلسَّبِيلِ ۝

13 And because of their breaking their covenant, We have cursed them and made hard their hearts. They change words from their context and forget a part of that whereof they were admonished. Thou wilt not cease to discover treachery from all, save a few of them. But bear with them and pardon them. Lo! Allah loveth the kindly.

فَبِمَا نَقْضِهِم مِّيثَٰقَهُمْ لَعَنَّٰهُمْ وَجَعَلْنَا قُلُوبَهُمْ قَٰسِيَةً يُحَرِّفُونَ ٱلْكَلِمَ عَن مَّوَاضِعِهِۦ وَنَسُوا۟ حَظًّا مِّمَّا ذُكِّرُوا۟ بِهِۦ وَلَا تَزَالُ تَطَّلِعُ عَلَىٰ خَآئِنَةٍ مِّنْهُمْ إِلَّا قَلِيلًا مِّنْهُمْ فَٱعْفُ عَنْهُمْ وَٱصْفَحْ إِنَّ ٱللَّهَ يُحِبُّ ٱلْمُحْسِنِينَ ۝

14 And with those who say: "Lo! we are Christians," We made a covenant, but they forgot a part of that whereof they were admonished. Therefore We have stirred up enmity and hatred among them till the Day of Resurrection, when Allah will inform them of their handiwork.

وَمِنَ ٱلَّذِينَ قَالُوٓا۟ إِنَّا نَصَٰرَىٰٓ أَخَذْنَا مِيثَٰقَهُمْ فَنَسُوا۟ حَظًّا مِّمَّا ذُكِّرُوا۟ بِهِۦ فَأَغْرَيْنَا بَيْنَهُمُ ٱلْعَدَاوَةَ وَٱلْبَغْضَآءَ إِلَىٰ يَوْمِ ٱلْقِيَٰمَةِ وَسَوْفَ يُنَبِّئُهُمُ ٱللَّهُ بِمَا كَانُوا۟ يَصْنَعُونَ ۝

15 O people of the Scripture! Now hath Our messenger come unto you, expounding unto you much of that which ye used to hide in the Scripture, and forgiving much. Now hath come unto you light from Allah and a plain Scripture;

يَٰٓأَهْلَ ٱلْكِتَٰبِ قَدْ جَآءَكُمْ رَسُولُنَا يُبَيِّنُ لَكُمْ كَثِيرًا مِّمَّا كُنتُمْ تُخْفُونَ مِنَ ٱلْكِتَٰبِ وَيَعْفُوا۟ عَن كَثِيرٍ قَدْ جَآءَكُم مِّنَ ٱللَّهِ نُورٌ وَكِتَٰبٌ مُّبِينٌ ۝

---

3. *i.e.* a loan without interest or thought of gain.

16 Whereby Allah guideth him who seeketh His good pleasure unto paths of peace. He bringeth them out of darkness unto light by His decree, and guideth them unto a straight path.

يَهْدِي بِهِ اللَّهُ مَنِ اتَّبَعَ رِضْوَانَهُ سُبُلَ السَّلَامِ وَيُخْرِجُهُم مِّنَ الظُّلُمَاتِ إِلَى النُّورِ بِإِذْنِهِ وَيَهْدِيهِمْ إِلَى صِرَاطٍ مُّسْتَقِيمٍ ۝

17 They indeed have disbelieved who say: Lo! Allah is the Messiah, son of Mary. Say: Who then can do aught against Allah, if He had willed to destroy the Messiah son of Mary, and his mother and everyone on earth? Allah's is the Sovereignty of the heavens and the earth and all that is between them. He createth what He will. And Allah is Able to do all things.

لَّقَدْ كَفَرَ الَّذِينَ قَالُوا إِنَّ اللَّهَ هُوَ الْمَسِيحُ ابْنُ مَرْيَمَ قُلْ فَمَن يَمْلِكُ مِنَ اللَّهِ شَيْئًا إِنْ أَرَادَ أَن يُهْلِكَ الْمَسِيحَ ابْنَ مَرْيَمَ وَأُمَّهُ وَمَن فِي الْأَرْضِ جَمِيعًا وَلِلَّهِ مُلْكُ السَّمَاوَاتِ وَالْأَرْضِ وَمَا بَيْنَهُمَا يَخْلُقُ مَا يَشَاءُ وَاللَّهُ عَلَى كُلِّ شَيْءٍ قَدِيرٌ ۝

18 The Jews and Christians say: We are sons of Allah and His loved ones. Say; Why then doth He chastise you for your sins? Nay, ye are but mortals of His creating. He forgiveth whom He will, and chastiseth whom He will. Allah's is the Sovereignty of the heavens and the earth and all that is between them, and unto Him is the journeying.

وَقَالَتِ الْيَهُودُ وَالنَّصَارَى نَحْنُ أَبْنَاءُ اللَّهِ وَأَحِبَّاؤُهُ قُلْ فَلِمَ يُعَذِّبُكُم بِذُنُوبِكُم بَلْ أَنتُم بَشَرٌ مِّمَّنْ خَلَقَ يَغْفِرُ لِمَن يَشَاءُ وَيُعَذِّبُ مَن يَشَاءُ وَلِلَّهِ مُلْكُ السَّمَاوَاتِ وَالْأَرْضِ وَمَا بَيْنَهُمَا وَإِلَيْهِ الْمَصِيرُ ۝

19 O people of the Scripture! Now hath Our messenger come unto you to make things plain unto you after an interval (of cessation) of the messengers, lest ye should say: There came not unto us a messenger of cheer nor any warner. Now hath a messenger of cheer and a warner come unto you. Allah is Able to do all things.

يَا أَهْلَ الْكِتَابِ قَدْ جَاءَكُمْ رَسُولُنَا يُبَيِّنُ لَكُمْ عَلَى فَتْرَةٍ مِّنَ الرُّسُلِ أَن تَقُولُوا مَا جَاءَنَا مِن بَشِيرٍ وَلَا نَذِيرٍ فَقَدْ جَاءَكُم بَشِيرٌ وَنَذِيرٌ وَاللَّهُ عَلَى كُلِّ شَيْءٍ قَدِيرٌ ۝

20 And (remember) when Moses said unto his people: O my people! Remember Allah's favour unto you, how He placed among you Prophets, and He made you Kings, and gave you that (which) He gave not to any (other) of (His) creatures.

وَإِذْ قَالَ مُوسَىٰ لِقَوْمِهِ يَٰقَوْمِ اذْكُرُوا نِعْمَةَ اللَّهِ عَلَيْكُمْ إِذْ جَعَلَ فِيكُمْ أَنۢبِيَآءَ وَجَعَلَكُم مُّلُوكًا وَءَاتَىٰكُم مَّا لَمْ يُؤْتِ أَحَدًا مِّنَ ٱلْعَٰلَمِينَ ﴿٢٠﴾

21 O my people! Go into the holy land which Allah hath ordained for you. Turn not in flight, for surely ye turn back as losers:

يَٰقَوْمِ ادْخُلُوا ٱلْأَرْضَ ٱلْمُقَدَّسَةَ ٱلَّتِي كَتَبَ ٱللَّهُ لَكُمْ وَلَا تَرْتَدُّوا عَلَىٰٓ أَدْبَارِكُمْ فَتَنقَلِبُوا خَٰسِرِينَ ﴿٢١﴾

22 They said: O Moses! Lo! a giant people (dwell) therein, and lo! we go not in till they go forth from thence. When they go forth from thence, then we will enter (not till then).

قَالُوا يَٰمُوسَىٰٓ إِنَّ فِيهَا قَوْمًا جَبَّارِينَ وَإِنَّا لَن نَّدْخُلَهَا حَتَّىٰ يَخْرُجُوا مِنْهَا فَإِن يَخْرُجُوا مِنْهَا فَإِنَّا دَٰخِلُونَ ﴿٢٢﴾

23 Then outspake two of those who feared (their Lord, men) unto whom Allah had been gracious: Enter in upon them by the gate, for if ye enter by it, lo! ye will be victorious. So put your trust (in Allah) if ye are indeed believers.

قَالَ رَجُلَانِ مِنَ ٱلَّذِينَ يَخَافُونَ أَنْعَمَ ٱللَّهُ عَلَيْهِمَا ادْخُلُوا عَلَيْهِمُ ٱلْبَابَ فَإِذَا دَخَلْتُمُوهُ فَإِنَّكُمْ غَٰلِبُونَ وَعَلَى ٱللَّهِ فَتَوَكَّلُوٓا إِن كُنتُم مُّؤْمِنِينَ ﴿٢٣﴾

24 They said: O Moses! We will never enter (the land) while they are in it. So go thou and thy Lord and fight! We will sit here.

قَالُوا يَٰمُوسَىٰٓ إِنَّا لَن نَّدْخُلَهَآ أَبَدًا مَّا دَامُوا فِيهَا فَاذْهَبْ أَنتَ وَرَبُّكَ فَقَٰتِلَآ إِنَّا هَٰهُنَا قَٰعِدُونَ ﴿٢٤﴾

25 He said: My Lord! I have control of none but myself and my brother, so distinguish between us and the wrongdoing folk.

قَالَ رَبِّ إِنِّي لَآ أَمْلِكُ إِلَّا نَفْسِي وَأَخِي فَٱفْرُقْ بَيْنَنَا وَبَيْنَ ٱلْقَوْمِ ٱلْفَٰسِقِينَ ﴿٢٥﴾

26 (Their Lord) said: For this the land will surely be forbidden them for forty years that they will wan-

قَالَ فَإِنَّهَا مُحَرَّمَةٌ عَلَيْهِمْ أَرْبَعِينَ سَنَةً

der in the earth, bewildered. So grieve not over the wrongdoing folk.

27 But recite unto them with truth the tale of the two sons of Adam, how they offered each a sacrifice, and it was accepted from the one of them and it was not accepted from the other. (The one) said: I will surely kill thee. (The other) answered: Allah accepteth only from those who ward off (evil).

28 Even if thou stretch out thy hand against me to kill me, I shall not stretch out my hand against thee to kill thee, lo! I fear Allah, the Lord of the Worlds.

29 Lo! I would rather thou shouldst bear the punishment of the sin against me and thine own sin and become one of the owners of the Fire. That is the reward of evil doers.

30 But (the other's) mind imposed on him the killing of his brother, so he slew him and became one of the losers.

31 Then Allah sent a raven scratching up the ground, to show him how to hide his brother's naked corpse. He said: Woe unto me! Am I not able to be as this raven and so hide my brother's naked corpse? And he became repentant.

بَيْتِهُونَ فِى ٱلْأَرْضِ فَلَا تَأْسَ عَلَى ٱلْقَوْمِ ٱلْفَٰسِقِينَ ۝

۞ وَٱتْلُ عَلَيْهِمْ نَبَأَ ٱبْنَىْ ءَادَمَ بِٱلْحَقِّ إِذْ قَرَّبَا قُرْبَانًا فَتُقُبِّلَ مِنْ أَحَدِهِمَا وَلَمْ يُتَقَبَّلْ مِنَ ٱلْءَاخَرِ قَالَ لَأَقْتُلَنَّكَ قَالَ إِنَّمَا يَتَقَبَّلُ ٱللَّهُ مِنَ ٱلْمُتَّقِينَ ۝

لَئِنۢ بَسَطتَ إِلَىَّ يَدَكَ لِتَقْتُلَنِى مَآ أَنَا۠ بِبَاسِطٍ يَدِىَ إِلَيْكَ لِأَقْتُلَكَ إِنِّىٓ أَخَافُ ٱللَّهَ رَبَّ ٱلْعَٰلَمِينَ ۝

إِنِّىٓ أُرِيدُ أَن تَبُوٓأَ بِإِثْمِى وَإِثْمِكَ فَتَكُونَ مِنْ أَصْحَٰبِ ٱلنَّارِ وَذَٰلِكَ جَزَٰٓؤُا۟ ٱلظَّٰلِمِينَ ۝

فَطَوَّعَتْ لَهُۥ نَفْسُهُۥ قَتْلَ أَخِيهِ فَقَتَلَهُۥ فَأَصْبَحَ مِنَ ٱلْخَٰسِرِينَ ۝

فَبَعَثَ ٱللَّهُ غُرَابًا يَبْحَثُ فِى ٱلْأَرْضِ لِيُرِيَهُۥ كَيْفَ يُوَٰرِى سَوْءَةَ أَخِيهِ قَالَ يَٰوَيْلَتَىٰٓ أَعَجَزْتُ أَنْ أَكُونَ مِثْلَ هَٰذَا ٱلْغُرَابِ فَأُوَٰرِىَ سَوْءَةَ أَخِى فَأَصْبَحَ مِنَ ٱلنَّٰدِمِينَ ۝

32 For that cause We decreed for the Children of Israel that whosoever killeth a human being for other than manslaughter or corruption in the earth, it shall be as if be had killed all mankind, and whoso saveth the life of one, it shall be as if he had saved the life of all mankind. Our messengers came unto them of old with clear proofs (of Allah's sovereignty), but afterwards lo! many of them became prodigals in the earth.

مِنْ أَجْلِ ذٰلِكَ كَتَبْنَا عَلٰى بَنِىٓ إِسْرَآءِيلَ أَنَّهُۥ مَنْ قَتَلَ نَفْسًۢا بِغَيْرِ نَفْسٍ أَوْ فَسَادٍ فِى ٱلْأَرْضِ فَكَأَنَّمَا قَتَلَ ٱلنَّاسَ جَمِيعًا وَمَنْ أَحْيَاهَا فَكَأَنَّمَآ أَحْيَا ٱلنَّاسَ جَمِيعًا وَلَقَدْ جَآءَتْهُمْ رُسُلُنَا بِٱلْبَيِّنَٰتِ ثُمَّ إِنَّ كَثِيرًا مِّنْهُم بَعْدَ ذٰلِكَ فِى ٱلْأَرْضِ لَمُسْرِفُونَ ۝

33 The only reward of those who make war upon Allah and His messenger and strive after corruption in the land will be that they will be killed or crucified, or have their hands and feet on alternate sides cut off, or will be expelled out of the land. Such will be their degradation in the world, and in the Hereafter theirs will be an awful doom;

إِنَّمَا جَزٰٓؤُا۟ ٱلَّذِينَ يُحَارِبُونَ ٱللَّهَ وَرَسُولَهُۥ وَيَسْعَوْنَ فِى ٱلْأَرْضِ فَسَادًا أَن يُقَتَّلُوٓا۟ أَوْ يُصَلَّبُوٓا۟ أَوْ تُقَطَّعَ أَيْدِيهِمْ وَأَرْجُلُهُم مِّنْ خِلَٰفٍ أَوْ يُنفَوْا۟ مِنَ ٱلْأَرْضِ ذٰلِكَ لَهُمْ خِزْىٌ فِى ٱلدُّنْيَا وَلَهُمْ فِى ٱلْءَاخِرَةِ عَذَابٌ عَظِيمٌ ۝

34 Save those who repent before ye overpower them. For know that Allah is Forgiving, Merciful.

إِلَّا ٱلَّذِينَ تَابُوا۟ مِن قَبْلِ أَن تَقْدِرُوا۟ عَلَيْهِمْ فَٱعْلَمُوٓا۟ أَنَّ ٱللَّهَ غَفُورٌ رَّحِيمٌ ۝

35 O ye who believe! Be mindful of your duty to Allah, and seek the way of approach unto Him, and strive in His way in order that ye may succeed.

يَٰٓأَيُّهَا ٱلَّذِينَ ءَامَنُوا۟ ٱتَّقُوا۟ ٱللَّهَ وَٱبْتَغُوٓا۟ إِلَيْهِ ٱلْوَسِيلَةَ وَجَٰهِدُوا۟ فِى سَبِيلِهِۦ لَعَلَّكُمْ تُفْلِحُونَ ۝

36 As for those who disbelieve, lo! if all that is in the earth were theirs, and as much again therewith, to ransom them from the doom on the Day of Resurrection, it would not be accepted from them. Theirs will be a painful doom.

إِنَّ ٱلَّذِينَ كَفَرُوا۟ لَوْ أَنَّ لَهُم مَّا فِى ٱلْأَرْضِ جَمِيعًا وَمِثْلَهُۥ مَعَهُۥ لِيَفْتَدُوا۟ بِهِۦ مِنْ عَذَابِ يَوْمِ ٱلْقِيَٰمَةِ مَا تُقُبِّلَ مِنْهُمْ وَلَهُمْ عَذَابٌ أَلِيمٌ ۝

37 They will wish to come forth from the Fire, but they will not come forth from it. Theirs will be a lasting doom.

وَيُرِيدُونَ أَن يَخْرُجُوا مِنَ النَّارِ وَمَا هُم بِخَارِجِينَ مِنْهَا وَلَهُمْ عَذَابٌ مُّقِيمٌ ۝

38 As for the thief, both male and female, cut off their hands. It is the reward of their own deeds, an exemplary punishment from Allah. Allah is Mighty, Wise.

وَالسَّارِقُ وَالسَّارِقَةُ فَاقْطَعُوا أَيْدِيَهُمَا جَزَآءً بِمَا كَسَبَا نَكَالًا مِّنَ اللَّهِ وَاللَّهُ عَزِيزٌ حَكِيمٌ ۝

39 But whoso repenteth after his wrongdoing and amendeth, lo! Allah will relent toward him. Lo! Allah is Forgiving, Merciful.

فَمَن تَابَ مِنۢ بَعْدِ ظُلْمِهِ وَأَصْلَحَ فَإِنَّ اللَّهَ يَتُوبُ عَلَيْهِ إِنَّ اللَّهَ غَفُورٌ رَّحِيمٌ ۝

40 Knowest thou not that unto Allah belongeth the Sovereignty of the heavens and the earth? He punisheth whom He will, and forgiveth whom He will. Allah is Able to do all things.

أَلَمْ تَعْلَمْ أَنَّ اللَّهَ لَهُ مُلْكُ السَّمَوَاتِ وَالْأَرْضِ يُعَذِّبُ مَن يَشَآءُ وَيَغْفِرُ لِمَن يَشَآءُ وَاللَّهُ عَلَىٰ كُلِّ شَيْءٍ قَدِيرٌ ۝

41 O Messenger! Let not them grieve thee who vie one with another in the race to disbelief, of such as say with their mouths: "We believe," but their hearts believe not, and of the Jews: listeners for the sake of falsehood, listeners on behalf of other folk who come not unto thee, changing words from their context and saying: If this be given unto you, receive it, but if this be not given unto you, then beware! He whom Allah doometh unto sin, thou (by thine efforts) wilt avail him naught against Allah. Those are they for whom the will of Allah is that, He cleanse not their hearts. Theirs in the world will be ignominy, and in the Hereafter an awful doom;

۞ يَٰٓأَيُّهَا الرَّسُولُ لَا يَحْزُنكَ الَّذِينَ يُسَٰرِعُونَ فِي الْكُفْرِ مِنَ الَّذِينَ قَالُوٓا ءَامَنَّا بِأَفْوَٰهِهِمْ وَلَمْ تُؤْمِن قُلُوبُهُمْ وَمِنَ الَّذِينَ هَادُوا سَمَّٰعُونَ لِلْكَذِبِ سَمَّٰعُونَ لِقَوْمٍ ءَاخَرِينَ لَمْ يَأْتُوكَ يُحَرِّفُونَ الْكَلِمَ مِنۢ بَعْدِ مَوَاضِعِهِ يَقُولُونَ إِنْ أُوتِيتُمْ هَٰذَا فَخُذُوهُ وَإِن لَّمْ تُؤْتَوْهُ فَاحْذَرُوا وَمَن يُرِدِ اللَّهُ فِتْنَتَهُ فَلَن تَمْلِكَ لَهُ مِنَ اللَّهِ شَيْـًٔا أُوْلَٰٓئِكَ الَّذِينَ لَمْ يُرِدِ اللَّهُ أَن يُطَهِّرَ قُلُوبَهُمْ لَهُمْ فِي الدُّنْيَا خِزْيٌ وَلَهُمْ فِي الْآخِرَةِ عَذَابٌ عَظِيمٌ ۝

42 Listeners for the sake of false-hood! Eaters of illicit gain! If then they have recourse unto thee (Muhammad) judge between them or disclaim jurisdiction. If thou disclaimest jurisdiction, then they cannot harm thee at all. But if thou judgest, judge between them with equity. Lo! Allah loveth the equitable.

سَيَّعُوْنَ لِلْكَذِبِ أَكَّلُوْنَ لِلسُّحْتِ
فَإِنْ جَآءُوْكَ فَاحْكُمْ بَيْنَهُمْ أَوْ أَعْرِضْ عَنْهُمْ
وَإِنْ تُعْرِضْ عَنْهُمْ فَلَنْ يَّضُرُّوْكَ شَيْئًا
وَإِنْ حَكَمْتَ فَاحْكُمْ بَيْنَهُمْ بِالْقِسْطِ
إِنَّ اللّٰهَ يُحِبُّ الْمُقْسِطِيْنَ ﴿٤٢﴾

43 How come they unto thee for judgment when they have the Torah, wherein Allah hath delivered judgment (for them)? Yet even after that they turn away. Such (folk) are not believers.

وَكَيْفَ يُحَكِّمُوْنَكَ وَعِنْدَهُمُ التَّوْرٰةُ فِيْهَا حُكْمُ
اللّٰهِ ثُمَّ يَتَوَلَّوْنَ مِنْ بَعْدِ ذٰلِكَ
وَمَا أُولٰٓئِكَ بِالْمُؤْمِنِيْنَ ﴿٤٣﴾

44 Lo! We did reveal the Torah, wherein is guidance and a light, by which the Prophets who surrendered (unto Allah) judged the Jews, and the rabbis and the priests (judged) by such of Allah's Scripture as they were bidden to observe, and thereunto were they witnesses. So fear not mankind, but fear Me. And barter not My revelations for a little gain. Whoso judgeth not by that which Allah hath revealed: such are disbelievers.

إِنَّا أَنْزَلْنَا التَّوْرٰةَ فِيْهَا هُدًى وَّنُوْرٌ يَّحْكُمُ بِهَا
النَّبِيُّوْنَ الَّذِيْنَ أَسْلَمُوْا لِلَّذِيْنَ هَادُوْا
وَالرَّبَّانِيُّوْنَ وَالْأَحْبَارُ بِمَا اسْتُحْفِظُوْا
مِنْ كِتٰبِ اللّٰهِ وَكَانُوْا عَلَيْهِ شُهَدَآءَ فَلَا
تَخْشَوُا النَّاسَ وَاخْشَوْنِ وَلَا تَشْتَرُوْا
بِآيٰتِيْ ثَمَنًا قَلِيْلًا وَمَنْ لَّمْ يَحْكُمْ بِمَا أَنْزَلَ اللّٰهُ
فَأُولٰٓئِكَ هُمُ الْكٰفِرُوْنَ ﴿٤٤﴾

45 And We prescribed for them therein: The life for the life, and the eye for the eye, and the nose for the nose, and the ear for the ear, and the tooth for the tooth, and for wounds; retaliation. But whoso forgoeth it (in the way of charity) it

وَكَتَبْنَا عَلَيْهِمْ فِيْهَا أَنَّ النَّفْسَ بِالنَّفْسِ
وَالْعَيْنَ بِالْعَيْنِ وَالْأَنْفَ بِالْأَنْفِ
وَالْأُذُنَ بِالْأُذُنِ وَالسِّنَّ بِالسِّنِّ وَالْجُرُوْحَ
قِصَاصٌ فَمَنْ تَصَدَّقَ بِهِ فَهُوَ كَفَّارَةٌ

shall be expiation for him. Whoso judgeth not by that which Allah hath revealed: such are wrong-doers.

لَهُۥ وَمَن لَّمۡ يَحۡكُم بِمَآ أَنزَلَ ٱللَّهُ فَأُوْلَٰٓئِكَ هُمُ ٱلظَّٰلِمُونَ ٤٥

46 And We caused Jesus, son of Mary, to follow in their footsteps, confirming that which was (revealed) before him, and We bestowed on him the Gospel wherein is guidance and a light, confirming that which was (revealed) before it in the Torah—a guidance and an admonition unto those who ward off (evil).

وَقَفَّيۡنَا عَلَىٰٓ ءَاثَٰرِهِم بِعِيسَى ٱبۡنِ مَرۡيَمَ مُصَدِّقًا لِّمَا بَيۡنَ يَدَيۡهِ مِنَ ٱلتَّوۡرَىٰةِ وَءَاتَيۡنَٰهُ ٱلۡإِنجِيلَ فِيهِ هُدًى وَنُورٌ وَمُصَدِّقًا لِّمَا بَيۡنَ يَدَيۡهِ مِنَ ٱلتَّوۡرَىٰةِ وَهُدًى وَمَوۡعِظَةً لِّلۡمُتَّقِينَ ٤٦

47 Let the People of the Gospel judge by that which Allah hath revealed therein. Whoso judgeth not by that which Allah hath revealed; such are evil-livers.

وَلۡيَحۡكُمۡ أَهۡلُ ٱلۡإِنجِيلِ بِمَآ أَنزَلَ ٱللَّهُ فِيهِ وَمَن لَّمۡ يَحۡكُم بِمَآ أَنزَلَ ٱللَّهُ فَأُوْلَٰٓئِكَ هُمُ ٱلۡفَٰسِقُونَ ٤٧

48 And unto thee have We revealed the Scripture with the truth, confirming whatever Scripture was before it, and a watcher over it. So judge between them by that which Allah hath revealed, and follow not their desires away from the truth which hath come unto thee. For each We have appointed a divine law and a traced-out way. Had Allah willed He could have made you one community. But that He may try you by that which He hath given you (He hath made you as ye are). So vie one with another in good works. Unto Allah ye will all return, and He will then inform you of that wherein ye differ.

وَأَنزَلۡنَآ إِلَيۡكَ ٱلۡكِتَٰبَ بِٱلۡحَقِّ مُصَدِّقًا لِّمَا بَيۡنَ يَدَيۡهِ مِنَ ٱلۡكِتَٰبِ وَمُهَيۡمِنًا عَلَيۡهِ فَٱحۡكُم بَيۡنَهُم بِمَآ أَنزَلَ ٱللَّهُ وَلَا تَتَّبِعۡ أَهۡوَآءَهُمۡ عَمَّا جَآءَكَ مِنَ ٱلۡحَقِّ لِكُلٍّ جَعَلۡنَا مِنكُمۡ شِرۡعَةً وَمِنۡهَاجًا وَلَوۡ شَآءَ ٱللَّهُ لَجَعَلَكُمۡ أُمَّةً وَٰحِدَةً وَلَٰكِن لِّيَبۡلُوَكُمۡ فِى مَآ ءَاتَىٰكُمۡ فَٱسۡتَبِقُوا۟ ٱلۡخَيۡرَٰتِ إِلَى ٱللَّهِ مَرۡجِعُكُمۡ جَمِيعًا فَيُنَبِّئُكُم بِمَا كُنتُمۡ فِيهِ تَخۡتَلِفُونَ ٤٨

49 So judge between them by that
which Allah hath revealed, and follow not their desires, but beware of
them lest they seduce thee from
some part of that which Allah hath
revealed unto thee. And if they turn
away, then know that Allah's will
is to smite them for some sin of
theirs. Lo! many of mankind are
evil-livers.

وَأَنِ احْكُم بَيْنَهُم بِمَا أَنزَلَ ٱللَّهُ وَلَا تَتَّبِعْ أَهْوَآءَهُمْ
وَٱحْذَرْهُمْ أَن يَفْتِنُوكَ عَنْ بَعْضِ مَآ أَنزَلَ ٱللَّهُ
إِلَيْكَ فَإِن تَوَلَّوْاْ فَٱعْلَمْ أَنَّمَا يُرِيدُ ٱللَّهُ أَن يُصِيبَهُم بِبَعْضِ
ذُنُوبِهِمْ وَإِنَّ كَثِيرًا مِّنَ ٱلنَّاسِ لَفَٰسِقُونَ ۝

50 Is it a judgment of the time of
(pagan) ignorance that they are
seeking? Who is better than Allah
for judgment to a people who have
certainty (in their belief)?

أَفَحُكْمَ ٱلْجَٰهِلِيَّةِ يَبْغُونَ وَمَنْ أَحْسَنُ مِنَ ٱللَّهِ
حُكْمًا لِّقَوْمٍ يُوقِنُونَ ۝

51 O ye who believe! Take not the
Jews and Christians for friends.
They are friends one to another. He
among you who taketh them for
friends is (one) of them. Lo! Allah
guideth not wrongdoing folk.

۞ يَٰٓأَيُّهَا ٱلَّذِينَ ءَامَنُواْ لَا تَتَّخِذُواْ ٱلْيَهُودَ وَٱلنَّصَٰرَىٰٓ
أَوْلِيَآءَ بَعْضُهُمْ أَوْلِيَآءُ بَعْضٍ وَمَن يَتَوَلَّهُم مِّنكُمْ فَإِنَّهُۥ
مِنْهُمْ إِنَّ ٱللَّهَ لَا يَهْدِى ٱلْقَوْمَ ٱلظَّٰلِمِينَ ۝

52 And thou seest those in whose
heart is a disease race toward them,
saying: We fear lest a change of
fortune befall us. And it may happen that Allah will vouchsafe (unto
thee) the victory, or a commandment from His presence. Then will
they repent of their secret thoughts.

فَتَرَى ٱلَّذِينَ فِى قُلُوبِهِم مَّرَضٌ يُسَٰرِعُونَ فِيهِمْ
يَقُولُونَ نَخْشَىٰٓ أَن تُصِيبَنَا دَآئِرَةٌ فَعَسَى ٱللَّهُ أَن يَأْتِىَ
بِٱلْفَتْحِ أَوْ أَمْرٍ مِّنْ عِندِهِۦ فَيُصْبِحُواْ عَلَىٰ مَآ أَسَرُّواْ
فِىٓ أَنفُسِهِمْ نَٰدِمِينَ ۝

53 Then will the believers say
(unto the people of the Scripture):
Are these they who swore by Allah
their most binding oaths that they
were surely with you? Their works
have failed, and they have become
the losers.

وَيَقُولُ ٱلَّذِينَ ءَامَنُوٓاْ أَهَٰٓؤُلَآءِ ٱلَّذِينَ أَقْسَمُواْ بِٱللَّهِ
جَهْدَ أَيْمَٰنِهِمْ إِنَّهُمْ لَمَعَكُمْ حَبِطَتْ أَعْمَٰلُهُمْ
فَأَصْبَحُواْ خَٰسِرِينَ ۝

54 O ye who believe! Whoso of you becometh a renegade from his religion, (know that in his stead) Allah will bring a people whom He loveth and who love Him, humble toward believers, stern toward disbelievers, striving in the way of Allah and fearing not the blame of any blamer. Such is the grace of Allah which He giveth unto whom He will. Allah is All Embracing, All Knowing.

يَا أَيُّهَا الَّذِينَ ءَامَنُوا مَن يَرْتَدَّ مِنكُمْ عَن دِينِهِ فَسَوْفَ يَأْتِي اللَّهُ بِقَوْمٍ يُحِبُّهُمْ وَيُحِبُّونَهُ أَذِلَّةٍ عَلَى الْمُؤْمِنِينَ أَعِزَّةٍ عَلَى الْكَافِرِينَ يُجَاهِدُونَ فِي سَبِيلِ اللَّهِ وَلَا يَخَافُونَ لَوْمَةَ لَآئِمٍ ذَلِكَ فَضْلُ اللَّهِ يُؤْتِيهِ مَن يَشَاءُ وَاللَّهُ وَاسِعٌ عَلِيمٌ ۝

55 Your friend can be only Allah; and His messenger and those who believe, who establish worship and pay the poor due, and bow down (in prayer).

إِنَّمَا وَلِيُّكُمُ اللَّهُ وَرَسُولُهُ وَالَّذِينَ ءَامَنُوا الَّذِينَ يُقِيمُونَ الصَّلَوٰةَ وَيُؤْتُونَ الزَّكَوٰةَ وَهُمْ رَاكِعُونَ ۝

56 And whoso taketh Allah and His messenger and those who believe for friend (will know that), lo! the party of Allah, they are the victorious.

وَمَن يَتَوَلَّ اللَّهَ وَرَسُولَهُ وَالَّذِينَ ءَامَنُوا فَإِنَّ حِزْبَ اللَّهِ هُمُ الْغَالِبُونَ ۝

57 O ye who believe! Choose not for friends such of those who received the Scripture before you, and of the disbelievers, as make a jest and sport of your religion. But keep your duty to Allah if ye are true believers.

يَا أَيُّهَا الَّذِينَ ءَامَنُوا لَا تَتَّخِذُوا الَّذِينَ اتَّخَذُوا دِينَكُمْ هُزُوًا وَلَعِبًا مِنَ الَّذِينَ أُوتُوا الْكِتَابَ مِن قَبْلِكُمْ وَالْكُفَّارَ أَوْلِيَاءَ وَاتَّقُوا اللَّهَ إِن كُنتُم مُؤْمِنِينَ ۝

58 And when ye call to prayer they take it for a jest and sport. That is because they are a folk who understand not.

وَإِذَا نَادَيْتُمْ إِلَى الصَّلَوٰةِ اتَّخَذُوهَا هُزُوًا وَلَعِبًا ذَلِكَ بِأَنَّهُمْ قَوْمٌ لَا يَعْقِلُونَ ۝

59 Say: O, People of the Scripture! Do ye blame us for aught else than that we believe in Allah and that which is revealed unto us and that which was revealed aforetime, and because most of you are evil-livers?

قُلْ يَا أَهْلَ الْكِتَابِ هَلْ تَنقِمُونَ مِنَّا إِلَّا أَنْ ءَامَنَّا بِاللَّهِ وَمَا أُنزِلَ إِلَيْنَا وَمَا أُنزِلَ مِن قَبْلُ وَأَنَّ أَكْثَرَكُمْ فَاسِقُونَ ۝

60 Shall I tell thee of a worse (case) than theirs for retribution with Allah? Worse (is the case of him) whom Allah hath cursed, him on whom His wrath hath fallen! Worse is he of whose sort Allah hath turned some to apes and swine, and who serveth idols. Such are in worse plight and further astray from the plain road.

قُلْ هَلْ أُنَبِّئُكُمْ بِشَرٍّ مِنْ ذَٰلِكَ مَثُوبَةً عِنْدَ اللّٰهِ مَنْ لَعَنَهُ اللّٰهُ وَغَضِبَ عَلَيْهِ وَجَعَلَ مِنْهُمُ الْقِرَدَةَ وَالْخَنَازِيرَ وَعَبَدَ الطَّاغُوتَ أُولَٰئِكَ شَرٌّ مَكَانًا وَأَضَلُّ عَنْ سَوَآءِ السَّبِيلِ ﴿٦٠﴾

61 When they come unto you (Muslims), they say: We believe; but they came in unbelief and they went out in the same; and Allah knoweth best what they were hiding.

وَإِذَا جَآءُوكُمْ قَالُوٓا۟ءَامَنَّا وَقَدْ دَخَلُوا۟ بِالْكُفْرِ وَهُمْ قَدْ خَرَجُوا۟ بِهِ وَاللّٰهُ أَعْلَمُ بِمَا كَانُوا۟ يَكْتُمُونَ ﴿٦١﴾

62 And thou seest many of them vying one with another in sin and transgression and their devouring of illicit gain. Verily evil is what they do.

وَتَرَىٰ كَثِيرًا مِنْهُمْ يُسَارِعُونَ فِي الْإِثْمِ وَالْعُدْوَٰنِ وَأَكْلِهِمُ السُّحْتَ لَبِئْسَ مَا كَانُوا۟ يَعْمَلُونَ ﴿٦٢﴾

63 Why do not the rabbis and the priests forbid their evil speaking and their devouring of illicit gain? Verily evil is their handiwork.

لَوْلَا يَنْهَاهُمُ الرَّبَّانِيُّونَ وَالْأَحْبَارُ عَنْ قَوْلِهِمُ الْإِثْمَ وَأَكْلِهِمُ السُّحْتَ لَبِئْسَ مَا كَانُوا۟ يَصْنَعُونَ ﴿٦٣﴾

64 The Jews say: Allah's hand is fettered. Their hands are fettered and they are accursed for saying so. Nay, but both His hands are spread out wide in bounty. He bestoweth as He will. That which hath been revealed unto thee from thy Lord is certain to increase the contumacy and disbelief of many of them, and We have cast among them enmity and hatred till the Day of Resur-

وَقَالَتِ الْيَهُودُ يَدُ اللّٰهِ مَغْلُولَةٌ غُلَّتْ أَيْدِيهِمْ وَلُعِنُوا۟ بِمَا قَالُوا۟ بَلْ يَدَاهُ مَبْسُوطَتَانِ يُنْفِقُ كَيْفَ يَشَآءُ وَلَيَزِيدَنَّ كَثِيرًا مِنْهُمْ مَآ أُنْزِلَ إِلَيْكَ مِنْ رَبِّكَ طُغْيَانًا وَكُفْرًا وَأَلْقَيْنَا بَيْنَهُمُ الْعَدَاوَةَ وَالْبَغْضَآءَ إِلَىٰ يَوْمِ

rection. As often as they light a fire for war, Allah extinguisheth it. Their effort is for corruption in the land, and Allah loveth not corrupters.

ٱلْقِيَمَةِ كُلَّمَآ أَوْقَدُوا نَارًا لِّلْحَرْبِ أَطْفَأَهَا ٱللَّهُ وَيَسْعَوْنَ فِي ٱلْأَرْضِ فَسَادًا وَٱللَّهُ لَا يُحِبُّ ٱلْمُفْسِدِينَ ۝

65 If only the People of the Scripture would believe and ward off (evil), surely We should remit their sins from them and surely We should bring them into Gardens of Delight.

وَلَوْ أَنَّ أَهْلَ ٱلْكِتَٰبِ ءَامَنُوا وَٱتَّقَوْا لَكَفَّرْنَا عَنْهُمْ سَيِّـَٔاتِهِمْ وَلَأَدْخَلْنَٰهُمْ جَنَّٰتِ ٱلنَّعِيمِ ۝

66 If they had observed the Torah and the Gospel and that which was revealed unto them from their Lord, they would surely have been nourished from above them and from beneath their feet. Among them there are people who are moderate, but many of them are of evil conduct.

وَلَوْ أَنَّهُمْ أَقَامُوا ٱلتَّوْرَىٰةَ وَٱلْإِنجِيلَ وَمَآ أُنزِلَ إِلَيْهِم مِّن رَّبِّهِمْ لَأَكَلُوا مِن فَوْقِهِمْ وَمِن تَحْتِ أَرْجُلِهِمْ مِّنْهُمْ أُمَّةٌ مُّقْتَصِدَةٌ وَكَثِيرٌ مِّنْهُمْ سَآءَ مَا يَعْمَلُونَ ۝

67 O Messenger! Make known that which hath been revealed unto thee from thy Lord, for if thou do it not, thou will not have conveyed His message. Allah will protect thee from mankind. Lo! Allah guideth not the disbelieving folk.

۞ يَٰٓأَيُّهَا ٱلرَّسُولُ بَلِّغْ مَآ أُنزِلَ إِلَيْكَ مِن رَّبِّكَ وَإِن لَّمْ تَفْعَلْ فَمَا بَلَّغْتَ رِسَالَتَهُۥ وَٱللَّهُ يَعْصِمُكَ مِنَ ٱلنَّاسِ إِنَّ ٱللَّهَ لَا يَهْدِي ٱلْقَوْمَ ٱلْكَٰفِرِينَ ۝

68 Say: O People of the Scripture! Ye have naught (of guidance) till ye observe the Torah and the Gospel and that which was revealed unto you from your Lord. That which is revealed unto thee (Muhammad) from thy Lord is certain to increase the contumacy and disbelief of many of them. But grieve not for the disbelieving folk.

قُلْ يَٰٓأَهْلَ ٱلْكِتَٰبِ لَسْتُمْ عَلَىٰ شَيْءٍ حَتَّىٰ تُقِيمُوا ٱلتَّوْرَىٰةَ وَٱلْإِنجِيلَ وَمَآ أُنزِلَ إِلَيْكُم مِّن رَّبِّكُمْ وَلَيَزِيدَنَّ كَثِيرًا مِّنْهُم مَّآ أُنزِلَ إِلَيْكَ مِن رَّبِّكَ طُغْيَٰنًا وَكُفْرًا فَلَا تَأْسَ عَلَى ٱلْقَوْمِ ٱلْكَٰفِرِينَ ۝

69 Lo! those who believe, and those who are Jews, and Sabaeans, and Christians—Whosoever believeth in Allah and the Last Day and doeth right—there shall no fear come upon them neither shall they grieve.[4]

إِنَّ ٱلَّذِينَ ءَامَنُوا۟ وَٱلَّذِينَ هَادُوا۟ وَٱلصَّٰبِـُٔونَ وَٱلنَّصَٰرَىٰ مَنْ ءَامَنَ بِٱللَّهِ وَٱلْيَوْمِ ٱلْءَاخِرِ وَعَمِلَ صَٰلِحًا فَلَا خَوْفٌ عَلَيْهِمْ وَلَا هُمْ يَحْزَنُونَ ۝

70 We made a covenant of old with the Children of Israel and We sent unto them messengers. As often as a messenger came unto them with that which their souls desired not (they became rebellious). Some (of them) they denied and some they slew.

لَقَدْ أَخَذْنَا مِيثَٰقَ بَنِىٓ إِسْرَٰٓءِيلَ وَأَرْسَلْنَآ إِلَيْهِمْ رُسُلًا كُلَّمَا جَآءَهُمْ رَسُولٌۢ بِمَا لَا تَهْوَىٰٓ أَنفُسُهُمْ فَرِيقًا كَذَّبُوا۟ وَفَرِيقًا يَقْتُلُونَ ۝

71 They thought no harm would come of it, so they were wilfully blind and deaf. And afterward Allah turned (in mercy) toward them. Now (even after that) are many of them wilfully blind and deaf. Allah is Seer of what they do.

وَحَسِبُوٓا۟ أَلَّا تَكُونَ فِتْنَةٌ فَعَمُوا۟ وَصَمُّوا۟ ثُمَّ تَابَ ٱللَّهُ عَلَيْهِمْ ثُمَّ عَمُوا۟ وَصَمُّوا۟ كَثِيرٌ مِّنْهُمْ وَٱللَّهُ بَصِيرٌۢ بِمَا يَعْمَلُونَ ۝

72 They surely disbelieve who say: Lo! Allah is the Messiah, son of Mary. The Messiah (himself) said: O Children of Israel, worship Allah, my Lord and your Lord. Lo! whoso ascribeth partners unto Allah, for him Allah hath forbidden Paradise. His abode is the Fire. For evil-doers there will be no helpers.

لَقَدْ كَفَرَ ٱلَّذِينَ قَالُوٓا۟ إِنَّ ٱللَّهَ هُوَ ٱلْمَسِيحُ ٱبْنُ مَرْيَمَ وَقَالَ ٱلْمَسِيحُ يَٰبَنِىٓ إِسْرَٰٓءِيلَ ٱعْبُدُوا۟ ٱللَّهَ رَبِّى وَرَبَّكُمْ إِنَّهُۥ مَن يُشْرِكْ بِٱللَّهِ فَقَدْ حَرَّمَ ٱللَّهُ عَلَيْهِ ٱلْجَنَّةَ وَمَأْوَىٰهُ ٱلنَّارُ وَمَا لِلظَّٰلِمِينَ مِنْ أَنصَارٍ ۝

73 They surely disbelieve who say: Lo! Allah is the third of three;

لَقَدْ كَفَرَ ٱلَّذِينَ قَالُوٓا۟ إِنَّ ٱللَّهَ ثَالِثُ ثَلَٰثَةٍ

---

4. Almost identical with Sūrah 2: 62.

when there is no God save the One God. If they desist not from so saying a painful doom will fall on those of them who disbelieve.

وَمَا مِنْ إِلَهٍ إِلَّا إِلَهٌ وَاحِدٌ وَإِن لَّمْ يَنتَهُوا عَمَّا يَقُولُونَ لَيَمَسَّنَّ الَّذِينَ كَفَرُوا مِنْهُمْ عَذَابٌ أَلِيمٌ ۝

74 Will they not rather turn unto Allah and seek forgiveness of Him? For Allah is Forgiving, Merciful.

أَفَلَا يَتُوبُونَ إِلَى اللَّهِ وَيَسْتَغْفِرُونَهُ وَاللَّهُ غَفُورٌ رَّحِيمٌ ۝

75 The Messiah, son of Mary, was no other than a messenger, messengers (the like of whom) had passed away before him. And his mother was a saintly woman. And they both used to eat (earthly) food. See how we make the revelations clear for them, and see how they are turned away!

مَّا الْمَسِيحُ ابْنُ مَرْيَمَ إِلَّا رَسُولٌ قَدْ خَلَتْ مِن قَبْلِهِ الرُّسُلُ وَأُمُّهُ صِدِّيقَةٌ كَانَا يَأْكُلَانِ الطَّعَامَ انظُرْ كَيْفَ نُبَيِّنُ لَهُمُ الْآيَاتِ ثُمَّ انظُرْ أَنَّى يُؤْفَكُونَ ۝

76 Say: Serve ye in place of Allah that which possesseth for you neither hurt nor use? Allah it is Who is the Hearer, the Knower.

قُلْ أَتَعْبُدُونَ مِن دُونِ اللَّهِ مَا لَا يَمْلِكُ لَكُمْ ضَرًّا وَلَا نَفْعًا وَاللَّهُ هُوَ السَّمِيعُ الْعَلِيمُ ۝

77 Say: O People of the Scripture! Stress not in your religion other than the truth, and follow not the vain desires of folk who erred of old and led many astray, and erred from a plain road.

قُلْ يَا أَهْلَ الْكِتَابِ لَا تَغْلُوا فِي دِينِكُمْ غَيْرَ الْحَقِّ وَلَا تَتَّبِعُوا أَهْوَاءَ قَوْمٍ قَدْ ضَلُّوا مِن قَبْلُ وَأَضَلُّوا كَثِيرًا وَضَلُّوا عَن سَوَاءِ السَّبِيلِ ۝

78 Those of the children of Israel who went astray were cursed by the tongue of David, and of Jesus, son of Mary. That was because they rebelled and used to transgress.

لُعِنَ الَّذِينَ كَفَرُوا مِن بَنِي إِسْرَائِيلَ عَلَى لِسَانِ دَاوُودَ وَعِيسَى ابْنِ مَرْيَمَ ذَلِكَ بِمَا عَصَوا وَّكَانُوا يَعْتَدُونَ ۝

79 They restrained not one another from the wickedness they did. Verily evil was that they used to do!

كَانُوا لَا يَتَنَاهَوْنَ عَن مُّنكَرٍ فَعَلُوهُ لَبِئْسَ مَا كَانُوا يَفْعَلُونَ ۝

80 Thou seest many of them making friends with those who disbelieve. Surely ill for them is that which they themselves send on before them: that Allah will be wroth with them and in the doom they will abide.

تَرَىٰ كَثِيرًا مِّنْهُمْ يَتَوَلَّوْنَ الَّذِينَ كَفَرُوا ۚ لَبِئْسَ مَا قَدَّمَتْ لَهُمْ أَنفُسُهُمْ أَن سَخِطَ اللَّهُ عَلَيْهِمْ وَفِي الْعَذَابِ هُمْ خَالِدُونَ ۝

81 If they believed in Allah and the Prophet and that which is revealed unto him, they would not choose them for their friends. But many of them are of evil conduct.

وَلَوْ كَانُوا يُؤْمِنُونَ بِاللَّهِ وَالنَّبِيِّ وَمَا أُنزِلَ إِلَيْهِ مَا اتَّخَذُوهُمْ أَوْلِيَاءَ وَلَٰكِنَّ كَثِيرًا مِّنْهُمْ فَاسِقُونَ ۝

82 Thou wilt find the most vehement of mankind in hostility to those who believe (to be) the Jews and the idolaters. And thou wilt find the nearest of them in affection to those who believe (to be) those who say: Lo! We are Christians. That is because there are among them priests and monks,[5] and because they are not proud.

۞ لَتَجِدَنَّ أَشَدَّ النَّاسِ عَدَاوَةً لِّلَّذِينَ آمَنُوا الْيَهُودَ وَالَّذِينَ أَشْرَكُوا ۖ وَلَتَجِدَنَّ أَقْرَبَهُم مَّوَدَّةً لِّلَّذِينَ آمَنُوا الَّذِينَ قَالُوا إِنَّا نَصَارَىٰ ۚ ذَٰلِكَ بِأَنَّ مِنْهُمْ قِسِّيسِينَ وَرُهْبَانًا وَأَنَّهُمْ لَا يَسْتَكْبِرُونَ ۝

83 When they listen to that which hath been revealed unto the messenger, thou seest their eyes overflow with tears because of their recognition of the Truth. They say: Our Lord, we believe. Inscribe us as among the witnesses.

وَإِذَا سَمِعُوا مَا أُنزِلَ إِلَى الرَّسُولِ تَرَىٰ أَعْيُنَهُمْ تَفِيضُ مِنَ الدَّمْعِ مِمَّا عَرَفُوا مِنَ الْحَقِّ ۖ يَقُولُونَ رَبَّنَا آمَنَّا فَاكْتُبْنَا مَعَ الشَّاهِدِينَ ۝

84 How should we not believe in Allah and that which hath come unto us of the Truth. And (how should we not) hope that our Lord will bring us in along with righteous folk?

وَمَا لَنَا لَا نُؤْمِنُ بِاللَّهِ وَمَا جَاءَنَا مِنَ الْحَقِّ وَنَطْمَعُ أَن يُدْخِلَنَا رَبُّنَا مَعَ الْقَوْمِ الصَّالِحِينَ ۝

---

5. *i.e.* persons entirely devoted to the service of God, as were Muslims.

85 Allah hath rewarded them for that their saying—Gardens underneath which rivers flow, wherein they will abide forever. That is the reward of the good.

فَأَثَابَهُمُ اللّٰهُ بِمَا قَالُوْا جَنّٰتٍ تَجْرِىْ مِنْ تَحْتِهَا الْأَنْهٰرُ خٰلِدِيْنَ فِيْهَا ؕ وَذٰلِكَ جَزَآءُ الْمُحْسِنِيْنَ ۝

86 But those who disbelieve and deny Our revelations, they are owners of hell fire.

وَالَّذِيْنَ كَفَرُوْا وَكَذَّبُوْا بِاٰيٰتِنَآ أُولٰٓئِكَ أَصْحٰبُ الْجَحِيْمِ ۝

87 O ye who believe! Forbid not the good things which Allah hath made lawful for you, and transgress not. Lo! Allah loveth not transgressors.

يٰٓأَيُّهَا الَّذِيْنَ اٰمَنُوْا لَا تُحَرِّمُوْا طَيِّبٰتِ مَآ أَحَلَّ اللّٰهُ لَكُمْ وَلَا تَعْتَدُوْا ؕ إِنَّ اللّٰهَ لَا يُحِبُّ الْمُعْتَدِيْنَ ۝

88 Eat of that which Allah hath bestowed on you as food lawful and good, and keep your duty to Allah in Whom ye are believers.

وَكُلُوْا مِمَّا رَزَقَكُمُ اللّٰهُ حَلٰلًا طَيِّبًا ۖ وَّاتَّقُوا اللّٰهَ الَّذِيْ أَنْتُمْ بِهِ مُؤْمِنُوْنَ ۝

89 Allah will not take you to task for that which is unintentional in your oaths, but He will take you to task for the oaths which ye swear in earnest. The expiation thereof is the feeding of ten of the needy with the average of that wherewith ye feed your own folk, or the clothing of them, or the liberation of a slave, and for him who findeth not (the wherewithal to do so) then a three days fast. This is the expiation of your oaths when ye have sworn; and keep your oaths. Thus Allah expoundeth unto you His revelations in order that ye may give thanks.

لَا يُؤَاخِذُكُمُ اللّٰهُ بِاللَّغْوِ فِيْ أَيْمَانِكُمْ وَلٰكِنْ يُّؤَاخِذُكُمْ بِمَا عَقَّدْتُّمُ الْأَيْمَانَ ۚ فَكَفَّارَتُهُ إِطْعَامُ عَشَرَةِ مَسٰكِيْنَ مِنْ أَوْسَطِ مَا تُطْعِمُوْنَ أَهْلِيْكُمْ أَوْ كِسْوَتُهُمْ أَوْ تَحْرِيْرُ رَقَبَةٍ ؕ فَمَنْ لَّمْ يَجِدْ فَصِيَامُ ثَلٰثَةِ أَيَّامٍ ؕ ذٰلِكَ كَفَّارَةُ أَيْمَانِكُمْ إِذَا حَلَفْتُمْ ؕ وَاحْفَظُوْا أَيْمَانَكُمْ ؕ كَذٰلِكَ يُبَيِّنُ اللّٰهُ لَكُمْ اٰيٰتِهِ لَعَلَّكُمْ تَشْكُرُوْنَ ۝

90 O ye who believe! Strong drink and games of chance and idols and divining arrows are only an infamy of Satan's handiwork. Leave it aside in order that ye may succeed.

91 Satan seeketh only to cast among you enmity and hatred by means of strong drink and games of chance, and to turn you from remembrance of Allah and from (His) worship. Will ye then have done?

92 Obey Allah and obey the messenger, and beware! But if ye turn away, then know that the duty of Our messenger is only plain conveyance (of the message).

93 There shall be no sin (imputed) unto those who believe and do good works for what they may have eaten (in the past), when they did their duty (to Allah), believed (in Him) and did good works; and again were mindful of their duty (to Allah) and believed; and once again were mindful of their duty (to Allah) and did right, Allah loveth the good.

94 O ye who believe! Allah will surely try you somewhat (in the matter) of the game which ye take with your hands and your spears, that Allah may know him who feareth Him in secret. Whoso transgresseth after this, for him there is a painful doom.

يَٰٓأَيُّهَا ٱلَّذِينَ ءَامَنُوٓا۟ إِنَّمَا ٱلْخَمْرُ وَٱلْمَيْسِرُ وَٱلْأَنصَابُ وَٱلْأَزْلَٰمُ رِجْسٌ مِّنْ عَمَلِ ٱلشَّيْطَٰنِ فَٱجْتَنِبُوهُ لَعَلَّكُمْ تُفْلِحُونَ ٩٠

إِنَّمَا يُرِيدُ ٱلشَّيْطَٰنُ أَن يُوقِعَ بَيْنَكُمُ ٱلْعَدَٰوَةَ وَٱلْبَغْضَآءَ فِى ٱلْخَمْرِ وَٱلْمَيْسِرِ وَيَصُدَّكُمْ عَن ذِكْرِ ٱللَّهِ وَعَنِ ٱلصَّلَوٰةِ فَهَلْ أَنتُم مُّنتَهُونَ ٩١

وَأَطِيعُوا۟ ٱللَّهَ وَأَطِيعُوا۟ ٱلرَّسُولَ وَٱحْذَرُوا۟ فَإِن تَوَلَّيْتُمْ فَٱعْلَمُوٓا۟ أَنَّمَا عَلَىٰ رَسُولِنَا ٱلْبَلَٰغُ ٱلْمُبِينُ ٩٢

لَيْسَ عَلَى ٱلَّذِينَ ءَامَنُوا۟ وَعَمِلُوا۟ ٱلصَّٰلِحَٰتِ جُنَاحٌ فِيمَا طَعِمُوٓا۟ إِذَا مَا ٱتَّقَوا۟ وَّءَامَنُوا۟ وَعَمِلُوا۟ ٱلصَّٰلِحَٰتِ ثُمَّ ٱتَّقَوا۟ وَّءَامَنُوا۟ ثُمَّ ٱتَّقَوا۟ وَّأَحْسَنُوا۟ وَٱللَّهُ يُحِبُّ ٱلْمُحْسِنِينَ ٩٣

يَٰٓأَيُّهَا ٱلَّذِينَ ءَامَنُوا۟ لَيَبْلُوَنَّكُمُ ٱللَّهُ بِشَىْءٍ مِّنَ ٱلصَّيْدِ تَنَالُهُ أَيْدِيكُمْ وَرِمَاحُكُمْ لِيَعْلَمَ ٱللَّهُ مَن يَخَافُهُ بِٱلْغَيْبِ فَمَنِ ٱعْتَدَىٰ بَعْدَ ذَٰلِكَ فَلَهُۥ عَذَابٌ أَلِيمٌ ٩٤

95 O ye who believe! Kill no wild game while ye are on the pilgrimage. Whoso of you killeth it of set purpose he shall pay its forfeit in the equivalent of that which he hath killed, of domestic animals, the judge to be two men among you known for justice, (the forfeit) to be brought as an offering to the Ka'bah; or, for expiation, he shall feed poor persons, or the equivalent thereof in fasting, that he may taste the evil consequences of his deed. Allah forgiveth whatever (of this kind) may have happened in the past, but whoso relapseth, Allah will take retribution from him. Allah is Mighty, Able to Requite (the wrong).

يَـٰٓأَيُّهَا ٱلَّذِينَ ءَامَنُوا۟ لَا تَقْتُلُوا۟ ٱلصَّيْدَ وَأَنتُمْ حُرُمٌ وَمَن قَتَلَهُۥ مِنكُم مُّتَعَمِّدًا فَجَزَآءٌ مِّثْلُ مَا قَتَلَ مِنَ ٱلنَّعَمِ يَحْكُمُ بِهِۦ ذَوَا عَدْلٍ مِّنكُمْ هَدْيًۢا بَٰلِغَ ٱلْكَعْبَةِ أَوْ كَفَّٰرَةٌ طَعَامُ مَسَٰكِينَ أَوْ عَدْلُ ذَٰلِكَ صِيَامًا لِّيَذُوقَ وَبَالَ أَمْرِهِۦ عَفَا ٱللَّهُ عَمَّا سَلَفَ وَمَنْ عَادَ فَيَنتَقِمُ ٱللَّهُ مِنْهُ وَٱللَّهُ عَزِيزٌ ذُو ٱنتِقَامٍ ٩٥

96 To hunt and to eat the fish of the sea is made lawful for you, a provision for you and for seafarers; but to hunt on land is forbidden to you so long as ye are on the pilgrimage. Be mindful of your duty to Allah, unto Whom ye will be gathered.

أُحِلَّ لَكُمْ صَيْدُ ٱلْبَحْرِ وَطَعَامُهُۥ مَتَٰعًا لَّكُمْ وَلِلسَّيَّارَةِ وَحُرِّمَ عَلَيْكُمْ صَيْدُ ٱلْبَرِّ مَا دُمْتُمْ حُرُمًا وَٱتَّقُوا۟ ٱللَّهَ ٱلَّذِىٓ إِلَيْهِ تُحْشَرُونَ ٩٦

97 Allah hath appointed the Ka'bah, the Sacred House, a standard for mankind, and the Sacred Month and the offerings and the garlands. That is so that ye may know that Allah knoweth whatsoever is in the heavens and whatsoever is in the earth, and that Allah is Knower of all things.

۞ جَعَلَ ٱللَّهُ ٱلْكَعْبَةَ ٱلْبَيْتَ ٱلْحَرَامَ قِيَٰمًا لِّلنَّاسِ وَٱلشَّهْرَ ٱلْحَرَامَ وَٱلْهَدْىَ وَٱلْقَلَٰٓئِدَ ذَٰلِكَ لِتَعْلَمُوٓا۟ أَنَّ ٱللَّهَ يَعْلَمُ مَا فِى ٱلسَّمَٰوَٰتِ وَمَا فِى ٱلْأَرْضِ وَأَنَّ ٱللَّهَ بِكُلِّ شَىْءٍ عَلِيمٌ ٩٧

98 Know that Allah is severe in punishment, but that Allah (also) is Forgiving, Merciful.

اَعْلَمُوٓاْ أَنَّ ٱللَّهَ شَدِيدُ ٱلْعِقَابِ وَأَنَّ ٱللَّهَ غَفُورٌ رَّحِيمٌ ۝

99 The duty of the messenger is only to convey (the message). Allah knoweth what ye proclaim and what ye hide.

مَّا عَلَى ٱلرَّسُولِ إِلَّا ٱلْبَلَـٰغُ وَٱللَّهُ يَعْلَمُ مَا تُبْدُونَ وَمَا تَكْتُمُونَ ۝

100 Say: The evil and the good are not alike even though the plenty of the evil attract thee. So be mindful of your duty to Allah, O men of understanding, that ye may succeed.

قُل لَّا يَسْتَوِى ٱلْخَبِيثُ وَٱلطَّيِّبُ وَلَوْ أَعْجَبَكَ كَثْرَةُ ٱلْخَبِيثِ فَٱتَّقُواْ ٱللَّهَ يَـٰٓأُوْلِى ٱلْأَلْبَـٰبِ لَعَلَّكُمْ تُفْلِحُونَ ۝

101 O ye who believe! Ask not of things which, if they were made known unto you, would trouble you; but if ye ask of them when the Qur'an is being revealed, they will be made known unto you. Allah pardoneth this, for Allah is Forgiving, Clement.

يَـٰٓأَيُّهَا ٱلَّذِينَ ءَامَنُواْ لَا تَسْـَٔلُواْ عَنْ أَشْيَآءَ إِن تُبْدَ لَكُمْ تَسُؤْكُمْ وَإِن تَسْـَٔلُواْ عَنْهَا حِينَ يُنَزَّلُ ٱلْقُرْءَانُ تُبْدَ لَكُمْ عَفَا ٱللَّهُ عَنْهَا وَٱللَّهُ غَفُورٌ حَلِيمٌ ۝

102 A folk before you asked (for such disclosures) and then disbelieved therein.

قَدْ سَأَلَهَا قَوْمٌ مِّن قَبْلِكُمْ ثُمَّ أَصْبَحُواْ بِهَا كَـٰفِرِينَ ۝

103 Allah hath not appointed anything in the nature of a *Baḥirah* or a *Sā'ibah* or a *Waṣilah* or a *Ḥāmi*,[6] but those who disbelieve invent a lie against Allah. Most of them have no sense.

مَا جَعَلَ ٱللَّهُ مِنۢ بَحِيرَةٍ وَلَا سَآئِبَةٍ وَلَا وَصِيلَةٍ وَلَا حَامٍ وَلَـٰكِنَّ ٱلَّذِينَ كَفَرُواْ يَفْتَرُونَ عَلَى ٱللَّهِ ٱلْكَذِبَ وَأَكْثَرُهُمْ لَا يَعْقِلُونَ ۝

104 And when it is said unto them: Come unto that which Allah hath revealed and unto the mes-

وَإِذَا قِيلَ لَهُمْ تَعَالَوْاْ إِلَىٰ مَآ أَنزَلَ ٱللَّهُ وَإِلَى

---

6. Different classes of cattle liberated in honour of idols and reverenced by the pagan Arabs.

senger, they say: Enough for us is that wherein we found our fathers. What! Even though their fathers had no knowledge whatsoever, and no guidance?

105   O ye who believe! Ye have charge of your own souls. He who erreth cannot injure you if ye are rightly guided. Unto Allah ye will all return; and then He will inform you of what ye used to do.

106   O ye who believe! Let there be witnesses between you when death draweth nigh unto one of you, at the time of bequest—two witnesses, just men from among you, or two others from another tribe, in case ye are campaigning in the land and the calamity of death befall you. Ye shall empanel them both after the prayer, and, if ye doubt, they shall be made to swear by Allah (saying): We will not take a bribe, even though it were (on behalf of) a near kinsman nor will we hide the testimony of Allah, for then indeed we should be of the sinful.

107   But then, if it is afterwards ascertained that both of them merit (the suspicion of) sin, let two others take their place of those nearly concerned, and let them swear by Allah, (saying): Verily our testimony is truer than their testimony and we have not transgressed (the bounds of duty), for then indeed we should be of the evil-doers.

ٱلرَّسُولِ قَالُوا حَسْبُنَا مَا وَجَدْنَا عَلَيْهِ ءَابَاءَنَا ۚ أَوَلَوْ كَانَ ءَابَاؤُهُمْ لَا يَعْلَمُونَ شَيْئًا وَلَا يَهْتَدُونَ ۝

يَٰٓأَيُّهَا ٱلَّذِينَ ءَامَنُوا عَلَيْكُمْ أَنفُسَكُمْ ۖ لَا يَضُرُّكُم مَّن ضَلَّ إِذَا ٱهْتَدَيْتُمْ ۚ إِلَى ٱللَّهِ مَرْجِعُكُمْ جَمِيعًا فَيُنَبِّئُكُم بِمَا كُنتُمْ تَعْمَلُونَ ۝

يَٰٓأَيُّهَا ٱلَّذِينَ ءَامَنُوا شَهَٰدَةُ بَيْنِكُمْ إِذَا حَضَرَ أَحَدَكُمُ ٱلْمَوْتُ حِينَ ٱلْوَصِيَّةِ ٱثْنَانِ ذَوَا عَدْلٍ مِّنكُمْ أَوْ ءَاخَرَانِ مِنْ غَيْرِكُمْ إِنْ أَنتُمْ ضَرَبْتُمْ فِى ٱلْأَرْضِ فَأَصَٰبَتْكُم مُّصِيبَةُ ٱلْمَوْتِ ۚ تَحْبِسُونَهُمَا مِنۢ بَعْدِ ٱلصَّلَوٰةِ فَيُقْسِمَانِ بِٱللَّهِ إِنِ ٱرْتَبْتُمْ لَا نَشْتَرِى بِهِۦ ثَمَنًا وَلَوْ كَانَ ذَا قُرْبَىٰ وَلَا نَكْتُمُ شَهَٰدَةَ ٱللَّهِ إِنَّا إِذًا لَّمِنَ ٱلْءَاثِمِينَ ۝

فَإِنْ عُثِرَ عَلَىٰٓ أَنَّهُمَا ٱسْتَحَقَّآ إِثْمًا فَـَٔاخَرَانِ يَقُومَانِ مَقَامَهُمَا مِنَ ٱلَّذِينَ ٱسْتَحَقَّ عَلَيْهِمُ ٱلْأَوْلَيَٰنِ فَيُقْسِمَانِ بِٱللَّهِ لَشَهَٰدَتُنَآ أَحَقُّ مِن شَهَٰدَتِهِمَا وَمَا ٱعْتَدَيْنَآ إِنَّآ إِذًا لَّمِنَ ٱلظَّٰلِمِينَ ۝

108   Thus it is more likely that they will bear true witness or fear that after their oaths the oaths (of others) will be taken. So be mindful of your duty (to Allah) and hearken. Allah guideth not the froward folk.

ذَٰلِكَ أَدْنَىٰٓ أَن يَأْتُوا۟ بِالشَّهَٰدَةِ عَلَىٰ وَجْهِهَآ أَوْ يَخَافُوٓا۟ أَن تُرَدَّ أَيْمَٰنٌۢ بَعْدَ أَيْمَٰنِهِمْ ۗ وَٱتَّقُوا۟ ٱللَّهَ وَٱسْمَعُوا۟ ۗ وَٱللَّهُ لَا يَهْدِى ٱلْقَوْمَ ٱلْفَٰسِقِينَ ۝

109   In the day when Allah gathereth together the messengers, and saith: What was your response (from mankind)? they say: We have no knowledge. Lo! Thou, only Thou art the Knower of Things Hidden.

۞ يَوْمَ يَجْمَعُ ٱللَّهُ ٱلرُّسُلَ فَيَقُولُ مَاذَآ أُجِبْتُمْ ۖ قَالُوا۟ لَا عِلْمَ لَنَآ ۖ إِنَّكَ أَنتَ عَلَّٰمُ ٱلْغُيُوبِ ۝

110   When Allah saith: O Jesus, son of Mary! Remember My favour unto thee and unto thy mother; how I strengthened thee with the holy Spirit, so that thou spakest unto mankind in the cradle as in maturity; and how I taught thee the Scripture and Wisdom and the Torah and the Gospel; and how thou didst shape of clay as it were the likeness of a bird by My permission, and didst blow upon it and it was a bird by My permission, and thou didst heal him who was born blind and the leper by My permission; and how thou didst raise the dead, by My permission; and how I restrained the Children of Israel from (harming) thee when thou camest unto them with clear proofs, and those of them who disbelieved exclaimed: This is naught else than evident magic;

إِذْ قَالَ ٱللَّهُ يَٰعِيسَى ٱبْنَ مَرْيَمَ ٱذْكُرْ نِعْمَتِى عَلَيْكَ وَعَلَىٰ وَٰلِدَتِكَ إِذْ أَيَّدتُّكَ بِرُوحِ ٱلْقُدُسِ تُكَلِّمُ ٱلنَّاسَ فِى ٱلْمَهْدِ وَكَهْلًا ۖ وَإِذْ عَلَّمْتُكَ ٱلْكِتَٰبَ وَٱلْحِكْمَةَ وَٱلتَّوْرَىٰةَ وَٱلْإِنجِيلَ ۖ وَإِذْ تَخْلُقُ مِنَ ٱلطِّينِ كَهَيْـَٔةِ ٱلطَّيْرِ بِإِذْنِى فَتَنفُخُ فِيهَا فَتَكُونُ طَيْرًۢا بِإِذْنِى ۖ وَتُبْرِئُ ٱلْأَكْمَهَ وَٱلْأَبْرَصَ بِإِذْنِى ۖ وَإِذْ تُخْرِجُ ٱلْمَوْتَىٰ بِإِذْنِى ۖ وَإِذْ كَفَفْتُ بَنِىٓ إِسْرَٰٓءِيلَ عَنكَ إِذْ جِئْتَهُم بِٱلْبَيِّنَٰتِ فَقَالَ ٱلَّذِينَ كَفَرُوا۟ مِنْهُمْ إِنْ هَٰذَآ إِلَّا سِحْرٌ مُّبِينٌ ۝

111   And when I inspired the disciples, (saying): Believe in Me and in My messenger, they said: We believe. Bear witness that we have surrendered[7] (unto Thee).

وَإِذْ أَوْحَيْتُ إِلَى الْحَوَارِيِّنَ أَنْ ءَامِنُوا بِى وَبِرَسُولِى قَالُوٓا ءَامَنَّا وَاشْهَدْ بِأَنَّنَا مُسْلِمُونَ ۝

112   When the disciples said: O Jesus, son of Mary! Is thy Lord able to send down for us a table spread with food from heaven? He said: Observe your duty to Allah, if ye are true believers.

إِذْ قَالَ الْحَوَارِيُّونَ يَٰعِيسَى ابْنَ مَرْيَمَ هَلْ يَسْتَطِيعُ رَبُّكَ أَن يُنَزِّلَ عَلَيْنَا مَآئِدَةً مِّنَ السَّمَآءِ قَالَ اتَّقُوا اللَّهَ إِن كُنتُم مُّؤْمِنِينَ ۝

113   (They said:) We wish to eat thereof, that our hearts may become satisfied and know that thou hast spoken truth to us, and that thereof we may be witnesses.

قَالُوا نُرِيدُ أَن نَّأْكُلَ مِنْهَا وَتَطْمَئِنَّ قُلُوبُنَا وَنَعْلَمَ أَن قَدْ صَدَقْتَنَا وَنَكُونَ عَلَيْهَا مِنَ الشَّٰهِدِينَ ۝

114   Jesus, son of Mary, said: O Allah, Lord of us! Send down for us a table spread with food from heaven, that it may be a feast for us, for the first of us and for the last of us, and a sign from Thee. Give us sustenance, for Thou art the Best of Sustainers.

قَالَ عِيسَى ابْنُ مَرْيَمَ اللَّهُمَّ رَبَّنَآ أَنزِلْ عَلَيْنَا مَآئِدَةً مِّنَ السَّمَآءِ تَكُونُ لَنَا عِيدًا لِّأَوَّلِنَا وَءَاخِرِنَا وَءَايَةً مِّنكَ وَارْزُقْنَا وَأَنتَ خَيْرُ الرَّٰزِقِينَ ۝

115   Allah said: Lo! I send it down for you. And whoso disbelieveth of you afterward, him surely will I punish with a punishment wherewith I have not punished any of (My) creatures.

قَالَ اللَّهُ إِنِّى مُنَزِّلُهَا عَلَيْكُمْ فَمَن يَكْفُرْ بَعْدُ مِنكُمْ فَإِنِّى أُعَذِّبُهُ عَذَابًا لَّا أُعَذِّبُهُ أَحَدًا مِّنَ الْعَٰلَمِينَ ۝

116   And when Allah saith: O Jesus, son of Mary! Didst thou say unto mankind: Take me and my

وَإِذْ قَالَ اللَّهُ يَٰعِيسَى ابْنَ مَرْيَمَ ءَأَنتَ قُلْتَ لِلنَّاسِ اتَّخِذُونِى وَأُمِّىَ إِلَٰهَيْنِ مِن دُونِ اللَّهِ

---

7. Or "are Muslims".

mother for two gods beside Allah?
he saith: Be glorified! It was not
mine to utter that to which I had no
right. If I had ever said it, then
Thou wouldst have known it. Thou
knowest what is in my mind, and I
know not what is in Thy mind. Lo!
Thou, only Thou art the Knower of
Things Hidden.

قَالَ سُبْحَانَكَ مَا يَكُونُ لِيْۤ أَنْ أَقُوْلَ مَا لَيْسَ لِيْ
بِحَقٍّ ۚ اِنْ كُنْتُ قُلْتُهٗ فَقَدْ عَلِمْتَهٗ ۚ تَعْلَمُ مَا فِيْ نَفْسِيْ
وَلَاۤ أَعْلَمُ مَا فِيْ نَفْسِكَ ۚ اِنَّكَ أَنْتَ عَلَّامُ الْغُيُوْبِ ﴿١١٦﴾

117   I spake unto them only that
which Thou commandedst me, (saying): Worship Allah, my Lord and
your Lord. I was a witness of them
while I dwelt among them, and
when Thou tookest me; Thou wast
the Watcher over them. Thou art
Witness over all things.

مَا قُلْتُ لَهُمْ اِلَّا مَاۤ أَمَرْتَنِيْ بِهٖۤ أَنِ اعْبُدُوا اللّٰهَ رَبِّيْ
وَرَبَّكُمْ ۚ وَكُنْتُ عَلَيْهِمْ شَهِيْدًا مَا دُمْتُ فِيْهِمْ ۚ
فَلَمَّا تَوَفَّيْتَنِيْ كُنْتَ أَنْتَ الرَّقِيْبَ عَلَيْهِمْ ۚ
وَأَنْتَ عَلٰى كُلِّ شَيْءٍ شَهِيْدٌ ﴿١١٧﴾

118   If Thou punish them, lo!
they are Thy slaves, and if Thou
forgive them (lo! they are Thy
slaves). Lo! Thou, only Thou art
the Mighty, the Wise.

اِنْ تُعَذِّبْهُمْ فَاِنَّهُمْ عِبَادُكَ ۚ وَاِنْ تَغْفِرْ لَهُمْ فَاِنَّكَ
أَنْتَ الْعَزِيْزُ الْحَكِيْمُ ﴿١١٨﴾

119   Allah saith: This is a day in
which their truthfulness profiteth
the truthful, for theirs are Gardens
underneath   which   rivers   flow,
wherein they are secure forever,
Allah taking pleasure in them and
they in Him. That is the great
triumph.

قَالَ اللّٰهُ هٰذَا يَوْمُ يَنْفَعُ الصَّادِقِيْنَ صِدْقُهُمْ ۚ
لَهُمْ جَنَّاتٌ تَجْرِيْ مِنْ تَحْتِهَا الْأَنْهَارُ خَالِدِيْنَ فِيْهَاۤ أَبَدًا ۚ
رَضِيَ اللّٰهُ عَنْهُمْ وَرَضُوْا عَنْهُ ۚ ذٰلِكَ الْفَوْزُ الْعَظِيْمُ ﴿١١٩﴾

120   Unto Allah belongeth the
Sovereignty of the heavens and the
earth and whatsoever is therein, and
He is Able to do all things.

لِلّٰهِ مُلْكُ السَّمٰوٰتِ وَالْأَرْضِ وَمَا فِيْهِنَّ ۚ
وَهُوَ عَلٰى كُلِّ شَيْءٍ قَدِيْرٌ ﴿١٢٠﴾

Sūrah 6

Al An'ām
(Cattle)

Al An'ām "Cattle," takes its name from a word in v. 137, repeated in vv. 139, 140, where cattle are mentioned in connection with superstitious practices condemned by Al-Islām.

With the possible exception of nine verses, which some authorities—e.g. Ibn Salāmah—ascribe to the Madīnah period, the whole of this sūrah belongs to the year before the Hijrah. It is related, on the authority of Ibn 'Abbās, that it was revealed in a single visitation. It is placed here on account of the subject, vindication of the Divine Unity, which fitly follows on the subjects of the previous sūrahs. The note of certain triumph is remarkable in the circumstances of its revelation, when the Prophet, after thirteen years of effort, saw himself obliged to flee from Makkah and seek help from strangers.

A late Makkan Sūrah.

In the name of Allah, the Beneficent, the Merciful.

1 Praise be to Allah, Who hath created the heavens and the earth, and hath appointed darkness and light. Yet those who disbelieve ascribe rivals unto their Lord.

2 He it is Who hath created you from clay, and hath decreed a term for you. A term is fixed with Him. Yet still ye doubt!

173

3   He is Allah in the heavens and in the earth. He knoweth both your secret and your utterance, and He knoweth what ye earn.

وَهُوَ اللَّهُ فِى السَّمٰوٰتِ وَفِى الْأَرْضِ يَعْلَمُ سِرَّكُمْ وَجَهْرَكُمْ وَيَعْلَمُ مَا تَكْسِبُوْنَ ۝

4   Never came there unto them a revelation of the revelations of Allah, but they did turn away from it.

وَمَا تَأْتِيْهِمْ مِّنْ ءَايَةٍ مِّنْ ءَايٰتِ رَبِّهِمْ إِلَّا كَانُوْا عَنْهَا مُعْرِضِيْنَ ۝

5   And they denied the truth when it came unto them. But there will come unto them the tidings of that which they used to deride.

فَقَدْ كَذَّبُوْا بِالْحَقِّ لَمَّا جَاءَهُمْ فَسَوْفَ يَأْتِيْهِمْ أَنْبٰٓؤُا مَا كَانُوْا بِهٖ يَسْتَهْزِءُوْنَ ۝

6   See they not how many a generation We destroyed before them, whom We had established in the earth more firmly than We have established you, and We shed on them abundant showers from the sky, and made the rivers flow beneath them. Yet We destroyed them for their sins, and created after them another generation.

أَلَمْ يَرَوْا كَمْ أَهْلَكْنَا مِنْ قَبْلِهِمْ مِّنْ قَرْنٍ مَّكَّنّٰهُمْ فِى الْأَرْضِ مَا لَمْ نُمَكِّنْ لَّكُمْ وَأَرْسَلْنَا السَّمَاءَ عَلَيْهِمْ مِّدْرَارًا وَّجَعَلْنَا الْأَنْهٰرَ تَجْرِيْ مِنْ تَحْتِهِمْ فَأَهْلَكْنٰهُمْ بِذُنُوْبِهِمْ وَأَنْشَأْنَا مِنْ بَعْدِهِمْ قَرْنًا ءَاخَرِيْنَ ۝

7   Had we sent down unto thee (Muḥammad) (actual) writing upon parchment, so that they could feel it with their hands, those who disbelieve would have said: This is naught else than mere magic.

وَلَوْ نَزَّلْنَا عَلَيْكَ كِتٰبًا فِىْ قِرْطَاسٍ فَلَمَسُوْهُ بِأَيْدِيْهِمْ لَقَالَ الَّذِيْنَ كَفَرُوْا إِنْ هٰذَا إِلَّا سِحْرٌ مُّبِيْنٌ ۝

8   They say: Why hath not an angel been sent down unto him? If We sent down an angel, then the matter would be judged; no further time would be allowed them (for reflection).

وَقَالُوْا لَوْلَا أُنْزِلَ عَلَيْهِ مَلَكٌ وَلَوْ أَنْزَلْنَا مَلَكًا لَّقُضِىَ الْأَمْرُ ثُمَّ لَا يُنْظَرُوْنَ ۝

9 Had We appointed an angel (Our messenger), We assuredly had made him (as) a man (that he might speak to men); and (thus) obscured for them (the truth) they (now) obscure.

وَلَوْ جَعَلْنَهُ مَلَكًا لَّجَعَلْنَهُ رَجُلًا وَلَلَبَسْنَا عَلَيْهِمْ مَا يَلْبِسُونَ ٩

10 Messengers (of Allah) have been derided before thee, but that whereat they scoffed surrounded such of them as did deride.

وَلَقَدِ اسْتُهْزِئَ بِرُسُلٍ مِّنْ قَبْلِكَ فَحَاقَ بِالَّذِينَ سَخِرُوا مِنْهُمْ مَّا كَانُوا بِهِ يَسْتَهْزِءُونَ ١٠

11 Say (unto the disbelievers): Travel in the land, and see the nature of the consequence for the rejecters!

قُلْ سِيرُوا فِي الْأَرْضِ ثُمَّ انْظُرُوا كَيْفَ كَانَ عَاقِبَةُ الْمُكَذِّبِينَ ١١

12 Say: Unto whom belongeth whatsoever is in the heavens and the earth? Say: Unto Allah. He hath prescribed for Himself mercy, that He may bring you all together to the Day of Resurrection whereof there is no doubt. Those who ruin their own souls will not believe.

قُلْ لِّمَنْ مَّا فِي السَّمَوَاتِ وَالْأَرْضِ قُلْ لِلَّهِ كَتَبَ عَلَى نَفْسِهِ الرَّحْمَةَ لَيَجْمَعَنَّكُمْ إِلَى يَوْمِ الْقِيَامَةِ لَا رَيْبَ فِيهِ الَّذِينَ خَسِرُوا أَنْفُسَهُمْ فَهُمْ لَا يُؤْمِنُونَ ١٢

13 Unto Him belongeth whatsoever resteth in the night and the day. He is the Hearer, the Knower.

۞ وَلَهُ مَا سَكَنَ فِي الَّيْلِ وَالنَّهَارِ وَهُوَ السَّمِيعُ الْعَلِيمُ ١٣

14 Say: Shall I choose for a protecting friend other than Allah, the Originator of the heavens and the earth? Who feedeth and is never fed! Say: I am ordered to be the first to surrender (unto Him). And be not thou (O Muḥammad) of the idolaters.

قُلْ أَغَيْرَ اللَّهِ أَتَّخِذُ وَلِيًّا فَاطِرِ السَّمَوَاتِ وَالْأَرْضِ وَهُوَ يُطْعِمُ وَلَا يُطْعَمُ قُلْ إِنِّي أُمِرْتُ أَنْ أَكُونَ أَوَّلَ مَنْ أَسْلَمَ وَلَا تَكُونَنَّ مِنَ الْمُشْرِكِينَ ١٤

15 Say: I fear, if I rebel against my Lord, the retribution of an Awful Day.

قُلْ إِنِّي أَخَافُ إِنْ عَصَيْتُ رَبِّي عَذَابَ يَوْمٍ عَظِيمٍ ١٥

16 He from whom (such retribution) is averted on that day (Allah) hath in truth had mercy on him. That will be the signal triumph.

مَن يُصْرَفْ عَنْهُ يَوْمَئِذٍ فَقَدْ رَحِمَهُ وَذَٰلِكَ الْفَوْزُ الْمُبِينُ ﴿١٦﴾

17 If Allah touch thee with affliction, there is none that can relieve therefrom save Him, and if He touch thee with good fortune (there is none that can impair it); for He is Able to do all things.

وَإِن يَمْسَسْكَ اللَّهُ بِضُرٍّ فَلَا كَاشِفَ لَهُ إِلَّا هُوَ وَإِن يَمْسَسْكَ بِخَيْرٍ فَهُوَ عَلَىٰ كُلِّ شَيْءٍ قَدِيرٌ ﴿١٧﴾

18 He is the Omnipotent over His slaves, and He is the Wise, the Knower.

وَهُوَ الْقَاهِرُ فَوْقَ عِبَادِهِ وَهُوَ الْحَكِيمُ الْخَبِيرُ ﴿١٨﴾

19 Say (O Muḥammad): What thing is of most weight in testimony? Say: Allah is witness between you and me. And this Qur'an hath been inspired in me, that I may warn therewith you and whomsoever it may reach. Do ye in truth bear witness that there are gods beside Allah? Say: I bear no such witness. Say: He is only One God. Lo! I am innocent of that which ye associate (with Him).

قُلْ أَيُّ شَيْءٍ أَكْبَرُ شَهَادَةً قُلِ اللَّهُ شَهِيدٌ بَيْنِي وَبَيْنَكُمْ وَأُوحِيَ إِلَيَّ هَٰذَا الْقُرْآنُ لِأُنذِرَكُم بِهِ وَمَن بَلَغَ أَئِنَّكُمْ لَتَشْهَدُونَ أَنَّ مَعَ اللَّهِ آلِهَةً أُخْرَىٰ قُل لَّا أَشْهَدُ قُلْ إِنَّمَا هُوَ إِلَٰهٌ وَاحِدٌ وَإِنَّنِي بَرِيءٌ مِّمَّا تُشْرِكُونَ ﴿١٩﴾

20 Those unto whom We gave the Scripture recognize (this Revelation) as they recognize their sons. Those who ruin their own souls will not believe.

الَّذِينَ آتَيْنَاهُمُ الْكِتَابَ يَعْرِفُونَهُ كَمَا يَعْرِفُونَ أَبْنَاءَهُمُ الَّذِينَ خَسِرُوا أَنفُسَهُمْ فَهُمْ لَا يُؤْمِنُونَ ﴿٢٠﴾

21 Who doth greater wrong than he who inventeth a lie against Allah or denieth His revelations? Lo! the wrong-doers will not be successful.

وَمَنْ أَظْلَمُ مِمَّنِ افْتَرَىٰ عَلَى اللَّهِ كَذِبًا أَوْ كَذَّبَ بِآيَاتِهِ إِنَّهُ لَا يُفْلِحُ الظَّالِمُونَ ﴿٢١﴾

22 And on the Day We gather them together We shall say unto those who ascribed partners (unto Allah): Where are (now) those partners of your make believe?

وَيَوْمَ نَحْشُرُهُمْ جَمِيعًا ثُمَّ نَقُولُ لِلَّذِينَ أَشْرَكُوٓا أَيْنَ شُرَكَآؤُكُمُ الَّذِينَ كُنتُمْ تَزْعُمُونَ ۝

23 Then will they have no contention save that they will say: By Allah, our Lord, we never were idolaters.

ثُمَّ لَمْ تَكُنْ فِتْنَتُهُمْ إِلَّآ أَن قَالُوا وَاللَّهِ رَبِّنَا مَا كُنَّا مُشْرِكِينَ ۝

24 See how they lie against themselves, and (how) the thing which they devised hath failed them!

انظُرْ كَيْفَ كَذَبُوا عَلَىٰٓ أَنفُسِهِمْ وَضَلَّ عَنْهُم مَّا كَانُوا يَفْتَرُونَ ۝

25 Of them are some who listen unto thee, but We have placed upon their hearts veils, lest they should understand, and in their ears a deafness. If they saw every token they would not believe therein; to the point that, when they come unto thee to argue with thee, the disbelievers say: This is naught else than fables of the men of old.

وَمِنْهُم مَّن يَسْتَمِعُ إِلَيْكَ وَجَعَلْنَا عَلَىٰ قُلُوبِهِمْ أَكِنَّةً أَن يَفْقَهُوهُ وَفِىٓ ءَاذَانِهِمْ وَقْرًا وَإِن يَرَوْا كُلَّ ءَايَةٍ لَّا يُؤْمِنُوا بِهَا حَتَّىٰٓ إِذَا جَآءُوكَ يُجَادِلُونَكَ يَقُولُ الَّذِينَ كَفَرُوٓا إِنْ هَٰذَآ إِلَّآ أَسَاطِيرُ الْأَوَّلِينَ ۝

26 And they forbid (men) from it and avoid it, and they ruin none save themselves, though they perceive not.

وَهُمْ يَنْهَوْنَ عَنْهُ وَيَنْأَوْنَ عَنْهُ وَإِن يُهْلِكُونَ إِلَّآ أَنفُسَهُمْ وَمَا يَشْعُرُونَ ۝

27 If thou couldst see when they are set before the Fire and say: Oh, would that we might return! Then would we not deny the revelations of our Lord, but we would be of the believers!

وَلَوْ تَرَىٰٓ إِذْ وُقِفُوا عَلَى النَّارِ فَقَالُوا يَٰلَيْتَنَا نُرَدُّ وَلَا نُكَذِّبَ بِـَٔايَٰتِ رَبِّنَا وَنَكُونَ مِنَ الْمُؤْمِنِينَ ۝

28 Nay, but that hath become clear unto them which before they used to hide. And if they were sent back;

بَلْ بَدَا لَهُم مَّا كَانُوا يُخْفُونَ مِن قَبْلُ وَلَوْ رُدُّوا لَعَادُوا

they would return unto that which they are forbidden. Lo! they are liars.

لِمَا نُهُوا عَنْهُ وَإِنَّهُمْ لَكَٰذِبُونَ ۝

29 And they say: There is naught save our life of the world, and we shall not be raised (again).

وَقَالُوٓا إِنْ هِيَ إِلَّا حَيَاتُنَا الدُّنْيَا وَمَا نَحْنُ بِمَبْعُوثِينَ ۝

30 If thou couldst see when they are set before their Lord! He will say: Is not this real? They will say: Yea, verily, by our Lord! He will say: Taste now the retribution for that ye used to disbelieve.

وَلَوْ تَرَىٰٓ إِذْ وُقِفُوا عَلَىٰ رَبِّهِمْ قَالَ أَلَيْسَ هَٰذَا بِالْحَقِّ قَالُوا بَلَىٰ وَرَبِّنَا قَالَ فَذُوقُوا الْعَذَابَ بِمَا كُنْتُمْ تَكْفُرُونَ ۝

31 They indeed are losers who deny their meeting with Allah until, when the hour cometh on them suddenly, they cry: Alas for us, that we neglected it! They bear upon their backs their burdens. Ah! Evil is that which they bear!

قَدْ خَسِرَ الَّذِينَ كَذَّبُوا بِلِقَاءِ اللَّهِ حَتَّىٰ إِذَا جَاءَتْهُمُ السَّاعَةُ بَغْتَةً قَالُوا يَا حَسْرَتَنَا عَلَىٰ مَا فَرَّطْنَا فِيهَا وَهُمْ يَحْمِلُونَ أَوْزَارَهُمْ عَلَىٰ ظُهُورِهِمْ أَلَا سَاءَ مَا يَزِرُونَ ۝

32 Naught is the life of the world save a pastime and a sport. Better far is the abode of the Hereafter for those who keep their duty (to Allah). Have ye then no sense?

وَمَا الْحَيَوٰةُ الدُّنْيَا إِلَّا لَعِبٌ وَلَهْوٌ وَلَلدَّارُ الْآخِرَةُ خَيْرٌ لِلَّذِينَ يَتَّقُونَ أَفَلَا تَعْقِلُونَ ۝

33 We know well how their talk grieveth thee, though in truth they deny not thee (Muhammad) but evil-doers flout the revelations of Allah.

قَدْ نَعْلَمُ إِنَّهُ لَيَحْزُنُكَ الَّذِي يَقُولُونَ فَإِنَّهُمْ لَا يُكَذِّبُونَكَ وَلَٰكِنَّ الظَّالِمِينَ بِآيَاتِ اللَّهِ يَجْحَدُونَ ۝

34 Messengers indeed have been denied before thee, and they were patient under the denial and the persecution till Our succour reached them. There is none to alter the decisions of Allah. Already there hath reached thee (somewhat) of the tidings of the messengers (We sent before).

وَلَقَدْ كُذِّبَتْ رُسُلٌ مِنْ قَبْلِكَ فَصَبَرُوا عَلَىٰ مَا كُذِّبُوا وَأُوذُوا حَتَّىٰ أَتَاهُمْ نَصْرُنَا وَلَا مُبَدِّلَ لِكَلِمَاتِ اللَّهِ وَلَقَدْ جَاءَكَ مِنْ نَبَإِ الْمُرْسَلِينَ ۝

35 And if their aversion is grievous unto thee, then, if thou canst, seek a way down into the earth or a ladder unto the sky that thou mayst bring unto them a portent (to convince them all)!—If Allah willed, He could have brought them all together to the guidance—So be not thou among the foolish ones.

وَإِن كَانَ كَبُرَ عَلَيْكَ إِعْرَاضُهُمْ فَإِنِ اسْتَطَعْتَ أَن تَبْتَغِيَ نَفَقًا فِي الْأَرْضِ أَوْ سُلَّمًا فِي السَّمَاءِ فَتَأْتِيَهُم بِآيَةٍ وَلَوْ شَاءَ اللَّهُ لَجَمَعَهُمْ عَلَى الْهُدَىٰ فَلَا تَكُونَنَّ مِنَ الْجَاهِلِينَ ﴿٣٥﴾

36 Only those can accept who hear. As for the dead, Allah will raise them up; then unto Him they will be returned.

۞ إِنَّمَا يَسْتَجِيبُ الَّذِينَ يَسْمَعُونَ وَالْمَوْتَىٰ يَبْعَثُهُمُ اللَّهُ ثُمَّ إِلَيْهِ يُرْجَعُونَ ﴿٣٦﴾

37 They say: Why hath no portent been sent down upon him from his Lord? Say: Lo! Allah is Able to send down a portent. But most of them know not.

وَقَالُوا لَوْلَا نُزِّلَ عَلَيْهِ ءَايَةٌ مِّن رَّبِّهِ قُلْ إِنَّ اللَّهَ قَادِرٌ عَلَىٰ أَن يُنَزِّلَ ءَايَةً وَلَٰكِنَّ أَكْثَرَهُمْ لَا يَعْلَمُونَ ﴿٣٧﴾

38 There is not an animal in the earth, nor a flying creature flying on two wings, but they are peoples like unto you. We have neglected nothing in the Book (of Our decrees). Then unto their Lord they will be gathered.

وَمَا مِن دَابَّةٍ فِي الْأَرْضِ وَلَا طَائِرٍ يَطِيرُ بِجَنَاحَيْهِ إِلَّا أُمَمٌ أَمْثَالُكُم مَّا فَرَّطْنَا فِي الْكِتَابِ مِن شَيْءٍ ثُمَّ إِلَىٰ رَبِّهِمْ يُحْشَرُونَ ﴿٣٨﴾

39 Those who deny our revelations are deaf and dumb in darkness. Whom Allah will He sendeth astray, and whom He will He placeth on a straight path.

وَالَّذِينَ كَذَّبُوا بِآيَاتِنَا صُمٌّ وَبُكْمٌ فِي الظُّلُمَاتِ مَن يَشَإِ اللَّهُ يُضْلِلْهُ وَمَن يَشَأْ يَجْعَلْهُ عَلَىٰ صِرَاطٍ مُّسْتَقِيمٍ ﴿٣٩﴾

40 Say: Can ye see yourselves, if the punishment of Allah come upon you or the Hour come upon you? Do ye then call (for help) to any other than Allah? (Answer that) if ye are truthful.

قُلْ أَرَأَيْتَكُمْ إِنْ أَتَاكُمْ عَذَابُ اللَّهِ أَوْ أَتَتْكُمُ السَّاعَةُ أَغَيْرَ اللَّهِ تَدْعُونَ إِن كُنتُمْ صَادِقِينَ ﴿٤٠﴾

41 Nay, but unto Him ye call, and He removeth that because of which ye call unto Him, if He will, and ye forget whatever partners ye ascribed unto Him.

بَلْ إِيَّاهُ تَدْعُونَ فَيَكْشِفُ مَا تَدْعُونَ إِلَيْهِ إِن شَآءَ وَتَنسَوْنَ مَا تُشْرِكُونَ ۝

42 We have sent already unto peoples that were before thee, and We visited them with tribulation and adversity, in order that they might grow humble.

وَلَقَدْ أَرْسَلْنَآ إِلَىٰ أُمَمٍ مِّن قَبْلِكَ فَأَخَذْنَٰهُم بِٱلْبَأْسَآءِ وَٱلضَّرَّآءِ لَعَلَّهُمْ يَتَضَرَّعُونَ ۝

43 If only, when our disaster came on them, they had been humble! But their hearts were hardened and the devil made all that they used to do seem fair unto them!

فَلَوْلَآ إِذْ جَآءَهُم بَأْسُنَا تَضَرَّعُوا۟ وَلَٰكِن قَسَتْ قُلُوبُهُمْ وَزَيَّنَ لَهُمُ ٱلشَّيْطَٰنُ مَا كَانُوا۟ يَعْمَلُونَ ۝

44 Then, when they forgot that whereof they had been reminded, We opened unto them the gates of all things till, even as they were rejoicing in that which they were given, We seized them unawares, and lo! they were dumbfounded.

فَلَمَّا نَسُوا۟ مَا ذُكِّرُوا۟ بِهِۦ فَتَحْنَا عَلَيْهِمْ أَبْوَٰبَ كُلِّ شَىْءٍ حَتَّىٰٓ إِذَا فَرِحُوا۟ بِمَآ أُوتُوٓا۟ أَخَذْنَٰهُم بَغْتَةً فَإِذَا هُم مُّبْلِسُونَ ۝

45 So of the people who did wrong the last remnant was cut off. Praise be to Allah, Lord of the Worlds!

فَقُطِعَ دَابِرُ ٱلْقَوْمِ ٱلَّذِينَ ظَلَمُوا۟ وَٱلْحَمْدُ لِلَّهِ رَبِّ ٱلْعَٰلَمِينَ ۝

46 Say: Have ye imagined, if Allah should take away your hearing and your sight and seal your hearts, who is the God who could restore it to you save Allah? See how We display the revelations unto them? Yet still they turn away.

قُلْ أَرَءَيْتُمْ إِنْ أَخَذَ ٱللَّهُ سَمْعَكُمْ وَأَبْصَٰرَكُمْ وَخَتَمَ عَلَىٰ قُلُوبِكُم مَّنْ إِلَٰهٌ غَيْرُ ٱللَّهِ يَأْتِيكُم بِهِۦٓ ٱنظُرْ كَيْفَ نُصَرِّفُ ٱلْءَايَٰتِ ثُمَّ هُمْ يَصْدِفُونَ ۝

47 Say: Can ye see yourselves, if the punishment of Allah come upon you unawares or openly? Would any perish save wrongdoing folk?

قُلْ أَرَءَيْتَكُمْ إِنْ أَتَىٰكُمْ عَذَابُ ٱللَّهِ بَغْتَةً أَوْ جَهْرَةً هَلْ يُهْلَكُ إِلَّا ٱلْقَوْمُ ٱلظَّٰلِمُونَ ۝

48 We send not the messengers save as bearers of good news and warners. Whoso believeth and doeth right, there shall no fear come upon them neither shall they grieve.

وَمَا نُرْسِلُ الْمُرْسَلِينَ إِلَّا مُبَشِّرِينَ وَمُنذِرِينَ فَمَنْ ءَامَنَ وَأَصْلَحَ فَلَا خَوْفٌ عَلَيْهِمْ وَلَا هُمْ يَحْزَنُونَ ٤٨

49 But as for those who deny Our revelations, torment will afflict them for that they used to disobey.

وَالَّذِينَ كَذَّبُوا بِـَٔايَٰتِنَا يَمَسُّهُمُ الْعَذَابُ بِمَا كَانُوا يَفْسُقُونَ ٤٩

50 Say (O Muhammad, to the disbelievers): I say not unto you (that) I possess the treasures of Allah, nor that I have knowledge of the Unseen; and I say not unto you: Lo! I am an angel. I follow only that which is inspired in me. Say: Are the blind man and the seer equal? Will ye not then take thought?

قُل لَّآ أَقُولُ لَكُمْ عِندِي خَزَآئِنُ اللَّهِ وَلَآ أَعْلَمُ الْغَيْبَ وَلَآ أَقُولُ لَكُمْ إِنِّي مَلَكٌ إِنْ أَتَّبِعُ إِلَّا مَا يُوحَىٰ إِلَيَّ قُلْ هَلْ يَسْتَوِي الْأَعْمَىٰ وَالْبَصِيرُ أَفَلَا تَتَفَكَّرُونَ ٥٠

51 Warn hereby those who fear (because they know) that they will be gathered unto their Lord, for whom there is no protecting friend nor intercessor beside Him, that they may ward off (evil).

وَأَنذِرْ بِهِ الَّذِينَ يَخَافُونَ أَن يُحْشَرُوا إِلَىٰ رَبِّهِمْ لَيْسَ لَهُم مِّن دُونِهِ وَلِيٌّ وَلَا شَفِيعٌ لَّعَلَّهُمْ يَتَّقُونَ ٥١

52 Repel not those who call upon their Lord at morn and evening, seeking His countenance. Thou art not accountable for them in aught, nor are they accountable for thee in aught, that thou shouldst repel them and be of the wrong-doers.

وَلَا تَطْرُدِ الَّذِينَ يَدْعُونَ رَبَّهُم بِالْغَدَوٰةِ وَالْعَشِيِّ يُرِيدُونَ وَجْهَهُۥ مَا عَلَيْكَ مِنْ حِسَابِهِم مِّن شَيْءٍ وَمَا مِنْ حِسَابِكَ عَلَيْهِم مِّن شَيْءٍ فَتَطْرُدَهُمْ فَتَكُونَ مِنَ الظَّٰلِمِينَ ٥٢

53 And even so do We try some of them by others, that they say: Are these they whom Allah favoureth among us? Is not Allah best aware of the thanksgivers?

وَكَذَٰلِكَ فَتَنَّا بَعْضَهُم بِبَعْضٍ لِّيَقُولُوٓا أَهَٰٓؤُلَآءِ مَنَّ اللَّهُ عَلَيْهِم مِّنۢ بَيْنِنَآ أَلَيْسَ اللَّهُ بِأَعْلَمَ بِالشَّٰكِرِينَ ٥٣

54 And when those who believe in
Our revelations come unto thee,
say: Peace be unto you! Your Lord
hath prescribed for Himself mercy,
that whoso of you doth evil through
ignorance and repenteth afterward
thereof and doeth right, (for him)
lo! Allah is Forgiving, Merciful.

وَإِذَا جَاءَكَ الَّذِينَ يُؤْمِنُونَ بِآيَاتِنَا فَقُلْ سَلَـٰمٌ
عَلَيْكُمْ كَتَبَ رَبُّكُمْ عَلَىٰ نَفْسِهِ الرَّحْمَةَ
أَنَّهُ مَنْ عَمِلَ مِنكُمْ سُوٓءًا بِجَهَـٰلَةٍ ثُمَّ تَابَ
مِنۢ بَعْدِهِ وَأَصْلَحَ فَأَنَّهُۥ غَفُورٌ رَّحِيمٌ ۝

55 Thus do We expound the revelations that the way of the unrighteous may be manifest.

وَكَذَٰلِكَ نُفَصِّلُ الْآيَـٰتِ وَلِتَسْتَبِينَ سَبِيلُ
الْمُجْرِمِينَ ۝

56 Say: I am forbidden to worship
those on whom ye call instead of
Allah. Say: I will not follow your
desires, for then should I go astray
and I should not be of the rightly
guided.

قُلْ إِنِّى نُهِيتُ أَنْ أَعْبُدَ الَّذِينَ تَدْعُونَ مِن دُونِ
اللَّهِ قُل لَّآ أَتَّبِعُ أَهْوَآءَكُمْ قَدْ ضَلَلْتُ إِذًا
وَمَآ أَنَا۠ مِنَ الْمُهْتَدِينَ ۝

57 Say: I am (relying) on clear
proof from my Lord, while ye deny
Him. I have not that for which ye
are impatient. The decision is for
Allah only. He telleth the truth and
He is the Best of Deciders.

قُلْ إِنِّى عَلَىٰ بَيِّنَةٍ مِّن رَّبِّى وَكَذَّبْتُم بِهِۦ
مَا عِندِى مَا تَسْتَعْجِلُونَ بِهِۦ إِنِ الْحُكْمُ
إِلَّا لِلَّهِ يَقُصُّ الْحَقَّ وَهُوَ خَيْرُ الْفَـٰصِلِينَ ۝

58 Say: If I had that for which ye
are impatient, then would the case
(ere this) have been decided between me and you. Allah is best
aware of the wrong-doers.

قُل لَّوْ أَنَّ عِندِى مَا تَسْتَعْجِلُونَ بِهِۦ لَقُضِىَ
الْأَمْرُ بَيْنِى وَبَيْنَكُمْ وَاللَّهُ أَعْلَمُ
بِالظَّـٰلِمِينَ ۝

59 And with Him are the keys of
the invisible. None but He knoweth
them. And He knoweth what is in
the land and the sea. Not a leaf
falleth but He knoweth it, not a
grain amid the darkness of the
earth, naught of wet or dry but (it
is noted) in a clear record.

۞ وَعِندَهُۥ مَفَاتِحُ الْغَيْبِ لَا يَعْلَمُهَآ إِلَّا هُوَ
وَيَعْلَمُ مَا فِى الْبَرِّ وَالْبَحْرِ وَمَا تَسْقُطُ مِن وَرَقَةٍ
إِلَّا يَعْلَمُهَا وَلَا حَبَّةٍ فِى ظُلُمَـٰتِ الْأَرْضِ
وَلَا رَطْبٍ وَلَا يَابِسٍ إِلَّا فِى كِتَـٰبٍ مُّبِينٍ ۝

60 He it is Who gathereth you at night and knoweth that which ye commit by day. Then He raiseth you again to life therein, that the term appointed (for you) may be accomplished. And afterward unto Him is your return. Then He will proclaim unto you what ye used to do.

وَهُوَ الَّذِى يَتَوَفَّىٰكُمْ بِالَّيْلِ وَيَعْلَمُ مَا جَرَحْتُمْ بِالنَّهَارِ ثُمَّ يَبْعَثُكُمْ فِيهِ لِيُقْضَىٰٓ أَجَلٌ مُّسَمًّى ثُمَّ إِلَيْهِ مَرْجِعُكُمْ ثُمَّ يُنَبِّئُكُم بِمَا كُنتُمْ تَعْمَلُونَ ۝

61 He is the Omnipotent over His slaves. He sendeth guardians over you until, when death cometh unto one of you, Our messengers[1] receive him, and they neglect not.

وَهُوَ الْقَاهِرُ فَوْقَ عِبَادِهِۦ وَيُرْسِلُ عَلَيْكُمْ حَفَظَةً حَتَّىٰٓ إِذَا جَآءَ أَحَدَكُمُ الْمَوْتُ تَوَفَّتْهُ رُسُلُنَا وَهُمْ لَا يُفَرِّطُونَ ۝

62 Then are they restored unto Allah, their Lord, the Just. Surely His is the judgment. And He is the most swift of reckoners.

ثُمَّ رُدُّوٓاْ إِلَى اللَّهِ مَوْلَىٰهُمُ الْحَقِّ أَلَا لَهُ الْحُكْمُ وَهُوَ أَسْرَعُ الْحَاسِبِينَ ۝

63 Say: Who delivereth you from the darkness of the land and the sea? Ye call upon Him humbly and in secret, (saying): If He delivers us from this (fear) we truly will be of the thankful.

قُلْ مَن يُنَجِّيكُم مِّن ظُلُمَاتِ الْبَرِّ وَالْبَحْرِ تَدْعُونَهُۥ تَضَرُّعًا وَخُفْيَةً لَّئِنْ أَنجَىٰنَا مِنْ هَٰذِهِۦ لَنَكُونَنَّ مِنَ الشَّاكِرِينَ ۝

64 Say: Allah delivereth you from this and from all afflictions. Yet ye attribute partners unto Him.

قُلِ اللَّهُ يُنَجِّيكُم مِّنْهَا وَمِن كُلِّ كَرْبٍ ثُمَّ أَنتُمْ تُشْرِكُونَ ۝

65 Say: He is able to send punishment upon you from above you or from beneath your feet, or to bewilder you with dissension and make you taste the tyranny one of another. See how We display the revelations so that they may understand.

قُلْ هُوَ الْقَادِرُ عَلَىٰٓ أَن يَبْعَثَ عَلَيْكُمْ عَذَابًا مِّن فَوْقِكُمْ أَوْ مِن تَحْتِ أَرْجُلِكُمْ أَوْ يَلْبِسَكُمْ شِيَعًا وَيُذِيقَ بَعْضَكُم بَأْسَ بَعْضٍ انظُرْ كَيْفَ نُصَرِّفُ الْآيَٰتِ لَعَلَّهُمْ يَفْقَهُونَ ۝

---

1. *i.e.* angels. The same word *rusul* is used for angels and for prophets.

66 Thy people (O Muhammad) have denied it, though it is the Truth. Say: I am not put in charge of you.

وَكَذَّبَ بِهِ قَوْمُكَ وَهُوَ الْحَقُّ قُلْ لَسْتُ عَلَيْكُم بِوَكِيلٍ ۝

67 For every announcement there is a term, and ye will come to know.

لِكُلِّ نَبَإٍ مُسْتَقَرٌّ وَسَوْفَ تَعْلَمُونَ ۝

68 And when thou seest those who meddle with Our revelations, withdraw from them until they meddle with another topic. And if the devil cause thee to forget, sit not, after the remembrance, with the congregation of wrong-doers.

وَإِذَا رَأَيْتَ الَّذِينَ يَخُوضُونَ فِي آيَاتِنَا فَأَعْرِضْ عَنْهُمْ حَتَّىٰ يَخُوضُوا فِي حَدِيثٍ غَيْرِهِ وَإِمَّا يُنسِيَنَّكَ الشَّيْطَانُ فَلَا تَقْعُدْ بَعْدَ الذِّكْرَىٰ مَعَ الْقَوْمِ الظَّالِمِينَ ۝

69 Those who ward off (evil) are not accountable for them in aught, but the Reminder (must be given them) that haply they (too) may ward off (evil).

وَمَا عَلَى الَّذِينَ يَتَّقُونَ مِنْ حِسَابِهِم مِّن شَيْءٍ وَلَٰكِن ذِكْرَىٰ لَعَلَّهُمْ يَتَّقُونَ ۝

70 And forsake those who take their religion for a pastime and a jest, and whom the life of the world beguileth. Remind (mankind) hereby lest a soul be destroyed by what it earneth. It hath beside Allah no friend nor intercessor, and though it offer every compensation it will not be accepted from it. Those are they who perish by their own deserts. For them is drink of boiling water and a painful doom, because they disbelieved.

وَذَرِ الَّذِينَ اتَّخَذُوا دِينَهُمْ لَعِبًا وَلَهْوًا وَغَرَّتْهُمُ الْحَيَاةُ الدُّنْيَا وَذَكِّرْ بِهِ أَن تُبْسَلَ نَفْسٌ بِمَا كَسَبَتْ لَيْسَ لَهَا مِن دُونِ اللَّهِ وَلِيٌّ وَلَا شَفِيعٌ وَإِن تَعْدِلْ كُلَّ عَدْلٍ لَّا يُؤْخَذْ مِنْهَا أُولَٰئِكَ الَّذِينَ أُبْسِلُوا بِمَا كَسَبُوا لَهُمْ شَرَابٌ مِّنْ حَمِيمٍ وَعَذَابٌ أَلِيمٌ بِمَا كَانُوا يَكْفُرُونَ ۝

71 Say: Shall we cry, instead of unto Allah, unto that which neither profiteth us nor hurteth us, and shall we turn back after Allah hath guided us, like one bewildered

قُلْ أَنَدْعُوا مِن دُونِ اللَّهِ مَا لَا يَنفَعُنَا وَلَا يَضُرُّنَا وَنُرَدُّ عَلَىٰ أَعْقَابِنَا بَعْدَ إِذْ هَدَانَا اللَّهُ كَالَّذِي

whom the devils have infatuated in the earth, who hath companions who invite him to the guidance (saying): Come unto us? Say: Lo! the guidance of Allah is Guidance, and we are ordered to surrender to the Lord of the Worlds;

اسْتَهْوَتْهُ الشَّيَاطِينُ فِي الْأَرْضِ حَيْرَانَ لَهُ أَصْحَابٌ يَدْعُونَهُ إِلَى الْهُدَى ائْتِنَا قُلْ إِنَّ هُدَى اللَّهِ هُوَ الْهُدَى وَأُمِرْنَا لِنُسْلِمَ لِرَبِّ الْعَالَمِينَ ﴿٧١﴾

72 And to establish worship and ward off (evil), and He it is unto Whom ye will be gathered.

وَأَنْ أَقِيمُوا الصَّلَاةَ وَاتَّقُوهُ وَهُوَ الَّذِي إِلَيْهِ تُحْشَرُونَ ﴿٧٢﴾

73 He it is Who created the heavens and the earth in truth. In that day when He saith: Be! it is. His word is the truth, and His will be the Sovereignty on the day when the trumpet is blown. Knower of the invisible and the visible, He is the Wise, the Aware.

وَهُوَ الَّذِي خَلَقَ السَّمَاوَاتِ وَالْأَرْضَ بِالْحَقِّ وَيَوْمَ يَقُولُ كُنْ فَيَكُونُ قَوْلُهُ الْحَقُّ وَلَهُ الْمُلْكُ يَوْمَ يُنْفَخُ فِي الصُّورِ عَالِمُ الْغَيْبِ وَالشَّهَادَةِ وَهُوَ الْحَكِيمُ الْخَبِيرُ ﴿٧٣﴾

74 (Remember) when Abraham said unto his father Azar: Takest thou idols for gods? Lo! I see thee and thy folk in error manifest.

۞ وَإِذْ قَالَ إِبْرَاهِيمُ لِأَبِيهِ آزَرَ أَتَتَّخِذُ أَصْنَامًا آلِهَةً إِنِّي أَرَاكَ وَقَوْمَكَ فِي ضَلَالٍ مُبِينٍ ﴿٧٤﴾

75 Thus did We show Abraham the kingdom of the heavens and the earth that he might be of those possessing certainty:

وَكَذَلِكَ نُرِي إِبْرَاهِيمَ مَلَكُوتَ السَّمَاوَاتِ وَالْأَرْضِ وَلِيَكُونَ مِنَ الْمُوقِنِينَ ﴿٧٥﴾

76 When the night grew dark upon him he beheld a star. He said: This is my Lord. But when it set, he said: I love not things that set.

فَلَمَّا جَنَّ عَلَيْهِ اللَّيْلُ رَأَى كَوْكَبًا قَالَ هَذَا رَبِّي فَلَمَّا أَفَلَ قَالَ لَا أُحِبُّ الْآفِلِينَ ﴿٧٦﴾

77 And when he saw the moon uprising, he exclaimed: This my Lord. But when it set, he said: Unless my Lord guide me, I surely shall become one of the folk who are astray.

فَلَمَّا رَأَى الْقَمَرَ بَازِغًا قَالَ هَذَا رَبِّي فَلَمَّا أَفَلَ قَالَ لَئِنْ لَمْ يَهْدِنِي رَبِّي لَأَكُونَنَّ مِنَ الْقَوْمِ الضَّالِّينَ ﴿٧٧﴾

78 And when he saw the sun uprising, he cried: This is my Lord! This is greater! And when it set he exclaimed: O my people! Lo! I am free from all that ye associate (with Him).

فَلَمَّا رَءَا الشَّمْسَ بَازِغَةً قَالَ هَذَا رَبِّى هَذَآ أَكْبَرُ فَلَمَّآ أَفَلَتْ قَالَ يَقَوْمِ إِنِّى بَرِىٓءٌ مِّمَّا تُشْرِكُونَ ۝

79 Lo! I have turned my face toward Him Who created the heavens and the earth, as one by nature upright, and I am not of the idolaters.

إِنِّى وَجَّهْتُ وَجْهِىَ لِلَّذِى فَطَرَ السَّمَوَاتِ وَالْأَرْضَ حَنِيفًا وَمَآ أَنَا۠ مِنَ الْمُشْرِكِينَ ۝

80 His people argued with him. He said: Dispute ye with me concerning Allah when He hath guided me? I fear not at all that which ye set beside Him unless my Lord willeth aught. My Lord includeth all things in His knowledge. Will ye not then remember?

وَحَآجَّهُ قَوْمُهُ قَالَ أَتُحَٰٓجُّوٓنِّى فِى اللَّهِ وَقَدْ هَدَانِ وَلَآ أَخَافُ مَا تُشْرِكُونَ بِهِۦٓ إِلَّآ أَن يَشَآءَ رَبِّى شَيْـًٔا وَسِعَ رَبِّى كُلَّ شَىْءٍ عِلْمًا أَفَلَا تَتَذَكَّرُونَ ۝

81 How should I fear that which ye set up beside Him, when ye fear not to set up beside Allah that for which He hath revealed unto you no warrant? Which of the two factions hath more right to safety? (Answer me that) if ye have knowledge.

وَكَيْفَ أَخَافُ مَآ أَشْرَكْتُمْ وَلَا تَخَافُونَ أَنَّكُمْ أَشْرَكْتُم بِاللَّهِ مَا لَمْ يُنَزِّلْ بِهِۦ عَلَيْكُمْ سُلْطَانًا فَأَىُّ الْفَرِيقَيْنِ أَحَقُّ بِالْأَمْنِ إِن كُنتُمْ تَعْلَمُونَ ۝

82 Those who believe and obscure not their belief by wrong-doing, theirs is safety; and they are rightly guided.

الَّذِينَ ءَامَنُوا وَلَمْ يَلْبِسُوٓا إِيمَٰنَهُم بِظُلْمٍ أُو۟لَٰٓئِكَ لَهُمُ الْأَمْنُ وَهُم مُّهْتَدُونَ ۝

83 That is Our argument. We gave it unto Abraham against his folk. We raise unto degrees (of wisdom) whom We will. Lo! thy Lord is Wise, Aware.

وَتِلْكَ حُجَّتُنَآ ءَاتَيْنَٰهَآ إِبْرَٰهِيمَ عَلَىٰ قَوْمِهِۦ نَرْفَعُ دَرَجَٰتٍ مَّن نَّشَآءُ إِنَّ رَبَّكَ حَكِيمٌ عَلِيمٌ ۝

84 And We bestowed upon him Isaac and Jacob; each of them We guided; and Noah did We guide aforetime; and of his seed (We guided) David and Solomon and Job and Joseph and Moses and Aaron. Thus do We reward the good.

وَوَهَبْنَا لَهٗٓ إِسْحَقَ وَيَعْقُوبَ ۚ كُلًّا هَدَيْنَا ۚ وَنُوحًا هَدَيْنَا مِنْ قَبْلُ وَمِنْ ذُرِّيَّتِهٖ دَاوٗدَ وَسُلَيْمٰنَ وَأَيُّوبَ وَيُوسُفَ وَمُوسٰى وَهٰرُوْنَ ۚ وَكَذٰلِكَ نَجْزِى الْمُحْسِنِيْنَ ۝

85 And Zachariah and John and Jesus and Elias. Each one (of them) was of the righteous.

وَزَكَرِيَّا وَيَحْيٰى وَعِيْسٰى وَإِلْيَاسَ ۚ كُلٌّ مِّنَ الصّٰلِحِيْنَ ۝

86 And Ishmael and Elisha and Jonah and Lot. Each one of them did We prefer above (Our) creatures;

وَإِسْمٰعِيْلَ وَالْيَسَعَ وَيُوْنُسَ وَلُوْطًا ۚ وَكُلًّا فَضَّلْنَا عَلَى الْعٰلَمِيْنَ ۝

87 With some of their forefathers and their offspring and their brethren; and We chose them and guided them unto a straight path.

وَمِنْ ءَابَآئِهِمْ وَذُرِّيّٰتِهِمْ وَإِخْوَانِهِمْ ۚ وَاجْتَبَيْنٰهُمْ وَهَدَيْنٰهُمْ إِلٰى صِرٰطٍ مُّسْتَقِيمٍ ۝

88 Such is the guidance of Allah wherewith He guideth whom He will of His bondmen. But if they had set up (for worship) aught beside Him, (all) that they did would have been vain.

ذٰلِكَ هُدَى اللّٰهِ يَهْدِيْ بِهٖ مَنْ يَّشَآءُ مِنْ عِبَادِهٖ ۚ وَلَوْ أَشْرَكُوا لَحَبِطَ عَنْهُمْ مَّا كَانُوْا يَعْمَلُوْنَ ۝

89 Those are they unto whom We gave the Scripture and Command and Prophethood. But if these disbelieve therein, then indeed We shall entrust it to a people who will not be disbelievers therein.

أُولٰٓئِكَ الَّذِيْنَ ءَاتَيْنٰهُمُ الْكِتٰبَ وَالْحُكْمَ وَالنُّبُوَّةَ ۚ فَإِنْ يَّكْفُرْ بِهَا هٰٓؤُلَآءِ فَقَدْ وَكَّلْنَا بِهَا قَوْمًا لَّيْسُوْا بِهَا بِكٰفِرِيْنَ ۝

90 Those are they whom Allah guideth, so follow their guidance. Say (O Muhammad, unto mankind): I ask of you no fee for it. Lo! it is naught but a Reminder to (His) creatures.

أُولٰٓئِكَ الَّذِيْنَ هَدَى اللّٰهُ ۚ فَبِهُدٰىهُمُ اقْتَدِهْ ۗ قُلْ لَّآ أَسْئَلُكُمْ عَلَيْهِ أَجْرًا ۚ إِنْ هُوَ إِلَّا ذِكْرٰى لِلْعٰلَمِيْنَ ۝

91 And they measure not the power
of Allah its true measure when they
say: Allah hath naught revealed
unto a human being. Say (unto the
Jews who speak thus): Who revealed the Book which Moses brought, a light and guidance for mankind, which ye have put on parch-
ments which ye show, but ye hide
much (thereof), and by which ye
were taught that which ye knew not
yourselves nor (did) your fathers
(know it)? Say: Allah. Then leave
them to their play of cavilling.

وَمَا قَدَرُوا اللَّهَ حَقَّ قَدْرِهِ إِذْ قَالُوا مَا أَنْزَلَ اللَّهُ عَلَى
بَشَرٍ مِنْ شَيْءٍ قُلْ مَنْ أَنْزَلَ الْكِتَبَ الَّذِي جَاءَ بِهِ
مُوسَى نُورًا وَهُدًى لِلنَّاسِ تَجْعَلُونَهُ قَرَاطِيسَ
تُبْدُونَهَا وَتُخْفُونَ كَثِيرًا وَعُلِّمْتُمْ مَا لَمْ تَعْلَمُوا أَنْتُمْ
وَلَا ءَابَاؤُكُمْ قُلِ اللَّهُ ثُمَّ ذَرْهُمْ فِي خَوْضِهِمْ
يَلْعَبُونَ ٩١

92 And this is a blessed Scripture
which We have revealed, confirming that which (was revealed)
before it, that thou mayst warn the
Mother of Villages[2] and those
around her. Those who believe in
the Hereafter believe herein, and
they are careful of their worship.

وَهَذَا كِتَبٌ أَنْزَلْنَهُ مُبَارَكٌ مُصَدِّقُ الَّذِي بَيْنَ
يَدَيْهِ وَلِتُنْذِرَ أُمَّ الْقُرَى وَمَنْ حَوْلَهَا وَالَّذِينَ يُؤْمِنُونَ
بِالْآخِرَةِ يُؤْمِنُونَ بِهِ وَهُمْ عَلَى صَلَاتِهِمْ
يُحَافِظُونَ ٩٢

93 Who is guilty of more wrong
than he who forgeth a lie against
Allah, or saith: I am inspired, when
he is not inspired in aught; and who
saith: I will reveal the like of that
which Allah hath revealed? If thou
couldst see, when the wrong-doers
reach the pangs of death and the
angels stretch their hands out, saying: Deliver up your souls. This day
ye are awarded doom of degra-

وَمَنْ أَظْلَمُ مِمَّنِ افْتَرَى عَلَى اللَّهِ كَذِبًا أَوْ قَالَ أُوحِيَ
إِلَيَّ وَلَمْ يُوحَ إِلَيْهِ شَيْءٌ وَمَنْ قَالَ سَأُنْزِلُ مِثْلَ مَا أَنْزَلَ
اللَّهُ وَلَوْ تَرَى إِذِ الظَّالِمُونَ فِي غَمَرَاتِ الْمَوْتِ
وَالْمَلَائِكَةُ بَاسِطُوا أَيْدِيهِمْ أَخْرِجُوا
أَنْفُسَكُمُ الْيَوْمَ تُجْزَوْنَ عَذَابَ الْهُونِ

---

2. *i.e.* Makkah.

dation for that ye spake concerning Allah other than the truth, and scorned His portents.

بِمَا كُنْتُمْ تَقُولُونَ عَلَى اللهِ غَيْرَ الْحَقِّ وَكُنْتُمْ عَنْ ءَايَتِهِ تَسْتَكْبِرُونَ ۝

94 Now have ye come unto Us solitary as We did create you at the first, and ye have left behind you all that We bestowed upon you, and We behold not with you those your intercessors, of whom ye claimed that they possessed a share in you. Now is the bond between you severed, and that which ye presumed hath failed you.

وَلَقَدْ جِئْتُمُونَا فُرَادَى كَمَا خَلَقْنَكُمْ أَوَّلَ مَرَّةٍ وَتَرَكْتُمْ مَّا خَوَّلْنَكُمْ وَرَآءَ ظُهُورِكُمْ وَمَا نَرَى مَعَكُمْ شُفَعَاءَكُمُ الَّذِينَ زَعَمْتُمْ أَنَّهُمْ فِيكُمْ شُرَكَؤُا لَقَدْ تَقَطَّعَ بَيْنَكُمْ وَضَلَّ عَنْكُمْ مَّا كُنْتُمْ تَزْعُمُونَ ۝

95 Lo! Allah (it is) who splitteth the grain of corn and the date stone (for sprouting). He bringeth forth the living from the dead, and is the bringer-forth of the dead from the living. Such is Allah. How then are ye perverted?

۞ إِنَّ اللهَ فَالِقُ الْحَبِّ وَالنَّوَى يُخْرِجُ الْحَىَّ مِنَ الْمَيِّتِ وَمُخْرِجُ الْمَيِّتِ مِنَ الْحَىِّ ذَلِكُمُ اللهُ فَأَنَّى تُؤْفَكُونَ ۝

96 He is the Cleaver of the Daybreak, and He hath appointed the night for stillness, and the sun and the moon for reckoning. That is the measuring of the Mighty, the Wise.

فَالِقُ الْإِصْبَاحِ وَجَعَلَ الَّيْلَ سَكَنًا وَالشَّمْسَ وَالْقَمَرَ حُسْبَانًا ذَلِكَ تَقْدِيرُ الْعَزِيزِ الْعَلِيمِ ۝

97 And He it is Who hath set for you the stars that ye may guide your course by them amid the darkness of the land and the sea. We have detailed Our revelations for a people who have knowledge.

وَهُوَ الَّذِى جَعَلَ لَكُمُ النُّجُومَ لِتَهْتَدُوا بِهَا فِى ظُلُمَتِ الْبَرِّ وَالْبَحْرِ قَدْ فَصَّلْنَا الْآيَتِ لِقَوْمٍ يَعْلَمُونَ ۝

98 And He it is Who hath produced you from a single being, and (hath given you) a habitation and a repository. We have detailed Our revelations for a people who have understanding.

وَهُوَ الَّذِى أَنشَأَكُم مِّن نَّفْسٍ وَحِدَةٍ فَمُسْتَقَرٌّ وَمُسْتَوْدَعٌ قَدْ فَصَّلْنَا الْآيَتِ لِقَوْمٍ يَفْقَهُونَ ۝

99 He it is Who sendeth down
water from the sky, and therewith
We bring forth buds of every kind;
We bring forth the green blade
from which we bring forth the
thick-clustered grain; and from the
date palm, from the pollen thereof,
spring pendant bunches; and (We
bring forth) gardens of grapes, and
the olive and the pomegranate, alike
and unlike. Look upon the fruit
thereof, when they bear fruit, and
upon its ripening. Lo! herein verily
are portents for a people who
believe.

وَهُوَ الَّذِىٓ أَنزَلَ مِنَ السَّمَآءِ مَآءً فَأَخْرَجْنَا بِهِۦ
نَبَاتَ كُلِّ شَىْءٍ فَأَخْرَجْنَا مِنْهُ خَضِرًا نُّخْرِجُ
مِنْهُ حَبًّا مُّتَرَاكِبًا وَمِنَ النَّخْلِ مِن طَلْعِهَا
قِنْوَانٌ دَانِيَةٌ وَجَنَّـٰتٍ مِّنْ أَعْنَابٍ وَالزَّيْتُونَ
وَالرُّمَّانَ مُشْتَبِهًا وَغَيْرَ مُتَشَـٰبِهٍ ٱنظُرُوٓا۟
إِلَىٰ ثَمَرِهِۦٓ إِذَآ أَثْمَرَ وَيَنْعِهِۦٓ إِنَّ فِى ذَٰلِكُمْ
لَءَايَـٰتٍ لِّقَوْمٍ يُؤْمِنُونَ ﴿٩٩﴾

100   Yet they ascribe as partners
unto Allah the Jinn, although He
did create them, and impute falsely,
without knowledge, sons and daughters unto Him. Glorified be He
and high exalted above (all) that
they ascribe (unto Him).

وَجَعَلُوا۟ لِلَّهِ شُرَكَآءَ الْجِنَّ وَخَلَقَهُمْ وَخَرَقُوا۟ لَهُۥ بَنِينَ
وَبَنَـٰتٍۭ بِغَيْرِ عِلْمٍ سُبْحَـٰنَهُۥ وَتَعَـٰلَىٰ عَمَّا
يَصِفُونَ ﴿١٠٠﴾

101   The Originator of the heavens and the earth! How can He
have a child, when there is for Him
no consort, when He created all
things and is Aware of all things?

بَدِيعُ السَّمَـٰوَٰتِ وَالْأَرْضِ أَنَّىٰ يَكُونُ لَهُۥ وَلَدٌ
وَلَمْ تَكُن لَّهُۥ صَـٰحِبَةٌ وَخَلَقَ كُلَّ شَىْءٍ
وَهُوَ بِكُلِّ شَىْءٍ عَلِيمٌ ﴿١٠١﴾

102   Such is Allah, your Lord.
There is no God save Him, the Cre-
ator of all things, so worship Him.
And He taketh care of all things.

ذَٰلِكُمُ اللَّهُ رَبُّكُمْ لَآ إِلَـٰهَ إِلَّا هُوَ خَـٰلِقُ كُلِّ
شَىْءٍ فَاعْبُدُوهُ وَهُوَ عَلَىٰ كُلِّ شَىْءٍ وَكِيلٌ ﴿١٠٢﴾

103   Vision comprehendeth Him
not, but He comprehendeth (all) vision. He is the Subtile, the Aware.

لَّا تُدْرِكُهُ الْأَبْصَـٰرُ وَهُوَ يُدْرِكُ الْأَبْصَـٰرَ
وَهُوَ اللَّطِيفُ الْخَبِيرُ ﴿١٠٣﴾

104   Proofs have come unto you
from your Lord, so whoso seeth, it

قَدْ جَآءَكُم بَصَآئِرُ مِن رَّبِّكُمْ فَمَنْ أَبْصَرَ فَلِنَفْسِهِۦ

is for his own good, and whoso is blind is blind to his own hurt. And I am not a keeper over you.

وَمَنْ عَمِيَ فَعَلَيْهَا وَمَاۤ أَنَا۠ عَلَيْكُم بِحَفِيظٍ ﴿١٠٤﴾

105   Thus do We display Our revelations that they may say (unto thee, Muḥammad): "Thou hast studied," and that We may make (it) clear for people who have knowledge.

وَكَذَٰلِكَ نُصَرِّفُ ٱلْأَيَٰتِ وَلِيَقُولُوا۟ دَرَسْتَ وَلِنُبَيِّنَهُ لِقَوْمٍ يَعْلَمُونَ ﴿١٠٥﴾

106   Follow that which is inspired in thee from thy Lord; there is no God save Him; and turn away from the idolaters.

ٱتَّبِعْ مَاۤ أُوحِىَ إِلَيْكَ مِن رَّبِّكَ لَاۤ إِلَٰهَ إِلَّا هُوَ وَأَعْرِضْ عَنِ ٱلْمُشْرِكِينَ ﴿١٠٦﴾

107   Had Allah is willed, they had not been idolatrous. We have not set thee as a keeper over them, nor art thou responsible for them.

وَلَوْ شَاۤءَ ٱللَّهُ مَاۤ أَشْرَكُوا۟ وَمَا جَعَلْنَٰكَ عَلَيْهِمْ حَفِيظًا وَمَاۤ أَنتَ عَلَيْهِم بِوَكِيلٍ ﴿١٠٧﴾

108   Revile not those unto whom they pray beside Allah, lest they wrongfully revile Allah through ignorance. Thus unto every nation have We made their deed seem fair. Then unto their Lord is their return, and He will tell them what they used to do.

وَلَا تَسُبُّوا۟ ٱلَّذِينَ يَدْعُونَ مِن دُونِ ٱللَّهِ فَيَسُبُّوا۟ ٱللَّهَ عَدْوًۢا بِغَيْرِ عِلْمٍ كَذَٰلِكَ زَيَّنَّا لِكُلِّ أُمَّةٍ عَمَلَهُمْ ثُمَّ إِلَىٰ رَبِّهِم مَّرْجِعُهُمْ فَيُنَبِّئُهُم بِمَا كَانُوا۟ يَعْمَلُونَ ﴿١٠٨﴾

109   And they swear a solemn oath by Allah that if there come unto them a portent they will believe therein. Say: Portents are with Allah and (so is) that which telleth you that if such came unto them they would not believe.

وَأَقْسَمُوا۟ بِٱللَّهِ جَهْدَ أَيْمَٰنِهِمْ لَئِن جَاۤءَتْهُمْ ءَايَةٌ لَّيُؤْمِنُنَّ بِهَا قُلْ إِنَّمَا ٱلْأَيَٰتُ عِندَ ٱللَّهِ وَمَا يُشْعِرُكُمْ أَنَّهَاۤ إِذَا جَاۤءَتْ لَا يُؤْمِنُونَ ﴿١٠٩﴾

110   We confound their hearts and their eyes. As they believed not therein at the first, We let them wander blindly on in their contumacy.

وَنُقَلِّبُ أَفْـِٔدَتَهُمْ وَأَبْصَٰرَهُمْ كَمَا لَمْ يُؤْمِنُوا۟ بِهِۦ أَوَّلَ مَرَّةٍ وَنَذَرُهُمْ فِى طُغْيَٰنِهِمْ يَعْمَهُونَ ﴿١١٠﴾

111   And though We should send down the angels unto them, and the dead should speak unto them, and We should gather against them all things in array, they would not believe unless Allah so willed. How-be-it, most of them are ignorant.

۞ وَلَوْ أَنَّنَا نَزَّلْنَا إِلَيْهِمُ الْمَلَٰٓئِكَةَ وَكَلَّمَهُمُ الْمَوْتَىٰ وَحَشَرْنَا عَلَيْهِمْ كُلَّ شَىْءٍ قُبُلًا مَّا كَانُوا لِيُؤْمِنُوٓا إِلَّا أَن يَشَآءَ اللَّهُ وَلَٰكِنَّ أَكْثَرَهُمْ يَجْهَلُونَ ۝

112   Thus have We appointed unto every Prophet an adversary— devils of humankind and jinn who inspire in one another plausible discourse through guile. If thy Lord willed, they would not do so; so leave them alone with their devising;

وَكَذَٰلِكَ جَعَلْنَا لِكُلِّ نَبِىٍّ عَدُوًّا شَيَٰطِينَ الْإِنسِ وَالْجِنِّ يُوحِى بَعْضُهُمْ إِلَىٰ بَعْضٍ زُخْرُفَ الْقَوْلِ غُرُورًا وَلَوْ شَآءَ رَبُّكَ مَا فَعَلُوهُ فَذَرْهُمْ وَمَا يَفْتَرُونَ ۝

113   That the hearts of those who believe not in the Hereafter may incline thereto, and that they may take pleasure therein, and that they may earn what they are earning.

وَلِتَصْغَىٰٓ إِلَيْهِ أَفْـِٔدَةُ الَّذِينَ لَا يُؤْمِنُونَ بِالْآخِرَةِ وَلِيَرْضَوْهُ وَلِيَقْتَرِفُوا مَا هُم مُّقْتَرِفُونَ ۝

114   Shall I seek other than Allah for judge, when He it is who hath revealed unto you (this) Scripture, fully explained? Those unto whom We gave the Scripture (aforetime) know that it is revealed from thy Lord in truth. So be not thou (O Muhammad) of the waverers.

أَفَغَيْرَ اللَّهِ أَبْتَغِى حَكَمًا وَهُوَ الَّذِىٓ أَنزَلَ إِلَيْكُمُ الْكِتَٰبَ مُفَصَّلًا وَالَّذِينَ ءَاتَيْنَٰهُمُ الْكِتَٰبَ يَعْلَمُونَ أَنَّهُ مُنَزَّلٌ مِّن رَّبِّكَ بِالْحَقِّ فَلَا تَكُونَنَّ مِنَ الْمُمْتَرِينَ ۝

115   Perfected is the Word of thy Lord in truth and justice. There is naught that can change His words. He is the Hearer, the Knower.

وَتَمَّتْ كَلِمَتُ رَبِّكَ صِدْقًا وَعَدْلًا لَّا مُبَدِّلَ لِكَلِمَٰتِهِ وَهُوَ السَّمِيعُ الْعَلِيمُ ۝

116   If thou obeyedst most of those on earth they would mislead thee far from Allah's way. They follow naught but an opinion, and they do but guess.

وَإِن تُطِعْ أَكْثَرَ مَن فِى الْأَرْضِ يُضِلُّوكَ عَن سَبِيلِ اللَّهِ إِن يَتَّبِعُونَ إِلَّا الظَّنَّ وَإِنْ هُمْ إِلَّا يَخْرُصُونَ ۝

117   Lo! thy Lord, He knoweth best who erreth from His way; and He knoweth best (who are) the rightly guided.

إِنَّ رَبَّكَ هُوَ أَعْلَمُ مَن يَضِلُّ عَن سَبِيلِهِ وَهُوَ أَعْلَمُ بِالْمُهْتَدِينَ ۝

118   Eat of that over which the name of Allah hath been mentioned, if ye are believers in His revelations.

فَكُلُوا مِمَّا ذُكِرَ اسْمُ اللَّهِ عَلَيْهِ إِن كُنتُم بِآيَاتِهِ مُؤْمِنِينَ ۝

119   How should ye not eat of that over which the name of Allah hath been mentioned, when He hath explained unto you that which is forbidden unto you, unless ye are compelled thereto. But lo! many lead astray (others) by their own lusts through ignorance. Lo! thy Lord, He is best aware of the transgressors.

وَمَا لَكُمْ أَلَّا تَأْكُلُوا مِمَّا ذُكِرَ اسْمُ اللَّهِ عَلَيْهِ وَقَدْ فَصَّلَ لَكُم مَّا حَرَّمَ عَلَيْكُمْ إِلَّا مَا اضْطُرِرْتُمْ إِلَيْهِ وَإِنَّ كَثِيرًا لَّيُضِلُّونَ بِأَهْوَائِهِم بِغَيْرِ عِلْمٍ إِنَّ رَبَّكَ هُوَ أَعْلَمُ بِالْمُعْتَدِينَ ۝

120   Forsake the outwardness of sin and the inwardness thereof. Lo! those who garner sin will be awarded that which they have earned.

وَذَرُوا ظَاهِرَ الْإِثْمِ وَبَاطِنَهُ إِنَّ الَّذِينَ يَكْسِبُونَ الْإِثْمَ سَيُجْزَوْنَ بِمَا كَانُوا يَقْتَرِفُونَ ۝

121   And eat not of that whereon Allah's name hath not been mentioned, for lo! it is abomination. Lo! the devils do inspire thee minions to dispute with you. But if ye obey them, ye will be in truth idolaters.

وَلَا تَأْكُلُوا مِمَّا لَمْ يُذْكَرِ اسْمُ اللَّهِ عَلَيْهِ وَإِنَّهُ لَفِسْقٌ وَإِنَّ الشَّيَاطِينَ لَيُوحُونَ إِلَىٰ أَوْلِيَائِهِمْ لِيُجَادِلُوكُمْ وَإِنْ أَطَعْتُمُوهُمْ إِنَّكُمْ لَمُشْرِكُونَ ۝

122   Is he who was dead and We have raised him unto life, and set for him a light wherein he walketh among men, as him whose similitude is in utter darkness whence he cannot emerge? Thus is their conduct made fair seeming for the disbelievers.

أَوَمَن كَانَ مَيْتًا فَأَحْيَيْنَاهُ وَجَعَلْنَا لَهُ نُورًا يَمْشِي بِهِ فِي النَّاسِ كَمَن مَّثَلُهُ فِي الظُّلُمَاتِ لَيْسَ بِخَارِجٍ مِّنْهَا كَذَٰلِكَ زُيِّنَ لِلْكَافِرِينَ مَا كَانُوا يَعْمَلُونَ ۝

123   And thus have We made in every city great ones of its wicked ones, that they should plot therein. They do but plot against themselves, though they perceive not.

وَكَذَٰلِكَ جَعَلْنَا فِى كُلِّ قَرْيَةٍ أَكَـٰبِرَ مُجْرِمِيهَا لِيَمْكُرُوا فِيهَا وَمَا يَمْكُرُونَ إِلَّا بِأَنفُسِهِمْ وَمَا يَشْعُرُونَ ۝

124   And when a token cometh unto them, they say: We will not believe till we are given that which Allah's messengers are given. Allah knoweth best with whom to place His message. Humiliation from Allah and heavy punishment will smite the guilty for their scheming.

وَإِذَا جَآءَتْهُمْ ءَايَةٌ قَالُوا لَن نُّؤْمِنَ حَتَّىٰ نُؤْتَىٰ مِثْلَ مَآ أُوتِىَ رُسُلُ اللَّهِ اللَّهُ أَعْلَمُ حَيْثُ يَجْعَلُ رِسَالَتَهُ سَيُصِيبُ الَّذِينَ أَجْرَمُوا صَغَارٌ عِندَ اللَّهِ وَعَذَابٌ شَدِيدٌ بِمَا كَانُوا يَمْكُرُونَ ۝

125   And whomsoever it is Allah's will to guide, He expandeth His bosom unto the Surrender,[3] and whomsoever it is His will to send astray, He maketh His bosom closed and narrow, as if he were engaged in sheer ascent in the sky. Thus Allah layeth ignominy upon those who believe not.

فَمَن يُرِدِ اللَّهُ أَن يَهْدِيَهُ يَشْرَحْ صَدْرَهُ لِلْإِسْلَـٰمِ وَمَن يُرِدْ أَن يُضِلَّهُ يَجْعَلْ صَدْرَهُ ضَيِّقًا حَرَجًا كَأَنَّمَا يَصَّعَّدُ فِى السَّمَآءِ كَذَٰلِكَ يَجْعَلُ اللَّهُ الرِّجْسَ عَلَى الَّذِينَ لَا يُؤْمِنُونَ ۝

126   This is the path of thy Lord, a straight path. We have detailed Our revelations for a people who take heed.

وَهَـٰذَا صِرَٰطُ رَبِّكَ مُسْتَقِيمًا قَدْ فَصَّلْنَا الْآيَـٰتِ لِقَوْمٍ يَذَّكَّرُونَ ۝

127   For them is the abode of peace with their Lord. He will be their Protecting Friend because of what they used to do.

۞ لَهُمْ دَارُ السَّلَـٰمِ عِندَ رَبِّهِمْ وَهُوَ وَلِيُّهُم بِمَا كَانُوا يَعْمَلُونَ ۝

128   In the day when He will gather them together (He will say): O ye assembly of the jinn! Many of

وَيَوْمَ يَحْشُرُهُمْ جَمِيعًا يَـٰمَعْشَرَ الْجِنِّ

---

3. Al-Islām.

humankind did ye seduce. And their adherents among humankind will say: Our Lord! We enjoyed one another, but now we have arrived at the appointed term which Thou appointedst for us. He will say: Fire is your home. Abide therein forever, save him whom Allah willeth (to deliver). Lo! thy Lord is Wise, Aware.

قَدِ اسْتَكْثَرْتُم مِّنَ الْإِنسِ وَقَالَ أَوْلِيَآؤُهُم مِّنَ الْإِنسِ رَبَّنَا اسْتَمْتَعَ بَعْضُنَا بِبَعْضٍ وَبَلَغْنَآ أَجَلَنَا الَّذِيٓ أَجَّلْتَ لَنَا قَالَ النَّارُ مَثْوَىٰكُمْ خَٰلِدِينَ فِيهَآ إِلَّا مَا شَآءَ اللَّهُ إِنَّ رَبَّكَ حَكِيمٌ عَلِيمٌ ۝

129 Thus We let some of the wrong-doers have power over others because of what they are wont to earn.

وَكَذَٰلِكَ نُوَلِّي بَعْضَ الظَّٰلِمِينَ بَعْضًۢا بِمَا كَانُواْ يَكْسِبُونَ ۝

130 O ye assembly of the jinn and humankind! Came there not unto you messengers of your own who recounted unto you My tokens and warned you of the meeting of this your Day? They will say: We testify against ourselves. And the life of the world beguiled them. And they testify against themselves that they were disbelievers.

يَٰمَعْشَرَ الْجِنِّ وَالْإِنسِ أَلَمْ يَأْتِكُمْ رُسُلٌ مِّنكُمْ يَقُصُّونَ عَلَيْكُمْ ءَايَٰتِي وَيُنذِرُونَكُمْ لِقَآءَ يَوْمِكُمْ هَٰذَا قَالُواْ شَهِدْنَا عَلَىٰٓ أَنفُسِنَا وَغَرَّتْهُمُ الْحَيَوٰةُ الدُّنْيَا وَشَهِدُواْ عَلَىٰٓ أَنفُسِهِمْ أَنَّهُمْ كَانُواْ كَٰفِرِينَ ۝

131 This is because thy Lord destroyeth not the townships arbitrarily while their people are unconscious (of the wrong they do).

ذَٰلِكَ أَن لَّمْ يَكُن رَّبُّكَ مُهْلِكَ الْقُرَىٰ بِظُلْمٍ وَأَهْلُهَا غَٰفِلُونَ ۝

132 For all there will be ranks from what they did. Thy Lord is not unaware of what they do.

وَلِكُلٍّ دَرَجَٰتٌ مِّمَّا عَمِلُواْ وَمَا رَبُّكَ بِغَٰفِلٍ عَمَّا يَعْمَلُونَ ۝

133 Thy Lord is the Absolute, the Lord of Mercy. If He will, He can remove you and can cause what He will to follow after you, even as He raised you from the seed of other folk.

وَرَبُّكَ الْغَنِيُّ ذُو الرَّحْمَةِ إِن يَشَأْ يُذْهِبْكُمْ وَيَسْتَخْلِفْ مِنۢ بَعْدِكُم مَّا يَشَآءُ كَمَآ أَنشَأَكُم مِّن ذُرِّيَّةِ قَوْمٍ ءَاخَرِينَ ۝

134   Lo! that which ye are promised will surely come to pass, and ye cannot escape.

إِنَّ مَا تُوعَدُونَ لَآتٍ وَمَا أَنتُم بِمُعْجِزِينَ ۝

135   Say (O Muhammad): O my people! Work according to your power. Lo! I too am working. Thus ye will come to know for which of us will be the happy sequel. Lo! the wrong-doers will not be successful.

قُلْ يَٰقَوْمِ ٱعْمَلُواْ عَلَىٰ مَكَانَتِكُمْ إِنِّى عَامِلٌ فَسَوْفَ تَعْلَمُونَ مَن تَكُونُ لَهُۥ عَٰقِبَةُ ٱلدَّارِ إِنَّهُۥ لَا يُفْلِحُ ٱلظَّٰلِمُونَ ۝

136   They assign unto Allah, of the crops and cattle which He created, a portion, and they say: "This is Allah's"—in their make believe—"and this is for (His) partners in regard to us." Thus that which (they assign) unto His partners in them reacheth not Allah and that which (they assign) unto Allah goeth to their (so called) partners. Evil is their ordinance.

وَجَعَلُواْ لِلَّهِ مِمَّا ذَرَأَ مِنَ ٱلْحَرْثِ وَٱلْأَنْعَٰمِ نَصِيبًا فَقَالُواْ هَٰذَا لِلَّهِ بِزَعْمِهِمْ وَهَٰذَا لِشُرَكَآئِنَا فَمَا كَانَ لِشُرَكَآئِهِمْ فَلَا يَصِلُ إِلَى ٱللَّهِ وَمَا كَانَ لِلَّهِ فَهُوَ يَصِلُ إِلَىٰ شُرَكَآئِهِمْ سَآءَ مَا يَحْكُمُونَ ۝

137   Thus have their (so called) partners (of Allah) made the killing of their children to seem fair unto many of the idolaters, that they may ruin them and make their faith obscure for them. Had Allah willed (it otherwise), they had not done so. So leave them alone with their devices.

وَكَذَٰلِكَ زَيَّنَ لِكَثِيرٍ مِّنَ ٱلْمُشْرِكِينَ قَتْلَ أَوْلَٰدِهِمْ شُرَكَآؤُهُمْ لِيُرْدُوهُمْ وَلِيَلْبِسُواْ عَلَيْهِمْ دِينَهُمْ وَلَوْ شَآءَ ٱللَّهُ مَا فَعَلُوهُ فَذَرْهُمْ وَمَا يَفْتَرُونَ ۝

138   And they say: Such cattle and crops are forbidden. No one is to eat of them save whom We will—in their make believe—cattle whose backs are forbidden, cattle over which they mention not the name of Allah. (All that is) a lie against Him. He will repay them for that which they invent.

وَقَالُواْ هَٰذِهِۦٓ أَنْعَٰمٌ وَحَرْثٌ حِجْرٌ لَّا يَطْعَمُهَآ إِلَّا مَن نَّشَآءُ بِزَعْمِهِمْ وَأَنْعَٰمٌ حُرِّمَتْ ظُهُورُهَا وَأَنْعَٰمٌ لَّا يَذْكُرُونَ ٱسْمَ ٱللَّهِ عَلَيْهَا ٱفْتِرَآءً عَلَيْهِ سَيَجْزِيهِم بِمَا كَانُواْ يَفْتَرُونَ ۝

139 And they say: That which is
in the bellies of such cattle is rese-
rved for our males and is forbidden
to our wives; but if it be born dead,
then they (all) may be partakers
thereof. He will reward them for
their attribution (of such ordinances
unto Him).[4] Lo, He is Wise, Aware.

وَقَالُوا۟ مَا فِى بُطُونِ هَٰذِهِ ٱلْأَنْعَٰمِ
خَالِصَةٌ لِّذُكُورِنَا وَمُحَرَّمٌ عَلَىٰٓ أَزْوَٰجِنَا
وَإِن يَكُن مَّيْتَةً فَهُمْ فِيهِ شُرَكَآءُ
سَيَجْزِيهِمْ وَصْفَهُمْ إِنَّهُۥ حَكِيمٌ عَلِيمٌ ﴿١٣٩﴾

140 They are losers who besot-
tedly have slain their children without knowledge,[5] and have forbidden
that which Allah bestowed upon
them, inventing a lie against Allah.
They indeed have gone astray and
are not guided.

قَدْ خَسِرَ ٱلَّذِينَ قَتَلُوٓا۟ أَوْلَٰدَهُمْ سَفَهًۢا بِغَيْرِ
عِلْمٍ وَحَرَّمُوا۟ مَا رَزَقَهُمُ ٱللَّهُ ٱفْتِرَآءً عَلَى ٱللَّهِ
قَدْ ضَلُّوا۟ وَمَا كَانُوا۟ مُهْتَدِينَ ﴿١٤٠﴾

141 He it is Who produceth gardens trellised and untrellised, and
the date palm, and crops of divers
flavour, and the olive and the pomegranate, like and unlike. Eat ye of
the fruit thereof when it fruiteth,
and pay the due thereof upon the
harvest day, and be not prodigal.
Lo! Allah loveth not the prodigals.

۞ وَهُوَ ٱلَّذِىٓ أَنشَأَ جَنَّٰتٍ مَّعْرُوشَٰتٍ وَغَيْرَ
مَعْرُوشَٰتٍ وَٱلنَّخْلَ وَٱلزَّرْعَ مُخْتَلِفًا أُكُلُهُۥ
وَٱلزَّيْتُونَ وَٱلرُّمَّانَ مُتَشَٰبِهًا وَغَيْرَ
مُتَشَٰبِهٍ كُلُوا۟ مِن ثَمَرِهِۦٓ إِذَآ أَثْمَرَ وَءَاتُوا۟
حَقَّهُۥ يَوْمَ حَصَادِهِۦ وَلَا تُسْرِفُوٓا۟ إِنَّهُۥ
لَا يُحِبُّ ٱلْمُسْرِفِينَ ﴿١٤١﴾

142 And of the cattle (He produceth) some for burdens, some for
food. Eat of that which Allah hath
bestowed upon you, and follow not
the footsteps of the devil, for lo! he
is an open foe to you.

وَمِنَ ٱلْأَنْعَٰمِ حَمُولَةً وَفَرْشًا كُلُوا۟
مِمَّا رَزَقَكُمُ ٱللَّهُ وَلَا تَتَّبِعُوا۟ خُطُوَٰتِ ٱلشَّيْطَٰنِ
إِنَّهُۥ لَكُمْ عَدُوٌّ مُّبِينٌ ﴿١٤٢﴾

---

4. vv. 139 and 140 refer to customs of pagan Arabs.

5. The reference is to the burial alive of female children who were deemed
superfluous, and the practice of human sacrifice to idols.

143   Eight in (four) pairs: Of the sheep twain, and of the goats twain. Say: Hath He forbidden the two males or the two females, or that which the wombs of the two females contain? Expound to me (the case) with knowledge, if ye are truthful.[6]

ثَمَنِيَةَ أَزْوَٰجٍ مِّنَ ٱلضَّأْنِ ٱثْنَيْنِ وَمِنَ ٱلْمَعْزِ ٱثْنَيْنِ قُلْ ءَآلذَّكَرَيْنِ حَرَّمَ أَمِ ٱلْأُنثَيَيْنِ أَمَّا ٱشْتَمَلَتْ عَلَيْهِ أَرْحَامُ ٱلْأُنثَيَيْنِ نَبِّئُونِي بِعِلْمٍ إِن كُنتُمْ صَٰدِقِينَ ۝

144   And of the camels twain and of the oxen twain. Say: Hath He forbidden the two males or the two females, or that which the wombs of the two females contain; or were ye by to witness when Allah commanded you (all) this? Then who doth greater wrong than he who deviseth a lie concerning Allah, that he may lead mankind astray without knowledge. Lo! Allah guideth not wrongdoing folk.

وَمِنَ ٱلْإِبِلِ ٱثْنَيْنِ وَمِنَ ٱلْبَقَرِ ٱثْنَيْنِ قُلْ ءَآلذَّكَرَيْنِ حَرَّمَ أَمِ ٱلْأُنثَيَيْنِ أَمَّا ٱشْتَمَلَتْ عَلَيْهِ أَرْحَامُ ٱلْأُنثَيَيْنِ أَمْ كُنتُمْ شُهَدَآءَ إِذْ وَصَّىٰكُمُ ٱللَّهُ بِهَٰذَا فَمَنْ أَظْلَمُ مِمَّنِ ٱفْتَرَىٰ عَلَى ٱللَّهِ كَذِبًا لِّيُضِلَّ ٱلنَّاسَ بِغَيْرِ عِلْمٍ إِنَّ ٱللَّهَ لَا يَهْدِى ٱلْقَوْمَ ٱلظَّٰلِمِينَ ۝

145   Say: I find not in that which is revealed unto me aught prohibited to an eater that he eat thereof, except it be carrion, or blood poured forth, or swineflesh—for that verily is foul—or the abomination which was immolated to the name of other than Allah. But whoso is compelled (thereto), neither craving nor transgressing, (for him) lo! your Lord is Forgiving, Merciful.

قُل لَّا أَجِدُ فِى مَآ أُوحِىَ إِلَىَّ مُحَرَّمًا عَلَىٰ طَاعِمٍ يَطْعَمُهُ إِلَّا أَن يَكُونَ مَيْتَةً أَوْ دَمًا مَّسْفُوحًا أَوْ لَحْمَ خِنزِيرٍ فَإِنَّهُ رِجْسٌ أَوْ فِسْقًا أُهِلَّ لِغَيْرِ ٱللَّهِ بِهِ فَمَنِ ٱضْطُرَّ غَيْرَ بَاغٍ وَلَا عَادٍ فَإِنَّ رَبَّكَ غَفُورٌ رَّحِيمٌ ۝

---

6. This and the following verses relate to superstitions of the pagan Arabs with regard to cattle used for food.

146   Unto those who are Jews We forbade every animal with claws. And of the oxen and the sheep forbade We unto them the fat thereof save that upon the backs or the entrails, or that which is mixed with the bone. That We awarded them for their rebellion. And lo! We verily are Truthful.

وَعَلَى ٱلَّذِينَ هَادُواْ حَرَّمْنَا كُلَّ ذِي ظُفُرٍ وَمِنَ ٱلْبَقَرِ وَٱلْغَنَمِ حَرَّمْنَا عَلَيْهِمْ شُحُومَهُمَا إِلَّا مَا حَمَلَتْ ظُهُورُهُمَا أَوِ ٱلْحَوَايَا أَوْ مَا ٱخْتَلَطَ بِعَظْمٍ ذَٰلِكَ جَزَيْنَاهُم بِبَغْيِهِمْ وَإِنَّا لَصَادِقُونَ ۝

147   So if they give the lie to thee (Muḥammad), say: Your Lord is a Lord of all embracing mercy, and His wrath will never be withdrawn from guilty folk.

فَإِن كَذَّبُوكَ فَقُل رَّبُّكُمْ ذُو رَحْمَةٍ وَٰسِعَةٍ وَلَا يُرَدُّ بَأْسُهُ عَنِ ٱلْقَوْمِ ٱلْمُجْرِمِينَ ۝

148   They who are idolaters will say: Had Allah willed, we had not ascribed (unto Him) partners neither had our fathers, nor had we forbidden aught. Thus did those who were before them give the lie (to Allah's messengers) till they tasted of the fear of Us. Say: Have ye any knowledge that ye can adduce for us? Lo! ye follow naught but an opinion. Lo! ye do but guess.

سَيَقُولُ ٱلَّذِينَ أَشْرَكُواْ لَوْ شَاءَ ٱللَّهُ مَا أَشْرَكْنَا وَلَا آبَاؤُنَا وَلَا حَرَّمْنَا مِن شَيْءٍ كَذَٰلِكَ كَذَّبَ ٱلَّذِينَ مِن قَبْلِهِمْ حَتَّىٰ ذَاقُواْ بَأْسَنَا قُلْ هَلْ عِندَكُم مِّنْ عِلْمٍ فَتُخْرِجُوهُ لَنَا إِن تَتَّبِعُونَ إِلَّا ٱلظَّنَّ وَإِنْ أَنتُمْ إِلَّا تَخْرُصُونَ ۝

149   Say—For Allah's is the final argument—Had He willed He could indeed have guided all of you.

قُلْ فَلِلَّهِ ٱلْحُجَّةُ ٱلْبَٰلِغَةُ فَلَوْ شَاءَ لَهَدَىٰكُمْ أَجْمَعِينَ ۝

150   Say: Come, bring your witnesses who can bear witness that Allah forbade (all) this. And if they bear witness, do not thou bear witness with them. Follow thou not the whims of those who deny Our revelations, those who believe not in the Hereafter and deem (others) equal with their Lord.

قُلْ هَلُمَّ شُهَدَاءَكُمُ ٱلَّذِينَ يَشْهَدُونَ أَنَّ ٱللَّهَ حَرَّمَ هَٰذَا فَإِن شَهِدُواْ فَلَا تَشْهَدْ مَعَهُمْ وَلَا تَتَّبِعْ أَهْوَاءَ ٱلَّذِينَ كَذَّبُواْ بِآيَٰتِنَا وَٱلَّذِينَ لَا يُؤْمِنُونَ بِٱلْآخِرَةِ وَهُم بِرَبِّهِمْ يَعْدِلُونَ ۝

151   Say: Come, I will recite unto you that which your Lord hath forbidden to you: that ye ascribe no thing as partner unto Him and that ye do good to parents, and that ye slay not your children because of penury—We provide for you and for them—and that ye draw not nigh to lewd things whether open or concealed. And that ye slay not the life which Allah hath made sacred, save in the course of justice. This He hath commanded you, in order that ye may discern.

﴾ قُلْ تَعَالَوْا أَتْلُ مَا حَرَّمَ رَبُّكُمْ عَلَيْكُمْ أَلَّا تُشْرِكُوا بِهِ شَيْئًا وَبِالْوَالِدَيْنِ إِحْسَانًا ۖ وَلَا تَقْتُلُوا أَوْلَادَكُمْ مِنْ إِمْلَاقٍ ۖ نَحْنُ نَرْزُقُكُمْ وَإِيَّاهُمْ ۖ وَلَا تَقْرَبُوا الْفَوَاحِشَ مَا ظَهَرَ مِنْهَا وَمَا بَطَنَ ۖ وَلَا تَقْتُلُوا النَّفْسَ الَّتِي حَرَّمَ اللَّهُ إِلَّا بِالْحَقِّ ۚ ذَٰلِكُمْ وَصَّاكُمْ بِهِ لَعَلَّكُمْ تَعْقِلُونَ ﴿١٥١﴾

152   And approach not the wealth of the orphan save with that which is better; till he reach maturity. Give full measure and full weight, in justice. We task not any soul beyond its scope. And if ye give your word, do justice thereunto, even though it be (against) a kinsman; and fulfil the covenant of Allah. This He commandeth you that haply ye may remember.

وَلَا تَقْرَبُوا مَالَ الْيَتِيمِ إِلَّا بِالَّتِي هِيَ أَحْسَنُ حَتَّىٰ يَبْلُغَ أَشُدَّهُ ۖ وَأَوْفُوا الْكَيْلَ وَالْمِيزَانَ بِالْقِسْطِ ۖ لَا نُكَلِّفُ نَفْسًا إِلَّا وُسْعَهَا ۖ وَإِذَا قُلْتُمْ فَاعْدِلُوا وَلَوْ كَانَ ذَا قُرْبَىٰ ۖ وَبِعَهْدِ اللَّهِ أَوْفُوا ۚ ذَٰلِكُمْ وَصَّاكُمْ بِهِ لَعَلَّكُمْ تَذَكَّرُونَ ﴿١٥٢﴾

153   And (He commandeth you, saying): This is My straight path, so follow it. Follow not other ways, lest ye be parted from His way. This hath He ordained for you, that ye may ward off (evil).

وَأَنَّ هَٰذَا صِرَاطِي مُسْتَقِيمًا فَاتَّبِعُوهُ ۖ وَلَا تَتَّبِعُوا السُّبُلَ فَتَفَرَّقَ بِكُمْ عَنْ سَبِيلِهِ ۚ ذَٰلِكُمْ وَصَّاكُمْ بِهِ لَعَلَّكُمْ تَتَّقُونَ ﴿١٥٣﴾

154   Again, We gave the Scripture unto Moses, complete for him who would do good, an explanation of all things, a guidance and a mercy, that they might believe in the meeting with their Lord.

ثُمَّ آتَيْنَا مُوسَى الْكِتَابَ تَمَامًا عَلَى الَّذِي أَحْسَنَ وَتَفْصِيلًا لِكُلِّ شَيْءٍ وَهُدًى وَرَحْمَةً لَعَلَّهُمْ بِلِقَاءِ رَبِّهِمْ يُؤْمِنُونَ ﴿١٥٤﴾

155   And this is a blessed Scripture which We have revealed. So follow it and ward off (evil), that ye may find mercy.

وَهَٰذَا كِتَٰبٌ أَنزَلْنَٰهُ مُبَارَكٌ فَٱتَّبِعُوهُ وَٱتَّقُوا لَعَلَّكُمْ تُرْحَمُونَ ۝

156   Lest ye should say: The Scripture was revealed only to two sects before us, and we in sooth were unaware of what they read;

أَن تَقُولُوٓا إِنَّمَآ أُنزِلَ ٱلْكِتَٰبُ عَلَىٰ طَآئِفَتَيْنِ مِن قَبْلِنَا وَإِن كُنَّا عَن دِرَاسَتِهِمْ لَغَٰفِلِينَ ۝

157   Or lest ye should say: If the Scripture had been revealed unto us, we surely had been better guided than are they. Now hath there come unto you a clear proof from your Lord, a guidance and a mercy; and who doeth greater wrong than he who denieth the revelations of Allah, and turneth away from them? We award unto those who turn away from Our revelations an evil doom because of their aversion.

أَوْ تَقُولُوا لَوْ أَنَّآ أُنزِلَ عَلَيْنَا ٱلْكِتَٰبُ لَكُنَّآ أَهْدَىٰ مِنْهُمْ فَقَدْ جَآءَكُم بَيِّنَةٌ مِّن رَّبِّكُمْ وَهُدًى وَرَحْمَةٌ فَمَنْ أَظْلَمُ مِمَّن كَذَّبَ بِـَٔايَٰتِ ٱللَّهِ وَصَدَفَ عَنْهَا سَنَجْزِى ٱلَّذِينَ يَصْدِفُونَ عَنْ ءَايَٰتِنَا سُوٓءَ ٱلْعَذَابِ بِمَا كَانُوا يَصْدِفُونَ ۝

158   Wait they, indeed, for nothing less than that the angels should come unto them, or thy Lord should come, or there should come one of the portents from thy Lord? In the day when one of the portents from thy Lord cometh, its belief availeth naught a soul which theretofore believed not, nor in its belief earned good (by works). Say: Wait ye! Lo! We (too) are waiting.

هَلْ يَنظُرُونَ إِلَّآ أَن تَأْتِيَهُمُ ٱلْمَلَٰٓئِكَةُ أَوْ يَأْتِىَ رَبُّكَ أَوْ يَأْتِىَ بَعْضُ ءَايَٰتِ رَبِّكَ يَوْمَ يَأْتِى بَعْضُ ءَايَٰتِ رَبِّكَ لَا يَنفَعُ نَفْسًا إِيمَٰنُهَا لَمْ تَكُنْ ءَامَنَتْ مِن قَبْلُ أَوْ كَسَبَتْ فِى إِيمَٰنِهَا خَيْرًا قُلِ ٱنتَظِرُوٓا إِنَّا مُنتَظِرُونَ ۝

159   Lo! As for those who sunder their religion and become schismatics, no concern at all hast thou with them. Their case will go to Allah, who then will tell them what they used to do.

إِنَّ ٱلَّذِينَ فَرَّقُوا دِينَهُمْ وَكَانُوا شِيَعًا لَّسْتَ مِنْهُمْ فِى شَىْءٍ إِنَّمَآ أَمْرُهُمْ إِلَى ٱللَّهِ ثُمَّ يُنَبِّئُهُم بِمَا كَانُوا يَفْعَلُونَ ۝

160   Whoso bringeth a good deed will receive tenfold the like thereof, while whoso bringeth an ill deed will be awarded but the like thereof; and they will not be wronged.

مَن جَآءَ بِٱلْحَسَنَةِ فَلَهُۥ عَشْرُ أَمْثَالِهَا ۖ وَمَن جَآءَ بِٱلسَّيِّئَةِ فَلَا يُجْزَىٰٓ إِلَّا مِثْلَهَا وَهُمْ لَا يُظْلَمُونَ ﴿١٦٠﴾

161   Say: Lo! As for me, my Lord hath guided me unto a straight path, a right religion, the community of Abraham, the upright, who was no idolater.

قُلْ إِنَّنِي هَدَىٰنِي رَبِّيٓ إِلَىٰ صِرَٰطٍ مُّسْتَقِيمٍ دِينًا قِيَمًا مِّلَّةَ إِبْرَٰهِيمَ حَنِيفًا ۚ وَمَا كَانَ مِنَ ٱلْمُشْرِكِينَ ﴿١٦١﴾

162   Say: Lo! my worship and my sacrifice and my living and my dying are for Allah, Lord of the Worlds.

قُلْ إِنَّ صَلَاتِي وَنُسُكِي وَمَحْيَايَ وَمَمَاتِي لِلَّهِ رَبِّ ٱلْعَٰلَمِينَ ﴿١٦٢﴾

163   He hath no partner. This am I commanded, and I am first of those who surrender (unto Him).

لَا شَرِيكَ لَهُۥ ۖ وَبِذَٰلِكَ أُمِرْتُ وَأَنَا۠ أَوَّلُ ٱلْمُسْلِمِينَ ﴿١٦٣﴾

164   Say: Shall I seek another than Allah for Lord, when He is Lord of all things? Each soul earneth only on its own account, nor doth any laden bear another's load. Then unto your Lord is your return and He will tell you that wherein ye differed.

قُلْ أَغَيْرَ ٱللَّهِ أَبْغِي رَبًّا وَهُوَ رَبُّ كُلِّ شَيْءٍ ۚ وَلَا تَكْسِبُ كُلُّ نَفْسٍ إِلَّا عَلَيْهَا ۚ وَلَا تَزِرُ وَازِرَةٌ وِزْرَ أُخْرَىٰ ۚ ثُمَّ إِلَىٰ رَبِّكُم مَّرْجِعُكُمْ فَيُنَبِّئُكُم بِمَا كُنتُمْ فِيهِ تَخْتَلِفُونَ ﴿١٦٤﴾

165   He it is who hath placed you as viceroys of the earth and hath exalted some of you in rank above others, that He may try you by (the test of) that which He hath given you. Lo! Thy Lord is swift in prosecution, and lo! He is Forgiving, Merciful.

وَهُوَ ٱلَّذِي جَعَلَكُمْ خَلَٰٓئِفَ ٱلْأَرْضِ وَرَفَعَ بَعْضَكُمْ فَوْقَ بَعْضٍ دَرَجَٰتٍ لِّيَبْلُوَكُمْ فِي مَآ ءَاتَىٰكُمْ ۗ إِنَّ رَبَّكَ سَرِيعُ ٱلْعِقَابِ وَإِنَّهُۥ لَغَفُورٌ رَّحِيمٌۢ ﴿١٦٥﴾

Al A'rāf
(The Heights)

Al A'rāf, "The Heights," takes its name from a word in v. 46, "And on the Heights are men who know them all by their marks." The best authorities assign the whole of it to about the same period as sūrah 6, *i.e.* the Prophet's last year in Makkah, though some consider vv. 163-167 to have been revealed at Al-Madīnah. The subject may be said to be the opponents of God's will and purpose, from Satan onward, through the history of Divine Guidance.

A late Makkan Sūrah.

In the name of Allah, the Beneficent, the Merciful.

1   Alif. Lām. Mīm. Sād.[1]

2   (It is) a Scripture that is revealed unto thee (Muhammad)—so let there be no heaviness in thy heart therefrom—that thou mayest warn thereby, and (it is) a Reminder unto believers.

3   (Saying): Follow that which is sent down unto you from your Lord, and follow no protecting friends beside Him. Little do ye recollect!

---

1. See Sūrah 2: 1, footnote.

4 How many a township have We destroyed! As a raid by night, or while they slept at noon, Our terror came unto them.

وَكَمْ مِّن قَرْيَةٍ أَهْلَكْنَاهَا فَجَاءَهَا بَأْسُنَا بَيَاتًا أَوْ هُمْ قَآئِلُونَ ٤

5 No plea had they, when Our terror came unto them, save that they said: Lo! We were wrong-doers.

فَمَا كَانَ دَعْوَاهُمْ إِذْ جَاءَهُم بَأْسُنَا إِلَّا أَن قَالُوٓا۟ إِنَّا كُنَّا ظَالِمِينَ ٥

6 Then verily We shall question those unto whom (Our message) hath been sent, and verily We shall question the messengers.

فَلَنَسْـَٔلَنَّ ٱلَّذِينَ أُرْسِلَ إِلَيْهِمْ وَلَنَسْـَٔلَنَّ ٱلْمُرْسَلِينَ ٦

7 Then verily We shall narrate unto them (the event) with knowledge, for verily We were not absent (when it came to pass).

فَلَنَقُصَّنَّ عَلَيْهِم بِعِلْمٍ وَمَا كُنَّا غَآئِبِينَ ٧

8 The weighing on that day is the true (weighing). As for those whose scale is heavy, they are the successful.

وَٱلْوَزْنُ يَوْمَئِذٍ ٱلْحَقُّ فَمَن ثَقُلَتْ مَوَٰزِينُهُۥ فَأُو۟لَٰٓئِكَ هُمُ ٱلْمُفْلِحُونَ ٨

9 And as for those whose scale is light: those are they who lose their souls because they disbelieved Our revelations.

وَمَنْ خَفَّتْ مَوَٰزِينُهُۥ فَأُو۟لَٰٓئِكَ ٱلَّذِينَ خَسِرُوٓا۟ أَنفُسَهُم بِمَا كَانُوا۟ بِـَٔايَٰتِنَا يَظْلِمُونَ ٩

10 And We have given you (mankind) power in the earth, and appointed for you therein a livelihood. Little give ye thanks!

وَلَقَدْ مَكَّنَّٰكُمْ فِى ٱلْأَرْضِ وَجَعَلْنَا لَكُمْ فِيهَا مَعَٰيِشَ قَلِيلًا مَّا تَشْكُرُونَ ١٠

11 And We created you, then fashioned you, then told the angels: Fall ye prostrate before Adam! And they fell prostrate, all save Iblīs, who was not of those who make prostration.

وَلَقَدْ خَلَقْنَٰكُمْ ثُمَّ صَوَّرْنَٰكُمْ ثُمَّ قُلْنَا لِلْمَلَٰٓئِكَةِ ٱسْجُدُوا۟ لِءَادَمَ فَسَجَدُوٓا۟ إِلَّآ إِبْلِيسَ لَمْ يَكُن مِّنَ ٱلسَّٰجِدِينَ ١١

12 He said: What hindered thee that thou didst not fall prostrate when I bade thee? (Iblis) said: I am better than him. Thou createdst me of fire while him Thou didst create of mud.

قَالَ مَا مَنَعَكَ أَلَّا تَسْجُدَ إِذْ أَمَرْتُكَ قَالَ أَنَا۠ خَيْرٌ مِّنْهُ خَلَقْتَنِي مِن نَّارٍ وَخَلَقْتَهُۥ مِن طِينٍ ﴿١٢﴾

13 He said: Then go down hence! It is not for thee to show pride here, so go forth! Lo! thou art of those degraded.

قَالَ فَاهْبِطْ مِنْهَا فَمَا يَكُونُ لَكَ أَن تَتَكَبَّرَ فِيهَا فَاخْرُجْ إِنَّكَ مِنَ ٱلصَّٰغِرِينَ ﴿١٣﴾

14 He said: Reprieve me till the day when they are raised (from the dead).

قَالَ أَنظِرْنِي إِلَىٰ يَوْمِ يُبْعَثُونَ ﴿١٤﴾

15 He said: Lo! thou art of those reprieved.

قَالَ إِنَّكَ مِنَ ٱلْمُنظَرِينَ ﴿١٥﴾

16 He said: Now, because Thou hast sent me astray, verily I shall lurk in ambush for them on Thy Right Path.

قَالَ فَبِمَآ أَغْوَيْتَنِي لَأَقْعُدَنَّ لَهُمْ صِرَٰطَكَ ٱلْمُسْتَقِيمَ ﴿١٦﴾

17 Then I shall come upon them from before them and from behind them and from their right hands and from their left hands, and Thou wilt not find most of them beholden (unto Thee).

ثُمَّ لَآتِيَنَّهُم مِّنۢ بَيْنِ أَيْدِيهِمْ وَمِنْ خَلْفِهِمْ وَعَنْ أَيْمَٰنِهِمْ وَعَن شَمَآئِلِهِمْ وَلَا تَجِدُ أَكْثَرَهُمْ شَٰكِرِينَ ﴿١٧﴾

18 He said: Go forth from hence, degraded, banished. As for such of them as follow thee, surely I will fill hell with all of you.

قَالَ ٱخْرُجْ مِنْهَا مَذْءُومًا مَّدْحُورًا لَّمَن تَبِعَكَ مِنْهُمْ لَأَمْلَأَنَّ جَهَنَّمَ مِنكُمْ أَجْمَعِينَ ﴿١٨﴾

19 And (unto man): O Adam! Dwell thou and thy wife in the Garden and eat from whence ye will, but come not nigh this tree lest ye become wrong-doers.

وَيَٰٓـَٔادَمُ ٱسْكُنْ أَنتَ وَزَوْجُكَ ٱلْجَنَّةَ فَكُلَا مِنْ حَيْثُ شِئْتُمَا وَلَا تَقْرَبَا هَٰذِهِ ٱلشَّجَرَةَ فَتَكُونَا مِنَ ٱلظَّٰلِمِينَ ﴿١٩﴾

20 Then Satan whispered to them
that he might manifest unto them
that which was hidden from them
of their shame, and he said: Your
Lord forbade you from this tree
only lest ye should become angels
or become of the immortals.

فَوَسْوَسَ لَهُمَا الشَّيْطَنُ لِيُبْدِيَ لَهُمَا مَا وُرِيَ
عَنْهُمَا مِنْ سَوْءَٰتِهِمَا وَقَالَ مَا نَهَىٰكُمَا رَبُّكُمَا
عَنْ هَٰذِهِ الشَّجَرَةِ إِلَّا أَن تَكُونَا مَلَكَيْنِ أَوْ تَكُونَا
مِنَ الْخَٰلِدِينَ ۝

21 And he swore unto them (saying):
Lo! I am a sincere adviser unto you.

وَقَاسَمَهُمَا إِنِّي لَكُمَا لَمِنَ النَّٰصِحِينَ ۝

22 Thus did he lead them on with
guile. And when they tasted of the
tree; their shame was manifest to
them and they began to hide (by
heaping) on themselves some of the
leaves of the Garden. And their Lord
called them, (saying): Did I not forbid you from that tree and tell you:
Lo! Satan is an open enemy to you?

فَدَلَّىٰهُمَا بِغُرُورٍ فَلَمَّا ذَاقَا الشَّجَرَةَ بَدَتْ لَهُمَا
سَوْءَٰتُهُمَا وَطَفِقَا يَخْصِفَانِ عَلَيْهِمَا مِن وَرَقِ الْجَنَّةِ
وَنَادَىٰهُمَا رَبُّهُمَا أَلَمْ أَنْهَكُمَا عَن تِلْكُمَا
الشَّجَرَةِ وَأَقُل لَّكُمَا إِنَّ الشَّيْطَنَ لَكُمَا عَدُوٌّ مُّبِينٌ ۝

23 They said: Our Lord! We have
wronged ourselves. If Thou forgive
us not and have not mercy on us,
surely we are of the lost!

قَالَا رَبَّنَا ظَلَمْنَا أَنفُسَنَا وَإِن لَّمْ تَغْفِرْ لَنَا وَتَرْحَمْنَا
لَنَكُونَنَّ مِنَ الْخَٰسِرِينَ ۝

24 He said: Go down (from hence),
some of you a foe unto others. There
will be for you on earth a habitation
and provision for a while.

قَالَ اهْبِطُوا بَعْضُكُمْ لِبَعْضٍ عَدُوٌّ
وَلَكُمْ فِي الْأَرْضِ مُسْتَقَرٌّ وَمَتَٰعٌ إِلَىٰ حِينٍ ۝

25 He said: There shall ye live, and
there shall ye die, and thence shall ye
be brought forth.

قَالَ فِيهَا تَحْيَوْنَ وَفِيهَا تَمُوتُونَ وَمِنْهَا
تُخْرَجُونَ ۝

26 O Children of Adam! We have
revealed unto you raiment to conceal
your shame, and splendid vesture, but
the raiment of restraint from evil,
that is best. This is of the revelations
of Allah, that they may remember.

يَٰبَنِي ءَادَمَ قَدْ أَنزَلْنَا عَلَيْكُمْ لِبَاسًا يُوَٰرِي سَوْءَٰتِكُمْ
وَرِيشًا وَلِبَاسُ التَّقْوَىٰ ذَٰلِكَ خَيْرٌ
ذَٰلِكَ مِنْ ءَايَٰتِ اللَّهِ لَعَلَّهُمْ يَذَّكَّرُونَ ۝

27 O Children of Adam! Let not Satan seduce you as he caused your (first) parents to go forth from the Garden and tore off from them their robe (of innocence) that he might manifest their shame to them. Lo! he seeth you, he and his tribe, from whence ye see him not. Lo! We have made the devils protecting friends for those who believe not.

يَٰبَنِىٓ ءَادَمَ لَا يَفْتِنَنَّكُمُ الشَّيْطَٰنُ كَمَآ أَخْرَجَ أَبَوَيْكُم مِّنَ الْجَنَّةِ يَنزِعُ عَنْهُمَا لِبَاسَهُمَا لِيُرِيَهُمَا سَوْءَٰتِهِمَآ إِنَّهُۥ يَرَىٰكُمْ هُوَ وَقَبِيلُهُۥ مِنْ حَيْثُ لَا تَرَوْنَهُمْ إِنَّا جَعَلْنَا الشَّيَٰطِينَ أَوْلِيَآءَ لِلَّذِينَ لَا يُؤْمِنُونَ ۝

28 And when they do some lewdness they say: We found our fathers doing it and Allah hath enjoined it on us. Say: Allah, verily, enjoineth not lewdness. Tell ye concerning Allah that which ye know not?

وَإِذَا فَعَلُوا۟ فَٰحِشَةً قَالُوا۟ وَجَدْنَا عَلَيْهَآ ءَابَآءَنَا وَاللَّهُ أَمَرَنَا بِهَا قُلْ إِنَّ اللَّهَ لَا يَأْمُرُ بِالْفَحْشَآءِ أَتَقُولُونَ عَلَى اللَّهِ مَا لَا تَعْلَمُونَ ۝

29 Say: My Lord enjoineth justice. And set your faces, upright (toward Him) at every place of worship and call upon Him, making religion pure for Him (only). As He brought you into being, so return ye (unto Him).

قُلْ أَمَرَ رَبِّى بِالْقِسْطِ وَأَقِيمُوا۟ وُجُوهَكُمْ عِندَ كُلِّ مَسْجِدٍ وَادْعُوهُ مُخْلِصِينَ لَهُ الدِّينَ كَمَا بَدَأَكُمْ تَعُودُونَ ۝

30 A party hath He led aright, while error hath just hold over (another) party, for lo! they choose the devils for protecting friends instead of Allah and deem that they are rightly guided.

فَرِيقًا هَدَىٰ وَفَرِيقًا حَقَّ عَلَيْهِمُ الضَّلَٰلَةُ إِنَّهُمُ اتَّخَذُوا۟ الشَّيَٰطِينَ أَوْلِيَآءَ مِن دُونِ اللَّهِ وَيَحْسَبُونَ أَنَّهُم مُّهْتَدُونَ ۝

31 O Children of Adam! Look to your adornment at every place of worship, and eat and drink, but be not prodigal. Lo! He loveth not the prodigals.

۞ يَٰبَنِىٓ ءَادَمَ خُذُوا۟ زِينَتَكُمْ عِندَ كُلِّ مَسْجِدٍ وَكُلُوا۟ وَاشْرَبُوا۟ وَلَا تُسْرِفُوٓا۟ إِنَّهُۥ لَا يُحِبُّ الْمُسْرِفِينَ ۝

32 Say: Who hath forbidden the adornment of Allah which He hath brought forth for His bondmen, and the good things of His providing? Say: Such, on the Day of Resurrection, will be only for those who believed during the life of the world. Thus do We detail Our revelations for people who have knowledge.

قُلْ مَنْ حَرَّمَ زِيْنَةَ اللّٰهِ الَّتِيْٓ اَخْرَجَ لِعِبَادِهٖ وَالطَّيِّبٰتِ مِنَ الرِّزْقِ قُلْ هِيَ لِلَّذِيْنَ اٰمَنُوْا فِي الْحَيٰوةِ الدُّنْيَا خَالِصَةً يَّوْمَ الْقِيٰمَةِ كَذٰلِكَ نُفَصِّلُ الْاٰيٰتِ لِقَوْمٍ يَّعْلَمُوْنَ ۝

33 Say: My Lord forbiddeth only indecencies, such of them as are apparent and such as are within, and sin and wrongful oppression, and that ye associate with Allah that for which no warrant hath been revealed, and that ye tell concerning Allah that which ye know not.

قُلْ اِنَّمَا حَرَّمَ رَبِّيَ الْفَوَاحِشَ مَا ظَهَرَ مِنْهَا وَمَا بَطَنَ وَالْاِثْمَ وَالْبَغْيَ بِغَيْرِ الْحَقِّ وَاَنْ تُشْرِكُوْا بِاللّٰهِ مَا لَمْ يُنَزِّلْ بِهٖ سُلْطٰنًا وَّاَنْ تَقُوْلُوْا عَلَى اللّٰهِ مَا لَا تَعْلَمُوْنَ ۝

34 And every nation hath its term, and when its term cometh, they cannot put it off an hour nor yet advance (it).

وَلِكُلِّ اُمَّةٍ اَجَلٌ فَاِذَا جَاءَ اَجَلُهُمْ لَا يَسْتَأْخِرُوْنَ سَاعَةً وَّلَا يَسْتَقْدِمُوْنَ ۝

35 O Children of Adam! If messengers of your own come unto you; who narrate unto you My revelations, then whosoever refraineth from evil and amendeth—there shall no fear come upon them neither shall they grieve.

يٰبَنِيْٓ اٰدَمَ اِمَّا يَأْتِيَنَّكُمْ رُسُلٌ مِّنْكُمْ يَقُصُّوْنَ عَلَيْكُمْ اٰيٰتِيْ فَمَنِ اتَّقٰى وَاَصْلَحَ فَلَا خَوْفٌ عَلَيْهِمْ وَلَا هُمْ يَحْزَنُوْنَ ۝

36 But they who deny Our revelations and scorn them—such are rightful owners of the Fire; they will abide therein.

وَالَّذِيْنَ كَذَّبُوْا بِاٰيٰتِنَا وَاسْتَكْبَرُوْا عَنْهَآ اُولٰٓئِكَ اَصْحٰبُ النَّارِ هُمْ فِيْهَا خٰلِدُوْنَ ۝

37 Who doeth greater wrong than he who inventeth a lie concerning Allah or denieth His tokens? (For

فَمَنْ اَظْلَمُ مِمَّنِ افْتَرٰى عَلَى اللّٰهِ كَذِبًا اَوْ كَذَّبَ بِاٰيٰتِهٖ

such) their appointed portion of the Book (of destiny) reacheth them till, when Our messengers[2] come to gather them, they say: Where (now) is that to which ye cried beside Allah? They say: They have departed from us. And they testify against themselves that they were disbelievers.

أُوْلَٰٓئِكَ يَنَالُهُمْ نَصِيبُهُم مِّنَ ٱلْكِتَٰبِ حَتَّىٰ إِذَا جَآءَتْهُمْ رُسُلُنَا يَتَوَفَّوْنَهُمْ قَالُوٓاْ أَيْنَ مَا كُنتُمْ تَدْعُونَ مِن دُونِ ٱللَّهِ قَالُواْ ضَلُّواْ عَنَّا وَشَهِدُواْ عَلَىٰٓ أَنفُسِهِمْ أَنَّهُمْ كَانُواْ كَٰفِرِينَ ٣٧

38 He saith: Enter into the Fire among nations of the jinn and humankind who passed away before you. Every time a nation entereth, it curseth its sister (nation) till, when they have all been made to follow one another thither, the last of them saith unto the first of them: Our Lord! These led us astray, so give them double torment of the Fire. He saith: For each one there is double (torment), but ye know not.

قَالَ ٱدْخُلُواْ فِىٓ أُمَمٍ قَدْ خَلَتْ مِن قَبْلِكُم مِّنَ ٱلْجِنِّ وَٱلْإِنسِ فِى ٱلنَّارِ كُلَّمَا دَخَلَتْ أُمَّةٌ لَّعَنَتْ أُخْتَهَا حَتَّىٰٓ إِذَا ٱدَّارَكُواْ فِيهَا جَمِيعًا قَالَتْ أُخْرَىٰهُمْ لِأُولَىٰهُمْ رَبَّنَا هَٰٓؤُلَآءِ أَضَلُّونَا فَـَٔاتِهِمْ عَذَابًا ضِعْفًا مِّنَ ٱلنَّارِ قَالَ لِكُلٍّ ضِعْفٌ وَلَٰكِن لَّا تَعْلَمُونَ ٣٨

39 And the first of them saith unto the last of them: Ye were no whit better than us, so taste the doom for what ye used to earn.

وَقَالَتْ أُولَىٰهُمْ لِأُخْرَىٰهُمْ فَمَا كَانَ لَكُمْ عَلَيْنَا مِن فَضْلٍ فَذُوقُواْ ٱلْعَذَابَ بِمَا كُنتُمْ تَكْسِبُونَ ٣٩

40 Lo! they who deny Our revelations and scorn them, for them the gates of Heaven will not be opened nor will they enter the Garden until the camel goeth through the needle's eye. Thus do We requite the guilty.

إِنَّ ٱلَّذِينَ كَذَّبُواْ بِـَٔايَٰتِنَا وَٱسْتَكْبَرُواْ عَنْهَا لَا تُفَتَّحُ لَهُمْ أَبْوَٰبُ ٱلسَّمَآءِ وَلَا يَدْخُلُونَ ٱلْجَنَّةَ حَتَّىٰ يَلِجَ ٱلْجَمَلُ فِى سَمِّ ٱلْخِيَاطِ وَكَذَٰلِكَ نَجْزِى ٱلْمُجْرِمِينَ ٤٠

41 Theirs will be a bed of Hell, and over them coverings (of Hell). Thus do We requite wrong-doers.

لَهُم مِّن جَهَنَّمَ مِهَادٌ وَمِن فَوْقِهِمْ غَوَاشٍ وَكَذَٰلِكَ نَجْزِى ٱلظَّٰلِمِينَ ٤١

---

2. *i.e.* Angels.

42 But (as for) those who believe
and do good works—We tax not any
soul beyond its scope—Such are
rightful owners of the Garden. They
abide therein.

وَالَّذِينَ ءَامَنُوا وَعَمِلُوا الصَّٰلِحَٰتِ
لَا نُكَلِّفُ نَفْسًا إِلَّا وُسْعَهَا أُولَٰٓئِكَ أَصْحَٰبُ
الْجَنَّةِ هُمْ فِيهَا خَٰلِدُونَ ﴿٤٢﴾

43 And We remove whatever rancour may be in their hearts. Rivers
flow beneath them. And they say:
The praise to Allah, Who hath guided us to this. We could not truly
have been led aright if Allah had not
guided us. Verily the messengers of
our Lord did bring the Truth. And it
is cried unto them: This is the Garden. Ye inherit it for what ye used to
do.

وَنَزَعْنَا مَا فِي صُدُورِهِم مِّنْ غِلٍّ تَجْرِي مِن تَحْتِهِمُ
الْأَنْهَٰرُ وَقَالُوا الْحَمْدُ لِلَّهِ الَّذِي هَدَىٰنَا لِهَٰذَا
وَمَا كُنَّا لِنَهْتَدِيَ لَوْلَا أَنْ هَدَىٰنَا اللَّهُ لَقَدْ جَاءَتْ
رُسُلُ رَبِّنَا بِالْحَقِّ وَنُودُوا أَن تِلْكُمُ الْجَنَّةُ
أُورِثْتُمُوهَا بِمَا كُنتُمْ تَعْمَلُونَ ﴿٤٣﴾

44 And the dwellers of the Garden
cry unto the dwellers of the Fire: We
have found that which our Lord promised us (to be) the Truth. Have ye
(too) found that which your Lord
promised the Truth? They say: Yea,
verily. And a crier in between them
crieth: The curse of Allah is on evil-
doers;

وَنَادَىٰ أَصْحَٰبُ الْجَنَّةِ أَصْحَٰبَ النَّارِ أَن قَدْ وَجَدْنَا
مَا وَعَدَنَا رَبُّنَا حَقًّا فَهَلْ وَجَدتُّم مَّا وَعَدَ رَبُّكُمْ حَقًّا
قَالُوا نَعَمْ فَأَذَّنَ مُؤَذِّنٌ بَيْنَهُمْ أَن لَّعْنَةُ اللَّهِ
عَلَى الظَّٰلِمِينَ ﴿٤٤﴾

45 Who debar (men) from the path
of Allah and would have it crooked,
and who are disbelievers in the Last
Day.

الَّذِينَ يَصُدُّونَ عَن سَبِيلِ اللَّهِ وَيَبْغُونَهَا عِوَجًا وَهُم
بِالْآخِرَةِ كَٰفِرُونَ ﴿٤٥﴾

46 Between them is a veil. And on
the Heights are men who know them
all by their marks. And they call
unto the dwellers of the Garden:
Peace be unto you! They enter it not
although they hope (to enter).

وَبَيْنَهُمَا حِجَابٌ وَعَلَى الْأَعْرَافِ رِجَالٌ يَعْرِفُونَ كُلًّا
بِسِيمَٰهُمْ وَنَادَوْا أَصْحَٰبَ الْجَنَّةِ أَن سَلَٰمٌ عَلَيْكُمْ
لَمْ يَدْخُلُوهَا وَهُمْ يَطْمَعُونَ ﴿٤٦﴾

47 And when their eyes are turned
toward the dwellers of the Fire,

۞ وَإِذَا صُرِفَتْ أَبْصَٰرُهُمْ تِلْقَاءَ أَصْحَٰبِ النَّارِ قَالُوا رَبَّنَا

they say: Our Lord! Place us not with the wrongdoing folk.

لَا تَجْعَلْنَا مَعَ الْقَوْمِ الظَّالِمِينَ ۝

48 And the dwellers on the Heights call unto men whom they know by their marks, (saying): What did your multitude and that in which ye took your pride avail you?

وَنَادَىٰ أَصْحَبُ الْأَعْرَافِ رِجَالًا يَعْرِفُوْنَهُمْ بِسِيمَاهُمْ قَالُوْا مَا أَغْنَىٰ عَنْكُمْ جَمْعُكُمْ وَمَا كُنْتُمْ تَسْتَكْبِرُوْنَ ۝

49 Are these they of whom ye swore that Allah would not show them mercy? (Unto them it hath been said): Enter the Garden. No fear shall come upon you nor is it ye who will grieve.

أَهَؤُلَاءِ الَّذِيْنَ أَقْسَمْتُمْ لَا يَنَالُهُمُ اللّٰهُ بِرَحْمَةٍ ادْخُلُوا الْجَنَّةَ لَا خَوْفٌ عَلَيْكُمْ وَلَا أَنْتُمْ تَحْزَنُوْنَ ۝

50 And the dwellers of the Fire cry out unto the dwellers of the Garden; Pour on us some water or some of that wherewith Allah hath provided you. They say: Lo! Allah hath forbidden both to the disbelievers.

وَنَادَىٰ أَصْحَبُ النَّارِ أَصْحَبَ الْجَنَّةِ أَنْ أَفِيضُوْا عَلَيْنَا مِنَ الْمَاءِ أَوْ مِمَّا رَزَقَكُمُ اللّٰهُ قَالُوْا إِنَّ اللّٰهَ حَرَّمَهُمَا عَلَى الْكَفِرِيْنَ ۝

51 Who took their religion for a sport and pastime, and whom the life of the world beguiled. So this day We have forgotten them even as they forgot the meeting of this day of theirs and as they used to deny Our tokens.

الَّذِيْنَ اتَّخَذُوا دِيْنَهُمْ لَهْوًا وَلَعِبًا وَغَرَّتْهُمُ الْحَيٰوةُ الدُّنْيَا فَالْيَوْمَ نَنْسَاهُمْ كَمَا نَسُوْا لِقَاءَ يَوْمِهِمْ هَذَا وَمَا كَانُوْا بِآيَاتِنَا يَجْحَدُوْنَ ۝

52 Verily We have brought them a Scripture which We expound with knowledge, a guidance and a mercy for a people who believe.

وَلَقَدْ جِئْنَاهُمْ بِكِتَابٍ فَصَّلْنَاهُ عَلَى عِلْمٍ هُدًى وَرَحْمَةً لِقَوْمٍ يُؤْمِنُوْنَ ۝

53 Await they aught save the fulfillment thereof? On the day when the fulfillment thereof cometh, those who were before forgetful thereof will say: The messengers of our

هَلْ يَنْظُرُوْنَ إِلَّا تَأْوِيْلَهُ يَوْمَ يَأْتِيْ تَأْوِيْلُهُ يَقُوْلُ الَّذِيْنَ نَسُوْهُ مِنْ قَبْلُ قَدْ جَاءَتْ رُسُلُ رَبِّنَا

Lord did bring the Truth! Have we any intercessors, that they may intercede for us? Or can we be returned (to life on earth), that we may act otherwise than we used to act? They have lost their souls, and that which they devised hath failed them.

بِالْحَقِّ فَهَلْ لَّنَا مِنْ شُفَعَآءَ فَيَشْفَعُوا لَنَآ أَوْنُرَدُّ فَنَعْمَلَ غَيْرَ الَّذِى كُنَّا نَعْمَلُ قَدْ خَسِرُوٓا أَنْفُسَهُمْ وَضَلَّ عَنْهُمْ مَّا كَانُوا يَفْتَرُونَ ۝

54 Lo! your Lord is Allah Who created the heavens and the earth in six Days, then mounted He the Throne. He covereth the night with the day, which is in haste to follow it, and hath made the sun and the moon and the stars subservient by His command. His verily is all creation and commandment. Blessed be Allah, the Lord of the Worlds!

إِنَّ رَبَّكُمُ اللّهُ الَّذِى خَلَقَ السَّمَوَٰتِ وَالْأَرْضَ فِى سِتَّةِ أَيَّامٍ ثُمَّ اسْتَوَىٰ عَلَى الْعَرْشِ يُغْشِى الَّيْلَ النَّهَارَ يَطْلُبُهُ حَثِيثًا وَالشَّمْسَ وَالْقَمَرَ وَالنُّجُومَ مُسَخَّرَٰتٍۢ بِأَمْرِهِ أَلَا لَهُ الْخَلْقُ وَالْأَمْرُ تَبَارَكَ اللّهُ رَبُّ الْعَالَمِينَ ۝

55 (O mankind!) Call upon your Lord humbly and in secret. Lo! He loveth not aggressors.

ادْعُوا رَبَّكُمْ تَضَرُّعًا وَخُفْيَةً إِنَّهُ لَا يُحِبُّ الْمُعْتَدِينَ ۝

56 Work not confusion in the earth after the fair ordering (thereof), and call on Him in fear and hope. Lo! the mercy of Allah is nigh unto the good.

وَلَا تُفْسِدُوا فِى الْأَرْضِ بَعْدَ إِصْلَٰحِهَا وَادْعُوهُ خَوْفًا وَطَمَعًا إِنَّ رَحْمَتَ اللّهِ قَرِيبٌ مِّنَ الْمُحْسِنِينَ ۝

57 And He it is Who sendeth the winds as tidings heralding His mercy, till, when they bear a cloud heavy (with rain), We lead it to a dead land, and then cause water to descend thereon, and thereby bring forth fruits of every kind. Thus bring We forth the dead. Haply ye may remember.

وَهُوَ الَّذِى يُرْسِلُ الرِّيَٰحَ بُشْرًۢا بَيْنَ يَدَىْ رَحْمَتِهِ حَتَّىٰٓ إِذَآ أَقَلَّتْ سَحَابًا ثِقَالًا سُقْنَٰهُ لِبَلَدٍ مَّيِّتٍ فَأَنْزَلْنَا بِهِ الْمَآءَ فَأَخْرَجْنَا بِهِ مِنْ كُلِّ الثَّمَرَٰتِ كَذَٰلِكَ نُخْرِجُ الْمَوْتَىٰ لَعَلَّكُمْ تَذَكَّرُونَ ۝

58 As for the good land, its vegetation cometh forth by permission of its Lord; while as for that which is bad, only evil cometh forth (from it). Thus do We recount the tokens for people who give thanks.

وَالْبَلَدُ الطَّيِّبُ يَخْرُجُ نَبَاتُهُ بِإِذْنِ رَبِّهِ وَالَّذِى خَبُثَ لَا يَخْرُجُ إِلَّا نَكِدًا كَذَلِكَ نُصَرِّفُ الْآيَاتِ لِقَوْمٍ يَشْكُرُونَ ۝

59 We sent Noah (of old) unto his people, and he said: O my people! Serve Allah. Ye have no other God save Him. Lo! I fear for you the retribution of an Awful Day.

لَقَدْ أَرْسَلْنَا نُوحًا إِلَى قَوْمِهِ فَقَالَ يَقَوْمِ اعْبُدُوا اللَّهَ مَالَكُمْ مِنْ إِلَهٍ غَيْرُهُ إِنِّى أَخَافُ عَلَيْكُمْ عَذَابَ يَوْمٍ عَظِيمٍ ۝

60 The chieftains of his people said: Lo! we see thee surely in plain error.

قَالَ الْمَلَأُ مِن قَوْمِهِ إِنَّا لَنَرَىكَ فِى ضَلَلٍ مُّبِينٍ ۝

61 He said: O my people! There is no error in me, but I am a messenger from the Lord of the Worlds.

قَالَ يَقَوْمِ لَيْسَ بِى ضَلَلَةٌ وَلَكِنِّى رَسُولٌ مِّن رَّبِّ الْعَلَمِينَ ۝

62 I convey unto you the messages of my Lord and give good counsel unto you, and know from Allah that which ye know not.

أُبَلِّغُكُمْ رِسَلَتِ رَبِّى وَأَنصَحُ لَكُمْ وَأَعْلَمُ مِنَ اللَّهِ مَا لَا تَعْلَمُونَ ۝

63 Marvel ye that there should come unto you a Reminder from your Lord by means of a man among you, that he may warn you, and that ye may keep from evil, and that haply ye may find mercy.

أَوَعَجِبْتُمْ أَن جَآءَكُمْ ذِكْرٌ مِّن رَّبِّكُمْ عَلَى رَجُلٍ مِّنكُمْ لِيُنذِرَكُمْ وَلِتَتَّقُوا وَلَعَلَّكُمْ تُرْحَمُونَ ۝

64 But they denied him, so We saved him and those with him in the ship, and We drowned those who denied Our tokens. Lo! they were blind folk.

فَكَذَّبُوهُ فَأَنجَيْنَهُ وَالَّذِينَ مَعَهُ فِى الْفُلْكِ وَأَغْرَقْنَا الَّذِينَ كَذَّبُوا بِآيَاتِنَا إِنَّهُمْ كَانُوا قَوْمًا عَمِينَ ۝

65 And unto (the tribe of) 'Ād (We sent) their brother, Hūd.[3] He said: O my people! Serve Allah. Ye have no other God save Him. Will ye not ward off (evil)?

٦٥ وَإِلَىٰ عَادٍ أَخَاهُمْ هُودًا ۗ قَالَ يَٰقَوْمِ اعْبُدُوا اللَّهَ مَا لَكُم مِّنْ إِلَٰهٍ غَيْرُهُ ۚ أَفَلَا تَتَّقُونَ ۝

66 The chieftains of his people, who were disbelieving, said: Lo! we surely see thee in foolishness, and lo! we deem thee of the liars.

٦٦ قَالَ الْمَلَأُ الَّذِينَ كَفَرُوا مِن قَوْمِهِ إِنَّا لَنَرَاكَ فِي سَفَاهَةٍ وَإِنَّا لَنَظُنُّكَ مِنَ الْكَاذِبِينَ ۝

67 He said: O my people; There is no foolishness in me, but I am a messenger from the Lord of the Worlds.

٦٧ قَالَ يَٰقَوْمِ لَيْسَ بِي سَفَاهَةٌ وَلَٰكِنِّي رَسُولٌ مِّن رَّبِّ الْعَالَمِينَ ۝

68 I convey unto you the messages of my Lord and am for you a true adviser.

٦٨ أُبَلِّغُكُمْ رِسَالَاتِ رَبِّي وَأَنَا لَكُمْ نَاصِحٌ أَمِينٌ ۝

69 Marvel ye that there should come unto you a Reminder from your Lord by means of a man among you, that he may warn you? Remember how He made you viceroys after Noah's folk, and gave you growth of stature. Remember (all) the bounties of your Lord, that haply ye may be successful.

٦٩ أَوَعَجِبْتُمْ أَن جَاءَكُمْ ذِكْرٌ مِّن رَّبِّكُمْ عَلَىٰ رَجُلٍ مِّنكُمْ لِيُنذِرَكُمْ ۚ وَاذْكُرُوا إِذْ جَعَلَكُمْ خُلَفَاءَ مِن بَعْدِ قَوْمِ نُوحٍ وَزَادَكُمْ فِي الْخَلْقِ بَسْطَةً ۖ فَاذْكُرُوا آلَاءَ اللَّهِ لَعَلَّكُمْ تُفْلِحُونَ ۝

70 They said: Hast come unto us that we should serve Allah alone, and forsake what our fathers worshipped? Then bring upon us that wherewith thou threatenest us if thou art of the truth.

٧٠ قَالُوا أَجِئْتَنَا لِنَعْبُدَ اللَّهَ وَحْدَهُ وَنَذَرَ مَا كَانَ يَعْبُدُ آبَاؤُنَا ۖ فَأْتِنَا بِمَا تَعِدُنَا إِن كُنتَ مِنَ الصَّادِقِينَ ۝

---

3. An ancient Arab prophet.

71 He said: Terror and wrath from your Lord have already fallen on you. Would ye wrangle with me over names which ye have named, ye and your fathers, for which no warrant from Allah hath been revealed? Then await (the consequence), lo! I (also) am of those awaiting (it).

قَالَ قَدْ وَقَعَ عَلَيْكُمْ مِّنْ رَّبِّكُمْ رِجْسٌ وَّعَضَبٌ ۚ أَتُجَادِلُونَنِي فِي أَسْمَاءٍ سَمَّيْتُمُوهَا أَنْتُمْ وَءَابَاؤُكُمْ مَّا نَزَّلَ اللَّهُ بِهَا مِنْ سُلْطَانٍ ۚ فَانْتَظِرُوْا إِنِّي مَعَكُمْ مِّنَ الْمُنْتَظِرِينَ ۝

72 And We saved him and those with him by a mercy from Us, and We cut the root of those who denied Our revelations and were not believers.

فَأَنْجَيْنَاهُ وَالَّذِينَ مَعَهُ بِرَحْمَةٍ مِّنَّا وَقَطَعْنَا دَابِرَ الَّذِينَ كَذَّبُوْا بِآيَاتِنَا ۖ وَمَا كَانُوْا مُؤْمِنِينَ ۝

73 And to (the tribe of) Thamūd (We sent) their brother Sālih.[4] He said: O my people! Serve Allah. Ye have no other God save Him. A wonder from your Lord hath come unto you. Lo! this is the camel of Allah, a token unto you; so let her feed in Allah's earth, and touch her not with hurt lest painful torment seize you.

وَإِلَى ثَمُودَ أَخَاهُمْ صَالِحًا ۗ قَالَ يَا قَوْمِ اعْبُدُوا اللَّهَ مَا لَكُمْ مِّنْ إِلَهٍ غَيْرُهُ ۖ قَدْ جَاءَتْكُمْ بَيِّنَةٌ مِّنْ رَّبِّكُمْ ۖ هَذِهِ نَاقَةُ اللَّهِ لَكُمْ ءَايَةً ۖ فَذَرُوهَا تَأْكُلْ فِي أَرْضِ اللَّهِ وَلَا تَمَسُّوهَا بِسُوءٍ فَيَأْخُذَكُمْ عَذَابٌ أَلِيمٌ ۝

74 And remember how He made you viceroys after 'Ād and gave you station in the earth. Ye choose castles in the plains and hew the mountains into dwellings. So remember (all) the bounties of Allah and do not evil, making mischief in the earth.

وَاذْكُرُوا إِذْ جَعَلَكُمْ خُلَفَاءَ مِنْ بَعْدِ عَادٍ وَّبَوَّأَكُمْ فِي الْأَرْضِ تَتَّخِذُونَ مِنْ سُهُولِهَا قُصُورًا وَّتَنْحِتُونَ الْجِبَالَ بُيُوتًا ۖ فَاذْكُرُوا ءَالَاءَ اللَّهِ وَلَا تَعْثَوْا فِي الْأَرْضِ مُفْسِدِينَ ۝

---

4. An ancient Arab prophet.

75 The chieftains of his people, who were scornful, said unto those whom they despised, unto such of them as believed: Know ye that Sāliḥ is one sent from his Lord? They said: Lo! In that wherewith he hath been sent we are believers.

قَالَ الْمَلَأُ الَّذِينَ اسْتَكْبَرُوْا مِنْ قَوْمِهٖ لِلَّذِينَ اسْتُضْعِفُوْا لِمَنْ اٰمَنَ مِنْهُمْ أَتَعْلَمُوْنَ أَنَّ صٰلِحًا مُّرْسَلٌ مِّنْ رَّبِّهٖ ۚ قَالُوْۤا إِنَّا بِمَاۤ أُرْسِلَ بِهٖ مُؤْمِنُوْنَ ۝

76 Those who were scornful said: Lo! in that which ye believe we are disbelievers.

قَالَ الَّذِينَ اسْتَكْبَرُوْۤا إِنَّا بِالَّذِيْۤ اٰمَنْتُمْ بِهٖ كٰفِرُوْنَ ۝

77 So they hamstrung the she-camel, and they flouted the commandment of their Lord, and they said: O Sāliḥ! Bring upon us that thou threatenest if thou art indeed of those sent (from Allah).

فَعَقَرُوا النَّاقَةَ وَعَتَوْا عَنْ أَمْرِ رَبِّهِمْ وَقَالُوْا يٰصٰلِحُ ائْتِنَا بِمَا تَعِدُنَاۤ إِنْ كُنْتَ مِنَ الْمُرْسَلِيْنَ ۝

78 So the earthquake seized them, and morning found them prostrate in their dwelling place.

فَأَخَذَتْهُمُ الرَّجْفَةُ فَأَصْبَحُوْا فِيْ دَارِهِمْ جٰثِمِيْنَ ۝

79 And Sāliḥ turned from them and said: O my people! I delivered my Lord's message unto you and gave you good advice, but ye love not good advisers.

فَتَوَلّٰى عَنْهُمْ وَقَالَ يٰقَوْمِ لَقَدْ أَبْلَغْتُكُمْ رِسَالَةَ رَبِّيْ وَنَصَحْتُ لَكُمْ وَلٰكِنْ لَّا تُحِبُّوْنَ النّٰصِحِيْنَ ۝

80 And Lot! (Remember) when he said unto his folk: Will ye commit abomination such as no creature ever did before you?

وَلُوْطًا إِذْ قَالَ لِقَوْمِهٖۤ أَتَأْتُوْنَ الْفَاحِشَةَ مَا سَبَقَكُمْ بِهَا مِنْ أَحَدٍ مِّنَ الْعٰلَمِيْنَ ۝

81 Lo! ye come with lust unto men instead of women. Nay, but ye are wanton folk.

إِنَّكُمْ لَتَأْتُوْنَ الرِّجَالَ شَهْوَةً مِّنْ دُوْنِ النِّسَاءِ ۚ بَلْ أَنْتُمْ قَوْمٌ مُّسْرِفُوْنَ ۝

82 And the answer of his people was only that they said (one to another): Turn them out of your town-

وَمَا كَانَ جَوَابَ قَوْمِهٖۤ إِلَّاۤ أَنْ قَالُوْۤا أَخْرِجُوْهُمْ مِّنْ قَرْيَتِكُمْ ۚ إِنَّهُمْ أُنَاسٌ

يَطَّهَّرُونَ ۝

ship.[5] They are folk, forsooth, who keep pure.

فَأَنجَيْنَٰهُ وَأَهْلَهُۥٓ إِلَّا ٱمْرَأَتَهُۥ كَانَتْ مِنَ ٱلْغَٰبِرِينَ ۝

83 And We rescued him and his household, save his wife, who was of those who stayed behind.

وَأَمْطَرْنَا عَلَيْهِم مَّطَرًا فَٱنظُرْ كَيْفَ كَانَ عَٰقِبَةُ ٱلْمُجْرِمِينَ ۝

84 And We rained a rain upon them. See now the nature of the consequence for evil-doers!

وَإِلَىٰ مَدْيَنَ أَخَاهُمْ شُعَيْبًا قَالَ يَٰقَوْمِ ٱعْبُدُوا۟ ٱللَّهَ مَا لَكُم مِّنْ إِلَٰهٍ غَيْرُهُۥ قَدْ جَآءَتْكُم بَيِّنَةٌ مِّن رَّبِّكُمْ فَأَوْفُوا۟ ٱلْكَيْلَ وَٱلْمِيزَانَ وَلَا تَبْخَسُوا۟ ٱلنَّاسَ أَشْيَآءَهُمْ وَلَا تُفْسِدُوا۟ فِى ٱلْأَرْضِ بَعْدَ إِصْلَٰحِهَا ذَٰلِكُمْ خَيْرٌ لَّكُمْ إِن كُنتُم مُّؤْمِنِينَ ۝

85 And unto Madyan (We sent) their brother, Shu'ayb.[6] He said: O my people! Serve Allah. Ye have no other God save Him. Lo! a clear proof hath come unto you from your Lord; so give full measure and full weight and wrong not mankind in their goods, and work not confusion in the earth after the fair ordering thereof. That will be better for you, if ye are believers.

وَلَا تَقْعُدُوا۟ بِكُلِّ صِرَٰطٍ تُوعِدُونَ وَتَصُدُّونَ عَن سَبِيلِ ٱللَّهِ مَنْ ءَامَنَ بِهِۦ وَتَبْغُونَهَا عِوَجًا وَٱذْكُرُوٓا۟ إِذْ كُنتُمْ قَلِيلًا فَكَثَّرَكُمْ وَٱنظُرُوا۟ كَيْفَ كَانَ عَٰقِبَةُ ٱلْمُفْسِدِينَ ۝

86 Lurk not on every road to threaten (wayfarers), and to turn away from Allah's path him who believeth in Him, and to seek to make it crooked. And remember, when ye were but few, how He did multiply you. And see the nature of the consequence for the corrupters!

وَإِن كَانَ طَآئِفَةٌ مِّنكُمْ ءَامَنُوا۟ بِٱلَّذِىٓ أُرْسِلْتُ بِهِۦ وَطَآئِفَةٌ لَّمْ يُؤْمِنُوا۟ فَٱصْبِرُوا۟ حَتَّىٰ

87 And if there is a party of you which believeth in that wherewith I have been sent, and there is a party which believeth not, then have pati-

---

5. The Arabic word *Qariah* means originally a setded community, polity or civilisation.

6. Identified with Jethro.

ence until Allah judge between us.
He is the best of all who deal in
judgment.

88 The chieftains of his people,
who were scornful, said: Surely we
will drive thee out, O Shu'ayb, and
those who believe with thee, from
our township, unless ye return to
our religion. He said: Even though
we hate it?

89 We should have invented a lie
against Allah if we returned to your
religion after Allah hath rescued us
from it. It is not for us to return to
it unless Allah should (so) will. Our
Lord comprehendeth all things in
knowledge. In Allah do we put our
trust. Our Lord! Decide with truth
between us and our folk, for Thou
art the best of those who make
decision.

90 But the chieftains of his people,
who were disbelieving, said: If ye
follow Shu'ayb, then truly we shall
be the losers.

91 So the earthquake seized them,
and morning found them prostrate
in their dwelling place.

92 Those who denied Shu'ayb became as though they had not dwelt
there. Those who denied Shu'ayb,
they were the losers.

93 So he turned from them and
said: O my people! I delivered my
Lord's messages unto you and gave

يَحْكُمَ اللّٰهُ بَيْنَنَا وَهُوَ خَيْرُ الْحَاكِمِينَ ۞

۞ قَالَ الْمَلَأُ الَّذِينَ اسْتَكْبَرُوا مِن قَوْمِهِ لَنُخْرِجَنَّكَ
يَشُعَيْبُ وَالَّذِينَ ءَامَنُوا مَعَكَ مِن قَرْيَتِنَا أَوْ لَتَعُودُنَّ
فِي مِلَّتِنَا قَالَ أَوَلَوْ كُنَّا كَارِهِينَ ۞

قَدِ افْتَرَيْنَا عَلَى اللّٰهِ كَذِبًا إِنْ عُدْنَا فِي مِلَّتِكُم
بَعْدَ إِذْ نَجَّىٰنَا اللّٰهُ مِنْهَا وَمَا يَكُونُ لَنَا أَن نَّعُودَ فِيهَا
إِلَّا أَن يَشَاءَ اللّٰهُ رَبُّنَا وَسِعَ رَبُّنَا كُلَّ شَيْءٍ عِلْمًا
عَلَى اللّٰهِ تَوَكَّلْنَا رَبَّنَا افْتَحْ بَيْنَنَا وَبَيْنَ قَوْمِنَا
بِالْحَقِّ وَأَنتَ خَيْرُ الْفَاتِحِينَ ۞

وَقَالَ الْمَلَأُ الَّذِينَ كَفَرُوا مِن قَوْمِهِ لَئِنِ اتَّبَعْتُمْ
شُعَيْبًا إِنَّكُمْ إِذًا لَّخَاسِرُونَ ۞
فَأَخَذَتْهُمُ الرَّجْفَةُ فَأَصْبَحُوا فِي دَارِهِمْ
جَاثِمِينَ ۞

الَّذِينَ كَذَّبُوا شُعَيْبًا كَأَن لَّمْ يَغْنَوْا فِيهَا الَّذِينَ
كَذَّبُوا شُعَيْبًا كَانُوا هُمُ الْخَاسِرِينَ ۞

فَتَوَلَّىٰ عَنْهُمْ وَقَالَ يَٰقَوْمِ لَقَدْ أَبْلَغْتُكُمْ
رِسَالَاتِ رَبِّي وَنَصَحْتُ لَكُمْ فَكَيْفَ ءَاسَىٰ

you good advice; then how can I sorrow for a people that rejected (truth)?

94 And We sent no prophet unto any township but We did afflict its folk with tribulation and adversity that haply they might grow humble.

95 Then changed We the evil plight for good till they grew affluent and said: Tribulation and distress did touch our fathers. Then We seized them unawares, when they perceived not.

96 And if the people of the townships had believed and kept from evil, surely We should have opened for them blessings from the sky and from the earth. But (unto every messenger) they gave the lie, and so We seized them on account of what they used to earn.

97 Are the people of the townships then secure from the coming of Our wrath upon them as a night-raid while they sleep?

98 Or are the people of the townships then secure from the coming of Our wrath upon them in the day-time while they play?

99 Are they then secure from Allah's scheme? None deemeth himself secure from Allah's scheme save folk that perish.

100 Is it not an indication to those who inherit the land after its

عَلَىٰ قَوْمٍ كَٰفِرِينَ ۝

وَمَآ أَرْسَلْنَا فِى قَرْيَةٍ مِّن نَّبِىٍّ إِلَّآ أَخَذْنَآ أَهْلَهَا بِٱلْبَأْسَآءِ وَٱلضَّرَّآءِ لَعَلَّهُمْ يَضَّرَّعُونَ ۝

ثُمَّ بَدَّلْنَا مَكَانَ ٱلسَّيِّئَةِ ٱلْحَسَنَةَ حَتَّىٰ عَفَوا۟ وَّقَالُوا۟ قَدْ مَسَّ ءَابَآءَنَا ٱلضَّرَّآءُ وَٱلسَّرَّآءُ فَأَخَذْنَٰهُم بَغْتَةً وَّهُمْ لَا يَشْعُرُونَ ۝

وَلَوْ أَنَّ أَهْلَ ٱلْقُرَىٰٓ ءَامَنُوا۟ وَٱتَّقَوْا۟ لَفَتَحْنَا عَلَيْهِم بَرَكَٰتٍ مِّنَ ٱلسَّمَآءِ وَٱلْأَرْضِ وَلَٰكِن كَذَّبُوا۟ فَأَخَذْنَٰهُم بِمَا كَانُوا۟ يَكْسِبُونَ ۝

أَفَأَمِنَ أَهْلُ ٱلْقُرَىٰٓ أَن يَأْتِيَهُم بَأْسُنَا بَيَٰتًا وَهُمْ نَآئِمُونَ ۝

أَوَأَمِنَ أَهْلُ ٱلْقُرَىٰٓ أَن يَأْتِيَهُم بَأْسُنَا ضُحًى وَهُمْ يَلْعَبُونَ ۝

أَفَأَمِنُوا۟ مَكْرَ ٱللَّهِ فَلَا يَأْمَنُ مَكْرَ ٱللَّهِ إِلَّا ٱلْقَوْمُ ٱلْخَٰسِرُونَ ۝

أَوَلَمْ يَهْدِ لِلَّذِينَ يَرِثُونَ ٱلْأَرْضَ مِنۢ بَعْدِ

people (who thus reaped the consequence of evil-doing) that, if We will, We can smite them for their sins and print upon their hearts so that they hear not?

أَهْلِهَا أَن لَّوْ نَشَآءُ أَصَبْنَهُم بِذُنُوبِهِمْ وَنَطْبَعُ عَلَىٰ قُلُوبِهِمْ فَهُمْ لَا يَسْمَعُونَ ﴿١٠٠﴾

101   Such were the townships. We relate some tidings of them unto thee (Muhammad). Their messengers verily came unto them with clear proofs (of Allah's Sovereignty), but they could not believe because they had before denied. Thus doth Allah print upon the hearts of disbelievers (that they hear not).

تِلْكَ ٱلْقُرَىٰ نَقُصُّ عَلَيْكَ مِنْ أَنۢبَآئِهَا وَلَقَدْ جَآءَتْهُمْ رُسُلُهُم بِٱلْبَيِّنَٰتِ فَمَا كَانُوا لِيُؤْمِنُوا بِمَا كَذَّبُوا مِن قَبْلُ كَذَٰلِكَ يَطْبَعُ ٱللَّهُ عَلَىٰ قُلُوبِ ٱلْكَٰفِرِينَ ﴿١٠١﴾

102   We found no (loyalty to any) covenant in most of them. Nay, most of them We found wrong-doers.

وَمَا وَجَدْنَا لِأَكْثَرِهِم مِّنْ عَهْدٍ وَإِن وَجَدْنَآ أَكْثَرَهُمْ لَفَٰسِقِينَ ﴿١٠٢﴾

103   Then, after them, We sent Moses with our tokens unto Pharaoh and his chiefs, but they repelled them. Now, see the nature of the consequence for the corrupters!

ثُمَّ بَعَثْنَا مِنۢ بَعْدِهِم مُّوسَىٰ بِآيَٰتِنَآ إِلَىٰ فِرْعَوْنَ وَمَلَإِيْهِ فَظَلَمُوا بِهَا فَٱنظُرْ كَيْفَ كَانَ عَٰقِبَةُ ٱلْمُفْسِدِينَ ﴿١٠٣﴾

104   Moses said: O Pharaoh! Lo! I am a messenger from the Lord of the Worlds;

وَقَالَ مُوسَىٰ يَٰفِرْعَوْنُ إِنِّي رَسُولٌ مِّن رَّبِّ ٱلْعَٰلَمِينَ ﴿١٠٤﴾

105   Approved upon condition that I speak concerning Allah nothing but the truth. I come unto you (lords of Egypt) with a clear proof from your Lord. So let the Children of Israel go with me.

حَقِيقٌ عَلَىٰٓ أَن لَّآ أَقُولَ عَلَى ٱللَّهِ إِلَّا ٱلْحَقَّ قَدْ جِئْتُكُم بِبَيِّنَةٍ مِّن رَّبِّكُمْ فَأَرْسِلْ مَعِيَ بَنِيٓ إِسْرَٰٓءِيلَ ﴿١٠٥﴾

106   (Pharaoh) said: If thou comest with a token, then produce it, if thou art of those who speak the truth.

قَالَ إِن كُنتَ جِئْتَ بِآيَةٍ فَأْتِ بِهَآ إِن كُنتَ مِنَ ٱلصَّٰدِقِينَ ﴿١٠٦﴾

107   Then he flung down his staff and lo! it was a serpent manifest;

فَأَلْقَىٰ عَصَاهُ فَإِذَا هِيَ ثُعْبَانٌ مُّبِينٌ ۝

108   And he drew forth his hand (from his bosom); and lo! it was white for the beholders.

وَنَزَعَ يَدَهُ فَإِذَا هِيَ بَيْضَآءُ لِلنَّـٰظِرِينَ ۝

109   The chiefs of Pharaoh's people said: Lo! this is some knowing wizard;

قَالَ الْمَلَأُ مِن قَوْمِ فِرْعَوْنَ إِنَّ هَـٰذَا لَسَـٰحِرٌ عَلِيمٌ ۝

110   Who would expel you from your land. Now what do ye advise?

يُرِيدُ أَن يُخْرِجَكُم مِّنْ أَرْضِكُمْ فَمَاذَا تَأْمُرُونَ ۝

111   They said (unto Pharaoh): Put him off (a while)—him and his brother—and send into the cities summoners;

قَالُوٓا أَرْجِهْ وَأَخَاهُ وَأَرْسِلْ فِى الْمَدَآئِنِ حَـٰشِرِينَ ۝

112   To bring each knowing wizard unto thee.

يَأْتُوكَ بِكُلِّ سَـٰحِرٍ عَلِيمٍ ۝

113   And the wizards came to Pharaoh, saying: Surely there will be a reward for us if we are victors.

وَجَآءَ السَّحَرَةُ فِرْعَوْنَ قَالُوٓا إِنَّ لَنَا لَأَجْرًا إِن كُنَّا نَحْنُ الْغَـٰلِبِينَ ۝

114   He answered: Yea, and surely ye shall be of those brought near (to me).

قَالَ نَعَمْ وَإِنَّكُمْ لَمِنَ الْمُقَرَّبِينَ ۝

115   They said: O Moses! Either throw (first) or let us be the first throwers?

قَالُوا يَـٰمُوسَىٰ إِمَّآ أَن تُلْقِىَ وَإِمَّآ أَن نَّكُونَ نَحْنُ الْمُلْقِينَ ۝

116   He said: Throw! And when they threw they cast a spell upon the people's eyes, and overawed them, and produced a mighty spell.

قَالَ أَلْقُوا فَلَمَّآ أَلْقَوْا سَحَرُوٓا أَعْيُنَ النَّاسِ وَاسْتَرْهَبُوهُمْ وَجَآءُو بِسِحْرٍ عَظِيمٍ ۝

117   And We inspired Moses (saying): Throw thy staff! And lo! it swallowed up their lying show.

وَأَوْحَيْنَآ إِلَىٰ مُوسَىٰٓ أَنْ أَلْقِ عَصَاكَ فَإِذَا هِيَ تَلْقَفُ مَا يَأْفِكُونَ ۝

118   Thus was the Truth vindicated and that which they were doing was made vain.

فَوَقَعَ الْحَقُّ وَبَطَلَ مَا كَانُوا يَعْمَلُونَ ۝

119   Thus were they there defeated and brought low.

فَغُلِبُوا هُنَالِكَ وَانقَلَبُوا صَاغِرِينَ ۝

120   And the wizards fell down prostrate;

وَأُلْقِيَ السَّحَرَةُ سَاجِدِينَ ۝

121   Crying: We believe in the Lord of the Worlds;

قَالُوا ءَامَنَّا بِرَبِّ الْعَالَمِينَ ۝

122   The Lord of Moses and Aaron.

رَبِّ مُوسَى وَهَارُونَ ۝

123   Pharaoh said: Ye believe in Him before I give you leave! Lo! this is the plot that ye have plotted in the city that ye may drive its people hence. But ye shall come to know!

قَالَ فِرْعَوْنُ ءَامَنتُم بِهِ قَبْلَ أَن ءَاذَنَ لَكُمْ إِنَّ هَـٰذَا لَمَكْرٌ مَّكَرْتُمُوهُ فِي الْمَدِينَةِ لِتُخْرِجُوا مِنْهَا أَهْلَهَا فَسَوْفَ تَعْلَمُونَ ۝

124   Surely I shall have your hands and feet cut off upon alternate sides. Then I shall crucify you every one.

لَأُقَطِّعَنَّ أَيْدِيَكُمْ وَأَرْجُلَكُم مِّنْ خِلَافٍ ثُمَّ لَأُصَلِّبَنَّكُمْ أَجْمَعِينَ ۝

125   They said: Lo! We are about to return unto our Lord!

قَالُوا إِنَّا إِلَىٰ رَبِّنَا مُنقَلِبُونَ ۝

126   Thou takest vengeance on us only for as much as we believed the tokens of our Lord when they came unto us. Our Lord! Vouchsafe unto us steadfastness and make us die as men who have surrendered (unto Thee).

وَمَا تَنقِمُ مِنَّا إِلَّا أَنْ ءَامَنَّا بِـَٔايَـٰتِ رَبِّنَا لَمَّا جَآءَتْنَا رَبَّنَا أَفْرِغْ عَلَيْنَا صَبْرًا وَتَوَفَّنَا مُسْلِمِينَ ۝

127   The chiefs of Pharaoh's people said: (O King), wilt thou suffer Moses and his people to make mischief in the land, and flout thee and thy gods? He said: We will slay their sons and spare their women, for lo! we are in power over them.

وَقَالَ الْمَلَأُ مِن قَوْمِ فِرْعَوْنَ أَتَذَرُ مُوسَىٰ وَقَوْمَهُ لِيُفْسِدُوا فِي الْأَرْضِ وَيَذَرَكَ وَءَالِهَتَكَ قَالَ سَنُقَتِّلُ أَبْنَآءَهُمْ وَنَسْتَحْيِ نِسَآءَهُمْ وَإِنَّا فَوْقَهُمْ قَاهِرُونَ ۝

128   And Moses said unto his
people: Seek help in Allah and
endure. Lo! the earth is Allah's. He
giveth it for an inheritance to whom
He will. And lo! the sequel is for
those who keep their duty (unto
Him).

قَالَ مُوسَىٰ لِقَوْمِهِ ٱسْتَعِينُوا بِٱللَّهِ وَٱصْبِرُوٓا
إِنَّ ٱلْأَرْضَ لِلَّهِ يُورِثُهَا مَن يَشَآءُ
مِنْ عِبَادِهِۦ ۖ وَٱلْعَٰقِبَةُ لِلْمُتَّقِينَ ۝

129   They said: We suffered hurt
before thou camest unto us, and
since thou hast come unto us. He
said: It may be that your Lord is
going to destroy your adversary and
make you viceroys in the earth, that
He may see how ye behave.

قَالُوٓا أُوذِينَا مِن قَبْلِ أَن تَأْتِيَنَا وَمِنۢ بَعْدِ
مَا جِئْتَنَا ۚ قَالَ عَسَىٰ رَبُّكُمْ أَن يُهْلِكَ
عَدُوَّكُمْ وَيَسْتَخْلِفَكُمْ فِى ٱلْأَرْضِ
فَيَنظُرَ كَيْفَ تَعْمَلُونَ ۝

130   And We straitened Pharaoh's
folk with famine and the dearth of
fruits, that peradventure they might
heed.

وَلَقَدْ أَخَذْنَآ ءَالَ فِرْعَوْنَ بِٱلسِّنِينَ وَنَقْصٍ
مِّنَ ٱلثَّمَرَٰتِ لَعَلَّهُمْ يَذَّكَّرُونَ ۝

131   But whenever good befell
them, they said: This is ours; and
whenever evil smote them they
ascribed it to the evil auspices of
Moses and those with him. Surely
their evil auspice was only with
Allah. But most of them knew not.

فَإِذَا جَآءَتْهُمُ ٱلْحَسَنَةُ قَالُوا لَنَا هَٰذِهِۦ ۖ وَإِن تُصِبْهُمْ
سَيِّئَةٌ يَطَّيَّرُوا بِمُوسَىٰ وَمَن مَّعَهُۥٓ ۗ أَلَآ إِنَّمَا
طَٰٓئِرُهُمْ عِندَ ٱللَّهِ وَلَٰكِنَّ أَكْثَرَهُمْ
لَا يَعْلَمُونَ ۝

132   And they said: Whatever
portent thou bringest wherewith to
bewitch us, we shall not put faith in
thee.

وَقَالُوا مَهْمَا تَأْتِنَا بِهِۦ مِنْ ءَايَةٍ لِّتَسْحَرَنَا بِهَا فَمَا
نَحْنُ لَكَ بِمُؤْمِنِينَ ۝

133   So We sent them the flood
and the locusts and the vermin and
the frogs and the blood—a succession of clear signs. But they were
arrogant and became a guilty folk.

فَأَرْسَلْنَا عَلَيْهِمُ ٱلطُّوفَانَ وَٱلْجَرَادَ وَٱلْقُمَّلَ
وَٱلضَّفَادِعَ وَٱلدَّمَ ءَايَٰتٍ مُّفَصَّلَٰتٍ فَٱسْتَكْبَرُوا
وَكَانُوا قَوْمًا مُّجْرِمِينَ ۝

134   And when the terror fell on them they cried: O Moses! Pray for us unto thy Lord, because He hath a covenant with thee. If thou removest the terror from us; we verily will trust thee and will let the Children of Israel go with thee.

وَلَمَّا وَقَعَ عَلَيْهِمُ الرِّجْزُ قَالُوا يَا مُوسَى ادْعُ لَنَا رَبَّكَ بِمَا عَهِدَ عِنْدَكَ لَئِنْ كَشَفْتَ عَنَّا الرِّجْزَ لَنُؤْمِنَنَّ لَكَ وَلَنُرْسِلَنَّ مَعَكَ بَنِى إِسْرَٰءِيلَ ﴿١٣٤﴾

135   But when We did remove from them the terror for a term which they must reach, behold! they broke their covenant.

فَلَمَّا كَشَفْنَا عَنْهُمُ الرِّجْزَ إِلَىٰ أَجَلٍ هُمْ بَٰلِغُوهُ إِذَا هُمْ يَنْكُثُونَ ﴿١٣٥﴾

136   Therefore We took retribution from them; therefore We drowned them in the sea: because they denied Our revelations and were heedless of them.

فَٱنْتَقَمْنَا مِنْهُمْ فَأَغْرَقْنَاهُمْ فِى الْيَمِّ بِأَنَّهُمْ كَذَّبُوا بِٱيَٰتِنَا وَكَانُوا عَنْهَا غَٰفِلِينَ ﴿١٣٦﴾

137   And We caused the folk who were despised to inherit the eastern parts of the land and the western parts thereof which We had blessed. And the fair word of the Lord was fulfilled for the Children of Israel because of their endurance; and We annihilated (all) that Pharaoh and his folk had done and that they had contrived.

وَأَوْرَثْنَا الْقَوْمَ الَّذِينَ كَانُوا يُسْتَضْعَفُونَ مَشَٰرِقَ الْأَرْضِ وَمَغَٰرِبَهَا الَّتِى بَٰرَكْنَا فِيهَا وَتَمَّتْ كَلِمَتُ رَبِّكَ الْحُسْنَىٰ عَلَىٰ بَنِى إِسْرَٰءِيلَ بِمَا صَبَرُوا وَدَمَّرْنَا مَا كَانَ يَصْنَعُ فِرْعَوْنُ وَقَوْمُهُ وَمَا كَانُوا يَعْرِشُونَ ﴿١٣٧﴾

138   And We brought the Children of Israel across the sea, and they came unto a people who were given up to idols which they had. They said: O Moses! Make for us a god even as they have gods. He said: Lo! ye are a folk who know not.

وَجَٰوَزْنَا بِبَنِى إِسْرَٰءِيلَ الْبَحْرَ فَأَتَوْا عَلَىٰ قَوْمٍ يَعْكُفُونَ عَلَىٰ أَصْنَامٍ لَهُمْ قَالُوا يَا مُوسَى اجْعَل لَنَا إِلَٰهًا كَمَا لَهُمْ ءَالِهَةٌ قَالَ إِنَّكُمْ قَوْمٌ تَجْهَلُونَ ﴿١٣٨﴾

139   Lo! as for these, their way will be destroyed and all that they are doing is in vain.

إِنَّ هَٰؤُلَاءِ مُتَبَّرٌ مَّا هُمْ فِيهِ وَبَٰطِلٌ مَّا كَانُوا يَعْمَلُونَ ﴿١٣٩﴾

140　He said: Shall I seek for you a god other than Allah when He hath favoured you above (all) creatures?

قَالَ أَغَيْرَ اللّٰهِ أَبْغِيكُمْ إِلٰهًا وَّهُوَ فَضَّلَكُمْ عَلَى الْعٰلَمِيْنَ ۝

141　And (remember) when We did deliver you from Pharaoh's folk who were afflicting you with dreadful torment, slaughtering your sons and sparing your women. That was a tremendous trial from your Lord.

وَإِذْ أَنْجَيْنٰكُمْ مِّنْ اٰلِ فِرْعَوْنَ يَسُوْمُوْنَكُمْ سُوْٓءَ الْعَذَابِ ۚ يُقَتِّلُوْنَ أَبْنَآءَكُمْ وَيَسْتَحْيُوْنَ نِسَآءَكُمْ ۚ وَفِيْ ذٰلِكُمْ بَلَآءٌ مِّنْ رَّبِّكُمْ عَظِيْمٌ ۝

142　And when We did appoint for Moses thirty nights (of solitude), and added to them ten, and he completed the whole time appointed by his Lord of forty nights; and Moses said unto his brother, Aaron: Take my place among the people. Do right, and follow not the way of mischief-makers.

۞ وَوَاعَدْنَا مُوْسٰى ثَلٰثِيْنَ لَيْلَةً وَّأَتْمَمْنٰهَا بِعَشْرٍ فَتَمَّ مِيْقَاتُ رَبِّهٖ أَرْبَعِيْنَ لَيْلَةً ۚ وَقَالَ مُوْسٰى لِأَخِيْهِ هٰرُوْنَ اخْلُفْنِيْ فِيْ قَوْمِيْ وَأَصْلِحْ وَلَا تَتَّبِعْ سَبِيْلَ الْمُفْسِدِيْنَ ۝

143　And when Moses came to Our appointed tryst and his Lord had spoken unto him, he said: My Lord! Show me (Thy self), that I may gaze upon Thee. He said: Thou wilt not see Me, but gaze upon the mountain! If it stand still in its place, then thou wilt see Me. And when his Lord revealed (His) glory to the mountain; He sent it crashing down. And Moses fell down senseless. And when he woke he said: Glory unto Thee! I turn unto Thee repentant, and I am the first of (true) believers.

وَلَمَّا جَآءَ مُوْسٰى لِمِيْقَاتِنَا وَكَلَّمَهٗ رَبُّهٗ ۙ قَالَ رَبِّ أَرِنِيْ أَنْظُرْ إِلَيْكَ ۚ قَالَ لَنْ تَرٰنِيْ وَلٰكِنِ انْظُرْ إِلَى الْجَبَلِ فَإِنِ اسْتَقَرَّ مَكَانَهٗ فَسَوْفَ تَرٰنِيْ ۚ فَلَمَّا تَجَلّٰى رَبُّهٗ لِلْجَبَلِ جَعَلَهٗ دَكًّا وَّخَرَّ مُوْسٰى صَعِقًا ۚ فَلَمَّآ أَفَاقَ قَالَ سُبْحٰنَكَ تُبْتُ إِلَيْكَ وَأَنَا أَوَّلُ الْمُؤْمِنِيْنَ ۝

144   He said: O Moses! I have
preferred thee above mankind by
My messages and by My speaking
(unto thee). So hold that which I
have given thee, and be among the
thankful.

قَالَ يَٰمُوسَىٰٓ إِنِّى ٱصْطَفَيْتُكَ عَلَى ٱلنَّاسِ بِرِسَٰلَٰتِى
وَبِكَلَٰمِى فَخُذْ مَآ ءَاتَيْتُكَ
وَكُن مِّنَ ٱلشَّٰكِرِينَ ۝

145   And We wrote for him, upon
the tablets, the lesson to be drawn
from all things and the explanation
of all things, then (bade him): Hold
it fast; and command thy people
(saying): Take the better (course
made clear) therein. I shall show
thee the abode of evil-livers.

وَكَتَبْنَا لَهُۥ فِى ٱلْأَلْوَاحِ مِن كُلِّ شَىْءٍ
مَّوْعِظَةً وَتَفْصِيلًا لِّكُلِّ شَىْءٍ فَخُذْهَا بِقُوَّةٍ
وَأْمُرْ قَوْمَكَ يَأْخُذُوا۟ بِأَحْسَنِهَا ۚ سَأُو۟رِيكُمْ
دَارَ ٱلْفَٰسِقِينَ ۝

146   I shall turn away from My
revelations those who magnify
themselves wrongfully in the earth,
and if they see each token believe it
not, and if they see the way of righteousness, choose it not for (their)
way, and if they see the way of
error, choose it for (their) way.
That is because they deny Our revelations and are used to disregard
them.

سَأَصْرِفُ عَنْ ءَايَٰتِىَ ٱلَّذِينَ يَتَكَبَّرُونَ فِى ٱلْأَرْضِ
بِغَيْرِ ٱلْحَقِّ وَإِن يَرَوْا۟ كُلَّ ءَايَةٍ لَّا يُؤْمِنُوا۟
بِهَا وَإِن يَرَوْا۟ سَبِيلَ ٱلرُّشْدِ لَا يَتَّخِذُوهُ سَبِيلًا
وَإِن يَرَوْا۟ سَبِيلَ ٱلْغَىِّ يَتَّخِذُوهُ سَبِيلًا ۚ ذَٰلِكَ
بِأَنَّهُمْ كَذَّبُوا۟ بِـَٔايَٰتِنَا وَكَانُوا۟ عَنْهَا غَٰفِلِينَ ۝

147   Those who deny Our revelations and the meeting of the Hereafter, their works are fruitless. Are
they requited aught save what they
used to do?

وَٱلَّذِينَ كَذَّبُوا۟ بِـَٔايَٰتِنَا وَلِقَآءِ ٱلْءَاخِرَةِ
حَبِطَتْ أَعْمَٰلُهُمْ ۚ هَلْ يُجْزَوْنَ إِلَّا مَا كَانُوا۟
يَعْمَلُونَ ۝

148   And the folk of Moses, after
(he had left them), chose a calf (for
worship), (made) out of their orna-

وَٱتَّخَذَ قَوْمُ مُوسَىٰ مِنۢ بَعْدِهِۦ مِنْ حُلِيِّهِمْ عِجْلًا

ments a calf (of saffron hue)[7] a
body which gave a lowing sound.
Saw they not that it spake not unto
them nor guided them to any way?
They chose it, and became wrong-
doers.

149 And when they feared the
consequences thereof and saw that
they had gone astray, they said: Unless our Lord have mercy on us and
forgive us, we verily are of the lost.

150 And when Moses returned
unto his people, angry and grieved,
he said: Evil is that (course) which
ye took after I had left you. Would
ye hasten on the judgment of your
Lord? And he cast down the tablets,
and he seized his brother by the
head, dragging him toward him. He
said: Son of my mother! Lo! the
folk did judge me weak and almost
killed me. Oh, make not mine enemies to triumph over me and place
me not among the evil-doers!

151 He said: My Lord! Have
mercy on me and on my brother;
bring us into Thy mercy and Thou
art the Most Merciful of all who
show mercy.

152 Lo! those who chose the calf
(for worship), terror from their
Lord and humiliation will come

جَسَدًا لَّهُ خُوَارٌ أَلَمْ يَرَوْا أَنَّهُ لَا يُكَلِّمُهُمْ
وَلَا يَهْدِيهِمْ سَبِيلًا اتَّخَذُوهُ
وَكَانُوا ظَالِمِينَ ﴿١٤٨﴾

وَلَمَّا سُقِطَ فِي أَيْدِيهِمْ وَرَأَوْا أَنَّهُمْ قَدْ ضَلُّوا
قَالُوا لَئِن لَّمْ يَرْحَمْنَا رَبُّنَا وَيَغْفِرْ لَنَا
لَنَكُونَنَّ مِنَ الْخَاسِرِينَ ﴿١٤٩﴾

وَلَمَّا رَجَعَ مُوسَىٰ إِلَىٰ قَوْمِهِ غَضْبَانَ أَسِفًا قَالَ بِئْسَمَا
خَلَفْتُمُونِي مِن بَعْدِي أَعَجِلْتُمْ أَمْرَ رَبِّكُمْ وَأَلْقَى
الْأَلْوَاحَ وَأَخَذَ بِرَأْسِ أَخِيهِ يَجُرُّهُ إِلَيْهِ قَالَ ابْنَ أُمَّ
إِنَّ الْقَوْمَ اسْتَضْعَفُونِي وَكَادُوا يَقْتُلُونَنِي
فَلَا تُشْمِتْ بِيَ الْأَعْدَاءَ وَلَا تَجْعَلْنِي مَعَ الْقَوْمِ
الظَّالِمِينَ ﴿١٥٠﴾

قَالَ رَبِّ اغْفِرْ لِي وَلِأَخِي وَأَدْخِلْنَا
فِي رَحْمَتِكَ وَأَنتَ أَرْحَمُ الرَّاحِمِينَ ﴿١٥١﴾

إِنَّ الَّذِينَ اتَّخَذُوا الْعِجْلَ سَيَنَالُهُمْ غَضَبٌ
مِّن رَّبِّهِمْ وَذِلَّةٌ فِي الْحَيَوٰةِ الدُّنْيَا وَكَذَٰلِكَ

---

7. Or a *body*. But, as the word in the Arabic (*jasad*) can only mean a body of flesh
and blood, the meaning "saffron-coloured" better fits the context.

upon them in the life of the world.
Thus do We requite those who invent a lie.

153   But those who do ill deeds
and afterward repent and believe—lo! for them, afterward, Allah
is Forgiving, Merciful.

154   Then, when the anger of
Moses abated, he took up the tablets, and in their inscription there
was guidance and mercy for all
those who fear their Lord.

155   And Moses chose of his
people seventy men for Our appointed tryst and, when the trembling
came on them, he said: My Lord! If
thou hadst willed Thou hadst destroyed them long before, and me
with them. Wilt thou destroy us for
that which the ignorant among us
did? It is but Thy trial (of us). Thou
sendest whom Thou wilt astray and
guidest whom Thou wilt. Thou art
our Protecting Friend, therefore
forgive us and have mercy on us,
Thou, the Best of all who show
forgiveness.

156   And ordain for us in this
world that which is good, and in the
Hereafter (that which is good). Lo!
We have turned unto Thee. He said:
I smite with My punishment whom
I will, and My mercy embraceth all
things, therefore I shall ordain it for
those who ward off (evil) and pay
the poor-due, and those who believe
Our revelations;

نَجْزِى الْمُفْتَرِينَ ۝

وَالَّذِينَ عَمِلُوا السَّيِّئَاتِ ثُمَّ تَابُوا مِنْ بَعْدِهَا
وَءَامَنُوا إِنَّ رَبَّكَ مِنْ بَعْدِهَا لَغَفُورٌ رَحِيمٌ ۝

وَلَمَّا سَكَتَ عَنْ مُّوسَى الْغَضَبُ أَخَذَ الْأَلْوَاحَ
وَفِى نُسْخَتِهَا هُدًى وَرَحْمَةٌ لِلَّذِينَ هُمْ
لِرَبِّهِمْ يَرْهَبُونَ ۝

وَاخْتَارَ مُوسَى قَوْمَهُ سَبْعِينَ رَجُلًا لِمِيقَاتِنَا فَلَمَّا
أَخَذَتْهُمُ الرَّجْفَةُ قَالَ رَبِّ لَوْ شِئْتَ أَهْلَكْتَهُمْ
مِنْ قَبْلُ وَإِيَّايَ أَتُهْلِكُنَا بِمَا فَعَلَ السُّفَهَاءُ مِنَّا إِنْ هِيَ
إِلَّا فِتْنَتُكَ تُضِلُّ بِهَا مَنْ تَشَاءُ وَتَهْدِى مَنْ تَشَاءُ
أَنْتَ وَلِيُّنَا فَاغْفِرْ لَنَا وَارْحَمْنَا وَأَنْتَ خَيْرُ الْغَافِرِينَ ۝

وَاكْتُبْ لَنَا فِى هَذِهِ الدُّنْيَا حَسَنَةً وَفِى
الْآخِرَةِ إِنَّا هُدْنَا إِلَيْكَ قَالَ عَذَابِى أُصِيبُ بِهِ
مَنْ أَشَاءُ وَرَحْمَتِى وَسِعَتْ كُلَّ شَىْءٍ
فَسَأَكْتُبُهَا لِلَّذِينَ يَتَّقُونَ وَيُؤْتُونَ
الزَّكَوٰةَ وَالَّذِينَ هُمْ بِآيَاتِنَا يُؤْمِنُونَ ۝

157   Those who follow the messenger, the Prophet who can neither read nor write, whom they will find described in the Torah and the Gospel (which are) with them. He will enjoin on them that which is right and forbid them that which is wrong. He will make lawful for them all good things and prohibit for them only the foul; and he will relieve them of their burden and the fetters that they used to wear. Then those who believe in him, and honour him, and help him, and follow the light which is sent down with him; they are the successful.

الَّذِينَ يَتَّبِعُونَ الرَّسُولَ النَّبِيَّ الْأُمِّيَّ الَّذِي يَجِدُونَهُ مَكْتُوبًا عِنْدَهُمْ فِي التَّوْرَىةِ وَالْإِنْجِيلِ يَأْمُرُهُمْ بِالْمَعْرُوفِ وَيَنْهَىهُمْ عَنِ الْمُنْكَرِ وَيُحِلُّ لَهُمُ الطَّيِّبَتِ وَيُحَرِّمُ عَلَيْهِمُ الْخَبَٰئِثَ وَيَضَعُ عَنْهُمْ إِصْرَهُمْ وَالْأَغْلَلَ الَّتِي كَانَتْ عَلَيْهِمْ فَالَّذِينَ ءَامَنُوا بِهِ وَعَزَّرُوهُ وَنَصَرُوهُ وَاتَّبَعُوا النُّورَ الَّذِي أُنْزِلَ مَعَهُ أُولَٰئِكَ هُمُ الْمُفْلِحُونَ ۝

158   Say (O Muhammad): O mankind! Lo! I am the messenger of Allah to you all—(the messenger of) Him unto whom belongeth the Sovereignty of the heavens and the earth. There is no God save Him. He quickeneth and He giveth death. So believe in Allah and His messenger, the Prophet who can neither read nor write,[8] who believeth in Allah and in His words and follow him that haply ye may be led aright.

قُلْ يَٰأَيُّهَا النَّاسُ إِنِّي رَسُولُ اللَّهِ إِلَيْكُمْ جَمِيعًا الَّذِي لَهُ مُلْكُ السَّمَٰوَٰتِ وَالْأَرْضِ لَا إِلَٰهَ إِلَّا هُوَ يُحْيِۦ وَيُمِيتُ فَآمِنُوا بِاللَّهِ وَرَسُولِهِ النَّبِيِّ الْأُمِّيِّ الَّذِي يُؤْمِنُ بِاللَّهِ وَكَلِمَٰتِهِ وَاتَّبِعُوهُ لَعَلَّكُمْ تَهْتَدُونَ ۝

159   And of Moses' folk there is a community who lead with truth and establish justice therewith.

وَمِن قَوْمِ مُوسَىٰ أُمَّةٌ يَهْدُونَ بِالْحَقِّ وَبِهِ يَعْدِلُونَ ۝

---

8. I give the usual rendering. Some modern criticism, while not denying the comparative illiteracy of the Prophet, would prefer the rendering " who is not of those who read the Scriptures" or "Gentile."

160   We divided them into twelve tribes, nations; and We inspired Moses, when his people asked him for water, saying: Smite with thy staff the rock! And there gushed forth therefrom twelve springs, so that each tribe knew their drinking place. And we caused the white cloud to overshadow them and sent down for them the manna and the quails (saying): Eat of the good things wherewith We have provided you. They wronged Us not, but they were wont to wrong themselves.

وَقَطَّعْنَاهُمُ اثْنَتَيْ عَشْرَةَ أَسْبَاطًا أُمَمًا وَأَوْحَيْنَا إِلَى مُوسَى إِذِ اسْتَسْقَاهُ قَوْمُهُ أَنِ اضْرِبْ بِعَصَاكَ الْحَجَرَ فَانْبَجَسَتْ مِنْهُ اثْنَتَا عَشْرَةَ عَيْنًا قَدْ عَلِمَ كُلُّ أُنَاسٍ مَشْرَبَهُمْ وَظَلَّلْنَا عَلَيْهِمُ الْغَمَامَ وَأَنْزَلْنَا عَلَيْهِمُ الْمَنَّ وَالسَّلْوَى كُلُوا مِنْ طَيِّبَاتِ مَا رَزَقْنَاكُمْ وَمَا ظَلَمُونَا وَلَكِنْ كَانُوا أَنْفُسَهُمْ يَظْلِمُونَ ﴿١٦٠﴾

161   And when it was said unto them: Dwell in this township and eat therefrom whence ye will, and say "Repentance,"[9] and enter the gate prostrate; We shall forgive you your sins; We shall increase (reward) for the right-doers.

وَإِذْ قِيلَ لَهُمُ اسْكُنُوا هَذِهِ الْقَرْيَةَ وَكُلُوا مِنْهَا حَيْثُ شِئْتُمْ وَقُولُوا حِطَّةٌ وَادْخُلُوا الْبَابَ سُجَّدًا نَغْفِرْ لَكُمْ خَطِيئَتِكُمْ سَنَزِيدُ الْمُحْسِنِينَ ﴿١٦١﴾

162   But those of them who did wrong changed the word which had been told them for another saying, and We sent down upon them wrath from heaven for their wrongdoing.

فَبَدَّلَ الَّذِينَ ظَلَمُوا مِنْهُمْ قَوْلًا غَيْرَ الَّذِي قِيلَ لَهُمْ فَأَرْسَلْنَا عَلَيْهِمْ رِجْزًا مِنَ السَّمَاءِ بِمَا كَانُوا يَظْلِمُونَ ﴿١٦٢﴾

163   Ask them (O Muhammad) of the township that was by the sea, how they did break the sabbath, how their big fish came unto them visibly upon their sabbath day and on a day when they did not keep sabbath came they not unto them. Thus did We try them for that they were evil-livers.

وَسْأَلْهُمْ عَنِ الْقَرْيَةِ الَّتِي كَانَتْ حَاضِرَةَ الْبَحْرِ إِذْ يَعْدُونَ فِي السَّبْتِ إِذْ تَأْتِيهِمْ حِيتَانُهُمْ يَوْمَ سَبْتِهِمْ شُرَّعًا وَيَوْمَ لَا يَسْبِتُونَ لَا تَأْتِيهِمْ كَذَلِكَ نَبْلُوهُمْ بِمَا كَانُوا يَفْسُقُونَ ﴿١٦٣﴾

---

9. Sūrah 2: 58, footnote.

164   And when a community among them said: Why preach ye to a folk whom Allah is about to destroy and punish with an awful doom, they said: In order to be free from guilt before your Lord, and that haply they may ward off (evil).

165   And when they forgot that whereof they had been reminded, We rescued those who forbade wrong, and visited those who did wrong with dreadful punishment because they were evil-livers.

166   So when they took pride in that which they had been forbidden, We said unto them: Be ye apes despised and loathed!

167   And (remember) when thy Lord proclaimed that He would raise against them till the Day of Resurrection those who would lay on them a cruel torment. Lo! verily thy Lord is swift in prosecution and lo! verily He is Forgiving, Merciful.

168   And We have sundered them in the earth as (separate) nations. Some of them are righteous, and some far from that. And We have tried them with good things and evil things that haply they might return.

169   And a generation hath succeeded them who inherited the Scriptures. They grasp the goods of this low life (as the price of evil-doing) and say: It will be forgiven us. And if there came to them (again) the

offer of the like, they would accept it (and would sin again). Hath not the covenant of the Scripture been taken on their behalf that they should not speak aught concerning Allah save the truth? And they have studied that which is therein. And the abode of the Hereafter is better, for those who ward off (evil). Have ye then no sense?

عَرَضٌ مِّثْلُهُ يَأْخُذُوهُ أَلَمْ يُؤْخَذْ عَلَيْهِمْ مِّيْثَقُ الْكِتَبِ
أَنْ لَّا يَقُولُوا عَلَى اللهِ إِلَّا الْحَقَّ وَدَرَسُوا مَا فِيهِ
وَالدَّارُ الْأَخِرَةُ خَيْرٌ لِّلَّذِينَ
يَتَّقُونَ أَفَلَا تَعْقِلُونَ ﴿١٦٩﴾

170   And as for those who make (men) keep the Scripture, and establish worship—lo! We squander not the wages of reformers.

وَالَّذِينَ يُمَسِّكُونَ بِالْكِتَبِ وَأَقَامُوا الصَّلَوةَ
إِنَّا لَا نُضِيعُ أَجْرَ الْمُصْلِحِينَ ﴿١٧٠﴾

171   And when We shook the Mount above them, as if it were a covering, and they supposed that it was going to fall upon them (and We said): Hold fast that which We have given you, and remember that which is therein, that ye may ward off (evil).

﴿وَإِذْ نَتَقْنَا الْجَبَلَ فَوْقَهُمْ كَأَنَّهُ ظُلَّةٌ وَظَنُّوا أَنَّهُ
وَاقِعٌ بِهِمْ خُذُوا مَا آتَيْنَكُمْ بِقُوَّةٍ وَاذْكُرُوا مَا فِيهِ
لَعَلَّكُمْ تَتَّقُونَ ﴿١٧١﴾

172   And (remember) when thy Lord brought forth from the Children of Adam, from their reins, their seed, and made them testify of themselves, (saying): Am I not your Lord? They said: Yea, verily; we testify. (That was) lest ye should say at the Day of Resurrection: Lo! of this we were unaware;

وَإِذْ أَخَذَ رَبُّكَ مِنْ بَنِي آدَمَ مِنْ ظُهُورِهِمْ ذُرِّيَّتَهُمْ
وَأَشْهَدَهُمْ عَلَى أَنْفُسِهِمْ أَلَسْتُ بِرَبِّكُمْ قَالُوا
بَلَى شَهِدْنَا أَنْ تَقُولُوا يَوْمَ الْقِيَمَةِ إِنَّا كُنَّا
عَنْ هَذَا غَفِلِينَ ﴿١٧٢﴾

173   Or lest ye should say: (It is) only (that) our fathers ascribed partners to Allah of old and we were (their) seed after them. Wilt Thou destroy us on account of that which those who follow falsehood did?

أَوْ تَقُولُوا إِنَّمَا أَشْرَكَ آبَاؤُنَا مِنْ قَبْلُ وَكُنَّا ذُرِّيَّةً
مِّنْ بَعْدِهِمْ أَفَتُهْلِكُنَا بِمَا فَعَلَ الْمُبْطِلُونَ ﴿١٧٣﴾

174 Thus We detail the signs, that haply they may return.

وَكَذَٰلِكَ نُفَصِّلُ ٱلْأَيَٰتِ وَلَعَلَّهُمْ يَرْجِعُونَ ۝

175 Recite unto them the tale of him to whom We gave Our revelations, but he sloughed them off, so Satan overtook him and he became of those who lead astray.

وَٱتْلُ عَلَيْهِمْ نَبَأَ ٱلَّذِىٓ ءَاتَيْنَٰهُ ءَايَٰتِنَا فَٱنسَلَخَ مِنْهَا فَأَتْبَعَهُ ٱلشَّيْطَٰنُ فَكَانَ مِنَ ٱلْغَاوِينَ ۝

176 And had We willed We could have raised him by their means, but he clung to the earth and followed his own lust. Therefor his likeness is as the likeness of a dog; if thou attackest him, he panteth with his tongue out; and if thou leavest him, he panteth with his tongue out. Such is the likeness of the people who deny Our revelations. Narrate unto them the history (of the men of old), that haply they may take thought.

وَلَوْ شِئْنَا لَرَفَعْنَٰهُ بِهَا وَلَٰكِنَّهُۥٓ أَخْلَدَ إِلَى ٱلْأَرْضِ وَٱتَّبَعَ هَوَىٰهُ فَمَثَلُهُۥ كَمَثَلِ ٱلْكَلْبِ إِن تَحْمِلْ عَلَيْهِ يَلْهَثْ أَوْ تَتْرُكْهُ يَلْهَث ذَّٰلِكَ مَثَلُ ٱلْقَوْمِ ٱلَّذِينَ كَذَّبُوا بِـَٔايَٰتِنَا فَٱقْصُصِ ٱلْقَصَصَ لَعَلَّهُمْ يَتَفَكَّرُونَ ۝

177 Evil as an example are the folk who denied Our revelations, and were wont to wrong themselves.

سَآءَ مَثَلًا ٱلْقَوْمُ ٱلَّذِينَ كَذَّبُوا بِـَٔايَٰتِنَا وَأَنفُسَهُمْ كَانُوا يَظْلِمُونَ ۝

178 He who Allah leadeth, he indeed is led aright, while he whom Allah sendeth astray—they indeed are losers.

مَن يَهْدِ ٱللَّهُ فَهُوَ ٱلْمُهْتَدِى وَمَن يُضْلِلْ فَأُو۟لَٰٓئِكَ هُمُ ٱلْخَٰسِرُونَ ۝

179 Already have We urged unto hell many of the jinn and humankind, having hearts wherewith they understand not, and having eyes wherewith they see not, and having ears wherewith they hear not. These are as the cattle—nay, but they are more astray! These are the neglectful.

وَلَقَدْ ذَرَأْنَا لِجَهَنَّمَ كَثِيرًا مِّنَ ٱلْجِنِّ وَٱلْإِنسِ لَهُمْ قُلُوبٌ لَّا يَفْقَهُونَ بِهَا وَلَهُمْ أَعْيُنٌ لَّا يُبْصِرُونَ بِهَا وَلَهُمْ ءَاذَانٌ لَّا يَسْمَعُونَ بِهَآ أُو۟لَٰٓئِكَ كَٱلْأَنْعَٰمِ بَلْ هُمْ أَضَلُّ أُو۟لَٰٓئِكَ هُمُ ٱلْغَٰفِلُونَ ۝

180   Allah's are the fairest names.
Invoke Him by them. And leave the
company of those who blaspheme
His names. They will be requited
what they do.

وَلِلّٰهِ الْأَسْمَآءُ الْحُسْنٰى فَادْعُوْهُ بِهَا ۖ وَذَرُوا الَّذِيْنَ
يُلْحِدُوْنَ فِيْۤ أَسْمَآئِهٖ ۚ سَيُجْزَوْنَ مَا كَانُوْا
يَعْمَلُوْنَ ۝

181   And of those whom We
created there is a nation who guide
with the Truth and establish justice
therewith.

وَمِمَّنْ خَلَقْنَاۤ أُمَّةٌ يَّهْدُوْنَ بِالْحَقِّ وَبِهٖ
يَعْدِلُوْنَ ۝

182   And those who deny Our
revelations—step by step We lead
them on from whence they know
not.

وَالَّذِيْنَ كَذَّبُوْا بِاٰيٰتِنَا سَنَسْتَدْرِجُهُمْ مِّنْ حَيْثُ
لَا يَعْلَمُوْنَ ۝

183   I give them rein (for) lo! My
scheme is strong.

وَأُمْلِيْ لَهُمْ ۚ إِنَّ كَيْدِيْ مَتِيْنٌ ۝

184   Have they not bethought
them (that) there is no madness in
their comrade? He is but a plain
warner.

أَوَلَمْ يَتَفَكَّرُوْا ۗ مَا بِصَاحِبِهِمْ مِّنْ جِنَّةٍ ۚ
إِنْ هُوَ إِلَّا نَذِيْرٌ مُّبِيْنٌ ۝

185   Have they not considered the
dominion of the heavens and the
earth, and what things Allah hath
created, and that it may be that
their own term draweth nigh? In
what fact after this will they believe?

أَوَلَمْ يَنْظُرُوْا فِيْ مَلَكُوْتِ السَّمٰوٰتِ وَالْأَرْضِ
وَمَا خَلَقَ اللّٰهُ مِنْ شَيْءٍ وَّأَنْ عَسٰۤى أَنْ يَّكُوْنَ قَدِ اقْتَرَبَ
أَجَلُهُمْ ۖ فَبِأَيِّ حَدِيْثٍ بَعْدَهٗ يُؤْمِنُوْنَ ۝

186   Those whom Allah sendeth
astray, there is no guide for them.
He leaveth them to wander blindly
on in their contumacy.

مَنْ يُّضْلِلِ اللّٰهُ فَلَا هَادِيَ لَهٗ ۖ وَيَذَرُهُمْ فِيْ طُغْيَانِهِمْ
يَعْمَهُوْنَ ۝

187   They ask thee of the (destined) Hour, when will it come to
port. Say: Knowledge thereof is
with my Lord only. He alone will
manifest it at its proper time. It is

يَسْئَلُوْنَكَ عَنِ السَّاعَةِ أَيَّانَ مُرْسٰهَا ۖ قُلْ إِنَّمَا عِلْمُهَا
عِنْدَ رَبِّيْ ۚ لَا يُجَلِّيْهَا لِوَقْتِهَاۤ إِلَّا هُوَ ۘ ثَقُلَتْ فِي السَّمٰوٰتِ

heavy in the heavens and the earth.
It cometh not to you save unawares.
They question thee as if thou couldst be well informed thereof. Say:
Knowledge thereof is with Allah
only, but most of mankind know
not.

188   Say: For myself I have no
power to benefit, nor power to hurt,
save that which Allah willeth. Had
I knowledge of the Unseen, I should have abundance of wealth, and
adversity would not touch me. I am
but a warner, and a bearer of good
tidings unto folk who believe.

189   He it is who did create you
from a single soul, and therefrom
did make his mate that he might
take rest in her. And when he covered her she bore a light burden,
and she passed (unnoticed) with it,
but when it became heavy they
cried unto Allah, their Lord, saying:
If thou givest unto us aright we
shall be of the thankful.

190   But when He gave unto
them aright, they ascribed unto Him
partners in respect of that which He
had given them. High is He exalted
above all that they associate (with
Him).

191   Attribute they as partners to
Allah, those who created naught,
but are themselves created;

192   And cannot give them help,
nor can they help themselves.

وَالْأَرْضِ لَا تَأْتِيكُمْ إِلَّا بَغْتَةً يَسْـَٔلُونَكَ كَأَنَّكَ حَفِيٌّ عَنْهَا قُلْ إِنَّمَا عِلْمُهَا عِندَ اللَّهِ وَلَٰكِنَّ أَكْثَرَ النَّاسِ لَا يَعْلَمُونَ ﴿١٨٧﴾

قُل لَّا أَمْلِكُ لِنَفْسِي نَفْعًا وَلَا ضَرًّا إِلَّا مَا شَاءَ اللَّهُ وَلَوْ كُنتُ أَعْلَمُ الْغَيْبَ لَاسْتَكْثَرْتُ مِنَ الْخَيْرِ وَمَا مَسَّنِيَ السُّوءُ إِنْ أَنَا إِلَّا نَذِيرٌ وَبَشِيرٌ لِّقَوْمٍ يُؤْمِنُونَ ﴿١٨٨﴾

۞ هُوَ الَّذِي خَلَقَكُم مِّن نَّفْسٍ وَاحِدَةٍ وَجَعَلَ مِنْهَا زَوْجَهَا لِيَسْكُنَ إِلَيْهَا فَلَمَّا تَغَشَّاهَا حَمَلَتْ حَمْلًا خَفِيفًا فَمَرَّتْ بِهِ فَلَمَّا أَثْقَلَت دَّعَوَا اللَّهَ رَبَّهُمَا لَئِنْ ءَاتَيْتَنَا صَالِحًا لَّنَكُونَنَّ مِنَ الشَّاكِرِينَ ﴿١٨٩﴾

فَلَمَّا ءَاتَىٰهُمَا صَالِحًا جَعَلَا لَهُ شُرَكَاءَ فِيمَا ءَاتَىٰهُمَا فَتَعَالَى اللَّهُ عَمَّا يُشْرِكُونَ ﴿١٩٠﴾

أَيُشْرِكُونَ مَا لَا يَخْلُقُ شَيْـًٔا وَهُمْ يُخْلَقُونَ ﴿١٩١﴾

وَلَا يَسْتَطِيعُونَ لَهُمْ نَصْرًا وَلَا أَنفُسَهُمْ يَنصُرُونَ ﴿١٩٢﴾

193   And if ye call them to the
Guidance, they follow you not.
Whether ye call them or are silent
is all one to them.

وَإِن تَدْعُوهُمْ إِلَى الْهُدَىٰ لَا يَتَّبِعُوكُمْ سَوَآءٌ عَلَيْكُمْ
أَدَعَوْتُمُوهُمْ أَمْ أَنتُمْ صَٰمِتُونَ ۝

194   Lo! those on whom ye call
beside Allah are slaves like unto
you. Call on them now, and let
them answer you, if ye are truthful!

إِنَّ الَّذِينَ تَدْعُونَ مِن دُونِ اللَّهِ عِبَادٌ
أَمْثَالُكُمْ فَادْعُوهُمْ فَلْيَسْتَجِيبُوا۟
لَكُمْ إِن كُنتُمْ صَٰدِقِينَ ۝

195   Have they feet wherewith
they walk, or have they hands wherewith they hold, or have they eyes
wherewith they see, or have they
ears wherewith they hear? Say: Call
upon your (so called) partners (of
Allah), and then contrive against
me, spare me not!

أَلَهُمْ أَرْجُلٌ يَمْشُونَ بِهَآ أَمْ لَهُمْ أَيْدٍ يَبْطِشُونَ
بِهَآ أَمْ لَهُمْ أَعْيُنٌ يُبْصِرُونَ بِهَآ أَمْ لَهُمْ ءَاذَانٌ
يَسْمَعُونَ بِهَا قُلِ ادْعُوا۟ شُرَكَآءَكُمْ ثُمَّ كِيدُونِ
فَلَا تُنظِرُونِ ۝

196   Lo! my Protecting Friend is
Allah who revealeth the Scripture.
He befriendeth the righteous.

إِنَّ وَلِيِّيَ اللَّهُ الَّذِي نَزَّلَ الْكِتَٰبَ وَهُوَ يَتَوَلَّى
الصَّٰلِحِينَ ۝

197   They on whom ye call beside Him have no power to help
you, nor can they help themselves.

وَالَّذِينَ تَدْعُونَ مِن دُونِهِ لَا يَسْتَطِيعُونَ
نَصْرَكُمْ وَلَآ أَنفُسَهُمْ يَنصُرُونَ ۝

198   And if ye (Muslims) call
them to the Guidance, they hear
not; and thou (Muhammad) seest
them looking toward thee, but they
see not.

وَإِن تَدْعُوهُمْ إِلَى الْهُدَىٰ لَا يَسْمَعُوا۟ وَتَرَىٰهُمْ
يَنظُرُونَ إِلَيْكَ وَهُمْ لَا يُبْصِرُونَ ۝

199   Keep to forgiveness (O
Muhammad), and enjoin kindness,
and turn away from the ignorant.

خُذِ الْعَفْوَ وَأْمُرْ بِالْعُرْفِ وَأَعْرِضْ
عَنِ الْجَٰهِلِينَ ۝

200   And if a slander from the
devil wound thee, then seek refuge
in Allah. Lo! He is Hearer,
Knower.

وَإِمَّا يَنزَغَنَّكَ مِنَ الشَّيْطَٰنِ نَزْغٌ فَاسْتَعِذْ
بِاللَّهِ إِنَّهُ سَمِيعٌ عَلِيمٌ ۝

201   Lo! those who ward off (evil), when a glamour from the devil troubleth them, they do but remember (Allah's guidance) and behold them seers!

202   Their brethren plunge them further into error and cease not.

203   And when thou bringest not a verse for them they say: Why hast thou not chosen it? Say: I follow only that which is inspired in me from my Lord. This (Qur'an) is insight from your Lord, and a guidance and a mercy for a people that believe.

204   And when the Qur'an is recited, give ear to it and pay heed, that ye may obtain mercy.

205   And do thou (O Muhammad) remember thy Lord within thyself humbly and with awe, below thy breath, at morn and evening. And be thou not of the neglectful.

206   Lo! those who are with thy Lord are not too proud to do Him service, but they praise Him and adore Him.

إِنَّ ٱلَّذِينَ ٱتَّقَوْا إِذَا مَسَّهُمْ طَٰٓئِفٌ مِّنَ ٱلشَّيْطَٰنِ تَذَكَّرُوا فَإِذَا هُم مُّبْصِرُونَ ۝

وَإِخْوَٰنُهُمْ يَمُدُّونَهُمْ فِى ٱلْغَىِّ ثُمَّ لَا يُقْصِرُونَ ۝

وَإِذَا لَمْ تَأْتِهِم بِـَٔايَةٍ قَالُوا لَوْلَا ٱجْتَبَيْتَهَا قُلْ إِنَّمَآ أَتَّبِعُ مَا يُوحَىٰٓ إِلَىَّ مِن رَّبِّى هَٰذَا بَصَآئِرُ مِن رَّبِّكُمْ وَهُدًى وَرَحْمَةٌ لِّقَوْمٍ يُؤْمِنُونَ ۝

وَإِذَا قُرِئَ ٱلْقُرْءَانُ فَٱسْتَمِعُوا لَهُۥ وَأَنصِتُوا لَعَلَّكُمْ تُرْحَمُونَ ۝

وَٱذْكُر رَّبَّكَ فِى نَفْسِكَ تَضَرُّعًا وَخِيفَةً وَدُونَ ٱلْجَهْرِ مِنَ ٱلْقَوْلِ بِٱلْغُدُوِّ وَٱلْءَاصَالِ وَلَا تَكُن مِّنَ ٱلْغَٰفِلِينَ ۝

إِنَّ ٱلَّذِينَ عِندَ رَبِّكَ لَا يَسْتَكْبِرُونَ عَنْ عِبَادَتِهِۦ وَيُسَبِّحُونَهُۥ وَلَهُۥ يَسْجُدُونَ ۩ ۝

Al Anfāl
(Spoils of War)

Al Anfāl, "The Spoils," takes its name from the first verse by which it is proclaimed that property in war belongs "to Allah and His messenger"—that is to say, to the theocratic State, to be used for the common weal. The date of the revelation of this sūrah is established, from the nature of the contents, as the time that elapsed between the battle of Badr and the division of the spoils—a space of only one month—in the second year of the Hijrah. The concluding verses are of later date and lead up to the subject of sūrah 9.

A Makkan caravan was returning from Syria, and its leader, Abū Sufyān, fearing an attack from Al-Madīnah, sent a camel-rider on to Makkah with a frantic appeal for help; which must have come too late, considering the distances, if, as some writers even among Muslims have alleged, the Prophet had always intended to attack the caravan. Ibn Isḥāq (*apud* Ibn Hishām) when treating of the Tabūk expedition, says that the Prophet announced the destination on that occasion, whereas it was his custom to hide his real objective. Was not the real objective hidden in this first campaign? It is a fact that he only advanced when the army sent to protect the caravan, or rather (it is probable) to punish the Muslims for having plundered it, was approaching Al-Madīnah. His little army of three hundred and thirteen men, ill-armed and roughly equipped, traversed the desert for three days till, when they halted near the water of Badr, they had news that the army of Quraysh was approaching on the other side of the valley. Then rain fell-heavily upon Quraysh so that they could not advance further on account of the muddy state of the ground, lightly on the Muslims, who were able to advance to the water and secure it. At the same time Abū Sufyān, the leader of the caravan, which was also heading for the water of Badr, was warned by one of his scouts of the advance of the Muslims and turned back to the coast-plain. Before the battle against what must have appeared to all men overwhelming odds, the Prophet gave the Ansār, the men of Al-Madīnah, whose oath of allegiance had not included fighting in the field, the chance of returning if they wished; but they were only hurt by the suggestion that they could possibly forsake him. On the other hand, several of Quraysh, including the whole Zuhri clan, returned to Makkah when they heard the caravan was safe, having no grudge otherwise against the Prophet and his followers, whom they regarded as men who had been wronged.

Still the army of Quraysh outnumbered the Muslims by more than two to one, and was much better mounted and equipped, so that their leaders counted on an easy victory. When the Prophet saw them streaming down the sandhills, he cried: "O Allah! Here are Quraysh with all their chivalry and pomp, who oppose Thee and deny Thy messenger. O Allah! Thy help which Thou hast promised me! O Allah! Make them bow this day!"

The Muslims were successful in the single combats with which Arab battles opened. But the mêlèe at first went hard against them; and the Prophet stood and prayed under the shelter which they had put up to screen him from the sun, and cried: "O Allah, if this little company is destroyed, there will be none left in the land to worship Thee." Then he fell into a trance and, when he spoke again, he told Abū Bakr, who was with him, that the promised help had come. Thereupon he went out to encourage his people. Taking up a handful of gravel, he ran towards Quraysh and flung it at them, saying: "The faces are confounded!" on which the tide of battle turned in favour of the Muslims. The leader of Quraysh and several of their greatest men were killed, many were taken prisoner, and their baggage and camels were captured by the Muslims. It was indeed a day to be remembered in the early history of Al-Islām, and there was great rejoicing in Al-Madīnah. But the Muslims are warned in this sūrah that it is only the beginning of their struggle against heavy odds. In fact, in the following year at Mount Uhud (referred to in sūrah 3), the enemy came against them with an army of three thousand, and in the fifth year of the Hijrah, an allied army of the pagan clans, amounting to 10,000, besieged Al-Madīnah in the "War of the Trench" (see sūrah 33, "The Clans").

The date of revelation is the second year of the Hijrah for the most part. Some good Arabic authorities hold that vv. 30-40, or some of them, were revealed at Makkah just before the Hijrah.

In the name of Allah, the
Beneficent, the Merciful.

1   They ask thee (O Muhammad)
of the spoils of war. Say: The
spoils of war belong to Allah and
the messenger, so keep your duty to
Allah, and adjust the matter of your
difference, and obey Allah and His
messenger, if ye are (true) believers.

2   They only are the (true) believers whose hearts feel fear when
Allah is mentioned, and when the
revelations of Allah are recited unto
them they increase their faith, and
who trust in their Lord;

3   Who establish worship and
spend of that We have bestowed on
them.

4   Those are they who are in truth
believers. For them are grades (of
honour) with their Lord, and pardon, and a bountiful provision.

5   Even as thy Lord caused thee
(Muhammad) to go forth from thy
home with the Truth, and lo! a
party of the believers were averse
(to it);

6   Disputing with thee of the Truth after it had been made manifest, as if they were being driven to death visible.

يُجَٰدِلُونَكَ فِى ٱلْحَقِّ بَعْدَ مَا تَبَيَّنَ كَأَنَّمَا يُسَاقُونَ إِلَى ٱلْمَوْتِ وَهُمْ يَنظُرُونَ ٦

7   And when Allah promised you one of the two bands[1] (of the enemy) that it should be yours, and ye longed that other than the armed one might be yours. And Allah willed that He should cause the Truth to triumph by His words, and cut the root of the disbelievers;

وَإِذْ يَعِدُكُمُ ٱللَّهُ إِحْدَى ٱلطَّآئِفَتَيْنِ أَنَّهَا لَكُمْ وَتَوَدُّونَ أَنَّ غَيْرَ ذَاتِ ٱلشَّوْكَةِ تَكُونُ لَكُمْ وَيُرِيدُ ٱللَّهُ أَن يُحِقَّ ٱلْحَقَّ بِكَلِمَٰتِهِۦ وَيَقْطَعَ دَابِرَ ٱلْكَٰفِرِينَ ٧

8   That He might cause the Truth to triumph and bring vanity to naught, however much the guilty might oppose;

لِيُحِقَّ ٱلْحَقَّ وَيُبْطِلَ ٱلْبَٰطِلَ وَلَوْ كَرِهَ ٱلْمُجْرِمُونَ ٨

9   When ye sought help of your Lord and He answered you (saying): I will help you with a thousand of the angels, rank on rank.

إِذْ تَسْتَغِيثُونَ رَبَّكُمْ فَٱسْتَجَابَ لَكُمْ أَنِّى مُمِدُّكُم بِأَلْفٍ مِّنَ ٱلْمَلَٰٓئِكَةِ مُرْدِفِينَ ٩

10   Allah appointed it only as good tidings, and that your hearts thereby might be at rest. Victory cometh only by the help of Allah. Lo! Allah is Mighty, Wise.

وَمَا جَعَلَهُ ٱللَّهُ إِلَّا بُشْرَىٰ وَلِتَطْمَئِنَّ بِهِۦ قُلُوبُكُمْ وَمَا ٱلنَّصْرُ إِلَّا مِنْ عِندِ ٱللَّهِ إِنَّ ٱللَّهَ عَزِيزٌ حَكِيمٌ ١٠

11   When he made the slumber fall upon you as a reassurance from Him and sent down water from the sky upon you, that thereby He might purify you, and remove from you the fear of Satan, and make strong your hearts and firm (your) feet thereby.

إِذْ يُغَشِّيكُمُ ٱلنُّعَاسَ أَمَنَةً مِّنْهُ وَيُنَزِّلُ عَلَيْكُم مِّنَ ٱلسَّمَآءِ مَآءً لِّيُطَهِّرَكُم بِهِۦ وَيُذْهِبَ عَنكُمْ رِجْزَ ٱلشَّيْطَٰنِ وَلِيَرْبِطَ عَلَىٰ قُلُوبِكُمْ وَيُثَبِّتَ بِهِ ٱلْأَقْدَامَ ١١

---

1. Either the army or the caravan.

12 When thy Lord inspired the angels, (saying:) I am with you. So make those who believe stand firm. I will throw fear into the hearts of those who disbelieve. Then smite the necks and smite of them each finger.

إِذْ يُوحِى رَبُّكَ إِلَى ٱلْمَلَٰٓئِكَةِ أَنِّى مَعَكُمْ فَثَبِّتُوا۟ ٱلَّذِينَ ءَامَنُوا۟ سَأُلْقِى فِى قُلُوبِ ٱلَّذِينَ كَفَرُوا۟ ٱلرُّعْبَ فَٱضْرِبُوا۟ فَوْقَ ٱلْأَعْنَاقِ وَٱضْرِبُوا۟ مِنْهُمْ كُلَّ بَنَانٍ ١٢

13 That is because they opposed Allah and His messenger. Whoso opposeth Allah and His messenger, (for him) lo! Allah is severe in punishment.

ذَٰلِكَ بِأَنَّهُمْ شَآقُّوا۟ ٱللَّهَ وَرَسُولَهُۥ وَمَن يُشَاقِقِ ٱللَّهَ وَرَسُولَهُۥ فَإِنَّ ٱللَّهَ شَدِيدُ ٱلْعِقَابِ ١٣

14 That (is the award), so taste it, and (know) that for disbelievers is the torment of the Fire.

ذَٰلِكُمْ فَذُوقُوهُ وَأَنَّ لِلْكَٰفِرِينَ عَذَابَ ٱلنَّارِ ١٤

15 O ye who believe, When ye meet those who disbelieve in battle, turn not your backs to them.

يَٰٓأَيُّهَا ٱلَّذِينَ ءَامَنُوٓا۟ إِذَا لَقِيتُمُ ٱلَّذِينَ كَفَرُوا۟ زَحْفًا فَلَا تُوَلُّوهُمُ ٱلْأَدْبَارَ ١٥

16 Whoso on that day turneth his back to them, unless maneuvering for battle or intent to join a company, he truly hath incurred wrath from Allah, and his habitation will be hell, a hapless journey's end.

وَمَن يُوَلِّهِمْ يَوْمَئِذٍ دُبُرَهُۥٓ إِلَّا مُتَحَرِّفًا لِّقِتَالٍ أَوْ مُتَحَيِّزًا إِلَىٰ فِئَةٍ فَقَدْ بَآءَ بِغَضَبٍ مِّنَ ٱللَّهِ وَمَأْوَىٰهُ جَهَنَّمُ وَبِئْسَ ٱلْمَصِيرُ ١٦

17 Ye (Muslims) slew them not, but Allah slew them. And thou (Muhammad) threwest not when thou didst throw, but Allah threw, that He might test the believers by a fair test from Him. Lo! Allah is Hearer, Knower.

فَلَمْ تَقْتُلُوهُمْ وَلَٰكِنَّ ٱللَّهَ قَتَلَهُمْ وَمَا رَمَيْتَ إِذْ رَمَيْتَ وَلَٰكِنَّ ٱللَّهَ رَمَىٰ وَلِيُبْلِىَ ٱلْمُؤْمِنِينَ مِنْهُ بَلَآءً حَسَنًا إِنَّ ٱللَّهَ سَمِيعٌ عَلِيمٌ ١٧

18 That (is the case); and (know) that Allah (it is) who maketh weak the plan of disbelievers.

ذَٰلِكُمْ وَأَنَّ ٱللَّهَ مُوهِنُ كَيْدِ ٱلْكَٰفِرِينَ ١٨

19 (O Quraysh!) If ye sought a judgment, now hath the judgment come unto you. And if ye cease (from persecuting the believers) it will be better for you, but if ye return (to the attack) We also shall return. And your host will avail you naught, however numerous it be, and (know) that Allah is with the believers (in His guidance).

إِن تَسْتَفْتِحُوا فَقَدْ جَاءَكُمُ الْفَتْحُ وَإِن تَنتَهُوا فَهُوَ خَيْرٌ لَّكُمْ وَإِن تَعُودُوا نَعُدْ وَلَن تُغْنِيَ عَنكُمْ فِئَتُكُمْ شَيْئًا وَلَوْ كَثُرَتْ وَأَنَّ اللَّهَ مَعَ الْمُؤْمِنِينَ ۝

20 O ye who believe! Obey Allah and His messenger, and turn not away from him when ye hear (him speak).

يَٰٓأَيُّهَا الَّذِينَ ءَامَنُوٓا أَطِيعُوا اللَّهَ وَرَسُولَهُ وَلَا تَوَلَّوْا عَنْهُ وَأَنتُمْ تَسْمَعُونَ ۝

21 Be not as those who say, We hear, and they hear not.

وَلَا تَكُونُوا كَالَّذِينَ قَالُوا سَمِعْنَا وَهُمْ لَا يَسْمَعُونَ ۝

22 Lo! the worst of beasts in Allah's sight are the deaf, the dumb, who have no sense.

إِنَّ شَرَّ الدَّوَابِّ عِندَ اللَّهِ الصُّمُّ الْبُكْمُ الَّذِينَ لَا يَعْقِلُونَ ۝

23 Had Allah Known of any good in them, He would have made them hear, but had He made them hear they would have turned away, averse.

وَلَوْ عَلِمَ اللَّهُ فِيهِمْ خَيْرًا لَّأَسْمَعَهُمْ وَلَوْ أَسْمَعَهُمْ لَتَوَلَّوا وَّهُم مُّعْرِضُونَ ۝

24 O ye who believe; respond to Allah and the messenger when He calleth you to that which quickeneth you, and know that Allah cometh in between the man and his own heart, and that He it is unto Whom ye will be gathered.

يَٰٓأَيُّهَا الَّذِينَ ءَامَنُوا اسْتَجِيبُوا لِلَّهِ وَلِلرَّسُولِ إِذَا دَعَاكُمْ لِمَا يُحْيِيكُمْ وَاعْلَمُوا أَنَّ اللَّهَ يَحُولُ بَيْنَ الْمَرْءِ وَقَلْبِهِ وَأَنَّهُ إِلَيْهِ تُحْشَرُونَ ۝

25 And guard yourselves against a chastisement which cannot fall exclusively on those of you who are wrong-doers, and know that Allah is severe in punishment.

وَاتَّقُوا فِتْنَةً لَّا تُصِيبَنَّ الَّذِينَ ظَلَمُوا مِنكُمْ خَاصَّةً وَاعْلَمُوا أَنَّ اللَّهَ شَدِيدُ الْعِقَابِ ۝

26 And remember, when ye were few and reckoned feeble in the land, and were in fear lest men should extirpate you, how He gave you refuge, and strengthened you with His help, and made provision of good things for you, that haply ye might be thankful.

27 O ye who believe! Betray not Allah and His messenger, nor knowingly betray your trusts.

28 And know that your possessions and your children are a test, and that with Allah is immense reward.

29 O ye who believe! If ye keep your duty to Allah, He will give you discrimination (between right and wrong) and will rid you of your evil thoughts and deeds, and will forgive you. Allah is of infinite bounty.

30 And when those who disbelieve plot against thee (O Muhammad) to wound thee fatally, or to kill thee or to drive thee forth; they plot, but Allah (also) plotteth; and Allah is the best of plotters.

31 And when Our revelations are recited unto them, they say: We have heard. If we wish we can speak the like of this. Lo! this is naught but fables of the men of old.

32 And when they said: O Allah! If this be indeed the truth from Thee, then rain down stones on us or bring on us some painful doom!

وَاذْكُرُوٓا إِذْ أَنتُمْ قَلِيلٌ مُّسْتَضْعَفُونَ فِى ٱلْأَرْضِ تَخَافُونَ أَن يَتَخَطَّفَكُمُ ٱلنَّاسُ فَـَٔاوَىٰكُمْ وَأَيَّدَكُم بِنَصْرِهِۦ وَرَزَقَكُم مِّنَ ٱلطَّيِّبَٰتِ لَعَلَّكُمْ تَشْكُرُونَ ﴿٢٦﴾

يَٰٓأَيُّهَا ٱلَّذِينَ ءَامَنُوا لَا تَخُونُوا ٱللَّهَ وَٱلرَّسُولَ وَتَخُونُوٓا أَمَٰنَٰتِكُمْ وَأَنتُمْ تَعْلَمُونَ ﴿٢٧﴾

وَٱعْلَمُوٓا أَنَّمَآ أَمْوَٰلُكُمْ وَأَوْلَٰدُكُمْ فِتْنَةٌ وَأَنَّ ٱللَّهَ عِندَهُۥٓ أَجْرٌ عَظِيمٌ ﴿٢٨﴾

يَٰٓأَيُّهَا ٱلَّذِينَ ءَامَنُوٓا إِن تَتَّقُوا ٱللَّهَ يَجْعَل لَّكُمْ فُرْقَانًا وَيُكَفِّرْ عَنكُمْ سَيِّـَٔاتِكُمْ وَيَغْفِرْ لَكُمْ وَٱللَّهُ ذُو ٱلْفَضْلِ ٱلْعَظِيمِ ﴿٢٩﴾

وَإِذْ يَمْكُرُ بِكَ ٱلَّذِينَ كَفَرُوا لِيُثْبِتُوكَ أَوْ يَقْتُلُوكَ أَوْ يُخْرِجُوكَ وَيَمْكُرُونَ وَيَمْكُرُ ٱللَّهُ وَٱللَّهُ خَيْرُ ٱلْمَٰكِرِينَ ﴿٣٠﴾

وَإِذَا تُتْلَىٰ عَلَيْهِمْ ءَايَٰتُنَا قَالُوا قَدْ سَمِعْنَا لَوْ نَشَآءُ لَقُلْنَا مِثْلَ هَٰذَآ إِنْ هَٰذَآ إِلَّآ أَسَٰطِيرُ ٱلْأَوَّلِينَ ﴿٣١﴾

وَإِذْ قَالُوا ٱللَّهُمَّ إِن كَانَ هَٰذَا هُوَ ٱلْحَقَّ مِنْ عِندِكَ فَأَمْطِرْ عَلَيْنَا حِجَارَةً مِّنَ ٱلسَّمَآءِ أَوِ ٱئْتِنَا بِعَذَابٍ أَلِيمٍ ﴿٣٢﴾

33 But Allah would not punish them while thou wast with them, nor will He punish them while they seek forgiveness.

وَمَا كَانَ اللّٰهُ لِيُعَذِّبَهُمْ وَأَنْتَ فِيهِمْ وَمَا كَانَ اللّٰهُ مُعَذِّبَهُمْ وَهُمْ يَسْتَغْفِرُوْنَ ۝

34 What (plea) have they that Allah should not punish them, when they debar (His servants) from the Inviolable Place of Worship, though they are not its fitting guardians. Its fitting guardians are those only who keep their duty to Allah. But most of them know not.

وَمَا لَهُمْ أَلَّا يُعَذِّبَهُمُ اللّٰهُ وَهُمْ يَصُدُّوْنَ عَنِ الْمَسْجِدِ الْحَرَامِ وَمَا كَانُوْا أَوْلِيَاءَهُ ۚ إِنْ أَوْلِيَاؤُهُ إِلَّا الْمُتَّقُوْنَ وَلٰكِنَّ أَكْثَرَهُمْ لَا يَعْلَمُوْنَ ۝

35 And their worship at the (holy) House is naught but whistling and hand clapping. Therefore (it is said unto them): Taste of the doom because ye disbelieve.

وَمَا كَانَ صَلَاتُهُمْ عِنْدَ الْبَيْتِ إِلَّا مُكَاءً وَتَصْدِيَةً ۚ فَذُوْقُوا الْعَذَابَ بِمَا كُنْتُمْ تَكْفُرُوْنَ ۝

36 Lo! those who disbelieve spend their wealth in order that they may debar (men) from the way of Allah. They will spend it, then it will become an anguish for them, then they will be conquered. And those who disbelieve will be gathered unto hell;

إِنَّ الَّذِيْنَ كَفَرُوْا يُنْفِقُوْنَ أَمْوَالَهُمْ لِيَصُدُّوْا عَنْ سَبِيْلِ اللّٰهِ ۚ فَسَيُنْفِقُوْنَهَا ثُمَّ تَكُوْنُ عَلَيْهِمْ حَسْرَةً ثُمَّ يُغْلَبُوْنَ ۗ وَالَّذِيْنَ كَفَرُوْا إِلٰى جَهَنَّمَ يُحْشَرُوْنَ ۝

37 That Allah may separate the wicked from the good. The wicked will He place piece upon piece, and heap them all together, and consign them unto hell. Such verily are the losers.

لِيَمِيْزَ اللّٰهُ الْخَبِيْثَ مِنَ الطَّيِّبِ وَيَجْعَلَ الْخَبِيْثَ بَعْضَهُ عَلٰى بَعْضٍ فَيَرْكُمَهُ جَمِيْعًا فَيَجْعَلَهُ فِيْ جَهَنَّمَ ۚ أُولٰئِكَ هُمُ الْخَاسِرُوْنَ ۝

38 Tell those who disbelieve that if they cease (from persecution of believers) that which is past will be forgiven them; but if they return (thereto) then the example of the

قُلْ لِلَّذِيْنَ كَفَرُوْا إِنْ يَنْتَهُوْا يُغْفَرْ لَهُمْ مَا قَدْ سَلَفَ ۚ وَإِنْ يَعُوْدُوْا فَقَدْ مَضَتْ سُنَّتُ

men of old hath already gone
(before them, for a warning).

39 And fight them until persecution
is no more, and religion is all for
Allah. But if they cease, then lo!
Allah is Seer of what they do.

40 And if they turn away, then
know that Allah is your Befri-
ender—a transcendent Patron, a
transcendent Helper!

41 And know that whatever ye take
as spoils of war, lo! a fifth thereof
is for Allah, and for the messenger[2]
and for the kinsman (who hath
need) and orphans and the needy
and the wayfarer; if ye believe in
Allah and that which We revealed
unto Our slave on the Day of Discrimination, the day when the two
armies met. And Allah is Able to
do all things.

42 When ye were on the near bank
(of the valley) and they were on the
yonder bank, and the caravan was
below you (on the coast plain). And
had ye trysted to meet one another,
ye surely would have failed to keep
the tryst, but (it happened, as it did,
without the forethought of either of
you) that Allah might conclude a
thing that must be done; that he
who perished (on that day) might
perish by a clear proof (of His

ٱلۡأَوَّلِينَ ۝

وَقَٰتِلُوهُمۡ حَتَّىٰ لَا تَكُونَ فِتۡنَةٌ وَيَكُونَ
ٱلدِّينُ كُلُّهُۥ لِلَّهِ فَإِنِ ٱنتَهَوۡاْ فَإِنَّ ٱللَّهَ
بِمَا يَعۡمَلُونَ بَصِيرٌ ۝

وَإِن تَوَلَّوۡاْ فَٱعۡلَمُوٓاْ أَنَّ ٱللَّهَ مَوۡلَىٰكُمۡ نِعۡمَ ٱلۡمَوۡلَىٰ
وَنِعۡمَ ٱلنَّصِيرُ ۝

۞ وَٱعۡلَمُوٓاْ أَنَّمَا غَنِمۡتُم مِّن شَىۡءٍ فَأَنَّ لِلَّهِ خُمُسَهُۥ
وَلِلرَّسُولِ وَلِذِى ٱلۡقُرۡبَىٰ وَٱلۡيَتَٰمَىٰ وَٱلۡمَسَٰكِينِ
وَٱبۡنِ ٱلسَّبِيلِ إِن كُنتُمۡ ءَامَنتُم بِٱللَّهِ وَمَآ أَنزَلۡنَا
عَلَىٰ عَبۡدِنَا يَوۡمَ ٱلۡفُرۡقَانِ يَوۡمَ ٱلۡتَقَى ٱلۡجَمۡعَانِ
وَٱللَّهُ عَلَىٰ كُلِّ شَىۡءٍ قَدِيرٌ ۝

إِذۡ أَنتُم بِٱلۡعُدۡوَةِ ٱلدُّنۡيَا وَهُم بِٱلۡعُدۡوَةِ ٱلۡقُصۡوَىٰ
وَٱلرَّكۡبُ أَسۡفَلَ مِنكُمۡ وَلَوۡ تَوَاعَدتُّمۡ
لَٱخۡتَلَفۡتُمۡ فِى ٱلۡمِيعَٰدِ وَلَٰكِن لِّيَقۡضِىَ ٱللَّهُ
أَمۡرًا كَانَ مَفۡعُولًا لِّيَهۡلِكَ مَنۡ هَلَكَ

---

2. *i.e.* for the State, to be used for the common weal.

sovereignty) and he who survived might survive by a clear proof (of His sovereignty). Lo! Allah in truth is Hearer, Knower.

عَنۢ بَيِّنَةٍ وَيَحْىَ مَنْ حَىَّ عَنۢ بَيِّنَةٍ وَإِنَّ اللَّهَ لَسَمِيعٌ عَلِيمٌ ۝

43 When Allah showed them unto thee (O Muhammad) in thy dream as few in number, and if He had shown them to thee as many, ye (Muslims) would have faltered and would have quarrelled over the affair. But Allah saved (you). Lo! He knoweth what is in the breasts (of men).

إِذْ يُرِيكَهُمُ اللَّهُ فِى مَنَامِكَ قَلِيلًا وَلَوْ أَرَىٰكَهُمْ كَثِيرًا لَّفَشِلْتُمْ وَلَتَنَٰزَعْتُمْ فِى الْأَمْرِ وَلَٰكِنَّ اللَّهَ سَلَّمَ إِنَّهُۥ عَلِيمٌ بِذَاتِ الصُّدُورِ ۝

44 And when He made you (Muslims), when ye met (them), see them with your eyes as few, and lessened you in their eyes, (it was) that Allah might conclude a thing that must be done. Unto Allah all things are brought back.

وَإِذْ يُرِيكُمُوهُمْ إِذِ الْتَقَيْتُمْ فِى أَعْيُنِكُمْ قَلِيلًا وَيُقَلِّلُكُمْ فِى أَعْيُنِهِمْ لِيَقْضِىَ اللَّهُ أَمْرًا كَانَ مَفْعُولًا وَإِلَى اللَّهِ تُرْجَعُ الْأُمُورُ ۝

45 O ye who believe! When ye meet an army, hold firm and think of Allah much, that ye may be successful.

يَٰٓأَيُّهَا الَّذِينَ ءَامَنُوٓا إِذَا لَقِيتُمْ فِئَةً فَاثْبُتُوا وَاذْكُرُوا اللَّهَ كَثِيرًا لَّعَلَّكُمْ تُفْلِحُونَ ۝

46 And obey Allah and His messenger, and dispute not one with another lest ye falter and your strength depart from you; but be steadfast! Lo! Allah is with the steadfast.

وَأَطِيعُوا اللَّهَ وَرَسُولَهُۥ وَلَا تَنَٰزَعُوا فَتَفْشَلُوا وَتَذْهَبَ رِيحُكُمْ وَاصْبِرُوٓا إِنَّ اللَّهَ مَعَ الصَّٰبِرِينَ ۝

47 Be not as those who came forth from their dwellings boastfully and to be seen of men, and debar (men) from the way of Allah, while Allah is surrounding all they do.

وَلَا تَكُونُوا كَالَّذِينَ خَرَجُوا مِن دِيَٰرِهِم بَطَرًا وَرِئَآءَ النَّاسِ وَيَصُدُّونَ عَن سَبِيلِ اللَّهِ وَاللَّهُ بِمَا يَعْمَلُونَ مُحِيطٌ ۝

48 And when Satan made their deeds seem fair to them and said: No one of mankind can conquer you this day, for I am your protector. But when the armies came in sight of one another, he took flight, saying: Lo! I am guiltless of you. Lo! I see that which ye see not. Lo! I fear Allah. And Allah is severe in punishment.

وَإِذْ زَيَّنَ لَهُمُ الشَّيْطَانُ أَعْمَالَهُمْ وَقَالَ لَا غَالِبَ لَكُمُ الْيَوْمَ مِنَ النَّاسِ وَإِنِّي جَارٌ لَكُمْ فَلَمَّا تَرَاءَتِ الْفِئَتَانِ نَكَصَ عَلَى عَقِبَيْهِ وَقَالَ إِنِّي بَرِيءٌ مِّنكُمْ إِنِّي أَرَى مَا لَا تَرَوْنَ إِنِّي أَخَافُ اللّٰهَ وَاللّٰهُ شَدِيدُ الْعِقَابِ ۝

49 When the hypocrites and those in whose hearts is a disease said: Their religion hath deluded these. Whoso putteth his trust in Allah (will find that) lo! Allah is Mighty, Wise.

إِذْ يَقُولُ الْمُنَافِقُونَ وَالَّذِينَ فِي قُلُوبِهِم مَّرَضٌ غَرَّ هٰؤُلَاءِ دِينُهُمْ وَمَن يَتَوَكَّلْ عَلَى اللّٰهِ فَإِنَّ اللّٰهَ عَزِيزٌ حَكِيمٌ ۝

50 If thou couldst see how the angels receive those who disbelieve, smiting their faces and their backs and (saying): Taste the punishment of burning!

وَلَوْ تَرَى إِذْ يَتَوَفَّى الَّذِينَ كَفَرُوا الْمَلَائِكَةُ يَضْرِبُونَ وُجُوهَهُمْ وَأَدْبَارَهُمْ وَذُوقُوا عَذَابَ الْحَرِيقِ ۝

51 This is for that which your own hands have sent before (to the Judgment), and (know) that Allah is not a tyrant to His slaves.

ذَٰلِكَ بِمَا قَدَّمَتْ أَيْدِيكُمْ وَأَنَّ اللّٰهَ لَيْسَ بِظَلَّامٍ لِّلْعَبِيدِ ۝

52 (Their way is) as the way of Pharaoh's folk and those before them; they disbelieved the revelations of Allah, and Allah took them in their sins. Lo! Allah is Strong, severe in punishment.

كَدَأْبِ آلِ فِرْعَوْنَ وَالَّذِينَ مِن قَبْلِهِمْ كَفَرُوا بِآيَاتِ اللّٰهِ فَأَخَذَهُمُ اللّٰهُ بِذُنُوبِهِمْ إِنَّ اللّٰهَ قَوِيٌّ شَدِيدُ الْعِقَابِ ۝

53 That is because Allah never changeth the grace He hath bestowed on any people until they first change that which is in their hearts, and (that is) because Allah is Hearer, Knower.

ذَٰلِكَ بِأَنَّ اللّٰهَ لَمْ يَكُ مُغَيِّرًا نِّعْمَةً أَنْعَمَهَا عَلَى قَوْمٍ حَتَّى يُغَيِّرُوا مَا بِأَنفُسِهِمْ وَأَنَّ اللّٰهَ سَمِيعٌ عَلِيمٌ ۝

54 (Their way is) as the way of Pharoah's folk and those before them; they denied the revelations of their Lord, so We destroyed them in their sins. And We drowned the folk of Pharaoh. All were evil-doers.

55 Lo! the worst of beasts in Allah's sight are the ungrateful who will not believe;

56 Those of them with whom thou madest a treaty, and then at every opportunity they break their treaty, and they keep not duty (to Allah).

57 If thou comest on them in the war, deal with them so as to strike fear in those who are behind them, that haply they may remember.

58 And if thou fearest treachery from any folk, then throw back to them (their treaty) fairly. Lo! Allah loveth not the treacherous.

59 And let not those who disbelieve suppose that they can outstrip (Allah's purpose). Lo! they cannot escape.

60 Make ready for them all thou canst of (armed) force and of horses tethered, that thereby ye may dismay the enemy of Allah and your enemy, and others beside them whom ye know not. Allah knoweth them. Whatsoever ye spend in the way of Allah it will be repaid to you in full, and ye will not be wronged.

61 And if they incline to peace, incline thou also to it, and trust in

كَدَأْبِ ءَالِ فِرْعَوْنَ وَالَّذِينَ مِن قَبْلِهِمْ كَذَّبُوا۟ بِـَٔايَٰتِ رَبِّهِمْ فَأَهْلَكْنَٰهُم بِذُنُوبِهِمْ وَأَغْرَقْنَآ ءَالَ فِرْعَوْنَ وَكُلٌّ كَانُوا۟ ظَٰلِمِينَ ۝

إِنَّ شَرَّ ٱلدَّوَآبِّ عِندَ ٱللَّهِ ٱلَّذِينَ كَفَرُوا۟ فَهُمْ لَا يُؤْمِنُونَ ۝

ٱلَّذِينَ عَٰهَدتَّ مِنْهُمْ ثُمَّ يَنقُضُونَ عَهْدَهُمْ فِى كُلِّ مَرَّةٍ وَهُمْ لَا يَتَّقُونَ ۝

فَإِمَّا تَثْقَفَنَّهُمْ فِى ٱلْحَرْبِ فَشَرِّدْ بِهِم مَّنْ خَلْفَهُمْ لَعَلَّهُمْ يَذَّكَّرُونَ ۝

وَإِمَّا تَخَافَنَّ مِن قَوْمٍ خِيَانَةً فَٱنۢبِذْ إِلَيْهِمْ عَلَىٰ سَوَآءٍ إِنَّ ٱللَّهَ لَا يُحِبُّ ٱلْخَآئِنِينَ ۝

وَلَا يَحْسَبَنَّ ٱلَّذِينَ كَفَرُوا۟ سَبَقُوٓا۟ إِنَّهُمْ لَا يُعْجِزُونَ ۝

وَأَعِدُّوا۟ لَهُم مَّا ٱسْتَطَعْتُم مِّن قُوَّةٍ وَمِن رِّبَاطِ ٱلْخَيْلِ تُرْهِبُونَ بِهِۦ عَدُوَّ ٱللَّهِ وَعَدُوَّكُمْ وَءَاخَرِينَ مِن دُونِهِمْ لَا تَعْلَمُونَهُمُ ٱللَّهُ يَعْلَمُهُمْ وَمَا تُنفِقُوا۟ مِن شَىْءٍ فِى سَبِيلِ ٱللَّهِ يُوَفَّ إِلَيْكُمْ وَأَنتُمْ لَا تُظْلَمُونَ ۝

۞ وَإِن جَنَحُوا۟ لِلسَّلْمِ فَٱجْنَحْ لَهَا وَتَوَكَّلْ عَلَى ٱللَّهِ

Allah. Lo! He is the Hearer, the Knower.

إِنَّهُ هُوَ السَّمِيعُ الْعَلِيمُ ﴿٦١﴾

62 And if they would deceive thee, then lo! Allah is sufficient for thee. He it is Who supporteth thee with His help and with the believers;

وَإِن يُرِيدُوا أَن يَخْدَعُوكَ فَإِنَّ حَسْبَكَ اللَّهُ هُوَ الَّذِي أَيَّدَكَ بِنَصْرِهِ وَبِالْمُؤْمِنِينَ ﴿٦٢﴾

63 And (as for the believers) hath attuned their hearts. If thou hadst spent all that is in the earth thou couldst not have attuned their hearts, but Allah hath attuned them. Lo! He is Mighty, Wise.

وَأَلَّفَ بَيْنَ قُلُوبِهِمْ لَوْ أَنفَقْتَ مَا فِي الْأَرْضِ جَمِيعًا مَّا أَلَّفْتَ بَيْنَ قُلُوبِهِمْ وَلَٰكِنَّ اللَّهَ أَلَّفَ بَيْنَهُمْ إِنَّهُ عَزِيزٌ حَكِيمٌ ﴿٦٣﴾

64 O Prophet! Allah is sufficient for thee and those who follow thee of the believers.

يَا أَيُّهَا النَّبِيُّ حَسْبُكَ اللَّهُ وَمَنِ اتَّبَعَكَ مِنَ الْمُؤْمِنِينَ ﴿٦٤﴾

65 O Prophet! Exhort the believers to fight. If there be of you twenty steadfast they shall overcome two hundred, and if there be of you a hundred steadfast, they shall overcome a thousand of those who disbelieve; because they (the disbelievers) are a folk without intelligence.

يَا أَيُّهَا النَّبِيُّ حَرِّضِ الْمُؤْمِنِينَ عَلَى الْقِتَالِ إِن يَكُن مِّنكُمْ عِشْرُونَ صَابِرُونَ يَغْلِبُوا مِائَتَيْنِ وَإِن يَكُن مِّنكُم مِّائَةٌ يَغْلِبُوا أَلْفًا مِّنَ الَّذِينَ كَفَرُوا بِأَنَّهُمْ قَوْمٌ لَّا يَفْقَهُونَ ﴿٦٥﴾

66 Now hath Allah lightened your burden, for He knoweth that there is weakness in you. So if there be of you a steadfast hundred they shall overcome two hundred, and if there be of you a thousand (steadfast) they shall overcome two thousand by permission of Allah. Allah is with the steadfast.

الْآنَ خَفَّفَ اللَّهُ عَنكُمْ وَعَلِمَ أَنَّ فِيكُمْ ضَعْفًا فَإِن يَكُن مِّنكُم مِّائَةٌ صَابِرَةٌ يَغْلِبُوا مِائَتَيْنِ وَإِن يَكُن مِّنكُمْ أَلْفٌ يَغْلِبُوا أَلْفَيْنِ بِإِذْنِ اللَّهِ وَاللَّهُ مَعَ الصَّابِرِينَ ﴿٦٦﴾

67 It is not for any Prophet to have captives until he hath made slaugh-

مَا كَانَ لِنَبِيٍّ أَن يَكُونَ لَهُ أَسْرَىٰ حَتَّىٰ يُثْخِنَ

ter in the land. Ye desire the lure of this world and Allah desireth (for you) the Hereafter, and Allah is Mighty, Wise.

فِى ٱلْأَرْضِ تُرِيدُونَ عَرَضَ ٱلدُّنْيَا وَٱللَّهُ يُرِيدُ ٱلْأَخِرَةَ وَٱللَّهُ عَزِيزٌ حَكِيمٌ ۝

68 Had it not been for an ordinance of Allah which had gone before, an awful doom had come upon you on account of what ye took.

لَّوْلَا كِتَٰبٌ مِّنَ ٱللَّهِ سَبَقَ لَمَسَّكُمْ فِيمَآ أَخَذْتُمْ عَذَابٌ عَظِيمٌ ۝

69 Now enjoy what ye have won, as lawful and good, and keep your duty to Allah. Lo! Allah is Forgiving, Merciful.[3]

فَكُلُوا۟ مِمَّا غَنِمْتُمْ حَلَٰلًا طَيِّبًا وَٱتَّقُوا۟ ٱللَّهَ إِنَّ ٱللَّهَ غَفُورٌ رَّحِيمٌ ۝

70 O Prophet, Say unto those captives who are in your hands: If Allah knoweth any good in your hearts He will give you better than that which hath been taken from you, and will forgive you. Lo! Allah is Forgiving, Merciful.

يَٰٓأَيُّهَا ٱلنَّبِىُّ قُل لِّمَن فِىٓ أَيْدِيكُم مِّنَ ٱلْأَسْرَىٰٓ إِن يَعْلَمِ ٱللَّهُ فِى قُلُوبِكُمْ خَيْرًا يُؤْتِكُمْ خَيْرًا مِّمَّآ أُخِذَ مِنكُمْ وَيَغْفِرْ لَكُمْ وَٱللَّهُ غَفُورٌ رَّحِيمٌ ۝

71 And if they would betray thee, they betrayed Allah before, and He gave (thee) power over them. Allah is knower, Wise.

وَإِن يُرِيدُوا۟ خِيَانَتَكَ فَقَدْ خَانُوا۟ ٱللَّهَ مِن قَبْلُ فَأَمْكَنَ مِنْهُمْ وَٱللَّهُ عَلِيمٌ حَكِيمٌ ۝

72 Lo! those who believed and left their homes and strove with their wealth and their lives for the cause of Allah, and those who took them in and helped them; these are protecting friends one of another. And

إِنَّ ٱلَّذِينَ ءَامَنُوا۟ وَهَاجَرُوا۟ وَجَٰهَدُوا۟ بِأَمْوَٰلِهِمْ وَأَنفُسِهِمْ فِى سَبِيلِ ٱللَّهِ وَٱلَّذِينَ ءَاوَوا۟ وَّنَصَرُوٓا۟ أُو۟لَٰٓئِكَ بَعْضُهُمْ أَوْلِيَآءُ بَعْضٍ وَٱلَّذِينَ ءَامَنُوا۟

---

3. vv. 67-69 were revealed when the Prophet had decided to spare the lives of the prisoners taken at Badr and hold them to ransom, against the wish of 'Umar, who would have executed them for their past crimes. The Prophet took the verses as a reproof, and they are generally understood to mean that no quarter ought to have been given in that first battle.

those who believed but did not leave their homes, ye have no duty to protect them till they leave their homes; but if they seek help from you in the matter of religion; then it is your duty to help (them) except against a folk between whom and you there is a treaty. Allah is Seer of what ye do.

73 And those who disbelieve are protectors one of another—If ye do not so, there will be confusion in the land, and great corruption.

74 Those who believed and left their homes and strove for the cause of Allah, and those who took them in and helped them—these are the believers in truth. For them is pardon, and a bountiful provision.

75 And those who afterwards believed and left their homes and strove along with you, they are of you; and those who are akin are nearer one to another in the ordinance of Allah. Lo! Allah is Knower of all things.

وَلَمْ يُهَاجِرُوا مَا لَكُم مِّن وَلَايَتِهِم مِّن شَىْءٍ حَتَّىٰ يُهَاجِرُوا وَإِنِ ٱسْتَنصَرُوكُمْ فِى ٱلدِّينِ فَعَلَيْكُمُ ٱلنَّصْرُ إِلَّا عَلَىٰ قَوْمٍ بَيْنَكُمْ وَبَيْنَهُم مِّيثَٰقٌ وَٱللَّهُ بِمَا تَعْمَلُونَ بَصِيرٌ ﴿٧٢﴾

وَٱلَّذِينَ كَفَرُوا بَعْضُهُمْ أَوْلِيَآءُ بَعْضٍ إِلَّا تَفْعَلُوهُ تَكُن فِتْنَةٌ فِى ٱلْأَرْضِ وَفَسَادٌ كَبِيرٌ ﴿٧٣﴾

وَٱلَّذِينَ ءَامَنُوا وَهَاجَرُوا وَجَٰهَدُوا فِى سَبِيلِ ٱللَّهِ وَٱلَّذِينَ ءَاوَوا وَّنَصَرُوٓا أُو۟لَٰٓئِكَ هُمُ ٱلْمُؤْمِنُونَ حَقًّا لَّهُم مَّغْفِرَةٌ وَرِزْقٌ كَرِيمٌ ﴿٧٤﴾

وَٱلَّذِينَ ءَامَنُوا مِنۢ بَعْدُ وَهَاجَرُوا وَجَٰهَدُوا مَعَكُمْ فَأُو۟لَٰٓئِكَ مِنكُمْ وَأُو۟لُوا ٱلْأَرْحَامِ بَعْضُهُمْ أَوْلَىٰ بِبَعْضٍ فِى كِتَٰبِ ٱللَّهِ إِنَّ ٱللَّهَ بِكُلِّ شَىْءٍ عَلِيمٌ ﴿٧٥﴾

At Tawbah
(Repentance)

At Tawbah, "Repentance," takes its name from v. 104. It is often called Al Barā'ah (The Immunity), from the first word. It is the only sūrah which is without the *Bi'smi'llāhi'r-Raḥmāni'r-Raḥīm* ("In the name of Allah, the Beneficent, the Merciful") which is generally considered to be on account of the stern commandments against idolaters which it contains. Vv. 1-12, forming the proclamation of immunity from obligation toward the idolaters, were revealed after the pilgrims had started for Makkah in the ninth year of the Hijrah and sent by special messenger to Abū Bakr, leader of the pilgrimage, to be read out by 'Alī to the multitudes at Makkah. It signified the end of idolatry in Arabia. The Christian Byzantine Empire had begun to move against the growing Muslim power, and this sūrah contains mention of a greater war to come, and instructions with regard to it. Vv. 38-99 refer to the Tabūk campaign, and especially to those Arab tribes who failed to join the Muslims in that campaign. The "Hypocrites," as the half-hearted supporters of Al-Islām were called, had long been a thorn in the side of the Muslims. They had even at one time gone the length in dissent of forming a congregation and building a mosque of their own surreptitiously. On the Prophet's return from Tabūk they invited him to visit that mosque. This is referred to in vv. 107 ff.

The date of revelation is the ninth year of the Hijrah.

1 Freedom from obligation (is proclaimed) from Allah and His messenger toward those of the idolaters with whom ye made a treaty:

بَرَآءَةٌ مِّنَ اللّٰهِ وَرَسُوْلِهٖۤ اِلَى الَّذِيْنَ عٰهَدْتُّمْ مِّنَ الْمُشْرِكِيْنَ ۟ ۚ ۞

2 Travel freely in the land four months, and know that ye cannot escape Allah and that Allah will confound the disbelievers (in His guidance).

فَسِيْحُوْا فِى الْاَرْضِ اَرْبَعَةَ اَشْهُرٍ وَّاعْلَمُوْۤا اَنَّكُمْ غَيْرُ مُعْجِزِى اللّٰهِ ۙ وَاَنَّ اللّٰهَ مُخْزِى الْكٰفِرِيْنَ ۟ ۞

3 And a proclamation from Allah and His messenger to all men on the day of the Greater Pilgrimage that Allah is free from obligation to the idolaters, and (so is) His messenger. So, if ye repent, it will be better for you; but if ye are averse, then know that ye cannot escape Allah. Give tidings (O Muḥammad) of a painful doom to those who disbelieve.

وَاَذَانٌ مِّنَ اللّٰهِ وَرَسُوْلِهٖۤ اِلَى النَّاسِ يَوْمَ الْحَجِّ الْاَكْبَرِ اَنَّ اللّٰهَ بَرِيْٓءٌ مِّنَ الْمُشْرِكِيْنَ ۙ وَرَسُوْلُهٗ ۚ فَاِنْ تُبْتُمْ فَهُوَ خَيْرٌ لَّكُمْ ۚ وَاِنْ تَوَلَّيْتُمْ فَاعْلَمُوْۤا اَنَّكُمْ غَيْرُ مُعْجِزِى اللّٰهِ ۚ وَبَشِّرِ الَّذِيْنَ كَفَرُوْا بِعَذَابٍ اَلِيْمٍ ۟ ۞

4 Excepting those of the idolaters with whom ye (Muslims) have a treaty, and who have since abated nothing of your right nor have supported anyone against you. (As for these), fulfil their treaty to them till their term. Lo! Allah loveth those who keep their duty (unto Him).

اِلَّا الَّذِيْنَ عٰهَدْتُّمْ مِّنَ الْمُشْرِكِيْنَ ثُمَّ لَمْ يَنْقُصُوْكُمْ شَيْئًا وَّلَمْ يُظَاهِرُوْا عَلَيْكُمْ اَحَدًا فَاَتِمُّوْۤا اِلَيْهِمْ عَهْدَهُمْ اِلَى مُدَّتِهِمْ ۚ اِنَّ اللّٰهَ يُحِبُّ الْمُتَّقِيْنَ ۟ ۞

5 Then, when the sacred months have passed, slay the idolaters wherever ye find them, and take

فَاِذَا انْسَلَخَ الْاَشْهُرُ الْحُرُمُ فَاقْتُلُوا الْمُشْرِكِيْنَ حَيْثُ وَجَدْتُّمُوْهُمْ وَخُذُوْهُمْ وَاحْصُرُوْهُمْ وَاقْعُدُوْا

them (captive), and besiege them, and prepare for them each ambush. But if they repent and establish worship and pay the poor-due, then leave their way free. Lo! Allah is Forgiving, Merciful.

لَهُمْ كُلَّ مَرْصَدٍ فَإِن تَابُوا وَأَقَامُوا الصَّلَوٰةَ وَءَاتَوُا الزَّكَوٰةَ فَخَلُّوا سَبِيلَهُمْ إِنَّ اللَّهَ غَفُورٌ رَّحِيمٌ ﴿٥﴾

6 And if anyone of the idolaters seeketh thy protection (O Muhammad), then protect him so that he may hear the word of Allah; and afterward convey him to his place of safety. That is because they are a folk who know not.

وَإِنْ أَحَدٌ مِّنَ الْمُشْرِكِينَ اسْتَجَارَكَ فَأَجِرْهُ حَتَّىٰ يَسْمَعَ كَلَٰمَ اللَّهِ ثُمَّ أَبْلِغْهُ مَأْمَنَهُ ذَٰلِكَ بِأَنَّهُمْ قَوْمٌ لَّا يَعْلَمُونَ ﴿٦﴾

7 How can there be a treaty with Allah and with His messenger for the idolaters save those with whom ye made a treaty at the Inviolable Place of Worship? So long as they are true to you, be true to them. Lo! Allah loveth those who keep their duty.

كَيْفَ يَكُونُ لِلْمُشْرِكِينَ عَهْدٌ عِندَ اللَّهِ وَعِندَ رَسُولِهِ إِلَّا الَّذِينَ عَٰهَدتُّمْ عِندَ الْمَسْجِدِ الْحَرَامِ فَمَا اسْتَقَٰمُوا لَكُمْ فَاسْتَقِيمُوا لَهُمْ إِنَّ اللَّهَ يُحِبُّ الْمُتَّقِينَ ﴿٧﴾

8 How (can there be any treaty for the others) when, if they have the upper hand of you, they regard not pact nor honour in respect of you? They satisfy you with their mouths, while their hearts refuse. And most of them are wrong-doers.

كَيْفَ وَإِن يَظْهَرُوا عَلَيْكُمْ لَا يَرْقُبُوا فِيكُمْ إِلًّا وَلَا ذِمَّةً يُرْضُونَكُم بِأَفْوَٰهِهِمْ وَتَأْبَىٰ قُلُوبُهُمْ وَأَكْثَرُهُمْ فَٰسِقُونَ ﴿٨﴾

9 They have purchased with the revelations of Allah a little gain, so they debar (men) from His way. Lo! evil is that which they are wont to do.

اشْتَرَوْا بِآيَٰتِ اللَّهِ ثَمَنًا قَلِيلًا فَصَدُّوا عَن سَبِيلِهِ إِنَّهُمْ سَاءَ مَا كَانُوا يَعْمَلُونَ ﴿٩﴾

10 And they observe toward a believer neither pact nor honour. These are they who are transgressors.

لَا يَرْقُبُونَ فِي مُؤْمِنٍ إِلًّا وَلَا ذِمَّةً وَأُوْلَٰئِكَ هُمُ الْمُعْتَدُونَ ﴿١٠﴾

11 But if they repent and establish worship and pay the poor-due, then are they your brethren in religion. We detail Our revelations for a people who have knowledge.

فَإِن تَابُوا۟ وَأَقَامُوا۟ الصَّلَوٰةَ وَءَاتَوُا۟ الزَّكَوٰةَ فَإِخْوَٰنُكُمْ فِى الدِّينِ ۗ وَنُفَصِّلُ الْءَايَٰتِ لِقَوْمٍ يَعْلَمُونَ ۝

12 And if they break their pledges after their treaty (hath been made with you) and assail your religion, then fight the heads of disbelief. Lo! they have no binding oaths; in order that they may desist.

وَإِن نَّكَثُوٓا۟ أَيْمَٰنَهُم مِّنۢ بَعْدِ عَهْدِهِمْ وَطَعَنُوا۟ فِى دِينِكُمْ فَقَٰتِلُوٓا۟ أَئِمَّةَ الْكُفْرِ ۙ إِنَّهُمْ لَآ أَيْمَٰنَ لَهُمْ لَعَلَّهُمْ يَنتَهُونَ ۝

13 Will ye not fight a folk who broke their solemn pledges, and purposed to drive out the messenger and did attack you first? What! Fear ye them? Now Allah hath more right that ye should fear Him, if ye are believers.

أَلَا تُقَٰتِلُونَ قَوْمًا نَّكَثُوٓا۟ أَيْمَٰنَهُمْ وَهَمُّوا۟ بِإِخْرَاجِ الرَّسُولِ وَهُم بَدَءُوكُمْ أَوَّلَ مَرَّةٍ ۚ أَتَخْشَوْنَهُمْ ۚ فَاللَّهُ أَحَقُّ أَن تَخْشَوْهُ إِن كُنتُم مُّؤْمِنِينَ ۝

14 Fight them! Allah will chastise them at your hands, and He will lay them low and give you victory over them, and He will heal the breasts of folk who are believers.

قَٰتِلُوهُمْ يُعَذِّبْهُمُ اللَّهُ بِأَيْدِيكُمْ وَيُخْزِهِمْ وَيَنصُرْكُمْ عَلَيْهِمْ وَيَشْفِ صُدُورَ قَوْمٍ مُّؤْمِنِينَ ۝

15 And He will remove the anger of their hearts. Allah relenteth toward whom He will. Allah is Knower, Wise.

وَيُذْهِبْ غَيْظَ قُلُوبِهِمْ ۗ وَيَتُوبُ اللَّهُ عَلَىٰ مَن يَشَآءُ ۗ وَاللَّهُ عَلِيمٌ حَكِيمٌ ۝

16 Or deemed ye that ye would be left (in peace) when Allah yet knoweth not those of you who strive, choosing for familiar none save Allah and His messenger and the believers? Allah is Informed of what ye do.

أَمْ حَسِبْتُمْ أَن تُتْرَكُوا۟ وَلَمَّا يَعْلَمِ اللَّهُ الَّذِينَ جَٰهَدُوا۟ مِنكُمْ وَلَمْ يَتَّخِذُوا۟ مِن دُونِ اللَّهِ وَلَا رَسُولِهِ وَلَا الْمُؤْمِنِينَ وَلِيجَةً ۚ وَاللَّهُ خَبِيرٌۢ بِمَا تَعْمَلُونَ ۝

17 It is not for the idolaters to tend Allah's sanctuaries, bearing witness against themselves of disbelief. As

مَا كَانَ لِلْمُشْرِكِينَ أَن يَعْمُرُوا۟ مَسَٰجِدَ اللَّهِ شَٰهِدِينَ عَلَىٰٓ أَنفُسِهِم بِالْكُفْرِ ۚ أُو۟لَٰٓئِكَ

for such, their works are vain and in the Fire they will abide.

حَبِطَتْ أَعْمَالُهُمْ وَفِى النَّارِهُمْ خَالِدُونَ ۝

18 He only shall tend Allah's sanctuaries who believeth in Allah and the Last Day and observeth proper worship and payeth the poor-due and feareth none save Allah. For such (only) is it possible that they can be of the rightly guided.

إِنَّمَا يَعْمُرُ مَسَاجِدَ اللَّهِ مَنْ ءَامَنَ بِاللَّهِ وَالْيَوْمِ الْأَخِرِ وَأَقَامَ الصَّلَوٰةَ وَءَاتَى الزَّكَوٰةَ وَلَمْ يَخْشَ إِلَّا اللَّهَ فَعَسَىٰٓ أُوْلَٰٓئِكَ أَن يَكُونُوا مِنَ الْمُهْتَدِينَ ۝

19 Count ye the slaking of a pilgrim's thirst and tendance of the Inviolable Place of Worship as (equal to the worth of him) who believeth in Allah and the Last Day, and striveth in the way of Allah? They are not equal in the sight of Allah. Allah guideth not wrongdoing folk.

۞ أَجَعَلْتُمْ سِقَايَةَ الْحَاجِّ وَعِمَارَةَ الْمَسْجِدِ الْحَرَامِ كَمَنْ ءَامَنَ بِاللَّهِ وَالْيَوْمِ الْأَخِرِ وَجَاهَدَ فِى سَبِيلِ اللَّهِ لَا يَسْتَوُونَ عِندَ اللَّهِ وَاللَّهُ لَا يَهْدِى الْقَوْمَ الظَّالِمِينَ ۝

20 Those who believe, and have left their homes and striven with their wealth and their lives in Allah's way are of much greater worth in Allah's sight. These are they who are triumphant.

الَّذِينَ ءَامَنُوا وَهَاجَرُوا وَجَاهَدُوا فِى سَبِيلِ اللَّهِ بِأَمْوَالِهِمْ وَأَنفُسِهِمْ أَعْظَمُ دَرَجَةً عِندَ اللَّهِ وَأُوْلَٰٓئِكَ هُمُ الْفَآئِزُونَ ۝

21 Their Lord giveth them good tidings of mercy from Him, and acceptance, and Gardens where enduring pleasure will be theirs;

يُبَشِّرُهُمْ رَبُّهُم بِرَحْمَةٍ مِّنْهُ وَرِضْوَانٍ وَجَنَّاتٍ لَّهُمْ فِيهَا نَعِيمٌ مُّقِيمٌ ۝

22 There they will abide forever. Lo! with Allah there is immense reward.

خَالِدِينَ فِيهَا أَبَدًا إِنَّ اللَّهَ عِندَهُ أَجْرٌ عَظِيمٌ ۝

23 O ye who believe! Choose not your fathers nor your brethren for friends if they take pleasure in dis-

يَٰٓأَيُّهَا الَّذِينَ ءَامَنُوا لَا تَتَّخِذُوٓا ءَابَآءَكُمْ وَإِخْوَانَكُمْ أَوْلِيَآءَ إِنِ اسْتَحَبُّوا الْكُفْرَ

belief rather than faith. Whoso of
you taketh them for friends, such
are wrong-doers.

24 Say: If your fathers, and your
sons, and your brethren, and your
wives, and your tribe, and the
wealth ye have acquired, and merchandise for which ye fear that there
will be no sale,[1] and dwellings ye
desire are dearer to you than Allah
and His messenger and striving in
His way: then wait till Allah bringeth His command to pass. Allah
guideth not wrongdoing folk.

25 Allah hath given you victory on
many fields and on the day of
Hunayn,[2] when ye exulted in your
multitude but it availed you naught,
and the earth, vast as it is, was
straitened for you; then ye turned
back in flight;

26 Then Allah sent His peace of
reassurance down upon His messenger and upon the believers, and
sent down hosts ye could not see,
and punished those who disbelieved.
Such is the reward of disbelievers.

27 Then afterward Allah will relent
toward whom He will; for Allah is
Forgiving, Merciful.

عَلَى الْإِيمَانِ وَمَن يَتَوَلَّهُم مِّنكُمْ فَأُوْلَٰٓئِكَ
هُمُ الظَّٰلِمُونَ ۝

قُلْ إِن كَانَ ءَابَآؤُكُمْ وَأَبْنَآؤُكُمْ وَإِخْوَٰنُكُمْ
وَأَزْوَٰجُكُمْ وَعَشِيرَتُكُمْ وَأَمْوَٰلٌ اقْتَرَفْتُمُوهَا
وَتِجَٰرَةٌ تَخْشَوْنَ كَسَادَهَا وَمَسَٰكِنُ تَرْضَوْنَهَآ
أَحَبَّ إِلَيْكُم مِّنَ اللَّهِ وَرَسُولِهِ وَجِهَادٍ
فِى سَبِيلِهِ فَتَرَبَّصُوا حَتَّىٰ يَأْتِيَ اللَّهُ بِأَمْرِهِ وَاللَّهُ
لَا يَهْدِى الْقَوْمَ الْفَٰسِقِينَ ۝

لَقَدْ نَصَرَكُمُ اللَّهُ فِى مَوَاطِنَ كَثِيرَةٍ وَيَوْمَ
حُنَيْنٍ إِذْ أَعْجَبَتْكُمْ كَثْرَتُكُمْ فَلَمْ تُغْنِ
عَنكُمْ شَيْئًا وَضَاقَتْ عَلَيْكُمُ
الْأَرْضُ بِمَا رَحُبَتْ ثُمَّ وَلَّيْتُم مُّدْبِرِينَ ۝

ثُمَّ أَنزَلَ اللَّهُ سَكِينَتَهُ عَلَىٰ رَسُولِهِ
وَعَلَى الْمُؤْمِنِينَ وَأَنزَلَ جُنُودًا لَّمْ تَرَوْهَا
وَعَذَّبَ الَّذِينَ كَفَرُوا وَذَٰلِكَ جَزَآءُ
الْكَٰفِرِينَ ۝

ثُمَّ يَتُوبُ اللَّهُ مِنۢ بَعْدِ ذَٰلِكَ عَلَىٰ مَن يَشَآءُ
وَاللَّهُ غَفُورٌ رَّحِيمٌ ۝

---

1. It was objected that, if idolaters were forbidden to make the pilgrimage, the trade
of Makkah would decline.

2. The Muslim army, ambushed at Ḥunayn, gained a great victory after being nearly
routed.

28 O ye who believe! The idolaters only are unclean. So let them not come near the Inviolable Place of Worship after this their year. If ye fear poverty (from the loss of their merchandise) Allah shall preserve you of His bounty if He will. Lo! Allah is Knower, Wise.

يَـٰٓأَيُّهَا ٱلَّذِينَ ءَامَنُوٓا إِنَّمَا ٱلْمُشْرِكُونَ نَجَسٌ فَلَا يَقْرَبُوا ٱلْمَسْجِدَ ٱلْحَرَامَ بَعْدَ عَامِهِمْ هَـٰذَا وَإِنْ خِفْتُمْ عَيْلَةً فَسَوْفَ يُغْنِيكُمُ ٱللَّهُ مِن فَضْلِهِ إِن شَآءَ إِنَّ ٱللَّهَ عَلِيمٌ حَكِيمٌ ۝

29 Fight against such of those who have been given the Scripture as believe not in Allah nor the Last Day, and forbid not that which Allah hath forbidden by His messenger, and follow not the religion of truth, until they pay the tribute readily, being brought low.

قَـٰتِلُوا ٱلَّذِينَ لَا يُؤْمِنُونَ بِٱللَّهِ وَلَا بِٱلْيَوْمِ ٱلْءَاخِرِ وَلَا يُحَرِّمُونَ مَا حَرَّمَ ٱللَّهُ وَرَسُولُهُ وَلَا يَدِينُونَ دِينَ ٱلْحَقِّ مِنَ ٱلَّذِينَ أُوتُوا ٱلْكِتَـٰبَ حَتَّىٰ يُعْطُوا ٱلْجِزْيَةَ عَن يَدٍ وَهُمْ صَـٰغِرُونَ ۝

30 And the Jews say: Ezra is the son of Allah, and the Christians say: The Messiah is the son of Allah. That is their saying with their mouths. They imitate the saying of those who disbelieved of old. Allah (himself) fighteth against them. How perverse are they!

وَقَالَتِ ٱلْيَهُودُ عُزَيْرٌ ٱبْنُ ٱللَّهِ وَقَالَتِ ٱلنَّصَـٰرَى ٱلْمَسِيحُ ٱبْنُ ٱللَّهِ ذَٰلِكَ قَوْلُهُم بِأَفْوَٰهِهِمْ يُضَـٰهِـُٔونَ قَوْلَ ٱلَّذِينَ كَفَرُوا مِن قَبْلُ قَـٰتَلَهُمُ ٱللَّهُ أَنَّىٰ يُؤْفَكُونَ ۝

31 They have taken as lords beside Allah their rabbis and their monks and the Messiah son of Mary, when they were bidden to worship only One God. There is no god save Him. Be He glorified from all that they ascribe as partner (unto Him)!

ٱتَّخَذُوٓا أَحْبَارَهُمْ وَرُهْبَـٰنَهُمْ أَرْبَابًا مِّن دُونِ ٱللَّهِ وَٱلْمَسِيحَ ٱبْنَ مَرْيَمَ وَمَآ أُمِرُوٓا إِلَّا لِيَعْبُدُوٓا إِلَـٰهًا وَٰحِدًا لَّآ إِلَـٰهَ إِلَّا هُوَ سُبْحَـٰنَهُ عَمَّا يُشْرِكُونَ ۝

32 Fain would they put out the light of Allah with their mouths, but Allah disdaineth (aught) save that He shall perfect His light, however much the disbelievers are averse.

يُرِيدُونَ أَن يُطْفِـُٔوا نُورَ ٱللَّهِ بِأَفْوَٰهِهِمْ وَيَأْبَى ٱللَّهُ إِلَّآ أَن يُتِمَّ نُورَهُ وَلَوْ كَرِهَ ٱلْكَـٰفِرُونَ ۝

33 He it is who hath sent His messenger with the guidance and the
Religion of Truth, that He may
cause it to prevail over all religion,
however much the idolaters may be
averse.

هُوَ الَّذِىٓ أَرْسَلَ رَسُولَهُۥ بِالْهُدَىٰ وَدِينِ
الْحَقِّ لِيُظْهِرَهُۥ عَلَى الدِّينِ كُلِّهِۦ وَلَوْ كَرِهَ
الْمُشْرِكُونَ ۝

34 O ye, who believe! Lo! many of
the (Jewish) rabbis and the (Christian) monks devour the wealth of
mankind wantonly and debar (men)
from the way of Allah. They who
hoard up gold and silver and spend
it not in the way of Allah, unto
them give tidings (O Muḥammad)
of a painful doom.

۞ يَـٰٓأَيُّهَا الَّذِينَ ءَامَنُوٓا إِنَّ كَثِيرًا
مِّنَ الْأَحْبَارِ وَالرُّهْبَانِ لَيَأْكُلُونَ أَمْوَٰلَ
النَّاسِ بِالْبَٰطِلِ وَيَصُدُّونَ عَن سَبِيلِ
اللَّهِ ۗ وَالَّذِينَ يَكْنِزُونَ الذَّهَبَ وَالْفِضَّةَ
وَلَا يُنفِقُونَهَا فِى سَبِيلِ اللَّهِ فَبَشِّرْهُم
بِعَذَابٍ أَلِيمٍ ۝

35 On the day when it will (all) be
heated in the fire of hell, and their
foreheads and their flanks and their
backs will be branded therewith
(and it will be said unto them):
Here is that which ye hoarded for
yourselves. Now taste of what ye
used to hoard.

يَوْمَ يُحْمَىٰ عَلَيْهَا فِى نَارِ جَهَنَّمَ فَتُكْوَىٰ بِهَا
جِبَاهُهُمْ وَجُنُوبُهُمْ وَظُهُورُهُمْ
هَـٰذَا مَا كَنَزْتُمْ لِأَنفُسِكُمْ فَذُوقُوا مَا كُنتُمْ
تَكْنِزُونَ ۝

36 Lo! the number of the months
with Allah is twelve months by
Allah's ordinance in the day that
He created the heavens and the
earth. Four of them are sacred: that
is the right religion. So wrong not
yourselves in them. And wage war
on all the idolaters as they are
waging war on all of you. And
know that Allah is with those who
keep their duty (unto Him).

إِنَّ عِدَّةَ الشُّهُورِ عِندَ اللَّهِ اثْنَا عَشَرَ شَهْرًا
فِى كِتَٰبِ اللَّهِ يَوْمَ خَلَقَ السَّمَٰوَٰتِ
وَالْأَرْضَ مِنْهَآ أَرْبَعَةٌ حُرُمٌ ۚ ذَٰلِكَ الدِّينُ
الْقَيِّمُ ۚ فَلَا تَظْلِمُوا فِيهِنَّ أَنفُسَكُمْ ۚ وَقَٰتِلُوا
الْمُشْرِكِينَ كَآفَّةً كَمَا يُقَٰتِلُونَكُمْ
كَآفَّةً ۚ وَاعْلَمُوٓا أَنَّ اللَّهَ مَعَ الْمُتَّقِينَ ۝

37 Postponement (of a sacred month)[3] is only an excess of disbelief whereby those who disbelieve are misled, they allow it one year and forbid it (another) year, that they may make up the number of the months which Allah hath hallowed, so that they allow that which Allah hath forbidden. The evil of their deeds is made fair seeming unto them. Allah guideth not the disbelieving folk.

إِنَّمَا النَّسِيءُ زِيَادَةٌ فِي الْكُفْرِ يُضَلُّ بِهِ الَّذِينَ كَفَرُوا يُحِلُّونَهُ عَامًا وَيُحَرِّمُونَهُ عَامًا لِّيُوَاطِئُوا عِدَّةَ مَا حَرَّمَ اللَّهُ فَيُحِلُّوا مَا حَرَّمَ اللَّهُ زُيِّنَ لَهُمْ سُوءُ أَعْمَالِهِمْ وَاللَّهُ لَا يَهْدِي الْقَوْمَ الْكَافِرِينَ ۝

38 O ye who believe! What aileth you that when it is said unto you: Go forth in the way of Allah, ye are bowed down to the ground with heaviness. Take ye pleasure in the life of the world rather than in the Hereafter? The comfort of the life of the world is but little in the Hereafter.

يَا أَيُّهَا الَّذِينَ آمَنُوا مَا لَكُمْ إِذَا قِيلَ لَكُمُ انْفِرُوا فِي سَبِيلِ اللَّهِ اثَّاقَلْتُمْ إِلَى الْأَرْضِ أَرَضِيتُم بِالْحَيَاةِ الدُّنْيَا مِنَ الْآخِرَةِ فَمَا مَتَاعُ الْحَيَاةِ الدُّنْيَا فِي الْآخِرَةِ إِلَّا قَلِيلٌ ۝

39 If ye go not forth, He will afflict you with a painful doom, and will choose instead of you a folk other then you. Ye cannot harm Him at all. Allah is Able to do all things.

إِلَّا تَنْفِرُوا يُعَذِّبْكُمْ عَذَابًا أَلِيمًا وَيَسْتَبْدِلْ قَوْمًا غَيْرَكُمْ وَلَا تَضُرُّوهُ شَيْئًا وَاللَّهُ عَلَى كُلِّ شَيْءٍ قَدِيرٌ ۝

40 If ye help him not, still Allah helped him when those who disbelieve drove him forth, the second of two; when they two[4] were in the cave, when he said unto his com-

إِلَّا تَنْصُرُوهُ فَقَدْ نَصَرَهُ اللَّهُ إِذْ أَخْرَجَهُ الَّذِينَ كَفَرُوا ثَانِيَ اثْنَيْنِ إِذْ هُمَا فِي الْغَارِ إِذْ يَقُولُ لِصَاحِبِهِ لَا تَحْزَنْ

---

3. The idolaters would postpone a sacred month in which war was forbidden, when they wanted to make war, and make up for it by hallowing another month.

4. The Prophet and Abū Bakr during the Flight from Makkah to Al-Madīnah.

rade: Grieve not. Lo! Allah is with us. Then Allah caused His peace of reassurance to descend upon him and supported him with hosts ye cannot see, and made the word of those who disbelieved the nethermost, while Allah's word it was that became the uppermost. Allah is Mighty, Wise.

41 Go forth, light-armed and heavy-armed, and strive with your wealth and your lives in the way of Allah! That is best for you if ye but knew.

42 Had it been a near adventure and an easy journey they had followed thee, but the distance seemed too far for them.[5] Yet will they swear by Allah (saying): If we had been able, we would surely have set out with you. They destroy their souls, and Allah knoweth that they verily are liars.

43 Allah forgive thee (O Muhammad)! Wherefore didst thou grant them leave ere those who told the truth were manifest to thee and thou didst know the liars?

44 Those who believe in Allah and the Last Day ask no leave of thee lest they should strive with their wealth and their lives. Allah is Aware of those who keep their duty (unto Him).

---

5. The reference is to the Tabūk expedition. Tabūk is half-way between Al-Madīnah and Damascus.

45 They alone ask leave of thee who believe not in Allah and the Last Day, and whose hearts feel doubt, so in their doubt they waver.

46 And if they had wished to go forth they would assuredly have made ready some equipment, but Allah was averse to their being sent forth and held them back and (it was said unto them): Sit ye with the sedentary!

47 Had they gone forth among you they had added to you naught save trouble and had hurried to and fro among you, seeking to cause sedition among you; and among you there are some who would have listened to them. Allah Is Aware of evil-doers.

48 Aforetime they sought to cause sedition and raised difficulties for thee till the Truth came and the decree of Allah was made manifest, though they were loth.

49 Of them is he who saith: Grant me leave (to stay at home) and tempt me not.[6] Surely it is into temptation that they (thus) have fallen. Lo! hell is all around the disbelievers.

50 If good befalleth thee (O Muhammad) it afflicteth them, and

إِنَّمَا يَسْتَأْذِنُكَ الَّذِينَ لَا يُؤْمِنُونَ بِاللَّهِ وَالْيَوْمِ الْآخِرِ وَارْتَابَتْ قُلُوبُهُمْ فَهُمْ فِى رَيْبِهِمْ يَتَرَدَّدُونَ ۝

۞ وَلَوْ أَرَادُوا الْخُرُوجَ لَأَعَدُّوا لَهُ عُدَّةً وَلَكِن كَرِهَ اللَّهُ انْبِعَاثَهُمْ فَثَبَّطَهُمْ وَقِيلَ اقْعُدُوا مَعَ الْقَاعِدِينَ ۝

لَوْ خَرَجُوا فِيكُم مَّا زَادُوكُمْ إِلَّا خَبَالًا وَلَأَوْضَعُوا خِلَالَكُمْ يَبْغُونَكُمُ الْفِتْنَةَ وَفِيكُمْ سَمَّاعُونَ لَهُمْ وَاللَّهُ عَلِيمٌ بِالظَّالِمِينَ ۝

لَقَدِ ابْتَغَوُا الْفِتْنَةَ مِن قَبْلُ وَقَلَّبُوا لَكَ الْأُمُورَ حَتَّى جَاءَ الْحَقُّ وَظَهَرَ أَمْرُ اللَّهِ وَهُمْ كَارِهُونَ ۝

وَمِنْهُم مَّن يَقُولُ ائْذَن لِّي وَلَا تَفْتِنِّي أَلَا فِى الْفِتْنَةِ سَقَطُوا وَإِنَّ جَهَنَّمَ لَمُحِيطَةٌ بِالْكَافِرِينَ ۝

إِن تُصِبْكَ حَسَنَةٌ تَسُؤْهُمْ

---

6. The temptation here referred to is generally explained as being the beauty of the women of Syria, the country against which the campaign was directed.

if calamity befalleth thee, they say: We took precaution, and they turn away well pleased.

وَإِن تُصِبۡكَ مُصِيبَةٌ يَقُولُواْ قَدۡ أَخَذۡنَاۤ أَمۡرَنَا مِن قَبۡلُ وَيَتَوَلَّواْ وَّهُمۡ فَرِحُونَ ﴿٥٠﴾

51 Say: Naught befalleth us save that which Allah hath decreed for us. He is our protecting Friend. In Allah let believers put their trust!

قُل لَّن يُصِيبَنَاۤ إِلَّا مَا كَتَبَ اللَّهُ لَنَا هُوَ مَوۡلَىٰنَا وَعَلَى اللَّهِ فَلۡيَتَوَكَّلِ الۡمُؤۡمِنُونَ ﴿٥١﴾

52 Say: Can ye await for us aught save one of two good things (death or victory in Allah's way)? while we await for you that Allah will afflict you with a doom from Him or at our hands. Await then! Lo! we are awaiting with you.

قُلۡ هَلۡ تَرَبَّصُونَ بِنَاۤ إِلَّاۤ إِحۡدَى الۡحُسۡنَيَيۡنِ وَنَحۡنُ نَتَرَبَّصُ بِكُمۡ أَن يُصِيبَكُمُ اللَّهُ بِعَذَابٍ مِّنۡ عِندِهِ أَوۡ بِأَيۡدِينَا فَتَرَبَّصُوۤاْ إِنَّا مَعَكُم مُّتَرَبِّصُونَ ﴿٥٢﴾

53 Say: Pay (your contribution), willingly or unwillingly, it will not be accepted from you. Lo! ye were ever froward folk.

قُلۡ أَنفِقُواْ طَوۡعًا أَوۡ كَرۡهًا لَّن يُتَقَبَّلَ مِنكُمۡ إِنَّكُمۡ كُنتُمۡ قَوۡمًا فَاسِقِينَ ﴿٥٣﴾

54 And naught preventeth that their contributions should be accepted from them save that they have disbelieved in Allah and in His messenger, and they come not to worship save as idlers, and pay not (their contribution) save reluctantly.

وَمَا مَنَعَهُمۡ أَن تُقۡبَلَ مِنۡهُمۡ نَفَقَٰتُهُمۡ إِلَّاۤ أَنَّهُمۡ كَفَرُواْ بِاللَّهِ وَبِرَسُولِهِ وَلَا يَأۡتُونَ الصَّلَوٰةَ إِلَّا وَهُمۡ كُسَالَىٰ وَلَا يُنفِقُونَ إِلَّا وَهُمۡ كَٰرِهُونَ ﴿٥٤﴾

55 So let not their riches nor their children please thee (O Muhammad). Allah thereby intendeth but to punish them in the life of the world and that their souls shall pass away while they are disbelievers

فَلَا تُعۡجِبۡكَ أَمۡوَٰلُهُمۡ وَلَاۤ أَوۡلَٰدُهُمۡ إِنَّمَا يُرِيدُ اللَّهُ لِيُعَذِّبَهُم بِهَا فِي الۡحَيَوٰةِ الدُّنۡيَا وَتَزۡهَقَ أَنفُسُهُمۡ وَهُمۡ كَٰفِرُونَ ﴿٥٥﴾

56 And they swear by Allah that they are in truth of you, when they are not of you, but they are folk who are afraid.

وَيَحۡلِفُونَ بِاللَّهِ إِنَّهُمۡ لَمِنكُمۡ وَمَا هُم مِّنكُمۡ وَلَٰكِنَّهُمۡ قَوۡمٌ يَفۡرَقُونَ ﴿٥٦﴾

57 Had they but found a refuge, or caverns, or a place to enter, they surely had resorted thither swift as runaways.

لَوْ يَجِدُوْنَ مَلْجَأً أَوْ مَغٰرٰتٍ أَوْ مُدَّخَلًا لَّوَلَّوْا إِلَيْهِ وَهُمْ يَجْمَحُوْنَ ۞

58 And of them is he who defameth thee in the matter of the alms. If they are given thereof they are content, and if they are not given thereof, behold! they are enraged.

وَمِنْهُمْ مَّنْ يَّلْمِزُكَ فِى الصَّدَقٰتِ ۚ فَإِنْ أُعْطُوْا مِنْهَا رَضُوْا وَإِنْ لَّمْ يُعْطَوْا مِنْهَا إِذَا هُمْ يَسْخَطُوْنَ ۞

59 (How much more seemly) had they been content with that which Allah and His messenger had given them and had said: Allah sufficeth us. Allah will give us of His bounty, and (also) His messenger. Unto Allah we are suppliants.

وَلَوْ أَنَّهُمْ رَضُوْا مَا آتٰهُمُ اللّٰهُ وَرَسُوْلُهُ ۙ وَقَالُوْا حَسْبُنَا اللّٰهُ سَيُؤْتِيْنَا اللّٰهُ مِنْ فَضْلِهِ وَرَسُوْلُهُ ۙ إِنَّا إِلَى اللّٰهِ رٰغِبُوْنَ ۞

60 The alms are only for the poor and the needy, and those who collect them, and those whose hearts are to be reconciled,[7] and to free the captives and the debtors, and for the cause of Allah, and (for) the wayfarers; a duty imposed by Allah. Allah is Knower, Wise.

۞ إِنَّمَا الصَّدَقٰتُ لِلْفُقَرَاءِ وَالْمَسٰكِيْنِ وَالْعٰمِلِيْنَ عَلَيْهَا وَالْمُؤَلَّفَةِ قُلُوْبُهُمْ وَفِى الرِّقَابِ وَالْغٰرِمِيْنَ وَفِيْ سَبِيْلِ اللّٰهِ وَابْنِ السَّبِيْلِ ۖ فَرِيْضَةً مِّنَ اللّٰهِ ۗ وَاللّٰهُ عَلِيْمٌ حَكِيْمٌ ۞

61 And of them are those who vex the Prophet and say: He is only a hearer. Say: A hearer of good for you, who believeth in Allah and is true to the believers, and a mercy for such of you as believe. Those who vex the messenger of Allah, for them there is a painful doom.

وَمِنْهُمُ الَّذِيْنَ يُؤْذُوْنَ النَّبِيَّ وَيَقُوْلُوْنَ هُوَ أُذُنٌ ۚ قُلْ أُذُنُ خَيْرٍ لَّكُمْ يُؤْمِنُ بِاللّٰهِ وَيُؤْمِنُ لِلْمُؤْمِنِيْنَ وَرَحْمَةٌ لِّلَّذِيْنَ آمَنُوْا مِنْكُمْ ۚ وَالَّذِيْنَ يُؤْذُوْنَ رَسُوْلَ اللّٰهِ لَهُمْ عَذَابٌ أَلِيْمٌ ۞

---

7. A special portion of the Alms was alloted to the people of Makkah, the former enemies of Al-Islām, who were converted en masse after the capture of the city, and whose "hearts were to be reconciled."

62 They swear by Allah to you (Muslims) to please you, but Allah, with His messenger, hath more right that they should please Him if they are believers.

يَحْلِفُوۡنَ بِاللّٰهِ لَكُمۡ لِيُرۡضُوۡكُمۡ ۚ وَاللّٰهُ وَرَسُوۡلُهٗۤ اَحَقُّ اَنۡ يُّرۡضُوۡهُ اِنۡ كَانُوۡا مُؤۡمِنِيۡنَ ۝

63 Know they not that whoso opposeth Allah and His messenger, his portion verily is hell, to abide therein? That is the extreme abasement.

اَلَمۡ يَعۡلَمُوۡۤا اَنَّهٗ مَنۡ يُّحَادِدِ اللّٰهَ وَرَسُوۡلَهٗ فَاَنَّ لَهٗ نَارَ جَهَنَّمَ خَالِدًا فِيۡهَا ۚ ذٰلِكَ الۡخِزۡيُ الۡعَظِيۡمُ ۝

64 The hypocrites fear lest a sūrah should be revealed concerning them, proclaiming what is in their hearts. Say: Scoff (your fill)! Lo! Allah is disclosing what ye fear.

يَحۡذَرُ الۡمُنٰفِقُوۡنَ اَنۡ تُنَزَّلَ عَلَيۡهِمۡ سُوۡرَةٌ تُنَبِّئُهُمۡ بِمَا فِيۡ قُلُوۡبِهِمۡ ۚ قُلِ اسۡتَهۡزِءُوۡا ۚ اِنَّ اللّٰهَ مُخۡرِجٌ مَّا تَحۡذَرُوۡنَ ۝

65 And if thou ask them (O Muhammad) they will say: We did but talk and jest. Say: was it at Allah and His revelations and His Messenger that ye did scoff?

وَلَئِنۡ سَاَلۡتَهُمۡ لَيَقُوۡلُنَّ اِنَّمَا كُنَّا نَخُوۡضُ وَنَلۡعَبُ ۚ قُلۡ اَبِاللّٰهِ وَاٰيٰتِهٖ وَرَسُوۡلِهٖ كُنۡتُمۡ تَسۡتَهۡزِءُوۡنَ ۝

66 Make no excuse. Ye have disbelieved after your (confession of) belief. If We forgive a party of you, a party of you We shall punish because they have been guilty.

لَا تَعۡتَذِرُوۡا قَدۡ كَفَرۡتُمۡ بَعۡدَ اِيۡمَانِكُمۡ ۚ اِنۡ نَّعۡفُ عَنۡ طَآئِفَةٍ مِّنۡكُمۡ نُعَذِّبۡ طَآئِفَةً ۢ بِاَنَّهُمۡ كَانُوۡا مُجۡرِمِيۡنَ ۝

67 The hypocrites, both men and women, proceed one from another. They enjoin the wrong, and they forbid the right, and they withhold their hands (from spending for the cause of Allah). They forget Allah, so He hath forgotten them. Lo! the hypocrites, they are the transgressors.

اَلۡمُنٰفِقُوۡنَ وَالۡمُنٰفِقٰتُ بَعۡضُهُمۡ مِّنۡ بَعۡضٍ ۚ يَاۡمُرُوۡنَ بِالۡمُنۡكَرِ وَيَنۡهَوۡنَ عَنِ الۡمَعۡرُوۡفِ وَيَقۡبِضُوۡنَ اَيۡدِيَهُمۡ ۚ نَسُوا اللّٰهَ فَنَسِيَهُمۡ ۚ اِنَّ الۡمُنٰفِقِيۡنَ هُمُ الۡفٰسِقُوۡنَ ۝

68 Allah promiseth the hypocrites, both men and women, and the disbelievers fire of hell to abide therein forever. It will suffice them. Allah curseth them, and theirs is lasting torment.

وَعَدَاللّٰهُ الْمُنٰفِقِيْنَ وَالْمُنٰفِقٰتِ وَالْكُفَّارَ نَارَجَهَنَّمَ خٰلِدِيْنَ فِيْهَا ۚ هِيَ حَسْبُهُمْ ۚ وَلَعَنَهُمُ اللّٰهُ ۚ وَلَهُمْ عَذَابٌ مُّقِيْمٌ ۝

69 Even as those before you were mightier than you in strength, and more affluent than you in wealth and children. They enjoyed their lot awhile, so ye enjoy your lot awhile even as those before you did enjoy their lot awhile. And ye prate even as they prated. Such are they whose works have perished in the world and the Hereafter. Such are they who are the losers.

كَالَّذِيْنَ مِنْ قَبْلِكُمْ كَانُوْٓا أَشَدَّ مِنْكُمْ قُوَّةً وَّأَكْثَرَ أَمْوَالًا وَّأَوْلَادًا ۚ فَاسْتَمْتَعُوْا بِخَلَاقِهِمْ فَاسْتَمْتَعْتُمْ بِخَلَاقِكُمْ كَمَا اسْتَمْتَعَ الَّذِيْنَ مِنْ قَبْلِكُمْ بِخَلَاقِهِمْ وَخُضْتُمْ كَالَّذِيْ خَاضُوْٓا ۚ أُولٰئِكَ حَبِطَتْ أَعْمَالُهُمْ فِي الدُّنْيَا وَالْآخِرَةِ ۚ وَأُولٰئِكَ هُمُ الْخٰسِرُوْنَ ۝

70 Hath not the fame of those before them reached them—the folk of Noah, 'Ād, Thamūd, the folk of Abraham, the dwellers of Madyan and the disasters (which befell them)? Their messengers (from Allah) came unto them with proofs (of Allah's sovereignty). So Allah surely wronged them not, but they did wrong themselves.

أَلَمْ يَأْتِهِمْ نَبَأُ الَّذِيْنَ مِنْ قَبْلِهِمْ قَوْمِ نُوْحٍ وَعَادٍ وَّثَمُوْدَ ۚ وَقَوْمِ إِبْرَاهِيْمَ وَأَصْحٰبِ مَدْيَنَ وَالْمُؤْتَفِكٰتِ ۚ أَتَتْهُمْ رُسُلُهُمْ بِالْبَيِّنٰتِ ۚ فَمَا كَانَ اللّٰهُ لِيَظْلِمَهُمْ وَلٰكِنْ كَانُوْٓا أَنْفُسَهُمْ يَظْلِمُوْنَ ۝

71 And the believers, men and women, are protecting friends one of another; they enjoin the right and forbid the wrong, and they establish worship and they pay the poor-due, and they obey Allah and His messenger. As for these, Allah will have mercy on them. Lo! Allah is Mighty, Wise.

وَالْمُؤْمِنُوْنَ وَالْمُؤْمِنٰتُ بَعْضُهُمْ أَوْلِيَاءُ بَعْضٍ ۚ يَأْمُرُوْنَ بِالْمَعْرُوْفِ وَيَنْهَوْنَ عَنِ الْمُنْكَرِ وَيُقِيْمُوْنَ الصَّلٰوةَ وَيُؤْتُوْنَ الزَّكٰوةَ وَيُطِيْعُوْنَ اللّٰهَ وَرَسُوْلَهُ ۚ أُولٰئِكَ سَيَرْحَمُهُمُ اللّٰهُ ۚ إِنَّ اللّٰهَ عَزِيْزٌ حَكِيْمٌ ۝

72 Allah promiseth to the believers, men and women, Gardens underneath which rivers flow, wherein they will abide—blessed dwellings in Gardens of Eden. And—greater (far)!—Acceptance from Allah. That is the supreme triumph.

وَعَدَ اللّٰهُ الْمُؤْمِنِيْنَ وَالْمُؤْمِنٰتِ جَنّٰتٍ تَجْرِيْ مِنْ تَحْتِهَا الْأَنْهٰرُ خٰلِدِيْنَ فِيْهَا وَمَسٰكِنَ طَيِّبَةً فِيْ جَنّٰتِ عَدْنٍ ۚ وَرِضْوَانٌ مِّنَ اللّٰهِ أَكْبَرُ ۚ ذٰلِكَ هُوَ الْفَوْزُ الْعَظِيْمُ ۝

73 O Prophet! Strive against the disbelievers and the hypocrites! Be harsh with them. Their ultimate abode is hell, a hapless journey's end.

يَاۤ أَيُّهَا النَّبِيُّ جَاهِدِ الْكُفَّارَ وَالْمُنٰفِقِيْنَ وَاغْلُظْ عَلَيْهِمْ ۚ وَمَأْوٰىهُمْ جَهَنَّمُ ۚ وَبِئْسَ الْمَصِيْرُ ۝

74 They swear by Allah that they said nothing (wrong), yet they did say the word of disbelief, and did disbelieve after their Surrender (to Allah). And they purposed that which they could not attain, and they sought revenge only because Allah and His messenger had enriched them of His bounty. If they repent it will be better for them; and if they turn away, Allah will afflict them with a painful doom in the world and the Hereafter, and they have no protecting friend nor helper in the earth.

يَحْلِفُوْنَ بِاللّٰهِ مَا قَالُوْا ۚ وَلَقَدْ قَالُوْا كَلِمَةَ الْكُفْرِ وَكَفَرُوْا بَعْدَ إِسْلَامِهِمْ وَهَمُّوْا بِمَا لَمْ يَنَالُوْا ۚ وَمَا نَقَمُوْا إِلَّاۤ أَنْ أَغْنٰىهُمُ اللّٰهُ وَرَسُوْلُهُ مِنْ فَضْلِهِ ۚ فَإِنْ يَّتُوْبُوْا يَكُ خَيْرًا لَّهُمْ ۚ وَإِنْ يَّتَوَلَّوْا يُعَذِّبْهُمُ اللّٰهُ عَذَابًا أَلِيْمًا فِي الدُّنْيَا وَالْآخِرَةِ ۚ وَمَا لَهُمْ فِي الْأَرْضِ مِنْ وَّلِيٍّ وَّلَا نَصِيْرٍ ۝

75 And of them is he who made a covenant with Allah (saying): If He give us of His bounty; we will give alms and become of the righteous.

وَمِنْهُمْ مَّنْ عٰهَدَ اللّٰهَ لَئِنْ آتٰىنَا مِنْ فَضْلِهِ لَنَصَّدَّقَنَّ وَلَنَكُوْنَنَّ مِنَ الصّٰلِحِيْنَ ۝

76 Yet when He gave them of His bounty, they hoarded it and turned away, averse.

فَلَمَّاۤ آتٰىهُمْ مِّنْ فَضْلِهِ بَخِلُوْا بِهِ وَتَوَلَّوْا وَّهُمْ مُّعْرِضُوْنَ ۝

77 So He hath made the consequence (to be) hypocrisy in their

فَأَعْقَبَهُمْ نِفَاقًا فِيْ قُلُوْبِهِمْ إِلٰى يَوْمِ يَلْقَوْنَهُ

hearts until the day when they shall
meet Him, because they broke their
word to Allah that they promised
Him, and because they lied.

بِمَآ أَخْلَفُوا اللّٰهَ مَا وَعَدُوهُ وَبِمَا كَانُوا
يَكْذِبُونَ ۝

78 Know they not that Allah knoweth both their secret and the thought
that they confide, and that Allah is
the Knower of Things Hidden?

أَلَمْ يَعْلَمُوٓا أَنَّ اللّٰهَ يَعْلَمُ سِرَّهُمْ وَنَجْوَىٰهُمْ
وَأَنَّ اللّٰهَ عَلَّامُ الْغُيُوبِ ۝

79 Those who point at such of the
believers as give the alms willingly
and such as can find naught to give
but their endeavours, and deride
them—Allah (Himself) derideth them. Theirs will be a painful doom.

الَّذِينَ يَلْمِزُونَ الْمُطَّوِّعِينَ
مِنَ الْمُؤْمِنِينَ فِى الصَّدَقَاتِ وَالَّذِينَ
لَا يَجِدُونَ إِلَّا جُهْدَهُمْ فَيَسْخَرُونَ مِنْهُمْ سَخِرَ اللّٰهُ
مِنْهُمْ وَلَهُمْ عَذَابٌ أَلِيمٌ ۝

80 Ask forgiveness for them (O
Muhammad), or ask not forgiveness
for them; though thou ask forgiveness for them seventy times; Allah
will not forgive them. That is because they disbelieved in Allah and
His messenger, and Allah guideth
not wrongdoing folk.

اسْتَغْفِرْ لَهُمْ أَوْ لَا تَسْتَغْفِرْ لَهُمْ إِنْ تَسْتَغْفِرْ لَهُمْ
سَبْعِينَ مَرَّةً فَلَنْ يَغْفِرَ اللّٰهُ لَهُمْ ذَٰلِكَ بِأَنَّهُمْ
كَفَرُوا بِاللّٰهِ وَرَسُولِهِ وَاللّٰهُ لَا يَهْدِى
الْقَوْمَ الْفَاسِقِينَ ۝

81 Those who were left behind
rejoiced at sitting still behind the
messenger of Allah, and were averse to striving with their wealth and
their lives in Allah's way. And they
said: Go not forth in the heat! Say:
The fire of hell is more intense of
heat, if they but understood.

فَرِحَ الْمُخَلَّفُونَ بِمَقْعَدِهِمْ خِلَافَ رَسُولِ
اللّٰهِ وَكَرِهُوٓا أَنْ يُجَاهِدُوا بِأَمْوَالِهِمْ وَأَنْفُسِهِمْ فِى سَبِيلِ
اللّٰهِ وَقَالُوا لَا تَنْفِرُوا فِى الْحَرِّ قُلْ نَارُ جَهَنَّمَ
أَشَدُّ حَرًّا لَوْ كَانُوا يَفْقَهُونَ ۝

82 Then let them laugh a little and
weep much, as the reward of what
they used to earn.

فَلْيَضْحَكُوا قَلِيلًا وَلْيَبْكُوا كَثِيرًا
جَزَآءً بِمَا كَانُوا يَكْسِبُونَ ۝

83 If Allah bring thee back (from the campaign) unto a party of them and they ask of thee leave to go out (to fight), then say unto them: Ye shall never more go out with me nor fight with me against a foe. Ye were content with sitting still the first time. So sit still with those who remain behind.

فَإِن رَّجَعَكَ ٱللَّهُ إِلَىٰ طَآئِفَةٍ مِّنۡهُمۡ فَٱسۡتَـٔۡذَنُوكَ لِلۡخُرُوجِ فَقُل لَّن تَخۡرُجُواۡ مَعِىَ أَبَدًا وَلَن تُقَـٰتِلُواۡ مَعِىَ عَدُوًّاۚ إِنَّكُمۡ رَضِيتُم بِٱلۡقُعُودِ أَوَّلَ مَرَّةٍ فَٱقۡعُدُواۡ مَعَ ٱلۡخَـٰلِفِينَ ﴿٨٣﴾

84 And never (O Muhammad) pray for one of them who dieth, nor stand by his grave. Lo! they disbelieved in Allah and His messenger, and they died while they were evil-doers.

وَلَا تُصَلِّ عَلَىٰٓ أَحَدٍ مِّنۡهُم مَّاتَ أَبَدًا وَلَا تَقُمۡ عَلَىٰ قَبۡرِهِۦٓ إِنَّهُمۡ كَفَرُواۡ بِٱللَّهِ وَرَسُولِهِۦ وَمَاتُواۡ وَهُمۡ فَـٰسِقُونَ ﴿٨٤﴾

85 Let not their wealth nor their children please thee! Allah purposeth only to punish them thereby in the world, and that their souls shall pass away while they are disbelievers.

وَلَا تُعۡجِبۡكَ أَمۡوَٰلُهُمۡ وَأَوۡلَـٰدُهُمۡۚ إِنَّمَا يُرِيدُ ٱللَّهُ أَن يُعَذِّبَهُم بِهَا فِى ٱلدُّنۡيَا وَتَزۡهَقَ أَنفُسُهُمۡ وَهُمۡ كَـٰفِرُونَ ﴿٨٥﴾

86 And when a sūrah is revealed (which saith): Believe in Allah and strive along with His messenger, the men of wealth among them still ask leave of thee and say: Suffer us to be with those who sit (at home).

وَإِذَآ أُنزِلَتۡ سُورَةٌ أَنۡ ءَامِنُواۡ بِٱللَّهِ وَجَـٰهِدُواۡ مَعَ رَسُولِهِ ٱسۡتَـٔۡذَنَكَ أُوۡلُواۡ ٱلطَّوۡلِ مِنۡهُمۡ وَقَالُواۡ ذَرۡنَا نَكُن مَّعَ ٱلۡقَـٰعِدِينَ ﴿٨٦﴾

87 They are content that they should be with those who remain behind and their hearts are sealed, so that they apprehend not.

رَضُواۡ بِأَن يَكُونُواۡ مَعَ ٱلۡخَوَالِفِ وَطُبِعَ عَلَىٰ قُلُوبِهِمۡ فَهُمۡ لَا يَفۡقَهُونَ ﴿٨٧﴾

88 But the messenger and those who believe with him strive with their wealth and their lives. Such are they for whom are the good things. Such are they who are the successful.

لَـٰكِنِ ٱلرَّسُولُ وَٱلَّذِينَ ءَامَنُواۡ مَعَهُۥ جَـٰهَدُواۡ بِأَمۡوَٰلِهِمۡ وَأَنفُسِهِمۡۚ وَأُوۡلَـٰٓئِكَ لَهُمُ ٱلۡخَيۡرَٰتُۖ وَأُوۡلَـٰٓئِكَ هُمُ ٱلۡمُفۡلِحُونَ ﴿٨٨﴾

89 Allah hath made ready for them Gardens underneath which rivers flow, wherein they will abide. That is the supreme triumph.

أَعَدَّ اللَّهُ لَهُمْ جَنَّاتٍ تَجْرِى مِن تَحْتِهَا الْأَنْهَارُ خَالِدِينَ فِيهَا ذَلِكَ الْفَوْزُ الْعَظِيمُ ﴿٨٩﴾

90 And those among the wandering Arabs who had an excuse came in order that permission might be granted them. And those who lied to Allah and His messenger; sat at home. A painful doom will fall on those of them who disbelieve.

وَجَاءَ الْمُعَذِّرُونَ مِنَ الْأَعْرَابِ لِيُؤْذَنَ لَهُمْ وَقَعَدَ الَّذِينَ كَذَبُوا اللَّهَ وَرَسُولَهُ سَيُصِيبُ الَّذِينَ كَفَرُوا مِنْهُمْ عَذَابٌ أَلِيمٌ ﴿٩٠﴾

91 Not unto the weak nor unto the sick nor unto those who can find naught to spend is any fault (to be imputed though they stay at home) if they are true to Allah and His messenger. Not unto the good is there any road (of blame). Allah is Forgiving, Merciful.

لَيْسَ عَلَى الضُّعَفَاءِ وَلَا عَلَى الْمَرْضَى وَلَا عَلَى الَّذِينَ لَا يَجِدُونَ مَا يُنفِقُونَ حَرَجٌ إِذَا نَصَحُوا لِلَّهِ وَرَسُولِهِ مَا عَلَى الْمُحْسِنِينَ مِن سَبِيلٍ وَاللَّهُ غَفُورٌ رَّحِيمٌ ﴿٩١﴾

92 Nor unto those whom, when they came to thee (asking) that thou shouldest mount them, thou didst tell: I cannot find whereon to mount you. They turned back with eyes flowing with tears, for sorrow that they could not find the means to spend.

وَلَا عَلَى الَّذِينَ إِذَا مَا أَتَوْكَ لِتَحْمِلَهُمْ قُلْتَ لَا أَجِدُ مَا أَحْمِلُكُمْ عَلَيْهِ تَوَلَّوْا وَّأَعْيُنُهُمْ تَفِيضُ مِنَ الدَّمْعِ حَزَنًا أَلَّا يَجِدُوا مَا يُنفِقُونَ ﴿٩٢﴾

93 The road (of blame) is only against those who ask for leave of thee (to stay at home) when they are rich. They are content to be with those who remain behind. Allah hath sealed their hearts so that they know not.

۞ إِنَّمَا السَّبِيلُ عَلَى الَّذِينَ يَسْتَأْذِنُونَكَ وَهُمْ أَغْنِيَاءُ رَضُوا بِأَن يَكُونُوا مَعَ الْخَوَالِفِ وَطَبَعَ اللَّهُ عَلَى قُلُوبِهِمْ فَهُمْ لَا يَعْلَمُونَ ﴿٩٣﴾

94 They will make excuse to you (Muslims) when ye return unto

يَعْتَذِرُونَ إِلَيْكُمْ إِذَا رَجَعْتُمْ إِلَيْهِمْ قُل

them. Say: Make no excuse, for we shall not believe you. Allah hath told us tidings of you. Allah and His messenger will see your conduct, and then ye will be brought back unto Him, Who knoweth the invisible as well as the visible, and He will tell you what ye used to do.

لَا تَعْتَذِرُوا لَنْ نُؤْمِنَ لَكُمْ قَدْ نَبَّأَنَا اللّٰهُ مِنْ أَخْبَارِكُمْ وَسَيَرَى اللّٰهُ عَمَلَكُمْ وَرَسُولُهُ ثُمَّ تُرَدُّونَ إِلَى عَالِمِ الْغَيْبِ وَالشَّهَادَةِ فَيُنَبِّئُكُمْ بِمَا كُنْتُمْ تَعْمَلُونَ ۝

95 They will swear by Allah unto you, when ye return unto them, that ye may let them be. Let them be, for lo! they are unclean, and their abode is hell as the reward for what they used to earn.

سَيَحْلِفُونَ بِاللّٰهِ لَكُمْ إِذَا انْقَلَبْتُمْ إِلَيْهِمْ لِتُعْرِضُوا عَنْهُمْ فَأَعْرِضُوا عَنْهُمْ إِنَّهُمْ رِجْسٌ وَمَأْوَاهُمْ جَهَنَّمُ جَزَآءً بِمَا كَانُوا يَكْسِبُونَ ۝

96 They swear unto you, that ye may accept them. Though ye accept them, Allah verily accepteth not wrongdoing folk.

يَحْلِفُونَ لَكُمْ لِتَرْضَوْا عَنْهُمْ فَإِنْ تَرْضَوْا عَنْهُمْ فَإِنَّ اللّٰهَ لَا يَرْضَى عَنِ الْقَوْمِ الْفَاسِقِينَ ۝

97 The wandering Arabs are more hard in disbelief and hypocrisy, and more likely to be ignorant of the limits which Allah hath revealed unto His messenger. And Allah is Knower, Wise.

الْأَعْرَابُ أَشَدُّ كُفْرًا وَنِفَاقًا وَأَجْدَرُ أَلَّا يَعْلَمُوا حُدُودَ مَآ أَنْزَلَ اللّٰهُ عَلَى رَسُولِهِ وَاللّٰهُ عَلِيمٌ حَكِيمٌ ۝

98 And of the wandering Arabs there is he who taketh that which he expendeth (for the cause of Allah), as a loss, and awaiteth (evil) turns of fortune for you (that he may be rid of it). The evil turn of fortune will be theirs. Allah is Hearer, Knower.

وَمِنَ الْأَعْرَابِ مَنْ يَتَّخِذُ مَا يُنْفِقُ مَغْرَمًا وَيَتَرَبَّصُ بِكُمُ الدَّوَائِرَ عَلَيْهِمْ دَآئِرَةُ السَّوْءِ وَاللّٰهُ سَمِيعٌ عَلِيمٌ ۝

99 And of the wandering Arabs there is he who believeth in Allah and the Last day, and taketh that which he expendeth and also the

وَمِنَ الْأَعْرَابِ مَنْ يُؤْمِنُ بِاللّٰهِ وَالْيَوْمِ الْآخِرِ وَيَتَّخِذُ مَا يُنْفِقُ قُرُبَاتٍ عِنْدَ اللّٰهِ

prayers of the messenger as acceptable offerings in the sight of Allah. Lo! verily it is an acceptable offering for them. Allah will bring them into His mercy. Lo! Allah is Forgiving, Merciful.

وَصَلَوَاتِ الرَّسُولِ أَلَا إِنَّهَا قُرْبَةٌ لَّهُمْ سَيُدْخِلُهُمُ اللّٰهُ فِى رَحْمَتِهِ إِنَّ اللّٰهَ غَفُورٌ رَّحِيمٌ ۝

100 And the first to lead the way, of the Muhājirūn[8] and the Ansār,[9] and those who followed them in goodness—Allah is well pleased with them and they are well pleased with Him, and He hath made ready for them Gardens underneath which rivers flow, wherein they will abide forever. That is the supreme triumph.

وَالسّٰبِقُونَ الْأَوَّلُونَ مِنَ الْمُهَاجِرِينَ وَالْأَنْصَارِ وَالَّذِينَ اتَّبَعُوهُم بِإِحْسَانٍ رَّضِىَ اللّٰهُ عَنْهُمْ وَرَضُوا عَنْهُ وَأَعَدَّ لَهُمْ جَنَّٰتٍ تَجْرِى تَحْتَهَا الْأَنْهَٰرُ خَٰلِدِينَ فِيهَا أَبَدًا ذَٰلِكَ الْفَوْزُ الْعَظِيمُ ۝

101 And among those around you of the wandering Arabs there are hypocrites, and among the townspeople of Al-Madīnah (there are some who) persist in hypocrisy whom thou (O Muhammad) knowest not. We, We know them, and We shall chastise them twice; then they will be relegated to a painful doom.

وَمِمَّنْ حَوْلَكُم مِّنَ الْأَعْرَابِ مُنَافِقُونَ وَمِنْ أَهْلِ الْمَدِينَةِ مَرَدُوا عَلَى النِّفَاقِ لَا تَعْلَمُهُمْ نَحْنُ نَعْلَمُهُمْ سَنُعَذِّبُهُم مَّرَّتَيْنِ ثُمَّ يُرَدُّونَ إِلَىٰ عَذَابٍ عَظِيمٍ ۝

102 And (there are) others who have acknowledged their faults. They mixed a righteous action with another that was bad. It may be that Allah will relent toward them. Lo! Allah is Relenting, Merciful.

وَآخَرُونَ اعْتَرَفُوا بِذُنُوبِهِمْ خَلَطُوا عَمَلًا صَٰلِحًا وَآخَرَ سَيِّئًا عَسَى اللّٰهُ أَن يَتُوبَ عَلَيْهِمْ إِنَّ اللّٰهَ غَفُورٌ رَّحِيمٌ ۝

---

8. The fugitives from Makkah to Al-Madīnah.

9. The Muslims of Al-Madīnah who welcomed the fugitives from Makkah and helped the Prophet with their wealth and defended him with thier lives.

103   Take alms of their wealth, wherewith thou mayst purify them and mayst make them grow, and pray for them. Lo! thy prayer is an assuagement for them. Allah is Hearer, Knower.

خُذْ مِنْ أَمْوَالِهِمْ صَدَقَةً تُطَهِّرُهُمْ وَتُزَكِّيهِمْ بِهَا وَصَلِّ عَلَيْهِمْ إِنَّ صَلَوٰتَكَ سَكَنٌ لَّهُمْ وَاللّٰهُ سَمِيعٌ عَلِيمٌ ﴿١٠٣﴾

104   Know they not that Allah is He Who accepteth repentance from His bondmen and taketh the alms, and that Allah is He, Who is the Relenting, the Merciful.

أَلَمْ يَعْلَمُوا أَنَّ اللّٰهَ هُوَ يَقْبَلُ التَّوْبَةَ عَنْ عِبَادِهِ وَيَأْخُذُ الصَّدَقَاتِ وَأَنَّ اللّٰهَ هُوَ التَّوَّابُ الرَّحِيمُ ﴿١٠٤﴾

105   And say (unto them): Act! Allah will behold your actions, and (so will) His messenger and the believers, and ye will be brought back to the Knower of the invisible and the visible, and He will tell you what ye used to do.

وَقُلِ اعْمَلُوا فَسَيَرَى اللّٰهُ عَمَلَكُمْ وَرَسُولُهُ وَالْمُؤْمِنُونَ وَسَتُرَدُّونَ إِلَى عَالِمِ الْغَيْبِ وَالشَّهَادَةِ فَيُنَبِّئُكُمْ بِمَا كُنْتُمْ تَعْمَلُونَ ﴿١٠٥﴾

106   And (there are) others who await Allah's decree, whether He will punish them or will forgive them. Allah is Knower, Wise.

وَءَاخَرُونَ مُرْجَوْنَ لِأَمْرِ اللّٰهِ إِمَّا يُعَذِّبُهُمْ وَإِمَّا يَتُوبُ عَلَيْهِمْ وَاللّٰهُ عَلِيمٌ حَكِيمٌ ﴿١٠٦﴾

107   And as for those who chose a place of worship out of opposition and disbelief, and in order to cause dissent among the believers, and as an outpost for those who warred against Allah and His messenger aforetime, they will surely swear: we purposed naught save good. Allah beareth witness that they verily are liars.

وَالَّذِينَ اتَّخَذُوا مَسْجِدًا ضِرَارًا وَكُفْرًا وَتَفْرِيقًا بَيْنَ الْمُؤْمِنِينَ وَإِرْصَادًا لِّمَنْ حَارَبَ اللّٰهَ وَرَسُولَهُ مِنْ قَبْلُ وَلَيَحْلِفُنَّ إِنْ أَرَدْنَا إِلَّا الْحُسْنَى وَاللّٰهُ يَشْهَدُ إِنَّهُمْ لَكَاذِبُونَ ﴿١٠٧﴾

108   Never stand (to pray) there. A place of worship which was founded on piety from the first day is more worthy that thou shouldst

لَا تَقُمْ فِيهِ أَبَدًا لَّمَسْجِدٌ أُسِّسَ عَلَى التَّقْوَى مِنْ أَوَّلِ يَوْمٍ أَحَقُّ أَنْ تَقُومَ فِيهِ فِيهِ رِجَالٌ

stand (to pray) therein, wherein are men who love to purify themselves. Allah loveth the purifiers.

109   Is he then who founded his building upon piety and His good pleasure better; or he who founded his building on the brink of a crumbling, overhanging precipice so that it toppled with him into the fire of hell? Allah guideth not wrongdoing folk.

110   The building which they built will never cease to be a misgiving in their hearts unless their hearts be torn to pieces. Allah is Knower, Wise.

111   Lo! Allah hath bought from the believers their lives and their wealth because the Garden will be theirs: they shall fight in the way of Allah and shall slay and be slain. It is a promise which is binding on Him in the Torah and the Gospel and the Qur'an. Who fulfilleth His covenant better than Allah? Rejoice then in your bargain that ye have made, for that is the supreme triumph.

112   (Triumphant) are those who turn repentant (to Allah), those who serve (Him), those who praise (Him), those who fast, those who bow down, those who fall prostrate (in worship), those who enjoin the right and who forbid the wrong and those who keep the limits (ordained) of Allah—And give glad tidings to believers!

يُحِبُّونَ أَن يَتَطَهَّرُوا ۚ وَٱللَّهُ يُحِبُّ ٱلْمُطَّهِّرِينَ ۝

أَفَمَنْ أَسَّسَ بُنْيَـٰنَهُ عَلَىٰ تَقْوَىٰ مِنَ ٱللَّهِ وَرِضْوَٰنٍ خَيْرٌ أَم مَّنْ أَسَّسَ بُنْيَـٰنَهُ عَلَىٰ شَفَا جُرُفٍ هَارٍ فَٱنْهَارَ بِهِۦ فِى نَارِ جَهَنَّمَ ۗ وَٱللَّهُ لَا يَهْدِى ٱلْقَوْمَ ٱلظَّـٰلِمِينَ ۝

لَا يَزَالُ بُنْيَـٰنُهُمُ ٱلَّذِى بَنَوْا۟ رِيبَةً فِى قُلُوبِهِمْ إِلَّآ أَن تَقَطَّعَ قُلُوبُهُمْ ۗ وَٱللَّهُ عَلِيمٌ حَكِيمٌ ۝

۞ إِنَّ ٱللَّهَ ٱشْتَرَىٰ مِنَ ٱلْمُؤْمِنِينَ أَنفُسَهُمْ وَأَمْوَٰلَهُم بِأَنَّ لَهُمُ ٱلْجَنَّةَ ۚ يُقَـٰتِلُونَ فِى سَبِيلِ ٱللَّهِ فَيَقْتُلُونَ وَيُقْتَلُونَ ۖ وَعْدًا عَلَيْهِ حَقًّا فِى ٱلتَّوْرَىٰةِ وَٱلْإِنجِيلِ وَٱلْقُرْءَانِ ۚ وَمَنْ أَوْفَىٰ بِعَهْدِهِۦ مِنَ ٱللَّهِ ۚ فَٱسْتَبْشِرُوا۟ بِبَيْعِكُمُ ٱلَّذِى بَايَعْتُم بِهِۦ ۚ وَذَٰلِكَ هُوَ ٱلْفَوْزُ ٱلْعَظِيمُ ۝

ٱلتَّـٰٓئِبُونَ ٱلْعَـٰبِدُونَ ٱلْحَـٰمِدُونَ ٱلسَّـٰٓئِحُونَ ٱلرَّٰكِعُونَ ٱلسَّـٰجِدُونَ ٱلْءَامِرُونَ بِٱلْمَعْرُوفِ وَٱلنَّاهُونَ عَنِ ٱلْمُنكَرِ وَٱلْحَـٰفِظُونَ لِحُدُودِ ٱللَّهِ ۗ وَبَشِّرِ ٱلْمُؤْمِنِينَ ۝

113 It is not for the Prophet, and those who believe, to pray for the forgiveness of idolaters even though they may be near of kin (to them) after it hath become clear that they are people of hell fire.

مَا كَانَ لِلنَّبِيِّ وَالَّذِينَ ءَامَنُوٓاۡ أَن يَسۡتَغۡفِرُواۡ لِلۡمُشۡرِكِينَ وَلَوۡ كَانُوٓاۡ أُوْلِي قُرۡبَىٰ مِنۢ بَعۡدِ مَا تَبَيَّنَ لَهُمۡ أَنَّهُمۡ أَصۡحَٰبُ ٱلۡجَحِيمِ ۝

114 The prayer of Abraham for the forgiveness of his father was only because of a promise he had promised him, but when it had become clear unto him that he (his father) was an enemy to Allah he (Abraham) disowned him. Lo! Abraham was soft of heart, forbearing.

وَمَا كَانَ ٱسۡتِغۡفَارُ إِبۡرَٰهِيمَ لِأَبِيهِ إِلَّا عَن مَّوۡعِدَةٍ وَعَدَهَآ إِيَّاهُ فَلَمَّا تَبَيَّنَ لَهُۥٓ أَنَّهُۥ عَدُوٌّ لِّلَّهِ تَبَرَّأَ مِنۡهُ إِنَّ إِبۡرَٰهِيمَ لَأَوَّٰهٌ حَلِيمٌ ۝

115 It was never Allah's (part) that he should send a folk astray after He had guided them until He had made clear unto them what they should avoid. Lo! Allah is Aware of all things.

وَمَا كَانَ ٱللَّهُ لِيُضِلَّ قَوۡمَۢا بَعۡدَ إِذۡ هَدَىٰهُمۡ حَتَّىٰ يُبَيِّنَ لَهُم مَّا يَتَّقُونَ إِنَّ ٱللَّهَ بِكُلِّ شَيۡءٍ عَلِيمٌ ۝

116 Lo ! Allah! Unto Him belongeth the sovereignty of the heavens and the earth. He quickeneth and He giveth death. And ye have, instead of Allah, no protecting friend nor helper.

إِنَّ ٱللَّهَ لَهُۥ مُلۡكُ ٱلسَّمَٰوَٰتِ وَٱلۡأَرۡضِ يُحۡيِۦ وَيُمِيتُ وَمَا لَكُم مِّن دُونِ ٱللَّهِ مِن وَلِيٍّ وَلَا نَصِيرٍ ۝

117 Allah hath turned in mercy to the Prophet, and to the Muhājirūn and the Ansār[10] who followed him in the hour of hardship. After the hearts of a party of them had almost swerved aside, then turned He unto them in mercy. Lo! He is Full of Pity, Merciful for them.

لَّقَد تَّابَ ٱللَّهُ عَلَى ٱلنَّبِيِّ وَٱلۡمُهَٰجِرِينَ وَٱلۡأَنصَارِ ٱلَّذِينَ ٱتَّبَعُوهُ فِي سَاعَةِ ٱلۡعُسۡرَةِ مِنۢ بَعۡدِ مَا كَادَ يَزِيغُ قُلُوبُ فَرِيقٍ مِّنۡهُمۡ ثُمَّ تَابَ عَلَيۡهِمۡ إِنَّهُۥ بِهِمۡ رَءُوفٌ رَّحِيمٌ ۝

---

10. See v. 100, footnotes.

118   And to the three also (did He turn in mercy) who were left behind, when the earth, vast as it is, became straitened for them, and their own souls were straitened for them till they bethought them that there is no refuge from Allah save toward Him. Then turned He unto them in mercy that they (too) might turn (repentant unto Him).[11] Lo! Allah! He is the Relenting, the Merciful.

وَعَلَى الثَّلَاثَةِ الَّذِينَ خُلِّفُوا حَتَّىٰ إِذَا ضَاقَتْ عَلَيْهِمُ الْأَرْضُ بِمَا رَحُبَتْ وَضَاقَتْ عَلَيْهِمْ أَنفُسُهُمْ وَظَنُّوا أَن لَّا مَلْجَأَ مِنَ اللَّهِ إِلَّا إِلَيْهِ ثُمَّ تَابَ عَلَيْهِمْ لِيَتُوبُوا إِنَّ اللَّهَ هُوَ التَّوَّابُ الرَّحِيمُ ۝

119   O ye who believe! Be careful of your duty to Allah, and be with the truthful.

يَا أَيُّهَا الَّذِينَ آمَنُوا اتَّقُوا اللَّهَ وَكُونُوا مَعَ الصَّادِقِينَ ۝

120   It is not for the townsfolk of Al-Madīnah and for those around them of the wandering Arabs to stay behind the messenger of Allah and prefer their lives to his life. That is because neither thirst nor toil nor hunger afflicteth them in the way of Allah, nor step they any step that angereth the disbelievers, nor gain they from the enemy a gain, but a good deed is recorded for them therefore. Lo! Allah loseth not the wages of the good.

مَا كَانَ لِأَهْلِ الْمَدِينَةِ وَمَنْ حَوْلَهُم مِّنَ الْأَعْرَابِ أَن يَتَخَلَّفُوا عَن رَّسُولِ اللَّهِ وَلَا يَرْغَبُوا بِأَنفُسِهِمْ عَن نَّفْسِهِ ذَٰلِكَ بِأَنَّهُمْ لَا يُصِيبُهُمْ ظَمَأٌ وَلَا نَصَبٌ وَلَا مَخْمَصَةٌ فِي سَبِيلِ اللَّهِ وَلَا يَطَئُونَ مَوْطِئًا يَغِيظُ الْكُفَّارَ وَلَا يَنَالُونَ مِنْ عَدُوٍّ نَّيْلًا إِلَّا كُتِبَ لَهُم بِهِ عَمَلٌ صَالِحٌ إِنَّ اللَّهَ لَا يُضِيعُ أَجْرَ الْمُحْسِنِينَ ۝

121   Nor spend they any spending, small or great, nor do they cross a valley, but it is recorded for them, that Allah may repay them the best of what they used to do.

وَلَا يُنفِقُونَ نَفَقَةً صَغِيرَةً وَلَا كَبِيرَةً وَلَا يَقْطَعُونَ وَادِيًا إِلَّا كُتِبَ لَهُمْ لِيَجْزِيَهُمُ اللَّهُ أَحْسَنَ مَا كَانُوا يَعْمَلُونَ ۝

---

11. The reference is to three men of Al-Madīnah who were ostracised on account of a misdeed, but afterwards repented and were forgiven.

122   And the believers should not
all go out to fight. Of every troop
of them, a party only should go
forth, that they (who are left behind) may gain sound knowledge in
religion, and that they may warn
their folk when they return to them,
so that they may beware.

﷽ وَمَا كَانَ الْمُؤْمِنُونَ لِيَنْفِرُوا كَآفَّةً
فَلَوْلَا نَفَرَ مِنْ كُلِّ فِرْقَةٍ مِّنْهُمْ طَآئِفَةٌ لِّيَتَفَقَّهُوا
فِي الدِّينِ وَلِيُنْذِرُوا قَوْمَهُمْ إِذَا رَجَعُوا إِلَيْهِمْ
لَعَلَّهُمْ يَحْذَرُونَ ﴿١٢٢﴾

123   O ye who believe! Fight
those of the disbelievers who are
near to you, and let them find hars-
hness in you, and know that Allah
is with those who keep their duty
(unto Him).

يَا أَيُّهَا الَّذِينَ آمَنُوا قَاتِلُوا الَّذِينَ يَلُونَكُمْ
مِّنَ الْكُفَّارِ وَلْيَجِدُوا فِيكُمْ غِلْظَةً
وَاعْلَمُوا أَنَّ اللَّهَ مَعَ الْمُتَّقِينَ ﴿١٢٣﴾

124   And whenever a sūrah is
revealed there are some of them
who say: The faith of which one of
you hath this increased? As for
those who believe, it hath increased
them in faith and they rejoice
(therefore).

وَإِذَا مَا أُنْزِلَتْ سُورَةٌ فَمِنْهُمْ مَّنْ يَقُولُ أَيُّكُمْ
زَادَتْهُ هَذِهِ إِيمَانًا فَأَمَّا الَّذِينَ آمَنُوا
فَزَادَتْهُمْ إِيمَانًا وَهُمْ يَسْتَبْشِرُونَ ﴿١٢٤﴾

125   But as for those in whose
hearts is disease, it only addeth
wickedness to their wickedness, and
they die while they are disbelievers.

وَأَمَّا الَّذِينَ فِي قُلُوبِهِمْ مَّرَضٌ فَزَادَتْهُمْ
رِجْسًا إِلَى رِجْسِهِمْ وَمَاتُوا وَهُمْ
كَافِرُونَ ﴿١٢٥﴾

126   See they not that they are
tested once or twice in every year?
Still they turn not in repentance,
neither pay they heed.

أَوَلَا يَرَوْنَ أَنَّهُمْ يُفْتَنُونَ فِي كُلِّ عَامٍ
مَّرَّةً أَوْ مَرَّتَيْنِ ثُمَّ لَا يَتُوبُونَ وَلَا هُمْ
يَذَّكَّرُونَ ﴿١٢٦﴾

127   And whenever a sūrah is
revealed, they look one at another
(as who should say): Doth anybody
see you? Then they turn away.
Allah turneth away their hearts
because they are a folk who understand not.

وَإِذَا مَا أُنْزِلَتْ سُورَةٌ نَّظَرَ بَعْضُهُمْ إِلَى بَعْضٍ
هَلْ يَرَاكُمْ مِّنْ أَحَدٍ ثُمَّ انْصَرَفُوا
صَرَفَ اللَّهُ قُلُوبَهُمْ بِأَنَّهُمْ قَوْمٌ لَا يَفْقَهُونَ ﴿١٢٧﴾

128 There hath come unto you a messenger, (one) of yourselves, unto whom aught that ye are overburdened is grievous, full of concern for you, for the believers full of pity, merciful.

لَقَدْ جَآءَكُمْ رَسُولٌ مِّنْ أَنفُسِكُمْ عَزِيزٌ عَلَيْهِ مَا عَنِتُّمْ حَرِيصٌ عَلَيْكُم بِالْمُؤْمِنِينَ رَءُوفٌ رَّحِيمٌ ﴿١٢٨﴾

129 Now, if they turn away (O Muhammad) say: Allah sufficeth me. There is no God save Him. In Him have I put my trust, and He is Lord of the Tremendous Throne.

فَإِن تَوَلَّوْاْ فَقُلْ حَسْبِيَ اللَّهُ لَا إِلَٰهَ إِلَّا هُوَ عَلَيْهِ تَوَكَّلْتُ وَهُوَ رَبُّ الْعَرْشِ الْعَظِيمِ ﴿١٢٩﴾

Yūnus
(Jonah)

Derives its title from v. 99: "If only there had been a community (of those that were) destroyed of old that believed and profited by its belief as did the folk of Jonah!"; As is the case with nearly all the Makkan sūrahs, the date of revelation is uncertain, on account of the dearth of historical allusion. All that can with certainty be said is, that it belongs to the latest group of Makkan sūrahs, and must therefore have been revealed at some time during the last four years before the Hijrah.

A late Makkan sūrah, with the exception of three verses revealed at Al-Madīnah.

In the name of Allah, the Beneficent, the Merciful.

بِسْمِ اللَّهِ الرَّحْمَنِ الرَّحِيمِ

1   Alif. Lām. Rā.[1] These are verses of the Wise Scripture.

الَرَ تِلْكَ ءَايَتُ ٱلْكِتَبِ ٱلْحَكِيمِ ﴿١﴾

2   Is it a wonder for mankind that We have inspired a man among them, saying: Warn mankind and bring unto those who believe the good tidings that they have a sure footing with their Lord? The disbelievers say: Lo! this is a mere wizard.

أَكَانَ لِلنَّاسِ عَجَبًا أَنْ أَوْحَيْنَآ إِلَى رَجُلٍ مِّنْهُمْ أَنْ أَنذِرِ ٱلنَّاسَ وَبَشِّرِ ٱلَّذِينَ ءَامَنُوٓا أَنَّ لَهُمْ قَدَمَ صِدْقٍ عِندَ رَبِّهِمْ قَالَ ٱلْكَفِرُونَ إِنَّ هَذَا لَسَحِرٌ مُّبِينٌ ﴿٢﴾

---

1. See Sūrah 2, v. 1, footnote.

3 Lo! your Lord is Allah Who created the heavens and the earth in six days,[2] then He established Himself upon the Throne, directing all things. There is no intercessor (with Him) save after His permission. That is Allah, your Lord, so worship Him. Oh, will ye not mind?

إِنَّ رَبَّكُمُ اللَّهُ الَّذِى خَلَقَ السَّمَوَاتِ وَالْأَرْضَ فِى سِتَّةِ أَيَّامٍ ثُمَّ اسْتَوَىٰ عَلَى الْعَرْشِ يُدَبِّرُ الْأَمْرَ مَا مِن شَفِيعٍ إِلَّا مِنْ بَعْدِ إِذْنِهِ ذَٰلِكُمُ اللَّهُ رَبُّكُمْ فَاعْبُدُوهُ أَفَلَا تَذَكَّرُونَ ۝

4 Unto Him is the return of all of you; it is a promise of Allah in truth. Lo! He produceth creation, then reproduceth it, that He may reward those who believe and do good works with equity; while, as for those who disbelieve, theirs will be a boiling drink and painful doom because they disbelieved.

إِلَيْهِ مَرْجِعُكُمْ جَمِيعًا وَعْدَ اللَّهِ حَقًّا إِنَّهُ يَبْدَؤُا الْخَلْقَ ثُمَّ يُعِيدُهُ لِيَجْزِىَ الَّذِينَ ءَامَنُوا وَعَمِلُوا الصَّٰلِحَٰتِ بِالْقِسْطِ وَالَّذِينَ كَفَرُوا لَهُمْ شَرَابٌ مِّنْ حَمِيمٍ وَعَذَابٌ أَلِيمٌ بِمَا كَانُوا يَكْفُرُونَ ۝

5 He it is who appointed the sun a splendour and the moon a light, and measured for her stages, that ye might know the number of the years, and the reckoning. Allah created not (all) that save in truth. He detaileth the revelations for people who have knowledge.

هُوَ الَّذِى جَعَلَ الشَّمْسَ ضِيَآءً وَالْقَمَرَ نُورًا وَقَدَّرَهُ مَنَازِلَ لِتَعْلَمُوا عَدَدَ السِّنِينَ وَالْحِسَابَ مَا خَلَقَ اللَّهُ ذَٰلِكَ إِلَّا بِالْحَقِّ يُفَصِّلُ الْآيَٰتِ لِقَوْمٍ يَعْلَمُونَ ۝

6 Lo! in the difference of day and night and all that Allah hath created in the heavens and the earth are portents, verily, for folk who ward off (evil).

إِنَّ فِى اخْتِلَٰفِ الَّيْلِ وَالنَّهَارِ وَمَا خَلَقَ اللَّهُ فِى السَّمَٰوَٰتِ وَالْأَرْضِ لَآيَٰتٍ لِّقَوْمٍ يَتَّقُونَ ۝

7 Lo! those who expect not the meeting with Us, but desire the life of the world and feel secure therein,

إِنَّ الَّذِينَ لَا يَرْجُونَ لِقَآءَنَا وَرَضُوا بِالْحَيَوٰةِ الدُّنْيَا

2. See (22: 47), (32: 5) and (70: 4).

and those who are neglectful of Our revelations;

8 Their home will be the Fire because of what they used to earn.

9 Lo! those who believe and do good works, their Lord guideth them by their faith. Rivers will flow beneath them in the Gardens of Delight;

10 Their prayer therein will be: Glory be to Thee, O Allah! and their greeting therein will be: Peace. And the conclusion of their prayer will be: Praise be to Allah, Lord of the Worlds!

11 If Allah were to hasten on for men the ill (that they have earned) as they would hasten on the good, their respite would already have expired. But We suffer those who look not for the meeting with Us, to wander blindly on in their contumacy.

12 And if misfortune touch a man he crieth unto Us, (while reclining) on his side, or sitting or standing, but when We have relieved him of the misfortune he goeth his way as though he had not cried unto Us because of a misfortune that afflicted him. Thus have the deeds of the transgressors been made fairseeming to the prodigal.

13 We destroyed the generations before you when they did wrong; and their messengers (from Allah) came unto them with clear proofs

وَاطْمَأَنُّوا بِهَا وَالَّذِينَ هُمْ عَنْ ءَايَٰتِنَا غَٰفِلُونَ ۝

أُو۟لَٰٓئِكَ مَأْوَىٰهُمُ النَّارُ بِمَا كَانُوا۟ يَكْسِبُونَ ۝

إِنَّ الَّذِينَ ءَامَنُوا۟ وَعَمِلُوا۟ الصَّٰلِحَٰتِ يَهْدِيهِمْ رَبُّهُم بِإِيمَٰنِهِمْ تَجْرِى مِن تَحْتِهِمُ الْأَنْهَٰرُ فِى جَنَّٰتِ النَّعِيمِ ۝

دَعْوَىٰهُمْ فِيهَا سُبْحَٰنَكَ اللَّٰهُمَّ وَتَحِيَّتُهُمْ فِيهَا سَلَٰمٌ وَءَاخِرُ دَعْوَىٰهُمْ أَنِ الْحَمْدُ لِلَّٰهِ رَبِّ الْعَٰلَمِينَ ۝

۞ وَلَوْ يُعَجِّلُ اللَّٰهُ لِلنَّاسِ الشَّرَّ اسْتِعْجَالَهُم بِالْخَيْرِ لَقُضِىَ إِلَيْهِمْ أَجَلُهُمْ فَنَذَرُ الَّذِينَ لَا يَرْجُونَ لِقَآءَنَا فِى طُغْيَٰنِهِمْ يَعْمَهُونَ ۝

وَإِذَا مَسَّ الْإِنسَٰنَ الضُّرُّ دَعَانَا لِجَنبِهِۦٓ أَوْ قَاعِدًا أَوْ قَآئِمًا فَلَمَّا كَشَفْنَا عَنْهُ ضُرَّهُۥ مَرَّ كَأَن لَّمْ يَدْعُنَآ إِلَىٰ ضُرٍّ مَّسَّهُۥ كَذَٰلِكَ زُيِّنَ لِلْمُسْرِفِينَ مَا كَانُوا۟ يَعْمَلُونَ ۝

وَلَقَدْ أَهْلَكْنَا الْقُرُونَ مِن قَبْلِكُمْ لَمَّا ظَلَمُوا۟ وَجَآءَتْهُمْ رُسُلُهُم بِالْبَيِّنَٰتِ وَمَا كَانُوا۟ لِيُؤْمِنُوا۟

(of His Sovereignty) but they would not believe. Thus do We reward the guilty folk:

14 Then We appointed you viceroys in the earth after them, that We might see how ye behave.

15 And when Our clear revelations are recited unto them they who look not for the meeting with Us say: Bring a Lecture[3] other than this, or change it. Say (O Muhammad): It is not for me to change it of my own accord. I only follow that which is inspired in me. Lo! If I disobey my Lord, I fear the retribution of an awful Day.

16 Say: If Allah had so willed I should not have recited it to you nor would He have made it known to you. I dwelt among you a whole lifetime before it (came to me). Have ye then no sense?

17 Who doeth greater wrong than he who inventeth a lie concerning Allah and denieth His revelations? Lo! the guilty never are successful.

18 They worship beside Allah that which neither hurteth them nor profiteth them, and they say: These are our intercessors with Allah. Say: Would ye inform Allah of (something) that He knoweth not in the heavens or in the earth? Praised be

كَذَٰلِكَ نَجْزِى ٱلْقَوْمَ ٱلْمُجْرِمِينَ ۝

ثُمَّ جَعَلْنَٰكُمْ خَلَٰٓئِفَ فِى ٱلْأَرْضِ مِنۢ بَعْدِهِمْ لِنَنظُرَ كَيْفَ تَعْمَلُونَ ۝

وَإِذَا تُتْلَىٰ عَلَيْهِمْ ءَايَاتُنَا بَيِّنَٰتٍ قَالَ ٱلَّذِينَ لَا يَرْجُونَ لِقَآءَنَا ٱئْتِ بِقُرْءَانٍ غَيْرِ هَٰذَآ أَوْ بَدِّلْهُ قُلْ مَا يَكُونُ لِىٓ أَنْ أُبَدِّلَهُۥ مِن تِلْقَآئِ نَفْسِىٓ إِنْ أَتَّبِعُ إِلَّا مَا يُوحَىٰٓ إِلَىَّ إِنِّىٓ أَخَافُ إِنْ عَصَيْتُ رَبِّى عَذَابَ يَوْمٍ عَظِيمٍ ۝

قُل لَّوْ شَآءَ ٱللَّهُ مَا تَلَوْتُهُۥ عَلَيْكُمْ وَلَآ أَدْرَىٰكُم بِهِۦ فَقَدْ لَبِثْتُ فِيكُمْ عُمُرًا مِّن قَبْلِهِۦٓ أَفَلَا تَعْقِلُونَ ۝

فَمَنْ أَظْلَمُ مِمَّنِ ٱفْتَرَىٰ عَلَى ٱللَّهِ كَذِبًا أَوْ كَذَّبَ بِـَٔايَٰتِهِۦٓ إِنَّهُۥ لَا يُفْلِحُ ٱلْمُجْرِمُونَ ۝

وَيَعْبُدُونَ مِن دُونِ ٱللَّهِ مَا لَا يَضُرُّهُمْ وَلَا يَنفَعُهُمْ وَيَقُولُونَ هَٰٓؤُلَآءِ شُفَعَٰٓؤُنَا عِندَ ٱللَّهِ قُلْ أَتُنَبِّئُونَ ٱللَّهَ بِمَا لَا يَعْلَمُ فِى ٱلسَّمَٰوَٰتِ وَلَا فِى ٱلْأَرْضِ سُبْحَٰنَهُۥ وَتَعَٰلَىٰ

---

3. Ar. *Qur'an.*

عَمَّا يُشْرِكُونَ ۞

He and high exalted above all that ye associate (with Him)!

19 Mankind were but one community; then they differed; and had it not been for a word that had already gone forth from thy Lord, it had been judged between them in respect of that wherein they differ.

وَمَا كَانَ ٱلنَّاسُ إِلَّا أُمَّةً وَٰحِدَةً فَٱخۡتَلَفُوا۟ وَلَوۡلَا كَلِمَةٌ سَبَقَتۡ مِن رَّبِّكَ لَقُضِيَ بَيۡنَهُمۡ فِيمَا فِيهِ يَخۡتَلِفُونَ ۞

20 And they will say: If only a portent were sent down upon him from his Lord! Then say (O Muḥammad): The Unseen belongeth to Allah. So wait! Lo, I am waiting with you.

وَيَقُولُونَ لَوۡلَآ أُنزِلَ عَلَيۡهِ ءَايَةٌ مِّن رَّبِّهِۦ فَقُلۡ إِنَّمَا ٱلۡغَيۡبُ لِلَّهِ فَٱنتَظِرُوٓا۟ إِنِّي مَعَكُم مِّنَ ٱلۡمُنتَظِرِينَ ۞

21 And when We cause mankind to taste of mercy after some adversity which had afflicted them, behold! they have some plot against Our revelations. Say: Allah is more swift in plotting. Lo! Our messengers write down that which ye plot.

وَإِذَآ أَذَقۡنَا ٱلنَّاسَ رَحۡمَةً مِّنۢ بَعۡدِ ضَرَّآءَ مَسَّتۡهُمۡ إِذَا لَهُم مَّكۡرٌ فِيٓ ءَايَاتِنَا قُلِ ٱللَّهُ أَسۡرَعُ مَكۡرًا إِنَّ رُسُلَنَا يَكۡتُبُونَ مَا تَمۡكُرُونَ ۞

22 He it is Who maketh you to go on the land and the sea till, when ye are in the ships and they sail with them with a fair breeze and they are glad therein, a storm-wind reacheth them and the wave cometh unto them from every side and they deem that they are overwhelmed therein; (then) they cry unto Allah, making their faith pure for Him only; If Thou deliver us from this, we truly will be of the thankful.

هُوَ ٱلَّذِي يُسَيِّرُكُمۡ فِي ٱلۡبَرِّ وَٱلۡبَحۡرِ حَتَّىٰٓ إِذَا كُنتُمۡ فِي ٱلۡفُلۡكِ وَجَرَيۡنَ بِهِم بِرِيحٍ طَيِّبَةٍ وَفَرِحُوا۟ بِهَا جَآءَتۡهَا رِيحٌ عَاصِفٌ وَجَآءَهُمُ ٱلۡمَوۡجُ مِن كُلِّ مَكَانٍ وَظَنُّوٓا۟ أَنَّهُمۡ أُحِيطَ بِهِمۡ دَعَوُا۟ ٱللَّهَ مُخۡلِصِينَ لَهُ ٱلدِّينَ لَئِنۡ أَنجَيۡتَنَا مِنۡ هَٰذِهِۦ لَنَكُونَنَّ مِنَ ٱلشَّٰكِرِينَ ۞

23 Yet when He hath delivered them, behold! they rebel in the earth wrongfully. O mankind! Your rebellion is only against yourselves.

فَلَمَّآ أَنجَىٰهُمۡ إِذَا هُمۡ يَبۡغُونَ فِي ٱلۡأَرۡضِ بِغَيۡرِ ٱلۡحَقِّ يَٰٓأَيُّهَا ٱلنَّاسُ إِنَّمَا بَغۡيُكُمۡ عَلَىٰٓ أَنفُسِكُم

(Ye have) enjoyment of the life of the world; then unto Us is your return and We shall proclaim unto you what ye used to do.

مَتَاعَ ٱلْحَيَوٰةِ ٱلدُّنْيَا ثُمَّ إِلَيْنَا مَرْجِعُكُمْ فَنُنَبِّئُكُمْ بِمَا كُنْتُمْ تَعْمَلُونَ ۝

24 The similitude of the life of the world is only as water which We send down from the sky, then the earth's growth of that which men and cattle eat mingleth with it till, when the earth hath taken on her ornaments and is embellished, and her people deem that they are masters of her, Our commandment cometh by night or by day and we make it as reaped corn as if it had not flourished yesterday. Thus do We expound the revelations for people who reflect.

إِنَّمَا مَثَلُ ٱلْحَيَوٰةِ ٱلدُّنْيَا كَمَاءٍ أَنزَلْنَٰهُ مِنَ ٱلسَّمَاءِ فَٱخْتَلَطَ بِهِۦ نَبَاتُ ٱلْأَرْضِ مِمَّا يَأْكُلُ ٱلنَّاسُ وَٱلْأَنْعَٰمُ حَتَّىٰٓ إِذَآ أَخَذَتِ ٱلْأَرْضُ زُخْرُفَهَا وَٱزَّيَّنَتْ وَظَنَّ أَهْلُهَآ أَنَّهُمْ قَٰدِرُونَ عَلَيْهَآ أَتَىٰهَآ أَمْرُنَا لَيْلًا أَوْ نَهَارًا فَجَعَلْنَٰهَا حَصِيدًا كَأَن لَّمْ تَغْنَ بِٱلْأَمْسِ كَذَٰلِكَ نُفَصِّلُ ٱلْآيَٰتِ لِقَوْمٍ يَتَفَكَّرُونَ ۝

25 And Allah summoneth to the abode of peace, and leadeth whom He will to a straight path.

وَٱللَّهُ يَدْعُوٓا۟ إِلَىٰ دَارِ ٱلسَّلَٰمِ وَيَهْدِى مَن يَشَآءُ إِلَىٰ صِرَٰطٍ مُّسْتَقِيمٍ ۝

26 For those who do good is the best (reward) and more (thereto). Neither dust nor ignominy cometh near their faces. Such are rightful owners of the Garden; they will abide therein.

لِّلَّذِينَ أَحْسَنُوا۟ ٱلْحُسْنَىٰ وَزِيَادَةٌ وَلَا يَرْهَقُ وُجُوهَهُمْ قَتَرٌ وَلَا ذِلَّةٌ أُو۟لَٰٓئِكَ أَصْحَٰبُ ٱلْجَنَّةِ هُمْ فِيهَا خَٰلِدُونَ ۝

27 And those who earn ill deeds, (for them) requital of each ill deed by the like thereof; and ignominy overtaketh them—They have no protector from Allah—as if their faces had been covered with a cloak of darkest night. Such are rightful owners of the Fire; they will abide therein.

وَٱلَّذِينَ كَسَبُوا۟ ٱلسَّيِّئَاتِ جَزَآءُ سَيِّئَةٍ بِمِثْلِهَا وَتَرْهَقُهُمْ ذِلَّةٌ مَّا لَهُم مِّنَ ٱللَّهِ مِنْ عَاصِمٍ كَأَنَّمَآ أُغْشِيَتْ وُجُوهُهُمْ قِطَعًا مِّنَ ٱلَّيْلِ مُظْلِمًا أُو۟لَٰٓئِكَ أَصْحَٰبُ ٱلنَّارِ هُمْ فِيهَا خَٰلِدُونَ ۝

28 On the day when We gather them all together, then We say unto those who ascribed partners (unto Us): Stand back, ye and your (pretended) partners (of Allah)! And We separate them, the one from the other, and their (pretended) partners say: It was not us ye worshipped.

وَيَوْمَ نَحْشُرُهُمْ جَمِيعًا ثُمَّ نَقُولُ لِلَّذِينَ أَشْرَكُوا مَكَانَكُمْ أَنْتُمْ وَشُرَكَاؤُكُمْ فَزَيَّلْنَا بَيْنَهُمْ وَقَالَ شُرَكَاؤُهُم مَّا كُنْتُمْ إِيَّانَا تَعْبُدُونَ ﴿٢٨﴾

29 Allah sufficeth as a witness between us and you, that we were unaware of your worship.

فَكَفَىٰ بِاللَّهِ شَهِيدًا بَيْنَنَا وَبَيْنَكُمْ إِن كُنَّا عَنْ عِبَادَتِكُمْ لَغَافِلِينَ ﴿٢٩﴾

30 There doth every soul experience that which it did aforetime, and they are returned unto Allah, their rightful Lord, and that which they used to invent hath failed them.

هُنَالِكَ تَبْلُو كُلُّ نَفْسٍ مَّا أَسْلَفَتْ وَرُدُّوا إِلَى اللَّهِ مَوْلَاهُمُ الْحَقِّ وَضَلَّ عَنْهُم مَّا كَانُوا يَفْتَرُونَ ﴿٣٠﴾

31 Say (unto them, O Muhammad): Who provideth for you from the sky and the earth, or Who owneth hearing and sight; and Who bringeth forth the living from the dead and bringeth forth the dead from the living; and Who directeth the course? They will say: Allah. Then say: Will ye not then keep your duty (unto Him)?

قُلْ مَن يَرْزُقُكُم مِّنَ السَّمَاءِ وَالْأَرْضِ أَمَّن يَمْلِكُ السَّمْعَ وَالْأَبْصَارَ وَمَن يُخْرِجُ الْحَيَّ مِنَ الْمَيِّتِ وَيُخْرِجُ الْمَيِّتَ مِنَ الْحَيِّ وَمَن يُدَبِّرُ الْأَمْرَ فَسَيَقُولُونَ اللَّهُ فَقُلْ أَفَلَا تَتَّقُونَ ﴿٣١﴾

32 Such then is Allah, your rightful Lord. After the Truth what is there saving error? How then are ye turned away!

فَذَٰلِكُمُ اللَّهُ رَبُّكُمُ الْحَقُّ فَمَاذَا بَعْدَ الْحَقِّ إِلَّا الضَّلَالُ فَأَنَّىٰ تُصْرَفُونَ ﴿٣٢﴾

33 Thus is the Word of thy Lord justified concerning those who do wrong; that they believe not.

كَذَٰلِكَ حَقَّتْ كَلِمَتُ رَبِّكَ عَلَى الَّذِينَ فَسَقُوا أَنَّهُمْ لَا يُؤْمِنُونَ ﴿٣٣﴾

34 Say: Is there of your partners (whom ye ascribe unto Allah) one that produceth Creation and then reproduceth it? Say: Allah produceth creation, then reproduceth it. How then, are ye misled!

قُلْ هَلْ مِنْ شُرَكَآئِكُمْ مَّنْ يَبْدَؤُا الْخَلْقَ ثُمَّ يُعِيدُهُ ۚ قُلِ اللهُ يَبْدَؤُا الْخَلْقَ ثُمَّ يُعِيدُهُ ۖ فَأَنَّىٰ تُؤْفَكُونَ ۝

35 Say: Is there of your partners (whom ye ascribe unto Allah) one that leadeth to the Truth? Say: Allah leadeth to the Truth. Is He Who leadeth to the Truth more deserving that He should be followed, or he who findeth not the way unless he (himself) be guided. What aileth you? How judge ye?

قُلْ هَلْ مِنْ شُرَكَآئِكُمْ مَّنْ يَهْدِىٓ إِلَى الْحَقِّ ۚ قُلِ اللهُ يَهْدِى لِلْحَقِّ ۗ أَفَمَنْ يَهْدِىٓ إِلَى الْحَقِّ أَحَقُّ أَنْ يُتَّبَعَ أَمَّنْ لَّا يَهِدِّىٓ إِلَّآ أَنْ يُهْدَىٰ ۖ فَمَا لَكُمْ ۖ كَيْفَ تَحْكُمُونَ ۝

36 Most of them follow naught but conjecture. Assuredly conjecture can by no means take the place of truth. Lo! Allah is Aware of what they do.

وَمَا يَتَّبِعُ أَكْثَرُهُمْ إِلَّا ظَنًّا ۚ إِنَّ الظَّنَّ لَا يُغْنِى مِنَ الْحَقِّ شَيْئًا ۚ إِنَّ اللهَ عَلِيمٌ بِمَا يَفْعَلُونَ ۝

37 And this Qur'an is not such as could ever be invented in despite of Allah; but it is a confirmation of that which was before it and an exposition of that which is decreed for mankind. Therein is no doubt from the Lord of the Worlds.

وَمَا كَانَ هَٰذَا الْقُرْآنُ أَنْ يُفْتَرَىٰ مِنْ دُونِ اللهِ وَلَٰكِنْ تَصْدِيقَ الَّذِى بَيْنَ يَدَيْهِ وَتَفْصِيلَ الْكِتَابِ لَا رَيْبَ فِيهِ مِنْ رَّبِّ الْعَالَمِينَ ۝

38 Or say they: He hath invented it? Say: Then bring a sūrah like unto it, and call (for help) on all ye can besides Allah, if ye are truthful.

أَمْ يَقُولُونَ افْتَرَاهُ ۖ قُلْ فَأْتُوا بِسُورَةٍ مِّثْلِهِ وَادْعُوا مَنِ اسْتَطَعْتُمْ مِّنْ دُونِ اللهِ إِنْ كُنْتُمْ صَادِقِينَ ۝

39 Nay, but they denied that, the knowledge whereof they could not compass, and whereof the interpretation (in events) hath not yet come unto them. Even so did those before them deny. Then see what was the consequence for the wrong-doers!

بَلْ كَذَّبُوا بِمَا لَمْ يُحِيطُوا بِعِلْمِهِ وَلَمَّا يَأْتِهِمْ تَأْوِيلُهُ ۚ كَذَٰلِكَ كَذَّبَ الَّذِينَ مِنْ قَبْلِهِمْ ۖ فَانْظُرْ كَيْفَ كَانَ عَاقِبَةُ الظَّالِمِينَ ۝

40 And of them is he who believeth therein, and of them is he who
believeth not therein, and thy Lord
is best aware of the corrupters.

وَمِنْهُمْ مَّنْ يُؤْمِنُ بِهِ وَمِنْهُمْ مَّنْ لَّا يُؤْمِنُ بِهِ
وَرَبُّكَ أَعْلَمُ بِالْمُفْسِدِينَ ﴿٤٠﴾

41 And if they deny thee, say:
Unto me my work, and unto you
your work. Ye are innocent of what
I do, and I am innocent of what ye
do.

وَإِنْ كَذَّبُوكَ فَقُل لِّي عَمَلِي وَلَكُمْ عَمَلُكُمْ
أَنتُم بَرِيُونَ مِمَّا أَعْمَلُ وَأَنَا بَرِيٓءٌ مِّمَّا تَعْمَلُونَ ﴿٤١﴾

42 And of them are some who listen unto thee. But canst thou make
the deaf to hear even though they
apprehend not?

وَمِنْهُم مَّن يَسْتَمِعُونَ إِلَيْكَ أَفَأَنتَ تُسْمِعُ الصُّمَّ
وَلَوْ كَانُوا لَا يَعْقِلُونَ ﴿٤٢﴾

43 And of them is he who looketh
toward thee. But canst thou guide
the blind even though they see not?

وَمِنْهُم مَّن يَنظُرُ إِلَيْكَ أَفَأَنتَ تَهْدِي الْعُمْيَ
وَلَوْ كَانُوا لَا يُبْصِرُونَ ﴿٤٣﴾

44 Lo! Allah wrongeth not mankind in aught; but mankind wrong
themselves.

إِنَّ اللَّهَ لَا يَظْلِمُ النَّاسَ شَيْئًا وَلَكِنَّ النَّاسَ
أَنفُسَهُمْ يَظْلِمُونَ ﴿٤٤﴾

45 And on the day when He shall
gather them together, (when it will
seem) as though they had tarried
but an hour of the day, recognising
one another, those will verily have
perished who denied the meeting
with Allah and were not guided.

وَيَوْمَ يَحْشُرُهُمْ كَأَن لَّمْ يَلْبَثُوا إِلَّا سَاعَةً مِّنَ النَّهَارِ
يَتَعَارَفُونَ بَيْنَهُمْ قَدْ خَسِرَ الَّذِينَ كَذَّبُوا بِلِقَاءِ اللَّهِ
وَمَا كَانُوا مُهْتَدِينَ ﴿٤٥﴾

46 Whether We let thee (O
Muhammad) behold something of
that which We promise them or
(whether We) cause thee to die, still
unto Us is their return, and Allah,
moreover, is Witness over what
they do.

وَإِمَّا نُرِيَنَّكَ بَعْضَ الَّذِي نَعِدُهُمْ أَوْ نَتَوَفَّيَنَّكَ فَإِلَيْنَا
مَرْجِعُهُمْ ثُمَّ اللَّهُ شَهِيدٌ عَلَى مَا يَفْعَلُونَ ﴿٤٦﴾

47 And for every nation there is a
messenger. And when their mes-

وَلِكُلِّ أُمَّةٍ رَّسُولٌ فَإِذَا جَاءَ رَسُولُهُمْ قُضِيَ

senger cometh (on the Day of Judgment) it will be judged between them fairly, and they will not be wronged.

بَيْنَهُمْ بِالْقِسْطِ وَهُمْ لَا يُظْلَمُونَ ۝

48 And they say: When will this promise be fulfilled, if ye are truthful?

وَيَقُولُونَ مَتَىٰ هَٰذَا الْوَعْدُ إِنْ كُنْتُمْ صَادِقِينَ ۝

49 Say: I have no power to hurt or benefit myself, save that which Allah willeth. For every nation there is an appointed time. When their time cometh, then they cannot put it off an hour, nor hasten (it).

قُلْ لَا أَمْلِكُ لِنَفْسِي ضَرًّا وَلَا نَفْعًا إِلَّا مَا شَاءَ اللَّهُ لِكُلِّ أُمَّةٍ أَجَلٌ إِذَا جَاءَ أَجَلُهُمْ فَلَا يَسْتَأْخِرُونَ سَاعَةً وَلَا يَسْتَقْدِمُونَ ۝

50 Say: Have ye thought: When His doom cometh unto you as a raid by night, or in the (busy) day; what is there of it that the guilty ones desire to hasten?

قُلْ أَرَأَيْتُمْ إِنْ أَتَاكُمْ عَذَابُهُ بَيَاتًا أَوْ نَهَارًا مَاذَا يَسْتَعْجِلُ مِنْهُ الْمُجْرِمُونَ ۝

51 Is it (only) then, when it hath befallen you, that ye will believe? What! (Believe) now, when (until now) ye have been hastening it on (through disbelief)?

أَثُمَّ إِذَا مَا وَقَعَ آمَنْتُمْ بِهِ آلْآنَ وَقَدْ كُنْتُمْ بِهِ تَسْتَعْجِلُونَ ۝

52 Then will it be said unto those who dealt unjustly: Taste the torment of eternity. Are ye requited aught save what ye used to earn?

ثُمَّ قِيلَ لِلَّذِينَ ظَلَمُوا ذُوقُوا عَذَابَ الْخُلْدِ هَلْ تُجْزَوْنَ إِلَّا بِمَا كُنْتُمْ تَكْسِبُونَ ۝

53 And they ask thee to inform them (saying): Is it true? Say: Yea, by my Lord, verily it is true, and ye cannot escape.

وَيَسْتَنْبِئُونَكَ أَحَقٌّ هُوَ قُلْ إِي وَرَبِّي إِنَّهُ لَحَقٌّ وَمَا أَنْتُمْ بِمُعْجِزِينَ ۝

54 And if each soul that doeth wrong had all that is in the earth it would seek to ransom itself therewith; and they will feel remorse

وَلَوْ أَنَّ لِكُلِّ نَفْسٍ ظَلَمَتْ مَا فِي الْأَرْضِ لَافْتَدَتْ بِهِ وَأَسَرُّوا النَّدَامَةَ لَمَّا رَأَوُا الْعَذَابَ وَقُضِيَ

within them, when they see the
doom. But it hath been judged between them fairly and they are not
wronged.

بَيْنَهُم بِالْقِسْطِ وَهُمْ لَا يُظْلَمُونَ ۝

55 Lo! verily all that is in the heavens and the earth is Allah's. Lo!
verily Allah's promise is true. But
most of them know not.

أَلَا إِنَّ لِلَّهِ مَا فِي السَّمَٰوَٰتِ وَالْأَرْضِ أَلَا إِنَّ وَعْدَ اللَّهِ
حَقٌّ وَلَٰكِنَّ أَكْثَرَهُمْ لَا يَعْلَمُونَ ۝

56 He quickeneth and giveth death,
and unto Him ye will be returned.

هُوَ يُحْيِۦ وَيُمِيتُ وَإِلَيْهِ تُرْجَعُونَ ۝

57 O mankind! There hath come
unto you an exhortation from your
Lord, a balm for that which is in
the breasts, a guidance and a mercy
for believers.

يَٰٓأَيُّهَا النَّاسُ قَدْ جَآءَتْكُم مَّوْعِظَةٌ مِّن رَّبِّكُمْ
وَشِفَآءٌ لِّمَا فِي الصُّدُورِ وَهُدًى
وَرَحْمَةٌ لِّلْمُؤْمِنِينَ ۝

58 Say: In the bounty of Allah and
in His mercy: therein let them
rejoice. It is better than what they
hoard.

قُلْ بِفَضْلِ اللَّهِ وَبِرَحْمَتِهِۦ فَبِذَٰلِكَ فَلْيَفْرَحُوا۟
هُوَ خَيْرٌ مِّمَّا يَجْمَعُونَ ۝

59 Say: Have ye considered what
provision Allah hath sent down for
you, how ye have made of it lawful
and unlawful? Say: Hath Allah permitted you, or do ye invent a lie
concerning Allah?

قُلْ أَرَءَيْتُم مَّآ أَنزَلَ اللَّهُ لَكُم مِّن رِّزْقٍ
فَجَعَلْتُم مِّنْهُ حَرَامًا وَحَلَٰلًا قُلْ ءَآللَّهُ أَذِنَ
لَكُمْ أَمْ عَلَى اللَّهِ تَفْتَرُونَ ۝

60 And what think those who
invent a lie concerning Allah (will
be their plight) upon the Day of
Resurrection? Lo! Allah truly is
Bountiful toward mankind, but most
of them give not thanks.

وَمَا ظَنُّ الَّذِينَ يَفْتَرُونَ عَلَى اللَّهِ الْكَذِبَ
يَوْمَ الْقِيَٰمَةِ إِنَّ اللَّهَ لَذُو فَضْلٍ عَلَى النَّاسِ
وَلَٰكِنَّ أَكْثَرَهُمْ لَا يَشْكُرُونَ ۝

61 And thou (Muhammad) art not
occupied with any business and

وَمَا تَكُونُ فِي شَأْنٍ وَمَا تَتْلُوا۟ مِنْهُ مِن قُرْءَانٍ

thou recitest not a lecture[4] from this (Scripture), and ye (mankind) perform no act, but We are Witness of you when ye are engaged therein. And not an atom's weight in the earth or in the sky escapeth your Lord, nor what is less than that or greater than that, but it is (written) in a clear Book.

وَلَا تَعْمَلُونَ مِنْ عَمَلٍ إِلَّا كُنَّا عَلَيْكُمْ شُهُودًا إِذْ تُفِيضُونَ فِيهِ وَمَا يَعْزُبُ عَنْ رَبِّكَ مِنْ مِثْقَالِ ذَرَّةٍ فِي الْأَرْضِ وَلَا فِي السَّمَاءِ وَلَا أَصْغَرَ مِنْ ذَلِكَ وَلَا أَكْبَرَ إِلَّا فِي كِتَابٍ مُبِينٍ ۝

62 Lo! verily the friends of Allah are (those) on whom fear (cometh) not, nor do they grieve.

أَلَا إِنَّ أَوْلِيَاءَ اللَّهِ لَا خَوْفٌ عَلَيْهِمْ وَلَا هُمْ يَحْزَنُونَ ۝

63 Those who believe and keep their duty (to Allah);

الَّذِينَ ءَامَنُوا وَكَانُوا يَتَّقُونَ ۝

64 Theirs are good tidings in the life of the world and in the Hereafter—There is no changing the Words of Allah, that is the Supreme Triumph.

لَهُمُ الْبُشْرَىٰ فِي الْحَيَوٰةِ الدُّنْيَا وَفِي الْآخِرَةِ لَا تَبْدِيلَ لِكَلِمَٰتِ اللَّهِ ذَٰلِكَ هُوَ الْفَوْزُ الْعَظِيمُ ۝

65 And let not their speech grieve thee (O Muhammad). Lo! power belongeth wholly to Allah. He is the Hearer, the Knower.

وَلَا يَحْزُنْكَ قَوْلُهُمْ إِنَّ الْعِزَّةَ لِلَّهِ جَمِيعًا هُوَ السَّمِيعُ الْعَلِيمُ ۝

66 Beware! To Allah belongeth whosoever is in the heavens and whosoever is in the earth. Those who follow aught instead of Allah follow not (His) partners. They follow only a conjecture and they do but guess.

أَلَا إِنَّ لِلَّهِ مَنْ فِي السَّمَٰوَٰتِ وَمَنْ فِي الْأَرْضِ وَمَا يَتَّبِعُ الَّذِينَ يَدْعُونَ مِنْ دُونِ اللَّهِ شُرَكَاءَ إِنْ يَتَّبِعُونَ إِلَّا الظَّنَّ وَإِنْ هُمْ إِلَّا يَخْرُصُونَ ۝

67 He it is who hath appointed for you the night that ye should rest therein and the day giving sight. Lo!

هُوَ الَّذِي جَعَلَ لَكُمُ الَّيْلَ لِتَسْكُنُوا فِيهِ وَالنَّهَارَ مُبْصِرًا إِنَّ فِي ذَلِكَ

---

4. Ar. *Qur'an*.

herein verily are portents for a folk that heed.

لَآيَٰتٍ لِّقَوۡمٍ يَسۡمَعُونَ ۝

68 They say: Allah hath taken (unto Him) a son. Glorified be He! He hath no needs! His is all that is in the heavens and all that is in the earth. Ye have no warrant for this. Tell ye concerning Allah that which ye know not?

قَالُوا۟ اتَّخَذَ اللَّهُ وَلَدًا ۗ سُبۡحَٰنَهُۥ ۖ هُوَ الۡغَنِيُّ ۖ لَهُۥ مَا فِي السَّمَٰوَٰتِ وَمَا فِي الۡأَرۡضِ ۚ إِنۡ عِندَكُم مِّن سُلۡطَٰنٍۭ بِهَٰذَآ ۚ أَتَقُولُونَ عَلَى اللَّهِ مَا لَا تَعۡلَمُونَ ۝

69 Say: Verily those who invent a lie concerning Allah will not succeed.

قُلۡ إِنَّ الَّذِينَ يَفۡتَرُونَ عَلَى اللَّهِ الۡكَذِبَ لَا يُفۡلِحُونَ ۝

70 This world's portion (will be theirs), then unto Us is their return. Then We make them taste a dreadful doom because they used to disbelieve.

مَتَٰعٌ فِي الدُّنۡيَا ثُمَّ إِلَيۡنَا مَرۡجِعُهُمۡ ثُمَّ نُذِيقُهُمُ الۡعَذَابَ الشَّدِيدَ بِمَا كَانُوا۟ يَكۡفُرُونَ ۝

71 Recite unto them the story of Noah, when he told his people: O my people! If my sojourn here and my reminding you of Allah's revelations are an offence unto you, in Allah have I put my trust, so decide upon your course of action, you and your partners. Let not your course of action be in doubt, for you. Then have at me, give me no respite.

۞ وَاتۡلُ عَلَيۡهِمۡ نَبَأَ نُوحٍ إِذۡ قَالَ لِقَوۡمِهِۦ يَٰقَوۡمِ إِن كَانَ كَبُرَ عَلَيۡكُم مَّقَامِي وَتَذۡكِيرِي بِـَٔايَٰتِ اللَّهِ فَعَلَى اللَّهِ تَوَكَّلۡتُ فَأَجۡمِعُوٓا۟ أَمۡرَكُمۡ وَشُرَكَآءَكُمۡ ثُمَّ لَا يَكُنۡ أَمۡرُكُمۡ عَلَيۡكُمۡ غُمَّةً ثُمَّ اقۡضُوٓا۟ إِلَيَّ وَلَا تُنظِرُونِ ۝

72 But if ye are averse I have asked of you no wage. My wage is the concern of Allah only, and I am commanded to be of those who surrender (unto Him).

فَإِن تَوَلَّيۡتُمۡ فَمَا سَأَلۡتُكُم مِّنۡ أَجۡرٍ ۖ إِنۡ أَجۡرِيَ إِلَّا عَلَى اللَّهِ ۖ وَأُمِرۡتُ أَنۡ أَكُونَ مِنَ الۡمُسۡلِمِينَ ۝

73 But they denied him, so We saved him and those with him in the ship, and made them viceroys (in the earth), while We drowned

فَكَذَّبُوهُ فَنَجَّيۡنَٰهُ وَمَن مَّعَهُۥ فِي الۡفُلۡكِ وَجَعَلۡنَٰهُمۡ خَلَٰٓئِفَ وَأَغۡرَقۡنَا الَّذِينَ كَذَّبُوا۟ بِـَٔايَٰتِنَا ۖ فَانظُرۡ

those who denied Our revelations.
See then the nature of the consequence for those who had been
warned.

74 Then, after him, We sent messengers unto their folk, and they
brought them clear proofs. But they
were not ready to believe in that
which they before denied. Thus
print We on the hearts of the transgressors.

75 Then, after them, We sent
Moses and Aaron unto Pharaoh and
his chiefs with Our revelations, but
they were arrogant and were a
guilty folk.

76 And when the Truth from Our
presence came unto them, they said:
This is mere magic.

77 Moses said: Speak ye (so) of the
Truth when it hath come unto you?
Is this magic? Now magicians
thrive not.

78 They said: Hast thou come unto
us to pervert us from that (faith) in
which we found our fathers, and
that you two may own the place of
greatness in the land? We will not
believe you two.

79 And Pharaoh said: Bring every
cunning wizard unto me.

80 And when the wizards came,
Moses said unto them: Cast your
cast!

كَيْفَ كَانَ عَاقِبَةُ الْمُنْذَرِينَ ۝

ثُمَّ بَعَثْنَا مِنْ بَعْدِهِ رُسُلًا إِلَىٰ قَوْمِهِمْ فَجَآءُوهُمْ
بِالْبَيِّنَاتِ فَمَا كَانُوا لِيُؤْمِنُوا بِمَا كَذَّبُوا بِهِ مِنْ قَبْلُ
كَذَٰلِكَ نَطْبَعُ عَلَىٰ قُلُوبِ الْمُعْتَدِينَ ۝

ثُمَّ بَعَثْنَا مِنْ بَعْدِهِمْ مُوسَىٰ وَهَارُونَ إِلَىٰ فِرْعَوْنَ
وَمَلَإِيْهِ بِآيَاتِنَا فَاسْتَكْبَرُوا وَكَانُوا قَوْمًا
مُّجْرِمِينَ ۝

فَلَمَّا جَآءَهُمُ الْحَقُّ مِنْ عِنْدِنَا قَالُوا
إِنَّ هَٰذَا لَسِحْرٌ مُّبِينٌ ۝

قَالَ مُوسَىٰ أَتَقُولُونَ لِلْحَقِّ لَمَّا جَآءَكُمْ
أَسِحْرٌ هَٰذَا وَلَا يُفْلِحُ السَّاحِرُونَ ۝

قَالُوا أَجِئْتَنَا لِتَلْفِتَنَا عَمَّا وَجَدْنَا عَلَيْهِ آبَآءَنَا
وَتَكُونَ لَكُمَا الْكِبْرِيَآءُ فِي الْأَرْضِ وَمَا نَحْنُ لَكُمَا
بِمُؤْمِنِينَ ۝

وَقَالَ فِرْعَوْنُ ائْتُونِي بِكُلِّ سَاحِرٍ عَلِيمٍ ۝

فَلَمَّا جَآءَ السَّحَرَةُ قَالَ لَهُمْ مُوسَىٰ أَلْقُوا مَآ أَنْتُم
مُّلْقُونَ ۝

81 And when they had cast, Moses
said: That which ye have brought is
magic. Lo! Allah will make it vain.
Lo! Allah upholdeth not the work
of mischief makers.

82 And Allah will vindicate the
Truth by His words, however much
the guilty be averse.

83 But none believed in Moses save
some scions of his people, (and they
were) in fear of Pharaoh and their
chiefs that he would persecute them.
Lo! Pharaoh was verily a tyrant in
the land, and lo! he verily was of
the wanton.

84 And Moses said: O my people!
If ye have believed in Allah then
put trust in Him, if ye have indeed
surrendered (unto Him)!

85 They said: In Allah we put trust.
Our Lord! Oh, make us not a lure
for the wrongdoing folk;

86 And, of Thy mercy, save us
from the folk that disbelieve.

87 And We inspired Moses and his
brother, (saying): Appoint houses
for your people in Egypt and make
your houses oratories, and establish
worship. And give good news to
the believers.

88 And Moses said: Our Lord! Lo!
Thou hast given Pharaoh and his
chiefs splendour and riches in the
life of the world, Our Lord! that
they may lead men astray from Thy

فَلَمَّآ أَلْقَوْا قَالَ مُوسَىٰ مَا جِئْتُم بِهِ ٱلسِّحْرُ إِنَّ ٱللَّهَ
سَيُبْطِلُهُۥٓ إِنَّ ٱللَّهَ لَا يُصْلِحُ عَمَلَ ٱلْمُفْسِدِينَ ﴿٨١﴾

وَيُحِقُّ ٱللَّهُ ٱلْحَقَّ بِكَلِمَٰتِهِۦ وَلَوْ كَرِهَ
ٱلْمُجْرِمُونَ ﴿٨٢﴾

فَمَآ ءَامَنَ لِمُوسَىٰٓ إِلَّا ذُرِّيَّةٌ مِّن قَوْمِهِۦ عَلَىٰ خَوْفٍ
مِّن فِرْعَوْنَ وَمَلَإِيْهِمْ أَن يَفْتِنَهُمْ وَإِنَّ فِرْعَوْنَ
لَعَالٍ فِى ٱلْأَرْضِ وَإِنَّهُۥ لَمِنَ ٱلْمُسْرِفِينَ ﴿٨٣﴾

وَقَالَ مُوسَىٰ يَٰقَوْمِ إِن كُنتُمْ ءَامَنتُم بِٱللَّهِ فَعَلَيْهِ تَوَكَّلُوٓا
إِن كُنتُم مُّسْلِمِينَ ﴿٨٤﴾

فَقَالُوا عَلَى ٱللَّهِ تَوَكَّلْنَا رَبَّنَا لَا تَجْعَلْنَا فِتْنَةً لِّلْقَوْمِ
ٱلظَّٰلِمِينَ ﴿٨٥﴾

وَنَجِّنَا بِرَحْمَتِكَ مِنَ ٱلْقَوْمِ ٱلْكَٰفِرِينَ ﴿٨٦﴾

وَأَوْحَيْنَآ إِلَىٰ مُوسَىٰ وَأَخِيهِ أَن تَبَوَّءَا لِقَوْمِكُمَا
بِمِصْرَ بُيُوتًا وَٱجْعَلُوا بُيُوتَكُمْ قِبْلَةً
وَأَقِيمُوا ٱلصَّلَوٰةَ وَبَشِّرِ ٱلْمُؤْمِنِينَ ﴿٨٧﴾

وَقَالَ مُوسَىٰ رَبَّنَآ إِنَّكَ ءَاتَيْتَ فِرْعَوْنَ
وَمَلَأَهُۥ زِينَةً وَأَمْوَٰلًا فِى ٱلْحَيَوٰةِ ٱلدُّنْيَا رَبَّنَا
لِيُضِلُّوا عَن سَبِيلِكَ رَبَّنَا ٱطْمِسْ عَلَىٰٓ أَمْوَٰلِهِمْ

way. Our Lord! Destroy their riches and harden their hearts so that they believe not till they see the painful doom.

89 He said: Your prayer is heard. Do ye twain keep to the straight path, and follow not the road of those who have no knowledge.

90 And We brought the Children of Israel across the sea, and Pharaoh with his hosts pursued them in rebellion and transgression, till, when the (fate of) drowning overtook him, he exclaimed: I believe that there is no God save Him in whom the Children of Israel believe, and I am of those who surrender (unto Him).

91 What! Now! When hitherto thou hast rebelled and been of the wrongdoers?

92 But this day We save thee in thy body that thou mayest be a portent for those after thee. Lo! most of mankind are heedless of Our portents.

93 And We verily did allot unto the Children of Israel a fixed abode, and did provide them with good things; and they differed not until knowledge came unto them. Lo! thy Lord will judge between them on the Day of Resurrection concerning that wherein they used to differ.

94 And if thou (Muhammad) art in doubt concerning that which We reveal unto thee, then question

وَٱشْدُدْ عَلَىٰ قُلُوبِهِمْ فَلَا يُؤْمِنُوا۟ حَتَّىٰ يَرَوُا۟ ٱلْعَذَابَ ٱلْأَلِيمَ ﴿٨٨﴾

قَالَ قَدْ أُجِيبَت دَّعْوَتُكُمَا فَٱسْتَقِيمَا وَلَا تَتَّبِعَآنِّ سَبِيلَ ٱلَّذِينَ لَا يَعْلَمُونَ ﴿٨٩﴾

۞ وَجَٰوَزْنَا بِبَنِىٓ إِسْرَٰٓءِيلَ ٱلْبَحْرَ فَأَتْبَعَهُمْ فِرْعَوْنُ وَجُنُودُهُۥ بَغْيًا وَعَدْوًا حَتَّىٰٓ إِذَآ أَدْرَكَهُ ٱلْغَرَقُ قَالَ ءَامَنتُ أَنَّهُۥ لَآ إِلَٰهَ إِلَّا ٱلَّذِىٓ ءَامَنَتْ بِهِۦ بَنُوٓا۟ إِسْرَٰٓءِيلَ وَأَنَا۠ مِنَ ٱلْمُسْلِمِينَ ﴿٩٠﴾

ءَآلْـَٰٔنَ وَقَدْ عَصَيْتَ قَبْلُ وَكُنتَ مِنَ ٱلْمُفْسِدِينَ ﴿٩١﴾

فَٱلْيَوْمَ نُنَجِّيكَ بِبَدَنِكَ لِتَكُونَ لِمَنْ خَلْفَكَ ءَايَةً وَإِنَّ كَثِيرًا مِّنَ ٱلنَّاسِ عَنْ ءَايَٰتِنَا لَغَٰفِلُونَ ﴿٩٢﴾

وَلَقَدْ بَوَّأْنَا بَنِىٓ إِسْرَٰٓءِيلَ مُبَوَّأَ صِدْقٍ وَرَزَقْنَٰهُم مِّنَ ٱلطَّيِّبَٰتِ فَمَا ٱخْتَلَفُوا۟ حَتَّىٰ جَآءَهُمُ ٱلْعِلْمُ إِنَّ رَبَّكَ يَقْضِى بَيْنَهُمْ يَوْمَ ٱلْقِيَٰمَةِ فِيمَا كَانُوا۟ فِيهِ يَخْتَلِفُونَ ﴿٩٣﴾

فَإِن كُنتَ فِى شَكٍّ مِّمَّآ أَنزَلْنَآ إِلَيْكَ فَسْـَٔلِ ٱلَّذِينَ

those who read the Scripture (that was) before thee. Verily the Truth from thy Lord hath come unto thee. So be not thou of the waverers.

95 And be not thou of those who deny the revelations of Allah, for then wert thou of the losers.

96 Lo! those for whom the word of thy Lord (concerning sinners) hath effect will not believe;

97. Though every token come unto them, till they see the painful doom.

98 If only there had been a community (of all those that were destroyed of old) that believed and profited by its belief as did the folk of Jonah! When they believed, We drew off from them the torment of disgrace in the life of the world and gave them comfort for a while.

99 And if thy Lord willed, all who are in the earth would have believed together. Wouldst thou (Muhammad) compel men until they are believers?

100   It is not for any soul to believe save by the permission of Allah. He hath set uncleanness upon those who have no sense.

101   Say: Behold what is in the heavens and the earth! But revelations and warnings avail not folk who will not believe.

102   What expect they save the like of the days of those who passed away before them? Say: Expect

يَقْرَءُونَ الْكِتَٰبَ مِن قَبْلِكَ لَقَدْ جَآءَكَ
الْحَقُّ مِن رَّبِّكَ فَلَا تَكُونَنَّ مِنَ الْمُمْتَرِينَ ٩٤

وَلَا تَكُونَنَّ مِنَ الَّذِينَ كَذَّبُوا۟ بِـَٔايَٰتِ اللَّهِ
فَتَكُونَ مِنَ الْخَٰسِرِينَ ٩٥

إِنَّ الَّذِينَ حَقَّتْ عَلَيْهِمْ كَلِمَتُ رَبِّكَ
لَا يُؤْمِنُونَ ٩٦

وَلَوْ جَآءَتْهُمْ كُلُّ ءَايَةٍ حَتَّىٰ يَرَوُا۟ الْعَذَابَ
الْأَلِيمَ ٩٧

فَلَوْلَا كَانَتْ قَرْيَةٌ ءَامَنَتْ فَنَفَعَهَآ إِيمَٰنُهَآ إِلَّا قَوْمَ
يُونُسَ لَمَّآ ءَامَنُوا۟ كَشَفْنَا عَنْهُمْ عَذَابَ الْخِزْيِ
فِى الْحَيَوٰةِ الدُّنْيَا وَمَتَّعْنَٰهُمْ إِلَىٰ حِينٍ ٩٨

وَلَوْ شَآءَ رَبُّكَ لَءَامَنَ مَن فِى الْأَرْضِ كُلُّهُمْ
جَمِيعًا أَفَأَنتَ تُكْرِهُ النَّاسَ حَتَّىٰ يَكُونُوا۟
مُؤْمِنِينَ ٩٩

وَمَا كَانَ لِنَفْسٍ أَن تُؤْمِنَ إِلَّا بِإِذْنِ اللَّهِ
وَيَجْعَلُ الرِّجْسَ عَلَى الَّذِينَ لَا يَعْقِلُونَ ١٠٠

قُلِ انظُرُوا۟ مَاذَا فِى السَّمَٰوَٰتِ وَالْأَرْضِ وَمَا تُغْنِى
الْءَايَٰتُ وَالنُّذُرُ عَن قَوْمٍ لَّا يُؤْمِنُونَ ١٠١

فَهَلْ يَنتَظِرُونَ إِلَّا مِثْلَ أَيَّامِ الَّذِينَ خَلَوْا۟
مِن قَبْلِهِمْ قُلْ فَانتَظِرُوا۟ إِنِّى مَعَكُم

then! I am with you among the expectant.

مِنَ ٱلْمُنتَظِرِينَ ۝

103 Then shall We save Our messengers and the believers, in like manner (as of old). It is incumbent upon Us to save believers.

ثُمَّ نُنَجِّى رُسُلَنَا وَٱلَّذِينَ ءَامَنُوٱ كَذَٰلِكَ حَقًّا عَلَيْنَا نُنجِ ٱلْمُؤْمِنِينَ ۝

104 Say (O Muḥammad): O mankind! If ye are in doubt of my religion, then (know that) I worship not those whom ye worship instead of Allah, but I worship Allah who causeth you to die, and I have been commanded to be of the believers.

قُلْ يَٰٓأَيُّهَا ٱلنَّاسُ إِن كُنتُمْ فِى شَكٍّ مِّن دِينِى فَلَآ أَعْبُدُ ٱلَّذِينَ تَعْبُدُونَ مِن دُونِ ٱللَّهِ وَلَٰكِنْ أَعْبُدُ ٱللَّهَ ٱلَّذِى يَتَوَفَّىٰكُمْ وَأُمِرْتُ أَنْ أَكُونَ مِنَ ٱلْمُؤْمِنِينَ ۝

105 And, (O Muḥammad) set thy purpose resolutely for religion, as a man by nature upright, and be not of those who ascribe partners (to Allah).

وَأَنْ أَقِمْ وَجْهَكَ لِلدِّينِ حَنِيفًا وَلَا تَكُونَنَّ مِنَ ٱلْمُشْرِكِينَ ۝

106 And cry not, beside Allah, unto that which cannot profit thee nor hurt thee, for if thou didst so then wert thou of the wrong-doers.

وَلَا تَدْعُ مِن دُونِ ٱللَّهِ مَا لَا يَنفَعُكَ وَلَا يَضُرُّكَ فَإِن فَعَلْتَ فَإِنَّكَ إِذًا مِّنَ ٱلظَّٰلِمِينَ ۝

107 If Allah afflicteth thee with some hurt, there is none who can remove it save Him; and if He desireth good for thee, there is none who can repel His bounty. He striketh with it whom He will of His bondmen. He is the Forgiving, the Merciful.

وَإِن يَمْسَسْكَ ٱللَّهُ بِضُرٍّ فَلَا كَاشِفَ لَهُۥٓ إِلَّا هُوَ وَإِن يُرِدْكَ بِخَيْرٍ فَلَا رَآدَّ لِفَضْلِهِۦ يُصِيبُ بِهِۦ مَن يَشَآءُ مِنْ عِبَادِهِۦ وَهُوَ ٱلْغَفُورُ ٱلرَّحِيمُ ۝

108 Say: O mankind! Now hath the Truth from your Lord come unto you. So whosoever is guided, is guided only for (the good of) his soul, and whosoever erreth, erreth

قُلْ يَٰٓأَيُّهَا ٱلنَّاسُ قَدْ جَآءَكُمُ ٱلْحَقُّ مِن رَّبِّكُمْ فَمَنِ ٱهْتَدَىٰ فَإِنَّمَا يَهْتَدِى لِنَفْسِهِۦ وَمَن ضَلَّ

only against it. And I am not a
warder over you.

109   And (O Muhammad) follow
that which is inspired in thee, and
forbear until Allah give judgment.
And He is the Best of Judges.

Hūd

Takes its name from v. 50, which begins the story of Hūd, of the tribe of ʿĀd, one of the prophets of Arabia who is not mentioned in the Hebrew Scriptures. The sūrah also contains the stories of two other Arab prophets, Sālih, of the tribe of Thamūd, and Shuʿayb of Madyan (identified with Jethro), which, with those of Noah and Moses, are quoted as part of the history of Divine Revelation, the truth of which is here vindicated, in a manner supplementary to sūrah 10.

A late Makkan sūrah, except v. 114 f., revealed at Al-Madīnah.

In the name of Allah, the Beneficent, the Merciful.

1   Alif. Lām. Rā.[1] (This is) a Scripture the revelations whereof are perfected and then expounded. (It cometh) from One Wise, Aware.

2   (Saying): Serve none but Allah. Lo! I am unto you from Him a warner and a bringer of good tidings.

3   And (bidding you): Ask pardon of your Lord and turn to Him repentant. He will cause you to enjoy a fair estate until a time appointed. He giveth His bounty unto every bountiful one. But if ye turn away, lo!

---

1. See Sūrah 2, v. 1, footnote.

وَإِن تَوَلَّوۡاْ فَإِنِّيٓ أَخَافُ عَلَيۡكُمۡ عَذَابَ يَوۡمٍ كَبِيرٍ ۝

(then) I fear for you the retribution of an awful Day.

إِلَى ٱللَّهِ مَرۡجِعُكُمۡۖ وَهُوَ عَلَىٰ كُلِّ شَىۡءٍ قَدِيرٌ ۝

4   Unto Allah is your return, and He is able to do all things.

أَلَآ إِنَّهُمۡ يَثۡنُونَ صُدُورَهُمۡ لِيَسۡتَخۡفُواْ مِنۡهُۚ أَلَا حِينَ يَسۡتَغۡشُونَ ثِيَابَهُمۡ يَعۡلَمُ مَا يُسِرُّونَ وَمَا يُعۡلِنُونَۚ إِنَّهُۥ عَلِيمٌۢ بِذَاتِ ٱلصُّدُورِ ۝

5   Lo! now they fold up their breasts that they may hide (their thoughts) from Him. At the very moment when they cover themselves with their clothing, Allah knoweth that which they keep hidden and that which they proclaim. Lo! He is Aware of what is in the breasts (of men).

۞ وَمَا مِن دَآبَّةٍ فِى ٱلۡأَرۡضِ إِلَّا عَلَى ٱللَّهِ رِزۡقُهَا وَيَعۡلَمُ مُسۡتَقَرَّهَا وَمُسۡتَوۡدَعَهَاۚ كُلٌّ فِى كِتَٰبٍ مُّبِينٍ ۝

6   And there is not a beast in the earth but the sustenance thereof dependeth on Allah. He knoweth its habitation and its repository. All is in a clear record.

وَهُوَ ٱلَّذِى خَلَقَ ٱلسَّمَٰوَٰتِ وَٱلۡأَرۡضَ فِى سِتَّةِ أَيَّامٍ وَكَانَ عَرۡشُهُۥ عَلَى ٱلۡمَآءِ لِيَبۡلُوَكُمۡ أَيُّكُمۡ أَحۡسَنُ عَمَلًاۗ وَلَئِن قُلۡتَ إِنَّكُم مَّبۡعُوثُونَ مِنۢ بَعۡدِ ٱلۡمَوۡتِ لَيَقُولَنَّ ٱلَّذِينَ كَفَرُوٓاْ إِنۡ هَٰذَآ إِلَّا سِحۡرٌ مُّبِينٌ ۝

7   And He it is Who created the heavens and the earth in six Days[2] and His Throne was upon the water that He might try you, which of you is best in conduct. Yet if thou (O Muhammad) sayest: Lo! ye will be raised again after death! those who disbelieve will surely say: This is not but evident magic.

وَلَئِنۡ أَخَّرۡنَا عَنۡهُمُ ٱلۡعَذَابَ إِلَىٰٓ أُمَّةٍ مَّعۡدُودَةٍ لَّيَقُولُنَّ مَا يَحۡبِسُهُۥٓۗ أَلَا يَوۡمَ يَأۡتِيهِمۡ لَيۡسَ مَصۡرُوفًا عَنۡهُمۡ وَحَاقَ بِهِم مَّا كَانُواْ بِهِۦ يَسۡتَهۡزِءُونَ ۝

8   And if We delay for them the doom until a reckoned time, they will surely say: What withholdeth it? Verily on the day when it cometh unto them, it cannot be averted from them, and that which they derided will surround them.

---

2. See (22: 47), (32: 5) and (70: 4).

9 And if We cause man to taste some mercy from Us and afterward withdraw it from him, lo! he is despairing, thankless.

وَلَئِنْ أَذَقْنَا الْإِنسَانَ مِنَّا رَحْمَةً ثُمَّ نَزَعْنَاهَا مِنْهُ إِنَّهُ لَيَئُوسٌ كَفُورٌ ۝

10 And if We cause him to taste grace after some misfortune that had befallen him, he saith: The ills have gone from me. Lo! he is exultant, boastful;

وَلَئِنْ أَذَقْنَاهُ نَعْمَاءَ بَعْدَ ضَرَّاءَ مَسَّتْهُ لَيَقُولَنَّ ذَهَبَ السَّيِّئَاتُ عَنِّي إِنَّهُ لَفَرِحٌ فَخُورٌ ۝

11 Save those who persevere and do good works. Theirs will be forgiveness and a great reward.

إِلَّا الَّذِينَ صَبَرُوا وَعَمِلُوا الصَّالِحَاتِ أُولَٰئِكَ لَهُم مَّغْفِرَةٌ وَأَجْرٌ كَبِيرٌ ۝

12 A likely thing, that thou wouldst forsake aught of that which hath been revealed unto thee, and that thy breast should be straitened for it, because they say: Why hath not a treasure been sent down for him, or an angel come with him? Thou art but a warner, and Allah is in charge of all things.

فَلَعَلَّكَ تَارِكٌ بَعْضَ مَا يُوحَىٰ إِلَيْكَ وَضَائِقٌ بِهِ صَدْرُكَ أَن يَقُولُوا لَوْلَا أُنزِلَ عَلَيْهِ كَنزٌ أَوْ جَاءَ مَعَهُ مَلَكٌ إِنَّمَا أَنتَ نَذِيرٌ وَاللَّهُ عَلَىٰ كُلِّ شَيْءٍ وَكِيلٌ ۝

13 Or they say: He hath invented it. Say: Then bring ten sūrahs, the like thereof, invented, and call on everyone ye can beside Allah, if ye are truthful!

أَمْ يَقُولُونَ افْتَرَاهُ قُلْ فَأْتُوا بِعَشْرِ سُوَرٍ مِّثْلِهِ مُفْتَرَيَاتٍ وَادْعُوا مَنِ اسْتَطَعْتُم مِّن دُونِ اللَّهِ إِن كُنتُمْ صَادِقِينَ ۝

14 And if they answer not your prayer, then know that it is revealed only in the knowledge of Allah; and that there is no God save Him. Will ye then be (of) those who surrender?[3]

فَإِلَّمْ يَسْتَجِيبُوا لَكُمْ فَاعْلَمُوا أَنَّمَا أُنزِلَ بِعِلْمِ اللَّهِ وَأَن لَّا إِلَٰهَ إِلَّا هُوَ فَهَلْ أَنتُم مُّسْلِمُونَ ۝

---

3. Ar. *Muslimīn*.

15 Whoso desireth the life of the world and its pomp, We shall repay them their deeds herein, and therein they will not be wronged.

مَنْ كَانَ يُرِيدُ الْحَيَوٰةَ الدُّنْيَا وَزِينَتَهَا نُوَفِّ إِلَيْهِمْ أَعْمَالَهُمْ فِيهَا وَهُمْ فِيهَا لَا يُبْخَسُونَ ۝

16 Those are they for whom is naught in the Hereafter save the Fire. (All) that they contrive here is vain and (all) that they are wont to do is fruitless.

أُولٰٓئِكَ الَّذِينَ لَيْسَ لَهُمْ فِي الْأَخِرَةِ إِلَّا النَّارُ وَحَبِطَ مَا صَنَعُوا فِيهَا وَبَٰطِلٌ مَّا كَانُوا يَعْمَلُونَ ۝

17 Is he (to be counted equal with them) who relieth on a clear proof from his Lord, and a witness from Him reciteth it, and before it was the Book of Moses, an example and a mercy? Such believe therein, and whoso disbelieveth therein of the clans, the Fire is his appointed place. So be not thou in doubt concerning it. Lo! it is the Truth from thy Lord; but most of mankind believe not.

أَفَمَنْ كَانَ عَلَىٰ بَيِّنَةٍ مِّن رَّبِّهِ وَيَتْلُوهُ شَاهِدٌ مِّنْهُ وَمِن قَبْلِهِ كِتَٰبُ مُوسَىٰ إِمَامًا وَرَحْمَةً أُولٰٓئِكَ يُؤْمِنُونَ بِهِ وَمَن يَكْفُرْ بِهِ مِنَ الْأَحْزَابِ فَالنَّارُ مَوْعِدُهُ فَلَا تَكُ فِي مِرْيَةٍ مِّنْهُ إِنَّهُ الْحَقُّ مِن رَّبِّكَ وَلَٰكِنَّ أَكْثَرَ النَّاسِ لَا يُؤْمِنُونَ ۝

18 Who doeth greater wrong than he who inventeth a lie concerning Allah? Such will be brought before their Lord, and the witnesses will say: These are they who lied concerning their Lord. Now the curse of Allah is upon wrong-doers;

وَمَنْ أَظْلَمُ مِمَّنِ افْتَرَىٰ عَلَى اللَّهِ كَذِبًا أُولٰٓئِكَ يُعْرَضُونَ عَلَىٰ رَبِّهِمْ وَيَقُولُ الْأَشْهَٰدُ هَٰٓؤُلَاءِ الَّذِينَ كَذَبُوا عَلَىٰ رَبِّهِمْ أَلَا لَعْنَةُ اللَّهِ عَلَى الظَّٰلِمِينَ ۝

19 Who debar (men) from the way of Allah and would have it crooked, and who are disbelievers in the Hereafter.

الَّذِينَ يَصُدُّونَ عَن سَبِيلِ اللَّهِ وَيَبْغُونَهَا عِوَجًا وَهُم بِالْأَخِرَةِ هُمْ كَٰفِرُونَ ۝

20 Such will not escape in the earth, nor have they any protecting friends beside Allah. For them the torment will be double. They could

أُولٰٓئِكَ لَمْ يَكُونُوا مُعْجِزِينَ فِي الْأَرْضِ وَمَا كَانَ لَهُم مِّن دُونِ اللَّهِ مِنْ أَوْلِيَاءَ يُضَٰعَفُ لَهُمُ الْعَذَابُ

not bear to hear, and they used not to see. مَا كَانُوا يَسْتَطِيعُونَ السَّمْعَ وَمَا كَانُوا يُبْصِرُونَ ۝

21 Such are they who have lost their souls, and that which they used to invent hath failed them. أُولَٰئِكَ الَّذِينَ خَسِرُوا أَنْفُسَهُمْ وَضَلَّ عَنْهُم مَّا كَانُوا يَفْتَرُونَ ۝

22 Assuredly in the Hereafter they will be the greatest losers. لَا جَرَمَ أَنَّهُمْ فِي الْآخِرَةِ هُمُ الْأَخْسَرُونَ ۝

23 Lo! those who believe and do good works and humble themselves before their Lord: such are rightful owners of the Garden; they will abide therein. إِنَّ الَّذِينَ آمَنُوا وَعَمِلُوا الصَّالِحَاتِ وَأَخْبَتُوا إِلَىٰ رَبِّهِمْ أُولَٰئِكَ أَصْحَابُ الْجَنَّةِ هُمْ فِيهَا خَالِدُونَ ۝

24 The similitude of the two parties is as the blind and the deaf and the seer and the hearer. Are they equal in similitude? Will ye not then be admonished? ۞ مَثَلُ الْفَرِيقَيْنِ كَالْأَعْمَىٰ وَالْأَصَمِّ وَالْبَصِيرِ وَالسَّمِيعِ هَلْ يَسْتَوِيَانِ مَثَلًا أَفَلَا تَذَكَّرُونَ ۝

25 And We sent Noah unto his folk (and he said): I am a plain warner unto you. وَلَقَدْ أَرْسَلْنَا نُوحًا إِلَىٰ قَوْمِهِ إِنِّي لَكُمْ نَذِيرٌ مُّبِينٌ ۝

26 That ye serve none, save Allah. Lo! I fear for you the retribution of a painful Day. أَن لَّا تَعْبُدُوا إِلَّا اللَّهَ إِنِّي أَخَافُ عَلَيْكُمْ عَذَابَ يَوْمٍ أَلِيمٍ ۝

27 The chieftains of his folk, who disbelieved, said: We see thee but a mortal like us, and we see not that any follow thee save the most abject among us, without reflection. We behold in you no merit above us—nay, we deem you liars. فَقَالَ الْمَلَأُ الَّذِينَ كَفَرُوا مِن قَوْمِهِ مَا نَرَاكَ إِلَّا بَشَرًا مِّثْلَنَا وَمَا نَرَاكَ اتَّبَعَكَ إِلَّا الَّذِينَ هُمْ أَرَاذِلُنَا بَادِيَ الرَّأْيِ وَمَا نَرَىٰ لَكُمْ عَلَيْنَا مِن فَضْلٍ بَلْ نَظُنُّكُمْ كَاذِبِينَ ۝

28 He said: O my people! Bethink you, if I rely on a clear proof from my Lord and there hath come unto me a mercy from His presence, and it hath been made obscure to you, قَالَ يَا قَوْمِ أَرَأَيْتُمْ إِن كُنتُ عَلَىٰ بَيِّنَةٍ مِّن رَّبِّي وَآتَانِي رَحْمَةً مِّنْ عِندِهِ فَعُمِّيَتْ عَلَيْكُمْ

can we compel you to accept it
when ye are averse thereto?

أَنُلْزِمُكُمُوهَا وَأَنْتُمْ لَهَا كَارِهُونَ ۝

29 And O my people! I ask of you
no wealth therefore. My reward is
the concern only of Allah, and I am
not going to thrust away those who
believe—Lo! they have to meet
their Lord, but I see you a folk that
are ignorant.

وَيَا قَوْمِ لَا أَسْأَلُكُمْ عَلَيْهِ مَالًا إِنْ أَجْرِيَ
إِلَّا عَلَى اللَّهِ وَمَا أَنَا بِطَارِدِ الَّذِينَ آمَنُوا إِنَّهُم
مُلَاقُوا رَبِّهِمْ وَلَكِنِّيَ أَرَاكُمْ قَوْمًا تَجْهَلُونَ ۝

30 And, O my people! who would
deliver me from Allah if I thrust
them away? Will ye not then reflect?

وَيَا قَوْمِ مَنْ يَنْصُرُنِي مِنَ اللَّهِ إِنْ طَرَدْتُهُمْ
أَفَلَا تَذَكَّرُونَ ۝

31 I say not unto you: "I have the
treasures of Allah" nor "I have
knowledge of the Unseen," nor say
I: "Lo! I am an angel!" Nor say I
unto those whom your eyes scorn
that Allah will not give them good,
Allah knoweth best what is their
hearts, lo! then indeed I should be
of the wrong-doers.

وَلَا أَقُولُ لَكُمْ عِنْدِي خَزَائِنُ اللَّهِ وَلَا أَعْلَمُ الْغَيْبَ
وَلَا أَقُولُ إِنِّي مَلَكٌ وَلَا أَقُولُ لِلَّذِينَ تَزْدَرِي
أَعْيُنُكُمْ لَنْ يُؤْتِيَهُمُ اللَّهُ خَيْرًا اللَّهُ أَعْلَمُ بِمَا
فِي أَنْفُسِهِمْ إِنِّي إِذًا لَمِنَ الظَّالِمِينَ ۝

32 They said: O Noah! Thou hast
disputed with us and multiplied dis-
putation with us; now bring upon us
that wherewith thou threatenest us,
if thou art of the truthful.

قَالُوا يَا نُوحُ قَدْ جَادَلْتَنَا فَأَكْثَرْتَ جِدَالَنَا
فَأْتِنَا بِمَا تَعِدُنَا إِنْ كُنْتَ مِنَ الصَّادِقِينَ ۝

33 He said: Only Allah will bring
it upon you if He will, and ye can
by no means escape.

قَالَ إِنَّمَا يَأْتِيكُمْ بِهِ اللَّهُ إِنْ شَاءَ
وَمَا أَنْتُمْ بِمُعْجِزِينَ ۝

34 My counsel will not profit you
if I were minded to advise you, if
Allah's will is to keep you astray.
He is your Lord and unto Him ye
will be brought back.

وَلَا يَنْفَعُكُمْ نُصْحِي إِنْ أَرَدْتُ أَنْ أَنْصَحَ لَكُمْ إِنْ كَانَ
اللَّهُ يُرِيدُ أَنْ يُغْوِيَكُمْ هُوَ رَبُّكُمْ وَإِلَيْهِ
تُرْجَعُونَ ۝

35 Or say they (again): He hath invented it? Say: If I have invented it, upon me be my crimes, but I am innocent of (all) that ye commit.

أَمْ يَقُولُونَ افْتَرَاهُ قُلْ إِنِ افْتَرَيْتُهُ فَعَلَيَّ إِجْرَامِى وَأَنَا بَرِىءٌ مِّمَّا تُجْرِمُونَ ۝

36 And it was inspired in Noah, (saying): No one of thy folk will believe save him who hath believed already. Be not distressed because of what they do.

وَأُوحِىَ إِلَىٰ نُوحٍ أَنَّهُ لَن يُؤْمِنَ مِن قَوْمِكَ إِلَّا مَن قَدْ ءَامَنَ فَلَا تَبْتَئِسْ بِمَا كَانُوا يَفْعَلُونَ ۝

37 Build the ship under Our Eyes and by Our Inspiration, and speak not unto Me on behalf of those who do wrong. Lo! they will be drowned.

وَاصْنَعِ الْفُلْكَ بِأَعْيُنِنَا وَوَحْيِنَا وَلَا تُخَاطِبْنِى فِى الَّذِينَ ظَلَمُوا إِنَّهُم مُّغْرَقُونَ ۝

38 And he was building the ship, and every time that chieftains of his people passed him, they made mock of him. He said: Though ye make mock of us, yet we mock at you even as ye mock;

وَيَصْنَعُ الْفُلْكَ وَكُلَّمَا مَرَّ عَلَيْهِ مَلَأٌ مِّن قَوْمِهِ سَخِرُوا مِنْهُ قَالَ إِن تَسْخَرُوا مِنَّا فَإِنَّا نَسْخَرُ مِنكُمْ كَمَا تَسْخَرُونَ ۝

39 And ye shall know to whom a punishment that will confound him cometh, and upon whom a lasting doom will fall.

فَسَوْفَ تَعْلَمُونَ مَن يَأْتِيهِ عَذَابٌ يُخْزِيهِ وَيَحِلُّ عَلَيْهِ عَذَابٌ مُّقِيمٌ ۝

40 (Thus it was) till, when Our commandment came to pass and the oven gushed forth water,[4] We said: Load therein two of every kind, a pair (the male and female), and thy household, save him against whom the word hath gone forth already, and those who believe. And but a few were they who believed with him.

حَتَّىٰ إِذَا جَاءَ أَمْرُنَا وَفَارَ التَّنُّورُ قُلْنَا احْمِلْ فِيهَا مِن كُلٍّ زَوْجَيْنِ اثْنَيْنِ وَأَهْلَكَ إِلَّا مَن سَبَقَ عَلَيْهِ الْقَوْلُ وَمَنْ ءَامَنَ وَمَا ءَامَنَ مَعَهُ إِلَّا قَلِيلٌ ۝

---

4. This was a sign of the deluge, water gushing up from underground as well as falling from the sky.

41 And he said: Embark therein! In the name of Allah be its course and its mooring. Lo! my Lord is Forgiving, Merciful.

وَقَالَ ارْكَبُوا فِيهَا بِسْمِ اللَّهِ مَجْرٜىٰهَا وَمُرْسَىٰهَا إِنَّ رَبِّى لَغَفُورٌ رَّحِيمٌ ﴿٤١﴾

42 And it sailed with them amid waves like mountains, and Noah cried unto his son and he was standing aloof: O my son! Come ride with us, and be not with the disbelievers.

وَهِىَ تَجْرِى بِهِمْ فِى مَوْجٍ كَالْجِبَالِ وَنَادَىٰ نُوحٌ ابْنَهُ وَكَانَ فِى مَعْزِلٍ يَٰبُنَىَّ ارْكَب مَّعَنَا وَلَا تَكُن مَّعَ الْكَٰفِرِينَ ﴿٤٢﴾

43 He said: I shall betake me to some mountain that will save me from the water. (Noah) said: This day there is none that saveth from the commandment of Allah save him on whom He hath had mercy. And the wave came in between them, so he was among the drowned.

قَالَ سَـَٔاوِى إِلَىٰ جَبَلٍ يَعْصِمُنِى مِنَ الْمَآءِ قَالَ لَا عَاصِمَ الْيَوْمَ مِنْ أَمْرِ اللَّهِ إِلَّا مَن رَّحِمَ وَحَالَ بَيْنَهُمَا الْمَوْجُ فَكَانَ مِنَ الْمُغْرَقِينَ ﴿٤٣﴾

44 And it was said: O earth! Swallow thy water and, O sky! be cleared of clouds! And the water was made to subside. And the commandment was fulfilled. And it (the ship) came to rest upon (the mount) Al-Jūdī and it was said: A far removal for wrongdoing folk!

وَقِيلَ يَٰأَرْضُ ابْلَعِى مَآءَكِ وَيَٰسَمَآءُ أَقْلِعِى وَغِيضَ الْمَآءُ وَقُضِىَ الْأَمْرُ وَاسْتَوَتْ عَلَى الْجُودِىِّ وَقِيلَ بُعْدًا لِّلْقَوْمِ الظَّٰلِمِينَ ﴿٤٤﴾

45 And Noah cried unto his Lord and said: My Lord! Lo! my son is of my household! Surely Thy promise is the Truth and Thou art the Most Just of Judges.

وَنَادَىٰ نُوحٌ رَّبَّهُ فَقَالَ رَبِّ إِنَّ ابْنِى مِنْ أَهْلِى وَإِنَّ وَعْدَكَ الْحَقُّ وَأَنتَ أَحْكَمُ الْحَٰكِمِينَ ﴿٤٥﴾

46 He said: O Noah! Lo! he is not of thy household; lo! he is of evil conduct, so ask not of Me that whereof thou hast no knowledge. I admonish thee lest thou be among the ignorant.

قَالَ يَٰنُوحُ إِنَّهُ لَيْسَ مِنْ أَهْلِكَ إِنَّهُ عَمَلٌ غَيْرُ صَٰلِحٍ فَلَا تَسْـَٔلْنِ مَا لَيْسَ لَكَ بِهِ عِلْمٌ إِنِّى أَعِظُكَ أَن تَكُونَ مِنَ الْجَٰهِلِينَ ﴿٤٦﴾

47 He said: My Lord! Lo! in Thee do I seek refuge (from the sin) that I should ask of Thee that whereof I have no knowledge. Unless Thou forgive me and have mercy on me, I shall he among the lost.

قَالَ رَبِّ إِنِّى أَعُوذُ بِكَ أَنْ أَسْئَلَكَ مَا لَيْسَ لِى بِهِ عِلْمٌ وَإِلَّا تَغْفِرْ لِى وَتَرْحَمْنِى أَكُن مِّنَ الْخَاسِرِينَ ۝

48 It was said (unto him): O Noah! Go thou down (from the mountain) with peace from Us and blessings upon thee and some nations (that will spring) from those with thee. (There will be other) nations unto whom We shall give enjoyment a long while and then a painful doom from Us will overtake them.

قِيلَ يَانُوحُ اهْبِطْ بِسَلَامٍ مِّنَّا وَبَرَكَاتٍ عَلَيْكَ وَعَلَى أُمَمٍ مِّمَّن مَّعَكَ وَأُمَمٌ سَنُمَتِّعُهُمْ ثُمَّ يَمَسُّهُم مِّنَّا عَذَابٌ أَلِيمٌ ۝

49 This is of the tidings of the Unseen which We inspire in thee (Muhammad). Thou thyself knewest it not, nor did thy folk (know it) before this. Then have patience. Lo! the sequel is for those who ward off (evil).

تِلْكَ مِنْ أَنْبَاءِ الْغَيْبِ نُوحِيهَا إِلَيْكَ مَا كُنتَ تَعْلَمُهَا أَنتَ وَلَا قَوْمُكَ مِن قَبْلِ هَٰذَا فَاصْبِرْ إِنَّ الْعَاقِبَةَ لِلْمُتَّقِينَ ۝

50 And unto (the tribe of) 'Ād (We sent) their brother, Hūd. He said: O my people! Serve Allah! Ye have no other God save Him. Lo! ye do but invent!

وَإِلَى عَادٍ أَخَاهُمْ هُودًا قَالَ يَاقَوْمِ اعْبُدُوا اللَّهَ مَا لَكُم مِّنْ إِلَٰهٍ غَيْرُهُ إِنْ أَنتُمْ إِلَّا مُفْتَرُونَ ۝

51 O my people! I ask of you no reward for it. Lo! my reward is the concern only of Him who made me. Have ye then no sense?

يَاقَوْمِ لَا أَسْئَلُكُمْ عَلَيْهِ أَجْرًا إِنْ أَجْرِىَ إِلَّا عَلَى الَّذِى فَطَرَنِى أَفَلَا تَعْقِلُونَ ۝

52 And, O my people! Ask forgiveness of your Lord, then turn unto Him repentant; He will cause the sky to rain abundance on you and will add unto you strength to your strength. Turn not away, guilty!

وَيَاقَوْمِ اسْتَغْفِرُوا رَبَّكُمْ ثُمَّ تُوبُوا إِلَيْهِ يُرْسِلِ السَّمَاءَ عَلَيْكُم مِّدْرَارًا وَيَزِدْكُمْ قُوَّةً إِلَى قُوَّتِكُمْ وَلَا تَتَوَلَّوْا مُجْرِمِينَ ۝

53 They said: O Hūd! Thou hast brought us no clear proof and we are not going to forsake our gods on thy (mere) saying, and we are not believers in thee.

قَالُوا يَا هُودُ مَا جِئْتَنَا بِبَيِّنَةٍ وَمَا نَحْنُ بِتَارِكِي ءَالِهَتِنَا عَن قَوْلِكَ وَمَا نَحْنُ لَكَ بِمُؤْمِنِينَ ۝

54 We say naught save that one of our gods hath possessed thee in an evil way. He said: I call Allah to witness, and do ye (too) bear witness, that I am innocent of (all) that ye ascribe as partners (to Allah);

إِن نَّقُولُ إِلَّا اعْتَرَاكَ بَعْضُ ءَالِهَتِنَا بِسُوٓءٍ قَالَ إِنِّي أُشْهِدُ اللَّهَ وَاشْهَدُوٓا أَنِّي بَرِيٓءٌ مِّمَّا تُشْرِكُونَ ۝

55 Beside Him. So (try to) circumvent me, all of you, give me no respite.

مِن دُونِهِ فَكِيدُونِي جَمِيعًا ثُمَّ لَا تُنظِرُونِ ۝

56 Lo! I have put my trust in Allah, my Lord and your Lord. Not an animal but He doth grasp it by the forelock! Lo! my Lord is on a straight path.

إِنِّي تَوَكَّلْتُ عَلَى اللَّهِ رَبِّي وَرَبِّكُم مَّا مِن دَآبَّةٍ إِلَّا هُوَ ءَاخِذٌ بِنَاصِيَتِهَآ إِنَّ رَبِّي عَلَىٰ صِرَاطٍ مُّسْتَقِيمٍ ۝

57 And if ye turn away, still I have conveyed unto you that wherewith I was sent unto you, and my Lord will set in place of you a folk other than you. Ye cannot injure Him at all. Lo! my Lord is Guardian over all things.

فَإِن تَوَلَّوْا فَقَدْ أَبْلَغْتُكُم مَّآ أُرْسِلْتُ بِهِ إِلَيْكُمْ وَيَسْتَخْلِفُ رَبِّي قَوْمًا غَيْرَكُمْ وَلَا تَضُرُّونَهُ شَيْئًا إِنَّ رَبِّي عَلَىٰ كُلِّ شَيْءٍ حَفِيظٌ ۝

58 And when Our commandment came to pass, We saved Hūd and those who believed with him by a mercy from Us; We saved them from a harsh doom.

وَلَمَّا جَآءَ أَمْرُنَا نَجَّيْنَا هُودًا وَالَّذِينَ ءَامَنُوا مَعَهُ بِرَحْمَةٍ مِّنَّا وَنَجَّيْنَاهُم مِّنْ عَذَابٍ غَلِيظٍ ۝

59 And such were 'Ād. They denied the revelations of their Lord and flouted His messengers and followed the command of every froward potentate.

وَتِلْكَ عَادٌ جَحَدُوا بِـَٔايَاتِ رَبِّهِمْ وَعَصَوْا رُسُلَهُ وَاتَّبَعُوٓا أَمْرَ كُلِّ جَبَّارٍ عَنِيدٍ ۝

60 And a curse was made to follow them in the world and on the Day of Resurrection. Lo! 'Ād disbelieved in their Lord. A far removal for 'Ād, the folk of Hūd!

وَأُتْبِعُوا۟ فِى هَٰذِهِ ٱلدُّنْيَا لَعْنَةً وَيَوْمَ ٱلْقِيَٰمَةِ ۚ أَلَآ إِنَّ عَادًا كَفَرُوا۟ رَبَّهُمْ ۗ أَلَا بُعْدًا لِّعَادٍ قَوْمِ هُودٍ ۝

61 And unto (the tribe of) Thamūd (We sent) their brother Salīh. He said: O my people! Serve Allah, Ye have no other God save Him. He brought you forth from the earth and hath made you husband it. So ask forgiveness of Him and turn unto Him repentant. Lo, my Lord is Nigh, Responsive.

۞ وَإِلَىٰ ثَمُودَ أَخَاهُمْ صَٰلِحًا ۚ قَالَ يَٰقَوْمِ ٱعْبُدُوا۟ ٱللَّهَ مَا لَكُم مِّنْ إِلَٰهٍ غَيْرُهُ ۖ هُوَ أَنشَأَكُم مِّنَ ٱلْأَرْضِ وَٱسْتَعْمَرَكُمْ فِيهَا فَٱسْتَغْفِرُوهُ ثُمَّ تُوبُوٓا۟ إِلَيْهِ ۚ إِنَّ رَبِّى قَرِيبٌ مُّجِيبٌ ۝

62 They said: O Salīh! Thou hast been among us hitherto as that wherein our hope was placed. Dost thou ask us not to worship what our fathers worshipped? Lo! we verily are in grave doubt concerning that to which thou callest us.

قَالُوا۟ يَٰصَٰلِحُ قَدْ كُنتَ فِينَا مَرْجُوًّا قَبْلَ هَٰذَآ ۖ أَتَنْهَىٰنَآ أَن نَّعْبُدَ مَا يَعْبُدُ ءَابَآؤُنَا وَإِنَّنَا لَفِى شَكٍّ مِّمَّا تَدْعُونَآ إِلَيْهِ مُرِيبٍ ۝

63 He said: O my people! Bethink you: if I am (acting) on clear proof from my Lord and there hath come unto me a mercy from Him, who will save me from Allah if I disobey Him? Ye would add to me naught save perdition.

قَالَ يَٰقَوْمِ أَرَءَيْتُمْ إِن كُنتُ عَلَىٰ بَيِّنَةٍ مِّن رَّبِّى وَءَاتَىٰنِى مِنْهُ رَحْمَةً فَمَن يَنصُرُنِى مِنَ ٱللَّهِ إِنْ عَصَيْتُهُ ۖ فَمَا تَزِيدُونَنِى غَيْرَ تَخْسِيرٍ ۝

64 O my people! This is the camel of Allah, a token unto you, so suffer her to feed in Allah's earth, and touch her not with harm lest a near torment seize you.

وَيَٰقَوْمِ هَٰذِهِۦ نَاقَةُ ٱللَّهِ لَكُمْ ءَايَةً فَذَرُوهَا تَأْكُلْ فِىٓ أَرْضِ ٱللَّهِ وَلَا تَمَسُّوهَا بِسُوٓءٍ فَيَأْخُذَكُمْ عَذَابٌ قَرِيبٌ ۝

65 But they hamstrung her, and then he said: Enjoy life in your dwelling place three days! This is a threat that will not be belied.

فَعَقَرُوهَا فَقَالَ تَمَتَّعُوا۟ فِى دَارِكُمْ ثَلَٰثَةَ أَيَّامٍ ۖ ذَٰلِكَ وَعْدٌ غَيْرُ مَكْذُوبٍ ۝

66 So, when Our commandment came to pass, We saved Salih, and those who believed with him, by a mercy from Us, from the ignominy of that day. Lo, thy Lord! He is the Strong, the Mighty.

فَلَمَّا جَآءَ أَمْرُنَا نَجَّيْنَا صَٰلِحًا وَالَّذِينَ ءَامَنُواْ مَعَهُۥ بِرَحْمَةٍ مِّنَّا وَمِنْ خِزْيِ يَوْمِئِذٍ إِنَّ رَبَّكَ هُوَ الْقَوِيُّ الْعَزِيزُ ٦٦

67 And the (Awful) Cry overtook those who did wrong, so that morning found them prostrate in their dwellings;

وَأَخَذَ الَّذِينَ ظَلَمُواْ الصَّيْحَةُ فَأَصْبَحُواْ فِى دِيَٰرِهِمْ جَٰثِمِينَ ٦٧

68 As though they had not dwelt there. Lo! Thamūd disbelieved in their Lord. A far removal for Thamūd!

كَأَن لَّمْ يَغْنَوْاْ فِيهَآ أَلَآ إِنَّ ثَمُودَاْ كَفَرُواْ رَبَّهُمْ أَلَا بُعْدًا لِّثَمُودَ ٦٨

69 And Our messengers came unto Abraham with good news. They said: Peace! He answered: Peace! and delayed not to bring a roasted calf.

وَلَقَدْ جَآءَتْ رُسُلُنَآ إِبْرَٰهِيمَ بِالْبُشْرَىٰ قَالُواْ سَلَٰمًا قَالَ سَلَٰمٌ فَمَا لَبِثَ أَن جَآءَ بِعِجْلٍ حَنِيذٍ ٦٩

70 And when he saw their hands reached not to it, he mistrusted them and conceived a fear of them. They said: Fear not! Lo! we are sent unto the folk of Lot.

فَلَمَّا رَءَآ أَيْدِيَهُمْ لَا تَصِلُ إِلَيْهِ نَكِرَهُمْ وَأَوْجَسَ مِنْهُمْ خِيفَةً قَالُواْ لَا تَخَفْ إِنَّآ أُرْسِلْنَآ إِلَىٰ قَوْمِ لُوطٍ ٧٠

71 And his wife, standing by, laughed when We gave her good tidings (of the birth) of Isaac, and, after Isaac, of Jacob.

وَامْرَأَتُهُۥ قَآئِمَةٌ فَضَحِكَتْ فَبَشَّرْنَٰهَا بِإِسْحَٰقَ وَمِن وَرَآءِ إِسْحَٰقَ يَعْقُوبَ ٧١

72 She said: Oh, woe is me! Shall I bear a child when I am an old woman, and this my husband is an old man? Lo! this is a strange thing!

قَالَتْ يَٰوَيْلَتَىٰٓ ءَأَلِدُ وَأَنَا۠ عَجُوزٌ وَهَٰذَا بَعْلِى شَيْخًا إِنَّ هَٰذَا لَشَىْءٌ عَجِيبٌ ٧٢

73 They said: Wonderest thou at the commandment of Allah? The mercy of Allah and His blessings be upon you, O people of the house! Lo! He is Owner of Praise, Owner of Glory!

قَالُوٓاْ أَتَعْجَبِينَ مِنْ أَمْرِ اللَّهِ رَحْمَتُ اللَّهِ وَبَرَكَٰتُهُۥ عَلَيْكُمْ أَهْلَ الْبَيْتِ إِنَّهُۥ حَمِيدٌ مَّجِيدٌ ٧٣

74 And when the awe departed from Abraham, and the glad news reached him, he pleaded with Us on behalf of the folk of Lot.

فَلَمَّا ذَهَبَ عَنْ إِبْرَٰهِيمَ ٱلرَّوْعُ وَجَآءَتْهُ ٱلْبُشْرَىٰ يُجَٰدِلُنَا فِى قَوْمِ لُوطٍ ۝

75 Lo! Abraham was mild, imploring, penitent.

إِنَّ إِبْرَٰهِيمَ لَحَلِيمٌ أَوَّٰهٌ مُّنِيبٌ ۝

76 (It was said) O Abraham! Forsake this! Lo! thy Lord's commandment hath gone forth, and lo! there cometh unto them a doom which cannot be repelled.

يَٰٓإِبْرَٰهِيمُ أَعْرِضْ عَنْ هَٰذَآ إِنَّهُۥ قَدْ جَآءَ أَمْرُ رَبِّكَ وَإِنَّهُمْ ءَاتِيهِمْ عَذَابٌ غَيْرُ مَرْدُودٍ ۝

77 And when Our messengers came unto Lot, he was distressed and knew not how to protect them. He said: This is a distressful day.

وَلَمَّا جَآءَتْ رُسُلُنَا لُوطًا سِىٓءَ بِهِمْ وَضَاقَ بِهِمْ ذَرْعًا وَقَالَ هَٰذَا يَوْمٌ عَصِيبٌ ۝

78 And his people came unto him, running towards him—and before then they used to commit abominations—he said: O my people! Here are my daughters! They are purer for you. Beware of Allah, and degrade me not in (the person of) my guests. Is there not among you any upright man?

وَجَآءَهُۥ قَوْمُهُۥ يُهْرَعُونَ إِلَيْهِ وَمِن قَبْلُ كَانُوا۟ يَعْمَلُونَ ٱلسَّيِّـَٔاتِ قَالَ يَٰقَوْمِ هَٰٓؤُلَآءِ بَنَاتِى هُنَّ أَطْهَرُ لَكُمْ فَٱتَّقُوا۟ ٱللَّهَ وَلَا تُخْزُونِ فِى ضَيْفِىٓ أَلَيْسَ مِنكُمْ رَجُلٌ رَّشِيدٌ ۝

79 They said: Well thou knowest that we have no right to thy daughters, and well thou knowest what we want.

قَالُوا۟ لَقَدْ عَلِمْتَ مَا لَنَا فِى بَنَاتِكَ مِنْ حَقٍّ وَإِنَّكَ لَتَعْلَمُ مَا نُرِيدُ ۝

80 He said: Would that I had strength to resist you or had some strong support (among you)!

قَالَ لَوْ أَنَّ لِى بِكُمْ قُوَّةً أَوْ ءَاوِىٓ إِلَىٰ رُكْنٍ شَدِيدٍ ۝

81 (The messengers) said: O Lot! Lo! we are messengers of thy Lord; they shall not reach thee. So travel with thy people in a part of the

قَالُوا۟ يَٰلُوطُ إِنَّا رُسُلُ رَبِّكَ لَن يَصِلُوٓا۟ إِلَيْكَ فَأَسْرِ بِأَهْلِكَ بِقِطْعٍ مِّنَ ٱلَّيْلِ وَلَا يَلْتَفِتْ

night, and let not one of you turn
round—(all) save thy wife. Lo! that
which smiteth them will smite her
(also). Lo! their tryst is (for) the
morning. Is not the morning nigh?

82 So when Our commandment
came to pass, We overthrew (that
township) and rained upon it stones
of clay, one after another;

83 Marked with fire in the providence of thy Lord (for the destruction of the wicked). And they are
never far from the wrong-doers.

84 And unto Madyan (We sent)
their brother Shu'ayb. He said: O
my people! Serve Allah. Ye have
no other God save Him! And give
not short measure and short weight.
Lo! I see you well-to-do, and lo! I
fear for you the doom of a beset-
ting Day.

85 O my people! Give full measure
and full weight in justice, and
wrong not people in respect of their
goods. And do not evil in the earth,
causing corruption.

86 That which Allah leaveth with
you is better for you if ye are believers; and I am not a keeper over
you.

87 They said: O Shu'ayb! Doth thy
way of prayer command thee that
we should forsake that which our
fathers (used to) worship, or that
we (should leave off) doing what

مِنكُمْ أَحَدٌ إِلَّا ٱمْرَأَتَكَ إِنَّهُۥ مُصِيبُهَا
مَآ أَصَابَهُمْ إِنَّ مَوْعِدَهُمُ ٱلصُّبْحُ
أَلَيْسَ ٱلصُّبْحُ بِقَرِيبٍ ۝

فَلَمَّا جَآءَ أَمْرُنَا جَعَلْنَا عَٰلِيَهَا سَافِلَهَا
وَأَمْطَرْنَا عَلَيْهَا حِجَارَةً مِّن سِجِّيلٍ
مَّنضُودٍ ۝

مُّسَوَّمَةً عِندَ رَبِّكَ وَمَا هِىَ مِنَ ٱلظَّٰلِمِينَ
بِبَعِيدٍ ۝

۞ وَإِلَىٰ مَدْيَنَ أَخَاهُمْ شُعَيْبًا قَالَ يَٰقَوْمِ ٱعْبُدُوا۟
ٱللَّهَ مَا لَكُم مِّنْ إِلَٰهٍ غَيْرُهُۥ وَلَا تَنقُصُوا۟
ٱلْمِكْيَالَ وَٱلْمِيزَانَ إِنِّىٓ أَرَىٰكُم بِخَيْرٍ
وَإِنِّىٓ أَخَافُ عَلَيْكُمْ عَذَابَ يَوْمٍ مُّحِيطٍ ۝

وَيَٰقَوْمِ أَوْفُوا۟ ٱلْمِكْيَالَ وَٱلْمِيزَانَ بِٱلْقِسْطِ
وَلَا تَبْخَسُوا۟ ٱلنَّاسَ أَشْيَآءَهُمْ وَلَا تَعْثَوْا۟
فِى ٱلْأَرْضِ مُفْسِدِينَ ۝

بَقِيَّتُ ٱللَّهِ خَيْرٌ لَّكُمْ إِن كُنتُم مُّؤْمِنِينَ
وَمَآ أَنَا۠ عَلَيْكُم بِحَفِيظٍ ۝

قَالُوا۟ يَٰشُعَيْبُ أَصَلَوٰتُكَ تَأْمُرُكَ أَن نَّتْرُكَ
مَا يَعْبُدُ ءَابَآؤُنَآ أَوْ أَن نَّفْعَلَ فِىٓ أَمْوَٰلِنَا

we will with our own property. Lo! thou are the mild, the guide to right behaviour.

88 He said: O my people! Bethink you: if I am (acting) on a clear proof from my Lord and He sustaineth me with fair sustenance from Him (how can I concede aught to you)? I desire not to do behind your backs that which I ask you not to do. I desire naught save reform so far as I am able. My welfare is only in Allah. In Him I trust and unto Him I turn (repentant).

89 And, O my people! Let not the schism with me cause you to sin so that there befall you that which befell the folk of Noah or the folk of Hūd, or the folk of Ṣāliḥ; and the folk of Lot are not far off from you.

90 Ask pardon of your Lord and then turn unto Him (repentant). Lo! my Lord is Merciful, Loving.

91 They said: O Shuʿayb! We understand not much of that thou tellest, and lo! we do behold thee weak among us. But for thy family, we should have stoned thee, for thou art not strong against us.

92 He said: O my people! Is my family more to be honoured by you than Allah? And ye put Him behind you, neglected! Lo! my Lord surroundeth what ye do.

مَا نَشَـٰٓؤُاْ إِنَّكَ لَأَنتَ ٱلۡحَلِيمُ ٱلرَّشِيدُ ۝

قَالَ يَـٰقَوۡمِ أَرَءَيۡتُمۡ إِن كُنتُ عَلَىٰ بَيِّنَةٍ مِّن رَّبِّى وَرَزَقَنِى مِنۡهُ رِزۡقًا حَسَنًا وَمَآ أُرِيدُ أَنۡ أُخَالِفَكُمۡ إِلَىٰ مَآ أَنۡهَىٰكُمۡ عَنۡهُ إِنۡ أُرِيدُ إِلَّا ٱلۡإِصۡلَٰحَ مَا ٱسۡتَطَعۡتُ وَمَا تَوۡفِيقِىٓ إِلَّا بِٱللَّهِ عَلَيۡهِ تَوَكَّلۡتُ وَإِلَيۡهِ أُنِيبُ ۝

وَيَـٰقَوۡمِ لَا يَجۡرِمَنَّكُمۡ شِقَاقِىٓ أَن يُصِيبَكُم مِّثۡلُ مَآ أَصَابَ قَوۡمَ نُوحٍ أَوۡ قَوۡمَ هُودٍ أَوۡ قَوۡمَ صَٰلِحٍ وَمَا قَوۡمُ لُوطٍ مِّنكُم بِبَعِيدٍ ۝

وَٱسۡتَغۡفِرُواْ رَبَّكُمۡ ثُمَّ تُوبُوٓاْ إِلَيۡهِ إِنَّ رَبِّى رَحِيمٌ وَدُودٌ ۝

قَالُواْ يَـٰشُعَيۡبُ مَا نَفۡقَهُ كَثِيرًا مِّمَّا تَقُولُ وَإِنَّا لَنَرَىٰكَ فِينَا ضَعِيفًا وَلَوۡلَا رَهۡطُكَ لَرَجَمۡنَٰكَ وَمَآ أَنتَ عَلَيۡنَا بِعَزِيزٍ ۝

قَالَ يَـٰقَوۡمِ أَرَهۡطِىٓ أَعَزُّ عَلَيۡكُم مِّنَ ٱللَّهِ وَٱتَّخَذۡتُمُوهُ وَرَآءَكُمۡ ظِهۡرِيًّا إِنَّ رَبِّى بِمَا تَعۡمَلُونَ مُحِيطٌ ۝

93 And, O my people! Act according to your power, lo! I (too) am acting. Ye will soon know on whom there cometh a doom that will abase him, and who it is that lieth. And watch! Lo! I am watcher with you.

وَيَٰقَوْمِ اعْمَلُوا عَلَىٰ مَكَانَتِكُمْ إِنِّي عَامِلٌ
سَوْفَ تَعْلَمُونَ مَن يَأْتِيهِ عَذَابٌ يُخْزِيهِ
وَمَنْ هُوَ كَاذِبٌ وَارْتَقِبُوا
إِنِّي مَعَكُمْ رَقِيبٌ ۝

94 And when Our commandment came to pass; We saved Shu'ayb and those who believed with Him by a mercy from Us; and the (Awful) Cry seized those who did injustice, and morning found them prostrate in their dwellings;

وَلَمَّا جَاءَ أَمْرُنَا نَجَّيْنَا شُعَيْبًا وَالَّذِينَ آمَنُوا
مَعَهُ بِرَحْمَةٍ مِّنَّا وَأَخَذَتِ الَّذِينَ ظَلَمُوا الصَّيْحَةُ
فَأَصْبَحُوا فِي دِيَارِهِمْ جَاثِمِينَ ۝

95 As though they had not dwelt there. A far removal for Madyan, even as Thamūd had been removed afar!

كَأَن لَّمْ يَغْنَوْا فِيهَا أَلَا بُعْدًا لِّمَدْيَنَ كَمَا بَعِدَتْ
ثَمُودُ ۝

96 And verily We sent Moses with Our revelations and a clear warrant;

وَلَقَدْ أَرْسَلْنَا مُوسَىٰ بِآيَاتِنَا وَسُلْطَانٍ مُّبِينٍ ۝

97 Unto Pharaoh and his chiefs, but they did follow the command of Pharaoh, and the command of Pharaoh was no right guide.

إِلَىٰ فِرْعَوْنَ وَمَلَإِيهِ فَاتَّبَعُوا أَمْرَ فِرْعَوْنَ
وَمَا أَمْرُ فِرْعَوْنَ بِرَشِيدٍ ۝

98 He will go before his people on the Day of Resurrection and will lead them to the Fire for watering-place. Ah, hapless is the watering-place (whither they are) led.

يَقْدُمُ قَوْمَهُ يَوْمَ الْقِيَامَةِ فَأَوْرَدَهُمُ النَّارَ
وَبِئْسَ الْوِرْدُ الْمَوْرُودُ ۝

99 A curse is made to follow them in the world and on the Day of Resurrection. Hapless is the gift (that will be) given (them).

وَأُتْبِعُوا فِي هَٰذِهِ لَعْنَةً وَيَوْمَ الْقِيَامَةِ بِئْسَ
الرِّفْدُ الْمَرْفُودُ ۝

100 That is (something) of the tidings of the townships[5] (which were destroyed of old). We relate it unto thee (Muhammad). Some of them are standing and some (already) reaped.

ذَٰلِكَ مِنْ أَنبَآءِ ٱلْقُرَىٰ نَقُصُّهُۥ عَلَيْكَ مِنْهَا قَآئِمٌ وَحَصِيدٌ ۝

101 We wronged them not, but they did wrong themselves; and their gods on whom they call beside Allah availed them naught when came thy Lord's command; they added to them naught save ruin.

وَمَا ظَلَمْنَٰهُمْ وَلَٰكِن ظَلَمُوٓاْ أَنفُسَهُمْ فَمَآ أَغْنَتْ عَنْهُمْ ءَالِهَتُهُمُ ٱلَّتِى يَدْعُونَ مِن دُونِ ٱللَّهِ مِن شَىْءٍ لَّمَّا جَآءَ أَمْرُ رَبِّكَ وَمَا زَادُوهُمْ غَيْرَ تَتْبِيبٍ ۝

102 Even thus is the grasp of thy Lord when he graspeth the townships[6] while they are doing wrong. Lo! His grasp is painful, very strong.

وَكَذَٰلِكَ أَخْذُ رَبِّكَ إِذَآ أَخَذَ ٱلْقُرَىٰ وَهِىَ ظَٰلِمَةٌ إِنَّ أَخْذَهُۥٓ أَلِيمٌ شَدِيدٌ ۝

103 Lo! herein verily there is a portent for those who fear the doom of the Hereafter. That is a day unto which mankind will be gathered, and that is a day that will be witnessed.

إِنَّ فِى ذَٰلِكَ لَءَايَةً لِّمَنْ خَافَ عَذَابَ ٱلْءَاخِرَةِ ذَٰلِكَ يَوْمٌ مَّجْمُوعٌ لَّهُ ٱلنَّاسُ وَذَٰلِكَ يَوْمٌ مَّشْهُودٌ ۝

104 And We defer it only as a term already reckoned.

وَمَا نُؤَخِّرُهُۥٓ إِلَّا لِأَجَلٍ مَّعْدُودٍ ۝

105 On the day when it cometh no soul will speak except by His permission; some among them will be wretched, (others) glad.

يَوْمَ يَأْتِ لَا تَكَلَّمُ نَفْسٌ إِلَّا بِإِذْنِهِۦ فَمِنْهُمْ شَقِىٌّ وَسَعِيدٌ ۝

106 As for those who will be wretched (on that day), they will be in the Fire; sighing and wailing will be their portion therein.

فَأَمَّا ٱلَّذِينَ شَقُواْ فَفِى ٱلنَّارِ لَهُمْ فِيهَا زَفِيرٌ وَشَهِيقٌ ۝

---

5. Or *communities*.

6. Or *communities*.

107   Abiding there so long as the heavens and the earth endure save for that which thy Lord willeth. Lo! thy Lord is Doer of what He will.

108   And as for those who will be glad (that day), they will be in the Garden, abiding there so long as the heavens and the earth endure save for that which thy Lord willeth: a gift unfailing.

خَٰلِدِينَ فِيهَا مَا دَامَتِ ٱلسَّمَٰوَٰتُ وَٱلۡأَرۡضُ إِلَّا مَا شَآءَ رَبُّكَ إِنَّ رَبَّكَ فَعَّالٌ لِّمَا يُرِيدُ ۝

۞ وَأَمَّا ٱلَّذِينَ سُعِدُوا۟ فَفِى ٱلۡجَنَّةِ خَٰلِدِينَ فِيهَا مَا دَامَتِ ٱلسَّمَٰوَٰتُ وَٱلۡأَرۡضُ إِلَّا مَا شَآءَ رَبُّكَ عَطَآءً غَيۡرَ مَجۡذُوذٍ ۝

109   So be not thou in doubt concerning that which these (folk) worship. They worship only as their fathers worshipped aforetime. Lo! We shall pay them their whole due unabated.

فَلَا تَكُ فِى مِرۡيَةٍ مِّمَّا يَعۡبُدُ هَٰٓؤُلَآءِ مَا يَعۡبُدُونَ إِلَّا كَمَا يَعۡبُدُ ءَابَآؤُهُم مِّن قَبۡلُ وَإِنَّا لَمُوَفُّوهُمۡ نَصِيبَهُمۡ غَيۡرَ مَنقُوصٍ ۝

110   And We verily gave unto Moses the Scripture, and there was strife thereupon; and had it not been for a Word that had already gone forth from thy Lord, the case would have been judged between them, and lo! they are in grave doubt concerning it.

وَلَقَدۡ ءَاتَيۡنَا مُوسَى ٱلۡكِتَٰبَ فَٱخۡتُلِفَ فِيهِ وَلَوۡلَا كَلِمَةٌ سَبَقَتۡ مِن رَّبِّكَ لَقُضِىَ بَيۡنَهُمۡ وَإِنَّهُمۡ لَفِى شَكٍّ مِّنۡهُ مُرِيبٍ ۝

111   And lo! unto each thy Lord will verily repay his works in full. Lo! He is Aware of what they do.

وَإِنَّ كُلًّا لَّمَّا لَيُوَفِّيَنَّهُمۡ رَبُّكَ أَعۡمَٰلَهُمۡ إِنَّهُۥ بِمَا يَعۡمَلُونَ خَبِيرٌ ۝

112   So tread thou the straight path as thou art commanded, and those who turn (unto Allah) with thee, and transgress not. Lo! He is Seer of what ye do.

فَٱسۡتَقِمۡ كَمَآ أُمِرۡتَ وَمَن تَابَ مَعَكَ وَلَا تَطۡغَوۡا۟ إِنَّهُۥ بِمَا تَعۡمَلُونَ بَصِيرٌ ۝

113   And incline not toward those who do wrong lest the Fire touch you, and ye have no protecting

وَلَا تَرۡكَنُوٓا۟ إِلَى ٱلَّذِينَ ظَلَمُوا۟ فَتَمَسَّكُمُ ٱلنَّارُ وَمَا لَكُم مِّن دُونِ ٱللَّهِ مِنۡ أَوۡلِيَآءَ ثُمَّ

friends against Allah, and afterward ye would not be helped.

114 Establish worship at the two ends of the day and in some watches of the night. Lo! good deeds annul ill deeds. This is a reminder for the mindful.

115 And have patience, (O Muḥammad), for lo! Allah loseth not the wages of the good.

116 If only there had been among the generations before you men possessing a remnant (of good sense) to warn (their people) from corruption in the earth, as did a few of those whom We saved from them! The wrong-doers followed that by which they were made sapless, and were guilty.

117 In truth thy Lord destroyed not the townships tyrannously while their folk were doing right.

118 And if thy Lord had willed, He verily would have made mankind one nation, yet they cease not differing;

119 Save him on whom thy Lord hath mercy; and for that He did create them. And the Word of thy Lord hath been fulfilled: Verily I shall fill hell with the jinn and mankind together.

120 And all that We relate unto thee of the story of the messengers is in order that thereby We may

لَا تُنصَرُونَ ۝

وَأَقِمِ الصَّلَوٰةَ طَرَفَيِ النَّهَارِ وَزُلَفًا مِّنَ الَّيْلِ إِنَّ الْحَسَنَـٰتِ يُذْهِبْنَ السَّيِّئَاتِ ذَٰلِكَ ذِكْرَىٰ لِلذَّاكِرِينَ ۝

وَاصْبِرْ فَإِنَّ اللَّهَ لَا يُضِيعُ أَجْرَ الْمُحْسِنِينَ ۝

فَلَوْلَا كَانَ مِنَ الْقُرُونِ مِن قَبْلِكُمْ أُوْلُواْ بَقِيَّةٍ يَنْهَوْنَ عَنِ الْفَسَادِ فِي الْأَرْضِ إِلَّا قَلِيلًا مِّمَّنْ أَنجَيْنَا مِنْهُمْ وَاتَّبَعَ الَّذِينَ ظَلَمُواْ مَا أُتْرِفُواْ فِيهِ وَكَانُواْ مُجْرِمِينَ ۝

وَمَا كَانَ رَبُّكَ لِيُهْلِكَ الْقُرَىٰ بِظُلْمٍ وَأَهْلُهَا مُصْلِحُونَ ۝

وَلَوْ شَاءَ رَبُّكَ لَجَعَلَ النَّاسَ أُمَّةً وَٰحِدَةً وَلَا يَزَالُونَ مُخْتَلِفِينَ ۝

إِلَّا مَن رَّحِمَ رَبُّكَ وَلِذَٰلِكَ خَلَقَهُمْ وَتَمَّتْ كَلِمَةُ رَبِّكَ لَأَمْلَأَنَّ جَهَنَّمَ مِنَ الْجِنَّةِ وَالنَّاسِ أَجْمَعِينَ ۝

وَكُلًّا نَّقُصُّ عَلَيْكَ مِنْ أَنْبَاءِ الرُّسُلِ مَا نُثَبِّتُ بِهِ

make firm thy heart. And herein hath come unto thee the Truth and an exhortation and a reminder for believers.

121   And say unto those who believe not: Act according to your power. Lo! we (too) are acting.

122   And wait! Lo! we (too) are waiting.

123   And Allah's is the Invisible of the heavens and the earth, and unto Him the whole matter will be returned. So worship Him and put thy trust in Him. Lo! thy Lord is not unaware of what ye (mortals) do.

فُؤَادَكَ وَجَآءَكَ فِى هَٰذِهِ ٱلْحَقُّ وَمَوْعِظَةٌ وَذِكْرَىٰ لِلْمُؤْمِنِينَ ﴿١٢٠﴾

وَقُل لِّلَّذِينَ لَا يُؤْمِنُونَ ٱعْمَلُوا۟ عَلَىٰ مَكَانَتِكُمْ إِنَّا عَٰمِلُونَ ﴿١٢١﴾

وَٱنتَظِرُوٓا۟ إِنَّا مُنتَظِرُونَ ﴿١٢٢﴾

وَلِلَّهِ غَيْبُ ٱلسَّمَٰوَٰتِ وَٱلْأَرْضِ وَإِلَيْهِ يُرْجَعُ ٱلْأَمْرُ كُلُّهُ فَٱعْبُدْهُ وَتَوَكَّلْ عَلَيْهِ وَمَا رَبُّكَ بِغَٰفِلٍ عَمَّا تَعْمَلُونَ ﴿١٢٣﴾

Yūsuf
(Joseph)

Yūsuf takes its name from its subject which is the lifestory of Joseph. It differs from all other sūrahs in having only one subject. The differences from the Bible narrative are striking. Jacob is here a Prophet, who is not deceived by the story of his son's death, but is distressed because, through a suspension of his clairvoyance, he cannot see what has become of Joseph. The real importance of the narrative, its psychic burden, is emphasised throughout, and the manner of narration, though astonishing to Western readers, is vivid.

Tradition says that it was recited by the Prophet at Makkah to the first converts from Yathrib (Al-Madīnah), i.e. in the second year before the Hijrah; but that, as Nöldeke points out, does not mean that it was not revealed till then, but that it had been revealed by then.

A late Makkan sūrah.

In the name of Allah, the Beneficent, the Merciful.

1   Alif. Lām. Rā.[1] These are verses of the Scripture that maketh plain.

2   Lo! We have revealed it, a Lecture[2] in Arabic, that ye may understand.

---

1. See footnote, Sūrah 2, v. 1.

2. Ar. *Qur'an.*

We narrate unto thee (Muhammad) the best of narratives in that We have inspired in thee this Qur'an, though aforetime thou wast of the heedless.

4 When Joseph said unto his father: O my father! Lo! I saw in a dream eleven planets and the sun and the moon, I saw them prostrating themselves unto me.

5 He said: O my dear son! Tell not thy brethren of thy vision, lest they plot a plot against thee. Lo! Satan is for man an open foe.

6 Thus thy Lord will prefer thee and will teach thee the interpretation of events, and will perfect his grace upon thee and upon the family of Jacob as he perfected it upon thy forefathers, Abraham and Isaac. Lo! thy Lord is Knower, Wise.

7 Verily in Joseph and his brethren are signs (of Allah's Sovereignty) for the inquiring.

8 When they said: Verily Joseph and his brother are dearer to our father than we are, many though we be. Lo! our father is in plain aberration.

9 (One said): Kill Joseph or cast him to some (other) land, so that your father's favour may be all for you, and (that) ye may afterward be righteous folk.

نَحْنُ نَقُصُّ عَلَيْكَ أَحْسَنَ ٱلْقَصَصِ بِمَآ أَوْحَيْنَآ إِلَيْكَ هَٰذَا ٱلْقُرْءَانَ وَإِن كُنتَ مِن قَبْلِهِۦ لَمِنَ ٱلْغَٰفِلِينَ ٣

إِذْ قَالَ يُوسُفُ لِأَبِيهِ يَٰٓأَبَتِ إِنِّي رَأَيْتُ أَحَدَ عَشَرَ كَوْكَبًا وَٱلشَّمْسَ وَٱلْقَمَرَ رَأَيْتُهُمْ لِي سَٰجِدِينَ ٤

قَالَ يَٰبُنَيَّ لَا تَقْصُصْ رُءْيَاكَ عَلَىٰٓ إِخْوَتِكَ فَيَكِيدُوا۟ لَكَ كَيْدًا إِنَّ ٱلشَّيْطَٰنَ لِلْإِنسَٰنِ عَدُوٌّ مُّبِينٌ ٥

وَكَذَٰلِكَ يَجْتَبِيكَ رَبُّكَ وَيُعَلِّمُكَ مِن تَأْوِيلِ ٱلْأَحَادِيثِ وَيُتِمُّ نِعْمَتَهُۥ عَلَيْكَ وَعَلَىٰٓ ءَالِ يَعْقُوبَ كَمَآ أَتَمَّهَا عَلَىٰٓ أَبَوَيْكَ مِن قَبْلُ إِبْرَٰهِيمَ وَإِسْحَٰقَ إِنَّ رَبَّكَ عَلِيمٌ حَكِيمٌ ٦

۞ لَّقَدْ كَانَ فِي يُوسُفَ وَإِخْوَتِهِۦٓ ءَايَٰتٌ لِّلسَّآئِلِينَ ٧

إِذْ قَالُوا۟ لَيُوسُفُ وَأَخُوهُ أَحَبُّ إِلَىٰٓ أَبِينَا مِنَّا وَنَحْنُ عُصْبَةٌ إِنَّ أَبَانَا لَفِي ضَلَٰلٍ مُّبِينٍ ٨

ٱقْتُلُوا۟ يُوسُفَ أَوِ ٱطْرَحُوهُ أَرْضًا يَخْلُ لَكُمْ وَجْهُ أَبِيكُمْ وَتَكُونُوا۟ مِنۢ بَعْدِهِۦ قَوْمًا صَٰلِحِينَ ٩

10 One among them said: Kill not Joseph but, if ye must be doing, fling him into the depth of the pit; some caravan will find him.

قَالَ قَآئِلٌ مِّنْهُمْ لَا تَقْتُلُوا يُوْسُفَ وَأَلْقُوْهُ فِيْ غَيٰبَتِ الْجُبِّ يَلْتَقِطْهُ بَعْضُ السَّيَّارَةِ إِنْ كُنْتُمْ فٰعِلِيْنَ ۝

11 They said: O our father! Why wilt thou not trust us with Joseph, when lo! we are good friends to him?

قَالُوْا يٰٓأَبَانَا مَا لَكَ لَا تَأْمَنَّا عَلٰى يُوْسُفَ وَإِنَّا لَهُ لَنٰصِحُوْنَ ۝

12 Send him with us tomorrow that he may enjoy himself and play. And lo! we shall take good care of him.

أَرْسِلْهُ مَعَنَا غَدًا يَّرْتَعْ وَيَلْعَبْ وَإِنَّا لَهُ لَحٰفِظُوْنَ ۝

13 He said: Lo! in truth it saddens me that ye should take him with you, and I fear lest the wolf devour him while ye are heedless of him.

قَالَ إِنِّيْ لَيَحْزُنُنِيْ أَنْ تَذْهَبُوْا بِهِ وَأَخَافُ أَنْ يَّأْكُلَهُ الذِّئْبُ وَأَنْتُمْ عَنْهُ غٰفِلُوْنَ ۝

14 They said: If the wolf should devour him when we are (so strong) a band, then surely we should have already perished.

قَالُوْا لَئِنْ أَكَلَهُ الذِّئْبُ وَنَحْنُ عُصْبَةٌ إِنَّآ إِذًا لَّخٰسِرُوْنَ ۝

15 Then, when they led him off, and were of one mind that they should place him in the depth of the pit, We inspired in him: Thou wilt tell them of this deed of theirs when they know (thee) not.

فَلَمَّا ذَهَبُوْا بِهِ وَأَجْمَعُوْا أَنْ يَّجْعَلُوْهُ فِيْ غَيٰبَتِ الْجُبِّ وَأَوْحَيْنَآ إِلَيْهِ لَتُنَبِّئَنَّهُمْ بِأَمْرِهِمْ هٰذَا وَهُمْ لَا يَشْعُرُوْنَ ۝

16 And they came weeping to their father in the evening.

وَجَآءُوْ أَبَاهُمْ عِشَآءً يَّبْكُوْنَ ۝

17 Saying: O our father! We went racing one with another, and left Joseph by our things, and the wolf devoured him, and thou believest not our sayings even when we speak the truth.

قَالُوْا يٰٓأَبَانَآ إِنَّا ذَهَبْنَا نَسْتَبِقُ وَتَرَكْنَا يُوْسُفَ عِنْدَ مَتَاعِنَا فَأَكَلَهُ الذِّئْبُ وَمَآ أَنْتَ بِمُؤْمِنٍ لَّنَا وَلَوْ كُنَّا صٰدِقِيْنَ ۝

18 And they came with false blood
on his shirt. He said: Nay, but your
minds have beguiled you into something. (My course is) comely patience. And Allah it is whose help is
to be sought in that (predicament)
which ye describe.

وَجَاءُوْ عَلَىٰ قَمِيْصِهِ بِدَمٍ كَذِبٍ قَالَ بَلْ سَوَّلَتْ
لَكُمْ أَنْفُسُكُمْ أَمْرًا فَصَبْرٌ جَمِيْلٌ
وَاللّٰهُ الْمُسْتَعَانُ عَلَىٰ مَا تَصِفُوْنَ ۝

19 And there came a caravan, and
they sent their water drawer. He let
down his pail (into the pit). He
said: Good luck! Here is a youth.
And they hid him as a treasure, and
Allah was Aware of what they did.

وَجَاءَتْ سَيَّارَةٌ فَأَرْسَلُوْا وَارِدَهُمْ فَأَدْلَىٰ دَلْوَهُ قَالَ
يٰبُشْرٰى هٰذَا غُلٰمٌ وَأَسَرُّوْهُ بِضَاعَةً
وَاللّٰهُ عَلِيْمٌ بِمَا يَعْمَلُوْنَ ۝

20 And they sold him for a low
price, a number of silver coins; and
they attached no value to him.

وَشَرَوْهُ بِثَمَنٍ بَخْسٍ دَرَاهِمَ مَعْدُوْدَةٍ
وَكَانُوْا فِيْهِ مِنَ الزَّاهِدِيْنَ ۝

21 And he of Egypt who purchased
him said unto his wife: Receive him
honourably. Perchance he may prove useful to us or we may adopt
him as a son. Thus We established
Joseph in the land that We might
teach him the interpretation of events. And Allah was predominant in
his career, but most of mankind
know not.

وَقَالَ الَّذِى اشْتَرَاهُ مِنْ مِّصْرَ لِامْرَأَتِهِ أَكْرِمِى
مَثْوَاهُ عَسٰى أَنْ يَّنْفَعَنَا أَوْ نَتَّخِذَهُ وَلَدًا
وَكَذٰلِكَ مَكَّنَّا لِيُوْسُفَ فِى الْأَرْضِ
وَلِنُعَلِّمَهُ مِنْ تَأْوِيْلِ الْأَحَادِيْثِ وَاللّٰهُ غَالِبٌ
عَلٰى أَمْرِهِ وَلٰكِنَّ أَكْثَرَ النَّاسِ
لَا يَعْلَمُوْنَ ۝

22 And when he reached his prime,
We gave him wisdom and knowledge. Thus We reward the good.

وَلَمَّا بَلَغَ أَشُدَّهُ ءَاتَيْنَاهُ حُكْمًا وَعِلْمًا
وَكَذٰلِكَ نَجْزِى الْمُحْسِنِيْنَ ۝

23 And she, in whose house he
was, asked of him an evil act. She
bolted the doors and said: Come!
He said: I seek refuge in Allah! Lo!
he is my Lord, who hath treated me
honourably. Wrong-doers never prosper.

وَرَاوَدَتْهُ الَّتِى هُوَ فِى بَيْتِهَا عَنْ نَفْسِهِ وَغَلَّقَتِ
الْأَبْوَابَ وَقَالَتْ هَيْتَ لَكَ قَالَ مَعَاذَ اللّٰهِ
إِنَّهُ رَبِّى أَحْسَنَ مَثْوَاىَ إِنَّهُ لَا يُفْلِحُ
الظّٰلِمُوْنَ ۝

24 She verily desired him, and he would have desired her if it had not been that he saw the argument of his Lord. Thus it was, that We might ward off from him evil and lewdness. Lo! he was of Our chosen slaves.

وَلَقَدْ هَمَّتْ بِهِ ۖ وَهَمَّ بِهَا لَوْلَا أَن رَّءَا بُرْهَٰنَ رَبِّهِ ۚ كَذَٰلِكَ لِنَصْرِفَ عَنْهُ ٱلسُّوٓءَ وَٱلْفَحْشَآءَ ۚ إِنَّهُۥ مِنْ عِبَادِنَا ٱلْمُخْلَصِينَ ﴿٢٤﴾

25 And they raced with one another to the door, and she tore his shirt from behind, and they met her lord and master at the door. She said: What shall be his reward, who wisheth evil to thy folk, save prison or a painful doom?

وَٱسْتَبَقَا ٱلْبَابَ وَقَدَّتْ قَمِيصَهُۥ مِن دُبُرٍ وَأَلْفَيَا سَيِّدَهَا لَدَا ٱلْبَابِ ۚ قَالَتْ مَا جَزَآءُ مَنْ أَرَادَ بِأَهْلِكَ سُوٓءًا إِلَّآ أَن يُسْجَنَ أَوْ عَذَابٌ أَلِيمٌ ﴿٢٥﴾

26 (Joseph) said: She it was who asked of me an evil act. And a witness of her own folk testified: If his shirt is torn from the front, then she speaketh truth and he is of the liars.

قَالَ هِىَ رَٰوَدَتْنِى عَن نَّفْسِى ۚ وَشَهِدَ شَاهِدٌ مِّنْ أَهْلِهَآ إِن كَانَ قَمِيصُهُۥ قُدَّ مِن قُبُلٍ فَصَدَقَتْ وَهُوَ مِنَ ٱلْكَٰذِبِينَ ﴿٢٦﴾

27 And if his shirt is torn from behind, then she hath lied and he is of the truthful.

وَإِن كَانَ قَمِيصُهُۥ قُدَّ مِن دُبُرٍ فَكَذَبَتْ وَهُوَ مِنَ ٱلصَّٰدِقِينَ ﴿٢٧﴾

28 So when he saw his shirt torn from behind, he said: Lo! this is of the guile of you women. Lo! the guile of you is very great.

فَلَمَّا رَءَا قَمِيصَهُۥ قُدَّ مِن دُبُرٍ قَالَ إِنَّهُۥ مِن كَيْدِكُنَّ ۖ إِنَّ كَيْدَكُنَّ عَظِيمٌ ﴿٢٨﴾

29 O Joseph! Turn away from this, and thou, (O woman), ask forgiveness for thy sin. Lo! thou art of the sinful.

يُوسُفُ أَعْرِضْ عَنْ هَٰذَا ۚ وَٱسْتَغْفِرِى لِذَنۢبِكِ ۖ إِنَّكِ كُنتِ مِنَ ٱلْخَاطِئِينَ ﴿٢٩﴾

30 And women in the city said: The ruler's wife is asking of her slave-boy an ill deed. Indeed he has smitten her to the heart with love. We behold her in plain aberration.

۞ وَقَالَ نِسْوَةٌ فِى ٱلْمَدِينَةِ ٱمْرَأَتُ ٱلْعَزِيزِ تُرَٰوِدُ فَتَىٰهَا عَن نَّفْسِهِ ۖ قَدْ شَغَفَهَا حُبًّا ۖ إِنَّا لَنَرَىٰهَا فِى ضَلَٰلٍ مُّبِينٍ ﴿٣٠﴾

31 And when she heard of their sly talk, she sent to them and prepared for them a cushioned couch (to lie on at the feast) and gave to every one of them a knife and said (to Joseph): Come out unto them! And when they saw him they exalted him and cut their hands, exclaiming: Allah Blameless! This is not a human being. This is no other than some gracious angel.

فَلَمَّا سَمِعَتْ بِمَكْرِهِنَّ أَرْسَلَتْ إِلَيْهِنَّ وَأَعْتَدَتْ لَهُنَّ مُتَّكَأً وَآتَتْ كُلَّ وَاحِدَةٍ مِنْهُنَّ سِكِّينًا وَقَالَتِ اخْرُجْ عَلَيْهِنَّ فَلَمَّا رَأَيْنَهُ أَكْبَرْنَهُ وَقَطَّعْنَ أَيْدِيَهُنَّ وَقُلْنَ حَاشَ لِلّهِ مَا هَذَا بَشَرًا إِنْ هَذَا إِلَّا مَلَكٌ كَرِيمٌ ۝

32 She said: This is he on whose account ye blamed me. I asked of him an evil act, but he proved continent, but if he do not my behest he verily shall be imprisoned, and verily shall be of those brought low.

قَالَتْ فَذَلِكُنَّ الَّذِي لُمْتُنَّنِي فِيهِ وَلَقَدْ رَاوَدتُّهُ عَن نَّفْسِهِ فَاسْتَعْصَمَ وَلَئِن لَّمْ يَفْعَلْ مَا آمُرُهُ لَيُسْجَنَنَّ وَلَيَكُونًا مِّنَ الصَّاغِرِينَ ۝

33 He said: O my Lord! Prison is more dear than that unto which they urge me, and if Thou fend not off their wiles from me; I shall incline unto them and become of the foolish.

قَالَ رَبِّ السِّجْنُ أَحَبُّ إِلَيَّ مِمَّا يَدْعُونَنِي إِلَيْهِ وَإِلَّا تَصْرِفْ عَنِّي كَيْدَهُنَّ أَصْبُ إِلَيْهِنَّ وَأَكُن مِّنَ الْجَاهِلِينَ ۝

34 So his Lord heard his prayer and fended off their wiles from him. Lo! He is Hearer, Knower.

فَاسْتَجَابَ لَهُ رَبُّهُ فَصَرَفَ عَنْهُ كَيْدَهُنَّ إِنَّهُ هُوَ السَّمِيعُ الْعَلِيمُ ۝

35 And it seemed good to them (the men folk) after they had seen the signs (of his innocence) to imprison him for a time.

ثُمَّ بَدَا لَهُم مِّن بَعْدِ مَا رَأَوُا الْآيَاتِ لَيَسْجُنُنَّهُ حَتَّى حِينٍ ۝

36 And two young men went to prison with him. One of them said: I dreamed that I was pressing wine. The other said: I dreamed that I was carrying upon my head bread

وَدَخَلَ مَعَهُ السِّجْنَ فَتَيَانِ قَالَ أَحَدُهُمَا إِنِّي أَرَانِي أَعْصِرُ خَمْرًا وَقَالَ الْآخَرُ إِنِّي أَرَانِي أَحْمِلُ فَوْقَ رَأْسِي خُبْزًا تَأْكُلُ الطَّيْرُ مِنْهُ نَبِّئْنَا

whereof the birds were eating. Announce unto us the interpretation, for we see thee of those good (at interpretation).

37 He said: The food which ye are given (daily) shall not come unto you but I shall tell you the interpretation ere it cometh unto you. This is of that which my Lord hath taught me. Lo! I have forsaken the religion of folk who believe not in Allah and are disbelievers in the Hereafter.

38 And I have followed the religion of my fathers, Abraham and Isaac and Jacob. It never was for us to attribute aught as partner to Allah. This is of the bounty of Allah unto us (the seed of Abraham) and unto mankind; but most men give not thanks.

39 O my two fellow prisoners! Are divers lords better, or Allah the One, the Almighty?

40 Those whom ye worship beside Him are but names which ye have named, ye and your fathers. Allah hath revealed no sanction for them. The decision rests with Allah only, Who hath commanded you that ye worship none save Him. This is the right religion, but most men know not.

41 O my two fellow prisoners! As for one of you, he will pour out wine for his lord to drink; and as

بِتَأْوِيلِهِۦٓ إِنَّا نَرَىٰكَ مِنَ ٱلْمُحْسِنِينَ ﴿٣٦﴾

قَالَ لَا يَأْتِيكُمَا طَعَامٌ تُرْزَقَانِهِۦٓ إِلَّا نَبَّأْتُكُمَا بِتَأْوِيلِهِۦ قَبْلَ أَن يَأْتِيَكُمَا ذَٰلِكُمَا مِمَّا عَلَّمَنِي رَبِّىٓ إِنِّي تَرَكْتُ مِلَّةَ قَوْمٍ لَّا يُؤْمِنُونَ بِٱللَّهِ وَهُم بِٱلْأَخِرَةِ هُمْ كَٰفِرُونَ ﴿٣٧﴾

وَٱتَّبَعْتُ مِلَّةَ ءَابَآءِىٓ إِبْرَٰهِيمَ وَإِسْحَٰقَ وَيَعْقُوبَ مَا كَانَ لَنَآ أَن نُّشْرِكَ بِٱللَّهِ مِن شَىْءٍ ذَٰلِكَ مِن فَضْلِ ٱللَّهِ عَلَيْنَا وَعَلَى ٱلنَّاسِ وَلَٰكِنَّ أَكْثَرَ ٱلنَّاسِ لَا يَشْكُرُونَ ﴿٣٨﴾

يَٰصَٰحِبَىِ ٱلسِّجْنِ ءَأَرْبَابٌ مُّتَفَرِّقُونَ خَيْرٌ أَمِ ٱللَّهُ ٱلْوَٰحِدُ ٱلْقَهَّارُ ﴿٣٩﴾

مَا تَعْبُدُونَ مِن دُونِهِۦٓ إِلَّآ أَسْمَآءً سَمَّيْتُمُوهَآ أَنتُمْ وَءَابَآؤُكُم مَّآ أَنزَلَ ٱللَّهُ بِهَا مِن سُلْطَٰنٍ إِنِ ٱلْحُكْمُ إِلَّا لِلَّهِ أَمَرَ أَلَّا تَعْبُدُوٓا۟ إِلَّآ إِيَّاهُ ذَٰلِكَ ٱلدِّينُ ٱلْقَيِّمُ وَلَٰكِنَّ أَكْثَرَ ٱلنَّاسِ لَا يَعْلَمُونَ ﴿٤٠﴾

يَٰصَٰحِبَىِ ٱلسِّجْنِ أَمَّآ أَحَدُكُمَا فَيَسْقِى رَبَّهُۥ

for the other, he will be crucified so that the birds will eat from his head. Thus is the case judged concerning which ye did inquire.

42 And he said unto him of the twain who he knew would be released: Mention me in the presence of thy lord. But Satan caused him to forget to mention it to his lord, so he (Joseph) stayed in prison for some years.

43 And the king said: Lo! I saw in a dream seven fat kine which seven lean were eating, and seven green ears of corn and other (seven) dry. O notables! Expound for me my vision, if ye can interpret dreams.

44 They answered: Jumbled dreams! And we are not knowing in the interpretation of dreams.

45 And he of the two who was released, and (now) at length remembered, said: I am going to announce unto you the interpretation, therefore send me forth.

46 (And when he came to Joseph in the prison, he exclaimed): Joseph! O thou truthful one! Expound for us the seven fat kine which seven lean were eating and the seven green ears of corn and other (seven) dry, that I may return unto the people, so that they may know.

47 He said: Ye shall sow seven years as usual, but that which ye reap, leave it in the ear, all save a little which ye eat.

48 Then after that will come seven hard years which will devour all that ye have prepared for them, save a little of that which ye have stored.

ثُمَّ يَأْتِي مِنْ بَعْدِ ذَلِكَ سَبْعٌ شِدَادٌ يَأْكُلْنَ مَا قَدَّمْتُمْ لَهُنَّ إِلَّا قَلِيلًا مِّمَّا تُحْصِنُونَ ۝

49 Then, after that, will come a year when the people will have plenteous crops and when they will press (wine and oil).

ثُمَّ يَأْتِي مِنْ بَعْدِ ذَلِكَ عَامٌ فِيهِ يُغَاثُ النَّاسُ وَفِيهِ يَعْصِرُونَ ۝

50 And the king said: Bring him unto me. And when the messenger came unto him, he (Joseph) said: Return unto thy lord and ask him what was the case of the women who cut their hands. Lo! my lord knoweth their guile.

وَقَالَ الْمَلِكُ ائْتُونِي بِهِ ۖ فَلَمَّا جَاءَهُ الرَّسُولُ قَالَ ارْجِعْ إِلَى رَبِّكَ فَاسْأَلْهُ مَا بَالُ النِّسْوَةِ اللَّاتِي قَطَّعْنَ أَيْدِيَهُنَّ إِنَّ رَبِّي بِكَيْدِهِنَّ عَلِيمٌ ۝

51 He (the king, then sent for those women and) said: What happened when ye asked an evil act of Joseph? They answered: Allah Blameless! We know no evil of him. Said the wife of the ruler: Now the truth is out. I asked of him an evil act, and he is surely of the truthful.

قَالَ مَا خَطْبُكُنَّ إِذْ رَاوَدتُّنَّ يُوسُفَ عَن نَّفْسِهِ ۚ قُلْنَ حَاشَ لِلَّهِ مَا عَلِمْنَا عَلَيْهِ مِن سُوءٍ قَالَتِ امْرَأَتُ الْعَزِيزِ الْآنَ حَصْحَصَ الْحَقُّ أَنَا رَاوَدتُّهُ عَن نَّفْسِهِ وَإِنَّهُ لَمِنَ الصَّادِقِينَ ۝

52 (Then Joseph said: I asked for) this, that he (my lord) may know that I betrayed him not in secret, and that surely Allah guideth not the snare of the betrayers.

ذَلِكَ لِيَعْلَمَ أَنِّي لَمْ أَخُنْهُ بِالْغَيْبِ وَأَنَّ اللَّهَ لَا يَهْدِي كَيْدَ الْخَائِنِينَ ۝

53 I do not exculpate myself. Lo! the (human) soul enjoineth unto evil, save that whereon my Lord hath mercy. Lo! my Lord is Forgiving, Merciful.

وَمَا أُبَرِّئُ نَفْسِي إِنَّ النَّفْسَ لَأَمَّارَةٌ بِالسُّوءِ إِلَّا مَا رَحِمَ رَبِّي إِنَّ رَبِّي غَفُورٌ رَّحِيمٌ ۝

54 And the king said: Bring him unto me that I may attach him to my person. And when he had talked with him he said: Lo! thou art today in our presence established and trusted.

وَقَالَ ٱلْمَلِكُ ٱئْتُونِي بِهِ أَسْتَخْلِصْهُ لِنَفْسِي فَلَمَّا كَلَّمَهُ قَالَ إِنَّكَ ٱلْيَوْمَ لَدَيْنَا مَكِينٌ أَمِينٌ ۝

55 He said: Set me over the store-houses of the land. Lo! I am a skilled custodian.

قَالَ ٱجْعَلْنِي عَلَىٰ خَزَآئِنِ ٱلْأَرْضِ إِنِّي حَفِيظٌ عَلِيمٌ ۝

56 Thus gave We power to Joseph in the land. He was the owner of it where he pleased. We bestow Our mercy on whom We will. We lose not the reward of the good.

وَكَذَٰلِكَ مَكَّنَّا لِيُوسُفَ فِي ٱلْأَرْضِ يَتَبَوَّأُ مِنْهَا حَيْثُ يَشَآءُ نُصِيبُ بِرَحْمَتِنَا مَن نَّشَآءُ وَلَا نُضِيعُ أَجْرَ ٱلْمُحْسِنِينَ ۝

57 And the reward of the Hereafter is better, for those who believe and ward off (evil).

وَلَأَجْرُ ٱلْآخِرَةِ خَيْرٌ لِّلَّذِينَ ءَامَنُوا۟ وَكَانُوا۟ يَتَّقُونَ ۝

58 And Joseph's brethren came and presented themselves before him, and he knew them but they knew him not.

وَجَآءَ إِخْوَةُ يُوسُفَ فَدَخَلُوا۟ عَلَيْهِ فَعَرَفَهُمْ وَهُمْ لَهُۥ مُنكِرُونَ ۝

59 And when he provided them with their provision he said: Bring unto me a brother of yours from your father. See ye not that I fill up the measure and I am the best of hosts?

وَلَمَّا جَهَّزَهُم بِجَهَازِهِمْ قَالَ ٱئْتُونِي بِأَخٍ لَّكُم مِّنْ أَبِيكُمْ أَلَا تَرَوْنَ أَنِّي أُوفِي ٱلْكَيْلَ وَأَنَا۠ خَيْرُ ٱلْمُنزِلِينَ ۝

60 And if ye bring him not unto me, then there shall be no measure for you with me, nor shall ye draw near.

فَإِن لَّمْ تَأْتُونِي بِهِۦ فَلَا كَيْلَ لَكُمْ عِندِي وَلَا تَقْرَبُونِ ۝

61 They said: We will try to win him from his father; that we will surely do.

قَالُوا۟ سَنُرَٰوِدُ عَنْهُ أَبَاهُ وَإِنَّا لَفَاعِلُونَ ۝

62 He said unto his young men: Place their merchandise in their saddlebags, so that they may know it when they go back to their folk, and so will come again.

وَقَالَ لِفِتْيَـٰنِهِ اجْعَلُوا بِضَـٰعَتَهُمْ فِى رِحَالِهِمْ لَعَلَّهُمْ يَعْرِفُونَهَا إِذَا انْقَلَبُوا إِلَىٰ أَهْلِهِمْ لَعَلَّهُمْ يَرْجِعُونَ ۝

63 So when they went back to their father they said: O our father! The measure is denied us, so send with us our brother, that we may obtain the measure, surely we will guard him well.

فَلَمَّا رَجَعُوا إِلَىٰ أَبِيهِمْ قَالُوا يَـٰأَبَانَا مُنِعَ مِنَّا الْكَيْلُ فَأَرْسِلْ مَعَنَا أَخَانَا نَكْتَلْ وَإِنَّا لَهُ لَحَـٰفِظُونَ ۝

64 He said: Can I entrust him to you save as I entrusted his brother to you aforetime? Allah is better at guarding, and He is the Most Merciful of those who show mercy.

قَالَ هَلْ ءَامَنُكُمْ عَلَيْهِ إِلَّا كَمَا أَمِنْتُكُمْ عَلَىٰ أَخِيهِ مِن قَبْلُ فَاللَّهُ خَيْرٌ حَـٰفِظًا وَهُوَ أَرْحَمُ الرَّٰحِمِينَ ۝

65 And when they opened their belongings they discovered that their merchandise had been returned to them. They said: O our father! What (more) can we ask? Here is our merchandise returned to us. We shall get provision for our folk and guard our brother, and we shall have the extra measure of a camel (load). This (that we bring now) is a light measure.

وَلَمَّا فَتَحُوا مَتَـٰعَهُمْ وَجَدُوا بِضَـٰعَتَهُمْ رُدَّتْ إِلَيْهِمْ قَالُوا يَـٰأَبَانَا مَا نَبْغِى هَـٰذِهِ بِضَـٰعَتُنَا رُدَّتْ إِلَيْنَا وَنَمِيرُ أَهْلَنَا وَنَحْفَظُ أَخَانَا وَنَزْدَادُ كَيْلَ بَعِيرٍ ذَٰلِكَ كَيْلٌ يَسِيرٌ ۝

66 He said: I will not send him with you till ye give me an undertaking in the name of Allah that ye will bring him back to me, unless ye are surrounded. And when they gave him their undertaking he said: Allah is the Warden over what we say.

قَالَ لَنْ أُرْسِلَهُ مَعَكُمْ حَتَّىٰ تُؤْتُونِ مَوْثِقًا مِّنَ اللَّهِ لَتَأْتُنَّنِى بِهِ إِلَّا أَن يُحَاطَ بِكُمْ فَلَمَّا ءَاتَوْهُ مَوْثِقَهُمْ قَالَ اللَّهُ عَلَىٰ مَا نَقُولُ وَكِيلٌ ۝

67 And he said: O my sons! Go not in by one gate; go in by different gates. I can naught avail you as against Allah. Lo! the decision rests with Allah only. In Him do I put my trust, and in Him let all the trusting put their trust.

وَقَالَ يَٰبَنِيَّ لَا تَدْخُلُوا مِنْ بَابٍ وَاحِدٍ وَادْخُلُوا مِنْ أَبْوَابٍ مُّتَفَرِّقَةٍ وَمَا أُغْنِي عَنكُم مِّنَ اللَّهِ مِن شَيْءٍ إِنِ الْحُكْمُ إِلَّا لِلَّهِ عَلَيْهِ تَوَكَّلْتُ وَعَلَيْهِ فَلْيَتَوَكَّلِ الْمُتَوَكِّلُونَ ۝

68 And when they entered in the manner which their father had enjoined, it would have naught availed them as against Allah; it was but a need of Jacob's soul which he thus satisfied;[3] and lo! he was a lord of knowledge because We had taught him; but most of mankind know not.

وَلَمَّا دَخَلُوا مِنْ حَيْثُ أَمَرَهُمْ أَبُوهُم مَّا كَانَ يُغْنِي عَنْهُم مِّنَ اللَّهِ مِن شَيْءٍ إِلَّا حَاجَةً فِي نَفْسِ يَعْقُوبَ قَضَاهَا وَإِنَّهُ لَذُو عِلْمٍ لِّمَا عَلَّمْنَاهُ وَلَٰكِنَّ أَكْثَرَ النَّاسِ لَا يَعْلَمُونَ ۝

69 And when they went in before Joseph, he took his brother unto himself, saying: Lo; I, even I, am thy brother, therefore sorrow not for what they did.

وَلَمَّا دَخَلُوا عَلَىٰ يُوسُفَ ءَاوَىٰ إِلَيْهِ أَخَاهُ قَالَ إِنِّي أَنَا أَخُوكَ فَلَا تَبْتَئِسْ بِمَا كَانُوا يَعْمَلُونَ ۝

70 And when he provided them with their provision, he put the drinking cup in his brother's saddle-bag, and then a crier cried: O camel riders! Ye are surely thieves!

فَلَمَّا جَهَّزَهُم بِجَهَازِهِمْ جَعَلَ السِّقَايَةَ فِي رَحْلِ أَخِيهِ ثُمَّ أَذَّنَ مُؤَذِّنٌ أَيَّتُهَا الْعِيرُ إِنَّكُمْ لَسَارِقُونَ ۝

71 They cried, coming toward them: What is it ye have lost?

قَالُوا وَأَقْبَلُوا عَلَيْهِم مَّاذَا تَفْقِدُونَ ۝

72 They said: We have lost the king's cup, and he who bringeth it shall have a camel-load, and I (said Joseph) am answerable for it.

قَالُوا نَفْقِدُ صُوَاعَ الْمَلِكِ وَلِمَن جَاءَ بِهِ حِمْلُ بَعِيرٍ وَأَنَا بِهِ زَعِيمٌ ۝

---

3. There is a prevalent superstition in the East that the members of a large family ought not to appear all together, for fear of the ill luck that comes from envy in the hearts of others.

73 They said: By Allah, well ye know we came not to do evil in the land, and are no thieves.

قَالُوا تَاللَّهِ لَقَدْ عَلِمْتُمْ مَّا جِئْنَا لِنُفْسِدَ فِي الْأَرْضِ وَمَا كُنَّا سَارِقِينَ ﴿٧٣﴾

74 They said: And what shall be the penalty for it, if ye prove liars?

قَالُوا فَمَا جَزَاؤُهُ إِن كُنتُمْ كَاذِبِينَ ﴿٧٤﴾

75 They said: The penalty for it! He in whose bag (the cup) is found, he is the penalty for it. Thus we requite wrong-doers.

قَالُوا جَزَاؤُهُ مَن وُجِدَ فِي رَحْلِهِ فَهُوَ جَزَاؤُهُ كَذَلِكَ نَجْزِي الظَّالِمِينَ ﴿٧٥﴾

76 Then he (Joseph) began the search with their bags before his brother's bag, then he produced it from his brother's bag. Thus did We contrive for Joseph. He could not have taken his brother according to the king's law unless Allah willed. We raise by grades (of mercy) whom We will, and over every lord of knowledge there is one more knowing.

فَبَدَأَ بِأَوْعِيَتِهِمْ قَبْلَ وِعَاءِ أَخِيهِ ثُمَّ اسْتَخْرَجَهَا مِن وِعَاءِ أَخِيهِ كَذَلِكَ كِدْنَا لِيُوسُفَ مَا كَانَ لِيَأْخُذَ أَخَاهُ فِي دِينِ الْمَلِكِ إِلَّا أَن يَشَاءَ اللَّهُ نَرْفَعُ دَرَجَاتٍ مَّن نَّشَاءُ وَفَوْقَ كُلِّ ذِي عِلْمٍ عَلِيمٌ ﴿٧٦﴾

77 They said: If he stealeth, a brother of his stole before. But Joseph kept it secret in his soul and revealed it not unto them. He said (within himself): Ye are in worse case and Allah knoweth best (the truth of) that which ye allege.

۞ قَالُوا إِن يَسْرِقْ فَقَدْ سَرَقَ أَخٌ لَّهُ مِن قَبْلُ فَأَسَرَّهَا يُوسُفُ فِي نَفْسِهِ وَلَمْ يُبْدِهَا لَهُمْ قَالَ أَنتُمْ شَرٌّ مَّكَانًا وَاللَّهُ أَعْلَمُ بِمَا تَصِفُونَ ﴿٧٧﴾

78 They said: O ruler of the land! Lo! he hath an aged father, so take one of us instead of him. Lo! we behold thee of those who do kindness.

قَالُوا يَا أَيُّهَا الْعَزِيزُ إِنَّ لَهُ أَبًا شَيْخًا كَبِيرًا فَخُذْ أَحَدَنَا مَكَانَهُ إِنَّا نَرَاكَ مِنَ الْمُحْسِنِينَ ﴿٧٨﴾

79 He said: Allah forbid that we should seize save him with whom we found our property; then truly we should be wrong-doers.

قَالَ مَعَاذَ اللَّهِ أَن نَّأْخُذَ إِلَّا مَن وَجَدْنَا مَتَاعَنَا عِندَهُ إِنَّا إِذًا لَّظَالِمُونَ ﴿٧٩﴾

80 So, when they despaired of (moving) him, they conferred together apart. The eldest of them said: Know ye not how your father took an undertaking from you in Allah's name and how ye failed in the case of Joseph aforetime? Therefore I shall not go forth from the land until my father giveth leave or Allah judgeth for me. He is the Best of Judges.

فَلَمَّا اسْتَيْأَسُوا مِنْهُ خَلَصُوا نَجِيًّا قَالَ كَبِيرُهُمْ أَلَمْ تَعْلَمُوا أَنَّ أَبَاكُمْ قَدْ أَخَذَ عَلَيْكُمْ مَوْثِقًا مِنَ اللّهِ وَمِن قَبْلُ مَا فَرَّطتُمْ فِي يُوسُفَ فَلَنْ أَبْرَحَ الْأَرْضَ حَتَّى يَأْذَنَ لِي أَبِي أَوْ يَحْكُمَ اللّهُ لِي وَهُوَ خَيْرُ الْحَاكِمِينَ ۞

81 Return unto your father and say: O our father! Lo! thy son hath stolen. We testify only to that which we know; we are not guardians of the unseen.

ارْجِعُوا إِلَى أَبِيكُمْ فَقُولُوا يَا أَبَانَا إِنَّ ابْنَكَ سَرَقَ وَمَا شَهِدْنَا إِلَّا بِمَا عَلِمْنَا وَمَا كُنَّا لِلْغَيْبِ حَافِظِينَ ۞

82 Ask the township where we were, and the caravan with which we travelled hither. Lo! we speak the truth.

وَسْئَلِ الْقَرْيَةَ الَّتِي كُنَّا فِيهَا وَالْعِيرَ الَّتِي أَقْبَلْنَا فِيهَا وَإِنَّا لَصَادِقُونَ ۞

83 (And when they came unto their father and had spoken thus to him) he said: Nay, but your minds have beguiled you into something. (My course is) comely patience! It may be that Allah will bring them all unto me. Lo! He, only He, is the Knower, the Wise.

قَالَ بَلْ سَوَّلَتْ لَكُمْ أَنفُسُكُمْ أَمْرًا فَصَبْرٌ جَمِيلٌ عَسَى اللّهُ أَن يَأْتِيَنِي بِهِمْ جَمِيعًا إِنَّهُ هُوَ الْعَلِيمُ الْحَكِيمُ ۞

84 And he turned away from them and said: Alas, my grief for Joseph! And his eyes were whitened with the sorrow that he was suppressing.

وَتَوَلَّى عَنْهُمْ وَقَالَ يَا أَسَفَى عَلَى يُوسُفَ وَابْيَضَّتْ عَيْنَاهُ مِنَ الْحُزْنِ فَهُوَ كَظِيمٌ ۞

85 They said: By Allah, thou wilt never cease remembering Joseph till thy health is ruined or thou art of those who perish!

قَالُوا تَاللّهِ تَفْتَأُ تَذْكُرُ يُوسُفَ حَتَّى تَكُونَ حَرَضًا أَوْ تَكُونَ مِنَ الْهَالِكِينَ ۞

86 He said: I expose my distress and anguish only unto Allah, and I know from Allah that which ye know not.

قَالَ إِنَّمَا أَشْكُواْ بَثِّي وَحُزْنِي إِلَى اللهِ وَأَعْلَمُ مِنَ اللهِ مَا لَا تَعْلَمُونَ ﴿٨٦﴾

87 Go, O my sons, and ascertain concerning Joseph and his brother, and despair not of the Spirit of Allah. Lo! none despaireth of the Spirit of Allah save disbelieving folk.

يَبَنِيَّ اذْهَبُواْ فَتَحَسَّسُواْ مِن يُوسُفَ وَأَخِيهِ وَلَا تَأْيْئَسُواْ مِن رَّوْحِ اللهِ إِنَّهُ لَا يَأْيْئَسُ مِن رَّوْحِ اللهِ إِلَّا الْقَوْمُ الْكَٰفِرُونَ ﴿٨٧﴾

88 And when they came (again) before him (Joseph) they said: O ruler! Misfortune hath touched us and our folk, and we bring but poor merchandise, so fill for us the measure and be charitable unto us. Lo! Allah will requite the charitable.

فَلَمَّا دَخَلُواْ عَلَيْهِ قَالُواْ يَٰٓأَيُّهَا الْعَزِيزُ مَسَّنَا وَأَهْلَنَا الضُّرُّ وَجِئْنَا بِبِضَٰعَةٍ مُّزْجَىٰةٍ فَأَوْفِ لَنَا الْكَيْلَ وَتَصَدَّقْ عَلَيْنَآ إِنَّ اللهَ يَجْزِي الْمُتَصَدِّقِينَ ﴿٨٨﴾

89 He said: Know ye what ye did unto Joseph and his brother in your ignorance?

قَالَ هَلْ عَلِمْتُم مَّا فَعَلْتُم بِيُوسُفَ وَأَخِيهِ إِذْ أَنتُمْ جَٰهِلُونَ ﴿٨٩﴾

90 They said: Is it indeed thou who art Joseph? He said: I am Joseph and this is my brother. Allah hath shown us favour. Lo! he who wardeth off (evil) and endureth (findeth favour); for verily Allah loseth not the wages of the kindly.

قَالُواْ أَءِنَّكَ لَأَنتَ يُوسُفُ قَالَ أَنَا يُوسُفُ وَهَٰذَآ أَخِي قَدْ مَنَّ اللهُ عَلَيْنَآ إِنَّهُ مَن يَتَّقِ وَيَصْبِرْ فَإِنَّ اللهَ لَا يُضِيعُ أَجْرَ الْمُحْسِنِينَ ﴿٩٠﴾

91 They said: By Allah, verily Allah hath preferred thee above us, and we were indeed sinful.

قَالُواْ تَاللهِ لَقَدْ ءَاثَرَكَ اللهُ عَلَيْنَا وَإِن كُنَّا لَخَٰطِئِينَ ﴿٩١﴾

92 He said: Have no fear this day! May Allah forgive you, and He is the Most Merciful of those who show mercy.

قَالَ لَا تَثْرِيبَ عَلَيْكُمُ الْيَوْمَ يَغْفِرُ اللهُ لَكُمْ وَهُوَ أَرْحَمُ الرَّٰحِمِينَ ﴿٩٢﴾

93 Go with this shirt of mine and lay it on my father's face, he will become (again) a seer; and come to me with all your folk.

اذْهَبُوا بِقَمِيصِى هَذَا فَأَلْقُوهُ عَلَى وَجْهِ أَبِى يَأْتِ بَصِيرًا وَأْتُونِى بِأَهْلِكُمْ أَجْمَعِينَ ﴿٩٣﴾

94 When the caravan departed their father had said: Truly I am conscious of the breath of Joseph, though ye call me dotard.

وَلَمَّا فَصَلَتِ الْعِيرُ قَالَ أَبُوهُمْ إِنِّى لَأَجِدُ رِيحَ يُوسُفَ لَوْلَا أَن تُفَنِّدُونِ ﴿٩٤﴾

95 (Those around him) said: By Allah, lo! thou art in thine old aberration.

قَالُوا تَاللَّهِ إِنَّكَ لَفِى ضَلَالِكَ الْقَدِيمِ ﴿٩٥﴾

96 Then, when the bearer of glad tidings came, he laid it on his face and he became a seer once more. He said: Said I not unto you that I know from Allah that which ye know not?

فَلَمَّا أَن جَآءَ الْبَشِيرُ أَلْقَاهُ عَلَى وَجْهِهِ فَارْتَدَّ بَصِيرًا قَالَ أَلَمْ أَقُل لَّكُمْ إِنِّى أَعْلَمُ مِنَ اللَّهِ مَا لَا تَعْلَمُونَ ﴿٩٦﴾

97 They said: O our father! Ask forgiveness of our sins for us, for lo! we were sinful.

قَالُوا يَا أَبَانَا اسْتَغْفِرْ لَنَا ذُنُوبَنَا إِنَّا كُنَّا خَاطِئِينَ ﴿٩٧﴾

98 He said: I shall ask forgiveness for you of my Lord. Lo! He is the Forgiving, the Merciful.

قَالَ سَوْفَ أَسْتَغْفِرُ لَكُمْ رَبِّى إِنَّهُ هُوَ الْغَفُورُ الرَّحِيمُ ﴿٩٨﴾

99 And when they came in before Joseph, he took his parents unto him, and said: Come into Egypt safe, if Allah will!

فَلَمَّا دَخَلُوا عَلَى يُوسُفَ ءَاوَى إِلَيْهِ أَبَوَيْهِ وَقَالَ ادْخُلُوا مِصْرَ إِن شَآءَ اللَّهُ ءَامِنِينَ ﴿٩٩﴾

100   And he placed his parents on the daïs and they fell down before him prostrate, and he said: O my father! This is the interpretation of my dream of old. My Lord hath made it true, and He hath shown me kindness, since He took me out of the prison and hath brought you

وَرَفَعَ أَبَوَيْهِ عَلَى الْعَرْشِ وَخَرُّوا لَهُ سُجَّدًا وَقَالَ يَا أَبَتِ هَذَا تَأْوِيلُ رُؤْيَايَ مِن قَبْلُ قَدْ جَعَلَهَا رَبِّى حَقًّا وَقَدْ أَحْسَنَ بِى إِذْ أَخْرَجَنِى مِنَ السِّجْنِ

from the desert after Satan had made strife between me and my brethren. Lo! my Lord is tender unto whom He will. He is the Knower, the Wise.

وَجَآءَ بِكُم مِّنَ ٱلۡبَدۡوِ مِنۢ بَعۡدِ أَن نَّزَغَ ٱلشَّيۡطَٰنُ بَيۡنِي وَبَيۡنَ إِخۡوَتِيٓۚ إِنَّ رَبِّي لَطِيفٞ لِّمَا يَشَآءُۚ إِنَّهُۥ هُوَ ٱلۡعَلِيمُ ٱلۡحَكِيمُ ۝

101 O my Lord! Thou hast given me (something) of sovereignty and hast taught me (something) of the interpretation of events—Creator of the heavens and the earth! Thou art my Protecting Friend in the world and the Hereafter. Make me to die submissive (unto Thee), and join me to the righteous.

۞ رَبِّ قَدۡ ءَاتَيۡتَنِي مِنَ ٱلۡمُلۡكِ وَعَلَّمۡتَنِي مِن تَأۡوِيلِ ٱلۡأَحَادِيثِۚ فَاطِرَ ٱلسَّمَٰوَٰتِ وَٱلۡأَرۡضِ أَنتَ وَلِيِّۦ فِي ٱلدُّنۡيَا وَٱلۡأٓخِرَةِۖ تَوَفَّنِي مُسۡلِمٗا وَأَلۡحِقۡنِي بِٱلصَّٰلِحِينَ ۝

102 This is of the tidings of the Unseen which We inspire in thee (Muhammad). Thou wast not present with them when they fixed their plan and they were scheming.

ذَٰلِكَ مِنۡ أَنۢبَآءِ ٱلۡغَيۡبِ نُوحِيهِ إِلَيۡكَۖ وَمَا كُنتَ لَدَيۡهِمۡ إِذۡ أَجۡمَعُوٓاْ أَمۡرَهُمۡ وَهُمۡ يَمۡكُرُونَ ۝

103 And though thou try much, most men will not believe.

وَمَآ أَكۡثَرُ ٱلنَّاسِ وَلَوۡ حَرَصۡتَ بِمُؤۡمِنِينَ ۝

104 Thou askest them no fee for it. It is naught else than a reminder unto the peoples.

وَمَا تَسۡـَٔلُهُمۡ عَلَيۡهِ مِنۡ أَجۡرٍۚ إِنۡ هُوَ إِلَّا ذِكۡرٞ لِّلۡعَٰلَمِينَ ۝

105 How many a portent is there in the heavens and the earth which they pass by with face averted!

وَكَأَيِّن مِّنۡ ءَايَةٖ فِي ٱلسَّمَٰوَٰتِ وَٱلۡأَرۡضِ يَمُرُّونَ عَلَيۡهَا وَهُمۡ عَنۡهَا مُعۡرِضُونَ ۝

106 And most of them believe not in Allah except that they attribute partners (unto Him).

وَمَا يُؤۡمِنُ أَكۡثَرُهُم بِٱللَّهِ إِلَّا وَهُم مُّشۡرِكُونَ ۝

107 Deem they themselves secure from the coming on them of a pall of Allah's punishment, or the coming of the Hour suddenly while they are unaware?

أَفَأَمِنُوٓاْ أَن تَأۡتِيَهُمۡ غَٰشِيَةٞ مِّنۡ عَذَابِ ٱللَّهِ أَوۡ تَأۡتِيَهُمُ ٱلسَّاعَةُ بَغۡتَةٗ وَهُمۡ لَا يَشۡعُرُونَ ۝

108   Say: This is my Way: I call
on Allah with sure knowledge, I
and whosoever followeth me: Glory
be to Allah! and I am not of the
idolaters.

قُلْ هَٰذِهٖ سَبِيلِىٓ أَدْعُوٓاْ إِلَى اللّٰهِ عَلَىٰ بَصِيرَةٍ
أَنَا۠ وَمَنِ اتَّبَعَنِىۖ وَسُبْحَٰنَ اللّٰهِ
وَمَآ أَنَا۠ مِنَ الْمُشْرِكِينَ ﴿٨٨﴾

109   We sent not before thee (any
messengers) save men whom We
inspired from among the folk of the
townships—Have they not travelled
in the land and seen the nature of
the consequence for those who were
before them? And verily the abode
of the Hereafter, for those who ward
off (evil), is best. Have ye then no
sense?

وَمَآ أَرْسَلْنَا مِن قَبْلِكَ إِلَّا رِجَالًا نُّوحِىٓ إِلَيْهِم
مِّنْ أَهْلِ الْقُرَىٰٓ أَفَلَمْ يَسِيرُواْ فِى الْأَرْضِ
فَيَنظُرُواْ كَيْفَ كَانَ عَٰقِبَةُ الَّذِينَ مِن قَبْلِهِمْ
وَلَدَارُ الْآخِرَةِ خَيْرٌ لِّلَّذِينَ اتَّقَوْاۗ
أَفَلَا تَعْقِلُونَ ﴿١٠٩﴾

110   Till, when the messengers
despaired and thought that they
were denied, then came unto them
Our help, and whom We would was
saved. And our wrath cannot be
warded from the guilty.

حَتَّىٰٓ إِذَا اسْتَيْـَٔسَ الرُّسُلُ وَظَنُّوٓاْ أَنَّهُمْ
قَدْ كُذِبُواْ جَآءَهُمْ نَصْرُنَا فَنُجِّىَ مَن نَّشَآءُۖ
وَلَا يُرَدُّ بَأْسُنَا عَنِ الْقَوْمِ الْمُجْرِمِينَ ﴿١١٠﴾

111   In their history verily there
is a lesson for men of understanding. It is no invented story but a
confirmation of the existing (Scripture) and a detailed explanation of
everything, and a guidance and a
mercy for folk who believe.

لَقَدْ كَانَ فِى قَصَصِهِمْ عِبْرَةٌ لِّأُوْلِى الْأَلْبَٰبِۗ
مَا كَانَ حَدِيثًا يُفْتَرَىٰ وَلَٰكِن تَصْدِيقَ
الَّذِى بَيْنَ يَدَيْهِ وَتَفْصِيلَ كُلِّ شَىْءٍ
وَهُدًى وَرَحْمَةً لِّقَوْمٍ يُؤْمِنُونَ ﴿١١١﴾

Al Ra'd
(The Thunder)

Al Ra'd, "The Thunder," takes its name from a word in v. 13. The subject is Divine guidance in relation to the law of consequences, it being explained here, as elsewhere in the Qur'an, that there is no partiality or aversion on the part of God, but that reward and punishment are the result of obeying or rejecting natural (or Divine) laws. According to some ancient authorities, it is a Makkan sūrah with the exception of two verses revealed at Al-Madīnah; according to others, a Madīnan sūrah with the exception of two verses revealed at Makkah. The very fact of such wholesale difference of opinion favours the Makkan attribution because there could be no such doubt about a complete Madīnan sūrah, owing to the great number of witnesses. The Madīnan ascription may have arisen from the recognition of some verses by those witnesses as having been revealed at Al-Madīnah on a certain occasion.

A late Makkan sūrah for the most part.

In the name of Allah, the Beneficent, the Merciful.

1   Alif. Lām. Mīm. Rā.[1] These are verses of the Scripture. That which is revealed unto thee from thy Lord is the Truth, but most of mankind believe not.

---

1. See Sūrah 2, v. 1, footnote.

2   Allah it is who raised up the heavens without visible supports, then mounted the Throne, and compelled the sun and the moon to be of service, each runneth unto an appointed term; He ordereth the course; He detaileth the revelations, that haply ye may be certain of the meeting with your Lord.

اللّٰهُ الَّذِى رَفَعَ السَّمٰوٰتِ بِغَيْرِ عَمَدٍ تَرَوْنَهَا ثُمَّ اسْتَوٰى عَلَى الْعَرْشِ وَسَخَّرَ الشَّمْسَ وَالْقَمَرَ ۖ كُلٌّ يَجْرِى لِأَجَلٍ مُّسَمًّى ۚ يُدَبِّرُ الْأَمْرَ يُفَصِّلُ الْآيٰتِ لَعَلَّكُمْ بِلِقَآءِ رَبِّكُمْ تُوقِنُونَ ﴿٢﴾

3   And He it is who spread out the earth and placed therein firm hills and flowing streams, and of all fruits He placed therein two spouses (male and female). He covereth the night with the day. Lo! herein verily are portents for people who take thought.

وَهُوَ الَّذِى مَدَّ الْأَرْضَ وَجَعَلَ فِيْهَا رَوَاسِىَ وَأَنْهٰرًا ۖ وَمِنْ كُلِّ الثَّمَرٰتِ جَعَلَ فِيْهَا زَوْجَيْنِ اثْنَيْنِ ۖ يُغْشِى الَّيْلَ النَّهَارَ ۚ إِنَّ فِى ذٰلِكَ لَآيٰتٍ لِّقَوْمٍ يَتَفَكَّرُونَ ﴿٣﴾

4   And in the Earth are neighbouring tracts, vineyards and ploughed lands, and date-palms, like and unlike,[2] which are watered with one water. And We have made some of them to excel others in fruit. Lo! herein verily are portents for people who have sense.

وَفِى الْأَرْضِ قِطَعٌ مُّتَجٰوِرٰتٌ وَجَنّٰتٌ مِّنْ أَعْنٰبٍ وَّزَرْعٌ وَّنَخِيلٌ صِنْوَانٌ وَّغَيْرُ صِنْوَانٍ يُسْقٰى بِمَآءٍ وَّاحِدٍ ۖ وَنُفَضِّلُ بَعْضَهَا عَلٰى بَعْضٍ فِى الْأُكُلِ ۚ إِنَّ فِى ذٰلِكَ لَآيٰتٍ لِّقَوْمٍ يَعْقِلُونَ ﴿٤﴾

5   And if thou wonderest, then wondrous is their saying: When we are dust, are we then forsooth (to be raised) in a new creation? Such are they who disbelieve in their Lord; such have carcans on their necks; such are rightful owners of the Fire, they will abide therein.

۞ وَإِنْ تَعْجَبْ فَعَجَبٌ قَوْلُهُمْ أَءِذَا كُنَّا تُرٰبًا أَءِنَّا لَفِى خَلْقٍ جَدِيدٍ ۗ أُولٰئِكَ الَّذِينَ كَفَرُوا بِرَبِّهِمْ ۖ وَأُولٰئِكَ الْأَغْلٰلُ فِى أَعْنَاقِهِمْ ۖ وَأُولٰئِكَ أَصْحٰبُ النَّارِ ۖ هُمْ فِيْهَا خٰلِدُونَ ﴿٥﴾

---

2. Or it may be, "growing thickly or alone."

6 And they bid thee hasten on the evil rather than the good, when exemplary punishments have indeed occurred before them. But lo! thy Lord is rich in pardon for mankind despite their wrong, and lo! thy Lord is strong in punishment!

وَيَسْتَعْجِلُونَكَ بِالسَّيِّئَةِ قَبْلَ الْحَسَنَةِ وَقَدْ خَلَتْ مِن قَبْلِهِمُ الْمَثُلَاتُ وَإِنَّ رَبَّكَ لَذُو مَغْفِرَةٍ لِّلنَّاسِ عَلَى ظُلْمِهِمْ وَإِنَّ رَبَّكَ لَشَدِيدُ الْعِقَابِ ۝

7 Those who disbelieve say: If only some portent were sent down upon him from his Lord! Thou art a warner only, and for every folk a guide.

وَيَقُولُ الَّذِينَ كَفَرُوا لَوْلَا أُنزِلَ عَلَيْهِ ءَايَةٌ مِّن رَّبِّهِ إِنَّمَا أَنتَ مُنذِرٌ وَلِكُلِّ قَوْمٍ هَادٍ ۝

8 Allah knoweth that which every female beareth and that which the wombs absorb and that which they grow. And everything with Him is measured.

اللَّهُ يَعْلَمُ مَا تَحْمِلُ كُلُّ أُنثَى وَمَا تَغِيضُ الْأَرْحَامُ وَمَا تَزْدَادُ وَكُلُّ شَيْءٍ عِندَهُ بِمِقْدَارٍ ۝

9 He is the Knower of the invisible and the visible, the Great, the High Exalted.

عَالِمُ الْغَيْبِ وَالشَّهَادَةِ الْكَبِيرُ الْمُتَعَالِ ۝

10 Alike of you is he who hideth the saying and he who noiseth it abroad, he who lurketh in the night and he who goeth freely in the day-time.

سَوَاءٌ مِّنكُم مَّنْ أَسَرَّ الْقَوْلَ وَمَن جَهَرَ بِهِ وَمَنْ هُوَ مُسْتَخْفٍ بِالَّيْلِ وَسَارِبٌ بِالنَّهَارِ ۝

11 For him are angels ranged before him and behind him, who guard him by Allah's command.[3] Lo! Allah changeth not the condition of a folk until they (first) change that which is in their hearts; and if Allah willeth misfortune for a folk, there is

لَهُ مُعَقِّبَاتٌ مِّنۢ بَيْنِ يَدَيْهِ وَمِنْ خَلْفِهِ يَحْفَظُونَهُ مِنْ أَمْرِ اللَّهِ إِنَّ اللَّهَ لَا يُغَيِّرُ مَا بِقَوْمٍ حَتَّى يُغَيِّرُوا مَا بِأَنفُسِهِمْ وَإِذَا أَرَادَ اللَّهُ بِقَوْمٍ سُوءًا فَلَا مَرَدَّ لَهُ

---

3. This is taken by some commentators to refer to "him who goeth freely in the daytime" in the previous verse. In that case it would read: "for whom are guards before him and behind him as if to guard him against Allah's commandment."

none that can repel it, nor have they a defender beside Him.

12 He it is Who showeth you the lightning, a fear and a hope,[4] and raiseth the heavy clouds.

13 The thunder hymneth His praise and (so do) the angels for awe of Him. He launcheth the thunder bolts and smiteth with them whom He will while they dispute (in doubt) concerning Allah, and He is mighty in wrath.

14 Unto Him is the real prayer. Those unto whom they pray beside Allah respond to them not at all, save as (is the response to) one who stretcheth forth his hands toward water (asking) that it may come unto his mouth, and it will never reach it. The prayer of disbelievers goeth (far) astray.

15 And unto Allah falleth prostrate whosoever is in the heavens and the earth, willingly or unwillingly, as do their shadows in the morning and the evening hours.

16 Say (O Muhammad): Who is Lord of the heavens and the earth? Say: Allah! Say: Take ye then (others) beside Him for protectors, which, even for themselves, have neither benefit nor hurt? Say: Is the blind man equal to the seer, or is

---

4. The fear is of the lightning, and the hope is of rain.

darkness equal to light? Or assign they unto Allah partners who created the like of His creation so that the creation (which they made and His creation) seemed alike to them? Say: Allah is the Creator of all things, and He is the One, the Almighty.

اَلظُّلُمٰتُ وَالنُّوْرُ ۙ اَمْ جَعَلُوْا لِلّٰهِ شُرَكَآءَ خَلَقُوْا كَخَلْقِهٖ فَتَشَابَهَ الْخَلْقُ عَلَيْهِمْ ۚ قُلِ اللّٰهُ خَالِقُ كُلِّ شَيْءٍ وَّهُوَ الْوَاحِدُ الْقَهَّارُ ۞

17 He sendeth down water from the sky, so that valleys flow according to their measure, and the flood beareth (on its surface) swelling foam—from that which they smelt in the fire in order to make ornaments and tools riseth a foam like unto it—thus Allah coineth (the similitude of) the true and the false. Then, as for the foam, it passeth away as scum upon the banks, while, as for that which is of use to mankind, it remaineth in the earth. Thus Allah coineth the similitudes.

اَنْزَلَ مِنَ السَّمَآءِ مَآءً فَسَالَتْ اَوْدِيَةٌۢ بِقَدَرِهَا فَاحْتَمَلَ السَّيْلُ زَبَدًا رَّابِيًا ۚ وَمِمَّا يُوْقِدُوْنَ عَلَيْهِ فِي النَّارِ ابْتِغَآءَ حِلْيَةٍ اَوْ مَتَاعٍ زَبَدٌ مِّثْلُهٗ ۚ كَذٰلِكَ يَضْرِبُ اللّٰهُ الْحَقَّ وَالْبَاطِلَ ۚ فَاَمَّا الزَّبَدُ فَيَذْهَبُ جُفَآءً ۚ وَاَمَّا مَا يَنْفَعُ النَّاسَ فَيَمْكُثُ فِي الْاَرْضِ ۚ كَذٰلِكَ يَضْرِبُ اللّٰهُ الْاَمْثَالَ ۞

18 For those who answered Allah's call is bliss; and for those who answered not His call, if they had all that is in the earth, and therewith the like thereof, they would proffer it as ransom. Such will have a woeful reckoning, and their habitation will be hell, a dire abode.

لِلَّذِيْنَ اسْتَجَابُوْا لِرَبِّهِمُ الْحُسْنٰى ۖ وَالَّذِيْنَ لَمْ يَسْتَجِيْبُوْا لَهٗ لَوْ اَنَّ لَهُمْ مَّا فِي الْاَرْضِ جَمِيْعًا وَّمِثْلَهٗ مَعَهٗ لَافْتَدَوْا بِهٖ ۚ اُولٰٓئِكَ لَهُمْ سُوْٓءُ الْحِسَابِ ۖ وَمَأْوٰىهُمْ جَهَنَّمُ ۚ وَبِئْسَ الْمِهَادُ ۞

19 Is he who knoweth that what is revealed unto thee from thy Lord is the truth like him who is blind? But only men of understanding heed;

اَفَمَنْ يَّعْلَمُ اَنَّمَآ اُنْزِلَ اِلَيْكَ مِنْ رَّبِّكَ الْحَقُّ كَمَنْ هُوَ اَعْمٰى ۚ اِنَّمَا يَتَذَكَّرُ اُولُوا الْاَلْبَابِ ۞

20 Such as keep the pact of Allah, and break not the covenant;

اَلَّذِيْنَ يُوْفُوْنَ بِعَهْدِ اللّٰهِ وَلَا يَنْقُضُوْنَ الْمِيْثَاقَ ۞

21 Such as unite that which Allah hath commanded should be joined, and fear their Lord, and dread a woeful reckoning;

وَٱلَّذِينَ يَصِلُونَ مَآ أَمَرَ ٱللَّهُ بِهِۦٓ أَن يُوصَلَ وَيَخْشَوْنَ رَبَّهُمْ وَيَخَافُونَ سُوٓءَ ٱلْحِسَابِ ۝

22 Such as persevere in seeking their Lord's countenance and are regular in prayer and spend of that which We bestow upon them secretly and openly, and overcome evil with good. Theirs will be the sequel of the (heavenly) Home;

وَٱلَّذِينَ صَبَرُوا۟ ٱبْتِغَآءَ وَجْهِ رَبِّهِمْ وَأَقَامُوا۟ ٱلصَّلَوٰةَ وَأَنفَقُوا۟ مِمَّا رَزَقْنَٰهُمْ سِرًّا وَعَلَانِيَةً وَيَدْرَءُونَ بِٱلْحَسَنَةِ ٱلسَّيِّئَةَ أُو۟لَٰٓئِكَ لَهُمْ عُقْبَى ٱلدَّارِ ۝

23 Gardens of Eden which they enter, along with all who do right of their fathers and their helpmeets and their seed. The angels enter unto them from every gate.

جَنَّٰتُ عَدْنٍ يَدْخُلُونَهَا وَمَن صَلَحَ مِنْ ءَابَآئِهِمْ وَأَزْوَٰجِهِمْ وَذُرِّيَّٰتِهِمْ وَٱلْمَلَٰٓئِكَةُ يَدْخُلُونَ عَلَيْهِم مِّن كُلِّ بَابٍ ۝

24 (Saying): Peace be unto you because ye persevered. Ah, passing sweet will be the sequel of the (heavenly) Home.

سَلَٰمٌ عَلَيْكُم بِمَا صَبَرْتُمْ فَنِعْمَ عُقْبَى ٱلدَّارِ ۝

25 And those who break the covenant of Allah after ratifying it, and sever that which Allah hath commanded should be joined, and make mischief in the earth: theirs is the curse and theirs the ill abode.

وَٱلَّذِينَ يَنقُضُونَ عَهْدَ ٱللَّهِ مِنۢ بَعْدِ مِيثَٰقِهِۦ وَيَقْطَعُونَ مَآ أَمَرَ ٱللَّهُ بِهِۦٓ أَن يُوصَلَ وَيُفْسِدُونَ فِى ٱلْأَرْضِ أُو۟لَٰٓئِكَ لَهُمُ ٱللَّعْنَةُ وَلَهُمْ سُوٓءُ ٱلدَّارِ ۝

26 Allah enlargeth livelihood for whom He will, and straiteneth (it for whom He will); and they rejoice in the life of the world, whereas the life of the world is but brief comfort as compared with the Hereafter.

ٱللَّهُ يَبْسُطُ ٱلرِّزْقَ لِمَن يَشَآءُ وَيَقْدِرُ وَفَرِحُوا۟ بِٱلْحَيَوٰةِ ٱلدُّنْيَا وَمَا ٱلْحَيَوٰةُ ٱلدُّنْيَا فِى ٱلْءَاخِرَةِ إِلَّا مَتَٰعٌ ۝

27 Those who disbelieve say: If only a portent were sent down upon him from his Lord! Say: Lo! Allah

وَيَقُولُ ٱلَّذِينَ كَفَرُوا۟ لَوْلَآ أُنزِلَ عَلَيْهِ ءَايَةٌ مِّن رَّبِّهِۦ

sendeth whom He will astray, and
guideth unto Himself all who turn
(unto Him);

28 Who have believed and whose
hearts have rest in the remembrance
of Allah. Verily in the remembrance of Allah do hearts find rest!

29 Those who believe and do right:
Joy is for them, and bliss (their)
journey's end.

30 Thus We send thee (O
Muhammad) unto a nation, before
whom other nations have passed
away, that thou mayst recite unto
them that which We have inspired
in thee, while they are disbelievers
in the Beneficent. Say: He is my
Lord; there is no God save Him. In
Him do I put my trust and unto
Him is my recourse.

31 Had it been possible for a
Lecture[5] to cause the mountains to
move, or the earth to be torn asunder, or the dead to speak, (this
Qur'an would have done so). Nay,
but Allah's is the whole command.
Do not those who believe know
that, had Allah willed, He could
have guided all mankind? As for
those who disbelieve, disaster cea-
seth not to strike them because of
what they do, or it dwelleth near
their home until the threat of Allah

قُلْ إِنَّ اللَّهَ يُضِلُّ مَن يَشَآءُ وَيَهْدِىٓ إِلَيْهِ
مَنْ أَنَابَ ۝

ٱلَّذِينَ ءَامَنُوا۟ وَتَطْمَئِنُّ قُلُوبُهُم بِذِكْرِ اللَّهِ
أَلَا بِذِكْرِ اللَّهِ تَطْمَئِنُّ ٱلْقُلُوبُ ۝

ٱلَّذِينَ ءَامَنُوا۟ وَعَمِلُوا۟ ٱلصَّٰلِحَٰتِ طُوبَىٰ
لَهُمْ وَحُسْنُ مَـَٔابٍ ۝

كَذَٰلِكَ أَرْسَلْنَٰكَ فِىٓ أُمَّةٍ قَدْ خَلَتْ مِن قَبْلِهَآ أُمَمٌ
لِّتَتْلُوَا۟ عَلَيْهِمُ ٱلَّذِىٓ أَوْحَيْنَآ إِلَيْكَ وَهُمْ يَكْفُرُونَ
بِٱلرَّحْمَٰنِ قُلْ هُوَ رَبِّى لَآ إِلَٰهَ إِلَّا هُوَ عَلَيْهِ تَوَكَّلْتُ
وَإِلَيْهِ مَتَابِ ۝

وَلَوْ أَنَّ قُرْءَانًا سُيِّرَتْ بِهِ ٱلْجِبَالُ أَوْ قُطِّعَتْ
بِهِ ٱلْأَرْضُ أَوْ كُلِّمَ بِهِ ٱلْمَوْتَىٰ بَل لِّلَّهِ ٱلْأَمْرُ جَمِيعًا
أَفَلَمْ يَا۟يْـَٔسِ ٱلَّذِينَ ءَامَنُوٓا۟ أَن لَّوْ يَشَآءُ ٱللَّهُ لَهَدَى
ٱلنَّاسَ جَمِيعًا وَلَا يَزَالُ ٱلَّذِينَ كَفَرُوا۟ تُصِيبُهُم
بِمَا صَنَعُوا۟ قَارِعَةٌ أَوْ تَحُلُّ قَرِيبًا مِّن دَارِهِمْ حَتَّىٰ يَأْتِىَ

---

5. Ar. *Qur'an*.

come to pass. Lo! Allah faileth not
to keep the tryst.

32 And verily messengers (of Allah)
were mocked before thee, but long I
bore with those who disbelieved. At
length I seized them, and how (awful) was My punishment!

33 Is He Who is aware of the deserts of every soul (as he who is
aware of nothing)? Yet they ascribe
unto Allah partners. Say: Name
them. Is it that ye would inform Him
of something which He knoweth not
in the earth? Or is it but a way of
speaking? Nay, but their contrivance
is made seeming fair for those who
disbelieve and they are kept from the
right road. He whom Allah sendeth
astray, for him there is no guide.

34 For them is torment in the life
of the world, and verily the doom
of the Hereafter is more painful,
and they have no defender from
Allah.

35 A similitude of the Garden
which is promised unto those who
keep their duty (to Allah): Underneath it rivers flow; its food is everlasting, and its shade; this is the
reward of those who keep their
duty, while the reward of disbelievers is the Fire.

36 Those unto whom We gave the
Scripture rejoice in that which is
revealed unto thee. And of the clans

وَعْدَ اللّٰهِ ۖ إِنَّ اللّٰهَ لَا يُخْلِفُ الْمِيعَادَ ﴿٣١﴾

وَلَقَدِ اسْتُهْزِئَ بِرُسُلٍ مِّن قَبْلِكَ فَأَمْلَيْتُ لِلَّذِينَ
كَفَرُوا ثُمَّ أَخَذْتُهُمْ ۖ فَكَيْفَ كَانَ عِقَابِ ﴿٣٢﴾

أَفَمَنْ هُوَ قَآئِمٌ عَلَىٰ كُلِّ نَفْسٍ بِمَا كَسَبَتْ ۗ وَجَعَلُوا
لِلّٰهِ شُرَكَآءَ قُلْ سَمُّوهُمْ ۚ أَمْ تُنَبِّئُونَهُ بِمَا لَا يَعْلَمُ
فِي الْأَرْضِ أَم بِظَاهِرٍ مِّنَ الْقَوْلِ ۗ بَلْ زُيِّنَ لِلَّذِينَ
كَفَرُوا مَكْرُهُمْ وَصُدُّوا عَنِ السَّبِيلِ ۗ
وَمَن يُضْلِلِ اللّٰهُ فَمَا لَهُ مِنْ هَادٍ ﴿٣٣﴾

لَّهُمْ عَذَابٌ فِي الْحَيَوٰةِ الدُّنْيَا ۖ وَلَعَذَابُ الْآخِرَةِ أَشَقُّ ۖ
وَمَا لَهُم مِّنَ اللّٰهِ مِن وَاقٍ ﴿٣٤﴾

۞ مَّثَلُ الْجَنَّةِ الَّتِي وُعِدَ الْمُتَّقُونَ ۖ تَجْرِي
مِن تَحْتِهَا الْأَنْهَارُ ۖ أُكُلُهَا دَآئِمٌ وَظِلُّهَا ۚ تِلْكَ
عُقْبَى الَّذِينَ اتَّقَوا ۖ وَّعُقْبَى الْكَافِرِينَ النَّارُ ﴿٣٥﴾

وَالَّذِينَ آتَيْنَاهُمُ الْكِتَابَ يَفْرَحُونَ بِمَا أُنزِلَ

there are who deny some of it. Say: I am commanded only that I serve Allah and ascribe unto Him no partner. Unto Him I cry, and unto Him is my return.

إِلَيْكَ وَمِنَ ٱلْأَحْزَابِ مَن يُنكِرُ بَعْضَهُۥ قُلْ إِنَّمَآ أُمِرْتُ أَنْ أَعْبُدَ ٱللَّهَ وَلَآ أُشْرِكَ بِهِۦٓ إِلَيْهِ أَدْعُوا۟ وَإِلَيْهِ مَتَابِ ﴿٣٦﴾

37 Thus have We revealed it, a decisive utterance in Arabic; and if thou shouldst follow their desires after that which hath come unto thee of knowledge, then truly wouldst thou have from Allah no protecting friend nor defender.

وَكَذَٰلِكَ أَنزَلْنَٰهُ حُكْمًا عَرَبِيًّا وَلَئِنِ ٱتَّبَعْتَ أَهْوَآءَهُم بَعْدَمَا جَآءَكَ مِنَ ٱلْعِلْمِ مَا لَكَ مِنَ ٱللَّهِ مِن وَلِيٍّ وَلَا وَاقٍ ﴿٣٧﴾

38 And verily We sent messengers (to mankind) before thee, and We appointed for them wives and offspring, and it was not (given) to any messenger that he should bring a portent save by Allah's leave. For everything there is a time prescribed.

وَلَقَدْ أَرْسَلْنَا رُسُلًا مِّن قَبْلِكَ وَجَعَلْنَا لَهُمْ أَزْوَٰجًا وَذُرِّيَّةً وَمَا كَانَ لِرَسُولٍ أَن يَأْتِيَ بِـَٔايَةٍ إِلَّا بِإِذْنِ ٱللَّهِ لِكُلِّ أَجَلٍ كِتَابٌ ﴿٣٨﴾

39 Allah effaceth what He will, and establisheth (what He will), and with Him is the source of ordinance.

يَمْحُوا۟ ٱللَّهُ مَا يَشَآءُ وَيُثْبِتُ وَعِندَهُۥٓ أُمُّ ٱلْكِتَٰبِ ﴿٣٩﴾

40 Whether We let thee see something of that which We have promised them, or make thee die (before its happening), thine is but conveyance (of the message), Ours the reckoning.

وَإِن مَّا نُرِيَنَّكَ بَعْضَ ٱلَّذِى نَعِدُهُمْ أَوْ نَتَوَفَّيَنَّكَ فَإِنَّمَا عَلَيْكَ ٱلْبَلَٰغُ وَعَلَيْنَا ٱلْحِسَابُ ﴿٤٠﴾

41 See they not how We visit the land, reducing it of its outlying

أَوَلَمْ يَرَوْا۟ أَنَّا نَأْتِى ٱلْأَرْضَ نَنقُصُهَا مِنْ أَطْرَافِهَا وَٱللَّهُ

parts?[6] (When) Allah doometh there is none that can postpone His doom, and He is swift at reckoning.

يَحْكُمُ لَا مُعَقِّبَ لِحُكْمِهِ وَهُوَ سَرِيعُ الْحِسَابِ ۝

42 Those who were before them plotted; but all plotting is Allah's. He knoweth that which each soul earneth. The disbelievers will come to know for whom will be the sequel of the (heavenly) Home.

وَقَدْ مَكَرَ الَّذِينَ مِن قَبْلِهِمْ فَلِلَّهِ الْمَكْرُ جَمِيعًا يَعْلَمُ مَا تَكْسِبُ كُلُّ نَفْسٍ وَسَيَعْلَمُ الْكُفَّرُ لِمَنْ عُقْبَى الدَّارِ ۝

43 They who disbelieve say: Thou art no messenger (of Allah). Say: Allah, and whosoever hath true knowledge of the Scripture, is sufficient witness between me and you.

وَيَقُولُ الَّذِينَ كَفَرُوا لَسْتَ مُرْسَلًا قُلْ كَفَى بِاللَّهِ شَهِيدًا بَيْنِي وَبَيْنَكُمْ وَمَنْ عِنْدَهُ عِلْمُ الْكِتَٰبِ ۝

---

6. If this is a Madīnah verse, the reference would be to the spread of Al-Islām, if a Makkan verse it would be to the Persian and the Eastern Roman empires encroaching on Arabia.

Ibrāhīm
(Abraham)

Ibrāhīm, so-called from Abraham's prayer in vv. 35-41, at the time when he was establishing his son Ishmael, the ancestor of the Arabs, in the "uncultivable valley" of Makkah. Otherwise the subject of the sūrah is the same as that of other Makkan sūrahs revealed during the last three years before the Hijrah. The reference in v. 46 to the plot of the idolaters makes it probable that it is among the last of the Makkan revelations.

A late Makkan sūrah; except vv. 28-30, revealed at Al-Madīnah.

In the name of Allah, the Beneficent, the Merciful.

1   Alif. Lām. Rā.[1] (This is) a Scripture which We have revealed unto thee (Muhammad) that thereby thou mayst bring forth mankind from darkness unto light, by the permission of their Lord, unto the path of the Mighty, the Owner of Praise.

2   Allah, unto Whom belongeth whatsoever is in the heavens and whatsoever is in the earth. And woe unto the disbelievers from an awful doom;

---

1. See Sūrah 2, v. 1, footnote.

3   Those who love the life of the
world more than the Hereafter, and
debar (men) from the way of Allah
and would have it crooked: such are
far astray.

اَلَّذِيْنَ يَسْتَحِبُّوْنَ الْحَيٰوةَ الدُّنْيَا عَلَى الْاٰخِرَةِ
وَيَصُدُّوْنَ عَنْ سَبِيْلِ اللّٰهِ وَيَبْغُوْنَهَا عِوَجًا ؕ
اُولٰٓئِكَ فِيْ ضَلٰلٍۭ بَعِيْدٍ ۞

4   And We never sent a messenger
save with the language of his folk,
that he might make (the message)
clear for them. Then Allah sendeth
whom He will astray, and guideth
whom He will. He is the Mighty,
the Wise.

وَمَاۤ اَرْسَلْنَا مِنْ رَّسُوْلٍ اِلَّا بِلِسَانِ قَوْمِهٖ
لِيُبَيِّنَ لَهُمْ ؕ فَيُضِلُّ اللّٰهُ مَنْ يَّشَاۤءُ وَيَهْدِيْ
مَنْ يَّشَاۤءُ ؕ وَهُوَ الْعَزِيْزُ الْحَكِيْمُ ۞

5   We verily sent Moses with Our
revelations, saying: Bring thy people forth from darkness unto light.
And remind them of the days of
Allah. Lo! therein are revelations
for each steadfast, thankful (heart).

وَلَقَدْ اَرْسَلْنَا مُوْسٰى بِاٰيٰتِنَاۤ
اَنْ اَخْرِجْ قَوْمَكَ مِنَ الظُّلُمٰتِ
اِلَى النُّوْرِ ۙ وَذَكِّرْهُمْ بِاَيّٰمِ اللّٰهِ ؕ اِنَّ
فِيْ ذٰلِكَ لَاٰيٰتٍ لِّكُلِّ صَبَّارٍ شَكُوْرٍ ۞

6   And (remind them) how Moses
said unto his people: Remember
Allah's favour unto you when He
delivered you from Pharaoh's folk
who were afflicting you with dreadful torment, and were slaying your
sons and sparing your women; that
was a tremendous trial from your
Lord.

وَاِذْ قَالَ مُوْسٰى لِقَوْمِهِ اذْكُرُوْا نِعْمَةَ اللّٰهِ
عَلَيْكُمْ اِذْ اَنْجٰىكُمْ مِّنْ اٰلِ فِرْعَوْنَ
يَسُوْمُوْنَكُمْ سُوْٓءَ الْعَذَابِ وَيُذَبِّحُوْنَ اَبْنَاۤءَكُمْ
وَيَسْتَحْيُوْنَ نِسَاۤءَكُمْ ؕ وَفِيْ ذٰلِكُمْ
بَلَاۤءٌ مِّنْ رَّبِّكُمْ عَظِيْمٌ ۞

7   And when your Lord proclaimed: If ye give thanks, I will give
you more; but if ye are thankless;
Lo! My punishment is dire.

وَاِذْ تَاَذَّنَ رَبُّكُمْ لَئِنْ شَكَرْتُمْ
لَاَزِيْدَنَّكُمْ وَلَئِنْ كَفَرْتُمْ اِنَّ عَذَابِيْ
لَشَدِيْدٌ ۞

8   And Moses said: Though ye and
all who are in the earth prove thankless, lo! Allah verily is Absolute,
Owner of Praise.

وَقَالَ مُوْسٰۤى اِنْ تَكْفُرُوْۤا اَنْتُمْ وَمَنْ فِى الْاَرْضِ جَمِيْعًا ۙ
فَاِنَّ اللّٰهَ لَغَنِيٌّ حَمِيْدٌ ۞

9 Hath not the history of those before you reached you: the folk of Noah, and (the tribes of) 'Ād and Thamūd, and those after them? None save Allah knoweth them. Their messengers came unto them with clear proofs, but they thrust their hands into their mouths, and said: Lo! we disbelieve in that wherewith ye have been sent, and lo! we are in grave doubt concerning that to which ye call us.

أَلَمْ يَأْتِكُمْ نَبَؤُا۟ ٱلَّذِينَ مِن قَبْلِكُمْ قَوْمِ نُوحٍ وَعَادٍ وَثَمُودَ وَٱلَّذِينَ مِنۢ بَعْدِهِمْ لَا يَعْلَمُهُمْ إِلَّا ٱللَّهُ جَآءَتْهُمْ رُسُلُهُم بِٱلْبَيِّنَٰتِ فَرَدُّوٓا۟ أَيْدِيَهُمْ فِىٓ أَفْوَٰهِهِمْ وَقَالُوٓا۟ إِنَّا كَفَرْنَا بِمَآ أُرْسِلْتُم بِهِۦ وَإِنَّا لَفِى شَكٍّ مِّمَّا تَدْعُونَنَآ إِلَيْهِ مُرِيبٍ ۝

10 Their messengers said: Can there be doubt concerning Allah, the Creator of the heavens and the earth? He calleth you that He may forgive you your sins and reprieve you unto an appointed term. They said: Ye are but mortals like us, who would fain turn us away from what our fathers used to worship. Then bring some clear warrant.

۞ قَالَتْ رُسُلُهُمْ أَفِى ٱللَّهِ شَكٌّ فَاطِرِ ٱلسَّمَٰوَٰتِ وَٱلْأَرْضِ يَدْعُوكُمْ لِيَغْفِرَ لَكُم مِّن ذُنُوبِكُمْ وَيُؤَخِّرَكُمْ إِلَىٰٓ أَجَلٍ مُّسَمًّى قَالُوٓا۟ إِنْ أَنتُمْ إِلَّا بَشَرٌ مِّثْلُنَا تُرِيدُونَ أَن تَصُدُّونَا عَمَّا كَانَ يَعْبُدُ ءَابَآؤُنَا فَأْتُونَا بِسُلْطَٰنٍ مُّبِينٍ ۝

11 Their messengers said unto them: We are but mortals like you, but Allah giveth grace unto whom He will of His slaves. It is not ours to bring you a warrant unless by the permission of Allah. In Allah let believers put their trust!

قَالَتْ لَهُمْ رُسُلُهُمْ إِن نَّحْنُ إِلَّا بَشَرٌ مِّثْلُكُمْ وَلَٰكِنَّ ٱللَّهَ يَمُنُّ عَلَىٰ مَن يَشَآءُ مِنْ عِبَادِهِۦ وَمَا كَانَ لَنَآ أَن نَّأْتِيَكُم بِسُلْطَٰنٍ إِلَّا بِإِذْنِ ٱللَّهِ وَعَلَى ٱللَّهِ فَلْيَتَوَكَّلِ ٱلْمُؤْمِنُونَ ۝

12 How should we not put our trust in Allah when He hath shown us our ways? We surely will endure that hurt ye do us. In Allah let the trusting put their trust!

وَمَا لَنَآ أَلَّا نَتَوَكَّلَ عَلَى ٱللَّهِ وَقَدْ هَدَىٰنَا سُبُلَنَا وَلَنَصْبِرَنَّ عَلَىٰ مَآ ءَاذَيْتُمُونَا وَعَلَى ٱللَّهِ فَلْيَتَوَكَّلِ ٱلْمُتَوَكِّلُونَ ۝

13 And those who disbelieved said unto their messengers: Verily we

وَقَالَ ٱلَّذِينَ كَفَرُوا۟ لِرُسُلِهِمْ لَنُخْرِجَنَّكُم

will drive you out from our land,
unless ye return to our religion.
Then their Lord inspired them, (saying): Verily We shall destroy the
wrong-doers;

14 And verily We shall make you
to dwell in the land after them. This
is for him who fearth My Majesty
and feareth My threats.

15 And they sought help (from
their Lord) and every froward potentate was brought to naught;

16 Hell is before him, and he is
made to drink a festering water.

17 Which he sippeth but can hardly
swallow, and death cometh unto
him from every side while yet he
cannot die, and before him is a
harsh doom.

18 A similitude of those who disbelieve in their Lord: Their works
are as ashes which the wind blow-
eth hard upon a stormy day. They
have no control of aught that they
have earned. That is the extreme
failure.

19 Hast thou not seen that Allah
hath created the heavens and the
earth with truth? If He will, He can
remove you and bring (in) some
new creation;

20 And that is no great matter for
Allah.

21 They all come forth unto their
Lord. Then those who were despi-

مِنْ أَرْضِنَآ أَوْ لَتَعُوْدُنَّ فِى مِلَّتِنَا ۖ فَأَوْحَىٰٓ إِلَيْهِمْ رَبُّهُمْ لَنُهْلِكَنَّ الظَّالِمِيْنَ ۝

وَلَنُسْكِنَنَّكُمُ الْأَرْضَ مِنْ بَعْدِهِمْ ۚ ذَٰلِكَ لِمَنْ خَافَ مَقَامِى وَخَافَ وَعِيْدِ ۝

وَاسْتَفْتَحُوْا وَخَابَ كُلُّ جَبَّارٍ عَنِيْدٍ ۝

مِّنْ وَّرَآئِهِ جَهَنَّمُ وَيُسْقَىٰ مِنْ مَّآءٍ صَدِيْدٍ ۝ يَّتَجَرَّعُهُ وَلَا يَكَادُ يُسِيْغُهُ وَيَأْتِيْهِ الْمَوْتُ مِنْ كُلِّ مَكَانٍ وَّمَا هُوَ بِمَيِّتٍ ۖ وَمِنْ وَّرَآئِهِ عَذَابٌ غَلِيْظٌ ۝

مَّثَلُ الَّذِيْنَ كَفَرُوْا بِرَبِّهِمْ أَعْمَالُهُمْ كَرَمَادٍ اشْتَدَّتْ بِهِ الرِّيْحُ فِى يَوْمٍ عَاصِفٍ ۖ لَا يَقْدِرُوْنَ مِمَّا كَسَبُوْا عَلَىٰ شَيْءٍ ۚ ذَٰلِكَ هُوَ الضَّلَالُ الْبَعِيْدُ ۝

أَلَمْ تَرَ أَنَّ اللَّهَ خَلَقَ السَّمَاوَاتِ وَالْأَرْضَ بِالْحَقِّ ۚ إِنْ يَّشَأْ يُذْهِبْكُمْ وَيَأْتِ بِخَلْقٍ جَدِيْدٍ ۝

وَمَا ذَٰلِكَ عَلَى اللَّهِ بِعَزِيْزٍ ۝

وَبَرَزُوْا لِلَّهِ جَمِيْعًا فَقَالَ الضُّعَفَاءُ لِلَّذِيْنَ

sed say unto those who were scornful: We were unto you a following, can ye then avert from us aught of Allah's doom? They say: Had Allah guided us, we should have guided you. Whether we rage or patiently endure is (now) all one for us: we have no place of refuge.

22 And Satan saith, when the matter hath been decided: Lo! Allah promised you a promise of truth; and I promised you, then failed you. And I had no power over you save that I called unto you and ye obeyed me. So blame me not, but blame yourselves. I cannot help you, nor can ye help me. Lo! I disbelieved in that which ye before ascribed to me. Lo! for wrong-doers is a painful doom.

23 And those who believed and did good works are made to enter Gardens underneath which rivers flow, therein abiding by permission of their Lord, their greeting therein: Peace!

24 Seest thou not how Allah coineth a similitude: A goodly saying, as a goodly tree, its root set firm, its branches reaching into heaven;

25 Giving its fruit at every season by permission of its Lord? Allah coineth the similitudes for mankind in order that they may reflect.

26 And the similitude of a bad saying is as a bad tree, up-rooted from

upon the earth, possessing no stability.

من فَوْقِ ٱلْأَرْضِ مَا لَهَا مِن قَرَارٍ ﴿٢٦﴾

27 Allah confirmeth those who believe by a firm saying in the life of the world and in the Hereafter, and Allah sendeth wrong-doers astray. And Allah doeth what He will.

يُثَبِّتُ ٱللَّهُ ٱلَّذِينَ ءَامَنُوا بِٱلْقَوْلِ ٱلثَّابِتِ فِي ٱلْحَيَوٰةِ ٱلدُّنْيَا وَفِي ٱلْأَخِرَةِ وَيُضِلُّ ٱللَّهُ ٱلظَّٰلِمِينَ وَيَفْعَلُ ٱللَّهُ مَا يَشَاءُ ﴿٢٧﴾

28 Hast thou not seen those who gave the grace of Allah in exchange for thanklessness and led their people down to the Abode of Loss;

أَلَمْ تَرَ إِلَى ٱلَّذِينَ بَدَّلُوا نِعْمَتَ ٱللَّهِ كُفْرًا وَأَحَلُّوا قَوْمَهُمْ دَارَ ٱلْبَوَارِ ﴿٢٨﴾

29 (Even to) hell? They are exposed thereto. A hapless end!

جَهَنَّمَ يَصْلَوْنَهَا وَبِئْسَ ٱلْقَرَارُ ﴿٢٩﴾

30 And they set up rivals to Allah that they may mislead (men) from His way. Say: Enjoy life (while ye may) for lo! your journey's end will be the Fire.

وَجَعَلُوا لِلَّهِ أَندَادًا لِّيُضِلُّوا عَن سَبِيلِهِ قُلْ تَمَتَّعُوا فَإِنَّ مَصِيرَكُمْ إِلَى ٱلنَّارِ ﴿٣٠﴾

31 Tell My bondmen who believe to establish worship and spend of that which We have given them, secretly and publicly, before a day cometh wherein there will be neither traffick nor befriending.

قُل لِّعِبَادِيَ ٱلَّذِينَ ءَامَنُوا يُقِيمُوا ٱلصَّلَوٰةَ وَيُنفِقُوا مِمَّا رَزَقْنَٰهُمْ سِرًّا وَعَلَانِيَةً مِّن قَبْلِ أَن يَأْتِيَ يَوْمٌ لَّا بَيْعٌ فِيهِ وَلَا خِلَٰلٌ ﴿٣١﴾

32 Allah is He Who created the heavens and the earth, and causeth water to descend from the sky, thereby producing fruits as food for you, and maketh the ships to be of service unto you, that they may run upon the sea at His command, and hath made of service unto you the rivers;

ٱللَّهُ ٱلَّذِي خَلَقَ ٱلسَّمَٰوَٰتِ وَٱلْأَرْضَ وَأَنزَلَ مِنَ ٱلسَّمَاءِ مَاءً فَأَخْرَجَ بِهِ مِنَ ٱلثَّمَرَٰتِ رِزْقًا لَّكُمْ وَسَخَّرَ لَكُمُ ٱلْفُلْكَ لِتَجْرِيَ فِي ٱلْبَحْرِ بِأَمْرِهِ وَسَخَّرَ لَكُمُ ٱلْأَنْهَٰرَ ﴿٣٢﴾

33 And maketh the sun and the moon, constant in their courses, to

وَسَخَّرَ لَكُمُ ٱلشَّمْسَ وَٱلْقَمَرَ دَائِبَيْنِ

be of service unto you, and hath
made of service unto you the night
and the day.

وَسَخَّرَ لَكُمُ الَّيۡلَ وَالنَّهَارَ ۞

34 And He giveth you of all ye ask
of Him, and if ye would count the
bounty of Allah ye cannot reckon
it. Lo! man is verily a wrong-doer,
an ingrate.

وَءَاتَىٰكُم مِّن كُلِّ مَا سَأَلۡتُمُوهُ وَإِن تَعُدُّواْ
نِعۡمَتَ اللّٰهِ لَا تُحۡصُوهَاۗ إِنَّ الۡإِنسَٰنَ لَظَلُومٌ
كَفَّارٌ ۞

35 And when Abraham said: My
Lord! Make safe this territory, and
preserve me and my sons from ser-
ving idols.

وَإِذۡ قَالَ إِبۡرَٰهِيمُ رَبِّ اجۡعَلۡ هَٰذَا الۡبَلَدَ ءَامِنًا
وَاجۡنُبۡنِي وَبَنِيَّ أَن نَّعۡبُدَ الۡأَصۡنَامَ ۞

36 My Lord! Lo! they have led
many of mankind astray. But whoso
followeth me, he verily is of me.
And whoso disobeyeth me—still
Thou art Forgiving, Merciful.

رَبِّ إِنَّهُنَّ أَضۡلَلۡنَ كَثِيرًا مِّنَ النَّاسِۖ فَمَن تَبِعَنِي فَإِنَّهُ
مِنِّيۖ وَمَنۡ عَصَانِي فَإِنَّكَ غَفُورٌ رَّحِيمٌ ۞

37 Our Lord! Lo! I have settled
some of my posterity in an uncultivable valley near unto Thy holy
House,[2] our Lord! that they may
establish proper worship; so incline
some hearts of men that they may
yearn toward them, and provide
Thou them with fruits in order that
they may be thankful.

رَّبَّنَا إِنِّي أَسۡكَنتُ مِن ذُرِّيَّتِي بِوَادٍ غَيۡرِ ذِي زَرۡعٍ
عِندَ بَيۡتِكَ الۡمُحَرَّمِ رَبَّنَا لِيُقِيمُواْ الصَّلَوٰةَ
فَاجۡعَلۡ أَفۡئِدَةً مِّنَ النَّاسِ تَهۡوِيٓ إِلَيۡهِمۡ
وَارۡزُقۡهُم مِّنَ الثَّمَرَٰتِ لَعَلَّهُمۡ يَشۡكُرُونَ ۞

38 Our Lord! Lo! Thou knowest
that which we hide and that which
we proclaim. Nothing in the earth
or in the heaven is hidden from
Allah.

رَبَّنَا إِنَّكَ تَعۡلَمُ مَا نُخۡفِي وَمَا نُعۡلِنُۗ وَمَا يَخۡفَىٰ عَلَى اللّٰهِ
مِن شَيۡءٍ فِي الۡأَرۡضِ وَلَا فِي السَّمَاءِ ۞

39 Praise be to Allah Who hath given me, in my old age, Ishmael and

الۡحَمۡدُ لِلّٰهِ الَّذِي وَهَبَ لِي عَلَى الۡكِبَرِ إِسۡمَٰعِيلَ

---

2. The Valley of Makkah.

Isaac! Lo! my Lord is indeed the Hearer of Prayer.

وَإِسْحَقَ إِنَّ رَبِّى لَسَمِيعُ الدُّعَاءِ ﴿٣٩﴾

40 My Lord! Make me to establish proper worship, and some of my posterity (also); our Lord! and accept the prayer.

رَبِّ اجْعَلْنِى مُقِيمَ الصَّلَوٰةِ وَمِن ذُرِّيَّتِى رَبَّنَا وَتَقَبَّلْ دُعَاءِ ﴿٤٠﴾

41 Our Lord! Forgive me and my parents and believers on the day when the account is cast.

رَبَّنَا اغْفِرْ لِى وَلِوَالِدَىَّ وَلِلْمُؤْمِنِينَ يَوْمَ يَقُومُ الْحِسَابُ ﴿٤١﴾

42 Deem not that Allah is unaware of what the wicked do. He but giveth them a respite till a day when eyes will stare (in terror);

وَلَا تَحْسَبَنَّ اللَّهَ غَٰفِلًا عَمَّا يَعْمَلُ الظَّٰلِمُونَ إِنَّمَا يُؤَخِّرُهُمْ لِيَوْمٍ تَشْخَصُ فِيهِ الْأَبْصَٰرُ ﴿٤٢﴾

43 As they come hurrying on in fear, their heads upraised, their gaze returning not to them, and their hearts as air.

مُهْطِعِينَ مُقْنِعِى رُءُوسِهِمْ لَا يَرْتَدُّ إِلَيْهِمْ طَرْفُهُمْ وَأَفْئِدَتُهُمْ هَوَاءٌ ﴿٤٣﴾

44 And warn mankind of a day when the doom will come upon them, and those who did wrong will say: Our Lord! Reprieve us for a little while. We will obey Thy call and will follow the messengers. (It will be answered): Did ye not swear before that there would be no end for you?

وَأَنذِرِ النَّاسَ يَوْمَ يَأْتِيهِمُ الْعَذَابُ فَيَقُولُ الَّذِينَ ظَلَمُوا رَبَّنَا أَخِّرْنَا إِلَىٰ أَجَلٍ قَرِيبٍ نُّجِبْ دَعْوَتَكَ وَنَتَّبِعِ الرُّسُلَ أَوَلَمْ تَكُونُوا أَقْسَمْتُم مِّن قَبْلُ مَا لَكُم مِّن زَوَالٍ ﴿٤٤﴾

45 And (have ye not) dwelt in the dwellings of those who wronged themselves (of old) and (hath it not) become plain to you how We dealt with them, and made examples for you?

وَسَكَنتُمْ فِى مَسَٰكِنِ الَّذِينَ ظَلَمُوا أَنفُسَهُمْ وَتَبَيَّنَ لَكُمْ كَيْفَ فَعَلْنَا بِهِمْ وَضَرَبْنَا لَكُمُ الْأَمْثَالَ ﴿٤٥﴾

46 Verily they have plotted their plot, and their plot is with Allah, though their plot were one whereby the mountains should be moved.

وَقَدْ مَكَرُوا مَكْرَهُمْ وَعِندَ اللَّهِ مَكْرُهُمْ وَإِن كَانَ مَكْرُهُمْ لِتَزُولَ مِنْهُ الْجِبَالُ ﴿٤٦﴾

47 So think not that Allah will fail to keep His promise to His messengers. Lo! Allah is Mighty, Able to Requite (the wrong).

48 On the day when the earth will be changed to other than the earth, and the heavens (also will be changed) and they will come forth unto Allah, the One, the Almighty.

49 Thou wilt see the guilty on that day linked together in chains.

50 Their raiment of pitch, and the Fire covering their faces;

51 That Allah may repay each soul what it hath earned. Lo! Allah is Swift at reckoning.

52 This is a clear message for mankind in order that they may be warned thereby, and that they may know that He is only One God, and that men of understanding may take heed.

فَلَا تَحْسَبَنَّ اللَّهَ مُخْلِفَ وَعْدِهِۦ رُسُلَهُۥٓ
إِنَّ اللَّهَ عَزِيزٌ ذُو انتِقَامٍ ۝

يَوْمَ تُبَدَّلُ الْأَرْضُ غَيْرَ الْأَرْضِ وَالسَّمَٰوَٰتُ
وَبَرَزُوا لِلَّهِ الْوَٰحِدِ الْقَهَّارِ ۝

وَتَرَى الْمُجْرِمِينَ يَوْمَئِذٍ
مُّقَرَّنِينَ فِي الْأَصْفَادِ ۝
سَرَابِيلُهُم مِّن قَطِرَانٍ وَتَغْشَىٰ
وُجُوهَهُمُ النَّارُ ۝
لِيَجْزِيَ اللَّهُ كُلَّ نَفْسٍ مَّا كَسَبَتْ
إِنَّ اللَّهَ سَرِيعُ الْحِسَابِ ۝

هَٰذَا بَلَٰغٌ لِّلنَّاسِ وَلِيُنذَرُوا بِهِۦ وَلِيَعْلَمُوٓا
أَنَّمَا هُوَ إِلَٰهٌ وَٰحِدٌ وَلِيَذَّكَّرَ أُو۟لُوا الْأَلْبَٰبِ ۝

Al Ḥijr

Al Ḥijr (which I take to be a place-name) is so called from vv. 80-84, where the fate of the dwellers at that place is described. The date of revelation is earlier than that of any of the Makkan sūrahs which precede it in the arrangement of the Book, though the subject and the tone are similar, which accounts for its position. Nöldeke places it in his middle group of Makkan sūrahs, that is (as far as one can judge from the inclusions), those revealed after the eighth year and before the third year before the Hijrah, and in so doing confirms the judgment of the best Muslim authorities, though some Muslim authorities would place it among the earliest revelations.

It belongs to the middle group of Makkan sūrahs.

In the name of Allah, the Beneficent, the Merciful.

1 Alif. Lām. Rā.[1] These are verses of the Scripture and a plain Reading.[2]

2 It may be that those who disbelieve wish ardently that they were Muslims.[3]

3 Let them eat and enjoy life, and let (false) hope beguile them. They will come to know!

---

1. See Sūrah 2, v. 1, footnote.

2. Ar. *Qur'an.*

3. Or "those who have surrendered."

4 And We destroyed no township but there was a known decree for it.

وَمَآ أَهْلَكْنَا مِن قَرْيَةٍ إِلَّا وَلَهَا كِتَابٌ مَّعْلُومٌ ﴿٤﴾

5 No nation can outstrip its term nor can they lag behind.

مَّا تَسْبِقُ مِنْ أُمَّةٍ أَجَلَهَا وَمَا يَسْتَـْٔخِرُونَ ﴿٥﴾

6 And they say: O thou unto whom the Reminder is revealed, lo! thou art indeed a madman!

وَقَالُوا يَـٰٓأَيُّهَا الَّذِى نُزِّلَ عَلَيْهِ الذِّكْرُ إِنَّكَ لَمَجْنُونٌ ﴿٦﴾

7 Why bringest thou not angels unto us, if thou art of the truthful?

لَّوْ مَا تَأْتِينَا بِالْمَلَـٰٓئِكَةِ إِن كُنتَ مِنَ الصَّـٰدِقِينَ ﴿٧﴾

8 We send not down the angels save with the Fact, and in that case (the disbelievers) would not be tolerated.

مَا نُنَزِّلُ الْمَلَـٰٓئِكَةَ إِلَّا بِالْحَقِّ وَمَا كَانُوٓا إِذًا مُّنظَرِينَ ﴿٨﴾

9 Lo! We, even We, reveal the Reminder, and lo! We verily are its Guardian.

إِنَّا نَحْنُ نَزَّلْنَا الذِّكْرَ وَإِنَّا لَهُۥ لَحَـٰفِظُونَ ﴿٩﴾

10 We verily sent (messengers) before thee among the factions of the men of old.

وَلَقَدْ أَرْسَلْنَا مِن قَبْلِكَ فِى شِيَعِ الْأَوَّلِينَ ﴿١٠﴾

11 And never came there unto them a messenger but they did mock him.

وَمَا يَأْتِيهِم مِّن رَّسُولٍ إِلَّا كَانُوا بِهِۦ يَسْتَهْزِءُونَ ﴿١١﴾

12 Thus do We make it traverse the hearts of the guilty:

كَذَٰلِكَ نَسْلُكُهُۥ فِى قُلُوبِ الْمُجْرِمِينَ ﴿١٢﴾

13 They believe not therein, though the example of the men of old hath gone before.

لَا يُؤْمِنُونَ بِهِۦ وَقَدْ خَلَتْ سُنَّةُ الْأَوَّلِينَ ﴿١٣﴾

14 And even if We opened unto them a Gate of Heaven and they kept mounting through it.

وَلَوْ فَتَحْنَا عَلَيْهِم بَابًا مِّنَ السَّمَآءِ فَظَلُّوا فِيهِ يَعْرُجُونَ ﴿١٤﴾

15 They would say: Our sight is wrong—nay, but we are folk bewitched.

لَقَالُوٓا إِنَّمَا سُكِّرَتْ أَبْصَـٰرُنَا بَلْ نَحْنُ قَوْمٌ مَّسْحُورُونَ ﴿١٥﴾

16 And verily in the heaven We have set mansions of the stars, and We have beautified it for beholders.

وَلَقَدْ جَعَلْنَا فِى السَّمَآءِ بُرُوجًا وَزَيَّنَّـٰهَا لِلنَّـٰظِرِينَ ﴿١٦﴾

17 And We have guarded it from every outcast devil;

وَحَفِظْنَاهَا مِنْ كُلِّ شَيْطَانٍ رَجِيمٍ ۝

18 Save him who stealeth the hearing, and them doth a clear flame pursue.

إِلَّا مَنِ اسْتَرَقَ السَّمْعَ فَأَتْبَعَهُ شِهَابٌ مُبِينٌ ۝

19 And the earth have We spread out, and placed therein firm hills, and caused each seemly thing to grow therein.

وَالْأَرْضَ مَدَدْنَاهَا وَأَلْقَيْنَا فِيهَا رَوَاسِيَ وَأَنْبَتْنَا فِيهَا مِنْ كُلِّ شَيْءٍ مَوْزُونٍ ۝

20 And We have given unto you livelihoods therein, and unto those for whom ye provide not.

وَجَعَلْنَا لَكُمْ فِيهَا مَعَايِشَ وَمَنْ لَسْتُمْ لَهُ بِرَازِقِينَ ۝

21 And there is not a thing but with Us are the stores thereof. And We send it not down save in appointed measure.

وَإِنْ مِنْ شَيْءٍ إِلَّا عِنْدَنَا خَزَائِنُهُ وَمَا نُنَزِّلُهُ إِلَّا بِقَدَرٍ مَعْلُومٍ ۝

22 And We send the winds fertilising, and cause water to descend from the sky, and We give it to you to drink. It is not ye who are the holders of the store thereof.

وَأَرْسَلْنَا الرِّيَاحَ لَوَاقِحَ فَأَنْزَلْنَا مِنَ السَّمَاءِ مَاءً فَأَسْقَيْنَاكُمُوهُ وَمَا أَنْتُمْ لَهُ بِخَازِنِينَ ۝

23 Lo! and it is We, even We, Who quicken and give death, and We are the Inheritors.

وَإِنَّا لَنَحْنُ نُحْيِي وَنُمِيتُ وَنَحْنُ الْوَارِثُونَ ۝

24 And verily We know those who go forward among you and verily We know the laggards.

وَلَقَدْ عَلِمْنَا الْمُسْتَقْدِمِينَ مِنْكُمْ وَلَقَدْ عَلِمْنَا الْمُسْتَأْخِرِينَ ۝

25 Lo! thy Lord will gather them together. Lo! He is Wise, Aware.

وَإِنَّ رَبَّكَ هُوَ يَحْشُرُهُمْ إِنَّهُ حَكِيمٌ عَلِيمٌ ۝

26 Verily We created man of potter's clay, of black mud altered;

وَلَقَدْ خَلَقْنَا الْإِنْسَانَ مِنْ صَلْصَالٍ مِنْ حَمَإٍ مَسْنُونٍ ۝

27 And the jinn did We create aforetime of essential fire.

وَالْجَانَّ خَلَقْنَاهُ مِنْ قَبْلُ مِنْ نَارِ السَّمُومِ ۝

28 And (remember) when thy Lord said unto the angels: Lo! I am creating a mortal out of potter's clay, of black mud altered;

وَإِذْ قَالَ رَبُّكَ لِلْمَلَٰٓئِكَةِ إِنِّى خَٰلِقٌۢ بَشَرًا مِّن صَلْصَٰلٍ مِّنْ حَمَإٍ مَّسْنُونٍ ﴿٢٨﴾

29 So, when I have made him and have breathed into him of My spirit, do ye fall down, prostrating yourselves unto him.

فَإِذَا سَوَّيْتُهُۥ وَنَفَخْتُ فِيهِ مِن رُّوحِى فَقَعُوا۟ لَهُۥ سَٰجِدِينَ ﴿٢٩﴾

30 So the angels fell prostrate, all of them together.

فَسَجَدَ ٱلْمَلَٰٓئِكَةُ كُلُّهُمْ أَجْمَعُونَ ﴿٣٠﴾

31 Save Iblīs. He refused to be among the prostrate.

إِلَّآ إِبْلِيسَ أَبَىٰٓ أَن يَكُونَ مَعَ ٱلسَّٰجِدِينَ ﴿٣١﴾

32 He said: O Iblīs! What aileth thee that thou art not among the prostrate?

قَالَ يَٰٓإِبْلِيسُ مَا لَكَ أَلَّا تَكُونَ مَعَ ٱلسَّٰجِدِينَ ﴿٣٢﴾

33 He said: I am not going to prostrate myself unto a mortal whom Thou hast created out of potter's clay, of black mud altered.

قَالَ لَمْ أَكُن لِّأَسْجُدَ لِبَشَرٍ خَلَقْتَهُۥ مِن صَلْصَٰلٍ مِّنْ حَمَإٍ مَّسْنُونٍ ﴿٣٣﴾

34 He said: Then go thou forth from hence, for verily thou art outcast.

قَالَ فَٱخْرُجْ مِنْهَا فَإِنَّكَ رَجِيمٌ ﴿٣٤﴾

35 And lo! the curse shall be upon thee till the Day of Judgment.

وَإِنَّ عَلَيْكَ ٱللَّعْنَةَ إِلَىٰ يَوْمِ ٱلدِّينِ ﴿٣٥﴾

36 He said: My Lord! Reprieve me till the day when they are raised.

قَالَ رَبِّ فَأَنظِرْنِىٓ إِلَىٰ يَوْمِ يُبْعَثُونَ ﴿٣٦﴾

37 He said: Then lo! thou art of those reprieved;

قَالَ فَإِنَّكَ مِنَ ٱلْمُنظَرِينَ ﴿٣٧﴾

38 Till an appointed time.

إِلَىٰ يَوْمِ ٱلْوَقْتِ ٱلْمَعْلُومِ ﴿٣٨﴾

39 He said: My Lord! Because Thou has sent me astray, I verily shall adorn the path of error for them in the earth, and shall mislead them every one.

قَالَ رَبِّ بِمَآ أَغْوَيْتَنِى لَأُزَيِّنَنَّ لَهُمْ فِى ٱلْأَرْضِ وَلَأُغْوِيَنَّهُمْ أَجْمَعِينَ ﴿٣٩﴾

40 Save such of them as are Thy perfectly devoted slaves.

إِلَّا عِبَادَكَ مِنْهُمُ الْمُخْلَصِينَ ۝

41 He said: This is a right course incumbent upon Me:

قَالَ هَذَا صِرَاطٌ عَلَيَّ مُسْتَقِيمٌ ۝

42 Lo! as for My slaves, thou hast no power over any of them save such of the froward as follow thee;

إِنَّ عِبَادِى لَيْسَ لَكَ عَلَيْهِمْ سُلْطَانٌ إِلَّا مَنِ اتَّبَعَكَ مِنَ الْغَاوِينَ ۝

43 And lo! for all such, hell will be the promised place.

وَإِنَّ جَهَنَّمَ لَمَوْعِدُهُمْ أَجْمَعِينَ ۝

44 It hath seven gates, and each gate hath an appointed portion.

لَهَا سَبْعَةُ أَبْوَابٍ لِكُلِّ بَابٍ مِنْهُمْ جُزْءٌ مَقْسُومٌ ۝

45 Lo! those who ward off (evil) are among gardens and watersprings.

إِنَّ الْمُتَّقِينَ فِى جَنَّاتٍ وَعُيُونٍ ۝

46 (And it is said unto them): Enter them in peace, secure.

ادْخُلُوهَا بِسَلَامٍ آمِنِينَ ۝

47 And We remove whatever rancour may be in their breasts. As brethren, face to face, (they rest) on couches raised.

وَنَزَعْنَا مَا فِى صُدُورِهِمْ مِنْ غِلٍّ إِخْوَانًا عَلَى سُرُرٍ مُتَقَابِلِينَ ۝

48 Toil cometh not unto them there, nor will they be expelled from thence.

لَا يَمَسُّهُمْ فِيهَا نَصَبٌ وَمَا هُمْ مِنْهَا بِمُخْرَجِينَ ۝

49 Announce, (O Muhammad) unto My slaves that verily I am the Forgiving, the Merciful;

نَبِّئْ عِبَادِى أَنِّى أَنَا الْغَفُورُ الرَّحِيمُ ۝

50 And that My doom is the dolorous doom.

وَأَنَّ عَذَابِى هُوَ الْعَذَابُ الْأَلِيمُ ۝

51 And tell them of Abraham's guests;

وَنَبِّئْهُمْ عَنْ ضَيْفِ إِبْرَاهِيمَ ۝

52 (How) when they came in unto him, and said: Peace. He said: Lo! we are afraid of you.

إِذْ دَخَلُوا عَلَيْهِ فَقَالُوا سَلَامًا قَالَ إِنَّا مِنْكُمْ وَجِلُونَ ۝

53 They said: Be not afraid! Lo! we bring thee good tidings of a boy possessing wisdom.

قَالُوا لَا تَوْجَلْ إِنَّا نُبَشِّرُكَ بِغُلَٰمٍ عَلِيمٍ ﴿٥٣﴾

54 He said: Bring ye me good tidings (of a son) when old age hath overtaken me? Of what then can ye bring good tidings?

قَالَ أَبَشَّرْتُمُونِي عَلَىٰ أَن مَّسَّنِيَ ٱلْكِبَرُ فَبِمَ تُبَشِّرُونَ ﴿٥٤﴾

55 They said: We bring thee good tidings in truth. So be not thou of the despairing.

قَالُوا بَشَّرْنَٰكَ بِٱلْحَقِّ فَلَا تَكُن مِّنَ ٱلْقَٰنِطِينَ ﴿٥٥﴾

56 He said: And who despaireth of the mercy of his Lord save those who are astray?

قَالَ وَمَن يَقْنَطُ مِن رَّحْمَةِ رَبِّهِ إِلَّا ٱلضَّآلُّونَ ﴿٥٦﴾

57 He said: And afterward what is your business, O ye messengers (of Allah)?

قَالَ فَمَا خَطْبُكُمْ أَيُّهَا ٱلْمُرْسَلُونَ ﴿٥٧﴾

58 They said: We have been sent unto a guilty folk.

قَالُوا إِنَّا أُرْسِلْنَا إِلَىٰ قَوْمٍ مُّجْرِمِينَ ﴿٥٨﴾

59 (All) save the family of Lot. Them we shall deliver everyone;

إِلَّا ءَالَ لُوطٍ إِنَّا لَمُنَجُّوهُمْ أَجْمَعِينَ ﴿٥٩﴾

60 Except his wife, of whom We had decreed that she should be of those who stay behind.

إِلَّا ٱمْرَأَتَهُ قَدَّرْنَا إِنَّهَا لَمِنَ ٱلْغَٰبِرِينَ ﴿٦٠﴾

61 And when the messengers came unto the family of Lot;

فَلَمَّا جَآءَ ءَالَ لُوطٍ ٱلْمُرْسَلُونَ ﴿٦١﴾

62 He said: Lo! ye are folk unknown (to me).

قَالَ إِنَّكُمْ قَوْمٌ مُّنكَرُونَ ﴿٦٢﴾

63 They said: Nay, but we bring thee that concerning which they keep disputing;

قَالُوا بَلْ جِئْنَٰكَ بِمَا كَانُوا فِيهِ يَمْتَرُونَ ﴿٦٣﴾

64 And bring thee the Truth, and lo! we are truth-tellers.

وَأَتَيْنَٰكَ بِٱلْحَقِّ وَإِنَّا لَصَٰدِقُونَ ﴿٦٤﴾

65 So travel with thy household in a portion of the night, and follow

فَأَسْرِ بِأَهْلِكَ بِقِطْعٍ مِّنَ ٱلَّيْلِ وَٱتَّبِعْ أَدْبَٰرَهُمْ

thou their backs. Let none of you turn round, but go whither ye are commanded.

وَلَا يَلْتَفِتْ مِنكُمْ أَحَدٌ وَامْضُوا حَيْثُ تُؤْمَرُونَ ۝

66 And We made plain the case to him, that the root of them (who did wrong) was to be cut at early morn.

وَقَضَيْنَآ إِلَيْهِ ذَٰلِكَ الْأَمْرَ أَنَّ دَابِرَ هَٰٓؤُلَآءِ مَقْطُوعٌ مُّصْبِحِينَ ۝

67 And the people of the city came, rejoicing at the news (of new arrivals).

وَجَآءَ أَهْلُ الْمَدِينَةِ يَسْتَبْشِرُونَ ۝

68 He said: Lo! they are my guests. Affront me not!

قَالَ إِنَّ هَٰٓؤُلَآءِ ضَيْفِي فَلَا تَفْضَحُونِ ۝

69 And keep your duty to Allah, and shame me not!

وَاتَّقُوا اللَّهَ وَلَا تُخْزُونِ ۝

70 They said: Have we not forbidden you from (entertaining) anyone?

قَالُوٓا أَوَلَمْ نَنْهَكَ عَنِ الْعَالَمِينَ ۝

71 He said: Here are my daughters, if ye must be doing (so).

قَالَ هَٰٓؤُلَآءِ بَنَاتِي إِن كُنتُمْ فَاعِلِينَ ۝

72 By thy life (O Muhammad) they moved blindly in the frenzy of approaching death.

لَعَمْرُكَ إِنَّهُمْ لَفِي سَكْرَتِهِمْ يَعْمَهُونَ ۝

73 Then the (Awful) Cry overtook them at the sunrise.

فَأَخَذَتْهُمُ الصَّيْحَةُ مُشْرِقِينَ ۝

74 And We turned it upside down, and We rained upon them stones of heated clay.

فَجَعَلْنَا عَالِيَهَا سَافِلَهَا وَأَمْطَرْنَا عَلَيْهِمْ حِجَارَةً مِّن سِجِّيلٍ ۝

75 Lo! therein verily are portents for those who read the signs.

إِنَّ فِي ذَٰلِكَ لَآيَاتٍ لِّلْمُتَوَسِّمِينَ ۝

76 And lo! it is upon a road still uneffaced.

وَإِنَّهَا لَبِسَبِيلٍ مُّقِيمٍ ۝

77 Lo! therein is indeed a portent for believers.

إِنَّ فِي ذَٰلِكَ لَآيَةً لِّلْمُؤْمِنِينَ ۝

78 And the dwellers in the wood[4] indeed were evil-doers.

وَإِن كَانَ أَصْحَٰبُ ٱلْأَيْكَةِ لَظَٰلِمِينَ ۝

79 So We took vengeance on them; and lo! they both are on a high road plain to see.

فَٱنتَقَمْنَا مِنْهُمْ وَإِنَّهُمَا لَبِإِمَامٍ مُّبِينٍ ۝

80 And the dwellers in Al-Ḥijr indeed denied (Our) messengers.

وَلَقَدْ كَذَّبَ أَصْحَٰبُ ٱلْحِجْرِ ٱلْمُرْسَلِينَ ۝

81 And We gave them Our revelations, but they were averse to them.

وَءَاتَيْنَٰهُمْ ءَايَٰتِنَا فَكَانُوا۟ عَنْهَا مُعْرِضِينَ ۝

82 And they used to hew out dwellings from the hills, (wherein they dwelt) secure.

وَكَانُوا۟ يَنْحِتُونَ مِنَ ٱلْجِبَالِ بُيُوتًا ءَامِنِينَ ۝

83 But the (Awful) Cry overtook them at the morning hour;

فَأَخَذَتْهُمُ ٱلصَّيْحَةُ مُصْبِحِينَ ۝

84 And that which they were wont to count as gain availed them not.

فَمَآ أَغْنَىٰ عَنْهُم مَّا كَانُوا۟ يَكْسِبُونَ ۝

85 We created not the heavens and the earth and all that is between them save with truth, and lo! the Hour is surely coming. So forgive, O Muhammad, with a gracious forgiveness.

وَمَا خَلَقْنَا ٱلسَّمَٰوَٰتِ وَٱلْأَرْضَ وَمَا بَيْنَهُمَآ إِلَّا بِٱلْحَقِّ وَإِنَّ ٱلسَّاعَةَ لَءَاتِيَةٌ فَٱصْفَحِ ٱلصَّفْحَ ٱلْجَمِيلَ ۝

86 Lo! Thy Lord! He is the All Wise Creator.

إِنَّ رَبَّكَ هُوَ ٱلْخَلَّٰقُ ٱلْعَلِيمُ ۝

87 We have given thee seven of the oft-repeated (verses)[5] and the great Qur'an.

وَلَقَدْ ءَاتَيْنَٰكَ سَبْعًا مِّنَ ٱلْمَثَانِي وَٱلْقُرْءَانَ ٱلْعَظِيمَ ۝

88 Strain not thine eyes toward that which We cause some wedded pairs

لَا تَمُدَّنَّ عَيْنَيْكَ إِلَىٰ مَا مَتَّعْنَا بِهِۦٓ أَزْوَٰجًا مِّنْهُمْ

---

4. Another name for Madyan.

5. According to a strong tradition, the reference is to Sūrah 1, which consists of seven verses and forms a part of every Muslim prayer.

among them to enjoy, and be not grieved on their account, and lower thy wing (in tenderness) for the believers.

وَلَا تَحْزَنْ عَلَيْهِمْ وَاخْفِضْ جَنَاحَكَ لِلْمُؤْمِنِينَ ۝

89 And say: Lo! I, even I, am a plain warner;

وَقُلْ إِنِّيٓ أَنَا النَّذِيرُ الْمُبِينُ ۝

90 Such as We send down for those who make division;

كَمَآ أَنْزَلْنَا عَلَى الْمُقْتَسِمِينَ ۝

91 Those who break the Qur'an into parts.

الَّذِينَ جَعَلُوا الْقُرْءَانَ عِضِينَ ۝

92 Them, by thy Lord, We shall question, every one;

فَوَرَبِّكَ لَنَسْـَٔلَنَّهُمْ أَجْمَعِينَ ۝

93 Of what they used to do.

عَمَّا كَانُوا يَعْمَلُونَ ۝

94 So proclaim that which thou art commanded, and withdraw from the idolaters.

فَاصْدَعْ بِمَا تُؤْمَرُ وَأَعْرِضْ عَنِ الْمُشْرِكِينَ ۝

95 Lo! We are Sufficient for thee against the scoffers.

إِنَّا كَفَيْنَاكَ الْمُسْتَهْزِءِينَ ۝

96 Who set some other god along with Allah. But they will come to know.

الَّذِينَ يَجْعَلُونَ مَعَ اللَّهِ إِلَهًا ءَاخَرَ فَسَوْفَ يَعْلَمُونَ ۝

97 Well know We that thy bosom is at times oppressed by what they say;

وَلَقَدْ نَعْلَمُ أَنَّكَ يَضِيقُ صَدْرُكَ بِمَا يَقُولُونَ ۝

98 But hymn the praise of thy Lord, and be of those who make prostration (unto Him).

فَسَبِّحْ بِحَمْدِ رَبِّكَ وَكُنْ مِنَ السَّاجِدِينَ ۝

99 And serve thy Lord till the inevitable[6] cometh unto thee.

وَاعْبُدْ رَبَّكَ حَتَّى يَأْتِيَكَ الْيَقِينُ ۝

---

6. *i.e.* death.

Al Naḥl
(The Bee)

Al Naḥl, "The Bee," takes its name from v. 68, where the activities of the Bee are mentioned as a type of duty and of usefulness. It calls attention to God's providence for creation, and to His guidance to mankind as a necessary part of it, and warns disbelievers in that guidance of a folly in rejecting it as great as would be the rejection of food and drink. The sūrah is ascribed to the last Makkan group, though some ancient authorities regard the ascription as valid only for vv. 1-40, and consider the whole latter portion as revealed at Al-Madīnah. The only verse in the sūrah which is self-evidently of Madīnan revelation is v. 110, where the fugitives from persecution are said to have fought; for in the Makkan period fighting was unlawful for the Muslims, though many of them fled from persecution, taking refuge in Abyssinia.

A late Makkan sūrah, with the exception of v. 110, which must have been revealed at Al-Madīnah not earlier than the year 2 A.H., and possibly many other verses toward the end.

In the name of Allah, the Beneficent, the Merciful.

1   The commandment of Allah will come to pass, so seek not ye to hasten it. Glorified and Exalted be He above all that they associate (with Him).

2   He sendeth down the angels with the Spirit of His command unto whom He will of His bond-

men, (saying): Warn mankind that
there is no god save Me, so keep
your duty unto Me.

عِبَادِهِ أَنْ أَنْذِرُوا أَنَّهُ لَا إِلَهَ إِلَّا أَنَا فَاتَّقُونِ ۝

3 He hath created the heavens and
the earth with truth. High be He
exalted above all that they associate
(with Him).

خَلَقَ السَّمَوَاتِ وَالْأَرْضَ بِالْحَقِّ تَعَالَى
عَمَّا يُشْرِكُونَ ۝

4 He hath created man from a
drop of fluid, yet behold! he is an
open opponent.

خَلَقَ الْإِنْسَانَ مِنْ نُطْفَةٍ فَإِذَا
هُوَ خَصِيمٌ مُبِينٌ ۝

5 And the cattle hath He created,
whence ye have warm clothing and
uses, and whereof ye eat.

وَالْأَنْعَامَ خَلَقَهَا لَكُمْ فِيهَا دِفْءٌ وَمَنَافِعُ
وَمِنْهَا تَأْكُلُونَ ۝

6 And wherein is beauty for you,
when ye bring them home, and
when ye take them out to pasture.

وَلَكُمْ فِيهَا جَمَالٌ حِينَ تُرِيحُونَ
وَحِينَ تَسْرَحُونَ ۝

7 And they bear your loads for
you unto a land ye could not reach
save with great trouble to yourselves. Lo! your Lord is Full of Pity,
Merciful.

وَتَحْمِلُ أَثْقَالَكُمْ إِلَى بَلَدٍ لَّمْ تَكُونُوا بَالِغِيهِ
إِلَّا بِشِقِّ الْأَنْفُسِ إِنَّ رَبَّكُمْ لَرَؤُوفٌ رَحِيمٌ ۝

8 And horses and mules and asses
(hath He created) that ye may ride
them, and for ornament. And He
createth that which ye know not.

وَالْخَيْلَ وَالْبِغَالَ وَالْحَمِيرَ لِتَرْكَبُوهَا وَزِينَةً
وَيَخْلُقُ مَا لَا تَعْلَمُونَ ۝

9 And Allah's is the direction of
the way, and some (roads) go not
straight. And had He willed He
would have led you all aright.

وَعَلَى اللَّهِ قَصْدُ السَّبِيلِ وَمِنْهَا جَائِرٌ وَلَوْ شَاءَ
لَهَدَاكُمْ أَجْمَعِينَ ۝

10 He it is Who sendeth down water from the sky, whence ye have
drink, and whence are trees on wh-

هُوَ الَّذِي أَنْزَلَ مِنَ السَّمَاءِ مَاءً لَكُمْ مِنْهُ

شَرَابٌ وَّمِنْهُ شَجَرٌ فِيهِ تُسِيمُوْنَ ۞

ich ye send your beasts to pasture.[1]

يُنْۢبِتُ لَكُمْ بِهِ الزَّرْعَ وَالزَّيْتُوْنَ وَالنَّخِيْلَ
وَالْأَعْنَابَ وَمِنْ كُلِّ الثَّمَرٰتِ ۗ إِنَّ فِيْ ذٰلِكَ
لَأٰيَةً لِّقَوْمٍ يَّتَفَكَّرُوْنَ ۞

11 Therewith He causeth crops to grow for you, and the olive and the date-palm and grapes and all kinds of fruit. Lo! herein is indeed a portent for people who reflect.

وَسَخَّرَ لَكُمُ الَّيْلَ وَالنَّهَارَ ۙ وَالشَّمْسَ وَالْقَمَرَ ۖ
وَالنُّجُوْمُ مُسَخَّرٰتٌ ۢ بِأَمْرِهٖ ۗ إِنَّ فِيْ ذٰلِكَ
لَأٰيٰتٍ لِّقَوْمٍ يَّعْقِلُوْنَ ۞

12 And he hath constrained the night and the day and the sun and the moon to be of service unto you, and the stars are made subservient by His command. Lo! herein indeed are portents for people who have sense.

وَمَا ذَرَأَ لَكُمْ فِي الْأَرْضِ مُخْتَلِفًا أَلْوَانُهٗ ۗ
إِنَّ فِيْ ذٰلِكَ لَأٰيَةً لِّقَوْمٍ يَّذَّكَّرُوْنَ ۞

13 And whatsoever He hath created for you in the earth of divers hues, lo! therein is indeed a portent for people who take heed.

وَهُوَ الَّذِيْ سَخَّرَ الْبَحْرَ لِتَأْكُلُوْا مِنْهُ
لَحْمًا طَرِيًّا وَّتَسْتَخْرِجُوْا مِنْهُ حِلْيَةً تَلْبَسُوْنَهَا ۚ
وَتَرَى الْفُلْكَ مَوَاخِرَ فِيْهِ وَلِتَبْتَغُوْا
مِنْ فَضْلِهٖ وَلَعَلَّكُمْ تَشْكُرُوْنَ ۞

14 And He it is Who hath constrained the sea to be of service that ye eat fresh meat from thence, and bring forth from thence ornaments which ye wear. And thou seest the ships ploughing it that ye (mankind) may seek of His bounty, and that haply ye may give thanks.

وَأَلْقٰى فِي الْأَرْضِ رَوَاسِيَ أَنْ تَمِيْدَ بِكُمْ
وَأَنْهٰرًا وَّسُبُلًا لَّعَلَّكُمْ تَهْتَدُوْنَ ۞

15 And He hath cast into the earth firm hills that it quake not with you, and streams and roads that ye may find a way.

وَعَلٰمٰتٍ ۚ وَبِالنَّجْمِ هُمْ يَهْتَدُوْنَ ۞

16 And landmarks (too), and by the star they find a way.

---

1. There being hardly any herbage in Arabia, the cattle eat the leaves of trees and shrubs.

17 Is He then Who createth as him who createth not? Will ye not then remember?

أَفَمَنْ يَخْلُقُ كَمَنْ لَا يَخْلُقُ أَفَلَا تَذَكَّرُونَ ۝

18 And if ye would count the favour of Allah ye cannot reckon it. Lo! Allah is indeed Forgiving, Merciful.

وَإِنْ تَعُدُّوا نِعْمَةَ اللّٰهِ لَا تُحْصُوهَا إِنَّ اللّٰهَ لَغَفُورٌ رَحِيمٌ ۝

19 And Allah knoweth that which ye keep hidden and that which ye proclaim.

وَاللّٰهُ يَعْلَمُ مَا تُسِرُّونَ وَمَا تُعْلِنُونَ ۝

20 Those unto whom they cry beside Allah created naught, but are themselves created.

وَالَّذِينَ يَدْعُونَ مِنْ دُونِ اللّٰهِ لَا يَخْلُقُونَ شَيْئًا وَهُمْ يُخْلَقُونَ ۝

21 (They are) dead, not living. And they know not when they will be raised.

أَمْوَاتٌ غَيْرُ أَحْيَاءٍ وَمَا يَشْعُرُونَ أَيَّانَ يُبْعَثُونَ ۝

22 Your God is One God. But as for those who believe not in the Hereafter, their hearts refuse to know; for they are proud.

إِلٰهُكُمْ إِلٰهٌ وَاحِدٌ فَالَّذِينَ لَا يُؤْمِنُونَ بِالْآخِرَةِ قُلُوبُهُمْ مُنْكِرَةٌ وَهُمْ مُسْتَكْبِرُونَ ۝

23 Assuredly Allah knoweth that which they keep hidden and that which they proclaim. Lo! He loveth not the proud.

لَا جَرَمَ أَنَّ اللّٰهَ يَعْلَمُ مَا يُسِرُّونَ وَمَا يُعْلِنُونَ إِنَّهُ لَا يُحِبُّ الْمُسْتَكْبِرِينَ ۝

24 And when it is said unto them: What hath your Lord revealed? they say: (Mere) fables of the men of old;

وَإِذَا قِيلَ لَهُمْ مَاذَا أَنْزَلَ رَبُّكُمْ قَالُوا أَسَاطِيرُ الْأَوَّلِينَ ۝

25 That they may bear their burdens undiminished on the Day of Resurrection, with somewhat of the burdens of those whom they mislead without knowledge. Ah! evil is that which they bear!

لِيَحْمِلُوا أَوْزَارَهُمْ كَامِلَةً يَوْمَ الْقِيَامَةِ وَمِنْ أَوْزَارِ الَّذِينَ يُضِلُّونَهُمْ بِغَيْرِ عِلْمٍ أَلَا سَاءَ مَا يَزِرُونَ ۝

26 Those before them plotted, so Allah struck at the foundations of their building, and then the roof fell down upon them from above them, and the doom came on them whence they knew not;

قَدْ مَكَرَ الَّذِيْنَ مِنْ قَبْلِهِمْ فَأَتَى اللّٰهُ بُنْيَانَهُمْ مِّنَ الْقَوَاعِدِ فَخَرَّ عَلَيْهِمُ السَّقْفُ مِنْ فَوْقِهِمْ وَأَتَاهُمُ الْعَذَابُ مِنْ حَيْثُ لَا يَشْعُرُوْنَ ۝

27 Then on the Day of Resurrection; He will disgrace them and will say: Where are My partners, for whose sake ye opposed (My Guidance)? Those who have been given knowledge will say: Disgrace this day and evil are upon the disbelievers;

ثُمَّ يَوْمَ الْقِيٰمَةِ يُخْزِيْهِمْ وَيَقُوْلُ أَيْنَ شُرَكَآءِىَ الَّذِيْنَ كُنْتُمْ تُشَاقُّوْنَ فِيْهِمْ قَالَ الَّذِيْنَ أُوْتُوا الْعِلْمَ إِنَّ الْخِزْىَ الْيَوْمَ وَالسُّوْٓءَ عَلَى الْكٰفِرِيْنَ ۝

28 Whom the angels cause to die while they are wronging themselves. Then will they make full submission (saying): We used not to do any wrong. Nay! Surely Allah is Knower of what ye used to do.

الَّذِيْنَ تَتَوَفّٰهُمُ الْمَلٰٓئِكَةُ ظَالِمِىْ أَنْفُسِهِمْ فَأَلْقَوُا السَّلَمَ مَا كُنَّا نَعْمَلُ مِنْ سُوْٓءٍ بَلٰى إِنَّ اللّٰهَ عَلِيْمٌ بِمَا كُنْتُمْ تَعْمَلُوْنَ ۝

29 So enter the gates of hell, to dwell therein forever. Woeful indeed will be the lodging of the arrogant.

فَادْخُلُوْٓا أَبْوَابَ جَهَنَّمَ خٰلِدِيْنَ فِيْهَا فَلَبِئْسَ مَثْوَى الْمُتَكَبِّرِيْنَ ۝

30 And it is said unto those who ward off (evil): What hath your Lord revealed? They say: Good. For those who do good in this world there is a good (reward) and the home of the Hereafter will be better. Pleasant indeed will be the home of those who ward off (evil).

وَقِيْلَ لِلَّذِيْنَ اتَّقَوْا مَاذَا أَنْزَلَ رَبُّكُمْ قَالُوْا خَيْرًا لِّلَّذِيْنَ أَحْسَنُوْا فِيْ هٰذِهِ الدُّنْيَا حَسَنَةٌ وَلَدَارُ الْأٰخِرَةِ خَيْرٌ وَلَنِعْمَ دَارُ الْمُتَّقِيْنَ ۝

31 Gardens of Eden which they enter, underneath which rivers flow, wherein they have what they will. Thus Allah repayeth those who ward off (evil).

جَنّٰتُ عَدْنٍ يَّدْخُلُوْنَهَا تَجْرِيْ مِنْ تَحْتِهَا الْأَنْهٰرُ لَهُمْ فِيْهَا مَا يَشَآءُوْنَ كَذٰلِكَ يَجْزِى اللّٰهُ الْمُتَّقِيْنَ ۝

ٱلَّذِينَ تَتَوَفَّىٰهُمُ ٱلْمَلَـٰٓئِكَةُ طَيِّبِينَ يَقُولُونَ سَلَـٰمٌ عَلَيْكُمُ ٱدْخُلُوا۟ ٱلْجَنَّةَ بِمَا كُنتُمْ تَعْمَلُونَ ۝

32 Those whom the angels cause to die (when they are) good. They say: Peace be unto you! Enter the Garden because of what ye used to do.

هَلْ يَنظُرُونَ إِلَّآ أَن تَأْتِيَهُمُ ٱلْمَلَـٰٓئِكَةُ أَوْ يَأْتِيَ أَمْرُ رَبِّكَ كَذَٰلِكَ فَعَلَ ٱلَّذِينَ مِن قَبْلِهِمْ وَمَا ظَلَمَهُمُ ٱللَّهُ وَلَـٰكِن كَانُوٓا۟ أَنفُسَهُمْ يَظْلِمُونَ ۝

33 Await they aught save that the angels should come unto them or thy Lord's command should come to pass? Even so did those before them. Allah wronged them not, but they did wrong themselves;

فَأَصَابَهُمْ سَيِّـَٔاتُ مَا عَمِلُوا۟ وَحَاقَ بِهِم مَّا كَانُوا۟ بِهِۦ يَسْتَهْزِءُونَ ۝

34 So that the evil of what they did smote them, and that which they used to mock surrounded them.

وَقَالَ ٱلَّذِينَ أَشْرَكُوا۟ لَوْ شَآءَ ٱللَّهُ مَا عَبَدْنَا مِن دُونِهِۦ مِن شَىْءٍ نَّحْنُ وَلَآ ءَابَآؤُنَا وَلَا حَرَّمْنَا مِن دُونِهِۦ مِن شَىْءٍ كَذَٰلِكَ فَعَلَ ٱلَّذِينَ مِن قَبْلِهِمْ فَهَلْ عَلَى ٱلرُّسُلِ إِلَّا ٱلْبَلَـٰغُ ٱلْمُبِينُ ۝

35 And the idolaters say: Had Allah willed neither we had worshipped aught beside Him, nor our fathers, nor had we forbidden aught without (command from) Him. Even so did those before them. Are the messengers charged with aught save plain conveyance (of the message)?

وَلَقَدْ بَعَثْنَا فِى كُلِّ أُمَّةٍ رَّسُولًا أَنِ ٱعْبُدُوا۟ ٱللَّهَ وَٱجْتَنِبُوا۟ ٱلطَّـٰغُوتَ فَمِنْهُم مَّنْ هَدَى ٱللَّهُ وَمِنْهُم مَّنْ حَقَّتْ عَلَيْهِ ٱلضَّلَـٰلَةُ فَسِيرُوا۟ فِى ٱلْأَرْضِ فَٱنظُرُوا۟ كَيْفَ كَانَ عَـٰقِبَةُ ٱلْمُكَذِّبِينَ ۝

36 And verily We have raised in every nation a messenger, (proclaiming): Serve Allah and shun false gods. Then some of them (there were) whom Allah guided, and some of them (there were) upon whom error had just hold. Do but travel in the land and see the nature of the consequence for the deniers!

إِن تَحْرِصْ عَلَىٰ هُدَىٰهُمْ فَإِنَّ ٱللَّهَ لَا يَهْدِى مَن يُضِلُّ وَمَا لَهُم مِّن نَّـٰصِرِينَ ۝

37 Even if thou (O Muḥammad) desirest their right guidance, still Allah assuredly will not guide him who misleadeth. Such have no helpers.

38 And they swear by Allah their most binding oaths (that) Allah will not raise up him who dieth. Nay, but it is a promise (binding) upon Him in truth, but most of mankind know not;

وَأَقْسَمُواْ بِٱللَّهِ جَهْدَ أَيْمَٰنِهِمْ لَا يَبْعَثُ ٱللَّهُ مَن يَمُوتُ بَلَىٰ وَعْدًا عَلَيْهِ حَقًّا وَلَٰكِنَّ أَكْثَرَ ٱلنَّاسِ لَا يَعْلَمُونَ ۝

39 That he may explain unto them that wherein they differ, and that those who disbelieved may know that they were liars.

لِيُبَيِّنَ لَهُمُ ٱلَّذِى يَخْتَلِفُونَ فِيهِ وَلِيَعْلَمَ ٱلَّذِينَ كَفَرُوٓاْ أَنَّهُمْ كَانُواْ كَٰذِبِينَ ۝

40 And Our word unto a thing, when We intend it, is only that We say unto it: Be! and it is.

إِنَّمَا قَوْلُنَا لِشَىْءٍ إِذَآ أَرَدْنَٰهُ أَن نَّقُولَ لَهُۥ كُن فَيَكُونُ ۝

41 And those who became fugitives for the cause of Allah after they had been oppressed, We verily shall give them goodly lodging in the world, and surely the reward of the Hereafter is greater, if they but knew;

وَٱلَّذِينَ هَاجَرُواْ فِى ٱللَّهِ مِنۢ بَعْدِ مَا ظُلِمُواْ لَنُبَوِّئَنَّهُمْ فِى ٱلدُّنْيَا حَسَنَةً وَلَأَجْرُ ٱلْأَخِرَةِ أَكْبَرُ لَوْ كَانُواْ يَعْلَمُونَ ۝

42 Such as are steadfast and put their trust in Allah.

ٱلَّذِينَ صَبَرُواْ وَعَلَىٰ رَبِّهِمْ يَتَوَكَّلُونَ ۝

43 And We sent not (as Our messengers) before thee other than men whom We inspired—Ask the followers of the Remembrance if ye know not!

وَمَآ أَرْسَلْنَا مِن قَبْلِكَ إِلَّا رِجَالًا نُّوحِىٓ إِلَيْهِمْ فَسْـَٔلُوٓاْ أَهْلَ ٱلذِّكْرِ إِن كُنتُمْ لَا تَعْلَمُونَ ۝

44 With clear proofs and writings; and We have revealed unto thee the Remembrance that thou mayst explain to mankind that which hath been revealed for them, and that haply they may reflect.

بِٱلْبَيِّنَٰتِ وَٱلزُّبُرِ وَأَنزَلْنَآ إِلَيْكَ ٱلذِّكْرَ لِتُبَيِّنَ لِلنَّاسِ مَا نُزِّلَ إِلَيْهِمْ وَلَعَلَّهُمْ يَتَفَكَّرُونَ ۝

45 Are they who plan ill deeds then secure that Allah will not cause the

أَفَأَمِنَ ٱلَّذِينَ مَكَرُواْ ٱلسَّيِّـَٔاتِ أَن يَخْسِفَ

earth to swallow them, or that the doom will not come on them whence they know not?

اللَّهُ بِهِمُ الْأَرْضَ أَوْ يَأْتِيَهُمُ الْعَذَابُ مِنْ حَيْثُ لَايَشْعُرُونَ ۝

46 Or that He will not seize them in their going to and fro so that there be no escape for them?

أَوَيَأْخُذَهُمْ فِي تَقَلُّبِهِمْ فَمَاهُمْ بِمُعْجِزِينَ ۝

47 Or that He will not seize them with a gradual wasting? Lo! thy Lord is indeed Full of Pity, Merciful!

أَوْ يَأْخُذَهُمْ عَلَى تَخَوُّفٍ فَإِنَّ رَبَّكُمْ لَرَءُوفٌ رَّحِيمٌ ۝

48 Have they not observed all things that Allah hath created, how their shadows incline to the right and to the left, making prostration unto Allah, and they are lowly?

أَوَلَمْ يَرَوْا إِلَى مَاخَلَقَ اللَّهُ مِنْ شَيْءٍ يَتَفَيَّؤُا ظِلَالُهُ عَنِ الْيَمِينِ وَالشَّمَائِلِ سُجَّدًا لِلَّهِ وَهُمْ دَاخِرُونَ ۝

49 And unto Allah maketh prostration whatsoever is in the heavens and whatsoever is in the earth of living creatures, and the angels (also), and they are not proud.

وَلِلَّهِ يَسْجُدُ مَا فِي السَّمَوَاتِ وَمَا فِي الْأَرْضِ مِنْ دَابَّةٍ وَالْمَلَائِكَةُ وَهُمْ لَا يَسْتَكْبِرُونَ ۝

50 They fear their Lord above them, and do what they are bidden.

يَخَافُونَ رَبَّهُمْ مِنْ فَوْقِهِمْ وَيَفْعَلُونَ مَا يُؤْمَرُونَ ۝

51 Allah hath said: Choose not two gods. There is only One God. So of Me, Me only, be in awe.

وَقَالَ اللَّهُ لَا تَتَّخِذُوا إِلَهَيْنِ اثْنَيْنِ إِنَّمَا هُوَ إِلَهٌ وَاحِدٌ فَإِيَّايَ فَارْهَبُونِ ۝

52 Unto Him belongeth whatsoever is in the heavens and the earth, and religion is His forever. Will ye then fear any other than Allah?

وَلَهُ مَا فِي السَّمَوَاتِ وَالْأَرْضِ وَلَهُ الدِّينُ وَاصِبًا أَفَغَيْرَ اللَّهِ تَتَّقُونَ ۝

53 And whatever of comfort ye enjoy, it is from Allah. Then, when misfortune reacheth you, unto Him ye cry for help.

وَمَا بِكُمْ مِنْ نِعْمَةٍ فَمِنَ اللَّهِ ثُمَّ إِذَا مَسَّكُمُ الضُّرُّ فَإِلَيْهِ تَجْأَرُونَ ۝

54 And afterward, when He hath rid you of the misfortune, behold! a

ثُمَّ إِذَا كَشَفَ الضُّرَّ عَنْكُمْ إِذَا فَرِيقٌ مِنْكُمْ بِرَبِّهِمْ

يُشْرِكُونَ ۝

set of you attribute partners to their Lord;

لِيَكْفُرُوا بِمَا آتَيْنَاهُمْ فَتَمَتَّعُوا فَسَوْفَ تَعْلَمُونَ ۝

55 So as to deny that which We have given them. Then enjoy life (while ye may), for ye will come to know.

وَيَجْعَلُونَ لِمَا لَا يَعْلَمُونَ نَصِيبًا مِّمَّا رَزَقْنَاهُمْ تَاللَّهِ لَتُسْئَلُنَّ عَمَّا كُنتُمْ تَفْتَرُونَ ۝

56 And they assign a portion of that which We have given them unto what they know not. By Allah! but ye will indeed be asked concerning (all) that ye used to invent.

وَيَجْعَلُونَ لِلَّهِ الْبَنَاتِ سُبْحَانَهُ وَلَهُم مَّا يَشْتَهُونَ ۝

57 And they assign unto Allah daughters—Be He glorified!—and unto themselves what they desire;

وَإِذَا بُشِّرَ أَحَدُهُم بِالْأُنثَى ظَلَّ وَجْهُهُ مُسْوَدًّا وَهُوَ كَظِيمٌ ۝

58 When if one of them receiveth tidings of the birth of a female, his face remaineth darkened, and he is wroth inwardly.

يَتَوَارَى مِنَ الْقَوْمِ مِن سُوءِ مَا بُشِّرَ بِهِ أَيُمْسِكُهُ عَلَى هُونٍ أَمْ يَدُسُّهُ فِي التُّرَابِ أَلَا سَاءَ مَا يَحْكُمُونَ ۝

59 He hideth himself from the folk because of the evil of that whereof he hath had tidings, (asking himself): Shall he keep it in contempt, or bury it beneath the dust. Verily evil is their judgment.

لِلَّذِينَ لَا يُؤْمِنُونَ بِالْآخِرَةِ مَثَلُ السَّوْءِ وَلِلَّهِ الْمَثَلُ الْأَعْلَى وَهُوَ الْعَزِيزُ الْحَكِيمُ ۝

60 For those who believe not in the Hereafter is an evil similitude, and Allah's is the Sublime Similitude. He is the Mighty, the Wise.

وَلَوْ يُؤَاخِذُ اللَّهُ النَّاسَ بِظُلْمِهِم مَّا تَرَكَ عَلَيْهَا مِن دَابَّةٍ وَلَكِن يُؤَخِّرُهُمْ إِلَى أَجَلٍ مُّسَمًّى فَإِذَا جَاءَ أَجَلُهُمْ لَا يَسْتَأْخِرُونَ سَاعَةً وَلَا يَسْتَقْدِمُونَ ۝

61 If Allah were to take mankind to task for their wrongdoing, He would not leave hereon a living creature, but He reprieveth them to an appointed term, and when their term cometh they cannot put (it) off an hour nor (yet) advance (it).

62 And they assign unto Allah that which they (themselves) dislike, and their tongues expound the lie that the better portion will be theirs. Assuredly theirs will be the Fire, and they will be abandoned.

وَيَجْعَلُونَ لِلّٰهِ مَا يَكْرَهُونَ وَتَصِفُ أَلْسِنَتُهُمُ الْكَذِبَ أَنَّ لَهُمُ الْحُسْنَىٰ لَا جَرَمَ أَنَّ لَهُمُ النَّارَ وَأَنَّهُم مُّفْرَطُونَ ۝

63 By Allah, We verily sent messengers unto the nations before thee, but the devil made their deeds fair-seeming unto them. So he is their patron this day, and theirs will be a painful doom.

تَاللّٰهِ لَقَدْ أَرْسَلْنَا إِلَىٰ أُمَمٍ مِّن قَبْلِكَ فَزَيَّنَ لَهُمُ الشَّيْطَانُ أَعْمَالَهُمْ فَهُوَ وَلِيُّهُمُ الْيَوْمَ وَلَهُمْ عَذَابٌ أَلِيمٌ ۝

64 And We have revealed the Scripture unto thee only that thou mayst explain unto them that wherein they differ, and (as) a guidance and a mercy for a people who believe.

وَمَا أَنزَلْنَا عَلَيْكَ الْكِتَابَ إِلَّا لِتُبَيِّنَ لَهُمُ الَّذِي اخْتَلَفُوا فِيهِ وَهُدًى وَرَحْمَةً لِّقَوْمٍ يُؤْمِنُونَ ۝

65 Allah sendeth down water from the sky and therewith reviveth the earth after her death! Lo! herein is indeed a portent for a folk who hear.

وَاللّٰهُ أَنزَلَ مِنَ السَّمَاءِ مَاءً فَأَحْيَا بِهِ الْأَرْضَ بَعْدَ مَوْتِهَا إِنَّ فِي ذَٰلِكَ لَآيَةً لِّقَوْمٍ يَسْمَعُونَ ۝

66 And lo! in the cattle there is a lesson for you. We give you to drink of that which is in their bellies, from betwixt the refuse and the blood, pure milk palatable to the drinkers.

وَإِنَّ لَكُمْ فِي الْأَنْعَامِ لَعِبْرَةً نُّسْقِيكُم مِّمَّا فِي بُطُونِهِ مِن بَيْنِ فَرْثٍ وَدَمٍ لَّبَنًا خَالِصًا سَائِغًا لِّلشَّارِبِينَ ۝

67 And of the fruits of the date-palm, and grapes, whence ye derive strong drink and (also) good nourishment. Lo! therein, is indeed a portent for people who have sense.

وَمِن ثَمَرَاتِ النَّخِيلِ وَالْأَعْنَابِ تَتَّخِذُونَ مِنْهُ سَكَرًا وَرِزْقًا حَسَنًا إِنَّ فِي ذَٰلِكَ لَآيَةً لِّقَوْمٍ يَعْقِلُونَ ۝

68 And thy Lord inspired the bee, saying: Choose thou habitations in the hills and in the trees and in that which they thatch;

وَأَوْحَىٰ رَبُّكَ إِلَى النَّحْلِ أَنِ اتَّخِذِي مِنَ الْجِبَالِ بُيُوتًا وَمِنَ الشَّجَرِ وَمِمَّا يَعْرِشُونَ ۝

69 Then eat of all fruits, and follow
the ways of thy Lord, made smooth
(for thee). There cometh forth from
their bellies a drink diverse of hues,
wherein is healing for mankind. Lo!
herein is indeed a portent for people
who reflect.

ثُمَّ كُلِى مِنْ كُلِّ الثَّمَرٰتِ فَاسْلُكِى سُبُلَ رَبِّكِ ذُلُلاً ۗ
يَخْرُجُ مِنْ بُطُونِهَا شَرَابٌ مُّخْتَلِفٌ أَلْوَانُهُ ۖ فِيهِ
شِفَآءٌ لِّلنَّاسِ ۗ إِنَّ فِى ذٰلِكَ لَآيَةً لِّقَوْمٍ يَتَفَكَّرُونَ ۝

70 And Allah createth you, then
causeth you to die, and among you
is he who is brought back to the
most abject stage of life, so that he
knoweth nothing after (having had)
knowledge. Lo! Allah is Knower,
Powerful.

وَاللّٰهُ خَلَقَكُمْ ثُمَّ يَتَوَفَّىٰكُمْ ۚ وَمِنْكُمْ مَّنْ يُّرَدُّ إِلَىٰٓ أَرْذَلِ الْعُمُرِ
لِكَىْ لَا يَعْلَمَ بَعْدَ عِلْمٍ شَيْئًا ۚ إِنَّ اللّٰهَ عَلِيمٌ قَدِيرٌ ۝

71 And Allah hath favoured some
of you above others in provision.
Now those who are more favoured
will by no means hand over their
provision to those (slaves) whom
their right hands possess, so that
they may be equal with them in respect thereof. Is it then the grace of
Allah that they deny?

وَاللّٰهُ فَضَّلَ بَعْضَكُمْ عَلَىٰ بَعْضٍ فِى الرِّزْقِ ۚ فَمَا الَّذِينَ
فُضِّلُوا بِرَآدِّى رِزْقِهِمْ عَلَىٰ مَا مَلَكَتْ أَيْمَانُهُمْ
فَهُمْ فِيهِ سَوَآءٌ ۚ أَفَبِنِعْمَةِ اللّٰهِ يَجْحَدُونَ ۝

72 And Allah hath given you wives
of your own kind, and hath given
you, from your wives, sons and
grandsons, and hath made provision
of good things for you. Is it then in
vanity that they believe and in the
grace of Allah that they disbelieve?

وَاللّٰهُ جَعَلَ لَكُمْ مِّنْ أَنْفُسِكُمْ أَزْوَاجًا وَّجَعَلَ لَكُمْ
مِّنْ أَزْوَاجِكُمْ بَنِينَ وَحَفَدَةً وَّرَزَقَكُمْ
مِّنَ الطَّيِّبَاتِ ۚ أَفَبِالْبَاطِلِ يُؤْمِنُونَ وَبِنِعْمَتِ اللّٰهِ
هُمْ يَكْفُرُونَ ۝

73 And they worship beside Allah
that which owneth no provision
whatsoever for them from the heavens or the earth, nor have they
(whom they worship) any power.

وَيَعْبُدُونَ مِنْ دُونِ اللّٰهِ مَا لَا يَمْلِكُ لَهُمْ رِزْقًا
مِّنَ السَّمٰوٰتِ وَالْأَرْضِ شَيْئًا وَّلَا يَسْتَطِيعُونَ ۝

74 So coin not similitudes for Allah. Lo! Allah knoweth; ye know not.

75 Allah coineth a similitude: (on the one hand) a (mere) chattel slave, who hath control of nothing, and (on the other hand) one on whom We have bestowed a fair provision from Us, and he spendeth thereof secretly and openly. Are they equal? Praise be to Allah! But most of them know not.

76 And Allah coineth a similitude Two men, one of them dumb, having control of nothing, and he is a burden on his owner; whithersoever he directeth him to go, he bringeth no good. Is he equal with one who enjoineth justice and followeth a straight path (of conduct)?

77 And unto Allah belongeth the Unseen of the heavens and the earth, and the matter of the Hour (of Doom) is but as a twinkling of the eye, or it is nearer still. Lo! Allah is Able to do all things.

78 And Allah brought you forth from the wombs of your mothers knowing nothing, and gave you hearing and sight and hearts that haply ye might give thanks.

79 Have they not seen the birds obedient[2] in mid-air? None holdeth

فَلَا تَضْرِبُوا لِلَّهِ الْأَمْثَالَ إِنَّ اللَّهَ يَعْلَمُ وَأَنْتُمْ لَا تَعْلَمُونَ ۞

۞ ضَرَبَ اللَّهُ مَثَلًا عَبْدًا مَمْلُوكًا لَا يَقْدِرُ عَلَىٰ شَيْءٍ وَمَنْ رَزَقْنَاهُ مِنَّا رِزْقًا حَسَنًا فَهُوَ يُنْفِقُ مِنْهُ سِرًّا وَجَهْرًا هَلْ يَسْتَوُونَ الْحَمْدُ لِلَّهِ بَلْ أَكْثَرُهُمْ لَا يَعْلَمُونَ ۞

وَضَرَبَ اللَّهُ مَثَلًا رَجُلَيْنِ أَحَدُهُمَا أَبْكَمُ لَا يَقْدِرُ عَلَىٰ شَيْءٍ وَهُوَ كَلٌّ عَلَىٰ مَوْلَاهُ أَيْنَمَا يُوَجِّهْهُ لَا يَأْتِ بِخَيْرٍ هَلْ يَسْتَوِي هُوَ وَمَنْ يَأْمُرُ بِالْعَدْلِ وَهُوَ عَلَىٰ صِرَاطٍ مُسْتَقِيمٍ ۞

وَلِلَّهِ غَيْبُ السَّمَاوَاتِ وَالْأَرْضِ وَمَا أَمْرُ السَّاعَةِ إِلَّا كَلَمْحِ الْبَصَرِ أَوْ هُوَ أَقْرَبُ إِنَّ اللَّهَ عَلَىٰ كُلِّ شَيْءٍ قَدِيرٌ ۞

وَاللَّهُ أَخْرَجَكُمْ مِنْ بُطُونِ أُمَّهَاتِكُمْ لَا تَعْلَمُونَ شَيْئًا وَجَعَلَ لَكُمُ السَّمْعَ وَالْأَبْصَارَ وَالْأَفْئِدَةَ لَعَلَّكُمْ تَشْكُرُونَ ۞

أَلَمْ يَرَوْا إِلَى الطَّيْرِ مُسَخَّرَاتٍ فِي جَوِّ

---

2. Lit. made subservient - i.e. to the Law of Allah.

ٱلسَّمَآءِ مَا يُمْسِكُهُنَّ إِلَّا ٱللَّهُ إِنَّ فِى ذَٰلِكَ لَأَيَـٰتٍ لِّقَوْمٍ يُؤْمِنُونَ ﴿٧٩﴾

them save Allah. Lo! herein, verily, are portents for a people who believe.

80 And Allah hath given you in your houses an abode, and hath given you (also), of the hides of cattle, houses[3] which ye find light (to carry) on the day of migration and on the day of pitching camp; and of their wool and their fur and their hair, caparison and comfort for a while.

وَٱللَّهُ جَعَلَ لَكُم مِّنۢ بُيُوتِكُمْ سَكَنًا وَجَعَلَ لَكُم مِّن جُلُودِ ٱلْأَنْعَـٰمِ بُيُوتًا تَسْتَخِفُّونَهَا يَوْمَ ظَعْنِكُمْ وَيَوْمَ إِقَامَتِكُمْ وَمِنْ أَصْوَافِهَا وَأَوْبَارِهَا وَأَشْعَارِهَا أَثَـٰثًا وَمَتَـٰعًا إِلَىٰ حِينٍ ﴿٨٠﴾

81 And Allah hath given you, of that which He hath created, shelter from the sun; and hath given you places of refuge in the mountains, and hath given you coats to ward off the heat from you, and coats (of armour) to save you from your own foolhardiness. Thus doth He perfect His favour unto you, in order that ye may surrender (unto Him).

وَٱللَّهُ جَعَلَ لَكُم مِّمَّا خَلَقَ ظِلَـٰلًا وَجَعَلَ لَكُم مِّنَ ٱلْجِبَالِ أَكْنَـٰنًا وَجَعَلَ لَكُمْ سَرَٰبِيلَ تَقِيكُمُ ٱلْحَرَّ وَسَرَٰبِيلَ تَقِيكُم بَأْسَكُمْ كَذَٰلِكَ يُتِمُّ نِعْمَتَهُ عَلَيْكُمْ لَعَلَّكُمْ تُسْلِمُونَ ﴿٨١﴾

82 Then, if they turn away, thy duty (O Muhammad) is but plain conveyance (of the message).

فَإِن تَوَلَّوْا فَإِنَّمَا عَلَيْكَ ٱلْبَلَـٰغُ ٱلْمُبِينُ ﴿٨٢﴾

83 They know the favour of Allah and then deny it. Most of them are ingrates.

يَعْرِفُونَ نِعْمَتَ ٱللَّهِ ثُمَّ يُنكِرُونَهَا وَأَكْثَرُهُمُ ٱلْكَـٰفِرُونَ ﴿٨٣﴾

84 And (bethink you of) the day when We raise up of every nation a witness, then there is no leave for disbelievers, nor are they allowed to make amends.

وَيَوْمَ نَبْعَثُ مِن كُلِّ أُمَّةٍ شَهِيدًا ثُمَّ لَا يُؤْذَنُ لِلَّذِينَ كَفَرُوا وَلَا هُمْ يُسْتَعْتَبُونَ ﴿٨٤﴾

---

3. *i.e.* tents.

85 And when those who did wrong behold the doom, it will not be made light for them, nor will they be reprieved.

86 And when those who ascribed partners to Allah behold those partners of theirs, they will say: Our Lord! these are our partners unto whom we used to cry instead of Thee. But they will fling to them the saying: Lo! ye verily are liars!

87 And they proffer unto Allah submission on that day, and all that they used to invent hath failed them.

88 For those who disbelieve and debar (men) from the way of Allah, We add doom to doom because they wrought corruption.

89 And (bethink you of) the day when We raise in every nation a witness against them of their own folk, and We bring thee (Muhammad) as a witness against these. And We reveal the Scripture unto thee as an exposition of all things, and a guidance and a mercy and good tidings for those who have surrendered (to Allah).

90 Lo! Allah enjoineth justice and kindness, and giving to kinsfolk, and forbiddeth lewdness and abomination and wickedness. He exhorteth

وَإِذَا رَأَى الَّذِينَ ظَلَمُوا الْعَذَابَ فَلَا يُخَفَّفُ عَنْهُمْ وَلَا هُمْ يُنْظَرُونَ ﴿٨٥﴾

وَإِذَا رَأَى الَّذِينَ أَشْرَكُوا شُرَكَاءَهُمْ قَالُوا رَبَّنَا هَٰؤُلَاءِ شُرَكَاؤُنَا الَّذِينَ كُنَّا نَدْعُوا مِن دُونِكَ فَأَلْقَوْا إِلَيْهِمُ الْقَوْلَ إِنَّكُمْ لَكَاذِبُونَ ﴿٨٦﴾

وَأَلْقَوْا إِلَى اللَّهِ يَوْمَئِذٍ السَّلَمَ وَضَلَّ عَنْهُم مَّا كَانُوا يَفْتَرُونَ ﴿٨٧﴾

الَّذِينَ كَفَرُوا وَصَدُّوا عَن سَبِيلِ اللَّهِ زِدْنَاهُمْ عَذَابًا فَوْقَ الْعَذَابِ بِمَا كَانُوا يُفْسِدُونَ ﴿٨٨﴾

وَيَوْمَ نَبْعَثُ فِي كُلِّ أُمَّةٍ شَهِيدًا عَلَيْهِم مِّنْ أَنفُسِهِمْ وَجِئْنَا بِكَ شَهِيدًا عَلَىٰ هَٰؤُلَاءِ وَنَزَّلْنَا عَلَيْكَ الْكِتَابَ تِبْيَانًا لِّكُلِّ شَيْءٍ وَهُدًى وَرَحْمَةً وَبُشْرَىٰ لِلْمُسْلِمِينَ ﴿٨٩﴾

۞ إِنَّ اللَّهَ يَأْمُرُ بِالْعَدْلِ وَالْإِحْسَانِ وَإِيتَاءِ ذِي الْقُرْبَىٰ وَيَنْهَىٰ عَنِ الْفَحْشَاءِ وَالْمُنكَرِ

you in order that ye may take heed.[4]

91 Fulfill the covenant of Allah when ye have covenanted, and break not your oaths after the asseveration of them, and after ye have made Allah surety over you. Lo! Allah knoweth what ye do.

92 And be not like unto her who unravelleth the thread, after she hath made it strong, to thin filaments, making your oaths a deceit between you because of a nation being more numerous than (another) nation. Allah only trieth you thereby, and He verily will explain to you on the Day of Resurrection that wherein ye differed.

93 Had Allah willed He could have made you (all) one nation, but He sendeth whom He will astray and guideth whom He will, and ye will indeed be asked of what ye used to do.

94 Make not your oaths a deceit between you, lest a foot should slip after being firmly planted and ye should taste evil forasmuch as ye debarred (men) from the way of Allah, and yours should be an awful doom.

95 And purchase not a small gain at the price of Allah's covenant.

وَٱلۡبَغۡیُ یَعِظُكُمۡ لَعَلَّكُمۡ تَذَكَّرُونَ ۝

وَأَوۡفُواْ بِعَهۡدِ ٱللَّهِ إِذَا عَٰهَدتُّمۡ وَلَا تَنقُضُواْ ٱلۡأَیۡمَٰنَ بَعۡدَ تَوۡكِیدِهَا وَقَدۡ جَعَلۡتُمُ ٱللَّهَ عَلَیۡكُمۡ كَفِیلًا إِنَّ ٱللَّهَ یَعۡلَمُ مَا تَفۡعَلُونَ ۝

وَلَا تَكُونُواْ كَٱلَّتِی نَقَضَتۡ غَزۡلَهَا مِنۢ بَعۡدِ قُوَّةٍ أَنكَٰثًا تَتَّخِذُونَ أَیۡمَٰنَكُمۡ دَخَلًۢا بَیۡنَكُمۡ أَن تَكُونَ أُمَّةٌ هِیَ أَرۡبَىٰ مِنۡ أُمَّةٍ إِنَّمَا یَبۡلُوكُمُ ٱللَّهُ بِهِۦ وَلَیُبَیِّنَنَّ لَكُمۡ یَوۡمَ ٱلۡقِیَٰمَةِ مَا كُنتُمۡ فِیهِ تَخۡتَلِفُونَ ۝

وَلَوۡ شَآءَ ٱللَّهُ لَجَعَلَكُمۡ أُمَّةً وَٰحِدَةً وَلَٰكِن یُضِلُّ مَن یَشَآءُ وَیَهۡدِی مَن یَشَآءُ وَلَتُسۡـَٔلُنَّ عَمَّا كُنتُمۡ تَعۡمَلُونَ ۝

وَلَا تَتَّخِذُوٓاْ أَیۡمَٰنَكُمۡ دَخَلًۢا بَیۡنَكُمۡ فَتَزِلَّ قَدَمٌۢ بَعۡدَ ثُبُوتِهَا وَتَذُوقُواْ ٱلسُّوٓءَ بِمَا صَدَدتُّمۡ عَن سَبِیلِ ٱللَّهِ وَلَكُمۡ عَذَابٌ عَظِیمٌ ۝

وَلَا تَشۡتَرُواْ بِعَهۡدِ ٱللَّهِ ثَمَنًا قَلِیلًا إِنَّمَا عِندَ ٱللَّهِ

---

4. Since the time of 'Umar II the Umayyad, this verse has been recited at the end of every weekly sermon in all Sunni congregations.

Lo! that which Allah hath is better for you, if ye did but know.

هُوَخَيْرٌلَّكُمْ إِن كُنتُمْ تَعْلَمُونَ ۝

96 That which ye have wasteth away, and that which Allah hath remaineth. And verily We shall pay those who are steadfast a recompense in proportion to the best of what they used to do.

مَاعِندَكُمْ يَنفَدُ وَمَاعِندَاللَّهِ بَاقٍ وَلَنَجْزِيَنَّ الَّذِينَ صَبَرُوٓاْ أَجْرَهُم بِأَحْسَنِ مَاكَانُواْ يَعْمَلُونَ ۝

97 Whosoever doeth right, whether male or female, and is a believer, him verily We shall quicken with good life, and We shall pay them a recompense in proportion to the best of what they used to do.

مَنْ عَمِلَ صَٰلِحًا مِّن ذَكَرٍ أَوْ أُنثَىٰ وَهُوَ مُؤْمِنٌ فَلَنُحْيِيَنَّهُۥ حَيَوٰةً طَيِّبَةً وَلَنَجْزِيَنَّهُمْ أَجْرَهُم بِأَحْسَنِ مَاكَانُواْ يَعْمَلُونَ ۝

98 And when thou recitest the Qur'an, seek refuge in Allah from Satan the outcast.

فَإِذَا قَرَأْتَ الْقُرْءَانَ فَاسْتَعِذْ بِاللَّهِ مِنَ الشَّيْطَٰنِ الرَّجِيمِ ۝

99 Lo! he hath no power over those who believe and put trust in their Lord.

إِنَّهُۥ لَيْسَ لَهُۥ سُلْطَٰنٌ عَلَى الَّذِينَ ءَامَنُواْ وَعَلَىٰ رَبِّهِمْ يَتَوَكَّلُونَ ۝

100 His power is only over those who make a friend of him, and those who ascribe partners unto Him (Allah).

إِنَّمَا سُلْطَٰنُهُۥ عَلَى الَّذِينَ يَتَوَلَّوْنَهُۥ وَالَّذِينَ هُم بِهِۦ مُشْرِكُونَ ۝

101 And when We put a revelation in place of (another) revelation, and Allah knoweth best what He revealeth—they say: Lo! thou art but inventing. Most of them know not.

وَإِذَا بَدَّلْنَآ ءَايَةً مَّكَانَ ءَايَةٍ وَاللَّهُ أَعْلَمُ بِمَا يُنَزِّلُ قَالُوٓاْ إِنَّمَآ أَنتَ مُفْتَرٍ بَلْ أَكْثَرُهُمْ لَا يَعْلَمُونَ ۝

102 Say: The holy Spirit[5] hath revealed it from thy Lord with

قُلْ نَزَّلَهُۥ رُوحُ الْقُدُسِ مِن رَّبِّكَ بِالْحَقِّ

---

5. *i.e.* Gabriel.

truth, that it may confirm (the faith of) those who believe, and as guidance and good tidings for those who have surrendered[6] (to Allah).

لِيُثَبِّتَ ٱلَّذِينَ ءَامَنُوا۟ وَهُدًى وَبُشْرَىٰ لِلْمُسْلِمِينَ ﴿١٠٢﴾

103   And We know well that they say: Only a man teacheth him. The speech of him at whom they falsely hint is outlandish, and this is clear Arabic speech.[7]

وَلَقَدْ نَعْلَمُ أَنَّهُمْ يَقُولُونَ إِنَّمَا يُعَلِّمُهُ بَشَرٌ لِّسَانُ ٱلَّذِى يُلْحِدُونَ إِلَيْهِ أَعْجَمِىٌّ وَهَـٰذَا لِسَانٌ عَرَبِىٌّ مُّبِينٌ ﴿١٠٣﴾

104   Lo! those who disbelieve the revelations of Allah, Allah guideth them not and theirs will be a painful doom.

إِنَّ ٱلَّذِينَ لَا يُؤْمِنُونَ بِـَٔايَـٰتِ ٱللَّهِ لَا يَهْدِيهِمُ ٱللَّهُ وَلَهُمْ عَذَابٌ أَلِيمٌ ﴿١٠٤﴾

105   Only they invent falsehood who believe not Allah's revelations, and (only) they are the liars.

إِنَّمَا يَفْتَرِى ٱلْكَذِبَ ٱلَّذِينَ لَا يُؤْمِنُونَ بِـَٔايَـٰتِ ٱللَّهِ وَأُو۟لَـٰٓئِكَ هُمُ ٱلْكَـٰذِبُونَ ﴿١٠٥﴾

106   Whoso disbelieveth in Allah after his belief—save him who is forced thereto and whose heart is still content with Faith—but whoso findeth ease in disbelief: On them is wrath from Allah. Theirs will be an awful doom.

مَن كَفَرَ بِٱللَّهِ مِنۢ بَعْدِ إِيمَـٰنِهِۦٓ إِلَّا مَنْ أُكْرِهَ وَقَلْبُهُۥ مُطْمَئِنٌّۢ بِٱلْإِيمَـٰنِ وَلَـٰكِن مَّن شَرَحَ بِٱلْكُفْرِ صَدْرًا فَعَلَيْهِمْ غَضَبٌ مِّنَ ٱللَّهِ وَلَهُمْ عَذَابٌ عَظِيمٌ ﴿١٠٦﴾

107   That is because they have chosen the life of the world rather than the Hereafter, and because Allah guideth not the disbelieving folk.

ذَٰلِكَ بِأَنَّهُمُ ٱسْتَحَبُّوا۟ ٱلْحَيَوٰةَ ٱلدُّنْيَا عَلَى ٱلْءَاخِرَةِ وَأَنَّ ٱللَّهَ لَا يَهْدِى ٱلْقَوْمَ ٱلْكَـٰفِرِينَ ﴿١٠٧﴾

108   Such are they whose hearts and ears and eyes Allah hath sealed.

أُو۟لَـٰٓئِكَ ٱلَّذِينَ طَبَعَ ٱللَّهُ عَلَىٰ قُلُوبِهِمْ وَسَمْعِهِمْ وَأَبْصَـٰرِهِمْ وَأُو۟لَـٰٓئِكَ هُمُ

---

6. Ar. *Muslimīn*.

7. Among the various attempts of the idolaters to deride the Qur'an was the charge that a Christian slave among the earliest converts taught it to the Prophet. The same slave suffered cruel persecution for his belief in the divine inspiration of the Qur'an.

And such are the heedless.

109   Assuredly in the Hereafter they are the losers.

110   Then lo! thy Lord—for those who become fugitives after they had been persecuted, and then fought and were steadfast—lo! thy Lord afterward is (for them) indeed Forgiving, Merciful;

111   On the Day when every soul will come pleading for itself, and every soul will be repaid what it did, and they will not be wronged.

112   Allah coineth a similitude: a township that dwelt secure and well content, its provision coming to it in abundance from every side, but it disbelieved in Allah's favours, so Allah made it experience the garb of dearth and fear because of what they used to do.

113   And verily there had come unto them a messenger from among them, but they had denied him, and so the torment seized them while they were wrong-doers.

114   So eat of the lawful and good food which Allah hath provided for you, and thank the bounty of your Lord if it is Him ye serve.

115   He hath forbidden for you only carrion and blood and swine-flesh and that which hath been immolated in the name of any other than Allah; but he who is driven

الْغَافِلُونَ ۝

لَا جَرَمَ أَنَّهُمْ فِي الْآخِرَةِ هُمُ الْخَاسِرُونَ ۝

ثُمَّ إِنَّ رَبَّكَ لِلَّذِينَ هَاجَرُوا مِنْ بَعْدِ مَا فُتِنُوا ثُمَّ جَاهَدُوا وَصَبَرُوا إِنَّ رَبَّكَ مِنْ بَعْدِهَا لَغَفُورٌ رَحِيمٌ ۝

۞ يَوْمَ تَأْتِي كُلُّ نَفْسٍ تُجَادِلُ عَن نَّفْسِهَا وَتُوَفَّى كُلُّ نَفْسٍ مَّا عَمِلَتْ وَهُمْ لَا يُظْلَمُونَ ۝

وَضَرَبَ اللَّهُ مَثَلًا قَرْيَةً كَانَتْ آمِنَةً مُّطْمَئِنَّةً يَأْتِيهَا رِزْقُهَا رَغَدًا مِّن كُلِّ مَكَانٍ فَكَفَرَتْ بِأَنْعُمِ اللَّهِ فَأَذَاقَهَا اللَّهُ لِبَاسَ الْجُوعِ وَالْخَوْفِ بِمَا كَانُوا يَصْنَعُونَ ۝

وَلَقَدْ جَاءَهُمْ رَسُولٌ مِّنْهُمْ فَكَذَّبُوهُ فَأَخَذَهُمُ الْعَذَابُ وَهُمْ ظَالِمُونَ ۝

فَكُلُوا مِمَّا رَزَقَكُمُ اللَّهُ حَلَالًا طَيِّبًا وَاشْكُرُوا نِعْمَتَ اللَّهِ إِن كُنتُمْ إِيَّاهُ تَعْبُدُونَ ۝

إِنَّمَا حَرَّمَ عَلَيْكُمُ الْمَيْتَةَ وَالدَّمَ وَلَحْمَ الْخِنزِيرِ وَمَا أُهِلَّ لِغَيْرِ اللَّهِ بِهِ فَمَنِ اضْطُرَّ

thereto, neither craving nor transgressing, lo! then Allah is Forgiving, Merciful.

116 And speak not, concerning that which your own tongues qualify (as clean or unclean), the falsehood: "This is lawful, and this is forbidden," so that ye invent a lie against Allah. Lo! those who invent a lie against Allah will not succeed.

117 A brief enjoyment (will be theirs); and theirs a painful doom.

118 And unto those who are Jews We have forbidden that which We have already related unto thee. And We wronged them not, but they were wont to wrong themselves.

119 Then lo! thy Lord—for those who do evil in ignorance and afterward repent and amend—lo! (for them) thy Lord is afterward indeed Forgiving, Merciful.

120 Lo! Abraham was a nation obedient to Allah, by nature upright, and he was not of the idolaters;

121 Thankful for His bounties; He chose him and He guided him unto a straight path.

122 And We gave him good in the world, and in the Hereafter he is among the righteous.

123 And afterward We inspired thee (Muḥammad, saying): Follow the religion of Abraham, as one by nature upright. He was not of the idolaters.

غَيْرَ بَاغٍ وَلَا عَادٍ فَإِنَّ اللَّهَ غَفُورٌ رَّحِيمٌ ﴿١١٥﴾

وَلَا تَقُولُوا لِمَا تَصِفُ أَلْسِنَتُكُمُ الْكَذِبَ هَٰذَا حَلَالٌ وَهَٰذَا حَرَامٌ لِّتَفْتَرُوا عَلَى اللَّهِ الْكَذِبَ إِنَّ الَّذِينَ يَفْتَرُونَ عَلَى اللَّهِ الْكَذِبَ لَا يُفْلِحُونَ ﴿١١٦﴾

مَتَاعٌ قَلِيلٌ وَلَهُمْ عَذَابٌ أَلِيمٌ ﴿١١٧﴾

وَعَلَى الَّذِينَ هَادُوا حَرَّمْنَا مَا قَصَصْنَا عَلَيْكَ مِن قَبْلُ وَمَا ظَلَمْنَاهُمْ وَلَٰكِن كَانُوا أَنفُسَهُمْ يَظْلِمُونَ ﴿١١٨﴾

ثُمَّ إِنَّ رَبَّكَ لِلَّذِينَ عَمِلُوا السُّوءَ بِجَهَالَةٍ ثُمَّ تَابُوا مِن بَعْدِ ذَٰلِكَ وَأَصْلَحُوا إِنَّ رَبَّكَ مِن بَعْدِهَا لَغَفُورٌ رَّحِيمٌ ﴿١١٩﴾

إِنَّ إِبْرَاهِيمَ كَانَ أُمَّةً قَانِتًا لِّلَّهِ حَنِيفًا وَلَمْ يَكُ مِنَ الْمُشْرِكِينَ ﴿١٢٠﴾

شَاكِرًا لِّأَنْعُمِهِ اجْتَبَاهُ وَهَدَاهُ إِلَىٰ صِرَاطٍ مُّسْتَقِيمٍ ﴿١٢١﴾

وَآتَيْنَاهُ فِي الدُّنْيَا حَسَنَةً وَإِنَّهُ فِي الْآخِرَةِ لَمِنَ الصَّالِحِينَ ﴿١٢٢﴾

ثُمَّ أَوْحَيْنَا إِلَيْكَ أَنِ اتَّبِعْ مِلَّةَ إِبْرَاهِيمَ حَنِيفًا وَمَا كَانَ مِنَ الْمُشْرِكِينَ ﴿١٢٣﴾

124   The Sabbath was appointed
only for those who differed concerning it, and lo! thy Lord will judge
between them on the Day of Resurrection concerning that wherein they
used to differ.

إِنَّمَا جُعِلَ السَّبْتُ عَلَى الَّذِينَ اخْتَلَفُوا فِيهِ
وَإِنَّ رَبَّكَ لَيَحْكُمُ بَيْنَهُمْ يَوْمَ الْقِيَٰمَةِ فِيمَا
كَانُوا فِيهِ يَخْتَلِفُونَ ۝

125   Call unto the way of thy
Lord with wisdom and fair exhortation, and reason with them in the
better way. Lo! thy Lord is best
aware of him who strayeth from His
way, and He is Best Aware of those
who go aright.

ادْعُ إِلَىٰ سَبِيلِ رَبِّكَ بِالْحِكْمَةِ وَالْمَوْعِظَةِ
الْحَسَنَةِ وَجَٰدِلْهُم بِالَّتِي هِيَ أَحْسَنُ إِنَّ رَبَّكَ
هُوَ أَعْلَمُ بِمَن ضَلَّ عَن سَبِيلِهِ وَهُوَ أَعْلَمُ
بِالْمُهْتَدِينَ ۝

126   If ye punish, then punish
with the like of that wherewith ye
were afflicted. But if ye endure patiently, verily it is better for the patient.

وَإِنْ عَاقَبْتُمْ فَعَاقِبُوا بِمِثْلِ مَا عُوقِبْتُم بِهِ
وَلَئِن صَبَرْتُمْ لَهُوَ خَيْرٌ لِّلصَّٰبِرِينَ ۝

127   Endure thou patiently (O
Muhammad). Thine endurance is
only by (the help of) Allah. Grieve
not for them, and be not in distress
because of that which they devise.

وَاصْبِرْ وَمَا صَبْرُكَ إِلَّا بِاللَّهِ وَلَا تَحْزَنْ عَلَيْهِمْ
وَلَا تَكُ فِي ضَيْقٍ مِّمَّا يَمْكُرُونَ ۝

128   Lo! Allah is with those who
keep their duty unto Him and those
who are doers of good.

إِنَّ اللَّهَ مَعَ الَّذِينَ اتَّقَوا وَّالَّذِينَ هُم
مُّحْسِنُونَ ۝

Banī Isrā'īl or Al Isrā'
(The Children of Israel or The Night Journey)

Banī Isrā'īl, "The Children of Israel," begins and ends with references to the Israelites. V. 1 relates to the Prophet's vision, in which he was carried by night upon a heavenly steed to the Temple of Jerusalem, whence he was caught up through the seven heavens to the very presence of God. The sūrah may be taken as belonging to the middle group of Makkan sūrahs, except v. 81, or, according to other commentators vv. 76-82, revealed at Al-Madīnah.

In the name of Allah, the Beneficent, the Merciful.

1 Glorified be He Who carried His servant by night from the Inviolable Place of Worship[1] to the Far Distant Place of Worship[2] the neighbourhood whereof We have blessed, that We might show him of Our tokens! Lo! He, only He, is the Hearer, the Seer.

سُبْحَٰنَ ٱلَّذِىٓ أَسْرَىٰ بِعَبْدِهِۦ لَيْلًا مِّنَ ٱلْمَسْجِدِ ٱلْحَرَامِ إِلَى ٱلْمَسْجِدِ ٱلْأَقْصَا ٱلَّذِى بَٰرَكْنَا حَوْلَهُۥ لِنُرِيَهُۥ مِنْ ءَايَٰتِنَآ إِنَّهُۥ هُوَ ٱلسَّمِيعُ ٱلْبَصِيرُ ١

2 We gave unto Moses the Scripture, and We appointed it a guidance for the Children of Israel, saying: Choose no guardian beside Me.

وَءَاتَيْنَا مُوسَى ٱلْكِتَٰبَ وَجَعَلْنَٰهُ هُدًى لِّبَنِىٓ إِسْرَٰٓءِيلَ أَلَّا تَتَّخِذُوا۟ مِن دُونِى وَكِيلًا ٢

---

1. Makkah.

2. Jerusalem.

3 (They were) the seed of those whom We carried (in the ship) along with Noah. Lo! he was a grateful slave.

ذُرِّيَّةَ مَنْ حَمَلْنَا مَعَ نُوحٍ إِنَّهُ كَانَ عَبْدًا شَكُورًا ٣

4 And We decreed for the Children of Israel in the scripture: Ye verily will work corruption in the earth twice, and ye will become great tyrants.

وَقَضَيْنَا إِلَىٰ بَنِى إِسْرَٰٓءِيلَ فِى ٱلْكِتَٰبِ لَتُفْسِدُنَّ فِى ٱلْأَرْضِ مَرَّتَيْنِ وَلَتَعْلُنَّ عُلُوًّا كَبِيرًا ٤

5 So when the time for the first of the two came, We roused against you slaves of Ours of great might who ravaged (your) country, and it was a threat performed.

فَإِذَا جَآءَ وَعْدُ أُولَىٰهُمَا بَعَثْنَا عَلَيْكُمْ عِبَادًا لَّنَآ أُو۟لِى بَأْسٍ شَدِيدٍ فَجَاسُوا۟ خِلَٰلَ ٱلدِّيَارِ وَكَانَ وَعْدًا مَّفْعُولًا ٥

6 Then we gave you once again your turn against them, and We aided you with wealth and children and made you more in soldiery;

ثُمَّ رَدَدْنَا لَكُمُ ٱلْكَرَّةَ عَلَيْهِمْ وَأَمْدَدْنَٰكُم بِأَمْوَٰلٍ وَبَنِينَ وَجَعَلْنَٰكُمْ أَكْثَرَ نَفِيرًا ٦

7 (Saying): If ye do good, ye do good for your own souls, and if ye do evil, it is for them (in like manner). So, when the time for the second (of the judgments) came (We roused against you others of Our slaves) to ravage you, and to enter the Temple even as they entered it the first time, and to lay waste all that they conquered with an utter wasting.

إِنْ أَحْسَنتُمْ أَحْسَنتُمْ لِأَنفُسِكُمْ وَإِنْ أَسَأْتُمْ فَلَهَا فَإِذَا جَآءَ وَعْدُ ٱلْءَاخِرَةِ لِيَسُوٓءُوا۟ وُجُوهَكُمْ وَلِيَدْخُلُوا۟ ٱلْمَسْجِدَ كَمَا دَخَلُوهُ أَوَّلَ مَرَّةٍ وَلِيُتَبِّرُوا۟ مَا عَلَوْا۟ تَتْبِيرًا ٧

8 It may be that your Lord will have mercy on you, but if ye repeat (the crime) We shall repeat (the punishment), and We have appointed hell a dungeon for the disbelievers.

عَسَىٰ رَبُّكُمْ أَن يَرْحَمَكُمْ وَإِنْ عُدتُّمْ عُدْنَا وَجَعَلْنَا جَهَنَّمَ لِلْكَٰفِرِينَ حَصِيرًا ٨

9 Lo! this Qur'an guideth unto that which is straightest, and giveth

إِنَّ هَٰذَا ٱلْقُرْءَانَ يَهْدِى لِلَّتِى هِىَ أَقْوَمُ وَيُبَشِّرُ

tidings unto the believers who do good works that theirs will be a great reward.

اَلْمُؤْمِنِيْنَ الَّذِيْنَ يَعْمَلُوْنَ الصّٰلِحٰتِ اَنَّ لَهُمْ اَجْرًا كَبِيْرًا ۞

10 And that those who believe not in the Hereafter, for them We have prepared a painful doom.

وَاَنَّ الَّذِيْنَ لَا يُؤْمِنُوْنَ بِالْاٰخِرَةِ اَعْتَدْنَا لَهُمْ عَذَابًا اَلِيْمًا ۞

11 Man prayeth for evil as he prayeth for good; for man was ever hasty.

وَيَدْعُ الْاِنْسَانُ بِالشَّرِّ دُعَاءَهُ بِالْخَيْرِ وَكَانَ الْاِنْسَانُ عَجُوْلًا ۞

12 And we appoint the night and the day two portents. Then We efface the portent of the night, and We make the portent of the day sight-giving, that ye may seek bounty from your Lord, and that ye may know the computation of the years, and the reckoning; and everything have We expounded with a clear expounding.

وَجَعَلْنَا الَّيْلَ وَالنَّهَارَ اٰيَتَيْنِ فَمَحَوْنَا اٰيَةَ الَّيْلِ وَجَعَلْنَا اٰيَةَ النَّهَارِ مُبْصِرَةً لِّتَبْتَغُوْا فَضْلًا مِّنْ رَّبِّكُمْ وَلِتَعْلَمُوْا عَدَدَ السِّنِيْنَ وَالْحِسَابَ وَكُلَّ شَيْءٍ فَصَّلْنٰهُ تَفْصِيْلًا ۞

13 And every man's augury have We fastened to his own neck, and We shall bring forth for him on the Day of Resurrection a book which he will find wide open.

وَكُلَّ اِنْسَانٍ اَلْزَمْنٰهُ طٰٓئِرَهُ فِيْ عُنُقِهِ وَنُخْرِجُ لَهُ يَوْمَ الْقِيٰمَةِ كِتٰبًا يَّلْقٰهُ مَنْشُوْرًا ۞

14 (And it will be said unto him): Read thy book. Thy soul sufficeth as reckoner against thee this day.

اِقْرَأْ كِتٰبَكَ كَفٰى بِنَفْسِكَ الْيَوْمَ عَلَيْكَ حَسِيْبًا ۞

15 Whosoever goeth right, it is only for (the good of) his own soul that he goeth right, and whosoever erreth, erreth only to its hurt. No laden soul can bear another's load. We never punish until We have sent a messenger.

مَنِ اهْتَدٰى فَاِنَّمَا يَهْتَدِيْ لِنَفْسِهِ وَمَنْ ضَلَّ فَاِنَّمَا يَضِلُّ عَلَيْهَا وَلَا تَزِرُ وَازِرَةٌ وِّزْرَ اُخْرٰى وَمَا كُنَّا مُعَذِّبِيْنَ حَتّٰى نَبْعَثَ رَسُوْلًا ۞

16 And when We decide to destroy
a township, We send commandment
to its folk who live at ease, and
afterward they commit abomination
therein, and so the Word (of doom)
hath effect for it, and We annihilate
it with complete annihilation.

وَإِذَآ أَرَدْنَآ أَن نُّهْلِكَ قَرْيَةً أَمَرْنَا مُتْرَفِيهَا فَفَسَقُوا فِيهَا
فَحَقَّ عَلَيْهَا الْقَوْلُ فَدَمَّرْنَاهَا تَدْمِيرًا ﴿١٦﴾

17 How many generations have we
destroyed since Noah! And Allah
sufficeth as knower and Beholder of
the sins of His slaves.

وَكَمْ أَهْلَكْنَا مِنَ الْقُرُونِ مِنۢ بَعْدِ نُوحٍ وَكَفَىٰ بِرَبِّكَ
بِذُنُوبِ عِبَادِهِ خَبِيرًۢا بَصِيرًا ﴿١٧﴾

18 Whoso desireth that (life) which
hasteneth away, We hasten for him
therein that which We will for
whom We please. And afterward
We have appointed for him hell; he
will endure the heat thereof, condemned, rejected.

مَّن كَانَ يُرِيدُ الْعَاجِلَةَ عَجَّلْنَا لَهُۥ فِيهَا مَا نَشَآءُ
لِمَن نُّرِيدُ ثُمَّ جَعَلْنَا لَهُۥ جَهَنَّمَ يَصْلَىٰهَا مَذْمُومًا
مَّدْحُورًا ﴿١٨﴾

19 And whoso desireth the Hereafter and striveth for it with the effort necessary, being a believer; for
such, their effort findeth favour
(with their Lord).

وَمَنْ أَرَادَ الْءَاخِرَةَ وَسَعَىٰ لَهَا سَعْيَهَا وَهُوَ مُؤْمِنٌ
فَأُو۟لَٰٓئِكَ كَانَ سَعْيُهُم مَّشْكُورًا ﴿١٩﴾

20 Each do We supply, both these
and those, from the bounty of thy
Lord. And the bounty of thy Lord
can never be walled up.

كُلًّا نُّمِدُّ هَٰٓؤُلَآءِ وَهَٰٓؤُلَآءِ مِنْ عَطَآءِ رَبِّكَ
وَمَا كَانَ عَطَآءُ رَبِّكَ مَحْظُورًا ﴿٢٠﴾

21 See how We prefer one above
another, and verily the Hereafter
will be greater in degrees and greater in preferment.

انظُرْ كَيْفَ فَضَّلْنَا بَعْضَهُمْ عَلَىٰ بَعْضٍ وَلَلْءَاخِرَةُ
أَكْبَرُ دَرَجَٰتٍ وَأَكْبَرُ تَفْضِيلًا ﴿٢١﴾

22 Set not up with Allah any other
god (O man) lest thou sit down
reproved, forsaken.

لَّا تَجْعَلْ مَعَ اللَّهِ إِلَٰهًا ءَاخَرَ فَتَقْعُدَ مَذْمُومًا
مَّخْذُولًا ﴿٢٢﴾

23 Thy Lord hath decreed, that ye worship none save Him, and (that ye show) kindness to parents. If one of them or both of them to attain old age with thee, say not "Fie" unto them nor repulse them, but speak unto them a gracious word.

۞ وَقَضَىٰ رَبُّكَ أَلَّا تَعْبُدُوٓاْ إِلَّآ إِيَّاهُ وَبِٱلْوَٰلِدَيْنِ إِحْسَٰنًا ۚ إِمَّا يَبْلُغَنَّ عِندَكَ ٱلْكِبَرَ أَحَدُهُمَآ أَوْ كِلَاهُمَا فَلَا تَقُل لَّهُمَآ أُفٍّ وَلَا تَنْهَرْهُمَا وَقُل لَّهُمَا قَوْلًا كَرِيمًا ۝

24 And lower unto them the wing of submission through mercy, and say: My Lord! Have mercy on them both as they did care for me when I was little.

وَٱخْفِضْ لَهُمَا جَنَاحَ ٱلذُّلِّ مِنَ ٱلرَّحْمَةِ وَقُل رَّبِّ ٱرْحَمْهُمَا كَمَا رَبَّيَانِي صَغِيرًا ۝

25 Your Lord is best aware of what is in your minds. If ye are righteous, then lo! He was ever Forgiving unto those who turn (unto Him).

رَّبُّكُمْ أَعْلَمُ بِمَا فِى نُفُوسِكُمْ ۚ إِن تَكُونُوا۟ صَٰلِحِينَ فَإِنَّهُ كَانَ لِلْأَوَّٰبِينَ غَفُورًا ۝

26 Give the kinsman his due, and the needy, and the wayfarer, and squander not (thy wealth) in wantonness.

وَءَاتِ ذَا ٱلْقُرْبَىٰ حَقَّهُ وَٱلْمِسْكِينَ وَٱبْنَ ٱلسَّبِيلِ وَلَا تُبَذِّرْ تَبْذِيرًا ۝

27 Lo! the squanderers were ever brothers of the devils, and the devil was ever an ingrate to his Lord.

إِنَّ ٱلْمُبَذِّرِينَ كَانُوٓا۟ إِخْوَٰنَ ٱلشَّيَٰطِينِ ۖ وَكَانَ ٱلشَّيْطَٰنُ لِرَبِّهِ كَفُورًا ۝

28 But if thou turn away from them, seeking mercy from thy Lord, for which thou hopest, then speak unto them a reasonable word.

وَإِمَّا تُعْرِضَنَّ عَنْهُمُ ٱبْتِغَآءَ رَحْمَةٍ مِّن رَّبِّكَ تَرْجُوهَا فَقُل لَّهُمْ قَوْلًا مَّيْسُورًا ۝

29 And let not thy hand be chained to thy neck nor open it with a complete opening, lest thou sit down rebuked, denuded.

وَلَا تَجْعَلْ يَدَكَ مَغْلُولَةً إِلَىٰ عُنُقِكَ وَلَا تَبْسُطْهَا كُلَّ ٱلْبَسْطِ فَتَقْعُدَ مَلُومًا مَّحْسُورًا ۝

30 Lo! thy Lord enlargeth the provision for whom He will, and straiteneth (it for whom He will). Lo, He was ever Knower, Seer of His slaves.

إِنَّ رَبَّكَ يَبْسُطُ ٱلرِّزْقَ لِمَن يَشَآءُ وَيَقْدِرُ ۚ إِنَّهُ كَانَ بِعِبَادِهِ خَبِيرًا بَصِيرًا ۝

31 Slay not your children, fearing a fall to poverty, We shall provide for them and for you. Lo! the slaying of them is great sin.

32 And come not near unto adultery. Lo! it is an abomination and an evil way.

33 And slay not the life which Allah hath forbidden save with right. Whoso is slain wrongfully, We have given power unto his heir, but let him not commit excess in slaying. Lo! he will be helped.

34 Come not near the wealth of the orphan save with that which is better till he come to strength; and keep the covenant. Lo! of the covenant it will be asked.

35 Fill the measure when ye measure, and weigh with a right balance; that is meet, and better in the end.

36 (O man), follow not that whereof thou hast no knowledge. Lo! the hearing and the sight and the heart; of each of these it will be asked.

37 And walk not in the earth exultant. Lo! thou canst not rend the earth, nor canst thou stretch to the height of the hills.

38 The evil of all that is hateful in the sight of thy Lord.

39 This is (part) of that wisdom wherewith thy Lord hath inspired thee (O Muhammad). And set not

وَلَا تَقْتُلُوٓا أَوْلَٰدَكُمْ خَشْيَةَ إِمْلَٰقٍ نَّحْنُ نَرْزُقُهُمْ وَإِيَّاكُمْ إِنَّ قَتْلَهُمْ كَانَ خِطْـًٔا كَبِيرًا ۝

وَلَا تَقْرَبُوا الزِّنَىٰٓ إِنَّهُ كَانَ فَٰحِشَةً وَسَآءَ سَبِيلًا ۝

وَلَا تَقْتُلُوا النَّفْسَ الَّتِي حَرَّمَ اللَّهُ إِلَّا بِالْحَقِّ وَمَن قُتِلَ مَظْلُومًا فَقَدْ جَعَلْنَا لِوَلِيِّهِ سُلْطَٰنًا فَلَا يُسْرِف فِّي الْقَتْلِ إِنَّهُ كَانَ مَنصُورًا ۝

وَلَا تَقْرَبُوا مَالَ الْيَتِيمِ إِلَّا بِالَّتِي هِيَ أَحْسَنُ حَتَّىٰ يَبْلُغَ أَشُدَّهُ وَأَوْفُوا بِالْعَهْدِ إِنَّ الْعَهْدَ كَانَ مَسْـُٔولًا ۝

وَأَوْفُوا الْكَيْلَ إِذَا كِلْتُمْ وَزِنُوا بِالْقِسْطَاسِ الْمُسْتَقِيمِ ذَٰلِكَ خَيْرٌ وَأَحْسَنُ تَأْوِيلًا ۝

وَلَا تَقْفُ مَا لَيْسَ لَكَ بِهِ عِلْمٌ إِنَّ السَّمْعَ وَالْبَصَرَ وَالْفُؤَادَ كُلُّ أُوْلَٰئِكَ كَانَ عَنْهُ مَسْـُٔولًا ۝

وَلَا تَمْشِ فِي الْأَرْضِ مَرَحًا إِنَّكَ لَن تَخْرِقَ الْأَرْضَ وَلَن تَبْلُغَ الْجِبَالَ طُولًا ۝

كُلُّ ذَٰلِكَ كَانَ سَيِّئُهُ عِندَ رَبِّكَ مَكْرُوهًا ۝

ذَٰلِكَ مِمَّا أَوْحَىٰ إِلَيْكَ رَبُّكَ مِنَ الْحِكْمَةِ وَلَا تَجْعَلْ

up with Allah any other god, lest thou be cast into hell, reproved, abandoned.

40 Hath your Lord then distinguished you (O men of Makkah) by giving you sons, and hath chosen for Himself females from among the angels? Lo! verily ye speak an awful word!

مَعَ اللّٰهِ إِلٰهًا اٰخَرَ فَتُلْقٰى فِىْ جَهَنَّمَ مَلُوْمًا مَّدْحُوْرًا ۝

أَفَأَصْفٰكُمْ رَبُّكُمْ بِالْبَنِيْنَ وَاتَّخَذَ مِنَ الْمَلٰٓئِكَةِ إِنَاثًا ۚ إِنَّكُمْ لَتَقُوْلُوْنَ قَوْلًا عَظِيْمًا ۝

41 We verily have displayed (Our warnings) in this Qur'an that they may take heed, but it increaseth them in naught save aversion.

وَلَقَدْ صَرَّفْنَا فِىْ هٰذَا الْقُرْاٰنِ لِيَذَّكَّرُوْا ۚ وَمَا يَزِيْدُهُمْ إِلَّا نُفُوْرًا ۝

42 Say (O Muhammad, to the disbelievers): If there were other gods along with Him, as they say, then had they sought a way against the Lord of the Throne.

قُلْ لَّوْ كَانَ مَعَهُ اٰلِهَةٌ كَمَا يَقُوْلُوْنَ إِذًا لَّابْتَغَوْا إِلٰى ذِى الْعَرْشِ سَبِيْلًا ۝

43 Glorified is He, and High Exalted above what they say!

سُبْحٰنَهُ وَتَعٰلٰى عَمَّا يَقُوْلُوْنَ عُلُوًّا كَبِيْرًا ۝

44 The seven heavens and the earth and all that is therein, praise Him; and there is not a thing but hymneth his praise; but ye understand not their praise. Lo! He is ever Clement, Forgiving.

تُسَبِّحُ لَهُ السَّمٰوٰتُ السَّبْعُ وَالْأَرْضُ وَمَنْ فِيْهِنَّ ۚ وَإِنْ مِّنْ شَىْءٍ إِلَّا يُسَبِّحُ بِحَمْدِهِ وَلٰكِنْ لَّا تَفْقَهُوْنَ تَسْبِيْحَهُمْ ۚ إِنَّهُ كَانَ حَلِيْمًا غَفُوْرًا ۝

45 And when thou recitest the Qur'an We place between thee, and those who believe not in the Hereafter a hidden barrier;

وَإِذَا قَرَأْتَ الْقُرْاٰنَ جَعَلْنَا بَيْنَكَ وَبَيْنَ الَّذِيْنَ لَا يُؤْمِنُوْنَ بِالْاٰخِرَةِ حِجَابًا مَّسْتُوْرًا ۝

46 And We place upon their hearts veils lest they should understand it, and in their ears a deafness; and when thou makest mention of thy Lord alone in the Qur'an, they turn their backs in aversion.

وَجَعَلْنَا عَلٰى قُلُوْبِهِمْ أَكِنَّةً أَنْ يَّفْقَهُوْهُ وَفِىْ اٰذَانِهِمْ وَقْرًا ۚ وَإِذَا ذَكَرْتَ رَبَّكَ فِى الْقُرْاٰنِ وَحْدَهُ وَلَّوْا عَلٰى أَدْبَارِهِمْ نُفُوْرًا ۝

47 We are best aware of what they wish to hear when they give ear to thee and when they take secret counsel, when the evil-doers say: Ye follow but a man bewitched.

48 See what similitudes they coin for thee, and thus are all astray, and cannot find a road!

49 And they say: When we are bones and fragments, shall we, forsooth, be raised up as a new creation?

50 Say: Be ye stones or iron;

51 Or some created thing that is yet greater in your thoughts! Then they will say: Who shall bring us back (to life). Say: He who created you at the first. Then will they shake their heads at thee, and say: When will it be? Say: It will perhaps be soon;

52 A day when He will call you and ye will answer with His praise, and ye will think that ye have tarried but a little while.

53 Tell My bondmen to speak that which is kindlier. Lo! the devil soweth discord among them. Lo! the devil is for man an open foe.

54 Your Lord is best aware of you. If He will, He will have mercy on you, or if He will, He will punish you. We have not sent thee (O Muhammad) as a warden over them.

نَحْنُ أَعْلَمُ بِمَا يَسْتَمِعُونَ بِهِ إِذْ يَسْتَمِعُونَ إِلَيْكَ وَإِذْ هُمْ نَجْوَى إِذْ يَقُولُ الظَّالِمُونَ إِن تَتَّبِعُونَ إِلَّا رَجُلًا مَّسْحُورًا ۝

انظُرْ كَيْفَ ضَرَبُوا لَكَ الْأَمْثَالَ فَضَلُّوا فَلَا يَسْتَطِيعُونَ سَبِيلًا ۝

وَقَالُوا أَءِذَا كُنَّا عِظَامًا وَرُفَاتًا أَءِنَّا لَمَبْعُوثُونَ خَلْقًا جَدِيدًا ۝

۞ قُلْ كُونُوا حِجَارَةً أَوْ حَدِيدًا ۝

أَوْ خَلْقًا مِّمَّا يَكْبُرُ فِي صُدُورِكُمْ فَسَيَقُولُونَ مَن يُعِيدُنَا قُلِ الَّذِي فَطَرَكُمْ أَوَّلَ مَرَّةٍ فَسَيُنْغِضُونَ إِلَيْكَ رُءُوسَهُمْ وَيَقُولُونَ مَتَى هُوَ قُلْ عَسَى أَن يَكُونَ قَرِيبًا ۝

يَوْمَ يَدْعُوكُمْ فَتَسْتَجِيبُونَ بِحَمْدِهِ وَتَظُنُّونَ إِن لَّبِثْتُمْ إِلَّا قَلِيلًا ۝

وَقُل لِّعِبَادِي يَقُولُوا الَّتِي هِيَ أَحْسَنُ إِنَّ الشَّيْطَانَ يَنزَغُ بَيْنَهُمْ إِنَّ الشَّيْطَانَ كَانَ لِلْإِنسَانِ عَدُوًّا مُّبِينًا ۝

رَّبُّكُمْ أَعْلَمُ بِكُمْ إِن يَشَأْ يَرْحَمْكُمْ أَوْ إِن يَشَأْ يُعَذِّبْكُمْ وَمَا أَرْسَلْنَاكَ عَلَيْهِمْ وَكِيلًا ۝

55 And thy Lord is best aware of all who are in the heavens and the earth. And we preferred some of the Prophets above others, and unto David We gave the Psalms.

وَرَبُّكَ أَعْلَمُ بِمَن فِى ٱلسَّمَٰوَٰتِ وَٱلْأَرْضِ وَلَقَدْ فَضَّلْنَا بَعْضَ ٱلنَّبِيِّـۧنَ عَلَىٰ بَعْضٍ وَءَاتَيْنَا دَاوُۥدَ زَبُورًا ۝

56 Say: Cry unto those (saints and angels) whom ye assume (to be gods) beside Him, yet they have no power to rid you of misfortune nor to change.

قُلِ ٱدْعُوا۟ ٱلَّذِينَ زَعَمْتُم مِّن دُونِهِۦ فَلَا يَمْلِكُونَ كَشْفَ ٱلضُّرِّ عَنكُمْ وَلَا تَحْوِيلًا ۝

57 Those unto whom they cry seek the way of approach to their Lord, which of them shall be the nearest; they hope for His mercy and they fear His doom. Lo! the doom of thy Lord is to be shunned.

أُو۟لَٰٓئِكَ ٱلَّذِينَ يَدْعُونَ يَبْتَغُونَ إِلَىٰ رَبِّهِمُ ٱلْوَسِيلَةَ أَيُّهُمْ أَقْرَبُ وَيَرْجُونَ رَحْمَتَهُۥ وَيَخَافُونَ عَذَابَهُۥٓ إِنَّ عَذَابَ رَبِّكَ كَانَ مَحْذُورًا ۝

58 There is not a township[3] but We shall destroy it ere the Day of Resurrection, or punish it with dire punishment. That is set forth in the Book (of Our decrees).

وَإِن مِّن قَرْيَةٍ إِلَّا نَحْنُ مُهْلِكُوهَا قَبْلَ يَوْمِ ٱلْقِيَٰمَةِ أَوْ مُعَذِّبُوهَا عَذَابًا شَدِيدًا كَانَ ذَٰلِكَ فِى ٱلْكِتَٰبِ مَسْطُورًا ۝

59 Naught hindereth Us from sending portents save that the folk of old denied them. And We gave Thamūd the she-camel—a clear portent—but they did wrong in respect of her. We send not portents save to warn.

وَمَا مَنَعَنَآ أَن نُّرْسِلَ بِٱلْءَايَٰتِ إِلَّآ أَن كَذَّبَ بِهَا ٱلْأَوَّلُونَ وَءَاتَيْنَا ثَمُودَ ٱلنَّاقَةَ مُبْصِرَةً فَظَلَمُوا۟ بِهَا وَمَا نُرْسِلُ بِٱلْءَايَٰتِ إِلَّا تَخْوِيفًا ۝

60 And (it was a warning) when We told thee: Lo! thy Lord encompasseth mankind, and We appointed the vision[4] which We showed thee as an ordeal for mankind, and (like-

وَإِذْ قُلْنَا لَكَ إِنَّ رَبَّكَ أَحَاطَ بِٱلنَّاسِ وَمَا جَعَلْنَا ٱلرُّءْيَا ٱلَّتِىٓ أَرَيْنَٰكَ إِلَّا فِتْنَةً لِّلنَّاسِ وَٱلشَّجَرَةَ

---

3. Or *community*.

4. The Prophet's vision of his ascent through the seven heavens.

wise) the Accursed Tree in the Qur'an.[5] We warn them, but it increaseth them in naught save gross impiety.

61 And when We said unto the angels: Fall down prostrate before Adam and they fell prostrate all save Iblīs, he said: Shall I fall prostrate before that which Thou hast created of clay?

62 He said: Seest Thou this (creature) whom Thou hast honoured above me, if Thou give me grace until the Day of Resurrection, I verily will seize his seed, save but a few.

63 He said: Go, and whosoever of them followeth thee—lo! hell will be your payment, ample payment.

64 And excite any of them whom thou canst with thy voice, and urge thy horse and foot against them, and be a partner in their wealth and children, and promise them. Satan promiseth them only to deceive.

65 Lo! My (faithful) bondmen; over them thou hast no power, and thy Lord sufficeth as (their) guardian.

66 (O mankind), your Lord is He Who driveth for you the ship upon the sea that ye may seek of His bounty. Lo! He was ever Merciful toward you.

الْمَلْعُونَةَ فِي الْقُرْءَانِ وَنُخَوِّفُهُمْ فَمَا يَزِيدُهُمْ إِلَّا طُغْيَانًا كَبِيرًا ﴿٦٠﴾

وَإِذْ قُلْنَا لِلْمَلَٰٓئِكَةِ اسْجُدُوا لِآدَمَ فَسَجَدُوٓا إِلَّآ إِبْلِيسَ قَالَ ءَأَسْجُدُ لِمَنْ خَلَقْتَ طِينًا ﴿٦١﴾

قَالَ أَرَءَيْتَكَ هَٰذَا الَّذِي كَرَّمْتَ عَلَيَّ لَئِنْ أَخَّرْتَنِ إِلَىٰ يَوْمِ الْقِيَٰمَةِ لَأَحْتَنِكَنَّ ذُرِّيَّتَهُۥٓ إِلَّا قَلِيلًا ﴿٦٢﴾

قَالَ اذْهَبْ فَمَن تَبِعَكَ مِنْهُمْ فَإِنَّ جَهَنَّمَ جَزَآؤُكُمْ جَزَآءً مَّوْفُورًا ﴿٦٣﴾

وَاسْتَفْزِزْ مَنِ اسْتَطَعْتَ مِنْهُم بِصَوْتِكَ وَأَجْلِبْ عَلَيْهِم بِخَيْلِكَ وَرَجِلِكَ وَشَارِكْهُمْ فِي الْأَمْوَٰلِ وَالْأَوْلَٰدِ وَعِدْهُمْ وَمَا يَعِدُهُمُ الشَّيْطَٰنُ إِلَّا غُرُورًا ﴿٦٤﴾

إِنَّ عِبَادِي لَيْسَ لَكَ عَلَيْهِمْ سُلْطَٰنٌ وَكَفَىٰ بِرَبِّكَ وَكِيلًا ﴿٦٥﴾

رَّبُّكُمُ الَّذِي يُزْجِي لَكُمُ الْفُلْكَ فِي الْبَحْرِ لِتَبْتَغُوا مِن فَضْلِهِۦٓ إِنَّهُۥ كَانَ بِكُمْ رَحِيمًا ﴿٦٦﴾

---

5. See Sūrah 44, vv. 43-49.

67 And when harm toucheth you upon the sea, all unto whom ye cry (for succour) fail save Him (alone), but when He bringeth you safe to land, ye turn away, for man was ever thankless.

وَإِذَا مَسَّكُمُ الضُّرُّ فِي الْبَحْرِ ضَلَّ مَنْ تَدْعُوْنَ إِلَّا إِيَّاهُ فَلَمَّا نَجّىٰكُمْ إِلَى الْبَرِّ أَعْرَضْتُمْ وَكَانَ الْإِنْسَانُ كَفُوْرًا ۝

68 Feel ye then secure that He will not cause a slope of the land to engulf you, or send a sandstorm upon you, and then ye will find that ye have no protector?

أَفَأَمِنْتُمْ أَنْ يَّخْسِفَ بِكُمْ جَانِبَ الْبَرِّ أَوْ يُرْسِلَ عَلَيْكُمْ حَاصِبًا ثُمَّ لَا تَجِدُوْا لَكُمْ وَكِيْلًا ۝

69 Or feel ye secure that He will not return you to that (plight) a second time, and send against you a hurricane of wind and drown you for your thanklessness, and then ye will not find therein that ye have any avenger against Us?

أَمْ أَمِنْتُمْ أَنْ يُّعِيْدَكُمْ فِيْهِ تَارَةً أُخْرٰى فَيُرْسِلَ عَلَيْكُمْ قَاصِفًا مِّنَ الرِّيْحِ فَيُغْرِقَكُمْ بِمَا كَفَرْتُمْ ثُمَّ لَا تَجِدُوْا لَكُمْ عَلَيْنَا بِهِ تَبِيْعًا ۝

70 Verily We have honoured the children of Adam. We carry them on the land and the sea, and have made provision of good things for them, and have preferred them above many of those whom We created with a marked preferment.

۞ وَلَقَدْ كَرَّمْنَا بَنِيْ ءَادَمَ وَحَمَلْنَاهُمْ فِي الْبَرِّ وَالْبَحْرِ وَرَزَقْنَاهُمْ مِّنَ الطَّيِّبَاتِ وَفَضَّلْنَاهُمْ عَلَىٰ كَثِيْرٍ مِّمَّنْ خَلَقْنَا تَفْضِيْلًا ۝

71 On the day when We shall summon all men with their record, whoso is given his book in his right hand—such will read their book and they will not be wronged a shred.

يَوْمَ نَدْعُوْا كُلَّ أُنَاسٍ بِإِمَامِهِمْ فَمَنْ أُوْتِيَ كِتَابَهُ بِيَمِيْنِهِ فَأُولٰئِكَ يَقْرَءُوْنَ كِتَابَهُمْ وَلَا يُظْلَمُوْنَ فَتِيْلًا ۝

72 Whoso is blind here will be blind in the Hereafter, and yet further from the road.

وَمَنْ كَانَ فِيْ هٰذِهِ أَعْمٰى فَهُوَ فِي الْآخِرَةِ أَعْمٰى وَأَضَلُّ سَبِيْلًا ۝

73 And they indeed strove hard to beguile thee (Muhammad) away from that wherewith We have ins-

وَإِنْ كَادُوْا لَيَفْتِنُوْنَكَ عَنِ الَّذِيْ أَوْحَيْنَا

pired thee, that thou shouldst invent other than it against Us; and then would they have accepted thee as a friend.[6]

إِلَيْكَ لِتَفْتَرِىَ عَلَيْنَا غَيْرَهُ ۖ وَإِذًا لَّاتَّخَذُوكَ خَلِيلًا ۞

74 And if We had not made thee wholly firm thou mightest almost have inclined unto them a little.

وَلَوْلَاۤ أَن ثَبَّتْنَاكَ لَقَدْ كِدتَّ تَرْكَنُ إِلَيْهِمْ شَيْئًا قَلِيلًا ۞

75 Then had We made thee taste a double (punishment) of living and a double (punishment) of dying, then hadst thou found no helper against Us.

إِذًا لَّأَذَقْنَاكَ ضِعْفَ الْحَيَوٰةِ وَضِعْفَ الْمَمَاتِ ثُمَّ لَا تَجِدُ لَكَ عَلَيْنَا نَصِيرًا ۞

76 And they indeed wished to scare thee from the land that they might drive thee forth from thence, and then they would have stayed (there) but a little after thee.[7]

وَإِن كَادُواْ لَيَسْتَفِزُّونَكَ مِنَ الْأَرْضِ لِيُخْرِجُوكَ مِنْهَا وَإِذًا لَّا يَلْبَثُونَ خِلَافَكَ إِلَّا قَلِيلًا ۞

77 (Such was Our) method in the case of those whom We sent before thee (to mankind), and thou wilt not find for Our method aught of power to change.

سُنَّةَ مَن قَدْ أَرْسَلْنَا قَبْلَكَ مِن رُّسُلِنَا ۖ وَلَا تَجِدُ لِسُنَّتِنَا تَحْوِيلًا ۞

78 Establish worship at the going down of the sun until the dark of night, and (the recital of) the Qur'an at dawn. Lo! (the recital of) the Qur'an at dawn is ever witnessed.

أَقِمِ الصَّلَوٰةَ لِدُلُوكِ الشَّمْسِ إِلَىٰ غَسَقِ الَّيْلِ وَقُرْءَانَ الْفَجْرِ ۖ إِنَّ قُرْءَانَ الْفَجْرِ كَانَ مَشْهُودًا ۞

79 And some part of the night awake for it, a largess for thee. It may be that thy Lord will raise thee to a praised estate.

وَمِنَ الَّيْلِ فَتَهَجَّدْ بِهِ نَافِلَةً لَّكَ عَسَىٰٓ أَن يَبْعَثَكَ رَبُّكَ مَقَامًا مَّحْمُودًا ۞

---

6. The idolaters more then once offered to compromise with the Prophet.

7. If, as the Jalāleyn declare, vv. 76-82 were revealed at Al-Madīnah the reference here is to the plotting of the Jews and Hypocrites.

80 And say: My Lord! Cause me to come in with a firm incoming and to go out with a firm outgoing. And give me from Thy presence a sustaining Power.

وَقُلْ رَّبِّ أَدْخِلْنِي مُدْخَلَ صِدْقٍ وَأَخْرِجْنِي مُخْرَجَ صِدْقٍ وَاجْعَلْ لِّي مِنْ لَّدُنْكَ سُلْطَٰنًا نَّصِيرًا ۝

81 And say: Truth hath come and falsehood hath vanished away. Lo! falsehood is ever bound to vanish.[8]

وَقُلْ جَآءَ الْحَقُّ وَزَهَقَ الْبَٰطِلُ إِنَّ الْبَٰطِلَ كَانَ زَهُوقًا ۝

82 And We reveal of the Qur'an that which is a healing and a mercy for believers though it increase the evil-doers in naught save ruin.

وَنُنَزِّلُ مِنَ الْقُرْءَانِ مَا هُوَ شِفَآءٌ وَرَحْمَةٌ لِّلْمُؤْمِنِينَ وَلَا يَزِيدُ الظَّٰلِمِينَ إِلَّا خَسَارًا ۝

83 And when We make life pleasant unto man, he turneth away and is averse; and when ill toucheth him he is in despair.

وَإِذَآ أَنْعَمْنَا عَلَى الْإِنسَٰنِ أَعْرَضَ وَنَـَٔا بِجَانِبِهِ وَإِذَا مَسَّهُ الشَّرُّ كَانَ يَـُٔوسًا ۝

84 Say: Each one doth according to his rule of conduct, and thy Lord is best aware of him whose way is right.

قُلْ كُلٌّ يَعْمَلُ عَلَىٰ شَاكِلَتِهِ فَرَبُّكُمْ أَعْلَمُ بِمَنْ هُوَ أَهْدَىٰ سَبِيلًا ۝

85 They will ask thee concerning the Spirit. Say: The Spirit is by command of my Lord, and of knowledge ye have been vouchsafed but little.

وَيَسْـَٔلُونَكَ عَنِ الرُّوحِ قُلِ الرُّوحُ مِنْ أَمْرِ رَبِّي وَمَآ أُوتِيتُمْ مِّنَ الْعِلْمِ إِلَّا قَلِيلًا ۝

86 And if We willed We could withdraw that which We have revealed unto thee, then wouldst thou find no guardian for thee against Us in respect thereof.

وَلَئِنْ شِئْنَا لَنَذْهَبَنَّ بِالَّذِي أَوْحَيْنَآ إِلَيْكَ ثُمَّ لَا تَجِدُ لَكَ بِهِ عَلَيْنَا وَكِيلًا ۝

---

8. These words were recited by the Prophet when he witnessed the destruction of the idols round the Ka'bah after the conquest of Makkah.

87 (It is naught) save mercy from thy Lord. Lo! His kindness unto thee was ever great.[9]

إِلَّا رَحْمَةً مِّن رَّبِّكَ إِنَّ فَضْلَهُ كَانَ عَلَيْكَ كَبِيرًا ۝

88 Say: Verily, though mankind and the Jinn should assemble to produce the like of this Qur'an, they could not produce the like thereof though they were helpers one of another.

قُل لَّئِنِ اجْتَمَعَتِ الْإِنسُ وَالْجِنُّ عَلَىٰ أَن يَأْتُوا بِمِثْلِ هَٰذَا الْقُرْآنِ لَا يَأْتُونَ بِمِثْلِهِ وَلَوْ كَانَ بَعْضُهُمْ لِبَعْضٍ ظَهِيرًا ۝

89 And verily We have displayed for mankind in this Qur'an all kinds of similitudes, but most of mankind refuse aught save disbelief.

وَلَقَدْ صَرَّفْنَا لِلنَّاسِ فِى هَٰذَا الْقُرْآنِ مِن كُلِّ مَثَلٍ فَأَبَىٰ أَكْثَرُ النَّاسِ إِلَّا كُفُورًا ۝

90 And they say: We will not put faith in thee till thou cause a spring to gush forth from the earth for us;

وَقَالُوا لَن نُّؤْمِنَ لَكَ حَتَّىٰ تَفْجُرَ لَنَا مِنَ الْأَرْضِ يَنبُوعًا ۝

91 Or thou have a garden of date-palms and grapes, and cause rivers to gush forth therein abundantly;

أَوْ تَكُونَ لَكَ جَنَّةٌ مِّن نَّخِيلٍ وَعِنَبٍ فَتُفَجِّرَ الْأَنْهَارَ خِلَالَهَا تَفْجِيرًا ۝

92 Or thou cause the heaven to fall upon us piecemeal, as thou hast pretended, or bring Allah and the angels as a warrant;

أَوْ تُسْقِطَ السَّمَاءَ كَمَا زَعَمْتَ عَلَيْنَا كِسَفًا أَوْ تَأْتِىَ بِاللَّهِ وَالْمَلَائِكَةِ قَبِيلًا ۝

93 Thou have a house of gold; or thou ascend up into heaven, and even then we will put no faith in thine ascension till thou bring down for us a book that we can read. Say (O Muhammad): My Lord be glorified! Am I naught save a mortal messenger?

أَوْ يَكُونَ لَكَ بَيْتٌ مِّن زُخْرُفٍ أَوْ تَرْقَىٰ فِى السَّمَاءِ وَلَن نُّؤْمِنَ لِرُقِيِّكَ حَتَّىٰ تُنَزِّلَ عَلَيْنَا كِتَابًا نَّقْرَؤُهُ قُلْ سُبْحَانَ رَبِّى هَلْ كُنتُ إِلَّا بَشَرًا رَّسُولًا ۝

---

9. Vv. 85, 86 and 87 are said to have been revealed in answer to the third question which some Jewish rabbis prompted the idolaters to ask, the first two questions being answered in the following Sūrah.

94 And naught prevented mankind from believing when the guidance came unto them save that they said: Hath Allah sent a mortal as (His) messenger?

وَمَا مَنَعَ ٱلنَّاسَ أَن يُؤْمِنُوٓا۟ إِذْ جَآءَهُمُ ٱلْهُدَىٰٓ إِلَّآ أَن قَالُوٓا۟ أَبَعَثَ ٱللَّهُ بَشَرًا رَّسُولًا ۝

95 Say: If there were in the earth angels walking secure, We had sent down for them from heaven an angel as messenger.

قُل لَّوْ كَانَ فِى ٱلْأَرْضِ مَلَٰٓئِكَةٌ يَمْشُونَ مُطْمَئِنِّينَ لَنَزَّلْنَا عَلَيْهِم مِّنَ ٱلسَّمَآءِ مَلَكًا رَّسُولًا ۝

96 Say: Allah sufficeth for a witness between me and you. Lo! He is Knower, Seer of His slaves.

قُلْ كَفَىٰ بِٱللَّهِ شَهِيدًۢا بَيْنِى وَبَيْنَكُمْ إِنَّهُۥ كَانَ بِعِبَادِهِۦ خَبِيرًۢا بَصِيرًا ۝

97 And he whom Allah guideth, he is led aright; while, as for him whom He sendeth astray, for them thou wilt find no protecting friends beside Him, and We shall assemble them on the Day of Resurrection on their faces, blind, dumb and deaf; their habitation will be hell; whenever it abateth, We increase the flame for them.

وَمَن يَهْدِ ٱللَّهُ فَهُوَ ٱلْمُهْتَدِ وَمَن يُضْلِلْ فَلَن تَجِدَ لَهُمْ أَوْلِيَآءَ مِن دُونِهِۦ وَنَحْشُرُهُمْ يَوْمَ ٱلْقِيَٰمَةِ عَلَىٰ وُجُوهِهِمْ عُمْيًا وَبُكْمًا وَصُمًّا مَّأْوَىٰهُمْ جَهَنَّمُ كُلَّمَا خَبَتْ زِدْنَٰهُمْ سَعِيرًا ۝

98 That is their reward because they disbelieved Our revelations and said: When we are bones and fragments shall we, forsooth, be raised up as a new creation?

ذَٰلِكَ جَزَآؤُهُم بِأَنَّهُمْ كَفَرُوا۟ بِـَٔايَٰتِنَا وَقَالُوٓا۟ أَءِذَا كُنَّا عِظَٰمًا وَرُفَٰتًا أَءِنَّا لَمَبْعُوثُونَ خَلْقًا جَدِيدًا ۝

99 Have they not seen that Allah Who created the heavens and the earth is Able to create the like of them, and hath appointed for them an end whereof there is no doubt? But the wrong-doers refuse aught save disbelief.

۞ أَوَلَمْ يَرَوْا۟ أَنَّ ٱللَّهَ ٱلَّذِى خَلَقَ ٱلسَّمَٰوَٰتِ وَٱلْأَرْضَ قَادِرٌ عَلَىٰٓ أَن يَخْلُقَ مِثْلَهُمْ وَجَعَلَ لَهُمْ أَجَلًا لَّا رَيْبَ فِيهِ فَأَبَى ٱلظَّٰلِمُونَ إِلَّا كُفُورًا ۝

100 Say (unto them): If ye possessed the treasures of the mercy of

قُل لَّوْ أَنتُمْ تَمْلِكُونَ خَزَآئِنَ رَحْمَةِ رَبِّىٓ إِذًا

my Lord, ye would surely hold them back for fear of spending, for man was ever grudging.

لَأَمْسَكْتُمْ خَشْيَةَ ٱلْإِنْفَاقِ ۚ وَكَانَ ٱلْإِنسَٰنُ قَتُورًا ۝

101   And verily We gave unto Moses nine tokens, clear proofs (of Allah's Sovereignty). Do but ask the Children of Israel how he came unto them, then Pharaoh said unto him: Lo! I deem thee one bewitched, O Moses.

وَلَقَدْ ءَاتَيْنَا مُوسَىٰ تِسْعَ ءَايَٰتٍۭ بَيِّنَٰتٍ ۖ فَسْـَٔلْ بَنِىٓ إِسْرَٰٓءِيلَ إِذْ جَآءَهُمْ فَقَالَ لَهُۥ فِرْعَوْنُ إِنِّى لَأَظُنُّكَ يَٰمُوسَىٰ مَسْحُورًا ۝

102   He said: In truth thou knowest that none sent down these (portents) save the Lord of the heavens and the earth as proofs, and lo! (for my part) I deem thee lost, O Pharaoh.

قَالَ لَقَدْ عَلِمْتَ مَآ أَنزَلَ هَٰٓؤُلَآءِ إِلَّا رَبُّ ٱلسَّمَٰوَٰتِ وَٱلْأَرْضِ بَصَآئِرَ ۖ وَإِنِّى لَأَظُنُّكَ يَٰفِرْعَوْنُ مَثْبُورًا ۝

103   And he wished to scare them from the land, but We drowned him and those with him, all together.

فَأَرَادَ أَن يَسْتَفِزَّهُم مِّنَ ٱلْأَرْضِ فَأَغْرَقْنَٰهُ وَمَن مَّعَهُۥ جَمِيعًا ۝

104   And We said unto the Children of Israel after him: Dwell in the land; but when the promise of the Hereafter cometh to pass we shall bring you as a crowd gathered out of various nations.[10]

وَقُلْنَا مِنۢ بَعْدِهِۦ لِبَنِىٓ إِسْرَٰٓءِيلَ ٱسْكُنُوا۟ ٱلْأَرْضَ فَإِذَا جَآءَ وَعْدُ ٱلْءَاخِرَةِ جِئْنَا بِكُمْ لَفِيفًا ۝

105   With truth have We sent it down, and with truth hath it descended. And We have sent thee as naught else save a bearer of good tidings and a warner.

وَبِٱلْحَقِّ أَنزَلْنَٰهُ وَبِٱلْحَقِّ نَزَلَ ۗ وَمَآ أَرْسَلْنَٰكَ إِلَّا مُبَشِّرًا وَنَذِيرًا ۝

106   And (it is) a Qur'an that We have divided, that thou mayest re-

وَقُرْءَانًا فَرَقْنَٰهُ لِتَقْرَأَهُۥ عَلَى ٱلنَّاسِ عَلَىٰ مُكْثٍ

---

10. A reference to the dispersal of the Jews as the consequence of their own deeds after God had established them in the land.

cite it unto mankind at intervals,
and We have revealed it by (successive) revelation.

وَنَزَّلْنَـٰهُ تَنزِيلًا ۝

107   Say: Believe therein or believe not, lo! those who were given
knowledge before it, when it is read
unto them, fall down prostrate on
their faces, adoring;

قُلْ ءَامِنُوا۟ بِهِۦٓ أَوْ لَا تُؤْمِنُوٓا۟ إِنَّ ٱلَّذِينَ أُوتُوا۟ ٱلْعِلْمَ مِن قَبْلِهِۦٓ
إِذَا يُتْلَىٰ عَلَيْهِمْ يَخِرُّونَ لِلْأَذْقَانِ سُجَّدًا ۝

108   Saying: Glory to our Lord!
Verily the promise of our Lord
must be fulfilled.

وَيَقُولُونَ سُبْحَٰنَ رَبِّنَآ إِن كَانَ وَعْدُ رَبِّنَا لَمَفْعُولًا ۝

109   They fall down on their
faces, weeping, and it increaseth
humility in them.

وَيَخِرُّونَ لِلْأَذْقَانِ يَبْكُونَ وَيَزِيدُهُمْ
خُشُوعًا ۩ ۝

110   Say (unto mankind): Cry
unto Allah, or cry unto the Beneficent,[11] unto whichsoever ye cry (it
is the same). His are the most beautiful names. And thou
(Muhammad), be not loud voiced in
thy worship nor yet silent therein,
but follow a way between.

قُلِ ٱدْعُوا۟ ٱللَّهَ أَوِ ٱدْعُوا۟ ٱلرَّحْمَٰنَ أَيًّا مَّا تَدْعُوا۟ فَلَهُ
ٱلْأَسْمَآءُ ٱلْحُسْنَىٰ وَلَا تَجْهَرْ بِصَلَاتِكَ
وَلَا تُخَافِتْ بِهَا وَٱبْتَغِ بَيْنَ ذَٰلِكَ سَبِيلًا ۝

111   And say: Praise be to Allah,
Who hath not taken unto Himself a
son, and Who hath no partner in the
Sovereignty, nor hath He any protecting friend through dependence.
And magnify Him with all magnifi-
cence.

وَقُلِ ٱلْحَمْدُ لِلَّهِ ٱلَّذِى لَمْ يَتَّخِذْ وَلَدًا وَلَمْ يَكُن لَّهُۥ شَرِيكٌ
فِى ٱلْمُلْكِ وَلَمْ يَكُن لَّهُۥ وَلِىٌّ مِّنَ ٱلذُّلِّ وَكَبِّرْهُ تَكْبِيرًا ۝

---

11. The idolaters had a perculiar objection to the name *Ar-Rahmān*, "The
Beneficent," in the Qur'an. They said: "We do not know this Rahmān." Some of them
thought that Ar-Rahmān was a man living in Yamāmah.

Al Kahf
(The Cave)

Al Kahf, "The Cave," takes its name from the story of the youths who took refuge from persecution in a cave (vv. 10-27) and were preserved there as if asleep for a long period—a story which is generally identified by Western writers (e.g. Gibbon) with the legend of the Seven Sleepers of Ephesus. But a strong tradition in the Muslim world asserts that this story and that of Dhū'l Qarnayn ("The Two Horned One"), vv. 83-98, possibly also that of Moses and the angel, vv. 60-82, were revealed to the Prophet to enable him to answer the questions which the Jewish doctors of Yathrib had instructed the idolaters to ask him, as a test of Prophethood.

The questions were three: "Ask him," said the Rabbis, "of some youth who were of old, what was their fate, for they have a strange story; and ask him of a much-travelled man who reached the sunrise regions of the earth and the sunset regions thereof, what was his history; and ask him of the Spirit, what it is."

The tormentors of the Prophet, who had been to Yathrib to get hints from the Jews, on their return to Makkah put these questions to the Prophet, after having told the people that it was to be a crucial test. The Prophet said that he would surely answer them upon the morrow, without adding "if God will," as though he could command God's revelation. As a reproof for that omission, the wished-for revelation was withheld from him for some days, and when it came included the rebuke contained in verse 24.[1] There is no reason whatever to doubt the truth of the tradition which connects this chapter with three questions set by Jewish rabbis, and the answers must have been considered satisfying, or at least silencing, or the Jews would certainly have made fun of them when they were taunting the Prophet daily after his flight to Yathrib (Al-Madīnah). That being so, it would seem rash to identify the story with that of the Christian Seven Sleepers; it must belong, as the

---

1. Ibn Hishām (Cairo edition), Part I, pp. 102, 103.

story of the "Two Horned One" actually does belong, to rabbinical lore. The third of the question is answered in sūrah 17, vv. 85 ff.

It belongs to the middle group of Makkan sūrahs.

سُوْرَةُ الْكَهْفِ

In the name of Allah, the Beneficent, the Merciful.

بِسْمِ اللهِ الرَّحْمٰنِ الرَّحِيمِ

1 Praise be to Allah Who hath revealed the Scripture unto His slave, and hath not placed therein any crookedness;

ٱلْحَمْدُ لِلّٰهِ ٱلَّذِىٓ أَنزَلَ عَلَىٰ عَبْدِهِ ٱلْكِتَٰبَ وَلَمْ يَجْعَل لَّهُۥ عِوَجَاۜ ﴿١﴾

2 (But hath made it) straight, to give warning of stern punishment from Him, and to bring unto the believers who do good works the news that theirs will be a fair reward.

قَيِّمًا لِّيُنذِرَ بَأْسًا شَدِيدًا مِّن لَّدُنْهُ وَيُبَشِّرَ ٱلْمُؤْمِنِينَ ٱلَّذِينَ يَعْمَلُونَ ٱلصَّٰلِحَٰتِ أَنَّ لَهُمْ أَجْرًا حَسَنًا ﴿٢﴾

3 Wherein they will abide forever;

مَّٰكِثِينَ فِيهِ أَبَدًا ﴿٣﴾

4 And to warn those who say: Allah hath chosen a son;

وَيُنذِرَ ٱلَّذِينَ قَالُوا ٱتَّخَذَ ٱللَّهُ وَلَدًا ﴿٤﴾

5 (A thing) whereof they have no knowledge, nor (had) their fathers. Dreadful is the word that cometh out of their mouths. They speak naught but a lie.

مَّا لَهُم بِهِۦ مِنْ عِلْمٍ وَلَا لِءَابَآئِهِمْ كَبُرَتْ كَلِمَةً تَخْرُجُ مِنْ أَفْوَٰهِهِمْ إِن يَقُولُونَ إِلَّا كَذِبًا ﴿٥﴾

6 Yet it may be, if they believe not in this statement, that thou (Muhammad) wilt torment thy soul with grief over their footsteps.

فَلَعَلَّكَ بَٰخِعٌ نَّفْسَكَ عَلَىٰٓ ءَاثَٰرِهِمْ إِن لَّمْ يُؤْمِنُوا بِهَٰذَا ٱلْحَدِيثِ أَسَفًا ﴿٦﴾

7 Lo! We have placed all that is in the earth as an ornament thereof that we may try them: which of them is best in conduct.

إِنَّا جَعَلْنَا مَا عَلَى الْأَرْضِ زِينَةً لَّهَا لِنَبْلُوَهُمْ أَيُّهُمْ أَحْسَنُ عَمَلًا ۝

8 And lo! We shall make all that is therein a barren mound.

وَإِنَّا لَجَاعِلُونَ مَا عَلَيْهَا صَعِيدًا جُرُزًا ۝

9 Or deemest thou that the People of the Cave and the Inscription are a wonder among Our portents?

أَمْ حَسِبْتَ أَنَّ أَصْحَابَ الْكَهْفِ وَالرَّقِيمِ كَانُوا مِنْ ءَايَٰتِنَا عَجَبًا ۝

10 When the young men fled for refuge to the Cave and said: Our Lord! Give us mercy from Thy presence and shape for us right conduct in our plight.

إِذْ أَوَى الْفِتْيَةُ إِلَى الْكَهْفِ فَقَالُوا رَبَّنَا ءَاتِنَا مِن لَّدُنكَ رَحْمَةً وَهَيِّئْ لَنَا مِنْ أَمْرِنَا رَشَدًا ۝

11 Then We sealed up their hearing in the Cave for a number of years.

فَضَرَبْنَا عَلَى ءَاذَانِهِمْ فِي الْكَهْفِ سِنِينَ عَدَدًا ۝

12 And afterward We raised them up that We might know which of the two parties would best calculate the time that they had tarried.

ثُمَّ بَعَثْنَٰهُمْ لِنَعْلَمَ أَيُّ الْحِزْبَيْنِ أَحْصَىٰ لِمَا لَبِثُوا أَمَدًا ۝

13 We narrate unto thee their story with truth. Lo! they were young men who believed in their Lord, and We increased them in guidance.

نَّحْنُ نَقُصُّ عَلَيْكَ نَبَأَهُم بِالْحَقِّ إِنَّهُمْ فِتْيَةٌ ءَامَنُوا بِرَبِّهِمْ وَزِدْنَٰهُمْ هُدًى ۝

14 And We made firm their hearts when they stood forth and said: Our Lord is the Lord of the heavens and the earth. We cry unto no god beside Him, for then should we utter an enormity.

وَرَبَطْنَا عَلَىٰ قُلُوبِهِمْ إِذْ قَامُوا فَقَالُوا رَبُّنَا رَبُّ السَّمَٰوَٰتِ وَالْأَرْضِ لَن نَّدْعُوَا مِن دُونِهِ إِلَٰهًا لَّقَدْ قُلْنَا إِذًا شَطَطًا ۝

15 These, our people, have chosen (other) gods beside Him though they bring no clear warrant (vouchsafed) to them. And who doth greater wrong than he who inventeth a lie concerning Allah?

هَٰٓؤُلَآءِ قَوْمُنَا اتَّخَذُوا مِن دُونِهِ ءَالِهَةً لَّوْلَا يَأْتُونَ عَلَيْهِم بِسُلْطَٰنٍ بَيِّنٍ فَمَنْ أَظْلَمُ مِمَّنِ افْتَرَىٰ عَلَى اللَّهِ كَذِبًا ۝

16 And when ye withdraw from them and that which they worship except Allah, then seek refuge in the Cave; your Lord will spread for you of His mercy and will prepare for you a pillow in your plight.

وَإِذِ اعْتَزَلْتُمُوهُمْ وَمَا يَعْبُدُونَ إِلَّا اللّٰهَ فَأْوُوٓا إِلَى الْكَهْفِ يَنْشُرْ لَكُمْ رَبُّكُمْ مِنْ رَحْمَتِهِ وَيُهَيِّئْ لَكُمْ مِنْ أَمْرِكُمْ مِرْفَقًا ۝

17 And thou mightest have seen the sun when it rose move away from their cave to the right, and when it set go past them on the left, and they were in the cleft thereof. That was (one) of the portents of Allah. He whom Allah guideth, he indeed is led aright, and he whom He sendeth astray, for him thou wilt not find a guiding friend.

۞ وَتَرَى الشَّمْسَ إِذَا طَلَعَت تَّزَٰوَرُ عَن كَهْفِهِمْ ذَاتَ الْيَمِينِ وَإِذَا غَرَبَت تَّقْرِضُهُمْ ذَاتَ الشِّمَالِ وَهُمْ فِي فَجْوَةٍ مِّنْهُ ذَٰلِكَ مِنْ ءَايَٰتِ اللّٰهِ مَن يَهْدِ اللّٰهُ فَهُوَ الْمُهْتَدِ وَمَن يُضْلِلْ فَلَن تَجِدَ لَهُۥ وَلِيًّا مُّرْشِدًا ۝

18 And thou wouldst have deemed them waking though they were asleep, and we caused them to turn over to the right and the left, and their dog stretching out his paws on the threshold. If thou hadst observed them closely thou hadst assuredly turned away from them in flight, and hadst been filled with awe of them.

وَتَحْسَبُهُمْ أَيْقَاظًا وَهُمْ رُقُودٌ وَنُقَلِّبُهُمْ ذَاتَ الْيَمِينِ وَذَاتَ الشِّمَالِ وَكَلْبُهُم بَٰسِطٌ ذِرَاعَيْهِ بِالْوَصِيدِ لَوِ اطَّلَعْتَ عَلَيْهِمْ لَوَلَّيْتَ مِنْهُمْ فِرَارًا وَلَمُلِئْتَ مِنْهُمْ رُعْبًا ۝

19 And in like manner We awakened them that they might question one another. A speaker from among them said: How long have ye tarried? They said: We have tarried a day or some part of a day, (Others) said: Your Lord best knoweth what ye have tarried. Now send one of you, with this, your silver coin unto the city and let him see what food

وَكَذَٰلِكَ بَعَثْنَٰهُمْ لِيَتَسَآءَلُوا بَيْنَهُمْ قَالَ قَآئِلٌ مِّنْهُمْ كَمْ لَبِثْتُمْ قَالُوا لَبِثْنَا يَوْمًا أَوْ بَعْضَ يَوْمٍ قَالُوا رَبُّكُمْ أَعْلَمُ بِمَا لَبِثْتُمْ فَابْعَثُوٓا أَحَدَكُم بِوَرِقِكُمْ هَٰذِهِۦٓ إِلَى الْمَدِينَةِ فَلْيَنظُرْ أَيُّهَآ أَزْكَىٰ

is purest there and bring you a supply thereof. Let him be courteous
and let no man know of you.

20 For they, if they should come to
know of you, will stone you or turn
you back to their religion; then ye
will never prosper.

21 And in like manner We disclosed
them (to the people of the city) that
they might know that the promise of
Allah is true, and that, as for the
Hour, there is no doubt concerning
it. When (the people of the city) disputed of their case among themselves, they said: Build over them a
building; their Lord knoweth best
concerning them. Those who won
their point said: We verily shall
build a place of worship over them.

22 (Some) will say: They were
three, their dog the fourth, and
(some) say: Five, their dog the sixth,
guessing at random; and (some) say:
Seven, and their dog the eighth. Say
(O Muhammad): My Lord is best
aware of their number. None knoweth them save a few. So contend not
concerning them except with an outward contending, and ask not any of
them to pronounce concerning them.

23 And say not of anything: Lo! I
shall do that tomorrow;

24 Except if Allah will. And remember thy Lord when thou forgettest,
and say: It may be that my Lord

طَعَامًا فَلْيَأْتِكُمْ بِرِزْقٍ مِنْهُ وَلْيَتَلَطَّفْ
وَلَا يُشْعِرَنَّ بِكُمْ أَحَدًا ﴿١٩﴾

إِنَّهُمْ إِنْ يَظْهَرُوا عَلَيْكُمْ يَرْجُمُوكُمْ
أَوْ يُعِيدُوكُمْ فِي مِلَّتِهِمْ
وَلَنْ تُفْلِحُوا إِذًا أَبَدًا ﴿٢٠﴾

وَكَذَٰلِكَ أَعْثَرْنَا عَلَيْهِمْ لِيَعْلَمُوا أَنَّ وَعْدَ
اللَّهِ حَقٌّ وَأَنَّ السَّاعَةَ لَا رَيْبَ فِيهَا إِذْ يَتَنَازَعُونَ
بَيْنَهُمْ أَمْرَهُمْ فَقَالُوا ابْنُوا عَلَيْهِمْ بُنْيَانًا رَبُّهُمْ
أَعْلَمُ بِهِمْ قَالَ الَّذِينَ غَلَبُوا عَلَىٰ أَمْرِهِمْ
لَنَتَّخِذَنَّ عَلَيْهِمْ مَسْجِدًا ﴿٢١﴾

سَيَقُولُونَ ثَلَاثَةٌ رَابِعُهُمْ كَلْبُهُمْ وَيَقُولُونَ
خَمْسَةٌ سَادِسُهُمْ كَلْبُهُمْ رَجْمًا بِالْغَيْبِ وَيَقُولُونَ
سَبْعَةٌ وَثَامِنُهُمْ كَلْبُهُمْ قُلْ رَبِّي أَعْلَمُ بِعِدَّتِهِمْ
مَا يَعْلَمُهُمْ إِلَّا قَلِيلٌ فَلَا تُمَارِ فِيهِمْ إِلَّا مِرَاءً ظَاهِرًا
وَلَا تَسْتَفْتِ فِيهِمْ مِنْهُمْ أَحَدًا ﴿٢٢﴾

وَلَا تَقُولَنَّ لِشَيْءٍ إِنِّي فَاعِلٌ ذَٰلِكَ غَدًا ﴿٢٣﴾

إِلَّا أَنْ يَشَاءَ اللَّهُ وَاذْكُرْ رَبَّكَ إِذَا نَسِيتَ وَقُلْ

guideth me unto a nearer way of truth than this.

25 And (it is said) they tarried in their Cave three hundred years and add nine.

عَسَىٰٓ أَن يَهْدِيَنِ رَبِّى لِأَقْرَبَ مِنْ هَٰذَا رَشَدًا ﴿٢٤﴾

وَلَبِثُوا۟ فِى كَهْفِهِمْ ثَلَٰثَ مِا۟ئَةٍ سِنِينَ وَازْدَادُوا۟ تِسْعًا ﴿٢٥﴾

26 Say: Allah is best aware how long they tarried. His is the Invisible of the heavens and the earth. How clear of sight is He and keen of hearing! They have no protecting friend beside Him, and He maketh none to share in His government.

قُلِ ٱللَّهُ أَعْلَمُ بِمَا لَبِثُوا۟ لَهُۥ غَيْبُ ٱلسَّمَٰوَٰتِ وَٱلْأَرْضِ أَبْصِرْ بِهِۦ وَأَسْمِعْ مَا لَهُم مِّن دُونِهِۦ مِن وَلِىٍّ وَلَا يُشْرِكُ فِى حُكْمِهِۦٓ أَحَدًا ﴿٢٦﴾

27 And recite that which hath been revealed unto thee of the scripture of thy Lord. There is none who can change His words, and thou wilt find no refuge beside Him.

وَٱتْلُ مَآ أُوحِىَ إِلَيْكَ مِن كِتَابِ رَبِّكَ لَا مُبَدِّلَ لِكَلِمَٰتِهِۦ وَلَن تَجِدَ مِن دُونِهِۦ مُلْتَحَدًا ﴿٢٧﴾

28 Restrain thyself along with those who cry unto their Lord at morn and evening, seeking His countenance; and let not thine eyes overlook them, desiring the pomp of the life of the world; and obey not him whose heart We have made heedless of Our remembrance, who followeth his own lust and whose case hath been abandoned.

وَٱصْبِرْ نَفْسَكَ مَعَ ٱلَّذِينَ يَدْعُونَ رَبَّهُم بِٱلْغَدَوٰةِ وَٱلْعَشِىِّ يُرِيدُونَ وَجْهَهُۥ وَلَا تَعْدُ عَيْنَاكَ عَنْهُمْ تُرِيدُ زِينَةَ ٱلْحَيَوٰةِ ٱلدُّنْيَا وَلَا تُطِعْ مَنْ أَغْفَلْنَا قَلْبَهُۥ عَن ذِكْرِنَا وَٱتَّبَعَ هَوَىٰهُ وَكَانَ أَمْرُهُۥ فُرُطًا ﴿٢٨﴾

29 Say: (It is) the truth from the Lord of you (all). Then whosoever will, let him believe, and whosoever will, let him disbelieve. Lo! We have prepared for disbelievers Fire. Its tent encloseth them. If they ask for showers, they will be showered with water like to molten lead which burneth the faces. Calamitous

وَقُلِ ٱلْحَقُّ مِن رَّبِّكُمْ فَمَن شَآءَ فَلْيُؤْمِن وَمَن شَآءَ فَلْيَكْفُرْ إِنَّآ أَعْتَدْنَا لِلظَّٰلِمِينَ نَارًا أَحَاطَ بِهِمْ سُرَادِقُهَا وَإِن يَسْتَغِيثُوا۟ يُغَاثُوا۟ بِمَآءٍ كَٱلْمُهْلِ يَشْوِى ٱلْوُجُوهَ بِئْسَ ٱلشَّرَابُ

the drink and ill the resting-place!

30 Lo! as for those who believe and do good works—Lo! We suffer not the reward of one whose work is goodly to be lost.

وَسَآءَتْ مُرْتَفَقًا ۝

إِنَّ الَّذِينَ ءَامَنُوا وَعَمِلُوا الصَّٰلِحَٰتِ إِنَّا لَا نُضِيعُ أَجْرَ مَنْ أَحْسَنَ عَمَلًا ۝

31 As for such, theirs will be Gardens of Eden, wherein rivers flow beneath them; therein they will be given armlets of gold and will wear green robes of finest silk and gold embroidery, reclining upon thrones therein. Blest the reward, and fair the resting place!

أُولَٰٓئِكَ لَهُمْ جَنَّٰتُ عَدْنٍ تَجْرِى مِن تَحْتِهِمُ الْأَنْهَٰرُ يُحَلَّوْنَ فِيهَا مِنْ أَسَاوِرَ مِن ذَهَبٍ وَيَلْبَسُونَ ثِيَابًا خُضْرًا مِّن سُندُسٍ وَإِسْتَبْرَقٍ مُّتَّكِئِينَ فِيهَا عَلَى الْأَرَآئِكِ نِعْمَ الثَّوَابُ وَحَسُنَتْ مُرْتَفَقًا ۝

32 Coin for them a similitude: Two men, unto one of whom We had assigned two gardens of grapes, and We had surrounded both with date palms and had put between them tillage.

وَاضْرِبْ لَهُم مَّثَلًا رَّجُلَيْنِ جَعَلْنَا لِأَحَدِهِمَا جَنَّتَيْنِ مِنْ أَعْنَٰبٍ وَحَفَفْنَٰهُمَا بِنَخْلٍ وَجَعَلْنَا بَيْنَهُمَا زَرْعًا ۝

33 Each of the gardens gave its fruit and withheld naught thereof. And We caused a river to gush forth therein.

كِلْتَا الْجَنَّتَيْنِ ءَاتَتْ أُكُلَهَا وَلَمْ تَظْلِم مِّنْهُ شَيْئًا وَفَجَّرْنَا خِلَٰلَهُمَا نَهَرًا ۝

34 And he had fruit. And he said unto his comrade, when he spake with him: I am more than thee in wealth, and stronger in respect of men.

وَكَانَ لَهُۥ ثَمَرٌ فَقَالَ لِصَٰحِبِهِۦ وَهُوَ يُحَاوِرُهُۥٓ أَنَا۠ أَكْثَرُ مِنكَ مَالًا وَأَعَزُّ نَفَرًا ۝

35 And he went into his garden, while he (thus) wronged himself. He said: I think not that all this will ever perish.

وَدَخَلَ جَنَّتَهُۥ وَهُوَ ظَالِمٌ لِّنَفْسِهِۦ قَالَ مَآ أَظُنُّ أَن تَبِيدَ هَٰذِهِۦٓ أَبَدًا ۝

36 I think not that the Hour will ever come, and if indeed I am brought back unto my Lord, I surely shall find better than this as a resort.

وَمَآ أَظُنُّ السَّاعَةَ قَآئِمَةً وَلَئِن رُّدِدتُّ إِلَىٰ رَبِّى لَأَجِدَنَّ خَيْرًا مِّنْهَا مُنقَلَبًا ۝

37 And his comrade, while he disputed with him, exclaimed: Disbelievest thou in Him Who created thee of dust, then of a drop (of seed), and then fashioned thee a man?

قَالَ لَهُۥ صَاحِبُهُۥ وَهُوَ يُحَاوِرُهُۥٓ أَكَفَرْتَ بِٱلَّذِى خَلَقَكَ مِن تُرَابٍ ثُمَّ مِن نُّطْفَةٍ ثُمَّ سَوَّىٰكَ رَجُلًا ٣٧

38 But He is Allah, my Lord, and I ascribe unto my Lord no partner.

لَّكِنَّا۠ هُوَ ٱللَّهُ رَبِّى وَلَآ أُشْرِكُ بِرَبِّىٓ أَحَدًا ٣٨

39 If only, when thou enteredst thy garden, thou hadst said: That which Allah wilteth (will come to pass)! There is no strength save in Allah! Though thou seest me as less than thee in wealth and children.

وَلَوْلَآ إِذْ دَخَلْتَ جَنَّتَكَ قُلْتَ مَا شَآءَ ٱللَّهُ لَا قُوَّةَ إِلَّا بِٱللَّهِ إِن تَرَنِ أَنَا۠ أَقَلَّ مِنكَ مَالًا وَوَلَدًا ٣٩

40 Yet it may be that my Lord will give me better than thy garden, and will send on it a bolt from heaven, and some morning it will be a smooth hillside;

فَعَسَىٰ رَبِّىٓ أَن يُؤْتِيَنِ خَيْرًا مِّن جَنَّتِكَ وَيُرْسِلَ عَلَيْهَا حُسْبَانًا مِّنَ ٱلسَّمَآءِ فَتُصْبِحَ صَعِيدًا زَلَقًا ٤٠

41 Or some morning the water thereof will he lost in the earth so that thou canst not make search for it.

أَوْ يُصْبِحَ مَآؤُهَا غَوْرًا فَلَن تَسْتَطِيعَ لَهُۥ طَلَبًا ٤١

42 And his fruit was beset (with destruction). Then began he to wring his hands for all that he had spent upon it, when (now) it was all ruined on its trellises, and to say: Would that I had ascribed no partner to my Lord!

وَأُحِيطَ بِثَمَرِهِۦ فَأَصْبَحَ يُقَلِّبُ كَفَّيْهِ عَلَىٰ مَآ أَنفَقَ فِيهَا وَهِىَ خَاوِيَةٌ عَلَىٰ عُرُوشِهَا وَيَقُولُ يَٰلَيْتَنِى لَمْ أُشْرِكْ بِرَبِّىٓ أَحَدًا ٤٢

43 And he had no troop (of men) to help him against Allah, nor could he save himself.

وَلَمْ تَكُن لَّهُۥ فِئَةٌ يَنصُرُونَهُۥ مِن دُونِ ٱللَّهِ وَمَا كَانَ مُنتَصِرًا ٤٣

44 In this case is protection only from Allah, the True. He is best for reward, and best for consequence.

هُنَالِكَ ٱلْوَلَٰيَةُ لِلَّهِ ٱلْحَقِّ هُوَ خَيْرٌ ثَوَابًا وَخَيْرٌ عُقْبًا ٤٤

45 And coin for them the similitude of the life of the world as water which We send down from the sky, and the vegetation of the earth mingleth with it and then becometh dry twigs that the winds scatter. Allah is Able to do all things.

وَاضْرِبْ لَهُمْ مَثَلَ الْحَيَوةِ الدُّنْيَا كَمَاءٍ أَنْزَلْنَهُ مِنَ السَّمَاءِ فَاخْتَلَطَ بِهِ نَبَاتُ الْأَرْضِ فَأَصْبَحَ هَشِيمًا تَذْرُوهُ الرِّيَحُ وَكَانَ اللَّهُ عَلَى كُلِّ شَيْءٍ مُقْتَدِرًا ۝

46 Wealth and children are an ornament of life of the world. But the good deeds which endure are better in thy Lord's sight for reward, and better in respect of hope.

الْمَالُ وَالْبَنُونَ زِينَةُ الْحَيَوةِ الدُّنْيَا وَالْبَقِيَتُ الصَّلِحَتُ خَيْرٌ عِنْدَ رَبِّكَ ثَوَابًا وَخَيْرٌ أَمَلًا ۝

47 And (bethink you of) the Day when We remove the hills and ye see the earth emerging, and We gather them together so as to leave not one of them behind.

وَيَوْمَ نُسَيِّرُ الْجِبَالَ وَتَرَى الْأَرْضَ بَارِزَةً وَحَشَرْنَهُمْ فَلَمْ نُغَادِرْ مِنْهُمْ أَحَدًا ۝

48 And they are set before thy Lord in ranks (and it is said unto them): Now verily have ye come unto Us as We created you at the first. But ye thought that We had set no tryst for you.

وَعُرِضُوا عَلَى رَبِّكَ صَفًّا لَقَدْ جِئْتُمُونَا كَمَا خَلَقْنَكُمْ أَوَّلَ مَرَّةٍ بَلْ زَعَمْتُمْ أَلَّنْ نَجْعَلَ لَكُمْ مَوْعِدًا ۝

49 And the Book is placed, and thou seest the guilty fearful of that which is therein, and they say: What kind of a book is this that leaveth not a small thing nor a great thing but hath counted it! And they find all that they did confronting them, and thy Lord wrongeth no one.

وَوُضِعَ الْكِتَبُ فَتَرَى الْمُجْرِمِينَ مُشْفِقِينَ مِمَّا فِيهِ وَيَقُولُونَ يَوَيْلَتَنَا مَالِ هَذَا الْكِتَبِ لَا يُغَادِرُ صَغِيرَةً وَلَا كَبِيرَةً إِلَّا أَحْصَنَهَا وَوَجَدُوا مَا عَمِلُوا حَاضِرًا وَلَا يَظْلِمُ رَبُّكَ أَحَدًا ۝

50 And (remember) when We said unto the angels: Fall prostrate before Adam, and they fell prostrate,

وَإِذْ قُلْنَا لِلْمَلَئِكَةِ اسْجُدُوا لِأَدَمَ فَسَجَدُوا

all save Iblīs. He was of the Jinn,[2] so he rebelled against his Lord's command. Will ye choose him and his seed for your protecting friends instead of Me, when they are an enemy unto you? Calamitous is the exchange for evil-doers!

إِلَّا إِبْلِيسَ كَانَ مِنَ ٱلْجِنِّ فَفَسَقَ عَنْ أَمْرِ رَبِّهِۦٓ أَفَتَتَّخِذُونَهُۥ وَذُرِّيَّتَهُۥٓ أَوْلِيَآءَ مِن دُونِى وَهُمْ لَكُمْ عَدُوٌّۢ بِئْسَ لِلظَّـٰلِمِينَ بَدَلًا ٥٠

51 I made them not to witness the creation of the heavens and the earth, nor their own creation; nor choose I misleaders for (My) helpers.

۞ مَّآ أَشْهَدتُّهُمْ خَلْقَ ٱلسَّمَـٰوَٰتِ وَٱلْأَرْضِ وَلَا خَلْقَ أَنفُسِهِمْ وَمَا كُنتُ مُتَّخِذَ ٱلْمُضِلِّينَ عَضُدًا ٥١

52 And (be mindful of) the Day when He will say: Call those partners of Mine whom ye pretended. Then they will cry unto them, but they will not hear their prayer, and We shall set a gulf of doom between them.

وَيَوْمَ يَقُولُ نَادُوا شُرَكَآءِىَ ٱلَّذِينَ زَعَمْتُمْ فَدَعَوْهُمْ فَلَمْ يَسْتَجِيبُوا لَهُمْ وَجَعَلْنَا بَيْنَهُم مَّوْبِقًا ٥٢

53 And the guilty behold the Fire and know that they are about to fall therein, and they find no way of escape thence.

وَرَءَا ٱلْمُجْرِمُونَ ٱلنَّارَ فَظَنُّوٓا أَنَّهُم مُّوَاقِعُوهَا وَلَمْ يَجِدُوا عَنْهَا مَصْرِفًا ٥٣

54 And verily We have displayed for mankind in this Qur'an all manner of similitudes, but man is more than anything contentious.

وَلَقَدْ صَرَّفْنَا فِى هَـٰذَا ٱلْقُرْءَانِ لِلنَّاسِ مِن كُلِّ مَثَلٍ وَكَانَ ٱلْإِنسَـٰنُ أَكْثَرَ شَىْءٍ جَدَلًا ٥٤

55 And naught hindereth mankind from believing when the guidance cometh unto them, and from asking forgiveness of their Lord, unless (it

وَمَا مَنَعَ ٱلنَّاسَ أَن يُؤْمِنُوٓا إِذْ جَآءَهُمُ ٱلْهُدَىٰ وَيَسْتَغْفِرُوا رَبَّهُمْ إِلَّآ أَن تَأْتِيَهُمْ سُنَّةُ

---

2. The fact that Iblīs or Satan is of the Jinn and not of the angels, though he was among the latter, explains his disobedience; since Jinn, like men, can choose their path of conduct.

be that they wish) that the judgment of the men of old should come upon them or (that) they should be confronted with the Doom.

56 We send not the messengers save as bearers of good news and warners. Those who disbelieve contend with falsehood in order to refute the Truth thereby. And they take Our revelations and that wherewith they are threatened as a jest.

57 And who doth greater wrong than he who hath been reminded of the revelations of his Lord, yet turneth away from them and forgetteth what his hands send forward (to the Judgment)? Lo! on their hearts We have placed coverings so that they understand not, and in their ears a deafness. And though thou call them to the guidance, in that case they can never be led aright.

58 Thy Lord is the Forgiver, Full of Mercy. If He took them to task (now) for what they earn, He would hasten on the doom for them; but their is an appointed term from which they will find no escape.

59 And (all) those townships! We destroyed them when they did wrong, and We appointed a fixed time for their destruction.

60 And when Moses said unto his servant: I will not give up until I reach the point where the two rivers meet, though I march on for ages.

61 And when they reached the point where the two met, they forgot their fish, and it took its way into the waters, being free.

فَلَمَّا بَلَغَا مَجْمَعَ بَيْنِهِمَا نَسِيَا حُوتَهُمَا فَاتَّخَذَ سَبِيلَهُ فِى الْبَحْرِ سَرَبًا ۝

62 And when they had gone further, he said unto his servant: Bring us our breakfast. Verily we have found fatigue in this our journey.

فَلَمَّا جَاوَزَا قَالَ لِفَتَـٰهُ ءَاتِنَا غَدَآءَنَا لَقَدْ لَقِينَا مِن سَفَرِنَا هَـٰذَا نَصَبًا ۝

63 He said: Didst thou see, when we took refuge on the rock, and I forgot the fish and none but Satan caused me to forget to mention it; it took its way into the waters by a marvel.

قَالَ أَرَءَيْتَ إِذْ أَوَيْنَآ إِلَى الصَّخْرَةِ فَإِنِّى نَسِيتُ الْحُوتَ وَمَآ أَنسَىٰنِيهُ إِلَّا الشَّيْطَـٰنُ أَنْ أَذْكُرَهُ ۚ وَاتَّخَذَ سَبِيلَهُ فِى الْبَحْرِ عَجَبًا ۝

64 He said: This is that which we have been seeking. So they retraced their steps again.

قَالَ ذَٰلِكَ مَا كُنَّا نَبْغِ فَارْتَدَّا عَلَىٰٓ ءَاثَارِهِمَا قَصَصًا ۝

65 Then found they one of Our slaves, unto whom We had given mercy from Us, and had taught him knowledge from Our presence.

فَوَجَدَا عَبْدًا مِّنْ عِبَادِنَآ ءَاتَيْنَـٰهُ رَحْمَةً مِّنْ عِندِنَا وَعَلَّمْنَـٰهُ مِن لَّدُنَّا عِلْمًا ۝

66 Moses said unto him: May I follow thee, to the end that thou mayst teach me right conduct of that which thou hast been taught?

قَالَ لَهُ مُوسَىٰ هَلْ أَتَّبِعُكَ عَلَىٰٓ أَن تُعَلِّمَنِ مِمَّا عُلِّمْتَ رُشْدًا ۝

67 He said: Lo! thou canst not bear with me.

قَالَ إِنَّكَ لَن تَسْتَطِيعَ مَعِىَ صَبْرًا ۝

68 How canst thou bear with that whereof thou canst not compass any knowledge?

وَكَيْفَ تَصْبِرُ عَلَىٰ مَا لَمْ تُحِطْ بِهِ خُبْرًا ۝

69 He said: Allah willing, thou, shalt find me patient and I shall not in aught gainsay thee.

قَالَ سَتَجِدُنِى إِن شَآءَ اللَّهُ صَابِرًا وَلَآ أَعْصِى لَكَ أَمْرًا ۝

70 He said: Well, if thou go with me, ask me not concerning aught

قَالَ فَإِنِ اتَّبَعْتَنِى فَلَا تَسْـَٔلْنِى عَن شَىْءٍ

till I myself mention of it unto thee.

71 So the twain set out till, when they were in the ship, he made a hole therein. (Moses) said: Hast thou made a hole therein to drown the folk thereof? Thou verily hast done a dreadful thing.

72 He said: Did I not tell thee thou couldst not bear with me?

73 (Moses) said: Be not wroth with me that I forgot, and be not hard upon me for my fault.

74 So the twain journeyed on till, when they met a lad, he slew him. (Moses) said: What! Hast thou slain an innocent soul who hath slain no man? Verily thou hast done a horrid thing.

75 He said: Did I not tell thee that thou couldst not bear with me?

76 (Moses) said: If I ask thee after this concerning aught, keep not company with me. Thou hast received an excuse from me.

77 So they twain journeyed on till, when they came unto the folk of a certain township, they asked its folk for food, but they refused to make them guests. And they found therein a wall upon the point of falling into ruin, and he repaired it. (Moses) said: If thou hadst wished, thou couldst have taken payment for it.

78 He said: This is the parting between thee and me! I will announce

حَتّٰىٓ أُحْدِثَ لَكَ مِنْهُ ذِكْرًا ۝

فَانْطَلَقَا ۚ حَتّٰىٓ إِذَا رَكِبَا فِى السَّفِيْنَةِ خَرَقَهَا ۖ قَالَ أَخَرَقْتَهَا لِتُغْرِقَ أَهْلَهَا ۚ لَقَدْ جِئْتَ شَيْئًا إِمْرًا ۝

قَالَ أَلَمْ أَقُلْ إِنَّكَ لَنْ تَسْتَطِيعَ مَعِيَ صَبْرًا ۝

قَالَ لَا تُؤَاخِذْنِيْ بِمَا نَسِيْتُ وَلَا تُرْهِقْنِيْ مِنْ أَمْرِيْ عُسْرًا ۝

فَانْطَلَقَا ۚ حَتّٰىٓ إِذَا لَقِيَا غُلَامًا فَقَتَلَهُ ۖ قَالَ أَقَتَلْتَ نَفْسًا زَكِيَّةً بِغَيْرِ نَفْسٍ ۚ لَقَدْ جِئْتَ شَيْئًا نُكْرًا ۝

۞ قَالَ أَلَمْ أَقُلْ لَكَ إِنَّكَ لَنْ تَسْتَطِيعَ مَعِيَ صَبْرًا ۝

قَالَ إِنْ سَأَلْتُكَ عَنْ شَيْءٍ بَعْدَهَا فَلَا تُصَاحِبْنِيْ ۖ قَدْ بَلَغْتَ مِنْ لَدُنِّيْ عُذْرًا ۝

فَانْطَلَقَا ۚ حَتّٰىٓ إِذَآ أَتَيَآ أَهْلَ قَرْيَةٍ اسْتَطْعَمَآ أَهْلَهَا فَأَبَوْا أَنْ يُضَيِّفُوْهُمَا فَوَجَدَا فِيْهَا جِدَارًا يُرِيْدُ أَنْ يَنْقَضَّ فَأَقَامَهُ ۖ قَالَ لَوْ شِئْتَ لَتَّخَذْتَ عَلَيْهِ أَجْرًا ۝

قَالَ هٰذَا فِرَاقُ بَيْنِيْ وَبَيْنِكَ ۚ سَأُنَبِّئُكَ بِتَأْوِيْلِ

unto thee the interpretation of that thou couldst not bear with patience.

79 As for the ship, it belonged to poor people working on the river,[3] and I wished to mar it, for there was a king behind them who is taking every ship by force.

80 And as for the lad, his parents were believers and We feared lest he should oppress them by rebellion and disbelief.

81 And We intended that their Lord should change him for them for one better in purity and nearer to mercy.

82 And as for the wall, it belonged to two orphan boys in the city, and there was beneath it a treasure belonging to them and their father had been righteous, and thy Lord intended that they should come to their full strength and should bring forth their treasure as a mercy from their Lord; and I did it not upon my own command. Such is the interpretation of that wherewith thou couldst not bear.

83 They will ask thee of Dhū'l Qarnayn. Say: I shall recite unto you a remembrance of him.

84 Lo! We made him strong in the land and gave him unto everything a road.

85 And he followed a road;

مَا لَمْ تَسْتَطِعْ عَلَيْهِ صَبْرًا ۝

أَمَّا السَّفِينَةُ فَكَانَتْ لِمَسَاكِينَ يَعْمَلُونَ فِي الْبَحْرِ فَأَرَدْتُّ أَنْ أَعِيبَهَا وَكَانَ وَرَاءَهُمْ مَّلِكٌ يَأْخُذُ كُلَّ سَفِينَةٍ غَصْبًا ۝

وَأَمَّا الْغُلَامُ فَكَانَ أَبَوَاهُ مُؤْمِنَيْنِ فَخَشِينَآ أَنْ يُرْهِقَهُمَا طُغْيَانًا وَكُفْرًا ۝

فَأَرَدْنَآ أَنْ يُبْدِلَهُمَا رَبُّهُمَا خَيْرًا مِّنْهُ زَكَاةً وَأَقْرَبَ رُحْمًا ۝

وَأَمَّا الْجِدَارُ فَكَانَ لِغُلَامَيْنِ يَتِيمَيْنِ فِي الْمَدِينَةِ وَكَانَ تَحْتَهُ كَنْزٌ لَهُمَا وَكَانَ أَبُوهُمَا صَالِحًا فَأَرَادَ رَبُّكَ أَنْ يَبْلُغَا أَشُدَّهُمَا وَيَسْتَخْرِجَا كَنْزَهُمَا رَحْمَةً مِّنْ رَبِّكَ وَمَا فَعَلْتُهُ عَنْ أَمْرِي ذَلِكَ تَأْوِيلُ مَا لَمْ تَسْطِع عَّلَيْهِ صَبْرًا ۝

وَيَسْأَلُونَكَ عَنْ ذِي الْقَرْنَيْنِ قُلْ سَأَتْلُوا عَلَيْكُمْ مِّنْهُ ذِكْرًا ۝

إِنَّا مَكَّنَّا لَهُ فِي الْأَرْضِ وَآتَيْنَاهُ مِنْ كُلِّ شَيْءٍ سَبَبًا ۝

فَأَتْبَعَ سَبَبًا ۝

---

3. Or, it might be, "sea."

86 Till, when he reached the setting place of the sun, he found it setting in a muddy spring, and found a people thereabout: We said: O Dhū'l Qarnayn! Either punish or show them kindness.

حَتَّىٰٓ إِذَا بَلَغَ مَغْرِبَ ٱلشَّمْسِ وَجَدَهَا تَغْرُبُ فِى عَيْنٍ حَمِئَةٍ وَوَجَدَ عِندَهَا قَوْمًا قُلْنَا يَٰذَا ٱلْقَرْنَيْنِ إِمَّآ أَن تُعَذِّبَ وَإِمَّآ أَن تَتَّخِذَ فِيهِمْ حُسْنًا ﴿٨٦﴾

87 He said: As for him who doeth wrong, we shall punish him, and then he will be brought back unto his Lord, Who will punish him with awful punishment!

قَالَ أَمَّا مَن ظَلَمَ فَسَوْفَ نُعَذِّبُهُۥ ثُمَّ يُرَدُّ إِلَىٰ رَبِّهِۦ فَيُعَذِّبُهُۥ عَذَابًا نُّكْرًا ﴿٨٧﴾

88 But as for him who believeth and doeth right, good will be his reward, and We shall speak unto him a mild command.

وَأَمَّا مَنْ ءَامَنَ وَعَمِلَ صَٰلِحًا فَلَهُۥ جَزَآءً ٱلْحُسْنَىٰ وَسَنَقُولُ لَهُۥ مِنْ أَمْرِنَا يُسْرًا ﴿٨٨﴾

89 Then he followed a road;

ثُمَّ أَتْبَعَ سَبَبًا ﴿٨٩﴾

90 Till, when he reached the rising-place of the sun, he found it rising on a people for whom We had appointed no shelter therefrom.

حَتَّىٰٓ إِذَا بَلَغَ مَطْلِعَ ٱلشَّمْسِ وَجَدَهَا تَطْلُعُ عَلَىٰ قَوْمٍ لَّمْ نَجْعَل لَّهُم مِّن دُونِهَا سِتْرًا ﴿٩٠﴾

91 So (it was). And We knew all concerning him.

كَذَٰلِكَ وَقَدْ أَحَطْنَا بِمَا لَدَيْهِ خُبْرًا ﴿٩١﴾

92 Then he followed a road;

ثُمَّ أَتْبَعَ سَبَبًا ﴿٩٢﴾

93 Till, when he came between the two mountains, he found upon their hither side a folk that scarce could understand a saying.

حَتَّىٰٓ إِذَا بَلَغَ بَيْنَ ٱلسَّدَّيْنِ وَجَدَ مِن دُونِهِمَا قَوْمًا لَّا يَكَادُونَ يَفْقَهُونَ قَوْلًا ﴿٩٣﴾

94 They said: O Dhū'l Qarnayn! Lo! Gog and Magog are spoiling the land. So may we pay thee tribute on condition that thou set a barrier between us and them?

قَالُوا۟ يَٰذَا ٱلْقَرْنَيْنِ إِنَّ يَأْجُوجَ وَمَأْجُوجَ مُفْسِدُونَ فِى ٱلْأَرْضِ فَهَلْ نَجْعَلُ لَكَ خَرْجًا عَلَىٰٓ أَن تَجْعَلَ بَيْنَنَا وَبَيْنَهُمْ سَدًّا ﴿٩٤﴾

95 He said: That wherein my Lord hath established me better (than your tribute). Do but help me with

قَالَ مَا مَكَّنِّى فِيهِ رَبِّى خَيْرٌ فَأَعِينُونِى بِقُوَّةٍ أَجْعَلْ بَيْنَكُمْ

strength (of men), I will set between you and them a bank.

96 Give me pieces of iron—till, when he had levelled up (the gap) between the cliffs, he said: Blow!—till, when he had made it a fire, he said: Bring me molten copper to pour thereon.

97 And (Gog and Magog) were not able to surmount, nor could they pierce (it).

98 He said: This is a mercy from my Lord; but when the promise of my Lord cometh to pass, He will lay it low, for the promise of my Lord is true.

99 And on that day We shall let some of them surge against others, and the Trumpet will be blown. Then We shall gather them together in one gathering.

100 On that day We shall present hell to the disbelievers, plain to view;

101 Those whose eyes were hoodwinked from My reminder, and who could not bear to hear.

102 Do the disbelievers reckon that they can choose My bondmen as protecting friends beside Me? Lo! We have prepared hell as a welcome for the disbelievers.

103 Say: Shall We inform you who will be the greatest losers by their works?

وَبَيْنَهُمْ رَدْمًا ﴿٩٥﴾

ءَاتُونِى زُبَرَ ٱلْحَدِيدِ حَتَّىٰٓ إِذَا سَاوَىٰ بَيْنَ ٱلصَّدَفَيْنِ قَالَ ٱنفُخُوا حَتَّىٰٓ إِذَا جَعَلَهُۥ نَارًا قَالَ ءَاتُونِىٓ أُفْرِغْ عَلَيْهِ قِطْرًا ﴿٩٦﴾

فَمَا ٱسْطَٰعُوٓا أَن يَظْهَرُوهُ وَمَا ٱسْتَطَٰعُوا لَهُۥ نَقْبًا ﴿٩٧﴾

قَالَ هَٰذَا رَحْمَةٌ مِّن رَّبِّى فَإِذَا جَآءَ وَعْدُ رَبِّى جَعَلَهُۥ دَكَّآءَ وَكَانَ وَعْدُ رَبِّى حَقًّا ﴿٩٨﴾

۞ وَتَرَكْنَا بَعْضَهُمْ يَوْمَئِذٍ يَمُوجُ فِى بَعْضٍ وَنُفِخَ فِى ٱلصُّورِ فَجَمَعْنَٰهُمْ جَمْعًا ﴿٩٩﴾

وَعَرَضْنَا جَهَنَّمَ يَوْمَئِذٍ لِّلْكَٰفِرِينَ عَرْضًا ﴿١٠٠﴾

ٱلَّذِينَ كَانَتْ أَعْيُنُهُمْ فِى غِطَآءٍ عَن ذِكْرِى وَكَانُوا لَا يَسْتَطِيعُونَ سَمْعًا ﴿١٠١﴾

أَفَحَسِبَ ٱلَّذِينَ كَفَرُوٓا أَن يَتَّخِذُوا عِبَادِى مِن دُونِىٓ أَوْلِيَآءَ إِنَّآ أَعْتَدْنَا جَهَنَّمَ لِلْكَٰفِرِينَ نُزُلًا ﴿١٠٢﴾

قُلْ هَلْ نُنَبِّئُكُم بِٱلْأَخْسَرِينَ أَعْمَٰلًا ﴿١٠٣﴾

104   Those whose effort goeth astray in the life of the world, and yet they reckon that they do good work.

اَلَّذِيْنَ ضَلَّ سَعْيُهُمْ فِى الْحَيَوةِ الدُّنْيَا وَهُمْ يَحْسَبُوْنَ اَنَّهُمْ يُحْسِنُوْنَ صُنْعًا ۝

105   Those are they who disbelieve in the revelations of their Lord and in the meeting with Him. Therefore their works are vain, and on the Day of Resurrection We assign no weight to them.

اُولٰٓئِكَ الَّذِيْنَ كَفَرُوْا بِاٰيٰتِ رَبِّهِمْ وَلِقَآئِهٖ فَحَبِطَتْ اَعْمَالُهُمْ فَلَا نُقِيْمُ لَهُمْ يَوْمَ الْقِيٰمَةِ وَزْنًا ۝

106   That is their reward: hell, because they disbelieved, and made a jest of Our revelations and Our messengers.

ذٰلِكَ جَزَآؤُهُمْ جَهَنَّمُ بِمَا كَفَرُوْا وَاتَّخَذُوْا اٰيٰتِىْ وَرُسُلِىْ هُزُوًا ۝

107   Lo! those who believe and do good works, theirs are the Gardens of Paradise for welcome;

اِنَّ الَّذِيْنَ اٰمَنُوْا وَعَمِلُوا الصّٰلِحٰتِ كَانَتْ لَهُمْ جَنّٰتُ الْفِرْدَوْسِ نُزُلًا ۝

108   Wherein they will abide, with no desire to be removed from thence.

خٰلِدِيْنَ فِيْهَا لَا يَبْغُوْنَ عَنْهَا حِوَلًا ۝

109   Say: Though the sea became ink for the Words of my Lord, verily the sea would be used up before the Words of my Lord were exhausted, even though We brought the like thereof to help.

قُلْ لَّوْ كَانَ الْبَحْرُ مِدَادًا لِّكَلِمٰتِ رَبِّىْ لَنَفِدَ الْبَحْرُ قَبْلَ اَنْ تَنْفَدَ كَلِمٰتُ رَبِّىْ وَلَوْ جِئْنَا بِمِثْلِهٖ مَدَدًا ۝

110   Say: I am only a mortal like you. My Lord inspireth in me that your God is only One God. And whoever hopeth for the meeting with his Lord, let him do righteous work, and make none sharer of the worship due unto his Lord.

قُلْ اِنَّمَآ اَنَا بَشَرٌ مِّثْلُكُمْ يُوْحٰٓى اِلَىَّ اَنَّمَآ اِلٰهُكُمْ اِلٰهٌ وَّاحِدٌ فَمَنْ كَانَ يَرْجُوْا لِقَآءَ رَبِّهٖ فَلْيَعْمَلْ عَمَلًا صَالِحًا وَّلَا يُشْرِكْ بِعِبَادَةِ رَبِّهٖٓ اَحَدًا ۝

Maryam
(Mary)

Maryam takes its name from v. 16 ff. That it is of quite early Makkan revelation is established by the following tradition:

In the fifth year of the Prophet's mission (the ninth before the Hijrah, or Flight, to Al-Madīnah) a number of the poorer converts were allowed by the Prophet to emigrate to Abyssinia, a Christian country where they would not be subject to persecution for their worship of the One God. This is known as the first Hijrah. The rulers of Makkah sent ambassadors to ask the Negus for their extradition, accusing them of having left the religion of their own people without entering the Christian religion, and of having done wrong in their own country. The Negus (against the wish of the envoys) sent for the spokesmen of the refugees and, in the presence of the bishops of his realm, questioned them of their religion. Ja'far ibn Abī Tālib, cousin of the prophet, answered: (I translate from the account given by Ibn Ishāq.)[1]

"We were folk immersed in ignorance, worshipping idols, eating carrion, given to lewdness, severing the ties of kinship, bad neighbours, the strong among us preying the weak; thus were we till Allah sent to us a messenger of our own, whose lineage, honesty, trustworthiness and chastity we knew, and he called us to Allah that we should acknowledge His unity and worship Him and eschew all the stones and idols that we and our fathers used to worship beside Him; and ordered us to be truthful and to restore the pledge and observe the ties of kinship, and be good neighbours, and to abstain from things forbidden, and from blood, and forbade us lewdness and false speech, and to prey upon the wealth of orphans, and to accuse good women; and commanded us to worship Allah only, ascribing no thing unto Him as partner, and enjoined upon us prayer and legal alms and fasting. (And he enumerated for him the teachings of Islām.)

---

1. Ibn Hishām Sīrah (Cairo Edition), Part I, p. 116.

"So we trusted him and we believed in him and followed that which he had brought from Allah, and we worshipped Allah only, and ascribed no thing as partner unto Him. And we refrained from that which was forbidden to us, and indulged in that which was made lawful for us. And our people became hostile to us and tormented us, and sought to turn us from our religion that they might bring us back to the worship of idols from the worship of Allah Most High, and that we might indulge in those iniquities which before we had deemed lawful.

"And when they persecuted and oppressed us, and hemmed us in, and kept us from the practice of our religion, we came forth to thy land, and chose thee above all others, and sought thy protection, and hoped that we should not be troubled in thy land, O King!

"Then the Negus asked him: Hast with thee aught of that which he brought from Allah? Ja'far answered: Yes. Then the Negus said: Relate it to me, and Ja'far recited to him the beginning of Kāf, Hā, Yā, 'Ayn, Ṣād"—the Arabic letters with which this sūrah begins, such letters being generally used instead of titles by the early Muslims. Therefore this sūrah must have been revealed and well-known before the departure of the emigrants for Abyssinia."

An early Makkan sūrah, with the possible exception of vv. 59 and 60, which, according to some authorities, were revealed at Al-Madīnah.

سُوْرَةُ مَرْيَمَ

In the name of Allah, the Beneficent, the Merciful.

بِسْمِ اللهِ الرَّحْمٰنِ الرَّحِيمِ

1   Kāf. Hā. Yā. 'Ayn. Ṣād.[2]

كٓهٰیٰعٓصٓ ۟

2   A mention of the mercy of thy Lord unto His servant Zachariah.

ذِكْرُ رَحْمَتِ رَبِّكَ عَبْدَهُ زَكَرِيَّا ۟

3   When he cried unto his Lord a cry in secret;

إِذْ نَادٰى رَبَّهُ نِدَآءً خَفِيًّا ۟

4   Saying: My Lord! Lo! the bones of me wax feeble and my head is shining with grey hair, and I have never been unblest in prayer to Thee, my Lord.

قَالَ رَبِّ إِنِّي وَهَنَ الْعَظْمُ مِنِّي وَاشْتَعَلَ الرَّأْسُ شَيْبًا وَّلَمْ أَكُنْ بِدُعَآئِكَ رَبِّ شَقِيًّا ۟

5   Lo! I fear my kinsfolk after me, since my wife is barren. Oh, give me from Thy presence a successor;

وَإِنِّي خِفْتُ الْمَوَالِيَ مِنْ وَّرَآءِى وَكَانَتِ امْرَأَتِي عَاقِرًا فَهَبْ لِي مِنْ لَّدُنْكَ وَلِيًّا ۟

6   Who shall inherit of me and inherit (also) of the house of Jacob. And make him, my Lord, acceptable (unto Thee).

يَّرِثُنِي وَيَرِثُ مِنْ ءَالِ يَعْقُوبَ وَاجْعَلْهُ رَبِّ رَضِيًّا ۟

7   (It was said unto him): O Zachariah! Lo! We bring thee tidings of a son whose name is John;[3] We have given the same name to none before (him).

يٰزَكَرِيَّآ إِنَّا نُبَشِّرُكَ بِغُلٰمِ اسْمُهُ يَحْيٰى لَمْ نَجْعَلْ لَّهُ مِنْ قَبْلُ سَمِيًّا ۟

---

2. See Sūrah 2, v. 1, footnote.

3. Ar. *Yaḥya*.

8 He said: My Lord! How can I have a son when my wife is barren and I have reached infirm old age?

قَالَ رَبِّ أَنَّىٰ يَكُونُ لِي غُلَامٌ وَكَانَتِ امْرَأَتِي عَاقِرًا وَقَدْ بَلَغْتُ مِنَ الْكِبَرِ عِتِيًّا ۝

9 He said: So (it will be). Thy Lord saith: It is easy for Me, even as I created thee before, when thou wast naught.

قَالَ كَذَٰلِكَ قَالَ رَبُّكَ هُوَ عَلَيَّ هَيِّنٌ وَقَدْ خَلَقْتُكَ مِن قَبْلُ وَلَمْ تَكُ شَيْئًا ۝

10 He said: My Lord! Appoint for me some token. He said: Thy token is that thou, with no bodily defect, shalt not speak unto mankind three nights.

قَالَ رَبِّ اجْعَل لِّي آيَةً قَالَ آيَتُكَ أَلَّا تُكَلِّمَ النَّاسَ ثَلَاثَ لَيَالٍ سَوِيًّا ۝

11 Then he came forth unto his people from the sanctuary, and signified to them: Glorify your Lord at break of day and fall of night.

فَخَرَجَ عَلَىٰ قَوْمِهِ مِنَ الْمِحْرَابِ فَأَوْحَىٰ إِلَيْهِمْ أَن سَبِّحُوا بُكْرَةً وَعَشِيًّا ۝

12 (And it was said unto his son): O John! Hold fast the Scripture. And We gave him wisdom when a child.

يَٰيَحْيَىٰ خُذِ الْكِتَٰبَ بِقُوَّةٍ وَءَاتَيْنَٰهُ الْحُكْمَ صَبِيًّا ۝

13 And compassion from Our presence, and purity; and he was devout;

وَحَنَانًا مِّن لَّدُنَّا وَزَكَوٰةً وَكَانَ تَقِيًّا ۝

14 And dutiful toward his parents. And he was not arrogant, rebellious.

وَبَرًّۢا بِوَٰلِدَيْهِ وَلَمْ يَكُن جَبَّارًا عَصِيًّا ۝

15 Peace on him the day he was born, and the day he dieth and the day he shall be raised alive!

وَسَلَٰمٌ عَلَيْهِ يَوْمَ وُلِدَ وَيَوْمَ يَمُوتُ وَيَوْمَ يُبْعَثُ حَيًّا ۝

16 And make mention of Mary in the Scripture, when she had withdrawn from her people to a chamber looking East;

وَاذْكُرْ فِي الْكِتَٰبِ مَرْيَمَ إِذِ انتَبَذَتْ مِنْ أَهْلِهَا مَكَانًا شَرْقِيًّا ۝

17 And had chosen seclusion from them. Then We sent unto her Our

فَاتَّخَذَتْ مِن دُونِهِمْ حِجَابًا فَأَرْسَلْنَا

spirit and it assumed for her the likeness of a perfect man.

18 She said: Lo! I seek refuge in the Beneficent One from thee, if thou art God fearing.

19 He said: I am only a messenger of thy Lord, that I may bestow on thee a faultless son.

20 She said: How can I have a son when no mortal hath touched me, neither have I been unchaste?

21 He said: So (it will be). Thy Lord saith: It is easy for Me. And (it will be) that We may make of him a portent for mankind and a mercy from Us, and it is a thing ordained.

22 And she, conceived him, and she withdrew with him to a far place.

23 And the pangs of childbirth drove her unto the trunk of the palm tree. She said: Oh, would that I had died ere this and had become a thing of naught, forgotten!

24 Then (one) cried unto her from below her, saying: Grieve not! Thy Lord hath placed a rivulet beneath thee;

25 And shake the trunk of the palm tree toward thee, thou wilt cause ripe dates to fall upon thee.

26 So eat and drink and be consoled. And if thou meetest any mortal, say: Lo! I have vowed a fast

إِلَيْهَا رُوحَنَا فَتَمَثَّلَ لَهَا بَشَرًا سَوِيًّا ۝

قَالَتْ إِنِّي أَعُوذُ بِالرَّحْمَٰنِ مِنكَ إِن كُنتَ تَقِيًّا ۝

قَالَ إِنَّمَا أَنَا۠ رَسُولُ رَبِّكِ لِأَهَبَ لَكِ غُلَامًا زَكِيًّا ۝

قَالَتْ أَنَّىٰ يَكُونُ لِي غُلَامٌ وَلَمْ يَمْسَسْنِي بَشَرٌ وَلَمْ أَكُ بَغِيًّا ۝

قَالَ كَذَٰلِكِ قَالَ رَبُّكِ هُوَ عَلَيَّ هَيِّنٌ وَلِنَجْعَلَهُۥ ءَايَةً لِّلنَّاسِ وَرَحْمَةً مِّنَّا وَكَانَ أَمْرًا مَّقْضِيًّا ۝

فَحَمَلَتْهُ فَانتَبَذَتْ بِهِۦ مَكَانًا قَصِيًّا ۝

فَأَجَآءَهَا الْمَخَاضُ إِلَىٰ جِذْعِ النَّخْلَةِ قَالَتْ يَٰلَيْتَنِي مِتُّ قَبْلَ هَٰذَا وَكُنتُ نَسْيًا مَّنسِيًّا ۝

فَنَادَىٰهَا مِن تَحْتِهَآ أَلَّا تَحْزَنِي قَدْ جَعَلَ رَبُّكِ تَحْتَكِ سَرِيًّا ۝

وَهُزِّي إِلَيْكِ بِجِذْعِ النَّخْلَةِ تُسَٰقِطْ عَلَيْكِ رُطَبًا جَنِيًّا ۝

فَكُلِي وَاشْرَبِي وَقَرِّي عَيْنًا فَإِمَّا تَرَيِنَّ مِنَ الْبَشَرِ أَحَدًا فَقُولِي إِنِّي نَذَرْتُ لِلرَّحْمَٰنِ

unto the Beneficent, and may not speak this day to any mortal.

27 Then she brought him to her own folk, carrying him. They said: O Mary! Thou hast come with an amazing thing.

28 Oh sister of Aaron!⁴ Thy father was not a wicked man nor was thy mother a harlot.

29 Then she pointed to him. They said: How can we talk to one who is in the cradle, a young boy?

30 He spake: Lo! I am the slave of Allah. He hath given me the Scripture and hath appointed me a Prophet;

31 And hath made me blessed wheresoever I may be, and hath enjoined upon me prayer and alms giving so long as I remain alive;

32 And (hath made me) dutiful toward her who bore me, and hath not made me arrogant, unblest.

33 Peace on me the day I was born, and the day I die, and the day I shall be raised alive!

34 Such was Jesus, son of Mary: (this is) a statement of the truth concerning which they doubt.

35 It befitteth not (the Majesty of) Allah that He should take unto Himself a son. Glory be to Him! When

صَوْمًا فَلَنْ أُكَلِّمَ ٱلْيَوْمَ إِنسِيًّا ﴿٢٦﴾

فَأَتَتْ بِهِۦ قَوْمَهَا تَحْمِلُهُۥ قَالُوا۟ يَٰمَرْيَمُ لَقَدْ جِئْتِ شَيْـًٔا فَرِيًّا ﴿٢٧﴾

يَٰٓأُخْتَ هَٰرُونَ مَا كَانَ أَبُوكِ ٱمْرَأَ سَوْءٍ وَمَا كَانَتْ أُمُّكِ بَغِيًّا ﴿٢٨﴾

فَأَشَارَتْ إِلَيْهِ قَالُوا۟ كَيْفَ نُكَلِّمُ مَن كَانَ فِى ٱلْمَهْدِ صَبِيًّا ﴿٢٩﴾

قَالَ إِنِّى عَبْدُ ٱللَّهِ ءَاتَىٰنِىَ ٱلْكِتَٰبَ وَجَعَلَنِى نَبِيًّا ﴿٣٠﴾

وَجَعَلَنِى مُبَارَكًا أَيْنَ مَا كُنتُ وَأَوْصَٰنِى بِٱلصَّلَوٰةِ وَٱلزَّكَوٰةِ مَا دُمْتُ حَيًّا ﴿٣١﴾

وَبَرًّۢا بِوَٰلِدَتِى وَلَمْ يَجْعَلْنِى جَبَّارًا شَقِيًّا ﴿٣٢﴾

وَٱلسَّلَٰمُ عَلَىَّ يَوْمَ وُلِدتُّ وَيَوْمَ أَمُوتُ وَيَوْمَ أُبْعَثُ حَيًّا ﴿٣٣﴾

ذَٰلِكَ عِيسَى ٱبْنُ مَرْيَمَ قَوْلَ ٱلْحَقِّ ٱلَّذِى فِيهِ يَمْتَرُونَ ﴿٣٤﴾

مَا كَانَ لِلَّهِ أَن يَتَّخِذَ مِن وَلَدٍ سُبْحَٰنَهُۥ

---

4. See Sūrah 3, introduction.

He decreeth a thing, He saith unto it only: Be! and it is.

36 And lo! Allah is my Lord and your Lord. So serve Him. That is the right path.

37 The sects among them differ: but woe unto the disbelievers from the meeting of an awful Day.

38 How well will they hear and see on the Day they come unto Us! Yet the evil-doers are today in error manifest.

39 And warn them of the Day of anguish when the case hath been decided. Now they are in a state of carelessness, and they believe not.

40 Lo! We inherit the earth and all who are thereon, and unto Us they are returned.

41 And make mention (O Muḥammad) in the Scripture of Abraham. Lo! he was a saint, a Prophet.

42 When he said unto his father: O my father! Why worshippest thou that which heareth not nor seeth, nor can in aught avail thee?

43 O my father! Lo! there hath come unto me of knowledge that which came not unto thee. So follow me, and I will lead thee on a right path.

44 O my father! Serve not the devil. Lo! the devil is a rebel unto the Beneficent.

إِذَا قَضَىٰٓ أَمْرًا فَإِنَّمَا يَقُولُ لَهُۥ كُن فَيَكُونُ ﴿٣٥﴾

وَإِنَّ ٱللَّهَ رَبِّي وَرَبُّكُمْ فَٱعْبُدُوهُ هَٰذَا صِرَٰطٌ مُّسْتَقِيمٌ ﴿٣٦﴾

فَٱخْتَلَفَ ٱلْأَحْزَابُ مِنۢ بَيْنِهِمْ فَوَيْلٌ لِّلَّذِينَ كَفَرُوا۟ مِن مَّشْهَدِ يَوْمٍ عَظِيمٍ ﴿٣٧﴾

أَسْمِعْ بِهِمْ وَأَبْصِرْ يَوْمَ يَأْتُونَنَا لَٰكِنِ ٱلظَّٰلِمُونَ ٱلْيَوْمَ فِى ضَلَٰلٍ مُّبِينٍ ﴿٣٨﴾

وَأَنذِرْهُمْ يَوْمَ ٱلْحَسْرَةِ إِذْ قُضِىَ ٱلْأَمْرُ وَهُمْ فِى غَفْلَةٍ وَهُمْ لَا يُؤْمِنُونَ ﴿٣٩﴾

إِنَّا نَحْنُ نَرِثُ ٱلْأَرْضَ وَمَنْ عَلَيْهَا وَإِلَيْنَا يُرْجَعُونَ ﴿٤٠﴾

وَٱذْكُرْ فِى ٱلْكِتَٰبِ إِبْرَٰهِيمَ إِنَّهُۥ كَانَ صِدِّيقًا نَّبِيًّا ﴿٤١﴾

إِذْ قَالَ لِأَبِيهِ يَٰٓأَبَتِ لِمَ تَعْبُدُ مَا لَا يَسْمَعُ وَلَا يُبْصِرُ وَلَا يُغْنِى عَنكَ شَيْـًٔا ﴿٤٢﴾

يَٰٓأَبَتِ إِنِّى قَدْ جَآءَنِى مِنَ ٱلْعِلْمِ مَا لَمْ يَأْتِكَ فَٱتَّبِعْنِىٓ أَهْدِكَ صِرَٰطًا سَوِيًّا ﴿٤٣﴾

يَٰٓأَبَتِ لَا تَعْبُدِ ٱلشَّيْطَٰنَ إِنَّ ٱلشَّيْطَٰنَ كَانَ لِلرَّحْمَٰنِ عَصِيًّا ﴿٤٤﴾

45 O my father! Lo! I fear lest a punishment from the Beneficent overtake thee so that thou become a comrade of the devil.

يَـٰٓأَبَتِ إِنِّىٓ أَخَافُ أَن يَمَسَّكَ عَذَابٌ مِّنَ ٱلرَّحْمَٰنِ فَتَكُونَ لِلشَّيْطَٰنِ وَلِيًّا ﴿٤٥﴾

46 He said: Rejectest thou my gods, O Abraham? If thou cease not, I shall surely stone thee. Depart from me a long while!

قَالَ أَرَاغِبٌ أَنتَ عَنْ ءَالِهَتِى يَـٰٓإِبْرَٰهِيمُ لَئِن لَّمْ تَنتَهِ لَأَرْجُمَنَّكَ وَٱهْجُرْنِى مَلِيًّا ﴿٤٦﴾

47 He said: Peace be unto thee! I shall ask forgiveness of my Lord for thee. Lo! He was ever gracious unto me.

قَالَ سَلَٰمٌ عَلَيْكَ سَأَسْتَغْفِرُ لَكَ رَبِّىٓ إِنَّهُۥ كَانَ بِى حَفِيًّا ﴿٤٧﴾

48 I shall withdraw from you and that unto which ye pray beside Allah, and I shall pray unto my Lord. It may be that, in prayer unto my Lord, I shall not be unblest.

وَأَعْتَزِلُكُمْ وَمَا تَدْعُونَ مِن دُونِ ٱللَّهِ وَأَدْعُوا۟ رَبِّى عَسَىٰٓ أَلَّآ أَكُونَ بِدُعَآءِ رَبِّى شَقِيًّا ﴿٤٨﴾

49 So, when he had withdrawn from them and that which they were worshipping beside Allah, We gave him Isaac and Jacob. Each of them We made a Prophet.

فَلَمَّا ٱعْتَزَلَهُمْ وَمَا يَعْبُدُونَ مِن دُونِ ٱللَّهِ وَهَبْنَا لَهُۥٓ إِسْحَٰقَ وَيَعْقُوبَ وَكُلًّا جَعَلْنَا نَبِيًّا ﴿٤٩﴾

50 And We gave them of Our mercy, and assigned to them a high and true renown.

وَوَهَبْنَا لَهُم مِّن رَّحْمَتِنَا وَجَعَلْنَا لَهُمْ لِسَانَ صِدْقٍ عَلِيًّا ﴿٥٠﴾

51 And make mention in the Scripture of Moses. Lo! he was chosen, and he was a messenger (of Allah), a Prophet.

وَٱذْكُرْ فِى ٱلْكِتَٰبِ مُوسَىٰٓ إِنَّهُۥ كَانَ مُخْلَصًا وَكَانَ رَسُولًا نَّبِيًّا ﴿٥١﴾

52 We called him from the right slope of the Mount, and brought him nigh in communion.

وَنَٰدَيْنَٰهُ مِن جَانِبِ ٱلطُّورِ ٱلْأَيْمَنِ وَقَرَّبْنَٰهُ نَجِيًّا ﴿٥٢﴾

53 And We bestowed upon him of Our mercy his brother Aaron, a Prophet (likewise).

وَوَهَبْنَا لَهُۥ مِن رَّحْمَتِنَآ أَخَاهُ هَٰرُونَ نَبِيًّا ﴿٥٣﴾

54 And make mention in the Scripture of Ishmael. Lo! he was a keeper of his promise, and he was a messenger (of Allah), a Prophet.

وَاذْكُرْ فِي الْكِتَابِ إِسْمَٰعِيلَ إِنَّهُ كَانَ صَادِقَ الْوَعْدِ وَكَانَ رَسُولًا نَّبِيًّا ۝

55 He enjoined upon his people worship and almsgiving, and was acceptable in the sight of his Lord.

وَكَانَ يَأْمُرُ أَهْلَهُ بِالصَّلَوٰةِ وَالزَّكَوٰةِ وَكَانَ عِنْدَ رَبِّهِ مَرْضِيًّا ۝

56 And make mention in the Scripture of Idrīs.[5] Lo! he was a saint, a Prophet;

وَاذْكُرْ فِي الْكِتَابِ إِدْرِيسَ إِنَّهُ كَانَ صِدِّيقًا نَّبِيًّا ۝

57 And We raised him to high station.

وَرَفَعْنَاهُ مَكَانًا عَلِيًّا ۝

58 These are they unto whom Allah showed favour from among the Prophets, of the seed of Adam and of those whom We carried (in the ship) with Noah, and of the seed of Abraham and Israel, and from among those whom We guided and chose. When the revelations of the Beneficent were recited unto them, they fell down, adoring and weeping.

أُولَٰئِكَ الَّذِينَ أَنْعَمَ اللَّهُ عَلَيْهِمْ مِنَ النَّبِيِّنَ مِنْ ذُرِّيَّةِ ءَادَمَ وَمِمَّنْ حَمَلْنَا مَعَ نُوحٍ وَمِنْ ذُرِّيَّةِ إِبْرَٰهِيمَ وَإِسْرَٰئِيلَ وَمِمَّنْ هَدَيْنَا وَاجْتَبَيْنَا إِذَا تُتْلَىٰ عَلَيْهِمْ ءَايَٰتُ الرَّحْمَٰنِ خَرُّوا سُجَّدًا وَبُكِيًّا ۩ ۝

59 Now there hath succeeded them a later generation who have ruined worship and have followed lusts. But they will meet deception.

فَخَلَفَ مِنْ بَعْدِهِمْ خَلْفٌ أَضَاعُوا الصَّلَوٰةَ وَاتَّبَعُوا الشَّهَوَٰتِ فَسَوْفَ يَلْقَوْنَ غَيًّا ۝

60 Save him who shall repent and believe and do right. Such will enter the Garden and they will not be wronged in aught;

إِلَّا مَنْ تَابَ وَءَامَنَ وَعَمِلَ صَٰلِحًا فَأُولَٰئِكَ يَدْخُلُونَ الْجَنَّةَ وَلَا يُظْلَمُونَ شَيْئًا ۝

61 Gardens of Eden, which the Beneficent hath, promised to His sla-

جَنَّٰتِ عَدْنٍ الَّتِي وَعَدَ الرَّحْمَٰنُ عِبَادَهُ

---

5. Identified with Enoch.

ves in the Unseen. Lo! His promise is ever sure of fulfillment.

بِٱلۡغَيۡبِۚ إِنَّهُۥ كَانَ وَعۡدُهُۥ مَأۡتِيًّا ۝

62 They hear therein no idle talk, but only Peace; and therein they have food for morn and evening.

لَّا يَسۡمَعُونَ فِيهَا لَغۡوًا إِلَّا سَلَٰمًاۖ وَلَهُمۡ رِزۡقُهُمۡ فِيهَا بُكۡرَةً وَعَشِيًّا ۝

63 Such is the Garden which We cause the devout among Our bond-men to inherit.

تِلۡكَ ٱلۡجَنَّةُ ٱلَّتِي نُورِثُ مِنۡ عِبَادِنَا مَن كَانَ تَقِيًّا ۝

64 We (angels) come not down save by commandment of thy Lord. Unto Him belongeth all that is before us and all that is behind us and all that is between those two, and thy Lord was never forgetful;

وَمَا نَتَنَزَّلُ إِلَّا بِأَمۡرِ رَبِّكَۖ لَهُۥ مَا بَيۡنَ أَيۡدِينَا وَمَا خَلۡفَنَا وَمَا بَيۡنَ ذَٰلِكَۚ وَمَا كَانَ رَبُّكَ نَسِيًّا ۝

65 Lord of the heavens and the earth and all that is between them! Therefore, worship thou Him and be thou steadfast in His service. Knowest thou one that can be named along with Him?

رَّبُّ ٱلسَّمَٰوَٰتِ وَٱلۡأَرۡضِ وَمَا بَيۡنَهُمَا فَٱعۡبُدۡهُ وَٱصۡطَبِرۡ لِعِبَٰدَتِهِۦۚ هَلۡ تَعۡلَمُ لَهُۥ سَمِيًّا ۝

66 And man saith: When I am dead, shall I forsooth be brought forth alive?

وَيَقُولُ ٱلۡإِنسَٰنُ أَءِذَا مَا مِتُّ لَسَوۡفَ أُخۡرَجُ حَيًّا ۝

67 Doth not man remember that We created him before, when he was naught?

أَوَلَا يَذۡكُرُ ٱلۡإِنسَٰنُ أَنَّا خَلَقۡنَٰهُ مِن قَبۡلُ وَلَمۡ يَكُ شَيۡئًا ۝

68 And, by thy Lord, verily We shall assemble them and the devils, then We shall bring them, crouching, around hell.

فَوَرَبِّكَ لَنَحۡشُرَنَّهُمۡ وَٱلشَّيَٰطِينَ ثُمَّ لَنُحۡضِرَنَّهُمۡ حَوۡلَ جَهَنَّمَ جِثِيًّا ۝

69 Then We shall pluck out from every sect whichever of them was most stubborn in rebellion to the Beneficent.

ثُمَّ لَنَنزِعَنَّ مِن كُلِّ شِيعَةٍ أَيُّهُمۡ أَشَدُّ عَلَى ٱلرَّحۡمَٰنِ عِتِيًّا ۝

70 And surely We are best aware of those most worthy to be burned therein.

ثُمَّ لَنَحْنُ أَعْلَمُ بِالَّذِينَ هُمْ أَوْلَى بِهَا صِلِيًّا ۝

71 There is not one of you but shall approach it. That is a fixed ordinance of thy Lord.

وَإِنْ مِّنْكُمْ إِلَّا وَارِدُهَا كَانَ عَلَى رَبِّكَ حَتْمًا مَّقْضِيًّا ۝

72 Then We shall rescue those who kept from evil, and leave the evil-doers crouching there.

ثُمَّ نُنَجِّى الَّذِينَ اتَّقَوْا وَّنَذَرُ الظَّالِمِينَ فِيهَا جِثِيًّا ۝

73 And when Our clear revelations are recited unto them, those who disbelieve say unto those who believe: Which of the two parties (yours or ours) is better in position, and more imposing as an army?

وَإِذَا تُتْلَى عَلَيْهِمْ ءَايَاتُنَا بَيِّنَاتٍ قَالَ الَّذِينَ كَفَرُوا لِلَّذِينَ ءَامَنُوا أَيُّ الْفَرِيقَيْنِ خَيْرٌ مَّقَامًا وَّأَحْسَنُ نَدِيًّا ۝

74 How many a generation have We destroyed before them, who were more imposing in respect of gear and outward seeming!

وَكَمْ أَهْلَكْنَا قَبْلَهُمْ مِّنْ قَرْنٍ هُمْ أَحْسَنُ أَثَاثًا وَّرِءْيًا ۝

75 Say: As for him who is in error, the Beneficent will verily prolong his span of life until, when they behold that which they were promised, whether it be punishment (in the world), or the Hour (of Doom), they will know who is worse in position and who is weaker as an army.

قُلْ مَنْ كَانَ فِى الضَّلَالَةِ فَلْيَمْدُدْ لَهُ الرَّحْمَٰنُ مَدًّا حَتَّى إِذَا رَأَوْا مَا يُوعَدُونَ إِمَّا الْعَذَابَ وَإِمَّا السَّاعَةَ فَسَيَعْلَمُونَ مَنْ هُوَ شَرٌّ مَّكَانًا وَّأَضْعَفُ جُنْدًا ۝

76 Allah increaseth in right guidance those who walk aright, and the good deeds which endure are better in thy Lord's sight for reward, and better for resort.

وَيَزِيدُ اللَّهُ الَّذِينَ اهْتَدَوْا هُدًى وَالْبَاقِيَاتُ الصَّالِحَاتُ خَيْرٌ عِنْدَ رَبِّكَ ثَوَابًا وَّخَيْرٌ مَّرَدًّا ۝

77 Hast thou seen him who disbelieveth in Our revelations and saith:

أَفَرَأَيْتَ الَّذِى كَفَرَ بِئَايَاتِنَا وَقَالَ لَأُوتَيَنَّ

Assuredly I shall be given wealth and children?

مَالًا وَوَلَدًا ۝

78 Hath he perused the Unseen, or hath he made a pact with the Beneficent?

أَطَّلَعَ الْغَيْبَ أَمِ اتَّخَذَ عِندَ الرَّحْمَٰنِ عَهْدًا ۝

79 Nay, but We shall record that which he saith and prolong for him a span of torment.

كَلَّا ۚ سَنَكْتُبُ مَا يَقُولُ وَنَمُدُّ لَهُ مِنَ الْعَذَابِ مَدًّا ۝

80 And We shall inherit from him that whereof he spake, and he will come unto Us, alone (without his wealth and children).

وَنَرِثُهُ مَا يَقُولُ وَيَأْتِينَا فَرْدًا ۝

81 And they have chosen (other) gods beside Allah that they may be a power for them.

وَاتَّخَذُوا مِن دُونِ اللَّهِ آلِهَةً لِّيَكُونُوا لَهُمْ عِزًّا ۝

82 Nay, but they will deny their worship of them, and become opponents unto them.

كَلَّا ۚ سَيَكْفُرُونَ بِعِبَادَتِهِمْ وَيَكُونُونَ عَلَيْهِمْ ضِدًّا ۝

83 Seest thou not that We have set the devils on the disbelievers to confound them with confusion?

أَلَمْ تَرَ أَنَّا أَرْسَلْنَا الشَّيَاطِينَ عَلَى الْكَافِرِينَ تَؤُزُّهُمْ أَزًّا ۝

84 So make no haste against them (O Muhammad). We do but count out unto them a number (of days).

فَلَا تَعْجَلْ عَلَيْهِمْ ۖ إِنَّمَا نَعُدُّ لَهُمْ عَدًّا ۝

85 On the Day when We shall gather the righteous unto the Beneficent, a goodly company.

يَوْمَ نَحْشُرُ الْمُتَّقِينَ إِلَى الرَّحْمَٰنِ وَفْدًا ۝

86 And drive the guilty unto Hell, a weary herd;

وَنَسُوقُ الْمُجْرِمِينَ إِلَىٰ جَهَنَّمَ وِرْدًا ۝

87 They will have no power of intercession, save him who hath made a covenant with his Lord.

لَّا يَمْلِكُونَ الشَّفَاعَةَ إِلَّا مَنِ اتَّخَذَ عِندَ الرَّحْمَٰنِ عَهْدًا ۝

88 And they say: The Beneficent hath taken unto Himself a son.

وَقَالُوا اتَّخَذَ الرَّحْمَٰنُ وَلَدًا ۝

89 Assuredly ye utter a disastrous thing;

لَّقَدْ جِئْتُمْ شَيْئًا إِدًّا ۝

90 Whereby almost the heavens are torn, and the earth is split asunder and the mountains fall in ruins;

تَكَادُ السَّمٰوٰتُ يَتَفَطَّرْنَ مِنْهُ وَتَنْشَقُّ الْأَرْضُ وَتَخِرُّ الْجِبَالُ هَدًّا ۝

91 That they ascribe unto the Beneficent a son!

أَنْ دَعَوْا لِلرَّحْمٰنِ وَلَدًا ۝

92 When it is not meet for (the Majesty of) the Beneficent that He should choose a son.

وَمَا يَنْبَغِي لِلرَّحْمٰنِ أَنْ يَتَّخِذَ وَلَدًا ۝

93 There is none in the heavens and the earth but cometh unto the Beneficent as a slave.

إِنْ كُلُّ مَنْ فِي السَّمٰوٰتِ وَالْأَرْضِ إِلَّا ءَاتِي الرَّحْمٰنِ عَبْدًا ۝

94 Verily He knoweth them and numbereth them with (right) numbering.

لَقَدْ أَحْصٰهُمْ وَعَدَّهُمْ عَدًّا ۝

95 And each one of them will come unto Him on the Day of Resurrection, alone.

وَكُلُّهُمْ ءَاتِيهِ يَوْمَ الْقِيٰمَةِ فَرْدًا ۝

96 Lo! those who believe and do good works, the Beneficent will appoint for them love.

إِنَّ الَّذِينَ ءَامَنُوا وَعَمِلُوا الصّٰلِحٰتِ سَيَجْعَلُ لَهُمُ الرَّحْمٰنُ وُدًّا ۝

97 And We make (this Scripture) easy in thy tongue, (O Muhammad) only that thou mayst bear good tidings therewith unto those who ward off (evil), and warn therewith the froward folk.

فَإِنَّمَا يَسَّرْنٰهُ بِلِسَانِكَ لِتُبَشِّرَ بِهِ الْمُتَّقِينَ وَتُنْذِرَ بِهِ قَوْمًا لُّدًّا ۝

98 And how many a generation before them have We destroyed! Canst thou (Muhammad) see a single man of them, or hear from them the slightest sound?

وَكَمْ أَهْلَكْنَا قَبْلَهُمْ مِنْ قَرْنٍ هَلْ تُحِسُّ مِنْهُمْ مِنْ أَحَدٍ أَوْ تَسْمَعُ لَهُمْ رِكْزًا ۝

Ṭā Hā

Ṭā Hā takes its name from the Arabic letters which form the first verse. As in the case of sūrah 19, the early date of revelation is established by a strong tradition.

'Umar ibn al-Khaṭṭāb, who afterwards became Caliph, was among the bitterest opponents of Islām in early days. He set out one day, sword in hand, with the intention of killing the Prophet—"this Sabean who has split the unity of Quraysh, calls their ideals foolish and their religion shameful, and blasphemes their gods"—when a friend who met him dissuaded him, reminding him that if he slew the Prophet, he would have to reckon with the vengeance of a powerful clan: "Thinkest thou that the Banū 'Abd Manāf would let thee walk on the earth if thou hadst slain Muhammad?" for tribal pride survived religious difference. "Is it not better for thee to return to the folk of thine own house and keep them straight?" 'Umar asked: "Which of the folk of my house?" "Thy brother-in-law and cousin, Sa'īd ibn Zayd, and thy sister, Fātimah daughter of Al-Khaṭṭāb, for, by Allah, they have become Muslims and followers of Muhammad in his religion, so look thou to them." Then 'Umar returned, enraged against his sister and brother-in-law, and there was with them in the house Khubāb ibn Araat, having with him a leaf on which was written Ṭā Hā (this sūrah) which he was reading aloud to them. When they heard the noise of 'Umar's coming, Khubāb hid in a closet that they had in the house and Fātimah took the leaf and hid it under her thigh. But 'Umar had heard the sound of Khubāb's reading as he drew near the house, and when he entered he said: "What was that mumbling which I heard?" They said: " Thou heardest nothing." 'Umar said: "Yea, by Allah! And I have already been informed that ye have become followers of Muhammad in his religion." Then he attacked his brother-in-law Sa'īd ibn Zayd, but Fātimah sprang to keep him off her husband and he struck and wounded her. And when he had done that, his sister and his brother-in-law said to him: "Yes, we are Muslims and we believe in Allah and His messenger, so do what thou wilt!" But when 'Umar saw the blood upon his sister, he was sorry for what he had done, and he said to his sister: "Give me that leaf from which I heard you reading just now, that I may see what this is that Muḥammad has brought." And 'Umar was a scribe. When he said that, his sister said: "We fear to trust thee with it." He said: "Fear not!" and swore by his gods that he would return it to her when he had read it. And when he said that, she hoped for his conversion to Al-Islām, but said: "O my brother, thou art unclean on account of thine idolatry and none may touch it save the purified." Then 'Umar went out and washed himself, and she gave him the leaf on which Ṭā Hā was written and he read it. And when he had read it he said: "How excellent are these words!" and praised it highly. And when he heard that, Khubāb came out to him and said: "O 'Umar, I hope that Allah has brought you in answer to the prayer of the Prophet, for only yesterday I heard him saying: O Allah! Strengthen Al-Islām with Abū al Hakam ibn Hishām or 'Umar ibn Al-Khaṭṭāb; and Allah is Allah, O 'Umar!" At that he said: "O Khubāb, direct me to Muḥammad that I may go to him and make surrender."[1]

The conversion of 'Umar took place in the fifth year of the Prophet's mission (ninth before the Hijrah) soon after the departure of the emigrants to Abyssinia. At that time this sūrah was already written down and in circulation.

An early Makkan sūrah.

In the name of Allah, the Beneficent, the Merciful.

1 Ṭā Hā.

2 We have not revealed unto thee (Muhammad) this Qur'an that thou shouldst be distressed;

---

1. Ibn Hishām, Part I, pp. 119 and 120.

3   But as a reminder unto him who feareth;

إِلَّا تَذْكِرَةً لِّمَن يَخْشَىٰ ۞

4   A revelation from Him Who created the earth and the high heavens;

تَنزِيلًا مِّمَّنْ خَلَقَ ٱلْأَرْضَ وَٱلسَّمَٰوَٰتِ ٱلْعُلَى ۞

5   The Beneficent One, Who is established on the Throne.

ٱلرَّحْمَٰنُ عَلَى ٱلْعَرْشِ ٱسْتَوَىٰ ۞

6   Unto Him belongeth whatsoever is in the heavens and whatsoever is in the earth, and whatsoever is between them, and whatsoever is beneath the sod.

لَهُۥ مَا فِى ٱلسَّمَٰوَٰتِ وَمَا فِى ٱلْأَرْضِ وَمَا بَيْنَهُمَا وَمَا تَحْتَ ٱلثَّرَىٰ ۞

7   And if thou speakest aloud, then lo! He knoweth the secret (thought) and (that which is yet) more hidden.

وَإِن تَجْهَرْ بِٱلْقَوْلِ فَإِنَّهُۥ يَعْلَمُ ٱلسِّرَّ وَأَخْفَى ۞

8   Allah! There is no God save Him. His are the most beautiful names.

ٱللَّهُ لَا إِلَٰهَ إِلَّا هُوَ لَهُ ٱلْأَسْمَآءُ ٱلْحُسْنَى ۞

9   Hath there come unto thee the story of Moses?

وَهَلْ أَتَىٰكَ حَدِيثُ مُوسَىٰ ۞

10   When he saw a fire and said unto his folk: Wait! Lo! I see a fire afar off. Peradventure I may bring you a brand therefrom or may find guidance at the fire.

إِذْ رَءَا نَارًا فَقَالَ لِأَهْلِهِ ٱمْكُثُوٓا إِنِّىٓ ءَانَسْتُ نَارًا لَّعَلِّىٓ ءَاتِيكُم مِّنْهَا بِقَبَسٍ أَوْ أَجِدُ عَلَى ٱلنَّارِ هُدًى ۞

11   And when he reached it, he was called by name: O Moses!

فَلَمَّآ أَتَىٰهَا نُودِىَ يَٰمُوسَىٰٓ ۞

12   Lo! I, even I, am thy Lord. So take off thy shoes, for lo! thou art in the holy valley of Ṭuwā.

إِنِّىٓ أَنَا۠ رَبُّكَ فَٱخْلَعْ نَعْلَيْكَ إِنَّكَ بِٱلْوَادِ ٱلْمُقَدَّسِ طُوًى ۞

13   And I have chosen thee, so hearken unto that which is inspired.

وَأَنَا ٱخْتَرْتُكَ فَٱسْتَمِعْ لِمَا يُوحَىٰ ۞

14 Lo! I, even I, am Allah. There is no God save Me. So serve Me and establish worship for My remembrance.

إِنَّنِيٓ أَنَا ٱللَّهُ لَآ إِلَٰهَ إِلَّآ أَنَا۠ فَٱعْبُدْنِي وَأَقِمِ ٱلصَّلَوٰةَ لِذِكْرِيٓ ۝

15 Lo! the Hour is surely coming. But I will to keep it hidden, that every soul may be rewarded for that which it striveth (to achieve).

إِنَّ ٱلسَّاعَةَ ءَاتِيَةٌ أَكَادُ أُخْفِيهَا لِتُجْزَىٰ كُلُّ نَفْسٍ بِمَا تَسْعَىٰ ۝

16 Therefore, let not him turn thee aside from (the thought of) it who believeth not therein but followeth his own desire, lest thou perish.

فَلَا يَصُدَّنَّكَ عَنْهَا مَن لَّا يُؤْمِنُ بِهَا وَٱتَّبَعَ هَوَىٰهُ فَتَرْدَىٰ ۝

17 And what is that in thy right hand, O Moses?

وَمَا تِلْكَ بِيَمِينِكَ يَٰمُوسَىٰ ۝

18 He said: This is my staff whereon I lean, and wherewith I beat down branches for my sheep, and wherein I find other uses.

قَالَ هِيَ عَصَايَ أَتَوَكَّؤُا۟ عَلَيْهَا وَأَهُشُّ بِهَا عَلَىٰ غَنَمِي وَلِيَ فِيهَا مَـَٔارِبُ أُخْرَىٰ ۝

19 He said: Cast it down, O Moses!

قَالَ أَلْقِهَا يَٰمُوسَىٰ ۝

20 So he cast it down, and lo! it was a serpent, gliding.

فَأَلْقَىٰهَا فَإِذَا هِيَ حَيَّةٌ تَسْعَىٰ ۝

21 He said: Grasp it and fear not. We shall return it to its former state.

قَالَ خُذْهَا وَلَا تَخَفْ سَنُعِيدُهَا سِيرَتَهَا ٱلْأُولَىٰ ۝

22 And thrust thy hand within thine armpit, it will come forth white without hurt. (That will be) another token.

وَٱضْمُمْ يَدَكَ إِلَىٰ جَنَاحِكَ تَخْرُجْ بَيْضَآءَ مِنْ غَيْرِ سُوٓءٍ ءَايَةً أُخْرَىٰ ۝

23 That We may show thee (some) of Our greater portents;

لِنُرِيَكَ مِنْ ءَايَٰتِنَا ٱلْكُبْرَى ۝

24 Go thou unto Pharaoh! Lo! he hath transgressed (the bounds).

ٱذْهَبْ إِلَىٰ فِرْعَوْنَ إِنَّهُ طَغَىٰ ۝

25 (Moses) said: My Lord! Relieve my mind;

قَالَ رَبِّ ٱشْرَحْ لِي صَدْرِي ۝

26 And ease my task for me;

وَيَسِّرْ لِيٓ أَمْرِي ۝

27 And loose a knot from my tongue;

وَاحْلُلْ عُقْدَةً مِّنْ لِّسَانِي ۝

28 That they may understand my saying.

يَفْقَهُوْا قَوْلِي ۝

29 Appoint for me a henchman from my folk;

وَاجْعَلْ لِّيْ وَزِيْرًا مِّنْ أَهْلِيْ ۝

30 Aaron, my brother.

هَارُوْنَ أَخِي ۝

31 Confirm my strength with him.

اشْدُدْ بِهِ أَزْرِيْ ۝

32 And let him share my task;

وَأَشْرِكْهُ فِيْ أَمْرِيْ ۝

33 That we may glorify Thee much.

كَيْ نُسَبِّحَكَ كَثِيْرًا ۝

34 And much remember Thee.

وَّنَذْكُرَكَ كَثِيْرًا ۝

35 Lo! Thou art ever Seeing us.

إِنَّكَ كُنْتَ بِنَا بَصِيْرًا ۝

36 He said: Thou art granted thy request, O Moses.

قَالَ قَدْ أُوْتِيْتَ سُؤْلَكَ يَمُوْسٰى ۝

37 And indeed, another time, already We have shown thee favour;

وَلَقَدْ مَنَنَّا عَلَيْكَ مَرَّةً أُخْرَى ۝

38 When We inspired in thy mother that which is inspired;

إِذْ أَوْحَيْنَا إِلَى أُمِّكَ مَا يُوْحَى ۝

39 Saying: Throw him into the ark, and throw it into the river, then the river shall throw it on to the bank, and there an enemy to Me and an enemy to him shall take him. And I endued thee with love from Me that thou mightest be trained according to My will;

أَنِ اقْذِفِيْهِ فِي التَّابُوْتِ فَاقْذِفِيْهِ فِي الْيَمِّ فَلْيُلْقِهِ الْيَمُّ بِالسَّاحِلِ يَأْخُذْهُ عَدُوٌّ لِّيْ وَعَدُوٌّ لَّهُ ۚ وَأَلْقَيْتُ عَلَيْكَ مَحَبَّةً مِّنِّيْ ۚ وَلِتُصْنَعَ عَلَى عَيْنِيْ ۝

40 When thy sister went and said: Shall I show you one who will nurse him? and We restored thee to thy mother that her eyes might be refreshed and might not sorrow. And thou didst kill a man and We delivered thee from great distress, and tried thee with a heavy trial.

إِذْ تَمْشِيْ أُخْتُكَ فَتَقُوْلُ هَلْ أَدُلُّكُمْ عَلَى مَنْ يَّكْفُلُهُ ۖ فَرَجَعْنَاكَ إِلَى أُمِّكَ كَيْ تَقَرَّ عَيْنُهَا وَلَا تَحْزَنَ ۚ وَقَتَلْتَ نَفْسًا فَنَجَّيْنَاكَ مِنَ الْغَمِّ

And thou didst tarry years among the folk of Madyan. Then comest thou (hither) by (My) providence, O Moses;

وَفَتَنَّكَ فُتُوناً فَلَبِثْتَ سِنِينَ فِيٓ أَهْلِ مَدْيَنَ ثُمَّ جِئْتَ عَلَىٰ قَدَرٍ يَٰمُوسَىٰ ۝

41 And I have attached thee to Myself.

وَٱصْطَنَعْتُكَ لِنَفْسِي ۝

42 Go, thou and thy brother, with My tokens, and be not faint in remembrance of Me.

ٱذْهَبْ أَنتَ وَأَخُوكَ بِـَٔايَٰتِي وَلَا تَنِيَا فِي ذِكْرِي ۝

43 Go, both of you, unto Pharaoh. Lo! he hath transgressed (the bounds).

ٱذْهَبَآ إِلَىٰ فِرْعَوْنَ إِنَّهُۥ طَغَىٰ ۝

44 And speak unto him a gentle word, that peradventure he may heed or fear.

فَقُولَا لَهُۥ قَوْلاً لَّيِّناً لَّعَلَّهُۥ يَتَذَكَّرُ أَوْ يَخْشَىٰ ۝

45 They said: Our Lord! Lo! we fear that he may be beforehand with us or that he may play the tyrant.

قَالَا رَبَّنَآ إِنَّنَا نَخَافُ أَن يَفْرُطَ عَلَيْنَآ أَوْ أَن يَطْغَىٰ ۝

46 He said: Fear not. Lo! I am with you twain, Hearing and Seeing.

قَالَ لَا تَخَافَآ إِنَّنِي مَعَكُمَآ أَسْمَعُ وَأَرَىٰ ۝

47 So go ye unto him and say: Lo! we are two messengers of thy Lord. So let the Children of Israel go with us, and torment them not. We bring thee a token from thy Lord. And peace will be for him who followeth right guidance.

فَأْتِيَاهُ فَقُولَآ إِنَّا رَسُولَا رَبِّكَ فَأَرْسِلْ مَعَنَا بَنِيٓ إِسْرَٰٓءِيلَ وَلَا تُعَذِّبْهُمْ قَدْ جِئْنَٰكَ بِـَٔايَةٍ مِّن رَّبِّكَ وَٱلسَّلَٰمُ عَلَىٰ مَنِ ٱتَّبَعَ ٱلْهُدَىٰٓ ۝

48 Lo! it hath been revealed unto us that the doom will be for him who denieth and turneth away.

إِنَّا قَدْ أُوحِيَ إِلَيْنَآ أَنَّ ٱلْعَذَابَ عَلَىٰ مَن كَذَّبَ وَتَوَلَّىٰ ۝

49 (Pharaoh) said: Who then is the Lord of you twain, O Moses?

قَالَ فَمَن رَّبُّكُمَا يَٰمُوسَىٰ ۝

50 He said: Our Lord is He Who gave unto everything its nature, then guided it aright.

قَالَ رَبُّنَا ٱلَّذِيٓ أَعْطَىٰ كُلَّ شَيْءٍ خَلْقَهُۥ ثُمَّ هَدَىٰ ۝

51 He said: What then is the state of the generations of old?

قَالَ فَمَا بَالُ الْقُرُونِ الْأُولَى ۝

52 He said: The knowledge thereof is with my Lord in a Record. My Lord neither erreth nor forgetteth;

قَالَ عِلْمُهَا عِندَ رَبِّى فِى كِتَٰبٍ لَّا يَضِلُّ رَبِّى وَلَا يَنسَى ۝

53 Who hath appointed the earth as a bed and hath threaded roads for you therein and hath sent down water from the sky and thereby We have brought forth divers kinds of vegetation;

الَّذِى جَعَلَ لَكُمُ الْأَرْضَ مَهْدًا وَسَلَكَ لَكُمْ فِيهَا سُبُلًا وَأَنزَلَ مِنَ السَّمَاءِ مَاءً فَأَخْرَجْنَا بِهِ أَزْوَٰجًا مِّن نَّبَاتٍ شَتَّىٰ ۝

54 (Saying): Eat ye and feed your cattle. Lo! herein verily are portents for men of thought.

كُلُوا۟ وَارْعَوْا۟ أَنْعَٰمَكُمْ إِنَّ فِى ذَٰلِكَ لَءَايَٰتٍ لِّأُو۟لِى النُّهَىٰ ۝

55 Thereof We created you, and thereunto We return you and thence We bring you forth a second time.

۞ مِنْهَا خَلَقْنَٰكُمْ وَفِيهَا نُعِيدُكُمْ وَمِنْهَا نُخْرِجُكُمْ تَارَةً أُخْرَىٰ ۝

56 And We verily did show him all Our tokens, but he denied them and refused.

وَلَقَدْ أَرَيْنَٰهُ ءَايَٰتِنَا كُلَّهَا فَكَذَّبَ وَأَبَىٰ ۝

57 He said: Hast come to drive us out from our land by thy magic, O Moses?

قَالَ أَجِئْتَنَا لِتُخْرِجَنَا مِنْ أَرْضِنَا بِسِحْرِكَ يَٰمُوسَىٰ ۝

58 But we surely can bring to thee magic the like thereof; so appoint a tryst between us and you, which neither we nor thou shall fail to keep, at a place convenient (to us both).

فَلَنَأْتِيَنَّكَ بِسِحْرٍ مِّثْلِهِ فَاجْعَلْ بَيْنَنَا وَبَيْنَكَ مَوْعِدًا لَّا نُخْلِفُهُ نَحْنُ وَلَا أَنتَ مَكَانًا سُوًى ۝

59 (Moses) said: Your tryst shall be the day of the feast, and let the people assemble when the sun hath risen high.

قَالَ مَوْعِدُكُمْ يَوْمُ الزِّينَةِ وَأَن يُحْشَرَ النَّاسُ ضُحًى ۝

60 Then Pharaoh went and gathered his strength, then came (to the appointed tryst).

فَتَوَلَّىٰ فِرْعَوْنُ فَجَمَعَ كَيْدَهُ ثُمَّ أَتَىٰ ۝

61 Moses said unto them: Woe unto you! Invent not a lie against Allah, lest He extirpate you by some punishment. He who lieth faileth miserably.

قَالَ لَهُم مُّوسَى وَيْلَكُمْ لَا تَفْتَرُوا عَلَى اللهِ
كَذِبًا فَيُسْحِتَكُم بِعَذَابٍ
وَقَدْ خَابَ مَنِ افْتَرَى ۝

62 Then they debated one with another what they must do, and they kept their counsel secret.

فَتَنَازَعُوا أَمْرَهُم بَيْنَهُمْ وَأَسَرُّوا النَّجْوَى ۝

63 They said: Lo! these are two wizards who would drive you out from your country by their magic, and destroy your best traditions;

قَالُوا إِنْ هَذَانِ لَسَاحِرَانِ يُرِيدَانِ أَن يُخْرِجَاكُم
مِّنْ أَرْضِكُم بِسِحْرِهِمَا
وَيَذْهَبَا بِطَرِيقَتِكُمُ الْمُثْلَى ۝

64 So arrange your plan, and come in battle line. Whoso is uppermost this day will be indeed successful.

فَأَجْمِعُوا كَيْدَكُمْ ثُمَّ ائْتُوا صَفًّا
وَقَدْ أَفْلَحَ الْيَوْمَ مَنِ اسْتَعْلَى ۝

65 They said: O Moses! Either throw first, or let us be the first to throw?

قَالُوا يَا مُوسَى إِمَّا أَن تُلْقِيَ
وَإِمَّا أَن نَّكُونَ أَوَّلَ مَنْ أَلْقَى ۝

66 He said: Nay, do ye throw! Then lo! their cords and their staves, by their magic, appeared to him as though they ran.

قَالَ بَلْ أَلْقُوا فَإِذَا حِبَالُهُمْ وَعِصِيُّهُمْ
يُخَيَّلُ إِلَيْهِ مِن سِحْرِهِمْ أَنَّهَا تَسْعَى ۝

67 And Moses conceived a fear in his mind.

فَأَوْجَسَ فِي نَفْسِهِ خِيفَةً مُّوسَى ۝

68 We said: Fear not! Lo! thou art the higher.

قُلْنَا لَا تَخَفْ إِنَّكَ أَنتَ الْأَعْلَى ۝

69 Throw that which is in thy right hand! It will eat up that which they have made. Lo! that which they have made is but a wizard's artifice, and a wizard shall not be successful to whatever point (of skill) he may attain.

وَأَلْقِ مَا فِي يَمِينِكَ تَلْقَفْ مَا صَنَعُوا إِنَّمَا صَنَعُوا
كَيْدُ سَاحِرٍ وَلَا يُفْلِحُ السَّاحِرُ حَيْثُ أَتَى ۝

70 Then the wizards were (all) flung down prostrate, crying: We

فَأُلْقِيَ السَّحَرَةُ سُجَّدًا

believe in the Lord of Aaron and
Moses.

قَالُوٓاْ ءَامَنَّا بِرَبِّ هَٰرُونَ وَمُوسَىٰٓ ٧٠

71 (Pharaoh) said: Ye put faith in
him before I give you leave. Lo! he
is your chief who taught you magic.
Now surely I shall cut off your
hands and your feet alternately, and
I shall crucify you on the trunks of
palm trees, and ye shall know for
certain which of us hath sterner and
more lasting punishment.

قَالَ ءَامَنتُمْ لَهُۥ قَبْلَ أَنْ ءَاذَنَ لَكُمْ إِنَّهُۥ لَكَبِيرُكُمُ ٱلَّذِى
عَلَّمَكُمُ ٱلسِّحْرَ فَلَأُقَطِّعَنَّ أَيْدِيَكُمْ وَأَرْجُلَكُم
مِّنْ خِلَٰفٍ وَلَأُصَلِّبَنَّكُمْ فِى جُذُوعِ ٱلنَّخْلِ وَلَتَعْلَمُنَّ
أَيُّنَآ أَشَدُّ عَذَابًا وَأَبْقَىٰٓ ٧١

72 They said: We choose thee not
above the clear proofs that have
come unto us, and above Him Who
created us. So decree what thou wilt
decree. Thou wilt end for us only
the life of the world.

قَالُوا لَن نُّؤْثِرَكَ عَلَىٰ مَا جَآءَنَا مِنَ ٱلْبَيِّنَٰتِ وَٱلَّذِى
فَطَرَنَا فَٱقْضِ مَآ أَنتَ قَاضٍ إِنَّمَا تَقْضِى
هَٰذِهِ ٱلْحَيَوٰةَ ٱلدُّنْيَآ ٧٢

73 Lo! we believe in our Lord, that
He may forgive us our sins and the
magic unto which thou didst force
us. Allah is better and more lasting.

إِنَّآ ءَامَنَّا بِرَبِّنَا لِيَغْفِرَ لَنَا خَطَٰيَٰنَا وَمَآ أَكْرَهْتَنَا
عَلَيْهِ مِنَ ٱلسِّحْرِ وَٱللَّهُ خَيْرٌ وَأَبْقَىٰٓ ٧٣

74 Lo! whoso cometh guilty unto
his Lord, verily for him is hell.
There he will neither die nor live.

إِنَّهُۥ مَن يَأْتِ رَبَّهُۥ مُجْرِمًا
فَإِنَّ لَهُۥ جَهَنَّمَ لَا يَمُوتُ فِيهَا وَلَا يَحْيَىٰ ٧٤

75 But whoso cometh unto Him a
believer, having done good works,
for such are the high stations;

وَمَن يَأْتِهِ مُؤْمِنًا قَدْ عَمِلَ ٱلصَّٰلِحَٰتِ
فَأُو۟لَٰٓئِكَ لَهُمُ ٱلدَّرَجَٰتُ ٱلْعُلَىٰ ٧٥

76 Gardens of Eden underneath
which rivers flow, wherein they will
abide forever. That is the reward of
him who groweth.

جَنَّٰتُ عَدْنٍ تَجْرِى مِن تَحْتِهَا ٱلْأَنْهَٰرُ خَٰلِدِينَ فِيهَا
وَذَٰلِكَ جَزَآءُ مَن تَزَكَّىٰ ٧٦

77 And verily We inspired Moses,
saying: Take away My slaves by
night and strike for them a dry path

وَلَقَدْ أَوْحَيْنَآ إِلَىٰ مُوسَىٰٓ أَنْ أَسْرِ بِعِبَادِى فَٱضْرِبْ
لَهُمْ طَرِيقًا فِى ٱلْبَحْرِ يَبَسًا لَّا تَخَٰفُ دَرَكًا

in the sea, fearing not to be overtaken, neither being afraid (of the
sea).

78 Then Pharaoh followed with his
hosts and there covered them that
which did cover them of the sea.

وَلَا تَخْشَىٰ ۝

فَأَتْبَعَهُمْ فِرْعَوْنُ بِجُنُودِهِ
فَغَشِيَهُمْ مِنَ الْيَمِّ مَا غَشِيَهُمْ ۝

79 And Pharaoh led his folk astray,
he did not guide them.

وَأَضَلَّ فِرْعَوْنُ قَوْمَهُ وَمَا هَدَىٰ ۝

80 O Children of Israel! We delivered you from your enemy, and
We made a covenant with you on
the holy mountain's side, and sent
down on you the manna and the
quails;

يَبَنِي إِسْرَآءِيلَ قَدْ أَنجَيْنَٰكُم مِّنْ عَدُوِّكُمْ وَوَٰعَدْنَٰكُمْ جَانِبَ
الطُّورِ الْأَيْمَنَ وَنَزَّلْنَا عَلَيْكُمُ الْمَنَّ وَالسَّلْوَىٰ ۝

81 (Saying): Eat of the good things
wherewith We have provided you,
and transgress not in respect thereof
lest My wrath come upon you; and
he on whom My wrath cometh, he
is lost indeed.

كُلُوا مِن طَيِّبَٰتِ مَا رَزَقْنَٰكُمْ وَلَا تَطْغَوْا فِيهِ فَيَحِلَّ
عَلَيْكُمْ غَضَبِي وَمَن يَحْلِلْ عَلَيْهِ غَضَبِي
فَقَدْ هَوَىٰ ۝

82 And lo! verily I am Forgiving
toward him who repenteth and believeth and doeth good, and afterward walketh aright.

وَإِنِّي لَغَفَّارٌ لِّمَن تَابَ وَءَامَنَ وَعَمِلَ صَٰلِحًا
ثُمَّ اهْتَدَىٰ ۝

83 And (it was said): What hath
made thee hasten from thy folk, O
Moses?

۞ وَمَا أَعْجَلَكَ عَن قَوْمِكَ يَٰمُوسَىٰ ۝

84 He said: They are close upon
my track. I hastened unto Thee, my
Lord, that Thou mightest be well
pleased.

قَالَ هُمْ أُوْلَاءِ عَلَىٰ أَثَرِي وَعَجِلْتُ إِلَيْكَ
رَبِّ لِتَرْضَىٰ ۝

85 He said: Lo! We have tried thy
folk in thine absence, and As-Sāmirī
hath misled them.

قَالَ فَإِنَّا قَدْ فَتَنَّا قَوْمَكَ مِنۢ بَعْدِكَ وَأَضَلَّهُمُ
السَّامِرِيُّ ۝

86 Then Moses went back unto his folk, angry and sad, He said: O my people! Hath not your Lord promised you a fair promise? Did the time appointed then appear too long for you, or did ye wish that wrath from your Lord should come upon you, that ye broke tryst with me?

فَرَجَعَ مُوسَىٰٓ إِلَىٰ قَوْمِهِۦ غَضْبَٰنَ أَسِفًاۚ قَالَ يَٰقَوْمِ أَلَمْ يَعِدْكُمْ رَبُّكُمْ وَعْدًا حَسَنًاۚ أَفَطَالَ عَلَيْكُمُ ٱلْعَهْدُ أَمْ أَرَدتُّمْ أَن يَحِلَّ عَلَيْكُمْ غَضَبٌ مِّن رَّبِّكُمْ فَأَخْلَفْتُم مَّوْعِدِى ٨٦

87 They said: We broke not tryst with thee of our own will, but we were laden with burdens of ornaments of the folk, then cast them (in the fire), for thus As-Sāmirī proposed.

قَالُوا۟ مَآ أَخْلَفْنَا مَوْعِدَكَ بِمَلْكِنَا وَلَٰكِنَّا حُمِّلْنَآ أَوْزَارًا مِّن زِينَةِ ٱلْقَوْمِ فَقَذَفْنَٰهَا فَكَذَٰلِكَ أَلْقَى ٱلسَّامِرِىُّ ٨٧

88 Then he produced for them a calf, which gave forth a lowing sound. And they cried: This is your God and the God of Moses, but he hath forgotten.

فَأَخْرَجَ لَهُمْ عِجْلًا جَسَدًا لَّهُۥ خُوَارٌ فَقَالُوا۟ هَٰذَآ إِلَٰهُكُمْ وَإِلَٰهُ مُوسَىٰ فَنَسِىَ ٨٨

89 See they not, then, that it returneth no saying unto them and possesseth for them neither hurt nor use?

أَفَلَا يَرَوْنَ أَلَّا يَرْجِعُ إِلَيْهِمْ قَوْلًا وَلَا يَمْلِكُ لَهُمْ ضَرًّا وَلَا نَفْعًا ٨٩

90 And Aaron indeed had told them beforehand: O my people! Ye are but being seduced therewith, for lo! your Lord is the Beneficent, so follow me and obey my order.

وَلَقَدْ قَالَ لَهُمْ هَٰرُونُ مِن قَبْلُ يَٰقَوْمِ إِنَّمَا فُتِنتُم بِهِۦۖ وَإِنَّ رَبَّكُمُ ٱلرَّحْمَٰنُ فَٱتَّبِعُونِى وَأَطِيعُوٓا۟ أَمْرِى ٩٠

91 They said: We shall by no means cease to be its votaries till Moses return unto us.

قَالُوا۟ لَن نَّبْرَحَ عَلَيْهِ عَٰكِفِينَ حَتَّىٰ يَرْجِعَ إِلَيْنَا مُوسَىٰ ٩١

92 He (Moses) said: O Aaron! What held thee back when thou didst see them gone astray;

قَالَ يَٰهَٰرُونُ مَا مَنَعَكَ إِذْ رَأَيْتَهُمْ ضَلُّوٓا۟ ٩٢

93 That thou followedst me not? Hast thou then disobeyed my order?

أَلَّا تَتَّبِعَنِۖ أَفَعَصَيْتَ أَمْرِى ٩٣

94 He said: O son of my mother! Clutch not my beard nor my head! I feared lest thou shouldst say: Thou hast caused division among the Children of Israel, and hast not waited for my word.

قَالَ يَبْنَؤُمَّ لَا تَأْخُذْ بِلِحْيَتِي وَلَا بِرَأْسِيٓ إِنِّي خَشِيتُ أَن تَقُولَ فَرَّقْتَ بَيْنَ بَنِيٓ إِسْرَٰٓءِيلَ وَلَمْ تَرْقُبْ قَوْلِي ﴿٩٤﴾

95 (Moses) said: And what has thou to say, O Sāmirī?

قَالَ فَمَا خَطْبُكَ يَٰسَٰمِرِيُّ ﴿٩٥﴾

96 He said: I perceived what they perceived not, so I seized a handful from the footsteps of the messenger, and then threw it in. Thus my soul commended to me.[2]

قَالَ بَصُرْتُ بِمَا لَمْ يَبْصُرُوا۟ بِهِۦ فَقَبَضْتُ قَبْضَةً مِّنْ أَثَرِ ٱلرَّسُولِ فَنَبَذْتُهَا وَكَذَٰلِكَ سَوَّلَتْ لِي نَفْسِي ﴿٩٦﴾

97 (Moses) said: Then go! And lo! in this life it is for thee to say: Touch me not! and lo! there is for thee a tryst, which canst not be broken for thee. Now look upon thy god of which thou hast remained a votary. Verily we will burn it and will scatter its dust over the sea.

قَالَ فَٱذْهَبْ فَإِنَّ لَكَ فِي ٱلْحَيَوٰةِ أَن تَقُولَ لَا مِسَاسَ وَإِنَّ لَكَ مَوْعِدًا لَّن تُخْلَفَهُۥ وَٱنظُرْ إِلَىٰٓ إِلَٰهِكَ ٱلَّذِي ظَلْتَ عَلَيْهِ عَاكِفًا لَّنُحَرِّقَنَّهُۥ ثُمَّ لَنَنسِفَنَّهُۥ فِي ٱلْيَمِّ نَسْفًا ﴿٩٧﴾

98 Your God is only Allah, than Whom there is no other God. He embraceth all things in His knowledge.

إِنَّمَآ إِلَٰهُكُمُ ٱللَّهُ ٱلَّذِي لَآ إِلَٰهَ إِلَّا هُوَ وَسِعَ كُلَّ شَيْءٍ عِلْمًا ﴿٩٨﴾

99 Thus relate Who unto thee (Muhammad) some tidings of that which happened of old, and We have given thee from Our presence a Reminder.

كَذَٰلِكَ نَقُصُّ عَلَيْكَ مِنْ أَنۢبَآءِ مَا قَدْ سَبَقَ وَقَدْ ءَاتَيْنَٰكَ مِن لَّدُنَّا ذِكْرًا ﴿٩٩﴾

---

2. The explanation usually given is that As-Sāmirī had seen the angel Gabriel pass by, and had taken some of the dust which he had hallowed, and thrown it into the image of the calf, thus giving it a semblance of life. Others say that As-Sāmirī was an adept of the Egyptian idolatry who had believed for a little while and half-heartedly in the God of Moses.

100   Whoso turneth away from it, he verily will bear a burden on the Day of Resurrection;

مَّنْ أَعْرَضَ عَنْهُ فَإِنَّهُ يَحْمِلُ يَوْمَ الْقِيَمَةِ وِزْرًا ۝

101   Abiding under it—an evil burden for them on the Day of Resurrection;

خَٰلِدِينَ فِيهِ وَسَآءَ لَهُمْ يَوْمَ الْقِيَمَةِ حِمْلًا ۝

102   The day when the Trumpet is blown. On that day we assemble the guilty white-eyed (with terror);

يَوْمَ يُنفَخُ فِى الصُّورِ وَنَحْشُرُ الْمُجْرِمِينَ يَوْمَئِذٍ زُرْقًا ۝

103   Murmuring among themselves: Ye have tarried but ten (days).

يَتَخَٰفَتُونَ بَيْنَهُمْ إِن لَّبِثْتُمْ إِلَّا عَشْرًا ۝

104   We are best aware of what they utter when their best in conduct say: Ye have tarried but a day.

نَّحْنُ أَعْلَمُ بِمَا يَقُولُونَ إِذْ يَقُولُ أَمْثَلُهُمْ طَرِيقَةً إِن لَّبِثْتُمْ إِلَّا يَوْمًا ۝

105   They will ask thee of the mountains (on that day). Say: My Lord will break them into scattered dust.

وَيَسْـَٔلُونَكَ عَنِ الْجِبَالِ فَقُلْ يَنسِفُهَا رَبِّى نَسْفًا ۝

106   And leave it as an empty plain;

فَيَذَرُهَا قَاعًا صَفْصَفًا ۝

107   Wherein thou seest neither curve nor ruggedness.

لَّا تَرَىٰ فِيهَا عِوَجًا وَلَآ أَمْتًا ۝

108   On that day they follow the summoner who deceiveth not, and voices are hushed for the Beneficent, and thou hearest but a faint murmur.

يَوْمَئِذٍ يَتَّبِعُونَ الدَّاعِى لَا عِوَجَ لَهُ وَخَشَعَتِ الْأَصْوَاتُ لِلرَّحْمَٰنِ فَلَا تَسْمَعُ إِلَّا هَمْسًا ۝

109   On that Day no intercession availeth save (that of) him unto whom the Beneficent hath given leave and whose He accepteth.

يَوْمَئِذٍ لَّا تَنفَعُ الشَّفَٰعَةُ إِلَّا مَنْ أَذِنَ لَهُ الرَّحْمَٰنُ وَرَضِىَ لَهُ قَوْلًا ۝

110   He knoweth (all) that is before them and (all) that is behind

يَعْلَمُ مَا بَيْنَ أَيْدِيهِمْ وَمَا خَلْفَهُمْ وَلَا يُحِيطُونَ بِهِ

them, while they cannot compass it in knowledge.

111   And faces humble themselves before the Living, the Eternal. And he who beareth (a burden of) wrongdoing is indeed a failure (on that Day).

112   And he who hath done some good works, being a believer, he feareth not injustice nor begrudging (of his wage).

113   Thus We have revealed it as a Lecture[3] in Arabic, and have displayed therein certain threats, that peradventure they may keep from evil or that it may cause them to take heed.

114   Then exalted be Allah, the True King! And hasten not (O Muhammad) with the Qur'an ere its revelation hath been perfected unto thee, and say: My Lord! Increase me in knowledge.

115   And verily We made a covenant of old with Adam, but he forgot, and We found no constancy in him.

116   And when We said unto the angels: Fall prostrate before Adam, they fell prostrate (all) save Iblīs; he refused.

117   Therefore We said: O Adam! This is an enemy unto thee and unto

عِلْمًا ﴿١١٠﴾

۞ وَعَنَتِ الْوُجُوهُ لِلْحَيِّ الْقَيُّومِ ۖ وَقَدْ خَابَ مَنْ حَمَلَ ظُلْمًا ﴿١١١﴾

وَمَن يَعْمَلْ مِنَ الصَّالِحَاتِ وَهُوَ مُؤْمِنٌ فَلَا يَخَافُ ظُلْمًا وَلَا هَضْمًا ﴿١١٢﴾

وَكَذَٰلِكَ أَنزَلْنَاهُ قُرْآنًا عَرَبِيًّا وَصَرَّفْنَا فِيهِ مِنَ الْوَعِيدِ لَعَلَّهُمْ يَتَّقُونَ أَوْ يُحْدِثُ لَهُمْ ذِكْرًا ﴿١١٣﴾

فَتَعَالَى اللَّهُ الْمَلِكُ الْحَقُّ ۗ وَلَا تَعْجَلْ بِالْقُرْآنِ مِن قَبْلِ أَن يُقْضَىٰ إِلَيْكَ وَحْيُهُ ۖ وَقُل رَّبِّ زِدْنِي عِلْمًا ﴿١١٤﴾

وَلَقَدْ عَهِدْنَا إِلَىٰ آدَمَ مِن قَبْلُ فَنَسِيَ وَلَمْ نَجِدْ لَهُ عَزْمًا ﴿١١٥﴾

وَإِذْ قُلْنَا لِلْمَلَائِكَةِ اسْجُدُوا لِآدَمَ فَسَجَدُوا إِلَّا إِبْلِيسَ أَبَىٰ ﴿١١٦﴾

فَقُلْنَا يَا آدَمُ إِنَّ هَٰذَا عَدُوٌّ لَّكَ وَلِزَوْجِكَ

---

3. Ar. *Qur'an.*

thy wife, so let him not drive you both out of the Garden so that thou come to toil.

فَلَا يُخْرِجَنَّكُمَا مِنَ الْجَنَّةِ فَتَشْقَىٰ ۝

118   It is (vouchsafed) unto thee that thou hungerest not therein nor art naked;

إِنَّ لَكَ أَلَّا تَجُوعَ فِيهَا وَلَا تَعْرَىٰ ۝

119   And thou thirstest not therein nor art exposed to the sun's heat.

وَأَنَّكَ لَا تَظْمَؤُا فِيهَا وَلَا تَضْحَىٰ ۝

120   But the Devil whispered to him, saying: O Adam! Shall I show thee the tree of immortality and power that wasteth not away?

فَوَسْوَسَ إِلَيْهِ الشَّيْطَانُ قَالَ يَا آدَمُ هَلْ أَدُلُّكَ عَلَىٰ شَجَرَةِ الْخُلْدِ وَمُلْكٍ لَّا يَبْلَىٰ ۝

121   Then they twain ate thereof, so that their shame became apparent unto them, and they began to hide by heaping on themselves some of the leaves of the Garden. And Adam disobeyed his Lord, so went astray.[4]

فَأَكَلَا مِنْهَا فَبَدَتْ لَهُمَا سَوْآتُهُمَا وَطَفِقَا يَخْصِفَانِ عَلَيْهِمَا مِن وَرَقِ الْجَنَّةِ وَعَصَىٰ آدَمُ رَبَّهُ فَغَوَىٰ ۝

122   Then his Lord chose him, and relented toward him, and guided him.

ثُمَّ اجْتَبَاهُ رَبُّهُ فَتَابَ عَلَيْهِ وَهَدَىٰ ۝

123   He said: Go down hence, both of you, one of you a foe unto the other. But if there come unto you from Me a guidance, then whoso followeth My guidance, he will not go astray nor come to grief.[5]

قَالَ اهْبِطَا مِنْهَا جَمِيعًا بَعْضُكُمْ لِبَعْضٍ عَدُوٌّ فَإِمَّا يَأْتِيَنَّكُم مِّنِّي هُدًى فَمَنِ اتَّبَعَ هُدَايَ فَلَا يَضِلُّ وَلَا يَشْقَىٰ ۝

124   But he who turneth away from remembrance of Me, his will be a narrow life, and I shall bring

وَمَنْ أَعْرَضَ عَن ذِكْرِي فَإِنَّ لَهُ مَعِيشَةً ضَنكًا

---

4. Cf. Sūrah (7: 20) ff.

5. Cf. Sūrah (2: 38), and the passage leading up to it.

him blind to the assembly on the Day of Resurrection.

وَنَحْشُرُهُ يَوْمَ الْقِيَامَةِ أَعْمَىٰ ﴿١٢٤﴾

125   He will say: My Lord! Wherefore hast Thou gathered me (hither) blind, when I was wont to see?

قَالَ رَبِّ لِمَ حَشَرْتَنِىٓ أَعْمَىٰ وَقَدْ كُنتُ بَصِيرًا ﴿١٢٥﴾

126   He will say: So (it must be). Our revelations came unto thee but thou didst forget them. In like manner thou art forgotten this Day.

قَالَ كَذَٰلِكَ أَتَتْكَ ءَايَٰتُنَا فَنَسِيتَهَا ۖ وَكَذَٰلِكَ الْيَوْمَ تُنسَىٰ ﴿١٢٦﴾

127   Thus do We reward him who is prodigal and believeth not the revelations of his Lord; and verily the doom of the Hereafter will be sterner and more lasting.

وَكَذَٰلِكَ نَجْزِى مَنْ أَسْرَفَ وَلَمْ يُؤْمِنۢ بِـَٔايَٰتِ رَبِّهِ ۚ وَلَعَذَابُ الْءَاخِرَةِ أَشَدُّ وَأَبْقَىٰ ﴿١٢٧﴾

128   Is it not a guidance for them (to know) how many a generation We destroyed before them, amid whose dwellings they walk? Lo! therein verily are signs for men of thought.

أَفَلَمْ يَهْدِ لَهُمْ كَمْ أَهْلَكْنَا قَبْلَهُم مِّنَ الْقُرُونِ يَمْشُونَ فِى مَسَٰكِنِهِمْ ۚ إِنَّ فِى ذَٰلِكَ لَءَايَٰتٍ لِّأُولِى النُّهَىٰ ﴿١٢٨﴾

129   And but for a decree that had already gone forth from thy Lord, and a term already fixed, the judgment would (have) been inevitable (in this world).

وَلَوْلَا كَلِمَةٌ سَبَقَتْ مِن رَّبِّكَ لَكَانَ لِزَامًا وَأَجَلٌ مُّسَمًّى ﴿١٢٩﴾

130   Therefore (O Muhammad), bear with what they say, and celebrate the praises of thy Lord ere the rising of the sun and ere the going down thereof. And glorify Him some hours of the night and at the two ends of the day, that thou mayst be well pleased.

فَاصْبِرْ عَلَىٰ مَا يَقُولُونَ وَسَبِّحْ بِحَمْدِ رَبِّكَ قَبْلَ طُلُوعِ الشَّمْسِ وَقَبْلَ غُرُوبِهَا ۖ وَمِنْ ءَانَآئِ الَّيْلِ فَسَبِّحْ وَأَطْرَافَ النَّهَارِ لَعَلَّكَ تَرْضَىٰ ﴿١٣٠﴾

131   And strain not thine eyes toward that which We cause some wedded pairs among them to enjoy, the flower of the life of the world, that We may try them thereby. The provision of thy Lord is better and more lasting.

وَلَا تَمُدَّنَّ عَيْنَيْكَ إِلَىٰ مَا مَتَّعْنَا بِهِۦ أَزْوَاجًا مِّنْهُمْ زَهْرَةَ ٱلْحَيَوٰةِ ٱلدُّنْيَا لِنَفْتِنَهُمْ فِيهِ وَرِزْقُ رَبِّكَ خَيْرٌ وَأَبْقَىٰ ﴿١٣١﴾

132   And enjoin upon thy people worship, and be constant therein. We ask not of thee a provision: We provide for thee. And the sequel is for righteousness.

وَأْمُرْ أَهْلَكَ بِٱلصَّلَوٰةِ وَٱصْطَبِرْ عَلَيْهَا لَا نَسْـَٔلُكَ رِزْقًا نَّحْنُ نَرْزُقُكَ وَٱلْعَٰقِبَةُ لِلتَّقْوَىٰ ﴿١٣٢﴾

133   And they say: If only he would bring us a miracle from his Lord! Hath there not come unto them the proof of what is in the former Scriptures?

وَقَالُوا لَوْلَا يَأْتِينَا بِـَٔايَةٍ مِّن رَّبِّهِۦ أَوَلَمْ تَأْتِهِم بَيِّنَةُ مَا فِى ٱلصُّحُفِ ٱلْأُولَىٰ ﴿١٣٣﴾

134   And if We had destroyed them with some punishment before it, they would assuredly have said: Our Lord! If only Thou hadst sent unto us a messenger, so that we might have followed Thy revelations before we were (thus) humbled and disgraced!

وَلَوْ أَنَّا أَهْلَكْنَٰهُم بِعَذَابٍ مِّن قَبْلِهِۦ لَقَالُوا رَبَّنَا لَوْلَا أَرْسَلْتَ إِلَيْنَا رَسُولًا فَنَتَّبِعَ ءَايَٰتِكَ مِن قَبْلِ أَن نَّذِلَّ وَنَخْزَىٰ ﴿١٣٤﴾

135   Say: Each is awaiting; so await ye! Ye will come to know who are the owners of the path of equity, and who is right.

قُلْ كُلٌّ مُّتَرَبِّصٌ فَتَرَبَّصُوا فَسَتَعْلَمُونَ مَنْ أَصْحَٰبُ ٱلصِّرَٰطِ ٱلسَّوِيِّ وَمَنِ ٱهْتَدَىٰ ﴿١٣٥﴾

Al Anbiyā'
(The Prophets)

Al Anbiyā', "The Prophets," is named from its subject, the history of the former Prophets. The speaker in v. 4 and v. 112 is every Prophet. There is no historical reference or tradition to enable us to fix the date. It is undoubtedly of Makkan revelation, and lacks the characteristics of the latest and earliest Makkan sūrahs. It may, therefore, be taken as belonging to the middle group of Makkan sūrahs.

سُوْرَةُ الْأَنْبِيَاءِ

In the name of Allah, the Beneficent, the Merciful.

بِسْمِ اللهِ الرَّحْمٰنِ الرَّحِيمِ

1 Their reckoning draweth nigh for mankind, while they turn away in heedlessness.

اقْتَرَبَ لِلنَّاسِ حِسَابُهُمْ وَهُمْ فِى غَفْلَةٍ مُّعْرِضُونَ ۝

2 Never cometh there unto them a new reminder from their Lord but they listen to it while they play.

مَا يَأْتِيهِمْ مِّنْ ذِكْرٍ مِّنْ رَّبِّهِمْ مُّحْدَثٍ إِلَّا اسْتَمَعُوهُ وَهُمْ يَلْعَبُونَ ۝

3 With hearts preoccupied. And they confer in secret. The wrong-doers say: Is this other than a mortal like you? Will ye then succumb to magic when ye see (it)?

لَاهِيَةً قُلُوبُهُمْ وَأَسَرُّوا النَّجْوَى الَّذِينَ ظَلَمُوا هَلْ هٰذَا إِلَّا بَشَرٌ مِّثْلُكُمْ أَفَتَأْتُونَ السِّحْرَ وَأَنْتُمْ تُبْصِرُونَ ۝

4 He saith: My Lord knoweth what is spoken in the heaven and the earth. He is the Hearer, the Knower.

قَالَ رَبِّى يَعْلَمُ الْقَوْلَ فِى السَّمَاءِ وَالْأَرْضِ وَهُوَ السَّمِيعُ الْعَلِيمُ ۝

5 Nay, say they, (these are but) muddled dreams; nay, he hath but

بَلْ قَالُوا أَضْغَاثُ أَحْلَامٍ بَلِ افْتَرَاهُ بَلْ هُوَ

invented it; nay, he is but a poet.
Let him bring us a portent even as
those of old (who were God's messengers) were sent (with portents).

شَاعِرٌ فَلْيَأْتِنَا بِاٰيَةٍ كَمَآ أُرْسِلَ الْأَوَّلُوْنَ ۝

6   Not a township believed of those
which We destroyed before them
(though We sent them portents):
would they then believe?

مَآ اٰمَنَتْ قَبْلَهُمْ مِّنْ قَرْيَةٍ أَهْلَكْنٰهَا ۚ أَفَهُمْ
يُؤْمِنُوْنَ ۝

7   And We sent not (as Our messengers) before thee other than men
whom We inspired. Ask the followers of the Reminder[1] if ye know
not?

وَمَآ أَرْسَلْنَا قَبْلَكَ إِلَّا رِجَالًا نُّوْحِىٓ إِلَيْهِمْ فَسْـَٔلُوْٓا
أَهْلَ الذِّكْرِ إِنْ كُنْتُمْ لَا تَعْلَمُوْنَ ۝

8   We gave them not bodies that
would not eat food, nor were they
immortals.

وَمَا جَعَلْنٰهُمْ جَسَدًا لَّا يَأْكُلُوْنَ الطَّعَامَ
وَمَا كَانُوْا خٰلِدِيْنَ ۝

9   Then We fulfilled the promise
unto them. So We delivered them
and whom We would, and We destroyed the prodigals.

ثُمَّ صَدَقْنٰهُمُ الْوَعْدَ فَأَنْجَيْنٰهُمْ وَمَنْ نَّشَآءُ
وَأَهْلَكْنَا الْمُسْرِفِيْنَ ۝

10 Now We have revealed unto you
a Scripture wherein is your Reminder. Have ye then no sense?

لَقَدْ أَنْزَلْنَآ إِلَيْكُمْ كِتٰبًا فِيْهِ ذِكْرُكُمْ ۚ أَفَلَا
تَعْقِلُوْنَ ۝

11 How many a community that
dealt unjustly have We shattered, and
raised up after them another folk!

وَكَمْ قَصَمْنَا مِنْ قَرْيَةٍ كَانَتْ ظَالِمَةً
وَأَنْشَأْنَا بَعْدَهَا قَوْمًا اٰخَرِيْنَ ۝

12 And, when they felt Our might,
behold them fleeing from it!

فَلَمَّآ أَحَسُّوْا بَأْسَنَآ إِذَا هُمْ مِّنْهَا يَرْكُضُوْنَ ۝

13 (But it was said unto them): Flee
not, but return to that (existence)
which emasculated you and to your
dwellings, that ye may be questioned.

لَا تَرْكُضُوْا وَارْجِعُوْٓا إِلَىٰ مَآ أُتْرِفْتُمْ فِيْهِ
وَمَسٰكِنِكُمْ لَعَلَّكُمْ تُسْـَٔلُوْنَ ۝

---

1. *i.e.* the Jewish Scripture.

14 They cried: Alas for us! Lo! we were wrong-doers.

قَالُوا يَاوَيْلَنَا إِنَّا كُنَّا ظَٰلِمِينَ ۝

15 And this their crying ceased not till We made them as reaped corn, extinct.

فَمَا زَالَت تِّلْكَ دَعْوَىٰهُمْ حَتَّىٰ جَعَلْنَٰهُمْ حَصِيدًا خَٰمِدِينَ ۝

16 We created not the heaven and the earth and all that is between them in play.

وَمَا خَلَقْنَا السَّمَآءَ وَالْأَرْضَ وَمَا بَيْنَهُمَا لَٰعِبِينَ ۝

17 If We had wished to find a pastime, We could have found it in Our presence—if We ever did.

لَوْ أَرَدْنَآ أَن نَّتَّخِذَ لَهْوًا لَّاتَّخَذْنَٰهُ مِن لَّدُنَّآ إِن كُنَّا فَٰعِلِينَ ۝

18 Nay, but We hurl the true against the false, and it doth break its head and lo! it vanisheth. And yours will be woe for that which ye ascribe (unto Him).

بَلْ نَقْذِفُ بِالْحَقِّ عَلَى الْبَٰطِلِ فَيَدْمَغُهُ فَإِذَا هُوَ زَاهِقٌ وَلَكُمُ الْوَيْلُ مِمَّا تَصِفُونَ ۝

19 Unto Him belongeth whosoever is in the heavens and the earth. And those who dwell in His presence are not too proud to worship Him nor do they weary;

وَلَهُۥ مَن فِى السَّمَٰوَٰتِ وَالْأَرْضِ وَمَنْ عِندَهُۥ لَا يَسْتَكْبِرُونَ عَنْ عِبَادَتِهِۦ وَلَا يَسْتَحْسِرُونَ ۝

20 They glorify (Him) night and day; they flag not.

يُسَبِّحُونَ الَّيْلَ وَالنَّهَارَ لَا يَفْتُرُونَ ۝

21 Or have they chosen gods from the earth who raise the dead?

أَمِ اتَّخَذُوٓا ءَالِهَةً مِّنَ الْأَرْضِ هُمْ يُنشِرُونَ ۝

22 If there were therein gods beside Allah, then verily both (the heavens and the earth) had been disordered. Glorified be Allah, the Lord of the Throne, from all that they ascribe (unto Him).

لَوْ كَانَ فِيهِمَآ ءَالِهَةٌ إِلَّا اللَّهُ لَفَسَدَتَا فَسُبْحَٰنَ اللَّهِ رَبِّ الْعَرْشِ عَمَّا يَصِفُونَ ۝

23 He will not be questioned as to that which He doeth, but they will be questioned.

لَا يُسْـَٔلُ عَمَّا يَفْعَلُ وَهُمْ يُسْـَٔلُونَ ۝

24 Or have they chosen other gods beside Him? Say: Bring your proof (of their godhead). This is the Reminder of those with me and those before me, but most of them know not the Truth and so they are averse.

أَمِ ٱتَّخَذُوا مِن دُونِهِۦ ءَالِهَةً قُلْ هَاتُوا بُرْهَٰنَكُمْ هَٰذَا ذِكْرُ مَن مَّعِىَ وَذِكْرُ مَن قَبْلِى بَلْ أَكْثَرُهُمْ لَا يَعْلَمُونَ ٱلْحَقَّ فَهُم مُّعْرِضُونَ ٢٤

25 And We sent no messenger before thee but We inspired him, (saying): There is no God save Me (Allah), so worship Me.

وَمَا أَرْسَلْنَا مِن قَبْلِكَ مِن رَّسُولٍ إِلَّا نُوحِى إِلَيْهِ أَنَّهُ لَا إِلَٰهَ إِلَّا أَنَا۠ فَٱعْبُدُونِ ٢٥

26 And they say: The Beneficent hath taken unto Himself a son. Be He glorified! Nay, but (those whom they call sons) are honoured slaves;

وَقَالُوا ٱتَّخَذَ ٱلرَّحْمَٰنُ وَلَدًا سُبْحَٰنَهُۥ بَلْ عِبَادٌ مُّكْرَمُونَ ٢٦

27 They speak not until He hath spoken, and they act by His command.

لَا يَسْبِقُونَهُۥ بِٱلْقَوْلِ وَهُم بِأَمْرِهِۦ يَعْمَلُونَ ٢٧

28 He knoweth what is before them and what is behind them, and they cannot intercede except for him whom He accepteth, and they quake for awe of Him.

يَعْلَمُ مَا بَيْنَ أَيْدِيهِمْ وَمَا خَلْفَهُمْ وَلَا يَشْفَعُونَ إِلَّا لِمَنِ ٱرْتَضَىٰ وَهُم مِّنْ خَشْيَتِهِۦ مُشْفِقُونَ ٢٨

29 And one of them who should say: Lo! I am a God beside Him, that one We should repay with hell. Thus We repay wrong-doers.

۞ وَمَن يَقُلْ مِنْهُمْ إِنِّى إِلَٰهٌ مِّن دُونِهِۦ فَذَٰلِكَ نَجْزِيهِ جَهَنَّمَ كَذَٰلِكَ نَجْزِى ٱلظَّٰلِمِينَ ٢٩

30 Have not those who disbelieve known that the heavens and the earth were of one piece, then We parted them, and We made every living thing of water? Will they not then believe?

أَوَلَمْ يَرَ ٱلَّذِينَ كَفَرُوٓا أَنَّ ٱلسَّمَٰوَٰتِ وَٱلْأَرْضَ كَانَتَا رَتْقًا فَفَتَقْنَٰهُمَا وَجَعَلْنَا مِنَ ٱلْمَآءِ كُلَّ شَىْءٍ حَىٍّ أَفَلَا يُؤْمِنُونَ ٣٠

31 And We have placed in the earth firm hills lest it quake with them,

وَجَعَلْنَا فِى ٱلْأَرْضِ رَوَٰسِىَ أَن تَمِيدَ بِهِمْ وَجَعَلْنَا

and We have placed therein ravines as roads that haply they may find their way.

فِيهَا فِجَاجًا سُبُلًا لَّعَلَّهُمْ يَهْتَدُونَ ۝

32 And We have made the sky a roof withheld (from them). Yet they turn away from its portents.

وَجَعَلْنَا السَّمَاءَ سَقْفًا مَّحْفُوظًا وَهُمْ عَنْ آيَاتِهَا مُعْرِضُونَ ۝

33 And He it is Who created the night and the day, and the sun and the moon. They float, each in an orbit.

وَهُوَ الَّذِى خَلَقَ الَّيْلَ وَالنَّهَارَ وَالشَّمْسَ وَالْقَمَرَ كُلٌّ فِى فَلَكٍ يَسْبَحُونَ ۝

34 We appointed immortality for no mortal before thee. What! if thou diest, can they be immortal?

وَمَا جَعَلْنَا لِبَشَرٍ مِّنْ قَبْلِكَ الْخُلْدَ أَفَإِنْ مِتَّ فَهُمُ الْخَالِدُونَ ۝

35 Every soul must taste of death, and We try you with evil and with good, for ordeal. And unto Us ye will be returned.

كُلُّ نَفْسٍ ذَائِقَةُ الْمَوْتِ وَنَبْلُوكُمْ بِالشَّرِّ وَالْخَيْرِ فِتْنَةً وَإِلَيْنَا تُرْجَعُونَ ۝

36 And when those who disbelieve behold thee, they but choose thee out for mockery, (saying): Is this he who maketh mention of your gods? And they would deny all mention of the Beneficent.

وَإِذَا رَآكَ الَّذِينَ كَفَرُوا إِنْ يَتَّخِذُونَكَ إِلَّا هُزُوًا أَهَذَا الَّذِى يَذْكُرُ آلِهَتَكُمْ وَهُمْ بِذِكْرِ الرَّحْمَنِ هُمْ كَافِرُونَ ۝

37 Man is made of haste. I shall show you My portents, but ask Me not to hasten.

خُلِقَ الْإِنْسَانُ مِنْ عَجَلٍ سَأُورِيكُمْ آيَاتِى فَلَا تَسْتَعْجِلُونِ ۝

38 And they say: When will this promise (be fulfilled), if ye are truthful?

وَيَقُولُونَ مَتَى هَذَا الْوَعْدُ إِنْ كُنْتُمْ صَادِقِينَ ۝

39 If those who disbelieved but knew the time when they will not be able to drive off the fire from their faces and from their backs, and they will not be helped!

لَوْ يَعْلَمُ الَّذِينَ كَفَرُوا حِينَ لَا يَكُفُّونَ عَنْ وُجُوهِهِمُ النَّارَ وَلَا عَنْ ظُهُورِهِمْ وَلَا هُمْ يُنْصَرُونَ ۝

40 Nay, but it will come upon them unawares so that it will stupefy them, and they will be unable to repel it, neither will they be reprieved.

بَلْ تَأْتِيهِم بَغْتَةً فَتَبْهَتُهُمْ فَلَا يَسْتَطِيعُونَ رَدَّهَا وَلَا هُمْ يُنظَرُونَ ٤٠

41 Messengers before thee, indeed, were mocked, but that whereat they mocked surrounded those who scoffed at them.

وَلَقَدِ اسْتُهْزِئَ بِرُسُلٍ مِّن قَبْلِكَ فَحَاقَ بِالَّذِينَ سَخِرُوا مِنْهُم مَّا كَانُوا بِهِ يَسْتَهْزِءُونَ ٤١

42 Say: Who guardeth you in the night or in the day from the Beneficent? Nay, but they turn away from mention of their Lord!

قُلْ مَن يَكْلَؤُكُم بِالَّيْلِ وَالنَّهَارِ مِنَ الرَّحْمَٰنِ بَلْ هُمْ عَن ذِكْرِ رَبِّهِم مُّعْرِضُونَ ٤٢

43 Or have they gods who can shield them from Us? They cannot help themselves nor can they be defended from Us.

أَمْ لَهُمْ ءَالِهَةٌ تَمْنَعُهُم مِّن دُونِنَا لَا يَسْتَطِيعُونَ نَصْرَ أَنفُسِهِمْ وَلَا هُم مِّنَّا يُصْحَبُونَ ٤٣

44 Nay, but We gave these and their fathers ease until life grew long for them. See they not how we visit the land, reducing it of its outlying parts?[2] Can they then be the victors?

بَلْ مَتَّعْنَا هَٰؤُلَاءِ وَءَابَاءَهُمْ حَتَّىٰ طَالَ عَلَيْهِمُ الْعُمُرُ أَفَلَا يَرَوْنَ أَنَّا نَأْتِي الْأَرْضَ نَنقُصُهَا مِنْ أَطْرَافِهَا أَفَهُمُ الْغَٰلِبُونَ ٤٤

45 Say (O Muḥammad, unto mankind): I warn you only by the Inspiration. But the deaf hear not the call when they are warned.

قُلْ إِنَّمَا أُنذِرُكُم بِالْوَحْيِ وَلَا يَسْمَعُ الصُّمُّ الدُّعَاءَ إِذَا مَا يُنذَرُونَ ٤٥

46 And if a breath of thy Lord's punishment were to touch them, they assuredly would say: Alas for us! Lo! we were wrong-doers.

وَلَئِن مَّسَّتْهُمْ نَفْحَةٌ مِّنْ عَذَابِ رَبِّكَ لَيَقُولُنَّ يَٰوَيْلَنَا إِنَّا كُنَّا ظَٰلِمِينَ ٤٦

47 And We set a just balance for the Day of Resurrection so that no

وَنَضَعُ الْمَوَٰزِينَ الْقِسْطَ لِيَوْمِ الْقِيَٰمَةِ فَلَا تُظْلَمُ

---

2. See (13: 41), note.

soul is wronged in aught. Though it be of the weight of a grain of mustard seed, We bring it. And We suffice for reckoners.

نَفْسٌ شَيْئًا وَإِن كَانَ مِثْقَالَ حَبَّةٍ مِّنْ خَرْدَلٍ أَتَيْنَا بِهَا وَكَفَى بِنَا حَاسِبِينَ ۝

48 And We verily gave Moses and Aaron the Criterion (of right and wrong) and a light and a Reminder for those who keep from evil;

وَلَقَدْ ءَاتَيْنَا مُوسَى وَهَارُونَ الْفُرْقَانَ وَضِيَآءً وَذِكْرًا لِّلْمُتَّقِينَ ۝

49 Those who fear their Lord in secret and who dread the Hour (of doom).

الَّذِينَ يَخْشَوْنَ رَبَّهُم بِالْغَيْبِ وَهُم مِّنَ السَّاعَةِ مُشْفِقُونَ ۝

50 This is a blessed Reminder that We have revealed: Will ye then reject it?

وَهَذَا ذِكْرٌ مُّبَارَكٌ أَنزَلْنَاهُ أَفَأَنتُمْ لَهُ مُنكِرُونَ ۝

51 And We verily gave Abraham of old his proper course, and We were Aware of him;

۞ وَلَقَدْ ءَاتَيْنَا إِبْرَاهِيمَ رُشْدَهُ مِن قَبْلُ وَكُنَّا بِهِ عَالِمِينَ ۝

52 When he said unto his father and his folk: What are these images unto which ye pay devotion?

إِذْ قَالَ لِأَبِيهِ وَقَوْمِهِ مَا هَذِهِ التَّمَاثِيلُ الَّتِي أَنتُمْ لَهَا عَاكِفُونَ ۝

53 They said: We found our fathers worshippers of them.

قَالُوا وَجَدْنَا ءَابَآءَنَا لَهَا عَابِدِينَ ۝

54 He said: Verily ye and your fathers were in plain error.

قَالَ لَقَدْ كُنتُمْ أَنتُمْ وَءَابَآؤُكُمْ فِي ضَلَالٍ مُّبِينٍ ۝

55 They said: Bringest thou unto us the truth, or art thou some jester?

قَالُوا أَجِئْتَنَا بِالْحَقِّ أَمْ أَنتَ مِنَ اللَّاعِبِينَ ۝

56 He said: Nay, but your Lord is the Lord of the heavens and the earth, Who created them; and I am of those who testify unto that.

قَالَ بَل رَّبُّكُمْ رَبُّ السَّمَوَاتِ وَالْأَرْضِ الَّذِي فَطَرَهُنَّ وَأَنَا عَلَى ذَلِكُم مِّنَ الشَّاهِدِينَ ۝

57 And, by Allah, I shall circumvent your idols after ye have gone away and turned your backs.

وَتَاللَّهِ لَأَكِيدَنَّ أَصْنَامَكُم بَعْدَ أَن تُوَلُّوا مُدْبِرِينَ ۝

58 Then he reduced them to fragments, all save the chief of them, that haply they might have recourse to it.

فَجَعَلَهُمْ جُذَاذًا إِلَّا كَبِيرًا لَّهُمْ لَعَلَّهُمْ إِلَيْهِ يَرْجِعُونَ ۝

59 They said: Who hath done this to our gods? Surely it must be some evil-doer.

قَالُوا مَن فَعَلَ هَٰذَا بِآلِهَتِنَا إِنَّهُ لَمِنَ الظَّالِمِينَ ۝

60 They said: We heard a youth make mention of them, who is called Abraham.

قَالُوا سَمِعْنَا فَتًى يَذْكُرُهُمْ يُقَالُ لَهُ إِبْرَاهِيمُ ۝

61 They said: Then bring him (hither) before the people's eyes that they may testify.

قَالُوا فَأْتُوا بِهِ عَلَىٰ أَعْيُنِ النَّاسِ لَعَلَّهُمْ يَشْهَدُونَ ۝

62 They said: Is it thou who hast done this to our gods, O Abraham?

قَالُوا أَأَنتَ فَعَلْتَ هَٰذَا بِآلِهَتِنَا يَا إِبْرَاهِيمُ ۝

63 He said: But this, their chief hath done it. So question them, if they can speak.

قَالَ بَلْ فَعَلَهُ كَبِيرُهُمْ هَٰذَا فَاسْأَلُوهُمْ إِن كَانُوا يَنطِقُونَ ۝

64 Then gathered they apart and said: Lo! ye yourselves are the wrong-doers.

فَرَجَعُوا إِلَىٰ أَنفُسِهِمْ فَقَالُوا إِنَّكُمْ أَنتُمُ الظَّالِمُونَ ۝

65 And they were utterly confounded, and they said: Well thou knowest that these speak not.

ثُمَّ نُكِسُوا عَلَىٰ رُءُوسِهِمْ لَقَدْ عَلِمْتَ مَا هَٰؤُلَاءِ يَنطِقُونَ ۝

66 He said: Worship ye then instead of Allah that which cannot profit you at all, nor harm you?

قَالَ أَفَتَعْبُدُونَ مِن دُونِ اللَّهِ مَا لَا يَنفَعُكُمْ شَيْئًا وَلَا يَضُرُّكُمْ ۝

67 Fie on you and all that ye worship instead of Allah! Have ye then no sense?

أُفٍّ لَّكُمْ وَلِمَا تَعْبُدُونَ مِن دُونِ اللَّهِ أَفَلَا تَعْقِلُونَ ۝

68 They cried: Burn him and stand by your gods, if ye will be doing.

قَالُوا حَرِّقُوهُ وَانصُرُوا آلِهَتَكُمْ إِن كُنتُمْ فَاعِلِينَ ۝

69 We said: O fire, be coolness and peace for Abraham.

قُلْنَا يَا نَارُ كُونِي بَرْدًا وَسَلَامًا عَلَىٰ إِبْرَاهِيمَ ۝

70 And they wished to set a snare for him, but We made them the greater losers.

وَأَرَادُوا بِهِ كَيْدًا فَجَعَلْنَٰهُمُ الْأَخْسَرِينَ ۝

71 And We rescued him and Lot (and brought them) to the land which We have blessed for (all) peoples.

وَنَجَّيْنَٰهُ وَلُوطًا إِلَى الْأَرْضِ الَّتِي بَٰرَكْنَا فِيهَا لِلْعَٰلَمِينَ ۝

72 And We bestowed upon him Isaac, and Jacob as a grandson. Each of them We made righteous.

وَوَهَبْنَا لَهُ إِسْحَٰقَ وَيَعْقُوبَ نَافِلَةً وَكُلًّا جَعَلْنَا صَٰلِحِينَ ۝

73 And We made them chiefs who guide by Our command, and We inspired in them the doing of good deeds and the right establishment of worship and the giving of alms, and they were worshippers of Us (alone).

وَجَعَلْنَٰهُمْ أَئِمَّةً يَهْدُونَ بِأَمْرِنَا وَأَوْحَيْنَا إِلَيْهِمْ فِعْلَ الْخَيْرَٰتِ وَإِقَامَ الصَّلَوٰةِ وَإِيتَاءَ الزَّكَوٰةِ وَكَانُوا لَنَا عَٰبِدِينَ ۝

74 And unto Lot We gave judgment and knowledge, and We delivered him from the community that did abominations. Lo! they were folk of evil, lewd.

وَلُوطًا ءَاتَيْنَٰهُ حُكْمًا وَعِلْمًا وَنَجَّيْنَٰهُ مِنَ الْقَرْيَةِ الَّتِي كَانَت تَّعْمَلُ الْخَبَٰئِثَ إِنَّهُمْ كَانُوا قَوْمَ سَوْءٍ فَٰسِقِينَ ۝

75 And We brought him in unto Our mercy. Lo! he was of the righteous.

وَأَدْخَلْنَٰهُ فِي رَحْمَتِنَا إِنَّهُ مِنَ الصَّٰلِحِينَ ۝

76 And Noah, when he cried of old, We heard his prayer and saved him and his household from the great affliction.

وَنُوحًا إِذْ نَادَىٰ مِن قَبْلُ فَاسْتَجَبْنَا لَهُ فَنَجَّيْنَٰهُ وَأَهْلَهُ مِنَ الْكَرْبِ الْعَظِيمِ ۝

77 And delivered him from the people who denied Our revelations. Lo! they were folk of evil, therefore did We drown them all.

وَنَصَرْنَٰهُ مِنَ الْقَوْمِ الَّذِينَ كَذَّبُوا بِـَٔايَٰتِنَا إِنَّهُمْ كَانُوا قَوْمَ سَوْءٍ فَأَغْرَقْنَٰهُمْ أَجْمَعِينَ ۝

78 And David and Solomon, when they gave judgment concerning the

وَدَاوُۥدَ وَسُلَيْمَٰنَ إِذْ يَحْكُمَانِ

field, when people's sheep had strayed and browsed therein by night; and We were witnesses to their judgment.

79 And We made Solomon to understand (the case); and unto each of them We gave judgment and knowledge. And We subdued the hills and the birds to hymn (His) praise along with David. We were the doers (thereof).

80 And We taught him the art of making garments (of mail) to protect you in your daring. Are ye then thankful?

81 And unto Solomon (We subdued) the wind in its raging. It set by His command toward the land which We had blessed. And of everything We are aware.

82 And of the evil ones[3] (subdued We unto him) some who dived (for pearls) for him and did other work, and We were warders unto them.

83 And Job, when he cried unto his Lord, (saying): Lo! adversity afflicteth me, and Thou art Most Merciful of all who show mercy.

84 Then We heard his prayer and removed that adversity from which he suffered, and We gave him his household (that he had lost) and the

في الْحَرْثِ إِذْ نَفَشَتْ فِيهِ غَنَمُ الْقَوْمِ وَكُنَّا لِحُكْمِهِمْ شَاهِدِينَ ۝

فَفَهَّمْنَاهَا سُلَيْمَانَ وَكُلًّا ءَاتَيْنَا حُكْمًا وَعِلْمًا وَسَخَّرْنَا مَعَ دَاوُدَ الْجِبَالَ يُسَبِّحْنَ وَالطَّيْرَ وَكُنَّا فَاعِلِينَ ۝

وَعَلَّمْنَاهُ صَنْعَةَ لَبُوسٍ لَّكُمْ لِتُحْصِنَكُمْ مِنْ بَأْسِكُمْ فَهَلْ أَنتُمْ شَاكِرُونَ ۝

وَلِسُلَيْمَانَ الرِّيحَ عَاصِفَةً تَجْرِي بِأَمْرِهِ إِلَى الْأَرْضِ الَّتِي بَارَكْنَا فِيهَا وَكُنَّا بِكُلِّ شَيْءٍ عَالِمِينَ ۝

وَمِنَ الشَّيَاطِينِ مَن يَغُوصُونَ لَهُ وَيَعْمَلُونَ عَمَلًا دُونَ ذَلِكَ وَكُنَّا لَهُمْ حَافِظِينَ ۝

وَأَيُّوبَ إِذْ نَادَى رَبَّهُ أَنِّي مَسَّنِيَ الضُّرُّ وَأَنتَ أَرْحَمُ الرَّاحِمِينَ ۝

فَاسْتَجَبْنَا لَهُ فَكَشَفْنَا مَا بِهِ مِن ضُرٍّ وَءَاتَيْنَاهُ أَهْلَهُ وَمِثْلَهُم مَّعَهُمْ رَحْمَةً

---

3. Ar. *Shayātīn*, lit. "devils."

like thereof along with them, a mercy from Our store, and a remembrance for the worshippers;

85 And (mention) Ishmael, and Idrīs, and Dhū'l Kifl.[4] All were of the steadfast.

86 And We brought them in unto Our mercy. Lo! they are among the righteous.

87 And (mention) Dhū'n Nūn,[5] when he went off in anger and deemed that We had no power over him, but he cried out in the darkness, saying: There is no God save Thee. Be Thou glorified! Lo! I have been a wrong-doer.

88 Then We heard his prayer and saved him from the anguish. Thus We save believers.

89 And Zachariah, when he cried unto his Lord: My Lord! Leave me not childless, though Thou art the best of inheritors.

90 Then We heard his prayer, and bestowed upon him John, and adjusted his wife (to bear a child) for him. Lo! they used to vie one with the other in good deeds, and they cried unto Us in longing and in fear, and were submissive unto Us.

مِنْ عِنْدِنَا وَذِكْرَى لِلْعَبِدِينَ ۞

وَإِسْمَعِيلَ وَإِدْرِيسَ وَذَا الْكِفْلِ كُلٌّ مِّنَ الصَّبِرِينَ ۞

وَأَدْخَلْنَهُمْ فِي رَحْمَتِنَا إِنَّهُم مِّنَ الصَّلِحِينَ ۞

وَذَا النُّونِ إِذ ذَّهَبَ مُغَضِبًا فَظَنَّ أَن لَّن نَّقْدِرَ عَلَيْهِ فَنَادَى فِي الظُّلُمَتِ أَن لَّا إِلَهَ إِلَّا أَنتَ سُبْحَنَكَ إِنِّي كُنتُ مِنَ الظَّلِمِينَ ۞

فَاسْتَجَبْنَا لَهُ وَنَجَّيْنَهُ مِنَ الْغَمِّ وَكَذَلِكَ نُـجِي الْمُؤْمِنِينَ ۞

وَزَكَرِيَّا إِذ نَادَى رَبَّهُ رَبِّ لَا تَذَرْنِي فَرْدًا وَأَنتَ خَيْرُ الْوَرِثِينَ ۞

فَاسْتَجَبْنَا لَهُ وَوَهَبْنَا لَهُ يَحْيَى وَأَصْلَحْنَا لَهُ زَوْجَهُ إِنَّهُمْ كَانُوا يُسَرِعُونَ فِي الْخَيْرَتِ وَيَدْعُونَنَا رَغَبًا وَرَهَبًا وَكَانُوا لَنَا خَشِعِينَ ۞

---

4. A prophet famous among the Arabs, whose story resembles that of Ezekiel.

5. Lit. "Lord of the Fish" = Jonah.

91 And she who was chaste,[6] therefore We breathed into her (something) of Our spirit and made her and her son a token for (all) peoples.

وَالَّتِيَ أَحْصَنَتْ فَرْجَهَا فَنَفَخْنَا فِيهَا مِن رُّوحِنَا وَجَعَلْنَاهَا وَابْنَهَآ ءَايَةً لِّلْعَـٰلَمِينَ ۞

92 Lo! this, your religion, is one religion, and I am your Lord, so worship Me.

إِنَّ هَـٰذِهِۦٓ أُمَّتُكُمْ أُمَّةً وَٰحِدَةً وَأَنَا۠ رَبُّكُمْ فَٱعْبُدُونِ ۞

93 And they have broken their religion (into fragments) among them, (yet) all are returning unto Us.

وَتَقَطَّعُوٓا أَمْرَهُم بَيْنَهُمْ كُلٌّ إِلَيْنَا رَٰجِعُونَ ۞

94 Then whoso doeth good works and is a believer, there will be no rejection of his effort. Lo! We record (it) for him.

فَمَن يَعْمَلْ مِنَ ٱلصَّـٰلِحَـٰتِ وَهُوَ مُؤْمِنٌ فَلَا كُفْرَانَ لِسَعْيِهِۦ وَإِنَّا لَهُۥ كَـٰتِبُونَ ۞

95 And there is a ban upon any community which We have destroyed: that they shall not return;

وَحَرَٰمٌ عَلَىٰ قَرْيَةٍ أَهْلَكْنَـٰهَآ أَنَّهُمْ لَا يَرْجِعُونَ ۞

96 Until, when Gog and Magog are let loose, and they hasten out of every mound.

حَتَّىٰٓ إِذَا فُتِحَتْ يَأْجُوجُ وَمَأْجُوجُ وَهُم مِّن كُلِّ حَدَبٍ يَنسِلُونَ ۞

97 And the True Promise draweth nigh; then behold them, staring wide (in terror), the eyes of those who disbelieve! (They say): Alas for us! We (lived) in forgetfulness of this. Ah! But we were wrong-doers!

وَٱقْتَرَبَ ٱلْوَعْدُ ٱلْحَقُّ فَإِذَا هِيَ شَـٰخِصَةٌ أَبْصَـٰرُ ٱلَّذِينَ كَفَرُوا۟ يَـٰوَيْلَنَا قَدْ كُنَّا فِي غَفْلَةٍ مِّنْ هَـٰذَا بَلْ كُنَّا ظَـٰلِمِينَ ۞

98 Lo! ye (idolaters) and that which ye worship beside Allah are fuel of hell. Thereunto ye will come.

إِنَّكُمْ وَمَا تَعْبُدُونَ مِن دُونِ ٱللَّهِ حَصَبُ جَهَنَّمَ أَنتُمْ لَهَا وَٰرِدُونَ ۞

99 If these had been gods they would not have come thither, but all wilt abide therein.

لَوْ كَانَ هَـٰٓؤُلَآءِ ءَالِهَةً مَّا وَرَدُوهَا وَكُلٌّ فِيهَا خَـٰلِدُونَ ۞

---

6. The reference here is to the Virgin Mary.

100 Therein wailing is their portion, and therein they hear not.

لَهُمْ فِيهَا زَفِيرٌ وَهُمْ فِيهَا لَا يَسْمَعُونَ ۝

101 Lo! those unto whom kindness hath gone forth before from Us, they will be far removed from thence.

إِنَّ الَّذِينَ سَبَقَتْ لَهُمْ مِّنَّا الْحُسْنَىٰ أُولَٰئِكَ عَنْهَا مُبْعَدُونَ ۝

102 They will not hear the slightest sound thereof, while they abide in that which their souls desire.

لَا يَسْمَعُونَ حَسِيسَهَا وَهُمْ فِي مَا اشْتَهَتْ أَنْفُسُهُمْ خَالِدُونَ ۝

103 The Supreme Horror will not grieve them, and the angels will welcome them, (saying): This is your Day which ye were promised;

لَا يَحْزُنُهُمُ الْفَزَعُ الْأَكْبَرُ وَتَتَلَقَّاهُمُ الْمَلَائِكَةُ هَٰذَا يَوْمُكُمُ الَّذِي كُنْتُمْ تُوعَدُونَ ۝

104 The Day when We shall roll up the heavens as a recorder rolleth up a written scroll. As We began the first creation, We shall repeat it. (It is) a promise (binding) upon Us. Lo! We are to perform it.

يَوْمَ نَطْوِي السَّمَاءَ كَطَيِّ السِّجِلِّ لِلْكُتُبِ كَمَا بَدَأْنَا أَوَّلَ خَلْقٍ نُعِيدُهُ وَعْدًا عَلَيْنَا إِنَّا كُنَّا فَاعِلِينَ ۝

105 And verily We have written in the Scripture, after the Reminder: My righteous slaves will inherit the earth:

وَلَقَدْ كَتَبْنَا فِي الزَّبُورِ مِنْ بَعْدِ الذِّكْرِ أَنَّ الْأَرْضَ يَرِثُهَا عِبَادِيَ الصَّالِحُونَ ۝

106 Lo! there is a plain statement for folk who are devout.

إِنَّ فِي هَٰذَا لَبَلَاغًا لِّقَوْمٍ عَابِدِينَ ۝

107 We sent thee not save as a mercy for the peoples.

وَمَا أَرْسَلْنَاكَ إِلَّا رَحْمَةً لِّلْعَالَمِينَ ۝

108 Say: It is only inspired in me that your God is One God. Will ye then surrender (unto Him)?

قُلْ إِنَّمَا يُوحَىٰ إِلَيَّ أَنَّمَا إِلَٰهُكُمْ إِلَٰهٌ وَاحِدٌ فَهَلْ أَنْتُمْ مُّسْلِمُونَ ۝

109   But if they are averse, then
say: I have warned you all alike,
although I know not whether nigh
or far is that which ye are promised.

فَإِن تَوَلَّوْا فَقُلْ ءَاذَنتُكُمْ عَلَىٰ سَوَآءٍ ۖ
وَإِنْ أَدْرِىٓ أَقَرِيبٌ أَم بَعِيدٌ مَّا تُوعَدُونَ ﴿١٠٩﴾

110   Lo! He knoweth that which
is said openly, and that which ye
conceal.

إِنَّهُۥ يَعْلَمُ ٱلْجَهْرَ مِنَ ٱلْقَوْلِ وَيَعْلَمُ
مَا تَكْتُمُونَ ﴿١١٠﴾

111   And I know not but that this
may be a trial for you, and enjoyment for a while.

وَإِنْ أَدْرِى لَعَلَّهُۥ فِتْنَةٌ لَّكُمْ وَمَتَٰعٌ إِلَىٰ حِينٍ ﴿١١١﴾

112   He saith: My Lord! Judge
Thou with truth. Our Lord is the
Beneficent, whose help is to be
implored against that which ye
ascribe (unto Him).

قَٰلَ رَبِّ ٱحْكُم بِٱلْحَقِّ ۗ وَرَبُّنَا ٱلرَّحْمَٰنُ ٱلْمُسْتَعَانُ
عَلَىٰ مَا تَصِفُونَ ﴿١١٢﴾

Al Ḥajj
(The Pilgrimage)

Al Ḥajj, "The Pilgrimage," takes its name from vv. 26-38 relating to the pilgrimage to Makkah. This sūrah is ascribed by some authorities to the Makkan, by others to the Madīnah period. The copy of the Qur'an which I have followed throughout has the Madīnah ascription, and, as it was copied long before the days of "higher" criticism, and was authorised for use throughout the Ottoman Empire, I retain that ascription. Vv. 11-13, 25-30, 39-41 and 58-60 were, according to all authorities, revealed at Al-Madīnah. Nöldeke, greatest of the "higher" critics, says that the ascription is justified on account of the importance of the verses in this sūrah which must, from the nature of their contents, have been revealed at Al-Madīnah, while holding that much of the sūrah belongs to the last Makkan period.

In the name of Allah, the Beneficent, the Merciful.

1 O mankind! Fear your Lord. Lo! the earthquake of the Hour (of Doom) is a tremendous thing.

2 On the day when ye behold it, every nursing mother will forget her nursling and every pregnant one will be delivered of her burden, and thou (Muḥammad) wilt see mankind as drunken, yet they will not be drunken, but the Doom of Allah will be strong (upon them).

يَـٰٓأَيُّهَا ٱلنَّاسُ ٱتَّقُوا۟ رَبَّكُمْ إِنَّ زَلْزَلَةَ ٱلسَّاعَةِ شَىْءٌ عَظِيمٌ ۝

يَوْمَ تَرَوْنَهَا تَذْهَلُ كُلُّ مُرْضِعَةٍ عَمَّآ أَرْضَعَتْ وَتَضَعُ كُلُّ ذَاتِ حَمْلٍ حَمْلَهَا وَتَرَى ٱلنَّاسَ سُكَـٰرَىٰ وَمَا هُم بِسُكَـٰرَىٰ وَلَـٰكِنَّ عَذَابَ ٱللَّهِ شَدِيدٌ ۝

3   Among mankind is he who disputeth concerning Allah without
knowledge, and followeth each froward devil;

وَمِنَ النَّاسِ مَن يُجَادِلُ فِي اللَّهِ بِغَيْرِ عِلْمٍ
وَيَتَّبِعُ كُلَّ شَيْطَانٍ مَرِيدٍ ٣

4   For him it is decreed that whoso
taketh him for friend, he verily will
mislead him and will guide him to
the punishment of the Flame.

كُتِبَ عَلَيْهِ أَنَّهُ مَن تَوَلَّاهُ فَأَنَّهُ يُضِلُّهُ
وَيَهْدِيهِ إِلَىٰ عَذَابِ السَّعِيرِ ٤

5   O mankind! if ye are in doubt
concerning the Resurrection, then
lo! We have created you from dust,
then from a drop of seed, then from
a clot, then from a little lump of
flesh shapely and shapeless, that We
may make (it) clear for you. And
We cause what We will to remain
in the wombs for an appointed time,
and afterward We bring you forth
as infants, then (give you growth)
that ye attain your full strength.
And among you there is he who
dieth (young), and among you there
is he who is brought back to the
most abject time of life, so that,
after knowledge, he knoweth naught. And thou (Muhammad) seest
the earth barren, but when We send
down water thereon, it doth thrill
and swell and put forth every lovely
kind[1] (of growth).

يَـٰٓأَيُّهَا النَّاسُ إِن كُنتُمْ فِي رَيْبٍ مِّنَ الْبَعْثِ فَإِنَّا
خَلَقْنَاكُم مِّن تُرَابٍ ثُمَّ مِن نُّطْفَةٍ ثُمَّ مِنْ عَلَقَةٍ
ثُمَّ مِن مُّضْغَةٍ مُّخَلَّقَةٍ وَغَيْرِ مُخَلَّقَةٍ لِّنُبَيِّنَ لَكُمْ
وَنُقِرُّ فِي الْأَرْحَامِ مَا نَشَاءُ إِلَىٰ أَجَلٍ مُّسَمًّى
ثُمَّ نُخْرِجُكُمْ طِفْلًا ثُمَّ لِتَبْلُغُوٓا أَشُدَّكُمْ
وَمِنكُم مَّن يُتَوَفَّىٰ وَمِنكُم مَّن يُرَدُّ
إِلَىٰ أَرْذَلِ الْعُمُرِ لِكَيْلَا يَعْلَمَ مِنۢ بَعْدِ عِلْمٍ
شَيْـًٔا وَتَرَى الْأَرْضَ هَامِدَةً فَإِذَآ أَنزَلْنَا عَلَيْهَا
الْمَآءَ اهْتَزَّتْ وَرَبَتْ وَأَنۢبَتَتْ
مِن كُلِّ زَوْجٍ بَهِيجٍ ٥

---

1. Or "every lovely pair." Prof. Ghamrawi who helped me in the revision of the text
kept exclaiming on the sublety and wealth of the meaning of every expression used in the
Qur'an concerning natural phenomena. Thus the word "pair" occurs often in the sense of
"species," commemorating that fact that every growth of the earth exists as male and
female. See particularly (36: 35).-Tr.

6 That is because Allah, He is the Truth. Lo! He quickeneth the dead, and lo! He is Able to do all things;

ذٰلِكَ بِأَنَّ اللّٰهَ هُوَ الْحَقُّ وَأَنَّهُ يُحْيِ الْمَوْتٰى وَأَنَّهُ عَلٰى كُلِّ شَيْءٍ قَدِيرٌ ۟

7 And because the Hour will come, there is no doubt thereof; and because Allah will raise those who are in the graves.

وَأَنَّ السَّاعَةَ اٰتِيَةٌ لَّا رَيْبَ فِيهَا وَأَنَّ اللّٰهَ يَبْعَثُ مَنْ فِي الْقُبُورِ ۟

8 And among mankind is he who disputeth concerning Allah without knowledge or guidance or a Scripture giving light.

وَمِنَ النَّاسِ مَنْ يُّجَادِلُ فِي اللّٰهِ بِغَيْرِ عِلْمٍ وَلَا هُدًى وَلَا كِتٰبٍ مُّنِيرٍ ۟

9 Turning away in pride to beguile (men) from the way of Allah. For him in this world is ignominy, and on the Day of Resurrection, We make him taste the doom of burning.

ثَانِيَ عِطْفِهِ لِيُضِلَّ عَنْ سَبِيلِ اللّٰهِ لَهُ فِي الدُّنْيَا خِزْيٌ وَّنُذِيقُهُ يَوْمَ الْقِيٰمَةِ عَذَابَ الْحَرِيقِ ۟

10 (And unto him it will be said): This is for that which thy two hands have sent before, and because Allah is no oppressor of His slaves.

ذٰلِكَ بِمَا قَدَّمَتْ يَدَاكَ وَأَنَّ اللّٰهَ لَيْسَ بِظَلَّامٍ لِّلْعَبِيدِ ۟

11 And among mankind is he who worshippeth Allah upon a narrow marge so that if good befalleth him he is content therewith, but if a trial befalleth him, he falleth away utterly. He loseth both the world and the Hereafter. That is the sheer loss.[2]

وَمِنَ النَّاسِ مَنْ يَّعْبُدُ اللّٰهَ عَلٰى حَرْفٍ فَإِنْ أَصَابَهُ خَيْرٌ اطْمَأَنَّ بِهِ وَإِنْ أَصَابَتْهُ فِتْنَةٌ انْقَلَبَ عَلٰى وَجْهِهِ خَسِرَ الدُّنْيَا وَالْاٰخِرَةَ ذٰلِكَ هُوَ الْخُسْرَانُ الْمُبِينُ ۟

12 He calleth, beside Allah, unto that which hurteth him not nor

يَدْعُوا مِنْ دُونِ اللّٰهِ مَا لَا يَضُرُّهُ

---

2. Tradition says that the reference is to certain Arabs who came to the Prophet at Al-Madīnah and professed Al-Islām: then, if they prospered in a worldly sense, they were content, but if they had to suffer at all they relapsed to idolatry.

benefiteth him. That is the far error.

وَمَا لَا يَنفَعُهُ ۚ ذَٰلِكَ هُوَ الضَّلَٰلُ الْبَعِيدُ ۝

13 He calleth unto him whose harm
is nearer than his benefit; verily an
evil patron and verily an evil friend!

يَدْعُوا لَمَن ضَرُّهُۥٓ أَقْرَبُ مِن نَّفْعِهِۦ ۚ لَبِئْسَ الْمَوْلَىٰ
وَلَبِئْسَ الْعَشِيرُ ۝

14 Lo! Allah causeth those who
believe and do good works to enter
the Gardens underneath which rivers
flow. Lo! Allah doth what He intendeth.

إِنَّ اللَّهَ يُدْخِلُ الَّذِينَ ءَامَنُوا وَعَمِلُوا الصَّٰلِحَٰتِ
جَنَّٰتٍ تَجْرِى مِن تَحْتِهَا الْأَنْهَٰرُ ۚ إِنَّ اللَّهَ
يَفْعَلُ مَا يُرِيدُ ۝

15 Whoso is wont to think (through
envy) that Allah will not give him
(Muhammad) victory in the world
and the Hereafter (and is enraged at
the thought of his victory), let him
stretch a rope up to the roof (of his
dwelling), and let him hang himself. Then let him see whether his
strategy dispelleth that whereat he
rageth![3]

مَن كَانَ يَظُنُّ أَن لَّن يَنصُرَهُ اللَّهُ فِى الدُّنْيَا وَالْآخِرَةِ
فَلْيَمْدُدْ بِسَبَبٍ إِلَى السَّمَآءِ ثُمَّ لْيَقْطَعْ فَلْيَنظُرْ
هَلْ يُذْهِبَنَّ كَيْدُهُۥ مَا يَغِيظُ ۝

16 Thus We reveal it as plain revelations, and verily Allah guideth
whom He will.

وَكَذَٰلِكَ أَنزَلْنَٰهُ ءَايَٰتٍ بَيِّنَٰتٍ
وَأَنَّ اللَّهَ يَهْدِى مَن يُرِيدُ ۝

17 Lo! those who believe (this
Revelation), and those who are
Jews, and the Sabeans and the
Christians and the Magians and the
idolaters—Lo! Allah will decide
between them on the Day of Resurrection. Lo! Allah is Witness over
all things.

إِنَّ الَّذِينَ ءَامَنُوا وَالَّذِينَ هَادُوا وَالصَّٰبِئِينَ
وَالنَّصَٰرَىٰ وَالْمَجُوسَ وَالَّذِينَ أَشْرَكُوٓا
إِنَّ اللَّهَ يَفْصِلُ بَيْنَهُمْ يَوْمَ الْقِيَٰمَةِ ۚ إِنَّ اللَّهَ
عَلَىٰ كُلِّ شَىْءٍ شَهِيدٌ ۝

---

3. The meaning is that Allah will undoubtedly cause the Prophet to triumph in both
worlds, and therefore his opponents have no strategy save that of despair.

18 Hast thou not seen that unto Allah payeth adoration whosoever is in the heavens and whosoever is in the earth, and the sun, and the moon, and the stars, and the hills, and the trees, and the beasts, and many of mankind, while there are many unto whom the doom is justly due. He whom Allah scorneth, there is none to give him honour. Lo! Allah doeth what He will.

أَلَمْ تَرَ أَنَّ ٱللَّهَ يَسْجُدُ لَهُۥ مَن فِى ٱلسَّمَٰوَٰتِ وَمَن فِى ٱلْأَرْضِ وَٱلشَّمْسُ وَٱلْقَمَرُ وَٱلنُّجُومُ وَٱلْجِبَالُ وَٱلشَّجَرُ وَٱلدَّوَآبُّ وَكَثِيرٌ مِّنَ ٱلنَّاسِ وَكَثِيرٌ حَقَّ عَلَيْهِ ٱلْعَذَابُ وَمَن يُهِنِ ٱللَّهُ فَمَا لَهُۥ مِن مُّكْرِمٍ إِنَّ ٱللَّهَ يَفْعَلُ مَا يَشَآءُ ۩ ⑱

19 These twain (the believers and the disbelievers) are two opponents who contend concerning their Lord. But as for those who disbelieve, garments of fire will be cut out for them; boiling fluid will be poured down on their heads.

۞ هَٰذَانِ خَصْمَانِ ٱخْتَصَمُوا۟ فِى رَبِّهِمْ فَٱلَّذِينَ كَفَرُوا۟ قُطِّعَتْ لَهُمْ ثِيَابٌ مِّن نَّارٍ يُصَبُّ مِن فَوْقِ رُءُوسِهِمُ ٱلْحَمِيمُ ⑲

20 Whereby that which is in their bellies, and their skins too, will be melted;

يُصْهَرُ بِهِۦ مَا فِى بُطُونِهِمْ وَٱلْجُلُودُ ⑳

21 And for them are hooked rods of iron.

وَلَهُم مَّقَٰمِعُ مِنْ حَدِيدٍ ㉑

22 Whenever, in their anguish, they would go forth from thence they are driven back therein and (it is said unto them): Taste the doom of burning.

كُلَّمَآ أَرَادُوٓا۟ أَن يَخْرُجُوا۟ مِنْهَا مِنْ غَمٍّ أُعِيدُوا۟ فِيهَا وَذُوقُوا۟ عَذَابَ ٱلْحَرِيقِ ㉒

23 Lo! Allah will cause those who believe and do good works to enter Gardens underneath which rivers flow, wherein they will be allowed armlets of gold, and pearls, and their raiment therein will be silk.

إِنَّ ٱللَّهَ يُدْخِلُ ٱلَّذِينَ ءَامَنُوا۟ وَعَمِلُوا۟ ٱلصَّٰلِحَٰتِ جَنَّٰتٍ تَجْرِى مِن تَحْتِهَا ٱلْأَنْهَٰرُ يُحَلَّوْنَ فِيهَا مِنْ أَسَاوِرَ مِن ذَهَبٍ وَلُؤْلُؤًا وَلِبَاسُهُمْ فِيهَا حَرِيرٌ ㉓

24 They are guided unto gentle speech; they are guided unto the

وَهُدُوٓا۟ إِلَى ٱلطَّيِّبِ مِنَ ٱلْقَوْلِ وَهُدُوٓا۟

إِلَىٰ صِرَٰطِ ٱلْحَمِيدِ ﴿٢٤﴾

path of the Glorious One.

إِنَّ ٱلَّذِينَ كَفَرُواْ وَيَصُدُّونَ عَن سَبِيلِ ٱللَّهِ
وَٱلْمَسْجِدِ ٱلْحَرَامِ ٱلَّذِى جَعَلْنَٰهُ لِلنَّاسِ سَوَآءً
ٱلْعَٰكِفُ فِيهِ وَٱلْبَادِ وَمَن يُرِدْ فِيهِ
بِإِلْحَادِۭ بِظُلْمٍ نُّذِقْهُ مِنْ عَذَابٍ أَلِيمٍ ﴿٢٥﴾

25 Lo! those who disbelieve and bar
(men) from the way of Allah and
from the Inviolable Place of Worship, which We have appointed for
mankind together, the dweller therein and the nomad; whosoever seeketh wrongful partiality therein, him
We shall cause to taste a painful
doom.

وَإِذْ بَوَّأْنَا لِإِبْرَٰهِيمَ مَكَانَ ٱلْبَيْتِ أَن
لَّا تُشْرِكْ بِى شَيْـًٔا وَطَهِّرْ بَيْتِىَ لِلطَّآئِفِينَ
وَٱلْقَآئِمِينَ وَٱلرُّكَّعِ ٱلسُّجُودِ ﴿٢٦﴾

26 And (remember) when We prepared for Abraham the place of the
(holy) House, saying: Ascribe thou
no thing as partner unto Me, and
purify My House for those who
make the round (thereof) and those
who stand and those who bow and
make prostration.

وَأَذِّن فِى ٱلنَّاسِ بِٱلْحَجِّ يَأْتُوكَ رِجَالًا وَعَلَىٰ
كُلِّ ضَامِرٍ يَأْتِينَ مِن كُلِّ فَجٍّ عَمِيقٍ ﴿٢٧﴾

27 And proclaim unto mankind the
Pilgrimage.[4] They will come unto
thee on foot and on every lean
camel; they will come from every
deep ravine.

لِّيَشْهَدُواْ مَنَٰفِعَ لَهُمْ وَيَذْكُرُواْ ٱسْمَ ٱللَّهِ
فِىٓ أَيَّامٍ مَّعْلُومَٰتٍ عَلَىٰ مَا رَزَقَهُم مِّنۢ بَهِيمَةِ
ٱلْأَنْعَٰمِ فَكُلُواْ مِنْهَا وَأَطْعِمُواْ
ٱلْبَآئِسَ ٱلْفَقِيرَ ﴿٢٨﴾

28 That they may witness things
that are of benefit to them, and mention the name of Allah on appointed
days over the beast of cattle that He
hath bestowed upon them. Then eat
thereof and feed therewith the poor
unfortunate.

ثُمَّ لْيَقْضُواْ تَفَثَهُمْ وَلْيُوفُواْ
نُذُورَهُمْ وَلْيَطَّوَّفُواْ بِٱلْبَيْتِ ٱلْعَتِيقِ ﴿٢٩﴾

29 Then let them make an end of
their unkemptness and pay their
vows and go around the ancient
House.

---

4. (2: 196) ff.

30 That (is the command). And whoso magnifieth the sacred things of Allah, it will be well for him in the sight of his Lord. The cattle are lawful unto you save that which hath been told you. So shun the filth of idols, and shun lying speech.

ذٰلِكَ وَمَنْ يُّعَظِّمْ حُرُمٰتِ اللّٰهِ فَهُوَ خَيْرٌ لَّهٗ عِنْدَ رَبِّهٖ ۗ وَأُحِلَّتْ لَكُمُ الْأَنْعَامُ إِلَّا مَا يُتْلٰى عَلَيْكُمْ فَاجْتَنِبُوا الرِّجْسَ مِنَ الْأَوْثَانِ وَاجْتَنِبُوا قَوْلَ الزُّورِ ۝

31 Turning unto Allah (only), not ascribing partners unto Him; for whoso ascribeth partners unto Allah, it is as if he had fallen from the sky and the birds had snatched him or the wind had blown him to a far-off place.

حُنَفَاءَ لِلّٰهِ غَيْرَ مُشْرِكِينَ بِهٖ ۗ وَمَنْ يُّشْرِكْ بِاللّٰهِ فَكَأَنَّمَا خَرَّ مِنَ السَّمَاءِ فَتَخْطَفُهُ الطَّيْرُ أَوْ تَهْوِي بِهِ الرِّيحُ فِي مَكَانٍ سَحِيقٍ ۝

32 That (is the command). And whoso magnifieth the offerings consecrated to Allah, it surely is from devotion of the hearts.

ذٰلِكَ وَمَنْ يُّعَظِّمْ شَعَائِرَ اللّٰهِ فَإِنَّهَا مِنْ تَقْوَى الْقُلُوبِ ۝

33 Therein are benefits for you for an appointed term; and afterward they are brought for sacrifice[5] unto the ancient House.

لَكُمْ فِيهَا مَنَافِعُ إِلٰى أَجَلٍ مُّسَمًّى ثُمَّ مَحِلُّهَا إِلَى الْبَيْتِ الْعَتِيقِ ۝

34 And for every nation have We appointed a ritual, that they may mention the name of Allah over the beast of cattle that He hath given them (for food);[6] and your God is

وَلِكُلِّ أُمَّةٍ جَعَلْنَا مَنْسَكًا لِّيَذْكُرُوا اسْمَ اللّٰهِ عَلٰى مَا رَزَقَهُمْ مِّنْ بَهِيمَةِ الْأَنْعَامِ فَإِلٰهُكُمْ

---

5. The slaughter of animals for food for the poor which is one of the ceremonies of the Muslim pilgrimage is not a propitiatory sacrifice, but is in commemoration of the sacrifice of Abraham which marked the end of human sacrifices for the Semitic race, and which made it clear that the only sacrifice which God requires of man is the Surrender of his will and purpose—i.e. Al-Islām.

6. In order that they may realise the awfulness of taking life, and the solemn nature of the trust which Allah has imposed on them in the permission to eat animal food.

One God, therefore surrender unto Him. And give good tidings (O Muhammad) to the humble;

إِلَٰهٌ وَاحِدٌ فَلَهُۥٓ أَسْلِمُوا۟ وَبَشِّرِ ٱلْمُخْبِتِينَ ٣٤

35 Whose hearts fear when Allah is mentioned, and the patient of whatever may befall them, and those who establish worship and who spend of that We have bestowed on them.

ٱلَّذِينَ إِذَا ذُكِرَ ٱللَّهُ وَجِلَتْ قُلُوبُهُمْ وَٱلصَّٰبِرِينَ عَلَىٰ مَآ أَصَابَهُمْ وَٱلْمُقِيمِى ٱلصَّلَوٰةِ وَمِمَّا رَزَقْنَٰهُمْ يُنفِقُونَ ٣٥

36 And the camels! We have appointed them among the ceremonies of Allah. Therein ye have much good. So mention the name of Allah over them when they are drawn up in lines. Then when their flanks fall (dead), eat thereof and feed the beggar and the suppliant. Thus have We made them subject unto you, that haply ye may give thanks.

وَٱلْبُدْنَ جَعَلْنَٰهَا لَكُم مِّن شَعَٰٓئِرِ ٱللَّهِ لَكُمْ فِيهَا خَيْرٌ فَٱذْكُرُوا۟ ٱسْمَ ٱللَّهِ عَلَيْهَا صَوَآفَّ فَإِذَا وَجَبَتْ جُنُوبُهَا فَكُلُوا۟ مِنْهَا وَأَطْعِمُوا۟ ٱلْقَانِعَ وَٱلْمُعْتَرَّ كَذَٰلِكَ سَخَّرْنَٰهَا لَكُمْ لَعَلَّكُمْ تَشْكُرُونَ ٣٦

37 Their flesh and their blood reach not Allah, but the devotion from you reacheth Him. Thus have We made them subject unto you that ye may magnify Allah that He hath guided you. And give good tidings (O Muhammad) to the good.

لَن يَنَالَ ٱللَّهَ لُحُومُهَا وَلَا دِمَآؤُهَا وَلَٰكِن يَنَالُهُ ٱلتَّقْوَىٰ مِنكُمْ كَذَٰلِكَ سَخَّرَهَا لَكُمْ لِتُكَبِّرُوا۟ ٱللَّهَ عَلَىٰ مَا هَدَىٰكُمْ وَبَشِّرِ ٱلْمُحْسِنِينَ ٣٧

38 Lo! Allah defendeth those who are true. Lo! Allah loveth not each treacherous ingrate.

۞ إِنَّ ٱللَّهَ يُدَٰفِعُ عَنِ ٱلَّذِينَ ءَامَنُوٓا۟ إِنَّ ٱللَّهَ لَا يُحِبُّ كُلَّ خَوَّانٍ كَفُورٍ ٣٨

39 Sanction (to fight) is given unto those who are fought against, because they have been wronged; and Allah is indeed Able to give them victory;

أُذِنَ لِلَّذِينَ يُقَٰتَلُونَ بِأَنَّهُمْ ظُلِمُوا۟ وَإِنَّ ٱللَّهَ عَلَىٰ نَصْرِهِمْ لَقَدِيرٌ ٣٩

40 Those who have been driven from their homes unjustly only because they said: Our Lord is Allah—For had it not been for Allah's repelling some men by means of others, cloisters and churches and oratories and mosques, wherein the name of Allah is oft mentioned, would assuredly have been pulled down. Verily Allah helpeth one who helpeth Him. Lo! Allah is Strong, Almighty.

الَّذِينَ أُخْرِجُوا مِن دِيَارِهِم بِغَيْرِ حَقٍّ إِلَّا أَن يَقُولُوا رَبُّنَا اللَّهُ وَلَوْلَا دَفْعُ اللَّهِ النَّاسَ بَعْضَهُم بِبَعْضٍ لَّهُدِّمَتْ صَوَامِعُ وَبِيَعٌ وَصَلَوَاتٌ وَمَسَاجِدُ يُذْكَرُ فِيهَا اسْمُ اللَّهِ كَثِيرًا وَلَيَنصُرَنَّ اللَّهُ مَن يَنصُرُهُ إِنَّ اللَّهَ لَقَوِيٌّ عَزِيزٌ ۝

41 Those who, if We give them power in the land, establish worship and pay the poor-due and enjoin kindness and forbid iniquity. And Allah's is the sequel of events.

الَّذِينَ إِن مَّكَّنَّاهُمْ فِي الْأَرْضِ أَقَامُوا الصَّلَوٰةَ وَآتَوُا الزَّكَوٰةَ وَأَمَرُوا بِالْمَعْرُوفِ وَنَهَوْا عَنِ الْمُنكَرِ وَلِلَّهِ عَاقِبَةُ الْأُمُورِ ۝

42 If they deny thee (Muhammad), even so the folk of Noah, and (the tribes of) 'Ād and Thamūd, before thee, denied (Our messengers);

وَإِن يُكَذِّبُوكَ فَقَدْ كَذَّبَتْ قَبْلَهُمْ قَوْمُ نُوحٍ وَعَادٌ وَثَمُودُ ۝

43 And the folk of Abraham and the folk of Lot;

وَقَوْمُ إِبْرَاهِيمَ وَقَوْمُ لُوطٍ ۝

44 (And) the dwellers in Madyan. And Moses was denied; but I indulged the disbelievers a long while, then I seized them, and how (terrible) was My abhorrence!

وَأَصْحَابُ مَدْيَنَ وَكُذِّبَ مُوسَىٰ فَأَمْلَيْتُ لِلْكَافِرِينَ ثُمَّ أَخَذْتُهُمْ فَكَيْفَ كَانَ نَكِيرِ ۝

45 How many a township have We destroyed while it was sinful, so that it lieth (to this day) in ruins, and (how many) a deserted well and lofty tower!

فَكَأَيِّن مِّن قَرْيَةٍ أَهْلَكْنَاهَا وَهِيَ ظَالِمَةٌ فَهِيَ خَاوِيَةٌ عَلَىٰ عُرُوشِهَا وَبِئْرٍ مُّعَطَّلَةٍ وَقَصْرٍ مَّشِيدٍ ۝

46 Have they not travelled in the land, so that they may have hearts wherewith to feel and ears where-

أَفَلَمْ يَسِيرُوا فِي الْأَرْضِ فَتَكُونَ لَهُمْ قُلُوبٌ يَعْقِلُونَ

with to hear? For indeed it is not the eyes that grow blind, but it is the hearts, which are within the bosoms, that grow blind.

بِهَا أَوْءَاذَانٌ يَسْمَعُونَ بِهَا فَإِنَّهَا لَا تَعْمَى الْأَبْصَارُ وَلَٰكِن تَعْمَى الْقُلُوبُ الَّتِي فِي الصُّدُورِ ۝

47 And they will bid thee hasten on the Doom, and Allah faileth not His promise, but lo! a Day with Allah is as a thousand years of what ye reckon.

وَيَسْتَعْجِلُونَكَ بِالْعَذَابِ وَلَن يُخْلِفَ اللَّهُ وَعْدَهُ وَإِنَّ يَوْمًا عِندَ رَبِّكَ كَأَلْفِ سَنَةٍ مِّمَّا تَعُدُّونَ ۝

48 And how many a township to which I gave respite though it was sinful! Than I grasped it. Unto Me is the return.

وَكَأَيِّن مِّن قَرْيَةٍ أَمْلَيْتُ لَهَا وَهِيَ ظَالِمَةٌ ثُمَّ أَخَذْتُهَا وَإِلَيَّ الْمَصِيرُ ۝

49 Say: O mankind! I am only a plain warner unto you.

قُلْ يَٰأَيُّهَا النَّاسُ إِنَّمَا أَنَا لَكُمْ نَذِيرٌ مُّبِينٌ ۝

50 Those who believe and do good works, for them is pardon and a rich provision;

فَالَّذِينَ ءَامَنُوا وَعَمِلُوا الصَّٰلِحَٰتِ لَهُم مَّغْفِرَةٌ وَرِزْقٌ كَرِيمٌ ۝

51 While those who strive to thwart Our revelations, such are rightful owners of the Fire.

وَالَّذِينَ سَعَوْا فِي ءَايَٰتِنَا مُعَٰجِزِينَ أُو۟لَٰئِكَ أَصْحَٰبُ الْجَحِيمِ ۝

52 Never sent We a messenger or a Prophet before thee but when He recited (the message) Satan proposed (opposition) in respect of that which he recited thereof. But Allah abolisheth that which Satan proposeth. Then Allah establisheth His revelations. Allah is Knower, Wise;

وَمَا أَرْسَلْنَا مِن قَبْلِكَ مِن رَّسُولٍ وَلَا نَبِيٍّ إِلَّا إِذَا تَمَنَّىٰ أَلْقَى الشَّيْطَٰنُ فِي أُمْنِيَّتِهِ فَيَنسَخُ اللَّهُ مَا يُلْقِي الشَّيْطَٰنُ ثُمَّ يُحْكِمُ اللَّهُ ءَايَٰتِهِ وَاللَّهُ عَلِيمٌ حَكِيمٌ ۝

53 That He may make that which the devil proposeth a temptation for those in whose hearts is a disease, and those whose hearts are hardened—Lo! the evil-doers are in open schism;

لِّيَجْعَلَ مَا يُلْقِي الشَّيْطَٰنُ فِتْنَةً لِّلَّذِينَ فِي قُلُوبِهِم مَّرَضٌ وَالْقَاسِيَةِ قُلُوبُهُمْ وَإِنَّ الظَّٰلِمِينَ لَفِي شِقَاقٍ بَعِيدٍ ۝

54 And that those who have been given knowledge may know that it is the truth from thy Lord, so that they may believe therein and their hearts may submit humbly unto Him. Lo! Allah verily is guiding those who believe unto a right path.

وَلِيَعْلَمَ الَّذِينَ أُوتُوا الْعِلْمَ أَنَّهُ الْحَقُّ مِن رَّبِّكَ فَيُؤْمِنُوا بِهِ فَتُخْبِتَ لَهُ قُلُوبُهُمْ وَإِنَّ اللَّهَ لَهَادِ الَّذِينَ ءَامَنُوا إِلَىٰ صِرَٰطٍ مُّسْتَقِيمٍ ۞

55 And those who disbelieve will not cease to be in doubt thereof until the Hour come upon them unawares, or there come unto them the doom of a disastrous day.

وَلَا يَزَالُ الَّذِينَ كَفَرُوا فِي مِرْيَةٍ مِّنْهُ حَتَّىٰ تَأْتِيَهُمُ السَّاعَةُ بَغْتَةً أَوْ يَأْتِيَهُمْ عَذَابُ يَوْمٍ عَقِيمٍ ۞

56 The Sovereignty on that day will be Allah's. He will judge between them. Then those who believed and did good works will be in Gardens of Delight;

الْمُلْكُ يَوْمَئِذٍ لِّلَّهِ يَحْكُمُ بَيْنَهُمْ فَالَّذِينَ ءَامَنُوا وَعَمِلُوا الصَّـٰلِحَـٰتِ فِي جَنَّـٰتِ النَّعِيمِ ۞

57 While those who disbelieved and denied Our revelations, for them will be a shameful doom.

وَالَّذِينَ كَفَرُوا وَكَذَّبُوا بِـَٔايَـٰتِنَا فَأُوْلَـٰئِكَ لَهُمْ عَذَابٌ مُّهِينٌ ۞

58 Those who fled their homes for the cause of Allah and then were slain or died, Allah verily will provide for them a good provision. Lo! Allah, He verily is Best of all who make provision.

وَالَّذِينَ هَاجَرُوا فِي سَبِيلِ اللَّهِ ثُمَّ قُتِلُوا أَوْ مَاتُوا لَيَرْزُقَنَّهُمُ اللَّهُ رِزْقًا حَسَنًا وَإِنَّ اللَّهَ لَهُوَ خَيْرُ الرَّٰزِقِينَ ۞

59 Assuredly He will cause them to enter by an entry that they will love. Lo! Allah verily is Knower, Indulgent.

لَيُدْخِلَنَّهُم مُّدْخَلًا يَرْضَوْنَهُ وَإِنَّ اللَّهَ لَعَلِيمٌ حَلِيمٌ ۞

60 That (is so). And whoso hath retaliated with the like of that which he was made to suffer and then hath (again) been wronged, Allah will succour him. Lo! Allah verily is Mild, Forgiving.

۞ ذَٰلِكَ وَمَنْ عَاقَبَ بِمِثْلِ مَا عُوقِبَ بِهِ ثُمَّ بُغِيَ عَلَيْهِ لَيَنصُرَنَّهُ اللَّهُ إِنَّ اللَّهَ لَعَفُوٌّ غَفُورٌ ۞

61 That is because Allah maketh
the night to pass into the day and
maketh the day to pass into the
night, and because Allah is Hearer,
Seer.

ذٰلِكَ بِاَنَّ اللّٰهَ يُوْلِجُ الَّيْلَ فِى النَّهَارِ
وَيُوْلِجُ النَّهَارَ فِى الَّيْلِ وَاَنَّ اللّٰهَ سَمِيْعٌ بَصِيْرٌ ۝

62 That is because Allah, He is the
True, and that whereon they call
instead of Him, it is the False, and
because Allah, He is the High, the
Great.

ذٰلِكَ بِاَنَّ اللّٰهَ هُوَ الْحَقُّ وَاَنَّ مَا يَدْعُوْنَ
مِنْ دُوْنِهٖ هُوَ الْبَاطِلُ وَاَنَّ اللّٰهَ
هُوَ الْعَلِيُّ الْكَبِيْرُ ۝

63 Seest thou not how Allah sendeth down water from the sky and
then the earth becometh green upon
the morrow? Lo! Allah is Subtile,
Aware.

اَلَمْ تَرَ اَنَّ اللّٰهَ اَنْزَلَ مِنَ السَّمَآءِ مَآءً فَتُصْبِحُ
الْاَرْضُ مُخْضَرَّةً اِنَّ اللّٰهَ لَطِيْفٌ خَبِيْرٌ ۝

64 Unto Him belongeth all that is
in the heavens and all that is in the
earth. Lo! Allah, He verily is the
Absolute, the Owner of Praise.

لَهٗ مَا فِى السَّمٰوٰتِ وَمَا فِى الْاَرْضِ
وَاِنَّ اللّٰهَ لَهُوَ الْغَنِيُّ الْحَمِيْدُ ۝

65 Hast thou not seen how Allah
hath made all that is in the earth
subservient unto you? And the ship
runneth upon the sea by His command, and He holdeth back the
heaven from falling on the earth
unless by His leave. Lo! Allah is,
for mankind, Full of Pity, Merciful.

اَلَمْ تَرَ اَنَّ اللّٰهَ سَخَّرَ لَكُمْ مَّا فِى الْاَرْضِ وَالْفُلْكَ تَجْرِىْ
فِى الْبَحْرِ بِاَمْرِهٖ وَيُمْسِكُ السَّمَآءَ اَنْ تَقَعَ
عَلَى الْاَرْضِ اِلَّا بِاِذْنِهٖ اِنَّ اللّٰهَ بِالنَّاسِ
لَرَءُوْفٌ رَّحِيْمٌ ۝

66 And He it is Who gave you life,
then He will cause you to die, and
then will give you life (again). Lo!
man is verily an ingrate.

وَهُوَ الَّذِىْ اَحْيَاكُمْ ثُمَّ يُمِيْتُكُمْ
ثُمَّ يُحْيِيْكُمْ اِنَّ الْاِنْسَانَ لَكَفُوْرٌ ۝

67 Unto each nation have We given
sacred rites which they are to perform; so let them not dispute with
thee of the matter, but summon

لِكُلِّ اُمَّةٍ جَعَلْنَا مَنْسَكًا هُمْ نَاسِكُوْهُ
فَلَا يُنَازِعُنَّكَ فِى الْاَمْرِ وَادْعُ اِلٰى رَبِّكَ اِنَّكَ لَعَلٰى

thou unto thy Lord. Lo! thou indeed followest right guidance.

هُدًى مُسْتَقِيمٍ ۝

68 And if they wrangle with thee,
say: Allah is best aware of what ye
do.

وَإِن جَـٰدَلُوكَ فَقُلِ اللَّهُ أَعْلَمُ بِمَا تَعْمَلُونَ ۝

69 Allah will judge between you on
the Day of Resurrection concerning
that wherein ye used to differ.

اللَّهُ يَحْكُمُ بَيْنَكُمْ يَوْمَ الْقِيَٰمَةِ
فِيمَا كُنتُمْ فِيهِ تَخْتَلِفُونَ ۝

70 Hast thou not known that Allah
knoweth all that is in the heaven
and the earth? Lo! it is in a record.
Lo! that is easy for Allah.

أَلَمْ تَعْلَمْ أَنَّ اللَّهَ يَعْلَمُ مَا فِى السَّمَآءِ وَالْأَرْضِ
إِنَّ ذَٰلِكَ فِى كِتَٰبٍ إِنَّ ذَٰلِكَ عَلَى اللَّهِ يَسِيرٌ ۝

71 And they worship instead of
Allah that for which no warrant hath
been revealed unto them, and that
whereof they have no knowledge.
For evil-doers there is no helper.

وَيَعْبُدُونَ مِن دُونِ اللَّهِ مَا لَمْ يُنَزِّلْ بِهِ سُلْطَٰنًا
وَمَا لَيْسَ لَهُم بِهِۦ عِلْمٌ وَمَا لِلظَّٰلِمِينَ مِن نَصِيرٍ ۝

72 And when Our revelations are
recited unto them, thou knowest the
denial in the faces of those who disbelieve; they all but attack those
who recite Our revelations unto
them. Say: Shall I proclaim unto
you worse than that? The Fire!
Allah hath promised it for those
who disbelieve. A hapless journey's
end!

وَإِذَا تُتْلَىٰ عَلَيْهِمْ ءَايَٰتُنَا بَيِّنَٰتٍ تَعْرِفُ فِى وُجُوهِ
الَّذِينَ كَفَرُوا الْمُنكَرَ يَكَادُونَ
يَسْطُونَ بِالَّذِينَ يَتْلُونَ عَلَيْهِمْ ءَايَٰتِنَا
قُلْ أَفَأُنَبِّئُكُم بِشَرٍّ مِّن ذَٰلِكُمُ النَّارُ وَعَدَهَا
اللَّهُ الَّذِينَ كَفَرُوا وَبِئْسَ الْمَصِيرُ ۝

73 O mankind! A similitude is
coined, so pay ye heed to it: Lo!
those on whom ye call beside Allah
will never create a fly though they
combine together for the purpose.
And if the fly took something from
them, they could not rescue it from
him. So weak are (both) the seeker
and the sought!

يَٰٓأَيُّهَا النَّاسُ ضُرِبَ مَثَلٌ فَاسْتَمِعُوا لَهُۥٓ
إِنَّ الَّذِينَ تَدْعُونَ مِن دُونِ اللَّهِ لَن يَخْلُقُوا
ذُبَابًا وَلَوِ اجْتَمَعُوا لَهُۥ وَإِن يَسْلُبْهُمُ الذُّبَابُ
شَيْئًا لَّا يَسْتَنقِذُوهُ مِنْهُ ضَعُفَ
الطَّالِبُ وَالْمَطْلُوبُ ۝

74 They measure not Allah His rightful measure. Lo! Allah is Strong, Almighty.

75 Allah chooseth from the angels messengers, and (also) from mankind. Lo! Allah is Hearer, Seer.

76 He knoweth all that is before them and all that is behind them, and unto Allah all things are returned.

77 O, ye who believe! Bow down and prostrate yourselves, and worship your Lord, and do good, that haply ye may prosper.

78 And strive for Allah with the endeavour which is His right. He hath chosen you and hath not laid upon you in religion any hardship; the faith of your father Abraham (is yours). He hath named you Muslims[7] of old time and in this (Scripture), that the messenger may be a witness against you, and that ye may be witnesses against mankind. So establish worship, pay the poor-due, and hold fast to Allah. He is your Protecting Friend. A blessed Patron and a blessed Helper!

مَا قَدَرُوا اللَّهَ حَقَّ قَدْرِهِ إِنَّ اللَّهَ لَقَوِيٌّ عَزِيزٌ ۝

اللَّهُ يَصْطَفِى مِنَ الْمَلَائِكَةِ رُسُلًا وَمِنَ النَّاسِ إِنَّ اللَّهَ سَمِيعٌ بَصِيرٌ ۝

يَعْلَمُ مَا بَيْنَ أَيْدِيهِمْ وَمَا خَلْفَهُمْ وَإِلَى اللَّهِ تُرْجَعُ الْأُمُورُ ۝

يَا أَيُّهَا الَّذِينَ آمَنُوا ارْكَعُوا وَاسْجُدُوا وَاعْبُدُوا رَبَّكُمْ وَافْعَلُوا الْخَيْرَ لَعَلَّكُمْ تُفْلِحُونَ ۩ ۝

وَجَاهِدُوا فِي اللَّهِ حَقَّ جِهَادِهِ هُوَ اجْتَبَاكُمْ وَمَا جَعَلَ عَلَيْكُمْ فِي الدِّينِ مِنْ حَرَجٍ مِلَّةَ أَبِيكُمْ إِبْرَاهِيمَ هُوَ سَمَّاكُمُ الْمُسْلِمِينَ مِنْ قَبْلُ وَفِي هَذَا لِيَكُونَ الرَّسُولُ شَهِيدًا عَلَيْكُمْ وَتَكُونُوا شُهَدَاءَ عَلَى النَّاسِ فَأَقِيمُوا الصَّلَاةَ وَآتُوا الزَّكَاةَ وَاعْتَصِمُوا بِاللَّهِ هُوَ مَوْلَاكُمْ فَنِعْمَ الْمَوْلَى وَنِعْمَ النَّصِيرُ ۝

---

7. "Those who have surrendered."

Al Mu'minūn
(The Believers)

Al Mu'minūn, "The Believers," is so named from a word occurring in the first verse or, it may be said, from its subject, which is the triumph of believers. It is considered to be the last of the sūrahs revealed at Makkah, immediately before the Prophet's flight to Yathrib (Al-Madīnah).

A late Makkan sūrah.

In the name of Allah, the Beneficent, the Merciful.

1 Successful indeed are the believers;

قَدْ أَفْلَحَ الْمُؤْمِنُونَ ۝

2 Who are humble in their prayers;

الَّذِينَ هُمْ فِي صَلَاتِهِمْ خَاشِعُونَ ۝

3 And who shun vain conversation;

وَالَّذِينَ هُمْ عَنِ اللَّغْوِ مُعْرِضُونَ ۝

4 And who are payers of the poor-due;

وَالَّذِينَ هُمْ لِلزَّكَاةِ فَاعِلُونَ ۝

5 And who guard their modesty;

وَالَّذِينَ هُمْ لِفُرُوجِهِمْ حَافِظُونَ ۝

6 Save from their wives or the (slaves) that their right hands possess, for then they are not blameworthy;

إِلَّا عَلَى أَزْوَاجِهِمْ أَوْ مَا مَلَكَتْ أَيْمَانُهُمْ فَإِنَّهُمْ غَيْرُ مَلُومِينَ ۝

7 But whoso craveth beyond that, such are transgressors;

فَمَنِ ابْتَغَى وَرَاءَ ذَلِكَ فَأُولَئِكَ هُمُ الْعَادُونَ ۝

8 And who are keepers of their pledge and their covenant;

وَالَّذِينَ هُمْ لِأَمَنَتِهِمْ وَعَهْدِهِمْ رَاعُونَ ۝

9 And who pay heed to their prayers.

وَالَّذِينَ هُمْ عَلَى صَلَوَتِهِمْ يُحَافِظُونَ ۝

10 These are the heirs;

أُولَٰئِكَ هُمُ الْوَٰرِثُونَ ۝

11 Who will inherit Paradise: There they will abide.

الَّذِينَ يَرِثُونَ الْفِرْدَوْسَ هُمْ فِيهَا خَٰلِدُونَ ۝

12 Verily We created man from a product of wet earth;

وَلَقَدْ خَلَقْنَا الْإِنْسَٰنَ مِن سُلَٰلَةٍ مِّن طِينٍ ۝

13 Then placed him as a drop (of seed) in a safe lodging;

ثُمَّ جَعَلْنَٰهُ نُطْفَةً فِى قَرَارٍ مَّكِينٍ ۝

14 Then fashioned We the drop a clot, then fashioned We the clot a little lump, then fashioned We the little lump bones, then clothed the bones with flesh, and then produced it as another creation. So blessed be Allah, the Best of Creators!

ثُمَّ خَلَقْنَا النُّطْفَةَ عَلَقَةً فَخَلَقْنَا الْعَلَقَةَ مُضْغَةً فَخَلَقْنَا الْمُضْغَةَ عِظَٰمًا فَكَسَوْنَا الْعِظَٰمَ لَحْمًا ثُمَّ أَنشَأْنَٰهُ خَلْقًا ءَاخَرَ فَتَبَارَكَ اللَّهُ أَحْسَنُ الْخَٰلِقِينَ ۝

15 Then lo! after that ye surely die.

ثُمَّ إِنَّكُم بَعْدَ ذَٰلِكَ لَمَيِّتُونَ ۝

16 Then lo! on the Day of Resurrection ye are raised (again).

ثُمَّ إِنَّكُمْ يَوْمَ الْقِيَٰمَةِ تُبْعَثُونَ ۝

17 And We have created above you seven paths, and We are never unmindful of creation.

وَلَقَدْ خَلَقْنَا فَوْقَكُمْ سَبْعَ طَرَائِقَ وَمَا كُنَّا عَنِ الْخَلْقِ غَٰفِلِينَ ۝

18 And We send down from the sky water in measure, and We cause it to settle in the earth, and lo! We are able to withdraw it.

وَأَنزَلْنَا مِنَ السَّمَاءِ مَاءً بِقَدَرٍ فَأَسْكَنَّٰهُ فِى الْأَرْضِ وَإِنَّا عَلَىٰ ذَهَابٍ بِهِ لَقَٰدِرُونَ ۝

19 Then We produce for you therewith gardens of date-palms and grapes, wherein is much fruit for you and whereof ye eat;

فَأَنشَأْنَا لَكُم بِهِ جَنَّٰتٍ مِّن نَّخِيلٍ وَأَعْنَٰبٍ لَّكُمْ فِيهَا فَوَٰكِهُ كَثِيرَةٌ وَمِنْهَا تَأْكُلُونَ ۝

20 And a tree that springeth forth from Mount Sinai that groweth oil and relish for the eaters.

وَشَجَرَةً تَخْرُجُ مِنْ طُورِ سَيْنَاءَ تَنْبُتُ بِالدُّهْنِ وَصِبْغٍ لِّلْآكِلِينَ ﴿٢٠﴾

21 And lo! in the cattle there is verily a lesson for you. We give you to drink of that which is in their bellies, and many uses have ye in them, and of them do ye eat;

وَإِنَّ لَكُمْ فِي الْأَنْعَامِ لَعِبْرَةً نُسْقِيكُم مِّمَّا فِي بُطُونِهَا وَلَكُمْ فِيهَا مَنَافِعُ كَثِيرَةٌ وَمِنْهَا تَأْكُلُونَ ﴿٢١﴾

22 And on them and on the ship we are carried.

وَعَلَيْهَا وَعَلَى الْفُلْكِ تُحْمَلُونَ ﴿٢٢﴾

23 And We verily sent Noah unto his folk, and he said: O my people! Serve Allah. Ye have no other god save Him. Will ye not ward off (evil)?

وَلَقَدْ أَرْسَلْنَا نُوحًا إِلَى قَوْمِهِ فَقَالَ يَا قَوْمِ اعْبُدُوا اللَّهَ مَا لَكُم مِّنْ إِلَهٍ غَيْرُهُ أَفَلَا تَتَّقُونَ ﴿٢٣﴾

24 But the chieftains of his folk, who disbelieved, said: This is only a mortal like you who would make himself superior to you. Had Allah willed, He surely could have sent down angels. We heard not of this in the case of our fathers of old.

فَقَالَ الْمَلَأُ الَّذِينَ كَفَرُوا مِن قَوْمِهِ مَا هَذَا إِلَّا بَشَرٌ مِّثْلُكُمْ يُرِيدُ أَن يَتَفَضَّلَ عَلَيْكُمْ وَلَوْ شَاءَ اللَّهُ لَأَنزَلَ مَلَائِكَةً مَّا سَمِعْنَا بِهَذَا فِي آبَائِنَا الْأَوَّلِينَ ﴿٢٤﴾

25 He is only a man in whom is a madness, so watch him for a while.

إِنْ هُوَ إِلَّا رَجُلٌ بِهِ جِنَّةٌ فَتَرَبَّصُوا بِهِ حَتَّى حِينٍ ﴿٢٥﴾

26 He said: My Lord! Help me because they deny me.

قَالَ رَبِّ انصُرْنِي بِمَا كَذَّبُونِ ﴿٢٦﴾

27 Then We inspired in him, saying: Make the ship under Our eyes and Our inspiration. Then, when Our command cometh and the oven gusheth water, introduce therein of every (kind) two spouses, and thy household save him thereof against whom the Word hath already gone forth. And plead not with Me on

فَأَوْحَيْنَا إِلَيْهِ أَنِ اصْنَعِ الْفُلْكَ بِأَعْيُنِنَا وَوَحْيِنَا فَإِذَا جَاءَ أَمْرُنَا وَفَارَ التَّنُّورُ فَاسْلُكْ فِيهَا مِن كُلٍّ زَوْجَيْنِ اثْنَيْنِ وَأَهْلَكَ إِلَّا مَن سَبَقَ عَلَيْهِ الْقَوْلُ مِنْهُمْ وَلَا تُخَاطِبْنِي فِي الَّذِينَ ظَلَمُوا

behalf of those who have done
wrong. Lo! they will be drowned.

إِنَّهُم مُّغْرَقُونَ ۝

28 And when thou art on board the
ship, thou and whoso is with thee,
then say: Praise be to Allah Who
hath saved us from the wrongdoing
folk!

فَإِذَا اسْتَوَيْتَ أَنتَ وَمَن مَّعَكَ عَلَى الْفُلْكِ فَقُلِ الْحَمْدُ لِلَّهِ
الَّذِى نَجَّانَا مِنَ الْقَوْمِ الظَّالِمِينَ ۝

29 And say: My Lord! Cause me to
land at a blessed landing-place, for
Thou art best of all who bring to
land.

وَقُل رَّبِّ أَنزِلْنِى مُنزَلًا مُّبَارَكًا وَأَنتَ خَيْرُ الْمُنزِلِينَ ۝

30 Lo! herein verily are portents,
for lo! We are ever putting (mankind) to the test.

إِنَّ فِى ذَلِكَ لَآيَاتٍ وَإِن كُنَّا لَمُبْتَلِينَ ۝

31 Then, after them, We brought
forth another generation;

ثُمَّ أَنشَأْنَا مِن بَعْدِهِمْ قَرْنًا آخَرِينَ ۝

32 And We sent among them a
messenger of their own, saying:
Serve Allah. Ye have no other god
save Him. Will ye not ward off
(evil)?

فَأَرْسَلْنَا فِيهِمْ رَسُولًا مِّنْهُمْ أَنِ اعْبُدُوا اللَّهَ
مَا لَكُم مِّنْ إِلَهٍ غَيْرُهُ أَفَلَا تَتَّقُونَ ۝

33 And the chieftains of his folk,
who disbelieved and denied the
meeting of the Hereafter, and whom
We had made soft in the life of the
world, said: This is only a mortal
like you, who eateth of that whereof
ye eat and drinketh of that ye drink.

وَقَالَ الْمَلَأُ مِن قَوْمِهِ الَّذِينَ كَفَرُوا وَكَذَّبُوا بِلِقَاءِ
الْآخِرَةِ وَأَتْرَفْنَاهُمْ فِى الْحَيَاةِ الدُّنْيَا
مَا هَذَا إِلَّا بَشَرٌ مِّثْلُكُمْ يَأْكُلُ مِمَّا تَأْكُلُونَ مِنْهُ
وَيَشْرَبُ مِمَّا تَشْرَبُونَ ۝

34 If ye were to obey a mortal like
yourselves, ye surely would be
losers.

وَلَئِنْ أَطَعْتُم بَشَرًا مِّثْلَكُمْ إِنَّكُمْ إِذًا لَّخَاسِرُونَ ۝

35 Doth he promise you that you,
when ye are dead and have become
dust and bones, will (again) be
brought forth?

أَيَعِدُكُمْ أَنَّكُمْ إِذَا مِتُّمْ وَكُنتُمْ تُرَابًا وَعِظَامًا
أَنَّكُم مُّخْرَجُونَ ۝

36 Begone, begone, with that which ye are promised!

هَيْهَاتَ هَيْهَاتَ لِمَا تُوعَدُونَ ۝

37 There is naught but our life of the world; we die and we live, and we shall not be raised (again).

إِنْ هِيَ إِلَّا حَيَاتُنَا الدُّنْيَا نَمُوتُ وَنَحْيَا وَمَا نَحْنُ بِمَبْعُوثِينَ ۝

38 He is only a man who hath invented a lie about Allah. We are not going to put faith in him.

إِنْ هُوَ إِلَّا رَجُلٌ افْتَرَى عَلَى اللَّهِ كَذِبًا وَمَا نَحْنُ لَهُ بِمُؤْمِنِينَ ۝

39 He said: My Lord! Help me because they deny me;

قَالَ رَبِّ انْصُرْنِي بِمَا كَذَّبُونِ ۝

40 He said: In a little while they surely will become repentant.

قَالَ عَمَّا قَلِيلٍ لَّيُصْبِحُنَّ نَادِمِينَ ۝

41 So the (Awful) Cry overtook them rightfully, and We made them like as wreckage (that a torrent hurleth). A far removal for wrong-doing folk!

فَأَخَذَتْهُمُ الصَّيْحَةُ بِالْحَقِّ فَجَعَلْنَاهُمْ غُثَاءً فَبُعْدًا لِّلْقَوْمِ الظَّالِمِينَ ۝

42 Then after them We brought forth other generations.

ثُمَّ أَنْشَأْنَا مِنْ بَعْدِهِمْ قُرُونًا آخَرِينَ ۝

43 No nation can outstrip its term, nor yet postpone it.

مَا تَسْبِقُ مِنْ أُمَّةٍ أَجَلَهَا وَمَا يَسْتَأْخِرُونَ ۝

44 Then We sent our messengers one after another. Whenever its messenger came unto a nation, they denied him; so We caused them to follow one another (to disaster) and We made them bywords. A far removal for folk who believe not!

ثُمَّ أَرْسَلْنَا رُسُلَنَا تَتْرَا كُلَّ مَا جَاءَ أُمَّةً رَّسُولُهَا كَذَّبُوهُ فَأَتْبَعْنَا بَعْضَهُمْ بَعْضًا وَجَعَلْنَاهُمْ أَحَادِيثَ فَبُعْدًا لِّقَوْمٍ لَّا يُؤْمِنُونَ ۝

45 Then We sent Moses and his brother Aaron with Our tokens and a clear warrant;

ثُمَّ أَرْسَلْنَا مُوسَى وَأَخَاهُ هَارُونَ بِآيَاتِنَا وَسُلْطَانٍ مُّبِينٍ ۝

46 Unto Pharaoh and his chiefs, but they scorned (them) and they were despotic folk.

إِلَى فِرْعَوْنَ وَمَلَائِهِ فَاسْتَكْبَرُوا وَكَانُوا قَوْمًا عَالِينَ ۝

47 And they said: Shall we put
faith in two mortals like ourselves,
and whose folk are servile unto us?

فَقَالُوٓا أَنُؤۡمِنُ لِبَشَرَيۡنِ مِثۡلِنَا
وَقَوۡمُهُمَا لَنَا عَٰبِدُونَ ۝

48 So they denied them, and became of those who were destroyed.

فَكَذَّبُوهُمَا فَكَانُوا مِنَ ٱلۡمُهۡلَكِينَ ۝

49 And we verily gave Moses the
Scripture, that haply they might go
aright.

وَلَقَدۡ ءَاتَيۡنَا مُوسَى ٱلۡكِتَٰبَ لَعَلَّهُمۡ يَهۡتَدُونَ ۝

50 And We made the son of Mary
and his mother a portent, and We
gave them refuge on a height, a
place of flocks and water-springs.

وَجَعَلۡنَا ٱبۡنَ مَرۡيَمَ وَأُمَّهُۥٓ ءَايَةً وَءَاوَيۡنَٰهُمَآ
إِلَىٰ رَبۡوَةٍ ذَاتِ قَرَارٍ وَمَعِينٍ ۝

51 O ye messengers! Eat of the
good things, and do right. Lo! I am
Aware of what ye do.

يَٰٓأَيُّهَا ٱلرُّسُلُ كُلُوا مِنَ ٱلطَّيِّبَٰتِ وَٱعۡمَلُوا صَٰلِحًا
إِنِّي بِمَا تَعۡمَلُونَ عَلِيمٌ ۝

52 And lo! this your religion is one
religion and I am your Lord, so
keep your duty unto Me.

وَإِنَّ هَٰذِهِۦٓ أُمَّتُكُمۡ أُمَّةً وَٰحِدَةً وَأَنَا۠ رَبُّكُمۡ
فَٱتَّقُونِ ۝

53 But they (mankind) have broken
their religion among them into sects,
each sect rejoicing in its tenets.

فَتَقَطَّعُوٓا أَمۡرَهُم بَيۡنَهُمۡ زُبُرًا كُلُّ حِزۡبٍ بِمَا لَدَيۡهِمۡ
فَرِحُونَ ۝

54 So leave them in their error till
a time.

فَذَرۡهُمۡ فِي غَمۡرَتِهِمۡ حَتَّىٰ حِينٍ ۝

55 Think they that in the wealth
and sons wherewith We provide
them;

أَيَحۡسَبُونَ أَنَّمَا نُمِدُّهُم بِهِۦ مِن مَّالٍ وَبَنِينَ ۝

56 We hasten unto them with good
things? Nay, but they perceive not.

نُسَارِعُ لَهُمۡ فِي ٱلۡخَيۡرَٰتِ بَل لَّا يَشۡعُرُونَ ۝

57 Lo! those who go in awe for
fear of their Lord;

إِنَّ ٱلَّذِينَ هُم مِّنۡ خَشۡيَةِ رَبِّهِم مُّشۡفِقُونَ ۝

58 And those who believe in the
revelations of their Lord;

وَٱلَّذِينَ هُم بِـَٔايَٰتِ رَبِّهِمۡ يُؤۡمِنُونَ ۝

59 And those who ascribe not partners unto their Lord;

وَٱلَّذِينَ هُم بِرَبِّهِمۡ لَا يُشۡرِكُونَ ۝

60 And those who give that which they give with hearts afraid because they are about to return unto their Lord;

وَٱلَّذِينَ يُؤۡتُونَ مَآ ءَاتَوا وَّقُلُوبُهُمۡ وَجِلَةٌ أَنَّهُمۡ إِلَىٰ رَبِّهِمۡ رَٰجِعُونَ ۝

61 These race for the good things, and they shall win them in the race.

أُوْلَـٰٓئِكَ يُسَـٰرِعُونَ فِى ٱلۡخَيۡرَٰتِ وَهُمۡ لَهَا سَـٰبِقُونَ ۝

62 And We task not any soul beyond its scope, and with Us is a Record which speaketh the truth, and they will not be wronged.

وَلَا نُكَلِّفُ نَفۡسًا إِلَّا وُسۡعَهَا وَلَدَيۡنَا كِتَٰبٌ يَنطِقُ بِٱلۡحَقِّ وَهُمۡ لَا يُظۡلَمُونَ ۝

63 Nay, but their hearts are in ignorance of this (Qur'an), and they have other works, besides, which they are doing;

بَلۡ قُلُوبُهُمۡ فِى غَمۡرَةٍ مِّنۡ هَـٰذَا وَلَهُمۡ أَعۡمَـٰلٌ مِّن دُونِ ذَٰلِكَ هُمۡ لَهَا عَـٰمِلُونَ ۝

64 Till when We grasp their luxurious ones with the punishment, behold! they supplicate.

حَتَّىٰٓ إِذَآ أَخَذۡنَا مُتۡرَفِيهِم بِٱلۡعَذَابِ إِذَا هُمۡ يَجۡـَٔرُونَ ۝

65 Supplicate not this day! Assuredly ye will not be helped by Us.

لَا تَجۡـَٔرُوا ٱلۡيَوۡمَ إِنَّكُم مِّنَّا لَا تُنصَرُونَ ۝

66 My revelations were recited unto you, but ye used to turn back on your heels;

قَدۡ كَانَتۡ ءَايَٰتِى تُتۡلَىٰ عَلَيۡكُمۡ فَكُنتُمۡ عَلَىٰٓ أَعۡقَـٰبِكُمۡ تَنكِصُونَ ۝

67 In scorn thereof. Nightly did ye rave together.

مُسۡتَكۡبِرِينَ بِهِۦ سَـٰمِرًا تَهۡجُرُونَ ۝

68 Have they not pondered the Word, or hath that come unto them which came not unto their fathers of old?

أَفَلَمۡ يَدَّبَّرُوا ٱلۡقَوۡلَ أَمۡ جَآءَهُم مَّا لَمۡ يَأۡتِ ءَابَآءَهُمُ ٱلۡأَوَّلِينَ ۝

69 Or know they not their messenger, and so reject him?

أَمۡ لَمۡ يَعۡرِفُوا رَسُولَهُمۡ فَهُمۡ لَهُۥ مُنكِرُونَ ۝

70 Or say they: There is a madness in him? Nay, but he bringeth them the Truth; and most of them are haters of the Truth.

أَمۡ يَقُولُونَ بِهِۦ جِنَّةٌۢ بَلۡ جَآءَهُم بِٱلۡحَقِّ وَأَكۡثَرُهُمۡ لِلۡحَقِّ كَٰرِهُونَ ۝

71 And if the Truth had followed their desires, verily the heavens and the earth and whosoever is therein had been corrupted. Nay, We have brought them their Reminder, but from their Reminder they now turn away.

وَلَوِ اتَّبَعَ الْحَقُّ أَهْوَآءَهُمْ لَفَسَدَتِ السَّمٰوٰتُ وَالْأَرْضُ وَمَنْ فِيهِنَّ ۚ بَلْ أَتَيْنٰهُمْ بِذِكْرِهِمْ فَهُمْ عَنْ ذِكْرِهِمْ مُّعْرِضُوْنَ ۝

72 Or dost thou ask of them (O Muhammad) any tribute? But the bounty of thy Lord is better, for He is best of all who make provision.

أَمْ تَسْئَلُهُمْ خَرْجًا فَخَرَاجُ رَبِّكَ خَيْرٌ ۖ وَهُوَ خَيْرُ الرّٰزِقِيْنَ ۝

73 And lo! thou summonest them indeed unto a right path.

وَإِنَّكَ لَتَدْعُوهُمْ إِلٰى صِرٰطٍ مُّسْتَقِيْمٍ ۝

74 And lo! those who believe not in the Hereafter are indeed astray from the path.

وَإِنَّ الَّذِيْنَ لَا يُؤْمِنُوْنَ بِالْأَخِرَةِ عَنِ الصِّرٰطِ لَنٰكِبُوْنَ ۝

75 Though We had mercy on them and relieved them of the harm afflicting them, they still would wander blindly on in their contumacy.

وَلَوْ رَحِمْنٰهُمْ وَكَشَفْنَا مَا بِهِمْ مِّنْ ضُرٍّ لَّلَجُّوْا فِيْ طُغْيَانِهِمْ يَعْمَهُوْنَ ۝

76 Already have We grasped them with punishment, but they humble not themselves unto their Lord, nor do they pray;

وَلَقَدْ أَخَذْنٰهُمْ بِالْعَذَابِ فَمَا اسْتَكَانُوْا لِرَبِّهِمْ وَمَا يَتَضَرَّعُوْنَ ۝

77 Until, when We open for them the gate of extreme punishment, behold! they are aghast thereat.

حَتّٰى إِذَا فَتَحْنَا عَلَيْهِمْ بَابًا ذَا عَذَابٍ شَدِيْدٍ إِذَا هُمْ فِيْهِ مُبْلِسُوْنَ ۝

78 He it is Who hath created for you ears and eyes and hearts. Small thanks give ye!

وَهُوَ الَّذِيْ أَنْشَأَ لَكُمُ السَّمْعَ وَالْأَبْصَارَ وَالْأَفْئِدَةَ ۚ قَلِيْلًا مَّا تَشْكُرُوْنَ ۝

79 And He it is Who hath sown you broadcast in the earth, and unto Him ye will be gathered.

وَهُوَ الَّذِيْ ذَرَأَكُمْ فِي الْأَرْضِ وَإِلَيْهِ تُحْشَرُوْنَ ۝

80 And He it is Who giveth life and causeth death, and His is the

وَهُوَ الَّذِيْ يُحْيِي وَيُمِيْتُ وَلَهُ اخْتِلَافُ

difference of night and day. Have ye then no sense?

اَلَّيْلِ وَالنَّهَارِ أَفَلَا تَعْقِلُونَ ۞

81 Nay, but they say the like of that which said the men of old;

بَلْ قَالُوْا مِثْلَ مَا قَالَ الْأَوَّلُوْنَ ۞

82 They say: When we are dead and have become (mere) dust and bones, shall we then, forsooth, be raised again?

قَالُوْا أَءِذَا مِتْنَا وَكُنَّا تُرَابًا وَعِظَامًا أَءِنَّا لَمَبْعُوْثُوْنَ ۞

83 We were already promised this, we and our forefathers. Lo! this is naught but fables of the men of old.

لَقَدْ وُعِدْنَا نَحْنُ وَءَابَآؤُنَا هَذَا مِنْ قَبْلُ إِنْ هَذَا إِلَّا أَسَاطِيْرُ الْأَوَّلِيْنَ ۞

84 Say: Unto Whom (belongeth) the earth and whosoever is therein, if ye have knowledge?

قُلْ لِّمَنِ الْأَرْضُ وَمَنْ فِيْهَا إِنْ كُنْتُمْ تَعْلَمُوْنَ ۞

85 They will say: Unto Allah. Say: Will ye not then remember?

سَيَقُوْلُوْنَ لِلَّهِ قُلْ أَفَلَا تَذَكَّرُوْنَ ۞

86 Say: Who is Lord of the seven heavens, and Lord of the Tremendous Throne?

قُلْ مَنْ رَّبُّ السَّمَوَاتِ السَّبْعِ وَرَبُّ الْعَرْشِ الْعَظِيْمِ ۞

87 They will say: Unto Allah (all that belongeth). Say: Will ye not then keep duty (unto Him)?

سَيَقُوْلُوْنَ لِلَّهِ قُلْ أَفَلَا تَتَّقُوْنَ ۞

88 Say: In Whose hand is the dominion over all things and He protecteth, while against Him there is no protection, if ye have knowledge?

قُلْ مَنْ بِيَدِهِ مَلَكُوْتُ كُلِّ شَيْءٍ وَهُوَ يُجِيْرُ وَلَا يُجَارُ عَلَيْهِ إِنْ كُنْتُمْ تَعْلَمُوْنَ ۞

89 They will say: Unto Allah (all that belongeth). Say: How then are ye bewitched?

سَيَقُوْلُوْنَ لِلَّهِ قُلْ فَأَنَّى تُسْحَرُوْنَ ۞

90 Nay, but We have brought them the Truth, and lo! they are liars.

بَلْ أَتَيْنَاهُمْ بِالْحَقِّ وَإِنَّهُمْ لَكَاذِبُوْنَ ۞

91 Allah hath not chosen any son, nor is there any god along with Him; else would each god have assuredly championed that which he

مَا اتَّخَذَ اللَّهُ مِنْ وَلَدٍ وَمَا كَانَ مَعَهُ مِنْ إِلَهٍ إِذًا لَّذَهَبَ كُلُّ إِلَهٍ بِمَا خَلَقَ وَلَعَلَا بَعْضُهُمْ

created, and some of them would assuredly have overcome others. Glorified be Allah above all that they allege.

عَلَىٰ بَعْضٍ سُبْحَٰنَ ٱللَّهِ عَمَّا يَصِفُونَ ۞

92 Knower of the invisible and the visible! and exalted be He over all that they ascribe as partners (unto Him)!

عَٰلِمِ ٱلْغَيْبِ وَٱلشَّهَٰدَةِ فَتَعَٰلَىٰ عَمَّا يُشْرِكُونَ ۞

93 Say: My Lord! If thou shouldst show me that which they are promised;

قُل رَّبِّ إِمَّا تُرِيَنِّى مَا يُوعَدُونَ ۞

94 My Lord! then set me not among the wrongdoing folk.

رَبِّ فَلَا تَجْعَلْنِى فِى ٱلْقَوْمِ ٱلظَّٰلِمِينَ ۞

95 And verily We are Able to show thee that which We have promised them.

وَإِنَّا عَلَىٰٓ أَن نُّرِيَكَ مَا نَعِدُهُمْ لَقَٰدِرُونَ ۞

96 Repel evil with that which is better. We are best Aware of that which they allege.

ٱدْفَعْ بِٱلَّتِى هِىَ أَحْسَنُ ٱلسَّيِّئَةَ نَحْنُ أَعْلَمُ بِمَا يَصِفُونَ ۞

97 And say: My Lord! I seek refuge in Thee from suggestions of the evil ones;

وَقُل رَّبِّ أَعُوذُ بِكَ مِنْ هَمَزَٰتِ ٱلشَّيَٰطِينِ ۞

98 And I seek refuge in Thee, my Lord, lest they be present with me;

وَأَعُوذُ بِكَ رَبِّ أَن يَحْضُرُونِ ۞

99 Until, when death cometh unto one of them, he saith: My Lord! send me back;

حَتَّىٰٓ إِذَا جَآءَ أَحَدَهُمُ ٱلْمَوْتُ قَالَ رَبِّ ٱرْجِعُونِ ۞

100 That I may do right in that which I have left behind! But nay! It is but a word that he speaketh; and behind them is a barrier until the day when they are raised.

لَعَلِّىٓ أَعْمَلُ صَٰلِحًا فِيمَا تَرَكْتُ كَلَّآ إِنَّهَا كَلِمَةٌ هُوَ قَآئِلُهَا وَمِن وَرَآئِهِم بَرْزَخٌ إِلَىٰ يَوْمِ يُبْعَثُونَ ۞

101 And when the trumpet is blown there will be no kinship

فَإِذَا نُفِخَ فِى ٱلصُّورِ فَلَآ أَنسَابَ بَيْنَهُمْ يَوْمَئِذٍ

among them that day, nor will they ask of one another.

 وَلَا يَتَسَآءَلُونَ ۞

102   Then those whose scales are heavy, they are the successful.

فَمَن ثَقُلَتْ مَوَازِينُهُ فَأُولَٰٓئِكَ هُمُ الْمُفْلِحُونَ ۞

103   And those whose scales are light are those who lose their souls, in hell abiding.

وَمَنْ خَفَّتْ مَوَازِينُهُ فَأُولَٰٓئِكَ الَّذِينَ خَسِرُوٓا أَنفُسَهُمْ فِى جَهَنَّمَ خَٰلِدُونَ ۞

104   The fire burneth their faces, and they are glum therein.

تَلْفَحُ وُجُوهَهُمُ النَّارُ وَهُمْ فِيهَا كَٰلِحُونَ ۞

105   (It will be said): Were not My revelations recited unto you, and then ye used to deny them?

أَلَمْ تَكُنْ ءَايَٰتِى تُتْلَىٰ عَلَيْكُمْ فَكُنتُم بِهَا تُكَذِّبُونَ ۞

106   They will say: Our Lord! Our evil fortune conquered us, and we were erring folk.

قَالُوا۟ رَبَّنَا غَلَبَتْ عَلَيْنَا شِقْوَتُنَا وَكُنَّا قَوْمًا ضَآلِّينَ ۞

107   Our Lord! Oh, bring us forth from hence! If we return (to evil) then indeed we shall be wrongdoers.

رَبَّنَآ أَخْرِجْنَا مِنْهَا فَإِنْ عُدْنَا فَإِنَّا ظَٰلِمُونَ ۞

108   He saith: Begone therein, and speak not unto Me.

قَالَ اخْسَـُٔوا۟ فِيهَا وَلَا تُكَلِّمُونِ ۞

109   Lo! there was a party of My slaves who said: Our Lord! We believe, therefore forgive us and have mercy on us for Thou art best of all who show mercy;

إِنَّهُ كَانَ فَرِيقٌ مِّنْ عِبَادِى يَقُولُونَ رَبَّنَآ ءَامَنَّا فَاغْفِرْ لَنَا وَارْحَمْنَا وَأَنتَ خَيْرُ الرَّٰحِمِينَ ۞

110   But ye chose them from a laughing-stock until they caused you to forget remembrance of Me, while ye laughed at them.

فَاتَّخَذْتُمُوهُمْ سِخْرِيًّا حَتَّىٰٓ أَنسَوْكُمْ ذِكْرِى وَكُنتُم مِّنْهُمْ تَضْحَكُونَ ۞

111   Lo! I have rewarded them this day as they were steadfast; and they verily are the triumphant.

إِنِّى جَزَيْتُهُمُ الْيَوْمَ بِمَا صَبَرُوٓا أَنَّهُمْ هُمُ الْفَآئِزُونَ ۞

112   He will say: How long tarried ye in the earth, counting by years?

قَٰلَ كَمْ لَبِثْتُمْ فِى ٱلْأَرْضِ عَدَدَ سِنِينَ ﴿١١٢﴾

113   They will say: We tarried but a day or part of a day. Ask of those who keep count!

قَالُوا۟ لَبِثْنَا يَوْمًا أَوْ بَعْضَ يَوْمٍ فَسْـَٔلِ ٱلْعَآدِّينَ ﴿١١٣﴾

114   He will say: Ye tarried but a little if ye only knew.

قَٰلَ إِن لَّبِثْتُمْ إِلَّا قَلِيلًا لَّوْ أَنَّكُمْ كُنتُمْ تَعْلَمُونَ ﴿١١٤﴾

115   Deemed ye then that We had created you for naught, and that ye would not be returned unto Us?

أَفَحَسِبْتُمْ أَنَّمَا خَلَقْنَٰكُمْ عَبَثًا وَأَنَّكُمْ إِلَيْنَا لَا تُرْجَعُونَ ﴿١١٥﴾

116   Now Allah be exalted, the True King! There is no God save Him, the Lord of the Throne of Grace.

فَتَعَٰلَى ٱللَّهُ ٱلْمَلِكُ ٱلْحَقُّ لَا إِلَٰهَ إِلَّا هُوَ رَبُّ ٱلْعَرْشِ ٱلْكَرِيمِ ﴿١١٦﴾

117   He who crieth unto any other god along with Allah hath no proof thereof. His reckoning is only with his Lord. Lo! disbelievers will not be successful.

وَمَن يَدْعُ مَعَ ٱللَّهِ إِلَٰهًا ءَاخَرَ لَا بُرْهَٰنَ لَهُۥ بِهِۦ فَإِنَّمَا حِسَابُهُۥ عِندَ رَبِّهِۦٓ إِنَّهُۥ لَا يُفْلِحُ ٱلْكَٰفِرُونَ ﴿١١٧﴾

118   And (O Muhammad) say: My Lord! Forgive and have mercy, for Thou art best of all who show mercy.

وَقُل رَّبِّ ٱغْفِرْ وَٱرْحَمْ وَأَنتَ خَيْرُ ٱلرَّٰحِمِينَ ﴿١١٨﴾

An Nūr
(Light)

An Nūr, "Light," takes its name from vv. 35-40, descriptive of the Light of God as it should shine in the homes of believers, the greater part of the sūrah being legislation for the purifying of home life. All its verses were revealed at Al-Madīnah. Tradition says that vv. 11-20 relate to the slanderers of 'Ā'ishah in connection with an incident which occurred in the fifth year of the Hijrah when the Prophet was returning from the campaign against the Banū al Mustaliq, 'Ā'ishah, having been left behind on a march, and found and brought back by a young soldier who let her mount his camel and himself led the camel. A weaker tradition places the revelation of vv. 1-10 as late as the ninth year of the Hijrah.

The period of revelation is the fifth and sixth years of the Hijrah.

In the name of Allah, the Beneficent, the Merciful.

1   (Here is) a sūrah which We have revealed and enjoined, and wherein We have revealed plain tokens, that haply we may take heed.

2   The adulterer and the adulteress, scourge ye each one of them (with) a hundred stripes. And let not pity for the twain withhold you from obedience to Allah, if ye believe in Allah and the Last Day. And let a party of believers witness their punishment.

3 The adulterer shall not marry save an adulteress or an idolatress, and the adulteress none shall marry save an adulterer or an idolater. All that is forbidden unto believers.

الزَّانِى لَا يَنكِحُ إِلَّا زَانِيَةً أَوْ مُشْرِكَةً وَالزَّانِيَةُ لَا يَنكِحُهَا إِلَّا زَانٍ أَوْ مُشْرِكٌ وَحُرِّمَ ذَٰلِكَ عَلَى الْمُؤْمِنِينَ ۝

4 And those who accuse honourable women but bring not four witnesses, scourge them (with) eighty stripes and never (afterward) accept their testimony. They indeed are evil-doers.

وَالَّذِينَ يَرْمُونَ الْمُحْصَنَاتِ ثُمَّ لَمْ يَأْتُوا بِأَرْبَعَةِ شُهَدَاءَ فَاجْلِدُوهُمْ ثَمَانِينَ جَلْدَةً وَلَا تَقْبَلُوا لَهُمْ شَهَادَةً أَبَدًا وَأُولَٰئِكَ هُمُ الْفَاسِقُونَ ۝

5 Save those who afterward repent and make amends. (For such) lo! Allah is Forgiving, Merciful.

إِلَّا الَّذِينَ تَابُوا مِنْ بَعْدِ ذَٰلِكَ وَأَصْلَحُوا فَإِنَّ اللَّهَ غَفُورٌ رَحِيمٌ ۝

6 As for those who accuse their wives but have no witnesses except themselves; let the testimony of one of them be four testimonies, (swearing) by Allah that he is of those who speak the truth;

وَالَّذِينَ يَرْمُونَ أَزْوَاجَهُمْ وَلَمْ يَكُنْ لَهُمْ شُهَدَاءُ إِلَّا أَنفُسُهُمْ فَشَهَادَةُ أَحَدِهِمْ أَرْبَعُ شَهَادَاتٍ بِاللَّهِ إِنَّهُ لَمِنَ الصَّادِقِينَ ۝

7 And yet a fifth, invoking the curse of Allah on him if he is of those who lie.

وَالْخَامِسَةُ أَنَّ لَعْنَتَ اللَّهِ عَلَيْهِ إِن كَانَ مِنَ الْكَاذِبِينَ ۝

8 And it shall avert the punishment from her if she bear witness before Allah four times that the thing he saith is indeed false;

وَيَدْرَأُ عَنْهَا الْعَذَابَ أَن تَشْهَدَ أَرْبَعَ شَهَادَاتٍ بِاللَّهِ إِنَّهُ لَمِنَ الْكَاذِبِينَ ۝

9 And a fifth (time) that the wrath of Allah be upon her if he speaketh truth.

وَالْخَامِسَةَ أَنَّ غَضَبَ اللَّهِ عَلَيْهَا إِن كَانَ مِنَ الصَّادِقِينَ ۝

10 And had it not been for the grace of Allah and His mercy unto you, and that Allah is Clement, Wise, (ye had been undone).

وَلَوْلَا فَضْلُ اللَّهِ عَلَيْكُمْ وَرَحْمَتُهُ وَأَنَّ اللَّهَ تَوَّابٌ حَكِيمٌ ۝

11 Lo! they who spread the slander are a gang among you. Deem it not a bad thing for you; nay, it is good for you. Unto every man of them (will be paid) that which he hath earned of the sin; and as for him among them who had the greater share therein, his will be an awful doom.

إِنَّ الَّذِينَ جَاءُوا بِالْإِفْكِ عُصْبَةٌ مِّنكُمْ لَا تَحْسَبُوهُ شَرًّا لَّكُمْ بَلْ هُوَ خَيْرٌ لَّكُمْ لِكُلِّ امْرِئٍ مِّنْهُم مَّا اكْتَسَبَ مِنَ الْإِثْمِ وَالَّذِي تَوَلَّى كِبْرَهُ مِنْهُمْ لَهُ عَذَابٌ عَظِيمٌ ﴿١١﴾

12 Why did not the believers, men and women, when ye heard it, think good of their own folk; and say: It is a manifest untruth?

لَّوْلَا إِذْ سَمِعْتُمُوهُ ظَنَّ الْمُؤْمِنُونَ وَالْمُؤْمِنَاتُ بِأَنفُسِهِمْ خَيْرًا وَقَالُوا هَذَا إِفْكٌ مُّبِينٌ ﴿١٢﴾

13 Why did they not produce four witnesses? Since they produce not witnesses, they verily are liars in the sight of Allah.

لَّوْلَا جَاءُوا عَلَيْهِ بِأَرْبَعَةِ شُهَدَاءَ فَإِذْ لَمْ يَأْتُوا بِالشُّهَدَاءِ فَأُولَئِكَ عِندَ اللَّهِ هُمُ الْكَاذِبُونَ ﴿١٣﴾

14 Had it not been for the grace of Allah and His mercy unto you in the world and the Hereafter, an awful doom had overtaken you for that whereof ye murmured.

وَلَوْلَا فَضْلُ اللَّهِ عَلَيْكُمْ وَرَحْمَتُهُ فِي الدُّنْيَا وَالْآخِرَةِ لَمَسَّكُمْ فِي مَا أَفَضْتُمْ فِيهِ عَذَابٌ عَظِيمٌ ﴿١٤﴾

15 When ye welcomed it with your tongues, and uttered with your mouths that whereof ye had no knowledge, ye counted it a trifle. In the sight of Allah it is very great.

إِذْ تَلَقَّوْنَهُ بِأَلْسِنَتِكُمْ وَتَقُولُونَ بِأَفْوَاهِكُم مَّا لَيْسَ لَكُم بِهِ عِلْمٌ وَتَحْسَبُونَهُ هَيِّنًا وَهُوَ عِندَ اللَّهِ عَظِيمٌ ﴿١٥﴾

16 Wherefore, when ye heard it, said ye not: It is not for us to speak of this. Glory be to Thee (O Allah); This is awful calumny.

وَلَوْلَا إِذْ سَمِعْتُمُوهُ قُلْتُم مَّا يَكُونُ لَنَا أَن نَّتَكَلَّمَ بِهَذَا سُبْحَانَكَ هَذَا بُهْتَانٌ عَظِيمٌ ﴿١٦﴾

17 Allah admonisheth you that ye repeat not the like thereof ever, if ye are (in truth) believers.

يَعِظُكُمُ اللَّهُ أَن تَعُودُوا لِمِثْلِهِ أَبَدًا إِن كُنتُم مُّؤْمِنِينَ ﴿١٧﴾

18 And He expoundeth unto you
His revelations. Allah is Knower,
Wise.

وَيُبَيِّنُ اللّٰهُ لَكُمُ الْاٰيٰتِ وَاللّٰهُ عَلِيمٌ حَكِيمٌ ۝

19 Lo! those who love that slander
should be spread concerning those
who believe, theirs will be a painful
punishment in the world and the
Hereafter. Allah knoweth. Ye know
not.

إِنَّ الَّذِينَ يُحِبُّونَ أَنْ تَشِيعَ الْفَاحِشَةُ فِى الَّذِينَ
اٰمَنُوا لَهُمْ عَذَابٌ أَلِيمٌ فِى الدُّنْيَا وَالْاٰخِرَةِ
وَاللّٰهُ يَعْلَمُ وَأَنْتُمْ لَا تَعْلَمُونَ ۝

20 Had it not been for the grace of
Allah and His mercy unto you, and
that Allah is Clement, Merciful, (ye
had been undone).

وَلَوْلَا فَضْلُ اللّٰهِ عَلَيْكُمْ وَرَحْمَتُهُ وَأَنَّ اللّٰهَ
رَءُوفٌ رَحِيمٌ ۝

21 O ye who believe! Follow not
the footsteps of the devil. Unto
whomsoever followeth the footsteps
of the devil, lo! he commandeth
filthiness and wrong. Had it not
been for the grace of Allah and His
mercy unto you, not one of you
would ever have grown pure. But
Allah causeth whom He will to
grow. And Allah is Hearer, Knower.

يٰٓأَيُّهَا الَّذِينَ اٰمَنُوا لَا تَتَّبِعُوا خُطُوٰتِ الشَّيْطٰنِ
وَمَنْ يَتَّبِعْ خُطُوٰتِ الشَّيْطٰنِ فَإِنَّهُ يَأْمُرُ بِالْفَحْشَاءِ
وَالْمُنْكَرِ وَلَوْلَا فَضْلُ اللّٰهِ عَلَيْكُمْ وَرَحْمَتُهُ مَا زَكَىٰ
مِنْكُمْ مِنْ أَحَدٍ أَبَدًا وَلٰكِنَّ اللّٰهَ يُزَكِّى
مَنْ يَشَاءُ وَاللّٰهُ سَمِيعٌ عَلِيمٌ ۝

22 And let not those who possess
dignity and ease among you swear
not to give to the near of kin and to
the needy, and to fugitives for the
cause of Allah.[1] Let them forgive
and show indulgence. Yearn ye not
that Allah may forgive you? Allah
is Forgiving, Merciful.

وَلَا يَأْتَلِ أُولُوا الْفَضْلِ مِنْكُمْ وَالسَّعَةِ أَنْ يُؤْتُوا أُولِى
الْقُرْبَىٰ وَالْمَسٰكِينَ وَالْمُهٰجِرِينَ فِى سَبِيلِ اللّٰهِ
وَلْيَعْفُوا وَلْيَصْفَحُوا أَلَا تُحِبُّونَ أَنْ يَغْفِرَ اللّٰهُ لَكُمْ
وَاللّٰهُ غَفُورٌ رَحِيمٌ ۝

---

1. Tradition says that Abū Bakr, when he heard that a kinsman of his own whom he
had supported had been among the slanderers of his daughter 'Ā'ishah, swore no longer
to support him, and that this verse was revealed on that occasion.

23 Lo! as for those who traduce virtuous, believing women (who are) careless, cursed are they in the world and the Hereafter. Theirs will be an awful doom.

إِنَّ الَّذِينَ يَرْمُونَ الْمُحْصَنَاتِ الْغَافِلَاتِ الْمُؤْمِنَاتِ لُعِنُوا فِي الدُّنْيَا وَالْآخِرَةِ وَلَهُمْ عَذَابٌ عَظِيمٌ ۝

24 On the day when their tongues and their hands and their feet testify against them as to what they used to do;

يَوْمَ تَشْهَدُ عَلَيْهِمْ أَلْسِنَتُهُمْ وَأَيْدِيهِمْ وَأَرْجُلُهُم بِمَا كَانُوا يَعْمَلُونَ ۝

25 On that day Allah will pay them their just due, and they will know that Allah, He is the Manifest Truth.

يَوْمَئِذٍ يُوَفِّيهِمُ اللَّهُ دِينَهُمُ الْحَقَّ وَيَعْلَمُونَ أَنَّ اللَّهَ هُوَ الْحَقُّ الْمُبِينُ ۝

26 Vile women are for vile men, and vile men for vile women. Good women are for good men, and good men for good women; such are innocent of that which people say: For them is pardon and a bountiful provision.

الْخَبِيثَاتُ لِلْخَبِيثِينَ وَالْخَبِيثُونَ لِلْخَبِيثَاتِ وَالطَّيِّبَاتُ لِلطَّيِّبِينَ وَالطَّيِّبُونَ لِلطَّيِّبَاتِ أُولَٰئِكَ مُبَرَّؤُونَ مِمَّا يَقُولُونَ لَهُم مَّغْفِرَةٌ وَرِزْقٌ كَرِيمٌ ۝

27 O ye who believe! Enter not houses other than your own without first announcing your presence and invoking peace upon the folk thereof. That is better for you, that ye may be heedful.

يَا أَيُّهَا الَّذِينَ آمَنُوا لَا تَدْخُلُوا بُيُوتًا غَيْرَ بُيُوتِكُمْ حَتَّىٰ تَسْتَأْنِسُوا وَتُسَلِّمُوا عَلَىٰ أَهْلِهَا ذَٰلِكُمْ خَيْرٌ لَّكُمْ لَعَلَّكُمْ تَذَكَّرُونَ ۝

28 And if ye find no one therein, still enter not until permission hath been given. And if it be said unto you: Go back, then go back, for it is purer for you. Allah knoweth what ye do.

فَإِن لَّمْ تَجِدُوا فِيهَا أَحَدًا فَلَا تَدْخُلُوهَا حَتَّىٰ يُؤْذَنَ لَكُمْ وَإِن قِيلَ لَكُمُ ارْجِعُوا فَارْجِعُوا هُوَ أَزْكَىٰ لَكُمْ وَاللَّهُ بِمَا تَعْمَلُونَ عَلِيمٌ ۝

29 (It is) no sin for you to enter uninhabited houses wherein is comfort for you. Allah knoweth what ye proclaim and what ye hide.

لَّيْسَ عَلَيْكُمْ جُنَاحٌ أَن تَدْخُلُوا بُيُوتًا غَيْرَ مَسْكُونَةٍ فِيهَا مَتَاعٌ لَّكُمْ وَاللَّهُ يَعْلَمُ مَا تُبْدُونَ وَمَا تَكْتُمُونَ ۝

30 Tell the believing men to lower their gaze and be modest. That is purer for them. Lo! Allah is Aware of what they do.

قُل لِّلْمُؤْمِنِينَ يَغُضُّوا مِنْ أَبْصَٰرِهِمْ وَيَحْفَظُوا فُرُوجَهُمْ ذَٰلِكَ أَزْكَىٰ لَهُمْ إِنَّ ٱللَّهَ خَبِيرٌ بِمَا يَصْنَعُونَ ۝

31 And tell the believing women to lower their gaze and be modest, and to display of their adornment only that which is apparent, and to draw their veils over their bosoms, and not to reveal their adornment save to their own husbands or fathers or husbands' fathers, or their sons or their husbands' sons, or their brothers or their brothers' sons or sisters' sons, or their women, or their slaves, or male attendants who lack vigour, or children who know naught of women's nakedness. And let them not stamp their feet so as to reveal what they hide of their adornment. And turn unto Allah together, O believers, in order that ye may succeed.

وَقُل لِّلْمُؤْمِنَٰتِ يَغْضُضْنَ مِنْ أَبْصَٰرِهِنَّ وَيَحْفَظْنَ فُرُوجَهُنَّ وَلَا يُبْدِينَ زِينَتَهُنَّ إِلَّا مَا ظَهَرَ مِنْهَا وَلْيَضْرِبْنَ بِخُمُرِهِنَّ عَلَىٰ جُيُوبِهِنَّ وَلَا يُبْدِينَ زِينَتَهُنَّ إِلَّا لِبُعُولَتِهِنَّ أَوْ ءَابَآئِهِنَّ أَوْ ءَابَآءِ بُعُولَتِهِنَّ أَوْ أَبْنَآئِهِنَّ أَوْ أَبْنَآءِ بُعُولَتِهِنَّ أَوْ إِخْوَٰنِهِنَّ أَوْ بَنِىٓ إِخْوَٰنِهِنَّ أَوْ بَنِىٓ أَخَوَٰتِهِنَّ أَوْ نِسَآئِهِنَّ أَوْ مَا مَلَكَتْ أَيْمَٰنُهُنَّ أَوِ ٱلتَّٰبِعِينَ غَيْرِ أُو۟لِى ٱلْإِرْبَةِ مِنَ ٱلرِّجَالِ أَوِ ٱلطِّفْلِ ٱلَّذِينَ لَمْ يَظْهَرُوا۟ عَلَىٰ عَوْرَٰتِ ٱلنِّسَآءِ وَلَا يَضْرِبْنَ بِأَرْجُلِهِنَّ لِيُعْلَمَ مَا يُخْفِينَ مِن زِينَتِهِنَّ وَتُوبُوٓا۟ إِلَى ٱللَّهِ جَمِيعًا أَيُّهَ ٱلْمُؤْمِنُونَ لَعَلَّكُمْ تُفْلِحُونَ ۝

32 And marry such of you as are solitary and the pious of your slaves and maid-servants. If they be poor; Allah will enrich them of His bounty. Allah is of ample means, Aware.

وَأَنكِحُوا ٱلْأَيَٰمَىٰ مِنكُمْ وَٱلصَّٰلِحِينَ مِنْ عِبَادِكُمْ وَإِمَآئِكُمْ إِن يَكُونُوا۟ فُقَرَآءَ يُغْنِهِمُ ٱللَّهُ مِن فَضْلِهِ وَٱللَّهُ وَٰسِعٌ عَلِيمٌ ۝

33 And let those who cannot find a match keep chaste till Allah give them independence by His grace. And such of your slaves as seek a writing (of emancipation), write it for them if ye are aware of aught of good in them, and bestow upon

وَلْيَسْتَعْفِفِ ٱلَّذِينَ لَا يَجِدُونَ نِكَاحًا حَتَّىٰ يُغْنِيَهُمُ ٱللَّهُ مِن فَضْلِهِ وَٱلَّذِينَ يَبْتَغُونَ ٱلْكِتَٰبَ مِمَّا مَلَكَتْ أَيْمَٰنُكُمْ فَكَاتِبُوهُمْ إِنْ عَلِمْتُمْ فِيهِمْ خَيْرًا وَءَاتُوهُم

them of the wealth of Allah which He hath bestowed upon you. Force not your slave-girls to whoredom that ye may seek enjoyment of the life of the world, if they would preserve their chastity. And if one force them, then (unto them), after their compulsion, Lo! Allah will be Forgiving, Merciful.

مِّن مَّالِ اللَّهِ الَّذِيٓ ءَاتَىٰكُمْ ۚ وَلَا تُكْرِهُوا۟ فَتَيَٰتِكُمْ عَلَى الْبِغَآءِ إِنْ أَرَدْنَ تَحَصُّنًا لِّتَبْتَغُوا۟ عَرَضَ الْحَيَوٰةِ الدُّنْيَا ۚ وَمَن يُكْرِههُّنَّ فَإِنَّ اللَّهَ مِنۢ بَعْدِ إِكْرَٰهِهِنَّ غَفُورٌ رَّحِيمٌ ۞

34 And verily We have sent down for you revelations that make plain, and the example of those who passed away before you. An admonition unto those who ward off (evil).

وَلَقَدْ أَنزَلْنَآ إِلَيْكُمْ ءَايَٰتٍ مُّبَيِّنَٰتٍ وَمَثَلًا مِّنَ الَّذِينَ خَلَوْا۟ مِن قَبْلِكُمْ وَمَوْعِظَةً لِّلْمُتَّقِينَ ۞

35 Allah is the Light of the heavens and the earth. The similitude of His light is as a niche wherein is a lamp. The lamp is in a glass. The glass is as it were a shining star. (This lamp is) kindled from a blessed tree, an olive neither of the East nor of the West, whose oil would almost glow forth (of itself) though no fire touched it. Light upon light, Allah guideth unto His light whom He will. And Allah setteth forth for mankind similitudes, for Allah is Knower of all things.

۞ اللَّهُ نُورُ السَّمَٰوَٰتِ وَالْأَرْضِ ۚ مَثَلُ نُورِهِ كَمِشْكَوٰةٍ فِيهَا مِصْبَاحٌ ۖ الْمِصْبَاحُ فِي زُجَاجَةٍ ۖ الزُّجَاجَةُ كَأَنَّهَا كَوْكَبٌ دُرِّيٌّ يُوقَدُ مِن شَجَرَةٍ مُّبَٰرَكَةٍ زَيْتُونَةٍ لَّا شَرْقِيَّةٍ وَلَا غَرْبِيَّةٍ يَكَادُ زَيْتُهَا يُضِيٓءُ وَلَوْ لَمْ تَمْسَسْهُ نَارٌ ۚ نُّورٌ عَلَىٰ نُورٍ ۗ يَهْدِى اللَّهُ لِنُورِهِ مَن يَشَآءُ ۚ وَيَضْرِبُ اللَّهُ الْأَمْثَٰلَ لِلنَّاسِ ۗ وَاللَّهُ بِكُلِّ شَىْءٍ عَلِيمٌ ۞

36 (This lamp is found) in houses which Allah hath allowed to be exalted and that His name shall be remembered therein. Therein do offer praise to Him at morn and evening.

فِى بُيُوتٍ أَذِنَ اللَّهُ أَن تُرْفَعَ وَيُذْكَرَ فِيهَا اسْمُهُ يُسَبِّحُ لَهُ فِيهَا بِالْغُدُوِّ وَالْءَاصَالِ ۞

37 Men whom neither merchandise nor sale beguileth from remembrance of Allah and constancy in prayer and paying to the poor their due; who fear a day when hearts and eyeballs will be overturned;

رِجَالٌ لَّا تُلْهِيْهِمْ تِجَارَةٌ وَّلَا بَيْعٌ عَنْ ذِكْرِ اللّٰهِ وَاِقَامِ الصَّلٰوةِ وَاِيْتَآءِ الزَّكٰوةِ ۙ يَخَافُوْنَ يَوْمًا تَتَقَلَّبُ فِيْهِ الْقُلُوْبُ وَالْاَبْصَارُ ۙ ۞

38 That Allah may reward them with the best of what they did, and increase reward for them of His bounty. Allah giveth blessings without stint to whom He will.

لِيَجْزِيَهُمُ اللّٰهُ اَحْسَنَ مَا عَمِلُوْا وَيَزِيْدَهُمْ مِّنْ فَضْلِهٖ ۗ وَاللّٰهُ يَرْزُقُ مَنْ يَّشَآءُ بِغَيْرِ حِسَابٍ ۞

39 As for those who disbelieve, their deeds are as a mirage in a desert. The thirsty one supposeth it to be water till he cometh unto it and findeth it naught, and findeth, in the place thereof, Allah, Who payeth him his due; and Allah is swift at reckoning.

وَالَّذِيْنَ كَفَرُوْا اَعْمَالُهُمْ كَسَرَابٍ بِقِيْعَةٍ يَّحْسَبُهُ الظَّمْاٰنُ مَآءً ۗ حَتّٰى اِذَا جَآءَهٗ لَمْ يَجِدْهُ شَيْئًا وَّوَجَدَ اللّٰهَ عِنْدَهٗ فَوَفّٰىهُ حِسَابَهٗ ۗ وَاللّٰهُ سَرِيْعُ الْحِسَابِ ۞

40 Or as darkness on a vast, abysmal sea. There covereth him a wave, above which is a wave, above which is a cloud. Layer upon layer of darkness. When he holdeth out his hand he scarce can see it. And he for whom Allah hath not appointed light, for him there is no light.

اَوْ كَظُلُمٰتٍ فِيْ بَحْرٍ لُّجِّيٍّ يَّغْشٰهُ مَوْجٌ مِّنْ فَوْقِهٖ مَوْجٌ مِّنْ فَوْقِهٖ سَحَابٌ ۗ ظُلُمٰتٌ بَعْضُهَا فَوْقَ بَعْضٍ ۗ اِذَآ اَخْرَجَ يَدَهٗ لَمْ يَكَدْ يَرٰىهَا ۗ وَمَنْ لَّمْ يَجْعَلِ اللّٰهُ لَهٗ نُوْرًا فَمَا لَهٗ مِنْ نُّوْرٍ ۞

41 Hast thou not seen that Allah, He it is Whom all who are in the heavens and the earth praise; and the birds in their flight? Each one knoweth verily its worship and its praise; and Allah is Aware of what they do.

اَلَمْ تَرَ اَنَّ اللّٰهَ يُسَبِّحُ لَهٗ مَنْ فِي السَّمٰوٰتِ وَالْاَرْضِ وَالطَّيْرُ صٰٓفّٰتٍ ۗ كُلٌّ قَدْ عَلِمَ صَلَاتَهٗ وَتَسْبِيْحَهٗ ۗ وَاللّٰهُ عَلِيْمٌ بِمَا يَفْعَلُوْنَ ۞

42 And unto Allah belongeth the sovereignty of the heavens and the earth, and unto Allah is the journeying.

وَلِلَّهِ مُلْكُ السَّمَوَتِ وَالْأَرْضِ وَإِلَى اللَّهِ الْمَصِيرُ ﴿٤٢﴾

43 Hast thou not seen how Allah wafteth the clouds, then gathereth them, then maketh them layers, and thou seest the rain come forth from between them; He sendeth down from the heaven mountains wherein is hail, and smiteth therewith whom He will, and averteth it from whom He will. The flashing of His lightning all but snatcheth away the sight.

أَلَمْ تَرَ أَنَّ اللَّهَ يُزْجِي سَحَابًا ثُمَّ يُؤَلِّفُ بَيْنَهُ ثُمَّ يَجْعَلُهُ رُكَامًا فَتَرَى الْوَدْقَ يَخْرُجُ مِنْ خِلَلِهِ وَيُنَزِّلُ مِنَ السَّمَاءِ مِنْ جِبَالٍ فِيهَا مِنْ بَرَدٍ فَيُصِيبُ بِهِ مَنْ يَشَاءُ وَيَصْرِفُهُ عَنْ مَنْ يَشَاءُ يَكَادُ سَنَا بَرْقِهِ يَذْهَبُ بِالْأَبْصَارِ ﴿٤٣﴾

44 Allah causeth the revolution of the day and the night. Lo! herein is indeed a lesson for those who see.

يُقَلِّبُ اللَّهُ اللَّيْلَ وَالنَّهَارَ إِنَّ فِي ذَلِكَ لَعِبْرَةً لِأُولِي الْأَبْصَارِ ﴿٤٤﴾

45 Allah hath created every animal of water. Of them is (a kind) that goeth upon its belly and (a kind) that goeth upon two legs and (a kind) that goeth upon four. Allah createth what He will. Lo! Allah is Able to do all things.

وَاللَّهُ خَلَقَ كُلَّ دَابَّةٍ مِنْ مَاءٍ فَمِنْهُمْ مَنْ يَمْشِي عَلَى بَطْنِهِ وَمِنْهُمْ مَنْ يَمْشِي عَلَى رِجْلَيْنِ وَمِنْهُمْ مَنْ يَمْشِي عَلَى أَرْبَعٍ يَخْلُقُ اللَّهُ مَا يَشَاءُ إِنَّ اللَّهَ عَلَى كُلِّ شَيْءٍ قَدِيرٌ ﴿٤٥﴾

46 Verily We have sent down revelations and explained them. Allah guideth whom He will unto a straight path.

لَقَدْ أَنْزَلْنَا ءَايَتٍ مُبَيِّنَتٍ وَاللَّهُ يَهْدِي مَنْ يَشَاءُ إِلَى صِرَاطٍ مُسْتَقِيمٍ ﴿٤٦﴾

47 And they say: We believe in Allah and the messenger, and we obey; then after that a faction of them turn away. Such are not believers.

وَيَقُولُونَ ءَامَنَّا بِاللَّهِ وَبِالرَّسُولِ وَأَطَعْنَا ثُمَّ يَتَوَلَّى فَرِيقٌ مِنْهُمْ مِنْ بَعْدِ ذَلِكَ وَمَا أُولَئِكَ بِالْمُؤْمِنِينَ ﴿٤٧﴾

48 And when they are called unto Allah and His messenger to judge

وَإِذَا دُعُوا إِلَى اللَّهِ وَرَسُولِهِ لِيَحْكُمَ بَيْنَهُمْ إِذَا فَرِيقٌ

between them, lo! a faction of them are averse;

مِنْهُمْ مُّعْرِضُوْنَ ۝

49 But if right had been with them they would have come unto him willingly.

وَاِنْ يَّكُنْ لَّهُمُ الْحَقُّ يَأْتُوْٓا اِلَيْهِ مُذْعِنِيْنَ ۝

50 Is there in their hearts a disease, or have they doubts, or fear they lest Allah and His messenger should wrong them in judgment? Nay, but such are evil-doers.

اَفِىْ قُلُوْبِهِمْ مَّرَضٌ اَمِ ارْتَابُوْٓا اَمْ يَخَافُوْنَ اَنْ يَّحِيْفَ اللّٰهُ عَلَيْهِمْ وَرَسُوْلُهٗ ۚ بَلْ اُولٰٓئِكَ هُمُ الظّٰلِمُوْنَ ۝

51 The saying of (all true) believers when they are called unto Allah and His messenger to judge between them is only that they say: We hear and we obey. And such are the successful.

اِنَّمَا كَانَ قَوْلَ الْمُؤْمِنِيْنَ اِذَا دُعُوْٓا اِلَى اللّٰهِ وَرَسُوْلِهٖ لِيَحْكُمَ بَيْنَهُمْ اَنْ يَّقُوْلُوْا سَمِعْنَا وَاَطَعْنَا ۚ وَاُولٰٓئِكَ هُمُ الْمُفْلِحُوْنَ ۝

52 He who obeyeth Allah and His messenger, and feareth Allah, and keepeth duty (unto Him): such indeed are the victorious.

وَمَنْ يُّطِعِ اللّٰهَ وَرَسُوْلَهٗ وَيَخْشَ اللّٰهَ وَيَتَّقْهِ فَاُولٰٓئِكَ هُمُ الْفَآئِزُوْنَ ۝

53 They swear by Allah solemnly that, if thou order them, they will go forth. Say: Swear not; known obedience (is better). Lo! Allah is Aware of what ye do.

وَاَقْسَمُوْا بِاللّٰهِ جَهْدَ اَيْمَانِهِمْ لَئِنْ اَمَرْتَهُمْ لَيَخْرُجُنَّ ۚ قُلْ لَّا تُقْسِمُوْا ۚ طَاعَةٌ مَّعْرُوْفَةٌ ۚ اِنَّ اللّٰهَ خَبِيْرٌۢ بِمَا تَعْمَلُوْنَ ۝

54 Say: Obey Allah and obey the messenger. But if ye turn away, then (it is) for him (to do) only that wherewith he hath been charged, and for you (to do) only that wherewith ye have been charged. If ye obey him, ye will go aright. But the messenger hath no other charge than to convey (the message), plainly.

قُلْ اَطِيْعُوا اللّٰهَ وَاَطِيْعُوا الرَّسُوْلَ ۚ فَاِنْ تَوَلَّوْا فَاِنَّمَا عَلَيْهِ مَا حُمِّلَ وَعَلَيْكُمْ مَّا حُمِّلْتُمْ ۚ وَاِنْ تُطِيْعُوْهُ تَهْتَدُوْا ۚ وَمَا عَلَى الرَّسُوْلِ اِلَّا الْبَلٰغُ الْمُبِيْنُ ۝

55 Allah hath promised such of you as believe and do good works that

وَعَدَ اللّٰهُ الَّذِيْنَ اٰمَنُوْا مِنْكُمْ وَعَمِلُوا الصّٰلِحٰتِ

He will surely make them to succeed (the present rulers) in the earth even as He caused those who were before them to succeed others); and that He will surely establish for them their religion which He hath approved for them, and will give them in exchange safety after their fear. They serve Me. They ascribe no thing as partner unto Me. Those who disbelieve henceforth, they are the miscreants.

لَيَسْتَخْلِفَنَّهُمْ فِى الْأَرْضِ كَمَا اسْتَخْلَفَ الَّذِينَ مِن قَبْلِهِمْ وَلَيُمَكِّنَنَّ لَهُمْ دِينَهُمُ الَّذِى ارْتَضَىٰ لَهُمْ وَلَيُبَدِّلَنَّهُم مِّنۢ بَعْدِ خَوْفِهِمْ أَمْنًا يَعْبُدُونَنِى لَا يُشْرِكُونَ بِى شَيْئًا وَمَن كَفَرَ بَعْدَ ذَٰلِكَ فَأُولَٰٓئِكَ هُمُ الْفَٰسِقُونَ ۝

56 Establish worship and pay the poor-due and obey the messenger, that haply ye may find mercy.

وَأَقِيمُوا الصَّلَوٰةَ وَءَاتُوا الزَّكَوٰةَ وَأَطِيعُوا الرَّسُولَ لَعَلَّكُمْ تُرْحَمُونَ ۝

57 Think not that the disbelievers can escape in the land. Fire will be their home; a hapless journey's end!

لَا تَحْسَبَنَّ الَّذِينَ كَفَرُوا مُعْجِزِينَ فِى الْأَرْضِ وَمَأْوَىٰهُمُ النَّارُ وَلَبِئْسَ الْمَصِيرُ ۝

58 O ye who believe! Let your slaves, and those of you who have not come to puberty, ask leave of you at three times (before they come into your presence): Before the prayer of dawn, and when ye lay aside your raiment for the heat of noon, and after the prayer of night.[2] Three times of privacy for you. It is no sin for them or for you at other times, when some of you go round attendant upon others (if they come into your presence without leave). Thus Allah maketh clear the revelations for you. Allah is Knower, Wise.

يَٰٓأَيُّهَا الَّذِينَ ءَامَنُوا لِيَسْتَـْٔذِنكُمُ الَّذِينَ مَلَكَتْ أَيْمَٰنُكُمْ وَالَّذِينَ لَمْ يَبْلُغُوا الْحُلُمَ مِنكُمْ ثَلَٰثَ مَرَّٰتٍ مِّن قَبْلِ صَلَوٰةِ الْفَجْرِ وَحِينَ تَضَعُونَ ثِيَابَكُم مِّنَ الظَّهِيرَةِ وَمِنۢ بَعْدِ صَلَوٰةِ الْعِشَآءِ ثَلَٰثُ عَوْرَٰتٍ لَّكُمْ لَيْسَ عَلَيْكُمْ وَلَا عَلَيْهِمْ جُنَاحٌۢ بَعْدَهُنَّ طَوَّٰفُونَ عَلَيْكُم بَعْضُكُمْ عَلَىٰ بَعْضٍ كَذَٰلِكَ يُبَيِّنُ اللَّهُ لَكُمُ الْـَٔايَٰتِ وَاللَّهُ عَلِيمٌ حَكِيمٌ ۝

---

2. The prayer to be offered when the night has fully come.

59 And when the children among you come to puberty then let them ask leave even as those before them used to ask it. Thus Allah maketh clear His revelations for you. Allah is Knower, Wise.

وَإِذَا بَلَغَ الْأَطْفَالُ مِنكُمُ الْحُلُمَ فَلْيَسْتَـْذِنُوا كَمَا اسْتَـْذَنَ الَّذِينَ مِن قَبْلِهِمْ كَذَلِكَ يُبَيِّنُ اللَّهُ لَكُمْ ءَايَـٰتِهِ وَاللَّهُ عَلِيمٌ حَكِيمٌ ﴿٥٩﴾

60 As for women past child-bearing, who have no hope of marriage, it is no sin for them if they discard their (outer) clothing in such a way as not to show adornment. But to refrain is better for them. Allah is Hearer, Knower.

وَالْقَوَاعِدُ مِنَ النِّسَاءِ الَّتِي لَا يَرْجُونَ نِكَاحًا فَلَيْسَ عَلَيْهِنَّ جُنَاحٌ أَن يَضَعْنَ ثِيَابَهُنَّ غَيْرَ مُتَبَرِّجَاتٍ بِزِينَةٍ وَأَن يَسْتَعْفِفْنَ خَيْرٌ لَّهُنَّ وَاللَّهُ سَمِيعٌ عَلِيمٌ ﴿٦٠﴾

61 No blame is there upon the blind nor any blame upon the lame nor any blame upon the sick nor on yourselves if ye eat from your houses, or the houses of your fathers, or the houses of your mothers, or the houses of your brothers, or the houses of your sisters, or the houses of your fathers' brothers, or the houses of your fathers' sisters, or the houses of your mothers' brothers, or the houses of your mothers' sisters, or (from that) whereof ye hold the keys, or (from the house) of a friend. No sin shall it be for you whether ye eat together or apart. But when ye enter houses, salute one another with a greeting from Allah, blessed and sweet. Thus Allah maketh clear His revelations for you, that haply ye may understand.

لَّيْسَ عَلَى الْأَعْمَىٰ حَرَجٌ وَلَا عَلَى الْأَعْرَجِ حَرَجٌ وَلَا عَلَى الْمَرِيضِ حَرَجٌ وَلَا عَلَىٰ أَنفُسِكُمْ أَن تَأْكُلُوا مِن بُيُوتِكُمْ أَوْ بُيُوتِ ءَابَائِكُمْ أَوْ بُيُوتِ أُمَّهَاتِكُمْ أَوْ بُيُوتِ إِخْوَانِكُمْ أَوْ بُيُوتِ أَخَوَاتِكُمْ أَوْ بُيُوتِ أَعْمَامِكُمْ أَوْ بُيُوتِ عَمَّاتِكُمْ أَوْ بُيُوتِ أَخْوَالِكُمْ أَوْ بُيُوتِ خَالَاتِكُمْ أَوْ مَا مَلَكْتُم مَّفَاتِحَهُ أَوْ صَدِيقِكُمْ لَيْسَ عَلَيْكُمْ جُنَاحٌ أَن تَأْكُلُوا جَمِيعًا أَوْ أَشْتَاتًا فَإِذَا دَخَلْتُم بُيُوتًا فَسَلِّمُوا عَلَىٰ أَنفُسِكُمْ تَحِيَّةً مِّنْ عِندِ اللَّهِ مُبَارَكَةً طَيِّبَةً كَذَلِكَ يُبَيِّنُ اللَّهُ لَكُمُ الْآيَاتِ لَعَلَّكُمْ تَعْقِلُونَ ﴿٦١﴾

62 They only are the true believers
who believe in Allah and His messenger and, when they are with him
on some common errand, go not
away until they have asked leave of
him. Lo! those who ask leave of
thee, those are they who believe in
Allah and His messenger. So, if
they ask thy leave for some affair
of theirs, give leave to whom thou
wilt of them, and ask for them forgiveness of Allah. Lo! Allah is
Forgiving, Merciful.

إِنَّمَا الْمُؤْمِنُونَ الَّذِينَ ءَامَنُوا بِاللَّهِ وَرَسُولِهِ
وَإِذَا كَانُوا مَعَهُ عَلَىٰ أَمْرٍ جَامِعٍ لَّمْ يَذْهَبُوا
حَتَّىٰ يَسْتَـْٔذِنُوهُ إِنَّ الَّذِينَ يَسْتَـْٔذِنُونَكَ أُوْلَـٰٓئِكَ
الَّذِينَ يُؤْمِنُونَ بِاللَّهِ وَرَسُولِهِ ۚ فَإِذَا اسْتَـْٔذَنُوكَ
لِبَعْضِ شَأْنِهِمْ فَأْذَن لِّمَن شِئْتَ مِنْهُمْ
وَاسْتَغْفِرْ لَهُمُ اللَّهَ ۚ إِنَّ اللَّهَ غَفُورٌ رَّحِيمٌ ۝

63 Make not the calling of the messenger among you as your calling
one of another. Allah knoweth those
of you who steal away, hiding
themselves. And let those who conspire to evade orders beware lest
grief or painful punishment befall
them.

لَّا تَجْعَلُوا دُعَآءَ الرَّسُولِ بَيْنَكُمْ كَدُعَآءِ
بَعْضِكُم بَعْضًا ۚ قَدْ يَعْلَمُ اللَّهُ الَّذِينَ
يَتَسَلَّلُونَ مِنكُمْ لِوَاذًا ۚ فَلْيَحْذَرِ الَّذِينَ يُخَالِفُونَ
عَنْ أَمْرِهِ أَن تُصِيبَهُمْ فِتْنَةٌ أَوْ يُصِيبَهُمْ
عَذَابٌ أَلِيمٌ ۝

64 Lo! verily unto Allah belongeth
whatsoever is in the heavens and
the earth. He knoweth your condition. And (He knoweth) the Day
when they are returned unto Him so
that He may inform them of what
they did. Allah is Knower of all
things.

أَلَا إِنَّ لِلَّهِ مَا فِي السَّمَاوَاتِ وَالْأَرْضِ ۖ قَدْ يَعْلَمُ
مَا أَنتُمْ عَلَيْهِ وَيَوْمَ يُرْجَعُونَ إِلَيْهِ فَيُنَبِّئُهُم
بِمَا عَمِلُوا ۗ وَاللَّهُ بِكُلِّ شَيْءٍ عَلِيمٌ ۝

Al Furqān
(The Criterion)

Al Furqān, "The Criterion," takes its name from a word occurring in v. 1. The subject is the folly of superstition and the craving for miraculous events in face of the wonders of God's creation.

It belongs to the middle group of Makkan sūrahs, except vv. 68-70 which were revealed at Al-Madīnah.

In the name of Allah, the Beneficent, the Merciful.

1 Blessed is He Who hath revealed unto His slave the Criterion (of right and wrong), that he may be a warner to the peoples.

2 He unto Whom belongeth the sovereignty of the heavens and the earth. He hath chosen no son nor hath He any partner in the sovereignty. He hath created everything and hath meted out for it a measure.

3 Yet they choose beside Him other gods who create naught but are themselves created, and possess not hurt nor profit for themselves, and possess not death nor life, nor power to raise the dead.

502

4 Those who disbelieve say: This is naught but a lie that he hath invented, and other folk have helped him with it, so that they have produced a slander and a lie.

وَقَالَ الَّذِينَ كَفَرُوٓا إِنْ هَٰذَآ إِلَّآ إِفْكُ افْتَرَىٰهُ وَأَعَانَهُ عَلَيْهِ قَوْمٌ ءَاخَرُونَ فَقَدْ جَآءُو ظُلْمًا وَزُورًا ٤

5 And they say: Fables of the men of old which he hath had written down so that they are dictated to him morn and evening.

وَقَالُوٓا أَسَاطِيرُ الْأَوَّلِينَ اكْتَتَبَهَا فَهِيَ تُمْلَىٰ عَلَيْهِ بُكْرَةً وَأَصِيلًا ٥

6 Say (unto them, O Muhammad): He Who knoweth the secret of the heavens and the earth hath revealed it. Lo! He ever is Forgiving, Merciful.

قُلْ أَنزَلَهُ الَّذِي يَعْلَمُ السِّرَّ فِي السَّمَٰوَٰتِ وَالْأَرْضِ إِنَّهُ كَانَ غَفُورًا رَّحِيمًا ٦

7 And they say: What aileth this messenger (of Allah) that he eateth food and walketh in the markets? Why is not an angel sent down unto him, to be a warner with him.

وَقَالُوا مَالِ هَٰذَا الرَّسُولِ يَأْكُلُ الطَّعَامَ وَيَمْشِي فِي الْأَسْوَاقِ لَوْلَآ أُنزِلَ إِلَيْهِ مَلَكٌ فَيَكُونَ مَعَهُ نَذِيرًا ٧

8 Or (why is not) a treasure thrown down unto him, or why hath he not a paradise from whence to eat? And the evil-doers say: Ye are but following a man bewitched.

أَوْ يُلْقَىٰ إِلَيْهِ كَنزٌ أَوْ تَكُونُ لَهُ جَنَّةٌ يَأْكُلُ مِنْهَا وَقَالَ الظَّٰلِمُونَ إِن تَتَّبِعُونَ إِلَّا رَجُلًا مَّسْحُورًا ٨

9 See how they coin similitudes for thee, so that they are all astray and cannot find a road!

انظُرْ كَيْفَ ضَرَبُوا لَكَ الْأَمْثَٰلَ فَضَلُّوا فَلَا يَسْتَطِيعُونَ سَبِيلًا ٩

10 Blessed is He Who, if He will, will assign thee better than (all) that—Gardens underneath which rivers flow—and will assign thee mansions.

تَبَارَكَ الَّذِي إِن شَآءَ جَعَلَ لَكَ خَيْرًا مِّن ذَٰلِكَ جَنَّٰتٍ تَجْرِي مِن تَحْتِهَا الْأَنْهَٰرُ وَيَجْعَل لَّكَ قُصُورًا ١٠

11 Nay, but they deny (the coming of) the Hour, and for those who deny (the coming of) the Hour; We have prepared a flame.

بَلْ كَذَّبُوا بِالسَّاعَةِ وَأَعْتَدْنَا لِمَن كَذَّبَ بِالسَّاعَةِ سَعِيرًا ١١

12 When it seeth them from afar, they hear the crackling and the roar thereof.

إِذَا رَأَتْهُمْ مِّنْ مَّكَانٍ بَعِيدٍ سَمِعُوا لَهَا تَغَيُّظًا وَزَفِيرًا ۝

13 And when they are flung into a narrow place thereof, chained together, they pray for destruction there.

وَإِذَا أُلْقُوا مِنْهَا مَكَانًا ضَيِّقًا مُّقَرَّنِينَ دَعَوْا هُنَالِكَ ثُبُورًا ۝

14 Pray not that day for one destruction, but pray for many destructions!

لَّا تَدْعُوا الْيَوْمَ ثُبُورًا وَاحِدًا وَّادْعُوا ثُبُورًا كَثِيرًا ۝

15 Say: Is that (doom) better or the Garden of Immortality which is promised unto those who ward off (evil)? It will be their reward and journey's end.

قُلْ أَذَٰلِكَ خَيْرٌ أَمْ جَنَّةُ الْخُلْدِ الَّتِي وُعِدَ الْمُتَّقُونَ كَانَتْ لَهُمْ جَزَاءً وَّمَصِيرًا ۝

16 Therein abiding, they have all that they desire. It is for thy Lord a promise that must be fulfilled.

لَّهُمْ فِيهَا مَا يَشَاءُونَ خَالِدِينَ كَانَ عَلَىٰ رَبِّكَ وَعْدًا مَّسْئُولًا ۝

17 And on the day when He will assemble them and that which they worship instead of Allah and will say: Was it ye who misled these my slaves or did they (themselves) wander from the way?

وَيَوْمَ يَحْشُرُهُمْ وَمَا يَعْبُدُونَ مِن دُونِ اللَّهِ فَيَقُولُ أَأَنتُمْ أَضْلَلْتُمْ عِبَادِي هَٰؤُلَاءِ أَمْ هُمْ ضَلُّوا السَّبِيلَ ۝

18 They will say: Be Thou glorified! It was not for us to choose any protecting friends beside Thee; but Thou didst give them and their fathers ease till they forgot the warning and became lost folk.

قَالُوا سُبْحَانَكَ مَا كَانَ يَنْبَغِي لَنَا أَن نَّتَّخِذَ مِن دُونِكَ مِنْ أَوْلِيَاءَ وَلَٰكِن مَّتَّعْتَهُمْ وَآبَاءَهُمْ حَتَّىٰ نَسُوا الذِّكْرَ وَكَانُوا قَوْمًا بُورًا ۝

19 Thus they will give you the lie regarding what ye say, then ye can neither avert (the doom) nor obtain help. And whoso among you doeth wrong, We shall make him taste great torment.

فَقَدْ كَذَّبُوكُم بِمَا تَقُولُونَ فَمَا تَسْتَطِيعُونَ صَرْفًا وَلَا نَصْرًا وَمَن يَظْلِم مِّنكُمْ نُذِقْهُ عَذَابًا كَبِيرًا ۝

20 We never sent before thee any messengers but lo! they ate food and walked in the markets. And We have appointed some of you a test for others: Will ye be steadfast? And thy Lord is ever Seer.

وَمَآ أَرْسَلْنَا قَبْلَكَ مِنَ ٱلْمُرْسَلِينَ إِلَّآ إِنَّهُمْ لَيَأْكُلُونَ ٱلطَّعَامَ وَيَمْشُونَ فِى ٱلْأَسْوَاقِ وَجَعَلْنَا بَعْضَكُمْ لِبَعْضٍ فِتْنَةً أَتَصْبِرُونَ وَكَانَ رَبُّكَ بَصِيرًا ۝

21 And those who look not for a meeting with Us say: Why are angels not sent down unto us and (why) do we not see our Lord? Assuredly they think too highly of themselves and are scornful with great pride.

۞ وَقَالَ ٱلَّذِينَ لَا يَرْجُونَ لِقَآءَنَا لَوْلَآ أُنزِلَ عَلَيْنَا ٱلْمَلَٰٓئِكَةُ أَوْ نَرَىٰ رَبَّنَا لَقَدِ ٱسْتَكْبَرُوا۟ فِىٓ أَنفُسِهِمْ وَعَتَوْ عُتُوًّا كَبِيرًا ۝

22 On the day when they behold the angels, on that day there will be no good tidings for the guilty; and they will cry: A forbidding ban!

يَوْمَ يَرَوْنَ ٱلْمَلَٰٓئِكَةَ لَا بُشْرَىٰ يَوْمَئِذٍ لِّلْمُجْرِمِينَ وَيَقُولُونَ حِجْرًا مَّحْجُورًا ۝

23 And We shall turn unto the work they did and make it scattered motes.

وَقَدِمْنَآ إِلَىٰ مَا عَمِلُوا۟ مِنْ عَمَلٍ فَجَعَلْنَٰهُ هَبَآءً مَّنثُورًا ۝

24 Those who have earned the Garden on that day will be better in their home and happier in their place of noonday rest;

أَصْحَٰبُ ٱلْجَنَّةِ يَوْمَئِذٍ خَيْرٌ مُّسْتَقَرًّا وَأَحْسَنُ مَقِيلًا ۝

25 A day when the heaven with the clouds will be rent asunder and the angels will be sent down, a grand descent.

وَيَوْمَ تَشَقَّقُ ٱلسَّمَآءُ بِٱلْغَمَٰمِ وَنُزِّلَ ٱلْمَلَٰٓئِكَةُ تَنزِيلًا ۝

26 The Sovereignty on that day will be the True (Sovereignty) belonging to the Beneficent One, and it will be a hard day for disbelievers.

ٱلْمُلْكُ يَوْمَئِذٍ ٱلْحَقُّ لِلرَّحْمَٰنِ وَكَانَ يَوْمًا عَلَى ٱلْكَٰفِرِينَ عَسِيرًا ۝

27 On the day when the wrong-doer gnaweth his hands, he will say: Ah, would that I had chosen a way together with the messenger (of Allah)!

وَيَوْمَ يَعَضُّ ٱلظَّالِمُ عَلَىٰ يَدَيْهِ يَقُولُ يَٰلَيْتَنِى ٱتَّخَذْتُ مَعَ ٱلرَّسُولِ سَبِيلًا ۝

28 Alas for me! Ah, would that I had never taken such a one for friend!

29 He verily led me astray from the Reminder after it had reached me. Satan was ever man's deserter in the hour of need.

30 And the messenger saith: O my Lord! Lo! mine own folk make this Qur'an of no account.

31 Even so have We appointed unto every Prophet an opponent from among the guilty; but Allah sufficeth for a Guide and Helper.

32 And those who disbelieve say: Why is the Qur'an not revealed unto him all at once? (It is revealed) thus that We may strengthen thy heart therewith; and We have arranged it in right order.

33 And they bring thee no similitude but We bring thee the Truth (as against it), and better (than their similitude) as argument.

34 Those who will be gathered on their faces unto Hell: such are worse in plight and further from the right road.

35 We verily gave Moses the Scripture and placed with him his brother Aaron as henchman.

36 Then We said: Go together unto the folk who have denied Our revelations. Then We destroyed them, a complete destruction.

يَوَيْلَتَى لَيْتَنِى لَمْ أَتَّخِذْ فُلَانًا خَلِيلًا ۝

لَقَدْ أَضَلَّنِى عَنِ الذِّكْرِ بَعْدَ إِذْ جَآءَنِى وَكَانَ الشَّيْطَانُ لِلْإِنسَانِ خَذُولًا ۝

وَقَالَ الرَّسُولُ يَٰرَبِّ إِنَّ قَوْمِى اتَّخَذُوا هَٰذَا الْقُرْءَانَ مَهْجُورًا ۝

وَكَذَٰلِكَ جَعَلْنَا لِكُلِّ نَبِيٍّ عَدُوًّا مِّنَ الْمُجْرِمِينَ وَكَفَىٰ بِرَبِّكَ هَادِيًا وَنَصِيرًا ۝

وَقَالَ الَّذِينَ كَفَرُوا لَوْلَا نُزِّلَ عَلَيْهِ الْقُرْءَانُ جُمْلَةً وَاحِدَةً ۚ كَذَٰلِكَ لِنُثَبِّتَ بِهِ فُؤَادَكَ وَرَتَّلْنَٰهُ تَرْتِيلًا ۝

وَلَا يَأْتُونَكَ بِمَثَلٍ إِلَّا جِئْنَٰكَ بِالْحَقِّ وَأَحْسَنَ تَفْسِيرًا ۝

الَّذِينَ يُحْشَرُونَ عَلَىٰ وُجُوهِهِمْ إِلَىٰ جَهَنَّمَ أُو۟لَٰٓئِكَ شَرٌّ مَّكَانًا وَأَضَلُّ سَبِيلًا ۝

وَلَقَدْ ءَاتَيْنَا مُوسَى الْكِتَٰبَ وَجَعَلْنَا مَعَهُۥٓ أَخَاهُ هَٰرُونَ وَزِيرًا ۝

فَقُلْنَا اذْهَبَا إِلَى الْقَوْمِ الَّذِينَ كَذَّبُوا بِـَٔايَٰتِنَا فَدَمَّرْنَٰهُمْ تَدْمِيرًا ۝

37 And Noah's folk, when they denied the messengers, We drowned them and made of them a portent for mankind. We have prepared a painful doom for evil-doers.

وَقَوْمَ نُوحٍ لَّمَّا كَذَّبُوا الرُّسُلَ أَغْرَقْنَاهُمْ وَجَعَلْنَاهُمْ لِلنَّاسِ ءَايَةً وَأَعْتَدْنَا لِلظَّالِمِينَ عَذَابًا أَلِيمًا ۝

38 And (the tribes of) ʿĀd and Thamūd, and the dwellers in Ar-Rass,[1] and many generations in between.

وَعَادًا وَثَمُودَا۟ وَأَصْحَابَ الرَّسِّ وَقُرُونًا بَيْنَ ذَٰلِكَ كَثِيرًا ۝

39 Each (of them) We warned by examples, and each (of them) We brought to utter ruin.

وَكُلًّا ضَرَبْنَا لَهُ الْأَمْثَالَ وَكُلًّا تَبَّرْنَا تَتْبِيرًا ۝

40 And indeed they have passed by the township whereon was rained the fatal rain.[2] Can it be that they have not seen it? Nay, but they hope for no resurrection.

وَلَقَدْ أَتَوْا۟ عَلَى الْقَرْيَةِ الَّتِي أُمْطِرَتْ مَطَرَ السَّوْءِ أَفَلَمْ يَكُونُوا۟ يَرَوْنَهَا بَلْ كَانُوا۟ لَا يَرْجُونَ نُشُورًا ۝

41 And when they see thee (O Muhammad) they treat thee only as a jest (saying): Is this he whom Allah sendeth as a messenger?

وَإِذَا رَأَوْكَ إِن يَتَّخِذُونَكَ إِلَّا هُزُوًا أَهَٰذَا الَّذِي بَعَثَ اللَّهُ رَسُولًا ۝

42 He would have led us far away from our gods if we had not been staunch to them. They will know, when they behold the doom, who is more astray as to the road.

إِن كَادَ لَيُضِلُّنَا عَنْ ءَالِهَتِنَا لَوْلَا أَن صَبَرْنَا عَلَيْهَا وَسَوْفَ يَعْلَمُونَ حِينَ يَرَوْنَ الْعَذَابَ مَنْ أَضَلُّ سَبِيلًا ۝

43 Hast thou seen him who chooseth for his god his own lust? Wouldst thou then be guardian over him?

أَرَأَيْتَ مَنِ اتَّخَذَ إِلَٰهَهُ هَوَاهُ أَفَأَنتَ تَكُونُ عَلَيْهِ وَكِيلًا ۝

---

1. Said to have been a town in Yamāmah.

2. The great trade caravans from Makkah into Syria passed by the Dead sea.

44 Or deemest thou that most of them hear or understand? They are but as the cattle—nay, but they are farther astray!

أَمْ تَحْسَبُ أَنَّ أَكْثَرَهُمْ يَسْمَعُونَ أَوْ يَعْقِلُونَ إِنْ هُمْ إِلَّا كَالْأَنْعَامِ بَلْ هُمْ أَضَلُّ سَبِيلًا ﴿٤٤﴾

45 Hast thou not seen how thy Lord hath spread the shade—And if He willed He could have made it still—then We have made the sun its pilot;

أَلَمْ تَرَ إِلَى رَبِّكَ كَيْفَ مَدَّ الظِّلَّ وَلَوْ شَاءَ لَجَعَلَهُ سَاكِنًا ثُمَّ جَعَلْنَا الشَّمْسَ عَلَيْهِ دَلِيلًا ﴿٤٥﴾

46 Then We withdraw it unto Us, a gradual withdrawal?

ثُمَّ قَبَضْنَاهُ إِلَيْنَا قَبْضًا يَسِيرًا ﴿٤٦﴾

47 And He it is Who maketh night a covering for you, and sleep repose, and maketh day a resurrection.

وَهُوَ الَّذِي جَعَلَ لَكُمُ اللَّيْلَ لِبَاسًا وَالنَّوْمَ سُبَاتًا وَجَعَلَ النَّهَارَ نُشُورًا ﴿٤٧﴾

48 And He it is Who sendeth the winds, glad tidings heralding His mercy, and We send down purifying water from the sky.

وَهُوَ الَّذِي أَرْسَلَ الرِّيَاحَ بُشْرًا بَيْنَ يَدَيْ رَحْمَتِهِ وَأَنْزَلْنَا مِنَ السَّمَاءِ مَاءً طَهُورًا ﴿٤٨﴾

49 That We may give life thereby to a dead land, and We give many beasts and men that We have created to drink thereof.

لِنُحْيِيَ بِهِ بَلْدَةً مَيْتًا وَنُسْقِيَهُ مِمَّا خَلَقْنَا أَنْعَامًا وَأَنَاسِيَّ كَثِيرًا ﴿٤٩﴾

50 And verily We have repeated it among them that they may remember, but most of mankind begrudge aught save ingratitude.

وَلَقَدْ صَرَّفْنَاهُ بَيْنَهُمْ لِيَذَّكَّرُوا فَأَبَى أَكْثَرُ النَّاسِ إِلَّا كُفُورًا ﴿٥٠﴾

51 If We willed, We could raise up a warner in every village.

وَلَوْ شِئْنَا لَبَعَثْنَا فِي كُلِّ قَرْيَةٍ نَذِيرًا ﴿٥١﴾

52 So obey not the disbelievers, but strive against them herewith with a great endeavour.

فَلَا تُطِعِ الْكَافِرِينَ وَجَاهِدْهُمْ بِهِ جِهَادًا كَبِيرًا ﴿٥٢﴾

53 And He it is Who hath given independence to the two seas[3] (though they meet); one palatable, sweet, and the other saltish, bitter; and hath set a bar and a forbidding ban between them.

۞ وَهُوَ الَّذِى مَرَجَ الْبَحْرَيْنِ هَذَا عَذْبٌ فُرَاتٌ وَهَذَا مِلْحٌ أُجَاجٌ وَجَعَلَ بَيْنَهُمَا بَرْزَخًا وَحِجْرًا مَّحْجُورًا ﴿٥٣﴾

54 And He it is Who hath created man from water, and hath appointed for him kindred by blood and kindred by marriage; for thy Lord is ever Powerful.

وَهُوَ الَّذِى خَلَقَ مِنَ الْمَاءِ بَشَرًا فَجَعَلَهُ نَسَبًا وَصِهْرًا وَكَانَ رَبُّكَ قَدِيرًا ﴿٥٤﴾

55 Yet they worship instead of Allah that which can neither benefit them nor hurt them. The disbeliever was ever a partisan against his Lord.

وَيَعْبُدُونَ مِن دُونِ اللَّهِ مَا لَا يَنفَعُهُمْ وَلَا يَضُرُّهُمْ وَكَانَ الْكَافِرُ عَلَى رَبِّهِ ظَهِيرًا ﴿٥٥﴾

56 And We have sent thee (O Muhammad) only as a bearer of good tidings and a warner.

وَمَا أَرْسَلْنَاكَ إِلَّا مُبَشِّرًا وَنَذِيرًا ﴿٥٦﴾

57 Say: I ask of you no reward for this, save that whoso will may choose a way unto his Lord.

قُلْ مَا أَسْأَلُكُمْ عَلَيْهِ مِنْ أَجْرٍ إِلَّا مَن شَاءَ أَن يَتَّخِذَ إِلَى رَبِّهِ سَبِيلًا ﴿٥٧﴾

58 And trust thou in the Living One Who dieth not, and hymn His praise. He sufficeth as the Knower of His bondmen's sins;

وَتَوَكَّلْ عَلَى الْحَىِّ الَّذِى لَا يَمُوتُ وَسَبِّحْ بِحَمْدِهِ وَكَفَى بِهِ بِذُنُوبِ عِبَادِهِ خَبِيرًا ﴿٥٨﴾

59 Who created the heavens and the earth and all that is between them in six Days,[4] then He mounted the Throne. The Beneficent! Ask anyone informed concerning Him!

الَّذِى خَلَقَ السَّمَوَاتِ وَالْأَرْضَ وَمَا بَيْنَهُمَا فِى سِتَّةِ أَيَّامٍ ثُمَّ اسْتَوَى عَلَى الْعَرْشِ الرَّحْمَنُ فَاسْأَلْ بِهِ خَبِيرًا ﴿٥٩﴾

---

3. i.e. the two kinds of water in the earth.

4. See (22: 47), (32: 5), and (70: 4).

60 And when it is said unto them: Adore the Beneficent! they say: And what is the Beneficent? Are we to adore whatever thou (Muḥammad) biddest us? And it increaseth aversion in them.

وَإِذَا قِيلَ لَهُمُ اسْجُدُوا لِلرَّحْمَٰنِ قَالُوا وَمَا الرَّحْمَٰنُ أَنَسْجُدُ لِمَا تَأْمُرُنَا وَزَادَهُمْ نُفُورًا ۩ ۝

61 Blessed be He Who hath placed in the heaven mansions of the stars, and hath placed therein a great lamp and a moon giving light!

تَبَارَكَ الَّذِي جَعَلَ فِي السَّمَاءِ بُرُوجًا وَجَعَلَ فِيهَا سِرَاجًا وَقَمَرًا مُّنِيرًا ۝

62 And He it is Who hath appointed night and day in succession, for him who desireth to remember, or desireth thankfulness.

وَهُوَ الَّذِي جَعَلَ اللَّيْلَ وَالنَّهَارَ خِلْفَةً لِّمَنْ أَرَادَ أَن يَذَّكَّرَ أَوْ أَرَادَ شُكُورًا ۝

63 The (faithful) slaves of the Beneficent are they who walk upon the earth modestly, and when the foolish ones address them answer: Peace;

وَعِبَادُ الرَّحْمَٰنِ الَّذِينَ يَمْشُونَ عَلَى الْأَرْضِ هَوْنًا وَإِذَا خَاطَبَهُمُ الْجَاهِلُونَ قَالُوا سَلَامًا ۝

64 And who spend the night before their Lord, prostrate and standing;

وَالَّذِينَ يَبِيتُونَ لِرَبِّهِمْ سُجَّدًا وَقِيَامًا ۝

65 And who say: Our Lord! Avert from us the doom of hell; lo! the doom thereof is anguish;

وَالَّذِينَ يَقُولُونَ رَبَّنَا اصْرِفْ عَنَّا عَذَابَ جَهَنَّمَ إِنَّ عَذَابَهَا كَانَ غَرَامًا ۝

66 Lo! it is wretched as abode and station;

إِنَّهَا سَاءَتْ مُسْتَقَرًّا وَمُقَامًا ۝

67 And those who, when they spend, are neither prodigal nor grudging; and there is ever a firm station between the two;

وَالَّذِينَ إِذَا أَنفَقُوا لَمْ يُسْرِفُوا وَلَمْ يَقْتُرُوا وَكَانَ بَيْنَ ذَٰلِكَ قَوَامًا ۝

68 And those who cry not unto any other god along with Allah, nor take the life which Allah hath forbidden save in (course of) justice, nor commit adultery—and whoso doeth this shall pay the penalty;

وَالَّذِينَ لَا يَدْعُونَ مَعَ اللَّهِ إِلَٰهًا آخَرَ وَلَا يَقْتُلُونَ النَّفْسَ الَّتِي حَرَّمَ اللَّهُ إِلَّا بِالْحَقِّ وَلَا يَزْنُونَ وَمَن يَفْعَلْ ذَٰلِكَ يَلْقَ أَثَامًا ۝

69 The doom will be doubled for him on the Day of Resurrection, and he will abide therein disdained forever;

يُضَاعَفْ لَهُ الْعَذَابُ يَوْمَ الْقِيَٰمَةِ وَيَخْلُدْ فِيهِۦ مُهَانًا ۝

70 Save him who repenteth and believeth and doth righteous work; as for such, Allah will change their evil deeds to good deeds. Allah is ever Forgiving, Merciful.

إِلَّا مَن تَابَ وَءَامَنَ وَعَمِلَ عَمَلًا صَٰلِحًا فَأُوْلَٰٓئِكَ يُبَدِّلُ اللَّهُ سَيِّـَٔاتِهِمْ حَسَنَٰتٍ وَكَانَ اللَّهُ غَفُورًا رَّحِيمًا ۝

71 And whosoever repenteth and doeth good, he verily repenteth toward Allah with true repentance.

وَمَن تَابَ وَعَمِلَ صَٰلِحًا فَإِنَّهُۥ يَتُوبُ إِلَى اللَّهِ مَتَابًا ۝

72 And those who will not witness vanity, but when they pass near senseless play, pass by with dignity.

وَالَّذِينَ لَا يَشْهَدُونَ الزُّورَ وَإِذَا مَرُّوا بِاللَّغْوِ مَرُّوا كِرَامًا ۝

73 And those who, when they are reminded of the revelations of their Lord, fall not deaf and blind thereat.

وَالَّذِينَ إِذَا ذُكِّرُوا بِـَٔايَٰتِ رَبِّهِمْ لَمْ يَخِرُّوا عَلَيْهَا صُمًّا وَعُمْيَانًا ۝

74 And who say: Our Lord! Vouchsafe us comfort of our wives and of our offspring, and make us patterns for (all) those who ward off (evil).

وَالَّذِينَ يَقُولُونَ رَبَّنَا هَبْ لَنَا مِنْ أَزْوَٰجِنَا وَذُرِّيَّٰتِنَا قُرَّةَ أَعْيُنٍ وَاجْعَلْنَا لِلْمُتَّقِينَ إِمَامًا ۝

75 They will be awarded the high place forasmuch as they were steadfast, and they will be met therein with welcome and the word of peace;

أُوْلَٰٓئِكَ يُجْزَوْنَ الْغُرْفَةَ بِمَا صَبَرُوا وَيُلَقَّوْنَ فِيهَا تَحِيَّةً وَسَلَٰمًا ۝

76 Abiding there forever. Happy is it as abode and station!

خَٰلِدِينَ فِيهَا حَسُنَتْ مُسْتَقَرًّا وَمُقَامًا ۝

77 Say (O Muhammad, unto the disbelievers): My Lord would not concern himself with you but for your prayer. But now ye have denied (the Truth), therefore there will be judgment.

قُلْ مَا يَعْبَؤُا بِكُمْ رَبِّي لَوْلَا دُعَآؤُكُمْ فَقَدْ كَذَّبْتُمْ فَسَوْفَ يَكُونُ لِزَامًا ۝

Ash Shu'arā'
(The Poets)

Ash Shu'arā', "The Poets," takes its title from v. 224 ff., where the difference between poets and a Prophet is tersely pointed out; poets being those who say what they do not mean, while a Prophet always practises what he preaches. The pagan Arabs and their poets believed the poetic inspiration to be the work of Jinn.

The story of a number of former Prophets is here given to console the believers at a time of persecution, with the assurance that it is no new thing for a messenger of God to be persecuted, but that the persecutors always suffer in the end. It shows also that all the messengers of God came with the same message.

It belongs to the middle group of Makkan sūrahs, with the exception of vv. 224-227, which were revealed at Al-Madīnah.

In the name of Allah, the Beneficent, the Merciful.

1 Tā. Sīn. Mīm.[1]

2 These are revelations of the Scripture that maketh plain.

3 It may be that thou tormentest thyself (O Muḥammad) because they believe not.

---

1. See Sūrah 2, v. 1, footnote.

4 If We will, We can send down on them from the sky a portent so that their necks would remain bowed before it.

إِن نَّشَأْ نُنَزِّلْ عَلَيْهِم مِّنَ السَّمَاءِ ءَايَةً فَظَلَّتْ أَعْنَٰقُهُمْ لَهَا خَٰضِعِينَ ﴿٤﴾

5 Never cometh there unto them a fresh reminder from the Beneficent One, but they turn away from it.

وَمَا يَأْتِيهِم مِّن ذِكْرٍ مِّنَ الرَّحْمَٰنِ مُحْدَثٍ إِلَّا كَانُوا عَنْهُ مُعْرِضِينَ ﴿٥﴾

6 Now they have denied (the Truth); but there will come unto them tidings of that whereat they used to scoff.

فَقَدْ كَذَّبُوا فَسَيَأْتِيهِمْ أَنۢبَٰٓؤُا۟ مَا كَانُوا بِهِۦ يَسْتَهْزِءُونَ ﴿٦﴾

7 Have they not seen the earth, how much of every fruitful kind We make to grow therein?

أَوَلَمْ يَرَوْا إِلَى الْأَرْضِ كَمْ أَنۢبَتْنَا فِيهَا مِن كُلِّ زَوْجٍ كَرِيمٍ ﴿٧﴾

8 Lo! herein is indeed a portent; yet most of them are not believers.

إِنَّ فِى ذَٰلِكَ لَءَايَةً وَمَا كَانَ أَكْثَرُهُم مُّؤْمِنِينَ ﴿٨﴾

9 And lo! thy Lord! He is indeed the Mighty, the Merciful.

وَإِنَّ رَبَّكَ لَهُوَ الْعَزِيزُ الرَّحِيمُ ﴿٩﴾

10 And when thy Lord called Moses, saying: Go unto the wrong-doing folk;

وَإِذْ نَادَىٰ رَبُّكَ مُوسَىٰٓ أَنِ ائْتِ الْقَوْمَ الظَّٰلِمِينَ ﴿١٠﴾

11 The folk of Pharaoh. Will they not ward off (evil)?

قَوْمَ فِرْعَوْنَ أَلَا يَتَّقُونَ ﴿١١﴾

12 He said: My Lord! Lo! I fear that they will deny me;

قَالَ رَبِّ إِنِّىٓ أَخَافُ أَن يُكَذِّبُونِ ﴿١٢﴾

13 And I shall be embarrassed, and my tongue will not speak plainly, therefore send for Aaron (to help me).

وَيَضِيقُ صَدْرِى وَلَا يَنطَلِقُ لِسَانِى فَأَرْسِلْ إِلَىٰ هَٰرُونَ ﴿١٣﴾

14 And they have a crime against me, so I fear that they will kill me.

وَلَهُمْ عَلَىَّ ذَنۢبٌ فَأَخَافُ أَن يَقْتُلُونِ ﴿١٤﴾

15 He said: Nay, verily. So go ye twain with Our tokens. Lo! We shall be with you, Hearing.

قَالَ كَلَّا فَاذْهَبَا بِـَٔايَٰتِنَا إِنَّا مَعَكُم مُّسْتَمِعُونَ ﴿١٥﴾

16 And come together unto Pharaoh and say: Lo! we bear a message of the Lord of the Worlds;

فَأْتِيَا فِرْعَوْنَ فَقُولَا إِنَّا رَسُولُ رَبِّ الْعَالَمِينَ ﴿١٦﴾

17 (Saying): Let the Children of
Israel go with Us.

أَنْ أَرْسِلْ مَعَنَا بَنِي إِسْرَائِيلَ ﴿١٧﴾

18 (Pharaoh) said (unto Moses):
Did we not rear thee among us as a
child? And thou didst dwell many
years of thy life among us;

قَالَ أَلَمْ نُرَبِّكَ فِينَا وَلِيدًا وَلَبِثْتَ فِينَا
مِنْ عُمُرِكَ سِنِينَ ﴿١٨﴾

19 And thou didst that thy deed
which thou didst, and thou wast one
of the ingrates;

وَفَعَلْتَ فَعْلَتَكَ الَّتِي فَعَلْتَ
وَأَنْتَ مِنَ الْكَافِرِينَ ﴿١٩﴾

20 He said: I did it then, when I
was of those who are astray.

قَالَ فَعَلْتُهَا إِذًا وَأَنَا مِنَ الضَّالِّينَ ﴿٢٠﴾

21 Then I fled from you when I
feared you, and my Lord vouchsafed me a command and appointed
me (of the number) of those sent
(by Him).

فَفَرَرْتُ مِنكُمْ لَمَّا خِفْتُكُمْ فَوَهَبَ لِي رَبِّي حُكْمًا
وَجَعَلَنِي مِنَ الْمُرْسَلِينَ ﴿٢١﴾

22 And this is the past favour
wherewith thou reproachest me: that
thou hast enslaved the Children of
Israel.

وَتِلْكَ نِعْمَةٌ تَمُنُّهَا عَلَيَّ أَنْ عَبَّدتَّ بَنِي إِسْرَائِيلَ ﴿٢٢﴾

23 Pharaoh said: And what is the
Lord of the Worlds?

قَالَ فِرْعَوْنُ وَمَا رَبُّ الْعَالَمِينَ ﴿٢٣﴾

24 (Moses) said: Lord of the heavens and the earth and all that is
between them, if ye had but sure
belief.

قَالَ رَبُّ السَّمَاوَاتِ وَالْأَرْضِ وَمَا بَيْنَهُمَا
إِن كُنتُم مُّوقِنِينَ ﴿٢٤﴾

25 (Pharaoh) said unto those around
him: Hear ye not?

قَالَ لِمَنْ حَوْلَهُ أَلَا تَسْتَمِعُونَ ﴿٢٥﴾

26 He said: Your Lord and the Lord
of your fathers.

قَالَ رَبُّكُمْ وَرَبُّ آبَائِكُمُ الْأَوَّلِينَ ﴿٢٦﴾

27 (Pharaoh) said: Lo! your messenger who hath been sent unto you is indeed a madman!

قَالَ إِنَّ رَسُولَكُمُ الَّذِىٓ أُرْسِلَ إِلَيْكُمْ لَمَجْنُونٌ ۝

28 He said: Lord of the East and the West and all that is between them, if ye did but understand.

قَالَ رَبُّ الْمَشْرِقِ وَالْمَغْرِبِ وَمَا بَيْنَهُمَآ إِن كُنتُمْ تَعْقِلُونَ ۝

29 (Pharaoh) said: If thou choosest a god other than me, I assuredly shall place thee among the prisoners.

قَالَ لَئِنِ اتَّخَذْتَ إِلَٰهًا غَيْرِى لَأَجْعَلَنَّكَ مِنَ الْمَسْجُونِينَ ۝

30 He said: Even though I show thee something plain?

قَالَ أَوَلَوْ جِئْتُكَ بِشَىْءٍ مُّبِينٍ ۝

31 (Pharaoh) said: Produce it then, if thou art of the truthful!

قَالَ فَأْتِ بِهِۦٓ إِن كُنتَ مِنَ الصَّٰدِقِينَ ۝

32 Then he flung down his staff and it became a serpent manifest;

فَأَلْقَىٰ عَصَاهُ فَإِذَا هِىَ ثُعْبَانٌ مُّبِينٌ ۝

33 And he drew forth his hand and lo! it was white to the beholders.

وَنَزَعَ يَدَهُ فَإِذَا هِىَ بَيْضَآءُ لِلنَّٰظِرِينَ ۝

34 (Pharaoh) said unto the chiefs about him: Lo, this is verily a knowing wizard;

قَالَ لِلْمَلَإِ حَوْلَهُۥٓ إِنَّ هَٰذَا لَسَٰحِرٌ عَلِيمٌ ۝

35 Who would drive you out of your land by his magic. Now what counsel ye?

يُرِيدُ أَن يُخْرِجَكُم مِّنْ أَرْضِكُم بِسِحْرِهِۦ فَمَاذَا تَأْمُرُونَ ۝

36 They said: Put him off, (him) and his brother, and send them into the cities summoners;

قَالُوٓاْ أَرْجِهْ وَأَخَاهُ وَابْعَثْ فِى الْمَدَآئِنِ حَٰشِرِينَ ۝

37 Who shall bring unto thee every knowing wizard.

يَأْتُوكَ بِكُلِّ سَحَّارٍ عَلِيمٍ ۝

38 So the wizards were gathered together at a set time on a day appointed.

فَجُمِعَ السَّحَرَةُ لِمِيقَٰتِ يَوْمٍ مَّعْلُومٍ ۝

39 And it was said unto the people: Are ye (also) gathering?

وَقِيلَ لِلنَّاسِ هَلْ أَنتُم مُّجْتَمِعُونَ ۝

40 (They said): Aye, so that we
may follow the wizards if they are
the winners.

لَعَلَّنَا نَتَّبِعُ السَّحَرَةَ إِن كَانُوا هُمُ الْغَلِبِينَ ﴿٤٠﴾

41 And when the wizards came
they said unto Pharaoh: Will there
surely be a reward for us if we are
the winners?

فَلَمَّا جَآءَ السَّحَرَةُ قَالُوا لِفِرْعَوْنَ أَئِنَّ لَنَا لَأَجْرًا إِن كُنَّا نَحْنُ الْغَلِبِينَ ﴿٤١﴾

42 He said: Aye, and ye will then
surely be of those brought near (to
me).

قَالَ نَعَمْ وَإِنَّكُمْ إِذًا لَّمِنَ الْمُقَرَّبِينَ ﴿٤٢﴾

43 Moses said unto them: Throw
what ye are going to throw!

قَالَ لَهُم مُّوسَىٰٓ أَلْقُوا مَآ أَنتُم مُّلْقُونَ ﴿٤٣﴾

44 Then they threw down their
cords and their staves and said: By
Pharaoh's might, lo! we verily are
the winners.

فَأَلْقَوْا حِبَالَهُمْ وَعِصِيَّهُمْ وَقَالُوا بِعِزَّةِ فِرْعَوْنَ إِنَّا لَنَحْنُ الْغَلِبُونَ ﴿٤٤﴾

45 Then Moses threw his staff and
lo! it swallowed that which they did
falsely show.

فَأَلْقَىٰ مُوسَىٰ عَصَاهُ فَإِذَا هِيَ تَلْقَفُ مَا يَأْفِكُونَ ﴿٤٥﴾

46 And the wizards were flung
prostrate;

فَأُلْقِيَ السَّحَرَةُ سَاجِدِينَ ﴿٤٦﴾

47 Crying: We believe in the Lord
of the Worlds;

قَالُوٓا ءَامَنَّا بِرَبِّ الْعَالَمِينَ ﴿٤٧﴾

48 The Lord of Moses and Aaron.

رَبِّ مُوسَىٰ وَهَارُونَ ﴿٤٨﴾

49 (Pharaoh) said: Ye put your
faith in him before I give you leave.
Lo! he doubtless is your chief who
taught you magic! But verily ye
shall come to know. Verily I will
cut off your hands and your feet
alternately, and verily I will crucify
you every one.

قَالَ ءَامَنتُمْ لَهُ قَبْلَ أَنْ ءَاذَنَ لَكُمْ إِنَّهُ لَكَبِيرُكُمُ الَّذِي عَلَّمَكُمُ السِّحْرَ فَلَسَوْفَ تَعْلَمُونَ لَأُقَطِّعَنَّ أَيْدِيَكُمْ وَأَرْجُلَكُم مِّنْ خِلَافٍ وَلَأُصَلِّبَنَّكُمْ أَجْمَعِينَ ﴿٤٩﴾

50 They said: It is no hurt, for lo!
unto our Lord we shall return.

قَالُوا لَا ضَيْرَ إِنَّا إِلَىٰ رَبِّنَا مُنقَلِبُونَ ﴿٥٠﴾

51 Lo! we ardently hope that our Lord will forgive us our sins because we are the first of the believers.

إِنَّا نَطْمَعُ أَن يَغْفِرَ لَنَا رَبُّنَا خَطَايَانَا أَن كُنَّا أَوَّلَ ٱلْمُؤْمِنِينَ ﴿٥١﴾

52 And We inspired Moses, saying: Take away My slaves by night, for ye will be pursued.

۞ وَأَوْحَيْنَا إِلَىٰ مُوسَىٰٓ أَنْ أَسْرِ بِعِبَادِيٓ إِنَّكُم مُّتَّبَعُونَ ﴿٥٢﴾

53 Then Pharaoh sent into the cities summoners;

فَأَرْسَلَ فِرْعَوْنُ فِي ٱلْمَدَآئِنِ حَٰشِرِينَ ﴿٥٣﴾

54 (Who said): Lo! these indeed are but a little troop;

إِنَّ هَٰٓؤُلَآءِ لَشِرْذِمَةٌ قَلِيلُونَ ﴿٥٤﴾

55 And lo! they are offenders against us.

وَإِنَّهُمْ لَنَا لَغَآئِظُونَ ﴿٥٥﴾

56 And lo! we are a ready host.

وَإِنَّا لَجَمِيعٌ حَٰذِرُونَ ﴿٥٦﴾

57 Thus did We take them away from gardens and water springs;

فَأَخْرَجْنَٰهُم مِّن جَنَّٰتٍ وَعُيُونٍ ﴿٥٧﴾

58 And treasures and a fair estate.

وَكُنُوزٍ وَمَقَامٍ كَرِيمٍ ﴿٥٨﴾

59 Thus (were those things taken from them) and We caused the Children of Israel to inherit them.

كَذَٰلِكَ وَأَوْرَثْنَٰهَا بَنِىٓ إِسْرَٰٓءِيلَ ﴿٥٩﴾

60 And they overtook them at sunrise.

فَأَتْبَعُوهُم مُّشْرِقِينَ ﴿٦٠﴾

61 And when the two hosts saw each other, those with Moses said: Lo! we are indeed caught.

فَلَمَّا تَرَٰٓءَا ٱلْجَمْعَانِ قَالَ أَصْحَٰبُ مُوسَىٰٓ إِنَّا لَمُدْرَكُونَ ﴿٦١﴾

62 He said: Nay, verily! for lo! my Lord is with me. He will guide me.

قَالَ كَلَّآ إِنَّ مَعِىَ رَبِّى سَيَهْدِينِ ﴿٦٢﴾

63 Then We inspired Moses, saying: Smite the sea with thy staff. And it parted, and each part was as a mountain vast.

فَأَوْحَيْنَآ إِلَىٰ مُوسَىٰٓ أَنِ ٱضْرِب بِّعَصَاكَ ٱلْبَحْرَ فَٱنفَلَقَ فَكَانَ كُلُّ فِرْقٍ كَٱلطَّوْدِ ٱلْعَظِيمِ ﴿٦٣﴾

64 Then brought We near the others to that place.

وَأَزْلَفْنَا ثَمَّ ٱلْءَاخَرِينَ ﴿٦٤﴾

65 And We saved Moses and those with him, every one;

وَأَنجَيْنَا مُوسَىٰ وَمَن مَّعَهُۥٓ أَجْمَعِينَ ﴿٦٥﴾

66 We drowned the others.

ثُمَّ أَغْرَقْنَا ٱلْآخَرِينَ ﴿٦٦﴾

67 Lo! herein is indeed a portent, yet most of them are not believers.

إِنَّ فِى ذَٰلِكَ لَآيَةً وَمَا كَانَ أَكْثَرُهُم مُّؤْمِنِينَ ﴿٦٧﴾

68 And lo, thy Lord! He is indeed the Mighty, the Merciful.

وَإِنَّ رَبَّكَ لَهُوَ ٱلْعَزِيزُ ٱلرَّحِيمُ ﴿٦٨﴾

69 Recite unto them the story of Abraham:

وَٱتْلُ عَلَيْهِمْ نَبَأَ إِبْرَٰهِيمَ ﴿٦٩﴾

70 When he said unto his father and his folk: What worship ye?

إِذْ قَالَ لِأَبِيهِ وَقَوْمِهِۦ مَا تَعْبُدُونَ ﴿٧٠﴾

71 They said: We worship idols, and are ever devoted unto them.

قَالُوا۟ نَعْبُدُ أَصْنَامًا فَنَظَلُّ لَهَا عَٰكِفِينَ ﴿٧١﴾

72 He said: Do they hear you when ye cry?

قَالَ هَلْ يَسْمَعُونَكُمْ إِذْ تَدْعُونَ ﴿٧٢﴾

73 Or do they benefit or harm you?

أَوْ يَنفَعُونَكُمْ أَوْ يَضُرُّونَ ﴿٧٣﴾

74 They said: Nay, but we found our fathers acting on this wise.

قَالُوا۟ بَلْ وَجَدْنَآ ءَابَآءَنَا كَذَٰلِكَ يَفْعَلُونَ ﴿٧٤﴾

75 He said: See now that which ye worship;

قَالَ أَفَرَءَيْتُم مَّا كُنتُمْ تَعْبُدُونَ ﴿٧٥﴾

76 Ye and your forefathers!

أَنتُمْ وَءَابَآؤُكُمُ ٱلْأَقْدَمُونَ ﴿٧٦﴾

77 Lo! they are (all) an enemy unto me, save the Lord of the Worlds.

فَإِنَّهُمْ عَدُوٌّ لِّىٓ إِلَّا رَبَّ ٱلْعَٰلَمِينَ ﴿٧٧﴾

78 Who created me, and He doth guide me;

ٱلَّذِى خَلَقَنِى فَهُوَ يَهْدِينِ ﴿٧٨﴾

79 And Who feedeth me and watereth me.

وَٱلَّذِى هُوَ يُطْعِمُنِى وَيَسْقِينِ ﴿٧٩﴾

80 And when I sicken, then He healeth me,

وَإِذَا مَرِضْتُ فَهُوَ يَشْفِينِ ﴿٨٠﴾

81 And Who causeth me to die, then giveth me life (again);

وَٱلَّذِى يُمِيتُنِى ثُمَّ يُحْيِينِ ﴿٨١﴾

82 And Who, I ardently hope, will forgive me my sin on the Day of Judgement.

وَٱلَّذِىٓ أَطْمَعُ أَن يَغْفِرَ لِى خَطِيٓـَٔتِى يَوْمَ ٱلدِّينِ ﴿٨٢﴾

83 My Lord! Vouchsafe me wisdom and unite me to the righteous.

رَبِّ هَبْ لِي حُكْمًا وَأَلْحِقْنِي بِالصَّالِحِينَ ۝

84 And give unto me a good report in later generations.

وَاجْعَل لِّي لِسَانَ صِدْقٍ فِي الْآخِرِينَ ۝

85 And place me among the inheritors of the Garden of Delight;

وَاجْعَلْنِي مِن وَرَثَةِ جَنَّةِ النَّعِيمِ ۝

86 And forgive my father. Lo! he is of those who err.

وَاغْفِرْ لِأَبِي إِنَّهُ كَانَ مِنَ الضَّالِّينَ ۝

87 And abase me not on the day when they are raised;

وَلَا تُخْزِنِي يَوْمَ يُبْعَثُونَ ۝

88 The day when wealth and sons avail not (any man);

يَوْمَ لَا يَنفَعُ مَالٌ وَلَا بَنُونَ ۝

89 Save him who bringeth unto Allah a whole heart.

إِلَّا مَنْ أَتَى اللَّهَ بِقَلْبٍ سَلِيمٍ ۝

90 And the Garden will be brought nigh for those who ward off (evil).

وَأُزْلِفَتِ الْجَنَّةُ لِلْمُتَّقِينَ ۝

91 And hell will appear plainly to the erring.

وَبُرِّزَتِ الْجَحِيمُ لِلْغَاوِينَ ۝

92 And it will be said unto them: Where is (all) that ye used to worship;

وَقِيلَ لَهُمْ أَيْنَ مَا كُنتُمْ تَعْبُدُونَ ۝

93 Instead of Allah? Can they help you or help themselves?

مِن دُونِ اللَّهِ هَلْ يَنصُرُونَكُمْ أَوْ يَنتَصِرُونَ ۝

94 Then they will be hurled therein, they and the seducers,

فَكُبْكِبُوا فِيهَا هُمْ وَالْغَاوُونَ ۝

95 And the hosts of Iblīs, together.

وَجُنُودُ إِبْلِيسَ أَجْمَعُونَ ۝

96 And they will say, when they are quarrelling therein:

قَالُوا وَهُمْ فِيهَا يَخْتَصِمُونَ ۝

97 By Allah, of a truth we were in error manifest,

تَاللَّهِ إِن كُنَّا لَفِي ضَلَالٍ مُّبِينٍ ۝

98 When we made you equal with the Lord of the Worlds.

إِذْ نُسَوِّيكُم بِرَبِّ الْعَالَمِينَ ۝

99 It was but the guilty who misled us.

وَمَا أَضَلَّنَا إِلَّا الْمُجْرِمُونَ ۝

100 Now we have no inter-
cessors;

فَمَا لَنَا مِن شَٰفِعِينَ ۝

101 Nor any loving friend.

وَلَا صَدِيقٍ حَمِيمٍ ۝

102 Oh, that we had another turn
(on earth), that we might be of the
believers!

فَلَوْ أَنَّ لَنَا كَرَّةً فَنَكُونَ مِنَ ٱلْمُؤْمِنِينَ ۝

103 Lo! herein is indeed a portent, yet most of them are not
believers!

إِنَّ فِى ذَٰلِكَ لَءَايَةً وَمَا كَانَ أَكْثَرُهُم مُّؤْمِنِينَ ۝

104 And lo, thy Lord! He is
indeed the Mighty, the Merciful.

وَإِنَّ رَبَّكَ لَهُوَ ٱلْعَزِيزُ ٱلرَّحِيمُ ۝

105 Noah's folk denied the messengers (of Allah);

كَذَّبَتْ قَوْمُ نُوحٍ ٱلْمُرْسَلِينَ ۝

106 When their brother Noah said
unto them: Will ye not ward off
(evil)?

إِذْ قَالَ لَهُمْ أَخُوهُمْ نُوحٌ أَلَا تَتَّقُونَ ۝

107 Lo! I am a faithful messenger unto you;

إِنِّى لَكُمْ رَسُولٌ أَمِينٌ ۝

108 So keep your duty to Allah,
and obey me.

فَٱتَّقُوا ٱللَّهَ وَأَطِيعُونِ ۝

109 And I ask of you no wage
therefore; my wage is the concern
only of the Lord of the Worlds.

وَمَا أَسْـَٔلُكُمْ عَلَيْهِ مِنْ أَجْرٍ إِنْ أَجْرِىَ إِلَّا عَلَىٰ رَبِّ ٱلْعَٰلَمِينَ ۝

110 So keep your duty to Allah,
and obey me.

فَٱتَّقُوا ٱللَّهَ وَأَطِيعُونِ ۝

111 They said: Shall we put faith
in thee, when the lowest (of the
people) follow thee?

۞ قَالُوٓا أَنُؤْمِنُ لَكَ وَٱتَّبَعَكَ ٱلْأَرْذَلُونَ ۝

112 He said: And what knowledge have I of what they may have
been doing (in the past)?

قَالَ وَمَا عِلْمِى بِمَا كَانُوا۟ يَعْمَلُونَ ۝

113 Lo! their reckoning is my
Lord's concern, if ye but knew;

إِنْ حِسَابُهُمْ إِلَّا عَلَىٰ رَبِّى لَوْ تَشْعُرُونَ ۝

114 And I am not (here) to repulse believers.

وَمَآ أَنَا بِطَارِدِ الْمُؤْمِنِينَ ۝

115 I am only a plain warner.

إِنْ أَنَا إِلَّا نَذِيرٌ مُّبِينٌ ۝

116 They said: If thou cease not, O Noah, thou wilt surely be among those stoned (to death).

قَالُوا لَئِن لَّمْ تَنتَهِ يَنُوحُ لَتَكُونَنَّ مِنَ الْمَرْجُومِينَ ۝

117 He said: My Lord! Lo! my own folk deny me.

قَالَ رَبِّ إِنَّ قَوْمِي كَذَّبُونِ ۝

118 Therefore judge Thou between us, a (conclusive) judgement, and save me and those believers who are with me.

فَافْتَحْ بَيْنِي وَبَيْنَهُمْ فَتْحًا وَنَجِّنِي وَمَن مَّعِيَ مِنَ الْمُؤْمِنِينَ ۝

119 And We saved him and those with him in the laden ship.

فَأَنجَيْنَاهُ وَمَن مَّعَهُ فِي الْفُلْكِ الْمَشْحُونِ ۝

120 Then afterward We drowned the others.

ثُمَّ أَغْرَقْنَا بَعْدُ الْبَاقِينَ ۝

121 Lo! herein is indeed a portent, yet most of them are not believers.

إِنَّ فِي ذَٰلِكَ لَآيَةً وَمَا كَانَ أَكْثَرُهُم مُّؤْمِنِينَ ۝

122 And lo, thy Lord, He is indeed the Mighty, the Merciful.

وَإِنَّ رَبَّكَ لَهُوَ الْعَزِيزُ الرَّحِيمُ ۝

123 (The tribe of) 'Ād denied the messengers (of Allah);

كَذَّبَتْ عَادٌ الْمُرْسَلِينَ ۝

124 When their brother Hūd said unto them: Will ye not ward off (evil)?

إِذْ قَالَ لَهُمْ أَخُوهُمْ هُودٌ أَلَا تَتَّقُونَ ۝

125 Lo! I am a faithful messenger unto you;

إِنِّي لَكُمْ رَسُولٌ أَمِينٌ ۝

126 So keep your duty to Allah and obey me.

فَاتَّقُوا اللَّهَ وَأَطِيعُونِ ۝

127 And I ask of you no wage therefore; my wage is the concern only of the Lord of the Worlds.

وَمَا أَسْأَلُكُمْ عَلَيْهِ مِنْ أَجْرٍ إِنْ أَجْرِيَ إِلَّا عَلَىٰ رَبِّ الْعَالَمِينَ ۝

128   Build ye on every high place a monument for vain delight?

أَتَبْنُونَ بِكُلِّ رِيعٍ ءَايَةً تَعْبَثُونَ ۝

129   And seek ye out strongholds, that haply ye may last forever?

وَتَتَّخِذُونَ مَصَانِعَ لَعَلَّكُمْ تَخْلُدُونَ ۝

130   And if ye seize by force, seize ye as tyrants?

وَإِذَا بَطَشْتُم بَطَشْتُمْ جَبَّارِينَ ۝

131   Rather keep your duty to Allah, and obey me.

فَاتَّقُوا اللَّهَ وَأَطِيعُونِ ۝

132   Keep your duty toward Him who hath aided you with (the good things) that ye know;

وَاتَّقُوا الَّذِىٓ أَمَدَّكُم بِمَا تَعْلَمُونَ ۝

133   Hath aided you with cattle and sons.

أَمَدَّكُم بِأَنْعَٰمٍ وَبَنِينَ ۝

134   And gardens and water-springs.

وَجَنَّٰتٍ وَعُيُونٍ ۝

135   Lo! I fear for you the retribution of an awful day.

إِنِّىٓ أَخَافُ عَلَيْكُمْ عَذَابَ يَوْمٍ عَظِيمٍ ۝

136   They said: It is all one to us whether thou preachest or art not of those who preach;

قَالُوا سَوَآءٌ عَلَيْنَآ أَوَعَظْتَ أَمْ لَمْ تَكُن مِّنَ الْوَٰعِظِينَ ۝

137   This is but a fable of the men of old;

إِنْ هَٰذَآ إِلَّا خُلُقُ الْأَوَّلِينَ ۝

138   And we shall not be doomed.

وَمَا نَحْنُ بِمُعَذَّبِينَ ۝

139   And they denied him; therefore We destroyed them. Lo! herein is indeed a portent, yet most of them are not believers.

فَكَذَّبُوهُ فَأَهْلَكْنَٰهُمْ إِنَّ فِى ذَٰلِكَ لَءَايَةً وَمَا كَانَ أَكْثَرُهُم مُّؤْمِنِينَ ۝

140   And lo! thy Lord, He is indeed the Mighty, the Merciful.

وَإِنَّ رَبَّكَ لَهُوَ الْعَزِيزُ الرَّحِيمُ ۝

141   (The tribe of) Thamūd denied the messengers (of Allah);

كَذَّبَتْ ثَمُودُ الْمُرْسَلِينَ ۝

142   When their brother Ṣāliḥ said unto them: Will ye not ward off (evil)?

إِذْ قَالَ لَهُمْ أَخُوهُمْ صَٰلِحٌ أَلَا تَتَّقُونَ ۝

143 Lo! I am a faithful messenger unto you;

إِنِّي لَكُمْ رَسُولٌ أَمِينٌ ﴿١٤٣﴾

144 So keep your duty to Allah and obey me.

فَٱتَّقُوا۟ ٱللَّهَ وَأَطِيعُونِ ﴿١٤٤﴾

145 And I ask of you no wage therefore; my wage is the concern only of the Lord of the Worlds.

وَمَآ أَسْـَٔلُكُمْ عَلَيْهِ مِنْ أَجْرٍ إِنْ أَجْرِىَ إِلَّا عَلَىٰ رَبِّ ٱلْعَٰلَمِينَ ﴿١٤٥﴾

146 Will ye be left secure in that which is here before us;

أَتُتْرَكُونَ فِى مَا هَٰهُنَآ ءَامِنِينَ ﴿١٤٦﴾

147 In gardens and watersprings;

فِى جَنَّٰتٍ وَعُيُونٍ ﴿١٤٧﴾

148 And tilled fields and heavy-sheathed palm trees;

وَزُرُوعٍ وَنَخْلٍ طَلْعُهَا هَضِيمٌ ﴿١٤٨﴾

149 Though ye hew out dwellings in the mountain, being skilful?

وَتَنْحِتُونَ مِنَ ٱلْجِبَالِ بُيُوتًا فَٰرِهِينَ ﴿١٤٩﴾

150 Therefore keep your duty to Allah and obey me;

فَٱتَّقُوا۟ ٱللَّهَ وَأَطِيعُونِ ﴿١٥٠﴾

151 And obey not the command of the prodigal;

وَلَا تُطِيعُوٓا۟ أَمْرَ ٱلْمُسْرِفِينَ ﴿١٥١﴾

152 Who spread corruption in the earth, and reform not.

ٱلَّذِينَ يُفْسِدُونَ فِى ٱلْأَرْضِ وَلَا يُصْلِحُونَ ﴿١٥٢﴾

153 They said: Thou art but one of the bewitched;

قَالُوٓا۟ إِنَّمَآ أَنتَ مِنَ ٱلْمُسَحَّرِينَ ﴿١٥٣﴾

154 Thou art but a mortal like us. So bring some token if thou art of the truthful.

مَآ أَنتَ إِلَّا بَشَرٌ مِّثْلُنَا فَأْتِ بِـَٔايَةٍ إِن كُنتَ مِنَ ٱلصَّٰدِقِينَ ﴿١٥٤﴾

155 He said: (Behold) this she-camel. She hath the right to drink (at the well), and ye have the right to drink, (each) on an appointed day.

قَالَ هَٰذِهِۦ نَاقَةٌ لَّهَا شِرْبٌ وَلَكُمْ شِرْبُ يَوْمٍ مَّعْلُومٍ ﴿١٥٥﴾

156 And touch her not with ill lest there come on you the retribution of an awful day.

وَلَا تَمَسُّوهَا بِسُوٓءٍ فَيَأْخُذَكُمْ عَذَابُ يَوْمٍ عَظِيمٍ ﴿١٥٦﴾

157   But they hamstrung her, and then were penitent.

فَعَقَرُوهَا فَأَصْبَحُوا نَادِمِينَ ۝

158   So the retribution came on them. Lo! herein is indeed a portent, yet most of them are not believers.

فَأَخَذَهُمُ الْعَذَابُ إِنَّ فِي ذَٰلِكَ لَآيَةً وَمَا كَانَ أَكْثَرُهُم مُّؤْمِنِينَ ۝

159   And lo! thy Lord! He is indeed the Mighty, the Merciful.

وَإِنَّ رَبَّكَ لَهُوَ الْعَزِيزُ الرَّحِيمُ ۝

160   The folk of Lot denied the messengers (of Allah);

كَذَّبَتْ قَوْمُ لُوطٍ الْمُرْسَلِينَ ۝

161   When their brother Lot said unto them: Will ye not ward off (evil)?

إِذْ قَالَ لَهُمْ أَخُوهُمْ لُوطٌ أَلَا تَتَّقُونَ ۝

162   Lo! I am a faithful messenger unto you;

إِنِّي لَكُمْ رَسُولٌ أَمِينٌ ۝

163   So keep your duty to Allah and obey me.

فَاتَّقُوا اللَّهَ وَأَطِيعُونِ ۝

164   And I ask of you no wage therefore; my wage is the concern only of the Lord of the Worlds.

وَمَا أَسْأَلُكُمْ عَلَيْهِ مِنْ أَجْرٍ إِنْ أَجْرِيَ إِلَّا عَلَىٰ رَبِّ الْعَالَمِينَ ۝

165   What! Of all creatures do ye come unto the males;

أَتَأْتُونَ الذُّكْرَانَ مِنَ الْعَالَمِينَ ۝

166   And leave the wives your Lord created for you? Nay, but ye are froward folk.

وَتَذَرُونَ مَا خَلَقَ لَكُمْ رَبُّكُم مِّنْ أَزْوَاجِكُم بَلْ أَنتُمْ قَوْمٌ عَادُونَ ۝

167   They said: If thou cease not, O Lot, thou wilt soon be of the outcast.

قَالُوا لَئِن لَّمْ تَنتَهِ يَا لُوطُ لَتَكُونَنَّ مِنَ الْمُخْرَجِينَ ۝

168   He said: I am in truth of those who hate your conduct.

قَالَ إِنِّي لِعَمَلِكُم مِّنَ الْقَالِينَ ۝

169   My Lord! Save me and my household from what they do.

رَبِّ نَجِّنِي وَأَهْلِي مِمَّا يَعْمَلُونَ ۝

170   So We saved him and his household, every one;

فَنَجَّيْنَاهُ وَأَهْلَهُ أَجْمَعِينَ ۝

171 Save an old woman among those who stayed behind.

إِلَّا عَجُوزًا فِى ٱلْغَٰبِرِينَ ﴿١٧١﴾

172 Then afterward We destroyed the others.

ثُمَّ دَمَّرْنَا ٱلْءَاخَرِينَ ﴿١٧٢﴾

173 And We rained on them a rain. And dreadful is the rain of those who have been warned.

وَأَمْطَرْنَا عَلَيْهِم مَّطَرًا فَسَآءَ مَطَرُ ٱلْمُنذَرِينَ ﴿١٧٣﴾

174 Lo! herein is indeed a portent, yet most of them are not believers.

إِنَّ فِى ذَٰلِكَ لَءَايَةً وَمَا كَانَ أَكْثَرُهُم مُّؤْمِنِينَ ﴿١٧٤﴾

175 And lo! thy Lord, He is indeed the Mighty, the Merciful.

وَإِنَّ رَبَّكَ لَهُوَ ٱلْعَزِيزُ ٱلرَّحِيمُ ﴿١٧٥﴾

176 The dwellers in the wood (of Madyan) denied the messengers (of Allah);

كَذَّبَ أَصْحَٰبُ لْـَٔيْكَةِ ٱلْمُرْسَلِينَ ﴿١٧٦﴾

177 When Shuʻayb said unto them: Will ye not ward off (evil)?

إِذْ قَالَ لَهُمْ شُعَيْبٌ أَلَا تَتَّقُونَ ﴿١٧٧﴾

178 Lo! I am a faithful messenger unto you;

إِنِّى لَكُمْ رَسُولٌ أَمِينٌ ﴿١٧٨﴾

179 So keep your duty to Allah and obey me.

فَٱتَّقُوا۟ ٱللَّهَ وَأَطِيعُونِ ﴿١٧٩﴾

180 And I ask of you no wage for it; my wage is the concern only of the Lord of the Worlds.

وَمَآ أَسْـَٔلُكُمْ عَلَيْهِ مِنْ أَجْرٍ إِنْ أَجْرِىَ إِلَّا عَلَىٰ رَبِّ ٱلْعَٰلَمِينَ ﴿١٨٠﴾

181 Give full measure, and be not of those who give less (than the due).

۞ أَوْفُوا۟ ٱلْكَيْلَ وَلَا تَكُونُوا۟ مِنَ ٱلْمُخْسِرِينَ ﴿١٨١﴾

182 And weigh with the true balance.

وَزِنُوا۟ بِٱلْقِسْطَاسِ ٱلْمُسْتَقِيمِ ﴿١٨٢﴾

183 Wrong not mankind in their goods, and do not evil, making mischief, in the earth.

وَلَا تَبْخَسُوا۟ ٱلنَّاسَ أَشْيَآءَهُمْ وَلَا تَعْثَوْا۟ فِى ٱلْأَرْضِ مُفْسِدِينَ ﴿١٨٣﴾

184 And keep your duty unto Him Who created you and the generations of the men of old.

وَٱتَّقُوا۟ ٱلَّذِى خَلَقَكُمْ وَٱلْجِبِلَّةَ ٱلْأَوَّلِينَ ﴿١٨٤﴾

185   They said: Thou art but one of the bewitched;

قَالُوٓا إِنَّمَآ أَنتَ مِنَ ٱلْمُسَحَّرِينَ ﴿١٨٥﴾

186   Thou art but a mortal like us, and lo! we deem thee of the liars.

وَمَآ أَنتَ إِلَّا بَشَرٌ مِّثْلُنَا وَإِن نَّظُنُّكَ لَمِنَ ٱلْكَٰذِبِينَ ﴿١٨٦﴾

187   Then make fragments of the heaven fall upon us, if thou art of the truthful.

فَأَسْقِطْ عَلَيْنَا كِسَفًا مِّنَ ٱلسَّمَآءِ إِن كُنتَ مِنَ ٱلصَّٰدِقِينَ ﴿١٨٧﴾

188   He said: My Lord is best aware of what ye do.

قَالَ رَبِّيٓ أَعْلَمُ بِمَا تَعْمَلُونَ ﴿١٨٨﴾

189   But they denied him, so there came on them the retribution of the day of gloom. Lo! it was the retribution of an awful day.

فَكَذَّبُوهُ فَأَخَذَهُمْ عَذَابُ يَوْمِ ٱلظُّلَّةِ إِنَّهُۥ كَانَ عَذَابَ يَوْمٍ عَظِيمٍ ﴿١٨٩﴾

190   Lo! herein is indeed a portent; yet most of them are not believers.

إِنَّ فِى ذَٰلِكَ لَءَايَةً وَمَا كَانَ أَكْثَرُهُم مُّؤْمِنِينَ ﴿١٩٠﴾

191   And lo! thy Lord! He is indeed the Mighty, the Merciful.

وَإِنَّ رَبَّكَ لَهُوَ ٱلْعَزِيزُ ٱلرَّحِيمُ ﴿١٩١﴾

192   And lo! it is a revelation of the Lord of the Worlds;

وَإِنَّهُۥ لَتَنزِيلُ رَبِّ ٱلْعَٰلَمِينَ ﴿١٩٢﴾

193   Which the True Spirit hath brought down;

نَزَلَ بِهِ ٱلرُّوحُ ٱلْأَمِينُ ﴿١٩٣﴾

194   Upon thy heart, that thou mayest be (one) of the warners;

عَلَىٰ قَلْبِكَ لِتَكُونَ مِنَ ٱلْمُنذِرِينَ ﴿١٩٤﴾

195   In plain Arabic speech.

بِلِسَانٍ عَرَبِىٍّ مُّبِينٍ ﴿١٩٥﴾

196   And lo, it is in the Scriptures of the men of old.

وَإِنَّهُۥ لَفِى زُبُرِ ٱلْأَوَّلِينَ ﴿١٩٦﴾

197   Is it not a token for them that the doctors of the Children of Israel[2] know it?

أَوَلَمْ يَكُن لَّهُمْ ءَايَةً أَن يَعْلَمَهُۥ عُلَمَٰٓؤُا۟ بَنِىٓ إِسْرَٰٓءِيلَ ﴿١٩٧﴾

---

2. The Jews knew, from their Scripture, that a Prophet had been promised to the Arabs.

198 And if We had revealed it unto one of any other nation than the Arabs;

وَلَوْ نَزَّلْنَاهُ عَلَىٰ بَعْضِ الْأَعْجَمِينَ ﴿١٩٨﴾

199 And he had read it unto them, they would not have believed in it.

فَقَرَأَهُۥ عَلَيْهِم مَّا كَانُوا بِهِۦ مُؤْمِنِينَ ﴿١٩٩﴾

200 Thus do We make it traverse the hearts of the guilty.

كَذَٰلِكَ سَلَكْنَاهُ فِى قُلُوبِ الْمُجْرِمِينَ ﴿٢٠٠﴾

201 They will not believe in it till they behold the painful doom;

لَا يُؤْمِنُونَ بِهِۦ حَتَّىٰ يَرَوُا الْعَذَابَ الْأَلِيمَ ﴿٢٠١﴾

202 So that it will come upon them suddenly, when they perceive not.

فَيَأْتِيَهُم بَغْتَةً وَهُمْ لَا يَشْعُرُونَ ﴿٢٠٢﴾

203 Then they will say: Are we to be reprieved?

فَيَقُولُوا هَلْ نَحْنُ مُنظَرُونَ ﴿٢٠٣﴾

204 Would they (now) hasten on Our doom?

أَفَبِعَذَابِنَا يَسْتَعْجِلُونَ ﴿٢٠٤﴾

205 Hast thou then seen, if We content them for (long) years;

أَفَرَأَيْتَ إِن مَّتَّعْنَاهُمْ سِنِينَ ﴿٢٠٥﴾

206 And then cometh to them that which they were promised;

ثُمَّ جَاءَهُم مَّا كَانُوا يُوعَدُونَ ﴿٢٠٦﴾

207 (How) that wherewith they were contented naught availeth them?

مَا أَغْنَىٰ عَنْهُم مَّا كَانُوا يُمَتَّعُونَ ﴿٢٠٧﴾

208 And We destroyed no township but it had its warners;

وَمَا أَهْلَكْنَا مِن قَرْيَةٍ إِلَّا لَهَا مُنذِرُونَ ﴿٢٠٨﴾

209 For reminder, for We never were oppressors.

ذِكْرَىٰ وَمَا كُنَّا ظَالِمِينَ ﴿٢٠٩﴾

210 The devils did not bring it down.

وَمَا تَنَزَّلَتْ بِهِ الشَّيَاطِينُ ﴿٢١٠﴾

211   It is not meet for them, nor is it in their power;

وَمَا يَنۢبَغِى لَهُمْ وَمَا يَسْتَطِيعُونَ ۝

212   Lo! verily they are banished from the hearing.

إِنَّهُمْ عَنِ ٱلسَّمْعِ لَمَعْزُولُونَ ۝

213   Therefore invoke not with Allah another god, lest thou be one of the doomed.

فَلَا تَدْعُ مَعَ ٱللَّهِ إِلَٰهًا ءَاخَرَ فَتَكُونَ مِنَ ٱلْمُعَذَّبِينَ ۝

214   And warn thy tribe of near kindred;

وَأَنذِرْ عَشِيرَتَكَ ٱلْأَقْرَبِينَ ۝

215   And lower thy wing (in kindness) unto those believers who follow thee.

وَٱخْفِضْ جَنَاحَكَ لِمَنِ ٱتَّبَعَكَ مِنَ ٱلْمُؤْمِنِينَ ۝

216   And if they (thy kinsfolk) disobey thee, say: Lo! I am innocent of what they do.

فَإِنْ عَصَوْكَ فَقُلْ إِنِّى بَرِىٓءٌ مِّمَّا تَعْمَلُونَ ۝

217   And put thy trust in the Mighty, the Merciful.

وَتَوَكَّلْ عَلَى ٱلْعَزِيزِ ٱلرَّحِيمِ ۝

218   Who seeth thee when thou standest up (to pray);

ٱلَّذِى يَرَىٰكَ حِينَ تَقُومُ ۝

219   And (seeth) thine abasement among those who fall prostrate (in worship).

وَتَقَلُّبَكَ فِى ٱلسَّٰجِدِينَ ۝

220   Lo! He, only He, is the Hearer, the Knower.

إِنَّهُ هُوَ ٱلسَّمِيعُ ٱلْعَلِيمُ ۝

221   Shall I inform you upon whom the devils descend?

هَلْ أُنَبِّئُكُمْ عَلَىٰ مَن تَنَزَّلُ ٱلشَّيَٰطِينُ ۝

222   They descend on every sinful, false one.

تَنَزَّلُ عَلَىٰ كُلِّ أَفَّاكٍ أَثِيمٍ ۝

223   They listen eagerly, but most of them are liars.

يُلْقُونَ ٱلسَّمْعَ وَأَكْثَرُهُمْ كَٰذِبُونَ ۝

224 As for poets, the erring follow them.

وَالشُّعَرَآءُ يَتَّبِعُهُمُ الْغَاوُونَ ۝

225 Hast thou not seen how they stray in every valley;

أَلَمْ تَرَ أَنَّهُمْ فِى كُلِّ وَادٍ يَهِيمُونَ ۝

226 And how they say that which they do not?

وَأَنَّهُمْ يَقُولُونَ مَا لَا يَفْعَلُونَ ۝

227 Save those who believe and do good works, and remember Allah much, and vindicate themselves after they have been wronged. Those who do wrong will come to know by what a (great) reverse they will be overturned!

إِلَّا الَّذِينَ ءَامَنُوا وَعَمِلُوا الصَّٰلِحَٰتِ وَذَكَرُوا اللَّهَ كَثِيرًا وَانتَصَرُوا مِنۢ بَعْدِ مَا ظُلِمُوا ۗ وَسَيَعْلَمُ الَّذِينَ ظَلَمُوا أَىَّ مُنقَلَبٍ يَنقَلِبُونَ ۝

An Naml
(The Ant)

An Naml, "The Ant," takes its name from the ant mentioned in v. 18. Some commentators, objecting to the miraculous, seek to explain the ants, in the story of Solomon, as an old Arab tribe, the birds as cavalry, Hudhud (the hoopoe) as a man's name, and the Jinn as foreign troops.

It belongs to the middle group of Makkan sūrahs.

In the name of Allah, the Beneficent, the Merciful.

بِسْــــمِ ٱللَّهِ ٱلرَّحْمَنِ ٱلرَّحِيمِ

1   Tā. Sīn.[1] These are revelations of the Qur'an and a Scripture that maketh plain;

طسٓ تِلْكَ ءَايَتُ ٱلْقُرْءَانِ وَكِتَابٍ مُّبِينٍ ﴿١﴾

2   A guidance and good tidings for believers.

هُدًى وَبُشْرَىٰ لِلْمُؤْمِنِينَ ﴿٢﴾

3   Who establish worship and pay the poor-due and are sure of the Hereafter.

ٱلَّذِينَ يُقِيمُونَ ٱلصَّلَوٰةَ وَيُؤْتُونَ ٱلزَّكَوٰةَ وَهُم بِٱلْءَاخِرَةِ هُمْ يُوقِنُونَ ﴿٣﴾

4   Lo! as for those who believe not in the Hereafter, We have made their works fair-seeming unto them so that they are all astray.

إِنَّ ٱلَّذِينَ لَا يُؤْمِنُونَ بِٱلْءَاخِرَةِ زَيَّنَّا لَهُمْ أَعْمَالَهُمْ فَهُمْ يَعْمَهُونَ ﴿٤﴾

5   Those are they for whom is the worst of punishment, and in the Hereafter they will be the greatest losers.

أُوْلَٰٓئِكَ ٱلَّذِينَ لَهُمْ سُوٓءُ ٱلْعَذَابِ وَهُمْ فِى ٱلْءَاخِرَةِ هُمُ ٱلْأَخْسَرُونَ ﴿٥﴾

---

1. See Sūrah 2, v. 1, footnote.

6 Lo! as for thee (Muhammad), thou verily receivest the Qur'an from the presence of One Wise, Aware.

وَإِنَّكَ لَتُلَقَّى الْقُرْآنَ مِن لَّدُنْ حَكِيمٍ عَلِيمٍ ۝

7 (Remember) when Moses said unto his household: Lo! I spy afar off a fire; I will bring you tidings thence, or bring to you a borrowed flame that ye may warm yourselves.

إِذْ قَالَ مُوسَى لِأَهْلِهِ إِنِّي ءَانَسْتُ نَارًا سَآتِيكُم مِّنْهَا بِخَبَرٍ أَوْ ءَاتِيكُم بِشِهَابٍ قَبَسٍ لَّعَلَّكُمْ تَصْطَلُونَ ۝

8 But when he reached it, he was called, saying: Blessed is whosoever is in the fire and whosoever is round about it! And glorified be Allah, the Lord of the Worlds!

فَلَمَّا جَآءَهَا نُودِيَ أَن بُورِكَ مَن فِي النَّارِ وَمَنْ حَوْلَهَا وَسُبْحَانَ اللَّهِ رَبِّ الْعَالَمِينَ ۝

9 O Moses! Lo! it is I, Allah, the Mighty, the Wise.

يَا مُوسَى إِنَّهُ أَنَا اللَّهُ الْعَزِيزُ الْحَكِيمُ ۝

10 And throw down thy staff! But when he saw it writhing as it were a demon, he turned to flee headlong; (but it was said unto him): O Moses! Fear not! Lo! the emissaries fear not in My presence;

وَأَلْقِ عَصَاكَ فَلَمَّا رَآهَا تَهْتَزُّ كَأَنَّهَا جَآنٌّ وَلَّى مُدْبِرًا وَلَمْ يُعَقِّبْ يَا مُوسَى لَا تَخَفْ إِنِّي لَا يَخَافُ لَدَيَّ الْمُرْسَلُونَ ۝

11 Save him who hath done wrong and afterward hath changed evil for good.[2] And lo! I am Forgiving, Merciful.

إِلَّا مَن ظَلَمَ ثُمَّ بَدَّلَ حُسْنًا بَعْدَ سُوٓءٍ فَإِنِّي غَفُورٌ رَّحِيمٌ ۝

12 And put thy hand into the bosom of thy robe, it will come forth white but unhurt. (This will be one) among nine tokens unto Pharaoh and his people. Lo! they were ever evil-living folk.

وَأَدْخِلْ يَدَكَ فِي جَيْبِكَ تَخْرُجْ بَيْضَآءَ مِنْ غَيْرِ سُوٓءٍ فِي تِسْعِ ءَايَاتٍ إِلَى فِرْعَوْنَ وَقَوْمِهِ إِنَّهُمْ كَانُوا قَوْمًا فَاسِقِينَ ۝

---

2. Moses had been guilty of a crime in Egypt.

13 But when Our tokens came unto them, plain to see, they said: This is mere magic;

فَلَمَّا جَآءَتْهُمْ ءَايَٰتُنَا مُبْصِرَةً قَالُوا۟ هَٰذَا سِحْرٌ مُّبِينٌ ۝

14 And they denied them, though their souls acknowledged them, for spite and arrogance. Then see the nature of the consequence for the wrong-doers!

وَجَحَدُوا۟ بِهَا وَٱسْتَيْقَنَتْهَآ أَنفُسُهُمْ ظُلْمًا وَعُلُوًّا فَٱنظُرْ كَيْفَ كَانَ عَٰقِبَةُ ٱلْمُفْسِدِينَ ۝

15 And We verily gave knowledge unto David and Solomon, and they said: Praise be to Allah, Who hath preferred us above many of His believing slaves!

وَلَقَدْ ءَاتَيْنَا دَاوُۥدَ وَسُلَيْمَٰنَ عِلْمًا وَقَالَا ٱلْحَمْدُ لِلَّهِ ٱلَّذِى فَضَّلَنَا عَلَىٰ كَثِيرٍ مِّنْ عِبَادِهِ ٱلْمُؤْمِنِينَ ۝

16 And Solomon was David's heir. And he said: O mankind! Lo! we have been taught the language of birds, and have been given (abundance) of all things. This surely is evident favour.

وَوَرِثَ سُلَيْمَٰنُ دَاوُۥدَ وَقَالَ يَٰٓأَيُّهَا ٱلنَّاسُ عُلِّمْنَا مَنطِقَ ٱلطَّيْرِ وَأُوتِينَا مِن كُلِّ شَىْءٍ إِنَّ هَٰذَا لَهُوَ ٱلْفَضْلُ ٱلْمُبِينُ ۝

17 And there were gathered together unto Solomon his armies of the jinn and humankind, and of the birds, and they were set in battle order;

وَحُشِرَ لِسُلَيْمَٰنَ جُنُودُهُۥ مِنَ ٱلْجِنِّ وَٱلْإِنسِ وَٱلطَّيْرِ فَهُمْ يُوزَعُونَ ۝

18 Till, when they reached the Valley of the Ants, an ant exclaimed: O ants! Enter your dwellings lest Solomon and his armies crush you, unperceiving.

حَتَّىٰٓ إِذَآ أَتَوْا۟ عَلَىٰ وَادِ ٱلنَّمْلِ قَالَتْ نَمْلَةٌ يَٰٓأَيُّهَا ٱلنَّمْلُ ٱدْخُلُوا۟ مَسَٰكِنَكُمْ لَا يَحْطِمَنَّكُمْ سُلَيْمَٰنُ وَجُنُودُهُۥ وَهُمْ لَا يَشْعُرُونَ ۝

19 And (Solomon) smiled, laughing at her speech, and said: My Lord, arouse me to be thankful for Thy favour wherewith Thou hast favoured me and my parents, and to do good that shall be pleasing unto

فَتَبَسَّمَ ضَاحِكًا مِّن قَوْلِهَا وَقَالَ رَبِّ أَوْزِعْنِىٓ أَنْ أَشْكُرَ نِعْمَتَكَ ٱلَّتِىٓ أَنْعَمْتَ عَلَىَّ وَعَلَىٰ وَٰلِدَىَّ وَأَنْ أَعْمَلَ صَٰلِحًا تَرْضَىٰهُ وَأَدْخِلْنِى بِرَحْمَتِكَ

Thee, and include me in (the number of) Thy righteous slaves.

فِى عِبَادِكَ الصَّلِحِينَ ﴿١٩﴾

20 And he sought among the birds and said: How is it that I see not the hoopoe, or is he among the absent?

وَتَفَقَّدَ الطَّيْرَ فَقَالَ مَالِىَ لَآ أَرَى الْهُدْهُدَ أَمْ كَانَ مِنَ الْغَآئِبِينَ ﴿٢٠﴾

21 I verily will punish him with hard punishment or I verily will slay him, or he verily shall bring me a plain excuse.

لَأُعَذِّبَنَّهُ عَذَابًا شَدِيدًا أَوْ لَأَاذْبَحَنَّهُ أَوْ لَيَأْتِيَنِّى بِسُلْطَنٍ مُّبِينٍ ﴿٢١﴾

22 But he was not long in coming, and he said: I have found out (a thing) that thou apprehendest not, and I come unto thee from Sheba with sure tidings.

فَمَكَثَ غَيْرَ بَعِيدٍ فَقَالَ أَحَطتُ بِمَا لَمْ تُحِطْ بِهِ وَجِئْتُكَ مِن سَبَإٍ بِنَبَإٍ يَقِينٍ ﴿٢٢﴾

23 Lo! I found a woman ruling over them, and she hath been given (abundance) of all things, and hers is a mighty throne.

إِنِّى وَجَدتُّ امْرَأَةً تَمْلِكُهُمْ وَأُوتِيَتْ مِن كُلِّ شَىْءٍ وَلَهَا عَرْشٌ عَظِيمٌ ﴿٢٣﴾

24 I found her and her people worshipping the sun instead of Allah; and Satan maketh their works fair-seeming unto them, and debarreth them from the way (of Truth), so that they go not aright:

وَجَدتُّهَا وَقَوْمَهَا يَسْجُدُونَ لِلشَّمْسِ مِن دُونِ اللَّهِ وَزَيَّنَ لَهُمُ الشَّيْطَنُ أَعْمَلَهُمْ فَصَدَّهُمْ عَنِ السَّبِيلِ فَهُمْ لَا يَهْتَدُونَ ﴿٢٤﴾

25 So that they worship not Allah, Who bringeth forth the hidden in the heavens and the earth, and knoweth what ye hide and what ye proclaim;

أَلَّا يَسْجُدُوا لِلَّهِ الَّذِى يُخْرِجُ الْخَبْءَ فِى السَّمَوَتِ وَالْأَرْضِ وَيَعْلَمُ مَا تُخْفُونَ وَمَا تُعْلِنُونَ ﴿٢٥﴾

26 Allah; there is no God save Him, the Lord of the tremendous Throne.

اللَّهُ لَآ إِلَهَ إِلَّا هُوَ رَبُّ الْعَرْشِ الْعَظِيمِ ۩ ﴿٢٦﴾

27 (Solomon) said: We shall see whether thou speakest truth or whether thou art of the liars.

قَالَ سَنَنظُرُ أَصَدَقْتَ أَمْ كُنتَ مِنَ ٱلْكَٰذِبِينَ ۝

28 Go with this my letter and throw it down unto them; then turn away and see what (answer) they return,

ٱذْهَب بِّكِتَٰبِى هَٰذَا فَأَلْقِهْ إِلَيْهِمْ ثُمَّ تَوَلَّ عَنْهُمْ فَٱنظُرْ مَاذَا يَرْجِعُونَ ۝

29 (The Queen of Sheba) said (when she received the letter): O chieftains! Lo! there hath been thrown unto me a noble letter.

قَالَتْ يَٰٓأَيُّهَا ٱلْمَلَؤُاْ إِنِّىٓ أُلْقِىَ إِلَىَّ كِتَٰبٌ كَرِيمٌ ۝

30 Lo! it is from Solomon, and lo! it is: In the name of Allah the Beneficent, the Merciful;

إِنَّهُۥ مِن سُلَيْمَٰنَ وَإِنَّهُۥ بِسْمِ ٱللَّهِ ٱلرَّحْمَٰنِ ٱلرَّحِيمِ ۝

31 Exalt not yourselves against me, but come unto me as those who surrender.

أَلَّا تَعْلُواْ عَلَىَّ وَأْتُونِى مُسْلِمِينَ ۝

32 She said: O chieftains! Pronounce for me in my case. I decide no case till ye are present with me.

قَالَتْ يَٰٓأَيُّهَا ٱلْمَلَؤُاْ أَفْتُونِى فِىٓ أَمْرِى مَا كُنتُ قَاطِعَةً أَمْرًا حَتَّىٰ تَشْهَدُونِ ۝

33 They said: We are lords of might and lords of great prowess, but it is for thee to command; so consider what thou wilt command.

قَالُواْ نَحْنُ أُوْلُواْ قُوَّةٍ وَأُوْلُواْ بَأْسٍ شَدِيدٍ وَٱلْأَمْرُ إِلَيْكِ فَٱنظُرِى مَاذَا تَأْمُرِينَ ۝

34 She said: Lo! kings, when they enter a township, ruin it and make the honour of its people shame. Thus will they do.

قَالَتْ إِنَّ ٱلْمُلُوكَ إِذَا دَخَلُواْ قَرْيَةً أَفْسَدُوهَا وَجَعَلُوٓاْ أَعِزَّةَ أَهْلِهَآ أَذِلَّةً وَكَذَٰلِكَ يَفْعَلُونَ ۝

35 But lo! I am going to send a present unto them, and to see with what (answer) the messengers return.

وَإِنِّى مُرْسِلَةٌ إِلَيْهِم بِهَدِيَّةٍ فَنَاظِرَةٌۢ بِمَ يَرْجِعُ ٱلْمُرْسَلُونَ ۝

36 So when (the envoy) came unto Solomon, (the King) said: What! Would ye help me with wealth? But

فَلَمَّا جَآءَ سُلَيْمَٰنَ قَالَ أَتُمِدُّونَنِ بِمَالٍ فَمَآ ءَاتَىٰنِۦَ ٱللَّهُ

that which Allah hath given me is better than that which He hath given you. Nay it is ye (and not I) who exult in your gift.

37 Return unto them. We verily shall come unto them with hosts that they cannot resist, and we shall drive them out from thence with shame, and they will be abased.

خَيْرٌ مِّمَّا آتَاكُمُ بَلْ أَنتُم بِهَدِيَّتِكُمْ تَفْرَحُونَ ۝

ارْجِعْ إِلَيْهِمْ فَلَنَأْتِيَنَّهُم بِجُنُودٍ لَّا قِبَلَ لَهُم بِهَا وَلَنُخْرِجَنَّهُم مِّنْهَا أَذِلَّةً وَهُمْ صَاغِرُونَ ۝

38 He said: O chiefs! Which of you will bring me her throne before they come unto me, surrendering?

قَالَ يَٰٓأَيُّهَا الْمَلَؤُا۟ أَيُّكُمْ يَأْتِينِي بِعَرْشِهَا قَبْلَ أَن يَأْتُونِي مُسْلِمِينَ ۝

39 A stalwart of the Jinn said: I will bring it thee before thou canst rise from thy place. Lo! I verily am strong and trusty for such work.

قَالَ عِفْرِيتٌ مِّنَ الْجِنِّ أَنَا۠ آتِيكَ بِهِ قَبْلَ أَن تَقُومَ مِن مَّقَامِكَ وَإِنِّي عَلَيْهِ لَقَوِيٌّ أَمِينٌ ۝

40 One with whom was knowledge of the Scripture said: I will bring it thee before thy gaze returneth unto thee. And when he saw it set in his presence, (Solomon) said: This is of the bounty of my Lord, that He may try me whether I give thanks or am ungrateful. Whosoever giveth thanks he only giveth thanks for (the good of) his own soul: and whosoever is ungrateful (is ungrateful only to his own soul's hurt). For lo! my Lord is Absolute in independence, Bountiful.

قَالَ الَّذِي عِندَهُ عِلْمٌ مِّنَ الْكِتَٰبِ أَنَا۠ آتِيكَ بِهِ قَبْلَ أَن يَرْتَدَّ إِلَيْكَ طَرْفُكَ فَلَمَّا رَآهُ مُسْتَقِرًّا عِندَهُ قَالَ هَٰذَا مِن فَضْلِ رَبِّي لِيَبْلُوَنِي ءَأَشْكُرُ أَمْ أَكْفُرُ وَمَن شَكَرَ فَإِنَّمَا يَشْكُرُ لِنَفْسِهِ وَمَن كَفَرَ فَإِنَّ رَبِّي غَنِيٌّ كَرِيمٌ ۝

41 He said: Disguise her throne for her that we may see whether she will go aright or be of those not rightly guided.

قَالَ نَكِّرُوا لَهَا عَرْشَهَا نَنظُرْ أَتَهْتَدِىٓ أَمْ تَكُونُ مِنَ الَّذِينَ لَا يَهْتَدُونَ ۝

42 So, when she came, it was said (unto her): Is thy throne like this?

فَلَمَّا جَآءَتْ قِيلَ أَهَٰكَذَا عَرْشُكِ قَالَتْ كَأَنَّهُ هُوَ وَأُوتِينَا

She said: (It is) as though it were the very one. And (Solomon said): We were given the knowledge before her and we had surrendered (to Allah).

ٱلۡعِلۡمَ مِن قَبۡلِهَا وَكُنَّا مُسۡلِمِينَ ﴿٤٢﴾

43 And (all) that she was wont to worship instead of Allah hindered her, for she came of disbelieving folk.

وَصَدَّهَا مَا كَانَت تَّعۡبُدُ مِن دُونِ ٱللَّهِ إِنَّهَا كَانَتۡ مِن قَوۡمٖ كَٰفِرِينَ ﴿٤٣﴾

44 It was said unto her: Enter the hall. And when she saw it she deemed it a pool and bared her legs. (Solomon) said: Lo! it is a hall, made smooth, of glass. She said: My Lord! Lo! I have wronged myself, and I surrender with Solomon unto Allah, the Lord of the Worlds.

قِيلَ لَهَا ٱدۡخُلِي ٱلصَّرۡحَۖ فَلَمَّا رَأَتۡهُ حَسِبَتۡهُ لُجَّةٗ وَكَشَفَتۡ عَن سَاقَيۡهَاۚ قَالَ إِنَّهُۥ صَرۡحٞ مُّمَرَّدٞ مِّن قَوَارِيرَۗ قَالَتۡ رَبِّ إِنِّي ظَلَمۡتُ نَفۡسِي وَأَسۡلَمۡتُ مَعَ سُلَيۡمَٰنَ لِلَّهِ رَبِّ ٱلۡعَٰلَمِينَ ﴿٤٤﴾

45 And We verily sent unto Thamūd their brother Sāliḥ, saying: Worship Allah. And lo! they (then) became two parties quarrelling.

وَلَقَدۡ أَرۡسَلۡنَآ إِلَىٰ ثَمُودَ أَخَاهُمۡ صَٰلِحًا أَنِ ٱعۡبُدُواْ ٱللَّهَ فَإِذَا هُمۡ فَرِيقَانِ يَخۡتَصِمُونَ ﴿٤٥﴾

46 He said: O my people! Why will ye hasten on the evil rather than the good? Why will ye not ask pardon of Allah, that ye may receive mercy.

قَالَ يَٰقَوۡمِ لِمَ تَسۡتَعۡجِلُونَ بِٱلسَّيِّئَةِ قَبۡلَ ٱلۡحَسَنَةِۖ لَوۡلَا تَسۡتَغۡفِرُونَ ٱللَّهَ لَعَلَّكُمۡ تُرۡحَمُونَ ﴿٤٦﴾

47 They said: We augur evil of thee and those with thee. He said: Your evil augury is with Allah. Nay, but ye are folk that are being tested.

قَالُواْ ٱطَّيَّرۡنَا بِكَ وَبِمَن مَّعَكَۚ قَالَ طَٰٓئِرُكُمۡ عِندَ ٱللَّهِۖ بَلۡ أَنتُمۡ قَوۡمٞ تُفۡتَنُونَ ﴿٤٧﴾

48 And there were in the city nine persons who made mischief in the land and reformed not.

وَكَانَ فِي ٱلۡمَدِينَةِ تِسۡعَةُ رَهۡطٖ يُفۡسِدُونَ فِي ٱلۡأَرۡضِ وَلَا يُصۡلِحُونَ ﴿٤٨﴾

49 They said: Swear one to another by Allah that we verily will attack him and his household by night,

قَالُواْ تَقَاسَمُواْ بِٱللَّهِ لَنُبَيِّتَنَّهُۥ وَأَهۡلَهُۥ ثُمَّ لَنَقُولَنَّ

and afterward we will surely say unto his friend: We witnessed not the destruction of his household. And lo! we are truthtellers.

لِوَلِيِّهِۦ مَا شَهِدْنَا مَهْلِكَ أَهْلِهِۦ وَإِنَّا لَصَٰدِقُونَ ﴿٤٩﴾

50 So they plotted a plot: and We plotted a plot, while they perceived not.

وَمَكَرُوا۟ مَكْرًا وَمَكَرْنَا مَكْرًا وَهُمْ لَا يَشْعُرُونَ ﴿٥٠﴾

51 Then see the nature of the consequence of their plotting, for lo! We destroyed them and their people, every one.

فَٱنظُرْ كَيْفَ كَانَ عَٰقِبَةُ مَكْرِهِمْ أَنَّا دَمَّرْنَٰهُمْ وَقَوْمَهُمْ أَجْمَعِينَ ﴿٥١﴾

52 See, yonder are their dwellings empty and in ruins because they did wrong. Lo! herein is indeed a portent for a people who have knowledge.

فَتِلْكَ بُيُوتُهُمْ خَاوِيَةًۢ بِمَا ظَلَمُوٓا۟ إِنَّ فِى ذَٰلِكَ لَءَايَةً لِّقَوْمٍ يَعْلَمُونَ ﴿٥٢﴾

53 And we saved those who believed and used to ward off (evil).

وَأَنجَيْنَا ٱلَّذِينَ ءَامَنُوا۟ وَكَانُوا۟ يَتَّقُونَ ﴿٥٣﴾

54 And Lot! when he said unto his folk: will ye commit abomination knowingly?

وَلُوطًا إِذْ قَالَ لِقَوْمِهِۦٓ أَتَأْتُونَ ٱلْفَٰحِشَةَ وَأَنتُمْ تُبْصِرُونَ ﴿٥٤﴾

55 Must ye needs lust after men instead of women? Nay, but ye are folk who act senselessly.

أَئِنَّكُمْ لَتَأْتُونَ ٱلرِّجَالَ شَهْوَةً مِّن دُونِ ٱلنِّسَآءِ بَلْ أَنتُمْ قَوْمٌ تَجْهَلُونَ ﴿٥٥﴾

56 But the answer of his folk was naught save that they said: Expel the household of Lot from your township, for they (forsooth) are folk who would keep clean!

۞ فَمَا كَانَ جَوَابَ قَوْمِهِۦٓ إِلَّآ أَن قَالُوٓا۟ أَخْرِجُوٓا۟ ءَالَ لُوطٍ مِّن قَرْيَتِكُمْ إِنَّهُمْ أُنَاسٌ يَتَطَهَّرُونَ ﴿٥٦﴾

57 Then we saved him and his household save his wife; We destined her to be of those who stayed behind.

فَأَنجَيْنَٰهُ وَأَهْلَهُۥٓ إِلَّا ٱمْرَأَتَهُۥ قَدَّرْنَٰهَا مِنَ ٱلْغَٰبِرِينَ ﴿٥٧﴾

58 And We rained a rain upon them. Dreadful is the rain of those who have been warned.

وَأَمْطَرْنَا عَلَيْهِم مَّطَرًا فَسَآءَ مَطَرُ الْمُنذَرِينَ ۝

59 Say (O Muhammad): Praise be to Allah, and peace be on His slaves whom He hath chosen! Is Allah best, or (all) that ye ascribe as partners (unto Him)?

قُلِ الْحَمْدُ لِلَّهِ وَسَلَامٌ عَلَىٰ عِبَادِهِ الَّذِينَ اصْطَفَىٰٓ ءَآللَّهُ خَيْرٌ أَمَّا يُشْرِكُونَ ۝

60 Is not He (best) Who created the heavens and the earth, and sendeth down for you water from the sky wherewith We cause to spring forth joyous orchards, whose trees it never hath been yours to cause to grow. Is there any God beside Allah? Nay, but they are folk who ascribe equals (unto Him)!

أَمَّنْ خَلَقَ السَّمَاوَاتِ وَالْأَرْضَ وَأَنزَلَ لَكُم مِّنَ السَّمَاءِ مَآءً فَأَنبَتْنَا بِهِ حَدَآئِقَ ذَاتَ بَهْجَةٍ مَّا كَانَ لَكُمْ أَن تُنبِتُوا شَجَرَهَآ أَءِلَهٌ مَّعَ اللَّهِ بَلْ هُمْ قَوْمٌ يَعْدِلُونَ ۝

61 Is not He (best) Who made the earth a fixed abode, and placed rivers in the folds thereof, and placed firm hills therein, and hath set a barrier between the two seas? Is there any God beside Allah? Nay, but most of them know not!

أَمَّن جَعَلَ الْأَرْضَ قَرَارًا وَجَعَلَ خِلَالَهَآ أَنْهَارًا وَجَعَلَ لَهَا رَوَاسِيَ وَجَعَلَ بَيْنَ الْبَحْرَيْنِ حَاجِزًا أَءِلَهٌ مَّعَ اللَّهِ بَلْ أَكْثَرُهُمْ لَا يَعْلَمُونَ ۝

62 Is not He (best) Who answereth the wronged one when he crieth unto Him and removeth the evil, and hath made you viceroys of the earth? Is there any God beside Allah? Little do they reflect!

أَمَّن يُجِيبُ الْمُضْطَرَّ إِذَا دَعَاهُ وَيَكْشِفُ السُّوٓءَ وَيَجْعَلُكُمْ خُلَفَاءَ الْأَرْضِ أَءِلَهٌ مَّعَ اللَّهِ قَلِيلًا مَّا تَذَكَّرُونَ ۝

63 Is not He (best) Who guideth you in the darkness of the land and the sea, He Who sendeth the winds as heralds of His mercy? Is there any God beside Allah? High exalted

أَمَّن يَهْدِيكُمْ فِي ظُلُمَاتِ الْبَرِّ وَالْبَحْرِ وَمَن يُرْسِلُ الرِّيَاحَ بُشْرًا بَيْنَ يَدَيْ رَحْمَتِهِ

be Allah from all that they ascribe as partner (unto Him)!

أَءِلَٰهٌ مَّعَ اللَّهِ تَعَٰلَى اللَّهُ عَمَّا يُشْرِكُونَ ﴿٦٣﴾

64 Is not He (best), Who produceth creation, then reproduceth it, and Who provideth for you from the heaven and the earth? Is there any God beside Allah? Say: Bring your proof, if ye are truthful!

أَمَّنْ يَبْدَؤُا الْخَلْقَ ثُمَّ يُعِيدُهُ وَمَنْ يَرْزُقُكُمْ مِنَ السَّمَاءِ وَالْأَرْضِ أَءِلَٰهٌ مَّعَ اللَّهِ قُلْ هَاتُوا بُرْهَٰنَكُمْ إِنْ كُنْتُمْ صَٰدِقِينَ ﴿٦٤﴾

65 Say (O Muhammad): None in the heavens and the earth knoweth the Unseen save Allah; and they know not when they will be raised (again).

قُلْ لَا يَعْلَمُ مَنْ فِي السَّمَٰوَٰتِ وَالْأَرْضِ الْغَيْبَ إِلَّا اللَّهُ وَمَا يَشْعُرُونَ أَيَّانَ يُبْعَثُونَ ﴿٦٥﴾

66 Nay, but doth their knowledge reach to the Hereafter? Nay, for they are in doubt concerning it. Nay, for they cannot see it.

بَلِ ادَّٰرَكَ عِلْمُهُمْ فِي الْآخِرَةِ بَلْ هُمْ فِي شَكٍّ مِنْهَا بَلْ هُمْ مِنْهَا عَمُونَ ﴿٦٦﴾

67 Yet those who disbelieve say: When we have become dust like our fathers, shall we verily be brought forth (again)?

وَقَالَ الَّذِينَ كَفَرُوا أَءِذَا كُنَّا تُرَٰبًا وَءَابَاؤُنَا أَئِنَّا لَمُخْرَجُونَ ﴿٦٧﴾

68 We were promised this, forsooth, we and our fathers. (All) this is naught but fables of the men of old.

لَقَدْ وُعِدْنَا هَٰذَا نَحْنُ وَءَابَاؤُنَا مِنْ قَبْلُ إِنْ هَٰذَا إِلَّا أَسَٰطِيرُ الْأَوَّلِينَ ﴿٦٨﴾

69 Say (unto them, O Muhammad): Travel in the land and see the nature of the sequel for the guilty!

قُلْ سِيرُوا فِي الْأَرْضِ فَانْظُرُوا كَيْفَ كَانَ عَٰقِبَةُ الْمُجْرِمِينَ ﴿٦٩﴾

70 And grieve thou not for them, nor be in distress because of what they plot (against thee).

وَلَا تَحْزَنْ عَلَيْهِمْ وَلَا تَكُنْ فِي ضَيْقٍ مِمَّا يَمْكُرُونَ ﴿٧٠﴾

71 And they say: When (will) this promise (be fulfilled), if ye are truthful?

وَيَقُولُونَ مَتَىٰ هَٰذَا الْوَعْدُ إِنْ كُنْتُمْ صَٰدِقِينَ ﴿٧١﴾

72 Say: It may be that a part of that which ye would hasten on is close behind you.

قُلْ عَسَىٰٓ أَن يَكُونَ رَدِفَ لَكُم بَعْضُ ٱلَّذِى تَسْتَعْجِلُونَ ۝

73 Lo! thy Lord is full of bounty for mankind, but most of them do not give thanks.

وَإِنَّ رَبَّكَ لَذُو فَضْلٍ عَلَى ٱلنَّاسِ وَلَٰكِنَّ أَكْثَرَهُمْ لَا يَشْكُرُونَ ۝

74 Lo! thy Lord knoweth surely all that their bosoms hide, and all that they proclaim.

وَإِنَّ رَبَّكَ لَيَعْلَمُ مَا تُكِنُّ صُدُورُهُمْ وَمَا يُعْلِنُونَ ۝

75 And there is nothing hidden in the heaven or the earth but it is in a clear Record.

وَمَا مِنْ غَآئِبَةٍ فِى ٱلسَّمَآءِ وَٱلْأَرْضِ إِلَّا فِى كِتَٰبٍ مُّبِينٍ ۝

76 Lo! this Qur'an narrateth unto the Children of Israel most of that concerning which they differ.

إِنَّ هَٰذَا ٱلْقُرْءَانَ يَقُصُّ عَلَىٰ بَنِىٓ إِسْرَٰٓءِيلَ أَكْثَرَ ٱلَّذِى هُمْ فِيهِ يَخْتَلِفُونَ ۝

77 And lo! it is a guidance and a mercy for believers.

وَإِنَّهُۥ لَهُدًى وَرَحْمَةٌ لِّلْمُؤْمِنِينَ ۝

78 Lo! thy Lord will judge between them of His wisdom, and He is the Mighty, the Wise.

إِنَّ رَبَّكَ يَقْضِى بَيْنَهُم بِحُكْمِهِۦ وَهُوَ ٱلْعَزِيزُ ٱلْعَلِيمُ ۝

79 Therefore (O Muhammad) put thy trust in Allah, for thou (standest) on the plain Truth.

فَتَوَكَّلْ عَلَى ٱللَّهِ إِنَّكَ عَلَى ٱلْحَقِّ ٱلْمُبِينِ ۝

80 Lo! thou canst not make the dead to hear, nor canst thou make the deaf to hear the call when they have turned to flee;

إِنَّكَ لَا تُسْمِعُ ٱلْمَوْتَىٰ وَلَا تُسْمِعُ ٱلصُّمَّ ٱلدُّعَآءَ إِذَا وَلَّوْا۟ مُدْبِرِينَ ۝

81 Nor canst thou lead the blind out of their error. Thou canst make none to hear, save those who believe Our revelations and who have surrendered.

وَمَآ أَنتَ بِهَٰدِى ٱلْعُمْىِ عَن ضَلَٰلَتِهِمْ إِن تُسْمِعُ إِلَّا مَن يُؤْمِنُ بِـَٔايَٰتِنَا فَهُم مُّسْلِمُونَ ۝

82 And when the word is fulfilled concerning them, We shall bring forth a beast of the earth to speak

۞ وَإِذَا وَقَعَ ٱلْقَوْلُ عَلَيْهِمْ أَخْرَجْنَا لَهُمْ دَآبَّةً مِّنَ ٱلْأَرْضِ تُكَلِّمُهُمْ أَنَّ ٱلنَّاسَ كَانُوا۟ بِـَٔايَٰتِنَا

unto them because mankind had not
faith in Our revelations.

83 And (remind them of) the Day
when We shall gather out of every
nation a host of those who denied
Our revelations, and they will be
set in array;

84 Till, when they come (before
their Lord), He will say: Did ye
deny My revelations when ye could
not compass them in knowledge, or
what was it that ye did?

85 And the Word will be fulfilled
concerning them because they have
done wrong, and they will not
speak.

86 Have they not seen how We
have appointed the night that they
may rest therein, and the day sight-
giving? Lo! therein verily are portents for a people who believe.

87 And (remind them of) the Day
when the Trumpet will be blown,
and all who are in the heavens and
the earth will start in fear, save him
whom Allah willeth. And all come
unto Him, humbled.

88 And thou seest the hills thou
deemest them solid flying with the
flight of clouds: the doing of Allah
Who perfecteth all things. Lo! He is
Informed of what ye do.

89 Whoso bringeth a good deed
will have better than its worth; and
such are safe from fear that Day.

لَا يُوقِنُونَ ۝

وَيَوْمَ نَحْشُرُ مِن كُلِّ أُمَّةٍ فَوْجًا مِّمَّن يُكَذِّبُ
بِـَٔايَٰتِنَا فَهُمْ يُوزَعُونَ ۝

حَتَّىٰٓ إِذَا جَآءُو قَالَ أَكَذَّبْتُم بِـَٔايَٰتِي
وَلَمْ تُحِيطُواْ بِهَا عِلْمًا أَمَّاذَا كُنتُمْ تَعْمَلُونَ ۝

وَوَقَعَ ٱلْقَوْلُ عَلَيْهِم بِمَا ظَلَمُواْ فَهُمْ لَا يَنطِقُونَ ۝

أَلَمْ يَرَوْاْ أَنَّا جَعَلْنَا ٱلَّيْلَ لِيَسْكُنُواْ فِيهِ وَٱلنَّهَارَ
مُبْصِرًا إِنَّ فِي ذَٰلِكَ لَأَيَٰتٍ لِّقَوْمٍ يُؤْمِنُونَ ۝

وَيَوْمَ يُنفَخُ فِي ٱلصُّورِ فَفَزِعَ مَن فِي ٱلسَّمَٰوَٰتِ
وَمَن فِي ٱلْأَرْضِ إِلَّا مَن شَآءَ ٱللَّهُ وَكُلٌّ أَتَوْهُ
دَٰخِرِينَ ۝

وَتَرَى ٱلْجِبَالَ تَحْسَبُهَا جَامِدَةً وَهِيَ تَمُرُّ مَرَّ ٱلسَّحَابِ
صُنْعَ ٱللَّهِ ٱلَّذِىٓ أَتْقَنَ كُلَّ شَىْءٍ
إِنَّهُۥ خَبِيرٌۢ بِمَا تَفْعَلُونَ ۝

مَن جَآءَ بِٱلْحَسَنَةِ فَلَهُۥ خَيْرٌ مِّنْهَا وَهُم مِّن فَزَعٍ
يَوْمَئِذٍ ءَامِنُونَ ۝

90 And whoso bringeth an ill deed, such will be flung down on their faces in the Fire. Are ye rewarded aught save what ye did?

وَمَن جَآءَ بِٱلسَّيِّئَةِ فَكُبَّتْ وُجُوهُهُمْ فِى ٱلنَّارِ هَلْ تُجْزَوْنَ إِلَّا مَا كُنتُمْ تَعْمَلُونَ ۝

91 (Say): I (Muhammad) am commanded only to serve the Lord of this land which He hath hallowed, and unto Whom all things belong. And I am commanded to be of those who surrender (unto Him);

إِنَّمَآ أُمِرْتُ أَنْ أَعْبُدَ رَبَّ هَٰذِهِ ٱلْبَلْدَةِ ٱلَّذِى حَرَّمَهَا وَلَهُۥ كُلُّ شَىْءٍ وَأُمِرْتُ أَنْ أَكُونَ مِنَ ٱلْمُسْلِمِينَ ۝

92 And to recite the Qur'an. And whoso goeth right, goeth right only for (the good of) his own soul; and as for him who goeth astray—(Unto him) say: Lo! I am only a warner.

وَأَنْ أَتْلُوَاْ ٱلْقُرْءَانَ فَمَنِ ٱهْتَدَىٰ فَإِنَّمَا يَهْتَدِى لِنَفْسِهِۦ وَمَن ضَلَّ فَقُلْ إِنَّمَآ أَنَا۠ مِنَ ٱلْمُنذِرِينَ ۝

93 And say: Praise be to Allah Who will show you His portents so that ye shall know them. And thy Lord is not unaware of what ye (mortals) do.

وَقُلِ ٱلْحَمْدُ لِلَّهِ سَيُرِيكُمْ ءَايَٰتِهِۦ فَتَعْرِفُونَهَا وَمَا رَبُّكَ بِغَٰفِلٍ عَمَّا تَعْمَلُونَ ۝

Al Qaṣaṣ
(The Story)

Al Qaṣaṣ, "The Story," takes its name from a word in v. 25. The name is moreover justified by the nature of the sūrah, which consists mostly of the story of Moses, his early struggles and ultimate triumph, revealed at a time when the Prophet's case seemed desperate. It is one of the last Makkan sūrahs. Some Arabic writers even say that it was revealed during the Hijrah, while others are of opinion that v. 85 only was revealed during the flight.

A late Makkan sūrah, except v. 85 revealed during the Prophet's flight from Makkah to Al-Madīnah, and vv. 52-55 revealed at Al-Madīnah.[1]

سُورَةُ الْقَصَصِ

In the name of Allah, the Beneficent, the Mèrciful.

بِسْمِ اللَّهِ الرَّحْمَنِ الرَّحِيمِ

1 Ṭā. Sīn. Mīm.[2]

طسٓمّ ١

2 These are revelations of the Scripture that maketh plain.

تِلْكَ ءَايَٰتُ ٱلْكِتَٰبِ ٱلْمُبِينِ ٢

3 We narrate unto thee (somewhat) of the story of Moses and Pharaoh with truth, for folk who believe.

نَتْلُوا۟ عَلَيْكَ مِن نَّبَإِ مُوسَىٰ وَفِرْعَوْنَ بِٱلْحَقِّ لِقَوْمٍ يُؤْمِنُونَ ٣

4 Lo! Pharaoh exalted himself in the earth and made its people castes. A tribe among them he oppressed,

إِنَّ فِرْعَوْنَ عَلَا فِى ٱلْأَرْضِ وَجَعَلَ أَهْلَهَا شِيَعًا يَسْتَضْعِفُ طَآئِفَةً مِّنْهُمْ يُذَبِّحُ أَبْنَآءَهُمْ

---

1. *Tafsīr al-Jalāleyn.*

2. See Sūrah 2, v. 1, footnote.

killing their sons and sparing their women. Lo! he was of those who work corruption.

وَيَسْتَحْىِ نِسَآءَهُمْ إِنَّهُ كَانَ مِنَ الْمُفْسِدِينَ ۝

5 And We desired to show favour unto those who were oppressed in the earth, and to make them examples and to make them the inheritors;

وَنُرِيدُ أَنْ نَّمُنَّ عَلَى الَّذِينَ اسْتُضْعِفُوا فِى الْأَرْضِ وَنَجْعَلَهُمْ أَئِمَّةً وَنَجْعَلَهُمُ الْوَارِثِينَ ۝

6 And to establish them in the earth, and to show Pharaoh and Hāmān and their hosts that which they feared from them.

وَنُمَكِّنَ لَهُمْ فِى الْأَرْضِ وَنُرِىَ فِرْعَوْنَ وَهَامٰنَ وَجُنُودَهُمَا مِنْهُمْ مَّا كَانُوا يَحْذَرُونَ ۝

7 And We inspired the mother of Moses, saying: Suckle him and, when thou fearest for him, then cast him into the river and fear not nor grieve. Lo! We shall bring him back unto thee and shall make him (one) of Our messengers.

وَأَوْحَيْنَا إِلَى أُمِّ مُوسَى أَنْ أَرْضِعِيهِ فَإِذَا خِفْتِ عَلَيْهِ فَأَلْقِيهِ فِى الْيَمِّ وَلَا تَخَافِى وَلَا تَحْزَنِى إِنَّا رَآدُّوهُ إِلَيْكِ وَجَاعِلُوهُ مِنَ الْمُرْسَلِينَ ۝

8 And the family of Pharaoh took him up, that he might become for them an enemy and a sorrow. Lo! Pharaoh and Hāmān and their hosts were ever sinning.

فَالْتَقَطَهُ آلُ فِرْعَوْنَ لِيَكُونَ لَهُمْ عَدُوًّا وَحَزَنًا إِنَّ فِرْعَوْنَ وَهَامٰنَ وَجُنُودَهُمَا كَانُوا خَاطِئِينَ ۝

9 And the wife of Pharaoh said: (He will be) a consolation for me and for thee. Kill him not. Peradventure he may be of use to us, or we may choose him for a son. And they perceived not

وَقَالَتِ امْرَأَتُ فِرْعَوْنَ قُرَّتُ عَيْنٍ لِّى وَلَكَ لَا تَقْتُلُوهُ عَسَى أَنْ يَنْفَعَنَا أَوْ نَتَّخِذَهُ وَلَدًا وَهُمْ لَا يَشْعُرُونَ ۝

10 And the heart of the mother of Moses became void, and she would have betrayed him if We had not fortified her heart, that she might be of the believers.

وَأَصْبَحَ فُؤَادُ أُمِّ مُوسَى فَارِغًا إِنْ كَادَتْ لَتُبْدِى بِهِ لَوْلَا أَنْ رَبَطْنَا عَلَى قَلْبِهَا لِتَكُونَ مِنَ الْمُؤْمِنِينَ ۝

11 And she said unto his sister: Trace him. So she observed him from afar, and they perceived not.

وَقَالَتْ لِأُخْتِهِ قُصِّيهِ فَبَصُرَتْ بِهِ عَن جُنُبٍ وَهُمْ لَا يَشْعُرُونَ ۞

12 And We had before forbidden foster-mothers for him, so she said: Shall I show you a household who will rear him for you and take care of him?

۞ وَحَرَّمْنَا عَلَيْهِ الْمَرَاضِعَ مِن قَبْلُ فَقَالَتْ هَلْ أَدُلُّكُمْ عَلَىٰ أَهْلِ بَيْتٍ يَكْفُلُونَهُ لَكُمْ وَهُمْ لَهُۥ نَاصِحُونَ ۞

13 So We restored him to his mother that she might be comforted and not grieve, and that she might know that the promise of Allah is true. But most of them know not.

فَرَدَدْنَاهُ إِلَىٰ أُمِّهِ كَيْ تَقَرَّ عَيْنُهَا وَلَا تَحْزَنَ وَلِتَعْلَمَ أَنَّ وَعْدَ اللَّهِ حَقٌّ وَلَٰكِنَّ أَكْثَرَهُمْ لَا يَعْلَمُونَ ۞

14 And when he reached maturity and became full grown, We gave him wisdom and knowledge. Thus do We reward the good.

وَلَمَّا بَلَغَ أَشُدَّهُ وَاسْتَوَىٰ ءَاتَيْنَٰهُ حُكْمًا وَعِلْمًا وَكَذَٰلِكَ نَجْزِى الْمُحْسِنِينَ ۞

15 And he entered the city at a time of carelessness of its folk, and he found therein two men fighting, one of his own caste, and the other of his enemies; and he who was of his caste asked him for help against him who was of his enemies. So Moses struck him with his fist and killed him. He said: This is of the devil's doing. Lo! he is an enemy, a mere misleader.

وَدَخَلَ الْمَدِينَةَ عَلَىٰ حِينِ غَفْلَةٍ مِّنْ أَهْلِهَا فَوَجَدَ فِيهَا رَجُلَيْنِ يَقْتَتِلَانِ هَٰذَا مِن شِيعَتِهِ وَهَٰذَا مِنْ عَدُوِّهِ فَاسْتَغَٰثَهُ الَّذِى مِن شِيعَتِهِ عَلَى الَّذِى مِنْ عَدُوِّهِ فَوَكَزَهُۥ مُوسَىٰ فَقَضَىٰ عَلَيْهِ قَالَ هَٰذَا مِنْ عَمَلِ الشَّيْطَٰنِ إِنَّهُۥ عَدُوٌّ مُّضِلٌّ مُّبِينٌ ۞

16 He said: My Lord! Lo! I have wronged my soul, so forgive me. Then He forgave him. Lo! He is the Forgiving, the Merciful.

قَالَ رَبِّ إِنِّى ظَلَمْتُ نَفْسِى فَاغْفِرْ لِى فَغَفَرَ لَهُۥ إِنَّهُۥ هُوَ الْغَفُورُ الرَّحِيمُ ۞

17 He said: My Lord! Forasmuch as Thou hast favoured me, I will nevermore be a supporter of the guilty.

قَالَ رَبِّ بِمَا أَنْعَمْتَ عَلَىَّ فَلَنْ أَكُونَ ظَهِيرًا لِّلْمُجْرِمِينَ ۞

18 And morning found him in the city, fearing, vigilant, when behold! he who had appealed to him the day before cried out to him for help. Moses said unto him: Lo! thou art indeed a mere hothead.

19 And when he would have fallen upon the man who was an enemy unto them both, he said: O Moses! Wouldst thou kill me as thou didst kill a person yesterday. Thou wouldst be nothing but a tyrant in the land, thou wouldst not be of the reformers.

20 And a man came from the uttermost part of the city, running. He said: O Moses! Lo! the chiefs take counsel against thee to slay thee; therefore escape. Lo! I am of those who give thee good advice.

21 So he escaped from thence, fearing, vigilant. He said: My Lord! Deliver me from the wrongdoing folk.

22 And when he turned his face toward Madyan, he said: Peradventure my Lord will guide me in the right road.

23 And when he came unto the water of Madyan he found there a whole tribe of men, watering. And he found apart from them two women keeping, back (their flocks). He said: What aileth you? The two said: We cannot give (our flocks) to drink till the shepherds return from

فَأَصْبَحَ فِى ٱلْمَدِينَةِ خَآئِفًا يَتَرَقَّبُ فَإِذَا ٱلَّذِى ٱسْتَنصَرَهُۥ بِٱلْأَمْسِ يَسْتَصْرِخُهُۥ قَالَ لَهُۥ مُوسَىٰٓ إِنَّكَ لَغَوِىٌّ مُّبِينٌ ۝

فَلَمَّآ أَنْ أَرَادَ أَن يَبْطِشَ بِٱلَّذِى هُوَ عَدُوٌّ لَّهُمَا قَالَ يَٰمُوسَىٰٓ أَتُرِيدُ أَن تَقْتُلَنِى كَمَا قَتَلْتَ نَفْسًا بِٱلْأَمْسِ إِن تُرِيدُ إِلَّآ أَن تَكُونَ جَبَّارًا فِى ٱلْأَرْضِ وَمَا تُرِيدُ أَن تَكُونَ مِنَ ٱلْمُصْلِحِينَ ۝

وَجَآءَ رَجُلٌ مِّنْ أَقْصَا ٱلْمَدِينَةِ يَسْعَىٰ قَالَ يَٰمُوسَىٰٓ إِنَّ ٱلْمَلَأَ يَأْتَمِرُونَ بِكَ لِيَقْتُلُوكَ فَٱخْرُجْ إِنِّى لَكَ مِنَ ٱلنَّٰصِحِينَ ۝

فَخَرَجَ مِنْهَا خَآئِفًا يَتَرَقَّبُ قَالَ رَبِّ نَجِّنِى مِنَ ٱلْقَوْمِ ٱلظَّٰلِمِينَ ۝

وَلَمَّا تَوَجَّهَ تِلْقَآءَ مَدْيَنَ قَالَ عَسَىٰ رَبِّىٓ أَن يَهْدِيَنِى سَوَآءَ ٱلسَّبِيلِ ۝

وَلَمَّا وَرَدَ مَآءَ مَدْيَنَ وَجَدَ عَلَيْهِ أُمَّةً مِّنَ ٱلنَّاسِ يَسْقُونَ وَوَجَدَ مِن دُونِهِمُ ٱمْرَأَتَيْنِ تَذُودَانِ قَالَ مَا خَطْبُكُمَا قَالَتَا لَا نَسْقِى

the water; and our father is a very old man.

حَتَّىٰ يُصْدِرَ الرِّعَآءُ ۖ وَأَبُونَا شَيْخٌ كَبِيرٌ ٢٣

24 So he watered (their flock) for them. Then he turned aside into the shade, and said: My Lord! I am needy of whatever good thou sendest down for me.

فَسَقَىٰ لَهُمَا ثُمَّ تَوَلَّىٰ إِلَى الظِّلِّ فَقَالَ رَبِّ إِنِّي لِمَآ أَنزَلْتَ إِلَيَّ مِنْ خَيْرٍ فَقِيرٌ ٢٤

25 Then there came unto him one of the two women, walking shyly. She said: Lo! my father biddeth thee, that he may reward thee with a payment for that thou didst water (the flock) for us. Then, when he came unto him and told him the (whole) story, he said: Fear not! Thou hast escaped from the wrong-doing folk.

فَجَآءَتْهُ إِحْدَىٰهُمَا تَمْشِي عَلَى اسْتِحْيَآءٍ قَالَتْ إِنَّ أَبِي يَدْعُوكَ لِيَجْزِيَكَ أَجْرَ مَا سَقَيْتَ لَنَا ۚ فَلَمَّا جَآءَهُ وَقَصَّ عَلَيْهِ الْقَصَصَ قَالَ لَا تَخَفْ ۖ نَجَوْتَ مِنَ الْقَوْمِ الظَّالِمِينَ ٢٥

26 One of the two women said: O my father! Hire him! For the best (man) that thou canst hire is the strong, the trustworthy.

قَالَتْ إِحْدَىٰهُمَا يَٰٓأَبَتِ اسْتَٔجِرْهُ ۖ إِنَّ خَيْرَ مَنِ اسْتَٔجَرْتَ الْقَوِيُّ الْأَمِينُ ٢٦

27 He said: Lo! I fain would marry thee to one of these two daughters of mine on condition that thou hirest thyself to me for (the term of) eight pilgrimages. Then if thou completest ten it will be of thine own accord, for I would not make it hard for thee. Allah willing, thou wilt find me of the righteous.

قَالَ إِنِّي أُرِيدُ أَنْ أُنكِحَكَ إِحْدَى ابْنَتَيَّ هَٰتَيْنِ عَلَىٰٓ أَن تَأْجُرَنِي ثَمَٰنِيَ حِجَجٍ ۖ فَإِنْ أَتْمَمْتَ عَشْرًا فَمِنْ عِندِكَ ۖ وَمَآ أُرِيدُ أَنْ أَشُقَّ عَلَيْكَ ۚ سَتَجِدُنِي إِن شَآءَ اللَّهُ مِنَ الصَّٰلِحِينَ ٢٧

28 He said: That (is settled) between thee and me. Whichever of the two terms I fulfil, there will be no injustice to me, and Allah is Surety over what we say.

قَالَ ذَٰلِكَ بَيْنِي وَبَيْنَكَ ۖ أَيَّمَا الْأَجَلَيْنِ قَضَيْتُ فَلَا عُدْوَٰنَ عَلَيَّ ۖ وَاللَّهُ عَلَىٰ مَا نَقُولُ وَكِيلٌ ٢٨

29 Then, when Moses had fulfilled the term, and was traveling with his housefolk, he saw in the distance a fire and said unto his housefolk: Bide ye (here). Lo! I see in the distance a fire; peradventure I shall bring you tidings thence, or a brand from the fire that ye may warm yourselves.

﴿ فَلَمَّا قَضَىٰ مُوسَى ٱلْأَجَلَ وَسَارَ بِأَهْلِهِۦ ءَانَسَ مِن جَانِبِ ٱلطُّورِ نَارًا قَالَ لِأَهْلِهِ ٱمْكُثُوٓا۟ إِنِّىٓ ءَانَسْتُ نَارًا لَّعَلِّىٓ ءَاتِيكُم مِّنْهَا بِخَبَرٍ أَوْ جَذْوَةٍ مِّنَ ٱلنَّارِ لَعَلَّكُمْ تَصْطَلُونَ ﴾

30 And when he reached it, he was called from the rightside of the valley in the blessed field, from the tree: O Moses! Lo! I, even I, am Allah, the Lord of the Worlds;

فَلَمَّآ أَتَىٰهَا نُودِىَ مِن شَٰطِئِ ٱلْوَادِ ٱلْأَيْمَنِ فِى ٱلْبُقْعَةِ ٱلْمُبَٰرَكَةِ مِنَ ٱلشَّجَرَةِ أَن يَٰمُوسَىٰٓ إِنِّىٓ أَنَا ٱللَّهُ رَبُّ ٱلْعَٰلَمِينَ ﴿٣٠﴾

31 Throw down thy staff. And when he saw it writhing as if it were a serpent, he turned away retreating and looked not back, (and it was said unto him): O Moses! Draw nigh and fear not. Lo! thou art of those who are secure.

وَأَنْ أَلْقِ عَصَاكَ فَلَمَّا رَءَاهَا تَهْتَزُّ كَأَنَّهَا جَآنٌّ وَلَّىٰ مُدْبِرًا وَلَمْ يُعَقِّبْ يَٰمُوسَىٰٓ أَقْبِلْ وَلَا تَخَفْ إِنَّكَ مِنَ ٱلْءَامِنِينَ ﴿٣١﴾

32 Thrust thy hand into the bosom of thy robe, it will come forth white without hurt. And guard thy heart from fear. Then these shall be two proofs from your Lord unto Pharaoh and his chiefs: Lo! they are evil-living folk.

ٱسْلُكْ يَدَكَ فِى جَيْبِكَ تَخْرُجْ بَيْضَآءَ مِنْ غَيْرِ سُوٓءٍ وَٱضْمُمْ إِلَيْكَ جَنَاحَكَ مِنَ ٱلرَّهْبِ فَذَٰنِكَ بُرْهَٰنَانِ مِن رَّبِّكَ إِلَىٰ فِرْعَوْنَ وَمَلَإِيْهِۦٓ إِنَّهُمْ كَانُوا۟ قَوْمًا فَٰسِقِينَ ﴿٣٢﴾

33 He said: My Lord! Lo! I killed a man among them and I fear that they will kill me.

قَالَ رَبِّ إِنِّى قَتَلْتُ مِنْهُمْ نَفْسًا فَأَخَافُ أَن يَقْتُلُونِ ﴿٣٣﴾

34 My brother Aaron is more eloquent then me in speech. Therefore send him with me as a helper to confirm me. Lo! I fear that they will give the lie to me.

وَأَخِى هَٰرُونُ هُوَ أَفْصَحُ مِنِّى لِسَانًا فَأَرْسِلْهُ مَعِىَ رِدْءًا يُصَدِّقُنِىٓ إِنِّىٓ أَخَافُ أَن يُكَذِّبُونِ ﴿٣٤﴾

35 He said: We will strengthen thine arm with thy brother, and We will give unto you both power so that they cannot reach you for Our portents. Ye twain, and those who follow you, will be the winners.

قَالَ سَنَشُدُّ عَضُدَكَ بِأَخِيكَ وَنَجْعَلُ لَكُمَا سُلْطَانًا فَلَا يَصِلُونَ إِلَيْكُمَا بِآيَاتِنَا أَنْتُمَا وَمَنِ اتَّبَعَكُمَا الْغَالِبُونَ ۞

36 But when Moses came unto them with Our clear tokens, they said: This is naught but invented magic. We never heard of this among our fathers of old.

فَلَمَّا جَاءَهُم مُّوسَى بِآيَاتِنَا بَيِّنَاتٍ قَالُوا مَا هَذَا إِلَّا سِحْرٌ مُّفْتَرًى وَمَا سَمِعْنَا بِهَذَا فِي آبَائِنَا الْأَوَّلِينَ ۞

37 And Moses said: My Lord is best aware of him who bringeth guidance from His presence, and whose will be the sequel of the Home (of bliss). Lo! wrong-doers will not be successful.

وَقَالَ مُوسَى رَبِّي أَعْلَمُ بِمَن جَاءَ بِالْهُدَى مِنْ عِندِهِ وَمَن تَكُونُ لَهُ عَاقِبَةُ الدَّارِ إِنَّهُ لَا يُفْلِحُ الظَّالِمُونَ ۞

38 And Pharaoh said: O chiefs! I know not that ye have a god other than me, so kindle for me (a fire), O Hāmān, to bake the mud; and set up for me a lofty tower in order that I may survey the god of Moses; and lo! I deem him of the liars.

وَقَالَ فِرْعَوْنُ يَا أَيُّهَا الْمَلَأُ مَا عَلِمْتُ لَكُم مِّنْ إِلَهٍ غَيْرِي فَأَوْقِدْ لِي يَا هَامَانُ عَلَى الطِّينِ فَاجْعَل لِّي صَرْحًا لَّعَلِّي أَطَّلِعُ إِلَى إِلَهِ مُوسَى وَإِنِّي لَأَظُنُّهُ مِنَ الْكَاذِبِينَ ۞

39 And he and his hosts were haughty in the land without right, and deemed that they would never be brought back to Us.

وَاسْتَكْبَرَ هُوَ وَجُنُودُهُ فِي الْأَرْضِ بِغَيْرِ الْحَقِّ وَظَنُّوا أَنَّهُمْ إِلَيْنَا لَا يُرْجَعُونَ ۞

40 Therefore We seized him and his hosts, and abandoned them unto the sea. Behold the nature of the consequence for evil-doers!

فَأَخَذْنَاهُ وَجُنُودَهُ فَنَبَذْنَاهُمْ فِي الْيَمِّ فَانظُرْ كَيْفَ كَانَ عَاقِبَةُ الظَّالِمِينَ ۞

41 And We made them patterns that invite unto the Fire, and on the Day of Resurrection they will not be helped.

وَجَعَلْنَاهُمْ أَئِمَّةً يَدْعُونَ إِلَى النَّارِ وَيَوْمَ الْقِيَامَةِ لَا يُنصَرُونَ ۞

وَأَتْبَعْنَـٰهُمْ فِى هَـٰذِهِ ٱلدُّنْيَا لَعْنَةً ۖ
وَيَوْمَ ٱلْقِيَـٰمَةِ هُم مِّنَ ٱلْمَقْبُوحِينَ ۝

42 And We made a curse to follow them in this world, and on the Day of Resurrection they will be among the hateful.

وَلَقَدْ ءَاتَيْنَا مُوسَى ٱلْكِتَـٰبَ مِنۢ بَعْدِ
مَآ أَهْلَكْنَا ٱلْقُرُونَ ٱلْأُولَىٰ بَصَآئِرَ لِلنَّاسِ
وَهُدًى وَرَحْمَةً لَّعَلَّهُمْ يَتَذَكَّرُونَ ۝

43 And We verily gave the Scripture unto Moses after We had destroyed the generations of old; clear testimonies for mankind, and a guidance and a mercy, that haply they might reflect.

وَمَا كُنتَ بِجَانِبِ ٱلْغَرْبِىِّ إِذْ قَضَيْنَآ إِلَىٰ مُوسَى
ٱلْأَمْرَ وَمَا كُنتَ مِنَ ٱلشَّـٰهِدِينَ ۝

44 And thou (Muhammad) wast not on the western side (of the Mount) when We expounded unto Moses the commandment, and thou wast not among those present;

وَلَـٰكِنَّآ أَنشَأْنَا قُرُونًا فَتَطَاوَلَ عَلَيْهِمُ ٱلْعُمُرُ ۚ
وَمَا كُنتَ ثَاوِيًا فِىٓ أَهْلِ مَدْيَنَ تَتْلُوا۟
عَلَيْهِمْ ءَايَـٰتِنَا وَلَـٰكِنَّا كُنَّا مُرْسِلِينَ ۝

45 But We brought forth generations, and their lives dragged on for them. And thou wast not a dweller in Madyan, reciting unto them Our revelations, but We kept sending (messengers to men).

وَمَا كُنتَ بِجَانِبِ ٱلطُّورِ إِذْ نَادَيْنَا وَلَـٰكِن رَّحْمَةً
مِّن رَّبِّكَ لِتُنذِرَ قَوْمًا مَّآ أَتَـٰهُم مِّن نَّذِيرٍ
مِّن قَبْلِكَ لَعَلَّهُمْ يَتَذَكَّرُونَ ۝

46 And thou wast not beside the Mount when We did call; but (the knowledge of it is) a mercy from thy Lord that thou mayest warn a folk unto whom no warner came before thee, that haply they may give heed.

وَلَوْلَآ أَن تُصِيبَهُم مُّصِيبَةٌ بِمَا قَدَّمَتْ أَيْدِيهِمْ
فَيَقُولُوا۟ رَبَّنَا لَوْلَآ أَرْسَلْتَ إِلَيْنَا رَسُولًا فَنَتَّبِعَ
ءَايَـٰتِكَ وَنَكُونَ مِنَ ٱلْمُؤْمِنِينَ ۝

47 Otherwise, if disaster should afflict them because of that which their own hands have sent before (them), they might say: Our Lord! Why sentest Thou no messenger unto us, that we might have followed Thy revelations and been of the believers?

48 But when there came unto them the Truth from Our presence, they said: Why is he not given the like of what was given unto Moses? Did they not disbelieve in that which was given unto Moses of old? They say: Two magics[3] that support each other; and they say: Lo! in both we are disbelievers.

فَلَمَّا جَآءَهُمُ الْحَقُّ مِنْ عِنْدِنَا قَالُوا لَوْلَا أُوتِيَ مِثْلَ مَآ أُوتِيَ مُوسَى أَوَلَمْ يَكْفُرُوا بِمَآ أُوتِيَ مُوسَى مِنْ قَبْلُ قَالُوا سِحْرَانِ تَظَاهَرَا وَقَالُوا إِنَّا بِكُلٍّ كَافِرُونَ ۝

49 Say (unto them, O Muhammad): Then bring a Scripture from the presence of Allah that giveth clearer guidance than these two (that) I may follow it, if ye are truthful.

قُلْ فَأْتُوا بِكِتَابٍ مِّنْ عِنْدِ اللَّهِ هُوَ أَهْدَى مِنْهُمَآ أَتَّبِعْهُ إِن كُنتُمْ صَادِقِينَ ۝

50 And if they answer thee not, then know that what they follow is their lusts. And who goeth farther astray than he who followeth his lust without guidance from Allah. Lo! Allah guideth not wrongdoing folk.

فَإِن لَّمْ يَسْتَجِيبُوا لَكَ فَاعْلَمْ أَنَّمَا يَتَّبِعُونَ أَهْوَآءَهُمْ وَمَنْ أَضَلُّ مِمَّنِ اتَّبَعَ هَوَاهُ بِغَيْرِ هُدًى مِّنَ اللَّهِ إِنَّ اللَّهَ لَا يَهْدِي الْقَوْمَ الظَّالِمِينَ ۝

51 And now verily We have caused the Word to reach them, that haply they may give heed.

۞ وَلَقَدْ وَصَّلْنَا لَهُمُ الْقَوْلَ لَعَلَّهُمْ يَتَذَكَّرُونَ ۝

52 Those unto whom We gave the Scripture before it, they believe in it;

الَّذِينَ ءَاتَيْنَاهُمُ الْكِتَابَ مِن قَبْلِهِ هُم بِهِ يُؤْمِنُونَ ۝

53 And when it is recited unto them, they say: We believe in it. Lo! it is the Truth from our Lord. Lo! even before it we were of those who surrender (unto Him).

وَإِذَا يُتْلَى عَلَيْهِمْ قَالُوا ءَامَنَّا بِهِ إِنَّهُ الْحَقُّ مِن رَّبِّنَا إِنَّا كُنَّا مِن قَبْلِهِ مُسْلِمِينَ ۝

---

3. *i.e.* the Scripture of Moses and the Qur'an.

54 These will be given their reward twice over, because they are steadfast and repel evil with good, and spend of that wherewith We have provided them;

أُوْلَٰٓئِكَ يُؤْتَوْنَ أَجْرَهُم مَّرَّتَيْنِ بِمَا صَبَرُوا۟ وَيَدْرَءُونَ بِالْحَسَنَةِ السَّيِّئَةَ وَمِمَّا رَزَقْنَٰهُمْ يُنفِقُونَ ﴿٥٤﴾

55 And when they hear vanity they withdraw from it and say: Unto us our works and unto you your works. Peace be unto you! We desire not the ignorant.

وَإِذَا سَمِعُوا۟ اللَّغْوَ أَعْرَضُوا۟ عَنْهُ وَقَالُوا۟ لَنَآ أَعْمَٰلُنَا وَلَكُمْ أَعْمَٰلُكُمْ سَلَٰمٌ عَلَيْكُمْ لَا نَبْتَغِى الْجَٰهِلِينَ ﴿٥٥﴾

56 Lo! thou (O Muhammad) guidest not whom thou lovest, but Allah guideth whom He will. And He is best aware of those who walk aright.

إِنَّكَ لَا تَهْدِى مَنْ أَحْبَبْتَ وَلَٰكِنَّ اللَّهَ يَهْدِى مَن يَشَآءُ وَهُوَ أَعْلَمُ بِالْمُهْتَدِينَ ﴿٥٦﴾

57 And they say: If we were to follow the Guidance with thee we should be torn out of our land. Have We not established for them a sure sanctuary,[4] whereunto the produce of all things is brought (in trade), a provision from Our presence? But most of them know not.

وَقَالُوٓا۟ إِن نَّتَّبِعِ الْهُدَىٰ مَعَكَ نُتَخَطَّفْ مِنْ أَرْضِنَآ أَوَلَمْ نُمَكِّن لَّهُمْ حَرَمًا ءَامِنًا يُجْبَىٰٓ إِلَيْهِ ثَمَرَٰتُ كُلِّ شَىْءٍ رِّزْقًا مِّن لَّدُنَّا وَلَٰكِنَّ أَكْثَرَهُمْ لَا يَعْلَمُونَ ﴿٥٧﴾

58 And how many a community have We destroyed that was thankless for its means of livelihood! And yonder are their dwellings, which have not been inhabited after them save a little. And We, even We, were the inheritors.

وَكَمْ أَهْلَكْنَا مِن قَرْيَةٍ بَطِرَتْ مَعِيشَتَهَا فَتِلْكَ مَسَٰكِنُهُمْ لَمْ تُسْكَن مِّنۢ بَعْدِهِمْ إِلَّا قَلِيلًا وَكُنَّا نَحْنُ الْوَٰرِثِينَ ﴿٥٨﴾

59 And never did thy Lord destroy the townships, till He had raised up in their mother(-town) a messenger

وَمَا كَانَ رَبُّكَ مُهْلِكَ الْقُرَىٰ حَتَّىٰ يَبْعَثَ فِىٓ أُمِّهَا

---

4. The sacred territory of Makkah.

reciting unto them Our revelations. And never did We destroy the townships unless the folk thereof were evil-doers.

رَسُولًا يَتْلُوا عَلَيْهِمْ ءَايَٰتِنَا وَمَا كُنَّا مُهْلِكِى الْقُرَىٰ إِلَّا وَأَهْلُهَا ظَٰلِمُونَ ٥٩

60 And whatsoever ye have been given is a comfort of the life of the world and an ornament thereof; and that which Allah hath is better and more lasting. Have ye then no sense?

وَمَا أُوتِيتُم مِّن شَىْءٍ فَمَتَٰعُ الْحَيَوٰةِ الدُّنْيَا وَزِينَتُهَا وَمَا عِندَ اللَّهِ خَيْرٌ وَأَبْقَىٰ أَفَلَا تَعْقِلُونَ ٦٠

61 Is he whom We have promised a fair promise which he will find (true) like him whom We suffer to enjoy awhile the comfort of the life of the world, then on the Day of Resurrection he will be of those arraigned?

أَفَمَن وَعَدْنَٰهُ وَعْدًا حَسَنًا فَهُوَ لَٰقِيهِ كَمَن مَّتَّعْنَٰهُ مَتَٰعَ الْحَيَوٰةِ الدُّنْيَا ثُمَّ هُوَ يَوْمَ الْقِيَٰمَةِ مِنَ الْمُحْضَرِينَ ٦١

62 On the Day when He will call unto them and say: Where are My partners whom ye imagined?

وَيَوْمَ يُنَادِيهِمْ فَيَقُولُ أَيْنَ شُرَكَاءِىَ الَّذِينَ كُنتُمْ تَزْعُمُونَ ٦٢

63 Those concerning whom the Word will have come true will say: Our Lord! These are they whom we led astray. We led them astray even as we ourselves were astray. We declare our innocence before Thee: us they never worshipped.

قَالَ الَّذِينَ حَقَّ عَلَيْهِمُ الْقَوْلُ رَبَّنَا هَٰؤُلَاءِ الَّذِينَ أَغْوَيْنَا أَغْوَيْنَٰهُمْ كَمَا غَوَيْنَا تَبَرَّأْنَا إِلَيْكَ مَا كَانُوا إِيَّانَا يَعْبُدُونَ ٦٣

64 And it will be said: Cry unto your (so called) partners (of Allah). And they will cry unto them, and they will give no answer unto them, and they will see the Doom. Ah, if they had but been guided!

وَقِيلَ ادْعُوا شُرَكَاءَكُمْ فَدَعَوْهُمْ فَلَمْ يَسْتَجِيبُوا لَهُمْ وَرَأَوُا الْعَذَابَ لَوْ أَنَّهُمْ كَانُوا يَهْتَدُونَ ٦٤

65 And on the Day when He will call unto them and say: What answer gave ye to the messengers?

وَيَوْمَ يُنَادِيهِمْ فَيَقُولُ مَاذَا أَجَبْتُمُ الْمُرْسَلِينَ ٦٥

66 On that day (all) tidings will be dimmed for them, nor will they ask one of another;

فَعَمِيَتۡ عَلَيۡهِمُ الۡاَنۡبَآءُ يَوۡمَئِذٍ فَهُمۡ لَا يَتَسَآءَلُوۡنَ ۝

67 But as for him who shall repent and believe and do right, he haply may be one of the successful.

فَاَمَّا مَنۡ تَابَ وَاٰمَنَ وَعَمِلَ صَالِحًا فَعَسٰٓى اَنۡ يَّكُوۡنَ مِنَ الۡمُفۡلِحِيۡنَ ۝

68 Thy Lord createth what He willeth and chooseth. They have never any choice. Glorified be Allah and exalted above all that they associate (with Him)!

وَرَبُّكَ يَخۡلُقُ مَا يَشَآءُ وَيَخۡتَارُ ۖ مَا كَانَ لَهُمُ الۡخِيَرَةُ ۚ سُبۡحٰنَ اللّٰهِ وَتَعٰلٰى عَمَّا يُشۡرِكُوۡنَ ۝

69 And thy Lord knoweth what their breasts conceal, and what they publish.

وَرَبُّكَ يَعۡلَمُ مَا تُكِنُّ صُدُوۡرُهُمۡ وَمَا يُعۡلِنُوۡنَ ۝

70 And He is Allah; there is no God save Him. His is all praise in the former and the latter (state), and His is the command, and unto Him ye will be brought back.

وَهُوَ اللّٰهُ لَآ اِلٰهَ اِلَّا هُوَ ۖ لَهُ الۡحَمۡدُ فِى الۡاُوۡلٰى وَالۡاٰخِرَةِ ۖ وَلَهُ الۡحُكۡمُ وَاِلَيۡهِ تُرۡجَعُوۡنَ ۝

71 Say: Have ye thought, if Allah made night everlasting for you till the Day of Resurrection, who is a God beside Allah who could bring you light? Will ye not then hear?

قُلۡ اَرَءَيۡتُمۡ اِنۡ جَعَلَ اللّٰهُ عَلَيۡكُمُ الَّيۡلَ سَرۡمَدًا اِلٰى يَوۡمِ الۡقِيٰمَةِ مَنۡ اِلٰهٌ غَيۡرُ اللّٰهِ يَاۡتِيۡكُمۡ بِضِيَآءٍ ۖ اَفَلَا تَسۡمَعُوۡنَ ۝

72 Say: Have ye thought, if Allah made day everlasting for you till the Day of Resurrection, who is a God beside Allah who could bring you night wherein ye rest? Will ye not then see?

قُلۡ اَرَءَيۡتُمۡ اِنۡ جَعَلَ اللّٰهُ عَلَيۡكُمُ النَّهَارَ سَرۡمَدًا اِلٰى يَوۡمِ الۡقِيٰمَةِ مَنۡ اِلٰهٌ غَيۡرُ اللّٰهِ يَاۡتِيۡكُمۡ بِلَيۡلٍ تَسۡكُنُوۡنَ فِيۡهِ ۖ اَفَلَا تُبۡصِرُوۡنَ ۝

73 Of His mercy hath He appointed for you night and day, that therein ye may rest, and that ye may seek His bounty, and that haply ye may be thankful.

وَمِنۡ رَّحۡمَتِهٖ جَعَلَ لَكُمُ الَّيۡلَ وَالنَّهَارَ لِتَسۡكُنُوۡا فِيۡهِ وَلِتَبۡتَغُوۡا مِنۡ فَضۡلِهٖ وَلَعَلَّكُمۡ تَشۡكُرُوۡنَ ۝

74 And on the Day when He shall call unto them and say: Where are My partners whom ye pretended?

وَيَوْمَ يُنَادِيهِمْ فَيَقُولُ أَيْنَ شُرَكَآءِىَ الَّذِينَ كُنتُمْ تَزْعُمُونَ ٧٤

75 And We shall take out from every nation a witness and We shall say: Bring your proof. Then they will know that Allah hath the Truth, and all that they invented will have failed them.

وَنَزَعْنَا مِن كُلِّ أُمَّةٍ شَهِيدًا فَقُلْنَا هَاتُوا بُرْهَانَكُمْ فَعَلِمُوا أَنَّ الْحَقَّ لِلَّهِ وَضَلَّ عَنْهُم مَّا كَانُوا يَفْتَرُونَ ٧٥

76 Now Korah was of Moses' folk, but he oppressed them; and We gave him so much treasure that the stores thereof would verily have been a burden for a troop of mighty men. When his own folk said unto him: Exult not; lo! Allah loveth not the exultant;

إِنَّ قَارُونَ كَانَ مِن قَوْمِ مُوسَى فَبَغَى عَلَيْهِمْ وَءَاتَيْنَاهُ مِنَ الْكُنُوزِ مَا إِنَّ مَفَاتِحَهُ لَتَنُوأُ بِالْعُصْبَةِ أُولِي الْقُوَّةِ إِذْ قَالَ لَهُ قَوْمُهُ لَا تَفْرَحْ إِنَّ اللَّهَ لَا يُحِبُّ الْفَرِحِينَ ٧٦

77 But seek the abode of the Hereafter in that which Allah hath given thee and neglect not thy portion of the world, and be thou kind even as Allah hath been kind to thee, and seek not corruption in the earth; lo! Allah loveth not corrupters;

وَابْتَغِ فِيمَا ءَاتَاكَ اللَّهُ الدَّارَ الْءَاخِرَةَ وَلَا تَنسَ نَصِيبَكَ مِنَ الدُّنْيَا وَأَحْسِن كَمَا أَحْسَنَ اللَّهُ إِلَيْكَ وَلَا تَبْغِ الْفَسَادَ فِي الْأَرْضِ إِنَّ اللَّهَ لَا يُحِبُّ الْمُفْسِدِينَ ٧٧

78 He said: I have been given it only on account of knowledge I possess. Knew he not that Allah had destroyed already of the generations before him men who were mightier than Him in strength and greater in respect of following? The guilty are not questioned of their sins.

قَالَ إِنَّمَا أُوتِيتُهُ عَلَى عِلْمٍ عِندِي أَوَلَمْ يَعْلَمْ أَنَّ اللَّهَ قَدْ أَهْلَكَ مِن قَبْلِهِ مِنَ الْقُرُونِ مَنْ هُوَ أَشَدُّ مِنْهُ قُوَّةً وَأَكْثَرُ جَمْعًا وَلَا يُسْئَلُ عَن ذُنُوبِهِمُ الْمُجْرِمُونَ ٧٨

79 Then went he forth before his people in his pomp. Those who were desirous of the life of the

فَخَرَجَ عَلَى قَوْمِهِ فِي زِينَتِهِ قَالَ الَّذِينَ يُرِيدُونَ

world said: Ah, would that unto us had been given the like of what hath been given unto Korah! Lo! he is lord of rare good fortune.

ٱلْحَيَوٰةَ ٱلدُّنْيَا يَٰلَيْتَ لَنَا مِثْلَ مَآ أُوتِيَ قَٰرُونُ إِنَّهُۥ لَذُو حَظٍّ عَظِيمٍ ۝

80 But those who had been given knowledge said: Woe unto you! The reward of Allah for him who believeth and doeth right is better, and only the steadfast will obtain it.

وَقَالَ ٱلَّذِينَ أُوتُوا۟ ٱلْعِلْمَ وَيْلَكُمْ ثَوَابُ ٱللَّهِ خَيْرٌ لِّمَنْ ءَامَنَ وَعَمِلَ صَٰلِحًا وَلَا يُلَقَّىٰهَآ إِلَّا ٱلصَّٰبِرُونَ ۝

81 So We caused the earth to swallow him and his dwelling place. Then he had no host to help him against Allah, nor was he of those who can save themselves.

فَخَسَفْنَا بِهِۦ وَبِدَارِهِ ٱلْأَرْضَ فَمَا كَانَ لَهُۥ مِن فِئَةٍ يَنصُرُونَهُۥ مِن دُونِ ٱللَّهِ وَمَا كَانَ مِنَ ٱلْمُنتَصِرِينَ ۝

82 And morning found those who had coveted his place but yesterday crying: Ah, welladay! Allah enlargeth the provision for whom He will of His slaves and straiteneth it (for whom He will). If Allah had not been gracious unto us, He would have caused it to swallow us (also). Ah, welladay! the disbelievers never prosper.

وَأَصْبَحَ ٱلَّذِينَ تَمَنَّوْا۟ مَكَانَهُۥ بِٱلْأَمْسِ يَقُولُونَ وَيْكَأَنَّ ٱللَّهَ يَبْسُطُ ٱلرِّزْقَ لِمَن يَشَآءُ مِنْ عِبَادِهِۦ وَيَقْدِرُ لَوْلَآ أَن مَّنَّ ٱللَّهُ عَلَيْنَا لَخَسَفَ بِنَا وَيْكَأَنَّهُۥ لَا يُفْلِحُ ٱلْكَٰفِرُونَ ۝

83 As for that Abode of the Hereafter We assign it unto those who seek not oppression in the earth, nor yet corruption. The sequel is for those who ward off (evil).

تِلْكَ ٱلدَّارُ ٱلْأَخِرَةُ نَجْعَلُهَا لِلَّذِينَ لَا يُرِيدُونَ عُلُوًّا فِى ٱلْأَرْضِ وَلَا فَسَادًا وَٱلْعَٰقِبَةُ لِلْمُتَّقِينَ ۝

84 Whoso bringeth a good deed, he will have better than the same; while as for him who bringeth an ill deed, those who do ill deeds will be requited only what they did.

مَن جَآءَ بِٱلْحَسَنَةِ فَلَهُۥ خَيْرٌ مِّنْهَا وَمَن جَآءَ بِٱلسَّيِّئَةِ فَلَا يُجْزَى ٱلَّذِينَ عَمِلُوا۟ ٱلسَّيِّئَاتِ إِلَّا مَا كَانُوا۟ يَعْمَلُونَ ۝

85 Lo! He Who hath given thee the Qur'an for a law will surely bring thee home again.[5] Say: My Lord is best aware of him who bringeth guidance and him who is in error manifest.

إِنَّ الَّذِى فَرَضَ عَلَيْكَ الْقُرْءَانَ لَرَآدُّكَ إِلَى مَعَادٍ قُل رَّبِّى أَعْلَمُ مَن جَآءَ بِالْهُدَى وَمَنْ هُوَ فِى ضَلَٰلٍ مُّبِينٍ ۝

86 Thou hadst no hope that the Scripture would be inspired in thee; but it is a mercy from thy Lord, so never be a helper to the disbelievers.

وَمَا كُنتَ تَرْجُوٓاْ أَن يُلْقَىٰٓ إِلَيْكَ الْكِتَٰبُ إِلَّا رَحْمَةً مِّن رَّبِّكَ فَلَا تَكُونَنَّ ظَهِيرًا لِّلْكَٰفِرِينَ ۝

87 And let them not divert thee from the revelations of Allah after they have been sent down unto thee; but call (mankind) unto thy Lord, and be not of those who ascribe partners (unto Him).

وَلَا يَصُدُّنَّكَ عَنْ ءَايَٰتِ اللَّهِ بَعْدَ إِذْ أُنزِلَتْ إِلَيْكَ وَادْعُ إِلَىٰ رَبِّكَ وَلَا تَكُونَنَّ مِنَ الْمُشْرِكِينَ ۝

88 And cry not unto any other god along with Allah. There is no God save Him. Everything will perish save His countenance. His is the command, and unto Him ye will be brought back.

وَلَا تَدْعُ مَعَ اللَّهِ إِلَٰهًا ءَاخَرَ لَآ إِلَٰهَ إِلَّا هُوَ كُلُّ شَىْءٍ هَالِكٌ إِلَّا وَجْهَهُ لَهُ الْحُكْمُ وَإِلَيْهِ تُرْجَعُونَ ۝

---

5. A tradition says that this verse was revealed during the Prophet's flight from Makkah to Al-Madīnah.

Al 'Ankabūt
(The Spider)

Al 'Ankabūt, "The Spider," takes its name from v. 41 where false
beliefs are likened to the spider's web for frailty. Most of this sūrah
belongs to the middle or last Makkan period. Some authorities consider
vv. 7 and 8, others the whole latter portion of the sūrah,[1] to have been
revealed at Al-Madīnah. It gives comfort to the Muslims in a time of
persecution.

A late Makkan sūrah.

*In the name of Allah, the
Beneficent, the Merciful.*

بِسْمِ اللهِ الرَّحْمَنِ الرَّحِيمِ

1   Alif. Lām. Mīm.[2]

الٓمٓ ﴿١﴾

2   Do men imagine that they will
be left (at ease) because they say,
We believe, and will not be tested
with affliction?

أَحَسِبَ النَّاسُ أَن يُتْرَكُوٓاْ أَن يَقُولُوٓاْ ءَامَنَّا وَهُمْ
لَا يُفْتَنُونَ ﴿٢﴾

3   Lo! We tested those who were
before them. Thus Allah knoweth
those who are sincere, and knoweth
those who feign.

وَلَقَدْ فَتَنَّا الَّذِينَ مِن قَبْلِهِمْ فَلَيَعْلَمَنَّ اللهُ الَّذِينَ
صَدَقُواْ وَلَيَعْلَمَنَّ الْكَٰذِبِينَ ﴿٣﴾

4   Or do those who do ill deeds
imagine that they can outstrip Us?

أَمْ حَسِبَ الَّذِينَ يَعْمَلُونَ السَّيِّئَاتِ أَن يَسْبِقُونَا

---

1. *An-Nāsikh wal-Mansūkh* by Ibn Salāmah.

2. See Sūrah 2, v. 1, footnote.

Evil (for them) is that which they decide.

سَآءَ مَا يَحۡكُمُونَ ۞

5 Whoso looketh forward to the meeting with Allah (let him know that) Allah's reckoning is surely nigh, and He is the Hearer, the Knower.

مَن كَانَ يَرۡجُواْ لِقَآءَ ٱللَّهِ فَإِنَّ أَجَلَ ٱللَّهِ لَأَتٍ وَهُوَ ٱلسَّمِيعُ ٱلۡعَلِيمُ ۞

6 And whosoever striveth, striveth only for himself, for lo! Allah is altogether Independent of (His) creatures.

وَمَن جَٰهَدَ فَإِنَّمَا يُجَٰهِدُ لِنَفۡسِهِۦٓ إِنَّ ٱللَّهَ لَغَنِيٌّ عَنِ ٱلۡعَٰلَمِينَ ۞

7 And as for those who believe and do good works, We shall remit from them their evil deeds and shall repay them the best that they did.

وَٱلَّذِينَ ءَامَنُواْ وَعَمِلُواْ ٱلصَّٰلِحَٰتِ لَنُكَفِّرَنَّ عَنۡهُمۡ سَيِّـَٔاتِهِمۡ وَلَنَجۡزِيَنَّهُمۡ أَحۡسَنَ ٱلَّذِي كَانُواْ يَعۡمَلُونَ ۞

8 We have enjoined on man kindness to parents; but if they strive to make thee join with Me that of which thou hast no knowledge, then obey them not. Unto Me is your return and I shall tell you what ye used to do.

وَوَصَّيۡنَا ٱلۡإِنسَٰنَ بِوَٰلِدَيۡهِ حُسۡنًا وَإِن جَٰهَدَاكَ لِتُشۡرِكَ بِي مَا لَيۡسَ لَكَ بِهِۦ عِلۡمٌ فَلَا تُطِعۡهُمَآ إِلَيَّ مَرۡجِعُكُمۡ فَأُنَبِّئُكُم بِمَا كُنتُمۡ تَعۡمَلُونَ ۞

9 And as for those who believe and do good works, We verily shall make them enter in among the righteous.

وَٱلَّذِينَ ءَامَنُواْ وَعَمِلُواْ ٱلصَّٰلِحَٰتِ لَنُدۡخِلَنَّهُمۡ فِي ٱلصَّٰلِحِينَ ۞

10 Of mankind is he who saith: We believe in Allah, but, if he be made to suffer for the sake of Allah, he mistaketh the persecution of mankind for Allah's punishment; and then, if victory cometh from thy Lord, will say: Lo! we were with you (all the while). Is not Allah best aware of what is in the bosoms of (His) creatures?

وَمِنَ ٱلنَّاسِ مَن يَقُولُ ءَامَنَّا بِٱللَّهِ فَإِذَآ أُوذِيَ فِي ٱللَّهِ جَعَلَ فِتۡنَةَ ٱلنَّاسِ كَعَذَابِ ٱللَّهِ وَلَئِن جَآءَ نَصۡرٌ مِّن رَّبِّكَ لَيَقُولُنَّ إِنَّا كُنَّا مَعَكُمۡ أَوَلَيۡسَ ٱللَّهُ بِأَعۡلَمَ بِمَا فِي صُدُورِ ٱلۡعَٰلَمِينَ ۞

11 Verily Allah knoweth those who believe, and verily He knoweth the hypocrites.

وَلَيَعْلَمَنَّ اللّٰهُ الَّذِينَ ءَامَنُوا وَلَيَعْلَمَنَّ الْمُنٰفِقِينَ ﴿١١﴾

12 Those who disbelieve say unto those who believe: Follow our way (of religion) and we verily will bear your sins (for you). They cannot bear aught of their sins. Lo! they verily are liars.

وَقَالَ الَّذِينَ كَفَرُوا لِلَّذِينَ ءَامَنُوا اتَّبِعُوا سَبِيلَنَا وَلْنَحْمِلْ خَطٰيٰكُمْ وَمَا هُمْ بِحٰمِلِينَ مِنْ خَطٰيٰهُمْ مِّنْ شَىْءٍ إِنَّهُمْ لَكٰذِبُونَ ﴿١٢﴾

13 But they verily will bear their own loads and other loads beside their own, and they verily will be questioned on the Day of resurrection concerning that which they invented.

وَلَيَحْمِلُنَّ أَثْقَالَهُمْ وَأَثْقَالًا مَّعَ أَثْقَالِهِمْ وَلَيُسْـَٔلُنَّ يَوْمَ الْقِيٰمَةِ عَمَّا كَانُوا يَفْتَرُونَ ﴿١٣﴾

14 And verily We sent Noah (as Our messenger) unto his folk, and he continued with them for a thousand years save fifty years; and the flood engulfed them, for they were wrong-doers.

وَلَقَدْ أَرْسَلْنَا نُوحًا إِلَى قَوْمِهِ فَلَبِثَ فِيهِمْ أَلْفَ سَنَةٍ إِلَّا خَمْسِينَ عَامًا فَأَخَذَهُمُ الطُّوفَانُ وَهُمْ ظٰلِمُونَ ﴿١٤﴾

15 And We rescued him and those with him in the ship, and made of it a portent for the peoples.

فَأَنجَيْنٰهُ وَأَصْحٰبَ السَّفِينَةِ وَجَعَلْنٰهَا ءَايَةً لِّلْعٰلَمِينَ ﴿١٥﴾

16 And Abraham! (Remember) when he said unto his folk: Serve Allah, and keep your duty unto Him; that is better for you if ye did but know.

وَإِبْرٰهِيمَ إِذْ قَالَ لِقَوْمِهِ اعْبُدُوا اللّٰهَ وَاتَّقُوهُ ذٰلِكُمْ خَيْرٌ لَّكُمْ إِن كُنتُمْ تَعْلَمُونَ ﴿١٦﴾

17 Ye serve instead of Allah only idols, and ye only invent a lie. Lo! those whom ye serve instead of Allah own no provision for you. So seek your provision from Allah, and serve Him, and give thanks unto

إِنَّمَا تَعْبُدُونَ مِن دُونِ اللّٰهِ أَوْثٰنًا وَتَخْلُقُونَ إِفْكًا إِنَّ الَّذِينَ تَعْبُدُونَ مِن دُونِ اللّٰهِ لَا يَمْلِكُونَ لَكُمْ رِزْقًا فَابْتَغُوا عِندَ اللّٰهِ الرِّزْقَ

Him, (for) unto Him ye will be brought back.

18 But if ye deny, then nations have denied before you. The messenger is only to convey (the Message) plainly.

19 See they not how Allah produceth creation, then reproduceth it? Lo! for Allah that is easy.

20 Say (O Muhammad): Travel in the land and see how He originated creation, then Allah bringeth forth the later growth. Lo! Allah is Able to do all things.

21 He punisheth whom He will and showeth mercy unto whom He will, and unto Him ye will be turned.

22 Ye cannot escape (from Him) in the earth or in the sky, and beside Allah there is for you no friend nor helper.

23 Those who disbelieve in the revelations of Allah and in (their) Meeting with Him, such have no hope of My mercy. For such there is a painful doom.

24 But the answer of his folk was only that they said: "Kill him" or "Burn him." Then Allah saved him from the fire. Lo! herein verily are portents for folk who believe.

25 He said: Ye have chosen idols instead of Allah. The love between you is only in the life of the world. Then on the Day of Resurrection ye

will deny each other and curse each other, and your abode will be the Fire, and ye will have no helpers.

26 And Lot believed him, and said: Lo! I am a fugitive unto my Lord. Lo! He, only He, is the Mighty, the Wise.

27 And We bestowed on him Isaac and Jacob, and We established the Prophethood and the Scripture among his seed, and We gave him his reward in the world, and lo! in the Hereafter he verily is among the righteous.

28 And Lot! (Remember) when he said unto his folk: Lo! ye commit lewdness such as no creature did before you.

29 For come ye not in unto males, and cut ye not the road (for travellers), and commit ye not abomination in your meetings? But the answer of his folk was only that they said: Bring Allah's doom upon us, if thou art a truth-teller!

30 He said: My Lord! Give me victory over folk who work corruption.

31 And when Our messengers brought Abraham the good news,[3] they said: Lo! we are about to destroy the people of that township, for its people are wrong-doers.

بَعْضُكُمْ بِبَعْضٍ وَيَلْعَنُ بَعْضُكُمْ بَعْضًا وَمَأْوَىٰكُمُ ٱلنَّارُ وَمَا لَكُم مِّن نَّـٰصِرِينَ ۝

۞ فَـَٔامَنَ لَهُۥ لُوطٌ وَقَالَ إِنِّى مُهَاجِرٌ إِلَىٰ رَبِّىٓ إِنَّهُۥ هُوَ ٱلْعَزِيزُ ٱلْحَكِيمُ ۝

وَوَهَبْنَا لَهُۥٓ إِسْحَـٰقَ وَيَعْقُوبَ وَجَعَلْنَا فِى ذُرِّيَّتِهِ ٱلنُّبُوَّةَ وَٱلْكِتَـٰبَ وَءَاتَيْنَـٰهُ أَجْرَهُۥ فِى ٱلدُّنْيَا وَإِنَّهُۥ فِى ٱلْءَاخِرَةِ لَمِنَ ٱلصَّـٰلِحِينَ ۝

وَلُوطًا إِذْ قَالَ لِقَوْمِهِۦٓ إِنَّكُمْ لَتَأْتُونَ ٱلْفَـٰحِشَةَ مَا سَبَقَكُم بِهَا مِنْ أَحَدٍ مِّنَ ٱلْعَـٰلَمِينَ ۝

أَئِنَّكُمْ لَتَأْتُونَ ٱلرِّجَالَ وَتَقْطَعُونَ ٱلسَّبِيلَ وَتَأْتُونَ فِى نَادِيكُمُ ٱلْمُنكَرَ فَمَا كَانَ جَوَابَ قَوْمِهِۦٓ إِلَّآ أَن قَالُوا۟ ٱئْتِنَا بِعَذَابِ ٱللَّهِ إِن كُنتَ مِنَ ٱلصَّـٰدِقِينَ ۝

قَالَ رَبِّ ٱنصُرْنِى عَلَى ٱلْقَوْمِ ٱلْمُفْسِدِينَ ۝

وَلَمَّا جَآءَتْ رُسُلُنَآ إِبْرَٰهِيمَ بِٱلْبُشْرَىٰ قَالُوٓا۟ إِنَّا مُهْلِكُوٓا۟ أَهْلِ هَـٰذِهِ ٱلْقَرْيَةِ إِنَّ أَهْلَهَا كَانُوا۟ ظَـٰلِمِينَ ۝

---

3. That he was to have a son.

32 He said: Lo! Lot is there. They said: We are best aware of who is there. We are to deliver him and his household, all save his wife, who is of those who stay behind.

قَالَ إِنَّ فِيهَا لُوطًا قَالُوا نَحْنُ أَعْلَمُ بِمَن فِيهَا لَنُنَجِّيَنَّهُ وَأَهْلَهُ إِلَّا امْرَأَتَهُ كَانَتْ مِنَ الْغَابِرِينَ ﴿٣٢﴾

33 And when Our messengers came unto Lot, he was troubled upon their account, for he could not protect them; but they said: Fear not, nor grieve! Lo! we are to deliver thee and thy household, (all) save thy wife, who is of those who stay behind.

وَلَمَّا أَن جَاءَتْ رُسُلُنَا لُوطًا سِيءَ بِهِمْ وَضَاقَ بِهِمْ ذَرْعًا وَقَالُوا لَا تَخَفْ وَلَا تَحْزَنْ إِنَّا مُنَجُّوكَ وَأَهْلَكَ إِلَّا امْرَأَتَكَ كَانَتْ مِنَ الْغَابِرِينَ ﴿٣٣﴾

34 Lo! We are about to bring down upon folk of this township a fury from the sky because they are evil-livers.

إِنَّا مُنزِلُونَ عَلَى أَهْلِ هَذِهِ الْقَرْيَةِ رِجْزًا مِّنَ السَّمَاءِ بِمَا كَانُوا يَفْسُقُونَ ﴿٣٤﴾

35 And verily of that We have left a clear sign for people who have sense.

وَلَقَد تَّرَكْنَا مِنْهَا آيَةً بَيِّنَةً لِّقَوْمٍ يَعْقِلُونَ ﴿٣٥﴾

36 And unto Madyan We sent Shu'ayb, their brother. He said: O my people! Serve Allah, and look forward to the Last Day, and do not evil, making mischief, in the earth.

وَإِلَى مَدْيَنَ أَخَاهُمْ شُعَيْبًا فَقَالَ يَا قَوْمِ اعْبُدُوا اللَّهَ وَارْجُوا الْيَوْمَ الْآخِرَ وَلَا تَعْثَوْا فِي الْأَرْضِ مُفْسِدِينَ ﴿٣٦﴾

37 But they denied him, and the dreadful earthquake took them, and morning found them prostrate in their dwelling place.

فَكَذَّبُوهُ فَأَخَذَتْهُمُ الرَّجْفَةُ فَأَصْبَحُوا فِي دَارِهِمْ جَاثِمِينَ ﴿٣٧﴾

38 And (the tribes of) 'Ād and Thamūd! (Their fate) is manifest unto you from their (ruined and deserted) dwellings. Satan made their deeds seem fair unto them and so debarred them from the Way, though they were keen observers.

وَعَادًا وَثَمُودَ وَقَد تَّبَيَّنَ لَكُم مِّن مَّسَاكِنِهِمْ وَزَيَّنَ لَهُمُ الشَّيْطَانُ أَعْمَالَهُمْ فَصَدَّهُمْ عَنِ السَّبِيلِ وَكَانُوا مُسْتَبْصِرِينَ ﴿٣٨﴾

39 And Korah, Pharaoh and Hāmān!
Moses came unto them with clear
proofs (of Allah's sovereignty), but
they were boastful in the land. And
they were not winners (in the race).

وَقَٰرُونَ وَفِرْعَوْنَ وَهَٰمَٰنَ وَلَقَدْ جَآءَهُم
مُّوسَىٰ بِٱلْبَيِّنَٰتِ فَٱسْتَكْبَرُواْ فِى ٱلْأَرْضِ
وَمَا كَانُواْ سَٰبِقِينَ ﴿٣٩﴾

40 So We took each one in his sin;
of them was he on whom We sent a
hurricane, and of them was he who
was overtaken by the (Awful) Cry,
and of them was he whom We
caused the earth to swallow, and of
them was he whom We drowned. It
was not for Allah to wrong them,
but they wronged themselves.

فَكُلًّا أَخَذْنَا بِذَنۢبِهِۦ فَمِنْهُم مَّنْ أَرْسَلْنَا عَلَيْهِ
حَاصِبًا وَمِنْهُم مَّنْ أَخَذَتْهُ ٱلصَّيْحَةُ
وَمِنْهُم مَّنْ خَسَفْنَا بِهِ ٱلْأَرْضَ
وَمِنْهُم مَّنْ أَغْرَقْنَا وَمَا كَانَ ٱللَّهُ لِيَظْلِمَهُمْ
وَلَٰكِن كَانُوٓاْ أَنفُسَهُمْ يَظْلِمُونَ ﴿٤٠﴾

41 The likeness of those who
choose other patrons than Allah is
as the likeness of the spider when
she taketh unto herself a house, and
lo! the frailest of all houses is the
spider's house, if they but knew.

مَثَلُ ٱلَّذِينَ ٱتَّخَذُواْ مِن دُونِ ٱللَّهِ أَوْلِيَآءَ
كَمَثَلِ ٱلْعَنكَبُوتِ ٱتَّخَذَتْ بَيْتًا
وَإِنَّ أَوْهَنَ ٱلْبُيُوتِ لَبَيْتُ ٱلْعَنكَبُوتِ
لَوْ كَانُواْ يَعْلَمُونَ ﴿٤١﴾

42 Lo! Allah knoweth what thing
they invoke instead of Him. He is
the Mighty, the Wise.

إِنَّ ٱللَّهَ يَعْلَمُ مَا يَدْعُونَ مِن دُونِهِۦ مِن شَىْءٍ
وَهُوَ ٱلْعَزِيزُ ٱلْحَكِيمُ ﴿٤٢﴾

43 As for these similitudes, We coin
them for mankind, but none will
grasp their meaning save the wise.

وَتِلْكَ ٱلْأَمْثَٰلُ نَضْرِبُهَا لِلنَّاسِ
وَمَا يَعْقِلُهَآ إِلَّا ٱلْعَٰلِمُونَ ﴿٤٣﴾

44 Allah created the heavens and
the earth with truth. Lo! therein is
indeed a portent for believers.

خَلَقَ ٱللَّهُ ٱلسَّمَٰوَٰتِ وَٱلْأَرْضَ بِٱلْحَقِّ
إِنَّ فِى ذَٰلِكَ لَءَايَةً لِّلْمُؤْمِنِينَ ﴿٤٤﴾

45 Recite that which hath been
inspired in thee of the Scripture, and
establish worship. Lo! worship pre-
serveth from lewdness and iniquity,
but verily remembrance of Allah is
more important. And Allah knoweth
what ye do.

ٱتْلُ مَآ أُوحِىَ إِلَيْكَ مِنَ ٱلْكِتَٰبِ وَأَقِمِ ٱلصَّلَوٰةَ
إِنَّ ٱلصَّلَوٰةَ تَنْهَىٰ عَنِ ٱلْفَحْشَآءِ
وَٱلْمُنكَرِ وَلَذِكْرُ ٱللَّهِ أَكْبَرُ وَٱللَّهُ
يَعْلَمُ مَا تَصْنَعُونَ ﴿٤٥﴾

46 And argue not with the People of the Scripture unless it be in (a way) that is better, save with such of them as do wrong; and say: We believe in that which hath been revealed unto us and revealed unto you; our God and your God is One, and unto Him we surrender.

﴿ وَلَا تُجَـٰدِلُوٓا أَهْلَ ٱلْكِتَـٰبِ إِلَّا بِٱلَّتِى هِىَ أَحْسَنُ إِلَّا ٱلَّذِينَ ظَلَمُوا مِنْهُمْ وَقُولُوٓا ءَامَنَّا بِٱلَّذِىٓ أُنزِلَ إِلَيْنَا وَأُنزِلَ إِلَيْكُمْ وَإِلَـٰهُنَا وَإِلَـٰهُكُمْ وَٰحِدٌ وَنَحْنُ لَهُۥ مُسْلِمُونَ ﴿٤٦﴾

47 In like manner We have revealed unto thee the Scripture, and those unto whom We gave the Scripture aforetime will believe therein; and of these (also)[4] there are some who believe therein. And none deny our revelations save the disbelievers.

وَكَذَٰلِكَ أَنزَلْنَآ إِلَيْكَ ٱلْكِتَـٰبَ فَٱلَّذِينَ ءَاتَيْنَـٰهُمُ ٱلْكِتَـٰبَ يُؤْمِنُونَ بِهِۦ وَمِنْ هَـٰٓؤُلَآءِ مَن يُؤْمِنُ بِهِۦ وَمَا يَجْحَدُ بِـَٔايَـٰتِنَآ إِلَّا ٱلْكَـٰفِرُونَ ﴿٤٧﴾

48 And thou (O Muhammad) wast not a reader of any scripture before it, nor didst thou write it with thy right hand, for then might those have doubted, who follow falsehood.

وَمَا كُنتَ تَتْلُوا۟ مِن قَبْلِهِۦ مِن كِتَـٰبٍ وَلَا تَخُطُّهُۥ بِيَمِينِكَ إِذًا لَّٱرْتَابَ ٱلْمُبْطِلُونَ ﴿٤٨﴾

49 But it is clear revelations in the hearts of those who have been given knowledge, and none deny our revelations save wrong-doers.

بَلْ هُوَ ءَايَـٰتٌ بَيِّنَـٰتٌ فِى صُدُورِ ٱلَّذِينَ أُوتُوا۟ ٱلْعِلْمَ وَمَا يَجْحَدُ بِـَٔايَـٰتِنَآ إِلَّا ٱلظَّـٰلِمُونَ ﴿٤٩﴾

50 And they say: Why are not portents sent down upon him from his Lord? Say: Portents are with Allah only, and I am but a plain warner.

وَقَالُوا۟ لَوْلَآ أُنزِلَ عَلَيْهِ ءَايَـٰتٌ مِّن رَّبِّهِۦ قُلْ إِنَّمَا ٱلْـَٔايَـٰتُ عِندَ ٱللَّهِ وَإِنَّمَآ أَنَا۠ نَذِيرٌ مُّبِينٌ ﴿٥٠﴾

51 Is it not enough for them that We have sent down unto thee the Scripture which is read unto them? Lo! herein verily is mercy, and a reminder for folk who believe.

أَوَلَمْ يَكْفِهِمْ أَنَّآ أَنزَلْنَا عَلَيْكَ ٱلْكِتَـٰبَ يُتْلَىٰ عَلَيْهِمْ إِنَّ فِى ذَٰلِكَ لَرَحْمَةً وَذِكْرَىٰ لِقَوْمٍ يُؤْمِنُونَ ﴿٥١﴾

---

4. *i.e.* the people of Makkah.

52 Say (unto them, O Muhammad): Allah sufficeth for witness between me and you. He knoweth whatsoever is in the heavens and the earth. And those who believe in vanity and disbelieve in Allah, they it is who are the losers.

قُلْ كَفَىٰ بِاللَّهِ بَيْنِي وَبَيْنَكُمْ شَهِيدًا يَعْلَمُ مَا فِي السَّمَٰوَٰتِ وَالْأَرْضِ وَالَّذِينَ ءَامَنُوا بِالْبَٰطِلِ وَكَفَرُوا بِاللَّهِ أُو۟لَٰٓئِكَ هُمُ الْخَٰسِرُونَ ۝

53 They bid thee hasten on the doom (of Allah). And if a term had not been appointed, the doom would assuredly have come unto them (ere now). And verily it will come upon them suddenly when they perceive not.

وَيَسْتَعْجِلُونَكَ بِالْعَذَابِ وَلَوْلَآ أَجَلٌ مُّسَمًّى لَّجَآءَهُمُ الْعَذَابُ وَلَيَأْتِيَنَّهُم بَغْتَةً وَهُمْ لَا يَشْعُرُونَ ۝

54 They bid thee hasten on the doom, when lo! hell verily will encompass the disbelievers.

يَسْتَعْجِلُونَكَ بِالْعَذَابِ وَإِنَّ جَهَنَّمَ لَمُحِيطَةٌۢ بِالْكَٰفِرِينَ ۝

55 On the day when the doom will overwhelm them from above them and from underneath their feet, and He will say: Taste what ye used to do!

يَوْمَ يَغْشَٰهُمُ الْعَذَابُ مِن فَوْقِهِمْ وَمِن تَحْتِ أَرْجُلِهِمْ وَيَقُولُ ذُوقُوا مَا كُنتُمْ تَعْمَلُونَ ۝

56 O my bondmen who believe! Lo! My earth is spacious. Therefore serve Me only.

يَٰعِبَادِيَ الَّذِينَ ءَامَنُوٓا إِنَّ أَرْضِي وَٰسِعَةٌ فَإِيَّٰيَ فَاعْبُدُونِ ۝

57 Every soul will taste of death. Then unto Us ye will be returned.

كُلُّ نَفْسٍ ذَآئِقَةُ الْمَوْتِ ثُمَّ إِلَيْنَا تُرْجَعُونَ ۝

58 Those who believe and do good works, them verily We shall house in lofty dwellings of the Garden underneath which rivers flow. There they will dwell secure. How sweet the guerdon of the toilers;

وَالَّذِينَ ءَامَنُوا وَعَمِلُوا الصَّٰلِحَٰتِ لَنُبَوِّئَنَّهُم مِّنَ الْجَنَّةِ غُرَفًا تَجْرِي مِن تَحْتِهَا الْأَنْهَٰرُ خَٰلِدِينَ فِيهَا نِعْمَ أَجْرُ الْعَٰمِلِينَ ۝

59 Who persevere, and put their trust in their Lord!

الَّذِينَ صَبَرُوا وَعَلَىٰ رَبِّهِمْ يَتَوَكَّلُونَ ۝

60 And how many an animal there is that beareth not its own provision! Allah provideth for it and for you. He is the Hearer, the Knower.

وَكَأَيِّن مِّن دَآبَّةٍ لَّا تَحۡمِلُ رِزۡقَهَا ٱللَّهُ يَرۡزُقُهَا وَإِيَّاكُمۡ وَهُوَ ٱلسَّمِيعُ ٱلۡعَلِيمُ ٦٠

61 And if thou wert to ask them: Who created the heavens and the earth, and constrained the sun and the moon (to their appointed work)? they would say: Allah. How then are they turned away?

وَلَئِن سَأَلۡتَهُم مَّنۡ خَلَقَ ٱلسَّمَٰوَٰتِ وَٱلۡأَرۡضَ وَسَخَّرَ ٱلشَّمۡسَ وَٱلۡقَمَرَ لَيَقُولُنَّ ٱللَّهُ فَأَنَّىٰ يُؤۡفَكُونَ ٦١

62 Allah maketh the provision wide for whom He will of His bondmen, and straiteneth it for whom (He will). Lo! Allah is Aware of all things.

ٱللَّهُ يَبۡسُطُ ٱلرِّزۡقَ لِمَن يَشَآءُ مِنۡ عِبَادِهِۦ وَيَقۡدِرُ لَهُۥٓ إِنَّ ٱللَّهَ بِكُلِّ شَيۡءٍ عَلِيمٌ ٦٢

63 And if thou wert to ask them: Who causeth water to come down from the sky, and therewith reviveth the earth after its death? they verily would say: Allah. Say: Praise be to Allah! But most of them have no sense.

وَلَئِن سَأَلۡتَهُم مَّن نَّزَّلَ مِنَ ٱلسَّمَآءِ مَآءً فَأَحۡيَا بِهِ ٱلۡأَرۡضَ مِنۢ بَعۡدِ مَوۡتِهَا لَيَقُولُنَّ ٱللَّهُ قُلِ ٱلۡحَمۡدُ لِلَّهِ بَلۡ أَكۡثَرُهُمۡ لَا يَعۡقِلُونَ ٦٣

64 This life of the world is but a pastime and a game. Lo! the home of the Hereafter; that is Life, if they but knew.

وَمَا هَٰذِهِ ٱلۡحَيَوٰةُ ٱلدُّنۡيَآ إِلَّا لَهۡوٌ وَلَعِبٌ وَإِنَّ ٱلدَّارَ ٱلۡأٓخِرَةَ لَهِيَ ٱلۡحَيَوَانُ لَوۡ كَانُوا۟ يَعۡلَمُونَ ٦٤

65 And when they mount upon the ships they pray to Allah, making their faith pure for Him only, but when He bringeth them safe to land, behold! they ascribe partners (unto Him);

فَإِذَا رَكِبُوا۟ فِى ٱلۡفُلۡكِ دَعَوُا۟ ٱللَّهَ مُخۡلِصِينَ لَهُ ٱلدِّينَ فَلَمَّا نَجَّىٰهُمۡ إِلَى ٱلۡبَرِّ إِذَا هُمۡ يُشۡرِكُونَ ٦٥

66 That they may be ungrateful for what We have given them and that they may enjoy it. But they will come to know.

لِيَكۡفُرُوا۟ بِمَآ ءَاتَيۡنَٰهُمۡ وَلِيَتَمَتَّعُوا۟ فَسَوۡفَ يَعۡلَمُونَ ٦٦

67 Have they not seen that We
have appointed a sanctuary immune
(from violence),[5] while mankind are
ravaged all around them? Do they
then believe in falsehood and disbelieve in the bounty of Allah?

أَوَلَمْ يَرَوْا أَنَّا جَعَلْنَا حَرَمًا آمِنًا وَيُتَخَطَّفُ
النَّاسُ مِنْ حَوْلِهِمْ أَفَبِالْبَاطِلِ يُؤْمِنُونَ
وَبِنِعْمَةِ اللَّهِ يَكْفُرُونَ ﴿٦٧﴾

68 Who doeth greater wrong than
he who inventeth a lie concerning
Allah, or denieth the truth when it
cometh unto him? Is not there a
home in hell for disbelievers?

وَمَنْ أَظْلَمُ مِمَّنِ افْتَرَىٰ عَلَى اللَّهِ كَذِبًا أَوْ كَذَّبَ
بِالْحَقِّ لَمَّا جَاءَهُ أَلَيْسَ فِي جَهَنَّمَ مَثْوًى
لِلْكَافِرِينَ ﴿٦٨﴾

69 As for those who strive in Us,
We surely guide them to Our paths,
and lo! Allah is with the good.

وَالَّذِينَ جَاهَدُوا فِينَا لَنَهْدِيَنَّهُمْ سُبُلَنَا
وَإِنَّ اللَّهَ لَمَعَ الْمُحْسِنِينَ ﴿٦٩﴾

---

5. The territory of Makkah.

Ar Rūm
(The Romans)

Ar Rūm, "The Romans," takes its name from a word in the first verse.

The armies of the Eastern Roman Empire had been defeated by the Persians in all the territories near Arabia. In the year A.D. 613 Jerusalem and Damascus fell, and in the following year Egypt. A Persian army invaded Anatolia and was threatening Constantinople itself in the year A.D. 615 or 616 (the sixth or seventh year before the Hijrah) when, according to the best authorities, this sūrah was revealed at Makkah. The pagan Arabs triumphed in the news of Persian victories over the Romans, because the Christian Romans were believers in the One God, whereas the Persians were not. They argued that the power of Allah could not be supreme and absolute, as the Prophet kept proclaiming it to be, since the forces of a pagan empire had been able to defeat His worshippers.

The Prophet's answer was provided for him in this grand assertion of Theocracy, which shows the folly of all those who think of Allah as a partisan. It opens with two prophecies: that the Romans would be victorious over the Persians, and that the little persecuted company of Muslims in Arabia would have reason to rejoice, "within ten years."[1] In fact, in A.D. 624 the Roman armies entered purely Persian territory, and in the same year a little army of Muslims, led by the Prophet, overthrew the flower of Arab chivalry upon the field of Badr.

But the prophecies are only the prelude to a proclamation of God's universal kingdom, which is shown to be an actual Sovereignty. The laws of nature are expounded as the laws of Allah in the physical sphere, and in the moral and political spheres mankind is informed that there are similar laws of life and death, of good and evil, action and inaction, and their consequences—laws which no one can escape by

---

1. The word in the Arabic (*biḍ'un*) implies a space of not less than three, and not more than nine, years.

wisdom or by cunning. His mercy, like His law, surrounds all things, and the standard of His judgment is the same for all. He is not remote or indifferent, partial or capricious. Those who do good earn His favour, and those who do ill earn His wrath, no matter what may be their creed or race; and no one, by the lip profession of a creed, is able to escape His law of consequences.

It belongs to the middle group of Makkan sūrahs.

سُوْرَةُ الرُّوْمِ

In the name of Allah, the Beneficent, the Merciful.   بِسْمِ اللهِ الرَّحْمٰنِ الرَّحِيْمِ

1   Alif. Lām. Mīm.[2]   الٓمّٓ ۚ ١

2   The Romans have been defeated;   غُلِبَتِ الرُّوْمُ ۙ ٢

3   In the nearer land, and they, after their defeat will be victorious

فِىٓ أَدْنَى الْأَرْضِ وَهُمْ مِّنْ بَعْدِ غَلَبِهِمْ

سَيَغْلِبُوْنَ ۙ ٣

4   In a few (less then ten) years; Allah's is the command in the former case and in the latter; and in that day believers will rejoice;

فِىْ بِضْعِ سِنِيْنَ ۗ لِلّٰهِ الْأَمْرُ مِنْ قَبْلُ وَمِنْ بَعْدُ ۚ

وَيَوْمَئِذٍ يَّفْرَحُ الْمُؤْمِنُوْنَ ۙ ٤

5   In Allah's help to victory. He helpeth to victory whom He will. He is the Mighty, the Merciful.

بِنَصْرِ اللهِ ۗ يَنْصُرُ مَنْ يَّشَاءُ ۗ وَهُوَ الْعَزِيْزُ

الرَّحِيْمُ ٥

6   It is a promise of Allah. Allah faileth not His promise, but most of mankind know not.

وَعْدَ اللهِ ۗ لَا يُخْلِفُ اللهُ وَعْدَهُ وَلٰكِنَّ أَكْثَرَ النَّاسِ

لَا يَعْلَمُوْنَ ٦

---

2. See Sūrah 2, v. 1, footnote.

7 They know only some appearance of the life of the world, and are heedless of the Hereafter.

يَعْلَمُونَ ظَاهِرًا مِّنَ الْحَيَوةِ الدُّنْيَا وَهُمْ عَنِ الْأَخِرَةِ هُمْ غَفِلُونَ ۝

8 Have they not pondered upon themselves? Allah created not the heavens and the earth, and that which is between them, save with truth and for a destined end. But truly many of mankind are disbelievers in the meeting with their Lord.

أَوَلَمْ يَتَفَكَّرُوا فِي أَنْفُسِهِمْ مَا خَلَقَ اللّٰهُ السَّمٰوٰتِ وَالْأَرْضَ وَمَا بَيْنَهُمَا إِلَّا بِالْحَقِّ وَأَجَلٍ مُّسَمًّى وَإِنَّ كَثِيرًا مِّنَ النَّاسِ بِلِقَآيِ رَبِّهِمْ لَكٰفِرُونَ ۝

9 Have they not travelled in the land and seen the nature of the consequence for those who were before them?[3] They were stronger than these in power, and they dug the earth and built upon it more than these have built. Messengers of their own came unto them with clear proofs (of Allah's Sovereignty). Surely Allah wronged them not, but they did wrong themselves.

أَوَلَمْ يَسِيرُوا فِي الْأَرْضِ فَيَنْظُرُوا كَيْفَ كَانَ عَاقِبَةُ الَّذِينَ مِنْ قَبْلِهِمْ كَانُوا أَشَدَّ مِنْهُمْ قُوَّةً وَأَثَارُوا الْأَرْضَ وَعَمَرُوهَا أَكْثَرَ مِمَّا عَمَرُوهَا وَجَآءَتْهُمْ رُسُلُهُمْ بِالْبَيِّنٰتِ فَمَا كَانَ اللّٰهُ لِيَظْلِمَهُمْ وَلٰكِنْ كَانُوا أَنْفُسَهُمْ يَظْلِمُونَ ۝

10 Then evil was the consequence to those who dealt in evil, because they denied the revelations of Allah and made a mock of them.

ثُمَّ كَانَ عَاقِبَةَ الَّذِينَ أَسَاءُوا السُّوأَى أَنْ كَذَّبُوا بِآيٰتِ اللّٰهِ وَكَانُوا بِهَا يَسْتَهْزِءُونَ ۝

11 Allah produceth creation, then He reproduceth it, then unto Him ye will be returned.

اَللّٰهُ يَبْدَؤُا الْخَلْقَ ثُمَّ يُعِيدُهُ ثُمَّ إِلَيْهِ تُرْجَعُونَ ۝

12 And in the day when the Hour riseth the unrighteous will despair.

وَيَوْمَ تَقُومُ السَّاعَةُ يُبْلِسُ الْمُجْرِمُونَ ۝

---

3. To those who journeyed out from Makkah, northward into Mesopotamia and Syria, or southward to the Yaman and Haḍramaut, appeared the ruins of the old civilisation which, tradition said, had been destroyed on account of their corruption and disobedience to the will of God.

13 There will be none to intercede for them of those whom they made equal with Allah. And they will reject their partners (whom they ascribed unto Him).

وَلَمْ يَكُن لَّهُم مِّن شُرَكَآئِهِمْ شُفَعَـٰٓؤُاْ وَكَانُواْ بِشُرَكَآئِهِمْ كَـٰفِرِينَ ۝

14 In the day when the Hour cometh, in that day they will be sundered.

وَيَوْمَ تَقُومُ ٱلسَّاعَةُ يَوْمَئِذٍ يَتَفَرَّقُونَ ۝

15 As for those who believed and did good works, they will be made happy in a Garden.

فَأَمَّا ٱلَّذِينَ ءَامَنُواْ وَعَمِلُواْ ٱلصَّـٰلِحَـٰتِ فَهُمْ فِى رَوْضَةٍ يُحْبَرُونَ ۝

16 But as for those who disbelieved and denied Our revelations, and denied the meeting of the Hereafter, such will be brought to doom.

وَأَمَّا ٱلَّذِينَ كَفَرُواْ وَكَذَّبُواْ بِـَٔايَـٰتِنَا وَلِقَآئِ ٱلْأٓخِرَةِ فَأُوْلَـٰٓئِكَ فِى ٱلْعَذَابِ مُحْضَرُونَ ۝

17 So glory be to Allah when ye enter the night and when ye enter the morning;

فَسُبْحَـٰنَ ٱللَّهِ حِينَ تُمْسُونَ وَحِينَ تُصْبِحُونَ ۝

18 Unto Him be praise in the heavens and the earth!—and at the sun's decline and in the noonday.

وَلَهُ ٱلْحَمْدُ فِى ٱلسَّمَـٰوَٰتِ وَٱلْأَرْضِ وَعَشِيًّا وَحِينَ تُظْهِرُونَ ۝

19 He bringeth forth the living from the dead, and He bringeth forth the dead from the living, and He reviveth the earth after her death. And even so will ye be brought forth.

يُخْرِجُ ٱلْحَىَّ مِنَ ٱلْمَيِّتِ وَيُخْرِجُ ٱلْمَيِّتَ مِنَ ٱلْحَىِّ وَيُحْىِ ٱلْأَرْضَ بَعْدَ مَوْتِهَا وَكَذَٰلِكَ تُخْرَجُونَ ۝

20 And of His signs is this: He created you of dust, and behold you human beings, ranging widely!

وَمِنْ ءَايَـٰتِهِۦٓ أَنْ خَلَقَكُم مِّن تُرَابٍ ثُمَّ إِذَآ أَنتُم بَشَرٌ تَنتَشِرُونَ ۝

21 And of His signs is this: He created for you helpmeets from yourselves that ye might find rest in them, and He ordained between you

وَمِنْ ءَايَـٰتِهِۦٓ أَنْ خَلَقَ لَكُم مِّنْ أَنفُسِكُمْ أَزْوَٰجًا لِّتَسْكُنُوٓاْ إِلَيْهَا وَجَعَلَ بَيْنَكُم مَّوَدَّةً وَرَحْمَةً

love and mercy. Lo, herein indeed
are portents for folk who reflect.

إِنَّ فِى ذَٰلِكَ لَأَيَٰتٍ لِّقَوۡمٍ يَتَفَكَّرُونَ ۝

22 And of His signs is the creation
of the heavens and the earth, and
the difference of your languages
and colours. Lo! herein indeed are
portents for men of knowledge.

وَمِنۡ ءَايَٰتِهِۦ خَلۡقُ ٱلسَّمَٰوَٰتِ وَٱلۡأَرۡضِ وَٱخۡتِلَٰفُ
أَلۡسِنَتِكُمۡ وَأَلۡوَٰنِكُمۡ إِنَّ فِى ذَٰلِكَ
لَأَيَٰتٍ لِّلۡعَٰلِمِينَ ۝

23 And of His signs is your slumber by night and by day, and your
seeking of His bounty. Lo! herein
indeed are portents for folk who
heed.

وَمِنۡ ءَايَٰتِهِۦ مَنَامُكُم بِٱلَّيۡلِ وَٱلنَّهَارِ وَٱبۡتِغَآؤُكُم
مِّن فَضۡلِهِۦٓ إِنَّ فِى ذَٰلِكَ لَأَيَٰتٍ
لِّقَوۡمٍ يَسۡمَعُونَ ۝

24 And of His signs is this: He
showeth you the lightning for a fear
and for a hope, and sendeth down
water from the sky, and thereby
quickeneth the earth after her death.
Lo! herein indeed are portents for
folk who understand.

وَمِنۡ ءَايَٰتِهِۦ يُرِيكُمُ ٱلۡبَرۡقَ خَوۡفًا وَطَمَعًا
وَيُنَزِّلُ مِنَ ٱلسَّمَآءِ مَآءً فَيُحۡىِۦ بِهِ ٱلۡأَرۡضَ
بَعۡدَ مَوۡتِهَآ إِنَّ فِى ذَٰلِكَ لَأَيَٰتٍ لِّقَوۡمٍ
يَعۡقِلُونَ ۝

25 And of His signs is this: The
heavens and the earth stand fast by
His command, and afterward, when
He calleth you, lo! from the earth
ye will emerge.

وَمِنۡ ءَايَٰتِهِۦٓ أَن تَقُومَ ٱلسَّمَآءُ وَٱلۡأَرۡضُ بِأَمۡرِهِۦ
ثُمَّ إِذَا دَعَاكُمۡ دَعۡوَةً مِّنَ ٱلۡأَرۡضِ إِذَآ أَنتُمۡ تَخۡرُجُونَ ۝

26 Unto Him belongeth whosoever
is in the heavens and in the earth.
All are obedient unto Him.

وَلَهُۥ مَن فِى ٱلسَّمَٰوَٰتِ وَٱلۡأَرۡضِ
كُلٌّ لَّهُۥ قَٰنِتُونَ ۝

27 He it is who produceth creation,
then reproduceth it, and it is easier
for Him. His is the Sublime Similitude in the heavens and in the earth.
He is the Mighty, the Wise.

وَهُوَ ٱلَّذِى يَبۡدَؤُاْ ٱلۡخَلۡقَ ثُمَّ يُعِيدُهُۥ وَهُوَ أَهۡوَنُ
عَلَيۡهِ وَلَهُ ٱلۡمَثَلُ ٱلۡأَعۡلَىٰ فِى ٱلسَّمَٰوَٰتِ وَٱلۡأَرۡضِ
وَهُوَ ٱلۡعَزِيزُ ٱلۡحَكِيمُ ۝

28 He coineth for you a similitude
of yourselves. Have ye, from among
those whom your right hands pos-

ضَرَبَ لَكُم مَّثَلًا مِّنۡ أَنفُسِكُمۡ هَل لَّكُم
مِّن مَّا مَلَكَتۡ أَيۡمَٰنُكُم مِّن شُرَكَآءَ

sess,[4] partners in the wealth We have bestowed upon you, equal with you in respect thereof, so that ye fear them as ye fear each other (that ye ascribe unto Us partners out of that which We created)? Thus We display the revelations for people who have sense.

29 Nay, but those who do wrong follow their own lusts without knowledge. Who is able to guide him whom Allah hath sent astray? For such there are no helpers.

30 So set thy purpose (O Muhammad) for religion as a man by nature upright—the nature (framed) of Allah, in which He hath created man. There is no altering (the laws of) Allah's creation. That is the right religion, but most men know not;

31 Turning unto Him (only); and be careful of your duty unto Him, and establish worship, and be not of those who ascribe partners (unto Him);

32 Of those who split up their religion and became schismatics, each sect exulting in what they have.

33 And when harm toucheth men they cry unto their Lord, turning to Him in repentance; then, when they

في مَا رَزَقْنَـٰكُمْ فَأَنتُمْ فِيهِ سَوَآءٌ تَخَافُونَهُمْ كَخِيفَتِكُمْ أَنفُسَكُمْ كَذَٰلِكَ نُفَصِّلُ ٱلْأَيَٰتِ لِقَوْمٍ يَعْقِلُونَ ﴿٢٨﴾

بَلِ ٱتَّبَعَ ٱلَّذِينَ ظَلَمُوٓاْ أَهْوَآءَهُم بِغَيْرِ عِلْمٍ فَمَن يَهْدِى مَنْ أَضَلَّ ٱللَّهُ وَمَا لَهُم مِّن نَّٰصِرِينَ ﴿٢٩﴾

فَأَقِمْ وَجْهَكَ لِلدِّينِ حَنِيفًا فِطْرَتَ ٱللَّهِ ٱلَّتِى فَطَرَ ٱلنَّاسَ عَلَيْهَا لَا تَبْدِيلَ لِخَلْقِ ٱللَّهِ ذَٰلِكَ ٱلدِّينُ ٱلْقَيِّمُ وَلَٰكِنَّ أَكْثَرَ ٱلنَّاسِ لَا يَعْلَمُونَ ﴿٣٠﴾

۞ مُنِيبِينَ إِلَيْهِ وَٱتَّقُوهُ وَأَقِيمُواْ ٱلصَّلَوٰةَ وَلَا تَكُونُواْ مِنَ ٱلْمُشْرِكِينَ ﴿٣١﴾

مِنَ ٱلَّذِينَ فَرَّقُواْ دِينَهُمْ وَكَانُواْ شِيَعًا كُلُّ حِزْبٍ بِمَا لَدَيْهِمْ فَرِحُونَ ﴿٣٢﴾

وَإِذَا مَسَّ ٱلنَّاسَ ضُرٌّ دَعَوْاْ رَبَّهُم مُّنِيبِينَ إِلَيْهِ

---

4. *i.e.* the slaves.

have tasted of His mercy, behold! some of them attribute partners to their Lord.

34 So as to disbelieve in that which We have given them. (Unto such it is said): Enjoy yourselves awhile, but ye will come to know.

35 Or have We revealed unto them any warrant which speaketh of that which they associate with Him?

36 And when We cause mankind to taste of mercy they rejoice therein; but if an evil thing befall them as the consequence of their own deeds, lo! they are in despair!

37 See they not that Allah enlargeth the provision for whom He will, and straiteneth (it for whom He will). Lo! herein indeed are portents for folk who believe.

38 So give to the kinsman his due, and to the needy, and to the way-farer. That is best for those who seek Allah's countenance. And such are they who are successful.

39 That which ye give in usury in order that it may increase on (other) people's property hath no increase with Allah; but that which ye give in charity, seeking Allah's coun-tenance, hath increase manifold.

40 Allah is He Who created you and then sustained you, then causeth you to die, then giveth life to you again. Is there any of your (so called) partners (of Allah) that doeth

من ذَٰلِكُم مِّن شَىْءٍ سُبْحَٰنَهُۥ وَتَعَٰلَىٰ
عَمَّا يُشْرِكُونَ ﴿٤٠﴾

aught of that? Praised and exalted be He above what they associate (with Him)!

ظَهَرَ الْفَسَادُ فِى الْبَرِّ وَالْبَحْرِ بِمَا كَسَبَتْ
أَيْدِى النَّاسِ لِيُذِيقَهُم بَعْضَ الَّذِى عَمِلُوا۟
لَعَلَّهُمْ يَرْجِعُونَ ﴿٤١﴾

41 Corruption doth appear on land and sea because of (the evil) which men's hands have done, that He may make them taste a part of that which they have done, in order that they may return.

قُلْ سِيرُوا۟ فِى الْأَرْضِ فَانظُرُوا۟ كَيْفَ كَانَ عَٰقِبَةُ
الَّذِينَ مِن قَبْلُ ۚ كَانَ أَكْثَرُهُم مُّشْرِكِينَ ﴿٤٢﴾

42 Say (O Muhammad, to the disbelievers): Travel in the land, and see the nature of the consequence for those who were before you! Most of them were idolaters.

فَأَقِمْ وَجْهَكَ لِلدِّينِ الْقَيِّمِ مِن قَبْلِ أَن يَأْتِىَ
يَوْمٌ لَّا مَرَدَّ لَهُۥ مِنَ اللَّهِ ۖ يَوْمَئِذٍ يَصَّدَّعُونَ ﴿٤٣﴾

43 So set thy purpose resolutely for the right religion, before the inevitable day cometh from Allah. On that day mankind will be sundered;

مَن كَفَرَ فَعَلَيْهِ كُفْرُهُۥ ۖ وَمَنْ عَمِلَ صَٰلِحًا
فَلِأَنفُسِهِمْ يَمْهَدُونَ ﴿٤٤﴾

44 Whoso disbelieveth must (then) bear the consequences of his disbelief, while those who do right make provision for themselves;

لِيَجْزِىَ الَّذِينَ ءَامَنُوا۟ وَعَمِلُوا۟ الصَّٰلِحَٰتِ
مِن فَضْلِهِۦٓ ۚ إِنَّهُۥ لَا يُحِبُّ الْكَٰفِرِينَ ﴿٤٥﴾

45 That He may reward out of His bounty those who believe and do good works. Lo! He loveth not the disbelievers (in His guidance).

وَمِنْ ءَايَٰتِهِۦٓ أَن يُرْسِلَ الرِّيَاحَ مُبَشِّرَٰتٍ وَلِيُذِيقَكُم
مِّن رَّحْمَتِهِۦ وَلِتَجْرِىَ الْفُلْكُ بِأَمْرِهِۦ
وَلِتَبْتَغُوا۟ مِن فَضْلِهِۦ وَلَعَلَّكُمْ تَشْكُرُونَ ﴿٤٦﴾

46 And of His signs is this: He sendeth herald winds to make you taste His mercy, and that the ships may sail at His command, and that ye may seek His favour, and that haply ye may be thankful.

وَلَقَدْ أَرْسَلْنَا مِن قَبْلِكَ رُسُلًا إِلَىٰ قَوْمِهِمْ فَجَآءُوهُم وَهُم

47 Verily We sent before thee (Muhammad) messengers to their

own folk. They brought them clear proofs (of Allah's Sovereignty). Then We took vengeance upon those who were guilty (in regard to them). To help believers is incumbent upon Us.

48 Allah is He who sendeth the winds so that they raise clouds, and spreadeth them along the sky as pleaseth Him, and causeth them to break and thou seest the rain down-pouring from within them. And when He maketh it to fall on whom He will of His bondmen, lo! they rejoice;

49 Though before that, even before it was sent down upon them, they were in despair.

50 Look, therefore, at the prints of Allah's mercy (in creation): how He quickeneth the earth after her death. Lo! He verily is the Quickener of the Dead, and He is Able to do all things.

51 And if We sent a wind and they beheld it yellow; they verily would still continue in their disbelief.

52 For verily thou (Muhammad) canst not make the dead to hear, nor canst thou make the deaf to hear the call when they have turned to flee.

53 Nor canst thou guide the blind out of their error. Thou canst make none to hear save those who believe in Our revelations so that they surrender (unto Him).

بِالْبَيِّنَٰتِ فَانتَقَمْنَا مِنَ ٱلَّذِينَ أَجْرَمُوا ۚ وَكَانَ حَقًّا عَلَيْنَا نَصْرُ ٱلْمُؤْمِنِينَ ﴿٤٧﴾

ٱللَّهُ ٱلَّذِى يُرْسِلُ ٱلرِّيَٰحَ فَتُثِيرُ سَحَابًا فَيَبْسُطُهُۥ فِى ٱلسَّمَآءِ كَيْفَ يَشَآءُ وَيَجْعَلُهُۥ كِسَفًا فَتَرَى ٱلْوَدْقَ يَخْرُجُ مِنْ خِلَٰلِهِۦ ۖ فَإِذَآ أَصَابَ بِهِۦ مَن يَشَآءُ مِنْ عِبَادِهِۦٓ إِذَا هُمْ يَسْتَبْشِرُونَ ﴿٤٨﴾

وَإِن كَانُوا۟ مِن قَبْلِ أَن يُنَزَّلَ عَلَيْهِم مِّن قَبْلِهِۦ لَمُبْلِسِينَ ﴿٤٩﴾

فَٱنظُرْ إِلَىٰٓ ءَاثَٰرِ رَحْمَتِ ٱللَّهِ كَيْفَ يُحْىِ ٱلْأَرْضَ بَعْدَ مَوْتِهَآ ۚ إِنَّ ذَٰلِكَ لَمُحْىِ ٱلْمَوْتَىٰ ۖ وَهُوَ عَلَىٰ كُلِّ شَىْءٍ قَدِيرٌ ﴿٥٠﴾

وَلَئِنْ أَرْسَلْنَا رِيحًا فَرَأَوْهُ مُصْفَرًّا لَّظَلُّوا۟ مِنۢ بَعْدِهِۦ يَكْفُرُونَ ﴿٥١﴾

فَإِنَّكَ لَا تُسْمِعُ ٱلْمَوْتَىٰ وَلَا تُسْمِعُ ٱلصُّمَّ ٱلدُّعَآءَ إِذَا وَلَّوْا۟ مُدْبِرِينَ ﴿٥٢﴾

وَمَآ أَنتَ بِهَٰدِ ٱلْعُمْىِ عَن ضَلَٰلَتِهِمْ ۖ إِن تُسْمِعُ إِلَّا مَن يُؤْمِنُ بِـَٔايَٰتِنَا فَهُم مُّسْلِمُونَ ﴿٥٣﴾

54 Allah is He who shaped you out of weakness, then appointed after weakness strength, then, after strength, appointed weakness and grey hair. He createth what He will. He is the Knower, the Mighty.

۞ اللّٰهُ الَّذِىْ خَلَقَكُمْ مِّنْ ضَعْفٍ ثُمَّ جَعَلَ مِنْ بَعْدِ ضَعْفٍ قُوَّةً ثُمَّ جَعَلَ مِنْ بَعْدِ قُوَّةٍ ضَعْفًا وَّشَيْبَةً ۚ يَخْلُقُ مَا يَشَآءُ ۚ وَهُوَ الْعَلِيْمُ الْقَدِيْرُ ﴿٥٤﴾

55 And on the day when the Hour riseth the guilty will vow that they did tarry but an hour—thus were they ever deceived.

وَيَوْمَ تَقُوْمُ السَّاعَةُ يُقْسِمُ الْمُجْرِمُوْنَ ۙ مَا لَبِثُوْا غَيْرَ سَاعَةٍ ۚ كَذٰلِكَ كَانُوْا يُؤْفَكُوْنَ ﴿٥٥﴾

56 But those to whom knowledge and faith are given will say: The truth is, ye have tarried, by Allah's decree, until the Day of Resurrection. This is the Day of Resurrection, but ye used not to know.

وَقَالَ الَّذِيْنَ أُوْتُوا الْعِلْمَ وَالْإِيْمَانَ لَقَدْ لَبِثْتُمْ فِىْ كِتٰبِ اللّٰهِ إِلٰى يَوْمِ الْبَعْثِ ۖ فَهٰذَا يَوْمُ الْبَعْثِ وَلٰكِنَّكُمْ كُنْتُمْ لَا تَعْلَمُوْنَ ﴿٥٦﴾

57 In that day their excuses will not profit those who did injustice, nor will they be allowed to make amends.

فَيَوْمَئِذٍ لَّا يَنْفَعُ الَّذِيْنَ ظَلَمُوْا مَعْذِرَتُهُمْ وَلَا هُمْ يُسْتَعْتَبُوْنَ ﴿٥٧﴾

58 Verily, We have coined for mankind in this Qur'an all kinds of similitudes; and indeed if thou camest unto them with a miracle, those who disbelieve would verily exclaim: Ye are but tricksters!

وَلَقَدْ ضَرَبْنَا لِلنَّاسِ فِىْ هٰذَا الْقُرْاٰنِ مِنْ كُلِّ مَثَلٍ ۚ وَلَئِنْ جِئْتَهُمْ بِاٰيَةٍ لَّيَقُوْلَنَّ الَّذِيْنَ كَفَرُوْا إِنْ أَنْتُمْ إِلَّا مُبْطِلُوْنَ ﴿٥٨﴾

59 Thus doth Allah seal the hearts of those who know not.

كَذٰلِكَ يَطْبَعُ اللّٰهُ عَلٰى قُلُوْبِ الَّذِيْنَ لَا يَعْلَمُوْنَ ﴿٥٩﴾

60 So have patience (O Muhammad)! Allah's promise is the very truth, and let not those who have no certainty make thee impatient.

فَاصْبِرْ إِنَّ وَعْدَ اللّٰهِ حَقٌّ ۖ وَّلَا يَسْتَخِفَّنَّكَ الَّذِيْنَ لَا يُوْقِنُوْنَ ﴿٦٠﴾

Luqmān

Luqmān takes its name from v. 12 ff., which contain mention of the wisdom of Luqmān, a sage whose memory the Arabs reverenced, but who is unknown to Jewish Scripture. He is said to have been a negro slave and the fables associated with his name are so like those of Aesop that the usual identification seems justified. The sūrah conveys assurance of success to the Muslims at a time of persecution.

It belongs to the middle or last group of Makkan sūrahs; except vv. 27 and 28 which were revealed at Al-Madīnah.

سُوۡرَةُ لُقۡمَان

In the name of Allah, the Beneficent, the Merciful.

بِسۡمِ ٱللَّهِ ٱلرَّحۡمَٰنِ ٱلرَّحِيمِ

1   Alif. Lām. Mīm.[1]

2   These are revelations of the wise Scripture;

3   A guidance and a mercy for the good;

4   Those who establish worship and pay the poor-due and have sure faith in the Hereafter.

5   Such have guidance from their Lord. Such are the successful.

6   And of mankind is he who payeth for mere pastime of discourse, that he may mislead from

الٓمٓ ۝

تِلۡكَ ءَايَٰتُ ٱلۡكِتَٰبِ ٱلۡحَكِيمِ ۝

هُدٗى وَرَحۡمَةٗ لِّلۡمُحۡسِنِينَ ۝

ٱلَّذِينَ يُقِيمُونَ ٱلصَّلَوٰةَ وَيُؤۡتُونَ ٱلزَّكَوٰةَ وَهُم بِٱلۡأٓخِرَةِ هُمۡ يُوقِنُونَ ۝

أُوْلَٰٓئِكَ عَلَىٰ هُدٗى مِّن رَّبِّهِمۡ وَأُوْلَٰٓئِكَ هُمُ ٱلۡمُفۡلِحُونَ ۝

وَمِنَ ٱلنَّاسِ مَن يَشۡتَرِي لَهۡوَ ٱلۡحَدِيثِ

---

1. See Sūrah 2, v. 1, footnote.

Allah's way without knowledge, and maketh it the butt of mockery. For such there is a shameful doom.

7 And when Our revelations are recited unto him, he turneth away in his pride as if he heard them not, as if there were a deafness in his ears. So give him tidings of a painful doom.

8 Lo! those who believe and do good works, for them are gardens of delight;

9 Wherein they will abide. It is a promise of Allah in truth. He is the Mighty, the Wise.

10 He hath created the heavens without supports that ye can see, and hath cast into the earth firm hills, so that it quake not with you; and He hath dispersed therein all kinds of beasts. And We send down water from the sky and We cause (plants) of every goodly kind to grow therein.

11 This is the Creation of Allah. Now show me that which those (ye worship) beside Him have created. Nay, but the wrong-doers are in error manifest!

12 And verily We gave Luqmān wisdom, saying: Give thanks unto Allah; and whosoever giveth thanks, he giveth thanks for (the good of) his soul. And whosoever refuseth. Lo! Allah is Absolute, Owner of Praise.

لِيُضِلَّ عَنْ سَبِيلِ اللّٰهِ بِغَيْرِ عِلْمٍ وَّيَتَّخِذَهَا هُزُوًا ۚ أُولٰٓئِكَ لَهُمْ عَذَابٌ مُّهِينٌ ۝

وَإِذَا تُتْلَىٰ عَلَيْهِ ءَايٰتُنَا وَلّٰى مُسْتَكْبِرًا كَأَنْ لَّمْ يَسْمَعْهَا كَأَنَّ فِىٓ أُذُنَيْهِ وَقْرًا ۖ فَبَشِّرْهُ بِعَذَابٍ أَلِيمٍ ۝

إِنَّ الَّذِينَ ءَامَنُوا وَعَمِلُوا الصّٰلِحٰتِ لَهُمْ جَنّٰتُ النَّعِيمِ ۝

خٰلِدِينَ فِيهَا ۖ وَعْدَ اللّٰهِ حَقًّا ۚ وَهُوَ الْعَزِيزُ الْحَكِيمُ ۝

خَلَقَ السَّمٰوٰتِ بِغَيْرِ عَمَدٍ تَرَوْنَهَا ۖ وَأَلْقَىٰ فِى الْأَرْضِ رَوَاسِىَ أَن تَمِيدَ بِكُمْ وَبَثَّ فِيهَا مِن كُلِّ دَابَّةٍ ۚ وَأَنزَلْنَا مِنَ السَّمَآءِ مَآءً فَأَنبَتْنَا فِيهَا مِن كُلِّ زَوْجٍ كَرِيمٍ ۝

هٰذَا خَلْقُ اللّٰهِ فَأَرُونِى مَاذَا خَلَقَ الَّذِينَ مِن دُونِهِ ۚ بَلِ الظّٰلِمُونَ فِى ضَلٰلٍ مُّبِينٍ ۝

وَلَقَدْ ءَاتَيْنَا لُقْمٰنَ الْحِكْمَةَ أَنِ اشْكُرْ لِلّٰهِ ۚ وَمَن يَشْكُرْ فَإِنَّمَا يَشْكُرُ لِنَفْسِهِ ۖ وَمَن كَفَرَ فَإِنَّ اللّٰهَ غَنِىٌّ حَمِيدٌ ۝

13 And (remember) when Luqmān said unto his son, when he was exhorting him: O my dear son! Ascribe no partners unto Allah. Lo! to ascribe partners (unto Him) is a tremendous wrong;

وَإِذْ قَالَ لُقْمَانُ لِابْنِهِ وَهُوَ يَعِظُهُ يَبُنَيَّ لَا تُشْرِكْ بِاللَّهِ إِنَّ الشِّرْكَ لَظُلْمٌ عَظِيمٌ ۝

14 And We have enjoined upon man concerning his parents—His mother beareth him in weakness upon weakness, and his weaning is in two years. Give thanks unto Me and unto thy parents. Unto Me is the journeying.

وَوَصَّيْنَا الْإِنْسَانَ بِوَالِدَيْهِ حَمَلَتْهُ أُمُّهُ وَهْنًا عَلَى وَهْنٍ وَفِصَالُهُ فِي عَامَيْنِ أَنِ اشْكُرْ لِي وَلِوَالِدَيْكَ إِلَيَّ الْمَصِيرُ ۝

15 But if they strive with thee to make thee ascribe unto Me as partner that of which thou hast no knowledge, then obey them not. Consort with them in the world kindly, and follow the path of him who repenteth unto Me. Then unto Me will be your return, and I shall tell you what ye used to do.

وَإِنْ جَاهَدَاكَ عَلَى أَنْ تُشْرِكَ بِي مَا لَيْسَ لَكَ بِهِ عِلْمٌ فَلَا تُطِعْهُمَا وَصَاحِبْهُمَا فِي الدُّنْيَا مَعْرُوفًا وَاتَّبِعْ سَبِيلَ مَنْ أَنَابَ إِلَيَّ ثُمَّ إِلَيَّ مَرْجِعُكُمْ فَأُنَبِّئُكُمْ بِمَا كُنْتُمْ تَعْمَلُونَ ۝

16 O my dear son! Lo! though it be but the weight of a grain of mustard seed, and though it be in a rock, or in the heavens, or in the earth, Allah will bring it forth. Lo! Allah is Subtile, Aware.

يَبُنَيَّ إِنَّهَا إِنْ تَكُ مِثْقَالَ حَبَّةٍ مِنْ خَرْدَلٍ فَتَكُنْ فِي صَخْرَةٍ أَوْ فِي السَّمَاوَاتِ أَوْ فِي الْأَرْضِ يَأْتِ بِهَا اللَّهُ إِنَّ اللَّهَ لَطِيفٌ خَبِيرٌ ۝

17 O my dear son! Establish worship and enjoin kindness and forbid iniquity, and persevere whatever may befall thee. Lo! that is an affair of great resolution.

يَبُنَيَّ أَقِمِ الصَّلَاةَ وَأْمُرْ بِالْمَعْرُوفِ وَانْهَ عَنِ الْمُنْكَرِ وَاصْبِرْ عَلَى مَا أَصَابَكَ إِنَّ ذَلِكَ مِنْ عَزْمِ الْأُمُورِ ۝

18 Turn not thy cheek in scorn toward folk, nor walk with pertness

وَلَا تُصَعِّرْ خَدَّكَ لِلنَّاسِ وَلَا تَمْشِ فِي الْأَرْضِ

in the land. Lo! Allah loveth not
each braggart boaster.

مَرَحًا إِنَّ اللّٰهَ لَا يُحِبُّ كُلَّ مُخْتَالٍ فَخُورٍ ۞

19 Be modest in thy bearing and
subdue thy voice. Lo! the harshest
of all voices is the voice of the ass.

وَاقْصِدْ فِي مَشْيِكَ وَاغْضُضْ مِنْ صَوْتِكَ
إِنَّ أَنْكَرَ الْأَصْوَاتِ لَصَوْتُ الْحَمِيرِ ۞

20 See ye not how Allah hath made
serviceable unto you whatsoever is
in the skies and whatsoever is in the
earth and hath loaded you with His
favours both without and within?
Yet of mankind is he who disputeth
concerning Allah, without knowledge or guidance or a Scripture
giving light.

أَلَمْ تَرَوْا أَنَّ اللّٰهَ سَخَّرَ لَكُمْ مَّا فِي السَّمٰوٰتِ وَمَا فِي الْأَرْضِ
وَأَسْبَغَ عَلَيْكُمْ نِعَمَهُ ظَاهِرَةً وَبَاطِنَةً وَمِنَ النَّاسِ
مَنْ يُّجَادِلُ فِي اللّٰهِ بِغَيْرِ عِلْمٍ وَلَا هُدًى
وَلَا كِتٰبٍ مُّنِيرٍ ۞

21 And if it be said unto them:
Follow that which Allah hath revealed, they say: Nay, but we follow
that wherein we found our fathers.
What! Even though the devil were
inviting them unto the doom of
flame?

وَإِذَا قِيلَ لَهُمُ اتَّبِعُوا مَا أَنْزَلَ اللّٰهُ قَالُوا بَلْ نَتَّبِعُ
مَا وَجَدْنَا عَلَيْهِ آبَاءَنَا أَوَلَوْ كَانَ
الشَّيْطٰنُ يَدْعُوهُمْ إِلَى عَذَابِ السَّعِيرِ ۞

22 Whosoever surrendereth his purpose to Allah while doing good, he
verily hath grasped the firm hand-
hold. Unto Allah belongeth the
sequel of all things.

وَمَنْ يُّسْلِمْ وَجْهَهُ إِلَى اللّٰهِ وَهُوَ مُحْسِنٌ
فَقَدِ اسْتَمْسَكَ بِالْعُرْوَةِ الْوُثْقٰى
وَإِلَى اللّٰهِ عَاقِبَةُ الْأُمُورِ ۞

23 And whosoever disbelieveth, let
not his disbelief afflict thee (O
Muhammad). Unto Us is their
return, and We shall tell them what
they did. Lo! Allah is Aware of
what is in the breasts (of men).

وَمَنْ كَفَرَ فَلَا يَحْزُنْكَ كُفْرُهُ إِلَيْنَا مَرْجِعُهُمْ
فَنُنَبِّئُهُمْ بِمَا عَمِلُوا إِنَّ اللّٰهَ عَلِيمٌ بِذَاتِ الصُّدُورِ ۞

24 We give them comfort for a
little, and then We drive them to a
heavy doom.

نُمَتِّعُهُمْ قَلِيلًا ثُمَّ نَضْطَرُّهُمْ
إِلَى عَذَابٍ غَلِيظٍ ۞

25 If thou shouldst ask them: Who created the heavens and the earth? they would answer: Allah. Say: Praise be to Allah! But most of them know not.

وَلَئِن سَأَلْتَهُم مَّنْ خَلَقَ السَّمَوَٰتِ وَالْأَرْضَ لَيَقُولُنَّ اللَّهُ قُلِ الْحَمْدُ لِلَّهِ بَلْ أَكْثَرُهُمْ لَا يَعْلَمُونَ ٢٥

26 Unto Allah belongeth whatsoever is in the heavens and the earth. Lo! Allah, He is the Absolute, the Owner of Praise.

لِلَّهِ مَا فِي السَّمَوَٰتِ وَالْأَرْضِ إِنَّ اللَّهَ هُوَ الْغَنِيُّ الْحَمِيدُ ٢٦

27 And if all the trees in the earth were pens, and the sea, with seven more seas to help it, (were ink), the words of Allah could not be exhausted. Lo! Allah is Mighty, Wise.

وَلَوْ أَنَّمَا فِي الْأَرْضِ مِن شَجَرَةٍ أَقْلَامٌ وَالْبَحْرُ يَمُدُّهُ مِنۢ بَعْدِهِ سَبْعَةُ أَبْحُرٍ مَّا نَفِدَتْ كَلِمَٰتُ اللَّهِ إِنَّ اللَّهَ عَزِيزٌ حَكِيمٌ ٢٧

28 Your creation and your raising (from the dead) are only as (the creation and the raising of) a single soul. Lo! Allah is Hearer, Knower.

مَّا خَلْقُكُمْ وَلَا بَعْثُكُمْ إِلَّا كَنَفْسٍ وَٰحِدَةٍ إِنَّ اللَّهَ سَمِيعٌ بَصِيرٌ ٢٨

29 Hast thou not seen how Allah causeth the night to pass into the day and causeth the day to pass into the night, and hath subdued the sun and the moon (to do their work), each running unto an appointed term; and that Allah is Aware of what ye do.

أَلَمْ تَرَ أَنَّ اللَّهَ يُولِجُ الَّيْلَ فِي النَّهَارِ وَيُولِجُ النَّهَارَ فِي الَّيْلِ وَسَخَّرَ الشَّمْسَ وَالْقَمَرَ كُلٌّ يَجْرِي إِلَىٰ أَجَلٍ مُّسَمًّى وَأَنَّ اللَّهَ بِمَا تَعْمَلُونَ خَبِيرٌ ٢٩

30 That (is so) because Allah, He is the True, and that which they invoke beside Him is the False, and because Allah, He is the Sublime, the Great.

ذَٰلِكَ بِأَنَّ اللَّهَ هُوَ الْحَقُّ وَأَنَّ مَا يَدْعُونَ مِن دُونِهِ الْبَٰطِلُ وَأَنَّ اللَّهَ هُوَ الْعَلِيُّ الْكَبِيرُ ٣٠

31 Hast thou not seen how the ships glide on the sea by Allah's grace, that He may show you of His wonders? Lo! therein indeed are portents for every steadfast, grateful (heart).

أَلَمْ تَرَ أَنَّ الْفُلْكَ تَجْرِي فِي الْبَحْرِ بِنِعْمَتِ اللَّهِ لِيُرِيَكُم مِّنْ ءَايَٰتِهِ إِنَّ فِي ذَٰلِكَ لَأَيَٰتٍ لِّكُلِّ صَبَّارٍ شَكُورٍ ٣١

32 And if a wave enshroudeth them
like awnings, they cry unto Allah,
making their faith pure for Him
only. But when He bringeth them
safe to land, some of them compromise. None denieth Our signs
save every traitor ingrate.

وَإِذَا غَشِيَهُمْ مَّوْجٌ كَالظُّلَلِ دَعَوُا اللّٰهَ مُخْلِصِيْنَ
لَهُ الدِّيْنَ فَلَمَّا نَجّٰهُمْ إِلَى الْبَرِّ فَمِنْهُمْ مُّقْتَصِدٌ
وَمَا يَجْحَدُ بِاٰيٰتِنَا إِلَّا كُلُّ خَتَّارٍ كَفُوْرٍ ۝

33 O mankind! Keep your duty to
your Lord and fear a Day when the
parent will not be able to avail the
child in aught, nor the child to avail
the parent. Lo! Allah's promise is
the very truth. Let not the life of
the world beguile you, nor let the
deceiver beguile you, in regard to
Allah.

يٰٓاَيُّهَا النَّاسُ اتَّقُوْا رَبَّكُمْ وَاخْشَوْا يَوْمًا لَّا يَجْزِىْ
وَالِدٌ عَنْ وَّلَدِهٖ ۖ وَلَا مَوْلُوْدٌ هُوَ جَازٍ عَنْ وَّالِدِهٖ شَيْئًا
إِنَّ وَعْدَ اللّٰهِ حَقٌّ فَلَا تَغُرَّنَّكُمُ الْحَيٰوةُ
الدُّنْيَا ۖ وَلَا يَغُرَّنَّكُمْ بِاللّٰهِ الْغَرُوْرُ ۝

34 Lo! Allah! With Him is knowledge of the Hour. He sendeth down
the rain, and knoweth that which is
in the wombs. No soul knoweth
what it will earn tomorrow, and no
soul knoweth in what land it will
die. Lo! Allah is Knower, Aware.

إِنَّ اللّٰهَ عِنْدَهٗ عِلْمُ السَّاعَةِ ۖ وَيُنَزِّلُ الْغَيْثَ
وَيَعْلَمُ مَا فِى الْاَرْحَامِ ۖ وَمَا تَدْرِيْ نَفْسٌ
مَّاذَا تَكْسِبُ غَدًا ۖ وَمَا تَدْرِيْ نَفْسٌ بِاَيِّ اَرْضٍ
تَمُوْتُ ۚ إِنَّ اللّٰهَ عَلِيْمٌ خَبِيْرٌ ۝

As Sajdah
(The Prostration)

As Sajdah, "The Prostration," takes its name from a word in v. 15.

It belongs in the middle group of Makkan surahs.

In the name of Allah, the Beneficent, the Merciful.

1 Alif. Lām. Mīm.[1]

2 The revelation of the Scripture whereof there is no doubt is from the Lord of the Worlds.

3 Or say they: He hath invented it? Nay, but it is the Truth from thy Lord, that thou mayst warn a folk to whom no warner came before thee, that haply they may walk aright.

4 Allah it is Who created the heavens and the earth, and that which is between them, in six Days. Then He mounted the throne. Ye have not, beside Him, a protecting friend or mediator. Will ye not then remember?

---

1. See Sūrah 2, v. 1, footnote.

5   He directeth the ordinance from
the heaven unto the earth; then it
ascendeth unto Him in a Day,
whereof the measure is a thousand
years of that ye reckon.

يُدَبِّرُ الْأَمْرَ مِنَ السَّمَاءِ إِلَى الْأَرْضِ ثُمَّ يَعْرُجُ إِلَيْهِ
فِي يَوْمٍ كَانَ مِقْدَارُهُ أَلْفَ سَنَةٍ مِّمَّا تَعُدُّونَ ۝

6   Such is the Knower of the invisible and the visible, the Mighty,
the Merciful;

ذَٰلِكَ عَالِمُ الْغَيْبِ وَالشَّهَادَةِ الْعَزِيزُ الرَّحِيمُ ۝

7   Who made all things good
which He created, and He began the
creation of man from clay;

الَّذِي أَحْسَنَ كُلَّ شَيْءٍ خَلَقَهُ وَبَدَأَ خَلْقَ
الْإِنسَانِ مِن طِينٍ ۝

8   Then He made his seed from a
draught of despised fluid;

ثُمَّ جَعَلَ نَسْلَهُ مِن سُلَالَةٍ مِّن مَّاءٍ مَّهِينٍ ۝

9   Then He fashioned him and
breathed into him of His spirit; and
appointed for you hearing and sight
and hearts. Small thanks give ye!

ثُمَّ سَوَّاهُ وَنَفَخَ فِيهِ مِن رُّوحِهِ وَجَعَلَ لَكُمُ
السَّمْعَ وَالْأَبْصَارَ وَالْأَفْئِدَةَ قَلِيلًا
مَّا تَشْكُرُونَ ۝

10 And they say: When we are lost
in the earth, how can we then be
recreated? Nay but they are disbelievers in the meeting with their
Lord.

وَقَالُوا أَإِذَا ضَلَلْنَا فِي الْأَرْضِ أَإِنَّا لَفِي خَلْقٍ جَدِيدٍ
بَلْ هُم بِلِقَاءِ رَبِّهِمْ كَافِرُونَ ۝

11 Say: The angel of death, who
hath charge concerning you, will
gather you, and afterward unto your
Lord ye will be returned.

۞ قُلْ يَتَوَفَّاكُم مَّلَكُ الْمَوْتِ الَّذِي وُكِّلَ بِكُمْ
ثُمَّ إِلَى رَبِّكُمْ تُرْجَعُونَ ۝

12 Couldst thou but see when the
guilty hang their heads before their
Lord, (and say): Our Lord! We
have now seen and heard, so send
us back; we will do right, now we
are sure.

وَلَوْ تَرَىٰ إِذِ الْمُجْرِمُونَ نَاكِسُوا رُءُوسِهِمْ
عِندَ رَبِّهِمْ رَبَّنَا أَبْصَرْنَا وَسَمِعْنَا فَارْجِعْنَا
نَعْمَلْ صَالِحًا إِنَّا مُوقِنُونَ ۝

13 And if We had so willed, We
could have given every soul its guidance, but the word from Me con-

وَلَوْ شِئْنَا لَآتَيْنَا كُلَّ نَفْسٍ هُدَاهَا
وَلَٰكِنْ حَقَّ الْقَوْلُ مِنِّي لَأَمْلَأَنَّ جَهَنَّمَ

cerning evil-doers took effect: that I will fill hell with the jinn and mankind together.

مِنَ ٱلْجِنَّةِ وَٱلنَّاسِ أَجْمَعِينَ ۝

14 So taste (the evil of your deeds). Forasmuch as ye forgot the meeting of this your day, lo! We forget you. Taste the doom of immortality because of what ye used to do.

فَذُوقُوا بِمَا نَسِيتُمْ لِقَآءَ يَوْمِكُمْ هَٰذَآ إِنَّا نَسِينَٰكُمْ وَذُوقُوا عَذَابَ ٱلْخُلْدِ بِمَا كُنتُمْ تَعْمَلُونَ ۝

15 Only those believe in Our revelations who, when they are reminded of them, fall down prostrate and hymn the praise of their Lord, and they are not scornful;

إِنَّمَا يُؤْمِنُ بِـَٔايَٰتِنَا ٱلَّذِينَ إِذَا ذُكِّرُوا بِهَا خَرُّوا سُجَّدًا وَسَبَّحُوا بِحَمْدِ رَبِّهِمْ وَهُمْ لَا يَسْتَكْبِرُونَ ۩ ۝

16 Who forsake their beds to cry unto their Lord in fear and hope, and spend of what We have bestowed on them.

تَتَجَافَىٰ جُنُوبُهُمْ عَنِ ٱلْمَضَاجِعِ يَدْعُونَ رَبَّهُمْ خَوْفًا وَطَمَعًا وَمِمَّا رَزَقْنَٰهُمْ يُنفِقُونَ ۝

17 No soul knoweth what is kept hid for them of joy, as a reward for what they used to do.

فَلَا تَعْلَمُ نَفْسٌ مَّآ أُخْفِيَ لَهُم مِّن قُرَّةِ أَعْيُنٍ جَزَآءً بِمَا كَانُوا يَعْمَلُونَ ۝

18 Is he who is a believer like unto him who is an evil-liver? They are not alike.

أَفَمَن كَانَ مُؤْمِنًا كَمَن كَانَ فَاسِقًا لَّا يَسْتَوُۥنَ ۝

19 But as for those who believe and do good works, for them are the Gardens of Retreat, a welcome (in reward) for what they used to do.

أَمَّا ٱلَّذِينَ ءَامَنُوا وَعَمِلُوا ٱلصَّٰلِحَٰتِ فَلَهُمْ جَنَّٰتُ ٱلْمَأْوَىٰ نُزُلًا بِمَا كَانُوا يَعْمَلُونَ ۝

20 And as for those who do evil, their retreat is the Fire. Whenever they desire to issue forth from thence, they are brought back thither. Unto them it is said: Taste the torment of the Fire which ye used to deny.

وَأَمَّا ٱلَّذِينَ فَسَقُوا فَمَأْوَىٰهُمُ ٱلنَّارُ كُلَّمَآ أَرَادُوٓا أَن يَخْرُجُوا مِنْهَآ أُعِيدُوا فِيهَا وَقِيلَ لَهُمْ ذُوقُوا عَذَابَ ٱلنَّارِ ٱلَّذِى كُنتُم بِهِۦ تُكَذِّبُونَ ۝

21 And verily We make them taste the lower punishment[2] before the greater, that haply they may return.

وَلَنُذِيقَنَّهُم مِّنَ ٱلْعَذَابِ ٱلْأَدْنَىٰ دُونَ ٱلْعَذَابِ ٱلْأَكْبَرِ لَعَلَّهُمْ يَرْجِعُونَ ﴿٢١﴾

22 And who doth greater wrong than he who is reminded of the revelations of his Lord, then turneth from them. Lo! We shall requite the guilty.

وَمَنْ أَظْلَمُ مِمَّن ذُكِّرَ بِـَٔايَـٰتِ رَبِّهِۦ ثُمَّ أَعْرَضَ عَنْهَآ إِنَّا مِنَ ٱلْمُجْرِمِينَ مُنتَقِمُونَ ﴿٢٢﴾

23 We verily gave Moses the Scripture; so be not ye in doubt of his receiving it; and We appointed it a guidance for the Children of Israel.

وَلَقَدْ ءَاتَيْنَا مُوسَى ٱلْكِتَـٰبَ فَلَا تَكُن فِى مِرْيَةٍ مِّن لِّقَآئِهِۦ وَجَعَلْنَـٰهُ هُدًى لِّبَنِىٓ إِسْرَٰٓءِيلَ ﴿٢٣﴾

24 And when they became steadfast and believed firmly in Our revelations; We appointed from among them leaders who guided by Our command.

وَجَعَلْنَا مِنْهُمْ أَئِمَّةً يَهْدُونَ بِأَمْرِنَا لَمَّا صَبَرُوا۟ وَكَانُوا۟ بِـَٔايَـٰتِنَا يُوقِنُونَ ﴿٢٤﴾

25 Lo! thy Lord will judge between them on the Day of Resurrection concerning that wherein they used to differ.

إِنَّ رَبَّكَ هُوَ يَفْصِلُ بَيْنَهُمْ يَوْمَ ٱلْقِيَـٰمَةِ فِيمَا كَانُوا۟ فِيهِ يَخْتَلِفُونَ ﴿٢٥﴾

26 Is it not a guidance for them (to observe) how many generations We destroyed before them, amid whose dwelling places they do walk? Lo, therein verily are portents! Will they not then heed?

أَوَلَمْ يَهْدِ لَهُمْ كَمْ أَهْلَكْنَا مِن قَبْلِهِم مِّنَ ٱلْقُرُونِ يَمْشُونَ فِى مَسَـٰكِنِهِمْ إِنَّ فِى ذَٰلِكَ لَءَايَـٰتٍ أَفَلَا يَسْمَعُونَ ﴿٢٦﴾

27 Have they not seen how We lead the water to the barren land and therewith bring forth crops whereof their cattle eat, and they themselves? Will they not then see?

أَوَلَمْ يَرَوْا۟ أَنَّا نَسُوقُ ٱلْمَآءَ إِلَى ٱلْأَرْضِ ٱلْجُرُزِ فَنُخْرِجُ بِهِۦ زَرْعًا تَأْكُلُ مِنْهُ أَنْعَـٰمُهُمْ وَأَنفُسُهُمْ أَفَلَا يُبْصِرُونَ ﴿٢٧﴾

---

2. *i.e.* punishment in this world.

28 And they say: When cometh this victory (of yours) if ye are truthful?

وَيَقُولُونَ مَتَىٰ هَٰذَا الْفَتْحُ إِنْ كُنْتُمْ صَادِقِينَ ۝

29 Say (unto them): On the day of the victory the faith of those who disbelieve (and who then will believe) will not avail them, neither will they be reprieved.

قُلْ يَوْمَ الْفَتْحِ لَا يَنْفَعُ الَّذِينَ كَفَرُوا إِيمَانُهُمْ وَلَا هُمْ يُنْظَرُونَ ۝

30 So withdraw from them (O Muhammad), and await (the event). Lo! they also are awaiting (it).

فَأَعْرِضْ عَنْهُمْ وَانْتَظِرْ إِنَّهُمْ مُنْتَظِرُونَ ۝

Al Ahzāb
(The Clans)

Al Ahzāb, "The Clans," takes its name from the army of the allied clans which came against Yathrib (Al-Madīnah) in the fifth year of the Hijrah (vv. 9-25). Certain of the Banī Nadīr, a Jewish tribe whom the Prophet had expelled from Yathrib on the ground of treason (see sūrah 59), went first to the leaders of Quraysh in Makkah and then to the chiefs of the great desert tribe of Ghatafān, urging them to extirpate the Muslims and promising them help from the Jewish population of Yathrib. As a result of their efforts, Quraysh with all their clans, and Ghatafān with all their clans marched to destroy Yathrib.

When the Prophet had news of their design, he ordered a trench to be dug before the city and himself led the work of digging it. The trench was finished when the clans arrived, 10,000 strong. The Prophet went out against them with his army of 3000, the trench being between the two armies. For nearly a month the Muslims were exposed to showers of arrows, in constant expectation of attack by much superior forces; and, to make matters worse, news came that the Jewish tribe of Banī Qurayzah in their rear had broken their alliance with the Muslims and made common cause with Quraysh.

The women and children had been put in strongholds—towers like the peel-towers of Northern England, of which every family of note had one for refuge in time of raids. These were practically unguarded, and some of the Muslims asked permission of the Prophet to leave the battle front and go to guard them, though they were not then in danger because the Banī Qurayzah were not likely to show their treachery until the victory of the clans was certain.

The case of the Muslims seemed, humanly speaking, hopeless. But a secret sympathiser in the enemy camp managed to sow distrust between the Banī Qurayzah and the chiefs of the clans, making both feel uneasy. The obstacle of the trench was unexpected and seemed formidable; and when a fierce, bitter wind from the sea blew for three days and nights so furiously that they could not keep a shelter up, or light a fire, or boil a pot, Abū Sufyān, the leader of Quraysh, raised the siege in disgust. And when Ghatafān one morning found Quraysh had gone, they too departed for their homes.

On the very day when the Muslims returned from the trench, began the siege of the traitorous Banī Qurayẓah in their towers of refuge. It lasted for twenty-five days. When they at length surrendered some of the tribe of Aws, whose adherents they were, asked the Prophet to show them the same grace that he had shown to the tribe of Khazraj, in the case of Banī Naḍīr, in allowing them to intercede for their dependents.

The Prophet said: "Would you like that one of you should decide concerning them?" They said: "Yes," and he appointed Sa'd ibn Mu'ādh, a great chief of Aws, who had been wounded and was being cared for in the Mosque. Sa'd was sent for and he ordered their men to be put to death, their women and children to be made captive, and their property to be divided among the Muslims at the Prophet's will.

I have taken this account from the narrative of Ibn Khaldūn, which is concise, rather than from that in Ibn Hishām, which is exceedingly diffuse, the two accounts being in absolute agreement. Vv. 26 and 27 refer to the punishment of Banī Qurayẓah.

In v. 37 the reference is to the unhappy marriage of Zayd, the Prophet's freedman and adopted son, with Zaynab, the Prophet's cousin, a proud lady of Quraysh. The Prophet had arranged the marriage with the idea of breaking down the old barrier of pride of caste, and had shown but little consideration for Zaynab's feelings. Tradition says that both she and her brother were averse to the match, and that she had always wished to marry the Prophet. For Zayd, the marriage was nothing but a cause of embarrassment and humiliation. When the Prophet's attention was first called to their unhappiness, he urged Zayd to keep his wife and not divorce her, being apprehensive of the talk that would arise if it became known that a marriage arranged by him had proved unhappy. At last, Zayd did actually divorce Zaynab, and the Prophet was commanded to marry her in order, by his example, to disown the superstitious custom of the pagan Arabs, in such matters, of treating their adopted sons as their real sons, which was against the laws of God (i.e. the laws of nature); whereas in arranging a marriage, the woman's inclinations ought to be considered. Unhappy marriage was no part of Allah's ordinance, and was not to be held sacred in Islām.

The sūrah contains further references to the wives of the Prophet in connection with which it may be mentioned that from the age of twenty-five till the age of fifty he had only one wife, Khadījah, fifteen years his senior, to whom he was devotedly attached and whose memory he cherished till his dying day. With the exception of 'Ā'ishah, the daughter of his closest friend, Abū Bakr, whom he married at her father's request when she was still a child, all his later marriages were with widows whose state was pitiable for one reason or another. Some of them were widows of men killed in war. One was a captive, when he made the marriage the excuse for emancipating all the conquered tribe and restoring their property. Two were daughters of his enemies, and his alliance with them was a cause of peace. It is noteworthy that the period of these marriages was also the period of his greatest activity, when he had little rest from campaigning, and was always busy with the problems of a growing empire.

The period of revelation is between the end of the fifth and the end of the seventh years of the Hijrah.

In the name of Allah, the
Beneficent, the Merciful.

بِسْمِ اللَّهِ الرَّحْمَٰنِ الرَّحِيمِ

1 O Prophet! Keep thy duty to
Allah and obey not the disbelievers
and the hypocrites. Lo! Allah is
Knower, Wise.

يَٰٓأَيُّهَا ٱلنَّبِىُّ ٱتَّقِ ٱللَّهَ وَلَا تُطِعِ ٱلْكَٰفِرِينَ وَٱلْمُنَٰفِقِينَ
إِنَّ ٱللَّهَ كَانَ عَلِيمًا حَكِيمًا ١

2 And follow that which is inspired in thee from thy Lord. Lo!
Allah is Aware of what ye do.

وَٱتَّبِعْ مَا يُوحَىٰٓ إِلَيْكَ مِن رَّبِّكَ إِنَّ ٱللَّهَ كَانَ
بِمَا تَعْمَلُونَ خَبِيرًا ٢

3 And put thy trust in Allah, for
Allah is sufficient as Trustee.

وَتَوَكَّلْ عَلَى ٱللَّهِ وَكَفَىٰ بِٱللَّهِ وَكِيلًا ٣

4 Allah hath not assigned unto any
man two hearts within his body, nor
hath he made your wives whom ye
declare (to be your mothers) your
mothers,[1] nor hath he made those
whom ye claim (to be your sons)
your sons. This is but a saying of
your mouths. But Allah sayeth the
truth and He showeth the way.

مَّا جَعَلَ ٱللَّهُ لِرَجُلٍ مِّن قَلْبَيْنِ فِى جَوْفِهِۦ وَمَا جَعَلَ
أَزْوَٰجَكُمُ ٱلَّٰٓـِٔى تُظَٰهِرُونَ مِنْهُنَّ أُمَّهَٰتِكُمْ وَمَا جَعَلَ
أَدْعِيَآءَكُمْ أَبْنَآءَكُمْ ذَٰلِكُمْ قَوْلُكُم بِأَفْوَٰهِكُمْ وَٱللَّهُ
يَقُولُ ٱلْحَقَّ وَهُوَ يَهْدِى ٱلسَّبِيلَ ٤

5 Proclaim their real parentage.
That will be more equitable in the
sight of Allah. And if ye know not
their fathers, then (they are) your
brethren in the faith, and your
clients. And there is no sin for you

ٱدْعُوهُمْ لِءَابَآئِهِمْ هُوَ أَقْسَطُ عِندَ ٱللَّهِ
فَإِن لَّمْ تَعْلَمُوٓا۟ ءَابَآءَهُمْ فَإِخْوَٰنُكُمْ
فِى ٱلدِّينِ وَمَوَٰلِيكُمْ وَلَيْسَ عَلَيْكُمْ جُنَاحٌ

---

1. The reference is to a custom of the pagan Arabs by which a man could put away
his wife by merely saying: "Thy back is as my mother's back for me."

in the mistakes that ye make un-
intentionally, but what your hearts
purpose (that will be a sin for you).
Allah is Forgiving, Merciful.

فِيمَآ أَخْطَأْتُم بِهِ وَلَٰكِن مَّا تَعَمَّدَتْ قُلُوبُكُمْ
وَكَانَ ٱللَّهُ غَفُورًا رَّحِيمًا ٥

6 The Prophet is closer to the
believers than their selves, and his
wives are (as) their mothers. And
the owners of kinship are closer one
to another in the ordinance of Allah
than (other) believers and the fugitives (who fled from Makkah),
except that ye should do kindness to
your friends.[2] This is written in the
Book (of nature).

ٱلنَّبِيُّ أَوْلَىٰ بِٱلْمُؤْمِنِينَ مِنْ أَنفُسِهِمْ وَأَزْوَٰجُهُۥٓ
أُمَّهَٰتُهُمْ وَأُوْلُواْ ٱلْأَرْحَامِ بَعْضُهُمْ أَوْلَىٰ بِبَعْضٍ
فِى كِتَٰبِ ٱللَّهِ مِنَ ٱلْمُؤْمِنِينَ وَٱلْمُهَٰجِرِينَ
إِلَّآ أَن تَفْعَلُوٓاْ إِلَىٰٓ أَوْلِيَآئِكُم مَّعْرُوفًا
كَانَ ذَٰلِكَ فِى ٱلْكِتَٰبِ مَسْطُورًا ٦

7 And when We exacted a covenant from the Prophets, and from
thee (O Muhammad) and from
Noah and Abraham and Moses and
Jesus son of Mary. We took from
them a solemn covenant;

وَإِذْ أَخَذْنَا مِنَ ٱلنَّبِيِّـۧنَ مِيثَٰقَهُمْ وَمِنكَ وَمِن نُّوحٍ
وَإِبْرَٰهِيمَ وَمُوسَىٰ وَعِيسَى ٱبْنِ مَرْيَمَ وَأَخَذْنَا مِنْهُم
مِّيثَٰقًا غَلِيظًا ٧

8 That He may ask the loyal of
their loyalty. And He hath prepared
a painful doom for the unfaithful.

لِّيَسْـَٔلَ ٱلصَّٰدِقِينَ عَن صِدْقِهِمْ وَأَعَدَّ لِلْكَٰفِرِينَ
عَذَابًا أَلِيمًا ٨

9 O ye who believe! Remember
Allah's favour unto you when there
came against you hosts, and We
sent against them a great wind and
hosts ye could not see. And Allah is
ever Seer of what ye do.

يَٰٓأَيُّهَا ٱلَّذِينَ ءَامَنُواْ ٱذْكُرُواْ نِعْمَةَ ٱللَّهِ عَلَيْكُمْ
إِذْ جَآءَتْكُمْ جُنُودٌ فَأَرْسَلْنَا عَلَيْهِمْ رِيحًا وَجُنُودًا
لَّمْ تَرَوْهَا وَكَانَ ٱللَّهُ بِمَا تَعْمَلُونَ بَصِيرًا ٩

---

2. The Prophet had ordained brotherhood between individuals of the Anṣār (Muslims
of Al-Madīnah) and the Muhājirūn (fugitives from Makkah) a brotherhood which was
closer than kinship by blood. This verse abolished such brotherhood, in so far as
inheritance was concerned.

10 When they came upon you from above you and from below you, and when eyes grew wild and hearts reached to the throats, and ye were imagining vain thoughts concerning Allah.

إِذْ جَآءُوكُمْ مِّن فَوْقِكُمْ وَمِنْ أَسْفَلَ مِنكُمْ وَإِذْ زَاغَتِ الْأَبْصَٰرُ وَبَلَغَتِ الْقُلُوبُ الْحَنَاجِرَ وَتَظُنُّونَ بِاللَّهِ الظُّنُونَا ۝

11 There were the believers sorely tried, and shaken with a mighty shock.

هُنَالِكَ ابْتُلِيَ الْمُؤْمِنُونَ وَزُلْزِلُوا زِلْزَالًا شَدِيدًا ۝

12 And when the hypocrites, and those in whose hearts is a disease, were saying: Allah and His messenger promised us naught but delusion.

وَإِذْ يَقُولُ الْمُنَٰفِقُونَ وَالَّذِينَ فِى قُلُوبِهِم مَّرَضٌ مَّا وَعَدَنَا اللَّهُ وَرَسُولُهُ إِلَّا غُرُورًا ۝

13 And when a party of them said: O folk of Yathrib! There is no stand (possible) for you, therefore turn back. And certain of them (even) sought permission of the Prophet, saying: Our homes lie open (to the enemy). And they lay not open. They but wished to flee.

وَإِذْ قَالَت طَّآئِفَةٌ مِّنْهُمْ يَٰٓأَهْلَ يَثْرِبَ لَا مُقَامَ لَكُمْ فَارْجِعُوا وَيَسْتَـْٔذِنُ فَرِيقٌ مِّنْهُمُ النَّبِيَّ يَقُولُونَ إِنَّ بُيُوتَنَا عَوْرَةٌ وَمَا هِيَ بِعَوْرَةٍ إِن يُرِيدُونَ إِلَّا فِرَارًا ۝

14 If they had been approached from its sides and they had been exhorted to treachery, they would have committed it, and would have hesitated thereupon but little.

وَلَوْ دُخِلَتْ عَلَيْهِم مِّنْ أَقْطَارِهَا ثُمَّ سُئِلُوا الْفِتْنَةَ لَأَتَوْهَا وَمَا تَلَبَّثُوا بِهَا إِلَّا يَسِيرًا ۝

15 And verily they had already sworn unto Allah that they would not turn their backs (to the foe). An oath to Allah must be answered for.

وَلَقَدْ كَانُوا عَٰهَدُوا اللَّهَ مِن قَبْلُ لَا يُوَلُّونَ الْأَدْبَٰرَ وَكَانَ عَهْدُ اللَّهِ مَسْـُٔولًا ۝

16 Say: Flight will not avail you if ye flee from death or killing, and then ye will be made to enjoy yourselves but a little while.

قُل لَّن يَنفَعَكُمُ الْفِرَارُ إِن فَرَرْتُم مِّنَ الْمَوْتِ أَوِ الْقَتْلِ وَإِذًا لَّا تُمَتَّعُونَ إِلَّا قَلِيلًا ۝

17 Say: Who is he who can preserve you from Allah if He intendeth harm for you, or intendeth mercy for you. They will not find that they have any friend or helper other than Allah.

قُلْ مَنْ ذَا الَّذِي يَعْصِمُكُمْ مِّنَ اللّٰهِ إِنْ أَرَادَ بِكُمْ سُوْءًا أَوْ أَرَادَ بِكُمْ رَحْمَةً وَلَا يَجِدُوْنَ لَهُمْ مِّنْ دُوْنِ اللّٰهِ وَلِيًّا وَّلَا نَصِيْرًا ۝

18 Allah already knoweth those of you who hinder, and those who say unto their brethren: "Come ye hither unto us!" and they come not to the stress of battle save a little;

قَدْ يَعْلَمُ اللّٰهُ الْمُعَوِّقِيْنَ مِنْكُمْ وَالْقَائِلِيْنَ لِإِخْوَانِهِمْ هَلُمَّ إِلَيْنَا وَلَا يَأْتُوْنَ الْبَأْسَ إِلَّا قَلِيْلًا ۝

19 Being sparing of their help to you (believers). But when the fear cometh, then thou (Muhammad) seest them regarding thee with rolling eyes like one who fainteth unto death. Then, when the fear departeth, they scald you with sharp tongues in their greed for wealth (from the spoil). Such have not believed. Therefore Allah maketh their deeds fruitless. And that is easy for Allah.

أَشِحَّةً عَلَيْكُمْ فَإِذَا جَاءَ الْخَوْفُ رَأَيْتَهُمْ يَنْظُرُوْنَ إِلَيْكَ تَدُوْرُ أَعْيُنُهُمْ كَالَّذِي يُغْشَى عَلَيْهِ مِنَ الْمَوْتِ فَإِذَا ذَهَبَ الْخَوْفُ سَلَقُوْكُمْ بِأَلْسِنَةٍ حِدَادٍ أَشِحَّةً عَلَى الْخَيْرِ أُولَئِكَ لَمْ يُؤْمِنُوْا فَأَحْبَطَ اللّٰهُ أَعْمَالَهُمْ وَكَانَ ذَلِكَ عَلَى اللّٰهِ يَسِيْرًا ۝

20 They hold that the clans have not retired (for good); and if the clans should advance (again), they would fain be in the desert with the wandering Arabs, asking for the news of you and if they were among you, they would not give battle, save a little.

يَحْسَبُوْنَ الْأَحْزَابَ لَمْ يَذْهَبُوْا وَإِنْ يَأْتِ الْأَحْزَابُ يَوَدُّوْا لَوْ أَنَّهُمْ بَادُوْنَ فِي الْأَعْرَابِ يَسْأَلُوْنَ عَنْ أَنْبَائِكُمْ وَلَوْ كَانُوْا فِيْكُمْ مَّا قَاتَلُوْا إِلَّا قَلِيْلًا ۝

21 Verily in the messenger of Allah ye have a good example for him who looketh unto Allah and the Last Day, and remembereth Allah much.

لَقَدْ كَانَ لَكُمْ فِي رَسُوْلِ اللّٰهِ أُسْوَةٌ حَسَنَةٌ لِّمَنْ كَانَ يَرْجُو اللّٰهَ وَالْيَوْمَ الْآخِرَ وَذَكَرَ اللّٰهَ كَثِيْرًا ۝

22 And when the true believers saw the clans, they said: This is that which Allah and His messenger promised us. Allah and His messenger are true. It did but add to their faith and resignation.

وَلَمَّا رَءَا الْمُؤْمِنُونَ الْأَحْزَابَ قَالُوا هٰذَا مَا وَعَدَنَا اللّٰهُ وَرَسُولُهُ وَصَدَقَ اللّٰهُ وَرَسُولُهُ وَمَا زَادَهُمْ إِلَّا إِيمَانًا وَتَسْلِيمًا ۝

23 Of the believers are men who are true to that which they covenanted with Allah. Some of them have paid their vow by death (in battle), and some of them still are waiting; and they have not altered in the least;

مِنَ الْمُؤْمِنِينَ رِجَالٌ صَدَقُوا مَا عَاهَدُوا اللّٰهَ عَلَيْهِ فَمِنْهُمْ مَّنْ قَضَى نَحْبَهُ وَمِنْهُمْ مَّنْ يَنْتَظِرُ وَمَا بَدَّلُوا تَبْدِيلًا ۝

24 That Allah may reward the true men for their truth, and punish the hypocrites if He will, or relent toward them (if He will). Lo! Allah is Forgiving, Merciful.

لِيَجْزِيَ اللّٰهُ الصَّادِقِينَ بِصِدْقِهِمْ وَيُعَذِّبَ الْمُنَافِقِينَ إِنْ شَاءَ أَوْ يَتُوبَ عَلَيْهِمْ إِنَّ اللّٰهَ كَانَ غَفُورًا رَّحِيمًا ۝

25 And Allah repulsed the disbelievers in their wrath; they gained no good. Allah averted their attack from the believers. Allah is Strong, Mighty.

وَرَدَّ اللّٰهُ الَّذِينَ كَفَرُوا بِغَيْظِهِمْ لَمْ يَنَالُوا خَيْرًا وَكَفَى اللّٰهُ الْمُؤْمِنِينَ الْقِتَالَ وَكَانَ اللّٰهُ قَوِيًّا عَزِيزًا ۝

26 And He brought those of the People of the Scripture who supported them down from their strongholds, and cast panic into their hearts. Some ye slew, and ye made captive some.

وَأَنْزَلَ الَّذِينَ ظَاهَرُوهُمْ مِّنْ أَهْلِ الْكِتَابِ مِنْ صَيَاصِيهِمْ وَقَذَفَ فِي قُلُوبِهِمُ الرُّعْبَ فَرِيقًا تَقْتُلُونَ وَتَأْسِرُونَ فَرِيقًا ۝

27 And He caused you to inherit their land and their houses and their wealth, and land ye have not trodden. Allah is Able to do all things.

وَأَوْرَثَكُمْ أَرْضَهُمْ وَدِيَارَهُمْ وَأَمْوَالَهُمْ وَأَرْضًا لَّمْ تَطَئُوهَا وَكَانَ اللّٰهُ عَلَى كُلِّ شَيْءٍ قَدِيرًا ۝

28 O Prophet! Say unto thy wives: If ye desire the world's life and its adornment, come! I will content

يَا أَيُّهَا النَّبِيُّ قُلْ لِّأَزْوَاجِكَ إِنْ كُنْتُنَّ تُرِدْنَ الْحَيَاةَ الدُّنْيَا وَزِينَتَهَا فَتَعَالَيْنَ

you and will release you with a fair release.

29 But if ye desire Allah and His messenger and the abode of the Hereafter, then lo! Allah hath prepared for the good among you an immense reward.

30 O ye wives of the Prophet! Whosoever of you committeth manifest lewdness, the punishment for her will be doubled, and that is easy for Allah.

31 And whosoever of you is submissive unto Allah and His messenger and doeth right, We shall give her reward twice over, and We have prepared for her a rich provision.

32 O ye wives of the Prophet! Ye are not like any other women. If ye keep your duty (to Allah), then be not soft of speech, lest he in whose heart is a disease aspire (to you), but utter customary speech.

33 And stay in your houses. Bedizen not yourselves with the bedizenment of the Time of Ignorance. Be regular in prayer, and pay the poor-due, and obey Allah and His messenger. Allah's wish is but to remove uncleanness far from you, O Folk of the Household, and cleanse you with a thorough cleansing.

34 And bear in mind that which is recited in your houses of the reve-

أُمَتِّعْكُنَّ وَأُسَرِّحْكُنَّ سَرَاحًا جَمِيلًا ۝

وَإِن كُنتُنَّ تُرِدْنَ ٱللَّهَ وَرَسُولَهُۥ وَٱلدَّارَ ٱلْأَخِرَةَ فَإِنَّ ٱللَّهَ أَعَدَّ لِلْمُحْسِنَٰتِ مِنكُنَّ أَجْرًا عَظِيمًا ۝

يَٰنِسَآءَ ٱلنَّبِيِّ مَن يَأْتِ مِنكُنَّ بِفَٰحِشَةٍ مُّبَيِّنَةٍ يُضَٰعَفْ لَهَا ٱلْعَذَابُ ضِعْفَيْنِ وَكَانَ ذَٰلِكَ عَلَى ٱللَّهِ يَسِيرًا ۝

۞ وَمَن يَقْنُتْ مِنكُنَّ لِلَّهِ وَرَسُولِهِۦ وَتَعْمَلْ صَٰلِحًا نُّؤْتِهَآ أَجْرَهَا مَرَّتَيْنِ وَأَعْتَدْنَا لَهَا رِزْقًا كَرِيمًا ۝

يَٰنِسَآءَ ٱلنَّبِيِّ لَسْتُنَّ كَأَحَدٍ مِّنَ ٱلنِّسَآءِ إِنِ ٱتَّقَيْتُنَّ فَلَا تَخْضَعْنَ بِٱلْقَوْلِ فَيَطْمَعَ ٱلَّذِى فِى قَلْبِهِۦ مَرَضٌ وَقُلْنَ قَوْلًا مَّعْرُوفًا ۝

وَقَرْنَ فِى بُيُوتِكُنَّ وَلَا تَبَرَّجْنَ تَبَرُّجَ ٱلْجَٰهِلِيَّةِ ٱلْأُولَىٰ وَأَقِمْنَ ٱلصَّلَوٰةَ وَءَاتِينَ ٱلزَّكَوٰةَ وَأَطِعْنَ ٱللَّهَ وَرَسُولَهُۥٓ إِنَّمَا يُرِيدُ ٱللَّهُ لِيُذْهِبَ عَنكُمُ ٱلرِّجْسَ أَهْلَ ٱلْبَيْتِ وَيُطَهِّرَكُمْ تَطْهِيرًا ۝

وَٱذْكُرْنَ مَا يُتْلَىٰ فِى بُيُوتِكُنَّ مِنْ ءَايَٰتِ

lations of Allah and wisdom. Lo! Allah is Subtle, Aware.

اللَّهِ وَالْحِكْمَةِ إِنَّ اللَّهَ كَانَ لَطِيفًا خَبِيرًا ٣٤

35 Lo! men who surrender unto Allah, and women who surrender, and men who believe and women who believe, and men who obey and women who obey, and men who speak the truth and women who speak the truth, and men who persevere (in righteousness) and women who persevere, and men who are humble and women who are humble, and men who give alms and women who give alms, and men who fast and women who fast, and men who guard their modesty and women who guard (their modesty), and men who remember Allah much and women who remember; Allah hath prepared for them forgiveness and a vast reward.

إِنَّ الْمُسْلِمِينَ وَالْمُسْلِمَاتِ وَالْمُؤْمِنِينَ وَالْمُؤْمِنَاتِ وَالْقَانِتِينَ وَالْقَانِتَاتِ وَالصَّادِقِينَ وَالصَّادِقَاتِ وَالصَّابِرِينَ وَالصَّابِرَاتِ وَالْخَاشِعِينَ وَالْخَاشِعَاتِ وَالْمُتَصَدِّقِينَ وَالْمُتَصَدِّقَاتِ وَالصَّائِمِينَ وَالصَّائِمَاتِ وَالْحَافِظِينَ فُرُوجَهُمْ وَالْحَافِظَاتِ وَالذَّاكِرِينَ اللَّهَ كَثِيرًا وَالذَّاكِرَاتِ أَعَدَّ اللَّهُ لَهُم مَّغْفِرَةً وَأَجْرًا عَظِيمًا ٣٥

36 And it becometh not a believing man or a believing woman, when Allah and His messenger have decided an affair (for them), that they should (after that) claim any say in their affair; and whoso is rebellious to Allah and His messenger, he verily goeth astray in error manifest.

وَمَا كَانَ لِمُؤْمِنٍ وَلَا مُؤْمِنَةٍ إِذَا قَضَى اللَّهُ وَرَسُولُهُ أَمْرًا أَن يَكُونَ لَهُمُ الْخِيَرَةُ مِنْ أَمْرِهِمْ وَمَن يَعْصِ اللَّهَ وَرَسُولَهُ فَقَدْ ضَلَّ ضَلَالًا مُّبِينًا ٣٦

37 And when thou saidst unto him on whom Allah hath conferred favour and thou hast conferred favour: Keep thy wife to thyself, and fear Allah. And thou didst hide in thy mind that which Allah was to bring to light, and thou didst fear

وَإِذْ تَقُولُ لِلَّذِي أَنْعَمَ اللَّهُ عَلَيْهِ وَأَنْعَمْتَ عَلَيْهِ أَمْسِكْ عَلَيْكَ زَوْجَكَ وَاتَّقِ اللَّهَ وَتُخْفِي فِي نَفْسِكَ مَا اللَّهُ مُبْدِيهِ وَتَخْشَى النَّاسَ وَاللَّهُ

أَحَقُّ أَن تَخْشَهُ فَلَمَّا قَضَىٰ زَيْدٌ مِّنْهَا وَطَرًا زَوَّجْنَٰكَهَا لِكَىْ لَا يَكُونَ عَلَى ٱلْمُؤْمِنِينَ حَرَجٌ فِىٓ أَزْوَٰجِ أَدْعِيَآئِهِمْ إِذَا قَضَوْا۟ مِنْهُنَّ وَطَرًا وَكَانَ أَمْرُ ٱللَّهِ مَفْعُولًا ۝

mankind whereas Allah had a better right that thou shouldst fear Him. So when Zayd had performed the necessary formality (of divorce) from her, We gave her unto thee in marriage, so that (henceforth) there may be no sin for believers in respect of wives of their adopted sons, when the latter have performed the necessary formality (of release) from them. The commandment of Allah must be fulfilled.

مَّا كَانَ عَلَى ٱلنَّبِىِّ مِنْ حَرَجٍ فِيمَا فَرَضَ ٱللَّهُ لَهُ سُنَّةَ ٱللَّهِ فِى ٱلَّذِينَ خَلَوْا۟ مِن قَبْلُ وَكَانَ أَمْرُ ٱللَّهِ قَدَرًا مَّقْدُورًا ۝

38 There is no reproach for the Prophet in that which Allah maketh his due. That was Allah's way with those who passed away of old and the commandment of Allah is certain destiny;

ٱلَّذِينَ يُبَلِّغُونَ رِسَٰلَٰتِ ٱللَّهِ وَيَخْشَوْنَهُ وَلَا يَخْشَوْنَ أَحَدًا إِلَّا ٱللَّهَ وَكَفَىٰ بِٱللَّهِ حَسِيبًا ۝

39 Who delivered the messages of Allah and feared Him, and feared none save Allah. Allah keepeth good account.

مَّا كَانَ مُحَمَّدٌ أَبَآ أَحَدٍ مِّن رِّجَالِكُمْ وَلَٰكِن رَّسُولَ ٱللَّهِ وَخَاتَمَ ٱلنَّبِيِّـۧنَ وَكَانَ ٱللَّهُ بِكُلِّ شَىْءٍ عَلِيمًا ۝

40 Muhammad is not the father of any man among you, but he is the messenger of Allah and the Seal of the Prophets; and Allah is Aware of all things.

يَٰٓأَيُّهَا ٱلَّذِينَ ءَامَنُوا۟ ٱذْكُرُوا۟ ٱللَّهَ ذِكْرًا كَثِيرًا ۝

41 O ye who believe! Remember Allah with much remembrance.

وَسَبِّحُوهُ بُكْرَةً وَأَصِيلًا ۝

42 And glorify Him early and late.

هُوَ ٱلَّذِى يُصَلِّى عَلَيْكُمْ وَمَلَٰٓئِكَتُهُۥ لِيُخْرِجَكُم مِّنَ ٱلظُّلُمَٰتِ إِلَى ٱلنُّورِ وَكَانَ بِٱلْمُؤْمِنِينَ رَحِيمًا ۝

43 He it is who blesseth you, and His angels (bless you), that He may bring you forth from darkness unto light; and He is Merciful to the believers.

44 Their salutation on the day when they shall meet Him will be: Peace. And He hath prepared for them a goodly recompense.

تَحِيَّتُهُمْ يَوْمَ يَلْقَوْنَهُ سَلَامٌ وَأَعَدَّ لَهُمْ أَجْرًا كَرِيمًا ﴿٤٤﴾

45 O Prophet! Lo! We have sent thee as a witness and a bringer of good tidings and a warner.

يَا أَيُّهَا النَّبِيُّ إِنَّا أَرْسَلْنَاكَ شَاهِدًا وَمُبَشِّرًا وَنَذِيرًا ﴿٤٥﴾

46 And as a summoner unto Allah by His permission, and as a lamp that giveth light.

وَدَاعِيًا إِلَى اللَّهِ بِإِذْنِهِ وَسِرَاجًا مُنِيرًا ﴿٤٦﴾

47 And announce unto the believers the good tidings that they will have great bounty from Allah.

وَبَشِّرِ الْمُؤْمِنِينَ بِأَنَّ لَهُمْ مِنَ اللَّهِ فَضْلًا كَبِيرًا ﴿٤٧﴾

48 And incline not to the disbelievers and the hypocrites. Disregard their noxious talk, and put thy trust in Allah. Allah is sufficient as Trustee.

وَلَا تُطِعِ الْكَافِرِينَ وَالْمُنَافِقِينَ وَدَعْ أَذَاهُمْ وَتَوَكَّلْ عَلَى اللَّهِ وَكَفَى بِاللَّهِ وَكِيلًا ﴿٤٨﴾

49 O ye who believe! If ye wed believing women and divorce them before ye have touched them, then there is no period that ye should reckon. But content them and release them handsomely.

يَا أَيُّهَا الَّذِينَ آمَنُوا إِذَا نَكَحْتُمُ الْمُؤْمِنَاتِ ثُمَّ طَلَّقْتُمُوهُنَّ مِنْ قَبْلِ أَنْ تَمَسُّوهُنَّ فَمَا لَكُمْ عَلَيْهِنَّ مِنْ عِدَّةٍ تَعْتَدُّونَهَا فَمَتِّعُوهُنَّ وَسَرِّحُوهُنَّ سَرَاحًا جَمِيلًا ﴿٤٩﴾

50 O Prophet! Lo! We have made lawful unto thee thy wives unto whom thou hast paid their dowries, and those whom thy right hand possesseth of those whom Allah hath given thee as spoils of war, and the daughters of thine uncles on the father's side and the daughters of thine aunts on the father's side, and the daughters of thine uncles on the mother's side and the daughters of thine aunts on the mother's side

يَا أَيُّهَا النَّبِيُّ إِنَّا أَحْلَلْنَا لَكَ أَزْوَاجَكَ اللَّاتِي آتَيْتَ أُجُورَهُنَّ وَمَا مَلَكَتْ يَمِينُكَ مِمَّا أَفَاءَ اللَّهُ عَلَيْكَ وَبَنَاتِ عَمِّكَ وَبَنَاتِ عَمَّاتِكَ وَبَنَاتِ خَالِكَ وَبَنَاتِ خَالَاتِكَ اللَّاتِي هَاجَرْنَ

who emigrated with thee, and a
believing woman if she give herself
unto the Prophet and the Prophet
desire to ask her in marriage—a pri-
vilege for thee only, not for the
(rest of) believers—We are aware of
that which We enjoined upon them
concerning their wives and those
whom their right hands possess—that thou mayst be free from
blame, for Allah is Forgiving,
Merciful.

51 Thou canst defer whom thou
wilt of them and receive unto thee
whom thou wilt, and whomsoever
thou desirest of those whom thou
hast set aside (temporarily), it is no
sin for thee (to receive her again);
that is better; that they may be
comforted and not grieve, and may
all be pleased with what thou givest
them. Allah knoweth what is in
your hearts (O men) and Allah is
Forgiving, Clement.

52 It is not allowed thee to take
(other) women henceforth, nor that
thou shouldst change them for other
wives even though their beauty
pleased thee, save those whom thy
right hand possesseth. And Allah is
Watcher over all things.

53 O ye who believe! Enter not the
dwellings of the Prophet for a meal
without waiting for the proper time,
unless permission be granted you.
But if ye are invited, enter, and,

مَعَكَ وَامْرَأَةً مُّؤْمِنَةً إِن وَهَبَتْ نَفْسَهَا لِلنَّبِيِّ
إِنْ أَرَادَ النَّبِيُّ أَن يَسْتَنكِحَهَا خَالِصَةً لَّكَ
مِن دُونِ الْمُؤْمِنِينَ قَدْ عَلِمْنَا مَا فَرَضْنَا
عَلَيْهِمْ فِي أَزْوَاجِهِمْ وَمَا مَلَكَتْ
أَيْمَانُهُمْ لِكَيْلَا يَكُونَ عَلَيْكَ حَرَجٌ
وَكَانَ اللَّهُ غَفُورًا رَّحِيمًا ۝

۞ تُرْجِي مَن تَشَاءُ مِنْهُنَّ وَتُؤْوِي إِلَيْكَ مَن تَشَاءُ
وَمَنِ ابْتَغَيْتَ مِمَّنْ عَزَلْتَ فَلَا جُنَاحَ عَلَيْكَ ذَلِكَ
أَدْنَىٰ أَن تَقَرَّ أَعْيُنُهُنَّ وَلَا يَحْزَنَّ وَيَرْضَيْنَ
بِمَا آتَيْتَهُنَّ كُلُّهُنَّ وَاللَّهُ يَعْلَمُ مَا فِي قُلُوبِكُمْ
وَكَانَ اللَّهُ عَلِيمًا حَلِيمًا ۝

لَا يَحِلُّ لَكَ النِّسَاءُ مِنْ بَعْدُ وَلَا أَن تَبَدَّلَ بِهِنَّ
مِنْ أَزْوَاجٍ وَلَوْ أَعْجَبَكَ حُسْنُهُنَّ إِلَّا مَا مَلَكَتْ
يَمِينُكَ وَكَانَ اللَّهُ عَلَىٰ كُلِّ شَيْءٍ رَّقِيبًا ۝

يَا أَيُّهَا الَّذِينَ آمَنُوا لَا تَدْخُلُوا بُيُوتَ النَّبِيِّ
إِلَّا أَن يُؤْذَنَ لَكُمْ إِلَىٰ طَعَامٍ غَيْرَ نَاظِرِينَ إِنَاهُ
وَلَٰكِنْ إِذَا دُعِيتُمْ فَادْخُلُوا فَإِذَا طَعِمْتُمْ فَانتَشِرُوا

when your meal is ended, then disperse. Linger not for conversation. Lo! that would cause annoyance to the Prophet, and he would be shy of (asking) you (to go); but Allah is not shy of the truth. And when ye ask of them (the wives of the Prophet) anything, ask it of them from behind a curtain. That is purer for your hearts and for their hearts. And it is not for you to cause annoyance to the messenger of Allah, nor that ye should ever marry his wives after him. Lo! that in Allah's sight would be an enormity.

وَلَا مُسْتَأْنِسِينَ لِحَدِيثٍ إِنَّ ذَٰلِكُمْ كَانَ يُؤْذِى النَّبِىَّ فَيَسْتَحْىِۦ مِنكُمْ وَٱللَّهُ لَا يَسْتَحْىِۦ مِنَ ٱلْحَقِّ وَإِذَا سَأَلْتُمُوهُنَّ مَتَٰعًا فَسْـَٔلُوهُنَّ مِن وَرَآءِ حِجَابٍ ذَٰلِكُمْ أَطْهَرُ لِقُلُوبِكُمْ وَقُلُوبِهِنَّ وَمَا كَانَ لَكُمْ أَن تُؤْذُوا۟ رَسُولَ ٱللَّهِ وَلَآ أَن تَنكِحُوٓا۟ أَزْوَٰجَهُۥ مِنۢ بَعْدِهِۦٓ أَبَدًا إِنَّ ذَٰلِكُمْ كَانَ عِندَ ٱللَّهِ عَظِيمًا ﴿٥٣﴾

54 Whether ye divulge a thing or keep it hidden, lo! Allah is ever Knower of all things.

إِن تُبْدُوا۟ شَيْـًٔا أَوْ تُخْفُوهُ فَإِنَّ ٱللَّهَ كَانَ بِكُلِّ شَىْءٍ عَلِيمًا ﴿٥٤﴾

55 It is no sin for them (thy wives) (to converse freely) with their fathers, or their sons, or their brothers, or their brothers' sons, or the sons of their sisters or of their own women, or their slaves. O women! Keep your duty to Allah. Lo! Allah is Witness over all things.

لَّا جُنَاحَ عَلَيْهِنَّ فِىٓ ءَابَآئِهِنَّ وَلَآ أَبْنَآئِهِنَّ وَلَآ إِخْوَٰنِهِنَّ وَلَآ أَبْنَآءِ إِخْوَٰنِهِنَّ وَلَآ أَبْنَآءِ أَخَوَٰتِهِنَّ وَلَا نِسَآئِهِنَّ وَلَا مَا مَلَكَتْ أَيْمَٰنُهُنَّ وَٱتَّقِينَ ٱللَّهَ إِنَّ ٱللَّهَ كَانَ عَلَىٰ كُلِّ شَىْءٍ شَهِيدًا ﴿٥٥﴾

56 Lo! Allah and His angels shower blessings on the Prophet. O ye who believe! Ask blessings on him and salute him with a worthy salutation.

إِنَّ ٱللَّهَ وَمَلَٰٓئِكَتَهُۥ يُصَلُّونَ عَلَى ٱلنَّبِىِّ يَٰٓأَيُّهَا ٱلَّذِينَ ءَامَنُوا۟ صَلُّوا۟ عَلَيْهِ وَسَلِّمُوا۟ تَسْلِيمًا ﴿٥٦﴾

57 Lo! those who malign Allah and His messenger, Allah hath cursed them in the world and the Hereafter, and hath prepared for them an abasing doom.

إِنَّ ٱلَّذِينَ يُؤْذُونَ ٱللَّهَ وَرَسُولَهُۥ لَعَنَهُمُ ٱللَّهُ فِى ٱلدُّنْيَا وَٱلْءَاخِرَةِ وَأَعَدَّ لَهُمْ عَذَابًا مُّهِينًا ﴿٥٧﴾

58 And those who malign believing men and believing women undeservedly, they bear the guilt of slander and manifest sin.

وَالَّذِينَ يُؤْذُونَ الْمُؤْمِنِينَ وَالْمُؤْمِنَاتِ بِغَيْرِ مَا اكْتَسَبُوا فَقَدِ احْتَمَلُوا بُهْتَانًا وَإِثْمًا مُّبِينًا ۝

59 O Prophet! Tell thy wives and thy daughters and the women of the believers to draw their cloaks close round them (when they go abroad). That will be better, that so they may be recognised and not annoyed. Allah is ever Forgiving, Merciful.

يَا أَيُّهَا النَّبِيُّ قُل لِّأَزْوَاجِكَ وَبَنَاتِكَ وَنِسَاءِ الْمُؤْمِنِينَ يُدْنِينَ عَلَيْهِنَّ مِن جَلَابِيبِهِنَّ ذَلِكَ أَدْنَى أَن يُعْرَفْنَ فَلَا يُؤْذَيْنَ وَكَانَ اللَّهُ غَفُورًا رَّحِيمًا ۝

60 If the hypocrites, and those in whose hearts is a disease, and the alarmists in the city do not cease, We verily shall urge thee on against them, then they will be your neighbours in it but a little while.

لَّئِن لَّمْ يَنتَهِ الْمُنَافِقُونَ وَالَّذِينَ فِي قُلُوبِهِم مَّرَضٌ وَالْمُرْجِفُونَ فِي الْمَدِينَةِ لَنُغْرِيَنَّكَ بِهِمْ ثُمَّ لَا يُجَاوِرُونَكَ فِيهَا إِلَّا قَلِيلًا ۝

61 Accursed, they will be seized wherever found and slain with a (fierce) slaughter.

مَّلْعُونِينَ أَيْنَمَا ثُقِفُوا أُخِذُوا وَقُتِّلُوا تَقْتِيلًا ۝

62 That was the way of Allah in the case of those who passed away of old; thou wilt not find for the way of Allah aught of power to change.

سُنَّةَ اللَّهِ فِي الَّذِينَ خَلَوْا مِن قَبْلُ وَلَن تَجِدَ لِسُنَّةِ اللَّهِ تَبْدِيلًا ۝

63 Men ask you of the Hour. Say: The knowledge of it is with Allah only. What can convey (the knowledge) unto thee? It may be that the Hour is nigh.

يَسْأَلُكَ النَّاسُ عَنِ السَّاعَةِ قُلْ إِنَّمَا عِلْمُهَا عِندَ اللَّهِ وَمَا يُدْرِيكَ لَعَلَّ السَّاعَةَ تَكُونُ قَرِيبًا ۝

64 Lo! Allah hath cursed the disbelievers, and hath prepared for them a flaming fire;

إِنَّ اللَّهَ لَعَنَ الْكَافِرِينَ وَأَعَدَّ لَهُمْ سَعِيرًا ۝

65 Wherein they will abide forever. They will find (then) no protecting friend nor helper.

خَالِدِينَ فِيهَا أَبَدًا لَّا يَجِدُونَ وَلِيًّا وَلَا نَصِيرًا ۝

66 On the day when their faces are turned over in the fire, they say: Oh, would that we had obeyed Allah and had obeyed His messenger!

يَوْمَ تُقَلَّبُ وُجُوهُهُمْ فِى النَّارِ يَقُولُونَ يَٰلَيْتَنَآ أَطَعْنَا اللَّهَ وَأَطَعْنَا الرَّسُولَا ﴿٦٦﴾

67 And they say: Our Lord! Lo! we obeyed our princes and great men, and they misled us from the Way.

وَقَالُوا رَبَّنَآ إِنَّآ أَطَعْنَا سَادَتَنَا وَكُبَرَآءَنَا فَأَضَلُّونَا السَّبِيلَا ﴿٦٧﴾

68 Our Lord! Oh, give them double torment and curse them with a mighty curse.

رَبَّنَآ ءَاتِهِمْ ضِعْفَيْنِ مِنَ الْعَذَابِ وَالْعَنْهُمْ لَعْنًا كَبِيرًا ﴿٦٨﴾

69 O ye who believe! Be not as those who slandered Moses, but Allah proved his innocence of that which they alleged, and he was well esteemed in Allah's sight.

يَٰٓأَيُّهَا الَّذِينَ ءَامَنُوا لَا تَكُونُوا كَالَّذِينَ ءَاذَوْا مُوسَىٰ فَبَرَّأَهُ اللَّهُ مِمَّا قَالُوا وَكَانَ عِندَ اللَّهِ وَجِيهًا ﴿٦٩﴾

70 O ye who believe! Guard your duty to Allah, and speak words straight to the point;

يَٰٓأَيُّهَا الَّذِينَ ءَامَنُوا اتَّقُوا اللَّهَ وَقُولُوا قَوْلًا سَدِيدًا ﴿٧٠﴾

71 He will adjust your works for you and will forgive you your sins. Whosoever obeyeth Allah and His messenger, he verily hath gained a signal victory.

يُصْلِحْ لَكُمْ أَعْمَٰلَكُمْ وَيَغْفِرْ لَكُمْ ذُنُوبَكُمْ وَمَن يُطِعِ اللَّهَ وَرَسُولَهُ فَقَدْ فَازَ فَوْزًا عَظِيمًا ﴿٧١﴾

72 Lo! We offered the trust unto the heavens and the earth and the hills, but they shrank from bearing it and were afraid of it. And man assumed it. Lo! he hath proved a tyrant and a fool.

إِنَّا عَرَضْنَا الْأَمَانَةَ عَلَى السَّمَٰوَٰتِ وَالْأَرْضِ وَالْجِبَالِ فَأَبَيْنَ أَن يَحْمِلْنَهَا وَأَشْفَقْنَ مِنْهَا وَحَمَلَهَا الْإِنسَٰنُ إِنَّهُ كَانَ ظَلُومًا جَهُولًا ﴿٧٢﴾

73 So Allah punisheth hypocritical men and hypocritical women, and idolatrous men and idolatrous women. But Allah pardoneth believing men and believing women, and Allah is Forgiving, Merciful.

لِيُعَذِّبَ اللَّهُ الْمُنَٰفِقِينَ وَالْمُنَٰفِقَٰتِ وَالْمُشْرِكِينَ وَالْمُشْرِكَٰتِ وَيَتُوبَ اللَّهُ عَلَى الْمُؤْمِنِينَ وَالْمُؤْمِنَٰتِ وَكَانَ اللَّهُ غَفُورًا رَّحِيمًا ﴿٧٣﴾

Sabā'

Sabā', "Sheba," takes its name from v. 15 ff., where Sheba (Sabā'), a region in the Yaman, is mentioned as having been devastated by a flood. It warns of the effects of luxury.

An early Makkan sūrah.

In the name of Allah, the Beneficent, the Merciful.

1 Praise be to Allah, unto Whom belongeth whatsoever is in the heavens and whatsoever is in the earth. His is the praise in the Hereafter, and He is the Wise, the Aware.

2 He knoweth that which goeth down into the earth and that which cometh forth from it, and that which descendeth from the heaven and that which ascendeth into it. He is the Merciful, the Forgiving.

3 Those who disbelieve say: The Hour will never come unto us. Say: Nay, by my Lord, but it is coming unto you surely. (He is) the Knower of the Unseen. Not an atom's weight, or less than that or greater, escapeth Him in the heavens or in the earth, but it is in a clear Record;

606

4   That He may reward those who believe and do good works. For them is pardon and a rich provision.

5   But those who strive against Our revelations, challenging (Us), theirs will be a painful doom of wrath.

6   Those who have been given knowledge see that what is revealed unto thee from thy Lord is the truth and leadeth unto the path of the Mighty, the Owner of Praise.

7   Those who disbelieve say: Shall we show you a man who will tell you (that) when ye have become dispersed in dust with most complete dispersal, still, even then, ye will be created anew?

8   Hath he invented a lie concerning Allah, or is there in him a madness? Nay, but those who disbelieve in the Hereafter are in torment and far error.

9   Have they not observed what is before them and what is behind them of the sky and the earth? If We will, We can make the earth swallow them or cause a portion of the sky to fall on them. Lo! herein surely is a portent for every slave who turneth (to Allah) repentant.

10   And assuredly We gave David grace from Us, (saying): O ye hills and birds, echo his psalms of praise! And We made the iron supple unto him;

لِيَجْزِيَ الَّذِينَ ءَامَنُوا وَعَمِلُوا الصَّلِحَٰتِ أُوْلَٰٓئِكَ لَهُم مَّغْفِرَةٌ وَرِزْقٌ كَرِيمٌ ۝

وَالَّذِينَ سَعَوْا فِىٓ ءَايَٰتِنَا مُعَٰجِزِينَ أُوْلَٰٓئِكَ لَهُمْ عَذَابٌ مِّن رِّجْزٍ أَلِيمٌ ۝

وَيَرَى الَّذِينَ أُوتُوا الْعِلْمَ الَّذِىٓ أُنزِلَ إِلَيْكَ مِن رَّبِّكَ هُوَ الْحَقَّ وَيَهْدِىٓ إِلَىٰ صِرَٰطِ الْعَزِيزِ الْحَمِيدِ ۝

وَقَالَ الَّذِينَ كَفَرُوٓا هَلْ نَدُلُّكُمْ عَلَىٰ رَجُلٍ يُنَبِّئُكُمْ إِذَا مُزِّقْتُمْ كُلَّ مُمَزَّقٍ إِنَّكُمْ لَفِى خَلْقٍ جَدِيدٍ ۝

أَفْتَرَىٰ عَلَى اللَّهِ كَذِبًا أَم بِهِ جِنَّةٌ بَلِ الَّذِينَ لَا يُؤْمِنُونَ بِالْأَخِرَةِ فِى الْعَذَابِ وَالضَّلَٰلِ الْبَعِيدِ ۝

أَفَلَمْ يَرَوْا إِلَىٰ مَا بَيْنَ أَيْدِيهِمْ وَمَا خَلْفَهُم مِّنَ السَّمَاءِ وَالْأَرْضِ إِن نَّشَأْ نَخْسِفْ بِهِمُ الْأَرْضَ أَوْ نُسْقِطْ عَلَيْهِمْ كِسَفًا مِّنَ السَّمَاءِ إِنَّ فِى ذَٰلِكَ لَأَيَةً لِّكُلِّ عَبْدٍ مُّنِيبٍ ۝

۞ وَلَقَدْ ءَاتَيْنَا دَاوُۥدَ مِنَّا فَضْلًا يَٰجِبَالُ أَوِّبِى مَعَهُۥ وَالطَّيْرَ وَأَلَنَّا لَهُ الْحَدِيدَ ۝

11 Saying: Make thou long coats of mail and measure the links (thereof). And do ye right. Lo! I am Seer of what ye do.

أَنِ ٱعْمَلْ سَٰبِغَٰتٍ وَقَدِّرْ فِى ٱلسَّرْدِ وَٱعْمَلُوا۟ صَٰلِحًا إِنِّى بِمَا تَعْمَلُونَ بَصِيرٌ ۝

12 And unto Solomon (We gave) the wind, whereof the morning course was a month's journey and the evening course a month's journey, and We caused the fount of copper to gush forth for him, and (We gave him) certain of the jinn who worked before him by permission of his Lord. And such of them as deviated from Our command, them We caused to taste the punishment of flaming fire.

وَلِسُلَيْمَٰنَ ٱلرِّيحَ غُدُوُّهَا شَهْرٌ وَرَوَاحُهَا شَهْرٌ وَأَسَلْنَا لَهُۥ عَيْنَ ٱلْقِطْرِ وَمِنَ ٱلْجِنِّ مَن يَعْمَلُ بَيْنَ يَدَيْهِ بِإِذْنِ رَبِّهِۦ وَمَن يَزِغْ مِنْهُمْ عَنْ أَمْرِنَا نُذِقْهُ مِنْ عَذَابِ ٱلسَّعِيرِ ۝

13 They made for him what he willed: synagogues and statues, basins like wells and boilers built into the ground. Give thanks, O House of David! Few of My bondmen are thankful.

يَعْمَلُونَ لَهُۥ مَا يَشَآءُ مِن مَّحَٰرِيبَ وَتَمَٰثِيلَ وَجِفَانٍ كَٱلْجَوَابِ وَقُدُورٍ رَّاسِيَٰتٍ ٱعْمَلُوٓا۟ ءَالَ دَاوُۥدَ شُكْرًا وَقَلِيلٌ مِّنْ عِبَادِىَ ٱلشَّكُورُ ۝

14 And when We decreed death for him, nothing showed his death to them save a creeping creature of the earth which gnawed away his staff. And when he fell the jinn saw clearly how, if they had known the unseen, they would not have continued in humiliating torment.

فَلَمَّا قَضَيْنَا عَلَيْهِ ٱلْمَوْتَ مَا دَلَّهُمْ عَلَىٰ مَوْتِهِۦٓ إِلَّا دَآبَّةُ ٱلْأَرْضِ تَأْكُلُ مِنسَأَتَهُۥ فَلَمَّا خَرَّ تَبَيَّنَتِ ٱلْجِنُّ أَن لَّوْ كَانُوا۟ يَعْلَمُونَ ٱلْغَيْبَ مَا لَبِثُوا۟ فِى ٱلْعَذَابِ ٱلْمُهِينِ ۝

15 There was indeed a sign for Sheba in their dwelling place: Two gardens on the right hand and the left (as who should say): Eat of the provision of your Lord and render

لَقَدْ كَانَ لِسَبَإٍ فِى مَسْكَنِهِمْ ءَايَةٌ جَنَّتَانِ عَن يَمِينٍ وَشِمَالٍ كُلُوا۟ مِن رِّزْقِ رَبِّكُمْ وَٱشْكُرُوا۟ لَهُۥ بَلْدَةٌ

طَيِّبَةٌ وَرَبٌّ غَفُورٌ ۝

thanks to Him. A fair land and an indulgent Lord!

فَأَعْرَضُوا فَأَرْسَلْنَا عَلَيْهِمْ سَيْلَ الْعَرِمِ وَبَدَّلْنَاهُمْ بِجَنَّتَيْهِمْ جَنَّتَيْنِ ذَوَاتَيْ أُكُلٍ خَمْطٍ وَأَثْلٍ وَشَيْءٍ مِّن سِدْرٍ قَلِيلٍ ۝

16 But they were froward, so We sent on them the flood of 'Arim, and in exchange for their two gardens gave them two gardens bearing bitter fruit, the tamarisk and here and there a lote tree.

ذَٰلِكَ جَزَيْنَاهُم بِمَا كَفَرُوا وَهَلْ نُجَازِي إِلَّا الْكَفُورَ ۝

17 This We awarded them because of their ingratitude. Punish We ever any save the ingrates?

وَجَعَلْنَا بَيْنَهُمْ وَبَيْنَ الْقُرَى الَّتِي بَارَكْنَا فِيهَا قُرًى ظَاهِرَةً وَقَدَّرْنَا فِيهَا السَّيْرَ سِيرُوا فِيهَا لَيَالِيَ وَأَيَّامًا آمِنِينَ ۝

18 And We set, between them and the towns which We had blessed, towns easy to be seen, and We made the stage between them easy, (saying): Travel in them safely both by night and day.

فَقَالُوا رَبَّنَا بَاعِدْ بَيْنَ أَسْفَارِنَا وَظَلَمُوا أَنفُسَهُمْ فَجَعَلْنَاهُمْ أَحَادِيثَ وَمَزَّقْنَاهُمْ كُلَّ مُمَزَّقٍ إِنَّ فِي ذَٰلِكَ لَآيَاتٍ لِّكُلِّ صَبَّارٍ شَكُورٍ ۝

19 But they said: Our Lord! Make the stage between our journeys longer. And they wronged themselves, therefore We made them bywords (in the land) and scattered them abroad, a total scattering. Lo! herein verily are portents for each steadfast, grateful (heart).

وَلَقَدْ صَدَّقَ عَلَيْهِمْ إِبْلِيسُ ظَنَّهُ فَاتَّبَعُوهُ إِلَّا فَرِيقًا مِّنَ الْمُؤْمِنِينَ ۝

20 And Satan indeed found his calculation true concerning them, for they follow him, all save a group of true believers.

وَمَا كَانَ لَهُ عَلَيْهِم مِّن سُلْطَانٍ إِلَّا لِنَعْلَمَ مَن يُؤْمِنُ بِالْآخِرَةِ مِمَّنْ هُوَ مِنْهَا فِي شَكٍّ وَرَبُّكَ عَلَىٰ كُلِّ شَيْءٍ حَفِيظٌ ۝

21 And he had no warrant whatsoever against them, save that We would know him who believeth in the Hereafter from him who is in doubt thereof; and thy Lord (O Muhammad) taketh note of all things.

22 Say (O Muhammad): Call upon those whom ye set up beside Allah! They possess not an atom's weight either in the heavens or the earth, nor have they any share in either, nor hath He an auxiliary among them.

قُلِ ٱدۡعُواْ ٱلَّذِينَ زَعَمۡتُم مِّن دُونِ ٱللَّهِ لَا يَمۡلِكُونَ مِثۡقَالَ ذَرَّةٍ فِى ٱلسَّمَٰوَٰتِ وَلَا فِى ٱلۡأَرۡضِ وَمَا لَهُمۡ فِيهِمَا مِن شِرۡكٍ وَمَا لَهُۥ مِنۡهُم مِّن ظَهِيرٍ ۝

23 No intercession availeth with Him save for him whom He permitteth. Yet, when fear is banished from their hearts, they say: What was it that your Lord said? They say: The Truth. And He is the Sublime, the Great.

وَلَا تَنفَعُ ٱلشَّفَٰعَةُ عِندَهُۥٓ إِلَّا لِمَنۡ أَذِنَ لَهُۥ حَتَّىٰٓ إِذَا فُزِّعَ عَن قُلُوبِهِمۡ قَالُواْ مَاذَا قَالَ رَبُّكُمۡ قَالُواْ ٱلۡحَقَّ وَهُوَ ٱلۡعَلِىُّ ٱلۡكَبِيرُ ۝

24 Say: Who giveth you provision from the skies and the earth? Say: Allah. Lo! we or you assuredly are rightly guided or in error manifest.

۞ قُلۡ مَن يَرۡزُقُكُم مِّنَ ٱلسَّمَٰوَٰتِ وَٱلۡأَرۡضِ قُلِ ٱللَّهُ وَإِنَّآ أَوۡ إِيَّاكُمۡ لَعَلَىٰ هُدًى أَوۡ فِى ضَلَٰلٍ مُّبِينٍ ۝

25 Say: Ye will not be asked of what we committed, nor shall we be asked of what ye do.

قُل لَّا تُسۡـَٔلُونَ عَمَّآ أَجۡرَمۡنَا وَلَا نُسۡـَٔلُ عَمَّا تَعۡمَلُونَ ۝

26 Say: Our Lord will bring us all together, then He will judge between us with truth. He is the All-knowing Judge.

قُلۡ يَجۡمَعُ بَيۡنَنَا رَبُّنَا ثُمَّ يَفۡتَحُ بَيۡنَنَا بِٱلۡحَقِّ وَهُوَ ٱلۡفَتَّاحُ ٱلۡعَلِيمُ ۝

27 Say: Show me those whom ye have joined unto Him as partners. Nay (ye dare not)! For He is Allah, the Mighty, the Wise.

قُلۡ أَرُونِىَ ٱلَّذِينَ أَلۡحَقۡتُم بِهِۦ شُرَكَآءَ كَلَّا بَلۡ هُوَ ٱللَّهُ ٱلۡعَزِيزُ ٱلۡحَكِيمُ ۝

28 And We have not sent thee (O Muhammad) save as a bringer of good tidings and a warner unto all mankind; but most of mankind know not.

وَمَآ أَرۡسَلۡنَٰكَ إِلَّا كَآفَّةً لِّلنَّاسِ بَشِيرًا وَنَذِيرًا وَلَٰكِنَّ أَكۡثَرَ ٱلنَّاسِ لَا يَعۡلَمُونَ ۝

29 And they say: When is this promise (to be fulfilled) if ye are truthful?

وَيَقُولُونَ مَتَىٰ هَٰذَا ٱلْوَعْدُ إِن كُنتُمْ صَٰدِقِينَ ۝

30 Say (O Muḥammad): Yours is the promise of a Day which ye cannot postpone nor hasten by an hour.

قُل لَّكُم مِّيعَادُ يَوْمٍ لَّا تَسْتَـْٔخِرُونَ عَنْهُ سَاعَةً وَلَا تَسْتَقْدِمُونَ ۝

31 And those who disbelieve say: We believe not in this Qur'an nor in that which was before it; but oh, if thou couldst see, when the wrongdoers are brought up before their Lord, how they cast the blame one to another; how those who were despised (in the earth) say unto those who were proud: But for you, we should have been believers.

وَقَالَ ٱلَّذِينَ كَفَرُوٓا۟ لَن نُّؤْمِنَ بِهَٰذَا ٱلْقُرْءَانِ وَلَا بِٱلَّذِي بَيْنَ يَدَيْهِ وَلَوْ تَرَىٰٓ إِذِ ٱلظَّٰلِمُونَ مَوْقُوفُونَ عِندَ رَبِّهِمْ يَرْجِعُ بَعْضُهُمْ إِلَىٰ بَعْضٍ ٱلْقَوْلَ يَقُولُ ٱلَّذِينَ ٱسْتُضْعِفُوا۟ لِلَّذِينَ ٱسْتَكْبَرُوا۟ لَوْلَآ أَنتُمْ لَكُنَّا مُؤْمِنِينَ ۝

32 And those who were proud say unto those who were despised: Did we drive you away from the guidance after it had come unto you? Nay, but ye were guilty.

قَالَ ٱلَّذِينَ ٱسْتَكْبَرُوا۟ لِلَّذِينَ ٱسْتُضْعِفُوٓا۟ أَنَحْنُ صَدَدْنَٰكُمْ عَنِ ٱلْهُدَىٰ بَعْدَ إِذْ جَآءَكُم بَلْ كُنتُم مُّجْرِمِينَ ۝

33 Those who were despised say unto those who were proud: Nay but (it was your) scheming night and day, when ye commanded us to disbelieve in Allah and set up rivals unto Him. And they are filled with remorse when they behold the doom; and We place carcans on the necks of those who disbelieved. Are they requited aught save what they did?

وَقَالَ ٱلَّذِينَ ٱسْتُضْعِفُوا۟ لِلَّذِينَ ٱسْتَكْبَرُوا۟ بَلْ مَكْرُ ٱلَّيْلِ وَٱلنَّهَارِ إِذْ تَأْمُرُونَنَآ أَن نَّكْفُرَ بِٱللَّهِ وَنَجْعَلَ لَهُۥٓ أَندَادًا وَأَسَرُّوا۟ ٱلنَّدَامَةَ لَمَّا رَأَوُا۟ ٱلْعَذَابَ وَجَعَلْنَا ٱلْأَغْلَٰلَ فِىٓ أَعْنَاقِ ٱلَّذِينَ كَفَرُوا۟ هَلْ يُجْزَوْنَ إِلَّا مَا كَانُوا۟ يَعْمَلُونَ ۝

34 And We sent not unto any township a warner, but its pampered ones declared: Lo! we are disbelievers in that with which ye have been sent.

وَمَآ أَرْسَلْنَا فِى قَرْيَةٍ مِّن نَّذِيرٍ إِلَّا قَالَ مُتْرَفُوهَآ إِنَّا بِمَآ أُرْسِلْتُم بِهِۦ كَٰفِرُونَ ۝

35 And they say: We are more (than you) in wealth and children. We are not the punished!

وَقَالُوا نَحْنُ أَكْثَرُ أَمْوَالًا وَأَوْلَادًا وَمَا نَحْنُ بِمُعَذَّبِينَ ۝

36 Say (O Muhammad): Lo! my Lord enlargeth the provision for whom He will and narroweth it (for whom He will). But most of mankind know not.

قُلْ إِنَّ رَبِّي يَبْسُطُ الرِّزْقَ لِمَنْ يَشَاءُ وَيَقْدِرُ وَلَكِنَّ أَكْثَرَ النَّاسِ لَا يَعْلَمُونَ ۝

37 And it is not your wealth nor your children that will bring you near unto Us, but he who believeth and doeth good (he draweth near). As for such, theirs will be twofold reward for what they did, and they will dwell secure in lofty halls.

وَمَا أَمْوَالُكُمْ وَلَا أَوْلَادُكُمْ بِالَّتِي تُقَرِّبُكُمْ عِنْدَنَا زُلْفَى إِلَّا مَنْ آمَنَ وَعَمِلَ صَالِحًا فَأُولَئِكَ لَهُمْ جَزَاءُ الضِّعْفِ بِمَا عَمِلُوا وَهُمْ فِي الْغُرُفَاتِ آمِنُونَ ۝

38 And as for those who strive against Our revelations, challenging, they will be brought to the doom.

وَالَّذِينَ يَسْعَوْنَ فِي آيَاتِنَا مُعَاجِزِينَ أُولَئِكَ فِي الْعَذَابِ مُحْضَرُونَ ۝

39 Say: Lo! my Lord enlargeth the provision for whom He will of His bondmen, and narroweth (it) for him. And whatsoever ye spend (for good) He replaceth it. And He is the Best of Providers.

قُلْ إِنَّ رَبِّي يَبْسُطُ الرِّزْقَ لِمَنْ يَشَاءُ مِنْ عِبَادِهِ وَيَقْدِرُ لَهُ وَمَا أَنْفَقْتُمْ مِنْ شَيْءٍ فَهُوَ يُخْلِفُهُ وَهُوَ خَيْرُ الرَّازِقِينَ ۝

40 And on the day when He will gather them all together, He will say unto the angels: Did these worship you?

وَيَوْمَ يَحْشُرُهُمْ جَمِيعًا ثُمَّ يَقُولُ لِلْمَلَائِكَةِ أَهَؤُلَاءِ إِيَّاكُمْ كَانُوا يَعْبُدُونَ ۝

41 They will say: Be Thou glorified. Thou art our Protector from them! Nay, but they worshipped the jinn; most of them were believers in them.

قَالُوا سُبْحَانَكَ أَنْتَ وَلِيُّنَا مِنْ دُونِهِمْ بَلْ كَانُوا يَعْبُدُونَ الْجِنَّ أَكْثَرُهُمْ بِهِمْ مُؤْمِنُونَ ۝

42 That day ye will possess no use nor hurt one for another. And We

فَالْيَوْمَ لَا يَمْلِكُ بَعْضُكُمْ لِبَعْضٍ نَفْعًا وَلَا ضَرًّا

shall say unto those who did wrong:
Taste the doom of the Fire which
ye used to deny.

وَنَقُولُ لِلَّذِينَ ظَلَمُوا ذُوقُوا عَذَابَ
النَّارِ الَّتِي كُنتُم بِهَا تُكَذِّبُونَ ﴿٤٢﴾

43 And if Our revelations are
recited unto them in plain terms,
they say: This is naught else than a
man who would turn you away
from what your fathers used to worship; and they say: This is naught
else than an invented lie. Those
who disbelieve say of the truth
when it reacheth them: This is
naught else than mere magic.

وَإِذَا تُتْلَىٰ عَلَيْهِمْ ءَايَاتُنَا بَيِّنَاتٍ قَالُوا مَا هَٰذَا إِلَّا رَجُلٌ
يُرِيدُ أَن يَصُدَّكُمْ عَمَّا كَانَ يَعْبُدُ ءَابَاؤُكُمْ وَقَالُوا
مَا هَٰذَا إِلَّا إِفْكٌ مُّفْتَرًى وَقَالَ الَّذِينَ كَفَرُوا
لِلْحَقِّ لَمَّا جَاءَهُمْ إِنْ هَٰذَا إِلَّا سِحْرٌ مُّبِينٌ ﴿٤٣﴾

44 And We have given them no
Scriptures which they study, nor
sent We unto them, before thee, any
warner.

وَمَا ءَاتَيْنَاهُم مِّن كُتُبٍ يَدْرُسُونَهَا وَمَا أَرْسَلْنَا
إِلَيْهِم قَبْلَكَ مِن نَّذِيرٍ ﴿٤٤﴾

45 Those before them denied, and
these have not attained a tithe of
that which We bestowed on them
(of old); yet they denied My messengers. How intense then was My
abhorrence (of them)!

وَكَذَّبَ الَّذِينَ مِن قَبْلِهِمْ وَمَا بَلَغُوا مِعْشَارَ
مَا ءَاتَيْنَاهُمْ فَكَذَّبُوا رُسُلِي فَكَيْفَ كَانَ نَكِيرِ ﴿٤٥﴾

46 Say (unto them, O Muhammad):
I exhort you unto one thing only:
that ye awake, for Allah's sake, by
twos and singly, and then reflect:
There is no madness in your comrade. He is naught else than a warner unto you in face of a terrific
doom.

۞ قُلْ إِنَّمَا أَعِظُكُم بِوَاحِدَةٍ أَن تَقُومُوا لِلَّهِ مَثْنَىٰ
وَفُرَادَىٰ ثُمَّ تَتَفَكَّرُوا مَا بِصَاحِبِكُم مِّن جِنَّةٍ
إِنْ هُوَ إِلَّا نَذِيرٌ لَّكُم بَيْنَ يَدَيْ عَذَابٍ شَدِيدٍ ﴿٤٦﴾

47 Say: Whatever reward I might
have asked of you is yours. My
reward is the affair of Allah only.
He is Witness over all things.

قُلْ مَا سَأَلْتُكُم مِّنْ أَجْرٍ فَهُوَ لَكُمْ إِنْ أَجْرِيَ
إِلَّا عَلَى اللَّهِ وَهُوَ عَلَىٰ كُلِّ شَيْءٍ شَهِيدٌ ﴿٤٧﴾

48 Say: Lo! my Lord hurleth the
truth. (He is) the Knower of Things
Hidden.

قُلۡ إِنَّ رَبِّي يَقۡذِفُ بِٱلۡحَقِّ عَلَّٰمُ ٱلۡغُيُوبِ ۝

49 Say: The Truth hath come, and
falsehood showeth not its face and
will not return.

قُلۡ جَآءَ ٱلۡحَقُّ وَمَا يُبۡدِئُ ٱلۡبَٰطِلُ وَمَا يُعِيدُ ۝

50 Say: If I err, I err only to my
own loss, and if I am rightly guided
it is because of that which my Lord
hath revealed unto me. Lo! He is
Hearer, Nigh.

قُلۡ إِن ضَلَلۡتُ فَإِنَّمَآ أَضِلُّ عَلَىٰ نَفۡسِيۖ وَإِنِ ٱهۡتَدَيۡتُ
فَبِمَا يُوحِيٓ إِلَيَّ رَبِّيٓۚ إِنَّهُۥ سَمِيعٌ قَرِيبٌ ۝

51 Couldst thou but see when they
are terrified with no escape, and are
seized from near at hand.

وَلَوۡ تَرَىٰٓ إِذۡ فَزِعُواْ فَلَا فَوۡتَ وَأُخِذُواْ مِن مَّكَانٍ
قَرِيبٍ ۝

52 And say: We (now) believe
therein. But how can they reach
(faith) from afar off;

وَقَالُوٓاْ ءَامَنَّا بِهِۦ وَأَنَّىٰ لَهُمُ ٱلتَّنَاوُشُ مِن مَّكَانٍ
بَعِيدٍ ۝

53 When they disbelieved in it of
yore. They aim at the unseen from
afar off.

وَقَدۡ كَفَرُواْ بِهِۦ مِن قَبۡلُۖ وَيَقۡذِفُونَ
بِٱلۡغَيۡبِ مِن مَّكَانٍ بَعِيدٍ ۝

54 And a gulf is set between them
and that which they desire, as was
done for people of their kind of old.
Lo! they were in hopeless doubt.

وَحِيلَ بَيۡنَهُمۡ وَبَيۡنَ مَا يَشۡتَهُونَ كَمَا فُعِلَ بِأَشۡيَاعِهِم
مِّن قَبۡلُۚ إِنَّهُمۡ كَانُواْ فِي شَكٍّ مُّرِيبٍ ۝

Al Malā'ikah or Al Fāṭir
(The Angels or The Creator)

Al Malā'ikah, "The Angels," also called *Al Fāṭir*, "The Creator," takes its name in either case from a word in the first verse.

An early Makkan sūrah.

In the name of Allah, the Beneficent, the Merciful.

1   Praise be to Allah, the Creator of the heavens and the earth, who appointeth the angels messengers having wings two, three and four. He multiplieth in creation what He will. Lo! Allah is Able to do all things.

2   That which Allah openeth unto mankind of mercy none can withhold it; and that which He withholdeth none can release thereafter. He is the Mighty, the Wise.

3   O mankind! Remember Allah's grace toward you! Is there any creator other than Allah who provideth for you from the sky and the earth? There is no God save Him. Whither then are ye turned?

4   And if they deny thee, (O Muhammad), messengers (of Allah) were denied before thee. Unto Allah all things are brought back.

وَإِنْ يُكَذِّبُوكَ فَقَدْ كُذِّبَتْ رُسُلٌ مِّنْ قَبْلِكَ وَإِلَى اللَّهِ تُرْجَعُ الْأُمُورُ ۝

5   O mankind! Lo! the promise of Allah is true. So let not the life of the world beguile you, and let not the (avowed) beguiler beguile you with regard to Allah.

يَا أَيُّهَا النَّاسُ إِنَّ وَعْدَ اللَّهِ حَقٌّ فَلَا تَغُرَّنَّكُمُ الْحَيَوةُ الدُّنْيَا ۖ وَلَا يَغُرَّنَّكُم بِاللَّهِ الْغَرُورُ ۝

6   Lo! the devil is an enemy for you, so treat him as an enemy. He only summoneth his faction to be owners of the flaming Fire.

إِنَّ الشَّيْطَانَ لَكُمْ عَدُوٌّ فَاتَّخِذُوهُ عَدُوًّا إِنَّمَا يَدْعُوا حِزْبَهُ لِيَكُونُوا مِنْ أَصْحَابِ السَّعِيرِ ۝

7   Those who disbelieve, theirs will be an awful doom; and those who believe and do good works, theirs will be forgiveness and a great reward.

الَّذِينَ كَفَرُوا لَهُمْ عَذَابٌ شَدِيدٌ وَالَّذِينَ ءَامَنُوا وَعَمِلُوا الصَّالِحَاتِ لَهُم مَّغْفِرَةٌ وَأَجْرٌ كَبِيرٌ ۝

8   Is he, the evil of whose deeds is made fair-seeming unto him so that he deemeth it good, (other than Satan's dupe)? Allah verily sendeth whom He will astray, and guideth whom He will, so let not thy soul expire in sighings for them. Lo! Allah is Aware of what they do!

أَفَمَن زُيِّنَ لَهُ سُوءُ عَمَلِهِ فَرَءَاهُ حَسَنًا ۖ فَإِنَّ اللَّهَ يُضِلُّ مَن يَشَاءُ وَيَهْدِي مَن يَشَاءُ ۖ فَلَا تَذْهَبْ نَفْسُكَ عَلَيْهِمْ حَسَرَاتٍ ۚ إِنَّ اللَّهَ عَلِيمٌ بِمَا يَصْنَعُونَ ۝

9   And Allah it is who sendeth the winds and they raise a cloud; then We lead it unto a dead land and revive therewith the earth after its death. Such is the Resurrection.

وَاللَّهُ الَّذِي أَرْسَلَ الرِّيَاحَ فَتُثِيرُ سَحَابًا فَسُقْنَاهُ إِلَى بَلَدٍ مَّيِّتٍ فَأَحْيَيْنَا بِهِ الْأَرْضَ بَعْدَ مَوْتِهَا ۚ كَذَلِكَ النُّشُورُ ۝

10 Whoso desireth power (should know that) all power belongeth to Allah. Unto Him good words ascend, and the pious deed doth He exalt; but those who plot iniquities,

مَن كَانَ يُرِيدُ الْعِزَّةَ فَلِلَّهِ الْعِزَّةُ جَمِيعًا ۚ إِلَيْهِ يَصْعَدُ الْكَلِمُ الطَّيِّبُ وَالْعَمَلُ الصَّالِحُ يَرْفَعُهُ ۚ وَالَّذِينَ

theirs will be an awful doom; and the plotting of such (folk) will come to naught.

بَمْكُرُونَ السَّيِّئَاتِ لَهُمْ عَذَابٌ شَدِيدٌ
وَمَكْرُ أُوْلَئِكَ هُوَ يَبُورُ ١

11 Allah created you from dust, then from a little fluid, then He made you pairs (the male and female). No female beareth or bringeth forth save with His knowledge. And no one groweth old who groweth old, nor is aught lessened of his life, but it is recorded in a Book. Lo! that is easy for Allah.

وَاللَّهُ خَلَقَكُمْ مِّن تُرَابٍ ثُمَّ مِن نُّطْفَةٍ ثُمَّ جَعَلَكُمْ
أَزْوَاجًا وَمَا تَحْمِلُ مِنْ أُنثَى وَلَا تَضَعُ إِلَّا بِعِلْمِهِ
وَمَا يُعَمَّرُ مِن مُّعَمَّرٍ وَلَا يُنقَصُ مِنْ عُمُرِهِ
إِلَّا فِي كِتَابٍ إِنَّ ذَلِكَ عَلَى اللَّهِ يَسِيرٌ ١١

12 And two seas[1] are not alike: this, fresh, sweet, good to drink, this (other) bitter, salt. And from them both ye eat fresh meat and derive the ornament that ye wear. And thou seest the ship cleaving them with its prow that ye may seek of His bounty, and that haply ye may give thanks.

وَمَا يَسْتَوِي الْبَحْرَانِ هَذَا عَذْبٌ فُرَاتٌ سَائِغٌ
شَرَابُهُ وَهَذَا مِلْحٌ أُجَاجٌ وَمِن كُلٍّ تَأْكُلُونَ لَحْمًا
طَرِيًّا وَتَسْتَخْرِجُونَ حِلْيَةً تَلْبَسُونَهَا وَتَرَى
الْفُلْكَ فِيهِ مَوَاخِرَ لِتَبْتَغُوا مِن فَضْلِهِ
وَلَعَلَّكُمْ تَشْكُرُونَ ١٢

13 He maketh the night to pass into the day and He maketh the day to pass into the night. He hath subdued the sun and moon to service. Each runneth unto an appointed term. Such is Allah, your Lord; His is the Sovereignty; and those unto whom ye pray instead of Him own not so much as the white spot on a date-stone.

يُولِجُ الَّيْلَ فِي النَّهَارِ وَيُولِجُ النَّهَارَ فِي الَّيْلِ
وَسَخَّرَ الشَّمْسَ وَالْقَمَرَ كُلٌّ يَجْرِي
لِأَجَلٍ مُّسَمًّى ذَلِكُمُ اللَّهُ رَبُّكُمْ لَهُ الْمُلْكُ
وَالَّذِينَ تَدْعُونَ مِن دُونِهِ مَا يَمْلِكُونَ
مِن قِطْمِيرٍ ١٣

14 If ye pray unto them they hear not your prayer, and if they heard

إِن تَدْعُوهُمْ لَا يَسْمَعُوا دُعَاءَكُمْ وَلَوْ سَمِعُوا

---

1. *i.e.* the two kinds of water in the earth.

they could not grant it you. On the Day of Resurrection they will disown association with you. None can inform you like Him Who is Aware.

مَا ٱسْتَجَابُوا۟ لَكُمْ ۖ وَيَوْمَ ٱلْقِيَٰمَةِ يَكْفُرُونَ بِشِرْكِكُمْ ۚ وَلَا يُنَبِّئُكَ مِثْلُ خَبِيرٍ ﴿١٤﴾

15 O mankind! Ye are the poor in your relation to Allah. And Allah! He is the Absolute, the Owner of Praise.

۞ يَٰٓأَيُّهَا ٱلنَّاسُ أَنتُمُ ٱلْفُقَرَآءُ إِلَى ٱللَّهِ ۖ وَٱللَّهُ هُوَ ٱلْغَنِىُّ ٱلْحَمِيدُ ﴿١٥﴾

16 If He will, He can remove you and bring (instead of you) some new creation.

إِن يَشَأْ يُذْهِبْكُمْ وَيَأْتِ بِخَلْقٍ جَدِيدٍ ﴿١٦﴾

17 That is not a hard thing for Allah.

وَمَا ذَٰلِكَ عَلَى ٱللَّهِ بِعَزِيزٍ ﴿١٧﴾

18 And no burdened soul can bear another's burden, and if one heavy laden crieth for (help with) his load, naught of it will be lifted even though he (unto whom he crieth) be of kin. Thou warnest only those who fear their Lord in secret, and have established worship. He who groweth (in goodness), groweth only for himself, (he cannot by his merit redeem others). Unto Allah is the journeying.

وَلَا تَزِرُ وَازِرَةٌ وِزْرَ أُخْرَىٰ ۚ وَإِن تَدْعُ مُثْقَلَةٌ إِلَىٰ حِمْلِهَا لَا يُحْمَلْ مِنْهُ شَىْءٌ وَلَوْ كَانَ ذَا قُرْبَىٰٓ ۗ إِنَّمَا تُنذِرُ ٱلَّذِينَ يَخْشَوْنَ رَبَّهُم بِٱلْغَيْبِ وَأَقَامُوا۟ ٱلصَّلَوٰةَ ۚ وَمَن تَزَكَّىٰ فَإِنَّمَا يَتَزَكَّىٰ لِنَفْسِهِۦ ۚ وَإِلَى ٱللَّهِ ٱلْمَصِيرُ ﴿١٨﴾

19 The blind man is not equal with the seer;

وَمَا يَسْتَوِى ٱلْأَعْمَىٰ وَٱلْبَصِيرُ ﴿١٩﴾

20 Nor is darkness (tantamount to) light;

وَلَا ٱلظُّلُمَٰتُ وَلَا ٱلنُّورُ ﴿٢٠﴾

21 Nor is the shadow equal with the sun's full heat;

وَلَا ٱلظِّلُّ وَلَا ٱلْحَرُورُ ﴿٢١﴾

22 Nor are the living equal with the dead. Lo! Allah maketh whom He will to hear. Thou canst not reach those who are in the graves.

وَمَا يَسْتَوِى ٱلْأَحْيَآءُ وَلَا ٱلْأَمْوَٰتُ ۚ إِنَّ ٱللَّهَ يُسْمِعُ مَن يَشَآءُ ۖ وَمَآ أَنتَ بِمُسْمِعٍ مَّن فِى ٱلْقُبُورِ ﴿٢٢﴾

23 Thou art but a warner.

إِنْ أَنتَ إِلَّا نَذِيرٌ ۝

24 Lo! We have sent thee with the Truth, a bearer of glad tidings and a warner; and there is not a nation but a warner hath passed among them.

إِنَّآ أَرْسَلْنَٰكَ بِالْحَقِّ بَشِيرًا وَنَذِيرًا وَإِن مِّنْ أُمَّةٍ إِلَّا خَلَا فِيهَا نَذِيرٌ ۝

25 And if they deny thee: those before them also denied. Their messengers came unto them with clear proofs (of Allah's sovereignty), and with the Psalms and the Scripture giving light.

وَإِن يُكَذِّبُوكَ فَقَدْ كَذَّبَ الَّذِينَ مِن قَبْلِهِمْ جَآءَتْهُمْ رُسُلُهُم بِالْبَيِّنَٰتِ وَبِالزُّبُرِ وَبِالْكِتَٰبِ الْمُنِيرِ ۝

26 Then seized I those who disbelieved, and how intense was My abhorrence!

ثُمَّ أَخَذْتُ الَّذِينَ كَفَرُوا فَكَيْفَ كَانَ نَكِيرِ ۝

27 Hast thou not seen that Allah causeth water to fall from the sky, and We produce therewith fruit of divers hues; and among the hills are streaks white and red, of divers hues, and (others) raven-black;

أَلَمْ تَرَ أَنَّ اللَّهَ أَنزَلَ مِنَ السَّمَآءِ مَآءً فَأَخْرَجْنَا بِهِۦ ثَمَرَٰتٍ مُّخْتَلِفًا أَلْوَٰنُهَا وَمِنَ الْجِبَالِ جُدَدٌ بِيضٌ وَحُمْرٌ مُّخْتَلِفٌ أَلْوَٰنُهَا وَغَرَابِيبُ سُودٌ ۝

28 And of men and beasts and cattle, in like manner, divers hues? The erudite among His bondsmen fear Allah alone. Lo! Allah is Mighty, Forgiving.

وَمِنَ النَّاسِ وَالدَّوَآبِّ وَالْأَنْعَٰمِ مُخْتَلِفٌ أَلْوَٰنُهُۥ كَذَٰلِكَ إِنَّمَا يَخْشَى اللَّهَ مِنْ عِبَادِهِ الْعُلَمَٰؤُا۟ إِنَّ اللَّهَ عَزِيزٌ غَفُورٌ ۝

29 Lo! those who read the Scripture of Allah, and establish worship, and spend of that which We have bestowed on them secretly and openly, they look forward to imperishable gain;

إِنَّ الَّذِينَ يَتْلُونَ كِتَٰبَ اللَّهِ وَأَقَامُوا الصَّلَوٰةَ وَأَنفَقُوا مِمَّا رَزَقْنَٰهُمْ سِرًّا وَعَلَانِيَةً يَرْجُونَ تِجَٰرَةً لَّن تَبُورَ ۝

30 That He will pay them their wages and increase them of His grace. Lo! He is Forgiving, Responsive.

لِيُوَفِّيَهُمْ أُجُورَهُمْ وَيَزِيدَهُم مِّن فَضْلِهِۦٓ إِنَّهُۥ غَفُورٌ شَكُورٌ ۝

31 As for that which We inspire in thee of the Scripture, it is the Truth confirming that which was (revealed) before it. Lo! Allah is indeed Observer, Seer of his slaves.

وَالَّذِىٓ أَوْحَيْنَآ إِلَيْكَ مِنَ الْكِتَٰبِ هُوَ الْحَقُّ مُصَدِّقًا لِّمَا بَيْنَ يَدَيْهِ إِنَّ اللَّهَ بِعِبَادِهِ لَخَبِيرٌۢ بَصِيرٌ ۝

32 Then We gave the Scripture as inheritance unto those whom We elected of our bondmen. But of them are some who wrong themselves and of them are some who are lukewarm and of them are some who outstrip (others) through good deeds, by Allah's leave. That is the great favour!

ثُمَّ أَوْرَثْنَا الْكِتَٰبَ الَّذِينَ اصْطَفَيْنَا مِنْ عِبَادِنَا فَمِنْهُمْ ظَالِمٌ لِّنَفْسِهِ وَمِنْهُم مُّقْتَصِدٌ وَمِنْهُمْ سَابِقٌۢ بِالْخَيْرَٰتِ بِإِذْنِ اللَّهِ ذَٰلِكَ هُوَ الْفَضْلُ الْكَبِيرُ ۝

33 Gardens of Eden! They enter them wearing armlets of gold and pearl and their raiment therein is silk.

جَنَّٰتُ عَدْنٍ يَدْخُلُونَهَا يُحَلَّوْنَ فِيهَا مِنْ أَسَاوِرَ مِن ذَهَبٍ وَلُؤْلُؤًا وَلِبَاسُهُمْ فِيهَا حَرِيرٌ ۝

34 And they say: Praise be to Allah who hath put grief away from us. Lo! Our Lord is Forgiving, Bountiful;

وَقَالُوا الْحَمْدُ لِلَّهِ الَّذِىٓ أَذْهَبَ عَنَّا الْحَزَنَ إِنَّ رَبَّنَا لَغَفُورٌ شَكُورٌ ۝

35 Who, of His grace, hath installed us in the mansion of eternity, where toil toucheth us not nor can weariness affect us.

الَّذِىٓ أَحَلَّنَا دَارَ الْمُقَامَةِ مِن فَضْلِهِ لَا يَمَسُّنَا فِيهَا نَصَبٌ وَلَا يَمَسُّنَا فِيهَا لُغُوبٌ ۝

36 But as for those who disbelieve, for them is fire of hell; it taketh not complete effect upon them so that they can die, nor is its torment lightened for them. Thus We punish every ingrate.

وَالَّذِينَ كَفَرُوا لَهُمْ نَارُ جَهَنَّمَ لَا يُقْضَىٰ عَلَيْهِمْ فَيَمُوتُوا وَلَا يُخَفَّفُ عَنْهُم مِّنْ عَذَابِهَا كَذَٰلِكَ نَجْزِى كُلَّ كَفُورٍ ۝

37 And they cry for help there, (saying): Our Lord! Release us; we will do right, not (the wrong) that we used to do. Did not We grant

وَهُمْ يَصْطَرِخُونَ فِيهَا رَبَّنَآ أَخْرِجْنَا نَعْمَلْ صَٰلِحًا غَيْرَ الَّذِى كُنَّا نَعْمَلُ أَوَلَمْ نُعَمِّرْكُم

you a life long enough for him who reflected to reflect therein? And the warner came unto you. Now taste (the flavour of your deeds), for evildoers have no helper.

38 Lo! Allah is the Knower of the Unseen of the heavens and the earth. Lo! He is Aware of the secret of (men's) breasts.

39 He it is who hath made you regents in the earth; so he who disbelieveth, his disbelief be on his own head. Their disbelief increaseth for the disbelievers, in their Lord's sight, naught save abhorrence. Their disbelief increaseth for the disbelievers naught save loss.

40 Say: Have ye seen your partnergods to whom ye pray beside Allah? Show me what they created of the earth! Or have they any portion in the heavens? Or have We given them a Scripture so that they act on clear proof therefrom? Nay, the evil-doers promise one another only to deceive.

41 Lo! Allah graspeth the heavens and the earth that they deviate not, and if they were to deviate there is not one that could grasp them after Him. Lo! He is ever Clement, Forgiving.

42 And they swore by Allah, their most binding oath, that if a warner came unto them they would be more tractable than any of the nations;

yet, when a warner came unto them it aroused in them naught save repugnance;

مَا زَادَهُمْ إِلَّا نُفُورًا ۝

43 (Shown in their) behaving arrogantly in the land and plotting evil; and the evil plot encloseth but the men who make it. Then, can they expect aught save the treatment of the folk of old? Thou wilt not find for Allah's way of treatment any substitute, nor wilt thou find for Allah's way of treatment any change.

ٱسْتِكْبَارًا فِى ٱلْأَرْضِ وَمَكْرَ ٱلسَّيِّئِ وَلَا يَحِيقُ ٱلْمَكْرُ ٱلسَّيِّئُ إِلَّا بِأَهْلِهِ فَهَلْ يَنظُرُونَ إِلَّا سُنَّتَ ٱلْأَوَّلِينَ فَلَن تَجِدَ لِسُنَّتِ ٱللَّهِ تَبْدِيلًا وَلَن تَجِدَ لِسُنَّتِ ٱللَّهِ تَحْوِيلًا ۝

44 Have they not travelled in the land and seen the nature of the consequence for those who were before them, and they were mightier than these in power? Allah is not such that aught in the heavens or in the earth escapeth Him. Lo! He is the Wise, the Mighty.

أَوَلَمْ يَسِيرُوا۟ فِى ٱلْأَرْضِ فَيَنظُرُوا۟ كَيْفَ كَانَ عَٰقِبَةُ ٱلَّذِينَ مِن قَبْلِهِمْ وَكَانُوٓا۟ أَشَدَّ مِنْهُمْ قُوَّةً وَمَا كَانَ ٱللَّهُ لِيُعْجِزَهُۥ مِن شَىْءٍ فِى ٱلسَّمَٰوَٰتِ وَلَا فِى ٱلْأَرْضِ إِنَّهُۥ كَانَ عَلِيمًا قَدِيرًا ۝

45 If Allah took mankind to task for that which they earn, He would not leave a living creature on the surface of the earth; but He reprieveth them unto an appointed term, and when their term cometh; then verily (they will know that) Allah is ever Seer of His slaves.

وَلَوْ يُؤَاخِذُ ٱللَّهُ ٱلنَّاسَ بِمَا كَسَبُوا۟ مَا تَرَكَ عَلَىٰ ظَهْرِهَا مِن دَآبَّةٍ وَلَٰكِن يُؤَخِّرُهُمْ إِلَىٰٓ أَجَلٍ مُّسَمًّى فَإِذَا جَآءَ أَجَلُهُمْ فَإِنَّ ٱللَّهَ كَانَ بِعِبَادِهِۦ بَصِيرًا ۝

Yā Sīn

Yā Sīn takes its name from the two letters of the Arabic alphabet which stand as the first verse and are generally held to signify *Yā Insān* ("O Man"). This sūrah is regarded with special reverence, and is recited in times of adversity, illness, fasting and on the approach of death.

It belongs to the middle group of Makkan sūrahs.

In the name of Allah, the
Beneficent, the Merciful.

1 Yā Sīn.

2 By the wise Qur'an;

3 Lo! thou art of those sent;

4 On a straight path;

5 A revelation of the Mighty, the Merciful;

6 That thou mayst warn a folk whose fathers were not warned, so they are heedless.

7 Already hath the word proved true of most of them, so they believe not.

8 Lo! We have put on their necks carcans reaching unto the chins, so that they are made stiff-necked.

9 And We have set a bar before them and a bar behind them, and (thus) have covered them so that they see not.

10 Whether thou warn them or thou warn them not, it is alike for them, for they believe not.

11 Thou warnest only him who followeth the Reminder and feareth the Beneficent in secret. To him bear tidings of forgiveness and a rich reward.

12 Lo! We it is Who bring the dead to life. We record that which they send before (them), and their footprints. And all things We have kept in a clear register.

13 Coin for them a similitude: The people of the city when those sent (from Allah) came unto them;

14 When We sent unto them twain, and they denied them both, so We reinforced them with a third, and they said: Lo! we have been sent unto you.

15 They said: Ye are but mortals like unto us. The Beneficent hath naught revealed. Ye do but lie!

16 They answered: Our Lord knoweth that we are indeed sent unto you;

17 And our duty is but plain conveyance (of the message).

18 (The people of the city) said: We augur ill of you. If ye desist not, we shall surely stone you, and grievous torture will befall you at our hands.

وَسَوَآءٌ عَلَيْهِمْ ءَأَنذَرْتَهُمْ أَمْ لَمْ تُنذِرْهُمْ لَا يُؤْمِنُونَ ﴿١٠﴾

إِنَّمَا تُنذِرُ مَنِ اتَّبَعَ الذِّكْرَ وَخَشِيَ الرَّحْمَٰنَ بِالْغَيْبِ فَبَشِّرْهُ بِمَغْفِرَةٍ وَأَجْرٍ كَرِيمٍ ﴿١١﴾

إِنَّا نَحْنُ نُحْيِ الْمَوْتَىٰ وَنَكْتُبُ مَا قَدَّمُوا وَءَاثَارَهُمْ وَكُلَّ شَيْءٍ أَحْصَيْنَاهُ فِي إِمَامٍ مُّبِينٍ ﴿١٢﴾

وَاضْرِبْ لَهُم مَّثَلًا أَصْحَابَ الْقَرْيَةِ إِذْ جَاءَهَا الْمُرْسَلُونَ ﴿١٣﴾

إِذْ أَرْسَلْنَا إِلَيْهِمُ اثْنَيْنِ فَكَذَّبُوهُمَا فَعَزَّزْنَا بِثَالِثٍ فَقَالُوا إِنَّا إِلَيْكُم مُّرْسَلُونَ ﴿١٤﴾

قَالُوا مَا أَنتُمْ إِلَّا بَشَرٌ مِّثْلُنَا وَمَا أَنزَلَ الرَّحْمَٰنُ مِن شَيْءٍ إِنْ أَنتُمْ إِلَّا تَكْذِبُونَ ﴿١٥﴾

قَالُوا رَبُّنَا يَعْلَمُ إِنَّا إِلَيْكُمْ لَمُرْسَلُونَ ﴿١٦﴾

وَمَا عَلَيْنَا إِلَّا الْبَلَٰغُ الْمُبِينُ ﴿١٧﴾

قَالُوا إِنَّا تَطَيَّرْنَا بِكُمْ لَئِن لَّمْ تَنتَهُوا لَنَرْجُمَنَّكُمْ وَلَيَمَسَّنَّكُم مِّنَّا عَذَابٌ أَلِيمٌ ﴿١٨﴾

19 They said: Your evil augury be with you! Is it because ye are reminded (of the truth)? Nay, but ye are froward folk?

قَالُوا طَائِرُكُم مَّعَكُمْ أَيِن ذُكِّرْتُم بَلْ أَنتُمْ قَوْمٌ مُّسْرِفُونَ ۝

20 And there came from the uttermost part of the city a man running. He cried: O my people! Follow those who have been sent!

وَجَاءَ مِنْ أَقْصَا الْمَدِينَةِ رَجُلٌ يَسْعَى قَالَ يَٰقَوْمِ اتَّبِعُوا الْمُرْسَلِينَ ۝

21 Follow those who ask of you no fee, and who are rightly guided.

اتَّبِعُوا مَن لَّا يَسْأَلُكُمْ أَجْرًا وَهُم مُّهْتَدُونَ ۝

22 For what cause should I not serve Him Who hath created me, and unto Whom ye will be brought back?

وَمَالِيَ لَا أَعْبُدُ الَّذِي فَطَرَنِي وَإِلَيْهِ تُرْجَعُونَ ۝

23 Shall I take (other) gods in place of Him when, if the Beneficent should wish me any harm, their intercession will avail me naught, nor can they save?

ءَأَتَّخِذُ مِن دُونِهِ ءَالِهَةً إِن يُرِدْنِ الرَّحْمَٰنُ بِضُرٍّ لَّا تُغْنِ عَنِّي شَفَٰعَتُهُمْ شَيْئًا وَلَا يُنقِذُونِ ۝

24 Then truly I should be in error manifest.

إِنِّي إِذًا لَّفِي ضَلَٰلٍ مُّبِينٍ ۝

25 Lo! I have believed in your Lord, so hear me!

إِنِّي ءَامَنتُ بِرَبِّكُمْ فَاسْمَعُونِ ۝

26 It was said (unto him): Enter Paradise. He said: Would that my people knew;

قِيلَ ادْخُلِ الْجَنَّةَ قَالَ يَٰلَيْتَ قَوْمِي يَعْلَمُونَ ۝

27 With what (munificence) my Lord hath pardoned me and made me of the honoured ones!

بِمَا غَفَرَ لِي رَبِّي وَجَعَلَنِي مِنَ الْمُكْرَمِينَ ۝

28 We sent not down against his people after him a host from heaven, nor do We ever send.

۞ وَمَا أَنزَلْنَا عَلَىٰ قَوْمِهِ مِنۢ بَعْدِهِ مِن جُندٍ مِّنَ السَّمَاءِ وَمَا كُنَّا مُنزِلِينَ ۝

29 It was but one Shout, and lo! they were extinct.

إِن كَانَتْ إِلَّا صَيْحَةً وَٰحِدَةً فَإِذَا هُمْ خَٰمِدُونَ ۝

30 Ah, the anguish for the bond-men! Never came there unto them a messenger but they did mock him!

يَحَسْرَةً عَلَى الْعِبَادِ مَا يَأْتِيهِم
مِّنْ رَسُولٍ إِلَّا كَانُوا بِهِ يَسْتَهْزِءُونَ ۝

31 Have they not seen how many generations We destroyed before them, which indeed return not unto them;

أَلَمْ يَرَوْا كَمْ أَهْلَكْنَا قَبْلَهُم مِّنَ الْقُرُونِ
أَنَّهُمْ إِلَيْهِمْ لَا يَرْجِعُونَ ۝

32 But all, without exception, will be brought before Us.

وَإِن كُلٌّ لَّمَّا جَمِيعٌ لَّدَيْنَا مُحْضَرُونَ ۝

33 A token unto them is the dead earth. We revive it, and We bring forth from it grain so that they eat thereof;

وَءَايَةٌ لَّهُمُ الْأَرْضُ الْمَيْتَةُ أَحْيَيْنَاهَا
وَأَخْرَجْنَا مِنْهَا حَبًّا فَمِنْهُ يَأْكُلُونَ ۝

34 And We have placed therein gardens of the date-palm and grapes, and We have caused springs of water to gush forth therein:

وَجَعَلْنَا فِيهَا جَنَّاتٍ مِّن نَّخِيلٍ
وَأَعْنَابٍ وَفَجَّرْنَا فِيهَا مِنَ الْعُيُونِ ۝

35 That they may eat of the fruit thereof, and their hands made it not. Will they not, then, give thanks?

لِيَأْكُلُوا مِن ثَمَرِهِ وَمَا عَمِلَتْهُ
أَيْدِيهِمْ أَفَلَا يَشْكُرُونَ ۝

36 Glory be to Him Who created all the sexual pairs, of that which the earth groweth, and of them-selves, and of that which they know not!

سُبْحَانَ الَّذِي خَلَقَ الْأَزْوَاجَ كُلَّهَا مِمَّا تُنبِتُ
الْأَرْضُ وَمِنْ أَنفُسِهِمْ وَمِمَّا لَا يَعْلَمُونَ ۝

37 A token unto them is night. We strip it of the day, and lo! they are in darkness.

وَءَايَةٌ لَّهُمُ الَّيْلُ نَسْلَخُ مِنْهُ النَّهَارَ
فَإِذَا هُم مُّظْلِمُونَ ۝

38 And the sun runneth on unto a resting-place for him. That is the measuring of the Mighty, the Wise.

وَالشَّمْسُ تَجْرِي لِمُسْتَقَرٍّ لَّهَا
ذَلِكَ تَقْدِيرُ الْعَزِيزِ الْعَلِيمِ ۝

39 And for the moon We have appointed mansions till she return like an old shrivelled palm-leaf.

وَالْقَمَرَ قَدَّرْنَاهُ مَنَازِلَ حَتَّى عَادَ كَالْعُرْجُونِ
الْقَدِيمِ ۝

40 It is not for the sun to overtake the moon, nor doth the night outstrip the day. They float each in an orbit.

لَا الشَّمْسُ يَنۢبَغِى لَهَآ أَن تُدۡرِكَ الۡقَمَرَ وَلَا الَّيۡلُ سَابِقُ النَّهَارِ وَكُلٌّ فِى فَلَكٍ يَسۡبَحُونَ ۞

41 And a token unto them is that We bear their offspring in the laden ship;

وَءَايَةٌ لَّهُمۡ أَنَّا حَمَلۡنَا ذُرِّيَّتَهُمۡ فِى الۡفُلۡكِ الۡمَشۡحُونِ ۞

42 And have created for them of the like thereof whereon they ride.

وَخَلَقۡنَا لَهُم مِّن مِّثۡلِهِۦ مَا يَرۡكَبُونَ ۞

43 And if We will, We drown them, and there is no help for them, neither can they be saved;

وَإِن نَّشَأۡ نُغۡرِقۡهُمۡ فَلَا صَرِيخَ لَهُمۡ وَلَا هُمۡ يُنقَذُونَ ۞

44 Unless by mercy from Us and as comfort for a while.

إِلَّا رَحۡمَةً مِّنَّا وَمَتَـٰعًا إِلَىٰ حِينٍ ۞

45 When it is said unto them: Beware of that which is before you and that which is behind you, that haply ye may find mercy (they are heedless).

وَإِذَا قِيلَ لَهُمُ اتَّقُوا مَا بَيۡنَ أَيۡدِيكُمۡ وَمَا خَلۡفَكُمۡ لَعَلَّكُمۡ تُرۡحَمُونَ ۞

46 Never came a token of the tokens of their Lord to them, but they did turn away from it!

وَمَا تَأۡتِيهِم مِّنۡ ءَايَةٍ مِّنۡ ءَايَـٰتِ رَبِّهِمۡ إِلَّا كَانُوا عَنۡهَا مُعۡرِضِينَ ۞

47 And when it is said unto them: Spend of that wherewith Allah hath provided you, those who disbelieve say unto those who believe: Shall we feed those whom Allah, if He willed, would feed? Ye are in naught else than error manifest.

وَإِذَا قِيلَ لَهُمۡ أَنفِقُوا مِمَّا رَزَقَكُمُ اللَّهُ قَالَ الَّذِينَ كَفَرُوا لِلَّذِينَ ءَامَنُوا أَنُطۡعِمُ مَن لَّوۡ يَشَآءُ اللَّهُ أَطۡعَمَهُ إِنۡ أَنتُمۡ إِلَّا فِى ضَلَـٰلٍ مُّبِينٍ ۞

48 And they say: When will this promise be fulfilled, if ye are truthful?

وَيَقُولُونَ مَتَىٰ هَـٰذَا الۡوَعۡدُ إِن كُنتُمۡ صَـٰدِقِينَ ۞

49 They await but one Shout, which will surprise them while they are disputing.

مَا يَنظُرُونَ إِلَّا صَيۡحَةً وَٰحِدَةً تَأۡخُذُهُمۡ وَهُمۡ يَخِصِّمُونَ ۞

50 Then they cannot make bequest, nor can they return to their own folk.

فَلَا يَسْتَطِيعُونَ تَوْصِيَةً وَلَآ إِلَىٰٓ أَهْلِهِمْ يَرْجِعُونَ ۝

51 And the trumpet is blown and lo! from the graves they hie unto their Lord;

وَنُفِخَ فِى ٱلصُّورِ فَإِذَا هُم مِّنَ ٱلْأَجْدَاثِ إِلَىٰ رَبِّهِمْ يَنسِلُونَ ۝

52 Crying: Woe upon us! Who hath raised us from our place of sleep? This is that which the Beneficent did promise, and the messengers spoke truth;

قَالُوا۟ يَٰوَيْلَنَا مَنۢ بَعَثَنَا مِن مَّرْقَدِنَا ۗ هَٰذَا مَا وَعَدَ ٱلرَّحْمَٰنُ وَصَدَقَ ٱلْمُرْسَلُونَ ۝

53 It is but one Shout, and behold them brought together before Us!

إِن كَانَتْ إِلَّا صَيْحَةً وَٰحِدَةً فَإِذَا هُمْ جَمِيعٌ لَّدَيْنَا مُحْضَرُونَ ۝

54 This day no soul is wronged in aught; nor are ye requited aught save what ye used to do.

فَٱلْيَوْمَ لَا تُظْلَمُ نَفْسٌ شَيْـًٔا وَلَا تُجْزَوْنَ إِلَّا مَا كُنتُمْ تَعْمَلُونَ ۝

55 Lo! those who merit paradise this day are happily employed;

إِنَّ أَصْحَٰبَ ٱلْجَنَّةِ ٱلْيَوْمَ فِى شُغُلٍ فَٰكِهُونَ ۝

56 They and their wives, in pleasant shade, on thrones reclining;

هُمْ وَأَزْوَٰجُهُمْ فِى ظِلَٰلٍ عَلَى ٱلْأَرَآئِكِ مُتَّكِـُٔونَ ۝

57 Theirs the fruit (of their good deeds) and theirs (all) that they ask;

لَهُمْ فِيهَا فَٰكِهَةٌ وَلَهُم مَّا يَدَّعُونَ ۝

58 The word from a Merciful Lord (for them) is: Peace!

سَلَٰمٌ قَوْلًا مِّن رَّبٍّ رَّحِيمٍ ۝

59 But avaunt ye, O ye guilty, this day!

وَٱمْتَٰزُوا۟ ٱلْيَوْمَ أَيُّهَا ٱلْمُجْرِمُونَ ۝

60 Did I not charge you, O ye sons of Adam, that ye worship not the devil—Lo! he is your open foe!

۞ أَلَمْ أَعْهَدْ إِلَيْكُمْ يَٰبَنِىٓ ءَادَمَ أَن لَّا تَعْبُدُوا۟ ٱلشَّيْطَٰنَ ۖ إِنَّهُۥ لَكُمْ عَدُوٌّ مُّبِينٌ ۝

61 But that ye worship Me? That was the right path.

وَأَنِ ٱعْبُدُونِى ۚ هَٰذَا صِرَٰطٌ مُّسْتَقِيمٌ ۝

62 Yet he hath led astray of you a great multitude. Had ye then no sense?

وَلَقَدْ أَضَلَّ مِنكُمْ جِبِلًّا كَثِيرًا ۖ أَفَلَمْ تَكُونُوا۟ تَعْقِلُونَ ۝

63 This is hell which ye were promised (if ye followed him).

هَٰذِهِ جَهَنَّمُ الَّتِي كُنتُمْ تُوعَدُونَ ۝

64 Burn therein this day for that ye
disbelieved.

اصْلَوْهَا الْيَوْمَ بِمَا كُنتُمْ تَكْفُرُونَ ۝

65 This day We shall seal up their
mouths and their hands will speak
out to Us and feet bear witness as
to what they used to earn.

الْيَوْمَ نَخْتِمُ عَلَىٰ أَفْوَاهِهِمْ وَتُكَلِّمُنَا أَيْدِيهِمْ
وَتَشْهَدُ أَرْجُلُهُم بِمَا كَانُوا يَكْسِبُونَ ۝

66 And had We willed, We verily
could have quenched their eyesight
so that they should struggle for the
way. Then how could they have
seen?

وَلَوْ نَشَاءُ لَطَمَسْنَا عَلَىٰ أَعْيُنِهِمْ فَاسْتَبَقُوا
الصِّرَاطَ فَأَنَّىٰ يُبْصِرُونَ ۝

67 And had We willed, We verily
could have fixed them in their
place, making them powerless to go
forward or turn back.[1]

وَلَوْ نَشَاءُ لَمَسَخْنَاهُمْ عَلَىٰ مَكَانَتِهِمْ
فَمَا اسْتَطَاعُوا مُضِيًّا وَلَا يَرْجِعُونَ ۝

68 He whom We bring unto old
age, We reverse him in creation
(making him go back to weakness
after strength). Have ye then no
sense?

وَمَن نُّعَمِّرْهُ نُنَكِّسْهُ
فِي الْخَلْقِ أَفَلَا يَعْقِلُونَ ۝

69 And we have not taught him
(Muhammad) poetry, nor is it meet
for him. This is naught else than a
Reminder and a Lecture[2] making
plain;

وَمَا عَلَّمْنَاهُ الشِّعْرَ وَمَا يَنبَغِي
لَهُ إِنْ هُوَ إِلَّا ذِكْرٌ وَقُرْآنٌ مُّبِينٌ ۝

70 To warn whosoever liveth, and
that the word may be fulfilled
against the disbelievers.

لِّيُنذِرَ مَن كَانَ حَيًّا وَيَحِقَّ الْقَوْلُ
عَلَى الْكَافِرِينَ ۝

---

1. But they have sight and power of motion so can choose their way.

2. Ar. *Qur'an*.

71 Have they not seen how We have created for them of Our handiwork the cattle, so that they are their owners;

أَوَلَمْ يَرَوْا أَنَّا خَلَقْنَا لَهُم مِّمَّا عَمِلَتْ أَيْدِينَا أَنْعَـٰمًا فَهُمْ لَهَا مَـٰلِكُونَ ٧١

72 And have subdued them unto them, so that some of them they have for riding, some for food?

وَذَلَّلْنَـٰهَا لَهُمْ فَمِنْهَا رَكُوبُهُمْ وَمِنْهَا يَأْكُلُونَ ٧٢

73 Benefits and (divers) drinks have they from them. Will they not then give thanks?

وَلَهُمْ فِيهَا مَنَـٰفِعُ وَمَشَارِبُ أَفَلَا يَشْكُرُونَ ٧٣

74 And they have taken (other) gods beside Allah, in order that they may be helped.

وَاتَّخَذُوا مِن دُونِ اللَّهِ ءَالِهَةً لَّعَلَّهُمْ يُنصَرُونَ ٧٤

75 It is not in their power to help them; but they (the worshippers) are unto them a host in arms.

لَا يَسْتَطِيعُونَ نَصْرَهُمْ وَهُمْ لَهُمْ جُندٌ مُّحْضَرُونَ ٧٥

76 So let not their speech grieve thee (O Muḥammad). Lo! We know what they conceal and what proclaim.

فَلَا يَحْزُنكَ قَوْلُهُمْ إِنَّا نَعْلَمُ مَا يُسِرُّونَ وَمَا يُعْلِنُونَ ٧٦

77 Hath not man seen that We have created him from a drop of seed? Yet lo! he is an open opponent.

أَوَلَمْ يَرَ الْإِنسَـٰنُ أَنَّا خَلَقْنَـٰهُ مِن نُّطْفَةٍ فَإِذَا هُوَ خَصِيمٌ مُّبِينٌ ٧٧

78 And he hath coined for Us a similitude, and hath forgotten the fact of his creation, saying: Who will revive these bones when they have rotted away?

وَضَرَبَ لَنَا مَثَلًا وَنَسِيَ خَلْقَهُ قَالَ مَن يُحْيِ الْعِظَـٰمَ وَهِيَ رَمِيمٌ ٧٨

79 Say: He will revive them Who produced them at the first, for He is Knower of every creation;

قُلْ يُحْيِيهَا الَّذِي أَنشَأَهَا أَوَّلَ مَرَّةٍ وَهُوَ بِكُلِّ خَلْقٍ عَلِيمٌ ٧٩

80 Who hath appointed for you fire from the green tree, and behold! ye kindle from it.

الَّذِي جَعَلَ لَكُم مِّنَ الشَّجَرِ الْأَخْضَرِ نَارًا فَإِذَا أَنتُم مِّنْهُ تُوقِدُونَ ٨٠

81 Is not He Who created the heavens and the earth Able to create the like of them? Aye, that He is! for. He is the All Wise Creator;

أَوَلَيْسَ الَّذِى خَلَقَ السَّمَوَاتِ وَالْأَرْضَ بِقَدِرٍ عَلَى أَنْ يَخْلُقَ مِثْلَهُمْ بَلَى وَهُوَ الْخَلَّقُ الْعَلِيمُ ۞

82 But His command, when He intendeth a thing, is only that he saith unto it: Be! and it is.

إِنَّمَا أَمْرُهُ إِذَا أَرَادَ شَيْئًا أَنْ يَقُولَ لَهُ كُنْ فَيَكُونُ ۞

83 Therefore glory be to Him in Whose hand is the dominion over all things! Unto Him ye will be brought back.

فَسُبْحَانَ الَّذِى بِيَدِهِ مَلَكُوتُ كُلِّ شَيْءٍ وَإِلَيْهِ تُرْجَعُونَ ۞

Aṣ Ṣāffāt
(Those Who Set the Ranks)

Aṣ Ṣāffāt takes its name from a word in the first verse. The reference in the first three verses is to the angels, as is made clear by vv. 164-166, where the revealing angel speaks in person. Tradition says that soothsayers and astrologers throughout the East were bewildered at the time of the Prophet's coming by the appearance in the heavens of a comet and many meteors which baffled all their science and made them afraid to sit at nights on high peaks to watch the stars, as was their general custom. They told enquirers that their familiars could no longer guide them, being themselves completely at a loss and terrified. This is the explanation usually given of vv. 7-9, and of a passage of similar import in sūrah 72, vv. 8-10.

It stands early in the middle group of Makkan sūrahs.

سُورَةُ الصَّآفَّاتِ

In the name of Allah, the Beneficent, the Merciful.

بِسْمِ اللهِ الرَّحْمَنِ الرَّحِيمِ

1 By those who set the ranks in battle order

2 And those who drive away (the wicked) with reproof

3 And those who read (the Word) for a reminder,

4 Lo! thy Lord is surely One.

5 Lord of the heavens and of the earth and all that is between them, and Lord of the sun's risings.

وَالصَّافَّاتِ صَفًّا ﴿١﴾

فَالزَّاجِرَاتِ زَجْرًا ﴿٢﴾

فَالتَّالِيَاتِ ذِكْرًا ﴿٣﴾

إِنَّ إِلَهَكُمْ لَوَاحِدٌ ﴿٤﴾

رَبُّ السَّمَوَاتِ وَالْأَرْضِ وَمَا بَيْنَهُمَا وَرَبُّ الْمَشَارِقِ ﴿٥﴾

632

6 Lo! We have adorned the lowest heaven with an ornament, the planets:

إِنَّا زَيَّنَّا السَّمَآءَ الدُّنْيَا بِزِينَةٍ الْكَوَاكِبِ ۝

7 With security from every froward devil.

وَحِفْظًا مِّن كُلِّ شَيْطَٰنٍ مَّارِدٍ ۝

8 They cannot listen to the Highest Chiefs for they are pelted from every side;

لَّا يَسَّمَّعُونَ إِلَى الْمَلَإِ الْأَعْلَىٰ وَيُقْذَفُونَ مِن كُلِّ جَانِبٍ ۝

9 Outcast, and theirs is a perpetual torment;

دُحُورًا وَلَهُمْ عَذَابٌ وَاصِبٌ ۝

10 Save him who snatcheth a fragment, and there pursueth him a piercing flame.[1]

إِلَّا مَنْ خَطِفَ الْخَطْفَةَ فَأَتْبَعَهُ شِهَابٌ ثَاقِبٌ ۝

11 Then ask them (O Muḥammad): Are they stronger as a creation, or those (others) whom We have created? Lo! We created them of plastic clay.

فَاسْتَفْتِهِمْ أَهُمْ أَشَدُّ خَلْقًا أَم مَّنْ خَلَقْنَا إِنَّا خَلَقْنَاهُم مِّن طِينٍ لَّازِبٍ ۝

12 Nay, but thou dost marvel when they mock;

بَلْ عَجِبْتَ وَيَسْخَرُونَ ۝

13 And heed not when they are reminded;

وَإِذَا ذُكِّرُوا لَا يَذْكُرُونَ ۝

14 And seek to scoff when they behold a portent;

وَإِذَا رَأَوْا آيَةً يَسْتَسْخِرُونَ ۝

15 And they say: lo! this is mere magic;

وَقَالُوا إِنْ هَٰذَا إِلَّا سِحْرٌ مُّبِينٌ ۝

16 When we are dead and have become dust and bones, shall we then, forsooth, be raised (again)?

أَءِذَا مِتْنَا وَكُنَّا تُرَابًا وَعِظَامًا أَءِنَّا لَمَبْعُوثُونَ ۝

17 And our forefathers?

أَوَءَابَاؤُنَا الْأَوَّلُونَ ۝

---

1. See (72: 8-10); (67: 5).

18 Say (O Muhammad): Yea, in truth; and ye will be brought low.

قُلْ نَعَمْ وَأَنتُمْ دَٰخِرُونَ ۝

19 There is but one Shout, and lo! they behold

فَإِنَّمَا هِىَ زَجْرَةٌ وَٰحِدَةٌ فَإِذَا هُمْ يَنظُرُونَ ۝

20 And say: Ah, woe for us! This is the Day of Judgement.

وَقَالُوا يَٰوَيْلَنَا هَٰذَا يَوْمُ الدِّينِ ۝

21 This is the Day of Separation, which ye used to deny.

هَٰذَا يَوْمُ الْفَصْلِ الَّذِى كُنتُم بِهِ تُكَذِّبُونَ ۝

22 (And it is said unto the angels): Assemble those who did wrong, together with their wives and what they used to worship

۞ احْشُرُوا الَّذِينَ ظَلَمُوا وَأَزْوَٰجَهُمْ وَمَا كَانُوا يَعْبُدُونَ ۝

23 Instead of Allah, and lead them to the path to hell;

مِن دُونِ اللَّهِ فَاهْدُوهُمْ إِلَىٰ صِرَٰطِ الْجَحِيمِ ۝

24 And stop them, for they must be questioned.

وَقِفُوهُمْ إِنَّهُم مَّسْئُولُونَ ۝

25 What aileth you that ye help not one another?

مَا لَكُمْ لَا تَنَاصَرُونَ ۝

26 Nay, but this day they make full submission.

بَلْ هُمُ الْيَوْمَ مُسْتَسْلِمُونَ ۝

27 And some of them draw near unto others, mutually questioning.

وَأَقْبَلَ بَعْضُهُمْ عَلَىٰ بَعْضٍ يَتَسَآءَلُونَ ۝

28 They say: Lo! ye used to come unto us from the right side.

قَالُوا إِنَّكُمْ كُنتُمْ تَأْتُونَنَا عَنِ الْيَمِينِ ۝

29 They answer: Nay, but ye (yourselves) were not believers.

قَالُوا بَل لَّمْ تَكُونُوا مُؤْمِنِينَ ۝

30 We had no power over you, but ye were wayward folk.

وَمَا كَانَ لَنَا عَلَيْكُم مِّن سُلْطَٰنٍ بَلْ كُنتُمْ قَوْمًا طَٰغِينَ ۝

31 Now the Word of our Lord hath been fulfilled concerning us. Lo! we are about to taste (the doom).

فَحَقَّ عَلَيْنَا قَوْلُ رَبِّنَا إِنَّا لَذَآئِقُونَ ۝

32 Thus we misled you. Lo! we were (ourselves) astray.

فَأَغْوَيْنَٰكُمْ إِنَّا كُنَّا غَٰوِينَ ۝

33 Then lo! this day they (both) are sharers in the doom.

فَإِنَّهُمْ يَوْمَئِذٍ فِى ٱلْعَذَابِ مُشْتَرِكُونَ ۝

34 Lo! thus deal We with the guilty.

إِنَّا كَذَٰلِكَ نَفْعَلُ بِٱلْمُجْرِمِينَ ۝

35 For when it was said unto them, There is no god save Allah, they were scornful

إِنَّهُمْ كَانُوٓا۟ إِذَا قِيلَ لَهُمْ لَآ إِلَٰهَ إِلَّا ٱللَّهُ يَسْتَكْبِرُونَ ۝

36 And said: Shall we forsake our gods for a mad poet?

وَيَقُولُونَ أَئِنَّا لَتَارِكُوٓا۟ ءَالِهَتِنَا لِشَاعِرٍ مَّجْنُونٍۭ ۝

37 Nay, but he brought the Truth, and he confirmed those sent (before him).

بَلْ جَآءَ بِٱلْحَقِّ وَصَدَّقَ ٱلْمُرْسَلِينَ ۝

38 Lo! (now) verily ye taste the painful doom

إِنَّكُمْ لَذَآئِقُوا۟ ٱلْعَذَابِ ٱلْأَلِيمِ ۝

39 Ye are requited naught save what ye did

وَمَا تُجْزَوْنَ إِلَّا مَا كُنتُمْ تَعْمَلُونَ ۝

40 Save single minded slaves of Allah;

إِلَّا عِبَادَ ٱللَّهِ ٱلْمُخْلَصِينَ ۝

41 For them there is a known provision,

أُو۟لَٰٓئِكَ لَهُمْ رِزْقٌ مَّعْلُومٌ ۝

42 Fruits. And they will be honored

فَوَٰكِهُ وَهُم مُّكْرَمُونَ ۝

43 In the Gardens of delight,

فِى جَنَّٰتِ ٱلنَّعِيمِ ۝

44 On couches facing one another

عَلَىٰ سُرُرٍ مُّتَقَٰبِلِينَ ۝

45 A cup from a gushing spring is brought round for them,

يُطَافُ عَلَيْهِم بِكَأْسٍ مِّن مَّعِينٍۭ ۝

46 White, delicious to the drinkers,

بَيْضَآءَ لَذَّةٍ لِّلشَّٰرِبِينَ ۝

47 Wherein there is no headache nor are they made mad thereby.

لَا فِيهَا غَوْلٌ وَلَا هُمْ عَنْهَا يُنزَفُونَ ۝

48 And with them are those of modest gaze, with lovely eyes,

وَعِندَهُمْ قَٰصِرَٰتُ ٱلطَّرْفِ عِينٌ ۝

49 (Pure) as they were hidden eggs (of the ostrich).

كَأَنَّهُنَّ بَيْضٌ مَّكْنُونٌ ۝

50 And some of them draw near unto others, mutually questioning.

فَأَقْبَلَ بَعْضُهُمْ عَلَىٰ بَعْضٍ يَتَسَآءَلُونَ ۝

51 A speaker of them saith: Lo! I had a comrade

قَالَ قَآئِلٌ مِّنْهُمْ إِنِّي كَانَ لِي قَرِينٌ ۝

52 Who used to say: Art thou in truth of those who put faith (in his words)?

يَقُولُ أَءِنَّكَ لَمِنَ ٱلْمُصَدِّقِينَ ۝

53 Can we, when we are dead and have become mere dust and bones, can we (then) verily be brought to book?

أَءِذَا مِتْنَا وَكُنَّا تُرَابًا وَعِظَامًا أَءِنَّا لَمَدِينُونَ ۝

54 He saith: Will ye look?

قَالَ هَلْ أَنتُم مُّطَّلِعُونَ ۝

55 Then looketh he and seeth him in the depth of hell.

فَٱطَّلَعَ فَرَءَاهُ فِي سَوَآءِ ٱلْجَحِيمِ ۝

56 He saith: By Allah, thou verily didst all but cause my ruin,

قَالَ تَٱللَّهِ إِن كِدتَّ لَتُرْدِينِ ۝

57 And had it not been for the favour of my Lord, I too had been of those haled forth (to doom).

وَلَوْلَا نِعْمَةُ رَبِّي لَكُنتُ مِنَ ٱلْمُحْضَرِينَ ۝

58 Are we then not to die?

أَفَمَا نَحْنُ بِمَيِّتِينَ ۝

59 Saving our former death, and are we not to be punished?

إِلَّا مَوْتَتَنَا ٱلْأُولَىٰ وَمَا نَحْنُ بِمُعَذَّبِينَ ۝

60 Lo! this is the supreme triumph.

إِنَّ هَٰذَا لَهُوَ ٱلْفَوْزُ ٱلْعَظِيمُ ۝

61 For the like of this, then, let the workers work.

لِمِثْلِ هَٰذَا فَلْيَعْمَلِ ٱلْعَامِلُونَ ۝

62 Is this better as a welcome, or the tree of Zaqqūm?[2]

أَذَٰلِكَ خَيْرٌ نُّزُلًا أَمْ شَجَرَةُ ٱلزَّقُّومِ ۝

63 Lo! We have appointed it a torment for wrong-doers.

إِنَّا جَعَلْنَاهَا فِتْنَةً لِّلظَّالِمِينَ ۝

64 Lo! it is a tree that springeth in the heart of hell

إِنَّهَا شَجَرَةٌ تَخْرُجُ فِي أَصْلِ ٱلْجَحِيمِ ۝

2. (44: 43); (56: 52).

65 Its crop is as it were the heads of devils

طَلْعُهَا كَأَنَّهُۥ رُءُوسُ ٱلشَّيَـٰطِينِ ٦٥

66 And lo! they verily must eat thereof, and fill (their) bellies therewith.

فَإِنَّهُمْ لَأَكِلُونَ مِنْهَا فَمَالِئُونَ مِنْهَا ٱلْبُطُونَ ٦٦

67 And afterward, lo! thereupon they have a drink of boiling water

ثُمَّ إِنَّ لَهُمْ عَلَيْهَا لَشَوْبًا مِّنْ حَمِيمٍ ٦٧

68 And afterward, lo! their return is surely unto hell.

ثُمَّ إِنَّ مَرْجِعَهُمْ لَإِلَى ٱلْجَحِيمِ ٦٨

69 They indeed found their fathers astray,

إِنَّهُمْ أَلْفَوْا ءَابَآءَهُمْ ضَآلِّينَ ٦٩

70 But they make haste (to follow) in their footsteps.

فَهُمْ عَلَىٰٓ ءَاثَـٰرِهِمْ يُهْرَعُونَ ٧٠

71 And verily most of the men of old went astray before them,

وَلَقَدْ ضَلَّ قَبْلَهُمْ أَكْثَرُ ٱلْأَوَّلِينَ ٧١

72 And verily We sent among them warners.

وَلَقَدْ أَرْسَلْنَا فِيهِم مُّنذِرِينَ ٧٢

73 Then see the nature of the consequence for those warned,

فَٱنظُرْ كَيْفَ كَانَ عَـٰقِبَةُ ٱلْمُنذَرِينَ ٧٣

74 Save single-minded slaves of Allah.

إِلَّا عِبَادَ ٱللَّهِ ٱلْمُخْلَصِينَ ٧٤

75 And Noah verily prayed unto Us, and gracious was the Hearer of his prayer

وَلَقَدْ نَادَىٰنَا نُوحٌ فَلَنِعْمَ ٱلْمُجِيبُونَ ٧٥

76 And We saved him and his household from the great distress,

وَنَجَّيْنَـٰهُ وَأَهْلَهُۥ مِنَ ٱلْكَرْبِ ٱلْعَظِيمِ ٧٦

77 And made his seed the survivors,

وَجَعَلْنَا ذُرِّيَّتَهُۥ هُمُ ٱلْبَاقِينَ ٧٧

78 And left for him among the later folk (the salutation):

وَتَرَكْنَا عَلَيْهِ فِى ٱلْءَاخِرِينَ ٧٨

79 Peace be unto Noah among the peoples!

سَلَـٰمٌ عَلَىٰ نُوحٍ فِى ٱلْعَـٰلَمِينَ ٧٩

80 Lo! thus do We reward the good.

إِنَّا كَذَٰلِكَ نَجْزِى ٱلْمُحْسِنِينَ ٨٠

81 Lo! he is one of Our believing slaves.

إِنَّهُ مِنْ عِبَادِنَا الْمُؤْمِنِينَ ﴿٨١﴾

82 Then We did drown the others.

ثُمَّ أَغْرَقْنَا الْآخَرِينَ ﴿٨٢﴾

83 And lo! of his party verily was Abraham

وَإِنَّ مِنْ شِيعَتِهِ لَإِبْرَاهِيمَ ﴿٨٣﴾

84 When he came unto his Lord with a whole heart;

إِذْ جَآءَ رَبَّهُ بِقَلْبٍ سَلِيمٍ ﴿٨٤﴾

85 When he said unto his father and his folk: What is it that ye worship?

إِذْ قَالَ لِأَبِيهِ وَقَوْمِهِ مَاذَا تَعْبُدُونَ ﴿٨٥﴾

86 Is it a falsehood—gods beside Allah—that ye desire?

أَئِفْكًا آلِهَةً دُونَ اللَّهِ تُرِيدُونَ ﴿٨٦﴾

87 What then is your opinion of the Lord of the Worlds?

فَمَا ظَنُّكُمْ بِرَبِّ الْعَالَمِينَ ﴿٨٧﴾

88 And he glanced a glance at the stars

فَنَظَرَ نَظْرَةً فِي النُّجُومِ ﴿٨٨﴾

89 Then said: Lo! I feel sick!

فَقَالَ إِنِّي سَقِيمٌ ﴿٨٩﴾

90 And they turned their backs and went away from him

فَتَوَلَّوْا عَنْهُ مُدْبِرِينَ ﴿٩٠﴾

91 Then turned he to their gods and said: Will ye not eat?

فَرَاغَ إِلَى آلِهَتِهِمْ فَقَالَ أَلَا تَأْكُلُونَ ﴿٩١﴾

92 What aileth you that ye speak not?

مَا لَكُمْ لَا تَنْطِقُونَ ﴿٩٢﴾

93 Then he attacked them, striking with his right hand.

فَرَاغَ عَلَيْهِمْ ضَرْبًا بِالْيَمِينِ ﴿٩٣﴾

94 And (his people) came toward him, hastening.

فَأَقْبَلُوا إِلَيْهِ يَزِفُّونَ ﴿٩٤﴾

95 He said: Worship ye that which ye yourselves do carve

قَالَ أَتَعْبُدُونَ مَا تَنْحِتُونَ ﴿٩٥﴾

96 When Allah hath created you and what ye make?

وَاللَّهُ خَلَقَكُمْ وَمَا تَعْمَلُونَ ﴿٩٦﴾

97 They said: Build for him a building and fling him in the red hot fire.

قَالُوا ابْنُوا لَهُ بُنْيَانًا فَأَلْقُوهُ فِي الْجَحِيمِ ﴿٩٧﴾

98 And they designed a snare for him, but We made them the undermost.

فَأَرَادُوا بِهِ كَيْدًا فَجَعَلْنَهُمُ الْأَسْفَلِينَ ۝

99 And he said: Lo! I am going unto my Lord Who will guide me

وَقَالَ إِنِّي ذَاهِبٌ إِلَى رَبِّي سَيَهْدِينِ ۝

100 My Lord! Vouchsafe me of the righteous.

رَبِّ هَبْ لِي مِنَ الصَّالِحِينَ ۝

101 So We gave him tidings of a gentle son.

فَبَشَّرْنَهُ بِغُلَامٍ حَلِيمٍ ۝

102 And when (his son) was old enough to walk with him, (Abraham) said: O my dear son, I have seen in a dream that I must sacrifice thee. So look, what thinkest thou? He said: O my father! Do that which thou art commanded. Allah willing, thou shalt find me of the steadfast.

فَلَمَّا بَلَغَ مَعَهُ السَّعْيَ قَالَ يَبُنَيَّ إِنِّي أَرَى فِي الْمَنَامِ أَنِّي أَذْبَحُكَ فَانْظُرْ مَاذَا تَرَىٰ قَالَ يَأَبَتِ افْعَلْ مَا تُؤْمَرُ سَتَجِدُنِي إِن شَاءَ اللَّهُ مِنَ الصَّابِرِينَ ۝

103 Then, when they had both surrendered (to Allah), and he had flung him down upon his face,

فَلَمَّا أَسْلَمَا وَتَلَّهُ لِلْجَبِينِ ۝

104 We called unto him: O Abraham:

وَنَادَيْنَهُ أَن يَابِرَاهِيمُ ۝

105 Thou hast already fulfilled the vision. Lo! thus do We reward the good.

قَدْ صَدَّقْتَ الرُّؤْيَا إِنَّا كَذَلِكَ نَجْزِي الْمُحْسِنِينَ ۝

106 Lo! that verily was a clear test.

إِنَّ هَذَا لَهُوَ الْبَلَؤُا الْمُبِينُ ۝

107 Then We ransomed him with a tremendous victim.

وَفَدَيْنَهُ بِذِبْحٍ عَظِيمٍ ۝

108 And We left for him among the later folk (the salutation):

وَتَرَكْنَا عَلَيْهِ فِي الْآخِرِينَ ۝

109 Peace be unto Abraham!

سَلَامٌ عَلَى إِبْرَاهِيمَ ۝

110 Thus do We reward the good.

كَذَٰلِكَ نَجْزِى ٱلْمُحْسِنِينَ ﴿١١٠﴾

111 Lo! he is one of Our believing slaves.

إِنَّهُۥ مِنْ عِبَادِنَا ٱلْمُؤْمِنِينَ ﴿١١١﴾

112 And We gave him tidings of the birth of Isaac, a Prophet of the righteous.

وَبَشَّرْنَٰهُ بِإِسْحَٰقَ نَبِيًّا مِّنَ ٱلصَّٰلِحِينَ ﴿١١٢﴾

113 And We blessed him and Isaac. And of their seed are some who do good, and some who plainly wrong themselves.

وَبَٰرَكْنَا عَلَيْهِ وَعَلَىٰٓ إِسْحَٰقَ وَمِن ذُرِّيَّتِهِمَا مُحْسِنٌ وَظَالِمٌ لِّنَفْسِهِۦ مُبِينٌ ﴿١١٣﴾

114 And We verily gave grace unto Moses and Aaron,

وَلَقَدْ مَنَنَّا عَلَىٰ مُوسَىٰ وَهَٰرُونَ ﴿١١٤﴾

115 And saved them and their people from the great distress,

وَنَجَّيْنَٰهُمَا وَقَوْمَهُمَا مِنَ ٱلْكَرْبِ ٱلْعَظِيمِ ﴿١١٥﴾

116 And helped them so that they became the victors.

وَنَصَرْنَٰهُمْ فَكَانُوا۟ هُمُ ٱلْغَٰلِبِينَ ﴿١١٦﴾

117 And We gave them the clear Scripture

وَءَاتَيْنَٰهُمَا ٱلْكِتَٰبَ ٱلْمُسْتَبِينَ ﴿١١٧﴾

118 And showed them the right path.

وَهَدَيْنَٰهُمَا ٱلصِّرَٰطَ ٱلْمُسْتَقِيمَ ﴿١١٨﴾

119 And We left for them, among the later folk (the salutation):

وَتَرَكْنَا عَلَيْهِمَا فِى ٱلْءَاخِرِينَ ﴿١١٩﴾

120 Peace be unto Moses and Aaron!

سَلَٰمٌ عَلَىٰ مُوسَىٰ وَهَٰرُونَ ﴿١٢٠﴾

121 Lo! thus do We reward the good.

إِنَّا كَذَٰلِكَ نَجْزِى ٱلْمُحْسِنِينَ ﴿١٢١﴾

122 Lo! they are two of our believing slaves.

إِنَّهُمَا مِنْ عِبَادِنَا ٱلْمُؤْمِنِينَ ﴿١٢٢﴾

123 And lo! Elias was of those sent (to warn),

وَإِنَّ إِلْيَاسَ لَمِنَ ٱلْمُرْسَلِينَ ﴿١٢٣﴾

124 When he said unto his folk: Will ye not ward off (evil)?

إِذْ قَالَ لِقَوْمِهِۦٓ أَلَا تَتَّقُونَ ﴿١٢٤﴾

125 Will ye cry unto Ba'l and forsake the best of Creators,

أَنَدْعُونَ بَعْلًا وَتَذَرُونَ أَحْسَنَ الْخَالِقِينَ ۝

126 Allah, your Lord and Lord of your forefathers?

اللَّهَ رَبَّكُمْ وَرَبَّ ءَابَآئِكُمُ الْأَوَّلِينَ ۝

127 But they denied him, so they surely will be haled forth (to the doom)

فَكَذَّبُوهُ فَإِنَّهُمْ لَمُحْضَرُونَ ۝

128 Save single-minded slaves of Allah.

إِلَّا عِبَادَ اللَّهِ الْمُخْلَصِينَ ۝

129 And we left for him among the later folk (the salutation):

وَتَرَكْنَا عَلَيْهِ فِي الْآخِرِينَ ۝

130 Peace be unto Elias!

سَلَٰمٌ عَلَىٰٓ إِلْ يَاسِينَ ۝

131 Lo! thus do We reward the good.

إِنَّا كَذَٰلِكَ نَجْزِي الْمُحْسِنِينَ ۝

132 Lo! he is one of our believing slaves.

إِنَّهُۥ مِنْ عِبَادِنَا الْمُؤْمِنِينَ ۝

133 And lo! Lot verily was of those sent (to warn),

وَإِنَّ لُوطًا لَّمِنَ الْمُرْسَلِينَ ۝

134 When We saved him and his household, every one,

إِذْ نَجَّيْنَٰهُ وَأَهْلَهُۥٓ أَجْمَعِينَ ۝

135 Save an old woman among those who stayed behind;

إِلَّا عَجُوزًا فِي الْغَٰبِرِينَ ۝

136 Then We destroyed the others.

ثُمَّ دَمَّرْنَا الْآخَرِينَ ۝

137 And Lo! ye verily pass by (the ruin of) them in the morning

وَإِنَّكُمْ لَتَمُرُّونَ عَلَيْهِم مُّصْبِحِينَ ۝

138 And at night time; have ye then no sense?

وَبِالَّيْلِ أَفَلَا تَعْقِلُونَ ۝

139 And lo! Jonah verily was of those sent (to warn)

وَإِنَّ يُونُسَ لَمِنَ الْمُرْسَلِينَ ۝

140 When he fled unto the laden ship,

إِذْ أَبَقَ إِلَى الْفُلْكِ الْمَشْحُونِ ۝

141   And then drew lots and was
of those rejected;

فَسَاهَمَ فَكَانَ مِنَ ٱلْمُدْحَضِينَ ﴿١٤١﴾

142   And the fish swallowed him
while he was blameworthy;

فَٱلْتَقَمَهُ ٱلْحُوتُ وَهُوَ مُلِيمٌ ﴿١٤٢﴾

143   And had he not been one of
those who glorify (Allah)

فَلَوْلَآ أَنَّهُۥ كَانَ مِنَ ٱلْمُسَبِّحِينَ ﴿١٤٣﴾

144   He would have tarried in its
belly till the day when they are
raised;

لَلَبِثَ فِى بَطْنِهِۦٓ إِلَىٰ يَوْمِ يُبْعَثُونَ ﴿١٤٤﴾

145   Then We cast him on a
desert shore while he was sick;

۞ فَنَبَذْنَٰهُ بِٱلْعَرَآءِ وَهُوَ سَقِيمٌ ﴿١٤٥﴾

146   And We caused a tree of
gourd to grow above him;

وَأَنۢبَتْنَا عَلَيْهِ شَجَرَةً مِّن يَقْطِينٍ ﴿١٤٦﴾

147   And We sent him to a
hundred thousand (folk) or more

وَأَرْسَلْنَٰهُ إِلَىٰ مِائَةِ أَلْفٍ أَوْ يَزِيدُونَ ﴿١٤٧﴾

148   And they believed, therefore
We gave them comfort for a while.

فَـَٔامَنُوا۟ فَمَتَّعْنَٰهُمْ إِلَىٰ حِينٍ ﴿١٤٨﴾

149   Now ask them (O
Muhammad): Hath thy Lord
daughters whereas they have sons?

فَٱسْتَفْتِهِمْ أَلِرَبِّكَ ٱلْبَنَاتُ وَلَهُمُ ٱلْبَنُونَ ﴿١٤٩﴾

150   Or created We the angels
females while they were present?

أَمْ خَلَقْنَا ٱلْمَلَٰٓئِكَةَ إِنَٰثًا وَهُمْ
شَٰهِدُونَ ﴿١٥٠﴾

151   Lo! it is of their falsehood
that they say:

أَلَآ إِنَّهُم مِّنْ إِفْكِهِمْ لَيَقُولُونَ ﴿١٥١﴾

152   Allah hath begotten. And lo!
verily they tell a lie.

وَلَدَ ٱللَّهُ وَإِنَّهُمْ لَكَٰذِبُونَ ﴿١٥٢﴾

153   (And again of their falsehood): He hath preferred daughters
to sons

أَصْطَفَى ٱلْبَنَاتِ عَلَى ٱلْبَنِينَ ﴿١٥٣﴾

154   What aileth you? How judge
ye?

مَا لَكُمْ كَيْفَ تَحْكُمُونَ ﴿١٥٤﴾

155   Will ye not then reflect?

أَفَلَا تَذَكَّرُونَ ﴿١٥٥﴾

156   Or have ye a clear warrant?

أَمْ لَكُمْ سُلْطَٰنٌ مُّبِينٌ ﴿١٥٦﴾

157 Then produce your writ, if ye are truthful.

فَأْتُوا بِكِتَٰبِكُمْ إِن كُنتُمْ صَٰدِقِينَ ۝

158 And they imagine kinship between him and the jinn, whereas the jinn know well that they will be brought before (Him).

وَجَعَلُوا بَيْنَهُۥ وَبَيْنَ ٱلْجِنَّةِ نَسَبًا ۚ وَلَقَدْ عَلِمَتِ ٱلْجِنَّةُ إِنَّهُمْ لَمُحْضَرُونَ ۝

159 Glorified be Allah from that which they attribute (unto Him),

سُبْحَٰنَ ٱللَّهِ عَمَّا يَصِفُونَ ۝

160 Save single-minded slaves of Allah.

إِلَّا عِبَادَ ٱللَّهِ ٱلْمُخْلَصِينَ ۝

161 Lo! verily, ye and that which ye worship,

فَإِنَّكُمْ وَمَا تَعْبُدُونَ ۝

162 Ye cannot excite (anyone) against Him

مَا أَنتُمْ عَلَيْهِ بِفَٰتِنِينَ ۝

163 Save him who is to burn in hell.

إِلَّا مَنْ هُوَ صَالِ ٱلْجَحِيمِ ۝

164 There is not one of Us[3] but hath his known position.

وَمَا مِنَّآ إِلَّا لَهُۥ مَقَامٌ مَّعْلُومٌ ۝

165 Lo! We, even We are they who set the ranks.

وَإِنَّا لَنَحْنُ ٱلصَّآفُّونَ ۝

166 Lo! We, even We are they who hymn His praise

وَإِنَّا لَنَحْنُ ٱلْمُسَبِّحُونَ ۝

167 And indeed they used to say:

وَإِن كَانُوا لَيَقُولُونَ ۝

168 If we had but a reminder from the men of old

لَوْ أَنَّ عِندَنَا ذِكْرًا مِّنَ ٱلْأَوَّلِينَ ۝

169 We would be single-minded slaves of Allah.

لَكُنَّا عِبَادَ ٱللَّهِ ٱلْمُخْلَصِينَ ۝

170 Yet (now that it is come) they disbelieve therein; but they will come to know.

فَكَفَرُوا بِهِۦ ۖ فَسَوْفَ يَعْلَمُونَ ۝

---

3. Here the revealing angel speaks in person.

171   And verily Our word went forth of old unto Our bondmen sent (to warn)

وَلَقَدْ سَبَقَتْ كَلِمَتُنَا لِعِبَادِنَا ٱلْمُرْسَلِينَ ۝

172   That they verily would be helped,

إِنَّهُمْ لَهُمُ ٱلْمَنصُورُونَ ۝

173   And that Our host, they verily would be the victors.

وَإِنَّ جُندَنَا لَهُمُ ٱلْغَٰلِبُونَ ۝

174   So withdraw from them (O Muhammad) awhile,

فَتَوَلَّ عَنْهُمْ حَتَّىٰ حِينٍ ۝

175   And watch, for they will (soon) see.

وَأَبْصِرْهُمْ فَسَوْفَ يُبْصِرُونَ ۝

176   Would they hasten on Our doom?

أَفَبِعَذَابِنَا يَسْتَعْجِلُونَ ۝

177   But when it cometh home to them, then it will be a hapless morn for those who have been warned.

فَإِذَا نَزَلَ بِسَاحَتِهِمْ فَسَآءَ صَبَاحُ ٱلْمُنذَرِينَ ۝

178   Withdraw from them awhile

وَتَوَلَّ عَنْهُمْ حَتَّىٰ حِينٍ ۝

179   And watch, for they will (soon) see.

وَأَبْصِرْ فَسَوْفَ يُبْصِرُونَ ۝

180   Glorified be thy Lord, the Lord of Majesty, from that which they attribute (unto Him)

سُبْحَٰنَ رَبِّكَ رَبِّ ٱلْعِزَّةِ عَمَّا يَصِفُونَ ۝

181   And peace be unto those sent (to warn).

وَسَلَٰمٌ عَلَى ٱلْمُرْسَلِينَ ۝

182   And praise be to Allah, Lord of the Worlds!

وَٱلْحَمْدُ لِلَّهِ رَبِّ ٱلْعَٰلَمِينَ ۝

Ṣād

Ṣād. This sūrah takes its name from the letter of the Arabic Alphabet which stands alone as the first verse. Tradition says that the first ten verses were revealed when the leaders of Quraysh tried to persuade Abū Ṭālib to withdraw his protection from the Prophet, or when Abū Ṭālib died. The former is the more probable.

Its place is in the middle group of Makkan sūrahs.

In the name of Allah, the Beneficent, the Merciful.

1 Ṣād. By the renowned Qur'an,

2 Nay, but those who disbelieve are in false pride and schism.

3 How many a generation We destroyed before them, and they cried out when it was no longer the time for escape!

4 And they marvel that a warner from among themselves hath come unto them, and the disbelievers say: This is a wizard, a charlatan.

5 Maketh he the gods One God? Lo! that is an astounding thing.

6 The chiefs among them go about, exhorting: Go and be staunch to your gods! Lo! this is a thing designed.

645

7 We have not heard of this in later religion. This is naught but an invention.

8 Hath the reminder been revealed unto him (alone) among us? Nay, but they are in doubt concerning My reminder; nay but they have not yet tasted My doom.

9 Or are theirs the treasures of the mercy of thy Lord, the Mighty, the Bestower?

10 Or is the kingdom of the heavens and the earth and all that is between them theirs? Then let them ascend by ropes!

11 A defeated host are (all) the factions that are there.

12 The folk of Noah before them denied (their messenger) and (so did the tribe of) ʿĀd, and Pharaoh firmly planted,

13 And (the tribe of) Thamūd; and the folk of Lot, and the dwellers in the wood[1]: these were the factions.

14 Not one of them but did deny the messengers, therefore My doom was justified,

15 These wait for but one Shout, there will be no second thereto.

16 They say: Our Lord! Hasten on for us our fate before the Day of Reckoning.

 مَا سَمِعْنَا بِهَذَا فِى الْمِلَّةِ الْآخِرَةِ إِنْ هَذَآ إِلَّا اخْتِلَاقٌ ۝

أَءُنزِلَ عَلَيْهِ الذِّكْرُ مِنۢ بَيْنِنَا بَلْ هُمْ فِى شَكٍّ مِّن ذِكْرِى بَل لَّمَّا يَذُوقُوا عَذَابِ ۝

أَمْ عِندَهُمْ خَزَآئِنُ رَحْمَةِ رَبِّكَ الْعَزِيزِ الْوَهَّابِ ۝

أَمْ لَهُم مُّلْكُ السَّمَوَاتِ وَالْأَرْضِ وَمَا بَيْنَهُمَا فَلْيَرْتَقُوا فِى الْأَسْبَابِ ۝

جُندٌ مَّا هُنَالِكَ مَهْزُومٌ مِّنَ الْأَحْزَابِ ۝

كَذَّبَتْ قَبْلَهُمْ قَوْمُ نُوحٍ وَعَادٌ وَفِرْعَوْنُ ذُو الْأَوْتَادِ ۝

وَثَمُودُ وَقَوْمُ لُوطٍ وَأَصْحَابُ لْئَيْكَةِ أُوْلَئِكَ الْأَحْزَابُ ۝

إِن كُلٌّ إِلَّا كَذَّبَ الرُّسُلَ فَحَقَّ عِقَابِ ۝

وَمَا يَنظُرُ هَؤُلَآءِ إِلَّا صَيْحَةً وَاحِدَةً مَّا لَهَا مِن فَوَاقٍ ۝

وَقَالُوا رَبَّنَا عَجِّل لَّنَا قِطَّنَا قَبْلَ يَوْمِ الْحِسَابِ ۝

---

1. Madyan.

17 Bear with what they say, and remember Our bondman David, lord of might. Lo! he was ever turning in repentance (toward Allah).

أَصْبِرْ عَلَىٰ مَا يَقُولُونَ وَاذْكُرْ عَبْدَنَا دَاوُدَ ذَا الْأَيْدِ إِنَّهُ أَوَّابٌ ۝

18 Lo! We subdued the hills to hymn the praises (of their Lord) with him at nightfall and sunrise,

إِنَّا سَخَّرْنَا الْجِبَالَ مَعَهُ يُسَبِّحْنَ بِالْعَشِيِّ وَالْإِشْرَاقِ ۝

19 And the birds assembled; all were turning unto Him

وَالطَّيْرَ مَحْشُورَةً كُلٌّ لَّهُ أَوَّابٌ ۝

20 We made his kingdom strong and gave him wisdom and decisive speech.

وَشَدَدْنَا مُلْكَهُ وَآتَيْنَاهُ الْحِكْمَةَ وَفَصْلَ الْخِطَابِ ۝

21 And hath the story of the litigants come unto thee? How they climbed the wall into the royal chamber;

۞ وَهَلْ أَتَاكَ نَبَؤُا الْخَصْمِ إِذْ تَسَوَّرُوا الْمِحْرَابَ ۝

22 How they burst in upon David, and he was afraid of them. They said Be not afraid! (We are) two litigants, one of whom hath wronged the other, therefore judge aright between us; be not unjust; and show us the fair way.

إِذْ دَخَلُوا عَلَىٰ دَاوُدَ فَفَزِعَ مِنْهُمْ قَالُوا لَا تَخَفْ خَصْمَانِ بَغَىٰ بَعْضُنَا عَلَىٰ بَعْضٍ فَاحْكُمْ بَيْنَنَا بِالْحَقِّ وَلَا تُشْطِطْ وَاهْدِنَا إِلَىٰ سَوَاءِ الصِّرَاطِ ۝

23 Lo! this my brother hath ninety and nine ewes while I had one ewe; and he said: Entrust it to me, and he conquered me in speech.

إِنَّ هَٰذَا أَخِي لَهُ تِسْعٌ وَتِسْعُونَ نَعْجَةً وَلِيَ نَعْجَةٌ وَاحِدَةٌ فَقَالَ أَكْفِلْنِيهَا وَعَزَّنِي فِي الْخِطَابِ ۝

24 (David) said: He hath wronged thee in demanding thine ewe in addition to his ewes, and lo! many partners oppress one another, save such as believe and do good works, and they are few. And David guessed that We had tried him, and he sought forgiveness of his Lord, and he bowed himself and fell down prostrate and repented.

قَالَ لَقَدْ ظَلَمَكَ بِسُؤَالِ نَعْجَتِكَ إِلَىٰ نِعَاجِهِ وَإِنَّ كَثِيرًا مِّنَ الْخُلَطَاءِ لَيَبْغِي بَعْضُهُمْ عَلَىٰ بَعْضٍ إِلَّا الَّذِينَ آمَنُوا وَعَمِلُوا الصَّالِحَاتِ وَقَلِيلٌ مَّا هُمْ وَظَنَّ دَاوُدُ أَنَّمَا فَتَنَّاهُ فَاسْتَغْفَرَ رَبَّهُ وَخَرَّ رَاكِعًا وَأَنَابَ ۩ ۝

25 So We forgave him that; and lo! he had access to Our presence and a happy journey's end.

فَغَفَرْنَا لَهُ ذَٰلِكَ وَإِنَّ لَهُ عِنْدَنَا لَزُلْفَىٰ وَحُسْنَ مَـَٔابٍ ۝

26 (And it was said unto him): O David! Lo! We have set thee as a viceroy in the earth; therefore judge aright between mankind, and follow not desire that it beguile thee from the way of Allah. Lo! those who wander from the way of Allah have an awful doom, forasmuch as they forgot the Day of Reckoning.

يَـٰدَاوُدُ إِنَّا جَعَلْنَـٰكَ خَلِيفَةً فِى الْأَرْضِ فَاحْكُم بَيْنَ النَّاسِ بِالْحَقِّ وَلَا تَتَّبِعِ الْهَوَىٰ فَيُضِلَّكَ عَن سَبِيلِ اللَّهِ إِنَّ الَّذِينَ يَضِلُّونَ عَن سَبِيلِ اللَّهِ لَهُمْ عَذَابٌ شَدِيدٌۢ بِمَا نَسُوا يَوْمَ الْحِسَابِ ۝

27 And We created not the heaven and the earth and all that is between them in vain. That is the opinion of those who disbelieve. And woe unto those who disbelieve, from the Fire!

وَمَا خَلَقْنَا السَّمَاءَ وَالْأَرْضَ وَمَا بَيْنَهُمَا بَاطِلًا ذَٰلِكَ ظَنُّ الَّذِينَ كَفَرُوا فَوَيْلٌ لِّلَّذِينَ كَفَرُوا مِنَ النَّارِ ۝

28 Shall We treat those who believe and do good works as those who spread corruption in the earth; or shall We treat the Pious as the wicked?

أَمْ نَجْعَلُ الَّذِينَ ءَامَنُوا وَعَمِلُوا الصَّـٰلِحَـٰتِ كَالْمُفْسِدِينَ فِى الْأَرْضِ أَمْ نَجْعَلُ الْمُتَّقِينَ كَالْفُجَّارِ ۝

29 (This is) a Scripture that We have revealed unto thee, full of blessing, that they may ponder its revelations, and that men of understanding may reflect.

كِتَـٰبٌ أَنزَلْنَـٰهُ إِلَيْكَ مُبَـٰرَكٌ لِّيَدَّبَّرُوا ءَايَـٰتِهِ وَلِيَتَذَكَّرَ أُولُوا الْأَلْبَـٰبِ ۝

30 And We bestowed on David, Solomon. How excellent a slave! Lo! he was ever turning in repentance (toward Allah).

وَوَهَبْنَا لِدَاوُدَ سُلَيْمَـٰنَ نِعْمَ الْعَبْدُ إِنَّهُ أَوَّابٌ ۝

31 When there were shown to him at eventide light footed coursers

إِذْ عُرِضَ عَلَيْهِ بِالْعَشِىِّ الصَّـٰفِنَـٰتُ الْجِيَادُ ۝

32 And he said: Lo! I have preferred the good things (of the

فَقَالَ إِنِّى أَحْبَبْتُ حُبَّ الْخَيْرِ عَن ذِكْرِ رَبِّى

world) to the remembrance of my Lord; till they were taken out of sight behind the curtain.

حَتَّىٰ تَوَارَتْ بِالْحِجَابِ ﴿٣٢﴾

33 (Then he said): Bring them back to me, and fell to slashing (with his sword their) legs and necks.

رُدُّوهَا عَلَيَّ فَطَفِقَ مَسْحًا بِالسُّوقِ وَالْأَعْنَاقِ ﴿٣٣﴾

34 And verily We tried Solomon, and set upon his throne a (mere) body. Then did he repent.

وَلَقَدْ فَتَنَّا سُلَيْمَٰنَ وَأَلْقَيْنَا عَلَىٰ كُرْسِيِّهِ جَسَدًا ثُمَّ أَنَابَ ﴿٣٤﴾

35 He said: My Lord! Forgive me and bestow on me sovereignty such shall not belong to any after me. Lo! Thou art the Bestower.

قَالَ رَبِّ اغْفِرْ لِي وَهَبْ لِي مُلْكًا لَّا يَنْبَغِي لِأَحَدٍ مِّنْ بَعْدِي إِنَّكَ أَنتَ الْوَهَّابُ ﴿٣٥﴾

36 So We made the wind subservient unto him, setting fair by his command whithersoever he intended.

فَسَخَّرْنَا لَهُ الرِّيحَ تَجْرِي بِأَمْرِهِ رُخَاءً حَيْثُ أَصَابَ ﴿٣٦﴾

37 And the unruly,[2] every builder and diver (made We subservient),

وَالشَّيَاطِينَ كُلَّ بَنَّاءٍ وَغَوَّاصٍ ﴿٣٧﴾

38 And others linked together in chains,

وَءَاخَرِينَ مُقَرَّنِينَ فِي الْأَصْفَادِ ﴿٣٨﴾

39 (Saying): This is Our gift, so bestow thou, or withhold, without reckoning.

هَٰذَا عَطَاؤُنَا فَامْنُنْ أَوْ أَمْسِكْ بِغَيْرِ حِسَابٍ ﴿٣٩﴾

40 And lo! he hath favour with Us, and a happy journey's end.

وَإِنَّ لَهُ عِندَنَا لَزُلْفَىٰ وَحُسْنَ مَآبٍ ﴿٤٠﴾

41 And make mention (O Muhammad) of Our bondman Job, when he cried unto his Lord (saying): Lo! the devil doth afflict me with distress and torment.

وَاذْكُرْ عَبْدَنَا أَيُّوبَ إِذْ نَادَىٰ رَبَّهُ أَنِّي مَسَّنِيَ الشَّيْطَانُ بِنُصْبٍ وَعَذَابٍ ﴿٤١﴾

---

2. Lit. *devils*.

42 (And it was said unto him): Strike the ground with thy foot. This (spring) is a cool bath and a refreshing drink.

اركُضْ بِرِجْلِكَ هَذَا مُغْتَسَلٌ بَارِدٌ وَشَرَابٌ ۝

43 And We bestowed on him (again) his household and therewith the like thereof, a mercy from Us, and a memorial for men of understanding.

وَوَهَبْنَا لَهُ أَهْلَهُ وَمِثْلَهُم مَّعَهُمْ رَحْمَةً مِّنَّا وَذِكْرَىٰ لِأُولِي الْأَلْبَابِ ۝

44 And (it was said unto him): Take in thine hand a branch and smite therewith, and break not twine oath. Lo! We found him steadfast, how excellent a slave! Lo! he was ever turning in repentance (to his Lord).

وَخُذْ بِيَدِكَ ضِغْثًا فَاضْرِب بِّهِ وَلَا تَحْنَثْ إِنَّا وَجَدْنَاهُ صَابِرًا نِّعْمَ الْعَبْدُ إِنَّهُ أَوَّابٌ ۝

45 And make mention of our bondmen, Abraham, Isaac and Jacob, men of parts and vision.

وَاذْكُرْ عِبَادَنَا إِبْرَاهِيمَ وَإِسْحَقَ وَيَعْقُوبَ أُولِي الْأَيْدِي وَالْأَبْصَارِ ۝

46 Lo! We purified them with a pure thought, remembrance of the Home (of the Hereafter).

إِنَّا أَخْلَصْنَاهُم بِخَالِصَةٍ ذِكْرَى الدَّارِ ۝

47 Lo! in Our sight they are verily of the elect, the excellent.

وَإِنَّهُمْ عِندَنَا لَمِنَ الْمُصْطَفَيْنَ الْأَخْيَارِ ۝

48 And make mention of Ishmael and Elisha and Dhū'al Kifl.[3] All are of the chosen.

وَاذْكُرْ إِسْمَاعِيلَ وَالْيَسَعَ وَذَا الْكِفْلِ وَكُلٌّ مِّنَ الْأَخْيَارِ ۝

49 This is a reminder. And lo! for those who ward off (evil) is a happy journey's end,

هَذَا ذِكْرٌ وَإِنَّ لِلْمُتَّقِينَ لَحُسْنَ مَآبٍ ۝

50 Gardens of Eden, whereof the gates are opened for them.

جَنَّاتِ عَدْنٍ مُّفَتَّحَةً لَّهُمُ الْأَبْوَابُ ۝

---

3. A prophet of the Arabs whose story is like that of Ezekiel.

51 Wherein, reclining, they call for plenteous fruit and cool drink (that is) therein.

مُتَّكِئِينَ فِيهَا يَدْعُونَ فِيهَا بِفَاكِهَةٍ كَثِيرَةٍ وَشَرَابٍ ۝

52 And with them are those of modest gaze, companions.

وَعِنْدَهُمْ قَاصِرَاتُ الطَّرْفِ أَتْرَابٌ ۝

53 This it is that ye are promised for the Day of Reckoning.

هَذَا مَا تُوعَدُونَ لِيَوْمِ الْحِسَابِ ۝

54 Lo! this in truth is Our provision, which will never waste away.

إِنَّ هَذَا لَرِزْقُنَا مَا لَهُ مِنْ نَفَادٍ ۝

55 This (is for the righteous). And lo! for the transgressors there will be an evil journey's end,

هَذَا وَإِنَّ لِلطَّاغِينَ لَشَرَّ مَآبٍ ۝

56 Hell, where they will burn, an evil resting place.

جَهَنَّمَ يَصْلَوْنَهَا فَبِئْسَ الْمِهَادُ ۝

57 Here is a boiling and an ice cold draught, so let them taste it,

هَذَا فَلْيَذُوقُوهُ حَمِيمٌ وَغَسَّاقٌ ۝

58 And other (torment) of the kind in pairs (the two extremes)!

وَآخَرُ مِنْ شَكْلِهِ أَزْوَاجٌ ۝

59 Here is an army rushing blindly with you. (Those who are already in the fire say): No word of welcome for them. Lo! they will roast at the Fire.

هَذَا فَوْجٌ مُقْتَحِمٌ مَعَكُمْ لَا مَرْحَبًا بِهِمْ إِنَّهُمْ صَالُوا النَّارِ ۝

60 They say: Nay, but you (misleaders), for you there is no word of welcome. Ye prepared this for us (by your misleading). Now hapless is the plight.

قَالُوا بَلْ أَنْتُمْ لَا مَرْحَبًا بِكُمْ أَنْتُمْ قَدَّمْتُمُوهُ لَنَا فَبِئْسَ الْقَرَارُ ۝

61 They say: Our Lord! Whoever did prepare this for us, oh, give him double portion of the Fire!

قَالُوا رَبَّنَا مَنْ قَدَّمَ لَنَا هَذَا فَزِدْهُ عَذَابًا ضِعْفًا فِي النَّارِ ۝

62 And they say: What aileth us that we behold not men whom we were wont to count among the wicked?

وَقَالُوا مَا لَنَا لَا نَرَى رِجَالًا كُنَّا نَعُدُّهُمْ مِنَ الْأَشْرَارِ ۝

63 Did we take them (wrongly) for a laughing stock, or have our eyes missed them?

أَتَّخَذْنَٰهُمْ سِخْرِيًّا أَمْ زَاغَتْ عَنْهُمُ ٱلْأَبْصَٰرُ ﴿٦٣﴾

64 Lo! that is very truth: the wrangling of the dwellers in the Fire.

إِنَّ ذَٰلِكَ لَحَقٌّ تَخَاصُمُ أَهْلِ ٱلنَّارِ ﴿٦٤﴾

65 Say (unto them, O Muhammad): I am only a warner, and there is no God save Allah, the One, the Absolute,

قُلْ إِنَّمَآ أَنَا۠ مُنذِرٌ وَمَا مِنْ إِلَٰهٍ إِلَّا ٱللَّهُ ٱلْوَٰحِدُ ٱلْقَهَّارُ ﴿٦٥﴾

66 Lord of the heavens and the earth and all that is between them, the Mighty, the Pardoning.

رَبُّ ٱلسَّمَٰوَٰتِ وَٱلْأَرْضِ وَمَا بَيْنَهُمَا ٱلْعَزِيزُ ٱلْغَفَّٰرُ ﴿٦٦﴾

67 Say: It is tremendous tidings

قُلْ هُوَ نَبَؤٌا۟ عَظِيمٌ ﴿٦٧﴾

68 Whence ye turn away!

أَنتُمْ عَنْهُ مُعْرِضُونَ ﴿٦٨﴾

69 I had no knowledge of the Highest Chiefs when they disputed;

مَا كَانَ لِيَ مِنْ عِلْمٍ بِٱلْمَلَإِ ٱلْأَعْلَىٰٓ إِذْ يَخْتَصِمُونَ ﴿٦٩﴾

70 It is revealed unto me only that I may be a plain warner.

إِن يُوحَىٰٓ إِلَيَّ إِلَّآ أَنَّمَآ أَنَا۠ نَذِيرٌ مُّبِينٌ ﴿٧٠﴾

71 When thy Lord said unto the angels: lo! I am about to create a mortal out of mire,

إِذْ قَالَ رَبُّكَ لِلْمَلَٰٓئِكَةِ إِنِّى خَٰلِقٌۢ بَشَرًا مِّن طِينٍ ﴿٧١﴾

72 And when I have fashioned him and breathed into him of My spirit, then fall down before him prostrate,

فَإِذَا سَوَّيْتُهُۥ وَنَفَخْتُ فِيهِ مِن رُّوحِى فَقَعُوا۟ لَهُۥ سَٰجِدِينَ ﴿٧٢﴾

73 The angels fell down prostrate, every one.

فَسَجَدَ ٱلْمَلَٰٓئِكَةُ كُلُّهُمْ أَجْمَعُونَ ﴿٧٣﴾

74 Saving Iblīs, he was scornful and became one of the disbelievers.

إِلَّآ إِبْلِيسَ ٱسْتَكْبَرَ وَكَانَ مِنَ ٱلْكَٰفِرِينَ ﴿٧٤﴾

75 He said: O Iblīs! What hindereth thee from falling prostrate before that which I have created with both

قَالَ يَٰٓإِبْلِيسُ مَا مَنَعَكَ أَن تَسْجُدَ لِمَا خَلَقْتُ بِيَدَىَّ

My hands?[4] Art thou too proud or art thou of the high exalted?

أَسْتَكْبَرْتَ أَمْ كُنتَ مِنَ ٱلْعَالِينَ ﴿٧٥﴾

76 He said: I am better than him. Thou createdst me off fire, whilst him Thou didst create of clay.

قَالَ أَنَا۠ خَيْرٌ مِّنْهُ خَلَقْتَنِي مِن نَّارٍ وَخَلَقْتَهُ مِن طِينٍ ﴿٧٦﴾

77 He said: Go forth from hence, for lo! thou art outcast,

قَالَ فَٱخْرُجْ مِنْهَا فَإِنَّكَ رَجِيمٌ ﴿٧٧﴾

78 And lo! My curse is on thee till the Day of Judgement.

وَإِنَّ عَلَيْكَ لَعْنَتِي إِلَىٰ يَوْمِ ٱلدِّينِ ﴿٧٨﴾

79 He said: My Lord! Reprieve me till the day when they are raised.

قَالَ رَبِّ فَأَنظِرْنِي إِلَىٰ يَوْمِ يُبْعَثُونَ ﴿٧٩﴾

80 He said: Lo! thou art of those reprieved

قَالَ فَإِنَّكَ مِنَ ٱلْمُنظَرِينَ ﴿٨٠﴾

81 Until the day of the time appointed.

إِلَىٰ يَوْمِ ٱلْوَقْتِ ٱلْمَعْلُومِ ﴿٨١﴾

82 He said: Then, by Thy might, I surely will beguile them every one,

قَالَ فَبِعِزَّتِكَ لَأُغْوِيَنَّهُمْ أَجْمَعِينَ ﴿٨٢﴾

83 Save Thy single minded slaves among them.

إِلَّا عِبَادَكَ مِنْهُمُ ٱلْمُخْلَصِينَ ﴿٨٣﴾

84 He said: The Truth is, and the Truth I speak,

قَالَ فَٱلْحَقُّ وَٱلْحَقَّ أَقُولُ ﴿٨٤﴾

85 That I shall fill hell with thee and with such of them as follow thee, together.

لَأَمْلَأَنَّ جَهَنَّمَ مِنكَ وَمِمَّن تَبِعَكَ مِنْهُمْ أَجْمَعِينَ ﴿٨٥﴾

86 Say (O Muhammad, unto mankind): I ask of you no fee for this, and I am no impostor.

قُلْ مَآ أَسْـَٔلُكُمْ عَلَيْهِ مِنْ أَجْرٍ وَمَآ أَنَا۠ مِنَ ٱلْمُتَكَلِّفِينَ ﴿٨٦﴾

87 Lo! it is naught else than a reminder for all peoples

إِنْ هُوَ إِلَّا ذِكْرٌ لِّلْعَالَمِينَ ﴿٨٧﴾

88 And ye will come in time to know the truth thereof.

وَلَتَعْلَمُنَّ نَبَأَهُۥ بَعْدَ حِينٍ ﴿٨٨﴾

---

4. The Muslim mystics explain this as meaning with the both the glorious and the terrific attributes of God, whereas the angels were created by the exercise of only one class of attributes.

Az Zumar
(The Troops)

Az Zumar, "The Troops," takes its name from a peculiar word, meaning troops or companies, which occurs in v. 71, and again in v. 73. Some authorities think that vv. 53 and 54 were revealed at Al-Madīnah.

It seems manifestly to belong to the middle group of Makkan sūrahs, though Nöldeke places it in his last group.

In the name of Allah, the Beneficent, the Merciful.

1   The revelation of the Scripture is from Allah, the Mighty, the Wise.

2   Lo! We have revealed the Scripture unto thee (Muhammad) with truth; so worship Allah, making religion pure for Him (only).

3   Surely Pure religion is for Allah only. And those who choose protecting friends beside Him (say): We worship them only that they may bring us near unto Allah. Lo! Allah will judge between them concerning that wherein they differ. Lo! Allah guideth not him who is a liar, an ingrate.

4 If Allah had willed to choose a son, he could have chosen what he would of that which He hath created. Be He glorified! He is Allah, the One, the Absolute.

لَوْ أَرَادَ اللّٰهُ أَنْ يَتَّخِذَ وَلَدًا لَّاصْطَفٰى مِمَّا يَخْلُقُ مَا يَشَاءُ سُبْحَانَهُ هُوَ اللّٰهُ الْوَاحِدُ الْقَهَّارُ ۝

5 He hath created the heavens and the earth with truth. He maketh the night cover the day and He maketh the day cover the night, and He constraineth the sun and the moon to give service, each running on for an appointed term. Is not He the Mighty, the Forgiver?

خَلَقَ السَّمٰوٰتِ وَالْأَرْضَ بِالْحَقِّ يُكَوِّرُ الَّيْلَ عَلَى النَّهَارِ وَيُكَوِّرُ النَّهَارَ عَلَى الَّيْلِ وَسَخَّرَ الشَّمْسَ وَالْقَمَرَ كُلٌّ يَجْرِي لِأَجَلٍ مُّسَمًّى أَلَا هُوَ الْعَزِيزُ الْغَفَّارُ ۝

6 He created you from one being, then from that (being) He made its mate; and He hath provided for you of cattle eight kinds. He created you in the wombs of your mothers, creation after creation, in a three-fold gloom. Such is Allah, your Lord. His is the Sovereignty. There is no God save Him. How then are ye turned away?

خَلَقَكُمْ مِنْ نَفْسٍ وٰحِدَةٍ ثُمَّ جَعَلَ مِنْهَا زَوْجَهَا وَأَنْزَلَ لَكُمْ مِنَ الْأَنْعَامِ ثَمَانِيَةَ أَزْوَاجٍ يَخْلُقُكُمْ فِي بُطُونِ أُمَّهٰتِكُمْ خَلْقًا مِّنْ بَعْدِ خَلْقٍ فِي ظُلُمٰتٍ ثَلٰثٍ ذٰلِكُمُ اللّٰهُ رَبُّكُمْ لَهُ الْمُلْكُ لَا إِلٰهَ إِلَّا هُوَ فَأَنّٰى تُصْرَفُونَ ۝

7 If ye are thankless, yet Allah is Independent of you, though He is not pleased with thanklessness for His bondmen; and if ye are thankful He is pleased therewith for you. No laden soul will bear another's load. Then unto your Lord is your return; and He will tell you what ye used to do. Lo! He knoweth what is in the breasts (of men).

إِنْ تَكْفُرُوا فَإِنَّ اللّٰهَ غَنِيٌّ عَنْكُمْ وَلَا يَرْضٰى لِعِبَادِهِ الْكُفْرَ وَإِنْ تَشْكُرُوا يَرْضَهُ لَكُمْ وَلَا تَزِرُ وَازِرَةٌ وِزْرَ أُخْرٰى ثُمَّ إِلٰى رَبِّكُمْ مَّرْجِعُكُمْ فَيُنَبِّئُكُمْ بِمَا كُنْتُمْ تَعْمَلُونَ إِنَّهُ عَلِيمٌ بِذَاتِ الصُّدُورِ ۝

8 And then some hurt toucheth man, he crieth unto his Lord, turning unto Him (repentant). Then,

وَإِذَا مَسَّ الْإِنْسَانَ ضُرٌّ دَعَا رَبَّهُ مُنِيبًا إِلَيْهِ ثُمَّ إِذَا خَوَّلَهُ نِعْمَةً مِّنْهُ نَسِيَ مَا كَانَ يَدْعُوا إِلَيْهِ

when He granteth him a boon from Him he forgetteth that for which he cried unto Him before, and setteth up rivals to Allah that he may beguile (men) from His way. Say (O Muhammad, unto such an one): Take pleasure in thy disbelief a while. Lo! thou art of the owners of the Fire.

مِن قَبْلُ وَجَعَلَ لِلَّهِ أَندَادًا لِّيُضِلَّ عَن سَبِيلِهِ ۚ قُلْ تَمَتَّعْ بِكُفْرِكَ قَلِيلًا إِنَّكَ مِنْ أَصْحَٰبِ النَّارِ ۝

9 Is he who payeth adoration in the watches of the night, prostrate and standing, bewaring of the Hereafter and hoping for the mercy of his Lord, (to be accounted equal with a disbeliever)? Say (unto them, O Muhammad): Are those who know equal with those who know not? But only men of understanding will pay heed.

أَمَّنْ هُوَ قَٰنِتٌ ءَانَآءَ الَّيْلِ سَاجِدًا وَقَآئِمًا يَحْذَرُ الْءَاخِرَةَ وَيَرْجُوا۟ رَحْمَةَ رَبِّهِ ۗ قُلْ هَلْ يَسْتَوِى الَّذِينَ يَعْلَمُونَ وَالَّذِينَ لَا يَعْلَمُونَ ۗ إِنَّمَا يَتَذَكَّرُ أُو۟لُوا۟ الْأَلْبَٰبِ ۝

10 Say: O My bondmen who believe! Observe your duty to your Lord. For those who do good in this world there is good, and Allah's earth is spacious. Verily the steadfast will be paid their wages without stint.

قُلْ يَٰعِبَادِ الَّذِينَ ءَامَنُوا۟ اتَّقُوا۟ رَبَّكُمْ ۚ لِلَّذِينَ أَحْسَنُوا۟ فِى هَٰذِهِ الدُّنْيَا حَسَنَةٌ ۗ وَأَرْضُ اللَّهِ وَٰسِعَةٌ ۗ إِنَّمَا يُوَفَّى الصَّٰبِرُونَ أَجْرَهُم بِغَيْرِ حِسَابٍ ۝

11 Say (O Muhammad): Lo! I am commanded to worship Allah, making religion pure for Him (only).

قُلْ إِنِّى أُمِرْتُ أَنْ أَعْبُدَ اللَّهَ مُخْلِصًا لَّهُ الدِّينَ ۝

12 And I am commanded to be the first of those who surrender[1] (unto Him).

وَأُمِرْتُ لِأَنْ أَكُونَ أَوَّلَ الْمُسْلِمِينَ ۝

---

1. Ar. *Muslimin.*

13 Say: Lo! if I should disobey my Lord, I fear the doom of a tremendous Day.

قُلْ إِنِّيٓ أَخَافُ إِنْ عَصَيْتُ رَبِّي عَذَابَ يَوْمٍ عَظِيمٍ ۝

14 Say: Allah I worship, making my religion pure for Him (only).

قُلِ اللَّهَ أَعْبُدُ مُخْلِصًا لَّهُۥ دِينِي ۝

15 Then worship what ye will beside Him. Say: The losers will be those who lose themselves and their housefolk on the Day of Resurrection. Ah, that will be the manifest loss!

فَاعْبُدُوا۟ مَا شِئْتُم مِّن دُونِهِۦ ۗ قُلْ إِنَّ الْخَٰسِرِينَ الَّذِينَ خَسِرُوٓا۟ أَنفُسَهُمْ وَأَهْلِيهِمْ يَوْمَ الْقِيَٰمَةِ ۗ أَلَا ذَٰلِكَ هُوَ الْخُسْرَانُ الْمُبِينُ ۝

16 They have an awning of fire above them and beneath them a dais (of fire). With this doth Allah appal His bondmen. O My bondmen, therefore fear Me!

لَهُم مِّن فَوْقِهِمْ ظُلَلٌ مِّنَ النَّارِ وَمِن تَحْتِهِمْ ظُلَلٌ ۚ ذَٰلِكَ يُخَوِّفُ اللَّهُ بِهِۦ عِبَادَهُۥ ۚ يَٰعِبَادِ فَاتَّقُونِ ۝

17 And those who put away false gods lest they should worship them and turn to Allah in repentance, for them there are glad tidings. Therefore give good tidings (O Muhammad) to my bondmen

وَالَّذِينَ اجْتَنَبُوا۟ الطَّٰغُوتَ أَن يَعْبُدُوهَا وَأَنَابُوٓا۟ إِلَى اللَّهِ لَهُمُ الْبُشْرَىٰ ۚ فَبَشِّرْ عِبَادِ ۝

18 Who hear advice and follow the best thereof. Such are those whom Allah guideth, and such are men of understanding.

الَّذِينَ يَسْتَمِعُونَ الْقَوْلَ فَيَتَّبِعُونَ أَحْسَنَهُۥٓ ۚ أُو۟لَٰٓئِكَ الَّذِينَ هَدَىٰهُمُ اللَّهُ ۖ وَأُو۟لَٰٓئِكَ هُمْ أُو۟لُوا۟ الْأَلْبَٰبِ ۝

19 Is he on whom the word of doom is fulfilled (to be helped), and canst thou (O Muhammad) rescue him who is in the Fire?

أَفَمَنْ حَقَّ عَلَيْهِ كَلِمَةُ الْعَذَابِ أَفَأَنتَ تُنقِذُ مَن فِي النَّارِ ۝

20 But those who keep their duty to their Lord, for them are lofty halls with lofty halls above them, built (for them), beneath which rivers flow. (It is) a promise of Allah. Allah faileth not His promise.

لَٰكِنِ الَّذِينَ اتَّقَوْا۟ رَبَّهُمْ لَهُمْ غُرَفٌ مِّن فَوْقِهَا غُرَفٌ مَّبْنِيَّةٌ تَجْرِي مِن تَحْتِهَا الْأَنْهَٰرُ ۖ وَعْدَ اللَّهِ ۖ لَا يُخْلِفُ اللَّهُ الْمِيعَادَ ۝

21 Hast thou not seen how Allah hath sent down water from the sky and hath caused it to penetrate the earth as water springs, and afterward thereby produceth crops of divers hues; and afterward they wither and thou seest them turn yellow; then He maketh them chaff. Lo! herein verily is a reminder for men of understanding.

أَلَمْ تَرَ أَنَّ اللّٰهَ أَنزَلَ مِنَ السَّمَآءِ مَآءً فَسَلَكَهُ يَنَابِيعَ فِى الْأَرْضِ ثُمَّ يُخْرِجُ بِهِ زَرْعًا مُّخْتَلِفًا أَلْوَانُهُ ثُمَّ يَهِيجُ فَتَرَىٰهُ مُصْفَرًّا ثُمَّ يَجْعَلُهُ حُطَٰمًا إِنَّ فِى ذَٰلِكَ لَذِكْرَىٰ لِأُوْلِى الْأَلْبَٰبِ ﴿٢١﴾

22 Is he whose bosom Allah hath expanded for the Surrender[2] (unto Him), so that he followeth a light from His Lord, (as he who disbelieveth)? Then woe unto those whose hearts are hardened against remembrance of Allah. Such are in plain error.

أَفَمَن شَرَحَ اللّٰهُ صَدْرَهُ لِلْإِسْلَٰمِ فَهُوَ عَلَىٰ نُورٍ مِّن رَّبِّهِ فَوَيْلٌ لِّلْقَٰسِيَةِ قُلُوبُهُم مِّن ذِكْرِ اللّٰهِ أُوْلَٰٓئِكَ فِى ضَلَٰلٍ مُّبِينٍ ﴿٢٢﴾

23 Allah hath (now) revealed the fairest of statements, a Scripture consistent, (wherein promises of reward are) paired (with threats of punishment), whereat doth creep the flesh of those who fear their Lord, so that their flesh and their hearts soften to Allah's reminder. Such is Allah's guidance, wherewith He guideth whom He will. And him whom Allah sendeth astray, for him there is no guide.

اللّٰهُ نَزَّلَ أَحْسَنَ الْحَدِيثِ كِتَٰبًا مُّتَشَٰبِهًا مَّثَانِىَ تَقْشَعِرُّ مِنْهُ جُلُودُ الَّذِينَ يَخْشَوْنَ رَبَّهُمْ ثُمَّ تَلِينُ جُلُودُهُمْ وَقُلُوبُهُمْ إِلَىٰ ذِكْرِ اللّٰهِ ذَٰلِكَ هُدَى اللّٰهِ يَهْدِى بِهِ مَن يَشَآءُ وَمَن يُضْلِلِ اللّٰهُ فَمَا لَهُ مِنْ هَادٍ ﴿٢٣﴾

24 Is he then who wards off with his face that awful doom upon the Day of Resurrection (as he who

أَفَمَن يَتَّقِى بِوَجْهِهِ سُوٓءَ الْعَذَابِ يَوْمَ الْقِيَٰمَةِ

---

2. Ar. *Al-Islām.*

doeth right)? And it will be said unto the wrong-doers: Taste what ye used to earn.

وَقِيلَ لِلظَّالِمِينَ ذُوقُوا مَا كُنْتُمْ تَكْسِبُونَ ﴿٢٤﴾

25 Those before them denied, and so the doom came on them whence they knew not.

كَذَّبَ الَّذِينَ مِن قَبْلِهِمْ فَأَتَاهُمُ الْعَذَابُ مِنْ حَيْثُ لَا يَشْعُرُونَ ﴿٢٥﴾

26 Thus Allah made them taste humiliation in the life of the world, and verily the doom of the Here-after will be greater if they did but know.

فَأَذَاقَهُمُ اللَّهُ الْخِزْيَ فِي الْحَيَوةِ الدُّنْيَا وَلَعَذَابُ الْآخِرَةِ أَكْبَرُ لَوْ كَانُوا يَعْلَمُونَ ﴿٢٦﴾

27 And verily We have coined for mankind in this Qur'an all kinds of similitudes, that haply they may reflect;

وَلَقَدْ ضَرَبْنَا لِلنَّاسِ فِي هَذَا الْقُرْءَانِ مِن كُلِّ مَثَلٍ لَّعَلَّهُمْ يَتَذَكَّرُونَ ﴿٢٧﴾

28 A Lecture[3] in Arabic, containing no crookedness, that haply they may ward off (evil).

قُرْءَانًا عَرَبِيًّا غَيْرَ ذِي عِوَجٍ لَّعَلَّهُمْ يَتَّقُونَ ﴿٢٨﴾

29 Allah coineth a similitude: A man in relation to whom are several part-owners, quarrelling, and a man belonging wholly to one man. Are the two equal in similitude? Praise be to Allah! But most of them know not.

ضَرَبَ اللَّهُ مَثَلًا رَّجُلًا فِيهِ شُرَكَاءُ مُتَشَاكِسُونَ وَرَجُلًا سَلَمًا لِّرَجُلٍ هَلْ يَسْتَوِيَانِ مَثَلًا الْحَمْدُ لِلَّهِ بَلْ أَكْثَرُهُمْ لَا يَعْلَمُونَ ﴿٢٩﴾

30 Lo! thou wilt die, and lo! they will die;

إِنَّكَ مَيِّتٌ وَإِنَّهُم مَّيِّتُونَ ﴿٣٠﴾

31 Then lo! on the Day of Resurrection, before your Lord ye will dispute.

ثُمَّ إِنَّكُمْ يَوْمَ الْقِيَمَةِ عِندَ رَبِّكُمْ تَخْتَصِمُونَ ﴿٣١﴾

---

3. Ar. *Qur'an.*

32 And who doth greater wrong than he who telleth a lie against Allah, and denieth the truth when it reacheth him? Will not the home of disbelievers be in hell?

﴿ فَمَنْ أَظْلَمُ مِمَّن كَذَبَ عَلَى اللَّهِ وَكَذَّبَ بِالصِّدْقِ إِذْ جَاءَهُ ۚ أَلَيْسَ فِي جَهَنَّمَ مَثْوًى لِّلْكَافِرِينَ ۝

33 And whoso bringeth the truth and believeth therein—Such are the dutiful.

وَالَّذِي جَاءَ بِالصِّدْقِ وَصَدَّقَ بِهِ ۙ أُوْلَئِكَ هُمُ الْمُتَّقُونَ ۝

34 They shall have what they will of their Lord's bounty. That is the reward of the good:

لَهُم مَّا يَشَاءُونَ عِندَ رَبِّهِمْ ۚ ذَٰلِكَ جَزَاءُ الْمُحْسِنِينَ ۝

35 That Allah will remit from them the worst of what they did, and will pay them for reward the best they used to do.

لِيُكَفِّرَ اللَّهُ عَنْهُمْ أَسْوَأَ الَّذِي عَمِلُوا وَيَجْزِيَهُمْ أَجْرَهُم بِأَحْسَنِ الَّذِي كَانُوا يَعْمَلُونَ ۝

36 Will not Allah defend His slave? Yet they would frighten thee with those beside Him. He whom Allah sendeth astray, for him there is no guide.

أَلَيْسَ اللَّهُ بِكَافٍ عَبْدَهُ ۖ وَيُخَوِّفُونَكَ بِالَّذِينَ مِن دُونِهِ ۚ وَمَن يُضْلِلِ اللَّهُ فَمَا لَهُ مِنْ هَادٍ ۝

37 And he whom Allah guideth, for him there can be no misleader. Is not Allah Mighty, Able to Requite (the wrong)?

وَمَن يَهْدِ اللَّهُ فَمَا لَهُ مِن مُّضِلٍّ ۗ أَلَيْسَ اللَّهُ بِعَزِيزٍ ذِي انتِقَامٍ ۝

38 And verily, if thou shouldst ask them: Who created the heavens and the earth? they will say: Allah. Say: Bethink you then of those ye worship beside Allah, if Allah willed some hurt for me, could they remove from me His hurt; or if He willed some mercy for me, could they restrain His mercy? Say: Allah is my all. In Him do (all) the trusting put their trust.

وَلَئِن سَأَلْتَهُم مَّنْ خَلَقَ السَّمَاوَاتِ وَالْأَرْضَ لَيَقُولُنَّ اللَّهُ ۚ قُلْ أَفَرَأَيْتُم مَّا تَدْعُونَ مِن دُونِ اللَّهِ إِنْ أَرَادَنِيَ اللَّهُ بِضُرٍّ هَلْ هُنَّ كَاشِفَاتُ ضُرِّهِ أَوْ أَرَادَنِي بِرَحْمَةٍ هَلْ هُنَّ مُمْسِكَاتُ رَحْمَتِهِ ۚ قُلْ حَسْبِيَ اللَّهُ ۖ عَلَيْهِ يَتَوَكَّلُ الْمُتَوَكِّلُونَ ۝

39 Say: O my people! Act in your manner. I too am acting. Thus ye will come to know

قُل يَٰقَوْمِ اعْمَلُوا عَلَىٰ مَكَانَتِكُمْ إِنِّي عَٰمِلٌ فَسَوْفَ تَعْلَمُونَ ۝

40 Who it is unto whom cometh a doom that will abase him, and on whom there falleth everlasting doom.

مَن يَأْتِيهِ عَذَابٌ يُخْزِيهِ وَيَحِلُّ عَلَيْهِ عَذَابٌ مُّقِيمٌ ۝

41 Lo! We have revealed unto thee (Muhammad) the Scripture for mankind with truth. Then whosoever goeth right it is for his soul, and whosoever strayeth, strayeth only to its hurt. And thou art not a warder over them.

إِنَّا أَنزَلْنَا عَلَيْكَ الْكِتَٰبَ لِلنَّاسِ بِالْحَقِّ فَمَنِ اهْتَدَىٰ فَلِنَفْسِهِ وَمَن ضَلَّ فَإِنَّمَا يَضِلُّ عَلَيْهَا وَمَا أَنتَ عَلَيْهِم بِوَكِيلٍ ۝

42 Allah receiveth (men's) souls at the time of their death, and that (soul) which dieth not (yet) in its sleep. He keepeth that (soul) for which He hath ordained death and dismisseth the rest till an appointed term. Lo! herein verily are portents for people who take thought.

اللَّهُ يَتَوَفَّى الْأَنفُسَ حِينَ مَوْتِهَا وَالَّتِي لَمْ تَمُتْ فِي مَنَامِهَا فَيُمْسِكُ الَّتِي قَضَىٰ عَلَيْهَا الْمَوْتَ وَيُرْسِلُ الْأُخْرَىٰ إِلَىٰ أَجَلٍ مُّسَمًّى إِنَّ فِي ذَٰلِكَ لَآيَٰتٍ لِّقَوْمٍ يَتَفَكَّرُونَ ۝

43 Or choose they intercessors other than Allah? Say: What! Even though they have power over nothing and have no intelligence?

أَمِ اتَّخَذُوا مِن دُونِ اللَّهِ شُفَعَاءَ قُلْ أَوَلَوْ كَانُوا لَا يَمْلِكُونَ شَيْئًا وَلَا يَعْقِلُونَ ۝

44 Say: Unto Allah belongeth all intercession. His is the Sovereignty of the heavens and the earth. And afterward unto Him ye will be brought back.

قُل لِّلَّهِ الشَّفَٰعَةُ جَمِيعًا لَّهُ مُلْكُ السَّمَٰوَٰتِ وَالْأَرْضِ ثُمَّ إِلَيْهِ تُرْجَعُونَ ۝

45 And when Allah alone is mentioned, the hearts of those who believe not in the Hereafter are repelled, and when those (whom they worship) beside Him are mentioned, behold! they are glad.

وَإِذَا ذُكِرَ اللَّهُ وَحْدَهُ اشْمَأَزَّتْ قُلُوبُ الَّذِينَ لَا يُؤْمِنُونَ بِالْآخِرَةِ وَإِذَا ذُكِرَ الَّذِينَ مِن دُونِهِ إِذَا هُمْ يَسْتَبْشِرُونَ ۝

46 Say: O Allah! Creator of the
heavens and the earth! Knower of
the invisible and the visible! Thou
wilt judge between Thy slaves
concerning that wherein they used
to differ.

قُلِ اللّٰهُمَّ فَاطِرَ السَّمٰوٰتِ وَالْأَرْضِ عٰلِمَ الْغَيْبِ
وَالشَّهَادَةِ أَنْتَ تَحْكُمُ بَيْنَ عِبَادِكَ
فِيْ مَا كَانُوْا فِيْهِ يَخْتَلِفُوْنَ ۝

47 And though those who do
wrong possess all that is in the
earth, and therewith as much again,
they verily will seek to ransom
themselves therewith on the Day of
Resurrection from the awful doom;
and there will appear unto them,
from their Lord, that wherewith
they never reckoned.

وَلَوْ أَنَّ لِلَّذِيْنَ ظَلَمُوْا مَا فِي الْأَرْضِ جَمِيْعًا
وَمِثْلَهُ مَعَهُ لَافْتَدَوْا بِهِ مِنْ سُوْءِ الْعَذَابِ
يَوْمَ الْقِيٰمَةِ ۭ وَبَدَا لَهُمْ مِّنَ اللّٰهِ
مَا لَمْ يَكُوْنُوْا يَحْتَسِبُوْنَ ۝

48 And the evils that they earned
will appear unto them, and that
whereat they used to scoff will surround them.

وَبَدَا لَهُمْ سَيِّاٰتُ مَا كَسَبُوْا وَحَاقَ بِهِمْ
مَّا كَانُوْا بِهِ يَسْتَهْزِءُوْنَ ۝

49 Now when hurt toucheth a man
he crieth unto Us, and afterward
when We have granted him a boon
from Us, he saith: Only by force of
knowledge I obtained it. Nay, but it
is a test. But most of them know
not.

فَإِذَا مَسَّ الْإِنْسَانَ ضُرٌّ دَعَانَا ثُمَّ إِذَا خَوَّلْنٰهُ
نِعْمَةً مِّنَّا قَالَ إِنَّمَآ أُوْتِيْتُهُ عَلٰى عِلْمٍ ۭ
بَلْ هِيَ فِتْنَةٌ وَّلٰكِنَّ أَكْثَرَهُمْ لَا يَعْلَمُوْنَ ۝

50 Those before them said it, yet
(all) that they had earned availed
them not;

قَدْ قَالَهَا الَّذِيْنَ مِنْ قَبْلِهِمْ فَمَآ أَغْنٰى
عَنْهُمْ مَّا كَانُوْا يَكْسِبُوْنَ ۝

51 But the evils that they earned
smote them; and such of these as do
wrong, the evils that they earn will
smite them; they cannot escape.

فَأَصَابَهُمْ سَيِّاٰتُ مَا كَسَبُوْا ۭ وَالَّذِيْنَ ظَلَمُوْا
مِنْ هٰٓؤُلَاءِ سَيُصِيْبُهُمْ سَيِّاٰتُ مَا كَسَبُوْا
وَمَا هُمْ بِمُعْجِزِيْنَ ۝

52 Know they not that Allah enlargeth providence for whom He will, and straiteneth it (for whom He will). Lo! herein verily are portents for people who believe.

أَوَلَمْ يَعْلَمُوٓا أَنَّ ٱللَّهَ يَبْسُطُ ٱلرِّزْقَ لِمَن يَشَآءُ وَيَقْدِرُ إِنَّ فِى ذَٰلِكَ لَأَيَٰتٍ لِّقَوْمٍ يُؤْمِنُونَ ۞

53 Say: My slaves who have been prodigal to their own hurt! Despair not of the mercy of Allah, Lo! Allah forgiveth all sins. Lo! He is the Forgiving, the Merciful.

۞ قُلْ يَٰعِبَادِىَ ٱلَّذِينَ أَسْرَفُوا۟ عَلَىٰٓ أَنفُسِهِمْ لَا تَقْنَطُوا۟ مِن رَّحْمَةِ ٱللَّهِ إِنَّ ٱللَّهَ يَغْفِرُ ٱلذُّنُوبَ جَمِيعًا إِنَّهُۥ هُوَ ٱلْغَفُورُ ٱلرَّحِيمُ ۞

54 Turn unto your Lord repentant, and surrender unto Him, before there come unto you the doom, when ye cannot be helped.

وَأَنِيبُوٓا۟ إِلَىٰ رَبِّكُمْ وَأَسْلِمُوا۟ لَهُۥ مِن قَبْلِ أَن يَأْتِيَكُمُ ٱلْعَذَابُ ثُمَّ لَا تُنصَرُونَ ۞

55 And follow the better (guidance) of that which is revealed unto you from your Lord, before the doom cometh on you suddenly when ye know not,

وَٱتَّبِعُوٓا۟ أَحْسَنَ مَآ أُنزِلَ إِلَيْكُم مِّن رَّبِّكُم مِّن قَبْلِ أَن يَأْتِيَكُمُ ٱلْعَذَابُ بَغْتَةً وَأَنتُمْ لَا تَشْعُرُونَ ۞

56 Lest any soul should say: Alas, my grief that I was unmindful of Allah, and I was indeed among the scoffers!

أَن تَقُولَ نَفْسٌ يَٰحَسْرَتَىٰ عَلَىٰ مَا فَرَّطتُ فِى جَنۢبِ ٱللَّهِ وَإِن كُنتُ لَمِنَ ٱلسَّٰخِرِينَ ۞

57 Or should say: if Allah had but guided me I should have been among the dutiful!

أَوْ تَقُولَ لَوْ أَنَّ ٱللَّهَ هَدَىٰنِى لَكُنتُ مِنَ ٱلْمُتَّقِينَ ۞

58 Or should say, when it seeth the doom: Oh, that I had but a second chance that I might be among the righteous!

أَوْ تَقُولَ حِينَ تَرَى ٱلْعَذَابَ لَوْ أَنَّ لِى كَرَّةً فَأَكُونَ مِنَ ٱلْمُحْسِنِينَ ۞

59 (But now the answer will be): Nay, for My revelations came unto thee, but thou didst deny them and wast scornful and wast among the disbelievers.

بَلَىٰ قَدْ جَآءَتْكَ ءَايَٰتِى فَكَذَّبْتَ بِهَا وَٱسْتَكْبَرْتَ وَكُنتَ مِنَ ٱلْكَٰفِرِينَ ۞

60 And on the Day of Resurrection thou (Muḥammad) seest those who lied concerning Allah with their faces blackened. Is not the home of the scorners in hell?

وَيَوْمَ الْقِيَامَةِ تَرَى الَّذِينَ كَذَبُوا عَلَى اللَّهِ وُجُوهُهُم مُّسْوَدَّةٌ أَلَيْسَ فِي جَهَنَّمَ مَثْوًى لِّلْمُتَكَبِّرِينَ ۝

61 And Allah delivereth those who ward off (evil) because of their deserts. Evil toucheth them not, nor do they grieve.

وَيُنَجِّي اللَّهُ الَّذِينَ اتَّقَوْا بِمَفَازَتِهِمْ لَا يَمَسُّهُمُ السُّوءُ وَلَا هُمْ يَحْزَنُونَ ۝

62 Allah is Creator of all things, and He is Guardian over all things.

اللَّهُ خَالِقُ كُلِّ شَيْءٍ وَهُوَ عَلَى كُلِّ شَيْءٍ وَكِيلٌ ۝

63 His are the keys of the heavens and the earth, and they who disbelieve the revelations of Allah—such are they who are the losers.

لَّهُ مَقَالِيدُ السَّمَوَاتِ وَالْأَرْضِ وَالَّذِينَ كَفَرُوا بِآيَاتِ اللَّهِ أُولَئِكَ هُمُ الْخَاسِرُونَ ۝

64 Say (O Muḥammad, to the disbelievers): Do ye bid me serve other than Allah? O ye fools!

قُلْ أَفَغَيْرَ اللَّهِ تَأْمُرُونِّي أَعْبُدُ أَيُّهَا الْجَاهِلُونَ ۝

65 And verily it hath been revealed unto thee as unto those before thee (saying): If thou ascribe a partner to Allah thy work will fail and thou indeed wilt be among the losers.

وَلَقَدْ أُوحِيَ إِلَيْكَ وَإِلَى الَّذِينَ مِن قَبْلِكَ لَئِنْ أَشْرَكْتَ لَيَحْبَطَنَّ عَمَلُكَ وَلَتَكُونَنَّ مِنَ الْخَاسِرِينَ ۝

66 Nay, but Allah must thou serve, and be among the thankful!

بَلِ اللَّهَ فَاعْبُدْ وَكُن مِّنَ الشَّاكِرِينَ ۝

67 And they esteem not Allah as He hath the right to be esteemed, when the whole earth is His handful on the Day of Resurrection, and the heavens are rolled in His right hand. Glorified is He and High Exalted from all that they ascribe as partner (unto Him).

وَمَا قَدَرُوا اللَّهَ حَقَّ قَدْرِهِ وَالْأَرْضُ جَمِيعًا قَبْضَتُهُ يَوْمَ الْقِيَامَةِ وَالسَّمَوَاتُ مَطْوِيَّاتٌ بِيَمِينِهِ سُبْحَانَهُ وَتَعَالَى عَمَّا يُشْرِكُونَ ۝

68 And the trumpet is blown, and all who are in the heavens and the earth swoon away, save him whom Allah willeth. Then it is blown a second time, and behold them standing waiting!

69 And the earth shineth with the light of her Lord, and the Book is set up, and the Prophets and the witnesses are brought, and it is judged between them with truth, and they are not wronged.

70 And each soul is paid in full for what it did. And He is best aware of what they do.

71 And those who disbelieve are driven unto hell in troops till, when they reach it and the gates thereof are opened, and the warders thereof say unto them: Came there not unto you messengers of your own, reciting unto you the revelations of your Lord and warning you of the meeting of this your Day? They say Yea, verily. But the word of doom for disbelievers is fulfilled.

72 It is said (unto them): Enter ye the gates of hell to dwell therein. Thus hapless is the journey's end of the scorners.

73 And those who keep their duty to their Lord are driven unto the Garden in troops till, when they reach it, and the gates thereof are opened, and the warders thereof say

وَنُفِخَ فِى الصُّورِ فَصَعِقَ مَن فِى السَّمَـٰوَٰتِ وَمَن فِى الْأَرْضِ إِلَّا مَن شَاءَ اللَّهُ ثُمَّ نُفِخَ فِيهِ أُخْرَىٰ فَإِذَا هُمْ قِيَامٌ يَنظُرُونَ ﴿٦٨﴾

وَأَشْرَقَتِ الْأَرْضُ بِنُورِ رَبِّهَا وَوُضِعَ الْكِتَـٰبُ وَجِائَ بِالنَّبِيِّـۧنَ وَالشُّهَدَاءِ وَقُضِىَ بَيْنَهُم بِالْحَقِّ وَهُمْ لَا يُظْلَمُونَ ﴿٦٩﴾

وَوُفِّيَتْ كُلُّ نَفْسٍ مَّا عَمِلَتْ وَهُوَ أَعْلَمُ بِمَا يَفْعَلُونَ ﴿٧٠﴾

وَسِيقَ الَّذِينَ كَفَرُوٓا إِلَىٰ جَهَنَّمَ زُمَرًا حَتَّىٰٓ إِذَا جَاءُوهَا فُتِحَتْ أَبْوَٰبُهَا وَقَالَ لَهُمْ خَزَنَتُهَا أَلَمْ يَأْتِكُمْ رُسُلٌ مِّنكُمْ يَتْلُونَ عَلَيْكُمْ ءَايَـٰتِ رَبِّكُمْ وَيُنذِرُونَكُمْ لِقَاءَ يَوْمِكُمْ هَـٰذَا قَالُوا بَلَىٰ وَلَـٰكِنْ حَقَّتْ كَلِمَةُ الْعَذَابِ عَلَى الْكَـٰفِرِينَ ﴿٧١﴾

قِيلَ ادْخُلُوٓا أَبْوَٰبَ جَهَنَّمَ خَـٰلِدِينَ فِيهَا فَبِئْسَ مَثْوَى الْمُتَكَبِّرِينَ ﴿٧٢﴾

وَسِيقَ الَّذِينَ اتَّقَوْا رَبَّهُمْ إِلَى الْجَنَّةِ زُمَرًا حَتَّىٰٓ إِذَا جَاءُوهَا وَفُتِحَتْ أَبْوَٰبُهَا وَقَالَ لَهُمْ

unto them: Peace be unto you! Ye are good, so enter ye (the Garden of delight), to dwell therein;

74 They say: Praise be to Allah, Who hath fulfilled His promise unto us and hath made us inherit the land, sojourning in the Garden where we will! So bounteous is the wage of workers.

75 And thou (O Muhammad) seest the angels thronging round the Throne, hymning the praises of their Lord. And they are judged aright. And it is said: Praise be to Allah, the Lord of the Worlds!

خَزَنَتُهَا سَلَامٌ عَلَيْكُمْ طِبْتُمْ فَادْخُلُوهَا خَالِدِينَ ﴿٧٣﴾

وَقَالُوا الْحَمْدُ لِلَّهِ الَّذِي صَدَقَنَا وَعْدَهُ وَأَوْرَثَنَا الْأَرْضَ نَتَبَوَّأُ مِنَ الْجَنَّةِ حَيْثُ نَشَاءُ فَنِعْمَ أَجْرُ الْعَامِلِينَ ﴿٧٤﴾

وَتَرَى الْمَلَائِكَةَ حَافِّينَ مِنْ حَوْلِ الْعَرْشِ يُسَبِّحُونَ بِحَمْدِ رَبِّهِمْ وَقُضِيَ بَيْنَهُمْ بِالْحَقِّ وَقِيلَ الْحَمْدُ لِلَّهِ رَبِّ الْعَالَمِينَ ﴿٧٥﴾

Al Mu'min
(The Believer)

Al Mu'min, "The Believer," takes its name from vv. 28-45, which describe the attempt of a believer, in the house of Pharaoh, to dissuade his people from opposing Moses and Aaron. It is the first of seven sūrahs beginning with the Arabic letters Ḥā, Mīm, all of which are sometimes referred to as Ḥā, Mīm.

It belongs to the middle group of Makkan sūrahs. Some authorities hold vv. 56 and 57 to have been revealed at Al-Madīnah.

In the name of Allah, the Beneficent, the Merciful.

1 Ḥā. Mīm.[1]

2 The revelation of the Scripture is from Allah, the Mighty, the Knower,

3 The Forgiver of sin, the Acceptor of repentance, the Stern in punishment, the Bountiful. There is no God save Him. Unto Him is the journeying.

4 None argue concerning the revelations of Allah save those who disbelieve, so let not their turn of fortune in the land deceive thee (O Muhammad).

---

1. See Sūrah 2, v. 1, footnote.

667

5　The folk of Noah and the factions after them denied (their messengers) before these, and every nation purposed to seize their messenger and argued falsely, (thinking) thereby to refute the Truth. Then I seized them, and how (awful) was My punishment.

كَذَّبَتْ قَبْلَهُمْ قَوْمُ نُوحٍ وَالْأَحْزَابُ مِنْ بَعْدِهِمْ وَهَمَّتْ كُلُّ أُمَّةٍ بِرَسُولِهِمْ لِيَأْخُذُوهُ وَجَادَلُوا بِالْبَاطِلِ لِيُدْحِضُوا بِهِ الْحَقَّ فَأَخَذْتُهُمْ فَكَيْفَ كَانَ عِقَابِ ۝

6　Thus was the word of thy Lord concerning those who disbelieve fulfilled: that they are owners of the Fire.

وَكَذَلِكَ حَقَّتْ كَلِمَتُ رَبِّكَ عَلَى الَّذِينَ كَفَرُوا أَنَّهُمْ أَصْحَابُ النَّارِ ۝

7　Those who bear the Throne, and all who are round about it, hymn the praises of their Lord and believe in Him and ask forgiveness for those who believe (saying): Our Lord! Thou comprehendest all things in mercy and knowledge, therefore forgive those who repent and follow Thy way. Ward off from them the punishment of hell.

الَّذِينَ يَحْمِلُونَ الْعَرْشَ وَمَنْ حَوْلَهُ يُسَبِّحُونَ بِحَمْدِ رَبِّهِمْ وَيُؤْمِنُونَ بِهِ وَيَسْتَغْفِرُونَ لِلَّذِينَ آمَنُوا رَبَّنَا وَسِعْتَ كُلَّ شَيْءٍ رَحْمَةً وَعِلْمًا فَاغْفِرْ لِلَّذِينَ تَابُوا وَاتَّبَعُوا سَبِيلَكَ وَقِهِمْ عَذَابَ الْجَحِيمِ ۝

8　Our Lord! And make them enter the Gardens of Eden which thou hast promised them, with such of their fathers and their wives and their descendants as do right. Lo! Thou, only Thou, art the Mighty, the Wise.

رَبَّنَا وَأَدْخِلْهُمْ جَنَّاتِ عَدْنٍ الَّتِي وَعَدْتَهُمْ وَمَنْ صَلَحَ مِنْ آبَائِهِمْ وَأَزْوَاجِهِمْ وَذُرِّيَّاتِهِمْ إِنَّكَ أَنْتَ الْعَزِيزُ الْحَكِيمُ ۝

9　And ward off from them ill-deeds; and he from whom Thou wardest off ill deeds that day, him verily hast Thou taken into mercy. That is the supreme triumph.

وَقِهِمُ السَّيِّئَاتِ وَمَنْ تَقِ السَّيِّئَاتِ يَوْمَئِذٍ فَقَدْ رَحِمْتَهُ وَذَلِكَ هُوَ الْفَوْزُ الْعَظِيمُ ۝

10 Lo! (on that day) those who disbelieve are informed by proclamation: Verily Allah's abhorrence is more terrible than your abhorrence one of another, when ye were called unto the faith but did refuse.

إِنَّ الَّذِيْنَ كَفَرُوْا يُنَادَوْنَ لَمَقْتُ اللّٰهِ أَكْبَرُ مِنْ مَّقْتِكُمْ أَنْفُسَكُمْ إِذْ تُدْعَوْنَ إِلَى الْإِيْمَانِ فَتَكْفُرُوْنَ ۝

11 They say: Our Lord! Twice hast Thou made us die, and twice hast Thou made us live. Now we confess our sins. Is there any way to go out?

قَالُوْا رَبَّنَا أَمَتَّنَا اثْنَتَيْنِ وَأَحْيَيْتَنَا اثْنَتَيْنِ فَاعْتَرَفْنَا بِذُنُوْبِنَا فَهَلْ إِلَى خُرُوْجٍ مِّنْ سَبِيْلٍ ۝

12 (It is said unto them): This is (your plight) because, when Allah only was invoked, ye disbelieved, but when some partner was ascribed to Him ye were believing. But the command belongeth only to Allah, the Sublime, the Majestic.

ذٰلِكُمْ بِأَنَّهُ إِذَا دُعِيَ اللّٰهُ وَحْدَهُ كَفَرْتُمْ وَإِنْ يُّشْرَكْ بِهِ تُؤْمِنُوْا فَالْحُكْمُ لِلّٰهِ الْعَلِيِّ الْكَبِيْرِ ۝

13 He it is who showeth you His portents, and sendeth down for you provision from the sky. None payeth heed save him who turneth (unto Him) repentant.

هُوَ الَّذِيْ يُرِيْكُمْ اٰيٰتِهِ وَيُنَزِّلُ لَكُمْ مِّنَ السَّمَاءِ رِزْقًا وَمَا يَتَذَكَّرُ إِلَّا مَنْ يُّنِيْبُ ۝

14 Therefore (O believers) pray unto Allah, making religion pure for Him (only), however much the disbelievers be averse—

فَادْعُوا اللّٰهَ مُخْلِصِيْنَ لَهُ الدِّيْنَ وَلَوْ كَرِهَ الْكٰفِرُوْنَ ۝

15 The Exalter of Ranks, the Lord of the Throne. He casteth the Spirit of His command upon whom He will of His slaves, that He may warn of the Day of Meeting,

رَفِيْعُ الدَّرَجٰتِ ذُو الْعَرْشِ يُلْقِي الرُّوْحَ مِنْ أَمْرِهِ عَلَىٰ مَنْ يَّشَاءُ مِنْ عِبَادِهِ لِيُنْذِرَ يَوْمَ التَّلَاقِ ۝

16 The day when they come forth, nothing of them being hidden from Allah. Whose is the sovereignty this day? It is Allah's, the One, the Almighty.

يَوْمَ هُمْ بَارِزُوْنَ لَا يَخْفٰى عَلَى اللّٰهِ مِنْهُمْ شَيْءٌ لِّمَنِ الْمُلْكُ الْيَوْمَ لِلّٰهِ الْوَاحِدِ الْقَهَّارِ ۝

17 This day is each soul requited that which it hath earned; no wrong (is done) this day. Lo! Allah is swift at reckoning.

الْيَوْمَ تُجْزَىٰ كُلُّ نَفْسٍ بِمَا كَسَبَتْ لَا ظُلْمَ الْيَوْمَ إِنَّ اللَّهَ سَرِيعُ الْحِسَابِ ۝

18 Warn them (O Muhammad) of the Day of the approaching (doom), when the hearts will be choking the throats, (when) there will be no friend for the wrong-doers, nor any intercessor who will be heard.

وَأَنذِرْهُمْ يَوْمَ الْآزِفَةِ إِذِ الْقُلُوبُ لَدَى الْحَنَاجِرِ كَاظِمِينَ مَا لِلظَّالِمِينَ مِنْ حَمِيمٍ وَلَا شَفِيعٍ يُطَاعُ ۝

19 He knoweth the traitor of the eyes, and that which the bosoms hide.

يَعْلَمُ خَائِنَةَ الْأَعْيُنِ وَمَا تُخْفِي الصُّدُورُ ۝

20 Allah judgeth with truth, while those to whom they cry instead of Him judge not at all. Lo! Allah, He is the Hearer, the Seer.

وَاللَّهُ يَقْضِي بِالْحَقِّ وَالَّذِينَ يَدْعُونَ مِن دُونِهِ لَا يَقْضُونَ بِشَيْءٍ إِنَّ اللَّهَ هُوَ السَّمِيعُ الْبَصِيرُ ۝

21 Have they not travelled in the land to see the nature of the consequence for those who disbelieved before them? They were mightier than these in power and (in the) traces (which they left behind them) in the earth. Yet Allah seized them for their sins, and they had no protector from Allah.

أَوَلَمْ يَسِيرُوا فِي الْأَرْضِ فَيَنظُرُوا كَيْفَ كَانَ عَاقِبَةُ الَّذِينَ كَانُوا مِن قَبْلِهِمْ كَانُوا هُمْ أَشَدَّ مِنْهُمْ قُوَّةً وَآثَارًا فِي الْأَرْضِ فَأَخَذَهُمُ اللَّهُ بِذُنُوبِهِمْ وَمَا كَانَ لَهُم مِّنَ اللَّهِ مِن وَاقٍ ۝

22 That was because their messengers kept bringing them clear proofs (of Allah's sovereignty) but they disbelieved; so Allah seized them. Lo! He is Strong, Severe in punishment.

ذَٰلِكَ بِأَنَّهُمْ كَانَت تَّأْتِيهِمْ رُسُلُهُم بِالْبَيِّنَاتِ فَكَفَرُوا فَأَخَذَهُمُ اللَّهُ إِنَّهُ قَوِيٌّ شَدِيدُ الْعِقَابِ ۝

23 And verily We sent Moses with Our revelations and a clear warrant

وَلَقَدْ أَرْسَلْنَا مُوسَىٰ بِآيَاتِنَا وَسُلْطَانٍ مُّبِينٍ ۝

24 Unto Pharaoh and Hāmān and Korah, but they said: A lying sorcerer!

إِلَى فِرْعَوْنَ وَهَٰمَٰنَ وَقَٰرُونَ فَقَالُوا سَٰحِرٌ كَذَّابٌ ۝

25 And when he brought them the Truth from Our presence, they said: Slay the sons of those who believe with him, and spare their women. But the plot of disbelievers is in naught but error.

فَلَمَّا جَآءَهُم بِالْحَقِّ مِنْ عِندِنَا قَالُوا اقْتُلُوٓا أَبْنَآءَ الَّذِينَ ءَامَنُوا مَعَهُۥ وَاسْتَحْيُوا نِسَآءَهُمْ ۚ وَمَا كَيْدُ الْكَٰفِرِينَ إِلَّا فِى ضَلَٰلٍ ۝

26 And Pharaoh said: Suffer me to kill Moses, and let him cry unto his Lord. Lo! I fear that he will alter your religion or that he will cause confusion in the land.

وَقَالَ فِرْعَوْنُ ذَرُونِىٓ أَقْتُلْ مُوسَىٰ وَلْيَدْعُ رَبَّهُۥٓ إِنِّىٓ أَخَافُ أَن يُبَدِّلَ دِينَكُمْ أَوْ أَن يُظْهِرَ فِى الْأَرْضِ الْفَسَادَ ۝

27 Moses said: Lo! I seek refuge in my Lord and your Lord from every scorner who believeth not in a Day of Reckoning.

وَقَالَ مُوسَىٰٓ إِنِّى عُذْتُ بِرَبِّى وَرَبِّكُم مِّن كُلِّ مُتَكَبِّرٍ لَّا يُؤْمِنُ بِيَوْمِ الْحِسَابِ ۝

28 And a believing man of Pharaoh's family, who hid his faith, said: Would ye kill a man because he saith: My Lord is Allah, and hath brought you clear proofs from your Lord? If he is lying, then his lie is upon him; and if he is truthful then some of that wherewith he threateneth you will strike you. Lo! Allah guideth not one who is a prodigal, a liar.

وَقَالَ رَجُلٌ مُّؤْمِنٌ مِّنْ ءَالِ فِرْعَوْنَ يَكْتُمُ إِيمَٰنَهُۥٓ أَتَقْتُلُونَ رَجُلًا أَن يَقُولَ رَبِّىَ اللَّهُ وَقَدْ جَآءَكُم بِالْبَيِّنَٰتِ مِن رَّبِّكُمْ ۖ وَإِن يَكُ كَٰذِبًا فَعَلَيْهِ كَذِبُهُۥ ۖ وَإِن يَكُ صَادِقًا يُصِبْكُم بَعْضُ الَّذِى يَعِدُكُمْ ۖ إِنَّ اللَّهَ لَا يَهْدِى مَنْ هُوَ مُسْرِفٌ كَذَّابٌ ۝

29 O my people! Yours is the kingdom today, ye being uppermost in the land. But who would save us from the wrath of Allah should it reach us? Pharaoh said: I do but show you what I see, and I do but guide you to wise policy.

يَٰقَوْمِ لَكُمُ الْمُلْكُ الْيَوْمَ ظَٰهِرِينَ فِى الْأَرْضِ فَمَن يَنصُرُنَا مِنۢ بَأْسِ اللَّهِ إِن جَآءَنَا ۚ قَالَ فِرْعَوْنُ مَآ أُرِيكُمْ إِلَّا مَآ أَرَىٰ وَمَآ أَهْدِيكُمْ إِلَّا سَبِيلَ الرَّشَادِ ۝

30 And he who believed said: O my people! Lo! I fear for you a fate like that of the factions (of old);

وَقَالَ الَّذِىٓ ءَامَنَ يَٰقَوْمِ إِنِّىٓ أَخَافُ عَلَيْكُم مِّثْلَ يَوْمِ الْأَحْزَابِ ۝

31 A plight like that of Noah's folk, and 'Ād and Thamūd, and those after them, and Allah willeth no injustice for (His) slaves.

مِثْلَ دَأْبِ قَوْمِ نُوحٍ وَعَادٍ وَثَمُودَ وَالَّذِينَ مِنۢ بَعْدِهِمْ وَمَا اللَّهُ يُرِيدُ ظُلْمًا لِّلْعِبَادِ ۝

32 And, O my people! Lo! I fear for a Day of Summoning,

وَيَٰقَوْمِ إِنِّىٓ أَخَافُ عَلَيْكُمْ يَوْمَ التَّنَادِ ۝

33 A day when ye will turn to flee, having no preserver from Allah: and he whom Allah sendeth astray, for him there is no guide.

يَوْمَ تُوَلُّونَ مُدْبِرِينَ مَا لَكُم مِّنَ اللَّهِ مِنْ عَاصِمٍ وَمَن يُضْلِلِ اللَّهُ فَمَا لَهُۥ مِنْ هَادٍ ۝

34 And verily Joseph brought you of old clear proofs, yet ye ceased not to be in doubt concerning what he brought you till, when he died, he said: Allah will not send any messenger after him. Thus Allah deceiveth him who is a prodigal, a doubter.

وَلَقَدْ جَآءَكُمْ يُوسُفُ مِن قَبْلُ بِالْبَيِّنَٰتِ فَمَا زِلْتُمْ فِى شَكٍّ مِّمَّا جَآءَكُم بِهِۦ حَتَّىٰٓ إِذَا هَلَكَ قُلْتُمْ لَن يَبْعَثَ اللَّهُ مِنۢ بَعْدِهِۦ رَسُولًا كَذَٰلِكَ يُضِلُّ اللَّهُ مَنْ هُوَ مُسْرِفٌ مُّرْتَابٌ ۝

35 Those who wrangle concerning the revelations of Allah without any warrant that hath come unto them, it is greatly hateful in the sight of Allah and in the sight of those who believe. Thus doth Allah print on every arrogant, disdainful heart.

الَّذِينَ يُجَٰدِلُونَ فِىٓ ءَايَٰتِ اللَّهِ بِغَيْرِ سُلْطَٰنٍ أَتَىٰهُمْ كَبُرَ مَقْتًا عِندَ اللَّهِ وَعِندَ الَّذِينَ ءَامَنُوا۟ كَذَٰلِكَ يَطْبَعُ اللَّهُ عَلَىٰ كُلِّ قَلْبِ مُتَكَبِّرٍ جَبَّارٍ ۝

36 And Pharaoh said: O Hāmān! Build for me a tower that haply I may reach the means of access,

وَقَالَ فِرْعَوْنُ يَٰهَٰمَٰنُ ابْنِ لِى صَرْحًا لَّعَلِّىٓ أَبْلُغُ الْأَسْبَٰبَ ۝

37 The roads of the heavens, and may look upon the God of Moses, though verily I think him a liar.

أَسْبَٰبَ السَّمَٰوَٰتِ فَأَطَّلِعَ إِلَىٰٓ إِلَٰهِ مُوسَىٰ وَإِنِّى لَأَظُنُّهُۥ كَٰذِبًا وَكَذَٰلِكَ زُيِّنَ

Thus was the evil that he did made fair-seeming unto Pharaoh, and he was debarred from the (right) way. The plot of Pharaoh ended but in ruin.

لِفِرْعَوْنَ سُوٓءُ عَمَلِهٖ وَصُدَّ عَنِ السَّبِيلِ ۚ وَمَا كَيْدُ فِرْعَوْنَ إِلَّا فِى تَبَابٍ ﴿٣٧﴾

38 And he who believed said: O my people! Follow me. I will show you the way of right conduct.

وَقَالَ الَّذِىٓ ءَامَنَ يٰقَوْمِ اتَّبِعُونِ أَهْدِكُمْ سَبِيلَ الرَّشَادِ ﴿٣٨﴾

39 O my people! Lo! this life of the world is but a passing comfort, and lo! the Hereafter, that is the enduring home.

يٰقَوْمِ إِنَّمَا هٰذِهِ الْحَيٰوةُ الدُّنْيَا مَتَٰعٌ ۖ وَإِنَّ الْأَخِرَةَ هِىَ دَارُ الْقَرَارِ ﴿٣٩﴾

40 Whoso doeth an ill-deed, he will be repaid the like thereof, while whoso doeth right, whether male or female, and is a believer, (all) such will enter the Garden, where they will be nourished without stint.

مَنْ عَمِلَ سَيِّئَةً فَلَا يُجْزٰىٓ إِلَّا مِثْلَهَا ۖ وَمَنْ عَمِلَ صَٰلِحًا مِّن ذَكَرٍ أَوْ أُنثَىٰ وَهُوَ مُؤْمِنٌ فَأُولٰٓئِكَ يَدْخُلُونَ الْجَنَّةَ يُرْزَقُونَ فِيهَا بِغَيْرِ حِسَابٍ ﴿٤٠﴾

41 And, O my people! What aileth me that I call you unto deliverance when ye call me unto the Fire?

۞ وَيٰقَوْمِ مَا لِىٓ أَدْعُوكُمْ إِلَى النَّجَٰوةِ وَتَدْعُونَنِىٓ إِلَى النَّارِ ﴿٤١﴾

42 Ye call me to disbelieve in Allah and ascribe unto Him as partners that whereof I have no knowledge, while I call you unto the Mighty, the Forgiver.

تَدْعُونَنِى لِأَكْفُرَ بِاللّٰهِ وَأُشْرِكَ بِهٖ مَا لَيْسَ لِى بِهٖ عِلْمٌ وَأَنَا أَدْعُوكُمْ إِلَى الْعَزِيزِ الْغَفَّارِ ﴿٤٢﴾

43 Assuredly that whereunto ye call me hath no claim in the world or in the Hereafter, and our return will be unto Allah, and the prodigals will be owners of the fire.

لَا جَرَمَ أَنَّمَا تَدْعُونَنِىٓ إِلَيْهِ لَيْسَ لَهُ دَعْوَةٌ فِى الدُّنْيَا وَلَا فِى الْأَخِرَةِ وَأَنَّ مَرَدَّنَآ إِلَى اللّٰهِ وَأَنَّ الْمُسْرِفِينَ هُمْ أَصْحَٰبُ النَّارِ ﴿٤٣﴾

44 And ye will remember what I say unto you. I confide my cause unto Allah. Lo! Allah is Seer of (His) slaves.

فَسَتَذْكُرُونَ مَآ أَقُولُ لَكُمْ ۚ وَأُفَوِّضُ أَمْرِىٓ إِلَى اللّٰهِ ۚ إِنَّ اللّٰهَ بَصِيرٌ بِالْعِبَادِ ﴿٤٤﴾

45 So Allah warded off from him the evils which they plotted, while a dreadful doom encompassed Pharaoh's folk.

فَوَقَٮٰهُ ٱللَّهُ سَيِّئَاتِ مَا مَكَرُواْ ۖ وَحَاقَ بِـَٔالِ فِرْعَوْنَ سُوٓءُ ٱلْعَذَابِ ۝

46 The Fire; they are exposed to it morning and evening; and on the day when the Hour upriseth (it is said): Cause Pharaoh's folk to enter the most awful doom.

ٱلنَّارُ يُعْرَضُونَ عَلَيْهَا غُدُوًّا وَعَشِيًّا ۖ وَيَوْمَ تَقُومُ ٱلسَّاعَةُ أَدْخِلُوٓاْ ءَالَ فِرْعَوْنَ أَشَدَّ ٱلْعَذَابِ ۝

47 And when they wrangle in the fire, the weak say unto those who were proud: Lo! we were a following unto you: will ye therefore rid us of a portion of the Fire?

وَإِذْ يَتَحَآجُّونَ فِى ٱلنَّارِ فَيَقُولُ ٱلضُّعَفَٰٓؤُاْ لِلَّذِينَ ٱسْتَكْبَرُوٓاْ إِنَّا كُنَّا لَكُمْ تَبَعًا فَهَلْ أَنتُم مُّغْنُونَ عَنَّا نَصِيبًا مِّنَ ٱلنَّارِ ۝

48 Those who were proud say: Lo! we are all (together) herein. Lo! Allah hath judged between (His) slaves.

قَالَ ٱلَّذِينَ ٱسْتَكْبَرُوٓاْ إِنَّا كُلٌّ فِيهَآ إِنَّ ٱللَّهَ قَدْ حَكَمَ بَيْنَ ٱلْعِبَادِ ۝

49 And those in the Fire say unto the guards of hell: Entreat your Lord that He relieve us of a day of the torment.

وَقَالَ ٱلَّذِينَ فِى ٱلنَّارِ لِخَزَنَةِ جَهَنَّمَ ٱدْعُواْ رَبَّكُمْ يُخَفِّفْ عَنَّا يَوْمًا مِّنَ ٱلْعَذَابِ ۝

50 They say: Came not your messengers unto you with clear proofs? They say: Yea, verily. They say: Then do ye pray, although the prayer of disbelievers is in vain.

قَالُوٓاْ أَوَلَمْ تَكُ تَأْتِيكُمْ رُسُلُكُم بِٱلْبَيِّنَٰتِ قَالُواْ بَلَىٰ قَالُواْ فَٱدْعُواْ ۗ وَمَا دُعَٰٓؤُاْ ٱلْكَٰفِرِينَ إِلَّا فِى ضَلَٰلٍ ۝

51 Lo! We verily do help Our messengers, and those who believe, in the life of the world and on the day when the witnesses arise,

إِنَّا لَنَنصُرُ رُسُلَنَا وَٱلَّذِينَ ءَامَنُواْ فِى ٱلْحَيَوٰةِ ٱلدُّنْيَا وَيَوْمَ يَقُومُ ٱلْأَشْهَٰدُ ۝

52 The day when their excuse availeth not the evil-doers, and theirs is the curse, and theirs the ill abode.

يَوْمَ لَا يَنفَعُ ٱلظَّٰلِمِينَ مَعْذِرَتُهُمْ ۖ وَلَهُمُ ٱللَّعْنَةُ وَلَهُمْ سُوٓءُ ٱلدَّارِ ۝

53 And we verily gave Moses the guidance, and We caused the Children of Israel to inherit the Scripture,

ﻭَﻟَﻘَﺪْ ءَﺍﺗَﻴْﻨَﺎ ﻣُﻮﺳَﻰ ﺍﻟْﻬُﺪَﻯ ﻭَﺃَﻭْﺭَﺛْﻨَﺎ ﺑَﻨِﻰ ﺇِﺳْﺮَءِﻳﻞَ ﺍﻟْﻜِﺘَﺐَ ۝

54 A guide and a reminder for men of understanding.

ﻫُﺪًﻯ ﻭَﺫِﻛْﺮَﻯ ﻷُﻭْﻟِﻰ ﺍﻷَﻟْﺒَﺐِ ۝

55 Then have patience (O Muhammad). Lo! the promise of Allah is true. And ask forgiveness of thy sin, and hymn the praise of thy Lord at fall of night and in the early hours.

ﻓَﺎﺻْﺒِﺮْ ﺇِﻥَّ ﻭَﻋْﺪَ ﺍﻟﻠَّﻪِ ﺣَﻖٌّ ﻭَﺍﺳْﺘَﻐْﻔِﺮْ ﻟِﺬَﻧْﺒِﻚَ ﻭَﺳَﺒِّﺢْ ﺑِﺤَﻤْﺪِ ﺭَﺑِّﻚَ ﺑِﺎﻟْﻌَﺸِﻰِّ ﻭَﺍﻹِﺑْﻜَﺮِ ۝

56 Lo! those who wrangle concerning the revelations of Allah without a warrant having come unto them, there is naught else in their breasts save pride which they will never attain. So take thou refuge in Allah. Lo! He, only He, is the Hearer, the Seer.

ﺇِﻥَّ ﺍﻟَّﺬِﻳﻦَ ﻳُﺠَﺪِﻟُﻮﻥَ ﻓِﻰ ءَﺍﻳَﺖِ ﺍﻟﻠَّﻪِ ﺑِﻐَﻴْﺮِ ﺳُﻠْﻄَﻦٍ ﺃَﺗَﻬُﻢْ ﺇِﻥ ﻓِﻰ ﺻُﺪُﻭﺭِﻫِﻢْ ﺇِﻻَّ ﻛِﺒْﺮٌ ﻣَﺎ ﻫُﻢ ﺑِﺒَﻠِﻐِﻴﻪِ ﻓَﺎﺳْﺘَﻌِﺬْ ﺑِﺎﻟﻠَّﻪِ ﺇِﻧَّﻪُ ﻫُﻮَ ﺍﻟﺴَّﻤِﻴﻊُ ﺍﻟْﺒَﺼِﻴﺮُ ۝

57 Assuredly the creation of the heavens and the earth is greater than the creation of mankind; but most of mankind know not.

ﻟَﺨَﻠْﻖُ ﺍﻟﺴَّﻤَﻮَﺕِ ﻭَﺍﻷَﺭْﺽِ ﺃَﻛْﺒَﺮُ ﻣِﻦْ ﺧَﻠْﻖِ ﺍﻟﻨَّﺎﺱِ ﻭَﻟَﻜِﻦَّ ﺃَﻛْﺜَﺮَ ﺍﻟﻨَّﺎﺱِ ﻻ ﻳَﻌْﻠَﻤُﻮﻥَ ۝

58 And the blind man and the seer are not equal, neither are those who believe and do good works (equal with) the evil-doer. Little do ye reflect!

ﻭَﻣَﺎ ﻳَﺴْﺘَﻮِﻯ ﺍﻷَﻋْﻤَﻰ ﻭَﺍﻟْﺒَﺼِﻴﺮُ ﻭَﺍﻟَّﺬِﻳﻦَ ءَﺍﻣَﻨُﻮﺍ ﻭَﻋَﻤِﻠُﻮﺍ ﺍﻟﺼَّﻠِﺤَﺖِ ﻭَﻻ ﺍﻟْﻤُﺴِﻰءُ ﻗَﻠِﻴﻼ ﻣَﺎ ﺗَﺘَﺬَﻛَّﺮُﻭﻥَ ۝

59 Lo! the Hour is surely coming, there is no doubt thereof; yet most of mankind believe not.

ﺇِﻥَّ ﺍﻟﺴَّﺎﻋَﺔَ ﻵﺗِﻴَﺔٌ ﻻ ﺭَﻳْﺐَ ﻓِﻴﻬَﺎ ﻭَﻟَﻜِﻦَّ ﺃَﻛْﺜَﺮَ ﺍﻟﻨَّﺎﺱِ ﻻ ﻳُﺆْﻣِﻨُﻮﻥَ ۝

60 And your Lord hath said: Pray unto me and I will hear your prayer. Lo! those who scorn My service, they will enter hell, disgraced.

ﻭَﻗَﺎﻝَ ﺭَﺑُّﻜُﻢُ ﺍﺩْﻋُﻮﻧِﻰ ﺃَﺳْﺘَﺠِﺐْ ﻟَﻜُﻢْ ﺇِﻥَّ ﺍﻟَّﺬِﻳﻦَ ﻳَﺴْﺘَﻜْﺒِﺮُﻭﻥَ ﻋَﻦْ ﻋِﺒَﺎﺩَﺗِﻰ ﺳَﻴَﺪْﺧُﻠُﻮﻥَ ﺟَﻬَﻨَّﻢَ ﺩَﺍﺧِﺮِﻳﻦَ ۝

61 Allah it is Who hath appointed for you night that ye may rest therein, and day for seeing. Lo! Allah is a Lord of bounty for mankind, yet most of mankind give not thanks.

اللّٰهُ الَّذِىْ جَعَلَ لَكُمُ الَّيْلَ لِتَسْكُنُوْا فِيْهِ وَالنَّهَارَ مُبْصِرًا ۚ اِنَّ اللّٰهَ لَذُوْ فَضْلٍ عَلَى النَّاسِ وَلٰكِنَّ اَكْثَرَ النَّاسِ لَا يَشْكُرُوْنَ ۝

62 Such is Allah, your Lord, the Creator of all things. There is no God save Him. How then are ye perverted?

ذٰلِكُمُ اللّٰهُ رَبُّكُمْ خَالِقُ كُلِّ شَىْءٍ لَّا اِلٰهَ اِلَّا هُوَ ۖ فَاَنّٰى تُؤْفَكُوْنَ ۝

63 Thus are they perverted who deny the revelations of Allah.

كَذٰلِكَ يُؤْفَكُ الَّذِيْنَ كَانُوْا بِاٰيٰتِ اللّٰهِ يَجْحَدُوْنَ ۝

64 Allah it is Who appointed for you the earth for a dwelling place and the sky for a canopy, and fashioned you and perfected your shapes, and hath provided you with good things. Such is Allah, your Lord. Then blessed be Allah, the Lord of the Worlds!

اللّٰهُ الَّذِىْ جَعَلَ لَكُمُ الْاَرْضَ قَرَارًا وَّالسَّمَاءَ بِنَاءً وَّصَوَّرَكُمْ فَاَحْسَنَ صُوَرَكُمْ وَرَزَقَكُمْ مِّنَ الطَّيِّبٰتِ ذٰلِكُمُ اللّٰهُ رَبُّكُمْ ۖ فَتَبَارَكَ اللّٰهُ رَبُّ الْعٰلَمِيْنَ ۝

65 He is the Living One. There is no God save Him. So pray unto Him, making religion pure for Him (only). Praise be to Allah, the Lord of the Worlds!

هُوَ الْحَىُّ لَا اِلٰهَ اِلَّا هُوَ فَادْعُوْهُ مُخْلِصِيْنَ لَهُ الدِّيْنَ ۗ اَلْحَمْدُ لِلّٰهِ رَبِّ الْعٰلَمِيْنَ ۝

66 Say (O Muhammad): I am forbidden to worship those unto whom ye cry beside Allah since there have come unto me clear proofs from my Lord, and I am commanded to surrender to the Lord of the Worlds.

قُلْ اِنِّىْ نُهِيْتُ اَنْ اَعْبُدَ الَّذِيْنَ تَدْعُوْنَ مِنْ دُوْنِ اللّٰهِ لَمَّا جَاءَنِىَ الْبَيِّنٰتُ مِنْ رَّبِّىْ وَاُمِرْتُ اَنْ اُسْلِمَ لِرَبِّ الْعٰلَمِيْنَ ۝

67 He it is Who created you from dust, then from a drop (of seed) then from a clot, then bringeth you forth as a child, then (ordaineth)

هُوَ الَّذِىْ خَلَقَكُمْ مِّنْ تُرَابٍ ثُمَّ مِنْ نُّطْفَةٍ ثُمَّ مِنْ عَلَقَةٍ ثُمَّ يُخْرِجُكُمْ طِفْلًا ثُمَّ لِتَبْلُغُوْا

that ye attain full strength and afterward that ye become old men though some among you die before and that ye reach an appointed term, that haply ye may understand.

أَشُدَّكُمْ ثُمَّ لِتَكُونُوا شُيُوخًا وَمِنكُم مَّن يُتَوَفَّىٰ مِن قَبْلُ وَلِتَبْلُغُوا أَجَلًا مُّسَمًّى وَلَعَلَّكُمْ تَعْقِلُونَ ۝

68 He it is who quickeneth and giveth death. When He ordaineth a thing, He saith unto it only: Be! and it is.

هُوَ الَّذِى يُحْيِ وَيُمِيتُ فَإِذَا قَضَىٰ أَمْرًا فَإِنَّمَا يَقُولُ لَهُ كُن فَيَكُونُ ۝

69 Hast thou not seen those who wrangle concerning the revelations of Allah, how they are turned away?—

أَلَمْ تَرَ إِلَى الَّذِينَ يُجَادِلُونَ فِى ءَايَـٰتِ اللَّهِ أَنَّىٰ يُصْرَفُونَ ۝

70 Those who deny the Scripture and that wherewith We send Our messengers. But they will come to know,

الَّذِينَ كَذَّبُوا بِالْكِتَـٰبِ وَبِمَا أَرْسَلْنَا بِهِ رُسُلَنَا فَسَوْفَ يَعْلَمُونَ ۝

71 When carcans are about their necks and chains. They are dragged

إِذِ الْأَغْلَـٰلُ فِى أَعْنَـٰقِهِمْ وَالسَّلَـٰسِلُ يُسْحَبُونَ ۝

72 Through boiling waters; then they are thrust into the Fire.

فِى الْحَمِيمِ ثُمَّ فِى النَّارِ يُسْجَرُونَ ۝

73 Then it is said unto them: Where are (all) that ye used to make partners (in the Sovereignty)

ثُمَّ قِيلَ لَهُمْ أَيْنَ مَا كُنتُمْ تُشْرِكُونَ ۝

74 Beside Allah? They say: They have failed us: but we used not to pray to anything before. Thus doth Allah send astray the disbelievers (in His guidance).

مِن دُونِ اللَّهِ قَالُوا ضَلُّوا عَنَّا بَل لَّمْ نَكُن نَّدْعُوا مِن قَبْلُ شَيْـًٔا كَذَٰلِكَ يُضِلُّ اللَّهُ الْكَـٰفِرِينَ ۝

75 (And it is said unto them): This is because ye exulted in the earth without right, and because ye were petulant.

ذَٰلِكُم بِمَا كُنتُمْ تَفْرَحُونَ فِى الْأَرْضِ بِغَيْرِ الْحَقِّ وَبِمَا كُنتُمْ تَمْرَحُونَ ۝

76 Enter ye the gates of hell, to dwell therein forever. Evil is the habitation of the scornful.

ادْخُلُوا أَبْوَٰبَ جَهَنَّمَ خَـٰلِدِينَ فِيهَا فَبِئْسَ مَثْوَى الْمُتَكَبِّرِينَ ۝

77 Then have patience (O Muhammad). Lo! the promise of Allah is true. And whether We let thee see a part of that which We promise them, or (whether) We cause thee to die, still unto us they will be brought back.

فَاصۡبِرۡ اِنَّ وَعۡدَ اللّٰهِ حَقٌّ فَاِمَّا نُرِيَنَّكَ بَعۡضَ الَّذِىۡ نَعِدُهُمۡ اَوۡ نَتَوَفَّيَنَّكَ فَاِلَيۡنَا يُرۡجَعُوۡنَ ۝

78 Verily We sent messengers before thee, among them those of whom We have told thee, and some of whom We have not told thee; and it was not given to any messenger that he should bring a portent save by Allah's leave, but when Allah's commandment cometh (the cause) is judged aright, and the followers of vanity will then be lost.

وَلَقَدۡ اَرۡسَلۡنَا رُسُلًا مِّنۡ قَبۡلِكَ مِنۡهُمۡ مَّنۡ قَصَصۡنَا عَلَيۡكَ وَمِنۡهُمۡ مَّنۡ لَّمۡ نَقۡصُصۡ عَلَيۡكَ وَمَا كَانَ لِرَسُوۡلٍ اَنۡ يَّاۡتِيَ بِاٰيَةٍ اِلَّا بِاِذۡنِ اللّٰهِ فَاِذَا جَاۤءَ اَمۡرُ اللّٰهِ قُضِيَ بِالۡحَقِّ وَخَسِرَ هُنَالِكَ الۡمُبۡطِلُوۡنَ ۝

79 Allah it is Who hath appointed for you cattle, that ye may ride on some of them, and eat of some—

اَللّٰهُ الَّذِىۡ جَعَلَ لَكُمُ الۡاَنۡعَامَ لِتَرۡكَبُوۡا مِنۡهَا وَمِنۡهَا تَاۡكُلُوۡنَ ۝

80 (Many) benefits ye have from them and that ye may satisfy by their means a need that is in your breasts, and may be borne upon them as upon the ship.

وَلَكُمۡ فِيۡهَا مَنَافِعُ وَلِتَبۡلُغُوۡا عَلَيۡهَا حَاجَةً فِىۡ صُدُوۡرِكُمۡ وَعَلَيۡهَا وَعَلَى الۡفُلۡكِ تُحۡمَلُوۡنَ ۝

81 And He showeth you His tokens. Which, then, of the tokens of Allah do ye deny?

وَيُرِيۡكُمۡ اٰيٰتِهٖ فَاَىَّ اٰيٰتِ اللّٰهِ تُنۡكِرُوۡنَ ۝

82 Have they not travelled in the land to see the nature of the consequence for those before them? They were more numerous than these, and mightier in power and (in the)

اَفَلَمۡ يَسِيۡرُوۡا فِى الۡاَرۡضِ فَيَنۡظُرُوۡا كَيۡفَ كَانَ عَاقِبَةُ الَّذِيۡنَ مِنۡ قَبۡلِهِمۡ كَانُوۡا اَكۡثَرَ مِنۡهُمۡ وَاَشَدَّ قُوَّةً وَّاٰثَارًا فِى الۡاَرۡضِ فَمَا اَغۡنٰى عَنۡهُمۡ

traces (which they left behind them) in the earth. But all that they used to earn availed them not.

مَّا كَانُوْا يَكْسِبُوْنَ ۝

83 And when their messengers brought them clear proofs (of Allah's Sovereignty) they exulted in the knowledge they (themselves) possessed. And that which they were wont to mock befell them.

فَلَمَّا جَآءَتْهُمْ رُسُلُهُمْ بِالْبَيِّنَٰتِ فَرِحُوْا بِمَا عِنْدَهُمْ مِّنَ الْعِلْمِ وَحَاقَ بِهِمْ مَّا كَانُوْا بِهٖ يَسْتَهْزِءُوْنَ ۝

84 Then, when they saw Our doom, they said: We believe in Allah only and reject (all) that we used to associate (with Him).

فَلَمَّا رَأَوْا بَأْسَنَا قَالُوْٓا اٰمَنَّا بِاللّٰهِ وَحْدَهُ وَكَفَرْنَا بِمَا كُنَّا بِهٖ مُشْرِكِيْنَ ۝

85 But their faith could not avail them when they saw Our doom. This is Allah's law which hath ever taken course for his Bondsmen. And then the disbelievers will be ruined.

فَلَمْ يَكُ يَنْفَعُهُمْ إِيْمَانُهُمْ لَمَّا رَأَوْا بَأْسَنَا سُنَّتَ اللّٰهِ الَّتِيْ قَدْ خَلَتْ فِيْ عِبَادِهٖ وَخَسِرَ هُنَالِكَ الْكَٰفِرُوْنَ ۝

Fussilat
(They Are Expounded)

Fussilat, "They Are Expounded," derives its title from a word in v. 2. It is also often called *Hā, Mīm, As Sajdah*, from a word in v. 37, Hā Mīm being added to distinguish it from sūrah 32, which is called *As Sajdah*.

It belongs to the middle group of Makkan sūrahs.

In the name of Allah, the Beneficent, the Merciful.

1   Hā. Mīm.[1]

2   A revelation from the Beneficent, the Merciful,

3   A scripture whereof the verses are expounded, a Lecture[2] in Arabic for people who have knowledge.

4   Good tidings and a warning. But most of them turn away so that they hear not.

5   And they say: Our hearts are protected from that unto which thou (O Muhammad) callest us, and in our ears there is a deafness, and

---

1. See Sūrah 2, v. 1, footnote.

2. Ar. *Qur'an.*

between us and thee there is a veil.
Act, then. Lo! we also shall be
acting.

فَاعْمَلْ إِنَّنَا عَامِلُونَ ۝

6　Say (unto them O Muḥammad):
I am only a mortal like you. It is
inspired in me that your God is One
God, therefore take the straight path
unto Him and seek forgiveness of
Him. And woe unto the idolaters,

قُلْ إِنَّمَا أَنَا بَشَرٌ مِّثْلُكُمْ يُوحَى إِلَىَّ أَنَّمَا إِلَهُكُمْ
إِلَهٌ وَاحِدٌ فَاسْتَقِيمُوا إِلَيْهِ وَاسْتَغْفِرُوهُ وَوَيْلٌ
لِّلْمُشْرِكِينَ ۝

7　Who give not the poor due, and
who are disbelievers in the Hereafter.

الَّذِينَ لَا يُؤْتُونَ الزَّكَوةَ وَهُم بِالْآخِرَةِ
هُمْ كَافِرُونَ ۝

8　Lo! as for those who believe
and do good works, for them is a
reward enduring.

إِنَّ الَّذِينَ ءَامَنُوا وَعَمِلُوا الصَّالِحَاتِ لَهُمْ
أَجْرٌ غَيْرُ مَمْنُونٍ ۝

9　Say (O Muḥammad, unto the
idolaters): Disbelieve ye verily in
Him Who created the earth in two
Days,[3] and ascribe ye unto Him
rivals? He (and none else) is the
Lord of the Worlds.

۞ قُلْ أَئِنَّكُمْ لَتَكْفُرُونَ بِالَّذِي خَلَقَ الْأَرْضَ
فِي يَوْمَيْنِ وَتَجْعَلُونَ لَهُ أَندَادًا ذَلِكَ رَبُّ الْعَالَمِينَ ۝

10　He placed therein firm hills
rising above it, and blessed it and
measured therein its sustenance in
four Days, alike for (all) who ask;

وَجَعَلَ فِيهَا رَوَاسِيَ مِن فَوْقِهَا وَبَارَكَ فِيهَا وَقَدَّرَ فِيهَا
أَقْوَاتَهَا فِي أَرْبَعَةِ أَيَّامٍ سَوَاءً لِّلسَّائِلِينَ ۝

11　Then turned He to the heaven
when it was smoke, and said unto it
and unto the earth: Come both of
you, willingly or loth. They said:
We come, obedient.

ثُمَّ اسْتَوَى إِلَى السَّمَاءِ وَهِيَ دُخَانٌ فَقَالَ لَهَا وَلِلْأَرْضِ
ائْتِيَا طَوْعًا أَوْ كَرْهًا قَالَتَا أَتَيْنَا طَائِعِينَ ۝

12　Then He ordained them seven
heavens in two Days[4] and inspired

فَقَضَاهُنَّ سَبْعَ سَمَوَاتٍ فِي يَوْمَيْنِ وَأَوْحَى فِي كُلِّ

---

3. (22: 47); (32: 5); (70: 4).

4. (22: 47); (32: 5); (70: 4).

in each heaven its mandate; and we decked the nether heaven with lamps, and rendered it inviolable.[5] That is the measuring of the Mighty, the Knower.

13 But if they turn away, then say: I warn you of a thunderbolt like the thunderbolt (which fell of old upon the tribes) of 'Ād and Thamūd;

14 When their messengers came unto them from before them and behind them, saying: Worship none but Allah! they said: If our Lord had willed, He surely would have sent down angels (unto us), so lo! we are disbelievers in that wherewith ye have been sent.

15 As for 'Ād, they were arrogant in the land without right, and they said: Who is mightier than us in power? Could they not see that Allah Who created them, He was mightier than them in power? And they denied Our revelations.

16 Therefore We let loose on them a raging wind in evil days, that We might make them taste the torment of disgrace in the life of the world. And verily the doom of the Hereafter will be more shameful, and they will not be helped.

17 And as for Thamūd, We gave them guidance, but they preferred

سَمَآءٍ أَمْرَهَا وَزَيَّنَّا السَّمَآءَ الدُّنْيَا بِمَصَٰبِيحَ وَحِفْظًا ذَٰلِكَ تَقْدِيرُ الْعَزِيزِ الْعَلِيمِ ﴿١٢﴾

فَإِنْ أَعْرَضُوا فَقُلْ أَنذَرْتُكُمْ صَٰعِقَةً مِّثْلَ صَٰعِقَةِ عَادٍ وَثَمُودَ ﴿١٣﴾

إِذْ جَآءَتْهُمُ الرُّسُلُ مِن بَيْنِ أَيْدِيهِمْ وَمِنْ خَلْفِهِمْ أَلَّا تَعْبُدُوٓا إِلَّا اللَّهَ قَالُوا لَوْ شَآءَ رَبُّنَا لَأَنزَلَ مَلَٰٓئِكَةً فَإِنَّا بِمَآ أُرْسِلْتُم بِهِ كَٰفِرُونَ ﴿١٤﴾

فَأَمَّا عَادٌ فَاسْتَكْبَرُوا فِي الْأَرْضِ بِغَيْرِ الْحَقِّ وَقَالُوا مَنْ أَشَدُّ مِنَّا قُوَّةً أَوَلَمْ يَرَوْا أَنَّ اللَّهَ الَّذِي خَلَقَهُمْ هُوَ أَشَدُّ مِنْهُمْ قُوَّةً وَكَانُوا بِـَٔايَٰتِنَا يَجْحَدُونَ ﴿١٥﴾

فَأَرْسَلْنَا عَلَيْهِمْ رِيحًا صَرْصَرًا فِي أَيَّامٍ نَّحِسَاتٍ لِّنُذِيقَهُمْ عَذَابَ الْخِزْيِ فِي الْحَيَوٰةِ الدُّنْيَا وَلَعَذَابُ الْآخِرَةِ أَخْزَىٰ وَهُمْ لَا يُنصَرُونَ ﴿١٦﴾

وَأَمَّا ثَمُودُ فَهَدَيْنَٰهُمْ فَاسْتَحَبُّوا الْعَمَىٰ عَلَى الْهُدَىٰ

---

5. (37: 6-10); (72: 8-10).

blindness to the guidance, so the bolt of the doom of humiliation overtook them because of what they used to earn.

فَأَخَذَتْهُمْ صَاعِقَةُ الْعَذَابِ الْهُوْنِ بِمَاكَانُوْا يَكْسِبُوْنَ ۝

18 And We delivered those who believed and used to keep their duty to Allah.

وَنَجَّيْنَا الَّذِيْنَ اٰمَنُوْا وَكَانُوْا يَتَّقُوْنَ ۝

19 And (make mention of) the day when the enemies of Allah are gathered unto the Fire, they are driven on

وَيَوْمَ يُحْشَرُ أَعْدَاءُ اللّٰهِ إِلَى النَّارِ فَهُمْ يُوْزَعُوْنَ ۝

20 Till, when they reach it, their ears and their eyes and their skins testify against them as to what they used to do.

حَتّٰى إِذَا مَاجَاءُوْهَا شَهِدَ عَلَيْهِمْ سَمْعُهُمْ وَأَبْصَارُهُمْ وَجُلُوْدُهُمْ بِمَاكَانُوْا يَعْمَلُوْنَ ۝

21 And they say unto their skins: Why testify ye against us? They say: Allah hath given us speech Who giveth speech to all things, and Who created you at the first, and unto Whom ye are returned.

وَقَالُوْا لِجُلُوْدِهِمْ لِمَ شَهِدْتُمْ عَلَيْنَا قَالُوْا أَنْطَقَنَا اللّٰهُ الَّذِيْ أَنْطَقَ كُلَّ شَيْءٍ وَهُوَ خَلَقَكُمْ أَوَّلَ مَرَّةٍ وَإِلَيْهِ تُرْجَعُوْنَ ۝

22 Ye did not hide yourselves lest your ears and your eyes and your skins should testify against you, but ye deemed that Allah knew not much of what ye did.

وَمَاكُنْتُمْ تَسْتَتِرُوْنَ أَنْ يَشْهَدَ عَلَيْكُمْ سَمْعُكُمْ وَلَا أَبْصَارُكُمْ وَلَا جُلُوْدُكُمْ وَلٰكِنْ ظَنَنْتُمْ أَنَّ اللّٰهَ لَا يَعْلَمُ كَثِيْرًا مِّمَّا تَعْمَلُوْنَ ۝

23 That, your thought which ye did think about your Lord, hath ruined you; and ye find yourselves (this day) among the lost.

وَذٰلِكُمْ ظَنُّكُمُ الَّذِيْ ظَنَنْتُمْ بِرَبِّكُمْ أَرْدَاكُمْ فَأَصْبَحْتُمْ مِّنَ الْخَاسِرِيْنَ ۝

24 And though they are resigned, yet the Fire is still their home; and if they ask for favour, yet they are not of those unto whom favour can be shown.

فَإِنْ يَّصْبِرُوْا فَالنَّارُ مَثْوًى لَّهُمْ وَإِنْ يَّسْتَعْتِبُوْا فَمَاهُمْ مِّنَ الْمُعْتَبِيْنَ ۝

25 And We assigned them comrades (in the world), who made their present and their past fairseeming unto them. And the Word concerning nations of the jinn and humankind who passed away before them hath effect for them. Verily they are the losers.

وَقَيَّضْنَا لَهُمْ قُرَنَآءَ فَزَيَّنُوا لَهُمْ مَّا بَيْنَ أَيْدِيهِمْ وَمَا خَلْفَهُمْ وَحَقَّ عَلَيْهِمُ الْقَوْلُ فِىٓ أُمَمٍ قَدْ خَلَتْ مِن قَبْلِهِم مِّنَ الْجِنِّ وَالْإِنسِ إِنَّهُمْ كَانُوا خَاسِرِينَ ﴿٢٥﴾

26 Those who disbelieve say: Heed not this Qur'an, and drown the hearing of it; haply ye may conquer.

وَقَالَ الَّذِينَ كَفَرُوا لَا تَسْمَعُوا لِهَٰذَا الْقُرْءَانِ وَالْغَوْا فِيهِ لَعَلَّكُمْ تَغْلِبُونَ ﴿٢٦﴾

27 But verily We shall cause those who disbelieve to taste an awful doom, and verily We shall requite them the worst of what they used to do.

فَلَنُذِيقَنَّ الَّذِينَ كَفَرُوا عَذَابًا شَدِيدًا وَلَنَجْزِيَنَّهُمْ أَسْوَأَ الَّذِى كَانُوا يَعْمَلُونَ ﴿٢٧﴾

28 That is the reward of Allah's enemies: the Fire. Therein is their immortal home; payment forasmuch as they denied Our revelations.

ذَٰلِكَ جَزَآءُ أَعْدَآءِ اللَّهِ النَّارُ لَهُمْ فِيهَا دَارُ الْخُلْدِ جَزَآءً بِمَا كَانُوا بِـَٔايَٰتِنَا يَجْحَدُونَ ﴿٢٨﴾

29 And those who disbelieve will say: Our Lord! Show us these who beguiled us of the jinn and humankind. We will place them underneath our feet that they may be among the nethermost.

وَقَالَ الَّذِينَ كَفَرُوا رَبَّنَا أَرِنَا الَّذَيْنِ أَضَلَّانَا مِنَ الْجِنِّ وَالْإِنسِ نَجْعَلْهُمَا تَحْتَ أَقْدَامِنَا لِيَكُونَا مِنَ الْأَسْفَلِينَ ﴿٢٩﴾

30 Lo! those who say: Our Lord is Allah, and afterward are upright, the angels descend upon them, saying: Fear not nor grieve, but bear good tidings of the paradise which ye are promised.

إِنَّ الَّذِينَ قَالُوا رَبُّنَا اللَّهُ ثُمَّ اسْتَقَٰمُوا تَتَنَزَّلُ عَلَيْهِمُ الْمَلَٰٓئِكَةُ أَلَّا تَخَافُوا وَلَا تَحْزَنُوا وَأَبْشِرُوا بِالْجَنَّةِ الَّتِى كُنتُمْ تُوعَدُونَ ﴿٣٠﴾

31 We are your protecting friends in the life of the world and in the Hereafter. There ye will have (all)

نَحْنُ أَوْلِيَآؤُكُمْ فِى الْحَيَوٰةِ الدُّنْيَا وَفِى الْآخِرَةِ

that your souls desire, and there ye
will have (all) for which ye pray.

وَلَكُمْ فِيهَا مَا تَشْتَهِىٓ أَنفُسُكُمْ
وَلَكُمْ فِيهَا مَا تَدَّعُونَ ۞

32 A gift of welcome from the
Forgiving, the Merciful.

نُزُلًا مِّنْ غَفُورٍ رَّحِيمٍ ۞

33 And who is better in speech
than him who prayeth unto his Lord
and doeth right, and saith: Lo! I am
of those who surrender[6] (unto Him).

وَمَنْ أَحْسَنُ قَوْلًا مِّمَّن دَعَآ إِلَى ٱللَّهِ وَعَمِلَ
صَٰلِحًا وَقَالَ إِنَّنِى مِنَ ٱلْمُسْلِمِينَ ۞

34 The good deed and the evil deed
are not alike. Repel the evil deed
with one which is better, then lo!
he, between whom and thee there
was enmity (will become) as though
he was a bosom friend.

وَلَا تَسْتَوِى ٱلْحَسَنَةُ وَلَا ٱلسَّيِّئَةُ
ٱدْفَعْ بِٱلَّتِى هِىَ أَحْسَنُ فَإِذَا ٱلَّذِى
بَيْنَكَ وَبَيْنَهُۥ عَدَٰوَةٌ كَأَنَّهُۥ وَلِىٌّ حَمِيمٌ ۞

35 But none is granted it save those
who are steadfast, and none is
granted it save the owner of great
happiness.[7]

وَمَا يُلَقَّىٰهَآ إِلَّا ٱلَّذِينَ صَبَرُوا وَمَا يُلَقَّىٰهَآ
إِلَّا ذُو حَظٍّ عَظِيمٍ ۞

36 And if a whisper from the devil
reach thee (O Muhammad) then
seek refuge in Allah. Lo! He is the
Hearer, the Knower.

وَإِمَّا يَنزَغَنَّكَ مِنَ ٱلشَّيْطَٰنِ نَزْغٌ فَٱسْتَعِذْ بِٱللَّهِ
إِنَّهُۥ هُوَ ٱلسَّمِيعُ ٱلْعَلِيمُ ۞

37 And of His portents are the
night and the day and the sun and
the moon. Adore not the sun nor
the moon; but adore Allah Who
created them, if it is in truth Him
whom ye worship.

وَمِنْ ءَايَٰتِهِ ٱلَّيْلُ وَٱلنَّهَارُ وَٱلشَّمْسُ
وَٱلْقَمَرُ لَا تَسْجُدُوا لِلشَّمْسِ وَلَا لِلْقَمَرِ
وَٱسْجُدُوا لِلَّهِ ٱلَّذِى خَلَقَهُنَّ إِن كُنتُمْ
إِيَّاهُ تَعْبُدُونَ ۞

38 But if they are too proud still
those who are with thy Lord glorify
Him night and day, and tire not.

فَإِنِ ٱسْتَكْبَرُوا فَٱلَّذِينَ عِندَ رَبِّكَ يُسَبِّحُونَ
لَهُۥ بِٱلَّيْلِ وَٱلنَّهَارِ وَهُمْ لَا يَسْـَٔمُونَ ۩ ۞

---

6. Ar. *Muslimīn*.

7. *i.e.* not everyone is able to practise such forgiveness.

39 And of His portents (is this):
that thou seest the earth lowly, but
when We send down water thereon
it thrilleth and groweth. Lo! He who
quickeneth it is verily the Quickener
of the dead. Lo! He is Able to do
all things.

وَمِنْ ءَايَٰتِهِۦٓ أَنَّكَ تَرَى ٱلْأَرْضَ خَٰشِعَةً فَإِذَآ أَنزَلْنَا
عَلَيْهَا ٱلْمَآءَ ٱهْتَزَّتْ وَرَبَتْ إِنَّ ٱلَّذِىٓ أَحْيَاهَا
لَمُحْىِ ٱلْمَوْتَىٰٓ إِنَّهُۥ عَلَىٰ كُلِّ شَىْءٍ قَدِيرٌ ٣٩

40 Lo! those who distort Our
revelations are not hid from Us. Is
he who is hurled into the Fire
better, or he who cometh secure on
the Day of Resurrection? Do what
ye will. Lo! He is Seer of what ye
do.

إِنَّ ٱلَّذِينَ يُلْحِدُونَ فِىٓ ءَايَٰتِنَا لَا يَخْفَوْنَ عَلَيْنَآ أَفَمَن
يُلْقَىٰ فِى ٱلنَّارِ خَيْرٌ أَم مَّن يَأْتِىٓ ءَامِنًا يَوْمَ ٱلْقِيَٰمَةِ
ٱعْمَلُوا۟ مَا شِئْتُمْ إِنَّهُۥ بِمَا تَعْمَلُونَ بَصِيرٌ ٤٠

41 Lo! those who disbelieve in the
Reminder when it cometh unto them
(are guilty), for lo! it is an unassail-
able Scripture.

إِنَّ ٱلَّذِينَ كَفَرُوا۟ بِٱلذِّكْرِ لَمَّا جَآءَهُمْ
وَإِنَّهُۥ لَكِتَٰبٌ عَزِيزٌ ٤١

42 Falsehood cannot come at it
from before it or behind it. (It is) a
revelation from the Wise, the Owner
of Praise.

لَّا يَأْتِيهِ ٱلْبَٰطِلُ مِنۢ بَيْنِ يَدَيْهِ وَلَا مِنْ خَلْفِهِۦ تَنزِيلٌ
مِّنْ حَكِيمٍ حَمِيدٍ ٤٢

43 Naught is said unto thee
(Muhammad) save what was said
unto the messengers before thee. Lo!
thy Lord is Owner of forgiveness,
and Owner (also) of dire punishment.

مَّا يُقَالُ لَكَ إِلَّا مَا قَدْ قِيلَ لِلرُّسُلِ مِن قَبْلِكَ إِنَّ رَبَّكَ
لَذُو مَغْفِرَةٍ وَذُو عِقَابٍ أَلِيمٍ ٤٣

44 And if We had appointed it a
Lecture[8] in a foreign tongue they
would assuredly have said: If only
its verses were expounded (so that
we might understand)? What! A
foreign tongue and an Arab? Say

وَلَوْ جَعَلْنَٰهُ قُرْءَانًا أَعْجَمِيًّا لَّقَالُوا۟ لَوْلَا فُصِّلَتْ
ءَايَٰتُهُۥٓ ءَاعْجَمِىٌّ وَعَرَبِىٌّ قُلْ هُوَ لِلَّذِينَ ءَامَنُوا۟

---

8. Ar. *Qur'ān.*

unto them (O Muhammad): For those who believe it is a guidance and a healing; and as for those who disbelieve, there is a deafness in their ears, and it is blindness for them. Such are called to from afar.

هُدًى وَشِفَآءٌ ۚ وَالَّذِينَ لَا يُؤۡمِنُوۡنَ فِىۡٓ ءَاذَانِهِمۡ وَقۡرٌ وَّهُوَ عَلَيۡهِمۡ عَمًى ۚ أُولَٰٓئِكَ يُنَادَوۡنَ مِنۡ مَّكَانٍۭ بَعِيۡدٍ ﴿٤٤﴾

45 And We verily gave Moses the Scripture, but there hath been dispute concerning it; and but for a Word that had already gone forth from thy Lord, it would ere now have been judged between them; but lo! they are in hopeless doubt concerning it.

وَلَقَدۡ ءَاتَيۡنَا مُوۡسَى الۡكِتَٰبَ فَاخۡتُلِفَ فِيۡهِ ۚ وَلَوۡلَا كَلِمَةٌ سَبَقَتۡ مِنۡ رَّبِّكَ لَقُضِىَ بَيۡنَهُمۡ ۚ وَإِنَّهُمۡ لَفِىۡ شَكٍّ مِّنۡهُ مُرِيۡبٍ ﴿٤٥﴾

46 Whoso doeth right it is for his soul, and whoso doeth wrong it is against it. And thy Lord is not at all a tyrant to His slaves.

مَنۡ عَمِلَ صَالِحًا فَلِنَفۡسِهِ ۖ وَمَنۡ أَسَآءَ فَعَلَيۡهَا ۗ وَمَا رَبُّكَ بِظَلَّامٍ لِّلۡعَبِيۡدِ ﴿٤٦﴾

47 Unto Him is referred (all) knowledge of the Hour. And no fruits burst forth from their sheaths, and no female carrieth or bringeth forth but with His knowledge. And on the day when He calleth unto them: Where are now My partners? they will say: We confess unto Thee, not one of us is a witness (for them).

۞ إِلَيۡهِ يُرَدُّ عِلۡمُ السَّاعَةِ ۚ وَمَا تَخۡرُجُ مِنۡ ثَمَرَٰتٍ مِّنۡ أَكۡمَامِهَا وَمَا تَحۡمِلُ مِنۡ أُنۡثَى وَلَا تَضَعُ إِلَّا بِعِلۡمِهِ ۚ وَيَوۡمَ يُنَادِيۡهِمۡ أَيۡنَ شُرَكَآءِى قَالُوۡٓا ءَاذَنَّٰكَ مَا مِنَّا مِنۡ شَهِيۡدٍ ﴿٤٧﴾

48 And those to whom they used to cry of old have failed them, and they perceive they have no place of refuge.

وَضَلَّ عَنۡهُمۡ مَّا كَانُوۡا يَدۡعُوۡنَ مِنۡ قَبۡلُ ۖ وَظَنُّوۡا مَا لَهُمۡ مِّنۡ مَّحِيۡصٍ ﴿٤٨﴾

49 Man tireth not of praying for good, and if ill toucheth him, then he is disheartened, desperate.

لَا يَسۡـَٔمُ الۡإِنۡسَٰنُ مِنۡ دُعَآءِ الۡخَيۡرِ ۖ وَإِنۡ مَّسَّهُ الشَّرُّ فَيَـُٔوۡسٌ قَنُوۡطٌ ﴿٤٩﴾

50 And verily, if We cause him to taste mercy from Us after some hurt that hath touched him, he will say: This is my own; and I deem not that the Hour will ever rise, and if I am brought back to my Lord, I surely shall be better off with Him But We verily shall tell those who disbelieve (all) that they did, and We verily shall make them taste hard punishment

وَلَئِنْ أَذَقْنَٰهُ رَحْمَةً مِّنَّا مِنۢ بَعْدِ ضَرَّآءَ مَسَّتْهُ لَيَقُولَنَّ هَٰذَا لِى وَمَآ أَظُنُّ ٱلسَّاعَةَ قَآئِمَةً وَلَئِن رُّجِعْتُ إِلَىٰ رَبِّىٓ إِنَّ لِى عِندَهُۥ لَلْحُسْنَىٰ فَلَنُنَبِّئَنَّ ٱلَّذِينَ كَفَرُواْ بِمَا عَمِلُواْ وَلَنُذِيقَنَّهُم مِّنْ عَذَابٍ غَلِيظٍ ٥٠

51 When We show favour unto man, he withdraweth and turneth aside, but when ill toucheth him then he aboundeth in prayer.

وَإِذَآ أَنْعَمْنَا عَلَى ٱلْإِنسَٰنِ أَعْرَضَ وَنَـَٔا بِجَانِبِهِۦ وَإِذَا مَسَّهُ ٱلشَّرُّ فَذُو دُعَآءٍ عَرِيضٍ ٥١

52 Bethink you: If it is from Allah and ye reject it—Who is further astray than one who is at open feud (with Allah)?

قُلْ أَرَءَيْتُمْ إِن كَانَ مِنْ عِندِ ٱللَّهِ ثُمَّ كَفَرْتُم بِهِۦ مَنْ أَضَلُّ مِمَّنْ هُوَ فِى شِقَاقٍۭ بَعِيدٍ ٥٢

53 We shall show them Our portents on the horizons and within themselves until it will be manifest unto them that it is the Truth. Doth not thy Lord suffice, since He is Witness over all things?

سَنُرِيهِمْ ءَايَٰتِنَا فِى ٱلْءَافَاقِ وَفِىٓ أَنفُسِهِمْ حَتَّىٰ يَتَبَيَّنَ لَهُمْ أَنَّهُ ٱلْحَقُّ أَوَلَمْ يَكْفِ بِرَبِّكَ أَنَّهُۥ عَلَىٰ كُلِّ شَىْءٍ شَهِيدٌ ٥٣

54 Beware! They are still in doubt about the meeting with their Lord. Beware! He is surrounding all things?

أَلَآ إِنَّهُمْ فِى مِرْيَةٍ مِّن لِّقَآءِ رَبِّهِمْ أَلَآ إِنَّهُۥ بِكُلِّ شَىْءٍ مُّحِيطٌۢ ٥٤

Ash Shūrā
(Counsel)

Ash Shūrā, "Counsel," takes its name from a word in v. 38. It belongs to the middle group of Makkan sūrahs.

In the name of Allah, the Beneficent, the Merciful.

1 Ḥā. Mīm.[1]

2 'Ain. Sīn. Qāf.

3 Thus Allah the Mighty, the Knower inspireth thee (Muhammad) as (He inspired) those before thee.

4 Unto Him belongeth all that is in the heavens and all that is in the earth, and He is the Sublime, the Tremendous.

5 Almost might the heavens above be rent asunder while the angels hymn the praise of their Lord and ask forgiveness for those on the earth. Lo! Allah is the Forgiver, the Merciful.

6 And as for those who choose protecting friends beside Him, Allah

---

1. See Sūrah 2, v. 1, footnote.

is Warden over them, and thou art
in no wise a guardian over them.

عَلَيْهِمْ وَمَا أَنْتَ عَلَيْهِمْ بِوَكِيلٍ ۝

7   And thus we have inspired in
thee a Lecture[2] in Arabic, that thou
mayest warn the mother-town[3] and
those around it, and mayest warn of
a day of assembling whereof there
is no doubt. A host will be in the
Garden, and a host of them in the
Flame.

وَكَذَٰلِكَ أَوْحَيْنَا إِلَيْكَ قُرْآنًا عَرَبِيًّا لِتُنْذِرَ أُمَّ الْقُرَىٰ
وَمَنْ حَوْلَهَا وَتُنْذِرَ يَوْمَ الْجَمْعِ لَا رَيْبَ فِيهِ فَرِيقٌ
فِي الْجَنَّةِ وَفَرِيقٌ فِي السَّعِيرِ ۝

8   Had Allah willed, He could
have made them one community,
but Allah bringeth whom He will
into His mercy. And the wrong-
doers have no friend nor helper.

وَلَوْ شَاءَ اللَّهُ لَجَعَلَهُمْ أُمَّةً وَاحِدَةً وَلَٰكِنْ يُدْخِلُ
مَنْ يَشَاءُ فِي رَحْمَتِهِ ۚ وَالظَّالِمُونَ مَا لَهُمْ مِنْ وَلِيٍّ
وَلَا نَصِيرٍ ۝

9   Or have they chosen protecting
friends besides Him? But Allah, He
(alone) is the Protecting Friend. He
quickeneth the dead, and He is Able
to do all things.

أَمِ اتَّخَذُوا مِنْ دُونِهِ أَوْلِيَاءَ فَاللَّهُ هُوَ الْوَلِيُّ وَهُوَ يُحْيِ
الْمَوْتَىٰ وَهُوَ عَلَىٰ كُلِّ شَيْءٍ قَدِيرٌ ۝

10   And in whatsoever ye differ, the
verdict therein belongeth to Allah.
Such is my Lord, in Whom I put
my trust, and unto Whom I turn.

وَمَا اخْتَلَفْتُمْ فِيهِ مِنْ شَيْءٍ فَحُكْمُهُ إِلَى اللَّهِ ۚ
ذَٰلِكُمُ اللَّهُ رَبِّي عَلَيْهِ تَوَكَّلْتُ وَإِلَيْهِ أُنِيبُ ۝

11   The Creator of the heavens and
the earth. He hath made for you
pairs of yourselves, and of the
cattle also pairs, whereby He multiplieth you. Naught is as His likeness; and He is the Hearer, the
Seer.

فَاطِرُ السَّمَوَاتِ وَالْأَرْضِ ۚ جَعَلَ لَكُمْ مِنْ أَنْفُسِكُمْ
أَزْوَاجًا وَمِنَ الْأَنْعَامِ أَزْوَاجًا يَذْرَؤُكُمْ فِيهِ ۚ لَيْسَ
كَمِثْلِهِ شَيْءٌ ۖ وَهُوَ السَّمِيعُ الْبَصِيرُ ۝

---

2. Ar. *Qur'an*.

3. *i.e.* Makkah.

12 His are the keys of the heavens and the earth. He enlargeth providence for whom He will and straiteneth (it for whom He will). Lo! He is Knower of all things.

لَهُ مَقَالِيدُ السَّمٰوٰتِ وَالْأَرْضِ يَبْسُطُ الرِّزْقَ لِمَنْ يَّشَاءُ وَيَقْدِرُ اِنَّهُ بِكُلِّ شَيْءٍ عَلِيْمٌ ۝

13 He hath ordained for you that religion which He commended unto Noah, and that which We inspire in thee (Muhammad), and that which We commended unto Abraham and Moses and Jesus, saying: Establish the religion, and be not divided therein. Dreadful for the idolaters is that unto which thou callest them. Allah chooseth for Himself whom He will, and guideth unto Himself him who turneth (toward Him).

۞ شَرَعَ لَكُمْ مِّنَ الدِّيْنِ مَا وَصّٰى بِهٖ نُوْحًا وَّالَّذِيْ اَوْحَيْنَآ اِلَيْكَ وَمَا وَصَّيْنَا بِهٖ اِبْرٰهِيْمَ وَمُوْسٰى وَعِيْسٰٓى اَنْ اَقِيْمُوا الدِّيْنَ وَلَا تَتَفَرَّقُوْا فِيْهِ كَبُرَ عَلَى الْمُشْرِكِيْنَ مَا تَدْعُوْهُمْ اِلَيْهِ اَللّٰهُ يَجْتَبِيْٓ اِلَيْهِ مَنْ يَّشَاءُ وَيَهْدِيْٓ اِلَيْهِ مَنْ يُّنِيْبُ ۝

14 And they were not divided until after the knowledge came unto them, through rivalry among themselves; and had it not been for a Word that had already gone forth from thy Lord for an appointed term, it surely had been judged between them. And those who were made to inherit the Scripture after them are verily in hopeless doubt concerning it.

وَمَا تَفَرَّقُوْٓا اِلَّا مِنْ بَعْدِ مَا جَاءَهُمُ الْعِلْمُ بَغْيًا بَيْنَهُمْ وَلَوْلَا كَلِمَةٌ سَبَقَتْ مِنْ رَّبِّكَ اِلٰٓى اَجَلٍ مُّسَمًّى لَّقُضِيَ بَيْنَهُمْ وَاِنَّ الَّذِيْنَ اُوْرِثُوا الْكِتٰبَ مِنْ بَعْدِهِمْ لَفِيْ شَكٍّ مِّنْهُ مُرِيْبٍ ۝

15 Unto this, then, summon (O Muhammad). And be thou upright as thou art commanded, and follow not their lusts, but say: I believe in whatever Scripture Allah hath sent down, and I am commanded to be just among you. Allah is our Lord and your Lord. Unto us our works

فَلِذٰلِكَ فَادْعُ وَاسْتَقِمْ كَمَا اُمِرْتَ وَلَا تَتَّبِعْ اَهْوَاءَهُمْ وَقُلْ اٰمَنْتُ بِمَا اَنْزَلَ اللّٰهُ مِنْ كِتٰبٍ وَاُمِرْتُ لِاَعْدِلَ بَيْنَكُمُ اللّٰهُ رَبُّنَا وَرَبُّكُمْ ۝

and unto you your works; no argument between us and you. Allah will bring us together, and unto Him is the journeying.

لَنَآ أَعْمَالُنَا وَلَكُمْ أَعْمَالُكُمْ لَا حُجَّةَ بَيْنَنَا وَبَيْنَكُمْ اللّٰهُ يَجْمَعُ بَيْنَنَا وَإِلَيْهِ الْمَصِيرُ ﴿١٥﴾

16 And those who argue concerning Allah after He hath been acknowledged, their argument hath no weight with their Lord, and wrath is upon them and theirs will be an awful doom.

وَالَّذِينَ يُحَآجُّونَ فِى اللّٰهِ مِنْ بَعْدِ مَا اسْتُجِيبَ لَهُ حُجَّتُهُمْ دَاحِضَةٌ عِنْدَ رَبِّهِمْ وَعَلَيْهِمْ غَضَبٌ وَلَهُمْ عَذَابٌ شَدِيدٌ ﴿١٦﴾

17 Allah it is who hath revealed the Scripture with truth, and the Balance. How canst thou know? It may be that the Hour is nigh.

اللّٰهُ الَّذِيٓ أَنْزَلَ الْكِتَابَ بِالْحَقِّ وَالْمِيزَانَ وَمَا يُدْرِيكَ لَعَلَّ السَّاعَةَ قَرِيبٌ ﴿١٧﴾

18 Those who believe not therein seek to hasten it, while those who believe are fearful of it and know that it is the Truth. Beware! They who dispute concerning the Hour are far astray.

يَسْتَعْجِلُ بِهَا الَّذِينَ لَا يُؤْمِنُونَ بِهَا وَالَّذِينَ ءَامَنُوا مُشْفِقُونَ مِنْهَا وَيَعْلَمُونَ أَنَّهَا الْحَقُّ أَلَآ إِنَّ الَّذِينَ يُمَارُونَ فِى السَّاعَةِ لَفِى ضَلَالٍ بَعِيدٍ ﴿١٨﴾

19 Allah is gracious unto His slaves. He provideth for whom He will. And He is the Strong, the Mighty.

اللّٰهُ لَطِيفٌ بِعِبَادِهِ يَرْزُقُ مَنْ يَشَآءُ وَهُوَ الْقَوِىُّ الْعَزِيزُ ﴿١٩﴾

20 Whoso desireth the harvest of the Hereafter, We give him increase in its harvest. And Whoso desireth the harvest of the world, We give him thereof, and he hath no portion in the Hereafter.

مَنْ كَانَ يُرِيدُ حَرْثَ الْآخِرَةِ نَزِدْ لَهُ فِى حَرْثِهِ وَمَنْ كَانَ يُرِيدُ حَرْثَ الدُّنْيَا نُؤْتِهِ مِنْهَا وَمَا لَهُ فِى الْآخِرَةِ مِنْ نَصِيبٍ ﴿٢٠﴾

21 Or have they partners (of **Allah)** who have made lawful for them in religion that which Allah allowed not? And but for a decisive word (gone forth already), it would have

أَمْ لَهُمْ شُرَكَآؤُا شَرَعُوا لَهُمْ مِّنَ الدِّينِ مَا لَمْ يَأْذَنْ بِهِ اللّٰهُ وَلَوْلَا كَلِمَةُ الْفَصْلِ

been judged between them. Lo! for wrong-doers is a painful doom.

22 Thou seest the wrong-doers fearful of that which they have earned, and it will surely befall them; while those who believe and do good works (will be) in flowering meadows of the Gardens, having what they wish from their Lord. This is the great preferment.

23 This it is which Allah announceth unto His bondmen who believe and do good works. Say (O Muhammad, unto mankind): I ask of you no fee therefore, save loving kindness among kinsfolk. And whoso scoreth a good deed we add unto its good for him. Lo! Allah is Forgiving, Responsive.

24 Or say they: He hath invented a lie concerning Allah? If Allah willed, He could have sealed thy heart (against them). And Allah will wipe out the lie and will vindicate the truth by His words. Lo! He is Aware of what is hidden in the breasts (of men).

25 And He it is Who accepteth repentance from his bondmen, and pardoneth the evil deeds, and knoweth what ye do.

26 And accepteth those who believe and do good works and gives increase unto them of His bounty. And as for disbelievers, theirs will be an awful doom.

لَقُضِيَ بَيْنَهُمْ وَإِنَّ الظَّالِمِينَ لَهُمْ عَذَابٌ أَلِيمٌ ۜ ﴿٢١﴾

تَرَى الظَّالِمِينَ مُشْفِقِينَ مِمَّا كَسَبُوا وَهُوَ وَاقِعٌ بِهِمْ ۗ وَالَّذِينَ آمَنُوا وَعَمِلُوا الصَّالِحَاتِ فِي رَوْضَاتِ الْجَنَّاتِ ۖ لَهُمْ مَا يَشَاءُونَ عِنْدَ رَبِّهِمْ ۚ ذَٰلِكَ هُوَ الْفَضْلُ الْكَبِيرُ ﴿٢٢﴾

ذَٰلِكَ الَّذِي يُبَشِّرُ اللَّهُ عِبَادَهُ الَّذِينَ آمَنُوا وَعَمِلُوا الصَّالِحَاتِ ۗ قُلْ لَا أَسْأَلُكُمْ عَلَيْهِ أَجْرًا إِلَّا الْمَوَدَّةَ فِي الْقُرْبَىٰ ۗ وَمَنْ يَقْتَرِفْ حَسَنَةً نَزِدْ لَهُ فِيهَا حُسْنًا ۚ إِنَّ اللَّهَ غَفُورٌ شَكُورٌ ﴿٢٣﴾

أَمْ يَقُولُونَ افْتَرَىٰ عَلَى اللَّهِ كَذِبًا ۖ فَإِنْ يَشَأِ اللَّهُ يَخْتِمْ عَلَىٰ قَلْبِكَ ۗ وَيَمْحُ اللَّهُ الْبَاطِلَ وَيُحِقُّ الْحَقَّ بِكَلِمَاتِهِ ۚ إِنَّهُ عَلِيمٌ بِذَاتِ الصُّدُورِ ﴿٢٤﴾

وَهُوَ الَّذِي يَقْبَلُ التَّوْبَةَ عَنْ عِبَادِهِ وَيَعْفُو عَنِ السَّيِّئَاتِ وَيَعْلَمُ مَا تَفْعَلُونَ ﴿٢٥﴾

وَيَسْتَجِيبُ الَّذِينَ آمَنُوا وَعَمِلُوا الصَّالِحَاتِ وَيَزِيدُهُمْ مِنْ فَضْلِهِ ۚ وَالْكَافِرُونَ لَهُمْ عَذَابٌ شَدِيدٌ ﴿٢٦﴾

27 And if Allah were to enlarge the provision for His slaves they would surely rebel in the earth, but He sendeth down by measure as He willeth. Lo! He is Aware, a Seer of His bondmen.

وَلَوْ بَسَطَ ٱللَّهُ ٱلرِّزْقَ لِعِبَادِهِ لَبَغَوْا فِى ٱلْأَرْضِ وَلَٰكِن يُنَزِّلُ بِقَدَرٍ مَّا يَشَآءُ إِنَّهُۥ بِعِبَادِهِ خَبِيرٌ بَصِيرٌ ۝

28 And He it is Who sendeth down the saving rain after they have despaired, and spreadeth out His mercy. He is the Protecting Friend, the Praiseworthy.

وَهُوَ ٱلَّذِى يُنَزِّلُ ٱلْغَيْثَ مِنۢ بَعْدِ مَا قَنَطُوا۟ وَيَنشُرُ رَحْمَتَهُۥ وَهُوَ ٱلْوَلِىُّ ٱلْحَمِيدُ ۝

29 And of His portents is the creation of the heaven and the earth, and of whatever beasts He hath dispersed therein. And He is Able to gather them when He will.

وَمِنْ ءَايَٰتِهِۦ خَلْقُ ٱلسَّمَٰوَٰتِ وَٱلْأَرْضِ وَمَا بَثَّ فِيهِمَا مِن دَآبَّةٍ وَهُوَ عَلَىٰ جَمْعِهِمْ إِذَا يَشَآءُ قَدِيرٌ ۝

30 Whatever of misfortune striketh you, it is what your right hands have earned. And He forgiveth much.

وَمَآ أَصَٰبَكُم مِّن مُّصِيبَةٍ فَبِمَا كَسَبَتْ أَيْدِيكُمْ وَيَعْفُوا۟ عَن كَثِيرٍ ۝

31 Ye cannot escape in the earth, for beside Allah ye have no protecting friend nor any helper.

وَمَآ أَنتُم بِمُعْجِزِينَ فِى ٱلْأَرْضِ وَمَا لَكُم مِّن دُونِ ٱللَّهِ مِن وَلِىٍّ وَلَا نَصِيرٍ ۝

32 And of His portents are the ships, like banners on the sea;

وَمِنْ ءَايَٰتِهِ ٱلْجَوَارِ فِى ٱلْبَحْرِ كَٱلْأَعْلَٰمِ ۝

33 If He will He calmeth the wind so that they keep still upon its surface. Lo! herein verily are signs for every steadfast grateful (heart).

إِن يَشَأْ يُسْكِنِ ٱلرِّيحَ فَيَظْلَلْنَ رَوَاكِدَ عَلَىٰ ظَهْرِهِۦ إِنَّ فِى ذَٰلِكَ لَءَايَٰتٍ لِّكُلِّ صَبَّارٍ شَكُورٍ ۝

34 Or he causeth them to perish on account of that which they have earned—And He forgiveth much;

أَوْ يُوبِقْهُنَّ بِمَا كَسَبُوا۟ وَيَعْفُ عَن كَثِيرٍ ۝

35 And that those who argue concerning Our revelations may know they have no refuge.

وَيَعْلَمَ ٱلَّذِينَ يُجَٰدِلُونَ فِىٓ ءَايَٰتِنَا مَا لَهُم مِّن مَّحِيصٍ ۝

36 Now whatever ye have been given is but a passing comfort for the life of the world, and that which Allah hath is better and more lasting for those who believe and put their trust in their Lord.

فَمَآ أُوتِيتُم مِّن شَىۡءٍ فَمَتَٰعُ الۡحَيَوٰةِ الدُّنۡيَا وَمَا عِنۡدَ اللّٰهِ خَيۡرٌ وَأَبۡقَىٰ لِلَّذِينَ ءَامَنُوا وَعَلَىٰ رَبِّهِمۡ يَتَوَكَّلُونَ ۝

37 And those who shun the worst of sins and indecencies and, when they are wroth, forgive,

وَالَّذِينَ يَجۡتَنِبُونَ كَبَٰٓئِرَ الۡإِثۡمِ وَالۡفَوَٰحِشَ وَإِذَا مَا غَضِبُوا هُمۡ يَغۡفِرُونَ ۝

38 And those who answer the call of their Lord and establish worship, and whose affairs are a matter of counsel, and who spend of what We have bestowed on them,

وَالَّذِينَ اسۡتَجَابُوا لِرَبِّهِمۡ وَأَقَامُوا الصَّلَوٰةَ وَأَمۡرُهُمۡ شُورَىٰ بَيۡنَهُمۡ وَمِمَّا رَزَقۡنَٰهُمۡ يُنفِقُونَ ۝

39 And those who, when great wrong is done to them, defend themselves,

وَالَّذِينَ إِذَآ أَصَابَهُمُ الۡبَغۡيُ هُمۡ يَنتَصِرُونَ ۝

40 The guerdon of an ill deed is an ill the like thereof. But whosoever pardoneth and amendeth, his wage is the affair of Allah. Lo! He loveth not wrong-doers.

وَجَزَٰٓؤُاْ سَيِّئَةٍ سَيِّئَةٌ مِّثۡلُهَاۖ فَمَنۡ عَفَا وَأَصۡلَحَ فَأَجۡرُهُۥ عَلَى اللّٰهِۚ إِنَّهُۥ لَا يُحِبُّ الظَّٰلِمِينَ ۝

41 And whoso defendeth himself after he hath suffered wrong for such, there is no way (of blame) against them.

وَلَمَنِ انتَصَرَ بَعۡدَ ظُلۡمِهِۦ فَأُوْلَٰٓئِكَ مَا عَلَيۡهِم مِّن سَبِيلٍ ۝

42 The way (of blame) is only against those who oppress mankind, and wrongfully rebel in the earth. For such there is a painful doom.

إِنَّمَا السَّبِيلُ عَلَى الَّذِينَ يَظۡلِمُونَ النَّاسَ وَيَبۡغُونَ فِي الۡأَرۡضِ بِغَيۡرِ الۡحَقِّۚ أُوْلَٰٓئِكَ لَهُمۡ عَذَابٌ أَلِيمٌ ۝

43 And verily whoso is patient and forgiveth—lo! that, verily, is an affair of great resolution.

وَلَمَن صَبَرَ وَغَفَرَ إِنَّ ذَٰلِكَ لَمِنۡ عَزۡمِ الۡأُمُورِ ۝

44 He whom Allah sendeth astray, for him there is no protecting friend

وَمَن يُضۡلِلِ اللّٰهُ فَمَا لَهُۥ مِن وَلِيٍّ مِّنۢ بَعۡدِهِۦۗ وَتَرَى

after Him. And thou (Muḥammad) wilt see the evil-doers when they see the doom, (how) they say: Is there any way of return?

45 And thou wilt see them exposed to (the Fire), made humble by disgrace, and looking with veiled eyes. And those who believe will say: Lo! the (eternal) losers are they who lose themselves and their housefolk on the Day of Resurrection. Beware! The wrong-doers are in perpetual torment.

46 And they will have no protecting friends to help them instead of Allah. He whom Allah sendeth astray, for him there is no road.

47 Answer the call of your Lord before there cometh unto you from Allah a Day which there is no averting. Ye have no refuge on that Day, nor have ye any (power of) refusal.

48 But if they are averse, We have not sent thee as a warder over them. Thine is only to convey (the message). And lo! when We cause man to taste of mercy from Us he exulteth therefore. And if some evil striketh them because of that which their own hands have sent before, then lo! man is an ingrate.

49 Unto Allah belongeth the sovereignty of the heavens and the earth. He createth what He will. He bestoweth female (offspring) upon

ٱلظَّـٰلِمِينَ لَمَّا رَأَوُا۟ ٱلْعَذَابَ يَقُولُونَ هَلْ إِلَىٰ مَرَدٍّ مِّن سَبِيلٍ ﴿٤٤﴾

وَتَرَىٰهُمْ يُعْرَضُونَ عَلَيْهَا خَٰشِعِينَ مِنَ ٱلذُّلِّ يَنظُرُونَ مِن طَرْفٍ خَفِيٍّ وَقَالَ ٱلَّذِينَ ءَامَنُوٓا۟ إِنَّ ٱلْخَٰسِرِينَ ٱلَّذِينَ خَسِرُوٓا۟ أَنفُسَهُمْ وَأَهْلِيهِمْ يَوْمَ ٱلْقِيَـٰمَةِ أَلَآ إِنَّ ٱلظَّـٰلِمِينَ فِى عَذَابٍ مُّقِيمٍ ﴿٤٥﴾

وَمَا كَانَ لَهُم مِّنْ أَوْلِيَآءَ يَنصُرُونَهُم مِّن دُونِ ٱللَّهِ وَمَن يُضْلِلِ ٱللَّهُ فَمَا لَهُۥ مِن سَبِيلٍ ﴿٤٦﴾

ٱسْتَجِيبُوا۟ لِرَبِّكُم مِّن قَبْلِ أَن يَأْتِىَ يَوْمٌ لَّا مَرَدَّ لَهُۥ مِنَ ٱللَّهِ مَا لَكُم مِّن مَّلْجَإٍ يَوْمَئِذٍ وَمَا لَكُم مِّن نَّكِيرٍ ﴿٤٧﴾

فَإِنْ أَعْرَضُوا۟ فَمَآ أَرْسَلْنَٰكَ عَلَيْهِمْ حَفِيظًا إِنْ عَلَيْكَ إِلَّا ٱلْبَلَٰغُ وَإِنَّآ إِذَآ أَذَقْنَا ٱلْإِنسَٰنَ مِنَّا رَحْمَةً فَرِحَ بِهَا وَإِن تُصِبْهُمْ سَيِّئَةٌ بِمَا قَدَّمَتْ أَيْدِيهِمْ فَإِنَّ ٱلْإِنسَٰنَ كَفُورٌ ﴿٤٨﴾

لِلَّهِ مُلْكُ ٱلسَّمَٰوَٰتِ وَٱلْأَرْضِ يَخْلُقُ مَا يَشَآءُ يَهَبُ لِمَن يَشَآءُ إِنَٰثًا وَيَهَبُ لِمَن يَشَآءُ

whom He will, and bestoweth male (offspring) upon whom He will;

الذُّكُورَ ۝

50 Or He grants them males and females, and He maketh barren whom He will. Lo! He is Knower, Powerful.

أَوْ يُزَوِّجُهُمْ ذُكْرَانًا وَإِنَاثًا وَيَجْعَلُ مَنْ يَشَآءُ عَقِيمًا إِنَّهُ عَلِيمٌ قَدِيرٌ ۝

51 And it was not (vouchsafed) to any mortal that Allah should speak to him unless (it be) by revelation or from behind a veil, or (that) He sendeth a messenger to reveal what He will by His leave. Lo! He is Exalted, Wise.

۞ وَمَا كَانَ لِبَشَرٍ أَنْ يُكَلِّمَهُ اللهُ إِلَّا وَحْيًا أَوْ مِنْ وَرَآئِ حِجَابٍ أَوْ يُرْسِلَ رَسُولًا فَيُوحِيَ بِإِذْنِهِ مَا يَشَآءُ إِنَّهُ عَلِيٌّ حَكِيمٌ ۝

52 And thus have We inspired in thee (Muhammad) a Spirit of Our command. Thou knewest not what the Scripture was, nor what the Faith. But We have made it a light whereby We guide whom We will of Our bondmen. And lo! thou verily dost guide unto a right path.

وَكَذَٰلِكَ أَوْحَيْنَا إِلَيْكَ رُوحًا مِنْ أَمْرِنَا مَا كُنْتَ تَدْرِى مَا الْكِتَابُ وَلَا الْإِيمَانُ وَلَٰكِنْ جَعَلْنَاهُ نُورًا نَهْدِى بِهِ مَنْ نَشَآءُ مِنْ عِبَادِنَا وَإِنَّكَ لَتَهْدِى إِلَى صِرَاطٍ مُسْتَقِيمٍ ۝

53 The path of Allah, unto Whom belongeth whatsoever is in the heavens and whatsoever is in the earth. Beware! All things reach Allah at last.

صِرَاطِ اللهِ الَّذِى لَهُ مَا فِى السَّمَوَاتِ وَمَا فِى الْأَرْضِ أَلَا إِلَى اللهِ تَصِيرُ الْأُمُورُ ۝

Az Zukhruf
(Ornaments of Gold)

Az Zukhruf, "Ornaments of Gold," is the fourth of the *Hā. Mīm.* surahs. It takes its name from a word meaning golden ornaments which occurs in v. 35.

It belongs to the middle group of Makkan surahs.

In the name of Allah, the Beneficent, the Merciful.

1   Hā. Mīm.[1]

2   By the Scripture which maketh plain,

· 3   Lo! We have appointed it a Lecture[2] in Arabic that haply ye may understand.

4   And lo! in the Source of Decrees, which We possess, it is indeed sublime, decisive,

5   Shall We utterly ignore you because ye are a wanton folk?

6   How many a Prophet did We send among the men of old!

---

1. See Sūrah 2, v. 1, footnote.

2. Ar. *Qur'an*.

698

7 And never came there unto them a Prophet but they used to mock him.

8 Then We destroyed men mightier than these in prowess; and the example of the men of old hath gone (before them).

9 And if thou (Muhammad) ask them: Who created the heavens and the earth, they will surely answer: The Mighty, the Knower created them;

10 Who made the earth a resting place for you, and placed roads for you therein, that haply ye may find your way;

11 And who sendeth down water from the sky in (due) measure, and We revive a dead land therewith. Even so will ye be brought forth;

12 He who created all the pairs, and appointed for you ships and cattle whereupon ye ride.

13 That ye may mount upon their backs, and may remember your Lord's favour when ye mount thereon, and may say: Glorified be He Who hath subdued these unto us, and we were not capable (of subduing them);

14 And lo! unto our Lord we are returning.

15 And they allot to Him a portion of His bondmen! Lo! man is verily a mere ingrate.

وَمَا يَأْتِيهِم مِّن نَّبِيٍّ إِلَّا كَانُوا بِهِۦ يَسْتَهْزِءُونَ ۝

فَأَهْلَكْنَا أَشَدَّ مِنْهُم بَطْشًا وَمَضَىٰ مَثَلُ الْأَوَّلِينَ ۝

وَلَئِن سَأَلْتَهُم مَّنْ خَلَقَ السَّمَٰوَٰتِ وَالْأَرْضَ لَيَقُولُنَّ خَلَقَهُنَّ الْعَزِيزُ الْعَلِيمُ ۝

الَّذِي جَعَلَ لَكُمُ الْأَرْضَ مَهْدًا وَجَعَلَ لَكُمْ فِيهَا سُبُلًا لَّعَلَّكُمْ تَهْتَدُونَ ۝

وَالَّذِي نَزَّلَ مِنَ السَّمَآءِ مَآءً بِقَدَرٍ فَأَنشَرْنَا بِهِۦ بَلْدَةً مَّيْتًا كَذَٰلِكَ تُخْرَجُونَ ۝

وَالَّذِي خَلَقَ الْأَزْوَٰجَ كُلَّهَا وَجَعَلَ لَكُم مِّنَ الْفُلْكِ وَالْأَنْعَٰمِ مَا تَرْكَبُونَ ۝

لِتَسْتَوُۥا عَلَىٰ ظُهُورِهِۦ ثُمَّ تَذْكُرُوا نِعْمَةَ رَبِّكُمْ إِذَا اسْتَوَيْتُمْ عَلَيْهِ وَتَقُولُوا سُبْحَٰنَ الَّذِي سَخَّرَ لَنَا هَٰذَا وَمَا كُنَّا لَهُۥ مُقْرِنِينَ ۝

وَإِنَّا إِلَىٰ رَبِّنَا لَمُنقَلِبُونَ ۝

وَجَعَلُوا لَهُۥ مِنْ عِبَادِهِۦ جُزْءًا إِنَّ الْإِنسَٰنَ لَكَفُورٌ مُّبِينٌ ۝

16 Or chooseth He daughters of all that He hath created, and honoureth He you with sons?

17 And if one of them hath tidings of that which he likeneth to the Beneficent One,[3] his countenance becometh black and he is full of inward rage.

18 (Liken they then to Allah) that which is bred up in outward show, and in dispute cannot make itself plain?

19 And they make the angels, who are the slaves of the Beneficent, females. Did they witness their creation? Their testimony will be recorded and they will be questioned.

20 And they say: If the Beneficent One had (so) willed, we should not have worshipped them. They have no knowledge whatsoever of that. They do but guess.

21 Or have We given them any Scripture before (this Qur'an) so that they are holding fast thereto?

22 Nay, for they say only: Lo! we found our fathers following a religion, and we are guided by their footprints.

23 And even so We sent not a warner before thee (Muḥammad) into any township but its luxurious ones said: Lo! we found our fathers fol-

أَمِ اتَّخَذَ مِمَّا يَخْلُقُ بَنَاتٍ وَأَصْفَىٰكُم بِالْبَنِينَ ۝

وَإِذَا بُشِّرَ أَحَدُهُم بِمَا ضَرَبَ لِلرَّحْمَٰنِ مَثَلًا ظَلَّ وَجْهُهُۥ مُسْوَدًّا وَهُوَ كَظِيمٌ ۝

أَوَمَن يُنَشَّؤُاْ فِى الْحِلْيَةِ وَهُوَ فِى الْخِصَامِ غَيْرُ مُبِينٍ ۝

وَجَعَلُواْ الْمَلَٰٓئِكَةَ الَّذِينَ هُمْ عِبَٰدُ الرَّحْمَٰنِ إِنَٰثًا أَشَهِدُواْ خَلْقَهُمْ سَتُكْتَبُ شَهَٰدَتُهُمْ وَيُسْـَٔلُونَ ۝

وَقَالُواْ لَوْ شَآءَ الرَّحْمَٰنُ مَا عَبَدْنَٰهُم مَّا لَهُم بِذَٰلِكَ مِنْ عِلْمٍ إِنْ هُمْ إِلَّا يَخْرُصُونَ ۝

أَمْ ءَاتَيْنَٰهُمْ كِتَٰبًا مِّن قَبْلِهِۦ فَهُم بِهِۦ مُسْتَمْسِكُونَ ۝

بَلْ قَالُوٓاْ إِنَّا وَجَدْنَآ ءَابَآءَنَا عَلَىٰٓ أُمَّةٍ وَإِنَّا عَلَىٰٓ ءَاثَٰرِهِم مُّهْتَدُونَ ۝

وَكَذَٰلِكَ مَآ أَرْسَلْنَا مِن قَبْلِكَ فِى قَرْيَةٍ مِّن نَّذِيرٍ إِلَّا قَالَ مُتْرَفُوهَآ إِنَّا وَجَدْنَآ ءَابَآءَنَا عَلَىٰٓ أُمَّةٍ

---

3. *i.e.* tidings of the birth of a girl-child.

lowing a religion, and we are following their footprints.

24 (And the warner) said: What!
Even though I bring you better guidance than that ye found your
fathers following? They answered:
Lo! in what ye bring we are disbelievers.

25 So We requited them. Then see
the nature of the consequence for
the rejecters!

26 And when Abraham said unto
his father and his folk: Lo! I am
innocent of what ye worship

27 Save Him Who did create me,
for He will surely guide me.

28 And he made it a word enduring
among his seed, that haply they
might return.

29 Nay, but I let these and their
fathers enjoy life (only) till there
should come unto them the Truth
and a messenger making plain.

30 And now that the Truth hath
come unto them they say: This is
mere magic, and lo! we are disbelievers therein.

31 And they say: If only this
Qur'an had been revealed to some
great man of the two towns?[4]

32 Is it they who apportion thy
Lord's mercy? We have appor-

وَإِنَّا عَلَىٰ ءَاثَـٰرِهِم مُّقْتَدُونَ ﴿٢٣﴾

۞ قَـٰلَ أَوَلَوْ جِئْتُكُم بِأَهْدَىٰ مِمَّا وَجَدتُّمْ عَلَيْهِ
ءَابَآءَكُمْ قَالُوٓا۟ إِنَّا بِمَآ أُرْسِلْتُم بِهِۦ كَـٰفِرُونَ ﴿٢٤﴾

فَٱنتَقَمْنَا مِنْهُمْ فَٱنظُرْ كَيْفَ
كَانَ عَـٰقِبَةُ ٱلْمُكَذِّبِينَ ﴿٢٥﴾

وَإِذْ قَالَ إِبْرَٰهِيمُ لِأَبِيهِ وَقَوْمِهِۦٓ
إِنَّنِى بَرَآءٌ مِّمَّا تَعْبُدُونَ ﴿٢٦﴾

إِلَّا ٱلَّذِى فَطَرَنِى فَإِنَّهُۥ سَيَهْدِينِ ﴿٢٧﴾

وَجَعَلَهَا كَلِمَةًۢ بَاقِيَةً فِى عَقِبِهِۦ لَعَلَّهُمْ يَرْجِعُونَ ﴿٢٨﴾

بَلْ مَتَّعْتُ هَـٰٓؤُلَآءِ وَءَابَآءَهُمْ حَتَّىٰ جَآءَهُمُ
ٱلْحَقُّ وَرَسُولٌ مُّبِينٌ ﴿٢٩﴾

وَلَمَّا جَآءَهُمُ ٱلْحَقُّ قَالُوا۟ هَـٰذَا سِحْرٌ وَإِنَّا بِهِۦ كَـٰفِرُونَ ﴿٣٠﴾

وَقَالُوا۟ لَوْلَا نُزِّلَ هَـٰذَا ٱلْقُرْءَانُ عَلَىٰ رَجُلٍ
مِّنَ ٱلْقَرْيَتَيْنِ عَظِيمٍ ﴿٣١﴾

أَهُمْ يَقْسِمُونَ رَحْمَتَ رَبِّكَ نَحْنُ قَسَمْنَا بَيْنَهُم

---

4. The two towns were Makkah and Ṭā'if.

tioned among them their livelihood
in the life of the world, and raised
some of them above others in rank
that some of them may take labour
from others; and the mercy of thy
Lord is better than (the wealth) that
they amass.

مَعِيشَتَهُمْ فِى الْحَيَوٰةِ الدُّنْيَا وَرَفَعْنَا بَعْضَهُمْ فَوْقَ
بَعْضٍ دَرَجَتٍ لِيَتَّخِذَ بَعْضُهُمْ بَعْضًا سُخْرِيًّا ۗ
وَرَحْمَتُ رَبِّكَ خَيْرٌ مِّمَّا يَجْمَعُونَ ﴿٣٢﴾

33 And were it not that mankind
would have become one community,[5]
We might well have appointed, for
those who disbelieve in the Beneficent, roofs of silver for their houses
and stairs (of silver) whereby to
mount,

وَلَوْلَا أَن يَكُونَ النَّاسُ أُمَّةً وَٰحِدَةً لَّجَعَلْنَا
لِمَن يَكْفُرُ بِالرَّحْمَٰنِ لِبُيُوتِهِمْ سُقُفًا مِّن فِضَّةٍ
وَمَعَارِجَ عَلَيْهَا يَظْهَرُونَ ﴿٣٣﴾

34 And for their houses doors (of
silver) and couches of silver whereon to recline,

وَلِبُيُوتِهِمْ أَبْوَٰبًا وَسُرُرًا عَلَيْهَا يَتَّكِئُونَ ﴿٣٤﴾

35 And ornaments of gold. Yet all
that would have been but a provision of the life of the world. And
the Hereafter with your Lord would
have been for those who keep from
evil.

وَزُخْرُفًا ۚ وَإِن كُلُّ ذَٰلِكَ لَمَّا مَتَٰعُ الْحَيَوٰةِ الدُّنْيَا ۚ
وَالْآخِرَةُ عِندَ رَبِّكَ لِلْمُتَّقِينَ ﴿٣٥﴾

36 And he whose sight is dim to
the remembrance of the Beneficent,
We assign unto him a devil who
becometh his comrade;

وَمَن يَعْشُ عَن ذِكْرِ الرَّحْمَٰنِ نُقَيِّضْ لَهُ شَيْطَٰنًا
فَهُوَ لَهُ قَرِينٌ ﴿٣٦﴾

37 And lo! they surely turn them
from the way of Allah, and yet they
deem that they are rightly guided;

وَإِنَّهُمْ لَيَصُدُّونَهُمْ عَنِ السَّبِيلِ وَيَحْسَبُونَ
أَنَّهُم مُّهْتَدُونَ ﴿٣٧﴾

38 Till, when he cometh unto Us,
he saith (unto his comrade): Ah,
would that between me and thee

حَتَّىٰ إِذَا جَاءَنَا قَالَ يَٰلَيْتَ بَيْنِي وَبَيْنَكَ
بُعْدَ الْمَشْرِقَيْنِ فَبِئْسَ الْقَرِينُ ﴿٣٨﴾

---

5. Through love of riches.

there were the distance of the two horizons[6]—an evil comrade!

وَلَن يَنفَعَكُمُ الْيَوْمَ إِذ ظَّلَمْتُمْ أَنَّكُمْ فِى الْعَذَابِ مُشْتَرِكُونَ ۝

39 And it profiteth you not this day, because ye did wrong, that ye will be sharers in the doom.

أَفَأَنتَ تُسْمِعُ الصُّمَّ أَوْ تَهْدِى الْعُمْىَ وَمَن كَانَ فِى ضَلَٰلٍ مُّبِينٍ ۝

40 Canst thou (Muḥammad) make the deaf to hear, or canst thou guide the blind or him who is in error manifest?

فَإِمَّا نَذْهَبَنَّ بِكَ فَإِنَّا مِنْهُم مُّنتَقِمُونَ ۝

41 And if We take thee away, We surely shall take vengeance on them,

أَوْ نُرِيَنَّكَ الَّذِى وَعَدْنَٰهُمْ فَإِنَّا عَلَيْهِم مُّقْتَدِرُونَ ۝

42 Or (if) We show thee that wherewith We threaten them; for lo! We have complete command of them.

فَاسْتَمْسِكْ بِالَّذِىٓ أُوحِىَ إِلَيْكَ إِنَّكَ عَلَىٰ صِرَٰطٍ مُّسْتَقِيمٍ ۝

43 So hold thou fast to that which is inspired in thee. Lo! thou art on a right path.

وَإِنَّهُۥ لَذِكْرٌ لَّكَ وَلِقَوْمِكَ وَسَوْفَ تُسْـَٔلُونَ ۝

44 And lo! it is in truth a Reminder for thee and for thy folk; and ye will be questioned.

وَسْـَٔلْ مَنْ أَرْسَلْنَا مِن قَبْلِكَ مِن رُّسُلِنَآ أَجَعَلْنَا مِن دُونِ الرَّحْمَٰنِ ءَالِهَةً يُعْبَدُونَ ۝

45 And ask those of Our messengers whom We sent before thee: Did We ever appoint gods to be worshipped beside the Beneficent?

وَلَقَدْ أَرْسَلْنَا مُوسَىٰ بِـَٔايَٰتِنَآ إِلَىٰ فِرْعَوْنَ وَمَلَإِيْهِۦ فَقَالَ إِنِّى رَسُولُ رَبِّ الْعَٰلَمِينَ ۝

46 And verily We sent Moses with Our revelations unto Pharaoh and his chiefs, and he said: I am a messenger of the Lord of the Worlds.

---

6. Lit. the two Easts.

47 But when he brought them Our tokens, behold! they laughed at them.

فَلَمَّا جَآءَهُمْ بِاٰيٰتِنَآ إِذَا هُمْ مِّنْهَا يَضْحَكُوْنَ ۝

48 And every token that We showed them was greater than its sister (token), and we grasped them with the torment, that haply they might turn again.

وَمَا نُرِيْهِمْ مِّنْ اٰيَةٍ إِلَّا هِيَ أَكْبَرُ مِنْ أُخْتِهَا وَأَخَذْنٰهُمْ بِالْعَذَابِ لَعَلَّهُمْ يَرْجِعُوْنَ ۝

49 And they said: O wizard; Entreat thy Lord for us by the pact that He hath made with thee. Lo! we verily will walk aright.

وَقَالُوْا يٰٓاَيُّهَ السّٰحِرُ ادْعُ لَنَا رَبَّكَ بِمَا عَهِدَ عِنْدَكَ إِنَّنَا لَمُهْتَدُوْنَ ۝

50 But when We eased them of the torment, behold! they broke their word.

فَلَمَّا كَشَفْنَا عَنْهُمُ الْعَذَابَ إِذَا هُمْ يَنْكُثُوْنَ ۝

51 And Pharaoh caused a proclamation to be made among his people saying: O my people! Is not mine the sovereignty of Egypt and these rivers flowing under me? Can ye not then discern?

وَنَادٰى فِرْعَوْنُ فِيْ قَوْمِهٖ قَالَ يٰقَوْمِ أَلَيْسَ لِيْ مُلْكُ مِصْرَ وَهٰذِهِ الْأَنْهٰرُ تَجْرِيْ مِنْ تَحْتِيْ أَفَلَا تُبْصِرُوْنَ ۝

52 I am surely better than this fellow, who is despicable, and can hardly make (his meaning) plain!

أَمْ أَنَا خَيْرٌ مِّنْ هٰذَا الَّذِيْ هُوَ مَهِيْنٌ وَّلَا يَكَادُ يُبِيْنُ ۝

53 Why, then, have armlets of gold not been set upon him, nor the angels come along with him?

فَلَوْلَا أُلْقِيَ عَلَيْهِ أَسْوِرَةٌ مِّنْ ذَهَبٍ أَوْ جَآءَ مَعَهُ الْمَلٰٓئِكَةُ مُقْتَرِنِيْنَ ۝

54 Thus he persuaded his people to make light (of Moses), and they obeyed him. Lo! they were a wanton folk.

فَاسْتَخَفَّ قَوْمَهٗ فَأَطَاعُوْهُ إِنَّهُمْ كَانُوْا قَوْمًا فٰسِقِيْنَ ۝

55 So, when they angered Us, We punished them and drowned them every one.

فَلَمَّا اٰسَفُوْنَا انْتَقَمْنَا مِنْهُمْ فَأَغْرَقْنٰهُمْ أَجْمَعِيْنَ ۝

56 And We made them a thing past, and an example for those after (them).

فَجَعَلْنَاهُمْ سَلَفًا وَمَثَلًا لِّلْآخِرِينَ ۝

57 And when the son of Mary is quoted as an example, behold! the folk laugh out,

۞ وَلَمَّا ضُرِبَ ابْنُ مَرْيَمَ مَثَلًا إِذَا قَوْمُكَ مِنْهُ يَصِدُّونَ ۝

58 And say: Are our gods better, or is he? They raise not the objection save for argument. Nay! but they are a contentious folk.

وَقَالُوٓا ءَأَلِهَتُنَا خَيْرٌ أَمْ هُوَ مَا ضَرَبُوهُ لَكَ إِلَّا جَدَلًا بَلْ هُمْ قَوْمٌ خَصِمُونَ ۝

59 He is nothing but a slave[7] on whom We bestowed favour, and We made him a pattern for the Children of Israel.

إِنْ هُوَ إِلَّا عَبْدٌ أَنْعَمْنَا عَلَيْهِ وَجَعَلْنَاهُ مَثَلًا لِّبَنِىٓ إِسْرَٰٓءِيلَ ۝

60 And had We willed We could have set among you angels to be viceroys in the earth.

وَلَوْ نَشَآءُ لَجَعَلْنَا مِنكُم مَّلَٰٓئِكَةً فِى ٱلْأَرْضِ يَخْلُفُونَ ۝

61 And lo! verily there is knowledge of the Hour. So doubt ye not concerning it, but follow Me. This is the right path.

وَإِنَّهُۥ لَعِلْمٌ لِّلسَّاعَةِ فَلَا تَمْتَرُنَّ بِهَا وَٱتَّبِعُونِ هَٰذَا صِرَٰطٌ مُّسْتَقِيمٌ ۝

62 And let not Satan turn you aside. Lo! he is an open enemy for you.

وَلَا يَصُدَّنَّكُمُ ٱلشَّيْطَٰنُ إِنَّهُۥ لَكُمْ عَدُوٌّ مُّبِينٌ ۝

63 When Jesus came with clear proofs (of Allah's sovereignty), he said: I have come unto you with wisdom, and to make plain some of that concerning which ye differ. So keep your duty to Allah, and obey me.

وَلَمَّا جَآءَ عِيسَىٰ بِٱلْبَيِّنَٰتِ قَالَ قَدْ جِئْتُكُم بِٱلْحِكْمَةِ وَلِأُبَيِّنَ لَكُم بَعْضَ ٱلَّذِى تَخْتَلِفُونَ فِيهِ فَٱتَّقُوا۟ ٱللَّهَ وَأَطِيعُونِ ۝

---

7. 'Abd Allah, "slave of God," is a proud designation with the Muslims, bondage to Allah implying liberation from all earthly servitudes.

64 Lo! Allah, He is my Lord and your Lord. So worship Him. This is a right path.

إِنَّ اللّٰهَ هُوَ رَبِّيْ وَرَبُّكُمْ فَاعْبُدُوْهُ ۖ هٰذَا صِرَاطٌ مُّسْتَقِيْمٌ ۝

65 But the factions among them differed. Then woe unto those who do wrong from the doom of a painful day.

فَاخْتَلَفَ الْأَحْزَابُ مِنْ بَيْنِهِمْ ۖ فَوَيْلٌ لِّلَّذِيْنَ ظَلَمُوْا مِنْ عَذَابِ يَوْمٍ أَلِيْمٍ ۝

66 Await they aught save the Hour, that it shall come upon them suddenly, when they know not.

هَلْ يَنْظُرُوْنَ إِلَّا السَّاعَةَ أَنْ تَأْتِيَهُمْ بَغْتَةً وَّهُمْ لَا يَشْعُرُوْنَ ۝

67 Friends on that day will be foes one to another, save those who kept their duty (to Allah).

الْأَخِلَّاءُ يَوْمَئِذٍ بَعْضُهُمْ لِبَعْضٍ عَدُوٌّ إِلَّا الْمُتَّقِيْنَ ۝

68 O My slaves! For you there is no fear this day, nor is it ye who grieve;

يٰعِبَادِ لَا خَوْفٌ عَلَيْكُمُ الْيَوْمَ وَلَا أَنْتُمْ تَحْزَنُوْنَ ۝

69 (Ye) who believed Our revelations and were self-surrendered,

الَّذِيْنَ آمَنُوْا بِآيَاتِنَا وَكَانُوْا مُسْلِمِيْنَ ۝

70 Enter the Garden, ye and your wives, to be made glad.

ادْخُلُوا الْجَنَّةَ أَنْتُمْ وَأَزْوَاجُكُمْ تُحْبَرُوْنَ ۝

71 Therein are brought round for them trays of gold and goblets, and therein is all that souls desire and eyes find sweet. And ye are immortal therein.

يُطَافُ عَلَيْهِمْ بِصِحَافٍ مِّنْ ذَهَبٍ وَأَكْوَابٍ ۖ وَفِيْهَا مَا تَشْتَهِيْهِ الْأَنْفُسُ وَتَلَذُّ الْأَعْيُنُ ۖ وَأَنْتُمْ فِيْهَا خَالِدُوْنَ ۝

72 This is the Garden which ye are made to inherit because of what ye used to do.

وَتِلْكَ الْجَنَّةُ الَّتِيْ أُوْرِثْتُمُوْهَا بِمَا كُنْتُمْ تَعْمَلُوْنَ ۝

73 Therein for you is fruit in plenty whence to eat.

لَكُمْ فِيْهَا فَاكِهَةٌ كَثِيْرَةٌ مِّنْهَا تَأْكُلُوْنَ ۝

74 Lo! the guilty are immortal in hell's torment.

إِنَّ الْمُجْرِمِيْنَ فِيْ عَذَابِ جَهَنَّمَ خَالِدُوْنَ ۝

75 It is not relaxed for them, and they despair therein.

لَا يُفَتَّرُ عَنْهُمْ وَهُمْ فِيْهِ مُبْلِسُوْنَ ۝

76 We wronged them not, but they it was who did the wrong.

وَمَا ظَلَمْنَاهُمْ وَلَكِنْ كَانُوا هُمُ الظَّالِمِينَ ۝

77 And they cry: O Mālik! Let thy Lord make an end of us. He saith: Lo! here ye must remain.

وَنَادَوْا يَا مَالِكُ لِيَقْضِ عَلَيْنَا رَبُّكَ قَالَ إِنَّكُمْ مَاكِثُونَ ۝

78 We verily brought the Truth unto you, but ye were, most of you, averse to the Truth.

لَقَدْ جِئْنَاكُمْ بِالْحَقِّ وَلَكِنَّ أَكْثَرَكُمْ لِلْحَقِّ كَارِهُونَ ۝

79 Or do they determine any thing (against the Prophet)? Lo! We (also) are determining.

أَمْ أَبْرَمُوا أَمْرًا فَإِنَّا مُبْرِمُونَ ۝

80 Or deem they that We cannot hear their secret thoughts and private confidences? Nay, but Our envoys, present with them, do record.

أَمْ يَحْسَبُونَ أَنَّا لَا نَسْمَعُ سِرَّهُمْ وَنَجْوَاهُمْ بَلَى وَرُسُلُنَا لَدَيْهِمْ يَكْتُبُونَ ۝

81 Say (O Muḥammad): The Beneficent One hath no son. I am first among the worshippers.

قُلْ إِنْ كَانَ لِلرَّحْمَٰنِ وَلَدٌ فَأَنَا أَوَّلُ الْعَابِدِينَ ۝

82 Glorified be the Lord of the heavens and the earth, the Lord of the Throne, from that which they ascribe (unto Him)!

سُبْحَانَ رَبِّ السَّمَاوَاتِ وَالْأَرْضِ رَبِّ الْعَرْشِ عَمَّا يَصِفُونَ ۝

83 So let them flounder (in their talk) and play until they meet the Day which they are promised.

فَذَرْهُمْ يَخُوضُوا وَيَلْعَبُوا حَتَّى يُلَاقُوا يَوْمَهُمُ الَّذِي يُوعَدُونَ ۝

84 And He it is Who in the heaven is God, and in the earth God. He is the Wise, the Knower.

وَهُوَ الَّذِي فِي السَّمَاءِ إِلَٰهٌ وَفِي الْأَرْضِ إِلَٰهٌ وَهُوَ الْحَكِيمُ الْعَلِيمُ ۝

85 And blessed be He unto Whom belongeth the Sovereignty of the heavens and the earth and all that is between them, and with Whom is knowledge of the Hour, and unto Whom ye will be returned.

وَتَبَارَكَ الَّذِي لَهُ مُلْكُ السَّمَاوَاتِ وَالْأَرْضِ وَمَا بَيْنَهُمَا وَعِنْدَهُ عِلْمُ السَّاعَةِ وَإِلَيْهِ تُرْجَعُونَ ۝

86 And those unto whom they cry instead of Him possess no power of intercession, saving him who beareth witness unto the Truth knowingly.

وَلَا يَمْلِكُ الَّذِينَ يَدْعُونَ مِن دُونِهِ الشَّفَاعَةَ إِلَّا مَن شَهِدَ بِالْحَقِّ وَهُمْ يَعْلَمُونَ ۝

87 And if thou ask them who created them, they will surely say: Allah. How then are they turned away?

وَلَئِن سَأَلْتَهُم مَّنْ خَلَقَهُمْ لَيَقُولُنَّ اللَّهُ فَأَنَّىٰ يُؤْفَكُونَ ۝

88 And he saith: O my Lord! Lo! those are a folk who believe not.

وَقِيلِهِ يَا رَبِّ إِنَّ هَٰؤُلَاءِ قَوْمٌ لَّا يُؤْمِنُونَ ۝

89 Then bear with them (O Muhammad) and say: Peace. But they will come to know.

فَاصْفَحْ عَنْهُمْ وَقُلْ سَلَامٌ فَسَوْفَ يَعْلَمُونَ ۝

Ad Dukhān
(The Smoke)

Ad Dukhān, "The Smoke," takes its name from a word in v. 10. Tradition says that smoke here refers prophetically to the haze of dust which surrounded Makkah at the time of the great drought and famine which preceded the Muslim conquest of Makkah and facilitated it.

It belongs to the middle group of Makkan sūrahs.

In the name of Allah, the Beneficent, the Merciful.

بِسۡمِ ٱللَّهِ ٱلرَّحۡمَٰنِ ٱلرَّحِيمِ

1 Ḥā. Mīm.[1]

حمٓ ١

2 By the Scripture that maketh plain

وَٱلۡكِتَٰبِ ٱلۡمُبِينِ ٢

3 Lo! We revealed it on a blessed night—Lo! We are ever warning—

إِنَّآ أَنزَلۡنَٰهُ فِى لَيۡلَةٍ مُّبَٰرَكَةٍ إِنَّا كُنَّا مُنذِرِينَ ٣

4 Whereupon every wise command is made clear

فِيهَا يُفۡرَقُ كُلُّ أَمۡرٍ حَكِيمٍ ٤

5 As a command from Our presence—Lo! We are ever sending—

أَمۡرًا مِّنۡ عِندِنَآ إِنَّا كُنَّا مُرۡسِلِينَ ٥

6 A mercy from thy Lord. Lo! He is the Hearer, the Knower,

رَحۡمَةً مِّن رَّبِّكَ إِنَّهُۥ هُوَ ٱلسَّمِيعُ ٱلۡعَلِيمُ ٦

7 Lord of the heavens and the earth and all that is between them, if ye would be sure.

رَبِّ ٱلسَّمَٰوَٰتِ وَٱلۡأَرۡضِ وَمَا بَيۡنَهُمَآ إِن كُنتُم مُّوقِنِينَ ٧

---

1. See Sūrah 2, v. 1, footnote.

8   There is no God save Him. He quickeneth and giveth death; your Lord and Lord of your forefathers.

لَا إِلَٰهَ إِلَّا هُوَ يُحْيِۦ وَيُمِيتُ رَبُّكُمْ وَرَبُّ ءَابَآئِكُمُ ٱلْأَوَّلِينَ ۞

9   Nay, but they play in doubt.

بَلْ هُمْ فِى شَكٍّ يَلْعَبُونَ ۞

10   But watch thou (O Muhammad) for the day when the sky will produce visible smoke

فَٱرْتَقِبْ يَوْمَ تَأْتِى ٱلسَّمَآءُ بِدُخَانٍ مُّبِينٍ ۞

11   That will envelop the people.[2] This will be a painful torment.

يَغْشَى ٱلنَّاسَ هَٰذَا عَذَابٌ أَلِيمٌ ۞

12   (Then they will say): Our Lord relieve us of the torment. Lo! we are believers:

رَّبَّنَا ٱكْشِفْ عَنَّا ٱلْعَذَابَ إِنَّا مُؤْمِنُونَ ۞

13   How can there be remembrance for them, when a messenger making plain (the truth) had already come unto them,

أَنَّىٰ لَهُمُ ٱلذِّكْرَىٰ وَقَدْ جَآءَهُمْ رَسُولٌ مُّبِينٌ ۞

14   And they had turned away from him and said: One taught (by others), a madman?

ثُمَّ تَوَلَّوْا۟ عَنْهُ وَقَالُوا۟ مُعَلَّمٌ مَّجْنُونٌ ۞

15   Lo! We withdraw the torment a little. Lo! ye return (to disbelief).

إِنَّا كَاشِفُوا۟ ٱلْعَذَابِ قَلِيلًا إِنَّكُمْ عَآئِدُونَ ۞

16   On the day when We shall seize them with the greater seizure (then), in truth We shall punish.

يَوْمَ نَبْطِشُ ٱلْبَطْشَةَ ٱلْكُبْرَىٰ إِنَّا مُنتَقِمُونَ ۞

17   And verily We tried before them Pharaoh's folk, when there came unto them a noble messenger,

۞ وَلَقَدْ فَتَنَّا قَبْلَهُمْ قَوْمَ فِرْعَوْنَ وَجَآءَهُمْ رَسُولٌ كَرِيمٌ ۞

18   Saying: Give up to me the slaves of Allah. Lo! I am a faithful messenger unto you.

أَنْ أَدُّوٓا۟ إِلَىَّ عِبَادَ ٱللَّهِ إِنِّى لَكُمْ رَسُولٌ أَمِينٌ ۞

---

2. Of Makkah.

19 And saying: Be not proud against Allah. Lo! I bring you a clear warrant.

وَأَن لَّا تَعْلُوا عَلَى اللَّهِ إِنِّي ءَاتِيكُم بِسُلْطَنٍ مُّبِينٍ ﴿١٩﴾

20 And lo! I have sought refuge in my Lord and your Lord lest ye stone me to death.

وَإِنِّي عُذْتُ بِرَبِّي وَرَبِّكُمْ أَن تَرْجُمُونِ ﴿٢٠﴾

21 And if ye put no faith in me, then let me go.

وَإِن لَّمْ تُؤْمِنُوا لِي فَاعْتَزِلُونِ ﴿٢١﴾

22 And he cried unto his Lord (saying): These are a guilty folk.

فَدَعَا رَبَّهُ أَنَّ هَؤُلَاءِ قَوْمٌ مُّجْرِمُونَ ﴿٢٢﴾

23 Then (his Lord commanded) Take away my slaves by night. Lo! ye will be followed,

فَأَسْرِ بِعِبَادِي لَيْلًا إِنَّكُم مُّتَّبَعُونَ ﴿٢٣﴾

24 And leave the sea behind at rest, for lo! they are a drowned host.

وَاتْرُكِ الْبَحْرَ رَهْوًا إِنَّهُمْ جُندٌ مُّغْرَقُونَ ﴿٢٤﴾

25 How many were the gardens and the water springs that they left behind,

كَمْ تَرَكُوا مِن جَنَّاتٍ وَعُيُونٍ ﴿٢٥﴾

26 And the cornlands and the goodly sites

وَزُرُوعٍ وَمَقَامٍ كَرِيمٍ ﴿٢٦﴾

27 And pleasant things wherein they took delight!

وَنَعْمَةٍ كَانُوا فِيهَا فَكِهِينَ ﴿٢٧﴾

28 Even so (it was), and We made it an inheritance for other folk;

كَذَلِكَ وَأَوْرَثْنَاهَا قَوْمًا ءَاخَرِينَ ﴿٢٨﴾

29 And the heaven and the earth wept not for them, nor were they reprieved.

فَمَا بَكَتْ عَلَيْهِمُ السَّمَاءُ وَالْأَرْضُ وَمَا كَانُوا مُنظَرِينَ ﴿٢٩﴾

30 And We delivered the Children of Israel from the shameful doom;

وَلَقَدْ نَجَّيْنَا بَنِي إِسْرَائِيلَ مِنَ الْعَذَابِ الْمُهِينِ ﴿٣٠﴾

31 (We delivered them) from Pharaoh. Lo! he was a tyrant of the wanton ones.

مِن فِرْعَوْنَ إِنَّهُ كَانَ عَالِيًا مِنَ الْمُسْرِفِينَ ﴿٣١﴾

32 And We chose them, purposely, above (all) creatures.

وَلَقَدِ اخْتَرْنَاهُمْ عَلَى عِلْمٍ عَلَى الْعَالَمِينَ ﴿٣٢﴾

33 And We gave them portents wherein was a clear trial.

وَءَاتَيْنَٰهُم مِّنَ ٱلْءَايَٰتِ مَا فِيهِ بَلَٰٓؤٌا۟ مُّبِينٌ ۝

34 Lo! these, forsooth, are saying:

إِنَّ هَٰٓؤُلَآءِ لَيَقُولُونَ ۝

35 There is naught but our first death, and we shall not be raised again.

إِنْ هِىَ إِلَّا مَوْتَتُنَا ٱلْأُولَىٰ وَمَا نَحْنُ بِمُنشَرِينَ ۝

36 Bring back our fathers, if ye speak the truth!

فَأْتُوا۟ بِـَٔابَآئِنَآ إِن كُنتُمْ صَٰدِقِينَ ۝

37 Are they better, or the folk of Tubba'[3] and those before them? We destroyed them, for surely they were guilty.

أَهُمْ خَيْرٌ أَمْ قَوْمُ تُبَّعٍ وَٱلَّذِينَ مِن قَبْلِهِمْ أَهْلَكْنَٰهُمْ إِنَّهُمْ كَانُوا۟ مُجْرِمِينَ ۝

38 And We created not the heavens and the earth, and all that is between them, in play.

وَمَا خَلَقْنَا ٱلسَّمَٰوَٰتِ وَٱلْأَرْضَ وَمَا بَيْنَهُمَا لَٰعِبِينَ ۝

39 We created them not save with truth; but most of them know not.

مَا خَلَقْنَٰهُمَآ إِلَّا بِٱلْحَقِّ وَلَٰكِنَّ أَكْثَرَهُمْ لَا يَعْلَمُونَ ۝

40 Assuredly the Day of Decision is the term of all of them,

إِنَّ يَوْمَ ٱلْفَصْلِ مِيقَٰتُهُمْ أَجْمَعِينَ ۝

41 A day when friend can in naught avail friend, nor can they be helped,

يَوْمَ لَا يُغْنِى مَوْلًى عَن مَّوْلًى شَيْـًٔا وَلَا هُمْ يُنصَرُونَ ۝

42 Save him on whom Allah hath mercy. Lo! He is the Mighty, the Merciful.

إِلَّا مَن رَّحِمَ ٱللَّهُ إِنَّهُ هُوَ ٱلْعَزِيزُ ٱلرَّحِيمُ ۝

43 Lo! the tree of Zaqqūm,[4]

إِنَّ شَجَرَتَ ٱلزَّقُّومِ ۝

44 The food of the sinner!

طَعَامُ ٱلْأَثِيمِ ۝

45 Like molten brass, it seetheth in their bellies

كَٱلْمُهْلِ يَغْلِى فِى ٱلْبُطُونِ ۝

---

3. A name for many kings of Ḥimyar (the South Arabians), each of whom was called Tubba' just as every king of Egypt was called Pharaoh.

4. (27: 62); (56: 52).

46 As the seething of boiling water.

كَغَلِي ٱلْحَمِيمِ ﴿٤٦﴾

47 (And it will be said): Take him and drag him to the midst of hell,

خُذُوهُ فَٱعْتِلُوهُ إِلَىٰ سَوَآءِ ٱلْجَحِيمِ ﴿٤٧﴾

48 Then pour upon his head the torment of boiling water.

ثُمَّ صُبُّوا فَوْقَ رَأْسِهِ مِنْ عَذَابِ ٱلْحَمِيمِ ﴿٤٨﴾

49 (Saying): Taste! Lo! thou wast forsooth the mighty, the noble!

ذُقْ إِنَّكَ أَنتَ ٱلْعَزِيزُ ٱلْكَرِيمُ ﴿٤٩﴾

50 Lo! this is that whereof ye used to doubt.

إِنَّ هَٰذَا مَا كُنتُم بِهِۦ تَمْتَرُونَ ﴿٥٠﴾

51 Lo! those who kept their duty will be in a place secure

إِنَّ ٱلْمُتَّقِينَ فِي مَقَامٍ أَمِينٍ ﴿٥١﴾

52 Amid gardens and water springs,

فِي جَنَّٰتٍ وَعُيُونٍ ﴿٥٢﴾

53 Attired in silk and silk embroidery, facing one another.

يَلْبَسُونَ مِن سُندُسٍ وَإِسْتَبْرَقٍ مُّتَقَٰبِلِينَ ﴿٥٣﴾

54 Even so (it will be). And We shall wed them unto fair ones with wide, lovely eyes.

كَذَٰلِكَ وَزَوَّجْنَٰهُم بِحُورٍ عِينٍ ﴿٥٤﴾

55 They call therein for every fruit in safety.

يَدْعُونَ فِيهَا بِكُلِّ فَٰكِهَةٍ ءَامِنِينَ ﴿٥٥﴾

56 They taste not death therein, save the first death. And He hath saved them from the doom of hell,

لَا يَذُوقُونَ فِيهَا ٱلْمَوْتَ إِلَّا ٱلْمَوْتَةَ ٱلْأُولَىٰ وَوَقَىٰهُمْ عَذَابَ ٱلْجَحِيمِ ﴿٥٦﴾

57 A bounty from thy Lord. That is the supreme triumph.

فَضْلًا مِّن رَّبِّكَ ذَٰلِكَ هُوَ ٱلْفَوْزُ ٱلْعَظِيمُ ﴿٥٧﴾

58 And We have made (this Scripture) easy in thy language only that they may heed.

فَإِنَّمَا يَسَّرْنَٰهُ بِلِسَانِكَ لَعَلَّهُمْ يَتَذَكَّرُونَ ﴿٥٨﴾

59 Wait then (O Muhammad). Lo! they (too) are waiting.

فَٱرْتَقِبْ إِنَّهُم مُّرْتَقِبُونَ ﴿٥٩﴾

Al Jāthiyah
(Crouching)

Al Jāthiyah, "Crouching," takes its name from a word in v. 28. It belongs to the middle group of Makkan sūrahs.

In the name of Allah, the Beneficent, the Merciful.

1   Ḥā. Mīm.[1]

2   The revelation of the Scripture is from Allah, the Mighty, the Wise.

3   Lo! in the heavens and the earth are portents for believers.

4   And in your creation, and all the beasts that He scattered in the earth, are portents for a folk whose faith is sure.

5   And the difference of night and day and the provision that Allah sendeth down from the sky and thereby quickeneth the earth after her death, and the ordering of the winds, are portents for a people who have sense.

6   These are the portents of Allah which We recite unto thee

---

1. See Sūrah 2, v. 1, footnote.

714

(Muhammad) with truth. Then in what fact, after Allah and His portents, will they believe?

7 Woe unto each sinful liar,

8 Who heareth the revelations of Allah receive unto him, and then continueth in pride as though he heard them not. Give him tidings of a painful doom.

9 And when he knoweth aught of Our revelations he maketh it a jest. For such there is a shameful doom.

10 Beyond them there is hell, and that which they have earned will naught avail them, nor those whom they have chosen for protecting friends beside Allah. Theirs will be an awful doom.

11 This is guidance. And those who disbelieve the revelations of their Lord, for them there is a painful doom of wrath.

12 Allah it is Who hath made the sea of service unto you that the ships may run thereon by His command, and that ye may seek of His bounty, and that haply ye may be thankful;

13 And hath made of service unto you whatsoever is in the heavens and whatsoever is in the earth; it is all from Him. Lo! herein verily are portents for people who reflect.

14 Tell those who believe to forgive those who hope not for the

اللّٰهِ وَءَايٰتِهٖ يُؤْمِنُونَ ۞

وَيْلٌ لِّكُلِّ أَفَّاكٍ أَثِيمٍ ۞

يَسْمَعُ ءَايٰتِ اللّٰهِ تُتْلٰى عَلَيْهِ ثُمَّ يُصِرُّ مُسْتَكْبِرًا كَأَن لَّمْ يَسْمَعْهَا فَبَشِّرْهُ بِعَذَابٍ أَلِيمٍ ۞

وَإِذَا عَلِمَ مِنْ ءَايٰتِنَا شَيْئًا اتَّخَذَهَا هُزُوًا أُولٰئِكَ لَهُمْ عَذَابٌ مُّهِينٌ ۞

مِّن وَرَآئِهِمْ جَهَنَّمُ وَلَا يُغْنِى عَنْهُم مَّا كَسَبُوا شَيْئًا وَلَا مَا اتَّخَذُوا مِن دُونِ اللّٰهِ أَوْلِيَآءَ وَلَهُمْ عَذَابٌ عَظِيمٌ ۞

هٰذَا هُدًى وَالَّذِينَ كَفَرُوا بِآيٰتِ رَبِّهِمْ لَهُمْ عَذَابٌ مِّن رِّجْزٍ أَلِيمٌ ۞

۞ اللّٰهُ الَّذِى سَخَّرَ لَكُمُ الْبَحْرَ لِتَجْرِىَ الْفُلْكُ فِيهِ بِأَمْرِهٖ وَلِتَبْتَغُوا مِن فَضْلِهٖ وَلَعَلَّكُمْ تَشْكُرُونَ ۞

وَسَخَّرَ لَكُم مَّا فِى السَّمٰوٰتِ وَمَا فِى الْأَرْضِ جَمِيعًا مِّنْهُ إِنَّ فِى ذٰلِكَ لَآيٰتٍ لِّقَوْمٍ يَتَفَكَّرُونَ ۞

قُل لِّلَّذِينَ ءَامَنُوا يَغْفِرُوا لِلَّذِينَ لَا يَرْجُونَ

days of Allah; in order that He may requite folk what they used to earn.

أَيَّامَ اللّٰهِ لِيَجْزِيَ قَوْمًا بِمَا كَانُوا يَكْسِبُونَ ۝

15 Whoso doeth right, it is for his soul, and whoso doeth wrong, it is against it. And afterward unto your Lord ye will be brought back.

مَنْ عَمِلَ صَالِحًا فَلِنَفْسِهِ ۖ وَمَنْ أَسَاءَ فَعَلَيْهَا ۖ ثُمَّ إِلَىٰ رَبِّكُمْ تُرْجَعُونَ ۝

16 And verily We gave the Children of Israel the Scripture and the Command and the Prophethood, and provided them with good things and favoured them above (all) peoples;

وَلَقَدْ آتَيْنَا بَنِي إِسْرَآئِيلَ الْكِتَابَ وَالْحُكْمَ وَالنُّبُوَّةَ وَرَزَقْنَاهُم مِّنَ الطَّيِّبَاتِ وَفَضَّلْنَاهُمْ عَلَى الْعَالَمِينَ ۝

17 And gave them plain commandments. And they differed not until after the knowledge came unto them, through rivalry among themselves. Lo! thy Lord will judge between them on the Day of Resurrection concerning that wherein they used to differ.

وَآتَيْنَاهُم بَيِّنَاتٍ مِّنَ الْأَمْرِ ۖ فَمَا اخْتَلَفُوا إِلَّا مِن بَعْدِ مَا جَاءَهُمُ الْعِلْمُ بَغْيًا بَيْنَهُمْ ۚ إِنَّ رَبَّكَ يَقْضِي بَيْنَهُمْ يَوْمَ الْقِيَامَةِ فِيمَا كَانُوا فِيهِ يَخْتَلِفُونَ ۝

18 And now have We set thee (O Muhammad) on a clear road of (Our) commandment; so follow it, and follow not the whims of those who know not.

ثُمَّ جَعَلْنَاكَ عَلَىٰ شَرِيعَةٍ مِّنَ الْأَمْرِ فَاتَّبِعْهَا وَلَا تَتَّبِعْ أَهْوَاءَ الَّذِينَ لَا يَعْلَمُونَ ۝

19 Lo! they can avail thee naught against Allah. And lo! as for the wrong-doers, some of them are friends of others; and Allah is the Friend of those who ward off (evil).

إِنَّهُمْ لَن يُغْنُوا عَنكَ مِنَ اللّٰهِ شَيْئًا ۚ وَإِنَّ الظَّالِمِينَ بَعْضُهُمْ أَوْلِيَاءُ بَعْضٍ ۖ وَاللّٰهُ وَلِيُّ الْمُتَّقِينَ ۝

20 This is clear indication for mankind, and a guidance and a mercy for a folk whose faith is sure.

هَٰذَا بَصَائِرُ لِلنَّاسِ وَهُدًى وَرَحْمَةٌ لِّقَوْمٍ يُوقِنُونَ ۝

21 Or do those who commit ill deeds suppose that We shall make

أَمْ حَسِبَ الَّذِينَ اجْتَرَحُوا السَّيِّئَاتِ أَن نَّجْعَلَهُمْ

them as those who believe and do good works, the same life and death? Bad is their judgement!

كَالَّذِينَ ءَامَنُوا وَعَمِلُوا الصَّٰلِحَٰتِ سَوَآءً مَّحْيَاهُمْ وَمَمَاتُهُمْ سَآءَ مَا يَحْكُمُونَ ۝

22 And Allah hath created the heavens and the earth with truth, and that every soul may be repaid what it hath earned. And they will not be wronged.

وَخَلَقَ اللَّهُ السَّمَٰوَٰتِ وَالْأَرْضَ بِالْحَقِّ وَلِتُجْزَىٰ كُلُّ نَفْسٍ بِمَا كَسَبَتْ وَهُمْ لَا يُظْلَمُونَ ۝

23 Hast thou seen him who maketh his desire his god, and Allah sendeth him astray purposely, and sealeth up his hearing and his heart, and setteth on his sight a covering? Then who will lead him after Allah (hath condemned him)? Will ye not then heed?

أَفَرَءَيْتَ مَنِ اتَّخَذَ إِلَٰهَهُ هَوَىٰهُ وَأَضَلَّهُ اللَّهُ عَلَىٰ عِلْمٍ وَخَتَمَ عَلَىٰ سَمْعِهِ وَقَلْبِهِ وَجَعَلَ عَلَىٰ بَصَرِهِ غِشَٰوَةً فَمَن يَهْدِيهِ مِنۢ بَعْدِ اللَّهِ أَفَلَا تَذَكَّرُونَ ۝

24 And they say: There is naught but our life of the world; we die and we live, and naught destroyeth us save time; when they have no knowledge whatsoever of (all) that; they do but guess.

وَقَالُوا مَا هِيَ إِلَّا حَيَاتُنَا الدُّنْيَا نَمُوتُ وَنَحْيَا وَمَا يُهْلِكُنَا إِلَّا الدَّهْرُ وَمَا لَهُم بِذَٰلِكَ مِنْ عِلْمٍ إِنْ هُمْ إِلَّا يَظُنُّونَ ۝

25 And when Our clear revelations are recited unto them their only argument is that they say: Bring (back) our fathers then, if ye are truthful.

وَإِذَا تُتْلَىٰ عَلَيْهِمْ ءَايَٰتُنَا بَيِّنَٰتٍ مَّا كَانَ حُجَّتَهُمْ إِلَّا أَن قَالُوا ائْتُوا بِآبَائِنَا إِن كُنتُمْ صَٰدِقِينَ ۝

26 Say (unto them, O Muhammad): Allah giveth life to you, then causeth you to die, then gathereth you unto the Day of Resurrection whereof there is no doubt. But most of mankind know not.

قُلِ اللَّهُ يُحْيِيكُمْ ثُمَّ يُمِيتُكُمْ ثُمَّ يَجْمَعُكُمْ إِلَىٰ يَوْمِ الْقِيَٰمَةِ لَا رَيْبَ فِيهِ وَلَٰكِنَّ أَكْثَرَ النَّاسِ لَا يَعْلَمُونَ ۝

27 And unto Allah belongeth the Sovereignty of the heavens and the earth; and on the day when the

وَلِلَّهِ مُلْكُ السَّمَٰوَٰتِ وَالْأَرْضِ وَيَوْمَ تَقُومُ السَّاعَةُ

Hour riseth, on that day those who follow falsehood will be lost.

يَوْمَئِذٍ يَخْسَرُ ٱلْمُبْطِلُونَ ۝

28 And thou wilt see each nation crouching, each nation summoned to its record. (And it will be said unto them): This day ye are requited what ye used to do.

وَتَرَىٰ كُلَّ أُمَّةٍ جَاثِيَةً كُلُّ أُمَّةٍ تُدْعَىٰ إِلَىٰ كِتَٰبِهَا ٱلْيَوْمَ تُجْزَوْنَ مَا كُنتُمْ تَعْمَلُونَ ۝

29 This Our Book pronounceth against you with truth. Lo! We have caused (all) that ye did to be recorded.

هَٰذَا كِتَٰبُنَا يَنطِقُ عَلَيْكُم بِٱلْحَقِّ إِنَّا كُنَّا نَسْتَنسِخُ مَا كُنتُمْ تَعْمَلُونَ ۝

30 Then, as for those who believed and did good works, their Lord will bring them in unto His mercy. That is the evident triumph.

فَأَمَّا ٱلَّذِينَ ءَامَنُوا۟ وَعَمِلُوا۟ ٱلصَّٰلِحَٰتِ فَيُدْخِلُهُمْ رَبُّهُمْ فِى رَحْمَتِهِۦ ذَٰلِكَ هُوَ ٱلْفَوْزُ ٱلْمُبِينُ ۝

31 And as for those who disbelieved (it will be said unto them): Were not Our revelations recited unto you? But ye were scornful and became a guilty folk.

وَأَمَّا ٱلَّذِينَ كَفَرُوٓا۟ أَفَلَمْ تَكُنْ ءَايَٰتِى تُتْلَىٰ عَلَيْكُمْ فَٱسْتَكْبَرْتُمْ وَكُنتُمْ قَوْمًا مُّجْرِمِينَ ۝

32 And when it was said: Lo! Allah's promise is the truth, and there is no doubt of the Hour's coming, ye said: We know not what the Hour is. We deem it naught but a conjecture, and we are by no means convinced.

وَإِذَا قِيلَ إِنَّ وَعْدَ ٱللَّهِ حَقٌّ وَٱلسَّاعَةُ لَا رَيْبَ فِيهَا قُلْتُم مَّا نَدْرِى مَا ٱلسَّاعَةُ إِن نَّظُنُّ إِلَّا ظَنًّا وَمَا نَحْنُ بِمُسْتَيْقِنِينَ ۝

33 And the evils of what they did will appear unto them, and that which they used to deride will befall them:

وَبَدَا لَهُمْ سَيِّـَٔاتُ مَا عَمِلُوا۟ وَحَاقَ بِهِم مَّا كَانُوا۟ بِهِۦ يَسْتَهْزِءُونَ ۝

34 And it will be said: This day We forget you, even as ye forgot the meeting of this your day; and your habitation is the Fire, and there is none to help you.

وَقِيلَ ٱلْيَوْمَ نَنسَىٰكُمْ كَمَا نَسِيتُمْ لِقَآءَ يَوْمِكُمْ هَٰذَا وَمَأْوَىٰكُمُ ٱلنَّارُ وَمَا لَكُم مِّن نَّٰصِرِينَ ۝

35 This is because ye took the revelations of Allah as a jest, and the life of the world beguiled you. Therefore this day they come not forth from thence, nor can they make amends.

36 Then praise be to Allah, Lord of the heavens and Lord of the earth, the Lord of the Worlds.

37 And unto Him (alone) belongeth majesty in the heavens and the earth, and He is the Mighty, the Wise.

ذٰلِكُمْ بِأَنَّكُمُ اتَّخَذْتُمْ ءَايٰتِ اللهِ هُزُوًا وَغَرَّتْكُمُ الْحَيٰوةُ الدُّنْيَا فَالْيَوْمَ لَا يُخْرَجُونَ مِنْهَا وَلَا هُمْ يُسْتَعْتَبُونَ ۝

فَلِلّٰهِ الْحَمْدُ رَبِّ السَّمٰوٰتِ وَرَبِّ الْأَرْضِ رَبِّ الْعٰلَمِينَ ۝

وَلَهُ الْكِبْرِيَاءُ فِي السَّمٰوٰتِ وَالْأَرْضِ وَهُوَ الْعَزِيزُ الْحَكِيمُ ۝

Al Aḥqāf
(The Wind-Curved Sandhills)

Al Aḥqāf, "The Wind-Curved Sandhills" (a formation which will be familiar to all desert travellers, and which especially characterised the region in which the tribe of 'Ād were said originally to have lived), takes its name from a word in v. 21 and is the last of the *Hā Mīm* group.

It belongs to the middle group of Makkan sūrahs, with the exception of v. 10, vv. 15-18, and v. 35, which were revealed at Al-Madīnah.

سُورَةُ الأَحْقَافِ

In the name of Allah, the Beneficent, the Merciful.

بِسْمِ اللهِ الرَّحْمَنِ الرَّحِيمِ

1   Hā. Mīm.[1]

حمٓ ١

2   The revelation of the Scripture from Allah the Mighty, the Wise.

تَنْزِيلُ الْكِتَابِ مِنَ اللهِ الْعَزِيزِ الْحَكِيمِ ٢

3   We created not the heavens and the earth and all that is between them save with truth, and for a term appointed. But those who disbelieve turn away from that whereof they are warned.

مَا خَلَقْنَا السَّمَوَاتِ وَالأَرْضَ وَمَا بَيْنَهُمَا إِلَّا بِالْحَقِّ وَأَجَلٍ مُّسَمًّى وَالَّذِينَ كَفَرُوا عَمَّا أُنذِرُوا مُعْرِضُونَ ٣

4   Say (unto them, O Muhammad): Have ye thought on all that ye invoke beside Allah? Show me what they have created of the earth. Or

قُلْ أَرَأَيْتُم مَّا تَدْعُونَ مِن دُونِ اللهِ أَرُونِي مَاذَا خَلَقُوا مِنَ الأَرْضِ أَمْ لَهُمْ شِرْكٌ فِي السَّمَوَاتِ ائْتُونِي بِكِتَابٍ

---

1. See Sūrah 2, v. 1, footnote.

have they any portion in the heavens? Bring me a Scripture before this (Scripture), or some vestige of knowledge (in support of what ye say), if ye are truthful.

مِن قَبۡلِ هَٰذَآ أَوۡ أَثَٰرَةٖ مِّنۡ عِلۡمٍ إِن كُنتُمۡ صَٰدِقِينَ ﴿٤﴾

5   And who is further astray than those who, instead of Allah, pray unto such as hear not their prayer until the Day of Resurrection, and are unconscious of their prayer,

وَمَنۡ أَضَلُّ مِمَّن يَدۡعُواْ مِن دُونِ ٱللَّهِ مَن لَّا يَسۡتَجِيبُ لَهُۥٓ إِلَىٰ يَوۡمِ ٱلۡقِيَٰمَةِ وَهُمۡ عَن دُعَآئِهِمۡ غَٰفِلُونَ ﴿٥﴾

6   And when mankind are gathered (to the Judgement) they will become enemies for them, and will become deniers of having been worshipped by them.

وَإِذَا حُشِرَ ٱلنَّاسُ كَانُواْ لَهُمۡ أَعۡدَآءٗ وَكَانُواْ بِعِبَادَتِهِمۡ كَٰفِرِينَ ﴿٦﴾

7   And when Our clear revelations are recited unto them, those who disbelieve say of the Truth when it reacheth them: This is mere magic.

وَإِذَا تُتۡلَىٰ عَلَيۡهِمۡ ءَايَٰتُنَا بَيِّنَٰتٖ قَالَ ٱلَّذِينَ كَفَرُواْ لِلۡحَقِّ لَمَّا جَآءَهُمۡ هَٰذَا سِحۡرٞ مُّبِينٌ ﴿٧﴾

8   Or say they: He hath invented it? Say (O Muhammad): If I have invented it, still ye have no power to support me against Allah. He is best aware of what ye say among yourselves concerning it. He sufficeth for a witness between me and you. And He is the Forgiving, the Merciful.

أَمۡ يَقُولُونَ ٱفۡتَرَىٰهُ قُلۡ إِنِ ٱفۡتَرَيۡتُهُۥ فَلَا تَمۡلِكُونَ لِي مِنَ ٱللَّهِ شَيۡـًٔا هُوَ أَعۡلَمُ بِمَا تُفِيضُونَ فِيهِ كَفَىٰ بِهِۦ شَهِيدَۢا بَيۡنِي وَبَيۡنَكُمۡ وَهُوَ ٱلۡغَفُورُ ٱلرَّحِيمُ ﴿٨﴾

9   Say: I am no new thing among the messengers (of Allah), nor know I what will be done with me or with you. I do but follow that which is inspired in me, and I am but a plain warner.

قُلۡ مَا كُنتُ بِدۡعٗا مِّنَ ٱلرُّسُلِ وَمَآ أَدۡرِي مَا يُفۡعَلُ بِي وَلَا بِكُمۡ إِنۡ أَتَّبِعُ إِلَّا مَا يُوحَىٰٓ إِلَيَّ وَمَآ أَنَا۠ إِلَّا نَذِيرٞ مُّبِينٞ ﴿٩﴾

10 Bethink you: If it is from Allah and ye disbelieve therein, and a witness of the Children of Israel[2] hath already testified to the like thereof and hath believed, and ye are too proud (what plight is yours)? Lo! Allah, guideth not wrongdoing folk.

قُلۡ أَرَءَيۡتُمۡ إِن كَانَ مِنۡ عِندِ ٱللَّهِ وَكَفَرۡتُم بِهِۦ وَشَهِدَ شَاهِدٌ مِّنۢ بَنِىٓ إِسۡرَٰٓءِيلَ عَلَىٰ مِثۡلِهِۦ فَـَٔامَنَ وَٱسۡتَكۡبَرۡتُمۡ إِنَّ ٱللَّهَ لَا يَهۡدِى ٱلۡقَوۡمَ ٱلظَّٰلِمِينَ ١٠

11 And those who disbelieve say of those who believe: If it had been (any) good, they would not have been before us in attaining it. And since they will not be guided by it, they say: This is an ancient lie;

وَقَالَ ٱلَّذِينَ كَفَرُوا۟ لِلَّذِينَ ءَامَنُوا۟ لَوۡ كَانَ خَيۡرًا مَّا سَبَقُونَآ إِلَيۡهِ وَإِذۡ لَمۡ يَهۡتَدُوا۟ بِهِۦ فَسَيَقُولُونَ هَٰذَآ إِفۡكٌ قَدِيمٌ ١١

12 When before it there was the Scripture of Moses, an example and a mercy; and this is a confirming Scripture in the Arabic language, that it may warn those who do wrong and bring good tidings for the righteous.

وَمِن قَبۡلِهِۦ كِتَٰبُ مُوسَىٰٓ إِمَامًا وَرَحۡمَةً وَهَٰذَا كِتَٰبٌ مُّصَدِّقٌ لِّسَانًا عَرَبِيًّا لِّيُنذِرَ ٱلَّذِينَ ظَلَمُوا۟ وَبُشۡرَىٰ لِلۡمُحۡسِنِينَ ١٢

13 Lo! those who say: our Lord is Allah, and thereafter walk aright, there shall no fear come upon them neither shall they grieve.

إِنَّ ٱلَّذِينَ قَالُوا۟ رَبُّنَا ٱللَّهُ ثُمَّ ٱسۡتَقَٰمُوا۟ فَلَا خَوۡفٌ عَلَيۡهِمۡ وَلَا هُمۡ يَحۡزَنُونَ ١٣

14 Such are rightful owners of the Garden, immortal thereafter as a reward for what they used to do.

أُو۟لَٰٓئِكَ أَصۡحَٰبُ ٱلۡجَنَّةِ خَٰلِدِينَ فِيهَا جَزَآءًۢ بِمَا كَانُوا۟ يَعۡمَلُونَ ١٤

15 And We have commended unto man kindness toward parents. His mother beareth him with reluctance, and bringeth him forth with reluc-

وَوَصَّيۡنَا ٱلۡإِنسَٰنَ بِوَٰلِدَيۡهِ إِحۡسَٰنًا حَمَلَتۡهُ أُمُّهُۥ كُرۡهًا وَوَضَعَتۡهُ كُرۡهًا وَحَمۡلُهُۥ وَفِصَٰلُهُۥ ثَلَٰثُونَ شَهۡرًا

---

2. ʿAbdullah ibn Salām, a learned Jew of Al-Madīnah, who became a devout Muslim. This is the usual explanation, though the verse is still considered as a Makkan revelation.

tance, and the bearing of him and the weaning of him is thirty months, till, when he attaineth full strength and reacheth forty years, he saith: My Lord! Arouse me that I may give thanks for the favour wherewith Thou hast favoured me and my parents, and that I may do right acceptable unto Thee. And be gracious unto me in the matter of my seed. Lo! I have turned unto Thee repentant, and lo! I am of those who surrender[3] (unto Thee).

حَتَّىٰٓ إِذَا بَلَغَ أَشُدَّهُۥ وَبَلَغَ أَرۡبَعِينَ سَنَةً قَالَ رَبِّ أَوۡزِعۡنِىٓ أَنۡ أَشۡكُرَ نِعۡمَتَكَ ٱلَّتِىٓ أَنۡعَمۡتَ عَلَىَّ وَعَلَىٰ وَٰلِدَىَّ وَأَنۡ أَعۡمَلَ صَٰلِحٗا تَرۡضَىٰهُ وَأَصۡلِحۡ لِى فِى ذُرِّيَّتِىٓ إِنِّى تُبۡتُ إِلَيۡكَ وَإِنِّى مِنَ ٱلۡمُسۡلِمِينَ ۝

16 Those are they from whom We accept the best of what they do, and overlook their evil deeds. (They are) among the owners of the Garden. This is the true promise which they were promised (in the world).

أُوْلَٰٓئِكَ ٱلَّذِينَ نَتَقَبَّلُ عَنۡهُمۡ أَحۡسَنَ مَا عَمِلُواْ وَنَتَجَاوَزُ عَن سَيِّـَٔاتِهِمۡ فِىٓ أَصۡحَٰبِ ٱلۡجَنَّةِ وَعۡدَ ٱلصِّدۡقِ ٱلَّذِى كَانُواْ يُوعَدُونَ ۝

17 And whoso saith unto his parents: Fie upon you both! Do ye threaten me that I shall be brought forth (again) when generations before me have passed away? And they twain cry unto Allah for help (and say): Woe unto thee! Believe! Lo! the promise of Allah is true. But he saith: This is naught save fables of the men of old:

وَٱلَّذِى قَالَ لِوَٰلِدَيۡهِ أُفٍّ لَّكُمَآ أَتَعِدَانِنِىٓ أَنۡ أُخۡرَجَ وَقَدۡ خَلَتِ ٱلۡقُرُونُ مِن قَبۡلِى وَهُمَا يَسۡتَغِيثَانِ ٱللَّهَ وَيۡلَكَ ءَامِنۡ إِنَّ وَعۡدَ ٱللَّهِ حَقٌّ فَيَقُولُ مَا هَٰذَآ إِلَّآ أَسَٰطِيرُ ٱلۡأَوَّلِينَ ۝

18 Such are those on whom the Word concerning nations of the Jinn and mankind which have passed

أُوْلَٰٓئِكَ ٱلَّذِينَ حَقَّ عَلَيۡهِمُ ٱلۡقَوۡلُ فِىٓ أُمَمٍ قَدۡ خَلَتۡ

---

3. Ar. *Muslimūn.*

away before them hath effect. Lo! they are the losers.

من قَبْلِهِمْ مِنَ الْجِنِّ وَالْإِنْسِ إِنَّهُمْ كَانُوا خَاسِرِينَ ۝

19 And for all there will be ranks from what they do, that He may pay them for their deeds! and they will not be wronged.

وَلِكُلٍّ دَرَجَاتٌ مِّمَّا عَمِلُوا وَلِيُوَفِّيَهُمْ أَعْمَالَهُمْ وَهُمْ لَا يُظْلَمُونَ ۝

20 And on the day when those who disbelieve are exposed to the Fire (it will be said): Ye squandered your good things in your life of the world and sought comfort therein. Now this day ye are rewarded with the doom of ignominy because ye were disdainful in the land without a right and because ye used to transgress.

وَيَوْمَ يُعْرَضُ الَّذِينَ كَفَرُوا عَلَى النَّارِ أَذْهَبْتُمْ طَيِّبَاتِكُمْ فِي حَيَاتِكُمُ الدُّنْيَا وَاسْتَمْتَعْتُم بِهَا فَالْيَوْمَ تُجْزَوْنَ عَذَابَ الْهُونِ بِمَا كُنتُمْ تَسْتَكْبِرُونَ فِي الْأَرْضِ بِغَيْرِ الْحَقِّ وَبِمَا كُنتُمْ تَفْسُقُونَ ۝

21 And make mention (O Muhammad) of the brother of 'Ād[4] when he warned his folk among the wind-curved sandhills and verily warners came and went before and after him saying: Serve none but Allah. Lo! I fear for you the doom of a tremendous Day.

۞ وَاذْكُرْ أَخَا عَادٍ إِذْ أَنذَرَ قَوْمَهُ بِالْأَحْقَافِ وَقَدْ خَلَتِ النُّذُرُ مِنْ بَيْنِ يَدَيْهِ وَمِنْ خَلْفِهِ أَلَّا تَعْبُدُوا إِلَّا اللَّهَ إِنِّي أَخَافُ عَلَيْكُمْ عَذَابَ يَوْمٍ عَظِيمٍ ۝

22 They said: Hast come to turn us away from our gods? Then bring upon us that wherewith thou threatenest us, if thou art of the truthful.

قَالُوا أَجِئْتَنَا لِتَأْفِكَنَا عَنْ آلِهَتِنَا فَأْتِنَا بِمَا تَعِدُنَا إِن كُنتَ مِنَ الصَّادِقِينَ ۝

23 He said: The knowledge is with Allah only. I convey unto you that wherewith I have been sent, but I see you are a folk that know not.

قَالَ إِنَّمَا الْعِلْمُ عِندَ اللَّهِ وَأُبَلِّغُكُم مَّا أُرْسِلْتُ بِهِ وَلَكِنِّي أَرَاكُمْ قَوْمًا تَجْهَلُونَ ۝

---

4. The Prophet Hūd.

24 Then, when they beheld it as a dense cloud coming toward their valleys, they said; Here is a cloud bringing us rain. Nay, but it is that which ye did seek to hasten, a wind wherein is painful torment,

فَلَمَّا رَأَوْهُ عَارِضًا مُسْتَقْبِلَ أَوْدِيَتِهِمْ قَالُوا هٰذَا عَارِضٌ مُمْطِرُنَا بَلْ هُوَ مَا اسْتَعْجَلْتُمْ بِهِ رِيحٌ فِيهَا عَذَابٌ أَلِيمٌ ۝

25 Destroying all things by commandment of its Lord. And morning found them so that naught could be seen save their dwellings. Thus do We reward the guilty folk.

تُدَمِّرُ كُلَّ شَيْءٍ بِأَمْرِ رَبِّهَا فَأَصْبَحُوا لَا يُرَى إِلَّا مَسَاكِنُهُمْ كَذٰلِكَ نَجْزِي الْقَوْمَ الْمُجْرِمِينَ ۝

26 And verily We had empowered them with that wherewith We have not empowered you, and had assigned them ears and eyes and hearts; but their ears and eyes and hearts availed them naught since they denied the revelations of Allah; and what they used to mock befell them.

وَلَقَدْ مَكَّنَّاهُمْ فِيمَا إِنْ مَكَّنَّاكُمْ فِيهِ وَجَعَلْنَا لَهُمْ سَمْعًا وَأَبْصَارًا وَأَفْئِدَةً فَمَا أَغْنَى عَنْهُمْ سَمْعُهُمْ وَلَا أَبْصَارُهُمْ وَلَا أَفْئِدَتُهُمْ مِنْ شَيْءٍ إِذْ كَانُوا يَجْحَدُونَ بِآيَاتِ اللَّهِ وَحَاقَ بِهِمْ مَا كَانُوا بِهِ يَسْتَهْزِؤُونَ ۝

27 And verily We have destroyed townships round about you, and displayed (for them) Our revelation, that haply they might return.

وَلَقَدْ أَهْلَكْنَا مَا حَوْلَكُمْ مِنَ الْقُرَى وَصَرَّفْنَا الْآيَاتِ لَعَلَّهُمْ يَرْجِعُونَ ۝

28 Then why did those whom they had chosen for gods as a way of approach (unto Allah) not help them? Nay, but they did fail them utterly. And (all) that was their lie, and what they used to invent.

فَلَوْلَا نَصَرَهُمُ الَّذِينَ اتَّخَذُوا مِنْ دُونِ اللَّهِ قُرْبَانًا آلِهَةً بَلْ ضَلُّوا عَنْهُمْ وَذٰلِكَ إِفْكُهُمْ وَمَا كَانُوا يَفْتَرُونَ ۝

29 And when We inclined toward thee (Muhammad) certain of the Jinn, who wished to hear the Qur'an and, when they were in its presence, said: Give ear! and, when it was finished, turned back to their people, warning.

وَإِذْ صَرَفْنَا إِلَيْكَ نَفَرًا مِنَ الْجِنِّ يَسْتَمِعُونَ الْقُرْآنَ فَلَمَّا حَضَرُوهُ قَالُوا أَنْصِتُوا فَلَمَّا قُضِيَ وَلَّوْا إِلَى قَوْمِهِمْ مُنْذِرِينَ ۝

30 They said: O our people! Lo! we have heard a Scripture which hath been revealed after Moses,[5] confirming that which was before it, guiding unto the truth and a right road.

قَالُوا يَا قَوْمَنَا إِنَّا سَمِعْنَا كِتَابًا أُنزِلَ مِنۢ بَعْدِ مُوسَىٰ مُصَدِّقًا لِّمَا بَيْنَ يَدَيْهِ يَهْدِىٓ إِلَى ٱلْحَقِّ وَإِلَىٰ طَرِيقٍ مُّسْتَقِيمٍ ۝

31 O our people! respond to Allah's summoner and believe in Him. He will forgive you some of your sins and guard you from a painful doom.

يَا قَوْمَنَآ أَجِيبُوا دَاعِيَ ٱللَّهِ وَءَامِنُوا بِهِ يَغْفِرْ لَكُم مِّن ذُنُوبِكُمْ وَيُجِرْكُم مِّنْ عَذَابٍ أَلِيمٍ ۝

32 And whoso respondeth not to Allah's summoner he can nowise escape in the earth, and ye (can find) no protecting friends instead of Him. Such are in error manifest.

وَمَن لَّا يُجِبْ دَاعِيَ ٱللَّهِ فَلَيْسَ بِمُعْجِزٍ فِى ٱلْأَرْضِ وَلَيْسَ لَهُۥ مِن دُونِهِۦٓ أَوْلِيَآءُ أُوْلَٰٓئِكَ فِى ضَلَٰلٍ مُّبِينٍ ۝

33 Have they not seen that Allah, Who created the heavens and the earth and was not wearied by their creation, is Able to give life to the dead? Aye, He verily is Able to do all things.

أَوَلَمْ يَرَوْا أَنَّ ٱللَّهَ ٱلَّذِى خَلَقَ ٱلسَّمَٰوَٰتِ وَٱلْأَرْضَ وَلَمْ يَعْىَ بِخَلْقِهِنَّ بِقَٰدِرٍ عَلَىٰٓ أَن يُحْـِۧىَ ٱلْمَوْتَىٰ بَلَىٰٓ إِنَّهُۥ عَلَىٰ كُلِّ شَىْءٍ قَدِيرٌ ۝

34 And on the day when those who disbelieve are exposed to the Fire (they will be asked): Is not this real? They will say: Yea, by our Lord. He will say: Then taste the doom for that ye disbelieved.

وَيَوْمَ يُعْرَضُ ٱلَّذِينَ كَفَرُوا عَلَى ٱلنَّارِ أَلَيْسَ هَٰذَا بِٱلْحَقِّ قَالُوا بَلَىٰ وَرَبِّنَا قَالَ فَذُوقُوا ٱلْعَذَابَ بِمَا كُنتُمْ تَكْفُرُونَ ۝

---

5. From the mention of Moses it has been conjectured by some commentators that these Jinn were foreign (*i.e.* non-Arabian) Jews, the word *Jinn* in old Arabic being often applied to clever foreigners.

35 Then have patience (O Muhammad) even as the stout of heart among the messengers (of old) had patience, and seek not to hasten on the doom for them. On the day when they see that which they are promised (it will seem to them) as though they had tarried but an hour of daylight. A clear message. Shall any be destroyed save evil-living folk?

فَاصْبِرْ كَمَا صَبَرَ أُوْلُوا الْعَزْمِ مِنَ الرُّسُلِ وَلَا تَسْتَعْجِل لَّهُمْ كَأَنَّهُمْ يَوْمَ يَرَوْنَ مَا يُوعَدُونَ لَمْ يَلْبَثُوا إِلَّا سَاعَةً مِّن نَّهَارٍ بَلَغٌ فَهَلْ يُهْلَكُ إِلَّا الْقَوْمُ الْفَاسِقُونَ ۝

Muḥammad

Muḥammad. This surah takes its name from the mention of the Prophet by name in v. 2. Most commentators agree that v. 18 was revealed when the Prophet, forced to flee from Makkah, looked back, weeping, for a last sight of his native city. Some have considered the whole sūrah to be a Makkan revelation, but with no good reason.

It belongs to the first and second years after the Hijrah, with the exception of v. 18, which was revealed during the Hijrah.

In the name of Allah, the Beneficent, the Merciful.

1   Those who disbelieve and turn (men) from the way of Allah, He rendereth their actions vain.

اَلَّذِيْنَ كَفَرُوْا وَصَدُّوْا عَنْ سَبِيْلِ اللّٰهِ أَضَلَّ أَعْمَالَهُمْ ۝

2   And those who believe and do good works and believe in that which is revealed unto Muḥammad and it is the truth from their Lord. He riddeth them of their ill-deeds and improveth their state.

وَالَّذِيْنَ اٰمَنُوْا وَعَمِلُوا الصّٰلِحٰتِ وَاٰمَنُوْا بِمَا نُزِّلَ عَلٰى مُحَمَّدٍ وَّهُوَ الْحَقُّ مِنْ رَّبِّهِمْ كَفَّرَ عَنْهُمْ سَيِّاٰتِهِمْ وَأَصْلَحَ بَالَهُمْ ۝

3   That is because those who disbelieve follow falsehood and because those who believe follow the truth from their Lord. Thus Allah coineth their similitudes for mankind.

ذٰلِكَ بِأَنَّ الَّذِيْنَ كَفَرُوا اتَّبَعُوا الْبَاطِلَ وَأَنَّ الَّذِيْنَ اٰمَنُوا اتَّبَعُوا الْحَقَّ مِنْ رَّبِّهِمْ كَذٰلِكَ يَضْرِبُ اللّٰهُ لِلنَّاسِ أَمْثَالَهُمْ ۝

4   Now when ye meet in battle those who disbelieve, then it is

فَإِذَا لَقِيْتُمُ الَّذِيْنَ كَفَرُوْا فَضَرْبَ الرِّقَابِ حَتّٰى إِذَا أَثْخَنْتُمُوْهُمْ

smiting of the necks until, when ye have routed them, then making fast of bonds; and afterward either grace or ransom till the war lay down its burdens. That (is the ordinance). And if Allah willed He could have punished them (without you) but (thus it is ordained) that He may try some of you by means of others. And those who are slain in the way of Allah, He rendereth not their actions vain.

فَشَدُّوا الْوَثَاقَ فَإِمَّا مَنًّا بَعْدُ وَإِمَّا فِدَآءً حَتَّىٰ تَضَعَ الْحَرْبُ أَوْزَارَهَا ذَٰلِكَ وَلَوْ يَشَآءُ اللّٰهُ لَانْتَصَرَ مِنْهُمْ وَلَٰكِنْ لِيَبْلُوَا بَعْضَكُمْ بِبَعْضٍ وَالَّذِينَ قُتِلُوا فِي سَبِيلِ اللّٰهِ فَلَنْ يُضِلَّ أَعْمَالَهُمْ ۝

5 He will guide them and improve their state,

سَيَهْدِيهِمْ وَيُصْلِحُ بَالَهُمْ ۝

6 And bring them in unto the Garden which He hath made known to them.

وَيُدْخِلُهُمُ الْجَنَّةَ عَرَّفَهَا لَهُمْ ۝

7 O ye who believe! If ye help Allah, He will help you and will make your foothold firm.

يَٰٓأَيُّهَا الَّذِينَ ءَامَنُوٓا إِنْ تَنْصُرُوا اللّٰهَ يَنْصُرْكُمْ وَيُثَبِّتْ أَقْدَامَكُمْ ۝

8 And those who disbelieve, perdition is for them, and He will make their actions vain.

وَالَّذِينَ كَفَرُوا فَتَعْسًا لَهُمْ وَأَضَلَّ أَعْمَالَهُمْ ۝

9 That is because they are averse to that which Allah hath revealed, therefore maketh He their action fruitless.

ذَٰلِكَ بِأَنَّهُمْ كَرِهُوا مَآ أَنْزَلَ اللّٰهُ فَأَحْبَطَ أَعْمَالَهُمْ ۝

10 Have they not travelled in the land to see the nature of the consequence for those who were before them? Allah wiped them out. And for the disbelievers there will be the like thereof.

أَفَلَمْ يَسِيرُوا فِي الْأَرْضِ فَيَنْظُرُوا كَيْفَ كَانَ عَاقِبَةُ الَّذِينَ مِنْ قَبْلِهِمْ دَمَّرَ اللّٰهُ عَلَيْهِمْ وَلِلْكَافِرِينَ أَمْثَالُهَا ۝

11 That is because Allah is patron of those who believe, and because the disbelievers have no patron.

ذَٰلِكَ بِأَنَّ اللّٰهَ مَوْلَى الَّذِينَ ءَامَنُوا وَأَنَّ الْكَافِرِينَ لَا مَوْلَى لَهُمْ ۝

12 Lo! Allah will cause those who believe and do good works to enter Gardens underneath which rivers flow; while those who disbelieve take their comfort in this life and eat even as the cattle eat, and the Fire is their habitation.

إِنَّ ٱللَّهَ يُدْخِلُ ٱلَّذِينَ ءَامَنُواْ وَعَمِلُواْ ٱلصَّٰلِحَٰتِ جَنَّٰتٍ تَجْرِى مِن تَحْتِهَا ٱلْأَنْهَٰرُ وَٱلَّذِينَ كَفَرُواْ يَتَمَتَّعُونَ وَيَأْكُلُونَ كَمَا تَأْكُلُ ٱلْأَنْعَٰمُ وَٱلنَّارُ مَثْوًى لَّهُمْ ﴿١٢﴾

13 And how many a township stronger than thy township (O Muhammad) which hath cast thee out, have We destroyed, and they had no helper!

وَكَأَيِّن مِّن قَرْيَةٍ هِىَ أَشَدُّ قُوَّةً مِّن قَرْيَتِكَ ٱلَّتِىٓ أَخْرَجَتْكَ أَهْلَكْنَٰهُمْ فَلَا نَاصِرَ لَهُمْ ﴿١٣﴾

14 Is he who relieth on a clear proof from his Lord like those for whom the evil that they do is beautified while they follow their own lusts?

أَفَمَن كَانَ عَلَىٰ بَيِّنَةٍ مِّن رَّبِّهِۦ كَمَن زُيِّنَ لَهُۥ سُوٓءُ عَمَلِهِۦ وَٱتَّبَعُوٓاْ أَهْوَآءَهُم ﴿١٤﴾

15 A similitude of the Garden which those who keep their duty (to Allah) are promised: Therein are rivers of water unpolluted, and rivers of milk whereof the flavour changeth not, and rivers of wine delicious to the drinkers, and rivers of clear run honey; therein for them is every kind of fruit, with pardon from their Lord. (Are those who enjoy all this) like those who are immortal in the Fire and are given boiling water to drink so that it teareth their bowels?

مَّثَلُ ٱلْجَنَّةِ ٱلَّتِى وُعِدَ ٱلْمُتَّقُونَ فِيهَآ أَنْهَٰرٌ مِّن مَّآءٍ غَيْرِ ءَاسِنٍ وَأَنْهَٰرٌ مِّن لَّبَنٍ لَّمْ يَتَغَيَّرْ طَعْمُهُۥ وَأَنْهَٰرٌ مِّنْ خَمْرٍ لَّذَّةٍ لِّلشَّٰرِبِينَ وَأَنْهَٰرٌ مِّنْ عَسَلٍ مُّصَفًّى وَلَهُمْ فِيهَا مِن كُلِّ ٱلثَّمَرَٰتِ وَمَغْفِرَةٌ مِّن رَّبِّهِمْ كَمَنْ هُوَ خَٰلِدٌ فِى ٱلنَّارِ وَسُقُواْ مَآءً حَمِيمًا فَقَطَّعَ أَمْعَآءَهُمْ ﴿١٥﴾

16 Among them are some who give ear unto thee (Muhammad) till, when they go forth from thy presence, they say unto those who have been given knowledge: What was

وَمِنْهُم مَّن يَسْتَمِعُ إِلَيْكَ حَتَّىٰٓ إِذَا خَرَجُواْ مِنْ عِندِكَ قَالُواْ لِلَّذِينَ أُوتُواْ ٱلْعِلْمَ مَاذَا قَالَ ءَانِفًا قَالَ أُوْلَٰٓئِكَ ٱلَّذِينَ

that he said just now? Those are they whose hearts Allah hath sealed, and they follow their own lusts.

طَبَعَ اللّٰهُ عَلٰى قُلُوبِهِمْ وَاتَّبَعُوْٓا اَهْوَآءَهُمْ ۝

17 While as for those who walk aright, He addeth to their guidance, and giveth them their protection (against evil).

وَالَّذِيْنَ اهْتَدَوْا زَادَهُمْ هُدًى وَّاٰتٰهُمْ تَقْوٰىهُمْ ۝

18 Await they aught save the Hour, that it should come upon them unawares? And the beginnings thereof have already come. But how, when it hath come upon them, can they take their warning?

فَهَلْ يَنْظُرُوْنَ اِلَّا السَّاعَةَ اَنْ تَأْتِيَهُمْ بَغْتَةً فَقَدْ جَآءَ اَشْرَاطُهَا ۚ فَاَنّٰى لَهُمْ اِذَا جَآءَتْهُمْ ذِكْرٰىهُمْ ۝

19 So know (O Muhammad) that there is no God save Allah, and ask forgiveness for thy sin and for believing men and believing women. Allah knoweth (both) your place of turmoil and your place of rest.

فَاعْلَمْ اَنَّهٗ لَآ اِلٰهَ اِلَّا اللّٰهُ وَاسْتَغْفِرْ لِذَنْۢبِكَ وَلِلْمُؤْمِنِيْنَ وَالْمُؤْمِنٰتِ ۚ وَاللّٰهُ يَعْلَمُ مُتَقَلَّبَكُمْ وَمَثْوٰىكُمْ ۝

20 And those who believe say: If only a sūrah were revealed! But when a decisive sūrah is revealed and war is mentioned therein, thou seest those in whose hearts is a disease looking at thee with the look of men fainting unto death. Therefore woe unto them!

وَيَقُوْلُ الَّذِيْنَ اٰمَنُوْا لَوْلَا نُزِّلَتْ سُوْرَةٌ ۚ فَاِذَآ اُنْزِلَتْ سُوْرَةٌ مُّحْكَمَةٌ وَّذُكِرَ فِيْهَا الْقِتَالُ ۙ رَاَيْتَ الَّذِيْنَ فِيْ قُلُوْبِهِمْ مَّرَضٌ يَّنْظُرُوْنَ اِلَيْكَ نَظَرَ الْمَغْشِيِّ عَلَيْهِ مِنَ الْمَوْتِ ۚ فَاَوْلٰى لَهُمْ ۝

21 Obedience and a civil word. Then, when the matter is determined, if they are loyal to Allah it will be well for them.

طَاعَةٌ وَّقَوْلٌ مَّعْرُوْفٌ ۚ فَاِذَا عَزَمَ الْاَمْرُ ۚ فَلَوْ صَدَقُوا اللّٰهَ لَكَانَ خَيْرًا لَّهُمْ ۝

22 Would ye then, if ye were given the command, work corruption in the land and sever your ties of kinship?

فَهَلْ عَسَيْتُمْ اِنْ تَوَلَّيْتُمْ اَنْ تُفْسِدُوْا فِى الْاَرْضِ وَتُقَطِّعُوْٓا اَرْحَامَكُمْ ۝

23 Such are they whom Allah curseth so that he deafeneth them and maketh blind their eyes.

أُوْلَٰٓئِكَ ٱلَّذِينَ لَعَنَهُمُ ٱللَّهُ فَأَصَمَّهُمْ وَأَعْمَىٰٓ أَبْصَٰرَهُمْ ۝

24 Will they then not meditate on the Qur'an, or are there locks on the hearts?

أَفَلَا يَتَدَبَّرُونَ ٱلْقُرْءَانَ أَمْ عَلَىٰ قُلُوبٍ أَقْفَالُهَآ ۝

25 Lo! those who turn back after the guidance hath been manifested unto them, Satan hath seduced them, and He giveth them the rein.

إِنَّ ٱلَّذِينَ ٱرْتَدُّواْ عَلَىٰٓ أَدْبَٰرِهِم مِّنۢ بَعْدِ مَا تَبَيَّنَ لَهُمُ ٱلْهُدَى ٱلشَّيْطَٰنُ سَوَّلَ لَهُمْ وَأَمْلَىٰ لَهُمْ ۝

26 That is because they say unto those who hate what Allah hath revealed: We will obey you in some matters; and Allah knoweth their secret talk.

ذَٰلِكَ بِأَنَّهُمْ قَالُواْ لِلَّذِينَ كَرِهُواْ مَا نَزَّلَ ٱللَّهُ سَنُطِيعُكُمْ فِى بَعْضِ ٱلْأَمْرِ وَٱللَّهُ يَعْلَمُ إِسْرَارَهُمْ ۝

27 Then how (will it be with them) when the angels gather them, smiting their faces and their backs!

فَكَيْفَ إِذَا تَوَفَّتْهُمُ ٱلْمَلَٰٓئِكَةُ يَضْرِبُونَ وُجُوهَهُمْ وَأَدْبَٰرَهُمْ ۝

28 That will be because they followed that which angereth Allah, and hated that which pleaseth Him. Therefore He hath made their actions vain.

ذَٰلِكَ بِأَنَّهُمُ ٱتَّبَعُواْ مَآ أَسْخَطَ ٱللَّهَ وَكَرِهُواْ رِضْوَٰنَهُ فَأَحْبَطَ أَعْمَٰلَهُمْ ۝

29 Or do those in whose hearts is a disease deem that Allah will not bring to light their (secret) hates?

أَمْ حَسِبَ ٱلَّذِينَ فِى قُلُوبِهِم مَّرَضٌ أَن لَّن يُخْرِجَ ٱللَّهُ أَضْغَٰنَهُمْ ۝

30 And if We would, We could show them unto thee (Muhammad) so that thou shouldst know them surely by their marks. And thou shalt know them by the tone of their talk. And Allah knoweth your deeds.

وَلَوْ نَشَآءُ لَأَرَيْنَٰكَهُمْ فَلَعَرَفْتَهُم بِسِيمَٰهُمْ وَلَتَعْرِفَنَّهُمْ فِى لَحْنِ ٱلْقَوْلِ وَٱللَّهُ يَعْلَمُ أَعْمَٰلَكُمْ ۝

31 And verily We shall try you till We know those of you who strive hard (for the cause of Allah) and the steadfast, and till We test your record.

وَلَنَبْلُوَنَّكُمْ حَتَّىٰ نَعْلَمَ الْمُجَاهِدِينَ مِنكُمْ وَالصَّابِرِينَ وَنَبْلُوَا۟ أَخْبَارَكُمْ ﴿٣١﴾

32 Lo! those who disbelieve and turn from the way of Allah and oppose the messenger after the guidance hath been manifested unto them, they hurt Allah not a jot, and He will make their actions fruitless.

إِنَّ الَّذِينَ كَفَرُوا۟ وَصَدُّوا۟ عَن سَبِيلِ اللَّهِ وَشَآقُّوا۟ الرَّسُولَ مِنۢ بَعْدِ مَا تَبَيَّنَ لَهُمُ الْهُدَىٰ لَن يَضُرُّوا۟ اللَّهَ شَيْـًٔا وَسَيُحْبِطُ أَعْمَالَهُمْ ﴿٣٢﴾

33 O ye who believe! Obey Allah and obey the messenger, and render not your actions vain.

۞ يَـٰٓأَيُّهَا الَّذِينَ ءَامَنُوٓا۟ أَطِيعُوا۟ اللَّهَ وَأَطِيعُوا۟ الرَّسُولَ وَلَا تُبْطِلُوٓا۟ أَعْمَٰلَكُمْ ﴿٣٣﴾

34 Lo! those who disbelieve and turn from the way of Allah and then die disbelievers, Allah surely will not pardon them.

إِنَّ الَّذِينَ كَفَرُوا۟ وَصَدُّوا۟ عَن سَبِيلِ اللَّهِ ثُمَّ مَاتُوا۟ وَهُمْ كُفَّارٌ فَلَن يَغْفِرَ اللَّهُ لَهُمْ ﴿٣٤﴾

35 So do not falter and cry out for peace when ye (will be) the uppermost, and Allah is with you, and He will not grudge (the reward of) your actions.

فَلَا تَهِنُوا۟ وَتَدْعُوٓا۟ إِلَى السَّلْمِ وَأَنتُمُ الْأَعْلَوْنَ وَاللَّهُ مَعَكُمْ وَلَن يَتِرَكُمْ أَعْمَٰلَكُمْ ﴿٣٥﴾

36 The life of the world is but a sport and a pastime. And if ye believe and ward off (evil), He will give you your wages, and will not ask of you your worldly wealth.

إِنَّمَا الْحَيَوٰةُ الدُّنْيَا لَعِبٌ وَلَهْوٌ وَإِن تُؤْمِنُوا۟ وَتَتَّقُوا۟ يُؤْتِكُمْ أُجُورَكُمْ وَلَا يَسْـَٔلْكُمْ أَمْوَٰلَكُمْ ﴿٣٦﴾

37 If He should ask it of you and importune you, ye would hoard it, and He would bring to light your (secret) hates.

إِن يَسْـَٔلْكُمُوهَا فَيُحْفِكُمْ تَبْخَلُوا۟ وَيُخْرِجْ أَضْغَٰنَكُمْ ﴿٣٧﴾

38 Lo! ye are those who are called
to spend in the way of Allah, yet
among you there are some who
hoard. And as for him who hoardeth, he hoardeth only from his soul.
And Allah is the Rich, and ye are
the poor. And if ye turn away He
will exchange you for some other
folk, and they will not be the likes
of you.

هَآأَنتُمْ هَٰٓؤُلَآءِ تُدْعَوْنَ لِتُنفِقُوا۟ فِى سَبِيلِ ٱللَّهِ
فَمِنكُم مَّن يَبْخَلُ وَمَن يَبْخَلْ فَإِنَّمَا يَبْخَلُ
عَن نَّفْسِهِۦ وَٱللَّهُ ٱلْغَنِىُّ وَأَنتُمُ ٱلْفُقَرَآءُ
وَإِن تَتَوَلَّوْا۟ يَسْتَبْدِلْ قَوْمًا غَيْرَكُمْ
ثُمَّ لَا يَكُونُوٓا۟ أَمْثَٰلَكُم ۝

Al Fath
(Victory)

Al Fath takes its name from the word *Fath* meaning "Victory" which occurs several times, and refers, not to the conquest of Makkah, but to the truce of Al Ḥudaybiyah, which, though at the time it seemed a setback to the Muslims, proved in fact the greatest victory for Al Islām.

In the sixth year of the Hijrah, the Prophet set out with some 1400 Muslims from Al-Madīnah and the country round, in the garb of pilgrims, not for war but to visit the Ka'bah. When they drew near Makkah, they were warned that Quraysh had gathered their allies against them, and that their cavalry under Khālid ibn Al Walīd was on the road before them. Making a détour through gullies of the hills, they escaped the cavalry and, coming into the valley of Makkah, encamped at Al Ḥudaybiyah below the city. The Prophet resolutely refused to give battle and persisted in attempts to parley with Quraysh who had sworn not to let him reach the Ka'bah. The Muslims were all the while in a position of some danger. Finally 'Uthmān ibn 'Affān was sent into the city, as the man most likely to be well received on account of his relationships. 'Uthmān was detained by the Makkans, and news that he had been murdered reached the Muslims in their camp.[1]

It was then that the Prophet, sitting under a tree, took from his comrades the oath (referred to in v. 18) that they would hold together and fight to the death.[2] Then it became known that the rumour of 'Uthmān's death was false, and Quraysh at length agreed to a truce of which the terms were favourable to them. The Prophet and his multitude were to give up the project of visiting the sanctuary for that year, but were to make the pilgrimage the following year when the idolaters undertook to evacuate Makkah for three days to allow them to do so. Fugitives from Quraysh to the Muslims were to be returned, but not

---

1. Ibn Hishām, Part II, pp. 176-178.

2. Ibn Hishām, Part II, p. 179.

fugitives from the Muslims to Quraysh; and there was to be no hostility between the parties for ten years.

"And there was never a victory," says Ibn Khaldūn, "greater than this victory; for, as Az Zuhrī says, when it was war the peoples did not meet, but when the truce came and war laid down its burdens and people felt safe one with another, then they met and indulged in conversation and discussion. And no man spoke of Al Islām to another but the latter espoused it, so that there entered Al Islām in those two years (*i.e.*, between Al Ḥūdaybiyah and the breaking of the truce by Quraysh) as many as all those who had entered it before, or more."[3]

The date of revelation is the sixth year of the Hijrah.

In the name of Allah, the Beneficent, the Merciful.

1   Lo! We have given thee (O Muhammad) a signal victory;

2   That Allah may forgive thee of thy sin that which is past and that which is to come, and may perfect His favour unto thee, and may guide thee on a right path,

3   And that Allah may help thee with strong help,

4   He it is Who sent down peace of reassurance into the hearts of the believers that they might add faith

---

3. Ibn Khaldūn, *Tārīkh*. Supplement to Part II, Būlāq 1824, A.H. He follows Ibn Hishām.

unto their faith. Allah's are the hosts of the heavens and the earth, and Allah is ever Knower, Wise,

5 That He may bring the believing men and the believing women into Gardens underneath which rivers flow, wherein they will abide, and may remit from them their evil deeds. That, in the sight of Allah, is the supreme triumph,

6 And may punish the hypocritical men and the hypocritical women, and the idolatrous men and the idolatrous women, who think an evil thought concerning Allah. For them is the evil turn of fortune, and Allah is wroth against them and hath cursed them, and hath made ready for them hell, a hapless journey's end.

7 Allah's are the hosts of the heavens and the earth, and Allah is ever Mighty, Wise.

8 Lo! We have sent thee (O Muhammad) as a witness and a bearer of good tidings and a warner,

9 That ye (mankind) may believe in Allah and His messenger, and may honour Him, and may revere Him, and may glorify Him at early dawn and at the close of day.

10 Lo! those who swear allegiance unto thee (Muhammad), swear allegiance only unto Allah. The Hand of Allah is above their hands. So whosoever breaketh his oath, brea-

keth it only to his soul's hurt; while whosoever keepeth his covenant with Allah, on him will He bestow immense reward.

أَوْفَىٰ بِمَا عَاهَدَ عَلَيْهُ اللَّهَ فَسَيُؤْتِيهِ أَجْرًا عَظِيمًا ۝

11 Those of the wandering Arabs who were left behind will tell thee: Our possessions and our households occupied us, so ask forgiveness for us! They speak with their tongues that which is not in their hearts. Say: Who can avail you aught against Allah, if he intend you hurt or intend you profit? Nay, but Allah is ever Aware of what ye do.

سَيَقُولُ لَكَ الْمُخَلَّفُونَ مِنَ الْأَعْرَابِ شَغَلَتْنَا أَمْوَالُنَا وَأَهْلُونَا فَاسْتَغْفِرْ لَنَا يَقُولُونَ بِأَلْسِنَتِهِمْ مَا لَيْسَ فِى قُلُوبِهِمْ قُلْ فَمَنْ يَمْلِكُ لَكُمْ مِنَ اللَّهِ شَيْئًا إِنْ أَرَادَ بِكُمْ ضَرًّا أَوْ أَرَادَ بِكُمْ نَفْعًا بَلْ كَانَ اللَّهُ بِمَا تَعْمَلُونَ خَبِيرًا ۝

12 Nay, but ye deemed that the messenger and the believers would never return to their own folk, and that was made fair-seeming in your hearts, and ye did think an evil thought, and ye were worthless folk.

بَلْ ظَنَنْتُمْ أَنْ لَنْ يَنْقَلِبَ الرَّسُولُ وَالْمُؤْمِنُونَ إِلَىٰ أَهْلِيهِمْ أَبَدًا وَزُيِّنَ ذَلِكَ فِى قُلُوبِكُمْ وَظَنَنْتُمْ ظَنَّ السَّوْءِ وَكُنْتُمْ قَوْمًا بُورًا ۝

13 And as for him who believeth not in Allah and His messenger. Lo! We have prepared a flame for disbelievers.

وَمَنْ لَمْ يُؤْمِنْ بِاللَّهِ وَرَسُولِهِ فَإِنَّا أَعْتَدْنَا لِلْكَافِرِينَ سَعِيرًا ۝

14 And Allah's is the Sovereignty of the heavens and the earth. He forgiveth whom He will, and punisheth whom He will. And Allah is ever Forgiving, Merciful.

وَلِلَّهِ مُلْكُ السَّمَوَاتِ وَالْأَرْضِ يَغْفِرُ لِمَنْ يَشَاءُ وَيُعَذِّبُ مَنْ يَشَاءُ وَكَانَ اللَّهُ غَفُورًا رَحِيمًا ۝

15 Those who were left behind will say, when ye set forth to capture booty: Let us go with you. They fain would change the verdict of Allah. Say (unto them, O Muḥammad): Ye shall not go with

سَيَقُولُ الْمُخَلَّفُونَ إِذَا انْطَلَقْتُمْ إِلَىٰ مَغَانِمَ لِتَأْخُذُوهَا ذَرُونَا نَتَّبِعْكُمْ يُرِيدُونَ أَنْ يُبَدِّلُوا كَلَامَ اللَّهِ قُلْ لَنْ تَتَّبِعُونَا كَذَلِكُمْ

us. Thus hath Allah said before-hand. Then they will say: Ye are envious of us. Nay, but they understand not, save a little.

قَالَ اللهُ مِنْ قَبْلُ فَسَيَقُوْلُوْنَ بَلْ تَحْسُدُوْنَنَا ۚ بَلْ كَانُوْا لَا يَفْقَهُوْنَ إِلَّا قَلِيْلًا ۞

16 Say unto those of the wandering Arabs who were left behind: Ye will be called against a folk of mighty prowess,[4] to fight them until they surrender; and if ye obey, Allah will give you a fair reward; but if ye turn away as ye did turn away before, He will punish you with a painful doom.

قُلْ لِّلْمُخَلَّفِيْنَ مِنَ الْأَعْرَابِ سَتُدْعَوْنَ إِلَى قَوْمٍ أُولِي بَأْسٍ شَدِيْدٍ تُقَاتِلُوْنَهُمْ أَوْ يُسْلِمُوْنَ ۚ فَإِنْ تُطِيْعُوْا يُؤْتِكُمُ اللهُ أَجْرًا حَسَنًا ۚ وَإِنْ تَتَوَلَّوْا كَمَا تَوَلَّيْتُمْ مِّنْ قَبْلُ يُعَذِّبْكُمْ عَذَابًا أَلِيْمًا ۞

17 There is no blame for the blind, nor is there blame for the lame, nor is there blame for the sick (that they go not forth to war). And whoso obeyeth Allah and His messenger, He will make him enter Gardens underneath which rivers flow; and whoso turneth back, him will He punish with a painful doom.

لَيْسَ عَلَى الْأَعْمَى حَرَجٌ وَّلَا عَلَى الْأَعْرَجِ حَرَجٌ وَّلَا عَلَى الْمَرِيْضِ حَرَجٌ ۗ وَمَنْ يُّطِعِ اللهَ وَرَسُوْلَهُ يُدْخِلْهُ جَنّٰتٍ تَجْرِيْ مِنْ تَحْتِهَا الْأَنْهٰرُ ۚ وَمَنْ يَّتَوَلَّ يُعَذِّبْهُ عَذَابًا أَلِيْمًا ۞

18 Allah was well pleased with the believers when they swore allegiance unto thee beneath the tree, and He knew what was in their hearts, and He sent down peace of reassurance on them, and hath rewarded them with a near victory;

لَقَدْ رَضِيَ اللهُ عَنِ الْمُؤْمِنِيْنَ إِذْ يُبَايِعُوْنَكَ تَحْتَ الشَّجَرَةِ فَعَلِمَ مَا فِيْ قُلُوْبِهِمْ فَأَنْزَلَ السَّكِيْنَةَ عَلَيْهِمْ وَأَثَابَهُمْ فَتْحًا قَرِيْبًا ۞

19 And much booty that they will capture. Allah is ever Mighty, Wise.

وَّمَغَانِمَ كَثِيْرَةً يَّأْخُذُوْنَهَا ۚ وَكَانَ اللهُ عَزِيْزًا حَكِيْمًا ۞

---

4. This prophecy is taken to refer to the war with the Persian or the Byzantine empire.

20 Allah promiseth you much booty that ye will capture, and hath given you this in advance, and hath withheld men's hands from you, that it may be a token for the believers, and that He may guide you on a right path.

وَعَدَكُمُ اللّٰهُ مَغَانِمَ كَثِيرَةً تَأْخُذُونَهَا فَعَجَّلَ لَكُمْ هٰذِهِ وَكَفَّ أَيْدِيَ النَّاسِ عَنْكُمْ وَلِتَكُونَ ءَايَةً لِّلْمُؤْمِنِينَ وَيَهْدِيَكُمْ صِرَاطًا مُّسْتَقِيمًا ۝

21 And other (gain), which ye have not been able to achieve, Allah will compass it. Allah is Able to do all things.

وَأُخْرَىٰ لَمْ تَقْدِرُوا عَلَيْهَا قَدْ أَحَاطَ اللّٰهُ بِهَا وَكَانَ اللّٰهُ عَلَىٰ كُلِّ شَيْءٍ قَدِيرًا ۝

22 And if those who disbelieve join battle with you they will take to flight, and afterward they will find no protecting friend nor helper.

وَلَوْ قَاتَلَكُمُ الَّذِينَ كَفَرُوا لَوَلَّوُا الْأَدْبَارَ ثُمَّ لَا يَجِدُونَ وَلِيًّا وَلَا نَصِيرًا ۝

23 It is the law of Allah which hath taken course aforetime. Thou wilt not find in the law of Allah any change.

سُنَّةَ اللّٰهِ الَّتِي قَدْ خَلَتْ مِن قَبْلُ وَلَن تَجِدَ لِسُنَّةِ اللّٰهِ تَبْدِيلًا ۝

24 And He it is Who hath withheld men's hands from you, and hath withheld your hands from them, in the valley of Makkah, after He had made you victors over them. Allah is Seer of what ye do.

وَهُوَ الَّذِي كَفَّ أَيْدِيَهُمْ عَنْكُمْ وَأَيْدِيَكُمْ عَنْهُمْ بِبَطْنِ مَكَّةَ مِنْ بَعْدِ أَنْ أَظْفَرَكُمْ عَلَيْهِمْ وَكَانَ اللّٰهُ بِمَا تَعْمَلُونَ بَصِيرًا ۝

25 These it was who disbelieved and debarred you from the Inviolable Place of Worship, and debarred the offering from reaching its goal. And if it had not been for believing men and believing women, whom ye know not—lest ye should tread them under foot and thus incur guilt for them unknowingly; that Allah might bring into

هُمُ الَّذِينَ كَفَرُوا وَصَدُّوكُمْ عَنِ الْمَسْجِدِ الْحَرَامِ وَالْهَدْيَ مَعْكُوفًا أَن يَبْلُغَ مَحِلَّهُ وَلَوْلَا رِجَالٌ مُّؤْمِنُونَ وَنِسَاءٌ مُّؤْمِنَاتٌ لَّمْ تَعْلَمُوهُمْ أَن تَطَئُوهُمْ فَتُصِيبَكُم مِّنْهُم مَّعَرَّةٌ بِغَيْرِ عِلْمٍ لِّيُدْخِلَ اللّٰهُ

His mercy whom He will—If (the believers and the disbelievers) had been clearly separated, We verily had punished those of them who disbelieved with painful punishment.

فِى رَحْمَتِهِۦ مَن يَشَآءُ لَوْ تَزَيَّلُوا لَعَذَّبْنَا الَّذِينَ كَفَرُوا مِنْهُمْ عَذَابًا أَلِيمًا ۝

26 When those who disbelieve had set up in their hearts zealotry, the zealotry of the Age of Ignorance, then Allah sent down His peace of reassurance upon His messenger and upon the believers and imposed on them the word of self-restraint, for they were worthy of it and meet for it. And Allah is Aware of all things.

إِذْ جَعَلَ الَّذِينَ كَفَرُوا فِى قُلُوبِهِمُ الْحَمِيَّةَ حَمِيَّةَ الْجَـٰهِلِيَّةِ فَأَنزَلَ اللَّهُ سَكِينَتَهُۥ عَلَىٰ رَسُولِهِۦ وَعَلَى الْمُؤْمِنِينَ وَأَلْزَمَهُمْ كَلِمَةَ التَّقْوَىٰ وَكَانُوٓا أَحَقَّ بِهَا وَأَهْلَهَا وَكَانَ اللَّهُ بِكُلِّ شَىْءٍ عَلِيمًا ۝

27 Allah hath fulfilled the vision[5] for His messenger in very truth. Ye shall indeed enter the Inviolable Place of Worship, if Allah will, secure, (having your hair) shaven and cut, not fearing. But He knoweth that which ye know not, and hath given you a near victory beforehand.

لَّقَدْ صَدَقَ اللَّهُ رَسُولَهُ الرُّءْيَا بِالْحَقِّ لَتَدْخُلُنَّ الْمَسْجِدَ الْحَرَامَ إِن شَآءَ اللَّهُ ءَامِنِينَ مُحَلِّقِينَ رُءُوسَكُمْ وَمُقَصِّرِينَ لَا تَخَافُونَ فَعَلِمَ مَا لَمْ تَعْلَمُوا فَجَعَلَ مِن دُونِ ذَٰلِكَ فَتْحًا قَرِيبًا ۝

28 He it is Who hath sent His messenger with the guidance and the religion of truth, that He may cause it to prevail over all religion. And Allah sufficeth as a witness.

هُوَ الَّذِىٓ أَرْسَلَ رَسُولَهُۥ بِالْهُدَىٰ وَدِينِ الْحَقِّ لِيُظْهِرَهُۥ عَلَى الدِّينِ كُلِّهِۦ وَكَفَىٰ بِاللَّهِ شَهِيدًا ۝

---

5. The Prophet had had a vision that he was entering the Sanctuary at Makkah in peace and safety.

29 Muhammad is the messenger of Allah. And those with him are hard against the disbelievers and merciful among themselves. Thou (O Muhammad) seest them bowing and falling prostrate (in worship), seeking bounty from Allah and (His) acceptance. The mark of them is on their foreheads from the traces of prostration. Such is their likeness in the Torah and their likeness in the Gospel like as sown corn that sendeth forth its shoot and strengtheneth it and riseth firm upon its stalk, delighting the sowers that He may enrage the disbelievers with (the sight of) them. Allah hath promised, unto such of them as believe and do good works, forgiveness and immense reward.

مُّحَمَّدٌ رَّسُولُ اللّٰهِ وَالَّذِينَ مَعَهُ أَشِدَّاءُ عَلَى الْكُفَّارِ
رُحَمَاءُ بَيْنَهُمْ تَرَىٰهُمْ رُكَّعًا سُجَّدًا يَبْتَغُونَ فَضْلًا
مِّنَ اللّٰهِ وَرِضْوَانًا سِيمَاهُمْ فِى وُجُوهِهِم
مِّنْ أَثَرِ السُّجُودِ ذَٰلِكَ مَثَلُهُمْ فِى التَّوْرَىٰةِ وَمَثَلُهُمْ
فِى الْإِنجِيلِ كَزَرْعٍ أَخْرَجَ شَطْأَهُ فَآزَرَهُ
فَاسْتَغْلَظَ فَاسْتَوَىٰ عَلَىٰ سُوقِهِ يُعْجِبُ الزُّرَّاعَ
لِيَغِيظَ بِهِمُ الْكُفَّارَ وَعَدَ اللّٰهُ الَّذِينَ ءَامَنُوا وَعَمِلُوا
الصَّٰلِحَٰتِ مِنْهُم مَّغْفِرَةً وَأَجْرًا عَظِيمًا ۩

Al Ḥujurāt
(The Private Apartments)

Al Ḥujurāt takes its name from v. 4, which, with the following verse, is said to refer to the behaviour of a deputation at a time when deputations from all parts of Arabia were coming to Al-Madīnah to profess allegiance to the Prophet. The whole sūrah, dealing as it does with manners, and particularly with behaviour toward the Prophet, evidently belongs to a period when there were many seeking audience, among them many who were quite uncivilised.

The date of revelation is the ninth year of the Hijrah, "the year of deputations," as it is called.

In the name of Allah, the Beneficent, the Merciful.

بِسْمِ اللَّهِ الرَّحْمَنِ الرَّحِيمِ

1 O ye who believe! Be not forward in the presence of Allah and His messenger, and keep your duty to Allah. Lo! Allah is Hearer, Knower.

يَـٰٓأَيُّهَا ٱلَّذِينَ ءَامَنُوا۟ لَا تُقَدِّمُوا۟ بَيْنَ يَدَىِ ٱللَّهِ وَرَسُولِهِۦ ۖ وَٱتَّقُوا۟ ٱللَّهَ ۚ إِنَّ ٱللَّهَ سَمِيعٌ عَلِيمٌ ﴿١﴾

2 O ye who believe! Lift not up your voices above the voice of the Prophet, nor shout when speaking to him as ye shout one to another, lest your works be rendered vain while ye perceive not.

يَـٰٓأَيُّهَا ٱلَّذِينَ ءَامَنُوا۟ لَا تَرْفَعُوٓا۟ أَصْوَٰتَكُمْ فَوْقَ صَوْتِ ٱلنَّبِىِّ وَلَا تَجْهَرُوا۟ لَهُۥ بِٱلْقَوْلِ كَجَهْرِ بَعْضِكُمْ لِبَعْضٍ أَن تَحْبَطَ أَعْمَٰلُكُمْ وَأَنتُمْ لَا تَشْعُرُونَ ﴿٢﴾

3 Lo! they who subdue their voices in the presence of the messenger of Allah, those are they

إِنَّ ٱلَّذِينَ يَغُضُّونَ أَصْوَٰتَهُمْ عِندَ رَسُولِ ٱللَّهِ أُو۟لَـٰٓئِكَ ٱلَّذِينَ ٱمْتَحَنَ ٱللَّهُ قُلُوبَهُمْ لِلتَّقْوَىٰ ۚ

whose hearts Allah hath proven unto righteousness. Theirs will be forgiveness and immense reward.

لَهُمْ مَّغْفِرَةٌ وَّأَجْرٌ عَظِيمٌ ۝

4 Lo! those who call thee from behind the private apartments, most of them have no sense.

إِنَّ الَّذِينَ يُنَادُونَكَ مِنْ وَرَآءِ الْحُجُرَاتِ أَكْثَرُهُمْ لَا يَعْقِلُونَ ۝

5 And if they had patience till thou camest forth unto them, it had been better for them. And Allah is Forgiving, Merciful.

وَلَوْ أَنَّهُمْ صَبَرُوا حَتَّى تَخْرُجَ إِلَيْهِمْ لَكَانَ خَيْرًا لَّهُمْ وَاللّٰهُ غَفُورٌ رَّحِيمٌ ۝

6 O ye who believe! If an evil-liver bring you tidings,[1] verify it, lest ye smite some folk in ignorance and afterward repent of what ye did.

يَا أَيُّهَا الَّذِينَ آمَنُوا إِنْ جَاءَكُمْ فَاسِقٌ بِنَبَإٍ فَتَبَيَّنُوا أَنْ تُصِيبُوا قَوْمًا بِجَهَالَةٍ فَتُصْبِحُوا عَلَى مَا فَعَلْتُمْ نَادِمِينَ ۝

7 And know that the messenger of Allah is among you. If he were to obey you in many of the affairs, ye would surely be in trouble; but Allah hath endeared the faith to you and hath beautified it in your hearts, and hath made disbelief and lewdness and rebellion hateful unto you. Such are they who are rightly guided.

وَاعْلَمُوا أَنَّ فِيكُمْ رَسُولَ اللّٰهِ لَوْ يُطِيعُكُمْ فِي كَثِيرٍ مِّنَ الْأَمْرِ لَعَنِتُّمْ وَلَكِنَّ اللّٰهَ حَبَّبَ إِلَيْكُمُ الْإِيمَانَ وَزَيَّنَهُ فِي قُلُوبِكُمْ وَكَرَّهَ إِلَيْكُمُ الْكُفْرَ وَالْفُسُوقَ وَالْعِصْيَانَ أُولَٰئِكَ هُمُ الرَّاشِدُونَ ۝

8 (It is) a bounty and a grace from Allah; and Allah is Knower, Wise.

فَضْلًا مِّنَ اللّٰهِ وَنِعْمَةً وَاللّٰهُ عَلِيمٌ حَكِيمٌ ۝

9 And if two parties of believers fall to fighting, then make peace between them. And if one party of them doeth wrong to the other, fight

وَإِنْ طَائِفَتَانِ مِنَ الْمُؤْمِنِينَ اقْتَتَلُوا فَأَصْلِحُوا بَيْنَهُمَا فَإِنْ بَغَتْ إِحْدَاهُمَا عَلَى الْأُخْرَى فَقَاتِلُوا

---

1. The reference is to a man who brought false news of a revolt of the subject Jews of Khaybar.

ye that which doeth wrong till it return unto the ordinance of Allah; then, if it return, make peace between them justly, and act equitably. Lo! Allah loveth the equitable.

أَلَّتِي تَبْغِي حَتَّى تَفِيءَ إِلَىٰ أَمْرِ اللَّهِ فَإِن فَاءَتْ فَأَصْلِحُوا بَيْنَهُمَا بِالْعَدْلِ وَأَقْسِطُوا إِنَّ اللَّهَ يُحِبُّ الْمُقْسِطِينَ ﴿٩﴾

10 The believers are naught else than brothers. Therefore make peace between your brethren and observe your duty to Allah that haply ye may obtain mercy.

إِنَّمَا الْمُؤْمِنُونَ إِخْوَةٌ فَأَصْلِحُوا بَيْنَ أَخَوَيْكُمْ وَاتَّقُوا اللَّهَ لَعَلَّكُمْ تُرْحَمُونَ ﴿١٠﴾

11 O ye who believe! Let not a folk deride a folk who may be better than they (are), nor let women (deride) women who may be better than they are; neither defame one another, nor insult one another by nicknames. Bad is the name of lewdness after faith. And whoso turneth not in repentance, such are evil-doers.

يَٰٓأَيُّهَا الَّذِينَ ءَامَنُوا لَا يَسْخَرْ قَوْمٌ مِّن قَوْمٍ عَسَىٰ أَن يَكُونُوا خَيْرًا مِّنْهُمْ وَلَا نِسَآءٌ مِّن نِّسَآءٍ عَسَىٰ أَن يَكُنَّ خَيْرًا مِّنْهُنَّ وَلَا تَلْمِزُوا أَنفُسَكُمْ وَلَا تَنَابَزُوا بِالْأَلْقَٰبِ بِئْسَ الِاسْمُ الْفُسُوقُ بَعْدَ الْإِيمَٰنِ وَمَن لَّمْ يَتُبْ فَأُو۟لَٰٓئِكَ هُمُ الظَّٰلِمُونَ ﴿١١﴾

12 O ye who believe! Shun much suspicion; for lo! some suspicion is a crime. And spy not, neither backbite one another. Would one of you love to eat the flesh of his dead brother that ye would abhor it? And keep your duty (to Allah). Lo! Allah is Relenting, Merciful.

يَٰٓأَيُّهَا الَّذِينَ ءَامَنُوا اجْتَنِبُوا كَثِيرًا مِّنَ الظَّنِّ إِنَّ بَعْضَ الظَّنِّ إِثْمٌ وَلَا تَجَسَّسُوا وَلَا يَغْتَب بَّعْضُكُم بَعْضًا أَيُحِبُّ أَحَدُكُمْ أَن يَأْكُلَ لَحْمَ أَخِيهِ مَيْتًا فَكَرِهْتُمُوهُ وَاتَّقُوا اللَّهَ إِنَّ اللَّهَ تَوَّابٌ رَّحِيمٌ ﴿١٢﴾

13 O mankind! Lo! We have created you from a male and a female, and have made you nations and tribes that ye may know one another. Lo! the noblest of you, in the sight of Allah, is the best in conduct. Lo! Allah is Knower, Aware.

يَٰٓأَيُّهَا النَّاسُ إِنَّا خَلَقْنَٰكُم مِّن ذَكَرٍ وَأُنثَىٰ وَجَعَلْنَٰكُمْ شُعُوبًا وَقَبَآئِلَ لِتَعَارَفُوا إِنَّ أَكْرَمَكُمْ عِندَ اللَّهِ أَتْقَىٰكُمْ إِنَّ اللَّهَ عَلِيمٌ خَبِيرٌ ﴿١٣﴾

14 The wandering Arabs say: We believe. Say (unto them, O Muḥammad): Ye believe not, but rather say "We submit," for the faith hath not yet entered into your hearts. Yet, if ye obey Allah and His messenger, He will not withhold from you aught of (the reward of) your deeds. Lo! Allah is Forgiving, Merciful.

15 The (true) believers are those only who believe in Allah and His messenger and afterward doubt not, but strive with their wealth and their lives for the cause of Allah. Such are the truthful.

16 Say (unto them, O Muḥammad): Would ye teach Allah your religion, when Allah knoweth all that is in the heavens and all that is in the earth, and Allah is Aware of all things?

17 They make it favour unto thee (Muḥammad) that they have surrendered (unto Him). Say: Deem not your Surrender a favour unto me; nay, but Allah doth confer a favour on you, inasmuch as He hath led you to the Faith, if ye are truthful.

18 Lo! Allah knoweth the Unseen of the heavens and the earth. And Allah is Seer of what ye do.

۞ قَالَتِ ٱلْأَعْرَابُ ءَامَنَّا قُل لَّمْ تُؤْمِنُوا۟ وَلَٰكِن قُولُوٓا۟ أَسْلَمْنَا وَلَمَّا يَدْخُلِ ٱلْإِيمَٰنُ فِى قُلُوبِكُمْ وَإِن تُطِيعُوا۟ ٱللَّهَ وَرَسُولَهُۥ لَا يَلِتْكُم مِّنْ أَعْمَٰلِكُمْ شَيْـًٔا إِنَّ ٱللَّهَ غَفُورٌ رَّحِيمٌ ۝

إِنَّمَا ٱلْمُؤْمِنُونَ ٱلَّذِينَ ءَامَنُوا۟ بِٱللَّهِ وَرَسُولِهِۦ ثُمَّ لَمْ يَرْتَابُوا۟ وَجَٰهَدُوا۟ بِأَمْوَٰلِهِمْ وَأَنفُسِهِمْ فِى سَبِيلِ ٱللَّهِ أُو۟لَٰٓئِكَ هُمُ ٱلصَّٰدِقُونَ ۝

قُلْ أَتُعَلِّمُونَ ٱللَّهَ بِدِينِكُمْ وَٱللَّهُ يَعْلَمُ مَا فِى ٱلسَّمَٰوَٰتِ وَمَا فِى ٱلْأَرْضِ وَٱللَّهُ بِكُلِّ شَىْءٍ عَلِيمٌ ۝

يَمُنُّونَ عَلَيْكَ أَنْ أَسْلَمُوٓا۟ قُل لَّا تَمُنُّوا۟ عَلَىَّ إِسْلَٰمَكُم بَلِ ٱللَّهُ يَمُنُّ عَلَيْكُمْ أَنْ هَدَىٰكُمْ لِلْإِيمَٰنِ إِن كُنتُمْ صَٰدِقِينَ ۝

إِنَّ ٱللَّهَ يَعْلَمُ غَيْبَ ٱلسَّمَٰوَٰتِ وَٱلْأَرْضِ وَٱللَّهُ بَصِيرٌ بِمَا تَعْمَلُونَ ۝

Qāf

Qāf takes its name from the letter of the Arabic alphabet which stands alone at the beginning of the first verse.

It belongs to the middle group of Makkan sūrahs.

سُوْرَةُ قٓ

In the name of Allah, the Beneficent, the Merciful.

بِسْمِ اللَّهِ الرَّحْمَنِ الرَّحِيمِ

1 Qāf. By the glorious Qur'an,

قٓ وَالْقُرْآنِ الْمَجِيدِ ﴿١﴾

2 Nay, but they marvel that a warner of their own hath come unto them; and the disbelievers say: This is a strange thing:

بَلْ عَجِبُوا أَنْ جَاءَهُمْ مُنْذِرٌ مِنْهُمْ فَقَالَ الْكَافِرُونَ هَذَا شَيْءٌ عَجِيبٌ ﴿٢﴾

3 When we are dead and have become dust (shall we be brought back again)? That would be a far return!

أَءِذَا مِتْنَا وَكُنَّا تُرَابًا ذَلِكَ رَجْعٌ بَعِيدٌ ﴿٣﴾

4 We know that which the earth taketh of them[1], and with Us is a recording Book.

قَدْ عَلِمْنَا مَا تَنْقُصُ الْأَرْضُ مِنْهُمْ وَعِنْدَنَا كِتَابٌ حَفِيظٌ ﴿٤﴾

5 Nay, but they have denied the truth when it came unto them, therefore they are now in troubled case.

بَلْ كَذَّبُوا بِالْحَقِّ لَمَّا جَاءَهُمْ فَهُمْ فِي أَمْرٍ مَرِيجٍ ﴿٥﴾

6 Have they not then observed the sky above them, how We have

أَفَلَمْ يَنْظُرُوا إِلَى السَّمَاءِ فَوْقَهُمْ كَيْفَ بَنَيْنَاهَا

---

1. *i.e.* those of them who die and are buried in the earth.

747

وَزَيَّنَّاهَا وَمَا لَهَا مِن فُرُوجٍ ۝

constructed it and beautified it, and how there are no rifts therein?

وَالْأَرْضَ مَدَدْنَاهَا وَأَلْقَيْنَا فِيهَا رَوَاسِيَ وَأَنْبَتْنَا فِيهَا مِن كُلِّ زَوْجٍ بَهِيجٍ ۝

7 And the earth have We spread out, and have flung firm hills therein, and have caused of every lovely kind to grow thereon,

تَبْصِرَةً وَذِكْرَى لِكُلِّ عَبْدٍ مُّنِيبٍ ۝

8 A vision and a reminder for every penitent slave.

وَنَزَّلْنَا مِنَ السَّمَاءِ مَاءً مُّبَارَكًا فَأَنبَتْنَا بِهِ جَنَّاتٍ وَحَبَّ الْحَصِيدِ ۝

9 And We send down from the sky blessed water whereby We give growth unto gardens and the grain of crops,

وَالنَّخْلَ بَاسِقَاتٍ لَّهَا طَلْعٌ نَّضِيدٌ ۝

10 And lofty date-palms with ranged clusters,

رِزْقًا لِّلْعِبَادِ وَأَحْيَيْنَا بِهِ بَلْدَةً مَّيْتًا كَذَلِكَ الْخُرُوجُ ۝

11 Provision (made) for men; and therewith We quicken a dead land. Even so will be the resurrection of the dead.

كَذَّبَتْ قَبْلَهُمْ قَوْمُ نُوحٍ وَأَصْحَابُ الرَّسِّ وَثَمُودُ ۝

12 The folk of Noah denied (the truth) before them, and (so did) the dwellers at Ar-Rass and (the tribe of) Thamūd,

وَعَادٌ وَفِرْعَوْنُ وَإِخْوَانُ لُوطٍ ۝

13 And (the tribe of) ‘Ād, and Pharaoh, and the brethren of Lot,

وَأَصْحَابُ الْأَيْكَةِ وَقَوْمُ تُبَّعٍ كُلٌّ كَذَّبَ الرُّسُلَ فَحَقَّ وَعِيدِ ۝

14 And the dwellers in the wood,[2] and the folk of Tubba‘:[3] every one denied the messengers, therefore My threat took effect.

أَفَعَيِينَا بِالْخَلْقِ الْأَوَّلِ بَلْ هُمْ فِي لَبْسٍ مِّنْ خَلْقٍ جَدِيدٍ ۝

15 Were We then worn out by the first creation? Yet they are in doubt about a new creation.

---

2. Madyan.

3. The name of a famous dynasty in Al-Yaman.

16 We verily created a man and We know what his soul whispereth to him, and We are nearer to him than his jugular vein.

وَلَقَدْ خَلَقْنَا الْإِنسَانَ وَنَعْلَمُ مَا تُوَسْوِسُ بِهِ نَفْسُهُ ۖ وَنَحْنُ أَقْرَبُ إِلَيْهِ مِنْ حَبْلِ الْوَرِيدِ ۝

17 When the two Receivers receive (him), seated on the right hand and on the left,

إِذْ يَتَلَقَّى الْمُتَلَقِّيَانِ عَنِ الْيَمِينِ وَعَنِ الشِّمَالِ قَعِيدٌ ۝

18 He uttereth no word but there is with him an observer ready.

مَا يَلْفِظُ مِن قَوْلٍ إِلَّا لَدَيْهِ رَقِيبٌ عَتِيدٌ ۝

19 And the agony of death cometh in truth. (And it is said unto him): This is that which thou wast wont to shun.

وَجَآءَتْ سَكْرَةُ الْمَوْتِ بِالْحَقِّ ۖ ذَٰلِكَ مَا كُنتَ مِنْهُ تَحِيدُ ۝

20 And the trumpet is blown. This is the threatened Day.

وَنُفِخَ فِي الصُّورِ ۚ ذَٰلِكَ يَوْمُ الْوَعِيدِ ۝

21 And every soul cometh, along with it a driver and a witness

وَجَآءَتْ كُلُّ نَفْسٍ مَّعَهَا سَآئِقٌ وَشَهِيدٌ ۝

22 (And unto the evil-doer it is said): Thou wast in heedlessness of this. Now We have removed from thee thy covering, and piercing is thy sight this day.

لَّقَدْ كُنتَ فِي غَفْلَةٍ مِّنْ هَٰذَا فَكَشَفْنَا عَنكَ غِطَآءَكَ فَبَصَرُكَ الْيَوْمَ حَدِيدٌ ۝

23 And (unto the evil-doer) his comrade saith: This is that which I have ready (as testimony).

وَقَالَ قَرِينُهُ هَٰذَا مَا لَدَيَّ عَتِيدٌ ۝

24 (And it is said): Do ye twain[4] hurl to hell each rebel ingrate,

أَلْقِيَا فِي جَهَنَّمَ كُلَّ كَفَّارٍ عَنِيدٍ ۝

25 Hinderer of good, transgressor, doubter,

مَّنَّاعٍ لِّلْخَيْرِ مُعْتَدٍ مُّرِيبٍ ۝

26 Who setteth up another god along with Allah. Do ye twain hurl him to the dreadful doom.

الَّذِي جَعَلَ مَعَ اللَّهِ إِلَٰهًا آخَرَ فَأَلْقِيَاهُ فِي الْعَذَابِ الشَّدِيدِ ۝

---

4. The driver and the witness (v. 21) or the two Receivers (v.17).

27 His comrade saith: Our Lord! I did not cause him to rebel, but he was (himself) far gone in error.

28 He saith: Contend not in My presence, when I had already proffered unto you the warning.

29 The sentence that cometh from Me cannot be changed, and I am in no wise a tyrant unto the slaves.

30 On the day when We say unto hell: Art thou filled? and it saith: Can there be more to come?

31 And the Garden is brought nigh for those who kept from evil, no longer distant.

32 (And it is said): That is that which ye were promised. (It is) for every penitent and heedful one,

33 Who feareth the Beneficent in secret and cometh with a contrite heart.

34 Enter it in peace. This is the day of immortality.

35 There they have all that they desire, and there is more with Us.

36 And how many a generation We destroyed before them, who were mightier than these in prowess so that they overran the lands! Had they any place of refuge (when the judgement came)?

37 Lo! therein verily is a reminder for him who hath a heart, or giveth ear with full intelligence.

38 And verily We created the heavens and the earth, and all that is between them, in six days,[5] and naught of weariness touched Us.

وَلَقَدْ خَلَقْنَا السَّمَٰوَٰتِ وَالْأَرْضَ وَمَا بَيْنَهُمَا فِي سِتَّةِ أَيَّامٍ وَمَا مَسَّنَا مِن لُّغُوبٍ ﴿٣٨﴾

39 Therefore (O Muhammad) bear with what they say: and hymn the praise of thy Lord before the rising and before the setting of the sun;

فَاصْبِرْ عَلَىٰ مَا يَقُولُونَ وَسَبِّحْ بِحَمْدِ رَبِّكَ قَبْلَ طُلُوعِ الشَّمْسِ وَقَبْلَ الْغُرُوبِ ﴿٣٩﴾

40 And in the night time hymn His praise: And after the (prescribed) prostrations.

وَمِنَ اللَّيْلِ فَسَبِّحْهُ وَأَدْبَٰرَ السُّجُودِ ﴿٤٠﴾

41 And listen on the day when the crier crieth from a near place,

وَاسْتَمِعْ يَوْمَ يُنَادِ الْمُنَادِ مِن مَّكَانٍ قَرِيبٍ ﴿٤١﴾

42 The day when they will hear the (Awful) Cry in truth. That is the day of coming forth (from the graves).

يَوْمَ يَسْمَعُونَ الصَّيْحَةَ بِالْحَقِّ ذَٰلِكَ يَوْمُ الْخُرُوجِ ﴿٤٢﴾

43 Lo! We it is Who quicken and give death, and unto Us is the journeying.

إِنَّا نَحْنُ نُحْيِي وَنُمِيتُ وَإِلَيْنَا الْمَصِيرُ ﴿٤٣﴾

44 On the day when the earth splitteth asunder from them, hastening forth (they come). That is a gathering easy for Us (to make).

يَوْمَ تَشَقَّقُ الْأَرْضُ عَنْهُمْ سِرَاعًا ذَٰلِكَ حَشْرٌ عَلَيْنَا يَسِيرٌ ﴿٤٤﴾

45 We are best aware of what they say, and thou (O Muhammad) art in no wise a compeller over them. But warn by the Qur'an him who feareth My threat.

نَّحْنُ أَعْلَمُ بِمَا يَقُولُونَ وَمَا أَنتَ عَلَيْهِم بِجَبَّارٍ فَذَكِّرْ بِالْقُرْآنِ مَن يَخَافُ وَعِيدِ ﴿٤٥﴾

---

5. (22: 47); (32: 5); (70: 4).

Adh Dhāriyāt
(The Winnowing Winds)

Adh Dhāriyāt, "The Winnowing Winds," takes its name from a word in v. 1. I have followed the usual interpretation of the first four verses, but they may also be taken as all referring to winds or to angels.

An early Makkan sūrah.

In the name of Allah, the Beneficent, the Merciful.

1 By those that winnow with a winnowing

2 And those that bear the burden (of the rain)

3 And those that glide with ease (upon the sea)

4 And those who distribute (blessings) by command,

5 Lo! that wherewith ye are threatened is indeed true,

6 And lo! the judgement will indeed befall.

7 By the heaven full of paths,

8 Lo! ye, forsooth, are of various opinion (concerning the truth).

9 He is made to turn away from it who is (himself) averse.

752

قُتِلَ ٱلۡخَرَّصُونَ ۝

10 Accursed be the conjecturers.

ٱلَّذِينَ هُمۡ فِى غَمۡرَةٍ سَاهُونَ ۝

11 Who are careless in an abyss!

يَسۡـَٔلُونَ أَيَّانَ يَوۡمُ ٱلدِّينِ ۝

12 They ask: When is the Day of Judgement?

يَوۡمَ هُمۡ عَلَى ٱلنَّارِ يُفۡتَنُونَ ۝

13 (It is) the day when they will be tormented at the Fire,

ذُوقُوا۟ فِتۡنَتَكُمۡ هَٰذَا ٱلَّذِى كُنتُم بِهِۦ تَسۡتَعۡجِلُونَ ۝

14 (And it will be said unto them): Taste your torment (which ye inflicted). This is what ye sought to hasten.

إِنَّ ٱلۡمُتَّقِينَ فِى جَنَّٰتٍ وَعُيُونٍ ۝

15 Lo! those who keep from evil will dwell amid gardens and water-springs.

ءَاخِذِينَ مَآ ءَاتَىٰهُمۡ رَبُّهُمۡ إِنَّهُمۡ كَانُوا۟ قَبۡلَ ذَٰلِكَ مُحۡسِنِينَ ۝

16 Taking that which their Lord giveth them; for lo! aforetime they were doers of good;

كَانُوا۟ قَلِيلًا مِّنَ ٱلَّيۡلِ مَا يَهۡجَعُونَ ۝

17 They used to sleep but little of the night,

وَبِٱلۡأَسۡحَارِ هُمۡ يَسۡتَغۡفِرُونَ ۝

18 And ere the dawning of each day would seek forgiveness,

وَفِىٓ أَمۡوَٰلِهِمۡ حَقٌّ لِّلسَّآئِلِ وَٱلۡمَحۡرُومِ ۝

19 And in their wealth the beggar and the outcast had due share.

وَفِى ٱلۡأَرۡضِ ءَايَٰتٌ لِّلۡمُوقِنِينَ ۝

20 And in the earth are portents for those whose faith is sure,

وَفِىٓ أَنفُسِكُمۡ أَفَلَا تُبۡصِرُونَ ۝

21 And (also) in yourselves. Can ye then not see?

وَفِى ٱلسَّمَآءِ رِزۡقُكُمۡ وَمَا تُوعَدُونَ ۝

22 And in the heaven is your providence and that which ye are promised;

فَوَرَبِّ ٱلسَّمَآءِ وَٱلۡأَرۡضِ إِنَّهُۥ لَحَقٌّ مِّثۡلَ مَآ أَنَّكُمۡ تَنطِقُونَ ۝

23 And by the Lord of the heavens and the earth, it is the truth, even as (it is true) that ye speak.

24 Hath the story of Abraham's honoured guests reached thee (O Muhammad)?

هَلْ أَتَاكَ حَدِيثُ ضَيْفِ إِبْرَهِيمَ الْمُكْرَمِينَ ۝

25 When they came in unto him and said: Peace! he answered, Peace! (and thought): Folk unknown (to me).

إِذْ دَخَلُوا عَلَيْهِ فَقَالُوا سَلَمًا قَالَ سَلَمٌ قَوْمٌ مُّنكَرُونَ ۝

26 Then he went apart unto his housefolk so that they brought a fatted calf;

فَرَاغَ إِلَىٰ أَهْلِهِ فَجَآءَ بِعِجْلٍ سَمِينٍ ۝

27 And he set it before them, saying: Will ye not eat?

فَقَرَّبَهُ إِلَيْهِمْ قَالَ أَلَا تَأْكُلُونَ ۝

28 Then he conceived a fear of them. They said: Fear not! and gave him tidings of (the birth of) a wise son.

فَأَوْجَسَ مِنْهُمْ خِيفَةً قَالُوا لَا تَخَفْ وَبَشَّرُوهُ بِغُلَمٍ عَلِيمٍ ۝

29 Then his wife came forward, making moan, and smote her face, and cried: A barren old woman!

فَأَقْبَلَتِ امْرَأَتُهُ فِي صَرَّةٍ فَصَكَّتْ وَجْهَهَا وَقَالَتْ عَجُوزٌ عَقِيمٌ ۝

30 They said: Even so saith thy Lord. Lo! He is the Wise, the Knower.

قَالُوا كَذَٰلِكِ قَالَ رَبُّكِ إِنَّهُ هُوَ الْحَكِيمُ الْعَلِيمُ ۝

31 (Abraham) said: And (afterward) what is your errand, O ye sent (from Allah)?

۞ قَالَ فَمَا خَطْبُكُمْ أَيُّهَا الْمُرْسَلُونَ ۝

32 They said: Lo! we are sent unto a guilty folk,

قَالُوا إِنَّا أُرْسِلْنَا إِلَىٰ قَوْمٍ مُّجْرِمِينَ ۝

33 That we may send upon them stones of clay,

لِنُرْسِلَ عَلَيْهِمْ حِجَارَةً مِّن طِينٍ ۝

34 Marked by thy Lord for (the destruction of) the wanton.

مُّسَوَّمَةً عِندَ رَبِّكَ لِلْمُسْرِفِينَ ۝

35 Then We brought forth such believers as were there.

فَأَخْرَجْنَا مَن كَانَ فِيهَا مِنَ الْمُؤْمِنِينَ ۝

36 But We found there but one house of those surrendered[1] (to Allah).

فَمَا وَجَدْنَا فِيهَا غَيْرَ بَيْتٍ مِّنَ ٱلْمُسْلِمِينَ ۝

37 And We left behind therein a portent for those who fear a painful doom.

وَتَرَكْنَا فِيهَآ ءَايَةً لِّلَّذِينَ يَخَافُونَ ٱلْعَذَابَ ٱلْأَلِيمَ ۝

38 And in Moses (too, there is a portent) when We sent him unto Pharaoh with clear warrant,

وَفِى مُوسَىٰٓ إِذْ أَرْسَلْنَٰهُ إِلَىٰ فِرْعَوْنَ بِسُلْطَٰنٍ مُّبِينٍ ۝

39 But he withdrew (confiding) in his might, and said: A wizard or a madman.

فَتَوَلَّىٰ بِرُكْنِهِۦ وَقَالَ سَٰحِرٌ أَوْ مَجْنُونٌ ۝

40 So We seized him and his hosts and flung them in the sea, for he was reprobate.

فَأَخَذْنَٰهُ وَجُنُودَهُۥ فَنَبَذْنَٰهُمْ فِى ٱلْيَمِّ وَهُوَ مُلِيمٌ ۝

41 And in (the tribe of) ʿĀd (there is a portent) when We sent the fatal wind against them.

وَفِى عَادٍ إِذْ أَرْسَلْنَا عَلَيْهِمُ ٱلرِّيحَ ٱلْعَقِيمَ ۝

42 It spared naught that it reached, but made it (all) as dust.

مَا تَذَرُ مِن شَىْءٍ أَتَتْ عَلَيْهِ إِلَّا جَعَلَتْهُ كَٱلرَّمِيمِ ۝

43 And in (the tribe of) Thamūd (there is a portent) when it was told them: Take your ease awhile.

وَفِى ثَمُودَ إِذْ قِيلَ لَهُمْ تَمَتَّعُوا۟ حَتَّىٰ حِينٍ ۝

44 But they rebelled against their Lord's decree, and so the thunderbolt overtook them even while they gazed;

فَعَتَوْا۟ عَنْ أَمْرِ رَبِّهِمْ فَأَخَذَتْهُمُ ٱلصَّٰعِقَةُ وَهُمْ يَنظُرُونَ ۝

45 And they were unable to rise up, nor could they help themselves.

فَمَا ٱسْتَطَٰعُوا۟ مِن قِيَامٍ وَمَا كَانُوا۟ مُنتَصِرِينَ ۝

46 And the folk of Noah aforetime. Lo! they were licentious folk.

وَقَوْمَ نُوحٍ مِّن قَبْلُ إِنَّهُمْ كَانُوا۟ قَوْمًا فَٰسِقِينَ ۝

---

1. Ar. *Muslimīn.*

47 We have built the heaven with might, and We it is who make the vast extent (thereof).

وَالسَّمَآءَ بَنَيْنَاهَا بِأَيْدٍ وَإِنَّا لَمُوسِعُونَ ﴿٤٧﴾

48 And the earth have We laid out, how gracious was the Spreader (thereof)!

وَالْأَرْضَ فَرَشْنَاهَا فَنِعْمَ الْمَاهِدُونَ ﴿٤٨﴾

49 And all things We have created by pairs, that haply ye may reflect.

وَمِن كُلِّ شَيْءٍ خَلَقْنَا زَوْجَيْنِ لَعَلَّكُمْ تَذَكَّرُونَ ﴿٤٩﴾

50 Therefore flee unto Allah; lo! I² am a plain warner unto you from Him

فَفِرُّوٓا إِلَى اللَّهِ إِنِّى لَكُم مِّنْهُ نَذِيرٌ مُّبِينٌ ﴿٥٠﴾

51 And set not any other god along with Allah; lo! I am a plain warner unto you from Him.

وَلَا تَجْعَلُوا مَعَ اللَّهِ إِلَٰهًا ءَاخَرَ إِنِّى لَكُم مِّنْهُ نَذِيرٌ مُّبِينٌ ﴿٥١﴾

52 Even so there came no messenger unto those before them but they said: A wizard or a madman!

كَذَٰلِكَ مَآ أَتَى الَّذِينَ مِن قَبْلِهِم مِّن رَّسُولٍ إِلَّا قَالُوا سَاحِرٌ أَوْ مَجْنُونٌ ﴿٥٢﴾

53 Have they handed down (the saying) as an heirloom one unto another? Nay, but they are froward folk.

أَتَوَاصَوْا بِهِۦ بَلْ هُمْ قَوْمٌ طَاغُونَ ﴿٥٣﴾

54 So withdraw from them (O Muhammad), for thou art in no wise blameworthy,

فَتَوَلَّ عَنْهُمْ فَمَآ أَنتَ بِمَلُومٍ ﴿٥٤﴾

55 And warn, for warning profiteth believers.

وَذَكِّرْ فَإِنَّ الذِّكْرَىٰ تَنفَعُ الْمُؤْمِنِينَ ﴿٥٥﴾

56 I created the jinn and humankind only that they might worship Me.

وَمَا خَلَقْتُ الْجِنَّ وَالْإِنسَ إِلَّا لِيَعْبُدُونِ ﴿٥٦﴾

---

2. The revealing angel, it would appear.

57 I seek no livelihood from them, nor do I ask that they should feed Me.

مَآ أُرِيدُ مِنْهُم مِّن رِّزْقٍ وَمَآ أُرِيدُ أَن يُطْعِمُونِ ۝

58 Lo! Allah! He it is that giveth livelihood, the Lord of unbreakable might.

إِنَّ ٱللَّهَ هُوَ ٱلرَّزَّاقُ ذُو ٱلْقُوَّةِ ٱلْمَتِينُ ۝

59 And lo! for those who (now) do wrong there is an evil day like unto the evil day (which came for) their likes (of old); so let them not ask Me to hasten on (that day).

فَإِنَّ لِلَّذِينَ ظَلَمُوا ذَنُوبًا مِّثْلَ ذَنُوبِ أَصْحَٰبِهِمْ فَلَا يَسْتَعْجِلُونِ ۝

60 And woe unto those who disbelieve, from (that) their day which they are promised.

فَوَيْلٌ لِّلَّذِينَ كَفَرُوا مِن يَوْمِهِمُ ٱلَّذِي يُوعَدُونَ ۝

At Ṭūr
(The Mount)

At Ṭūr, "The Mount," takes name from the opening verse.

An early Makkan sūrah.

In the name of Allah, the Beneficent, the Merciful.

1 By the Mount,

2 And a Scripture inscribed

3 On fine parchment unrolled,

4 And the House frequented,

5 And the roof exalted,

6 And the sea kept filled,

7 Lo! the doom of thy Lord will surely come to pass;

8 There is none that can ward it off.

9 On the day when the heaven will heave with (awful) heaving,

10 And the mountains move away with (awful) movement,

11 Then woe that day unto the deniers

12 Who play in vain talk.

758

13 The day when they are thrust with a (disdainful) thrust, into the fire of hell.

يَوْمَ يُدَعُّونَ إِلَى نَارِ جَهَنَّمَ دَعًّا ۝

14 (And it is said unto them): This is the Fire which ye were wont to deny.

هَذِهِ النَّارُ الَّتِي كُنتُم بِهَا تُكَذِّبُونَ ۝

15 Is this magic, or do ye not see?

أَفَسِحْرٌ هَذَا أَمْ أَنتُمْ لَا تُبْصِرُونَ ۝

16 Endure the heat thereof, and whether ye are patient of it or impatient of it is all one for you. Ye are only being paid for what ye used to do.

اصْلَوْهَا فَاصْبِرُوا أَوْ لَا تَصْبِرُوا سَوَاءٌ عَلَيْكُمْ إِنَّمَا تُجْزَوْنَ مَا كُنتُمْ تَعْمَلُونَ ۝

17 Lo! those who kept their duty dwell in gardens and delight,

إِنَّ الْمُتَّقِينَ فِي جَنَّاتٍ وَنَعِيمٍ ۝

18 Happy because of what their Lord hath given them, and (because) their Lord hath warded off from them the torment of hell fire.

فَكِهِينَ بِمَا آتَاهُمْ رَبُّهُمْ وَوَقَاهُمْ رَبُّهُمْ عَذَابَ الْجَحِيمِ ۝

19 (And it is said unto them): Eat and drink in health (as reward) for what ye used to do,

كُلُوا وَاشْرَبُوا هَنِيئًا بِمَا كُنتُمْ تَعْمَلُونَ ۝

20 Reclining on ranged couches. And We wed them unto fair ones with wide, lovely eyes.

مُتَّكِئِينَ عَلَى سُرُرٍ مَّصْفُوفَةٍ وَزَوَّجْنَاهُم بِحُورٍ عِينٍ ۝

21 And they who believe and whose seed follow them in faith, We cause their seed to join them (there), and We deprive them of naught of their (life's) work. Every man is a pledge for that which he hath earned.

وَالَّذِينَ آمَنُوا وَاتَّبَعَتْهُمْ ذُرِّيَّتُهُم بِإِيمَانٍ أَلْحَقْنَا بِهِمْ ذُرِّيَّتَهُمْ وَمَا أَلَتْنَاهُم مِّنْ عَمَلِهِم مِّن شَيْءٍ كُلُّ امْرِئٍ بِمَا كَسَبَ رَهِينٌ ۝

22 And We provide them with fruit and meat such as they desire.

وَأَمْدَدْنَاهُم بِفَاكِهَةٍ وَلَحْمٍ مِّمَّا يَشْتَهُونَ ۝

23 There they pass from hand to hand a cup wherein is neither vanity nor cause of sin.

24 And there go round, waiting on them menservants of their own, as they were hidden pearls.

25 And some of them draw near unto others, questioning,

26 Saying: Lo! of old, when we were with our families, we were ever anxious;

27 But Allah hath been gracious unto us and hath preserved us from the torment of the breath of Fire.

28 Lo! we used to pray unto Him of old. Lo! He is the Benign, the Merciful.

29 Therefore warn (men, O Muhammad). By the grace of Allah thou art neither soothsayer nor madman.

30 Or say they: (He is) a poet, (one) for whom we may expect the accident of time?

31 Say (unto them): Expect (your fill)! Lo! I am with you among the expectant.

32 Do their minds command them to do this, or are they an outrageous folk?

33 Or say they: He hath invented it? Nay, but they will not believe!

34 Then let them produce speech the like thereof, if they are truthful.

يَتَنَازَعُونَ فِيهَا كَأْسًا لَّا لَغْوٌ فِيهَا وَلَا تَأْثِيمٌ ۝

۞ وَيَطُوفُ عَلَيْهِمْ غِلْمَانٌ لَّهُمْ كَأَنَّهُمْ لُؤْلُؤٌ مَّكْنُونٌ ۝

وَأَقْبَلَ بَعْضُهُمْ عَلَىٰ بَعْضٍ يَتَسَاءَلُونَ ۝

قَالُوٓا إِنَّا كُنَّا قَبْلُ فِىٓ أَهْلِنَا مُشْفِقِينَ ۝

فَمَنَّ ٱللَّهُ عَلَيْنَا وَوَقَىٰنَا عَذَابَ ٱلسَّمُومِ ۝

إِنَّا كُنَّا مِن قَبْلُ نَدْعُوهُ إِنَّهُ هُوَ ٱلْبَرُّ ٱلرَّحِيمُ ۝

فَذَكِّرْ فَمَآ أَنتَ بِنِعْمَتِ رَبِّكَ بِكَاهِنٍ وَلَا مَجْنُونٍ ۝

أَمْ يَقُولُونَ شَاعِرٌ نَّتَرَبَّصُ بِهِ رَيْبَ ٱلْمَنُونِ ۝

قُلْ تَرَبَّصُوا فَإِنِّى مَعَكُم مِّنَ ٱلْمُتَرَبِّصِينَ ۝

أَمْ تَأْمُرُهُمْ أَحْلَامُهُم بِهَٰذَآ أَمْ هُمْ قَوْمٌ طَاغُونَ ۝

أَمْ يَقُولُونَ تَقَوَّلَهُ بَل لَّا يُؤْمِنُونَ ۝

فَلْيَأْتُوا بِحَدِيثٍ مِّثْلِهِ إِن كَانُوا صَادِقِينَ ۝

35 Or were they created out of naught? Or are they the creators?

أَمْ خُلِقُوا مِنْ غَيْرِ شَيْءٍ أَمْ هُمُ الْخَالِقُونَ ۝

36 Or did they create the heavens and the earth? Nay, but they are sure of nothing!

أَمْ خَلَقُوا السَّمَوَاتِ وَالْأَرْضَ بَل لَّا يُوقِنُونَ ۝

37 Or do they own the treasures of thy Lord? Or have they been given charge (thereof)?

أَمْ عِنْدَهُمْ خَزَائِنُ رَبِّكَ أَمْ هُمُ الْمُصَيْطِرُونَ ۝

38 Or have they any stairway (unto heaven) by means of which they overhear (decrees). Then let their listener produce warrant manifest!

أَمْ لَهُمْ سُلَّمٌ يَسْتَمِعُونَ فِيهِ فَلْيَأْتِ مُسْتَمِعُهُم بِسُلْطَانٍ مُّبِينٍ ۝

39 Or hath He daughters whereas ye have sons?

أَمْ لَهُ الْبَنَاتُ وَلَكُمُ الْبَنُونَ ۝

40 Or askest thou (Muhammad) a fee from them so that they are plunged in debt?

أَمْ تَسْأَلُهُمْ أَجْرًا فَهُم مِّن مَّغْرَمٍ مُّثْقَلُونَ ۝

41 Or possess they the Unseen so that they can write (it) down?

أَمْ عِنْدَهُمُ الْغَيْبُ فَهُمْ يَكْتُبُونَ ۝

42 Or seek they to ensnare (the messenger)? But those who disbelieve, they are the ensnared!

أَمْ يُرِيدُونَ كَيْدًا فَالَّذِينَ كَفَرُوا هُمُ الْمَكِيدُونَ ۝

43 Or have they any god beside Allah? Glorified be Allah from all that they ascribe as partner (unto Him)!

أَمْ لَهُمْ إِلَهٌ غَيْرُ اللَّهِ سُبْحَانَ اللَّهِ عَمَّا يُشْرِكُونَ ۝

44 And if they were to see a fragment of the heaven falling, they would say: A heap of clouds.

وَإِن يَرَوْا كِسْفًا مِّنَ السَّمَاءِ سَاقِطًا يَقُولُوا سَحَابٌ مَّرْكُومٌ ۝

45 Then let them be (O Muhammad), till they meet their day, in which they will be thunderstricken,

فَذَرْهُمْ حَتَّى يُلَاقُوا يَوْمَهُمُ الَّذِي فِيهِ يُصْعَقُونَ ۝

46 A day in which their guile will naught avail them, nor will they be helped.

يَوْمَ لَا يُغْنِي عَنْهُمْ كَيْدُهُمْ شَيْئًا وَّلَا هُمْ يُنْصَرُوْنَ ۝

47 And verily, for those who do wrong, there is a punishment beyond that. But most of them know not.

وَإِنَّ لِلَّذِيْنَ ظَلَمُوْا عَذَابًا دُوْنَ ذٰلِكَ وَلٰكِنَّ اَكْثَرَهُمْ لَا يَعْلَمُوْنَ ۝

48 So wait patiently (O Muhammad) for thy Lord's decree, for surely thou art in Our sight; and hymn the praise of thy Lord when thou uprisest.

وَاصْبِرْ لِحُكْمِ رَبِّكَ فَإِنَّكَ بِأَعْيُنِنَا وَسَبِّحْ بِحَمْدِ رَبِّكَ حِيْنَ تَقُوْمُ ۝

49 And in the night time also hymn His praise, and at the setting of the stars.

وَمِنَ الَّيْلِ فَسَبِّحْهُ وَإِدْبَارَ النُّجُوْمِ ۝

An Najm
(The Star)

An Najm, "The Star," takes its name from a word in the first verse.

An early Makkan sūrah.

In the name of Allah, the
Beneficent, the Merciful.

1 By the Star when it setteth,

2 Your comrade erreth not, nor is
deceived;

3 Nor doth he speak of (his own)
desire.

4 It is naught save an inspiration
that is inspired,

5 Which one of mighty powers
hath taught him,

6 One vigorous; and he grew clear
to view[1]

7 When he was on the uppermost
horizon.

8 Then he drew nigh and came
down;

---

1. This and the five following verses are generally accepted as referring to the
Prophet's vision on Mount Hirā.

9   Till he was (distant) two bows length or even nearer,

فَكَانَ قَابَ قَوْسَيْنِ أَوْأَدْنَى ۝

10   And He revealed unto His slave that which He revealed.

فَأَوْحَى إِلَى عَبْدِهِ مَاأَوْحَى ۝

11   The heart lied not (in seeing) what it saw.

مَاكَذَبَ الْفُؤَادُ مَارَأَى ۝

12   Will ye then dispute with him concerning what he seeth?

أَفَتُمَارُونَهُ عَلَى مَايَرَى ۝

13   And verily he saw him, yet another time[2]

وَلَقَدْ رَءَاهُ نَزْلَةً أُخْرَى ۝

14   By the lote tree of the utmost boundary,

عِندَ سِدْرَةِ الْمُنتَهَى ۝

15   Nigh unto which is the Garden of Abode.

عِندَهَا جَنَّةُ الْمَأْوَى ۝

16   When that which shroudeth did enshroud the lote tree,

إِذْ يَغْشَى السِّدْرَةَ مَايَغْشَى ۝

17   The eye turned not aside nor yet was overbold.

مَازَاغَ الْبَصَرُ وَمَاطَغَى ۝

18   Verily he saw one of the greater portents of his Lord.

لَقَدْ رَأَى مِنْ ءَايَتِ رَبِّهِ الْكُبْرَى ۝

19   Have ye thought upon Al-Lāt[3] and Al-'Uzzā[4];

أَفَرَءَيْتُمُ اللَّتَ وَالْعُزَّى ۝

20   And Manāt,[5] the third, the other?

وَمَنَوةَ الثَّالِثَةَ الْأُخْرَى ۝

21   Are yours the males and His the females?[6]

أَلَكُمُ الذَّكَرُ وَلَهُ الْأُنثَى ۝

---

2. This is generally accepted as a reference to the Prophet's vision in which he ascended through the seven heavens.

3. An idol of the pagan Arabs.

4. An idol of the pagan Arabs.

5. An idol of the pagan Arabs.

6. The pagan Arabs pretended that their idols were daughters of Allah.

22 That indeed were an unfair division!

تِلْكَ إِذًا قِسْمَةٌ ضِيزَى ﴿٢٢﴾

23 They are but names which ye have named, ye and your fathers, for which Allah hath revealed no warrant. They follow but a guess and that which (they) themselves desire. And now the guidance from their Lord hath come unto them.

إِنْ هِيَ إِلَّآ أَسْمَآءٌ سَمَّيْتُمُوهَآ أَنتُمْ وَءَابَآؤُكُم مَّآ أَنزَلَ اللَّهُ بِهَا مِن سُلْطَنٍ إِن يَتَّبِعُونَ إِلَّا ٱلظَّنَّ وَمَا تَهْوَى ٱلْأَنفُسُ وَلَقَدْ جَآءَهُم مِّن رَّبِّهِمُ ٱلْهُدَى ﴿٢٣﴾

24 Or shall man have what he coveteth?

أَمْ لِلْإِنسَنِ مَا تَمَنَّى ﴿٢٤﴾

25 But unto Allah belongeth the after (life), and the former.

فَلِلَّهِ ٱلْآخِرَةُ وَٱلْأُولَى ﴿٢٥﴾

26 And how many angels are in the heavens whose intercession availeth naught save after Allah giveth leave to whom He chooseth and accepteth!

۞ وَكَم مِّن مَّلَكٍ فِي ٱلسَّمَوَتِ لَا تُغْنِي شَفَعَتُهُمْ شَيْئًا إِلَّا مِنۢ بَعْدِ أَن يَأْذَنَ ٱللَّهُ لِمَن يَشَآءُ وَيَرْضَى ﴿٢٦﴾

27 Lo! it is those who disbelieve in the Hereafter who name the angels with the names of females.

إِنَّ ٱلَّذِينَ لَا يُؤْمِنُونَ بِٱلْآخِرَةِ لَيُسَمُّونَ ٱلْمَلَئِكَةَ تَسْمِيَةَ ٱلْأُنثَى ﴿٢٧﴾

28 And they have no knowledge thereof. They follow but a guess, and lo! a guess can never take the place of the truth.

وَمَا لَهُم بِهِ مِنْ عِلْمٍ إِن يَتَّبِعُونَ إِلَّا ٱلظَّنَّ وَإِنَّ ٱلظَّنَّ لَا يُغْنِي مِنَ ٱلْحَقِّ شَيْئًا ﴿٢٨﴾

29 Then withdraw (O Muhammad) from him who fleeth from Our remembrance and desireth but the life of the world.

فَأَعْرِضْ عَن مَّن تَوَلَّى عَن ذِكْرِنَا وَلَمْ يُرِدْ إِلَّا ٱلْحَيَوٰةَ ٱلدُّنْيَا ﴿٢٩﴾

30 Such is their sum of knowledge. Lo! thy Lord is best Aware of him who strayeth from His path, and He is best aware of him who goeth right.

ذَلِكَ مَبْلَغُهُم مِّنَ ٱلْعِلْمِ إِنَّ رَبَّكَ هُوَ أَعْلَمُ بِمَن ضَلَّ عَن سَبِيلِهِ وَهُوَ أَعْلَمُ بِمَنِ ٱهْتَدَى ﴿٣٠﴾

31 And unto Allah belongeth whatsoever is in the heavens and whatsoever is in the earth, that He may reward those who do evil with that which they have done, and reward those who do good with goodness.

وَلِلّٰهِ مَا فِى السَّمٰوٰتِ وَمَا فِى الْأَرْضِ لِيَجْزِىَ الَّذِيْنَ أَسَآءُوْا بِمَا عَمِلُوْا وَيَجْزِىَ الَّذِيْنَ أَحْسَنُوْا بِالْحُسْنَى ۞

32 Those who avoid enormities of sin and abominations, save the unwilled offences (for them), lo! thy Lord is of vast mercy. He is best aware of you (from the time) when He created you from the earth, and when ye were hidden in the bellies of your mothers. Therefore ascribe not purity unto yourselves. He is best aware of him who wardeth off (evil).

الَّذِيْنَ يَجْتَنِبُوْنَ كَبٰٓئِرَ الْإِثْمِ وَالْفَوَاحِشَ إِلَّا اللَّمَمَ إِنَّ رَبَّكَ وَاسِعُ الْمَغْفِرَةِ هُوَ أَعْلَمُ بِكُمْ إِذْ أَنْشَأَكُمْ مِّنَ الْأَرْضِ وَإِذْ أَنْتُمْ أَجِنَّةٌ فِىْ بُطُوْنِ أُمَّهٰتِكُمْ فَلَا تُزَكُّوْٓا أَنْفُسَكُمْ هُوَ أَعْلَمُ بِمَنِ اتَّقَى ۞

33 Didst thou (O Muḥammad) observe him who turned away,

أَفَرَأَيْتَ الَّذِىْ تَوَلَّى ۞

34 And gave a little, then was grudging?

وَأَعْطَى قَلِيْلًا وَّأَكْدَى ۞

35 Hath he knowledge of the Unseen so that he seeth?

أَعِنْدَهُ عِلْمُ الْغَيْبِ فَهُوَ يَرَى ۞

36 Or hath he not bad news of what is in the books of Moses

أَمْ لَمْ يُنَبَّأْ بِمَا فِىْ صُحُفِ مُوْسَى ۞

37 And Abraham who paid his debt:

وَإِبْرٰهِيْمَ الَّذِىْ وَفّٰى ۞

38 That no laden one shall bear another's load,

أَلَّا تَزِرُ وَازِرَةٌ وِّزْرَ أُخْرَى ۞

39 And that man hath only that for which he maketh effort,

وَأَنْ لَّيْسَ لِلْإِنْسَانِ إِلَّا مَا سَعَى ۞

40 And that his effort will be seen,

وَأَنَّ سَعْيَهُ سَوْفَ يُرَى ۞

41 And afterward he will be repaid for it with fullest payment;

ثُمَّ يُجْزَىٰهُ الْجَزَاءَ الْأَوْفَىٰ ۝

42 And that thy Lord, He is the goal;

وَأَنَّ إِلَىٰ رَبِّكَ الْمُنْتَهَىٰ ۝

43 And that He it is Who maketh laugh, and maketh weep,

وَأَنَّهُ هُوَ أَضْحَكَ وَأَبْكَىٰ ۝

44 And that He it is Who giveth death and giveth life;

وَأَنَّهُ هُوَ أَمَاتَ وَأَحْيَا ۝

45 And that He createth the two spouses, the male and the female,

وَأَنَّهُ خَلَقَ الزَّوْجَيْنِ الذَّكَرَ وَالْأُنْثَىٰ ۝

46 From a drop (of seed) when it is poured forth;

مِنْ نُطْفَةٍ إِذَا تُمْنَىٰ ۝

47 And that He hath ordained the second bringing forth;

وَأَنَّ عَلَيْهِ النَّشْأَةَ الْأُخْرَىٰ ۝

48 And that He it is Who enricheth and contenteth:

وَأَنَّهُ هُوَ أَغْنَىٰ وَأَقْنَىٰ ۝

49 And that He it is Who is the Lord of Sirius;

وَأَنَّهُ هُوَ رَبُّ الشِّعْرَىٰ ۝

50 And that He destroyed the former (tribe of) 'Ād,[7]

وَأَنَّهُ أَهْلَكَ عَادًا الْأُولَىٰ ۝

51 And (the tribe of) Thamūd He spared not;

وَثَمُودَ فَمَا أَبْقَىٰ ۝

52 And the folk of Noah aforetime, lo! they were more unjust and more rebellious;

وَقَوْمَ نُوحٍ مِّنْ قَبْلُ إِنَّهُمْ كَانُوا هُمْ أَظْلَمَ وَأَطْغَىٰ ۝

53 And Al-Mu'tafikah[8] He destroyed

وَالْمُؤْتَفِكَةَ أَهْوَىٰ ۝

54 So that there covered them that which did cover.

فَغَشَّاهَا مَا غَشَّىٰ ۝

---

7. There was still in existence a tribe of that name.

8. Generally supposed to be a name for the villages of the people of Lot.

55 Concerning which then, of the bounties of thy Lord, canst thou dispute?

فَبِأَيِّ ءَالَآءِ رَبِّكَ تَتَمَارَىٰ ۝

56 This is a warner of the warners of old.

هَٰذَا نَذِيرٌ مِّنَ ٱلنُّذُرِ ٱلْأُولَىٰٓ ۝

57 The threatened Hour is nigh.

أَزِفَتِ ٱلْآزِفَةُ ۝

58 None beside Allah can disclose it.

لَيْسَ لَهَا مِن دُونِ ٱللَّهِ كَاشِفَةٌ ۝

59 Marvel ye then at this statement,

أَفَمِنْ هَٰذَا ٱلْحَدِيثِ تَعْجَبُونَ ۝

60 And laugh and not weep,

وَتَضْحَكُونَ وَلَا تَبْكُونَ ۝

61 While ye amuse yourselves?

وَأَنتُمْ سَٰمِدُونَ ۝

62 Rather prostrate yourselves before Allah and serve Him.

فَٱسْجُدُوا۟ لِلَّهِ وَٱعْبُدُوا۟ ۩ ۝

Al Qamar
(The Moon)

Al Qamar, "The Moon," takes its name from the first verse: "The hour drew nigh and the moon was rent in twain." A strange appearance of the moon in the sky, as if it had been torn asunder, is recorded in the traditions of several Companions of the Prophet as having astonished the people of Makkah about the time when the idolaters were beginning to persecute the Muslims.

An early Makkan sūrah.

In the name of Allah, the Beneficent, the Merciful.

1 The hour drew nigh and the moon was rent in twain.

2 And if they behold a portent they turn away and say: Prolonged illusion.

3 They denied (the Truth) and followed their own lusts. Yet everything will come to a decision

4 And surely there hath come unto them news whereof the purport should deter,

5 Effective wisdom; but warnings avail not.

769

6 So withdraw from them (O Muhammad) on the day when the Summoner summoneth unto a painful thing.

فَتَوَلَّ عَنْهُمْ يَوْمَ يَدْعُ الدَّاعِ إِلَىٰ شَىْءٍ نُكُرٍ ۝

7 With downcast eyes, they come forth from the graves as they were locusts spread abroad,

خُشَّعًا أَبْصَارُهُمْ يَخْرُجُونَ مِنَ الْأَجْدَاثِ كَأَنَّهُمْ جَرَادٌ مُّنْتَشِرٌ ۝

8 Hastening toward the Summoner; the disbelievers say: This is a hard day.

مُّهْطِعِينَ إِلَى الدَّاعِ يَقُولُ الْكَافِرُونَ هَٰذَا يَوْمٌ عَسِرٌ ۝

9 The folk of Noah denied before them, yea, they denied Our slave[1] and said: A madman; and he was repulsed.

۞ كَذَّبَتْ قَبْلَهُمْ قَوْمُ نُوحٍ فَكَذَّبُوا عَبْدَنَا وَقَالُوا مَجْنُونٌ وَازْدُجِرَ ۝

10 So he cried unto his Lord, saying: I am vanquished, so give help.

فَدَعَا رَبَّهُ أَنِّي مَغْلُوبٌ فَانتَصِرْ ۝

11 Then opened We the gates of heaven with pouring water

فَفَتَحْنَا أَبْوَابَ السَّمَاءِ بِمَاءٍ مُّنْهَمِرٍ ۝

12 And caused the earth to gush forth springs, so that the waters met for a predestined purpose.

وَفَجَّرْنَا الْأَرْضَ عُيُونًا فَالْتَقَى الْمَاءُ عَلَىٰ أَمْرٍ قَدْ قُدِرَ ۝

13 And We carried him upon a thing of planks and nails,

وَحَمَلْنَاهُ عَلَىٰ ذَاتِ أَلْوَاحٍ وَدُسُرٍ ۝

14 That ran (upon the waters) in Our sight, as a reward for him who was rejected.

تَجْرِي بِأَعْيُنِنَا جَزَاءً لِّمَن كَانَ كُفِرَ ۝

15 And verily We left it as a token; but is there any that remembereth?

وَلَقَد تَّرَكْنَاهَا آيَةً فَهَلْ مِن مُّدَّكِرٍ ۝

---

1. To be *'abd Allāh*, "a slave of God," is the proudest rank the Muslim can claim, bondage to Allah implying liberation from all other servitudes. All especially devoted men, all the chosen ones, are called slaves of Allah in the Qur'an.

16 Then see how (dreadful) was My punishment after My warnings!

فَكَيْفَ كَانَ عَذَابِي وَنُذُرِ ۝

17 And in truth, We have made the Qur'an easy to remember;[2] but is there any that remembered?

وَلَقَدْ يَسَّرْنَا الْقُرْآنَ لِلذِّكْرِ فَهَلْ مِن مُّدَّكِرٍ ۝

18 (The tribe of) 'Ād rejected warnings. Then how (dreadful) was My punishment after My warnings.

كَذَّبَتْ عَادٌ فَكَيْفَ كَانَ عَذَابِي وَنُذُرِ ۝

19 Lo! We let loose on them a raging wind on a day of constant calamity,

إِنَّا أَرْسَلْنَا عَلَيْهِمْ رِيحًا صَرْصَرًا فِي يَوْمِ نَحْسٍ مُّسْتَمِرٍّ ۝

20 Sweeping men away as though they were uprooted trunks of palm trees.

تَنزِعُ النَّاسَ كَأَنَّهُمْ أَعْجَازُ نَخْلٍ مُّنقَعِرٍ ۝

21 Then see how (dreadful) was My punishment after My warnings!

فَكَيْفَ كَانَ عَذَابِي وَنُذُرِ ۝

22 And in truth We have made the Qur'an easy to remember; but is there any that remembereth?

وَلَقَدْ يَسَّرْنَا الْقُرْآنَ لِلذِّكْرِ فَهَلْ مِن مُّدَّكِرٍ ۝

23 (The tribe of) Thamūd rejected warnings

كَذَّبَتْ ثَمُودُ بِالنُّذُرِ ۝

24 For they said: Is it a mortal man, alone among us, that we are to follow? Then indeed we should fall into error and madness.

فَقَالُوا أَبَشَرًا مِّنَّا وَاحِدًا نَّتَّبِعُهُ إِنَّا إِذًا لَّفِي ضَلَالٍ وَسُعُرٍ ۝

25 Hath the remembrance been given unto him alone among us? Nay, but he is a rash liar.

أَؤُلْقِيَ الذِّكْرُ عَلَيْهِ مِن بَيْنِنَا بَلْ هُوَ كَذَّابٌ أَشِرٌ ۝

---

2. It is a fact that the Qur'an is marvellously easy for believers to commit to memory. Thousands of people in the East know the whole book by heart. The translator, who finds great difficulty in remembering well-known English quotations accurately, can remember page after page of the Qur'an in Arabic with perfect accuracy.

26 (Unto their warner. it was said):
Tomorrow they will know who is
the rash liar.

سَيَعْلَمُونَ غَدًا مَّنِ ٱلْكَذَّابُ ٱلْأَشِرُ ۝

27 Lo! We are sending the she-
camel as a test for them; so watch
them and have patience;

إِنَّا مُرْسِلُواْ ٱلنَّاقَةِ فِتْنَةً لَّهُمْ فَٱرْتَقِبْهُمْ وَٱصْطَبِرْ ۝

28 And inform them that the water
is to be shared between (her and)
them. Every drinking will be witnessed.

وَنَبِّئْهُمْ أَنَّ ٱلْمَآءَ قِسْمَةٌ بَيْنَهُمْ كُلُّ شِرْبٍ مُّحْتَضَرٌ ۝

29 But they called their comrade
and he took and hamstrung (her).

فَنَادَوْاْ صَاحِبَهُمْ فَتَعَاطَىٰ فَعَقَرَ ۝

30 Then see how (dreadful) was
My punishment after My warnings!

فَكَيْفَ كَانَ عَذَابِى وَنُذُرِ ۝

31 Lo! We sent upon them one
Shout, and they became as the dry
twigs (rejected by) the builder of a
cattle fold.

إِنَّا أَرْسَلْنَا عَلَيْهِمْ صَيْحَةً وَٰحِدَةً فَكَانُواْ
كَهَشِيمِ ٱلْمُحْتَظِرِ ۝

32 And in truth We have made the
Qur'an easy to remember; but is
there any that remembereth?

وَلَقَدْ يَسَّرْنَا ٱلْقُرْءَانَ لِلذِّكْرِ فَهَلْ مِن مُّدَّكِرٍ ۝

33 The folk of Lot rejected warnings.

كَذَّبَتْ قَوْمُ لُوطٍ بِٱلنُّذُرِ ۝

34 Lo! We sent a storm of stones
upon them (all) save the family of
Lot, whom We rescued in the last
watch of the night,

إِنَّا أَرْسَلْنَا عَلَيْهِمْ حَاصِبًا إِلَّا ءَالَ لُوطٍ
نَّجَّيْنَٰهُم بِسَحَرٍ ۝

35 As grace from Us. Thus We
reward him who giveth thanks.

نِّعْمَةً مِّنْ عِندِنَا كَذَٰلِكَ نَجْزِى مَن شَكَرَ ۝

36 And he indeed had warned them
of Our blow, but they did doubt the
warnings.

وَلَقَدْ أَنذَرَهُم بَطْشَتَنَا فَتَمَارَوْاْ بِٱلنُّذُرِ ۝

37 They even asked of him his guests for an ill purpose. Then We blinded their eyes (and said): Taste now My punishment after My warnings!

وَلَقَدْ رَاوَدُوهُ عَن ضَيْفِهِ فَطَمَسْنَآ أَعْيُنَهُمْ فَذُوقُوا عَذَابِي وَنُذُرِ ۝

38 And in truth the punishment decreed befell them early in the morning.

وَلَقَدْ صَبَّحَهُم بُكْرَةً عَذَابٌ مُّسْتَقِرٌّ ۝

39 Now taste My punishment after My warnings!

فَذُوقُوا عَذَابِي وَنُذُرِ ۝

40 And in truth We have made the Qur'an easy to remember; but is there any that remembereth?

وَلَقَدْ يَسَّرْنَا الْقُرْءَانَ لِلذِّكْرِ فَهَلْ مِن مُّدَّكِرٍ ۝

41 And warnings came in truth unto the house of Pharaoh

وَلَقَدْ جَآءَ ءَالَ فِرْعَوْنَ النُّذُرُ ۝

42 Who denied Our revelations, every one. Therefore We grasped them with the grasp of the Mighty, the Powerful.

كَذَّبُوا بِـَٔايَٰتِنَا كُلِّهَا فَأَخَذْنَٰهُمْ أَخْذَ عَزِيزٍ مُّقْتَدِرٍ ۝

43 Are your disbelievers better than those, or have ye some immunity in the Scriptures?

أَكُفَّارُكُمْ خَيْرٌ مِّنْ أُوْلَٰٓئِكُمْ أَمْ لَكُم بَرَآءَةٌ فِي الزُّبُرِ ۝

44 Or say they: We are a host victorious?

أَمْ يَقُولُونَ نَحْنُ جَمِيعٌ مُّنتَصِرٌ ۝

45 The hosts will all be routed and will turn and flee.

سَيُهْزَمُ الْجَمْعُ وَيُوَلُّونَ الدُّبُرَ ۝

46 Nay, but the Hour (of doom) is their appointed tryst, and the Hour will be more wretched and more bitter (than their earthly failure).

بَلِ السَّاعَةُ مَوْعِدُهُمْ وَالسَّاعَةُ أَدْهَىٰ وَأَمَرُّ ۝

47 Lo! the guilty are in error and madness.

إِنَّ الْمُجْرِمِينَ فِي ضَلَٰلٍ وَسُعُرٍ ۝

48 On the day when they are dragged into the Fire upon their faces (it
is said unto them): Feel the touch of
hell.

يَوْمَ يُسْحَبُونَ فِي ٱلنَّارِ عَلَىٰ وُجُوهِهِمْ ذُوقُواْ مَسَّ سَقَرَ ۝

49 Lo! We have created every
thing by measure.

إِنَّا كُلَّ شَيْءٍ خَلَقْنَٰهُ بِقَدَرٍ ۝

50 And Our commandment is but
one (commandment), as the twinkling of an eye.

وَمَآ أَمْرُنَآ إِلَّا وَٰحِدَةٌ كَلَمْحٍ بِٱلْبَصَرِ ۝

51 And verily We have destroyed
your fellows; but is there any that
remembereth?

وَلَقَدْ أَهْلَكْنَآ أَشْيَاعَكُمْ فَهَلْ مِن مُّدَّكِرٍ ۝

52 And every thing they did is in
the Scriptures,

وَكُلُّ شَيْءٍ فَعَلُوهُ فِي ٱلزُّبُرِ ۝

53 And every small and great thing
is recorded.

وَكُلُّ صَغِيرٍ وَكَبِيرٍ مُّسْتَطَرٌ ۝

54 Lo! the righteous will dwell
among gardens and rivers,

إِنَّ ٱلْمُتَّقِينَ فِي جَنَّٰتٍ وَنَهَرٍ ۝

55 Firmly established in the favour
of a Mighty King.

فِي مَقْعَدِ صِدْقٍ عِندَ مَلِيكٍ مُّقْتَدِرٍ ۝

Ar Rahmān
(The Beneficent)

Ar Rahmān takes its name from the first verse. In the refrain: "Which is it, of the favours of your Lord, that ye deny?" *Ye* and the verb are in the dual form, and the question is generally believed to be addressed to mankind and the Jinn. Some have held that vv. 46-76 refer, not to the paradise hereafter, but to the later conquests of the Muslims, the four gardens being Egypt, Syria, Mesopotamia and Persia. There may well be a double meaning.

An early Makkan sūrah.

In the name of Allah, the Beneficent, the Merciful.

1 The Beneficent

2 Hath made known the Qur'an.

3 He hath created man.

4 He hath taught him utterance.

5 The sun and the moon are made punctual.

6 The stars and the trees adore.

7 And the sky He hath uplifted; and He hath set the measure,

8 That ye exceed not the measure,

9 But observe the measure strictly, nor fall short thereof.

10 And the earth hath He appointed for (His) creatures,

وَالْأَرْضَ وَضَعَهَا لِلْأَنَامِ ۝

11 Wherein are fruit and sheathed palm-trees,

فِيهَا فَاكِهَةٌ وَّالنَّخْلُ ذَاتُ الْأَكْمَامِ ۝

12 Husked grain and scented herb.

وَالْحَبُّ ذُو الْعَصْفِ وَالرَّيْحَانُ ۝

13 Which is it, of the favours of your Lord, that ye deny?

فَبِأَيِّ ءَالَآءِ رَبِّكُمَا تُكَذِّبَانِ ۝

14 He created man of clay like the potter's,

خَلَقَ الْإِنسَانَ مِن صَلْصَالٍ كَالْفَخَّارِ ۝

15 And the Jinn did He create of smokeless fire.

وَخَلَقَ الْجَانَّ مِن مَّارِجٍ مِّن نَّارٍ ۝

16 Which is it, of the favours of your Lord, that ye deny?

فَبِأَيِّ ءَالَآءِ رَبِّكُمَا تُكَذِّبَانِ ۝

17 Lord of the two Easts,[1] and Lord of the two Wests![2]

رَبُّ الْمَشْرِقَيْنِ وَرَبُّ الْمَغْرِبَيْنِ ۝

18 Which is it, of the favours of your Lord, that ye deny?

فَبِأَيِّ ءَالَآءِ رَبِّكُمَا تُكَذِّبَانِ ۝

19 He hath loosed the two seas,[3] flowing together (side by side).

مَرَجَ الْبَحْرَيْنِ يَلْتَقِيَانِ ۝

20 There is a barrier between them. They encroach not (one upon the other).

بَيْنَهُمَا بَرْزَخٌ لَّا يَبْغِيَانِ ۝

21 Which is it, of the favours of your Lord, that ye deny?

فَبِأَيِّ ءَالَآءِ رَبِّكُمَا تُكَذِّبَانِ ۝

22 There cometh forth from both of them the pearl and coral stone.

يَخْرُجُ مِنْهُمَا اللُّؤْلُؤُ وَالْمَرْجَانُ ۝

23 Which is it, of the favours of your Lord, that ye deny?

فَبِأَيِّ ءَالَآءِ رَبِّكُمَا تُكَذِّبَانِ ۝

---

1. The two points where the sun rises in winter and in summer.

2. The two points where the sun sets in winter and in summer.

3. *i.e.* the salt water and the sweet.

24 His are the ships displayed upon the sea, like banners.[4]

وَلَهُ الْجَوَارِ الْمُنْشَئَاتُ فِى الْبَحْرِ كَالْأَعْلَامِ ۝

25 Which is it, of the favours of your Lord, that ye deny?

فَبِأَىِّ ءَالَآءِ رَبِّكُمَا تُكَذِّبَانِ ۝

26 Everyone that is thereon will pass away;

كُلُّ مَنْ عَلَيْهَا فَانٍ ۝

27 There remaineth but the countenance of thy Lord of Might and Glory.

وَيَبْقَىٰ وَجْهُ رَبِّكَ ذُو الْجَلَالِ وَالْإِكْرَامِ ۝

28 Which is it, of the favours of your Lord, that ye deny?

فَبِأَىِّ ءَالَآءِ رَبِّكُمَا تُكَذِّبَانِ ۝

29 All that are in the heavens and the earth entreat Him. Every day He exerciseth (universal) power.

يَسْـَٔلُهُ مَن فِى السَّمَوَٰتِ وَالْأَرْضِ كُلَّ يَوْمٍ هُوَ فِى شَأْنٍ ۝

30 Which is it, of the favours of your Lord, that ye deny?

فَبِأَىِّ ءَالَآءِ رَبِّكُمَا تُكَذِّبَانِ ۝

31 We shall dispose of you, O ye two dependents (man and jinn).

سَنَفْرُغُ لَكُمْ أَيُّهَ الثَّقَلَانِ ۝

32 Which is it, of the favours of your Lord, that ye deny?

فَبِأَىِّ ءَالَآءِ رَبِّكُمَا تُكَذِّبَانِ ۝

33 O company of jinn and men, if ye have power to penetrate (all) regions of the heavens and the earth; then penetrate (them)! Ye will never penetrate them save with (Our) sanction.

يَٰمَعْشَرَ الْجِنِّ وَالْإِنسِ إِنِ اسْتَطَعْتُمْ أَن تَنفُذُوا مِنْ أَقْطَارِ السَّمَوَٰتِ وَالْأَرْضِ فَانفُذُوا لَا تَنفُذُونَ إِلَّا بِسُلْطَٰنٍ ۝

34 Which is it, of the favours of your Lord, that ye deny?

فَبِأَىِّ ءَالَآءِ رَبِّكُمَا تُكَذِّبَانِ ۝

35 There will be sent, against you both, heat of fire and flash of brass, and ye will not escape.

يُرْسَلُ عَلَيْكُمَا شُوَاظٌ مِّن نَّارٍ وَنُحَاسٌ فَلَا تَنتَصِرَانِ ۝

---

4. The usual explanation of the commentators is "built into the sea like mountains."

36 Which is it, of the favours of
your Lord, that ye deny?

فَبِأَيِّ ءَالَآءِ رَبِّكُمَا تُكَذِّبَانِ ۝

37 And when the heaven splitteth
asunder and becometh rosy like red
hide—

فَإِذَا ٱنشَقَّتِ ٱلسَّمَآءُ فَكَانَتْ وَرْدَةً كَٱلدِّهَانِ ۝

38 Which is it, of the favours of
your Lord, that ye deny?

فَبِأَيِّ ءَالَآءِ رَبِّكُمَا تُكَذِّبَانِ ۝

39 On that day neither man nor
jinn will be questioned of his sin.

فَيَوْمَئِذٍ لَّا يُسْـَٔلُ عَن ذَنۢبِهِۦٓ إِنسٌ وَلَا جَآنٌّ ۝

40 Which is it, of the favours of
your Lord, that ye deny?

فَبِأَيِّ ءَالَآءِ رَبِّكُمَا تُكَذِّبَانِ ۝

41 The guilty will be known by
their marks, and will he taken by
the forelocks and the feet.

يُعْرَفُ ٱلْمُجْرِمُونَ بِسِيمَٰهُمْ فَيُؤْخَذُ بِٱلنَّوَٰصِى
وَٱلْأَقْدَامِ ۝

42 Which is it, of the favours of
your Lord, that ye deny?

فَبِأَيِّ ءَالَآءِ رَبِّكُمَا تُكَذِّبَانِ ۝

43 This is Hell which the guilty
deny.

هَٰذِهِۦ جَهَنَّمُ ٱلَّتِى يُكَذِّبُ بِهَا ٱلْمُجْرِمُونَ ۝

44 They go circling round between
it and fierce, boiling water.

يَطُوفُونَ بَيْنَهَا وَبَيْنَ حَمِيمٍ ءَانٍ ۝

45 Which is it, of the favours of
your Lord, that ye deny?

فَبِأَيِّ ءَالَآءِ رَبِّكُمَا تُكَذِّبَانِ ۝

46 But for him who feareth the
standing before his Lord, there are
two gardens.

وَلِمَنْ خَافَ مَقَامَ رَبِّهِۦ جَنَّتَانِ ۝

47 Which is it, of the favours of
your Lord, that ye deny?

فَبِأَيِّ ءَالَآءِ رَبِّكُمَا تُكَذِّبَانِ ۝

48 Of spreading branches.

ذَوَاتَآ أَفْنَانٍ ۝

49 Which is it, of the favours of
your Lord, that ye deny?

فَبِأَيِّ ءَالَآءِ رَبِّكُمَا تُكَذِّبَانِ ۝

50 Wherein are two fountains
flowing.

فِيهِمَا عَيْنَانِ تَجْرِيَانِ ۝

51 Which is it, of the favours of
your Lord, that ye deny?

فَبِأَيِّ ءَالَآءِ رَبِّكُمَا تُكَذِّبَانِ ۝

52 Wherein is every kind of fruit in
pairs.

فِيهِمَا مِن كُلِّ فَٰكِهَةٍ زَوْجَانِ ۝

53 Which is it, of the favours of
your Lord, that ye deny?

فَبِأَيِّ ءَالَآءِ رَبِّكُمَا تُكَذِّبَانِ ۝

54 Reclining upon couches lined
with silk brocade, the fruit of both
gardens near to hand.

مُتَّكِئِينَ عَلَىٰ فُرُشٍ بَطَآئِنُهَا مِنْ إِسْتَبْرَقٍ
وَجَنَى ٱلْجَنَّتَيْنِ دَانٍ ۝

55 Which is it, of the favours of
your Lord, that ye deny?

فَبِأَيِّ ءَالَآءِ رَبِّكُمَا تُكَذِّبَانِ ۝

56 Therein are those of modest
gaze, whom neither man nor jinn
will have touched before them,

فِيهِنَّ قَٰصِرَٰتُ ٱلطَّرْفِ لَمْ يَطْمِثْهُنَّ إِنسٌ قَبْلَهُمْ
وَلَا جَآنٌّ ۝

57 Which is it, of the favours of
your Lord, that ye deny?

فَبِأَيِّ ءَالَآءِ رَبِّكُمَا تُكَذِّبَانِ ۝

58 (In beauty) like the jacynth and
the coral stone.

كَأَنَّهُنَّ ٱلْيَاقُوتُ وَٱلْمَرْجَانُ ۝

59 Which is it, of the favours of
your Lord, that ye deny?

فَبِأَيِّ ءَالَآءِ رَبِّكُمَا تُكَذِّبَانِ ۝

60 Is the reward of goodness aught
save goodness?

هَلْ جَزَآءُ ٱلْإِحْسَٰنِ إِلَّا ٱلْإِحْسَٰنُ ۝

61 Which is it, of the favours of
your Lord, that ye deny?

فَبِأَيِّ ءَالَآءِ رَبِّكُمَا تُكَذِّبَانِ ۝

62 And beside them are two other
gardens,

وَمِن دُونِهِمَا جَنَّتَانِ ۝

63 Which is it, of the favours of
your Lord, that ye deny?

فَبِأَيِّ ءَالَآءِ رَبِّكُمَا تُكَذِّبَانِ ۝

64 Dark green with foliage.

مُدْهَآمَّتَانِ ۝

65 Which is it, of the favours of
your Lord, that ye deny?

فَبِأَيِّ ءَالَآءِ رَبِّكُمَا تُكَذِّبَانِ ۝

66 Wherein are two abundant
springs.

فِيهِمَا عَيْنَانِ نَضَّاخَتَانِ ۝

67 Which is it, of the favours of
your Lord, that ye deny?

فَبِأَيِّ ءَالَآءِ رَبِّكُمَا تُكَذِّبَانِ ۝

68 Wherein is fruit, the date-palm
and pomegranate.

فِيهِمَا فَاكِهَةٌ وَنَخْلٌ وَرُمَّانٌ ۝

69 Which is it, of the favours of
your Lord, that ye deny?

فَبِأَيِّ ءَالَآءِ رَبِّكُمَا تُكَذِّبَانِ ۝

70 Wherein (are found) the good
and beautiful—

فِيهِنَّ خَيْرَٰتٌ حِسَانٌ ۝

71 Which is it, of the favours of
your Lord, that ye deny?

فَبِأَيِّ ءَالَآءِ رَبِّكُمَا تُكَذِّبَانِ ۝

72 Fair ones, close-guarded in
pavilions—

حُورٌ مَّقْصُورَٰتٌ فِى الْخِيَامِ ۝

73 Which is it, of the favours of
your Lord, that ye deny?

فَبِأَيِّ ءَالَآءِ رَبِّكُمَا تُكَذِّبَانِ ۝

74 Whom neither man nor jinn will
have touched before them—

لَمْ يَطْمِثْهُنَّ إِنسٌ قَبْلَهُمْ وَلَا جَانٌّ ۝

75 Which is it, of the favours of
your Lord, that ye deny?

فَبِأَيِّ ءَالَآءِ رَبِّكُمَا تُكَذِّبَانِ ۝

76 Reclining on green cushions and
fair carpets.

مُتَّكِئِينَ عَلَىٰ رَفْرَفٍ خُضْرٍ وَعَبْقَرِيٍّ حِسَانٍ ۝

77 Which is it, of the favours of
your Lord, that ye deny?

فَبِأَيِّ ءَالَآءِ رَبِّكُمَا تُكَذِّبَانِ ۝

78 Blessed be the name of thy
Lord, Mighty and Glorious!

تَبَٰرَكَ اسْمُ رَبِّكَ ذِى الْجَلَٰلِ وَالْإِكْرَامِ ۝

Al Wāqi'ah
(The Event)

Al Wāqi'ah, "The Event," takes its name from a word in verse 1.

An early Makkan sūrah.

In the name of Allah, the Beneficent, the Merciful.

1 When the event befalleth—

2 There is no denying that it will befall—

3 Abasing (some), exalting (others);

4 When the earth is shaken with a shock

5 And the hills are ground to powder;

6 So that they become a scattered dust,

7 And ye will be three kinds:

8 (First) those on the right hand; what of those on the right hand?

9 And (then) those on the left hand; what of those on the left hand?

10 And the foremost in the race, the foremost in the race:

781

11 Those are they who will be brought nigh

أُوْلَٰٓئِكَ ٱلْمُقَرَّبُونَ ۝

12 In gardens of delight;

فِى جَنَّٰتِ ٱلنَّعِيمِ ۝

13 A multitude of those of old

ثُلَّةٌ مِّنَ ٱلْأَوَّلِينَ ۝

14 And a few of those of later time,

وَقَلِيلٌ مِّنَ ٱلْءَاخِرِينَ ۝

15 On lined couches,

عَلَىٰ سُرُرٍ مَّوْضُونَةٍ ۝

16 Reclining therein face to face.

مُّتَّكِئِينَ عَلَيْهَا مُتَقَٰبِلِينَ ۝

17 There wait on them immortal youths

يَطُوفُ عَلَيْهِمْ وِلْدَٰنٌ مُّخَلَّدُونَ ۝

18 With bowls and ewers and a cup from a pure spring

بِأَكْوَابٍ وَأَبَارِيقَ وَكَأْسٍ مِّن مَّعِينٍ ۝

19 Wherefrom they get no aching of the head nor any madness,

لَّا يُصَدَّعُونَ عَنْهَا وَلَا يُنزِفُونَ ۝

20 And fruit that they prefer

وَفَٰكِهَةٍ مِّمَّا يَتَخَيَّرُونَ ۝

21 And flesh of fowls that they desire.

وَلَحْمِ طَيْرٍ مِّمَّا يَشْتَهُونَ ۝

22 And (there are) fair ones with wide, lovely eyes,

وَحُورٌ عِينٌ ۝

23 Like unto hidden pearls,

كَأَمْثَٰلِ ٱللُّؤْلُؤِ ٱلْمَكْنُونِ ۝

24 Reward for what they used to do.

جَزَآءً بِمَا كَانُوا۟ يَعْمَلُونَ ۝

25 There hear they no vain speaking nor recrimination

لَا يَسْمَعُونَ فِيهَا لَغْوًا وَلَا تَأْثِيمًا ۝

26 (Naught) but the saying: Peace, (and again) Peace.

إِلَّا قِيلًا سَلَٰمًا سَلَٰمًا ۝

27 And those on the right hand; what of those on the right hand?

وَأَصْحَٰبُ ٱلْيَمِينِ مَآ أَصْحَٰبُ ٱلْيَمِينِ ۝

28 Among thornless lote-trees

فِى سِدْرٍ مَّخْضُودٍ ۝

29 And clustered plantains,

وَطَلْحٍ مَّنضُودٍ ۝

30 And spreading shade,

وَظِلٍّ مَّمْدُودٍ ۝

31 And water gushing,

وَمَآءٍ مَّسْكُوبٍ ۝

32 And fruit in plenty

وَفَٰكِهَةٍ كَثِيرَةٍ ۝

33 Neither cut off nor forbidden,

لَّا مَقْطُوعَةٍ وَلَا مَمْنُوعَةٍ ۝

34 And raised couches;

وَفُرُشٍ مَّرْفُوعَةٍ ۝

35 Lo! We have created them a (new) creation

إِنَّا أَنشَأْنَاهُنَّ إِنشَاءً ۝

36 And made them virgins

فَجَعَلْنَاهُنَّ أَبْكَارًا ۝

37 Lovers, equal in age.

عُرُبًا أَتْرَابًا ۝

38 For those on the right hand;

لِّأَصْحَابِ الْيَمِينِ ۝

39 A multitude of those of old

ثُلَّةٌ مِّنَ الْأَوَّلِينَ ۝

40 And a multitude of those of later time.[1]

وَثُلَّةٌ مِّنَ الْآخِرِينَ ۝

41 And those on the left hand: What of those on the left hand?

وَأَصْحَابُ الشِّمَالِ مَا أَصْحَابُ الشِّمَالِ ۝

42 In scorching wind and scalding water

فِي سَمُومٍ وَحَمِيمٍ ۝

43 And shadow of black smoke,

وَظِلٍّ مِّن يَحْمُومٍ ۝

44 Neither cool nor refreshing.

لَّا بَارِدٍ وَلَا كَرِيمٍ ۝

45 Lo! heretofor they were effete with luxury

إِنَّهُمْ كَانُوا قَبْلَ ذَلِكَ مُتْرَفِينَ ۝

46 And used to persist in the awful sin.

وَكَانُوا يُصِرُّونَ عَلَى الْحِنثِ الْعَظِيمِ ۝

47 And they used to say: When we are dead and have become dust and bones, shall we then, forsooth, be raised again,

وَكَانُوا يَقُولُونَ أَئِذَا مِتْنَا وَكُنَّا تُرَابًا وَعِظَامًا أَئِنَّا لَمَبْعُوثُونَ ۝

48 And also our forefathers?

أَوَآبَاؤُنَا الْأَوَّلُونَ ۝

49 Say (unto them, O Muhammad): Lo! those of old and those of later time

قُلْ إِنَّ الْأَوَّلِينَ وَالْآخِرِينَ ۝

50 Will all be brought together to the tryst of an appointed day.

لَمَجْمُوعُونَ إِلَى مِيقَاتِ يَوْمٍ مَّعْلُومٍ ۝

---

1. This verse is said to have been revealed at Al-Madīnah.

51 Then lo! ye, the erring, the deniers,

ثُمَّ إِنَّكُمْ أَيُّهَا الضَّآلُّونَ الْمُكَذِّبُونَ ۝

52 Ye verily will eat of a tree called Zaqqūm

لَآكِلُونَ مِن شَجَرٍ مِّن زَقُّومٍ ۝

53 And will fill your bellies therewith;

فَمَالِئُونَ مِنْهَا الْبُطُونَ ۝

54 And thereon ye will drink of boiling water,

فَشَارِبُونَ عَلَيْهِ مِنَ الْحَمِيمِ ۝

55 Drinking even as the camel drinketh.

فَشَارِبُونَ شُرْبَ الْهِيمِ ۝

56 This will be their welcome on the Day of Judgement.

هَٰذَا نُزُلُهُمْ يَوْمَ الدِّينِ ۝

57 We created you. Will ye then admit the truth?

نَحْنُ خَلَقْنَاكُمْ فَلَوْلَا تُصَدِّقُونَ ۝

58 Have ye seen that which ye emit?

أَفَرَأَيْتُم مَّا تُمْنُونَ ۝

59 Do ye create it or are We the creator?

ءَأَنتُمْ تَخْلُقُونَهُ أَمْ نَحْنُ الْخَالِقُونَ ۝

60 We mete out death among you, and We are not to be outrun,

نَحْنُ قَدَّرْنَا بَيْنَكُمُ الْمَوْتَ وَمَا نَحْنُ بِمَسْبُوقِينَ ۝

61 That We may transfigure you and make you what ye know not.

عَلَىٰٓ أَن نُّبَدِّلَ أَمْثَالَكُمْ وَنُنشِئَكُمْ فِي مَا لَا تَعْلَمُونَ ۝

62 And verily ye know the first creation. Why, then, do ye not reflect?

وَلَقَدْ عَلِمْتُمُ النَّشْأَةَ الْأُولَىٰ فَلَوْلَا تَذَكَّرُونَ ۝

63 Have ye seen that which ye cultivate?

أَفَرَأَيْتُم مَّا تَحْرُثُونَ ۝

64 Is it ye who foster it, or are We the Fosterer?

ءَأَنتُمْ تَزْرَعُونَهُ أَمْ نَحْنُ الزَّارِعُونَ ۝

65 If We willed, We verily could make it chaff, then would ye cease not to exclaim:

لَوْ نَشَآءُ لَجَعَلْنَاهُ حُطَامًا فَظَلْتُمْ تَفَكَّهُونَ ۝

66 Lo! we are laden with debt!

إِنَّا لَمُغْرَمُونَ ۝

67 Nay, but we are deprived!

بَلْ نَحْنُ مَحْرُومُونَ ۝

68 Have ye observed the water which ye drink?

أَفَرَءَيْتُمُ الْمَاءَ الَّذِى تَشْرَبُونَ ۝

69 Is it ye who shed it from the rain cloud, or are We the shedder?

ءَأَنتُمْ أَنزَلْتُمُوهُ مِنَ الْمُزْنِ أَمْ نَحْنُ الْمُنزِلُونَ ۝

70 If We willed We verily could make it bitter. Why, then, give ye not thanks?

لَوْ نَشَاءُ جَعَلْنَاهُ أُجَاجًا فَلَوْلَا تَشْكُرُونَ ۝

71 Have ye observed the fire which ye strike out;

أَفَرَءَيْتُمُ النَّارَ الَّتِى تُورُونَ ۝

72 Was it ye who made the tree thereof to grow, or were We the grower?

ءَأَنتُمْ أَنشَأْتُمْ شَجَرَتَهَا أَمْ نَحْنُ الْمُنشِئُونَ ۝

73 We, even We, appointed it a memorial and a comfort for the dwellers in the wilderness.

نَحْنُ جَعَلْنَاهَا تَذْكِرَةً وَمَتَاعًا لِّلْمُقْوِينَ ۝

74 Therefore (O Muhammad), praise the name of thy Lord, the Tremendous.

فَسَبِّحْ بِاسْمِ رَبِّكَ الْعَظِيمِ ۝

75 Nay, I swear by the places of the stars—

فَلَا أُقْسِمُ بِمَوَاقِعِ النُّجُومِ ۝

76 And lo! that verily is a tremendous oath, if ye but knew—

وَإِنَّهُ لَقَسَمٌ لَّوْ تَعْلَمُونَ عَظِيمٌ ۝

77 That (this) is indeed a noble Qur'an

إِنَّهُ لَقُرْآنٌ كَرِيمٌ ۝

78 In a Book kept hidden

فِى كِتَابٍ مَّكْنُونٍ ۝

79 Which none toucheth save the purified,

لَّا يَمَسُّهُ إِلَّا الْمُطَهَّرُونَ ۝

80 A revelation from the Lord of the Worlds.

تَنزِيلٌ مِّن رَّبِّ الْعَالَمِينَ ۝

81 Is it this Statement that ye scorn,

أَفَبِهَذَا الْحَدِيثِ أَنتُم مُّدْهِنُونَ ۝

82 And make denial thereof your livelihood?

وَتَجْعَلُوْنَ رِزْقَكُمْ أَنَّكُمْ تُكَذِّبُوْنَ ۞

83 Why, then, when (the soul) cometh up to the throat (of the dying)

فَلَوْلَآ إِذَا بَلَغَتِ الْحُلْقُوْمَ ۞

84 And ye are at that moment looking—

وَأَنْتُمْ حِيْنَئِذٍ تَنْظُرُوْنَ ۞

85 And We are nearer unto him than ye are, but ye see not—

وَنَحْنُ أَقْرَبُ إِلَيْهِ مِنْكُمْ وَلٰكِنْ لَّا تُبْصِرُوْنَ ۞

86 Why then, if ye are not in bondage (unto Us),

فَلَوْلَآ إِنْ كُنْتُمْ غَيْرَ مَدِيْنِيْنَ ۞

87 Do ye not force it back, if ye are truthful?

تَرْجِعُوْنَهَآ إِنْ كُنْتُمْ صٰدِقِيْنَ ۞

88 Thus if he is of those brought nigh,

فَأَمَّآ إِنْ كَانَ مِنَ الْمُقَرَّبِيْنَ ۞

89 Then breath of life, and plenty, and a Garden of delight.

فَرَوْحٌ وَّرَيْحَانٌ ەوَّجَنَّتُ نَعِيْمٍ ۞

90 And if he is of those on the right hand,

وَأَمَّآ إِنْ كَانَ مِنْ أَصْحٰبِ الْيَمِيْنِ ۞

91 Then (the greeting) "Peace be unto thee" from those on the right hand.

فَسَلٰمٌ لَّكَ مِنْ أَصْحٰبِ الْيَمِيْنِ ۞

92 But if he is of the rejecters, the erring,

وَأَمَّآ إِنْ كَانَ مِنَ الْمُكَذِّبِيْنَ الضَّآلِّيْنَ ۞

93 Then the welcome will be boiling water

فَنُزُلٌ مِّنْ حَمِيْمٍ ۞

94 And roasting at hell fire.

وَتَصْلِيَةُ جَحِيْمٍ ۞

95 Lo! this is certain truth.

إِنَّ هٰذَا لَهُوَ حَقُّ الْيَقِيْنِ ۞

96 Therefore (O Muhammad) praise the name of thy Lord, the Tremendous.

فَسَبِّحْ بِاسْمِ رَبِّكَ الْعَظِيْمِ ۞

Al Ḥadīd
(Iron)

Al Ḥadīd, "Iron," takes its name from a word in v. 25.

The reference in the word "victory" in v. 10, is undoubtedly to the conquest of Makkah, though Nöldeke[1] takes it to refer to the battle of Badr, and so would place the sūrah in the fourth or fifth year of the Hijrah. The words of the verse are against such an assumption since no Muslims "spent and fought" before the battle at Badr, which was the beginning of their fighting.

The date of revelation must be the eighth or ninth year of the Hijrah.

In the name of Allah, the Beneficent, the Merciful.

بِسْمِ اللَّهِ الرَّحْمَٰنِ الرَّحِيمِ

1   All that is in the heavens and the earth glorifieth Allah and He is the Mighty, the Wise.

2   His is the Sovereignty of the heavens and the earth; He quickeneth and He giveth death; and He is Able to do all things.

3   He is the First and the Last, and the Outward and the Inward; and He is Knower of all things.

---

1. Th. Nöldeke, *Geschichte des Qorāns*, 2nd Ed., Part I, Leipzig, 1909, p. 195.

4   He it is Who created the heavens and the earth in six Days;[2] then He mounted the Throne. He knoweth all that entereth the earth and all that emergeth therefrom and all that cometh down from the sky and all that ascendeth therein; and He is with you wheresoever ye may be. And Allah is Seer of what ye do.

هُوَالَّذِى خَلَقَ السَّمَوَٰتِ وَالْأَرْضَ فِى سِتَّةِ أَيَّامٍ ثُمَّ اسْتَوَىٰ عَلَى الْعَرْشِ يَعْلَمُ مَا يَلِجُ فِى الْأَرْضِ وَمَا يَخْرُجُ مِنْهَا وَمَا يَنزِلُ مِنَ السَّمَآءِ وَمَا يَعْرُجُ فِيهَا وَهُوَ مَعَكُمْ أَيْنَ مَا كُنتُمْ وَاللَّهُ بِمَا تَعْمَلُونَ بَصِيرٌ ۝

5   His is the Sovereignty of the heavens and the earth and, unto Allah (all) things are brought back.

لَهُ مُلْكُ السَّمَوَٰتِ وَالْأَرْضِ وَإِلَى اللَّهِ تُرْجَعُ الْأُمُورُ ۝

6   He causeth the night to pass into the day, and He causeth the day to pass into the night, and He is Knower of all that is in the breasts.

يُولِجُ الَّيْلَ فِى النَّهَارِ وَيُولِجُ النَّهَارَ فِى الَّيْلِ وَهُوَ عَلِيمٌ بِذَاتِ الصُّدُورِ ۝

7   Believe in Allah and His messenger, and spend of that whereof He hath made you trustees; and such of you as believe and spend (aright), theirs will be a great reward,

ءَامِنُوا بِاللَّهِ وَرَسُولِهِ وَأَنفِقُوا مِمَّا جَعَلَكُم مُّسْتَخْلَفِينَ فِيهِ فَالَّذِينَ ءَامَنُوا مِنكُمْ وَأَنفَقُوا لَهُمْ أَجْرٌ كَبِيرٌ ۝

8   What aileth you that ye believe not in Allah, when the messenger calleth you to believe in your Lord, and He hath already made a covenant with you, if ye are believers?

وَمَا لَكُمْ لَا تُؤْمِنُونَ بِاللَّهِ وَالرَّسُولُ يَدْعُوكُمْ لِتُؤْمِنُوا بِرَبِّكُمْ وَقَدْ أَخَذَ مِيثَٰقَكُمْ إِن كُنتُم مُّؤْمِنِينَ ۝

9   He it is Who sendeth down clear revelations unto His slave, that He may bring you forth from darkness unto light; and lo! for you, Allah is Full of Pity, Merciful.

هُوَالَّذِى يُنَزِّلُ عَلَىٰ عَبْدِهِ ءَايَٰتٍ بَيِّنَٰتٍ لِّيُخْرِجَكُم مِّنَ الظُّلُمَٰتِ إِلَى النُّورِ وَإِنَّ اللَّهَ بِكُمْ لَرَءُوفٌ رَّحِيمٌ ۝

---

2. (22: 47); (32: 5); (70: 4).

10 And what aileth you that ye spend not in the way of Allah, when unto Allah belongeth the inheritance of the heavens and the earth? Those who spent and fought before the victory are not upon a level (with the rest of you). Such are greater in rank than those who spent and fought afterwards. Unto each hath Allah promised good. And Allah is Aware of what ye do.

وَمَا لَكُمْ أَلَّا تُنْفِقُوا فِى سَبِيلِ اللَّهِ وَلِلَّهِ مِيرَاثُ السَّمَوَاتِ وَالْأَرْضِ لَا يَسْتَوِى مِنكُم مَّنْ أَنفَقَ مِن قَبْلِ الْفَتْحِ وَقَاتَلَ أُوْلَـئِكَ أَعْظَمُ دَرَجَةً مِّنَ الَّذِينَ أَنفَقُوا مِنْ بَعْدُ وَقَاتَلُوا وَكُلًّا وَعَدَ اللَّهُ الْحُسْنَىٰ وَاللَّهُ بِمَا تَعْمَلُونَ خَبِيرٌ ۝

11 Who is he that will lend unto Allah a goodly loan,[3] that He may double it for him and his may be a rich reward?

مَن ذَا الَّذِى يُقْرِضُ اللَّهَ قَرْضًا حَسَنًا فَيُضَاعِفَهُ لَهُ وَلَهُ أَجْرٌ كَرِيمٌ ۝

12 On the day when thou (Muhammad) wilt see the believers, men and women, their light shining forth before them and on their right hands, (and wilt hear it said unto them): Glad news for you this day: Gardens underneath which rivers flow, wherein ye are immortal. That is the supreme triumph.

يَوْمَ تَرَى الْمُؤْمِنِينَ وَالْمُؤْمِنَاتِ يَسْعَىٰ نُورُهُم بَيْنَ أَيْدِيهِمْ وَبِأَيْمَانِهِم بُشْرَاكُمُ الْيَوْمَ جَنَّاتٌ تَجْرِى مِن تَحْتِهَا الْأَنْهَارُ خَالِدِينَ فِيهَا ذَلِكَ هُوَ الْفَوْزُ الْعَظِيمُ ۝

13 On the day when the hypocritical men and the hypocritical women will say unto those who believe: Look on us that we may borrow from your light! It will be said: Go back and seek for light! Then there will separate them a wall wherein is a gate, the inner side whereof containeth mercy, while the outer side thereof is toward the doom.

يَوْمَ يَقُولُ الْمُنَافِقُونَ وَالْمُنَافِقَاتُ لِلَّذِينَ ءَامَنُوا انظُرُونَا نَقْتَبِسْ مِن نُّورِكُمْ قِيلَ ارْجِعُوا وَرَاءَكُمْ فَالْتَمِسُوا نُورًا فَضُرِبَ بَيْنَهُم بِسُورٍ لَّهُ بَابٌ بَاطِنُهُ فِيهِ الرَّحْمَةُ وَظَاهِرُهُ مِن قِبَلِهِ الْعَذَابُ ۝

---

3. A loan without interest or any thought of gain or loss.

14 They will cry unto them
(saying): Were we not with you?
They will say: Yea, verily; but ye
tempted one another, and hesitated,
and doubted, and vain desires beguiled you till the ordinance of Allah
came to pass; and the deceiver
deceived you concerning Allah;

يُنَادُونَهُمْ أَلَمْ نَكُن مَّعَكُمْ قَالُوا بَلَىٰ وَلَٰكِنَّكُمْ فَتَنتُمْ
أَنفُسَكُمْ وَتَرَبَّصْتُمْ وَارْتَبْتُمْ وَغَرَّتْكُمُ الْأَمَانِيُّ
حَتَّىٰ جَاءَ أَمْرُ اللَّهِ وَغَرَّكُم بِاللَّهِ الْغَرُورُ ﴿١٤﴾

15 So this day no ransom can be
taken from you nor from those who
disbelieved. Your home is the Fire;
that is your patron, and a hapless
journey's end.

فَالْيَوْمَ لَا يُؤْخَذُ مِنكُمْ فِدْيَةٌ وَلَا مِنَ الَّذِينَ كَفَرُوا
مَأْوَاكُمُ النَّارُ هِيَ مَوْلَاكُمْ وَبِئْسَ الْمَصِيرُ ﴿١٥﴾

16 Is not the time ripe for the
hearts of those who believe to submit to Allah's reminder and to the
truth which is revealed, that they
become not as those who received
the Scripture of old but the term
was prolonged for them and so their
hearts were hardened, and many of
them are evil-livers.

۞ أَلَمْ يَأْنِ لِلَّذِينَ ءَامَنُوا أَن تَخْشَعَ قُلُوبُهُمْ لِذِكْرِ
اللَّهِ وَمَا نَزَلَ مِنَ الْحَقِّ وَلَا يَكُونُوا كَالَّذِينَ أُوتُوا
الْكِتَٰبَ مِن قَبْلُ فَطَالَ عَلَيْهِمُ الْأَمَدُ فَقَسَتْ
قُلُوبُهُمْ وَكَثِيرٌ مِّنْهُمْ فَٰسِقُونَ ﴿١٦﴾

17 Know that Allah quickeneth the
earth after its death. We have made
clear Our revelations for you, that
haply ye may understand.

اعْلَمُوا أَنَّ اللَّهَ يُحْيِ الْأَرْضَ بَعْدَ مَوْتِهَا قَدْ بَيَّنَّا
لَكُمُ الْآيَٰتِ لَعَلَّكُمْ تَعْقِلُونَ ﴿١٧﴾

18 Lo! those who give alms, both
men and women, and lend unto
Allah a goodly loan, it will be
doubled for them, and theirs will be
a rich reward.

إِنَّ الْمُصَّدِّقِينَ وَالْمُصَّدِّقَٰتِ وَأَقْرَضُوا اللَّهَ قَرْضًا
حَسَنًا يُضَٰعَفُ لَهُمْ وَلَهُمْ أَجْرٌ كَرِيمٌ ﴿١٨﴾

19 And those who believe in Allah
and His messengers, they are the
truthful; and the martyrs are with
their Lord; they have their reward

وَالَّذِينَ ءَامَنُوا بِاللَّهِ وَرُسُلِهِ أُولَٰئِكَ هُمُ الصِّدِّيقُونَ
وَالشُّهَدَاءُ عِندَ رَبِّهِمْ لَهُمْ أَجْرُهُمْ وَنُورُهُمْ

and their light; while as for those who disbelieve and deny Our revelations, they are owners of hell-fire.

20 Know that the life of this world is only play, and idle talk, and pageantry, and boasting among you, and rivalry in respect of wealth and children; as the likeness of vegetation after rain, whereof the growth is pleasing to the husbandman, but afterward it drieth up and thou seest it turning yellow then it becometh straw. And in the Hereafter there is grievous punishment, and (also) forgiveness from Allah and His good pleasure, whereas the life of the world is but matter of illusion.

21 Race one with another for forgiveness from your Lord and a Garden whereof the breadth is as the breadth of the heavens and the earth, which is in store for those who believe in Allah and His messengers. Such is the bounty of Allah, which He bestoweth upon whom He will, and Allah is of infinite bounty.

22 Naught of disaster befalleth in the earth or in yourselves but it is in a Book before We bring it into being—Lo! that is easy for Allah;

23 That ye grieve not for the sake of that which hath escaped you, nor yet exult because of what He has given you. Allah loveth not all prideful boasters,

وَالَّذِينَ كَفَرُوا وَكَذَّبُوا بِآيَاتِنَا أُولَٰئِكَ أَصْحَابُ الْجَحِيمِ ﴿١٩﴾

اعْلَمُوا أَنَّمَا الْحَيَاةُ الدُّنْيَا لَعِبٌ وَلَهْوٌ وَزِينَةٌ وَتَفَاخُرٌ بَيْنَكُمْ وَتَكَاثُرٌ فِي الْأَمْوَالِ وَالْأَوْلَادِ كَمَثَلِ غَيْثٍ أَعْجَبَ الْكُفَّارَ نَبَاتُهُ ثُمَّ يَهِيجُ فَتَرَاهُ مُصْفَرًّا ثُمَّ يَكُونُ حُطَامًا وَفِي الْآخِرَةِ عَذَابٌ شَدِيدٌ وَمَغْفِرَةٌ مِّنَ اللَّهِ وَرِضْوَانٌ وَمَا الْحَيَاةُ الدُّنْيَا إِلَّا مَتَاعُ الْغُرُورِ ﴿٢٠﴾

سَابِقُوا إِلَىٰ مَغْفِرَةٍ مِّن رَّبِّكُمْ وَجَنَّةٍ عَرْضُهَا كَعَرْضِ السَّمَاءِ وَالْأَرْضِ أُعِدَّتْ لِلَّذِينَ آمَنُوا بِاللَّهِ وَرُسُلِهِ ذَٰلِكَ فَضْلُ اللَّهِ يُؤْتِيهِ مَن يَشَاءُ وَاللَّهُ ذُو الْفَضْلِ الْعَظِيمِ ﴿٢١﴾

مَا أَصَابَ مِن مُّصِيبَةٍ فِي الْأَرْضِ وَلَا فِي أَنفُسِكُمْ إِلَّا فِي كِتَابٍ مِّن قَبْلِ أَن نَّبْرَأَهَا إِنَّ ذَٰلِكَ عَلَى اللَّهِ يَسِيرٌ ﴿٢٢﴾ لِّكَيْلَا تَأْسَوْا عَلَىٰ مَا فَاتَكُمْ وَلَا تَفْرَحُوا بِمَا آتَاكُمْ وَاللَّهُ لَا يُحِبُّ كُلَّ مُخْتَالٍ فَخُورٍ ﴿٢٣﴾

24 Who hoard and who enjoin upon the people avarice. And whosoever turneth away, still Allah is the Absolute, the Owner of Praise.

الَّذِينَ يَبْخَلُونَ وَيَأْمُرُونَ النَّاسَ بِالْبُخْلِ وَمَن يَتَوَلَّ فَإِنَّ اللَّهَ هُوَ الْغَنِيُّ الْحَمِيدُ ۝

25 We verily sent Our messengers with clear proofs, and revealed with them the Scripture and the Balance, that mankind may observe right measure; and We sent down iron, wherein is mighty power and (many) uses for mankind, and that Allah may know him who helpeth Him and His messengers, though unseen. Lo! Allah is Strong, Almighty.

لَقَدْ أَرْسَلْنَا رُسُلَنَا بِالْبَيِّنَاتِ وَأَنزَلْنَا مَعَهُمُ الْكِتَابَ وَالْمِيزَانَ لِيَقُومَ النَّاسُ بِالْقِسْطِ وَأَنزَلْنَا الْحَدِيدَ فِيهِ بَأْسٌ شَدِيدٌ وَمَنَافِعُ لِلنَّاسِ وَلِيَعْلَمَ اللَّهُ مَن يَنصُرُهُ وَرُسُلَهُ بِالْغَيْبِ إِنَّ اللَّهَ قَوِيٌّ عَزِيزٌ ۝

26 And We verily sent Noah and Abraham and placed the Prophethood and the Scripture among their seed, and among them there is he who goeth right, but many of them are evil-livers.

وَلَقَدْ أَرْسَلْنَا نُوحًا وَإِبْرَاهِيمَ وَجَعَلْنَا فِي ذُرِّيَّتِهِمَا النُّبُوَّةَ وَالْكِتَابَ فَمِنْهُم مُّهْتَدٍ وَكَثِيرٌ مِّنْهُمْ فَاسِقُونَ ۝

27 Then We caused Our messengers to follow in their footsteps; and We caused Jesus, son of Mary, to follow, and gave him the Gospel, and placed compassion and mercy in the hearts of those who followed him. But monasticism they invented—We ordained it not for them—Only seeking Allah's pleasure, and they observed it not with right observance. So We give those of them who believe their reward, but many of them are evil-livers.

ثُمَّ قَفَّيْنَا عَلَىٰ ءَاثَارِهِم بِرُسُلِنَا وَقَفَّيْنَا بِعِيسَى ابْنِ مَرْيَمَ وَءَاتَيْنَاهُ الْإِنجِيلَ وَجَعَلْنَا فِي قُلُوبِ الَّذِينَ اتَّبَعُوهُ رَأْفَةً وَرَحْمَةً وَرَهْبَانِيَّةً ابْتَدَعُوهَا مَا كَتَبْنَاهَا عَلَيْهِمْ إِلَّا ابْتِغَاءَ رِضْوَانِ اللَّهِ فَمَا رَعَوْهَا حَقَّ رِعَايَتِهَا فَآتَيْنَا الَّذِينَ ءَامَنُوا مِنْهُمْ أَجْرَهُمْ وَكَثِيرٌ مِّنْهُمْ فَاسِقُونَ ۝

28 O ye who believe! Be mindful
of your duty to Allah and put faith
in His messenger. He will give you
twofold of His mercy and will appoint for you a light wherein ye shall
walk, and will forgive you. Allah is
Forgiving, Merciful;

يَٰٓأَيُّهَا ٱلَّذِينَ ءَامَنُوا۟ ٱتَّقُوا۟ ٱللَّهَ وَءَامِنُوا۟ بِرَسُولِهِۦ
يُؤْتِكُمْ كِفْلَيْنِ مِن رَّحْمَتِهِۦ وَيَجْعَل لَّكُمْ نُورًا
تَمْشُونَ بِهِۦ وَيَغْفِرْ لَكُمْ وَٱللَّهُ غَفُورٌ رَّحِيمٌ ۝

29 That the People of the Scripture[4]
may know that they control naught
of the bounty of Allah, but that the
bounty is in Allah's hand to give to
whom He will. And Allah is of
infinite bounty.

لِّئَلَّا يَعْلَمَ أَهْلُ ٱلْكِتَٰبِ أَلَّا يَقْدِرُونَ
عَلَىٰ شَىْءٍ مِّن فَضْلِ ٱللَّهِ وَأَنَّ ٱلْفَضْلَ بِيَدِ ٱللَّهِ
يُؤْتِيهِ مَن يَشَآءُ وَٱللَّهُ ذُو ٱلْفَضْلِ ٱلْعَظِيمِ ۝

---

4. *i.e.* Jews and Christians.

Al Mujādilah
(She That Disputeth)

Al Mujādilah, "She That Disputeth," takes its name from a word in verse 1.

A woman had complained to the Prophet that her husband had put her away for no good reason by employing an old formula of the pagan Arabs, saying that her back was for him as the back of his mother, and she "disputed" with the Prophet because he would take no action against the man before this revelation came to him. There is a brief reference to the same method of getting rid of wives in sūrah 33, v. 4. This sūrah must therefore have been revealed before sūrah 33.

The date of revelation is the fourth or fifth year of the Hijrah.

In the name of Allah, the Beneficent, the Merciful.

1   Allah hath heard the saying of her that disputeth with thee (Muhammad) concerning her husband, and complaineth unto Allah. And Allah heareth your colloquy. Lo! Allah is Hearer, Knower.

2   Such of you as put away your wives (by saying they are as their mothers)—They are not their mothers;[1] none are their mothers

---

1. (33: 4).

except those who gave them birth—they indeed utter an ill word and a lie. And lo! Allah is Forgiving, Merciful.

3 Those who put away their wives (by saying they are as their mothers)[2] and afterward would go back on that which they have said; (the penalty) in that case (is) the freeing of a slave before they touch one another. Unto this ye are exhorted; and Allah is Aware of what ye do.

4 And he who findeth not (the wherewithal), let him fast for two successive months before they touch one another; and for him who is unable to do so (the penance is) the feeding of sixty needy ones. This, that ye may put trust in Allah and His messenger. Such are the limits (imposed by Allah); and for disbelievers is a painful doom.

5 Those who oppose Allah and His messenger will be abased even as those before them were abased; and We have sent down clear tokens, and for disbelievers is a shameful doom

6 On the day when Allah will raise them all together and inform them of what they did. Allah hath kept account of it while they forgot it. And Allah is Witness over all things.

وَإِنَّهُمْ لَيَقُولُونَ مُنكَرًا مِّنَ ٱلْقَوْلِ وَزُورًا ۚ وَإِنَّ ٱللَّهَ لَعَفُوٌّ غَفُورٌ ﴿٢﴾

وَٱلَّذِينَ يُظَٰهِرُونَ مِن نِّسَآئِهِمْ ثُمَّ يَعُودُونَ لِمَا قَالُواْ فَتَحْرِيرُ رَقَبَةٍ مِّن قَبْلِ أَن يَتَمَآسَّا ۚ ذَٰلِكُمْ تُوعَظُونَ بِهِۦ ۚ وَٱللَّهُ بِمَا تَعْمَلُونَ خَبِيرٌ ﴿٣﴾

فَمَن لَّمْ يَجِدْ فَصِيَامُ شَهْرَيْنِ مُتَتَابِعَيْنِ مِن قَبْلِ أَن يَتَمَآسَّا ۖ فَمَن لَّمْ يَسْتَطِعْ فَإِطْعَامُ سِتِّينَ مِسْكِينًا ۚ ذَٰلِكَ لِتُؤْمِنُواْ بِٱللَّهِ وَرَسُولِهِۦ ۚ وَتِلْكَ حُدُودُ ٱللَّهِ ۗ وَلِلْكَٰفِرِينَ عَذَابٌ أَلِيمٌ ﴿٤﴾

إِنَّ ٱلَّذِينَ يُحَآدُّونَ ٱللَّهَ وَرَسُولَهُۥ كُبِتُواْ كَمَا كُبِتَ ٱلَّذِينَ مِن قَبْلِهِمْ ۚ وَقَدْ أَنزَلْنَآ ءَايَٰتٍ بَيِّنَٰتٍ ۚ وَلِلْكَٰفِرِينَ عَذَابٌ مُّهِينٌ ﴿٥﴾

يَوْمَ يَبْعَثُهُمُ ٱللَّهُ جَمِيعًا فَيُنَبِّئُهُم بِمَا عَمِلُوٓاْ ۚ أَحْصَىٰهُ ٱللَّهُ وَنَسُوهُ ۚ وَٱللَّهُ عَلَىٰ كُلِّ شَىْءٍ شَهِيدٌ ﴿٦﴾

---

2. (33: 4).

7 Hast thou not seen that Allah knoweth all that is in the heavens and all that is in the earth? There is no secret conference of three but He is their fourth, nor of five but He is their sixth, nor of less than that or more but He is with them wheresoever they may be; and afterward, on the Day of Resurrection, He will inform them of what they did. Lo! Allah is Knower of all things.

أَلَمْ تَرَ أَنَّ اللّٰهَ يَعْلَمُ مَا فِى السَّمٰوٰتِ وَمَا فِى الْأَرْضِ مَا يَكُونُ مِنْ نَّجْوٰى ثَلٰثَةٍ إِلَّا هُوَ رَابِعُهُمْ وَلَا خَمْسَةٍ إِلَّا هُوَ سَادِسُهُمْ وَلَاۤ أَدْنٰى مِنْ ذٰلِكَ وَلَاۤ أَكْثَرَ إِلَّا هُوَ مَعَهُمْ أَيْنَ مَا كَانُوْا ۖ ثُمَّ يُنَبِّئُهُمْ بِمَا عَمِلُوْا يَوْمَ الْقِيٰمَةِ ۚ إِنَّ اللّٰهَ بِكُلِّ شَىْءٍ عَلِيمٌ ۝

8 Hast thou not observed those who were forbidden conspiracy and afterward returned to that which they had been forbidden, and (now) conspire together for crime and wrongdoing and disobedience toward the messenger? And when they come unto thee they greet thee with a greeting wherewith Allah greeteth thee not, and say within themselves: Why doth Allah punish us not for what we say? Hell will suffice them; they will feel the heat thereof. A hapless journey's end!

أَلَمْ تَرَ إِلَى الَّذِيْنَ نُهُوْا عَنِ النَّجْوٰى ثُمَّ يَعُوْدُوْنَ لِمَا نُهُوْا عَنْهُ وَيَتَنٰجَوْنَ بِالْإِثْمِ وَالْعُدْوَانِ وَمَعْصِيَتِ الرَّسُوْلِ وَإِذَا جَآءُوْكَ حَيَّوْكَ بِمَا لَمْ يُحَيِّكَ بِهِ اللّٰهُ وَيَقُوْلُوْنَ فِىْۤ أَنْفُسِهِمْ لَوْلَا يُعَذِّبُنَا اللّٰهُ بِمَا نَقُوْلُ ۚ حَسْبُهُمْ جَهَنَّمُ ۚ يَصْلَوْنَهَا ۚ فَبِئْسَ الْمَصِيْرُ ۝

9 O ye who believe! When ye conspire together, conspire not together for crime and wrongdoing and disobedience toward the messenger, but conspire together for righteousness and pity, and keep your duty, toward Allah, unto whom ye will be gathered.

يٰۤأَيُّهَا الَّذِيْنَ اٰمَنُوْۤا إِذَا تَنٰجَيْتُمْ فَلَا تَتَنٰجَوْا بِالْإِثْمِ وَالْعُدْوَانِ وَمَعْصِيَتِ الرَّسُوْلِ وَتَنٰجَوْا بِالْبِرِّ وَالتَّقْوٰى وَاتَّقُوا اللّٰهَ الَّذِىْۤ إِلَيْهِ تُحْشَرُوْنَ ۝

10 Lo! Conspiracy is only of the devil, that he may vex those who believe; but he can harm them not

إِنَّمَا النَّجْوٰى مِنَ الشَّيْطٰنِ لِيَحْزُنَ الَّذِيْنَ اٰمَنُوْا وَلَيْسَ بِضَآرِّهِمْ شَيْئًا إِلَّا بِإِذْنِ اللّٰهِ ۚ وَعَلَى اللّٰهِ

at all unless by Allah's leave. In Allah let believers put their trust.

فَلْيَتَوَكَّلِ الْمُؤْمِنُونَ ۝

11 O ye who believe! When it is said, Make room! in assemblies, then make room; Allah will make way for you (hereafter). And when it is said; Come up higher! Go up higher; Allah will exalt those who believe among you, and those who have knowledge, to high ranks. Allah is Informed of what ye do.

يَـٰٓأَيُّهَا الَّذِينَ ءَامَنُوٓا إِذَا قِيلَ لَكُمْ تَفَسَّحُوا فِى الْمَجَٰلِسِ فَافْسَحُوا يَفْسَحِ اللَّهُ لَكُمْ وَإِذَا قِيلَ انشُزُوا فَانشُزُوا يَرْفَعِ اللَّهُ الَّذِينَ ءَامَنُوا مِنكُمْ وَالَّذِينَ أُوتُوا الْعِلْمَ دَرَجَٰتٍ وَاللَّهُ بِمَا تَعْمَلُونَ خَبِيرٌ ۝

12 O ye who believe! When ye hold conference with the messenger, offer an alms before your conference. That is better and purer for you. But if ye cannot find (the wherewithal) then lo! Allah is Forgiving, Merciful.

يَـٰٓأَيُّهَا الَّذِينَ ءَامَنُوٓا إِذَا نَٰجَيْتُمُ الرَّسُولَ فَقَدِّمُوا بَيْنَ يَدَىْ نَجْوَىٰكُمْ صَدَقَةً ذَٰلِكَ خَيْرٌ لَّكُمْ وَأَطْهَرُ فَإِن لَّمْ تَجِدُوا فَإِنَّ اللَّهَ غَفُورٌ رَّحِيمٌ ۝

13 Fear ye to offer alms before your conference? Then, when ye do it not and Allah hath forgiven you, establish worship and pay the poor-due and obey Allah and His messenger. And Allah is Aware of what ye do.

ءَأَشْفَقْتُمْ أَن تُقَدِّمُوا بَيْنَ يَدَىْ نَجْوَىٰكُمْ صَدَقَٰتٍ فَإِذْ لَمْ تَفْعَلُوا وَتَابَ اللَّهُ عَلَيْكُمْ فَأَقِيمُوا الصَّلَوٰةَ وَءَاتُوا الزَّكَوٰةَ وَأَطِيعُوا اللَّهَ وَرَسُولَهُ وَاللَّهُ خَبِيرٌ بِمَا تَعْمَلُونَ ۝

14 Hast thou not seen those who take for friends a folk with whom Allah is wroth? They are neither of you nor of them, and they swear a false oath knowingly.

۞ أَلَمْ تَرَ إِلَى الَّذِينَ تَوَلَّوْا قَوْمًا غَضِبَ اللَّهُ عَلَيْهِم مَّا هُم مِّنكُمْ وَلَا مِنْهُمْ وَيَحْلِفُونَ عَلَى الْكَذِبِ وَهُمْ يَعْلَمُونَ ۝

15 Allah hath prepared for them a dreadful doom. Evil indeed is that which they are wont to do.

أَعَدَّ اللَّهُ لَهُمْ عَذَابًا شَدِيدًا إِنَّهُمْ سَآءَ مَا كَانُوا يَعْمَلُونَ ۝

16 They make a shelter of their oaths and turn (men) from the way

اتَّخَذُوٓا أَيْمَٰنَهُمْ جُنَّةً فَصَدُّوا عَن سَبِيلِ اللَّهِ فَلَهُمْ

of Allah; so theirs will be a shameful doom.

عَذَابٌ مُّهِينٌ ۝

17 Their wealth and their children
will avail them naught against
Allah. Such are rightful owners of
the Fire; they will abide therein.

لَن تُغْنِىَ عَنْهُمْ أَمْوَٰلُهُمْ وَلَآ أَوْلَٰدُهُم مِّنَ ٱللَّهِ
شَيْئًا أُوْلَٰٓئِكَ أَصْحَٰبُ ٱلنَّارِ هُمْ فِيهَا خَٰلِدُونَ ۝

18 On the day when Allah will
raise them all together, then will
they swear unto Him as they (now)
swear unto you, and they will fancy
that they have some standing.
Beware! Surely, it is they who are
the liars.

يَوْمَ يَبْعَثُهُمُ ٱللَّهُ جَمِيعًا فَيَحْلِفُونَ لَهُۥ كَمَا يَحْلِفُونَ لَكُمْ
وَيَحْسَبُونَ أَنَّهُمْ عَلَىٰ شَىْءٍ أَلَآ إِنَّهُمْ هُمُ ٱلْكَٰذِبُونَ ۝

19 The devil hath engrossed them
and so hath caused them to forget
remembrance of Allah. They are the
devil's party. Beware! Surely, it is
the devil's party who will be the
losers.

ٱسْتَحْوَذَ عَلَيْهِمُ ٱلشَّيْطَٰنُ فَأَنسَىٰهُمْ ذِكْرَ ٱللَّهِ أُوْلَٰٓئِكَ
حِزْبُ ٱلشَّيْطَٰنِ أَلَآ إِنَّ حِزْبَ ٱلشَّيْطَٰنِ هُمُ ٱلْخَٰسِرُونَ ۝

20 Lo! those who oppose Allah and
His messenger, they will be among
the lowest.

إِنَّ ٱلَّذِينَ يُحَآدُّونَ ٱللَّهَ وَرَسُولَهُۥٓ أُوْلَٰٓئِكَ فِى ٱلْأَذَلِّينَ ۝

21 Allah hath decreed: Lo! I verily
shall conquer, I and My messengers.
Lo! Allah is Strong, Almighty.

كَتَبَ ٱللَّهُ لَأَغْلِبَنَّ أَنَا۠ وَرُسُلِىٓ إِنَّ ٱللَّهَ
قَوِىٌّ عَزِيزٌ ۝

22 Thou wilt not find folk who
believe in Allah and the Last Day
loving those who oppose Allah and
His messenger: Even though they
be their fathers or, their sons or
their brethren or their clan. As for

لَّا تَجِدُ قَوْمًا يُؤْمِنُونَ بِٱللَّهِ وَٱلْيَوْمِ ٱلْأَخِرِ
يُوَآدُّونَ مَنْ حَآدَّ ٱللَّهَ وَرَسُولَهُۥ وَلَوْ كَانُوٓا۟
ءَابَآءَهُمْ أَوْ أَبْنَآءَهُمْ أَوْ إِخْوَٰنَهُمْ

such, He hath written faith upon their hearts and hath strengthened them with a Spirit from Him, and He will bring them into Gardens underneath which rivers flow, wherein they will abide. Allah is well pleased with them, and they are well pleased with Him. They are Allah's party. Beware! Surely, it is Allah's party who are the successful.

أُوْلَٰٓئِكَ كَتَبَ فِى قُلُوبِهِمُ اُوْعَشِيرَتَهُمْ
الْإِيمَٰنَ وَأَيَّدَهُم بِرُوحٍ مِّنْهُ وَيُدْخِلُهُمْ
جَنَّٰتٍ تَجْرِى مِن تَحْتِهَا الْأَنْهَٰرُ خَٰلِدِينَ فِيهَا
رَضِىَ اللَّهُ عَنْهُمْ وَرَضُواْ عَنْهُ أُوْلَٰٓئِكَ حِزْبُ اللَّهِ
أَلَآ إِنَّ حِزْبَ اللَّهِ هُمُ الْمُفْلِحُونَ ﴿٢٢﴾

Al Ḥashr
(Exile)

Al Ḥashr, "Exile," takes its name from vv. 2-17, which refer to the exile
of the Banī Nadīr, a Jewish tribe of Al-Madīnah (for treason and pro-
jected murder of the Prophet) and the confiscation of their property. The
"Hypocrites," as the lukewarm Muslims were called, had secretly
sympathised with these Jews, whose opposition had grown strong since
the Muslim reverse at Mount Uḥud, and had promised to side with them
if it came to a collision with the Muslims; and to emigrate with them
if they were forced to emigrate. But when the Muslims marched against
the Banī Nadīr, and the latter took refuge in their strong towers, the
Hypocrites did nothing. And when at length they were reduced and
exiled, the Hypocrites did not go with them into exile.

The date of revelation is the fourth year of the Hijrah.

سُوْرَةُ الْحَشْرِ

*In the name of Allah, the
Beneficent, the Merciful.*

بِسْمِ اللَّهِ الرَّحْمَنِ الرَّحِيمِ

1   All that is in the heavens and all
that is in the earth glorifieth Allah,
and He is the Mighty, the Wise.

سَبَّحَ لِلَّهِ مَا فِي السَّمَوَاتِ وَمَا فِي الْأَرْضِ
وَهُوَ الْعَزِيزُ الْحَكِيمُ ۝

2   He it is Who hath caused those
of the People of the Scripture[1] who
disbelieved to go forth from their
homes unto the first exile. Ye
deemed not that they would go

هُوَ الَّذِي أَخْرَجَ الَّذِينَ كَفَرُوا مِنْ أَهْلِ الْكِتَابِ
مِنْ دِيَارِهِمْ لِأَوَّلِ الْحَشْرِ مَا ظَنَنْتُمْ أَنْ يَخْرُجُوا

---

1. The term for Jews and Christians. In this case it refers to Jews.

forth, while they deemed that their strongholds would protect them from Allah. But Allah reached them from a place whereof they reckoned not, and cast terror in their hearts so that they ruined their houses with their own hands and the hands of the believers. So learn a lesson, O ye who have eyes!

3   And if Allah had not decreed migration for them, He verily would have punished them in this world, and theirs in the Hereafter is the punishment of the Fire.

4   That is because they were opposed to Allah and His messenger; and whoso is opposed to Allah, (for him) verily Allah is stern in reprisal.

5   Whatsoever palm-trees ye cut down or left standing on their roots, it was by Allah's leave, in order that He might confound the evil-livers.

6   And that which Allah gave as spoil unto His messenger from them, ye urged not any horse or riding camel for the sake thereof, but Allah giveth His messenger lordship over whom He will. Allah is Able to do all things.

7   That which Allah giveth as spoil unto His messenger from the people of the townships, it is for Allah and

وَظَنُّوٓا أَنَّهُم مَّانِعَتُهُمْ حُصُونُهُم مِّنَ ٱللَّهِ فَأَتَىٰهُمُ ٱللَّهُ مِنْ حَيْثُ لَمْ يَحْتَسِبُوا ۖ وَقَذَفَ فِى قُلُوبِهِمُ ٱلرُّعْبَ ۚ يُخْرِبُونَ بُيُوتَهُم بِأَيْدِيهِمْ وَأَيْدِى ٱلْمُؤْمِنِينَ فَٱعْتَبِرُوا يَٰٓأُو۟لِى ٱلْأَبْصَٰرِ ﴿٢﴾

وَلَوْلَآ أَن كَتَبَ ٱللَّهُ عَلَيْهِمُ ٱلْجَلَآءَ لَعَذَّبَهُمْ فِى ٱلدُّنْيَا ۖ وَلَهُمْ فِى ٱلْآخِرَةِ عَذَابُ ٱلنَّارِ ﴿٣﴾

ذَٰلِكَ بِأَنَّهُمْ شَآقُّوا ٱللَّهَ وَرَسُولَهُۥ ۖ وَمَن يُشَآقِّ ٱللَّهَ فَإِنَّ ٱللَّهَ شَدِيدُ ٱلْعِقَابِ ﴿٤﴾

مَا قَطَعْتُم مِّن لِّينَةٍ أَوْ تَرَكْتُمُوهَا قَآئِمَةً عَلَىٰٓ أُصُولِهَا فَبِإِذْنِ ٱللَّهِ وَلِيُخْزِىَ ٱلْفَٰسِقِينَ ﴿٥﴾

وَمَآ أَفَآءَ ٱللَّهُ عَلَىٰ رَسُولِهِۦ مِنْهُمْ فَمَآ أَوْجَفْتُمْ عَلَيْهِ مِنْ خَيْلٍ وَلَا رِكَابٍ وَلَٰكِنَّ ٱللَّهَ يُسَلِّطُ رُسُلَهُۥ عَلَىٰ مَن يَشَآءُ ۚ وَٱللَّهُ عَلَىٰ كُلِّ شَىْءٍ قَدِيرٌ ﴿٦﴾

مَّآ أَفَآءَ ٱللَّهُ عَلَىٰ رَسُولِهِۦ مِنْ أَهْلِ ٱلْقُرَىٰ فَلِلَّهِ وَلِلرَّسُولِ

His messenger[2] and for the near of kin and the orphans and the needy and the wayfarer, that it become not a commodity between the rich among you. And whatsoever the messenger giveth you, take it. And whatsoever he forbiddeth, abstain (from it). And keep your duty to Allah. Lo! Allah is stern in reprisal.

وَلِذِى الْقُرْبٰى وَالْيَتٰمٰى وَالْمَسٰكِيْنِ وَابْنِ السَّبِيْلِ ۙ كَيْ لَا يَكُوْنَ دُوْلَةًۢ بَيْنَ الْاَغْنِيَآءِ مِنْكُمْ ۚ وَمَآ اٰتٰىكُمُ الرَّسُوْلُ فَخُذُوْهُ ۚ وَمَا نَهٰىكُمْ عَنْهُ فَانْتَهُوْا ۚ وَاتَّقُوا اللّٰهَ ۗ اِنَّ اللّٰهَ شَدِيْدُ الْعِقَابِ ۘ ۷

8　And (it is) for the poor fugitives who have been driven out from their homes and their belongings, who seek bounty from Allah and help Allah and His messenger. They are the loyal.

لِلْفُقَرَآءِ الْمُهٰجِرِيْنَ الَّذِيْنَ اُخْرِجُوْا مِنْ دِيَارِهِمْ وَاَمْوَالِهِمْ يَبْتَغُوْنَ فَضْلًا مِّنَ اللّٰهِ وَرِضْوَانًا وَّيَنْصُرُوْنَ اللّٰهَ وَرَسُوْلَهٗ ۚ اُولٰٓئِكَ هُمُ الصّٰدِقُوْنَ ۚ ۸

9　Those who entered the city and the faith before them love those who flee unto them for refuge, and find in their breasts no need for that which hath been given them, but prefer (the fugitives) above themselves though poverty become their lot. And whoso is saved from his own avarice—such are they who are successful.

وَالَّذِيْنَ تَبَوَّءُو الدَّارَ وَالْاِيْمَانَ مِنْ قَبْلِهِمْ يُحِبُّوْنَ مَنْ هَاجَرَ اِلَيْهِمْ وَلَا يَجِدُوْنَ فِيْ صُدُوْرِهِمْ حَاجَةً مِّمَّآ اُوْتُوْا وَيُؤْثِرُوْنَ عَلٰٓى اَنْفُسِهِمْ وَلَوْ كَانَ بِهِمْ خَصَاصَةٌ ۚ وَمَنْ يُّوْقَ شُحَّ نَفْسِهٖ فَاُولٰٓئِكَ هُمُ الْمُفْلِحُوْنَ ۚ ۹

10 And those who came (into the faith) after them say: Our Lord! Forgive us and our brethren who were before us in the faith, and place not in our hearts any rancour toward those who believe. Our Lord! Thou art Full of Pity, Merciful.

وَالَّذِيْنَ جَآءُوْ مِنْۢ بَعْدِهِمْ يَقُوْلُوْنَ رَبَّنَا اغْفِرْ لَنَا وَلِاِخْوَانِنَا الَّذِيْنَ سَبَقُوْنَا بِالْاِيْمَانِ وَلَا تَجْعَلْ فِيْ قُلُوْبِنَا غِلًّا لِّلَّذِيْنَ اٰمَنُوْا رَبَّنَآ اِنَّكَ رَءُوْفٌ رَّحِيْمٌ ۚ ۱۰

---

2. *i.e.* for the State.

11 Hast thou not observed those who are hypocrites, (how) they tell their brethren who disbelieve among the People of the Scripture: If ye are driven out, we surely will go out with you, and we will never obey anyone against you, and if ye are attacked we verily will help you. And Allah beareth witness that they verily are liars.

بِسْمِ أَلَمْ تَرَ إِلَى الَّذِينَ نَافَقُوا يَقُولُونَ لِإِخْوَانِهِمُ الَّذِينَ كَفَرُوا مِنْ أَهْلِ الْكِتَٰبِ لَئِنْ أُخْرِجْتُمْ لَنَخْرُجَنَّ مَعَكُمْ وَلَا نُطِيعُ فِيكُمْ أَحَدًا أَبَدًا وَإِن قُوتِلْتُمْ لَنَنصُرَنَّكُمْ وَاللَّهُ يَشْهَدُ إِنَّهُمْ لَكَٰذِبُونَ ۝

12 (For) indeed if they are driven out they go not out with them, and indeed if they are attacked they help them not, and indeed if they had helped them they would have turned and fled, and then they would not have been victorious.

لَئِنْ أُخْرِجُوا لَا يَخْرُجُونَ مَعَهُمْ وَلَئِنْ قُوتِلُوا لَا يَنصُرُونَهُمْ وَلَئِنْ نَّصَرُوهُمْ لَيُوَلُّنَّ الْأَدْبَٰرَ ثُمَّ لَا يُنصَرُونَ ۝

13 Ye are more awful as a fear in their bosoms than Allah. That is because they are a folk who understand not.

لَأَنتُمْ أَشَدُّ رَهْبَةً فِى صُدُورِهِم مِّنَ اللَّهِ ذَٰلِكَ بِأَنَّهُمْ قَوْمٌ لَّا يَفْقَهُونَ ۝

14 They will not fight against you in a body save in fortified villages or from behind walls. Their fighting among themselves is very great. Ye think of them as a whole whereas their hearts are divers. That is because they are a folk who have no sense.

لَا يُقَٰتِلُونَكُمْ جَمِيعًا إِلَّا فِى قُرًى مُّحَصَّنَةٍ أَوْ مِن وَرَآءِ جُدُرٍ بَأْسُهُم بَيْنَهُمْ شَدِيدٌ تَحْسَبُهُمْ جَمِيعًا وَقُلُوبُهُمْ شَتَّىٰ ذَٰلِكَ بِأَنَّهُمْ قَوْمٌ لَّا يَعْقِلُونَ ۝

15 On the likeness of those (who suffered) a short time before them, they taste the ill effects of their conduct, and theirs is painful punishment.

كَمَثَلِ الَّذِينَ مِن قَبْلِهِمْ قَرِيبًا ذَاقُوا وَبَالَ أَمْرِهِمْ وَلَهُمْ عَذَابٌ أَلِيمٌ ۝

16 (And the hypocrites are) on the likeness of the devil when he telleth man to disbelieve, then, when he disbelieveth saith: Lo! I am quit of thee. Lo! I fear Allah, the Lord of the Worlds.

كَمَثَلِ ٱلشَّيْطَنِ إِذْ قَالَ لِلْإِنسَنِ ٱكْفُرْ فَلَمَّا كَفَرَ قَالَ إِنِّى بَرِىٓءٌ مِّنكَ إِنِّىٓ أَخَافُ ٱللَّهَ رَبَّ ٱلْعَـٰلَمِينَ ﴿١٦﴾

17 And the consequence for both will be that they are in the Fire, therein abiding. Such is the reward of evil-doers.

فَكَانَ عَـٰقِبَتَهُمَآ أَنَّهُمَا فِى ٱلنَّارِ خَـٰلِدَيْنِ فِيهَا وَذَٰلِكَ جَزَٰٓؤُاْ ٱلظَّـٰلِمِينَ ﴿١٧﴾

18 O ye who believe! Observe your duty to Allah. And let every soul look to that which it sendeth on before for the morrow. And observe your duty to Allah! Lo! Allah is Aware of what ye do.

يَـٰٓأَيُّهَا ٱلَّذِينَ ءَامَنُواْ ٱتَّقُواْ ٱللَّهَ وَلْتَنظُرْ نَفْسٌ مَّا قَدَّمَتْ لِغَدٍ وَٱتَّقُواْ ٱللَّهَ إِنَّ ٱللَّهَ خَبِيرٌۢ بِمَا تَعْمَلُونَ ﴿١٨﴾

19 And be not ye as those who forgot Allah, therefore He caused them to forget their souls. Such are the evil-doers.

وَلَا تَكُونُواْ كَٱلَّذِينَ نَسُواْ ٱللَّهَ فَأَنسَىٰهُمْ أَنفُسَهُمْ أُوْلَـٰٓئِكَ هُمُ ٱلْفَـٰسِقُونَ ﴿١٩﴾

20 Not equal are the owners of the Fire and the owners of the Garden. The owners of the Garden, they are the victorious.

لَا يَسْتَوِىٓ أَصْحَـٰبُ ٱلنَّارِ وَأَصْحَـٰبُ ٱلْجَنَّةِ أَصْحَـٰبُ ٱلْجَنَّةِ هُمُ ٱلْفَآئِزُونَ ﴿٢٠﴾

21 If We had caused this Qur'an to descend upon a mountain, thou (O Muhammad) verily hadst seen it humbled, rent asunder by the fear of Allah. Such similitudes coin We for mankind that haply they may reflect.

لَوْ أَنزَلْنَا هَـٰذَا ٱلْقُرْءَانَ عَلَىٰ جَبَلٍ لَّرَأَيْتَهُۥ خَـٰشِعًا مُّتَصَدِّعًا مِّنْ خَشْيَةِ ٱللَّهِ وَتِلْكَ ٱلْأَمْثَـٰلُ نَضْرِبُهَا لِلنَّاسِ لَعَلَّهُمْ يَتَفَكَّرُونَ ﴿٢١﴾

22 He is Allah, than whom there is no other God, the Knower of the invisible and the visible. He is the Beneficent, the Merciful.

هُوَ ٱللَّهُ ٱلَّذِى لَآ إِلَـٰهَ إِلَّا هُوَ عَـٰلِمُ ٱلْغَيْبِ وَٱلشَّهَـٰدَةِ هُوَ ٱلرَّحْمَـٰنُ ٱلرَّحِيمُ ﴿٢٢﴾

23 He is Allah, than whom there is no other God, the Sovereign Lord the Holy One, Peace, the Keeper of Faith, the Guardian, the Majestic, the Compeller, the Superb. Glorified be Allah from all that they ascribe as partner (unto Him).

هُوَ اللّٰهُ الَّذِىْ لَاۤ اِلٰهَ اِلَّا هُوَ ۚ اَلْمَلِكُ الْقُدُّوْسُ السَّلٰمُ الْمُؤْمِنُ الْمُهَيْمِنُ الْعَزِيْزُ الْجَبَّارُ الْمُتَكَبِّرُ ۚ سُبْحٰنَ اللّٰهِ عَمَّا يُشْرِكُوْنَ ۞

24 He is Allah, the Creator, the Shaper out of naught, the Fashioner. His are the most beautiful names. All that is in the heavens and the earth glorifieth Him, and He is the Mighty, the Wise.

هُوَ اللّٰهُ الْخَالِقُ الْبَارِئُ الْمُصَوِّرُ لَهُ الْاَسْمَآءُ الْحُسْنٰى ۚ يُسَبِّحُ لَهٗ مَا فِى السَّمٰوٰتِ وَالْاَرْضِ ۚ وَهُوَ الْعَزِيْزُ الْحَكِيْمُ ۞

Al Mumtaḥanah
(She That Is To Be Examined)

Al Mumtahanah, "She who is to be Examined," takes its name from v. 10, where the believers are told to examine women who come to them as fugitives from the idolaters and, if they find them sincere converts to Al-Islām, not to return them to the idolaters. This marked a modification in the terms of the Truce of Ḥudaybiyah, by which the Prophet had engaged to return all fugitives, male and female, while the idolaters were not obliged to give up renegades from Al-Islām. The more terrible persecution which women had to undergo, if extradited, and their helpless social condition were the causes of the change. Instead of giving up women refugees who were sincere, and not fugitives on account of crime or some family quarrel, the Muslims were to pay an indemnity for them; while as for Muslim husbands whose wives might flee to Quraysh, no indemnity was to be paid by the latter but, when some turn of fortune brought wealth to the Islamic State, they were to be repaid by the State what their wives had taken of their property. In v. 12 is the pledge which was to be taken from the women refugees after their examination.

The date of revelation is the eighth year of the Hijrah.

سُوْرَةُ الْمُمْتَحَنَةِ

In the name of Allah, the
Beneficent, the Merciful.

بِسْمِ اللهِ الرَّحْمٰنِ الرَّحِيْمِ

1   O ye who believe! Choose not
My enemy and your enemy for
friends. Ye give them friendship,
when they disbelieve in that truth
which hath come unto you, driving
out the messenger and you because
ye believe in Allah, your Lord? If
ye have come forth to strive in My
way and seeking My good pleasure,
(show them not friendship). Ye
show friendship unto them in
secret, when I am best Aware of
what ye hide and what ye proclaim?
And whosoever doeth it among
you, he verily hath strayed from the
right way.

يٰٓأَيُّهَا الَّذِيْنَ اٰمَنُوْا لَا تَتَّخِذُوْا عَدُوِّيْ وَعَدُوَّكُمْ أَوْلِيَآءَ
تُلْقُوْنَ إِلَيْهِمْ بِالْمَوَدَّةِ وَقَدْ كَفَرُوْا بِمَا جَآءَكُمْ
مِّنَ الْحَقِّ يُخْرِجُوْنَ الرَّسُوْلَ وَإِيَّاكُمْ أَنْ تُؤْمِنُوْا بِاللهِ
رَبِّكُمْ إِنْ كُنْتُمْ خَرَجْتُمْ جِهَادًا فِيْ سَبِيْلِيْ وَابْتِغَآءَ
مَرْضَاتِيْ تُسِرُّوْنَ إِلَيْهِمْ بِالْمَوَدَّةِ وَأَنَا أَعْلَمُ بِمَا أَخْفَيْتُمْ
وَمَآ أَعْلَنْتُمْ وَمَنْ يَّفْعَلْهُ مِنْكُمْ فَقَدْ ضَلَّ سَوَآءَ
السَّبِيْلِ ۝

2   If they have the upper hand of
you, they will be your foes, and
will stretch out their hands and
their tongues toward you with evil
(intent), and they long for you to
disbelieve.

إِنْ يَّثْقَفُوْكُمْ يَكُوْنُوْا لَكُمْ أَعْدَآءً وَّيَبْسُطُوْا إِلَيْكُمْ
أَيْدِيَهُمْ وَأَلْسِنَتَهُمْ بِالسُّوْءِ وَوَدُّوْا لَوْ تَكْفُرُوْنَ ۝

3   Your ties of kindred and your
children will avail you naught upon
the Day of Resurrection. He will
part you. Allah is Seer of what ye
do.

لَنْ تَنْفَعَكُمْ أَرْحَامُكُمْ وَلَا أَوْلَادُكُمْ يَوْمَ الْقِيٰمَةِ يَفْصِلُ
بَيْنَكُمْ وَاللهُ بِمَا تَعْمَلُوْنَ بَصِيْرٌ ۝

4   There is a goodly pattern for
you in Abraham and those with
him, when they told their folk: Lo!
we are guiltless of you and all that
ye worship beside Allah. We have
done with you. And there hath
arisen between us and you hostility
and hate forever until ye believe in
Allah only—save that which
Abraham promised his father (when
he said): I will ask forgiveness for
thee, though I own nothing for thee
from Allah Our Lord! In Thee we
put our trust, and unto Thee we
turn repentant, and unto Thee is the
journeying.

قَدْ كَانَتْ لَكُمْ أُسْوَةٌ حَسَنَةٌ فِىٓ إِبْرَٰهِيمَ وَٱلَّذِينَ مَعَهُۥٓ
إِذْ قَالُوا۟ لِقَوْمِهِمْ إِنَّا بُرَءَٰٓؤُا۟ مِنكُمْ وَمِمَّا تَعْبُدُونَ مِن دُونِ
ٱللَّهِ كَفَرْنَا بِكُمْ وَبَدَا بَيْنَنَا وَبَيْنَكُمُ ٱلْعَدَٰوَةُ وَٱلْبَغْضَآءُ
أَبَدًا حَتَّىٰ تُؤْمِنُوا۟ بِٱللَّهِ وَحْدَهُۥٓ إِلَّا قَوْلَ إِبْرَٰهِيمَ لِأَبِيهِ
لَأَسْتَغْفِرَنَّ لَكَ وَمَآ أَمْلِكُ لَكَ مِنَ ٱللَّهِ مِن شَىْءٍ
رَّبَّنَا عَلَيْكَ تَوَكَّلْنَا وَإِلَيْكَ أَنَبْنَا وَإِلَيْكَ ٱلْمَصِيرُ ۝

5   Our Lord! Make us not a prey
for those who disbelieve, and forgive us, our Lord! Lo! Thou, only
Thou, art the Mighty, the Wise.

رَبَّنَا لَا تَجْعَلْنَا فِتْنَةً لِّلَّذِينَ كَفَرُوا۟ وَٱغْفِرْ لَنَا
رَبَّنَآ إِنَّكَ أَنتَ ٱلْعَزِيزُ ٱلْحَكِيمُ ۝

6   Verily ye have in them a goodly
pattern for everyone who looketh to
Allah and the Last Day. And who-
soever may turn away, lo! still
Allah, He is the Absolute, the
Owner of Praise.

لَقَدْ كَانَ لَكُمْ فِيهِمْ أُسْوَةٌ حَسَنَةٌ لِّمَن كَانَ يَرْجُوا۟ ٱللَّهَ
وَٱلْيَوْمَ ٱلْءَاخِرَ وَمَن يَتَوَلَّ فَإِنَّ ٱللَّهَ هُوَ ٱلْغَنِىُّ ٱلْحَمِيدُ ۝

7   It may be that Allah will ordain
love between you and those of them
with whom ye are at enmity. Allah
is Mighty, and Allah is Forgiving,
Merciful.

۞ عَسَى ٱللَّهُ أَن يَجْعَلَ بَيْنَكُمْ وَبَيْنَ ٱلَّذِينَ عَادَيْتُم
مِّنْهُم مَّوَدَّةً وَٱللَّهُ قَدِيرٌ وَٱللَّهُ غَفُورٌ رَّحِيمٌ ۝

8   Allah forbiddeth you not those
who warred not against you on
account of religion and drove you
not out from your homes, that ye

لَّا يَنْهَىٰكُمُ ٱللَّهُ عَنِ ٱلَّذِينَ لَمْ يُقَٰتِلُوكُمْ فِى ٱلدِّينِ
وَلَمْ يُخْرِجُوكُم مِّن دِيَٰرِكُمْ أَن تَبَرُّوهُمْ وَتُقْسِطُوٓا۟ إِلَيْهِمْ

should show them kindness and deal justly with them. Lo! Allah loveth the just dealers.

إِنَّ ٱللَّهَ يُحِبُّ ٱلْمُقْسِطِينَ ۝

9 Allah forbiddeth you only those who warred against you on account of religion and have driven you out from your homes and helped to drive you out, that ye make friends of them. Whosoever maketh friends of them—(All) such are wrong-doers.

إِنَّمَا يَنْهَىٰكُمُ ٱللَّهُ عَنِ ٱلَّذِينَ قَٰتَلُوكُمْ فِى ٱلدِّينِ وَأَخْرَجُوكُم مِّن دِيَٰرِكُمْ وَظَٰهَرُوا عَلَىٰٓ إِخْرَاجِكُمْ أَن تَوَلَّوْهُمْ وَمَن يَتَوَلَّهُمْ فَأُو۟لَٰٓئِكَ هُمُ ٱلظَّٰلِمُونَ ۝

10 O ye who believe! When believing women come unto you as fugitives, examine them. Allah is best aware of their faith. Then, if ye know them for true believers, send them not back unto the disbelievers. These (women) are not lawful for them (the disbelievers) nor are they (the disbelievers) lawful for these (women). And give the disbelievers that which they have spent (upon them). And it is no sin for you to marry such women when ye have given them their dues. And hold not to the ties of disbelieving women; and ask for (the return of) that which ye have spent; and let the disbelievers ask for that which they have spent. That is the judgement of Allah. He judgeth between you. Allah is Knower, Wise.

يَٰٓأَيُّهَا ٱلَّذِينَ ءَامَنُوٓا إِذَا جَآءَكُمُ ٱلْمُؤْمِنَٰتُ مُهَٰجِرَٰتٍ فَٱمْتَحِنُوهُنَّ ٱللَّهُ أَعْلَمُ بِإِيمَٰنِهِنَّ فَإِنْ عَلِمْتُمُوهُنَّ مُؤْمِنَٰتٍ فَلَا تَرْجِعُوهُنَّ إِلَى ٱلْكُفَّارِ لَا هُنَّ حِلٌّ لَّهُمْ وَلَا هُمْ يَحِلُّونَ لَهُنَّ وَءَاتُوهُم مَّآ أَنفَقُوا وَلَا جُنَاحَ عَلَيْكُمْ أَن تَنكِحُوهُنَّ إِذَآ ءَاتَيْتُمُوهُنَّ أُجُورَهُنَّ وَلَا تُمْسِكُوا بِعِصَمِ ٱلْكَوَافِرِ وَسْـَٔلُوا مَآ أَنفَقْتُمْ وَلْيَسْـَٔلُوا مَآ أَنفَقُوا ذَٰلِكُمْ حُكْمُ ٱللَّهِ يَحْكُمُ بَيْنَكُمْ وَٱللَّهُ عَلِيمٌ حَكِيمٌ ۝

11 And if any of your wives have gone from you unto the disbelievers and afterward ye have your turn (of triumph), then give unto those

وَإِن فَاتَكُمْ شَىْءٌ مِّنْ أَزْوَٰجِكُمْ إِلَى ٱلْكُفَّارِ فَعَاقَبْتُمْ

whose wives have gone the like of
that which they have spent, and
keep your duty to Allah in whom
ye are believers.

12 O Prophet! If believing women
come unto thee, taking oath of
allegiance unto thee that they will
ascribe nothing as partner unto
Allah, and will neither steal nor
commit adultery nor kill their children, nor produce any lie that they
have devised between their hands
and feet, nor disobey thee in what is
right,[1] then accept their allegiance
and ask Allah to forgive them. Lo!
Allah is Forgiving, Merciful.

13 O ye who believe! Be not
friendly with a folk with whom
Allah is wroth, (a folk) who have
despaired of the Hereafter as the
disbelievers despair of those who
are in the graves.

فَاٰتُوا الَّذِيْنَ ذَهَبَتْ اَزْوَاجُهُمْ مِّثْلَ مَاۤ اَنْفَقُوْا ۚ
وَاتَّقُوا اللّٰهَ الَّذِيْۤ اَنْتُمْ بِهٖ مُؤْمِنُوْنَ ۞

يٰۤاَيُّهَا النَّبِيُّ اِذَا جَآءَكَ الْمُؤْمِنٰتُ يُبَايِعْنَكَ
عَلٰۤى اَنْ لَّا يُشْرِكْنَ بِاللّٰهِ شَيْئًا وَّلَا يَسْرِقْنَ
وَلَا يَزْنِيْنَ وَلَا يَقْتُلْنَ اَوْلَادَهُنَّ وَلَا يَأْتِيْنَ
بِبُهْتَانٍ يَّفْتَرِيْنَهٗ بَيْنَ اَيْدِيْهِنَّ وَاَرْجُلِهِنَّ
وَلَا يَعْصِيْنَكَ فِيْ مَعْرُوْفٍ فَبَايِعْهُنَّ
وَاسْتَغْفِرْ لَهُنَّ اللّٰهَ ۚ اِنَّ اللّٰهَ غَفُوْرٌ رَّحِيْمٌ ۞

يٰۤاَيُّهَا الَّذِيْنَ اٰمَنُوْا لَا تَتَوَلَّوْا قَوْمًا غَضِبَ
اللّٰهُ عَلَيْهِمْ قَدْ يَئِسُوْا مِنَ الْاٰخِرَةِ كَمَا يَئِسَ
الْكُفَّارُ مِنْ اَصْحٰبِ الْقُبُوْرِ ۞

---

1. This is called the women's oath of allegiance. It was the oath exacted from men
also until the second pact of Al-'Aqabah when the duty of defence was added to the
men's oath.

As Ṣaff
(The Ranks)

As Ṣaff, "The Ranks," takes its name from a word in v. 4. In the copy of the Qur'an which I have followed, it is stated to have been revealed at Makkah, though its contents evidently refer to the Madīnah period. It may have been revealed while the Prophet and his companions were encamped in the valley of Makkah during the negotiations of the Truce of Hudaybiyah, with which some of its verses are associated by tradition.

In that case the date of revelation would be the sixth year of the Hijrah.

In the name of Allah, the Beneficent, the Merciful.

1   All that is in the heavens and all that is in the earth glorifieth Allah, and He is the Mighty, the Wise.

2   O ye who believe! Why say ye that which ye do not?

3   It is most hateful in the sight of Allah that ye say that which ye do not.

4   Lo! Allah loveth those who battle for His cause in ranks, as if they were a solid structure.

5   And (remember) when Moses said unto his people: O my people! Why persecute ye me, when ye well know that I am Allah's messenger unto you? So when they went astray Allah sent their hearts astray. And Allah guideth not the evil-living folk.

وَإِذْ قَالَ مُوسَىٰ لِقَوْمِهِ يَـٰقَوْمِ لِمَ تُؤْذُونَنِي وَقَد تَّعْلَمُونَ أَنِّي رَسُولُ ٱللَّهِ إِلَيْكُمْ فَلَمَّا زَاغُوٓا۟ أَزَاغَ ٱللَّهُ قُلُوبَهُمْ وَٱللَّهُ لَا يَهْدِى ٱلْقَوْمَ ٱلْفَـٰسِقِينَ ۝

6   And when Jesus son of Mary said: O Children of Israel! Lo! I am the messenger of Allah unto you, confirming that which was (revealed) before me in the Torah,[1] and bringing good tidings of a messenger who cometh after me, whose name is the Praised One.[2] Yet when he hath come unto them with clear proofs, they say: This is mere magic.

وَإِذْ قَالَ عِيسَى ٱبْنُ مَرْيَمَ يَـٰبَنِىٓ إِسْرَٰٓءِيلَ إِنِّى رَسُولُ ٱللَّهِ إِلَيْكُم مُّصَدِّقًا لِّمَا بَيْنَ يَدَىَّ مِنَ ٱلتَّوْرَىٰةِ وَمُبَشِّرًۢا بِرَسُولٍ يَأْتِى مِنۢ بَعْدِى ٱسْمُهُۥٓ أَحْمَدُ فَلَمَّا جَآءَهُم بِٱلْبَيِّنَـٰتِ قَالُوا۟ هَـٰذَا سِحْرٌ مُّبِينٌ ۝

7   And who doth greater wrong than he who inventeth a lie against Allah when he is summoned unto Al-Islām?[3] And Allah guideth not wrongdoing folk.

وَمَنْ أَظْلَمُ مِمَّنِ ٱفْتَرَىٰ عَلَى ٱللَّهِ ٱلْكَذِبَ وَهُوَ يُدْعَىٰٓ إِلَى ٱلْإِسْلَـٰمِ وَٱللَّهُ لَا يَهْدِى ٱلْقَوْمَ ٱلظَّـٰلِمِينَ ۝

8   Fain would they put out the light of Allah with their mouths, but Allah will perfect His light however much the disbelievers are averse.

يُرِيدُونَ لِيُطْفِـُٔوا۟ نُورَ ٱللَّهِ بِأَفْوَٰهِهِمْ وَٱللَّهُ مُتِمُّ نُورِهِۦ وَلَوْ كَرِهَ ٱلْكَـٰفِرُونَ ۝

---

1. Books of Moses.

2. Ar. *Aḥmad*. A name of the Prophet of Arabia. The promised "Comforter" was believed by many Christian communities of the East to be a Prophet yet to come, and most of them accepted Muḥammad as that Prophet.

3   Lit. "The Surrender."

9 He it is who hath sent His messenger with the guidance and the religion of truth, that He may make it conqueror of all religion however much idolaters may be averse.

هُوَ الَّذِىٓ أَرْسَلَ رَسُولَهُ بِالْهُدَىٰ وَدِينِ الْحَقِّ لِيُظْهِرَهُ عَلَى الدِّينِ كُلِّهِ وَلَوْ كَرِهَ الْمُشْرِكُونَ ۝

10 O ye who believe! Shall I show you a commerce that will save you from a painful doom?

يَـٰٓأَيُّهَا الَّذِينَ ءَامَنُوٓا هَلْ أَدُلُّكُمْ عَلَىٰ تِجَـٰرَةٍ تُنجِيكُم مِّنْ عَذَابٍ أَلِيمٍ ۝

11 Ye should believe in Allah and His messenger, and should strive for the cause of Allah with your wealth and your lives. That is better for you, if ye did but know.

تُؤْمِنُونَ بِاللَّهِ وَرَسُولِهِ وَتُجَـٰهِدُونَ فِى سَبِيلِ اللَّهِ بِأَمْوَٰلِكُمْ وَأَنفُسِكُمْ ذَٰلِكُمْ خَيْرٌ لَّكُمْ إِن كُنتُمْ تَعْلَمُونَ ۝

12 He will forgive you your sins and bring you into Gardens underneath which rivers flow, and pleasant dwellings in Gardens of Eden. That is the supreme triumph.

يَغْفِرْ لَكُمْ ذُنُوبَكُمْ وَيُدْخِلْكُمْ جَنَّـٰتٍ تَجْرِى مِن تَحْتِهَا الْأَنْهَـٰرُ وَمَسَـٰكِنَ طَيِّبَةً فِى جَنَّـٰتِ عَدْنٍ ذَٰلِكَ الْفَوْزُ الْعَظِيمُ ۝

13 And (He will give you) another blessing which ye love: Help from Allah and a speedy victory. Give good tidings (O Muḥammad) to believers.

وَأُخْرَىٰ تُحِبُّونَهَا نَصْرٌ مِّنَ اللَّهِ وَفَتْحٌ قَرِيبٌ وَبَشِّرِ الْمُؤْمِنِينَ ۝

14 O ye who believe! Be Allah's helpers, even as Jesus son of Mary said unto the disciples: Who are my helpers for Allah? They said: We are Allah's helpers. And a party of the Children of Israel believed, while a party disbelieved. Then We strengthened those who believed against their foe, and they became the uppermost.

يَـٰٓأَيُّهَا الَّذِينَ ءَامَنُوا كُونُوٓا أَنصَارَ اللَّهِ كَمَا قَالَ عِيسَى ابْنُ مَرْيَمَ لِلْحَوَارِيِّـۧنَ مَنْ أَنصَارِىٓ إِلَى اللَّهِ قَالَ الْحَوَارِيُّونَ نَحْنُ أَنصَارُ اللَّهِ فَـَٔامَنَت طَّآئِفَةٌ مِّنۢ بَنِىٓ إِسْرَٰٓءِيلَ وَكَفَرَت طَّآئِفَةٌ فَأَيَّدْنَا الَّذِينَ ءَامَنُوا عَلَىٰ عَدُوِّهِمْ فَأَصْبَحُوا ظَـٰهِرِينَ ۝

Al Jumu'ah
(The Congregation)

Al Jumu'ah, "The Congregation," takes it name from a word in v. 9, where obedience to the call to congregational prayer is enjoined. Tradition says that vv. 9-11 refer to an occasion when a caravan entered Al-Madīnah with beating of drums at the time when the Prophet was preaching in the mosque, and that the congregation broke away to look at it except twelve men. If, as one version of the tradition says, the caravan was that of Daḥyah al-Kalbī, the incident must have occurred before the fifth year of the Hijrah, because Daḥyah was a Muslim in the fifth year A.H. The date of revelation is between the years 2 and 4 A.H.

In the name of Allah, the Beneficent, the Merciful.

1   All that is in the heavens and all that is in the earth glorifieth Allah, the Sovereign Lord, the Holy One, the Mighty, the Wise.

2   He it is Who hath sent among the unlettered ones a messenger of their own, to recite unto them His revelations and to make them grow, and to teach them the Scripture and Wisdom, though heretofore they were indeed in error manifest,

3   Along with others of them who have not yet joined them. He is the Mighty, the Wise.

4 That is the bounty of Allah; which he giveth unto whom He will. Allah is of infinite bounty.

ذَٰلِكَ فَضْلُ اللَّهِ يُؤْتِيهِ مَن يَشَاءُ وَاللَّهُ ذُو الْفَضْلِ الْعَظِيمِ ۝

5 The likeness of those who are entrusted with the Law of Moses, yet apply it not, is as the likeness of the ass carrying books. Wretched is the likeness of folk who deny the revelations of Allah. And Allah guideth not wrongdoing folk.

مَثَلُ الَّذِينَ حُمِّلُوا التَّوْرَاةَ ثُمَّ لَمْ يَحْمِلُوهَا كَمَثَلِ الْحِمَارِ يَحْمِلُ أَسْفَارًا بِئْسَ مَثَلُ الْقَوْمِ الَّذِينَ كَذَّبُوا بِآيَاتِ اللَّهِ وَاللَّهُ لَا يَهْدِي الْقَوْمَ الظَّالِمِينَ ۝

6 Say (O Muḥammad): O ye who are Jews! If ye claim that ye are favoured of Allah apart from (all) mankind, then long for death if ye are truthful.

قُلْ يَا أَيُّهَا الَّذِينَ هَادُوا إِن زَعَمْتُمْ أَنَّكُمْ أَوْلِيَاءُ لِلَّهِ مِن دُونِ النَّاسِ فَتَمَنَّوُا الْمَوْتَ إِن كُنتُمْ صَادِقِينَ ۝

7 But they will never long for it because of all that their own hands have sent before, and Allah is Aware of evil-doers.

وَلَا يَتَمَنَّوْنَهُ أَبَدًا بِمَا قَدَّمَتْ أَيْدِيهِمْ وَاللَّهُ عَلِيمٌ بِالظَّالِمِينَ ۝

8 Say (unto them, O Muḥammad): Lo! the death from which ye shrink will surely meet you, and afterward ye will be returned unto the Knower of the invisible and the visible, and He will tell you what ye used to do.

قُلْ إِنَّ الْمَوْتَ الَّذِي تَفِرُّونَ مِنْهُ فَإِنَّهُ مُلَاقِيكُمْ ثُمَّ تُرَدُّونَ إِلَى عَالِمِ الْغَيْبِ وَالشَّهَادَةِ فَيُنَبِّئُكُم بِمَا كُنتُمْ تَعْمَلُونَ ۝

9 O ye who believe! When the call is made for the prayer of the day of congregation, haste unto remembrance of Allah and leave your trading. That is better for you if ye did but know.

يَا أَيُّهَا الَّذِينَ آمَنُوا إِذَا نُودِيَ لِلصَّلَاةِ مِن يَوْمِ الْجُمُعَةِ فَاسْعَوْا إِلَى ذِكْرِ اللَّهِ وَذَرُوا الْبَيْعَ ذَٰلِكُمْ خَيْرٌ لَّكُمْ إِن كُنتُمْ تَعْلَمُونَ ۝

10 And when the prayer is ended, then disperse in the land and seek of Allah's bounty, and remember Allah much, that ye may be successful.

فَإِذَا قُضِيَتِ الصَّلَاةُ فَانتَشِرُوا فِي الْأَرْضِ وَابْتَغُوا مِن فَضْلِ اللَّهِ وَاذْكُرُوا اللَّهَ كَثِيرًا لَّعَلَّكُمْ تُفْلِحُونَ ۝

11 But when they spy some merchandise or pastime they break away to it and leave thee standing. Say: That which Allah hath is better than pastime and than merchandise, and Allah is the best of providers.

Al Munāfiqūn
(The Hypocrites)

Al Munāfiqūn, "The Hypocrites," takes its name from a word occuring in the first verse. Verse 8 refers to a remark of 'Abdullah ibn Ubayy, the "Hypocrite" leader, expressing the desire that the old aristocracy of Yathrib, of which he had been the acknowledged chief, might regain the ascendancy and turn out the refugees from Makkah, whom he regarded as intruders.

The date of the revelation is the fourth year of the Hijrah.

In the name of Allah, the Beneficent, the Merciful.

1 When the hypocrites come unto thee (O Muhammad), they say: We bear witness that thou art indeed Allah's messenger. And Allah knoweth that thou art indeed His messenger, and Allah beareth witness that the Hypocrites are speaking falsely.

إِذَا جَاءَكَ الْمُنَافِقُونَ قَالُوا نَشْهَدُ إِنَّكَ لَرَسُولُ اللَّهِ وَاللَّهُ يَعْلَمُ إِنَّكَ لَرَسُولُهُ وَاللَّهُ يَشْهَدُ إِنَّ الْمُنَافِقِينَ لَكَاذِبُونَ ۝

2 They make their faith a pretext that they may turn (men) from the way of Allah. Verily evil is that which they are wont to do,

اتَّخَذُوا أَيْمَانَهُمْ جُنَّةً فَصَدُّوا عَن سَبِيلِ اللَّهِ إِنَّهُمْ سَاءَ مَا كَانُوا يَعْمَلُونَ ۝

3 That is because they believed, then disbelieved, therefore their hearts are sealed so that they understand not.

ذَلِكَ بِأَنَّهُمْ ءَامَنُوا ثُمَّ كَفَرُوا فَطُبِعَ عَلَى قُلُوبِهِمْ فَهُمْ لَا يَفْقَهُونَ ۝

4   And when thou seest them their figures please thee; and if they speak thou givest ear unto their speech. (They are) as though they were blocks of wood in striped cloaks.[1] They deem every shout to be against them. They are the enemy, so beware of them. Allah confound them! How they are perverted!

وَإِذَا رَأَيْتَهُمْ تُعْجِبُكَ أَجْسَامُهُمْ وَإِن يَقُولُوا تَسْمَعْ لِقَوْلِهِمْ كَأَنَّهُمْ خُشُبٌ مُّسَنَّدَةٌ يَحْسَبُونَ كُلَّ صَيْحَةٍ عَلَيْهِمْ هُمُ الْعَدُوُّ فَاحْذَرْهُمْ قَاتَلَهُمُ اللَّهُ أَنَّى يُؤْفَكُونَ ۝

5   And when it is said unto them: Come! The messenger of Allah will ask forgiveness for you! They avert their heads and thou seest them turning away, disdainful.

وَإِذَا قِيلَ لَهُمْ تَعَالَوْا يَسْتَغْفِرْ لَكُمْ رَسُولُ اللَّهِ لَوَّوْا رُؤُوسَهُمْ وَرَأَيْتَهُمْ يَصُدُّونَ وَهُم مُّسْتَكْبِرُونَ ۝

6   Whether thou ask forgiveness for them or ask not forgiveness for them, Allah will not forgive them. Lo! Allah guideth not the evil-living folk.

سَوَاءٌ عَلَيْهِمْ أَسْتَغْفَرْتَ لَهُمْ أَمْ لَمْ تَسْتَغْفِرْ لَهُمْ لَن يَغْفِرَ اللَّهُ لَهُمْ إِنَّ اللَّهَ لَا يَهْدِي الْقَوْمَ الْفَاسِقِينَ ۝

7   They it is who say: Spend not on behalf of those (who dwell) with Allah's messenger that they may disperse (and go away from you); when Allah's are the treasures of the heavens and the earth; but the hypocrites comprehend not.

هُمُ الَّذِينَ يَقُولُونَ لَا تُنفِقُوا عَلَى مَنْ عِندَ رَسُولِ اللَّهِ حَتَّىٰ يَنفَضُّوا وَلِلَّهِ خَزَائِنُ السَّمَاوَاتِ وَالْأَرْضِ وَلَٰكِنَّ الْمُنَافِقِينَ لَا يَفْقَهُونَ ۝

8   They say: Surely, if we return to Al-Madīnah the mightier will soon drive out the weaker; when might belongeth to Allah and to His messenger and the believers; but the hypocrites know not.

يَقُولُونَ لَئِن رَّجَعْنَا إِلَى الْمَدِينَةِ لَيُخْرِجَنَّ الْأَعَزُّ مِنْهَا الْأَذَلَّ وَلِلَّهِ الْعِزَّةُ وَلِرَسُولِهِ وَلِلْمُؤْمِنِينَ وَلَٰكِنَّ الْمُنَافِقِينَ لَا يَعْلَمُونَ ۝

---

1. Or *propped-up blocks of wood.*

9 O ye who believe! Let not your wealth nor your children distract you from remembrance of Allah. Those who do so, they are the losers.

يَـٰٓأَيُّهَا ٱلَّذِينَ ءَامَنُوا۟ لَا تُلْهِكُمْ أَمْوَٰلُكُمْ وَلَآ أَوْلَٰدُكُمْ عَن ذِكْرِ ٱللَّهِ وَمَن يَفْعَلْ ذَٰلِكَ فَأُو۟لَٰٓئِكَ هُمُ ٱلْخَٰسِرُونَ ﴿٩﴾

10 And spend of that wherewith We have provided you before death cometh unto one of you and he saith: My Lord! If only thou wouldst reprieve me for a little while, then I would give alms and be among the righteous.

وَأَنفِقُوا۟ مِن مَّا رَزَقْنَٰكُم مِّن قَبْلِ أَن يَأْتِىَ أَحَدَكُمُ ٱلْمَوْتُ فَيَقُولَ رَبِّ لَوْلَآ أَخَّرْتَنِىٓ إِلَىٰٓ أَجَلٍ قَرِيبٍ فَأَصَّدَّقَ وَأَكُن مِّنَ ٱلصَّٰلِحِينَ ﴿١٠﴾

11 But Allah reprieveth no soul when its term cometh, and Allah is Aware of what ye do.

وَلَن يُؤَخِّرَ ٱللَّهُ نَفْسًا إِذَا جَآءَ أَجَلُهَا وَٱللَّهُ خَبِيرٌۢ بِمَا تَعْمَلُونَ ﴿١١﴾

At Taghābun
(Mutual Disillusion)

At Taghābun, "Mutual Disillusion," takes its name from a word in v. 9.

The date of revelation is possibly the year 1 A.H., though it is generally regarded as a late Makkan sūrah, vv. 14 ff. being taken as referring to the pressure brought to bear by wives and families to prevent Muslims leaving Makkah at the time of the Hijrah.

In the name of Allah, the Beneficent, the Merciful.

1   All that is in the heavens and all that is in the earth glorifieth Allah; unto Him belongeth sovereignty and unto Him belongeth praise, and He is Able to do all things.

2   He it is Who created you, but one of you is a disbeliever and one of you is a believer, and Allah is Seer of what ye do.

3   He created the heavens and the earth with truth, and He shaped you and made good your shapes, and unto Him is the journeying.

4   He knoweth all that is in the heavens and the earth, and He knoweth what ye conceal and what ye publish and Allah is Aware of what is in the breasts (of men).

5 Hath not the story reached you of those who disbelieved of old and so did taste the ill-effects of their conduct, and theirs will be a painful doom.

أَلَمْ يَأْتِكُمْ نَبَؤُاْ الَّذِينَ كَفَرُواْ مِن قَبْلُ فَذَاقُواْ وَبَالَ أَمْرِهِمْ وَلَهُمْ عَذَابٌ أَلِيمٌ ۝

6 That was because their messengers (from Allah) kept coming unto them with clear proofs (of Allah's sovereignty), but they said: Shall mere mortals guide us? So they disbelieved and turned away, and Allah was independent (of them). Allah is Absolute, Owner of Praise.

ذَٰلِكَ بِأَنَّهُۥ كَانَت تَّأْتِيهِمْ رُسُلُهُم بِالْبَيِّنَٰتِ فَقَالُوٓاْ أَبَشَرٌ يَهْدُونَنَا فَكَفَرُواْ وَتَوَلَّواْ وَاسْتَغْنَى اللَّهُ وَاللَّهُ غَنِيٌّ حَمِيدٌ ۝

7 Those who disbelieve assert that they will not be raised again. Say (unto them, O Muhammad): Yea, verily, by my Lord! ye will be raised again and then ye will be informed of what ye did; and that is easy for Allah.

زَعَمَ الَّذِينَ كَفَرُوٓاْ أَن لَّن يُبْعَثُواْ قُلْ بَلَىٰ وَرَبِّى لَتُبْعَثُنَّ ثُمَّ لَتُنَبَّؤُنَّ بِمَا عَمِلْتُمْ وَذَٰلِكَ عَلَى اللَّهِ يَسِيرٌ ۝

8 So believe in Allah and His messenger and the light which We have revealed. And Allah is Aware of what ye do.

فَـَٔامِنُواْ بِاللَّهِ وَرَسُولِهِۦ وَالنُّورِ الَّذِىٓ أَنزَلْنَا وَاللَّهُ بِمَا تَعْمَلُونَ خَبِيرٌ ۝

9 The day when He shall gather you unto the Day of Assembling, that will be a day of mutual disillusion. And whoso believeth in Allah and doeth right, He will remit from him his evil deeds and will bring him into Gardens underneath which rivers flow, therein to abide forever. That is the supreme triumph.

يَوْمَ يَجْمَعُكُمْ لِيَوْمِ الْجَمْعِ ذَٰلِكَ يَوْمُ التَّغَابُنِ وَمَن يُؤْمِنۢ بِاللَّهِ وَيَعْمَلْ صَٰلِحًا يُكَفِّرْ عَنْهُ سَيِّـَٔاتِهِۦ وَيُدْخِلْهُ جَنَّٰتٍ تَجْرِى مِن تَحْتِهَا الْأَنْهَٰرُ خَٰلِدِينَ فِيهَآ أَبَدًا ذَٰلِكَ الْفَوْزُ الْعَظِيمُ ۝

10 But those who disbelieve and deny Our revelations, such are owners of the Fire; they will abide therein a hapless journey's end!

وَالَّذِينَ كَفَرُوا وَكَذَّبُوا بِآيَاتِنَا أُوْلَٰئِكَ أَصْحَٰبُ النَّارِ خَٰلِدِينَ فِيهَا وَبِئْسَ الْمَصِيرُ ۝

11 No calamity befalleth save by Allah's leave. And whosoever believeth in Allah, He guideth his heart. And Allah is Knower of all things.

مَآ أَصَابَ مِن مُّصِيبَةٍ إِلَّا بِإِذْنِ اللَّهِ وَمَن يُؤْمِنۢ بِاللَّهِ يَهْدِ قَلْبَهُۥ وَاللَّهُ بِكُلِّ شَىْءٍ عَلِيمٌ ۝

12 Obey Allah and obey His messenger; but if ye turn away, then the duty of Our messenger is only to convey (the message) plainly.

وَأَطِيعُوا اللَّهَ وَأَطِيعُوا الرَّسُولَ فَإِن تَوَلَّيْتُمْ فَإِنَّمَا عَلَىٰ رَسُولِنَا الْبَلَٰغُ الْمُبِينُ ۝

13 Allah! There is no God save Him. In Allah, therefore, let believers put their trust.

اللَّهُ لَآ إِلَٰهَ إِلَّا هُوَ وَعَلَى اللَّهِ فَلْيَتَوَكَّلِ الْمُؤْمِنُونَ ۝

14 O ye who believe! Lo! among your wives and your children there are enemies for you, therefore beware of them. And if ye pardon and overlook and forgive, then lo! Allah is Forgiving, Merciful.

يَٰٓأَيُّهَا الَّذِينَ آمَنُوٓا إِنَّ مِنْ أَزْوَٰجِكُمْ وَأَوْلَٰدِكُمْ عَدُوًّا لَّكُمْ فَاحْذَرُوهُمْ وَإِن تَعْفُوا وَتَصْفَحُوا وَتَغْفِرُوا فَإِنَّ اللَّهَ غَفُورٌ رَّحِيمٌ ۝

15 Your wealth and your children are only a temptation, whereas Allah! with Him is an immense reward.

إِنَّمَآ أَمْوَٰلُكُمْ وَأَوْلَٰدُكُمْ فِتْنَةٌ وَاللَّهُ عِندَهُۥٓ أَجْرٌ عَظِيمٌ ۝

16 So keep your duty to Allah as best ye can, and listen, and obey, and spend; that is better for your souls. And whoso is saved from his own greed, such are the successful.

فَاتَّقُوا اللَّهَ مَا اسْتَطَعْتُمْ وَاسْمَعُوا وَأَطِيعُوا وَأَنفِقُوا خَيْرًا لِّأَنفُسِكُمْ وَمَن يُوقَ شُحَّ نَفْسِهِۦ فَأُوْلَٰئِكَ هُمُ الْمُفْلِحُونَ ۝

17 If ye lend unto Allah a goodly loan,[1] He will double it for you and will forgive you, for Allah is Responsive, Clement,

إِن تُقۡرِضُوا اللَّهَ قَرۡضًا حَسَنًا يُضَٰعِفۡهُ لَكُمۡ وَيَغۡفِرۡ لَكُمۡ وَاللَّهُ شَكُورٌ حَلِيمٌ ۝

18 Knower of the invisible and the visible, the Mighty, the Wise.

عَٰلِمُ الۡغَيۡبِ وَالشَّهَٰدَةِ الۡعَزِيزُ الۡحَكِيمُ ۝

---

1. *i.e.* a loan without interest or any thought of gain or loss.

At Ṭalāq
(Divorce)

At Ṭalāq, "Divorce," is so called from vv. 1-7, which contain an amendment to the laws of divorce which are set forth in sūrah 2. This is generally referred traditionally to a mistake made by Ibn 'Umar in divorcing his wife, which is said to have happened in the 6th year of the Hijrah. But others relate that the Prophet on that occasion only quoted this verse which had already been revealed.

The date of revelation is the sixth year of the Hijrah or a little earlier.

In the name of Allah, the Beneficent, the Merciful.

1   O Prophet! When ye (men) put away women, put them away for their (legal) period and reckon the period, and keep your duty to Allah, your Lord. Expel them not from their houses nor let them go forth unless they commit open immorality. Such are the limits (imposed by) Allah; and whoso transgresseth Allah's limits, he verily wrongeth his soul. Thou knowest not: it may be that Allah will afterward bring some new thing to pass.

يَٰٓأَيُّهَا ٱلنَّبِيُّ إِذَا طَلَّقْتُمُ ٱلنِّسَآءَ فَطَلِّقُوهُنَّ لِعِدَّتِهِنَّ وَأَحْصُوا۟ ٱلْعِدَّةَ وَٱتَّقُوا۟ ٱللَّهَ رَبَّكُمْ لَا تُخْرِجُوهُنَّ مِنۢ بُيُوتِهِنَّ وَلَا يَخْرُجْنَ إِلَّآ أَن يَأْتِينَ بِفَٰحِشَةٍ مُّبَيِّنَةٍ وَتِلْكَ حُدُودُ ٱللَّهِ وَمَن يَتَعَدَّ حُدُودَ ٱللَّهِ فَقَدْ ظَلَمَ نَفْسَهُۥ لَا تَدْرِى لَعَلَّ ٱللَّهَ يُحْدِثُ بَعْدَ ذَٰلِكَ أَمْرًا ١

2 Then, when they have reached their term, take them back in kindness or part from them in kindness, and call to witness two just men among you, and keep your testimony upright for Allah. Whoso believeth in Allah and the Last Day is exhorted to act thus. And whosoever keepeth his duty to Allah, Allah will appoint a way out for him,

فَإِذَا بَلَغْنَ أَجَلَهُنَّ فَأَمْسِكُوهُنَّ بِمَعْرُوفٍ أَوْ فَارِقُوهُنَّ بِمَعْرُوفٍ وَأَشْهِدُوا ذَوَيْ عَدْلٍ مِّنكُمْ وَأَقِيمُوا الشَّهَادَةَ لِلَّهِ ذَلِكُمْ يُوعَظُ بِهِ مَن كَانَ يُؤْمِنُ بِاللَّهِ وَالْيَوْمِ الْآخِرِ وَمَن يَتَّقِ اللَّهَ يَجْعَل لَّهُ مَخْرَجًا ۝

3 And will provide for him from (a quarter) whence he hath no expectation. And whosoever putteth his trust in Allah, He will suffice him. Lo! Allah bringeth His command to pass. Allah hath set a measure for all things.

وَيَرْزُقْهُ مِنْ حَيْثُ لَا يَحْتَسِبُ وَمَن يَتَوَكَّلْ عَلَى اللَّهِ فَهُوَ حَسْبُهُ إِنَّ اللَّهَ بَالِغُ أَمْرِهِ قَدْ جَعَلَ اللَّهُ لِكُلِّ شَيْءٍ قَدْرًا ۝

4 And for such of your women as despair of menstruation, if ye doubt, their period (of waiting) shall be three months along with those who have it not. And for those with child, their period shall be till they bring forth their burden. And whosoever keepeth his duty to Allah, He maketh his course easy for him.

وَاللَّائِي يَئِسْنَ مِنَ الْمَحِيضِ مِن نِّسَائِكُمْ إِنِ ارْتَبْتُمْ فَعِدَّتُهُنَّ ثَلَاثَةُ أَشْهُرٍ وَاللَّائِي لَمْ يَحِضْنَ وَأُولَاتُ الْأَحْمَالِ أَجَلُهُنَّ أَن يَضَعْنَ حَمْلَهُنَّ وَمَن يَتَّقِ اللَّهَ يَجْعَل لَّهُ مِنْ أَمْرِهِ يُسْرًا ۝

5 That is the commandment of Allah which He revealeth unto you. And whoso keepeth his duty to Allah, He will remit from him his evil deeds and magnify reward for him.

ذَلِكَ أَمْرُ اللَّهِ أَنزَلَهُ إِلَيْكُمْ وَمَن يَتَّقِ اللَّهَ يُكَفِّرْ عَنْهُ سَيِّئَاتِهِ وَيُعْظِمْ لَهُ أَجْرًا ۝

6 Lodge them where ye dwell, according to your wealth, and

أَسْكِنُوهُنَّ مِنْ حَيْثُ سَكَنتُم مِّن وُجْدِكُمْ وَلَا تُضَارُّوهُنَّ

harass them not so as to straiten life for them. And if they are with child, then spend for them till they bring forth their burden. Then, if they give suck for you, give them their due payment and consult together in kindness; but if ye make difficulties for one another, then let some other woman give suck for him (the father of the child).

لِتُضَيِّقُوا عَلَيْهِنَّ وَإِن كُنَّ أُوْلَاتِ حَمْلٍ فَأَنفِقُوا عَلَيْهِنَّ حَتَّىٰ يَضَعْنَ حَمْلَهُنَّ فَإِنْ أَرْضَعْنَ لَكُمْ فَـَٔاتُوهُنَّ أُجُورَهُنَّ وَأْتَمِرُوا بَيْنَكُم بِمَعْرُوفٍ وَإِن تَعَاسَرْتُمْ فَسَتُرْضِعُ لَهُۥٓ أُخْرَىٰ ٦

7   Let him who hath abundance spend of his abundance, and he whose provision is measured, let him spend of that which Allah hath given him. Allah asketh naught of any soul save that which He hath given it. Allah will vouchsafe, after hardship, ease.

لِيُنفِقْ ذُو سَعَةٍ مِّن سَعَتِهِۦ وَمَن قُدِرَ عَلَيْهِ رِزْقُهُۥ فَلْيُنفِقْ مِمَّآ ءَاتَىٰهُ ٱللَّهُ لَا يُكَلِّفُ ٱللَّهُ نَفْسًا إِلَّا مَآ ءَاتَىٰهَا سَيَجْعَلُ ٱللَّهُ بَعْدَ عُسْرٍ يُسْرًا ٧

8   And how many a community revolted against the ordinance of its Lord and His messenger, and We called it to a stern account and punished it with dire punishment,

وَكَأَيِّن مِّن قَرْيَةٍ عَتَتْ عَنْ أَمْرِ رَبِّهَا وَرُسُلِهِۦ فَحَاسَبْنَٰهَا حِسَابًا شَدِيدًا وَعَذَّبْنَٰهَا عَذَابًا نُّكْرًا ٨

9   So that it tasted the ill-effects of its conduct, and the consequence of its conduct was loss.

فَذَاقَتْ وَبَالَ أَمْرِهَا وَكَانَ عَٰقِبَةُ أَمْرِهَا خُسْرًا ٩

10   Allah hath prepared for them stern punishment; so keep your duty to Allah, O men of understanding! O ye who believe! Now Allah hath sent down unto you a reminder,

أَعَدَّ ٱللَّهُ لَهُمْ عَذَابًا شَدِيدًا فَٱتَّقُوا ٱللَّهَ يَٰٓأُوْلِي ٱلْأَلْبَٰبِ ٱلَّذِينَ ءَامَنُوا قَدْ أَنزَلَ ٱللَّهُ إِلَيْكُمْ ذِكْرًا ١٠

11   A messenger reciting unto you the revelations of Allah made plain, that He may bring forth those who

رَّسُولًا يَتْلُوا عَلَيْكُمْ ءَايَٰتِ ٱللَّهِ مُبَيِّنَٰتٍ لِّيُخْرِجَ ٱلَّذِينَ

believe and do good works from darkness unto light. And whosoever believeth in Allah and doeth right, He will bring him into Gardens underneath which rivers flow, therein to abide forever. Allah hath made good provision for him.

ءَامَنُوا۟ وَعَمِلُوا۟ ٱلصَّٰلِحَٰتِ مِنَ ٱلظُّلُمَٰتِ إِلَى ٱلنُّورِ وَمَن يُؤْمِنۢ بِٱللَّهِ وَيَعْمَلْ صَٰلِحًا يُدْخِلْهُ جَنَّٰتٍ تَجْرِى مِن تَحْتِهَا ٱلْأَنْهَٰرُ خَٰلِدِينَ فِيهَآ أَبَدًا قَدْ أَحْسَنَ ٱللَّهُ لَهُۥ رِزْقًا ﴿١١﴾

12 Allah it is who hath created seven heavens, and of the earth the like thereof. The commandment cometh down among them slowly, that ye may know that Allah is Able to do all things, and that Allah surroundeth all things in knowledge.

ٱللَّهُ ٱلَّذِى خَلَقَ سَبْعَ سَمَٰوَٰتٍ وَمِنَ ٱلْأَرْضِ مِثْلَهُنَّ يَتَنَزَّلُ ٱلْأَمْرُ بَيْنَهُنَّ لِتَعْلَمُوٓا۟ أَنَّ ٱللَّهَ عَلَىٰ كُلِّ شَىْءٍ قَدِيرٌ وَأَنَّ ٱللَّهَ قَدْ أَحَاطَ بِكُلِّ شَىْءٍ عِلْمًۢا ﴿١٢﴾

At Tahrīm
(Banning)

At Tahrīm, "Banning," takes its name from a word in v. 1. There are three traditions as to the occasion of vv. 1-4:

(1)　The Prophet was very fond of honey. One of his wives received a present of honey from a relative and by its means inveigled the Prophet into staying with her longer than was customary. The others felt aggrieved, and 'Ā'ishah devised a little plot. Knowing the Prophet's horror of unpleasant smells, she arranged with two other wives that they should hold their noses when he came to them after eating the honey, and accuse him of having eaten the produce of a very rank-smelling tree. When they accused him of having eaten *Maghāfīr* the Prophet said that he had eaten only honey. They said: "The bees had fed on *Maghāfīr*." The Prophet was dismayed and vowed to eat no more honey.

(2)　Hafsah found the Prophet in her room with Māriyah—the Coptic girl, presented to him by the ruler of Egypt, who became the mother of his only male child, Ibrahīm—on a day which custom had assigned to 'Ā'ishah. Moved by Hafsah's distress, the Prophet vowed that he would have no more to do with Māriyah, and asked her not to tell 'Ā'ishah. But Hafsah's distress had been largely feigned. No sooner had the Prophet gone, than she told 'Ā'ishah with glee how easily she had got rid of Māriyah.

(3)　Before Al-Islām women had had no standing in Arabia. The Qur'an gave them legal rights and an assured position, which some of them were inclined to exaggerate. 'Umar had to rebuke his wife for replying to him in a tone which he considered disrespectful. She assured him it was the tone in which his own daughter Hafsah, 'Ā'ishah and others of the Prophet's wives answered the Prophet. 'Umar went at once and remonstrated with Hafsah and with another of the Prophet's wives to whom he was related. He was told to mind his own business, which increased his horror and dismay. Soon afterwards the Prophet separated from his wives for a time, and it was thought that he was going to divorce them. Then 'Umar ventured to tell the story of his own vain effort to reform them, at which the Prophet laughed heartily.

Traditions (1) and (3) are the better authenticated and are alone adduced by the great traditionists. But the commentators generally prefer (2) as more explanatory of the text. All allude to a tendency on the part of some of the wives of the Prophet to presume on their new status and the Prophet's well known kindness—a tendency so marked that, if allowed to continue, it would have been of bad example to the whole community. The Qur'an first rebukes the Prophet for yielding to their desires to the extent of undertaking to forgo a thing which Allah had made lawful for him—in the case of (2), fulfilment of his vow involved a wrong to Māriyah and then reproves the women for their double-dealing and intrigue.

The above traditions have been made by some non-Muslim writers the text for strictures which appear irrelevant because their ideology is altogether un-Islamic. The Prophet has never been regarded by the Muslims as other than a human messenger of God; sanctity has never been identified with celibacy. For Christendom the strictest religious ideal has been celibacy, monogamy is already a concession to human nature. For Muslims, monogamy is the ideal, polygamy the concession to human nature. Polygamy is of the nature of some men in all countries, and of all men in some countries. Having set a great example of monogamic marriage, the Prophet was to set a great example of polygamic marriage, by following which men of that temperament could live righteous lives. He encountered all the difficulties inherent in the situation, and when he made mistakes the Qur'an helped him to retrieve them. Al-Islām did not institute polygamy. It restricted an existing institution by limiting the number of a man's legal wives, by giving to every woman a legal personality and legal rights which had to be respected, and making every man legally responsible for his conduct towards every woman. Whether monogamy or polygamy should prevail in a particular country or period is a matter of social and economic convenience. The Prophet himself was permitted to have more wives than were allowed to others because, as head of the State, he was responsible for the support of women who had no other protector. With the one exception of 'Ā'ishah, all his wives had been widows.

سُورَةُ التَّحْرِيمِ

*In the name of Allah, the
Beneficent, the Merciful.*

بِسْمِ اللهِ الرَّحْمٰنِ الرَّحِيمِ

1   O Prophet! Why bannest thou
that which Allah hath made lawful
for thee, seeking to please thy
wives? And Allah is Forgiving,
Merciful.

يٰٓأَيُّهَا النَّبِيُّ لِمَ تُحَرِّمُ مَآ أَحَلَّ اللهُ لَكَ تَبْتَغِي مَرْضَاتَ
أَزْوَاجِكَ وَاللهُ غَفُورٌ رَّحِيمٌ ۝

2   Allah hath made lawful for you
(Muslims) absolution from your
oaths (of such a kind), and Allah is
your Protector. He is the Knower,
the Wise.

قَدْ فَرَضَ اللهُ لَكُمْ تَحِلَّةَ أَيْمَانِكُمْ وَاللهُ مَوْلَىٰكُمْ
وَهُوَ الْعَلِيمُ الْحَكِيمُ ۝

3   When the Prophet confided a
fact unto one of his wives and when
she afterward divulged it and Allah
apprised him thereof, he made
known (to her) part thereof and
passed over part. And when he told
it her, she said: Who hath told thee?
He said: The Knower, the Aware
hath told me.

وَإِذْ أَسَرَّ النَّبِيُّ إِلَىٰ بَعْضِ أَزْوَاجِهِ حَدِيثًا فَلَمَّا نَبَّأَتْ بِهِ
وَأَظْهَرَهُ اللهُ عَلَيْهِ عَرَّفَ بَعْضَهُ وَأَعْرَضَ عَنۢ بَعْضٍ
فَلَمَّا نَبَّأَهَا بِهِ قَالَتْ مَنْ أَنۢبَأَكَ هٰذَا
قَالَ نَبَّأَنِيَ الْعَلِيمُ الْخَبِيرُ ۝

4   If ye twain turn unto Allah
repentant, (ye have cause to do so)
for your hearts desired (the ban);
and if ye aid one another against
him (Muhammad) then lo! Allah,
even He, is his protecting Friend,
and Gabriel and the righteous
among the believers; and further-
more the angels are his helpers.

إِن تَتُوبَآ إِلَى اللهِ فَقَدْ صَغَتْ قُلُوبُكُمَا وَإِن تَظَاهَرَا
عَلَيْهِ فَإِنَّ اللهَ هُوَ مَوْلَىٰهُ وَجِبْرِيلُ وَصَالِحُ الْمُؤْمِنِينَ
وَالْمَلَٰٓئِكَةُ بَعْدَ ذٰلِكَ ظَهِيرٌ ۝

5 It may happen that his Lord, if he divorce you, will give him in your stead wives better than you, submissive (to Allah), believing, pious, penitent, inclined to fasting, widows and maids.

عَسَىٰ رَبُّهُۥٓ إِن طَلَّقَكُنَّ أَن يُبْدِلَهُۥٓ أَزْوَٰجًا خَيْرًا مِّنكُنَّ مُسْلِمَٰتٍ مُّؤْمِنَٰتٍ قَٰنِتَٰتٍ تَٰٓئِبَٰتٍ عَٰبِدَٰتٍ سَٰٓئِحَٰتٍ ثَيِّبَٰتٍ وَأَبْكَارًا ۝

6 O ye who believe! Ward off from yourselves and your families a Fire whereof the fuel is men and stones, over which are set angels strong, severe, who resist not Allah in that which He commandeth them, but do that which they are commanded.

يَٰٓأَيُّهَا الَّذِينَ ءَامَنُوا۟ قُوٓا۟ أَنفُسَكُمْ وَأَهْلِيكُمْ نَارًا وَقُودُهَا ٱلنَّاسُ وَٱلْحِجَارَةُ عَلَيْهَا مَلَٰٓئِكَةٌ غِلَاظٌ شِدَادٌ لَّا يَعْصُونَ ٱللَّهَ مَآ أَمَرَهُمْ وَيَفْعَلُونَ مَا يُؤْمَرُونَ ۝

7 (Then it will be said): O ye who disbelieve! Make no excuses for yourselves this day. Ye are only being paid for what ye used to do.

يَٰٓأَيُّهَا الَّذِينَ كَفَرُوا۟ لَا تَعْتَذِرُوا۟ ٱلْيَوْمَ إِنَّمَا تُجْزَوْنَ مَا كُنتُمْ تَعْمَلُونَ ۝

8 O ye who believe! Turn unto Allah in sincere repentance! It may be that your Lord will remit from you your evil deeds and bring you into Gardens underneath which rivers flow, on the day when Allah will not abase the Prophet and those who believe with him. Their light will run before them and on their right hands: they will say: Our Lord! Perfect our light for us, and forgive us! Lo! Thou art Able to do all things.

يَٰٓأَيُّهَا الَّذِينَ ءَامَنُوا۟ تُوبُوٓا۟ إِلَى ٱللَّهِ تَوْبَةً نَّصُوحًا عَسَىٰ رَبُّكُمْ أَن يُكَفِّرَ عَنكُمْ سَيِّـَٔاتِكُمْ وَيُدْخِلَكُمْ جَنَّٰتٍ تَجْرِى مِن تَحْتِهَا ٱلْأَنْهَٰرُ يَوْمَ لَا يُخْزِى ٱللَّهُ ٱلنَّبِىَّ وَٱلَّذِينَ ءَامَنُوا۟ مَعَهُۥ نُورُهُمْ يَسْعَىٰ بَيْنَ أَيْدِيهِمْ وَبِأَيْمَٰنِهِمْ يَقُولُونَ رَبَّنَآ أَتْمِمْ لَنَا نُورَنَا وَٱغْفِرْ لَنَآ إِنَّكَ عَلَىٰ كُلِّ شَىْءٍ قَدِيرٌ ۝

9 O Prophet! Strive against the disbelievers and the hypocrites, and be stern with them. Hell will be their home, a hapless journey's end.

يَٰٓأَيُّهَا ٱلنَّبِىُّ جَٰهِدِ ٱلْكُفَّارَ وَٱلْمُنَٰفِقِينَ وَٱغْلُظْ عَلَيْهِمْ وَمَأْوَىٰهُمْ جَهَنَّمُ وَبِئْسَ ٱلْمَصِيرُ ۝

10 Allah citeth an example for those who disbelieve: the wife of Noah and the wife of Lot, who were under two of our righteous slaves yet betrayed them so that they (the husbands) availed them naught against Allah and it was said (unto them): Enter the Fire along with those who enter.

ضَرَبَ اللّٰهُ مَثَلًا لِّلَّذِينَ كَفَرُوا امْرَأَتَ نُوحٍ وَامْرَأَتَ لُوطٍ كَانَتَا تَحْتَ عَبْدَيْنِ مِنْ عِبَادِنَا صَالِحَيْنِ فَخَانَتَاهُمَا فَلَمْ يُغْنِيَا عَنْهُمَا مِنَ اللّٰهِ شَيْئًا وَقِيلَ ادْخُلَا النَّارَ مَعَ الدَّاخِلِينَ ۝

11 And Allah citeth an example for those who believe: the wife of Pharaoh when she said: My Lord! Build for me a home with thee in the Garden, and deliver me from Pharaoh and his work, and deliver me from evil-doing folk;

وَضَرَبَ اللّٰهُ مَثَلًا لِّلَّذِينَ امَنُوا امْرَأَتَ فِرْعَوْنَ إِذْ قَالَتْ رَبِّ ابْنِ لِي عِنْدَكَ بَيْتًا فِي الْجَنَّةِ وَنَجِّنِي مِنْ فِرْعَوْنَ وَعَمَلِهِ وَنَجِّنِي مِنَ الْقَوْمِ الظَّالِمِينَ ۝

12 And Mary, daughter of 'Imrān, whose body was chaste, therefore We breathed therein something of Our Spirit. And she put faith in the words of her Lord and His Scriptures, and was of the obedient.

وَمَرْيَمَ ابْنَتَ عِمْرَانَ الَّتِي أَحْصَنَتْ فَرْجَهَا فَنَفَخْنَا فِيهِ مِنْ رُوحِنَا وَصَدَّقَتْ بِكَلِمَاتِ رَبِّهَا وَكُتُبِهِ وَكَانَتْ مِنَ الْقَانِتِينَ ۝

Al Mulk
(The Sovereignty)

Al Mulk takes its name from a word in the first verse. It belongs to the middle group of Makkan sūrahs.

In the name of Allah, the
Beneficent, the Merciful.

بِسْمِ اللهِ الرَّحْمٰنِ الرَّحِيمِ

1 Blessed is He in Whose hand is the Sovereignty, and He is Able to do all things.

تَبَارَكَ الَّذِى بِيَدِهِ الْمُلْكُ وَهُوَ عَلَى كُلِّ شَىْءٍ قَدِيرٌ ۟

2 Who hath created life and death that He may try you, which of you is best in conduct; and He is the Mighty, Forgiving;

الَّذِى خَلَقَ الْمَوْتَ وَالْحَيٰوةَ لِيَبْلُوَكُمْ أَيُّكُمْ أَحْسَنُ عَمَلًا ۚ وَهُوَ الْعَزِيزُ الْغَفُورُ ۟

3 Who hath created seven heavens in harmony. Thou (Muḥammad) canst see no fault in the Beneficent One's creation; then look again: Canst thou see any rifts?

الَّذِى خَلَقَ سَبْعَ سَمٰوٰتٍ طِبَاقًا ۖ مَا تَرٰى فِى خَلْقِ الرَّحْمٰنِ مِن تَفٰوُتٍ ۖ فَارْجِعِ الْبَصَرَ هَلْ تَرٰى مِن فُطُورٍ ۟

4 Then look again and yet again, thy sight will return unto thee weakened and made dim.

ثُمَّ ارْجِعِ الْبَصَرَ كَرَّتَيْنِ يَنقَلِبْ إِلَيْكَ الْبَصَرُ خَاسِئًا وَهُوَ حَسِيرٌ ۟

5 And verily We have beautified the world's heaven with lamps, and We have made them missiles for

وَلَقَدْ زَيَّنَّا السَّمَاءَ الدُّنْيَا بِمَصٰبِيحَ وَجَعَلْنٰهَا رُجُومًا

833

the devils,[1] and for them We have
prepared the doom of flame.

6   And for those who disbelieve in
their Lord, there is the doom of
hell, a hapless journey's end!

7   When they are flung therein
they hear its roaring as it boileth up,

8   As it would burst with rage.
Whenever a (fresh) host is flung
therein the wardens thereof ask
them: Came there unto you no
warner?

9   They say: Yea, verily, a warner
came unto us; but we denied and
said: Allah hath naught revealed; ye
are in naught but a great error.

10 And they say: Had we been
wont to listen or have sense, we
had not been among the dwellers in
the flames.

11 So they acknowledge their sins;
but far removed (from mercy) are
the dwellers in the flames.

12 Lo! those who fear their Lord in
secret, theirs will be forgiveness
and a great reward.

13 And keep your opinion secret or
proclaim it, lo! He is Knower of all
that is in the breasts (of men).

لِلشَّيَاطِينِ وَأَعْتَدْنَا لَهُمْ عَذَابَ السَّعِيرِ ۝

وَلِلَّذِينَ كَفَرُوا بِرَبِّهِمْ عَذَابُ جَهَنَّمَ وَبِئْسَ الْمَصِيرُ ۝

إِذَا أُلْقُوا فِيهَا سَمِعُوا لَهَا شَهِيقًا وَهِيَ تَفُورُ ۝

تَكَادُ تَمَيَّزُ مِنَ الْغَيْظِ كُلَّمَا أُلْقِيَ فِيهَا فَوْجٌ سَأَلَهُمْ
خَزَنَتُهَا أَلَمْ يَأْتِكُمْ نَذِيرٌ ۝

قَالُوا بَلَى قَدْ جَاءَنَا نَذِيرٌ فَكَذَّبْنَا وَقُلْنَا مَا نَزَّلَ اللَّهُ مِنْ شَيْءٍ
إِنْ أَنْتُمْ إِلَّا فِي ضَلَالٍ كَبِيرٍ ۝

وَقَالُوا لَوْ كُنَّا نَسْمَعُ أَوْ نَعْقِلُ مَا كُنَّا فِي أَصْحَابِ السَّعِيرِ ۝

فَاعْتَرَفُوا بِذَنْبِهِمْ فَسُحْقًا لِأَصْحَابِ السَّعِيرِ ۝

إِنَّ الَّذِينَ يَخْشَوْنَ رَبَّهُمْ بِالْغَيْبِ لَهُمْ مَغْفِرَةٌ
وَأَجْرٌ كَبِيرٌ ۝

وَأَسِرُّوا قَوْلَكُمْ أَوِ اجْهَرُوا بِهِ إِنَّهُ عَلِيمٌ بِذَاتِ
الصُّدُورِ ۝

---

1. On the authority of a tradition going back to Ibn 'Abbās, the allusion is to the
soothsayers and astrologers who saw the source of good and evil in the stars. See sūrah
72, v. 9, footnote.

14 Should He not know what He created? And He is the Subtle, the Aware.

اَلَا يَعْلَمُ مَنْ خَلَقَ وَهُوَ اللَّطِيفُ الْخَبِيرُ ۝

15 He it is Who hath made the earth subservient unto you, so walk in the paths thereof and eat of His providence. And unto Him will be the resurrection (of the dead).

هُوَ الَّذِى جَعَلَ لَكُمُ الْأَرْضَ ذَلُولًا فَامْشُوا فِى مَنَاكِبِهَا وَكُلُوا مِنْ رِزْقِهِ وَإِلَيْهِ النُّشُورُ ۝

16 Have ye taken security from Him Who is in the heaven that He will not cause the earth to swallow you when lo! it is convulsed?

ءَأَمِنْتُمْ مَنْ فِى السَّمَاءِ أَنْ يَخْسِفَ بِكُمُ الْأَرْضَ فَإِذَا هِىَ تَمُورُ ۝

17 Or have ye taken security from Him Who is in the heaven that He will not let loose on you a hurricane? But ye shall know the manner of My warning.

أَمْ أَمِنْتُمْ مَنْ فِى السَّمَاءِ أَنْ يُرْسِلَ عَلَيْكُمْ حَاصِبًا فَسَتَعْلَمُونَ كَيْفَ نَذِيرِ ۝

18 And verily those before them denied, then (see) the manner of My wrath (with them)!

وَلَقَدْ كَذَّبَ الَّذِينَ مِنْ قَبْلِهِمْ فَكَيْفَ كَانَ نَكِيرِ ۝

19 Have they not seen the birds above them spreading out their wings and closing them? Naught upholdeth them save the Beneficent. Lo! He is Seer of all things.

أَوَلَمْ يَرَوْا إِلَى الطَّيْرِ فَوْقَهُمْ صَافَّاتٍ وَيَقْبِضْنَ مَا يُمْسِكُهُنَّ إِلَّا الرَّحْمَنُ إِنَّهُ بِكُلِّ شَىْءٍ بَصِيرٌ ۝

20 Or who is he that will be an army unto you to help you instead of the Beneficent? The disbelievers are in naught but illusion.

أَمَّنْ هَذَا الَّذِى هُوَ جُنْدٌ لَكُمْ يَنْصُرُكُمْ مِنْ دُونِ الرَّحْمَنِ إِنِ الْكَافِرُونَ إِلَّا فِى غُرُورٍ ۝

21 Or who is he that will provide for you if He should withhold His providence? Nay, but they are set in pride and frowardness.

أَمَّنْ هَذَا الَّذِى يَرْزُقُكُمْ إِنْ أَمْسَكَ رِزْقَهُ بَلْ لَجُّوا فِى عُتُوٍّ وَنُفُورٍ ۝

22 Is he who goeth groping on his face more rightly guided, or he who

أَفَمَنْ يَمْشِى مُكِبًّا عَلَى وَجْهِهِ أَهْدَى أَمَّنْ يَمْشِى سَوِيًّا

walketh upright on a beaten road?

عَلَىٰ صِرَاطٍ مُّسْتَقِيمٍ ۝

23 Say (unto them, O Muhammad): He it is Who gave you being, and hath assigned unto you ears and eyes and hearts. Small thanks give ye!

قُلْ هُوَ الَّذِىٓ أَنشَأَكُمْ وَجَعَلَ لَكُمُ السَّمْعَ وَالْأَبْصَٰرَ وَالْأَفْـِٔدَةَ قَلِيلًا مَّا تَشْكُرُونَ ۝

24 Say, He it is Who multiplieth you in the earth, and unto Whom ye will be gathered.

قُلْ هُوَ الَّذِى ذَرَأَكُمْ فِى الْأَرْضِ وَإِلَيْهِ تُحْشَرُونَ ۝

25 And they say: When (will) this promise (be fulfilled), if ye are truthful?

وَيَقُولُونَ مَتَىٰ هَٰذَا الْوَعْدُ إِن كُنتُمْ صَٰدِقِينَ ۝

26 Say: The knowledge is with Allah only, and I am but a plain warner;

قُلْ إِنَّمَا الْعِلْمُ عِندَ اللَّهِ وَإِنَّمَآ أَنَا۠ نَذِيرٌ مُّبِينٌ ۝

27 But when they see it nigh, the faces of those who disbelieve will be awry, and it will be said (unto them): This is that for which ye used to call.

فَلَمَّا رَأَوْهُ زُلْفَةً سِيٓئَتْ وُجُوهُ الَّذِينَ كَفَرُوا وَقِيلَ هَٰذَا الَّذِى كُنتُم بِهِۦ تَدَّعُونَ ۝

28 Say (O Muhammad): Have ye thought: If Allah causeth me (Muhammad) and those with me to perish or hath mercy on us, still, who will protect the disbelievers from a painful doom?

قُلْ أَرَءَيْتُمْ إِنْ أَهْلَكَنِىَ اللَّهُ وَمَن مَّعِىَ أَوْ رَحِمَنَا فَمَن يُجِيرُ الْكَٰفِرِينَ مِنْ عَذَابٍ أَلِيمٍ ۝

29 Say: He is the Beneficent. In Him we believe and in Him we put our trust. And ye will soon know who it is that is in error manifest.

قُلْ هُوَ الرَّحْمَٰنُ ءَامَنَّا بِهِۦ وَعَلَيْهِ تَوَكَّلْنَا فَسَتَعْلَمُونَ مَنْ هُوَ فِى ضَلَٰلٍ مُّبِينٍ ۝

30 Say: Have ye thought: If (all) your water were to disappear into the earth, who then could bring you gushing water?

قُلْ أَرَءَيْتُمْ إِنْ أَصْبَحَ مَآؤُكُمْ غَوْرًا فَمَن يَأْتِيكُم بِمَآءٍ مَّعِينٍ ۝

Al Qalam
(The Pen)

Al Qalam, "The Pen," takes its name from a word in the first verse. A very early Makkan sūrah.

In the name of Allah, the Beneficent, the Merciful.

1 Nūn.[1] By the pen and that which they write (therewith),

2 Thou art not, for thy Lord's favour unto thee, a madman.

3 And lo! thine verily will be a reward unfailing.

4 And lo! thou art on sublime morals.

5 And thou wilt see and they will see

6 Which of you is the demented.

7 Lo! thy Lord is best Aware of him who strayeth from his way, and He is best Aware of those who walk aright.

8 Therefore obey not thou the rejecters

---

1. See Sūrah 2, v. 1, footnote.

9 Who would have had thee compromise, that they may compromise.

10 Neither obey thou each feeble oath-monger,

11 Detractor, spreader abroad of slanders,

12 Hinderer of the good, transgressor, malefactor

13 Greedy, therewithal, intrusive.

14 It is because he is possessed of wealth and children;

15 That, when Our revelations are recited unto him, he saith: Mere fables of the men of old.

16 We shall brand him on the nose.

17 Lo! We have tried them as We tried the owners of the garden when they vowed they would pluck its fruit next morning.

18 And made no exception (for the will of Allah);[2]

19 Then a visitation came upon it from thy Lord while they slept.

20 And in the morning it was as if plucked.

21 And they cried out one unto another in the morning,

22 Saying: Run unto your field if ye would pluck (the fruit).

وَدُّوا۟ لَوْ تُدْهِنُ فَيُدْهِنُونَ ۝

وَلَا تُطِعْ كُلَّ حَلَّافٍ مَّهِينٍ ۝

هَمَّازٍ مَّشَّآءٍ بِنَمِيمٍ ۝

مَّنَّاعٍ لِّلْخَيْرِ مُعْتَدٍ أَثِيمٍ ۝

عُتُلٍّ بَعْدَ ذَٰلِكَ زَنِيمٍ ۝

أَن كَانَ ذَا مَالٍ وَبَنِينَ ۝

إِذَا تُتْلَىٰ عَلَيْهِ ءَايَٰتُنَا قَالَ أَسَٰطِيرُ الْأَوَّلِينَ ۝

سَنَسِمُهُ عَلَى الْخُرْطُومِ ۝

إِنَّا بَلَوْنَٰهُمْ كَمَا بَلَوْنَآ أَصْحَٰبَ الْجَنَّةِ إِذْ أَقْسَمُوا۟ لَيَصْرِمُنَّهَا مُصْبِحِينَ ۝

وَلَا يَسْتَثْنُونَ ۝

فَطَافَ عَلَيْهَا طَآئِفٌ مِّن رَّبِّكَ وَهُمْ نَآئِمُونَ ۝

فَأَصْبَحَتْ كَالصَّرِيمِ ۝

فَتَنَادَوْا۟ مُصْبِحِينَ ۝

أَنِ اغْدُوا۟ عَلَىٰ حَرْثِكُمْ إِن كُنتُمْ صَٰرِمِينَ ۝

---

2. *i.e.* they forgot to say: "If God wills."

23 So they went off, saying one unto another in low tones:

فَانطَلَقُوا وَهُمْ يَتَخَافَتُونَ ۝

24 No needy man shall enter it today against you.[3]

أَن لَّا يَدْخُلَنَّهَا الْيَوْمَ عَلَيْكُم مُّسْكِينٌ ۝

25 They went betimes, strong in (this) purpose.

وَغَدَوْا عَلَىٰ حَرْدٍ قَادِرِينَ ۝

26 But when they saw it, they said: Lo! we are in error!

فَلَمَّا رَأَوْهَا قَالُوٓا إِنَّا لَضَآلُّونَ ۝

27 Nay, but we are desolate!

بَلْ نَحْنُ مَحْرُومُونَ ۝

28 The best among them said: Said I not unto you: Why glorify ye not (Allah)?

قَالَ أَوْسَطُهُمْ أَلَمْ أَقُل لَّكُمْ لَوْلَا تُسَبِّحُونَ ۝

29 They said: Glorified be our Lord! Lo! we have been wrong-doers.

قَالُوا سُبْحَٰنَ رَبِّنَآ إِنَّا كُنَّا ظَٰلِمِينَ ۝

30 Then some of them drew near unto others, self-reproaching.

فَأَقْبَلَ بَعْضُهُمْ عَلَىٰ بَعْضٍ يَتَلَاوَمُونَ ۝

31 They said: Alas for us! In truth we were outrageous.

قَالُوا يَٰوَيْلَنَآ إِنَّا كُنَّا طَٰغِينَ ۝

32 It may be that our Lord will give us better than this in place thereof. Lo! we beseech our Lord.

عَسَىٰ رَبُّنَآ أَن يُبْدِلَنَا خَيْرًا مِّنْهَآ إِنَّآ إِلَىٰ رَبِّنَا رَاغِبُونَ ۝

33 Such was the punishment. And verily the punishment of the Here-after is greater if they did but know.

كَذَٰلِكَ الْعَذَابُ وَلَعَذَابُ الْآخِرَةِ أَكْبَرُ لَوْ كَانُوا يَعْلَمُونَ ۝

34 Lo! for those who keep from evil are gardens of bliss with their Lord.

إِنَّ لِلْمُتَّقِينَ عِندَ رَبِّهِمْ جَنَّٰتِ النَّعِيمِ ۝

---

3. It was a custom throughout the East to allow the poor a gleaning of all harvests.

35 Shall We then treat those who have surrendered[4] as We treat the guilty?

أَفَنَجْعَلُ الْمُسْلِمِينَ كَالْمُجْرِمِينَ ﴿٣٥﴾

36 What aileth you? How foolishly ye judge!

مَا لَكُمْ كَيْفَ تَحْكُمُونَ ﴿٣٦﴾

37 Or have ye a Scripture wherein ye learn

أَمْ لَكُمْ كِتَابٌ فِيهِ تَدْرُسُونَ ﴿٣٧﴾

38 That ye shall indeed have all that ye choose?

إِنَّ لَكُمْ فِيهِ لَمَا تَخَيَّرُونَ ﴿٣٨﴾

39 Or have ye a covenant on oath from Us that reacheth to the Day of Judgement, that yours shall be all that ye ordain?

أَمْ لَكُمْ أَيْمَانٌ عَلَيْنَا بَالِغَةٌ إِلَى يَوْمِ الْقِيَامَةِ إِنَّ لَكُمْ لَمَا تَحْكُمُونَ ﴿٣٩﴾

40 Ask them (O Muḥammad) which of them will vouch for that!

سَلْهُمْ أَيُّهُمْ بِذَلِكَ زَعِيمٌ ﴿٤٠﴾

41 Or have they other gods? Then let them bring their other gods if they are truthful;

أَمْ لَهُمْ شُرَكَاءُ فَلْيَأْتُوا بِشُرَكَائِهِمْ إِنْ كَانُوا صَادِقِينَ ﴿٤١﴾

42 On the day when the Shin shall be laid bare, and they are ordered to prostrate themselves but are not able,

يَوْمَ يُكْشَفُ عَنْ سَاقٍ وَيُدْعَوْنَ إِلَى السُّجُودِ فَلَا يَسْتَطِيعُونَ ﴿٤٢﴾

43 With eyes downcast, abasement stupefying them. And they had been summoned to prostrate themselves while they were yet unhurt.

خَاشِعَةً أَبْصَارُهُمْ تَرْهَقُهُمْ ذِلَّةٌ وَقَدْ كَانُوا يُدْعَوْنَ إِلَى السُّجُودِ وَهُمْ سَالِمُونَ ﴿٤٣﴾

44 Leave Me (to deal) with those who give the lie to this pronouncement. We shall lead them on by steps from whence they know not.

فَذَرْنِي وَمَنْ يُكَذِّبُ بِهَذَا الْحَدِيثِ سَنَسْتَدْرِجُهُمْ مِنْ حَيْثُ لَا يَعْلَمُونَ ﴿٤٤﴾

45 Yet I bear with them, for lo! My scheme is firm.

وَأُمْلِي لَهُمْ إِنَّ كَيْدِي مَتِينٌ ﴿٤٥﴾

4. Ar. *Muslimūn.*

46 Or dost thou (Muhammad) ask a fee from them so that they are heavily taxed?

أَمۡ تَسۡـَٔلُهُمۡ أَجۡرًا فَهُم مِّن مَّغۡرَمٍ مُّثۡقَلُونَ ﴿٤٦﴾

47 Or is the Unseen theirs that they can write (thereof)?

أَمۡ عِندَهُمُ ٱلۡغَيۡبُ فَهُمۡ يَكۡتُبُونَ ﴿٤٧﴾

48 But wait thou for thy Lord's decree, and be not like him of the fish,[5] who cried out in despair.

فَٱصۡبِرۡ لِحُكۡمِ رَبِّكَ وَلَا تَكُن كَصَاحِبِ ٱلۡحُوتِ إِذۡ نَادَىٰ وَهُوَ مَكۡظُومٌ ﴿٤٨﴾

49 Had it not been that favour from his Lord had reached him he surely had been cast into the wilderness while he was reprobate.

لَّوۡلَآ أَن تَدَٰرَكَهُۥ نِعۡمَةٌ مِّن رَّبِّهِۦ لَنُبِذَ بِٱلۡعَرَآءِ وَهُوَ مَذۡمُومٌ ﴿٤٩﴾

50 But his Lord chose him and placed him among the righteous.

فَٱجۡتَبَٰهُ رَبُّهُۥ فَجَعَلَهُۥ مِنَ ٱلصَّٰلِحِينَ ﴿٥٠﴾

51 And lo! those who disbelieve would fain disconcert thee with their eyes when they hear the Reminder, and they say: Lo! he is indeed mad;

وَإِن يَكَادُ ٱلَّذِينَ كَفَرُواْ لَيُزۡلِقُونَكَ بِأَبۡصَٰرِهِمۡ لَمَّا سَمِعُواْ ٱلذِّكۡرَ وَيَقُولُونَ إِنَّهُۥ لَمَجۡنُونٌ ﴿٥١﴾

52 When it is naught else than a Reminder to creation.

وَمَا هُوَ إِلَّا ذِكۡرٌ لِّلۡعَٰلَمِينَ ﴿٥٢﴾

---

5. *i.e.* Jonah.

Al Ḥāqqah
(The Reality)

Al Ḥāqqah takes its name from a word recurring in the first three verses.

It belongs to the middle group of Makkan sūrahs.

سُوْرَةُ الْحَاقَّةِ

In the name of Allah, the Beneficent, the Merciful.

بِسْمِ اللهِ الرَّحْمٰنِ الرَّحِيْمِ

1 The Reality!

ٱلْحَآقَّةُ ۝

2 What is the Reality?

مَا ٱلْحَآقَّةُ ۝

3 Ah, what will convey unto thee what the reality is!

وَمَآ أَدْرٰىكَ مَا ٱلْحَآقَّةُ ۝

4 (The tribes of) Thamūd and 'Ād disbelieved in the judgement to come.

كَذَّبَتْ ثَمُوْدُ وَعَادٌ بِٱلْقَارِعَةِ ۝

5 As for Thamūd, they were destroyed by the lightning.

فَأَمَّا ثَمُوْدُ فَأُهْلِكُوْا بِٱلطَّاغِيَةِ ۝

6 And as for 'Ād, they were destroyed by a fierce roaring wind;

وَأَمَّا عَادٌ فَأُهْلِكُوْا بِرِيْحٍ صَرْصَرٍ عَاتِيَةٍ ۝

7 Which He imposed on them for seven long nights and eight long days so that thou mightest have seen men lying overthrown, as they were hollow trunks of palm-trees.

سَخَّرَهَا عَلَيْهِمْ سَبْعَ لَيَالٍ وَثَمٰنِيَةَ أَيَّامٍ حُسُوْمًا فَتَرَى ٱلْقَوْمَ فِيْهَا صَرْعٰى كَأَنَّهُمْ أَعْجَازُ نَخْلٍ خَاوِيَةٍ ۝

8 Canst thou (O Muhammad) see any remnant of them?

فَهَلْ تَرٰى لَهُمْ مِّنْ بَاقِيَةٍ ۝

9 And Pharaoh and those before him, and the communities that were destroyed, brought error,

وَجَآءَ فِرْعَوْنُ وَمَن قَبْلَهُ وَالْمُؤْتَفِكَاتُ بِالْخَاطِئَةِ ۙ ٩

10 And they disobeyed the messenger of their Lord, therefore did He grip them with a tightening grip.

فَعَصَوْا رَسُولَ رَبِّهِمْ فَأَخَذَهُمْ أَخْذَةً رَّابِيَةً ۙ ١٠

11 Lo! when the waters rose, We carried you upon the ship.

إِنَّا لَمَّا طَغَا الْمَآءُ حَمَلْنَاكُمْ فِي الْجَارِيَةِ ۙ ١١

12 That We might make it a memorial for you, and that remembering ears (that heard the story) might remember.

لِنَجْعَلَهَا لَكُمْ تَذْكِرَةً وَّتَعِيَهَآ أُذُنٌ وَّاعِيَةٌ ۙ ١٢

13 And when the trumpet shall sound one blast

فَإِذَا نُفِخَ فِي الصُّورِ نَفْخَةٌ وَّاحِدَةٌ ۙ ١٣

14 And the earth with the mountains shall be lifted up and crushed with one crash,

وَحُمِلَتِ الْأَرْضُ وَالْجِبَالُ فَدُكَّتَا دَكَّةً وَّاحِدَةً ۙ ١٤

15 Then, on that day will the Event befall.

فَيَوْمَئِذٍ وَّقَعَتِ الْوَاقِعَةُ ۙ ١٥

16 And the heaven will split asunder, for that day it will be frail.

وَانْشَقَّتِ السَّمَآءُ فَهِيَ يَوْمَئِذٍ وَّاهِيَةٌ ۙ ١٦

17 And the angels will be on the sides thereof, and eight will uphold the Throne of thy Lord that day, above them.

وَالْمَلَكُ عَلَىٰ أَرْجَآئِهَا وَيَحْمِلُ عَرْشَ رَبِّكَ فَوْقَهُمْ يَوْمَئِذٍ ثَمَانِيَةٌ ۙ ١٧

18 On that day ye will be exposed; not a secret of you will be hidden.

يَوْمَئِذٍ تُعْرَضُونَ لَا تَخْفَىٰ مِنكُمْ خَافِيَةٌ ١٨

19 Then, as for him who is given his record in his right hand, he will say: Take, read my book!

فَأَمَّا مَنْ أُوتِيَ كِتَابَهُ بِيَمِينِهِ فَيَقُولُ هَآؤُمُ اقْرَءُوا كِتَابِيَهْ ۙ ١٩

20 Surely I knew that I should have to meet my reckoning.

إِنِّي ظَنَنتُ أَنِّي مُلَاقٍ حِسَابِيَهْ ۙ ٢٠

21 Then he will be in blissful state

فَهُوَ فِي عِيشَةٍ رَّاضِيَةٍ ۙ ٢١

22 In a high Garden

فِى جَنَّةٍ عَالِيَةٍ ۝

23 Whereof the clusters are in easy reach.

قُطُوفُهَا دَانِيَةٌ ۝

24 (And it will be said unto those therein): Eat and drink at ease for that which ye sent on before you in past days.

كُلُوا وَاشْرَبُوا هَنِيئًا بِمَآ أَسْلَفْتُمْ فِى الْأَيَّامِ الْخَالِيَةِ ۝

25 But as for him who is given his record in his left hand, he will say: Oh, would that I had not been given my book

وَأَمَّا مَنْ أُوتِىَ كِتَبَهُ بِشِمَالِهِ فَيَقُولُ يَلَيْتَنِى لَمْ أُوتَ كِتَبِيَهْ ۝

26 And knew not what my reckoning!

وَلَمْ أَدْرِ مَا حِسَابِيَهْ ۝

27 Oh, would that it had been death!

يَلَيْتَهَا كَانَتِ الْقَاضِيَةَ ۝

28 My wealth hath not availed me,

مَآ أَغْنَىٰ عَنِّى مَالِيَهْ ۝

29 My power hath gone from me.

هَلَكَ عَنِّى سُلْطَنِيَهْ ۝

30 (It will be said): Take him and fetter him

خُذُوهُ فَغُلُّوهُ ۝

31 And then expose him to hell-fire

ثُمَّ الْجَحِيمَ صَلُّوهُ ۝

32 And then insert him in a chain whereof the length is seventy cubits.

ثُمَّ فِى سِلْسِلَةٍ ذَرْعُهَا سَبْعُونَ ذِرَاعًا فَاسْلُكُوهُ ۝

33 Lo! he used not to believe in Allah the Tremendous,

إِنَّهُ كَانَ لَا يُؤْمِنُ بِاللَّهِ الْعَظِيمِ ۝

34 And urged not on the feeding of the wretched,

وَلَا يَحُضُّ عَلَىٰ طَعَامِ الْمِسْكِينِ ۝

35 Therefore hath he no lover here this day,

فَلَيْسَ لَهُ الْيَوْمَ هَهُنَا حَمِيمٌ ۝

36 Nor any food save filth

وَلَا طَعَامٌ إِلَّا مِنْ غِسْلِينٍ ۝

37 Which none but sinners eat.

لَا يَأْكُلُهُ إِلَّا الْخَاطِئُونَ ۝

38 But nay! I swear by all that ye see

فَلَا أُقْسِمُ بِمَا تُبْصِرُونَ ۝

وَمَا لَا تُبْصِرُونَ ﴿٣٩﴾

39 And all that ye see not

إِنَّهُ لَقَوْلُ رَسُولٍ كَرِيمٍ ﴿٤٠﴾

40 That it is indeed the speech of an illustrious messenger.

41 It is not poet's speech—little is it that ye believe!

وَمَا هُوَ بِقَوْلِ شَاعِرٍ قَلِيلًا مَّا تُؤْمِنُونَ ﴿٤١﴾

42 Nor diviner's speech—little is it that ye remember!

وَلَا بِقَوْلِ كَاهِنٍ قَلِيلًا مَّا تَذَكَّرُونَ ﴿٤٢﴾

43 It is a revelation from the Lord of the Worlds.

نَزِيلٌ مِّن رَّبِّ الْعَالَمِينَ ﴿٤٣﴾

44 And if he had invented false sayings concerning Us,

وَلَوْ تَقَوَّلَ عَلَيْنَا بَعْضَ الْأَقَاوِيلِ ﴿٤٤﴾

45 We assuredly had taken him by the right hand

لَأَخَذْنَا مِنْهُ بِالْيَمِينِ ﴿٤٥﴾

46 And then severed his life-artery,

ثُمَّ لَقَطَعْنَا مِنْهُ الْوَتِينَ ﴿٤٦﴾

47 And not one of you could have held Us off from him.

فَمَا مِنكُم مِّنْ أَحَدٍ عَنْهُ حَاجِزِينَ ﴿٤٧﴾

48 And lo! it is a warrant unto those who ward off (evil).

وَإِنَّهُ لَتَذْكِرَةٌ لِّلْمُتَّقِينَ ﴿٤٨﴾

49 And lo! We know that some among you will deny (it).

وَإِنَّا لَنَعْلَمُ أَنَّ مِنكُم مُّكَذِّبِينَ ﴿٤٩﴾

50 And lo! it is indeed an anguish for the disbelievers.

وَإِنَّهُ لَحَسْرَةٌ عَلَى الْكَافِرِينَ ﴿٥٠﴾

51 And lo! it is absolute truth.

وَإِنَّهُ لَحَقُّ الْيَقِينِ ﴿٥١﴾

52 So glorify the name of thy Tremendous Lord.

فَسَبِّحْ بِاسْمِ رَبِّكَ الْعَظِيمِ ﴿٥٢﴾

Al Ma'ārij
(The Ascending Stairways)

Al Ma'ārij takes its name from a word in verse 3. An early Makkan sūrah.

سُوْرَةُ الْمَعَارِج

In the name of Allah, the Beneficent, the Merciful.

1 A questioner questioned concerning the doom about to fall

سَأَلَ سَآئِلٌ بِعَذَابٍ وَاقِعٍ ۚ

2 Upon the disbelievers, which none can repel,

لِلْكَفِرِينَ لَيْسَ لَهُ دَافِعٌ ۚ

3 From Allah, Lord of the Ascending Stairways

مِّنَ اللّٰهِ ذِى الْمَعَارِجِ ۚ

4 (Whereby) the angels and the Spirit ascend unto Him in a Day whereof the span is fifty thousand years.

تَعْرُجُ الْمَلَٓئِكَةُ وَالرُّوحُ إِلَيْهِ فِى يَوْمٍ كَانَ مِقْدَارُهُ خَمْسِينَ أَلْفَ سَنَةٍ ۚ

5 But be patient (O Muhammad) with a patience fair to see.

فَاصْبِرْ صَبْرًا جَمِيلًا ۚ

6 Lo! they behold it afar off

إِنَّهُمْ يَرَوْنَهُ بَعِيدًا ۚ

7 While We behold it nigh:

وَنَرٰىهُ قَرِيبًا ۚ

8 The day when the sky will become as molten copper,

يَوْمَ تَكُونُ السَّمَآءُ كَالْمُهْلِ ۚ

9 And the hills become as flakes of wool,

وَتَكُونُ الْجِبَالُ كَالْعِهْنِ ۚ

846

10 And no familiar friend will ask a question of his friend

وَلَا يَسْئَلُ حَمِيمٌ حَمِيمًا ۞

11 Though they will be given sight of them. The guilty man will long be able to ransom himself from the punishment of that day at the price of his children

يُبَصَّرُونَهُمْ يَوَدُّ الْمُجْرِمُ لَوْ يَفْتَدِى مِنْ عَذَابِ يَوْمِئِذٍ بِبَنِيهِ ۞

12 And his spouse and his brother

وَصَاحِبَتِهِ وَأَخِيهِ ۞

13 And his kin that harboured him

وَفَصِيلَتِهِ الَّتِى تُؤْوِيهِ ۞

14 And all that are in the earth, if then it might deliver him.

وَمَنْ فِى الْأَرْضِ جَمِيعًا ثُمَّ يُنْجِيهِ ۞

15 But nay! for lo! it is the fire of hell

كَلَّا إِنَّهَا لَظَى ۞

16 Eager to roast;

نَزَّاعَةً لِلشَّوَى ۞

17 It calleth him who turned and fled (from truth),

تَدْعُوا مَنْ أَدْبَرَ وَتَوَلَّى ۞

18 And hoarded (wealth) and withheld it.

وَجَمَعَ فَأَوْعَى ۞

19 Lo! man was created anxious,

إِنَّ الْإِنْسَانَ خُلِقَ هَلُوعًا ۞

20 Fretful when evil befalleth him

إِذَا مَسَّهُ الشَّرُّ جَزُوعًا ۞

21 And, when good befalleth him, grudging;

وَإِذَا مَسَّهُ الْخَيْرُ مَنُوعًا ۞

22 Save worshippers

إِلَّا الْمُصَلِّينَ ۞

23 Who are constant at their worship

الَّذِينَ هُمْ عَلَى صَلَاتِهِمْ دَائِمُونَ ۞

24 And in whose wealth there is a right acknowledged

وَالَّذِينَ فِى أَمْوَالِهِمْ حَقٌّ مَعْلُومٌ ۞

25 For the beggar and the destitute;

لِلسَّائِلِ وَالْمَحْرُومِ ۞

26 And those who believe in the Day of Judgement,

وَالَّذِينَ يُصَدِّقُونَ بِيَوْمِ الدِّينِ ۞

27 And those who are fearful of their Lord's doom—

وَالَّذِينَ هُمْ مِنْ عَذَابِ رَبِّهِمْ مُشْفِقُونَ ۞

28 Lo! the doom of their Lord is that before which none can feel secure—

إِنَّ عَذَابَ رَبِّهِمْ غَيْرُ مَأْمُونٍ ۝

29 And those who preserve their chastity

وَالَّذِينَ هُمْ لِفُرُوجِهِمْ حَفِظُونَ ۝

30 Save with their wives and those whom their right hands possess, for thus they are not blameworthy;

إِلَّا عَلَى أَزْوَاجِهِمْ أَوْ مَا مَلَكَتْ أَيْمَنُهُمْ فَإِنَّهُمْ غَيْرُ مَلُومِينَ ۝

31 But whoso seeketh more than that, those are they who are transgressors;

فَمَنِ ابْتَغَى وَرَاءَ ذَلِكَ فَأُولَئِكَ هُمُ الْعَادُونَ ۝

32 And those who keep their pledges and their covenant.

وَالَّذِينَ هُمْ لِأَمَانَتِهِمْ وَعَهْدِهِمْ رَاعُونَ ۝

33 And those who stand by their testimony

وَالَّذِينَ هُمْ بِشَهَادَاتِهِمْ قَائِمُونَ ۝

34 And those who are attentive at their worship,

وَالَّذِينَ هُمْ عَلَى صَلَاتِهِمْ يُحَافِظُونَ ۝

35 These will dwell in Gardens, honoured.

أُولَئِكَ فِي جَنَّاتٍ مُّكْرَمُونَ ۝

36 What aileth those who disbelieve, that they keep staring toward thee (O Muhammad), open eyed,

فَمَالِ الَّذِينَ كَفَرُوا قِبَلَكَ مُهْطِعِينَ ۝

37 On the right and on the left, in groups?

عَنِ الْيَمِينِ وَعَنِ الشِّمَالِ عِزِينَ ۝

38 Doth every man among them hope to enter the Garden of Delight?

أَيَطْمَعُ كُلُّ امْرِئٍ مِّنْهُمْ أَن يُدْخَلَ جَنَّةَ نَعِيمٍ ۝

39 Nay, verily. Lo! We created them from what they know.

كَلَّا إِنَّا خَلَقْنَاهُم مِّمَّا يَعْلَمُونَ ۝

40 But nay! I swear by the Lord of the rising places and the setting places of the planets that We are Able

فَلَا أُقْسِمُ بِرَبِّ الْمَشَارِقِ وَالْمَغَارِبِ إِنَّا لَقَادِرُونَ ۝

41 To replace them by (others) better than them. And We are not to be outrun.

على أَن نُّبَدِّلَ خَيْرًا مِّنْهُمْ وَمَا نَحْنُ بِمَسْبُوقِينَ ۝

42 So let them chat and play until they meet their Day which they are promised,

فَذَرْهُمْ يَخُوضُوا وَيَلْعَبُوا حَتَّىٰ يُلَاقُوا يَوْمَهُمُ الَّذِى يُوعَدُونَ ۝

43 The day when they come forth from the graves in haste, as racing to a goal,

يَوْمَ يَخْرُجُونَ مِنَ الْأَجْدَاثِ سِرَاعًا كَأَنَّهُمْ إِلَىٰ نُصُبٍ يُوفِضُونَ ۝

44 With eyes aghast, abasement stupefying them: Such is the Day which they are promised.

خَاشِعَةً أَبْصَارُهُمْ تَرْهَقُهُمْ ذِلَّةٌ ذَٰلِكَ الْيَوْمُ الَّذِى كَانُوا يُوعَدُونَ ۝

Nūḥ
(Noah)

Takes its name from its subject, which is the preaching of the prophet Noah. An early Makkan sūrah.

In the name of Allah, the Beneficent, the Merciful.

1 Lo! We sent Noah unto his people (saying): Warn thy people ere the painful doom come unto them.

2 He said: O my people! Lo! I am a plain warner unto you

3 (Bidding you): Serve Allah and keep your duty unto Him and obey me,

4 That He may forgive you somewhat of your sins and respite you to an appointed term. Lo! the term of Allah, when it cometh, cannot be delayed, if ye but knew.

5 He said: My Lord! Lo! I have called unto my people night and day

6 But all my calling doth but add to their repugnance;

7 And lo! whenever I call unto them that Thou mayest pardon them they thrust their fingers in their ears and cover themselves with their garments and persist (in their refusal) and magnify themselves in pride.

وَإِنِّي كُلَّمَا دَعَوْتُهُمْ لِتَغْفِرَ لَهُمْ جَعَلُوٓا أَصَٰبِعَهُمْ فِىٓ ءَاذَانِهِمْ وَاسْتَغْشَوْا ثِيَابَهُمْ وَأَصَرُّوا وَاسْتَكْبَرُوا اسْتِكْبَارًا ۝

8 And lo! I have called unto them aloud,

ثُمَّ إِنِّي دَعَوْتُهُمْ جِهَارًا ۝

9 And lo! I have made public proclamation unto them, and I have appealed to them in private.

ثُمَّ إِنِّيٓ أَعْلَنتُ لَهُمْ وَأَسْرَرْتُ لَهُمْ إِسْرَارًا ۝

10 And I have said: Seek pardon of your Lord. Lo! He was ever Forgiving.

فَقُلْتُ اسْتَغْفِرُوا رَبَّكُمْ إِنَّهُۥ كَانَ غَفَّارًا ۝

11 He will let loose the sky for you in plenteous rain,

يُرْسِلِ السَّمَآءَ عَلَيْكُم مِّدْرَارًا ۝

12 And will help you with wealth and sons, and will assign unto you Gardens and will assign unto you rivers.

وَيُمْدِدْكُم بِأَمْوَٰلٍ وَبَنِينَ وَيَجْعَل لَّكُمْ جَنَّٰتٍ وَيَجْعَل لَّكُمْ أَنْهَٰرًا ۝

13 What aileth you that ye hope not toward Allah for dignity

مَّا لَكُمْ لَا تَرْجُونَ لِلَّهِ وَقَارًا ۝

14 When He created you by (divers) stages?

وَقَدْ خَلَقَكُمْ أَطْوَارًا ۝

15 See ye not how Allah hath created seven heavens in harmony,

أَلَمْ تَرَوْا كَيْفَ خَلَقَ اللَّهُ سَبْعَ سَمَٰوَٰتٍ طِبَاقًا ۝

16 And hath made the moon a light therein, and made the sun a lamp?

وَجَعَلَ الْقَمَرَ فِيهِنَّ نُورًا وَجَعَلَ الشَّمْسَ سِرَاجًا ۝

17 And Allah hath caused you to grow as a growth from the earth,

وَاللَّهُ أَنۢبَتَكُم مِّنَ الْأَرْضِ نَبَاتًا ۝

18 And afterward He maketh you return thereto, and He will bring you forth again, a (new) forth-bringing.

ثُمَّ يُعِيدُكُمْ فِيهَا وَيُخْرِجُكُمْ إِخْرَاجًا ۝

19 And Allah hath made the earth a wide expanse for you

وَاللَّهُ جَعَلَ لَكُمُ الْأَرْضَ بِسَاطًا ﴿١٩﴾

20 That ye may thread the valley-ways thereof.

لِتَسْلُكُوا مِنْهَا سُبُلًا فِجَاجًا ﴿٢٠﴾

21 Noah said: My Lord! they have disobeyed me and followed one whose wealth and children increase him in naught save ruin;

قَالَ نُوحٌ رَبِّ إِنَّهُمْ عَصَوْنِي وَاتَّبَعُوا مَنْ لَمْ يَزِدْهُ مَالُهُ وَوَلَدُهُ إِلَّا خَسَارًا ﴿٢١﴾

22 And they have plotted a mighty plot,

وَمَكَرُوا مَكْرًا كُبَّارًا ﴿٢٢﴾

23 And they have said: Forsake not your gods. Forsake not Wadd, nor Suwā', nor Yaghūth and Ya'ūq and Nasr.[1]

وَقَالُوا لَا تَذَرُنَّ آلِهَتَكُمْ وَلَا تَذَرُنَّ وَدًّا وَلَا سُوَاعًا وَلَا يَغُوثَ وَيَعُوقَ وَنَسْرًا ﴿٢٣﴾

24 And they have led many astray, and Thou increasest the wrong-doers in naught save error.

وَقَدْ أَضَلُّوا كَثِيرًا وَلَا تَزِدِ الظَّالِمِينَ إِلَّا ضَلَالًا ﴿٢٤﴾

25 Because of their sins they were drowned, then made to enter a Fire. And they found they had no helpers in place of Allah.

مِمَّا خَطِيئَاتِهِمْ أُغْرِقُوا فَأُدْخِلُوا نَارًا فَلَمْ يَجِدُوا لَهُمْ مِنْ دُونِ اللَّهِ أَنْصَارًا ﴿٢٥﴾

26 And Noah said: My Lord! Leave not one of the disbelievers in the land.

وَقَالَ نُوحٌ رَبِّ لَا تَذَرْ عَلَى الْأَرْضِ مِنَ الْكَافِرِينَ دَيَّارًا ﴿٢٦﴾

27 If Thou shouldst leave them, they will mislead Thy slaves and will beget none save lewd ingrates.

إِنَّكَ إِنْ تَذَرْهُمْ يُضِلُّوا عِبَادَكَ وَلَا يَلِدُوا إِلَّا فَاجِرًا كَفَّارًا ﴿٢٧﴾

28 My Lord! Forgive me and my parents and him who entereth my house believing, and believing men and believing women, and increase not the wrong-doers in aught save ruin.

رَبِّ اغْفِرْ لِي وَلِوَالِدَيَّ وَلِمَنْ دَخَلَ بَيْتِيَ مُؤْمِنًا وَلِلْمُؤْمِنِينَ وَالْمُؤْمِنَاتِ وَلَا تَزِدِ الظَّالِمِينَ إِلَّا تَبَارًا ﴿٢٨﴾

---

1. Idols of the pagan Arabs.

Al Jinn
(The Jinn)

Al Jinn takes its name from a word in the first verse, and also from the subject of verses 1-18. The meaning of the word *Jinn* in the Qur'an has exercised the minds of Muslim commentators, ancient and modern. Mr. Ya'qūb Hasan of Madras, in the first volume of a remarkable work in Urdu, *Kitābu'l-Hudā*, shows that it has at least three meanings in the Qur'an and that one of those meanings is something akin to "clever foreigners" as in the case of the *Jinn* who worked for Solomon. But undoubtedly the first and obvious meaning is "elemental spirits," to whom, as to mankind, the Qur'an came as a guidance. The incident is said to have occurred during the Prophet's return from his unsuccessful missionary journey to Tā'if.

A late Makkan sūrah.

In the name of Allah, the Beneficent, the Merciful.

1 Say (O Muḥammad): It is revealed unto me that a company of the Jinn gave ear, and they said: Lo! We have heard a marvellous Qur'an.

2 Which guideth unto righteousness, so we believe in it and we ascribe unto our Lord no partner.

3 And (we believe) that He— exalted be the glory of our Lord!— hath taken neither wife nor son,

4 And that the foolish one among us used to speak concerning Allah an atrocious lie.

وَأَنَّهُۥ كَانَ يَقُولُ سَفِيهُنَا عَلَى ٱللَّهِ شَطَطًا ۝

5 And lo! we had supposed that humankind and *Jinn* would not speak a lie concerning Allah—

وَأَنَّا ظَنَنَّآ أَن لَّن تَقُولَ ٱلْإِنسُ وَٱلْجِنُّ عَلَى ٱللَّهِ كَذِبًا ۝

6 And indeed (O Muhammad) individuals of humankind used to invoke the protection of individuals of the Jinn so that they increased them in revolt (against Allah);

وَأَنَّهُۥ كَانَ رِجَالٌ مِّنَ ٱلْإِنسِ يَعُوذُونَ بِرِجَالٍ مِّنَ ٱلْجِنِّ فَزَادُوهُمْ رَهَقًا ۝

7 And indeed they supposed, even as ye suppose, that Allah would not raise anyone (from the dead)—

وَأَنَّهُمْ ظَنُّوا۟ كَمَا ظَنَنتُمْ أَن لَّن يَبْعَثَ ٱللَّهُ أَحَدًا ۝

8 And (the Jinn who had listened to the Qur'an said): We had sought the heaven but had found it filled with strong warders and meteors.

وَأَنَّا لَمَسْنَا ٱلسَّمَآءَ فَوَجَدْنَٰهَا مُلِئَتْ حَرَسًا شَدِيدًا وَشُهُبًا ۝

9 And we used to sit on places (high) therein to listen. But he who listened now findeth a flame in wait for him;[1]

وَأَنَّا كُنَّا نَقْعُدُ مِنْهَا مَقَٰعِدَ لِلسَّمْعِ فَمَن يَسْتَمِعِ ٱلْآنَ يَجِدْ لَهُۥ شِهَابًا رَّصَدًا ۝

10 And we know not whether harm is boded unto all who are in the earth, or whether their Lord intendeth guidance for them.

وَأَنَّا لَا نَدْرِىٓ أَشَرٌّ أُرِيدَ بِمَن فِى ٱلْأَرْضِ أَمْ أَرَادَ بِهِمْ رَبُّهُمْ رَشَدًا ۝

11 And among us there are righteous folk and among us there are far from that. We are sects having different rules.

وَأَنَّا مِنَّا ٱلصَّٰلِحُونَ وَمِنَّا دُونَ ذَٰلِكَ كُنَّا طَرَآئِقَ قِدَدًا ۝

---

1. About the time of the Prophet's mission there were many meteors and other strange appearances in the heavens, which, tradition says, frightened the astrologers from the high observatories where they used to watch all night, and threw out all their calculations.

12 And we know that we cannot escape from Allah in the earth, nor can we escape by flight.

13 And when we heard the guidance, we believed therein, and whoso believeth in his Lord, he feareth neither loss nor oppression.

14 And there are among us some who have surrendered (to Allah) and there are among us some who are unjust. And whoso hath surrendered to Allah, such have taken the right path purposefully.

15 And as for those who are unjust, they are firewood for hell.

16 If they (the idolaters) tread the right path, We shall give them to drink of water in abundance

17 That We may test them thereby, and whoso turneth away from the remembrance of his Lord; He will thrust him into ever-growing torment.

18 And the places of worship are only for Allah, so pray not unto anyone along with Allah.

19 And when the slave of Allah[2] stood up in prayer to Him, they crowded on him, almost stifling.[3]

20 Say (unto them, O Muhammad): I pray unto Allah only, and ascribe unto Him no partner.

وَأَنَّا ظَنَنَّآ أَن لَّن نُّعۡجِزَ ٱللَّهَ فِى ٱلۡأَرۡضِ وَلَن نُّعۡجِزَهُۥ هَرَبٗا ۝

وَأَنَّا لَمَّا سَمِعۡنَا ٱلۡهُدَىٰٓ ءَامَنَّا بِهِۦۖ فَمَن يُؤۡمِنۢ بِرَبِّهِۦ فَلَا يَخَافُ بَخۡسٗا وَلَا رَهَقٗا ۝

وَأَنَّا مِنَّا ٱلۡمُسۡلِمُونَ وَمِنَّا ٱلۡقَٰسِطُونَۖ فَمَنۡ أَسۡلَمَ فَأُوْلَٰٓئِكَ تَحَرَّوۡاْ رَشَدٗا ۝

وَأَمَّا ٱلۡقَٰسِطُونَ فَكَانُواْ لِجَهَنَّمَ حَطَبٗا ۝

وَأَلَّوِ ٱسۡتَقَٰمُواْ عَلَى ٱلطَّرِيقَةِ لَأَسۡقَيۡنَٰهُم مَّآءً غَدَقٗا ۝

لِّنَفۡتِنَهُمۡ فِيهِۚ وَمَن يُعۡرِضۡ عَن ذِكۡرِ رَبِّهِۦ يَسۡلُكۡهُ عَذَابٗا صَعَدٗا ۝

وَأَنَّ ٱلۡمَسَٰجِدَ لِلَّهِ فَلَا تَدۡعُواْ مَعَ ٱللَّهِ أَحَدٗا ۝

وَأَنَّهُۥ لَمَّا قَامَ عَبۡدُ ٱللَّهِ يَدۡعُوهُ كَادُواْ يَكُونُونَ عَلَيۡهِ لِبَدٗا ۝

قُلۡ إِنَّمَآ أَدۡعُواْ رَبِّى وَلَآ أُشۡرِكُ بِهِۦٓ أَحَدٗا ۝

---

2. *i.e.* the Prophet.

3. Generally taken to be an allusion to the rough treatment which the Prophet received at the hands of the people of Ṭā'if.

21 Say: Lo! I control not hurt nor benefit for you.

قُلْ إِنِّى لَآ أَمْلِكُ لَكُمْ ضَرًّا وَلَا رَشَدًا ۝

22 Say: Lo! none can protect me from Allah, nor can I find any refuge beside Him

قُلْ إِنِّى لَن يُجِيرَنِى مِنَ اللَّهِ أَحَدٌ وَلَنْ أَجِدَ مِن دُونِهِ مُلْتَحَدًا ۝

23 (Mine is) but conveyance (of the truth) from Allah, and His messages; and whoso disobeyeth Allah and His messenger, lo! his is fire of hell, wherein such dwell forever.

إِلَّا بَلَٰغًا مِّنَ اللَّهِ وَرِسَٰلَٰتِهِۦ ۚ وَمَن يَعْصِ اللَّهَ وَرَسُولَهُۥ فَإِنَّ لَهُۥ نَارَ جَهَنَّمَ خَٰلِدِينَ فِيهَآ أَبَدًا ۝

24 Till (the day) when they shall behold that which they are promised (they may doubt); but then they will know for certain) who is weaker in allies and less in multitude.

حَتَّىٰٓ إِذَا رَأَوْا مَا يُوعَدُونَ فَسَيَعْلَمُونَ مَنْ أَضْعَفُ نَاصِرًا وَأَقَلُّ عَدَدًا ۝

25 Say (O Muhammad, unto the disbelievers): I know not whether that which ye are promised is nigh, or if my Lord hath set a distant term for it.

قُلْ إِنْ أَدْرِىٓ أَقَرِيبٌ مَّا تُوعَدُونَ أَمْ يَجْعَلُ لَهُۥ رَبِّىٓ أَمَدًا ۝

26 (He is) the knower of the Unseen, and He revealeth unto none His secret,

عَٰلِمُ الْغَيْبِ فَلَا يُظْهِرُ عَلَىٰ غَيْبِهِۦٓ أَحَدًا ۝

27 Save unto every messenger whom he hath chosen, and then He maketh a guard to go before him and a guard behind him

إِلَّا مَنِ ارْتَضَىٰ مِن رَّسُولٍ فَإِنَّهُۥ يَسْلُكُ مِنۢ بَيْنِ يَدَيْهِ وَمِنْ خَلْفِهِۦ رَصَدًا ۝

28 That He may know that they have indeed conveyed the messages of their Lord. He surroundeth all their doings, and He keepeth count of all things.

لِّيَعْلَمَ أَن قَدْ أَبْلَغُوا رِسَٰلَٰتِ رَبِّهِمْ وَأَحَاطَ بِمَا لَدَيْهِمْ وَأَحْصَىٰ كُلَّ شَىْءٍ عَدَدًا ۝

Al Muzzammil
(The Enshrouded One)

Al Muzzammil takes its title from a word in verse 1. After his first trance and vision, the Prophet went to his wife Khadījah and told her to wrap him up in cloaks, and that was afterwards his habit on such occasions, at any rate, in the early days at Makkah.

A very early Makkan revelation with the exception of the last verse, which all authorities assign to Al-Madīnah.

In the name of Allah, the Beneficent, the Merciful.

1 O thou wrapped up in thy raiment!

2 Keep vigil the night long, save a little—

3 A half thereof, or abate a little thereof

4 Or add (a little) thereto—and chant the Qur'an in measure,

5 For We shall charge thee with a word of weight.

6 Lo! the vigil of the night is (a time) when impression is more keen and speech more certain.

7 Lo! thou hast by day a chain of business.

857

8 So remember the name of thy Lord and devote thyself with a complete devotion—

وَاذْكُرِ اسْمَ رَبِّكَ وَتَبَتَّلْ إِلَيْهِ تَبْتِيلًا ۞

9 Lord of the East and the West; there is no God save Him; so choose thou Him alone for thy defender—

رَبُّ الْمَشْرِقِ وَالْمَغْرِبِ لَآ إِلَهَ إِلَّا هُوَ فَاتَّخِذْهُ وَكِيلًا ۞

10 And bear with patience what they utter, and part from them with a fair leave-taking.

وَاصْبِرْ عَلَى مَا يَقُولُونَ وَاهْجُرْهُمْ هَجْرًا جَمِيلًا ۞

11 Leave Me to deal with the deniers, lords of ease and comfort (in this life); and do thou respite them awhile.

وَذَرْنِي وَالْمُكَذِّبِينَ أُولِي النَّعْمَةِ وَمَهِّلْهُمْ قَلِيلًا ۞

12 Lo! with Us are heavy fetters and a raging fire,

إِنَّ لَدَيْنَآ أَنكَالًا وَجَحِيمًا ۞

13 And food which choketh (the partaker), and a painful doom

وَطَعَامًا ذَا غُصَّةٍ وَعَذَابًا أَلِيمًا ۞

14 On the day when the earth and the hills rock, and the hills become a heap of running sand.

يَوْمَ تَرْجُفُ الْأَرْضُ وَالْجِبَالُ وَكَانَتِ الْجِبَالُ كَثِيبًا مَّهِيلًا ۞

15 Lo! We have sent unto you a messenger as witness against you, even as We sent unto Pharaoh a messenger.

إِنَّآ أَرْسَلْنَآ إِلَيْكُمْ رَسُولًا شَاهِدًا عَلَيْكُمْ كَمَآ أَرْسَلْنَآ إِلَى فِرْعَوْنَ رَسُولًا ۞

16 But Pharaoh rebelled against the messenger, whereupon We seized him with no gentle grip.

فَعَصَى فِرْعَوْنُ الرَّسُولَ فَأَخَذْنَاهُ أَخْذًا وَبِيلًا ۞

17 Then how, if ye disbelieve, will ye protect yourselves upon the day which will turn children grey,

فَكَيْفَ تَتَّقُونَ إِنْ كَفَرْتُمْ يَوْمًا يَجْعَلُ الْوِلْدَانَ شِيبًا ۞

18 The very heaven being then rent asunder. His promise is to be fulfilled.

السَّمَآءُ مُنفَطِرٌ بِهِ كَانَ وَعْدُهُ مَفْعُولًا ۞

19 Lo! This is a Reminder. Let him who will, then, choose a way unto his Lord.

20 Lo! thy Lord knoweth how thou keepest vigil sometimes nearly two-thirds of the night, or (sometimes) half or a third thereof, as do a party of those with thee. Allah measureth the night and the day. He knoweth that ye count it not, and turneth unto you in mercy. Recite, then, of the Qur'an that which is easy for you. He knoweth that there are sick folk among you, while others travel in the land in search of Allah's bounty, and others (still) are fighting for the cause of Allah. So recite of it that which is easy (for you), and establish worship and pay the poor-due, and (so) lend unto Allah a goodly loan.[1] Whatsoever good ye send before you for your souls, ye will surely find it with Allah, better and greater in the recompense. And seek forgiveness of Allah. Lo! Allah is Forgiving, Merciful.

إِنَّ هَٰذِهِۦ تَذۡكِرَةٌ فَمَن شَآءَ ٱتَّخَذَ إِلَىٰ رَبِّهِۦ سَبِيلًا ۝

۞ إِنَّ رَبَّكَ يَعۡلَمُ أَنَّكَ تَقُومُ أَدۡنَىٰ مِن ثُلُثَيِ ٱلَّيۡلِ وَنِصۡفَهُۥ وَثُلُثَهُۥ وَطَآئِفَةٌ مِّنَ ٱلَّذِينَ مَعَكَ وَٱللَّهُ يُقَدِّرُ ٱلَّيۡلَ وَٱلنَّهَارَ عَلِمَ أَن لَّن تُحۡصُوهُ فَتَابَ عَلَيۡكُمۡ فَٱقۡرَءُوا۟ مَا تَيَسَّرَ مِنَ ٱلۡقُرۡءَانِ عَلِمَ أَن سَيَكُونُ مِنكُم مَّرۡضَىٰ وَءَاخَرُونَ يَضۡرِبُونَ فِى ٱلۡأَرۡضِ يَبۡتَغُونَ مِن فَضۡلِ ٱللَّهِ وَءَاخَرُونَ يُقَٰتِلُونَ فِى سَبِيلِ ٱللَّهِ فَٱقۡرَءُوا۟ مَا تَيَسَّرَ مِنۡهُ وَأَقِيمُوا۟ ٱلصَّلَوٰةَ وَءَاتُوا۟ ٱلزَّكَوٰةَ وَأَقۡرِضُوا۟ ٱللَّهَ قَرۡضًا حَسَنًا وَمَا تُقَدِّمُوا۟ لِأَنفُسِكُم مِّنۡ خَيۡرٍ تَجِدُوهُ عِندَ ٱللَّهِ هُوَ خَيۡرًا وَأَعۡظَمَ أَجۡرًا وَٱسۡتَغۡفِرُوا۟ ٱللَّهَ إِنَّ ٱللَّهَ غَفُورٌ رَّحِيمٌ ۝

---

1. *i.e.* a loan without interest or any thought of gain or loss.

Al Muddaththir
(The Cloaked One)

Al Muddaththir takes its name from a word in verse 1. The Prophet was accustomed to wrap himself in his cloak at the time of his trances. A tradition says that some time—about six months—elapsed between the first revelation (sūrah 96, vv. 1-5) and the second revelation in this sūrah. Then the Prophet suddenly again beheld the angel who had appeared to him on Mount Hirā, and wrapped himself in his cloak, whereupon this sūrah was revealed to him. Another opinion is that by this sūrah the Prophet was ordered to begin the public preaching of Al-Islām, his preaching having until then been done privately among his family and intimates. He is said to have begun his public preaching three years after his call.

In either case this is a very early Makkan sūrah.

In the name of Allah, the Beneficent, the Merciful.

1 O thou enveloped in thy cloak,

2 Arise and warn!

3 Thy Lord magnify,

4 Thy raiment purify,

5 Pollution shun!

6 And show not favour, seeking worldly gain!

7 For the sake of thy Lord, be patient!

8 For when the trumpet shall sound,

9 Surely that day will be a day of anguish,

فَذَٰلِكَ يَوْمَئِذٍ يَوْمٌ عَسِيرٌ ۝

10 Not of ease, for disbelievers.

عَلَى ٱلْكَٰفِرِينَ غَيْرُ يَسِيرٍ ۝

11 Leave Me (to deal) with him whom I created lonely,

ذَرْنِي وَمَنْ خَلَقْتُ وَحِيدًا ۝

12 And then bestowed upon him ample means,

وَجَعَلْتُ لَهُۥ مَالًا مَّمْدُودًا ۝

13 And sons abiding in his presence

وَبَنِينَ شُهُودًا ۝

14 And made (life) smooth for him.

وَمَهَّدتُّ لَهُۥ تَمْهِيدًا ۝

15 Yet he desireth that I should give more.

ثُمَّ يَطْمَعُ أَنْ أَزِيدَ ۝

16 Nay! For lo! he hath been stubborn to Our revelations.

كَلَّا ۖ إِنَّهُۥ كَانَ لِآيَٰتِنَا عَنِيدًا ۝

17 On him I shall impose a fearful doom.

سَأُرْهِقُهُۥ صَعُودًا ۝

18 For lo! he did consider; then he planned—

إِنَّهُۥ فَكَّرَ وَقَدَّرَ ۝

19 (Self) destroyed is he, how he planned!

فَقُتِلَ كَيْفَ قَدَّرَ ۝

20 Again (self) destroyed is he, how he planned!—

ثُمَّ قُتِلَ كَيْفَ قَدَّرَ ۝

21 Then looked he,

ثُمَّ نَظَرَ ۝

22 Then frowned he and showed displeasure.

ثُمَّ عَبَسَ وَبَسَرَ ۝

23 Then turned he away in pride

ثُمَّ أَدْبَرَ وَٱسْتَكْبَرَ ۝

24 And said: This is naught else than magic from of old;

فَقَالَ إِنْ هَٰذَآ إِلَّا سِحْرٌ يُؤْثَرُ ۝

25 This is naught else than speech of mortal man.

إِنْ هَٰذَآ إِلَّا قَوْلُ ٱلْبَشَرِ ۝

26 Him shall I fling unto the burning.

سَأُصْلِيهِ سَقَرَ ۝

27 Ah! What will convey unto thee what that burning is!—

وَمَآ أَدْرَىٰكَ مَا سَقَرُ ۝

28 I leaveth naught; it spareth
naught

29 It shrivelleth the man.

30 Above it are nineteen.

31 We have appointed only angels
to be wardens of the fire, and their
number have We made to be a
stumbling-block for those who
disbelieve; that those to whom the
scripture hath been given may have
certainty, and that believers may
increase in faith; and that those to
whom the Scripture hath been given
and believers may not doubt; and
that those in whose hearts there is
disease, and disbelievers, may say:
What meaneth Allah by this similitude? Thus Allah sendeth astray
whom He will, and whom He will
He guideth. None knoweth the hosts
of thy Lord save Him. This is naught
else than a Reminder unto mortals.

32 Nay, by the Moon

33 And the night when it withdraweth

34 And the dawn when it shineth
forth,

35 Lo! this is one of the greatest
(portents)

36 As a warning unto men,

37 Unto him of you who will
advance or hang back.

38 Every soul is a pledge for its
own deeds;

39 Save those who will stand on the right hand.

إِلَّآ أَصۡحَٰبَ ٱلۡيَمِينِ ﴿٣٩﴾

40 In gardens they will ask one another

فِى جَنَّٰتٖ يَتَسَآءَلُونَ ﴿٤٠﴾

41 Concerning the guilty:

عَنِ ٱلۡمُجۡرِمِينَ ﴿٤١﴾

42 What hath brought you to this burning?

مَا سَلَكَكُمۡ فِى سَقَرَ ﴿٤٢﴾

43 They will answer: We were not of those who prayed

قَالُواْ لَمۡ نَكُ مِنَ ٱلۡمُصَلِّينَ ﴿٤٣﴾

44 Nor did we feed the wretched.

وَلَمۡ نَكُ نُطۡعِمُ ٱلۡمِسۡكِينَ ﴿٤٤﴾

45 We used to wade (in vain dispute) with (all) waders,

وَكُنَّا نَخُوضُ مَعَ ٱلۡخَآئِضِينَ ﴿٤٥﴾

46 And we used to deny the Day of Judgement,

وَكُنَّا نُكَذِّبُ بِيَوۡمِ ٱلدِّينِ ﴿٤٦﴾

47 Till the inevitable came unto us.

حَتَّىٰٓ أَتَىٰنَا ٱلۡيَقِينُ ﴿٤٧﴾

48 The mediation of no mediators will avail them then.

فَمَا تَنفَعُهُمۡ شَفَٰعَةُ ٱلشَّٰفِعِينَ ﴿٤٨﴾

49 Why now turn they away from the Admonishment.

فَمَا لَهُمۡ عَنِ ٱلتَّذۡكِرَةِ مُعۡرِضِينَ ﴿٤٩﴾

50 As if they were frightened asses.

كَأَنَّهُمۡ حُمُرٞ مُّسۡتَنفِرَةٞ ﴿٥٠﴾

51 Fleeing from a lion?

فَرَّتۡ مِن قَسۡوَرَةِۭ ﴿٥١﴾

52 Nay, but everyone of them desireth that he should be given open pages (from Allah).

بَلۡ يُرِيدُ كُلُّ ٱمۡرِئٖ مِّنۡهُمۡ أَن يُؤۡتَىٰ صُحُفٗا مُّنَشَّرَةٗ ﴿٥٢﴾

53 Nay, verily. They fear not the Hereafter.

كَلَّآ بَل لَّا يَخَافُونَ ٱلۡأَخِرَةَ ﴿٥٣﴾

54 Nay, verily. Lo! this is an Admonishment.

كَلَّآ إِنَّهُۥ تَذۡكِرَةٞ ﴿٥٤﴾

55 So whosoever will may heed.

فَمَن شَآءَ ذَكَرَهُۥ ﴿٥٥﴾

56 And they will not heed unless Allah willeth (it). He is the fount of Fear. He is the fount of Mercy.

وَمَا يَذۡكُرُونَ إِلَّآ أَن يَشَآءَ ٱللَّهُۚ هُوَ أَهۡلُ ٱلتَّقۡوَىٰ وَأَهۡلُ ٱلۡمَغۡفِرَةِ ﴿٥٦﴾

Al Qiyāmah
(The Rising of the Dead)

Al Qiyāmah takes its name from a word in the first verse.

An early Makkan sūrah.

*In the name of Allah, the
Beneficent, the Merciful.*

1 Nay, I swear by the Day of Resurrection;

2 Nay, I swear by the accusing soul (that this Scripture is true).

3 Thinketh man that We shall not assemble his bones?

4 Yea, verily. Yea, We are able to restore his very fingers!

5 But man would fain deny what is before him.

6 He asketh: When will be this Day of Resurrection?

7 But when sight is confounded

8 And the moon is eclipsed

9 And sun and moon are united,

10 On that day man will cry: Whither to flee!

11 Alas! No refuge!

12 Unto thy Lord is the recourse that day.

إِلَىٰ رَبِّكَ يَوْمَئِذٍ ٱلْمُسْتَقَرُّ ۝

13 On that day man is told the tale of that which he hath sent before and left behind.

يُنَبَّؤُاْ ٱلْإِنسَٰنُ يَوْمَئِذٍ بِمَا قَدَّمَ وَأَخَّرَ ۝

14 Oh, but man is a telling witness against himself,

بَلِ ٱلْإِنسَٰنُ عَلَىٰ نَفْسِهِۦ بَصِيرَةٌ ۝

15 Although he tender his excuses.

وَلَوْ أَلْقَىٰ مَعَاذِيرَهُۥ ۝

16 Stir not thy tongue herewith to hasten it.[1]

لَا تُحَرِّكْ بِهِۦ لِسَانَكَ لِتَعْجَلَ بِهِۦٓ ۝

17 Lo! upon Us (resteth) the putting together thereof and the reading thereof.

إِنَّ عَلَيْنَا جَمْعَهُۥ وَقُرْءَانَهُۥ ۝

18 And when We read it, follow thou the reading;

فَإِذَا قَرَأْنَٰهُ فَٱتَّبِعْ قُرْءَانَهُۥ ۝

19 Then lo! upon Us (resteth) the explanation thereof.

ثُمَّ إِنَّ عَلَيْنَا بَيَانَهُۥ ۝

20 Nay, but ye do love the fleeting Now

كَلَّا بَلْ تُحِبُّونَ ٱلْعَاجِلَةَ ۝

21 And neglect the Hereafter.

وَتَذَرُونَ ٱلْءَاخِرَةَ ۝

22 That day will faces be resplendent,

وُجُوهٌ يَوْمَئِذٍ نَّاضِرَةٌ ۝

23 Looking toward their Lord;

إِلَىٰ رَبِّهَا نَاظِرَةٌ ۝

24 And that day will other faces be despondent,

وَوُجُوهٌ يَوْمَئِذٍ بَاسِرَةٌ ۝

25 Thou wilt know that some great disaster is about to fall on them.

تَظُنُّ أَن يُفْعَلَ بِهَا فَاقِرَةٌ ۝

26 Nay, but when the life cometh up to the throat

كَلَّآ إِذَا بَلَغَتِ ٱلتَّرَاقِيَ ۝

27 And it is said: Where is the wizard (who can save him now)?

وَقِيلَ مَنْ رَاقٍ ۝

---

1. *i.e.* the Qur'an, which was revealed gradually, piece by piece.

28 And he knoweth that it is the parting; ۝

29 And agony is heaped on agony; ۝

30 Unto thy Lord that day will be the driving. ۝

31 For he neither trusted, nor prayed. ۝

32 But he denied and flouted. ۝

33 Then went he to his folk with glee. ۝

34 Nearer unto thee and nearer, ۝

35 Again nearer unto thee and nearer (is the doom). ۝

36 Thinketh man that he is to be left aimless? ۝

37 Was he not a drop of fluid which gushed forth? ۝

38 Then he became a clot; then (Allah) shaped and fashioned ۝

39 And made of him a pair, the male and female. ۝

40 Is not He (who doeth so) able to bring the dead to life? ۝

وَظَنَّ أَنَّهُ الْفِرَاقُ ۝

وَالْتَفَّتِ السَّاقُ بِالسَّاقِ ۝

إِلَىٰ رَبِّكَ يَوْمَئِذٍ الْمَسَاقُ ۝

فَلَا صَدَّقَ وَلَا صَلَّىٰ ۝

وَلَٰكِنْ كَذَّبَ وَتَوَلَّىٰ ۝

ثُمَّ ذَهَبَ إِلَىٰ أَهْلِهِ يَتَمَطَّىٰ ۝

أَوْلَىٰ لَكَ فَأَوْلَىٰ ۝

ثُمَّ أَوْلَىٰ لَكَ فَأَوْلَىٰ ۝

أَيَحْسَبُ الْإِنْسَانُ أَنْ يُتْرَكَ سُدًى ۝

أَلَمْ يَكُ نُطْفَةً مِنْ مَنِيٍّ يُمْنَىٰ ۝

ثُمَّ كَانَ عَلَقَةً فَخَلَقَ فَسَوَّىٰ ۝

فَجَعَلَ مِنْهُ الزَّوْجَيْنِ الذَّكَرَ وَالْأُنْثَىٰ ۝

أَلَيْسَ ذَٰلِكَ بِقَادِرٍ عَلَىٰ أَنْ يُحْيِيَ الْمَوْتَىٰ ۝

Al Insān
(Man)

Al Insān or *Ad Dahr* is, in either case, so called from a word in the first verse. An early Makkan sūrah.

In the name of Allah, the Beneficent, the Merciful.

1 Hath there come upon man (ever) any period of time in which he was a thing unremembered?

إِنَّا خَلَقْنَا ٱلْإِنسَٰنَ مِن نُّطْفَةٍ أَمْشَاجٍ نَّبْتَلِيهِ فَجَعَلْنَٰهُ سَمِيعًۢا بَصِيرًا ١

2 Lo! We create man from a drop of thickened fluid to test him; so We make him hearing, knowing.

إِنَّا هَدَيْنَٰهُ ٱلسَّبِيلَ إِمَّا شَاكِرًا وَإِمَّا كَفُورًا ٢

3 Lo! We have shown him the way, whether he be grateful or ungrateful.

إِنَّآ أَعْتَدْنَا لِلْكَٰفِرِينَ سَلَٰسِلَا۟ وَأَغْلَٰلًا وَسَعِيرًا ٣

4 Lo! We have prepared for disbelievers manacles and carcans and a raging fire.

إِنَّ ٱلْأَبْرَارَ يَشْرَبُونَ مِن كَأْسٍ كَانَ مِزَاجُهَا كَافُورًا ٤

5 Lo! the righteous shall drink of a cup whereof the mixture is of water of Kāfūr,

عَيْنًا يَشْرَبُ بِهَا عِبَادُ ٱللَّهِ يُفَجِّرُونَهَا تَفْجِيرًا ٥

6 A spring wherefrom the slaves of Allah drink, making it gush forth abundantly,

7 (Because) they perform the vow and fear a day whereof the evil is wide-spreading,

يُوفُونَ بِالنَّذْرِ وَيَخَافُونَ يَوْمًا كَانَ شَرُّهُۥ مُسْتَطِيرًا ۝

8 And feed with food the needy wretch, the orphan and the prisoner, for love of Him,

وَيُطْعِمُونَ الطَّعَامَ عَلَىٰ حُبِّهِۦ مِسْكِينًا وَيَتِيمًا وَأَسِيرًا ۝

9 (Saying): We feed you, for the sake of Allah only. We wish for no reward nor thanks from you;

إِنَّمَا نُطْعِمُكُمْ لِوَجْهِ اللَّهِ لَا نُرِيدُ مِنكُمْ جَزَآءً وَلَا شُكُورًا ۝

10 Lo! we fear from our Lord a day of frowning and of fate.

إِنَّا نَخَافُ مِن رَّبِّنَا يَوْمًا عَبُوسًا قَمْطَرِيرًا ۝

11 Therefore Allah hath warded from them the evil of that day, and hath made them find brightness and joy;

فَوَقَىٰهُمُ اللَّهُ شَرَّ ذَٰلِكَ الْيَوْمِ وَلَقَّىٰهُمْ نَضْرَةً وَسُرُورًا ۝

12 And hath awarded them for all that they endured, a Garden and silk attire;

وَجَزَىٰهُم بِمَا صَبَرُوا جَنَّةً وَحَرِيرًا ۝

13 Reclining therein upon couches, they will find there neither (heat of) a sun nor bitter cold.

مُّتَّكِئِينَ فِيهَا عَلَى الْأَرَآئِكِ لَا يَرَوْنَ فِيهَا شَمْسًا وَلَا زَمْهَرِيرًا ۝

14 The shade thereof is close upon them and the clustered fruits thereof are made to bow down.

وَدَانِيَةً عَلَيْهِمْ ظِلَالُهَا وَذُلِّلَتْ قُطُوفُهَا تَذْلِيلًا ۝

15 Goblets of silver are brought round for them, and beakers (as) of glass

وَيُطَافُ عَلَيْهِم بِآنِيَةٍ مِّن فِضَّةٍ وَأَكْوَابٍ كَانَتْ قَوَارِيرَا۠ ۝

16 (Bright as) glass but (made) of silver, which they (themselves) have measured to the measure (of their deeds).

قَوَارِيرَ مِن فِضَّةٍ قَدَّرُوهَا تَقْدِيرًا ۝

17 There are they watered with a cup whereof the mixture is of Zanjabīl,

وَيُسْقَوْنَ فِيهَا كَأْسًا كَانَ مِزَاجُهَا زَنجَبِيلًا ۝

18 The water of a spring therein, named Salsabīl.

عَيْنًا فِيهَا تُسَمَّى سَلْسَبِيلًا ﴿١٨﴾

19 There serve them youths of everlasting youth, whom, when thou seest, thou wouldst take for scat-tered pearls.

۞ وَيَطُوفُ عَلَيْهِمْ وِلْدَانٌ مُّخَلَّدُونَ إِذَا رَأَيْتَهُمْ حَسِبْتَهُمْ لُؤْلُؤًا مَّنْثُورًا ﴿١٩﴾

20 When thou seest, thou wilt see there bliss and high estate.

وَإِذَا رَأَيْتَ ثَمَّ رَأَيْتَ نَعِيمًا وَمُلْكًا كَبِيرًا ﴿٢٠﴾

21 Their raiment will be fine green silk and gold embroidery. They will be adorned with bracelets of silver. Their Lord will slake their thirst with a pure drink.

عَالِيَهُمْ ثِيَابُ سُنْدُسٍ خُضْرٌ وَإِسْتَبْرَقٌ وَحُلُّوا أَسَاوِرَ مِنْ فِضَّةٍ وَسَقَاهُمْ رَبُّهُمْ شَرَابًا طَهُورًا ﴿٢١﴾

22 (And it will be said unto them): Lo! this is a reward for you. Your endeavour (upon earth) hath found acceptance.

إِنَّ هَذَا كَانَ لَكُمْ جَزَاءً وَكَانَ سَعْيُكُمْ مَّشْكُورًا ﴿٢٢﴾

23 Lo! We, even We, have reve-aled unto thee the Qur'an, a reve-lation;

إِنَّا نَحْنُ نَزَّلْنَا عَلَيْكَ الْقُرْآنَ تَنْزِيلًا ﴿٢٣﴾

24 So submit patiently to thy Lord's command, and obey not of them any guilty one or disbeliever.

فَاصْبِرْ لِحُكْمِ رَبِّكَ وَلَا تُطِعْ مِنْهُمْ آثِمًا أَوْ كَفُورًا ﴿٢٤﴾

25 Remember the name of thy Lord at morn and evening.

وَاذْكُرِ اسْمَ رَبِّكَ بُكْرَةً وَأَصِيلًا ﴿٢٥﴾

26 And worship Him (a portion) of the night. And glorify Him through the livelong night.

وَمِنَ الَّيْلِ فَاسْجُدْ لَهُ وَسَبِّحْهُ لَيْلًا طَوِيلًا ﴿٢٦﴾

27 Lo! these love fleeting life, and put behind them (the remembrance of) a grievous day.

إِنَّ هَؤُلَاءِ يُحِبُّونَ الْعَاجِلَةَ وَيَذَرُونَ وَرَاءَهُمْ يَوْمًا ثَقِيلًا ﴿٢٧﴾

28 We, even We, created them, and strengthened their frame. And when

نَحْنُ خَلَقْنَاهُمْ وَشَدَدْنَا أَسْرَهُمْ وَإِذَا شِئْنَا

We will, We can replace them, bringing others like them in their stead.

بَدَّلْنَآ أَمْثَالَهُمْ تَبْدِيلًا ۞

29 Lo! this is an Admonishment, that whosoever will may choose a way unto his Lord.

إِنَّ هَذِهِ تَذْكِرَةٌ فَمَنْ شَآءَ اتَّخَذَ إِلَىٰ رَبِّهِ سَبِيلًا ۞

30 Yet ye will not, unless Allah willeth. Lo! Allah is Knower, Wise.

وَمَا تَشَآءُونَ إِلَّا أَن يَشَآءَ اللَّهُ إِنَّ اللَّهَ كَانَ عَلِيمًا حَكِيمًا ۞

31 He maketh whom He will to enter His mercy, and for evil-doers hath prepared a painful doom.

يُدْخِلُ مَن يَشَآءُ فِي رَحْمَتِهِ وَالظَّالِمِينَ أَعَدَّ لَهُمْ عَذَابًا أَلِيمًا ۞

Al Mursalāt
(The Emissaries)

Al Mursalāt takes its name from a word in the first verse. Verses 1, 2 and 3 are taken to refer to winds, verses 4 and 5 to angels. An early Makkan sūrah.

In the name of Allah, the Beneficent, the Merciful.

1 By the emissary winds, (sent) one after another

2 By the raging hurricanes,

3 By those which cause earth's vegetation to revive;

4 By those who winnow with a winnowing,

5 By those who bring down the Reminder,

6 To excuse or to warn,

7 Surely that which ye are promised will befall.

8 So when the stars are put out,

9 And when the sky is riven asunder,

10 And when the mountains are blown away,

11 And when the messengers are brought unto their time appointed—

871

12 For what day is the time appointed?

لِأَيِّ يَوْمٍ أُجِّلَتْ ۝

13 For the Day of Decision.

لِيَوْمِ الْفَصْلِ ۝

14 And what will convey unto thee what the Day of Decision is!—

وَمَآ أَدْرَىٰكَ مَا يَوْمُ الْفَصْلِ ۝

15 Woe unto the repudiators on that day!

وَيْلٌ يَوْمَئِذٍ لِّلْمُكَذِّبِينَ ۝

16 Destroyed We not the former folk,

أَلَمْ نُهْلِكِ الْأَوَّلِينَ ۝

17 Then caused the latter folk to follow after?

ثُمَّ نُتْبِعُهُمُ الْآخِرِينَ ۝

18 Thus deal We ever with the guilty.

كَذَٰلِكَ نَفْعَلُ بِالْمُجْرِمِينَ ۝

19 Woe unto the repudiators on that day!

وَيْلٌ يَوْمَئِذٍ لِّلْمُكَذِّبِينَ ۝

20 Did We not create you from a base fluid?

أَلَمْ نَخْلُقكُّم مِّن مَّآءٍ مَّهِينٍ ۝

21 Which We laid up in a safe abode

فَجَعَلْنَٰهُ فِي قَرَارٍ مَّكِينٍ ۝

22 For a known term?

إِلَىٰ قَدَرٍ مَّعْلُومٍ ۝

23 Thus We determined (things). How excellent are We at determining?

فَقَدَرْنَا فَنِعْمَ الْقَٰدِرُونَ ۝

24 Woe unto the repudiators on that day!

وَيْلٌ يَوْمَئِذٍ لِّلْمُكَذِّبِينَ ۝

25 Have We not made the earth a receptacle

أَلَمْ نَجْعَلِ الْأَرْضَ كِفَاتًا ۝

26 Both for the living and the dead,

أَحْيَآءً وَأَمْوَٰتًا ۝

27 And placed therein high mountains and given you to drink sweet water therein?

وَجَعَلْنَا فِيهَا رَوَٰسِيَ شَٰمِخَٰتٍ وَأَسْقَيْنَٰكُم مَّآءً فُرَاتًا ۝

28 Woe unto the repudiators on that day!

وَيْلٌ يَوْمَئِذٍ لِّلْمُكَذِّبِينَ ۝

29 (It will be said unto them:) Depart unto that (doom) which ye used to deny;

أَنطَلِقُوٓاْ إِلَىٰ مَا كُنتُم بِهِۦ تُكَذِّبُونَ ﴿٢٩﴾

30 Depart unto the shadow falling threefold.

أَنطَلِقُوٓاْ إِلَىٰ ظِلٍّ ذِى ثَلَٰثِ شُعَبٍ ﴿٣٠﴾

31 (Which yet is) no relief nor shelter from the flame.

لَّا ظَلِيلٍ وَلَا يُغْنِى مِنَ ٱللَّهَبِ ﴿٣١﴾

32 Lo! it throweth up sparks like the castles,

إِنَّهَا تَرْمِى بِشَرَرٍ كَٱلْقَصْرِ ﴿٣٢﴾

33 (Or) as it might be camels of bright yellow hue.

كَأَنَّهُۥ جِمَٰلَتٌ صُفْرٌ ﴿٣٣﴾

34 Woe unto the repudiators on that day!

وَيْلٌ يَوْمَئِذٍ لِّلْمُكَذِّبِينَ ﴿٣٤﴾

35 This is a day wherein they speak not,

هَٰذَا يَوْمُ لَا يَنطِقُونَ ﴿٣٥﴾

36 Nor are they suffered to put forth excuses.

وَلَا يُؤْذَنُ لَهُمْ فَيَعْتَذِرُونَ ﴿٣٦﴾

37 Woe unto the repudiators on that day!

وَيْلٌ يَوْمَئِذٍ لِّلْمُكَذِّبِينَ ﴿٣٧﴾

38 This is the Day of Decision, We have brought you and the men of old together.

هَٰذَا يَوْمُ ٱلْفَصْلِ جَمَعْنَٰكُمْ وَٱلْأَوَّلِينَ ﴿٣٨﴾

39 If now ye have any wit, outwit Me.

فَإِن كَانَ لَكُمْ كَيْدٌ فَكِيدُونِ ﴿٣٩﴾

40 Woe unto the repudiators on that day!

وَيْلٌ يَوْمَئِذٍ لِّلْمُكَذِّبِينَ ﴿٤٠﴾

41 Lo! those who kept their duty are amid shade and fountains,

إِنَّ ٱلْمُتَّقِينَ فِى ظِلَٰلٍ وَعُيُونٍ ﴿٤١﴾

42 And fruits such as they desire.

وَفَوَٰكِهَ مِمَّا يَشْتَهُونَ ﴿٤٢﴾

43 (Unto them it is said:) Eat and drink pleasantly. O ye blessed, in return for what ye did.

كُلُوا۟ وَٱشْرَبُوا۟ هَنِيٓـًٔا بِمَا كُنتُمْ تَعْمَلُونَ ﴿٤٣﴾

44 Thus do We reward the good.

إِنَّا كَذَٰلِكَ نَجْزِى ٱلْمُحْسِنِينَ ﴿٤٤﴾

45 Woe unto the repudiators on that day!

وَيْلٌ يَوْمَئِذٍ لِّلْمُكَذِّبِينَ ﴿٤٥﴾

46 Eat and take your ease (on earth) a little. Lo! ye are guilty.

كُلُوا وَتَمَتَّعُوا قَلِيلًا إِنَّكُم مُّجْرِمُونَ ﴿٤٦﴾

47 Woe unto the repudiators on that day!

وَيْلٌ يَوْمَئِذٍ لِّلْمُكَذِّبِينَ ﴿٤٧﴾

48 When it is said unto them: Bow down, they bow not down!

وَإِذَا قِيلَ لَهُمُ ارْكَعُوا لَا يَرْكَعُونَ ﴿٤٨﴾

49 Woe unto the repudiators on that day!

وَيْلٌ يَوْمَئِذٍ لِّلْمُكَذِّبِينَ ﴿٤٩﴾

50 In what statement, after this, will they believe?

فَبِأَيِّ حَدِيثٍ بَعْدَهُ يُؤْمِنُونَ ﴿٥٠﴾

An Naba'
(The Tidings)

An Naba' takes its name from a word in the second verse.

An early Makkan sūrah.

In the name of Allah, the Beneficent, the Merciful.

1 Whereof do they question one another?

2 (It is) of the awful tidings,

3 Concerning which they are in disagreement.

4 Nay, but they will come to know!

5 Nay, again, but they will come to know!

6 Have We not made the earth an expanse,

7 And the high hills bulwarks?

8 And We have created you in pairs,

9 And have appointed your sleep for repose,

10 And have appointed the night as a cloak,

11 And have appointed the day for livelihood.

وَجَعَلْنَا النَّهَارَ مَعَاشًا ۝

12 And We have built above you seven strong (heavens),

وَبَنَيْنَا فَوْقَكُمْ سَبْعًا شِدَادًا ۝

13 And have appointed a dazzling lamp,

وَجَعَلْنَا سِرَاجًا وَهَّاجًا ۝

14 And have sent down from the rainy clouds abundant water,

وَأَنزَلْنَا مِنَ الْمُعْصِرَاتِ مَآءً ثَجَّاجًا ۝

15 Thereby to produce grain and plant,

لِنُخْرِجَ بِهِ حَبًّا وَنَبَاتًا ۝

16 And gardens of thick foliage.

وَجَنَّاتٍ أَلْفَافًا ۝

17 Lo! the Day of Decision is a fixed time,

إِنَّ يَوْمَ الْفَصْلِ كَانَ مِيقَاتًا ۝

18 A day when the trumpet is blown, and ye come in multitudes,

يَوْمَ يُنفَخُ فِي الصُّورِ فَتَأْتُونَ أَفْوَاجًا ۝

19 And the heaven is opened and becometh as gates,

وَفُتِحَتِ السَّمَآءُ فَكَانَتْ أَبْوَابًا ۝

20 And the hills are set in motion and become as a mirage.

وَسُيِّرَتِ الْجِبَالُ فَكَانَتْ سَرَابًا ۝

21 Lo! hell lurketh in ambush,

إِنَّ جَهَنَّمَ كَانَتْ مِرْصَادًا ۝

22 A home for the rebellious.

لِلطَّاغِينَ مَآبًا ۝

23 They will abide therein for ages.

لَّابِثِينَ فِيهَا أَحْقَابًا ۝

24 Therein taste they neither coolness nor (any) drink

لَّا يَذُوقُونَ فِيهَا بَرْدًا وَلَا شَرَابًا ۝

25 Save boiling water and a paralyzing cold:

إِلَّا حَمِيمًا وَغَسَّاقًا ۝

26 Reward proportioned (to their evil deeds).

جَزَآءً وِفَاقًا ۝

27 For lo! they looked not for a reckoning;

إِنَّهُمْ كَانُوا لَا يَرْجُونَ حِسَابًا ۝

28 They called Our revelations false with strong denial.

وَكَذَّبُوا بِآيَاتِنَا كِذَّابًا ۝

29 Everything have We recorded in a Book.

وَكُلَّ شَىْءٍ أَحْصَيْنَهُ كِتَبًا ۝

30 So taste (of that which ye have earned). No increase do We give you save of torment.

فَذُوقُوا فَلَن نَّزِيدَكُمْ إِلَّا عَذَابًا ۝

31 Lo! for the duteous is achievement—

إِنَّ لِلْمُتَّقِينَ مَفَازًا ۝

32 Gardens enclosed and vineyards,

حَدَآئِقَ وَأَعْنَٰبًا ۝

33 And maidens for companions,

وَكَوَاعِبَ أَتْرَابًا ۝

34 And a full cup.

وَكَأْسًا دِهَاقًا ۝

35 There hear they never vain discourse, nor lying—

لَّا يَسْمَعُونَ فِيهَا لَغْوًا وَلَا كِذَّٰبًا ۝

36 Requital from thy Lord—a gift in payment—

جَزَآءً مِّن رَّبِّكَ عَطَآءً حِسَابًا ۝

37 Lord of the heavens and the earth, and (all) that is between them, the Beneficent; with Whom none can converse.

رَّبِّ السَّمَٰوَٰتِ وَالْأَرْضِ وَمَا بَيْنَهُمَا الرَّحْمَٰنِ لَا يَمْلِكُونَ مِنْهُ خِطَابًا ۝

38 On the day when the angels and the Spirit stand arrayed, they speak not, saving him whom the Beneficent alloweth and who speaketh right.

يَوْمَ يَقُومُ الرُّوحُ وَالْمَلَٰئِكَةُ صَفًّا لَّا يَتَكَلَّمُونَ إِلَّا مَنْ أَذِنَ لَهُ الرَّحْمَٰنُ وَقَالَ صَوَابًا ۝

39 That is the True Day. So whoso will should seek recourse unto his Lord.

ذَٰلِكَ الْيَوْمُ الْحَقُّ فَمَن شَآءَ اتَّخَذَ إِلَىٰ رَبِّهِ مَـَٔابًا ۝

40 Lo! We warn you of a doom at hand, a day whereon a man will look on that which his own hands have sent before, and the disbeliever will cry: "Would that I were dust!"

إِنَّا أَنذَرْنَٰكُمْ عَذَابًا قَرِيبًا يَوْمَ يَنظُرُ الْمَرْءُ مَا قَدَّمَتْ يَدَاهُ وَيَقُولُ الْكَافِرُ يَٰلَيْتَنِي كُنتُ تُرَٰبًا ۝

An Nāzi'āt
(Those Who Drag Forth)

An Nāzi'āt takes its name from a word in the first verse.

An early Makkan sūrah.

سُوْرَةُ النَّازِعَاتِ

In the name of Allah, the
Beneficent, the Merciful.

بِسْمِ اللهِ الرَّحْمٰنِ الرَّحِيْمِ

1 By those who drag forth to
destruction,

وَالنّٰزِعٰتِ غَرْقًا ۙ١

2 By the meteors rushing,

وَالنّٰشِطٰتِ نَشْطًا ۙ٢

3 By the lone stars floating,[1]

وَالسّٰبِحٰتِ سَبْحًا ۙ٣

4 By the angels hastening,

فَالسّٰبِقٰتِ سَبْقًا ۙ٤

5 And those who govern the event,

فَالْمُدَبِّرٰتِ أَمْرًا ۚ٥

6 On the day when the first trump
resoundeth

يَوْمَ تَرْجُفُ الرَّاجِفَةُ ۙ٦

7 And the second followeth it,

تَتْبَعُهَا الرَّادِفَةُ ۙ٧

8 On that day hearts beat painfully

قُلُوْبٌ يَّوْمَئِذٍ وَّاجِفَةٌ ۙ٨

9 While eyes are downcast

أَبْصَارُهَا خَاشِعَةٌ ۘ٩

10 (Now) they are saying: Shall we
really be restored to our first state

يَقُوْلُوْنَ أَءِنَّا لَمَرْدُوْدُوْنَ فِى الْحَافِرَةِ ۙ١٠

11 Even after we are crumbled bones?

أَءِذَا كُنَّا عِظَامًا نَّخِرَةً ۗ١١

---

1. Some commentators take vv. 2 and 3 also referring to angels and explain them
thus: "By those who console (the spirits of the righteous) tenderly." "By those who come
floating (down from heaven with their Lord's command)." The rendering given in the text
above is more obvious.

12 They say: Then that would be a vain proceeding.

قَالُوا تِلْكَ إِذًا كَرَّةٌ خَاسِرَةٌ ﴿١٢﴾

13 Surely it will need but one shout,

فَإِنَّمَا هِيَ زَجْرَةٌ وَاحِدَةٌ ﴿١٣﴾

14 And lo! they will be awakened.

فَإِذَا هُمْ بِالسَّاهِرَةِ ﴿١٤﴾

15 Hath there come unto thee the history of Moses?

هَلْ أَتَاكَ حَدِيثُ مُوسَى ﴿١٥﴾

16 How his Lord called him in the holy vale of Ṭuwā,

إِذْ نَادَاهُ رَبُّهُ بِالْوَادِ الْمُقَدَّسِ طُوًى ﴿١٦﴾

17 (Saying:) Go thou unto Pharaoh—Lo! he hath rebelled—

اذْهَبْ إِلَى فِرْعَوْنَ إِنَّهُ طَغَى ﴿١٧﴾

18 And say (unto him): Hast thou (will) to grow (in grace)?

فَقُلْ هَلْ لَكَ إِلَى أَنْ تَزَكَّى ﴿١٨﴾

19 Then I will guide thee to thy Lord and thou shalt fear (Him).

وَأَهْدِيَكَ إِلَى رَبِّكَ فَتَخْشَى ﴿١٩﴾

20 And he showed him the tremendous token.

فَأَرَاهُ الْآيَةَ الْكُبْرَى ﴿٢٠﴾

21 But he denied and disobeyed,

فَكَذَّبَ وَعَصَى ﴿٢١﴾

22 Then turned he away in haste,

ثُمَّ أَدْبَرَ يَسْعَى ﴿٢٢﴾

23 Then gathered he and summoned

فَحَشَرَ فَنَادَى ﴿٢٣﴾

24 And proclaimed: "I (Pharaoh) am your Lord the Highest."

فَقَالَ أَنَا رَبُّكُمُ الْأَعْلَى ﴿٢٤﴾

25 So Allah seized him (and made him) an example for the after (life) and for the former.

فَأَخَذَهُ اللَّهُ نَكَالَ الْآخِرَةِ وَالْأُولَى ﴿٢٥﴾

26 Lo! herein is indeed a lesson for him who feareth.

إِنَّ فِي ذَلِكَ لَعِبْرَةً لِمَنْ يَخْشَى ﴿٢٦﴾

27 Are ye the harder to create, or is the heaven that He built?

أَأَنْتُمْ أَشَدُّ خَلْقًا أَمِ السَّمَاءُ بَنَاهَا ﴿٢٧﴾

28 He raised the height thereof and ordered it;

رَفَعَ سَمْكَهَا فَسَوَّاهَا ﴿٢٨﴾

29 And He made dark the night thereof, and He brought forth the morn thereof.

وَأَغْطَشَ لَيْلَهَا وَأَخْرَجَ ضُحَاهَا ﴿٢٩﴾

30 And after that He spread the earth,

وَالْأَرْضَ بَعْدَ ذَٰلِكَ دَحَهَآ ۝

31 And produced therefrom the water thereof and the pasture thereof,

أَخْرَجَ مِنْهَا مَآءَهَا وَمَرْعَٰهَا ۝

32 And He made fast the hills,

وَالْجِبَالَ أَرْسَٰهَا ۝

33 A provision for you and for your cattle.

مَتَٰعًا لَّكُمْ وَلِأَنْعَٰمِكُمْ ۝

34 But when the great disaster cometh,

فَإِذَا جَآءَتِ الطَّآمَّةُ الْكُبْرَىٰ ۝

35 The day when man will call to mind his (whole) endeavour,

يَوْمَ يَتَذَكَّرُ الْإِنسَٰنُ مَا سَعَىٰ ۝

36 And hell will stand forth visible to him who seeth,

وَبُرِّزَتِ الْجَحِيمُ لِمَن يَرَىٰ ۝

37 Then, as for him who rebelled

فَأَمَّا مَن طَغَىٰ ۝

38 And chose the life of the world,

وَءَاثَرَ الْحَيَوٰةَ الدُّنْيَا ۝

39 Lo! hell will be his home.

فَإِنَّ الْجَحِيمَ هِيَ الْمَأْوَىٰ ۝

40 But as for him who feared to stand before his Lord and restrained his soul from lust,

وَأَمَّا مَنْ خَافَ مَقَامَ رَبِّهِ وَنَهَى النَّفْسَ عَنِ الْهَوَىٰ ۝

41 Lo! the Garden will be his home.

فَإِنَّ الْجَنَّةَ هِيَ الْمَأْوَىٰ ۝

42 They ask thee of the Hour: When will it come to port?

يَسْئَلُونَكَ عَنِ السَّاعَةِ أَيَّانَ مُرْسَٰهَا ۝

43 Why (ask they)? What hast thou to tell thereof?

فِيمَ أَنتَ مِن ذِكْرَٰهَآ ۝

44 Unto thy Lord belongeth (knowledge of) the term thereof.

إِلَىٰ رَبِّكَ مُنتَهَٰهَآ ۝

45 Thou art but a warner unto him who feareth it.

إِنَّمَآ أَنتَ مُنذِرُ مَن يَخْشَٰهَا ۝

46 On the day when they behold it, it will be as if they had but tarried for an evening or the morn thereof.

كَأَنَّهُمْ يَوْمَ يَرَوْنَهَا لَمْ يَلْبَثُوٓاْ إِلَّا عَشِيَّةً أَوْ ضُحَٰهَا ۝

'Abasa
(He Frowned)

'Abasa, "He Frowned," takes its name from the first word. One day when the Prophet was in conversation with one of the great men of Quraysh (his own tribe), seeking to persuade him of the truth of Al-Islām, a blind man came and asked a question concerning the faith. The Prophet was annoyed at the interruption, frowned and turned away from the blind man. In this sūrah he is told that a man's importance is not to be judged from his appearance or worldly station.

An early Makkan sūrah.

In the name of Allah, the Beneficent, the Merciful.

1 He frowned and turned away

2 Because the blind man came unto him.

3 What could inform thee but that he might grow (in grace)

4 Or take heed and so the reminder might avail him?

5 As for him who thinketh himself independent,

6 Unto him thou payest regard.

7 Yet it is not thy concern if he grow not (in grace)

8 But as for him who cometh unto thee with earnest purpose

9 And hath fear, وَهُوَ يَخۡشَىٰ ۞

10 From him thou art distracted. فَأَنتَ عَنۡهُ تَلَهَّىٰ ۞

11 Nay, but verily it is an Admonishment, كَلَّا إِنَّهَا تَذۡكِرَةٌ ۞

12 So let whosoever will pay heed to it, فَمَن شَآءَ ذَكَرَهُ ۞

13 On honoured leaves فِى صُحُفٍ مُّكَرَّمَةٍ ۞

14 Exalted, purified, مَّرۡفُوعَةٍ مُّطَهَّرَةٍ ۞

15 (Set down) by scribes بِأَيۡدِى سَفَرَةٍ ۞

16 Noble and righteous. كِرَامٍ بَرَرَةٍ ۞

17 Woe to Man! How ungrateful is he! قُتِلَ ٱلۡإِنسَٰنُ مَآ أَكۡفَرَهُ ۞

18 From what thing doth He create him? مِنۡ أَىِّ شَىۡءٍ خَلَقَهُ ۞

19 From a drop of seed. He createth him and proportioneth him, مِن نُّطۡفَةٍ خَلَقَهُ فَقَدَّرَهُ ۞

20 Then maketh the way easy for him, ثُمَّ ٱلسَّبِيلَ يَسَّرَهُ ۞

21 Then causeth him to die, and burieth him; ثُمَّ أَمَاتَهُ فَأَقۡبَرَهُ ۞

22 Then, when He will, He bringeth him again to life. ثُمَّ إِذَا شَآءَ أَنشَرَهُ ۞

23 Nay, but (man) hath not done what He commanded him. كَلَّا لَمَّا يَقۡضِ مَآ أَمَرَهُ ۞

24 Let man consider his food: فَلۡيَنظُرِ ٱلۡإِنسَٰنُ إِلَىٰ طَعَامِهِ ۞

25 How We pour water in showers أَنَّا صَبَبۡنَا ٱلۡمَآءَ صَبًّا ۞

26 Then split the earth in clefts ثُمَّ شَقَقۡنَا ٱلۡأَرۡضَ شَقًّا ۞

27 And cause the grain to grow therein فَأَنۢبَتۡنَا فِيهَا حَبًّا ۞

28 And grapes and green fodder وَعِنَبًا وَقَضۡبًا ۞

29 And olive-trees and palm-trees وَزَيۡتُونًا وَنَخۡلًا ۞

30 And garden-closes of thick foliage وَحَدَآئِقَ غُلۡبًا ۞

31 And fruits and grasses:

وَفَٰكِهَةً وَأَبًّا ۝

32 Provision for you and your cattle.

مَّتَٰعًا لَّكُمْ وَلِأَنْعَٰمِكُمْ ۝

33 But when the Shout cometh

فَإِذَا جَآءَتِ ٱلصَّآخَّةُ ۝

34 On the day when a man fleeth from his brother

يَوْمَ يَفِرُّ ٱلْمَرْءُ مِنْ أَخِيهِ ۝

35 And his mother and his father

وَأُمِّهِۦ وَأَبِيهِ ۝

36 And his wife and his children,

وَصَٰحِبَتِهِۦ وَبَنِيهِ ۝

37 Every man that day will have concern enough to make him heedless (of others).

لِكُلِّ ٱمْرِئٍ مِّنْهُمْ يَوْمَئِذٍ شَأْنٌ يُغْنِيهِ ۝

38 On that day faces will be bright as dawn,

وُجُوهٌ يَوْمَئِذٍ مُّسْفِرَةٌ ۝

39 Laughing, rejoicing at good news;

ضَاحِكَةٌ مُّسْتَبْشِرَةٌ ۝

40 And other faces, on that day, with dust upon them,

وَوُجُوهٌ يَوْمَئِذٍ عَلَيْهَا غَبَرَةٌ ۝

41 Veiled in darkness,

تَرْهَقُهَا قَتَرَةٌ ۝

42 Those are the disbelievers, the wicked.

أُو۟لَٰٓئِكَ هُمُ ٱلْكَفَرَةُ ٱلْفَجَرَةُ ۝

At Takwīr
(The Overthrowing)

At Takwīr takes its name from a word in verse 1. Verses 8 and 9 contain an allusion to the practice of the pagan Arabs of burying alive girl-children whom they deemed superfluous. An early Makkan sūrah.

*In the name of Allah, the
Beneficent, the Merciful.*

1 When the sun is overthrown,

2 And when the stars fall,

3 And when the hills are moved,

4 And when the camels big with young are abandoned,

5 And when the wild beasts are herded together,

6 And when the seas rise,

7 And when souls are reunited,

8 And when the girl-child that was buried alive is asked

9 For what sin she was slain,

10 And when the pages are laid open,

11 And when the sky is torn away,

12 And when Hell is heated.

13 And when the garden is brought nigh,

14 (Then) every soul will know what it hath made ready.

عَلِمَتْ نَفْسٌ مَّا أَحْضَرَتْ ۝

15 Oh, but I call to witness the planets,

فَلَا أُقْسِمُ بِالْخُنَّسِ ۝

16 The stars which rise and set,

الْجَوَارِ الْكُنَّسِ ۝

17 And the close of night,[1]

وَالَّيْلِ إِذَا عَسْعَسَ ۝

18 And the breath of morning[2]

وَالصُّبْحِ إِذَا تَنَفَّسَ ۝

19 That this is in truth the word of an honoured messenger,

إِنَّهُ لَقَوْلُ رَسُولٍ كَرِيمٍ ۝

20 Mighty, established in the presence of the Lord of the Throne,

ذِى قُوَّةٍ عِندَ ذِى الْعَرْشِ مَكِينٍ ۝

21 (One) to be obeyed, and trustworthy;

مُّطَاعٍ ثَمَّ أَمِينٍ ۝

22 And your comrade is not mad.

وَمَا صَاحِبُكُم بِمَجْنُونٍ ۝

23 Surely he beheld him on the clear horizon.[3]

وَلَقَدْ رَءَاهُ بِالْأُفُقِ الْمُبِينِ ۝

24 And he is not avid of the Unseen.

وَمَا هُوَ عَلَى الْغَيْبِ بِضَنِينٍ ۝

25 Nor is this the utterance of a devil worthy to be stoned.

وَمَا هُوَ بِقَوْلِ شَيْطَانٍ رَّجِيمٍ ۝

26 Whither then go ye?

فَأَيْنَ تَذْهَبُونَ ۝

27 This is naught else than a reminder unto creation,

إِنْ هُوَ إِلَّا ذِكْرٌ لِّلْعَالَمِينَ ۝

28 Unto whomsoever of you willeth to walk straight.

لِمَن شَاءَ مِنكُمْ أَن يَسْتَقِيمَ ۝

29 And ye will not, unless (it be) that Allah willeth, the Lord of Creation.

وَمَا تَشَاءُونَ إِلَّا أَن يَشَاءَ اللَّهُ رَبُّ الْعَالَمِينَ ۝

---

1. Lit. "And the night when it closeth."

2. Lit. "And the morning when it breathes."

3. The reference is to the Prophet's vision at Mount Ḥirā.

Al Infitār
(The Cleaving)

*Al Infitār takes its name from a word in verse 1. An early Makkan
sūrah.*

*In the name of Allah, the
Beneficent, the Merciful.*

1 When the heaven is cleft
asunder,

2 When the planets are dispersed,

3 When the seas are poured forth,

4 And the sepulchres are overturned,

5 A soul will know what it hath
sent before (it) and what left behind.

6 O man! What hath made thee
careless concerning thy Lord, the
Bountiful,

7 Who created thee, then fashioned, then proportioned thee?

8 Into whatsover form He will, He
casteth thee.

9 Nay, but ye deny the Judgement.

10 Lo! there are above you guardians,

بِسْمِ اللَّهِ الرَّحْمَٰنِ الرَّحِيمِ

إِذَا السَّمَاءُ انفَطَرَتْ ۝

وَإِذَا الْكَوَاكِبُ انتَثَرَتْ ۝

وَإِذَا الْبِحَارُ فُجِّرَتْ ۝

وَإِذَا الْقُبُورُ بُعْثِرَتْ ۝

عَلِمَتْ نَفْسٌ مَّا قَدَّمَتْ وَأَخَّرَتْ ۝

يَٰٓأَيُّهَا الْإِنسَٰنُ مَا غَرَّكَ بِرَبِّكَ الْكَرِيمِ ۝

الَّذِى خَلَقَكَ فَسَوَّىٰكَ فَعَدَلَكَ ۝

فِىٓ أَىِّ صُورَةٍ مَّا شَاءَ رَكَّبَكَ ۝

كَلَّا بَلْ تُكَذِّبُونَ بِالدِّينِ ۝

وَإِنَّ عَلَيْكُمْ لَحَٰفِظِينَ ۝

11 Generous and recording,

كِرَامًا كَاتِبِينَ ﴿١١﴾

12 Who know (all) that ye do.

يَعْلَمُونَ مَا تَفْعَلُونَ ﴿١٢﴾

13 Lo! the righteous verily will be in delight.

إِنَّ الْأَبْرَارَ لَفِى نَعِيمٍ ﴿١٣﴾

14 And lo! the wicked verily will be in hell;

وَإِنَّ الْفُجَّارَ لَفِى جَحِيمٍ ﴿١٤﴾

15 They will burn therein on the Day of Judgement,

يَصْلَوْنَهَا يَوْمَ الدِّينِ ﴿١٥﴾

16 And will not be absent thence.

وَمَا هُمْ عَنْهَا بِغَائِبِينَ ﴿١٦﴾

17 Ah, what will convey unto thee what the Day of Judgement is!

وَمَا أَدْرَاكَ مَا يَوْمُ الدِّينِ ﴿١٧﴾

18 Again, what will convey unto thee what the Day of Judgement is!

ثُمَّ مَا أَدْرَاكَ مَا يَوْمُ الدِّينِ ﴿١٨﴾

19 A day on which no soul hath power at all for any (other) soul. The (absolute) command on that day is Allah's.

يَوْمَ لَا تَمْلِكُ نَفْسٌ لِّنَفْسٍ شَيْئًا وَالْأَمْرُ يَوْمَئِذٍ لِلَّهِ ﴿١٩﴾

Al Muṭaffifīn or At Taṭfīf
(The Dealers in Fraud or Defrauding)

At Taṭfīf, "Defrauding," takes its name from a word in verse 1. An early Makkan sūrah.

In the name of Allah, the Beneficent, the Merciful.

1   Woe unto the defrauders:

2   Those who when they take the measure from mankind demand it full,

3   But if they measure unto them or weigh for them, they cause them loss.

4   Do such (men) not consider that they will be raised again

5   Unto an awful Day,

6   The day when (all) mankind stand before the Lord of the Worlds?

7   Nay, but the record of the vile is in *Sijjīn*—

8   Ah! what will convey unto thee what *Sijjīn* is!—

9   A written record.

10 Woe unto the repudiators on that day!

888

11 Those who deny the Day of Judgement

12 Which none denieth save each criminal transgressor,

13 Who, when Our revelations are recited unto him, saith: (Mere) fables of the men of old.

14 Nay, but that which they have earned is rust upon their hearts.

15 Nay, but surely, on that day they will be screened off from (the mercy of) their Lord.

16 Then lo! they verily will burn in hell,

17 And it will be said (unto them): This is that which ye used to deny.

18 Nay, but the record of the righteous is in 'Illīyūn—

19 Ah, what will convey unto thee what 'Illīyūn is!—

20 A written record,

21 Those who are brought near (unto their Lord) witness it.

22 Lo! the righteous verily are in delight,

23 On couches, gazing,

24 Thou wilt know in their faces the radiance of delight.

25 They are given to drink of a pure wine, sealed,

26 Whose seal is musk—For this let (all) those strive who strive for bliss—

ٱلَّذِينَ يُكَذِّبُونَ بِيَوْمِ ٱلدِّينِ ۝

وَمَا يُكَذِّبُ بِهِۦٓ إِلَّا كُلُّ مُعْتَدٍ أَثِيمٍ ۝

إِذَا تُتْلَىٰ عَلَيْهِ ءَايَٰتُنَا قَالَ أَسَٰطِيرُ ٱلْأَوَّلِينَ ۝

كَلَّا بَلْ رَانَ عَلَىٰ قُلُوبِهِم مَّا كَانُوا۟ يَكْسِبُونَ ۝

كَلَّآ إِنَّهُمْ عَن رَّبِّهِمْ يَوْمَئِذٍ لَّمَحْجُوبُونَ ۝

ثُمَّ إِنَّهُمْ لَصَالُوا۟ ٱلْجَحِيمِ ۝

ثُمَّ يُقَالُ هَٰذَا ٱلَّذِى كُنتُم بِهِۦ تُكَذِّبُونَ ۝

كَلَّآ إِنَّ كِتَٰبَ ٱلْأَبْرَارِ لَفِى عِلِّيِّينَ ۝

وَمَآ أَدْرَىٰكَ مَا عِلِّيُّونَ ۝

كِتَٰبٌ مَّرْقُومٌ ۝

يَشْهَدُهُ ٱلْمُقَرَّبُونَ ۝

إِنَّ ٱلْأَبْرَارَ لَفِى نَعِيمٍ ۝

عَلَى ٱلْأَرَآئِكِ يَنظُرُونَ ۝

تَعْرِفُ فِى وُجُوهِهِمْ نَضْرَةَ ٱلنَّعِيمِ ۝

يُسْقَوْنَ مِن رَّحِيقٍ مَّخْتُومٍ ۝

خِتَٰمُهُۥ مِسْكٌ وَفِى ذَٰلِكَ فَلْيَتَنَافَسِ ٱلْمُتَنَٰفِسُونَ ۝

27 And mixed with water of Tasnīm,

وَمِزَاجُهُ مِن تَسْنِيمٍ ۝

28 A spring whence those brought near to Allah drink

عَيْنًا يَشْرَبُ بِهَا ٱلْمُقَرَّبُونَ ۝

29 Lo! the guilty used to laugh at those who believed,

إِنَّ ٱلَّذِينَ أَجْرَمُوا۟ كَانُوا۟ مِنَ ٱلَّذِينَ ءَامَنُوا۟ يَضْحَكُونَ ۝

30 And wink one to another when they passed them;

وَإِذَا مَرُّوا۟ بِهِمْ يَتَغَامَزُونَ ۝

31 And when they returned to their own folk, they returned jesting;

وَإِذَا ٱنقَلَبُوٓا۟ إِلَىٰٓ أَهْلِهِمُ ٱنقَلَبُوا۟ فَكِهِينَ ۝

32 And when they saw them they said: Lo! these have gone astray.

وَإِذَا رَأَوْهُمْ قَالُوٓا۟ إِنَّ هَٰٓؤُلَآءِ لَضَآلُّونَ ۝

33 Yet they were not sent as guardians over them.

وَمَآ أُرْسِلُوا۟ عَلَيْهِمْ حَٰفِظِينَ ۝

34 This day it is those who believe who have the laugh of disbelievers,

فَٱلْيَوْمَ ٱلَّذِينَ ءَامَنُوا۟ مِنَ ٱلْكُفَّارِ يَضْحَكُونَ ۝

35 On high couches, gazing.

عَلَى ٱلْأَرَآئِكِ يَنظُرُونَ ۝

36 Are not the disbelievers paid for what they used to do?

هَلْ ثُوِّبَ ٱلْكُفَّارُ مَا كَانُوا۟ يَفْعَلُونَ ۝

Al Inshiqāq
(The Sundering)

Al Inshiqāq, "The Sundering," takes its name from a word in verse 1. An early Makkan sūrah.

In the name of Allah, the Beneficent, the Merciful.

1 When the heaven is split asunder

2 And attentive to her Lord in fear,

3 And when the earth is spread out

4 And hath cast out all that was in her, and is empty

5 And attentive to her Lord in fear!

6 Thou, verily, O man, art working toward thy Lord a work which thou wilt meet (in His presence).

7 Then whoso is given his account in his right hand

8 He truly will receive an easy reckoning

9 And will return unto his folk in joy.

10 But whoso is given his account behind his back,

وَأَمَّا مَنْ أُوتِيَ كِتَٰبَهُۥ وَرَآءَ ظَهْرِهِۦ ۝

11 He surely will invoke destruction

فَسَوْفَ يَدْعُواْ ثُبُورًا ۝

12 And be thrown to scorching fire.

وَيَصْلَىٰ سَعِيرًا ۝

13 He verily lived joyous with his folk,

إِنَّهُۥ كَانَ فِىٓ أَهْلِهِۦ مَسْرُورًا ۝

14 He verily deemed that he would never return (unto Allah).

إِنَّهُۥ ظَنَّ أَن لَّن يَحُورَ ۝

15 Nay, but lo! his Lord is ever looking on him!

بَلَىٰٓ إِنَّ رَبَّهُۥ كَانَ بِهِۦ بَصِيرًا ۝

16 Oh, I swear by the afterglow of sunset,

فَلَآ أُقْسِمُ بِٱلشَّفَقِ ۝

17 And by the night and all that it enshroudeth,

وَٱلَّيْلِ وَمَا وَسَقَ ۝

18 And by the moon when she is at the full,

وَٱلْقَمَرِ إِذَا ٱتَّسَقَ ۝

19 That ye shall journey on from plane to plane.

لَتَرْكَبُنَّ طَبَقًا عَن طَبَقٍ ۝

20 What aileth them, then, that they believe not

فَمَا لَهُمْ لَا يُؤْمِنُونَ ۝

21 And, when the Qur'an is recited unto them, worship not (Allah)?

وَإِذَا قُرِئَ عَلَيْهِمُ ٱلْقُرْءَانُ لَا يَسْجُدُونَ ۩ ۝

22 Nay, but those who disbelieve will deny;

بَلِ ٱلَّذِينَ كَفَرُواْ يُكَذِّبُونَ ۝

23 And Allah knoweth best what they are hiding.

وَٱللَّهُ أَعْلَمُ بِمَا يُوعُونَ ۝

24 So give them tidings of a painful doom,

فَبَشِّرْهُم بِعَذَابٍ أَلِيمٍ ۝

25 Save those who believe and do good works, for theirs is a reward unfailing.

إِلَّا ٱلَّذِينَ ءَامَنُواْ وَعَمِلُواْ ٱلصَّٰلِحَٰتِ لَهُمْ أَجْرٌ غَيْرُ مَمْنُونٍ ۝

Al Burūj
(The Mansions of the Stars)

Al Burūj takes its name from a word in verse 1 which I have translated "mansions of the stars." The word has the meaning of towers or mansions and is applied to the signs of the Zodiac. Verses 4 to 7 are generally taken to refer to the massacre of the Christians of Najrān in Al-Yaman by a Jewish king Dhū Nawās, an event of great historical importance since it caused the intervention of the Negus and led to the Abyssinian supremacy in the Yaman which lasted until the War of the Elephant (sūrah 105) in the Prophet's year of birth. Professor Horowitz thinks that the words "owners of the ditch, of the fuel-fed fire" refer not to any historical event but to the condition of all persecutors in the hereafter.[1]

An early Makkan sūrah.

In the name of Allah, the Beneficent, the Merciful.

1 By the heaven, holding mansions of the stars,

2 And by the Promised Day.

3 And by the witness and that whereunto he beareth testimony,

4 Destruction overtook the owners of the ditch

---

1. See "Islamic Culture" (Hyderabad, Deccan), April 1929.

5 Of the fuel-fed fire,

ٱلنَّارِ ذَاتِ ٱلْوَقُودِ ﴿٥﴾

6 When they sat by it,

إِذْ هُمْ عَلَيْهَا قُعُودٌ ﴿٦﴾

7 And were themselves the witnesses of what they did to the believers.[2]

وَهُمْ عَلَىٰ مَا يَفْعَلُونَ بِٱلْمُؤْمِنِينَ شُهُودٌ ﴿٧﴾

8 They had naught against them save that they believed in Allah, the Mighty, the Owner of Praise,

وَمَا نَقَمُوا مِنْهُمْ إِلَّا أَن يُؤْمِنُوا بِٱللَّهِ ٱلْعَزِيزِ ٱلْحَمِيدِ ﴿٨﴾

9 Him unto Whom belongeth the Sovereignty of the heavens and the earth; and Allah is of all things the Witness.

ٱلَّذِى لَهُ مُلْكُ ٱلسَّمَٰوَٰتِ وَٱلْأَرْضِ وَٱللَّهُ عَلَىٰ كُلِّ شَىْءٍ شَهِيدٌ ﴿٩﴾

10 Lo! they who persecute believing men and believing women and repent not, theirs verily will be the doom of hell, and theirs the doom of burning.

إِنَّ ٱلَّذِينَ فَتَنُوا ٱلْمُؤْمِنِينَ وَٱلْمُؤْمِنَٰتِ ثُمَّ لَمْ يَتُوبُوا فَلَهُمْ عَذَابُ جَهَنَّمَ وَلَهُمْ عَذَابُ ٱلْحَرِيقِ ﴿١٠﴾

11 Lo! those who believe and do good works, theirs will be Gardens underneath which rivers flow. That is the Great Success.

إِنَّ ٱلَّذِينَ ءَامَنُوا وَعَمِلُوا ٱلصَّٰلِحَٰتِ لَهُمْ جَنَّٰتٌ تَجْرِى مِن تَحْتِهَا ٱلْأَنْهَٰرُ ذَٰلِكَ ٱلْفَوْزُ ٱلْكَبِيرُ ﴿١١﴾

12 Lo! the punishment of thy Lord is stern.

إِنَّ بَطْشَ رَبِّكَ لَشَدِيدٌ ﴿١٢﴾

13 Lo! He it is Who produceth, then reproduceth,

إِنَّهُ هُوَ يُبْدِئُ وَيُعِيدُ ﴿١٣﴾

14 And He is the Forgiving, the Loving,

وَهُوَ ٱلْغَفُورُ ٱلْوَدُودُ ﴿١٤﴾

15 Lord of the Throne of Glory,

ذُو ٱلْعَرْشِ ٱلْمَجِيدُ ﴿١٥﴾

16 Doer of what He will.

فَعَّالٌ لِّمَا يُرِيدُ ﴿١٦﴾

---

2. Or it might be: "(Self-)destroyed were the owners of the trench of fuel-fed fire (i.e. hell) when they took their ease on earth and were themselves the witnesses," etc.

17 Hath there come unto thee the story of the hosts

هَلْ أَتَاكَ حَدِيثُ الْجُنُودِ ۝

18 Of Pharaoh and (the tribe of) Thamūd?

فِرْعَوْنَ وَثَمُودَ ۝

19 Nay, but those who disbelieve live in denial

بَلِ الَّذِينَ كَفَرُوا فِي تَكْذِيبٍ ۝

20 And Allah surroundeth them on all sides.

وَاللَّهُ مِن وَرَائِهِم مُّحِيطٌ ۝

21 Nay, but it is a glorious Qur'an

بَلْ هُوَ قُرْآنٌ مَّجِيدٌ ۝

22 On a guarded tablet.

فِي لَوْحٍ مَّحْفُوظٍ ۝

Aṭ Ṭāriq
(The Morning Star)

Aṭ Ṭāriq takes its name from a word in verse 1. There are other meanings to the word *Ṭāriq*, but I have chosen that which must have occurred to every hearer of this sūrah, especially as in verse 3, it is stated that a star is meant. The Morning Star has here a mystic sense, and is taken to refer to the Prophet himself. Some have thought that it refers to a comet which alarmed the East about the time of the Prophet's call. Others believe that this and other introductory verses, hard to elucidate, hide scientific facts unimagined at the period of revelation, and are related to the verses following them. Ghamrāwi Bey, my collaborator in the revision of this work, informed me that the late Dr. Sidqi among others considered that the reference here is to the fertilising germ penetrating the ovary, the subject being the same as vv. 5-7.

An early Makkan sūrah.

In the name of Allah, the Beneficent, the Merciful.

1   By the heaven and the Morning Star[1]

2   —Ah, what will tell thee what the Morning Star is!

3   —The piercing Star!

---

1. The Arabic word means originally "that which comes at night" or "one who knocks at the door."

896

4 No human soul but hath a guardian over it.

إِن كُلُّ نَفْسٍ لَّمَّا عَلَيْهَا حَافِظٌ ۝

5 So let man consider from what he is created.

فَلْيَنظُرِ ٱلْإِنسَـٰنُ مِمَّ خُلِقَ ۝

6 He is created from a gushing fluid

خُلِقَ مِن مَّآءٍ دَافِقٍ ۝

7 That issued from between the loins and ribs.

يَخْرُجُ مِنۢ بَيْنِ ٱلصُّلْبِ وَٱلتَّرَآئِبِ ۝

8 Lo! He verily is Able to return him (unto life)

إِنَّهُۥ عَلَىٰ رَجْعِهِۦ لَقَادِرٌ ۝

9 On the day when hidden thoughts shall be searched out.

يَوْمَ تُبْلَى ٱلسَّرَآئِرُ ۝

10 Then will he have no might nor any helper.

فَمَا لَهُۥ مِن قُوَّةٍ وَلَا نَاصِرٍ ۝

11 By the heaven which giveth the returning rain,

وَٱلسَّمَآءِ ذَاتِ ٱلرَّجْعِ ۝

12 And the earth which splitteth (with the growth of trees and plants)

وَٱلْأَرْضِ ذَاتِ ٱلصَّدْعِ ۝

13 Lo! this (Qur'an) is a conclusive word,

إِنَّهُۥ لَقَوْلٌ فَصْلٌ ۝

14 It is no pleasantry.

وَمَا هُوَ بِٱلْهَزْلِ ۝

15 Lo! they plot a plot (against thee, O Muhammad)

إِنَّهُمْ يَكِيدُونَ كَيْدًا ۝

16 And I plot a plot (against them).

وَأَكِيدُ كَيْدًا ۝

17 So give a respite to the disbelievers. Deal thou gently with them for a while.

فَمَهِّلِ ٱلْكَافِرِينَ أَمْهِلْهُمْ رُوَيْدًۢا ۝

Al A'lā
(The Most High)

Al A'lā takes its name from a word in verse 1. An early Makkan sūrah.

*In the name of Allah, the
Beneficent, the Merciful.*

1 Praise the name of thy Lord the
Most High,

2 Who createth, then disposeth;

3 Who measureth, then guideth;

4 Who bringeth forth the pasturage,

5 Then turneth it to russet stubble.

6 We shall make thee read (O
Muhammad) so that thou shalt not
forget

7 Save that which Allah willeth.
Lo! He knoweth the disclosed and
that which still is hidden;

8 And We shall ease thy way unto
the state of ease.

9 Therefore remind (men), for of
use is the reminder.

10 He will heed who feareth,

11 But the most hapless will flout
it,

898

12 He who will be flung to the great fire

اَلَّذِى يَصْلَى النَّارَ الْكُبْرَىٰ ﴿١٢﴾

13 Wherein he will neither die nor live.

ثُمَّ لَا يَمُوتُ فِيهَا وَلَا يَحْيَىٰ ﴿١٣﴾

14 He is successful who groweth,

قَدْ أَفْلَحَ مَنْ تَزَكَّىٰ ﴿١٤﴾

15 And remembereth the name of his Lord, so prayeth.

وَذَكَرَ اسْمَ رَبِّهِ فَصَلَّىٰ ﴿١٥﴾

16 But ye prefer the life of the world

بَلْ تُؤْثِرُونَ الْحَيَوٰةَ الدُّنْيَا ﴿١٦﴾

17 Although the Hereafter is better and more lasting.

وَالْآخِرَةُ خَيْرٌ وَأَبْقَىٰ ﴿١٧﴾

18 Lo! This is in the former scrolls,

إِنَّ هَٰذَا لَفِى الصُّحُفِ الْأُولَىٰ ﴿١٨﴾

19 The Books of Abraham and Moses.

صُحُفِ إِبْرَاهِيمَ وَمُوسَىٰ ﴿١٩﴾

Al Ghāshiyah
(The Overwhelming)

Al Ghāshiyah takes its name from a word in verse 1. An early Makkan sūrah.

سُوْرَةُ الْغَاشِيَةِ

In the name of Allah, the Beneficent, the Merciful.

بِسْمِ اللهِ الرَّحْمٰنِ الرَّحِيْمِ

1 Hath there come unto thee tidings of the Overwhelming?

هَلْ أَتَاكَ حَدِيْثُ الْغَاشِيَةِ ۞

2 On that day (many) faces will be downcast,

وُجُوْهٌ يَّوْمَئِذٍ خَاشِعَةٌ ۞

3 Toiling, weary,

عَامِلَةٌ نَّاصِبَةٌ ۞

4 Scorched by burning fire,

تَصْلٰى نَارًا حَامِيَةً ۞

5 Drinking from a boiling spring,

تُسْقٰى مِنْ عَيْنٍ اٰنِيَةٍ ۞

6 No food for them save bitter thorn-fruit

لَّيْسَ لَهُمْ طَعَامٌ إِلَّا مِنْ ضَرِيْعٍ ۞

7 Which doth not nourish nor release from hunger.

لَّا يُسْمِنُ وَلَا يُغْنِيْ مِنْ جُوْعٍ ۞

8 In that day other faces will be calm,

وُجُوْهٌ يَّوْمَئِذٍ نَّاعِمَةٌ ۞

9 Glad for their effort past,

لِّسَعْيِهَا رَاضِيَةٌ ۞

10 In a high garden

فِيْ جَنَّةٍ عَالِيَةٍ ۞

11 Where they hear no idle speech,

لَّا تَسْمَعُ فِيْهَا لَاغِيَةً ۞

12 Wherein is a gushing spring,

فِيْهَا عَيْنٌ جَارِيَةٌ ۞

13 Wherein are couches raised

فِيْهَا سُرُرٌ مَّرْفُوْعَةٌ ۞

14 And goblets set at hand وَأَكْوَابٌ مَّوْضُوعَةٌ ۝

15 And cushions ranged وَنَمَارِقُ مَصْفُوفَةٌ ۝

16 And silken carpets spread. وَزَرَابِيُّ مَبْثُوثَةٌ ۝

17 Will they not regard the camels, how they are created? أَفَلَا يَنظُرُونَ إِلَى الْإِبِلِ كَيْفَ خُلِقَتْ ۝

18 And the heaven, how it is raised? وَإِلَى السَّمَاءِ كَيْفَ رُفِعَتْ ۝

19 And the hills, how they are set up? وَإِلَى الْجِبَالِ كَيْفَ نُصِبَتْ ۝

20 And the earth, how it is spread? وَإِلَى الْأَرْضِ كَيْفَ سُطِحَتْ ۝

21 Remind them, for thou art but a remembrancer, فَذَكِّرْ إِنَّمَا أَنتَ مُذَكِّرٌ ۝

22 Thou art not at all a warder over them. لَّسْتَ عَلَيْهِم بِمُصَيْطِرٍ ۝

23 But whoso is averse and disbelieveth, إِلَّا مَن تَوَلَّىٰ وَكَفَرَ ۝

24 Allah will punish him with direst punishment. فَيُعَذِّبُهُ اللَّهُ الْعَذَابَ الْأَكْبَرَ ۝

25 Lo! unto Us is their return إِنَّ إِلَيْنَا إِيَابَهُمْ ۝

26 And Ours their reckoning. ثُمَّ إِنَّ عَلَيْنَا حِسَابَهُم ۝

Al Fajr
(The Dawn)

Al Fajr takes its name from verse 1. A very early Makkan sūrah.

In the name of Allah, the Beneficent, the Merciful.

1 By the Dawn

2 And ten nights,[1]

3 And the Even and the Odd,

4 And the night when it departeth,

5 There surely is an oath for thinking man.

6 Dost thou not consider how thy Lord dealt with (the tribe of) 'Ād,

7 With many-columned[2] Iram,

8 The like of which was not created in the lands;

---

1. Of the month of pilgrimage.

2. I had written "many-columned," following the run of commentators, who take the word '*imād* to mean columns, pillars, when I happened upon Ibn Khaldūn's diatribe against that rendering and all the legends to which it has given rise, in the preface of the *Prolegomena*. The word meant "tent-poles" to the Arabs of the Prophet's day, as Ibn Khaldūn points out. In view of recent discoveries in the Yaman, however, I prefer the usual rendering.

9 And with (the tribe of) Thamūd, who clove the rocks in the valley;

وَثَمُوْدَ الَّذِيْنَ جَابُوا الصَّخْرَ بِالْوَادِ ۟

10 And with Pharaoh, firm of might,

وَفِرْعَوْنَ ذِي الْأَوْتَادِ ۟

11 Who (all) were rebellious (to Allah) in these lands,

الَّذِيْنَ طَغَوْا فِي الْبِلَادِ ۟

12 And multiplied inquiry therein?

فَأَكْثَرُوْا فِيْهَا الْفَسَادَ ۟

13 Therefore thy Lord poured on them the disaster of His punishment.

فَصَبَّ عَلَيْهِمْ رَبُّكَ سَوْطَ عَذَابٍ ۟

14 Lo! thy Lord is ever watchful.

إِنَّ رَبَّكَ لَبِالْمِرْصَادِ ۟

15 As for man, whenever his Lord trieth him by honouring him, and is gracious unto him, he saith: My Lord honoureth me.

فَأَمَّا الْإِنْسَانُ إِذَا مَا ابْتَلَاهُ رَبُّهُ فَأَكْرَمَهُ وَنَعَّمَهُ فَيَقُوْلُ رَبِّيْ أَكْرَمَنِ ۟

16 But whenever He trieth him by straitening his means of life, he saith: My Lord despiseth me.

وَأَمَّا إِذَا مَا ابْتَلَاهُ فَقَدَرَ عَلَيْهِ رِزْقَهُ فَيَقُوْلُ رَبِّيْ أَهَانَنِ ۟

17 Nay, but ye (for your part) honour not the orphan

كَلَّا بَلْ لَا تُكْرِمُوْنَ الْيَتِيْمَ ۟

18 And urge not on the feeding of the poor,

وَلَا تَحَاضُّوْنَ عَلَى طَعَامِ الْمِسْكِيْنِ ۟

19 And ye devour heritages with devouring greed

وَتَأْكُلُوْنَ التُّرَاثَ أَكْلًا لَّمًّا ۟

20 And love wealth with abounding love.

وَتُحِبُّوْنَ الْمَالَ حُبًّا جَمًّا ۟

21 Nay, but when the earth is ground to atoms, grinding, grinding,

كَلَّا إِذَا دُكَّتِ الْأَرْضُ دَكًّا دَكًّا ۟

22 And thy Lord shall come with angels, rank on rank,

وَجَاءَ رَبُّكَ وَالْمَلَكُ صَفًّا صَفًّا ۟

23 And hell is brought near that day; on that day man will remember, but how will the remembrance (then avail him)?

وَجِيْءَ يَوْمَئِذٍ بِجَهَنَّمَ يَوْمَئِذٍ يَتَذَكَّرُ الْإِنْسَانُ وَأَنَّى لَهُ الذِّكْرَى ۟

24 He will say: Ah, would that I had sent before me (some provision) for my life!　يَقُوْلُ يٰلَيْتَنِيْ قَدَّمْتُ لِحَيَاتِيْ ۝

25 None punisheth as He will punish on that day!　فَيَوْمَئِذٍ لَّا يُعَذِّبُ عَذَابَهٗٓ أَحَدٌ ۝

26 None bindeth as He then will bind.　وَّلَا يُوْثِقُ وَثَاقَهٗٓ أَحَدٌ ۝

27 But ah! thou soul at peace!　يٰٓأَيَّتُهَا النَّفْسُ الْمُطْمَئِنَّةُ ۝

28 Return unto thy Lord, content in His good pleasure!　اِرْجِعِيْٓ إِلٰى رَبِّكِ رَاضِيَةً مَّرْضِيَّةً ۝

29 Enter thou among My bondmen!　فَادْخُلِيْ فِيْ عِبٰدِيْ ۝

30 Enter thou My Garden!　وَادْخُلِيْ جَنَّتِيْ ۝

Al Balad
(The City)

Al Balad takes its name from a word in verse 1. A very early Makkan sūrah.

In the name of Allah, the
Beneficent, the Merciful.

1   Nay, I swear by this city—

2   And thou art an indweller of this city[1]—

3   And the begetter and that which he begat,

4   We verily have created man in an atmosphere:[2]

5   Thinketh he that none hath power over him?

6   And he saith: I have destroyed vast wealth:

7   Thinketh he that none beholdeth him?

8   Did We not assign unto him two eyes

9   And a tongue and two lips,

---

1. Or "when thou hast control over the city" (prophetically).

2. Or "in affliction."

10 And We guided him to the two ways.

وَهَدَيْنَاهُ النَّجْدَيْنِ ۝

11 But he hath not attempted the Ascent—

فَلَا اقْتَحَمَ الْعَقَبَةَ ۝

12 Ah, what will convey unto thee what the Ascent is!—

وَمَا أَدْرَاكَ مَا الْعَقَبَةُ ۝

13 (It is) to free a slave,

فَكُّ رَقَبَةٍ ۝

14 And to feed in the day of hunger

أَوْ إِطْعَامٌ فِي يَوْمٍ ذِي مَسْغَبَةٍ ۝

15 An orphan near of kin,

يَتِيمًا ذَا مَقْرَبَةٍ ۝

16 Or some poor wretch in misery,

أَوْ مِسْكِينًا ذَا مَتْرَبَةٍ ۝

17 And to be of those who believe and exhort one another to perseverance and exhort one another to pity.

ثُمَّ كَانَ مِنَ الَّذِينَ ءَامَنُوا وَتَوَاصَوْا بِالصَّبْرِ وَتَوَاصَوْا بِالْمَرْحَمَةِ ۝

18 Their place will be on the right hand.

أُوْلَـٰئِكَ أَصْحَابُ الْمَيْمَنَةِ ۝

19 But those who disbelieve Our revelations, their place will be on the left hand.　　　　　•

وَالَّذِينَ كَفَرُوا بِئَايَاتِنَا هُمْ أَصْحَابُ الْمَشْئَمَةِ ۝

20 Fire will be an awning over them.

عَلَيْهِمْ نَارٌ مُّؤْصَدَةٌ ۝

Ash Shams
(The Sun)

Ash Shams takes its name from a word in verse 1. A very early Makkan sūrah.

In the name of Allah, the
Beneficent, the Merciful.

1   By the sun and his brightness,

2   And the moon when she
followeth him,

3   And the day when it revealeth
him,

4   And the night when it enshroudeth him,

5   And the heaven and Him who
built it,

6   And the earth and Him who
spread it,

7   And a soul and Him who perfected it

8   And inspired it (with conscience
of) what is wrong for it and (what
is) right for it.

9   He is indeed successful who
causeth it to grow,

10 And he is indeed a failure who
stunteth it.

907

11 (The tribe of) Thamūd denied (the truth) in their rebellious pride.

كَذَّبَتْ ثَمُودُ بِطَغْوَاهَآ ۞

12 When the basest of them broke forth

إِذِ انۢبَعَثَ أَشْقَاهَا ۞

13 And the messenger of Allah said: It is the she-camel of Allah, so let her drink!

فَقَالَ لَهُمْ رَسُولُ اللّٰهِ نَاقَةَ اللّٰهِ وَسُقْيَاهَا ۞

14 But they denied him, and they hamstrung her, so Allah doomed them for their sin and razed (their dwellings).

فَكَذَّبُوهُ فَعَقَرُوهَا فَدَمْدَمَ عَلَيْهِمْ رَبُّهُمْ بِذَنْبِهِمْ فَسَوَّاهَا ۞

15 He dreadeth not the sequel (of events).

وَلَا يَخَافُ عُقْبَاهَا ۞

Al Layl
(The Night)

Al Layl takes its name from a word in verse 1. A very early Makkan
sūrah.

In the name of Allah, the
Beneficent, the Merciful.

1 By the night enshrouding

2 And the day resplendent

3 And Him Who hath created
male and female,

4 Lo! your effort is dispersed
(toward divers ends).

5 As for him who giveth and is
dutiful (toward Allah)

6 And believeth in goodness;

7 Surely We will ease his way
unto the state of ease.

8 But as for him who hoardeth
and deemeth himself independent,

9 And disbelieveth in goodness;

10 Surely We will ease his way
unto adversity.

11 His riches will not save him
when he perisheth.

12 Lo! Ours it is (to give) the guidance

إِنَّ عَلَيْنَا لَلْهُدَىٰ ۞

13 And lo! unto Us belong the latter portion and the former.

وَإِنَّ لَنَا لَلْآخِرَةَ وَالْأُولَىٰ ۞

14 Therefore have I warned you of the flaming Fire

فَأَنذَرْتُكُمْ نَارًا تَلَظَّىٰ ۞

15 Which only the most wretched must endure,

لَا يَصْلَىٰهَا إِلَّا الْأَشْقَى ۞

16 He who denieth and turneth away.

الَّذِي كَذَّبَ وَتَوَلَّىٰ ۞

17 Far removed from it will be the righteous

وَسَيُجَنَّبُهَا الْأَتْقَى ۞

18 Who giveth his wealth that he may grow (in goodness),

الَّذِي يُؤْتِي مَالَهُ يَتَزَكَّىٰ ۞

19 And none hath with him any favour for reward,

وَمَا لِأَحَدٍ عِندَهُ مِن نِّعْمَةٍ تُجْزَىٰ ۞

20 Except as seeking (to fulfil) the purpose of his Lord Most High.

إِلَّا ابْتِغَاءَ وَجْهِ رَبِّهِ الْأَعْلَىٰ ۞

21 He verily will be content.

وَلَسَوْفَ يَرْضَىٰ ۞

Ad Ḍuḥā
(The Morning Hours)

Ad Ḍuḥā, "The Morning Hours," takes its name from the first verse. There was an interval during which the Prophet received no revelation and the idolaters mocked him, saying: "Allah, of whom we used to hear so much, has forsaken poor Muhammad and now hates him." Then came this revelation. The Prophet had been a leading citizen of Makkah until he received his call. Now he was regarded as a madman. He was a man near fifty, and the prophecy in this sūrah that "the latter portion would be better for him than the former" must have seemed absurd to those who heard it. Yet the latter portion of the Prophet's life, the last ten years, is the most wonderful record of success in human history.

An early Makkan sūrah.

In the name of Allah, the Beneficent, the Merciful.

1   By the morning hours

2   And by the night when it is stillest,

3   Thy Lord hath not forsaken thee nor doth He hate thee,

4   And verily the latter portion will be better for thee than the former,

5   And verily thy Lord will give unto thee so that thou wilt be content.

6   Did He not find thee an orphan
and protect (thee)?

أَلَمْ يَجِدْكَ يَتِيمًا فَآوَى ۞

7   Did He not find thee wandering
and direct (thee)?

وَوَجَدَكَ ضَالًّا فَهَدَى ۞

8   Did He not find thee destitute
and enrich (thee)?

وَوَجَدَكَ عَآئِلًا فَأَغْنَى ۞

9   Therefore the orphan oppress
not,

فَأَمَّا الْيَتِيمَ فَلَا تَقْهَرْ ۞

10 Therefore the beggar drive not
away,

وَأَمَّا السَّآئِلَ فَلَا تَنْهَرْ ۞

11 Therefore of the bounty of thy
Lord be thy discourse.

وَأَمَّا بِنِعْمَةِ رَبِّكَ فَحَدِّثْ ۞

Al Sharḥ or Al Inshirāḥ
(The Expansion or Solace)

Al Inshirāḥ, "Solace," takes its name from a word in verse 1, and also from its subject, which is relief from anxiety. It was probably revealed upon the same occasion as sūrah 93; and, at a time when the Prophet was derided and shunned after having been respected and courted, must have struck the disbelievers as ridiculous. It refers to the inward assurance which the Prophet had received by revelation, and speaks of future events as accomplished, as is usual in the Qur'an, the revelation coming from a plane where time is not. Verse 4, speaking of his fame as exalted, must have seemed particularly absurd at that time of humiliation and persecution. But today, from every mosque in the world, the Prophet's name is cried, as that of the messenger of God, five times a day, and every Muslim prays for blessings on him when his name is mentioned.

An early Makkan sūrah.

In the name of Allah, the Beneficent, the Merciful.

1 Have We not caused thy bosom to dilate,

2 And eased thee of thy burden

3 Which weighed down thy back;

4 And exalted thy fame?

5 But lo! with hardship goeth ease,

6 Lo! with hardship goeth ease;

7 So when thou art relieved, still toil

8 And strive to please thy Lord.

At Tīn
(The Fig)

At Tīn, "The Fig," takes its name from a word in verse 1. The sense is mystical, referring to man in relation to the revealed Law of God and His judgement.

A very early Makkan sūrah.

In the name of Allah, the Beneficent, the Merciful.

1   By the fig and the olive,

2   By Mount Sinai,

3   And by this land made safe;

4   Surely We created man of the best stature

5   Then We reduced him to the lowest of the low,

6   Save those who believe and do good works, and theirs is a reward unfailing.

7   So who henceforth will give the lie to thee about the judgement?

8   Is not Allah the most conclusive of all judges?

914

Al 'Alaq
(The Clot)

Al 'Alaq takes its name from a word in verse 2. Verses 1-5 are the words which the Prophet received in the vision at Hirā, therefore the first of the Qur'an to be revealed.

A very early Makkan sūrah.

In the name of Allah, the Beneficent, the Merciful.

1 Read: In the name of thy Lord who createth,

2 Createth man from a clot.

3 Read: And thy Lord is the Most Bounteous,

4 Who teacheth by the pen,

5 Teacheth man that which he knew not.

6 Nay, but verily man is rebellious

7 That he thinketh himself independent!

8 Lo! unto thy Lord is the return.

9 Hast thou seen him who dissuadeth

10 A slave when he prayeth?

11 Hast thou seen if he (relieth) on the guidance (of Allah)

أَرَءَيْتَ إِن كَانَ عَلَى ٱلْهُدَىٰٓ ﴿١١﴾

12 Or enjoineth piety?

أَوْ أَمَرَ بِٱلتَّقْوَىٰٓ ﴿١٢﴾

13 Hast thou seen if he denieth (Allah's guidance) and is froward?

أَرَءَيْتَ إِن كَذَّبَ وَتَوَلَّىٰٓ ﴿١٣﴾

14 Is he then unaware that Allah seeth?

أَلَمْ يَعْلَم بِأَنَّ ٱللَّهَ يَرَىٰ ﴿١٤﴾

15 Nay, but if he cease not. We will seize him by the forelock—

كَلَّا لَئِن لَّمْ يَنتَهِ لَنَسْفَعًۢا بِٱلنَّاصِيَةِ ﴿١٥﴾

16 The lying, sinful forelock—

نَاصِيَةٍ كَاذِبَةٍ خَاطِئَةٍ ﴿١٦﴾

17 Then let him call upon his henchmen!

فَلْيَدْعُ نَادِيَهُ ﴿١٧﴾

18 We will call the guards of hell.

سَنَدْعُ ٱلزَّبَانِيَةَ ﴿١٨﴾

19 Nay! Obey not thou him. But prostrate thyself, and draw near (unto Allah).

كَلَّا لَا تُطِعْهُ وَٱسْجُدْ وَٱقْتَرِب ۩ ﴿١٩﴾

Al Qadr
(Power)

Al Qadr takes its name from a word in verse 1. It refers to the night (one of the last nights of Ramaḍān) on which the Prophet received his Call and the first verses of the Qur'an were revealed in the vision of Mount Hirā. It is said to be the night on which God's decrees for the year are brought down to the earthly plane.

A very early Makkan sūrah.

In the name of Allah, the Beneficent, the Merciful.

1 Lo! We revealed it on the Night of Power.

2 Ah, what will convey unto thee what the Night of Power is!

3 The Night of Power is better than a thousand months.

4 The angels and the Spirit[1] descend therein, by the permission of their Lord, with all decrees.

5 (That night is) Peace until the rising of the dawn.

---

1. *i.e.* Gabriel or, as some commentators think, a general term for angels of the highest rank.

Al Bayyinah
(The Clear Proof)

Al Bayyinah takes its name from a word in the first verse. There is no certainty as to the period of revelation. Many regard it as a late Makkan sūrah. I follow the attribution in the *Mushaf* which I have followed throughout.

The probable date of revelation is the year 1 A.H.

In the name of Allah, the Beneficent, the Merciful.

1 Those who disbelieve among the People of the Scripture and the idolaters could not have left off (erring) till the clear proof came unto them,

2 A messenger from Allah, reading purified pages

3 Containing correct scriptures.

4 Nor were the People of the Scripture divided until after the clear proof came unto them.

5 And they are ordered naught else than to serve Allah, keeping religion pure for Him, as men by nature upright, and to establish worship and to pay the poor-due. That is true religion.

918

6 Lo! those who disbelieve, among the People of the Scripture and the idolaters, will abide in fire of hell. They are the worst of created beings.

إِنَّ الَّذِينَ كَفَرُوا مِنْ أَهْلِ الْكِتَبِ وَالْمُشْرِكِينَ فِى نَارِ جَهَنَّمَ خَلِدِينَ فِيهَا ۚ أُولَٰٓئِكَ هُمْ شَرُّ الْبَرِيَّةِ ۝

7 (And) lo! those who believe and do good works are the best of created beings.

إِنَّ الَّذِينَ ءَامَنُوا وَعَمِلُوا الصَّلِحَتِ أُولَٰٓئِكَ هُمْ خَيْرُ الْبَرِيَّةِ ۝

8 Their reward is with their Lord: Gardens of Eden underneath which rivers flow, wherein they dwell forever. Allah hath pleasure in them and they have pleasure in Him. This is (in store) for him who feareth his Lord.

جَزَآؤُهُمْ عِنْدَ رَبِّهِمْ جَنَّتُ عَدْنٍ تَجْرِى مِن تَحْتِهَا الْأَنْهَرُ خَلِدِينَ فِيهَا أَبَدًا ۚ رَّضِىَ اللَّهُ عَنْهُمْ وَرَضُوا عَنْهُ ۚ ذَٰلِكَ لِمَنْ خَشِىَ رَبَّهُ ۝

Al Zalzalah
(The Earthquake)

Al Zalzalah takes its name from a word in verse 1. A very early Makkan sūrah.

In the name of Allah, the Beneficent, the Merciful.

1 When Earth is shaken with her (final) earthquake

2 And Earth yieldeth up her burdens,

3 And man saith: What aileth her?

4 That day she will relate her chronicles,

5 Because thy Lord inspireth her.

6 That day mankind will issue forth in scattered groups to be shown their deeds.

7 And whoso doeth good an atom's weight will see it then,

8 And whoso doeth ill an atom's weight will see it then.

Al 'Ādiyāt
(The Coursers)

Al 'Ādiyāt takes its name from a word in the first verse. A very early Makkan sūrah.

In the name of Allah, the Beneficent, the Merciful.

1 By the snorting coursers,

2 Striking sparks of fire

3 And scouring to the raid at dawn,

4 Then, therewith, with their trail of dust,

5 Cleaving, as one, the centre (of the foe),[1]

6 Lo! man is an ingrate unto his Lord

7 And lo! he is a witness unto that;

8 And lo! in the love of wealth he is violent.

---

1. The meaning of the first five verses is by no means clear. The above is a probable rendering.

9   Knoweth he not that, when the contents of the graves are poured forth

أَفَلَا يَعْلَمُ إِذَا بُعْثِرَ مَا فِي ٱلْقُبُورِ ۝

10 And the secrets of the breasts are made known.

وَحُصِّلَ مَا فِي ٱلصُّدُورِ ۝

11 On that day will their Lord be perfectly Aware concerning them.

إِنَّ رَبَّهُم بِهِمْ يَوْمَئِذٍ لَّخَبِيرُ ۝

Sūrah 101

Al Qāri'ah
(The Calamity)

Al Qāri'ah takes its name from a word in verse 1 recurring in the next
two verses.

*In the name of Allah, the
Beneficent, the Merciful.*

1 The Calamity!

2 What is the Calamity?

3 Ah, what will convey unto thee
what the Calamity is!

4 A day wherein mankind will be
as thickly-scattered moths

5 And the mountains will become
as carded wool.

6 Then, as for him whose scales
are heavy (with good works),

7 He will live a pleasant life.

8 But as for him whose scales are
light,

9 So his main abode will be the
abyss (of Hell).

10 Ah, what will convey unto thee
what she is!—

11 Raging fire.

923

At Takāthur
(Rivalry in Worldly Increase)

At Takāthur takes its name from a word in the first verse. A very early Makkan sūrah.

In the name of Allah, the Beneficent, the Merciful.

1 Rivalry in worldly increase distracteth you

2 Until ye come to the graves.

3 Nay, but ye will come to know!

4 Nay, but ye will come to know!

5 Nay, would that ye knew (now) with a sure knowledge!

6 For ye will behold hell-fire.

7 Aye, ye will behold it with sure vision.

8 Then, on that day, ye will be asked concerning pleasure

Al 'Asr
(The Declining Day)

Al 'Asr takes its name from a word in verse 1. A very early Makkan
sūrah.

In the name of Allah, the
Beneficent, the Merciful.

1 By the declining day,

2 Lo! man is in a state of loss,

3 Save those who believe and do
good works, and exhort one another
to truth and exhort one another to
endurance.

Sūrah 104

Al Humazah
(The Traducer)

Al Humazah takes its name from a word in verse 1. The idolaters waylaid all newcomers to Makkah and warned them against the Prophet, in order to prevent their listening to his preaching.

An early Makkan sūrah.

In the name of Allah, the Beneficent, the Merciful.

1 Woe unto every slandering traducer,

2 Who hath gathered wealth (of this world) and counted it.

3 He thinketh that his wealth will render him immortal.

4 Nay, but verily he will be flung to the Consuming One.

5 Ah, what will convey unto thee what the Consuming One is!

6 (It is) the fire of Allah, kindled,

7 Which leapeth up over the hearts (of men).

8 Lo! it is closed in on them

9 In outstretched columns.

Al Fīl
(The Elephant)

Al Fīl, "The Elephant," takes its name from a word in the first verse. The allusion is to the campaign of Abrahah, the Abyssinian ruler of Al-Yaman, against Makkah, with the purpose of destroying the Ka'bah in the year of the Prophet's birth. He had with him an elephant which much impressed the Arabs. Tradition says that the elephant refused to advance on the last stage of the march, and that swarms of flying creatures pelted the Abyssinians with stones. Another tradition says that they retired in disorder owing to an outbreak of smallpox in the camp. At the time when this sūrah was revealed, many men in Makkah must have known what happened. Dr. Krenkow, a sound Arabic scholar, is of the opinion that the flying creatures may well have been swarms of insects carrying infection. In any case the Ka'bah was saved from destruction after its defenders had despaired.

A very early Makkan sūrah.

In the name of Allah, the Beneficent, the Merciful.

1 Hast thou not seen how thy Lord dealt with the owners of the Elephant?

2 Did He not bring their stratagem to naught,

3 And send against them swarms of flying creatures,

4 Which pelted them with stones of baked clay,

5 And made them like straw eaten up (by cattle)?

Ash Shitā or *Quraysh*
(Winter or The Tribe of Quraysh)

Ash Shitā is so called from a word occurring in verse 2. It is also often called *Quraysh*. A very early Makkan sūrah.

In the name of Allah, the
Beneficent, the Merciful.

1   For the taming[1] of Quraysh

لِإِيلَٰفِ قُرَيْشٍ ۝

2   For their taming (We cause) the
caravans to set forth in winter and
summer.

إِۦلَٰفِهِمْ رِحْلَةَ ٱلشِّتَآءِ وَٱلصَّيْفِ ۝

3   So let them worship the Lord of
this House,

فَلْيَعْبُدُوا۟ رَبَّ هَٰذَا ٱلْبَيْتِ ۝

4   Who hath fed them against
hunger and hath made them safe
from fear.

ٱلَّذِىٓ أَطْعَمَهُم مِّن جُوعٍ وَءَامَنَهُم مِّنْ خَوْفٍۭ ۝

---

1. *i.e.* "civilising."

Al Māʿūn
(Small Kindnesses)

Al Māʿūn takes its name from a word in the last verse. An early Makkan revelation.

In the name of Allah, the Beneficent, the Merciful.

1 Hast thou observed him who belieth religion?

2 That is he who repelleth the orphan,

3 And urgeth not the feeding of the needy.

4 Ah, woe unto worshippers

5 Who are heedless of their prayer;

6 Who (only) make a show (of worship)

7 Yet refuse small kindnesses!

Sūrah 108

Al Kawthar
(Abundance)

Al Kawthar takes its name from a word in the first verse. The disbelievers used to taunt the Prophet with the fact that he had no son, and therefore none to uphold his religion after him.

In the name of Allah, the Beneficent, the Merciful.

1 Lo! We have given thee Abundance;

إِنَّآ أَعْطَيْنَاكَ ٱلْكَوْثَرَ ۝

2 So pray unto thy Lord, and sacrifice.

فَصَلِّ لِرَبِّكَ وَٱنْحَرْ ۝

3 Lo! It is thy insulter (and not thou) who is without posterity.

إِنَّ شَانِئَكَ هُوَ ٱلْأَبْتَرُ ۝

930

Sūrah 109

Al Kāfirūn
(The Disbelievers)

Al Kāfirūn takes its name from a word in verse 1. It was revealed at a time when the idolaters had asked the Prophet to compromise in matters of religion.

 شُوْرَةُ الْكَافِرُوْنَ

In the name of Allah, the Beneficent, the Merciful.

بِسْمِ اللهِ الرَّحْمٰنِ الرَّحِيمِ

1 Say: O disbelievers!

قُلْ يَـٰٓأَيُّهَا الْكَـٰفِرُونَ ۝

2 I worship not that which ye worship;

لَآ أَعْبُدُ مَا تَعْبُدُونَ ۝

3 Nor worship ye that which I worship.

وَلَآ أَنتُمْ عَـٰبِدُونَ مَآ أَعْبُدُ ۝

4 And I shall not worship that which ye worship.

وَلَآ أَنَا۠ عَابِدٌ مَّا عَبَدتُّمْ ۝

5 Nor will ye worship that which I worship.

وَلَآ أَنتُمْ عَـٰبِدُونَ مَآ أَعْبُدُ ۝

6 Unto you your religion, and unto me my religion.

لَكُمْ دِينُكُمْ وَلِىَ دِينِ ۝

931

An Naṣr
(Succour)

An Naṣr takes its name from a word in the first verse. It is one of the very last revelations, having come to the Prophet only a few weeks before his death. Though ascribed always to Al-Madīnah, tradition says that it was actually revealed at Makkah during the days the Prophet spent there when he made his farewell pilgrimage. It is described in Ibn Hishām and elsewhere as the first announcement that the Prophet received of his approaching death.

The date of revelation is the tenth year of the Hijrah.

In the name of Allah, the Beneficent, the Merciful.

1   When Allah's succour and the triumph cometh

2   And thou seest mankind entering the religion of Allah in troops,

3   Then hymn the praises of thy Lord, and seek forgiveness of Him. Lo! He is ever ready to show mercy.

Al Masad or Al Lahab
(Palm Fibre or The Flame)

Al Masad takes its name from a word (to the Arabs a very homely word) in the last verse. It is the only passage in the whole Qur'an where an opponent of the Prophet is denounced by name. Abū Lahab (The Father of Flame), whose real name was 'Abd al 'Uzzā, was an uncle of the Prophet and was the only member of his own clan who bitterly opposed the Prophet. He made it his business to torment the Prophet, and his wife took a pleasure in carrying thorn bushes and strewing them in the sand where she knew that the Prophet was sure to walk barefooted.

An early Makkan revelation.

In the name of Allah, the Beneficent, the Merciful.

بِسْمِ اللهِ الرَّحْمٰنِ الرَّحِيمِ

1 The power of Abū Lahab will perish, and he will perish.

تَبَّتْ يَدَآ أَبِي لَهَبٍ وَتَبَّ ۝

2 His wealth and gains will not exempt him.

مَآ أَغْنَىٰ عَنْهُ مَالُهُۥ وَمَا كَسَبَ ۝

3 He will be plunged in flaming fire,

سَيَصْلَىٰ نَارًا ذَاتَ لَهَبٍ ۝

4 And his wife, the wood-carrier,

وَامْرَأَتُهُۥ حَمَّالَةَ الْحَطَبِ ۝

5 Will have upon her neck a halter of palm-fibre.

فِي جِيدِهَا حَبْلٌ مِّن مَّسَدٍ ۝

At Tawḥīd or Al Ikhlāṣ
(The Unity or The Purity of Faith)

At Tawḥīd, "The Unity," takes its name from its subject. It has been called the essence of the Qur'an, of which it is really the last sūrah. Some authorities ascribe this sūrah to the Madīnah period, and think that it was revealed in answer to a question of some Jewish doctors concerning the nature of God.

It is generally held to be an early Makkan sūrah.

سُورَةُ الإِخْلاَصِ

In the name of Allah, the Beneficent, the Merciful.

بِسْمِ اللَّهِ الرَّحْمَٰنِ الرَّحِيمِ

1   Say: He is Allah, the One!

قُلْ هُوَ اللَّهُ أَحَدٌ ۝

2   Allah, the eternally Besought of all!

اللَّهُ الصَّمَدُ ۝

3   He begetteth not nor was begotten.

لَمْ يَلِدْ وَلَمْ يُولَدْ ۝

4   And there is none comparable unto Him.

وَلَمْ يَكُن لَّهُ كُفُوًا أَحَدٌ ۝

934

Sūrah 113

Al Falaq
(The Daybreak)

Al Falaq, "The Daybreak," takes its name from a word in the first verse. This and the following sūrah are prayers for protection, this one being for protection from fears proceeding from the unknown. The two sūrahs are known as *Al-Mu'awwadhateyn*, the two cries for refuge and protection.

An early Makkan sūrah.

In the name of Allah, the Beneficent, the Merciful.

1   Say: I seek refuge in the Lord of Daybreak

2   From the evil of that which He created;

3   From the evil of the darkness when it is intense,

4   And from the evil of malignant witchcraft,[1]

5   And from the evil of the envier when he envieth.

---

1. Lit. "from the evil of blowers (feminine) upon knots," it having been a common form of witchcraft in Arabia for women to tie knots in a cord and blow upon them with an imprecation.

935

Sūrah 114

An Nās
(Mankind)

An Nās, the second of the two cries for refuge and protection, takes its name from a recurring word which marks the rhythm in the Arabic. In this case protection is sought especially from the evil in a man's own heart and in the hearts of other men.

An early Makkan revelation.

In the name of Allah, the Beneficent, the Merciful.	بِسْمِ اللهِ الرَّحْمٰنِ الرَّحِيمِ
1 Say: I seek refuge in the Lord of mankind,	قُلْ أَعُوذُ بِرَبِّ النَّاسِ ۞
2 The King of mankind,	مَلِكِ النَّاسِ ۞
3 The God of mankind,	إِلٰهِ النَّاسِ ۞
4 From the evil of the sneaking whisperer,	مِنْ شَرِّ الْوَسْوَاسِ الْخَنَّاسِ ۞
5 Who whispereth in the hearts of mankind,	الَّذِى يُوَسْوِسُ فِى صُدُورِ النَّاسِ ۞
6 Of the jinn and of mankind.	مِنَ الْجِنَّةِ وَالنَّاسِ ۞

936

INDEX

INDEX OF LEGISLATION